THE TOOLS OF GOVERNMENT

THE TOOLS OF
GOVERNMENT

A Guide to the New Governance

Edited by

Lester M. Salamon

With the special assistance of

Odus V. Elliott

OXFORD
UNIVERSITY PRESS
2002

OXFORD
UNIVERSITY PRESS

Oxford New York
Athens Auckland Bangkok Bogotá Buenos Aires Calcutta
Cape Town Chennai Dar es Salaam Delhi Florence Hong Kong Istanbul
Karachi Kuala Lumpur Madrid Melbourne Mexico City Mumbai
Nairobi Paris São Paulo Shanghai Singapore Taipei Tokyo Toronto Warsaw
and associated companies in
Berlin Ibadan

Published by Oxford University Press, Inc.
198 Madison Avenue, New York, New York 10016
www.oup.com

Oxford is a registered trademark of Oxford University Press

Library of Congress Cataloging-in-Publication Data
The tools of government : a guide to the new governance / edited by Lester M. Salamon ;
with the special assistance of Odus V. Elliott.
p. cm.
Includes bibliographical references and index.
ISBN-13 978-0-19-513665-4
1. Political planning. 2. Public administration. 3. Intergovernmental cooperation. 4.
Public-private sector cooperation. 5. Contracting out. I. Salamon, Lester M. II. Elliott,
Odus V.
JP1525.P6 T66 2001   351—dc21   2001032134

7 9 8

Printed in the United States of America
on acid-free paper

CONTENTS

A political dispute has been raging throughout the world for at least the last two decades over the relative effectiveness of government and private action, and of different levels of government, in addressing public needs.

Largely overlooked in this dispute, however, has been the extent to which actual public problem solving has come to embrace the collaborative actions of governments at multiple levels and both government and private institutions. The vehicle for this has been the development and widespread adoption of a host of alternative instruments of public action through which governments at different levels and private organizations—both for-profit and nonprofit—have joined forces to meet human needs. Included here are grants, contracts, insurance, regulation, loan guarantees, vouchers, corrective fees, and tax expenditures. Taken together, these instruments have altered public management in rather fundamental ways, severing the financing of government action from the delivery of public services and creating complex networks that merge the activities of national and local governments and public and private organizations in increasingly inventive ways. Unfortunately, however, neither the training of public managers nor the popular discourse about government operations has yet come fully to terms with the resulting transformation.

It was this realization that led me, along with a handful of other analysts, to call more than two decades ago for the development of a more systematic body of knowledge about the varied "tools" of public action in widespread use, and about the system of "third-party government" to which they had given rise. Since then, considerable headway fortunately has been made in formulating such a "tools approach" and creating the base of knowledge required to put it into effect. At the same time, the proliferation and utilization of tools have clearly outpaced the formulation and dissemination of knowledge about their characteristics and demands. What is more, the deep ideological divide between supporters and opponents of state action has continued to foster a rhetoric that obscures the extent to which public and private action have fused. As a consequence, practitioners, policymakers, and the general public alike still find themselves ill equipped to cope with the challenges that public problem solving now entails.

This book is designed to take a major step toward filling this gap. It represents the most comprehensive effort yet attempted to pull together in one place a systematic description of the major tools now being used to address public problems both in the United States and, increasingly, around the world; to identify the major tasks that each of these tools entails, the circumstances for which each is best suited, and the kinds of challenges that each involves; and to examine the most important crosscutting issues that many of these tools pose. More than that, the book formulates a framework for coming to terms with the very different style of public problem solving that these different tools have made possible. Called "the new governance," this framework emphasizes the collaborative nature of modern efforts to meet human needs, the widespread use of tools of action that engage complex networks of public and private actors, and the resulting need for a different style of public management, and a different type of public sector, emphasizing collaboration and enablement rather than hierarchy and control.

While I am responsible for whatever shortcomings this volume may exhibit, numerous individuals and organizations share responsibility for any merits it may have. First and foremost is Dr. Paul Posner of the U.S. General Accounting Office, who first encouraged me to update and expand my earlier book on this topic, *Beyond Privatization: The Tools of Government Action,* which was published by the Urban Institute Press in 1989. Dr. Robert Long and the W. K. Kellogg Foundation, for which he works, saw the connection between this work and the broader initiative that Kellogg was launching in the area of nonprofit management and provided generous financial support that enabled this project to proceed. Scott Fosler, then of the National Academy of Public Administration; Dr. Richard Nathan of the State University of New York at Albany; Jonathan Breul, of the U.S. Office of Management and Budget; Melissa Middleton of the University of Minnesota; and former governor Michael Dukakis of Massachusetts agreed to serve on an advisory committee to oversee the project and assist me in identifying collaborating authors. An outstanding group of analysts familiar with the various "tools" of public action, although not always with the "tools concept," then agreed to prepare chapters on the different tools or on a variety of crosscutting themes that many of the newer tools have posed, and to take part in what turned out to be an extended "pro-seminar" on the nature, character, and implications of various tools conducted over more than a two-year period via e-mail, memorandum, and in-person meetings as drafts were developed, reviewed, and revised. Christopher Collins and his colleagues at Oxford University Press had the vision to understand the promise of the resulting product when it was still a glimmer in its creator's eye and to stand by the project through its extended gestation and development. Finally, helping me keep track of all this activity and ensure that the entire effort kept moving was Dr. Odus V. Elliott, a research associate of the Johns Hopkins Institute for Policy Studies. To all of them I owe my deepest gratitude.

The public sector is not widely credited as a source of innovation in society. Yet, the proliferation of forms of action linking governments at different levels and public and private actors that has occurred over the last forty to fifty years must certainly rank as one of the foremost social innovations of all time, making it possible to respond collectively to a wide range of human needs in a way that nevertheless engages private energies and capabilities. Surely this innovation and the challenges to which it has given rise deserve more attention than they have received thus far from practitioners, scholars, and the public at large. The dawn of a new millennium is a fitting time to come to terms, finally, with this "new governance." I hope that this book will provide the means to ensure that this occurs.

—Lester M. Salamon
Annapolis, Maryland
March 2001

EDITOR

Lester M. Salamon is a professor at Johns Hopkins University and director of the Johns Hopkins Center for Civil Society Studies. An expert on public management and the nonprofit sector, Dr. Salamon previously served as the founding director of the Johns Hopkins Institute for Policy Studies, as the director of the Center for Governance and Management Research at the Urban Institute in Washington, D.C., and as deputy associate director of the U.S. Office of Management and Budget. His recent books include *Global Civil Society: Dimensions of the Nonprofit Sector* (Johns Hopkins, 1999); *Defining the Nonprofit Sector* (Manchester University Press, 1997); *Partners in Public Service* (Johns Hopkins, 1995); and *Beyond Privatization: The Tools of Public Action* (Urban Institute Press, 1989). Dr. Salamon received his Ph.D. in government from Harvard University.
(CHAPTER 1, CHAPTER 4, CHAPTER 10, and CHAPTER 22)

ASSISTANT TO THE EDITOR

Odus V. Elliott is senior project administrator at the Johns Hopkins Institute for Policy Studies. He served formerly as academic officer of the Nebraska Coordinating Commission for Postsecondary Education, as senior program officer of the Fund for the Improvement of Postsecondary Education, and as associate director for academic and student affairs at the Arizona Board of Regents. Dr. Elliott earned his Ph.D. in education and political science at the University of Arizona.

CONTRIBUTORS

David R. Beam is director of the Masters of Public Administration Program and associate professor of political science at the Illinois Institute of Technology. Previously, he held research positions with the U.S. Advisory Commission on Intergovernmental Relations (ACIR), the Naisbitt Group, Northern Illinois University, and United Airlines. His publications include the ACIR studies *Categorical Grants: Their Role and Design* and *Improving Federal Grants Management*. Dr. Beam earned his Ph.D. in political science from Northern Illinois University.
(CHAPTER 11)

Timothy J. Conlan is professor of government and politics at George Mason University. Among other works, Professor Conlan is the author of *From New Federalism to Devolution: Twenty-five Years of Intergovernmental Reform* (The Brookings Institution, 1998) and coauthor with David Beam and Margaret Wrightson of *Taxing Choices: The Politics of Tax Reform* (Congressional Quarterly Press, 1990). Dr. Conlan earned his Ph.D. in government from Harvard University.
(CHAPTER 11)

Joseph J. Cordes is professor of economics and director of the Ph.D. Program in Public Policy at George Washington University. From 1989 to 1991, he was deputy assistant director for tax analysis at the Congressional Budget Office. He is a coeditor of the *Encyclopedia of Taxation and Tax Policy* (Urban Institute Press, 1999) and has published more than fifty articles on public policy and taxation. Dr. Cordes received his Ph.D. in economics from the University of Wisconsin–Madison.
(CHAPTER 8)

Ruth Hoogland DeHoog is professor of political science and director of the Master of Public Affairs (M.P.A.) program at the University of North Carolina at Greensboro. She wrote *Con-*

tracting Out for Human Services (SUNY Press, 1985) and coauthored *The Politics of Dissatisfaction* (M. E. Sharpe, 1992), as well as book chapters and journal articles on urban administration, privatization, and public service delivery. Dr. DeHoog earned her Ph.D. in political science from Michigan State University.
(CHAPTER 10)

Ron J. Feldman is assistant vice president at the Federal Reserve Bank of Minneapolis. A former analyst at the Congressional Budget Office (CBO), Dr. Feldman wrote CBO's *Controlling Losses of the Pension Benefit Guaranty Corporation.* He is also the author of the Federal Reserve Bank of Minneapolis's annual report essay *Fixing FDICIA: A Plan to Address the Too-Big-To-Fail Problem,* and *The Risks of Government Insurance Programs* for the World Bank. Mr. Feldman holds a master in public administration from the Maxwell School of Syracuse University.
(CHAPTER 6)

Christopher Howard is the David D. and Carolyn B. Wakefield Associate Professor of Government at the College of William and Mary. He is the author of *The Hidden Welfare State: Tax Expenditures and Social Policy in the United States* (Princeton University Press, 1997), as well as articles in the *Journal of Policy History, Political Science Quarterly, Public Administration Review, The American Prospect,* and other journals. He earned his Ph.D. in political science from the Massachusetts Institute of Technology.
(CHAPTER 13)

Helen Ingram holds the Warminton Endowed Chair of Social Ecology and is professor of social ecology and political science at the University of California, Irvine. She is coauthor of *Policy Design for Democracy* (University of Kansas Press, 1997) and coeditor of *Public Policy for Democracy* (The Brookings Institution, 1993). She earned her Ph.D. in public law and government from Columbia University.
(CHAPTER 20)

Steven J. Kelman is the Weatherhead Professor of Public Management at Harvard University's John F. Kennedy School of Government. He served as administrator of the Office of Federal Procurement Policy in the Office of Management and Budget, 1993–1997. Dr. Kelman is the author of *Making Public Policy: A Hopeful View of American Government* (Basic Books, 1988) and of other books and articles on the policymaking process and government management. He earned his Ph.D. in government from Harvard University.
(CHAPTER 9)

Donald F. Kettl is professor of public affairs and political science at the Robert M. La Follette School of Public Affairs at the University of Wisconsin–Madison. He is also Nonresident Senior Fellow at Washington's Brookings Institution. Among other works, he is the author of *The Global Public Management Revolution: A Report on the Transformation of Governance* (The Brookings Institution, 2000). Dr. Kettl earned his Ph.D. in political science from Yale University.
(CHAPTER 16)

Christopher K. Leman is a consultant based in Seattle, Washington. He has served as resident fellow at Resources for the Future, policy analyst at the U.S. Department of the Interior, and on the faculty of Brandeis University and the University of Washington. His writings have appeared in publications of the National Academy of Sciences, National Association of Regional Councils, the Urban Institute, and in many journals. Dr. Leman holds a Ph.D. in political science from Harvard University.
(CHAPTER 2)

John J. Lordan is senior vice president, chief financial officer, and treasurer of Fordham University and vice president emeritus of Johns Hopkins University. As a financial management official in the Office of Management and Budget, he developed and implemented regulations for administration of grants and contracts with state and local governments and nonprofit

organizations. Mr. Lordan holds a master of public administration from Harvard University and a master of business administration from Boston College.
(CHAPTER 17)

Peter J. May is professor of political science at the University of Washington. His research addresses policy design and implementation of social regulatory programs. He is the author of *Making Governments Plan: State Experiments in Managing Land Use* (Johns Hopkins University Press, 1997) and *Environmental Management and Governance* (Routledge, 1996). Dr. May earned his Ph.D. in political science from the University of California at Berkeley.
(CHAPTER 5)

Ronald C. Moe is the specialist in government organization and management of the Congressional Research Service, Library of Congress, and also a fellow of the Center for the Study of American Government, Johns Hopkins University. He is the author of numerous Congressional Research Service reports and of articles on government organization and management that have appeared in *Public Administration Review* and numerous other journals. Dr. Moe earned his Ph.D. in public law and government from Columbia University.
(CHAPTER 3)

B. Guy Peters is the Maurice Falk Professor of American Government at the University of Pittsburgh and distinguished research professor at the University of Strathclyde, Glasgow, Scotland. Among his recent publications are *Institutional Theory in Political Science* (Pinter, 1999) and *Governance, Politics and the State* (Macmillan, 2000). He holds a Ph.D. in political science from the Michigan State University.
(CHAPTER 19)

Paul L. Posner is director of budget issues for the U.S. General Accounting Office and adjunct professor at the Master of Arts in Policy Studies Program at Johns Hopkins and Georgetown Universities. He has published articles on public budgeting, federalism, and tax policy issues and is the author of *The Politics of Unfunded Mandates* (Georgetown University Press, 1998). He is a fellow in the National Academy of Public Administration and earned his Ph.D. in political science from Columbia University.
(CHAPTER 18)

Arthur B. Ringeling is professor of public administration at Erasmus University, Rotterdam, the Netherlands. He is coauthor of *Openbaar Bestuur*, 5th ed. (Sampson, 1996), *De instrumenten van het beleid* (Sampson, 1983), and *Het imago van de overheid* (VUGA, 1993). Dr. Ringeling earned his Ph.D. in social sciences from the University of Nijmegen, the Netherlands.
(CHAPTER 21)

Peter H. Schuck, J.D. and M.A. in government from Harvard University, is the Simeon E. Baldwin Professor of Law at Yale University. He served as principal Deputy Assistant Secretary for Planning and Evaluation at DHEW from 1977–1979. Recent books include *The Limits of Law: Essays on Democratic Governance* (Westview, 2000) and *Citizens, Strangers, and In-Betweens: Essays on Immigration and Citizenship* (Westview, 1998).
(CHAPTER 15)

Steven Rathgeb Smith is an associate professor at the Daniel J. Evans School of Public Affairs at the University of Washington where he directs the nonprofit management program. He is coeditor with Helen Ingram of *Public Policy for Democracy* (The Brookings Institution, 1993) and the coauthor of *Nonprofits for Hire* (Harvard University Press, 1993). He is the editor of *Nonprofit and Voluntary Sector Quarterly*. Dr. Smith earned his Ph.D. in political science from the Massachusetts Institute of Technology.
(CHAPTER 20)

Thomas Stanton is an attorney and a fellow of the Center for Study of American Government at Johns Hopkins University. He is chair of the Standing Panel on Executive Organization

and Management of the National Academy of Public Administration, is the author of *A State of Risk* (HarperCollins, 1991), and serves on the advisory board of *The Financier*. Mr. Stanton earned his M.A. at Yale University and a J.D. from the Harvard Law School.
(CHAPTER 3 and CHAPTER 12)

Eugene Steuerle is a senior fellow at the Urban Institute and author of a weekly column, "Economic Perspective," for *Tax Notes Magazine*. He has served in various positions in the Treasury Department under four different presidents, including Deputy Assistant Secretary of the Treasury for Tax Analysis. Recent books include *Vouchers and the Provision of Public Services* (The Brookings Institution, 2000), *Nonprofits and Government: Collaboration and Conflict* (Urban Institute Press, 1999), and *The Government We Deserve* (Urban Institute Press, 1998). Dr. Steuerle earned his Ph.D. in economics from the University of Wisconsin.
(CHAPTER 14)

Eric C. Twombly is a policy researcher at the Urban Institute. His numerous works include *Organizational Response in an Era of Welfare Reform: Exit and Entry Patterns of Nonprofit Human Service Providers* (George Washington University, 2000) and *Nonprofit Human Service Providers in an Era of Privatization: Toward a Theory of Economic and Political Response*, coauthored with Joseph J. Cordes and Jeffrey R. Henig (Quorem, 2000). He earned his Ph.D. in public policy from George Washington University.
(CHAPTER 14)

Janet A. Weiss is the Mary C. Bromage Collegiate Professor of Organizational Behavior and Public Policy and founder and director of the Nonprofit and Public Management Center at the University of Michigan. She has published widely in academic journals on the roles of information and ideas in the policy process. Dr. Weiss earned her Ph.D. in psychology from Harvard University.
(CHAPTER 7)

CHAPTER ONE

The New Governance and the Tools of Public Action: An Introduction

Lester M. Salamon

In economic life the possibilities for rational social action, for planning, for reform—in short, for solving problems—depend not upon our choice among mythical grand alternatives but largely upon choice among particular social techniques . . . techniques and not 'isms' are the kernal of rational social action in the Western world.[1]
—ROBERT DAHL AND CHARLES E. LINDBLOM, 1953

Far-reaching developments in the global economy have us revisiting basic questions about government: what its role should be, what it can and cannot do, and how best to do it.[2]
—WORLD BANK, 1997

I. INTRODUCTION: THE REVOLUTION THAT NO ONE NOTICED

A fundamental rethinking is currently under way throughout the world regarding how to cope with public problems.[3] Stimulated by popular frustrations with the cost and effectiveness of government programs and by a newfound faith in liberal economic theories, serious questions are being raised about the capabilities, and even the motivations, of public-sector institutions. Long a staple of American political discourse, such questioning has spread to other parts of the world as well, unleashing an extraordinary torrent of reform.[4] As a consequence, governments from the United States and Canada to Malaysia and New Zealand are being challenged to be reinvented, downsized, privatized, devolved, decentralized, deregulated, delayered, subjected to performance tests, and contracted out.

Underlying much of this reform surge is a set of theories that portrays government agencies as tightly structured hierarchies insulated from market forces and from effective citizen pressure and therefore free to serve the personal and institutional interests of bureaucrats instead.[5] Even defenders of government concede that we are saddled with the "wrong kind of governments" at the present time, industrial-era governments "with their sluggish, centralized bureaucracies, their preoccupation with rules and regulations, and their hierarchical chains of command. . . ."[6]

Largely overlooked in these accounts, however, is the extent to which the structure of modern government already embodies many of the features that these reforms seek to implement. In point of fact, a revolution has taken place in the "technology" of public action over the last fifty years, both in the United States and, increasingly, in other parts of the world.

The heart of this revolution has been a fundamental transformation not just in the scope and scale of government action, but in its basic *forms*. A massive proliferation has occurred in the *tools* of public action, in the *instruments* or means used to address

1

public problems. Whereas earlier government activity was largely restricted to the direct delivery of goods or services by government bureaucrats, it now embraces a dizzying array of loans, loan guarantees, grants, contracts, social regulation, economic regulation, insurance, tax expenditures, vouchers, and more.

What makes this development particularly significant is that each of these tools has its own operating procedures, skill requirements, and delivery mechanism, indeed its own "political economy." Therefore, each imparts its own "twist" to the operation of the programs that embody it. Loan guarantees, for example, rely on commercial banks to extend assisted credit to qualified borrowers. In the process, commercial lending officers become the implementing agents of government lending programs. Since private bankers have their own worldview, decision rules, and priorities, left to their own devices they will likely produce programs that differ markedly from those that would result from direct government lending, not to mention outright government grants.

Perhaps most important, like loan guarantees, many of these "newer" tools share a significant common feature: they are highly indirect. They rely heavily on a wide assortment of "third parties"—commercial banks, private hospitals, social service agencies, industrial corporations, universities, day-care centers, other levels of government, financiers, and construction firms—to deliver publicly financed services and pursue publicly authorized purposes. The upshot is an elaborate system of *third-party government* in which crucial elements of public authority are shared with a host of nongovernmental or other-governmental actors, frequently in complex collaborative systems that sometimes defy comprehension, let alone effective management and control. In a sense, the "public administration problem" has leaped beyond the borders of the public agency and now embraces a wide assortment of "third parties" that are intimately involved in the implementation, and often the management, of the public's business.

Take, for example, the system for delivery of publicly financed mental health services in Tucson, Arizona. Funding for such services comes from a variety of federal and state government programs. However, no federal or state bureaucrat ever comes in contact with any mentally ill person. Indeed, no federal or state bureaucrat even comes in contact with any local government official or private agency employee who actually delivers services to the mentally ill. Rather, the entire system is operated at two and three steps removed. The state of Arizona not only contracts out the delivery of mental health services, it also contracts out the contracting out of mental health services. It does so through a "master contract" with a private, nonprofit local mental health authority called ADAPT Inc. ADAPT, in turn, handles all dealings with more than twenty other local agencies that deliver mental health services in the Tucson area with funds provided by state and federal programs.[7] While this may be an extreme case, the pattern it exemplifies has been a central part of public-sector operations for well over a generation now.

What is involved here, moreover, is not simply the delegation of clearly defined ministerial duties to closely regulated agents of the state. That is a long-standing feature of government operations stretching back for generations. What is distinctive about many of the newer tools of public action is that they involve the sharing with third-party actors of a far more basic governmental function: the exercise of discretion over the use of public authority and the spending of public funds. Thanks to the nature of many of these tools and the sheer scale and complexity of current government operations, a major share—in many cases *the* major share—of the discretion over the operation of public programs routinely comes to rest not with the responsible governmental agencies, but with the third-party actors that actually carry the programs out.

This development has proceeded especially far in the United States, where hostility to government has long been a staple of political life, and where the expansion of governmental programs consequently has had to proceed in a highly circuitous way.[8] Contracting arrangements invented to fight the Revolutionary War and later elaborated to handle the far more complex tasks of product development during World War II were thus quickly expanded in the aftermath of that war to fields as diverse as agriculture, health, space exploration, and social services. Grants-in-aid, loan guarantees, social regulations, insurance, and other indirect instruments have expanded as well. As Donald Kettl has reminded us, "[E]very major policy initiative launched by the federal government since World War II—including Medicare and Medicaid, environmental cleanup and restoration, antipoverty programs and job training, interstate highways and sewage treatment plants—has been managed through public-private partnerships."[9]

Reflecting this, a study of a cross section of U.S. communities carried out by the present author in the early 1980s found that the majority of the government-financed human services available at the local level was already being delivered by private non-profit and for-profit organizations as of that date, and this was well before the advocates of "privatization," contracting out," and "reinventing government" had proposed it. In particular, as shown in Table 1-1, government agencies delivered only 40 percent of these publicly funded services, while private agencies—both nonprofit and for-profit— delivered 60 percent.[10]

Instead of the centralized hierarchical agencies delivering standardized services that is caricatured in much of the current reform literature and most of our political rhetoric, what exists in most spheres of policy is a dense mosaic of policy tools, many of them placing public agencies in complex, interdependent relationships with a host of third-party partners. Almost none of the federal government's more than $300 billion annual involvement in the housing field, for example, bears much resemblance to the classic picture of bureaucrats providing services to citizens. Rather, nearly $190 billion

TABLE 1-1 *Share of Government-Funded Human Services Delivered by Nonprofit, For-Profit, and Government Agencies in Sixteen Communities, 1982 (Weighted Average)**

	PROPORTION OF SERVICES DELIVERED BY			
Field	*Nonprofits*	*For-profits*	*Government*	*Total*
Social services	56%	4%	40%	100%
Employment/training	48	8	43	100
Housing/community development	5	7	88	100
Health	44	23	33	100
Arts/culture	51	a	49	100
All	42%	19%	39%	100%

* Figures are weighted by the scale of government spending in the sites. Percentages shown represent the share of all spending in all sites taken together that fall in the respective categories.

a Less than 0.5 percent.

SOURCE: Lester M. Salamon, *Partners in Public Service: Government-Nonprofit Relations in the Modern Welfare State* (Baltimore: Johns Hopkins University Press, 1995), p. 88.

takes the form of *loan guarantees* to underwrite mortgage credit extended by private commercial banks; another $114 billion takes the form of tax subsidies that flow to homeowners through the income tax system; and more than $20 billion takes the form of housing *vouchers* administered by semiautonomous *local* housing authorities to finance housing provided by private landlords (see Table 1-2).

More generally, as reflected in Table 1-3, the direct provision of goods or services by government bureaucrats accounts for only 5 percent of the activity of the U.S. federal government. Even with income transfers, direct loans, and interest payments counted as "direct government," the direct activities of the federal government amount to only 28 percent of its activities. Far larger in scale are other instruments of public action— contracting, grants-in-aid, vouchers, tax expenditures, loan guarantees, government-sponsored enterprises, insurance, and regulation, to name just a few. Including just the $376 billion in net additions to outstanding deposit insurance in 1999 and not the far larger amounts of pension, crop, and disaster insurance, a rough estimate would put the total monetary value of these activities in the neighborhood of $2.5 trillion as of fiscal year 1999, two and a half times higher than the roughly $1 trillion in direct activities in which the federal government is engaged, and one and a half times higher than the amounts recorded as outlays in the federal budget that year. This highlights another

TABLE 1-2 *U.S. Federal Housing Programs by Type of Tool, Fiscal Year 1999*

Type	Amount ($ bns)	% of Total
Expenditures		
Subsidies (Sec. 8)	21.1	6.3%
Mortgage credit	0.4	0.1%
Public housing	6.0	1.8%
Rural housing	0.6	0.2%
Veterans housing	1.6	0.5%
SUBTOTAL	29.7	8.9%
Other		
Loan guarantees	187.6	56.4%
Direct loans	1.1	0.3%
Tax expenditures	114.4	34.4%
SUBTOTAL	303.1	91.1%
GRAND TOTAL	332.8	100.0%

SOURCE: U.S. Office of Management and Budget, *Budget of the United States Government, Fiscal Year 2001; Analytical Perspectives* (Washington, D.C.: U.S. Government Printing Office, 2000), 109–111, 218–229, 230–236.

	Amt ($ bns)	Percent
Direct government		
Goods and services	186.8	5.2
Income support	550.4	15.4
Interest	229.7	6.4
Direct loans (obligations)	38.4	1.1
Subtotal, Direct	1005.3	28.1
Indirect government		
Contracting	198.8	5.6
Grants	286.4	8.0
Vouchers	251.0	7.0
Tax expenditures	602.0	16.8
Loan guarantees (commitments)	252.4	7.0
Government-sponsored enterprises (loans)	409.2	11.4
Deposit insurance (net additions)	376.1	10.5
Regulation	200.0	5.6
Subtotal, Indirect	2575.9	71.9
GRAND TOTAL	3581.2	100.0
Budget outlays	1703.1	47.6
Other activity	1878.1	52.4

SOURCE: Data on government contracting from General Services Administration, Federal Procurement Data System, "Federal Contract Actions and Dollars, FY 1999" (www.fpds.gsa.gov). Data on regulation from U.S. Office of Management and Budget, "Costs and Benefits of Regulation 2000" (www.whitehouse.gov/omb/inforeg/2000fedreg-charts.pdf). Data on tax expenditures, grants, loan guarantees, government-sponsored enterprises from U.S. Office of Management and Budget, *Analytical Perspectives, Budget of the United States Government, Fiscal Year 2001* (Washington, D.C.: U.S. Government Printing Office, 2000), 109–111, 184–185, 204, 230–237, 246. Data on deposit insurance from Federal Deposit Insurance Corporation Web site (www.fdic.gov/bank/statistical/statistics). All other data from U.S. Office of Management and Budget, *Budget of the United States Government, Fiscal Year 2001* (Washington, D.C.: U.S. Government Printing Office, 2000), 342–373.

interesting feature of many of these more indirect tools: they often do not show up on the government's budget, which further helps to explain their attractiveness.

This reliance on third parties to deliver publicly funded services is not an exclusively American phenomenon, however. It has also been a classic—if largely overlooked—

feature of the European welfare states, at least outside Scandinavia. In the Netherlands, for example, a fierce conflict between secular and religious communities in the late nineteenth century over control of public education was resolved early in the twentieth century by a compromise under which the state was called on to finance elementary and secondary education but to leave the actual provision in the hands of private schools, many of them religiously affiliated. As government was enlisted to assist in the provision of health care, social services, and even humanitarian assistance overseas, this same model was replicated in these other spheres, producing a widespread pattern known as "pillarization" under which state resources are used to finance services delivered by private institutions organized along religious and, later, ideological lines.[11] A similar phenomenon is also apparent in Germany, where the Catholic doctrine of "subsidiarity" has been enshrined in basic law, obliging the state to turn first to the "free welfare associations" to address social needs before enlisting state institutions.[12] Belgium, Ireland, Israel, and other nations also exhibit a similar pattern. Even France, long known for its centralized governmental structure and highly developed state welfare provision, dramatically increased its reliance on government contracts with private nonprofit institutions during the 1980s to implement a major decentralization of social welfare functions.[13] The upshot is that many countries in western Europe have nonprofit sectors quite a bit larger than that in the United States, financed largely through grants and contracts from the state, as reflected in Figure 1-1 below.[14]

II. THE NEED FOR A NEW PARADIGM

The proliferation of these new tools of public action has created new opportunities to tailor public action to the nature of public problems. It has also made it possible to enlist a wide assortment of different actors—governmental as well as nongovernmental—in meeting public needs. At the same time, however, this development has vastly complicated the task of public management. Instead of a single form of action, public managers must master a host of different "technologies" of public action, each with its own decision rules, rhythms, agents, and challenges. Policymakers must likewise weigh a far more elaborate set of considerations in deciding not just whether, but also *how*, to act, and then how to achieve some accountability for the results. And the public at large must somehow find ways to make sense of the disparate actions that are then taken on their behalf by complex networks of public and private actors. One of the central conclusions of the new field of "implementation studies" that emerged during the 1970s, in fact, was that the convoluted structure of many public programs was the source of many of the problems causing public programs to fall short of their promise.[15]

Regrettably, however, existing concepts of public administration and public policy offer little help in coming to terms with these dilemmas. *Traditional public administration* remains preoccupied with the internal operations of public agencies—their procedures for staff recruitment, budgeting, and task accomplishment. Indeed, a cardinal tenet of the field has been that the management of public affairs is best left to neutral professionals organized in public agencies that are arrayed in hierarchical fashion and therefore able to achieve the needed specialization of functions so crucial to effective operations and democratic control.[16] Such concepts leave little room for the proliferation of new forms of public action featuring the wholesale surrender of key elements of discretionary authority over the exercise of public authority and the spending of public funds to a host of nongovernmental or other-governmental actors. "Much of the time, when 'government' does something, it is the [government] employees who really take action," one recent text thus notes, conveniently overlooking the fact that

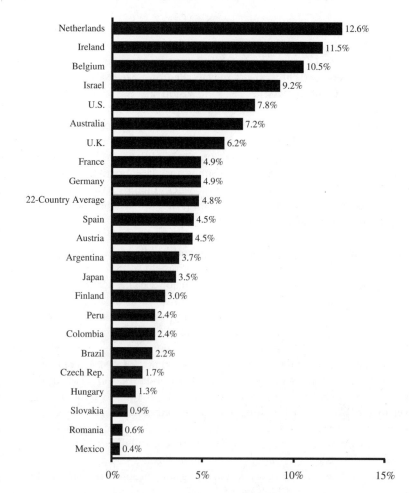

FIGURE 1-1 *Nonprofit share of total employment, by country; 22 countries; 1999.*
Source: Lester M. Salamon et al., Global Civil Society: Dimension of the
Nonprofit Sector *(Baltimore: Johns Hopkins Institute for Policy Studies,*
1999), p. 14.

in the current era it is mostly government's third-party partners that take the action
instead.[17]

Nor does the new field of *policy analysis* that recently has gained prominence offer
much help. The central preoccupation of this field has been the application of sophisticated techniques of microeconomics to the analysis of public problems. Of far less
concern has been the nitty-gritty of actual program operations. Indeed, the implementation of public programs has long been the "missing link" in the policy analysis worldview.[18]

Even the "new public management" and the "reinventing government" movement
that it helped spawn have failed to improve much on this record. To be sure, this line
of thinking has made the use of alternative instruments a major goal of public sector
reform.[19] However, to justify this prescription, as we have seen, reinventing enthusiasts
have embraced a caricature of current government operations that overlooks the extent
to which such instruments have already been adopted. In the process, they downplay
the immense difficulties that these instruments entail and the strong possibility that
the reforms they are espousing may be the source, rather than the cure, for the problems
they are seeking to remedy.

What this suggests is that government does not need to be "reinvented," as the new public management has suggested. That process is already well advanced. The great challenge now is to find a way to comprehend, and to manage, the reinvented government we have produced. For that, however, a new approach is needed, one that acknowledges the existence and likely persistence of "third-party government," and that focuses more coherently and explicitly on the distinctive challenges that it poses.

Fortunately, some progress has been made in developing such an approach. A half century ago, for example, Robert Dahl and Charles Lindblom called attention to the rapid innovation in techniques of social intervention already in evidence, referring to it as "perhaps the greatest political revolution of our times."[20] Frederick C. Mosher returned to this theme during the early 1980s, emphasizing our failure to take sufficient account of the extent to which the federal government in the United States had changed its role from one of doing to one of arranging.[21] The present author at around the same time proposed a wholly new focus for public management training and research concentrating on the distinctive tools or instruments through which the public sector increasingly operates.[22]

Despite some useful progress in formulating such a "tools framework,"[23] and the further proliferation in the use of diverse policy tools, however, most of our political rhetoric and much of our public administration training remains dominated by the image of the centralized bureaucratic state, as a recent survey of public administration textbooks makes clear.[24]

The purpose of this book is to remedy this situation, to bring the new tools of public action that are now in widespread use to the center of public and professional attention. To do so, the discussion builds on an earlier volume that first elaborated on the concept of tools of government.[25] Where that volume focused on only six tools, however, this one extends the analysis to many more. In addition, the present volume supplements the discussion of individual tools with an analysis of some of the overarching issues that the proliferation of tools of government action raises.

In the process, this book suggests a new approach to public problem solving for the era of "third-party government" in which we find ourselves. I call this approach "the new governance" to underline its two defining features. The *first* of these, signified by use of the term "governance" instead of "government," is an emphasis on what is perhaps the central reality of public problem solving for the foreseeable future—namely, its *collaborative nature,* its reliance on a wide array of third parties in addition to government to address public problems and pursue public purposes.[26] Such an approach is necessary, we will argue, because problems have become too complex for government to handle on its own, because disagreements exist about the proper ends of public action, and because government increasingly lacks the authority to enforce its will on other crucial actors without giving them a meaningful seat at the table. The *second* feature, signified by the use of the term "new," is a recognition that these collaborative approaches, while hardly novel, must now be approached in a new, more coherent way, one that more explicitly acknowledges the significant challenges that they pose as well as the important opportunities they create.

The balance of this introduction outlines this approach in more detail and introduces some of the basic concepts on which it rests. To do so, the discussion falls into three major sections. The first section introduces the major features that form the heart of this "new governance" paradigm and shows how they relate to existing conceptualizations in the field. The second section then spells out some of the basic analytics of the approach—what is meant by a "tool" of public action, how tools can be assessed, and what dimensions of tools are consequently most important. Finally, the third section examines the implications that flow from this analysis and explains the format of the rest of the book.

III. THE NEW GOVERNANCE PARADIGM

Like any new approach to a topic as old as public administration, the "new governance" is hardly entirely novel. Rather, it builds on a rich history of past thinking, changing emphases, and incorporating new elements, but hardly replacing all that has gone before. The result, however, is a new synthesis, a new paradigm, that brings prevailing realities into better focus and consequently makes more sense of some of the central dynamics at work. In particular, five key concepts form the core of this approach, as outlined in Table 1-4 below. In this section we examine these five concepts and show how they relate to existing approaches in the field.

From Agency and Program to Tool

At the heart of the new governance approach is a shift in the "unit of analysis" in policy analysis and public administration from the public agency or the individual public program to the distinctive *tools* or *instruments* through which public purposes are pursued. As we have seen, such instruments have mushroomed in both number and scale in recent decades. A central argument of the "new governance" is that this has altered the nature of public management and the pattern of public problem solving in rather fundamental ways, but ways that are only partly acknowledged in existing theories and approaches.

This focus on the tools or technologies of public action differentiates the new governance both from classical public administration and from the more recent "implementation" school that emerged during the 1970s. For the former, the central focus of public administration is on the operation of governmental agencies. This reflects the origins of the public administration field in the Progressive-era effort to legitimize government action to cope with the increasingly apparent shortcomings of the unfettered market system. As formulated by Woodrow Wilson, Max Weber, Frederick Taylor, Luther Gulick, and others, the classical theory posited a new type of institution, the democratic public agency, that would overcome the three major problems long associated with government bureaucracy in the American mind—that is, excessive administrative discretion, special-interest capture, and inefficiency. This was to be

TABLE 1-4 *The New Governance Paradigm*

Classical Public Administration	New Governance
Program/agency	Tool
Hierarchy	Network
Public vs. private	Public + private
Command and control	Negotiation and persuasion
Management skills	Enablement skills

achieved through three principal devices: first, the restriction of executive agencies to administration rather than policymaking; second, personnel recruitment on the basis of technical competence rather than political influence; and third, a set of "scientific" management principles designed to ensure the efficient conduct of administrative work.[27] Although subsequent work has refined and elaborated on these ideas, the basic principles have remained largely intact, fixing on public administration thinking a focus on the public agency as the basic unit of analysis, a sharp distinction between the public and private sectors, a separation between policy and administration, a preference for clear lines of administrative responsibility and control, and an emphasis on the skills of command and control.

While these ideas have provided a workable framework for the development of a relatively successful administrative apparatus in the American context, however,[28] they take as given that the funding and provision of public services are typically carried out by the same public entity. As a result, they apply most clearly to only one of a range of possible forms that public action can take (i.e., direct government). However, as we have seen, this is no longer the dominant form of public action at the present time.

This point became clear as early as the 1970s as efforts were made to explain why the Great Society social programs of the 1960s were not living up to their promise. The answer, a new school of implementation studies concluded, was not that the classical theory was wrong, but that the American political system was failing to supply the conditions necessary for it to work.[29] Instead of clear specification of program objectives, sufficient authority to put programs into effect, and reasonable attention to the management challenges that programs entailed, studies of program implementation revealed that administrators were often set adrift with only vague or conflicting guidance about program purposes, insufficient authority to act, and little attention to the administrative tasks that programs involved.[30] Especially problematic was the highly indirect character of many of the Great Society initiatives. The reason public programs were failing, students of implementation therefore concluded, was not that America adhered too closely to the Progressives' ideal and built too centralized an administrative state, as "privatization" advocates now contend, but that it departed too extensively from this ideal and created programs that resembled Rube Goldberg cartoons instead, with multiple actors linked together in often implausible decision sequences.

To remedy this, implementation theorists proposed to shift the unit of analysis in policy work from the public agency to the individual public program and to encourage clearer specification of program objectives and greater attention to program management. Far less clear, however, despite numerous case studies, was what improved management really entails and how this might vary systematically among the many types of programs that exist.[31]

The "new governance," by contrast, takes a significantly different approach. Rather than seeing programs as *sui generis,* the new governance finds commonalities flowing from the tools of public action that they employ. It thus shifts the unit of analysis from the individual program or agency to the distinctive tools or technologies that programs embody. Underlying this approach is the notion that the multitude of different government programs really embody a more limited number of basic tools or instruments of action that share common features regardless of the field in which they are deployed. Among other things, these tools define the set of actors who will be part of the cast during the all-important implementation process that follows program enactment, and they determine the roles that these actors will play. Since these different actors have their own perspectives, ethos, standard operating procedures, skills, and incentives, by determining the actors the choice of tool importantly influences the outcome of the process. Thus, this focus builds on the insight of the implementation studies that the division between policy and administration assumed in the classical theory does not seem to work in practice, and that the process of program design does not end with legislative enactment but rather continues into the implementation phase as well. Under these circumstances, it makes sense to focus attention on the decisions that shape which actors have significant roles in this stage of the process, and this is precisely what the "tools focus" of the new governance does. By shifting the focus from agencies or programs to underlying tools, therefore, the new governance provides a way to get a handle on the postenactment process that the implementation literature identifies as crucially important. Tool choices significantly structure this process and therefore affect its results.

Because of this, however, tool choices are also not just technical decisions. Rather, they are profoundly *political*: they give some actors, and therefore some perspectives, an advantage in determining how policies are carried out. This is especially critical given the degree of discretion that the implementation literature suggests is left to this stage of the process. The choice of tool thus helps determine how this discretion will be used and therefore which interests will be most advantaged as a result. For this reason, the choice of tool is often a central part of the political battle that shapes public programs. What is at stake in these battles is not simply the most efficient way to solve a particular public problem, but also the relative influence that various affected interests will have in shaping the program's postenactment evolution. Indeed, it may well be the case that the need to involve particular actors is what importantly determines which tool is chosen.

Such choices are also importantly shaped by cultural norms and ideological predispositions, and they, in turn, affect public attitudes toward the state.[32] A strong promarket bias underlies tool choices in the United States, for example, whereas western Europe is much more wary of the market and much more favorably inclined toward the state. At the same time, such cultural norms are hardly immutable. To the contrary, debates over the appropriate techniques of social intervention—over block grants vs. categorical grants, direct government vs. contracting out, public enterprise vs. economic regulation—forms the core of much of our political discourse.

If tool choices are fundamentally political choices, however, they are also operational choices with significant implications for the management of public affairs. Different tools involve different management tasks and therefore require different management knowledge and skills. The operation of a grant-in-aid program is significantly different from the operation of a regulatory program and this differs, in turn, from the operation of a voucher. Whatever generic skills of public management may exist, they must be supplemented by skills peculiar to the various tools being employed if public programs are to be effective. However, this requires a body of literature and a type of training that is geared to the characteristics of the different tools, which is precisely what the new governance seeks to provide.

From Hierarchy to Network

In shifting the focus in public problem solving from agencies and programs to generic tools, the *new governance* also shifts the attention from hierarchic agencies to *organizational networks*. The defining characteristic of many of the most widely used, and most rapidly expanding, tools, as we have seen, is their indirect character, their establishment of *interdependencies* between public agencies and a host of third-party actors. As a result, government gains important allies but loses the ability to exert complete control over the operation of its own programs. A variety of complex exchanges thus come into existence between government agencies and a wide variety of public and private institutions that are written into the operation of public programs. Under these circumstances, the traditional concerns of public administration with the internal operations of public agencies—their personnel systems, budgetary procedures, organizational structures, and institutional dynamics—have become far less central to program success. At least as important have become the internal dynamics and external relationships of the host of third parties—local governments, hospitals, universities, clinics, community development corporations, industrial corporations, landlords, commercial banks, and many more—that now also share with public authorities the responsibility for public programs operations.

Not only does this broadening of the focus from public agencies to "networks" of organizations differentiate the new governance from traditional public administration, it also differentiates it from the "privatization" and "reinventing government" perspectives that have surfaced in recent years.

Both of these schools of thought acknowledge the importance of indirect forms of government action. More than that, they both advocate it, the former as a way to replace government and the latter as a way to incentivize it.

In neither case, however, is the use of third parties viewed as particularly problematic. Privatization theories, for example, actually view reliance on the private sector to deliver public services as more likely to serve public interests than reliance on public agencies themselves. This is so, privatization advocates argue, because the civil service protections designed to insulate bureaucrats from political pressures insulate them as well from the citizens they are supposed to serve and consequently free them to pursue their self-interests instead.[33] Under these circumstances, "*the* key to effective government" becomes "privatization"—reducing the size of the public sector, shifting responsibilities to the private sector, and establishing "private sector alternatives that are more attractive to the current supporters of government programs."[34]

The reinvention school and the "new public management" of which it is a part take a different tack. For these theories, contracting out and other forms of indirect government are less ends in themselves than a means to improve internal agency management by forcing public managers to compete.[35] Reinventers thus have an incentive to downplay the extent to which such indirect devices are already being used and to minimize the difficulties to which they give rise. An internal contradiction thus creeps into the new public management prescription because managers are simultaneously encouraged to take more responsibility for the results of their activity and obliged to surrender significant shares of the authority for achieving those results to third-party implementers.

The "new governance," by contrast, shifts the focus of attention much more explicitly from the internal workings of public organizations to the networks of actors on which they increasingly depend. While acknowledging the advantages such networks can bring, however, it also acknowledges the considerable challenges they pose. As such it builds on two other bodies of theory: "principal-agent theory" and "network theory."

Principal-agent theory is part of a broader body of concepts designed to explain the existence of organizations in a market system.[36] What is relevant for our purposes here is the insight this theory provides into one of the central paradoxes that arises in relationships between principals and agents in contractual or other third-party arrangements of the sort that third-party government entails. Despite the apparent influence that the principals in such relationships wield by virtue of their control of the purse strings, it turns out that the agents frequently end up with the upper hand. This is so, principal-agent theory explains, because the agents in such relationships typically have more information than their principals about what they are doing with the discretion that is inevitably left in their hands. They therefore have significant opportunities to "shirk" their duties and subject the principals to the "moral hazard" of having to rely on agents whose competence and diligence the principal cannot fully know. The only way for principals to avoid this is to secure better information about how the agents are performing, but this involves costs. Therefore, every principal has to find an equilibrium between the level of control it would like and the level it can afford. Moreover, the more disparate the goals and characteristics of the principal and the agent, the more information will be needed and the more costly a given equilibrium is likely to be. Under these circumstances, "who pays the piper" may not really "call the tune" at all, at least not without considerable effort.

What *network theory* adds to this insight is the observation that the principals in such relationships may have difficulty getting their way even when the agents share their basic goals. This body of theory was developed to explain the complexities of policymaking in many modern democracies, where power is splintered among numerous divergent groups. However, it can also help explain the challenges of policy implementation as well, especially where indirect tools are used. In such situations, network theory argues, the standard relationship among actors is one of interdependence. As a consequence, no single actor, including the state, can enforce its will. This is especially true, network theory emphasizes, because of four crucial attributes that commonly characterize policy networks, making the tasks of network management in general, and the tasks of managing indirect tools in particular, especially demanding:[37]

- First, their *pluriformity*—the fact that they engage a diverse range of organizations and organizational types, many of which have limited experience cooperating with each other and limited knowledge of each other's operating styles;

- Second, their *self-referentiality*—the fact that each actor has its own interests and frame of reference and therefore approaches the relationship with a different set of perspectives and incentives;

- Third, their *asymmetric interdependencies*—the fact that all the actors in a network, including the state, are dependent on each other but rarely in a fully symmetrical way. Even when all the parties want the same thing, therefore, they may still not be able to cooperate fully because they may not all want it with the same urgency, in the same sequence, or at the same time; and

- *Finally,* their *dynamism*—the fact that all of these features change over time even as the network seeks to carry out its mission.

Far from automatically sharing the same objectives, as the privatization and reinventing paradigms tend to assume, the actors brought into the operation of public programs through indirect tools thus typically have goals, operating styles, skills, worldviews, incentives, and priorities that, even with the best of intentions, often differ widely from each other. As a consequence, the task of securing concerted action becomes a major administrative challenge. Under these circumstances, the hopeful assumptions of the reinventing government school that government can move easily from a "rowing" to a "steering" role are far from assured.[38]

What the "new governance" and its "tools approach" add to this network theory is a clearer understanding of the commonalities of various network arrangements. In a sense, tools significantly structure networks: they define the actors that are centrally involved in particular types of programs and the formal roles they will play. When policymakers choose a loan guarantee, for example, they choose a network that involves a structured interaction between a public agency and the commercial banking system. When they select a grant-in-aid, by contrast, they choose a different network that engages state and local governments. By shifting the focus from hierarchies to networks and specifying more precisely the kind of network a program embodies, the "tools approach" of the new governance thus can offer important clues about the kinds of management challenges that particular programs will confront.

From Public vs. Private to Public + Private

In moving the focus of public management and policy analysis from the program and the agency to the tool and the network, the *new governance* also brings a new perspective to the relationship between government and the other sectors. Traditional public management posits a tension between government and the private sector, both for-profit and nonprofit. The public sector is distinguished, in this view, by its monopoly on the legitimate use of force, which it acquires by virtue of its responsiveness to the democratic will of the people. Public agencies thus are imbued with sovereignty, the power to act on behalf of the public.[39] Many of the central precepts of classical public administration flow from this central premise and are designed to ensure that the administrative officials so empowered do in fact respond to the public's will and not the partial will of some private group. Without this clear differentiation, accountability for the spending of public funds and the exercise of public authority becomes impossible and the public sphere polluted by the intrusion of private interests. Keeping private interests and private organizations at arm's length thus becomes a central motivation of organizational design.

This notion of a sharp divide between the public and private sectors also figures prominently in the privatization theories. Here, however, it is the protection of the private sphere from the intrusion of the state that is the object of concern. In this view, the expansion of the state inevitably comes at the expense of the private sector, both for-profit and nonprofit. The best way to preserve a healthy market system and private voluntary sector therefore is to shrink the state and allow the private sector to take up the slack.[40]

Many of the new tools of public action defy these precepts rather fundamentally, however. Instead of a sharp division between the public and private spheres, they blend the two together. This is not to say that sectoral differences are blurred, as is often suggested. A central precept of network theory, after all, is that the participants in a network retain important elements of their individuality. However, *collaboration* replaces *competition* as the defining feature of sectoral relationships. Rather than seeing such collaboration as an aberration or a violation of appropriate administrative practice, moreover, the new governance views it as a desirable byproduct of the important complementarities that exist among the sectors, complementarities that can be built upon to help solve public problems.[41] For example, the state enjoys access to resources that are often critically needed by private, nonprofit groups. For their part, nonprofit groups are often already actively involved in fields that government is newly entering. By combining the actions of the two, utilizing the state for what it does best—raising resources and setting broad societal directions—while using nonprofit organizations for what they do best—delivering services at a human scale and innovating in new fields—important public advantages thus can be gained.

Similar synergies exist, moreover, with the private business sector.[42] So long as due attention is given to the management challenges they entail, cross-sectoral partnerships thus can yield important dividends in terms of effective public problem solving. Rather than viewing such interaction as a "fall from grace" that undermines the purity of the respective sectors, the "new governance" views it as a source of opportunity instead.

In emphasizing the shift from programs run by public agencies to cooperative action orchestrated through complex networks, the "new governance" also underlines the need for a new approach to public management. In this also it differs from both traditional public administration and the new privatization theories.

Traditional public management, with its focus on the operation of public agencies, emphasizes *command and control* as the modus operandi of public programs. This assumes that public action is carried out by hierarchically organized agencies whose central spinal chord is the chain of command. Such centralized control is, in fact, vital to the preservation of democratic accountability. Much of traditional public administration thus is preoccupied with clarifying lines of control and centralizing authority.

The privatization school, by contrast, downplays the need for administrative management altogether. Instead, it posits the market as a superior mechanism for achieving coordination and advancing public goals. Market competition, in this view, replaces public decisionmaking and obviates the need for administrative control.[43]

The "new governance" rejects both of these approaches and suggests a third route for achieving public purposes in the world of third-party government that now exists. Unlike the privatization school, it emphasizes the continued need for public management even when indirect tools are used. This is so because private markets cannot be relied on to give appropriate weight to public interests over private ones without active public involvement. "Government's relationships with the private sector are not self-administering," one expert on privatization has thus noted; "they require, rather, aggressive management by a strong, competent government."[44] Even the World Bank, long known for its market-oriented economic policies and endorsement of privatization, has had to acknowledge recently that "Institutions Matter," as the title of a recent World Bank publication puts it.[45] "An effective state," the World Bank noted in the 1997 edition of its influential *World Development Report*, "is vital for the provision of the goods and services—and the rules and institutions—that allow markets to flourish and people to lead healthier, happier lives. Without it, sustainable development, both economic and social, is impossible."[46] In fact, even the process of privatization itself has been found to require "strong political commitment and effective public management."[47]

While stressing the continued need for an active public role, however, the new governance acknowledges that command and control are not the appropriate administrative approach in the world of network relationships that increasingly exists. Given the pervasive interdependence that characterizes such networks, no entity, including the state, is in a position to enforce its will on the others over the long run. Under these circumstances, *negotiation and persuasion* replace command and control as the preferred management approach, not only in the setting of policy but in carrying it out.[48] Instead of issuing orders, public managers must learn how to create incentives for the outcomes they desire from actors over whom they have only imperfect control. Indeed, negotiation is even necessary over the *goals* that public action is to serve since part of the reason that third parties are often cut into the operation of public programs is that such clarity cannot be achieved at the point of enactment.

All of this suggests a new body of administrative "doctrine" that makes collaboration and negotiation legitimate components of public administrative routine rather than regrettable departures from expected practice. Reconciling such an approach with long-standing prohibitions against excessive administrative discretion will be no easy task, but interesting examples of how this can be done are already apparent in such approaches as negotiated regulation and cooperative contracting, as subsequent chapters of this book will show.

From Management Skills to Enablement Skills

Finally, because of the shift in emphasis from command and control to negotiation and persuasion, the world of third-party government necessitates a significantly different skill set on the part of public managers and those with whom they interact. Both traditional public administration and the "new public management" emphasize essentially *management* skills, the skills required to manipulate large numbers of people arrayed hierarchically in bureaucratic organizations. For traditional public administration, these are essentially the control skills summarized nicely by Luther Gulick in the classic administrative acronym POSDCORB—Planning, Organizing, Staffing, Directing, Coordinating, Reporting, and Budgeting.[49] The new public management moves the emphasis considerably from control to performance, but it remains preoccupied with internal agency management and with the manager as the key to success. Under this body of thought, the path to successful public-sector performance is to introduce business management practices into the public sector, freeing managers to manage but subjecting them to increased competition and holding them accountable for results.[50]

Unlike both traditional public administration and the new public management, the "new governance" shifts the emphasis from management skills and the control of large bureaucratic organizations to *enablement* skills, the skills required to engage partners arrayed horizontally in networks, to bring multiple stakeholders together for a common end in a situation of interdependence. Three rather different skills thus move into the center of attention as a consequence of this shift:

Activation Skills

In the first place, the new governance requires *activation skills,* the skills required to activate the networks of actors increasingly required to address public problems.[51] Many of the new governance tools create opportunities for third parties to take part in public problem solving but do not mandate that these opportunities be taken. Public managers therefore must perform a mobilization and activation role, marketing the new opportunities and encouraging the potential partners to step forward and play their roles. Thus, competent contractors must be identified and encouraged to bid in purchase-of-service programs; banks must be convinced to participate in loan guarantee schemes; and private individuals and corporations must be made aware of tax expenditures. In none of these cases can participation be taken for granted. Rather, it must often be coaxed and cajoled. One of the great challenges in purchase-of-service contracting, for example, has been to ensure an adequate supply of vendors willing to compete on the government's terms,[52] and similar problems have confronted loan guarantee programs as well. Those ultimately responsible for program success therefore often find themselves in the unaccustomed position not of withholding desired support but rather of trying to mobilize appropriate partners to accept it.

Moreover, the task of activating networks for public problem solving is not an exclusively governmental function. Other actors can also often take the initiative. In some cases, these are nonprofit organizations or community groups mobilized by grassroots activists who bring the other stakeholders to the table.[53] Increasingly, private foundations have played this role in the United States, either on their own or in cooperation with corporate and community partners. Rather than wait for government to act, in other words, private institutions are taking the initiative instead. This proliferation of a sense of responsibility for activating problem-solving networks is, in fact, one of the more hopeful facets of the "new governance."

In addition to activating networks, the new governance requires managers who can then sustain them. This calls for *orchestration* skills, the skills required of a symphony conductor. Essentially, a conductor's job is to get a group of skilled musicians to perform a given work in sync and on cue so that the result is a piece of music rather than a cacophony. Clearly, the conductor cannot do this by playing all of the instruments. Rather, he or she must tease the music out of the musicians, setting the tempo and conveying an interpretation, but nevertheless remaining within the bounds set by the physical capacities of the instruments (and the musicians) not to mention the melody prescribed in the score. The conductor thus is an enabler rather than a doer, but his or her interpretation and skill can nevertheless determine whether a given orchestra plays poorly or well.

Orchestration, therefore, does not mean command and control, nor is the orchestrating role an exclusively governmental one any more than is the activation one. Indeed, in major systems acquisition projects, government contracts out the orchestrating role to a general contractor who then mobilizes subcontractors to produce the components of the system. In recent years, this model has been applied as well to human service contracting. In fact, defense contractors such as Lockheed Martin have drawn on their experience in orchestrating the production of complex weapons system to bid successfully on contracts to orchestrate the complex networks of day care, drug abuse counseling, mental health service, job-search, health, job placement, and related service providers required to move welfare recipients into jobs and keep track of the results.[54] Beyond this, however, other actors can also lift the baton even without this kind of governmental *imprimatur*. What is needed to be effective is not simply command of resources—whether financial or legal—but also the intangibles of knowledge, vision, persuasiveness, and community respect.

Modulation Skills

Finally, the new governance requires the sensitive modulation of rewards and penalties in order to elicit the cooperative behavior required from the interdependent players in a complex tool network. Urban economic development specialists have referred to this as *enoughsmanship*—the provision of just enough subsidy to get private parties to make investments in run-down areas they might avoid, but not so much that it produces windfall profits for doing what the developers would have done anyway. Inevitably, as we have seen, third-party government leaves substantial discretion over the exercise of public authority and the spending of public funds in the hands of a variety of third parties over which public officials have at best limited control. Under these circumstances, the central challenge for public managers is to decide what combination of incentives and penalties to bring to bear to achieve the outcomes desired. Excessive use of authority can clearly backfire if partners choose not to "play" or to disguise their activities in ways that "principal-agent theory" predicts. On the other hand, insufficient accountability can invite complete disregard of public goals. Public managers in the era of the new governance are consequently perennially confronted with the dilemma of deciding how much authority or subsidy is "enough" and how much is too much.

Eugene Bardach and Robert Kagan recognized this point clearly in their classic analysis of the problem of regulatory enforcement. Rather than the classic "tough cop," Bardach and Kagan suggest regulatory enforcement may actually be more successful if it promotes the concept of the "good inspector," the inspector who understands when forbearance rather than rigid enforcement best achieves regulatory compliance, and who has the discretion to adjust regulatory enforcement accordingly.[55] Similar notions are also evident in endorsements of new types of contracting stressing cooperation as opposed to classic competitive bidding.[56] Instead of narrowing the range of administrative discretion left to the "street-level bureaucrat,"[57] in other words, the "new governance" calls for broadening that discretion and equipping the public official with the skills and understanding needed to exercise this discretion in a way that advances program objectives.

The growing use of entire "suites" of tools in particular programs only accentuates the need for this modulating, *enoughsmanship* approach to program implementation and enforcement. With rich medleys of instruments at their command, public managers can assemble highly targeted blends of incentives and disincentives specially tailored to the circumstances at hand. While this opens opportunities for abuse, it also creates the potential for truly effective management of public programs. To be effective, however, this approach requires site-level managers who can cope with the discretion involved, and who have a well-developed feel for what constitutes the appropriate mixture of penalties and rewards required to get a given job done.

Therefore, as with other facets of the new governance, the enablement skills required will vary with the type of tool being used. The task of securing the concurrence of industrial firms with the operation of an air pollution control program is likely to differ markedly from the task of enlisting financiers to take advantage of a tax credit for low-income housing. This points up again the importance of tool-specific knowledge to the operation of the third-party arrangements that now exist. However, it also underlines the fact that the new tools of public action, far from reducing the demands on public management, may increase them instead, necessitating more sophisticated management skills, requiring greater exercise of discretion, and calling for better information on performance and results. All of this suggests not the withering away of public administration, as privatization theories tend to assume, but its transformation and refinement instead.

Summary

In short, the proliferation of tools of public action has necessitated a new approach to public problem solving, a *new governance* that recognizes both the collaborative character of modern public action and the significant challenges that such collaboration entails. Central to this new governance is a shift in the basic paradigm guiding action on public problems. Instead of focusing exclusively on public agencies or public programs, the new governance moves the focus of attention to the distinctive tools or technologies used to address public problems. Underlying this shift is a recognition that different tools have their own characteristic features that impart a distinctive twist to the operation of public programs. Tools importantly structure the postenactment process of policy definition by specifying the network of actors that will play important roles and the nature of the roles they will perform. Under these circumstances, the whole character of public management has to change. Instead of command and control, it must emphasize negotiation and persuasion. In place of management skills, enablement skills are increasingly required instead. Far from simplifying the task of public problem solving, the proliferation of tools has importantly complicated it even while enlarging the range of options and the pool of resources potentially brought to bear. All of this makes the development of a systematic body of information about the dynamics and characteristics of the different tools of public action all the more urgent.

The *new governance* thus calls attention to the new world of public problem solving that has been ushered in by the proliferation of tools of public action over the past half century or more. Rather than resisting this trend, like the traditional public administration, or uncritically celebrating it, like the reinventing government school, however, the *new governance* calls for the development of a systematic body of knowledge that can help policymakers, public managers, and others engaged in the increasingly collaborative business of public problem solving take advantage of the special opportunities and cope with the special challenges that these new tools entail. In the process it directs our attention to the characteristic features of the different tools and at the often complex networks of interaction on which many of them depend.

But which features of the different tools are most important? How can tools be analyzed and compared? Which facets are likely to have the biggest effects? And which effects are most important? Clearly, if the "new governance" and the "tools framework" on which it rests are to be more than mere metaphors, they must offer meaningful answers to these questions. Therefore, it is necessary to turn from the rationale for the "new governance" and the general features that characterize it to a more detailed exploration of its analytical core.

Definition and Classification: The Basic Building Blocks

Basic Definition

As a first step in this direction, it may be useful to specify more precisely what is meant by a "tool" or "instrument" of public action.

This is no simple task since tools have multiple features and can be defined at any of a number of levels of abstraction. For our purposes here, however, the most basic descriptive level seems most appropriate. Therefore, as used here *a tool, or instrument, of public action can be defined as an identifiable method through which collective action is structured to address a public problem.*[58] Several features of this definition are particularly notable:

BOX 1-1 *A Tool of Public Action*

A tool of public action is an identifiable method through which collective action is structured to address a public problem.

- In the first place, each tool is assumed to have certain *common features* that make it "identifiable." This is not to say that all tools of a particular type share *all* features. In addition to their common, or *defining*, features, tools also have *design* features that can vary from one embodiment of the tool to another. For example, all grants-in-aid involve payments from one level of government to either another level of government or a private entity, but different grant programs can vary in the level of specificity with which they define eligible purposes, in the range of eligible recipients, in how funds are distributed, and in many other features.

- Second, tools "structure" action. What this means is that the relationships that tools foster are not free-form or transient. Rather, they are institutionalized. Thus, tools are "institutions" in the sense emphasized by students of the "new institutionalism" (i.e., they are regularized patterns of interaction among individuals or organizations).[59] They define who is involved in the operation of public programs, what their roles are, and how they relate to each other. Thus, they importantly shape the set of considerations that effectively come to bear in the all-important implementation phase of policy.

- Finally, the action that is structured by tools is "collective action" aimed at responding to "public problems." This is different from saying that tools structure only government action. Other entities are also often involved in the action that is structured by the tools of public action.

Given this definition, it is possible to distinguish *tools* from both *programs* and *policies,* two other concepts commonly used to discuss policy action. Tools are more general than programs. Programs thus embody tools, applying them to the circumstances of a particular field or problem. A single tool therefore can be used in many different programs in many different fields. Typically, a program embodies a single tool, although increasingly, as we will see below, programs are coming to embody entire suites of tools. A central premise of the tools approach is that particular tools impart similar pressures and have similar operating requirements wherever they happen to be applied.

If tools are typically more general than programs, they are typically less general than policies. Policies are essentially collections of programs operating in a similar field or aimed at some general objective. The programs comprising a policy can all utilize a single tool (e.g., multiple grants-in-aid) or multiple tools. An interesting question that tools analysis raises is whether some tools are more appropriate for some policy objectives than others, an issue we return to below.

One other distinction worth making is that between *internal* tools and *external* tools. Internal tools refer to the procedures that governments use to handle their own internal operations. Included here would be basic procedures for personnel recruitment, human resource management, budgeting, and procurement for the supplies that government needs to operate. External tools, by contrast, are those used to affect society at large, not just the government. The focus of this book, and of the "new governance" approach, is on the latter type of tools, those that seek to affect society and not just the internal workings of government.

Tools as Bundles of Attributes

From what has been said, it should be clear that while the concept of a tool of public action is relatively straightforward, in reality tools are often quite complex. Any given tool is really a "package" that contains a number of different elements. These include:

- *A type of good or activity* (e.g., a cash or in-kind payment, a restriction or prohibition, the provision of information);
- *A delivery vehicle for this good or activity* (e.g., through a loan, an outright grant, a voucher, the direct provision of a service, or the tax system);
- *A delivery system, that is, a set of organizations that are engaged in providing the good, service, or activity* (e.g., a government agency, a nonprofit organization, a local government, a for-profit corporation); and
- *A set of rules, whether formal or informal, defining the relationships among the entities that comprise the delivery system.*

These multiple facets naturally complicate the task of sorting and describing tools, as we will see more fully below. Tools can be classified according to any of the different facets—the nature of the good or service, the delivery vehicle, the nature of the delivery system. This means that no single classification of tools is possible. Classification schemes will differ depending on which facet is used as the basis. Table 1-5 illustrates this point by portraying how some of the most commonly used tools compare to each other descriptively in terms of these four features. Thus, for example, loan guarantees provide cash delivered through a loan by commercial banks operating according to a set of rules that stipulate the conditions under which the government will reimburse the bank if the loan becomes uncollectable. By contrast, direct loans provide cash through loans delivered by a government agency.

The Challenge of Classification

This multidimensionality of policy tools naturally complicates the task of describing and sorting them. This is particularly true in view of the fact that unlike tools in the physical world, such as hammers, saws, and screwdrivers, the tools of public action rarely appear in pure form. Rather, they come bundled in particular programs, many of which combine more than one tool, and all of which bring different approaches to the design issues that each program must address. Beyond this, there is occasionally ambiguity about which features of a tool are truly the *defining features* and which are the *design features* that can vary with particular manifestations. For example, some observers treat "block grants," a form of grant-in-aid that defines eligible purposes fairly broadly, as a separate tool from "categorical grants," which define eligible activities more narrowly. Other observers, however, consider this distinction inconsequential.[60]

Coupled with the considerable ingenuity that has characterized the design of public action in recent years, the multidimensionality of individual tools has made it difficult to reach consensus even on the number of tools that exist. Thus, Savas identified ten different arrangements that can be used just for the provision of public services, the U.S. Office of Management and Budget's *Catalog of Federal Assistance* identifies sixteen

TABLE 1-5 *Common Tools of Public Action: Defining Features*

Tool	Product/Activity	Vehicle	Delivery System
Direct government	Good or service	Direct provision	Public agency
Social regulation	Prohibition	Rule	Public agency/regulatee
Economic regulation	Fair prices	Entry and rate controls	Regulatory commission
Contracting	Good or service	Contract and cash payment	Business, nonprofit organization
Grant	Good or service	Grant award/cash payment	Lower level of government, nonprofit
Direct loan	Cash	Loan	Public agency
Loan guarantee	Cash	Loan	Commercial bank
Insurance	Protection	Insurance policy	Public agency
Tax expenditure	Cash, incentives	Tax	Tax system
Fees, charges	Financial penalty	Tax	Tax system
Liability law	Social protections	Tort law	Court system
Government corporations	Good or service	Direct provision/loan	Quasi-public agency
Vouchers	Good or service	Consumer subsidy	Public agency/consumer

distinct tools, Osborne and Gaebler recorded thirty-six, and E. S. Kirschen of the Netherlands identified no fewer than sixty-three.[61]

Complicating matters further is the fact that tools are often mislabeled, sometimes deliberately. For example, President Roosevelt insisted on including a symbolic employee contribution in the Social Security program so that this program could be characterized as "insurance," which was easier to sell politically, even though it lacks most of the defining features of insurance (current recipients receive their benefits from current wage earners not from their prior contributions to the trust fund). This mislabeling, whether deliberate or inadvertent, can play havoc with efforts to characterize tools and analyze their consequences.

All of this makes it difficult to reach clear consensus about the types of tools that exist. Several different classifications are available in the literature, but each uses a slightly different tool dimension as the basis for its grouping. Thus, Hood, in one of the earliest schemes, sorted tools in terms of two major dimensions: (1) the role of government for which they are used (i.e., detecting vs. effecting); and (2) the governmental resource they enlist (i.e., nodality, treasure, authority, or organization).[62] McDonnell and Elmore focused instead on the *strategy of intervention* that government uses, producing a fourfold division of tools into (1) mandates, (2) inducements, (3) capacity building, and (4) system changing.[63] Schneider and Ingram elaborated on this with a classification that focuses on the *behaviors* that programs seek to modify, leading to a fivefold distinction among: (1) authority tools, (2) incentive tools, (3) capacity tools, (4) symbolic or hortatory tools, and (5) learning tools.[64] Finally, Evert Vedung returned recently to a scheme first developed by F. C. J. van der Doelen and identified three classes of tools—carrots, sticks, and sermons—based on the extent of force that each involves.[65] Given this diversity, some analysts have begun to question whether the concept of a policy tool is rigorous enough to support any serious analysis.[66]

Our approach, by contrast, is to recognize this diversity not as a drawback of the tools approach, but as a strength. The fact is that tools have multiple dimensions in terms of which they can be compared and contrasted, and particular tools may be alike along some dimensions and different along others. This means that multiple classifications of tools are entirely appropriate since different classifications will highlight different facets. Thus, tools can be sorted in a two-step process: first, basic descriptive features can be used to define different tools; and second, various dimensions can then be identified in terms of which various tools so defined can be grouped together for analytical purposes.

But which dimensions are the most appropriate to use? Since the tools approach argues that various tool dimensions have significant consequences for how programs operate and what results they produce, the answer to this question depends, first, on which outcomes are of particular interest to us; and second, on which tool dimensions our theories suggest might affect them. Our approach to sorting tools therefore must be to focus on these two factors.

Evaluating Tools: The Criteria

So far as the first step in this process is concerned, the field of policy analysis has identified three criteria in terms of which public interventions are typically assessed: effectiveness, efficiency, and equity. The policy implementation and political science literature suggest two other criteria that also seem highly germane: manageability and political legitimacy. Taken together, this gives us five criteria in terms of which the consequences of tools can be assessed. Let us look briefly at each of these.

Effectiveness

Effectiveness is the most basic criterion for gauging the success of public action. It essentially measures the extent to which an activity achieves its intended objectives. Although considerations of cost can enter into this judgment, effectiveness judgments are typically made independent of costs. Using this criterion, the most effective tool is the one that most reliably allows action on a public problem to achieve its intended purposes.

Gauging the effectiveness of public action is far from easy, however. For one thing, as we have seen, program purposes are often quite ambiguous, either because precise indicators are technically difficult to locate or because conflicts exist about what really is the principal purpose. Indeed, such ambiguity is almost chronic in fragmented political systems like that in the United States, where multiple perspectives have ample opportunities to influence the definition of program objectives. This makes the choice of tool all the more important because ambiguity at the point of enactment pushes the specification of program purposes into the implementation process, where the choice of tool can have an even more decisive impact.

The effectiveness of different tools also varies with the circumstances. Not just the nature of the tool, but also the nature of the circumstances therefore must be considered when making tool choices. One of the major tasks of the tools approach, in fact, is to specify the circumstances under which particular tools are likely to be most effective. The tool of contracting has great advantages, for example, where a competitive market exists for the goods and services that government wants to buy. However, this is often not the case, so that the adoption of the contracting tool in such circumstances can lead to great disappointments. Since other considerations are often involved in tool choices, the new governance can hardly avoid such dilemmas. However, it can at least clarify the risks and point up the tradeoffs involved.

Efficiency

Where effectiveness focuses exclusively on results, a second criterion—efficiency— balances results against costs. The most efficient tool may not be the most effective one. Rather, it is the one that achieves the optimum balance between benefits and costs.

The costs that are relevant to a judgment about the efficiency of a tool are not only the ones that show up on the ledger of the government that authorizes the program, however. The costs imposed on nongovernmental institutions are also relevant, and for some tools these are far more immense. Regulation, for example, places heavy compliance costs on private businesses that never show up in the balance sheet of government. Indeed, with severe fiscal pressures on governments, there is a strong incentive to utilize tools that have precisely this effect. This suggests the need for a "double balance sheet" to assess the efficiency of various tools, one focused on the costs to government alone and one focused on the costs to other social actors as well.

Equity

A third crucial criterion in terms of which the consequences of tools can be judged is *equity*. The criterion of equity has two different meanings, however. The first of these involves basic fairness—the distribution of benefits and costs more or less evenly among all those eligible. A tool that facilitates the distribution of program benefits evenly across the country thus can be considered equitable in this "fairness" sense.

However, equity also has a different connotation relating to "redistribution," to channeling benefits disproportionately to those who lack them. Achieving such redistribution is, in fact, one of the principal rationales for public action. In this view, government exists in part to remedy past inequalities and ensure equal opportunity and access to all. Students of policy thus distinguish between *distributive* programs, which essentially distribute benefits evenly among a class of recipients; and *redistributive* programs, which tilt the benefits toward the disadvantaged.[67] Some tools might be more likely to serve such redistributive goals than others.

Manageability

In addition to the classic economic criteria of effectiveness, efficiency, and equity, recent research on program implementation suggests the importance of manageability, or "implementability," as an additional criterion in terms of which to assess tools. Implementability refers to the ease or difficulty involved in operating programs. The more complex and convoluted the tool, the more separate actors are involved, the more difficult it is likely to be to manage. Some tools are more cumbersome to operate than others. While they may promise great efficiency and effectiveness in theory, they are unlikely to deliver it in practice because of the managerial difficulties they pose. It was for this reason that Jeffrey Pressman and Aaron Wildavsky identified implementability as the "first rule" of program design.[68] Generally speaking, this presumably means choosing simpler, more direct tools.

Legitimacy and Political Feasibility

Finally, tool choices can also affect the political feasibility and perceived legitimacy of public action. They do this, in the first instance, by helping to determine which actors, and hence which interests, get to shape program implementation, and therefore which are most likely to support or oppose program passage. Clearly, no matter what the prospects for effectiveness, a program that cannot win political support cannot make headway.

Beyond this, tool choices can also affect broader public perceptions of the legitimacy of public action. As we have seen, some approaches are considered more legitimate than others in particular national settings regardless of their technical advantages.[69] Quite apart from such national styles, the choice of tool can affect the perceived legitimacy of public action in other ways as well. For one thing, some tools may facilitate accountability for the exercise of public authority or the spending of public funds better than others, a matter of some importance in a democratic society where such accountability is highly valued. So, too, the choice of tool can affect the extent to which the public can perceive a link between the taxes they pay and the services they receive. The more this link is attenuated or broken, the greater the degree of alienation between government and citizens and the greater the risk to democratic participation.[70] Tool choices thus can affect the overall sense of legitimacy that government enjoys in the eyes of citizens.

Key Tool Dimensions

Armed with this set of criteria, it is possible to identify more precisely which tool dimensions are likely to be most important, and therefore how best to classify tools for analytical purposes. Rather than focus on a single dimension that can work for all purposes, however, the discussion above suggests the need for a range of dimensions in terms of which tools can be compared and contrasted. Tools can differ from each other along one dimension and be similar along others. Only in this way will it be possible to clarify the full matrix of choices that policymakers face and the significant tradeoffs that exist among them.

More specifically, five key tool dimensions seem most likely to have implications for the kinds of consequences identified above. These are not, of course, the only tool dimensions that might be important. Nevertheless, they usefully illustrate the analytical power that the "new governance," and its tools framework, possess.

Degree of Coerciveness

Perhaps the most salient of these dimensions has to do with the nature of the activity that a tool embodies, and particularly with the degree of coercion that it utilizes.

Essentially, this dimension measures the *extent to which a tool restricts individual or group behavior as opposed to merely encouraging or discouraging it.*

This coerciveness dimension is probably the most common basis for classifying tools in the literature.[71] Economists in particular consider this dimension important since it essentially measures the

---

BOX 1-2 *Coercion*

Coercion measures the extent to which a tool restricts individual or group behavior as opposed to merely encouraging or discouraging it.

---

extent to which a tool involves a deviation from reliance on the market as a mechanism to allocate resources and settle social roles. Such deviations are commonly viewed by economists as inappropriate except where "market imperfections" make them imperative.[72]

The coerciveness of tools is also of concern to political scientists. This is so because coercion has implications not only for the operation of the market, but also for the operation of the political system, and especially for the preservation of democracy. Of particular concern is the degree of infringement on individual liberty that a tool entails. In a political democracy, all such infringements are viewed with skepticism and are expected to be undertaken only with clear popular authority. As we have seen, much of the classic theory of public administration, with its stress on the distinction between politics and administration, took shape in response to this concern to root administrative authority clearly in democratic decisionmaking. The more coercive the tool, the greater the infringement on individual liberty, the greater the potential threat to political legitimacy, and therefore the greater the burden of proof on those advocating the program embodying it.

Although almost all government action involves at least some degree of coercion, there are considerable differences among tools in the extent to which they rely on it. This is apparent in Table 1-6, which groups the various tools of public action in terms of the degree of coercion they utilize. Thus:

- At the low end of the coerciveness scale are tort liability, tax expenditures, and public information campaigns. All of these essentially rely on the voluntary cooperation of individuals and groups for their effects, although as Chapter 7 shows even information tools can involve considerable coercion if information crosses the border into indoctrination.

- In a "medium" category are a variety of tools that deliver subsidies of various sorts. The least coercive of these are vouchers, which deliver subsidies directly to consumers and leave it to them to do (or not do) what the program is seeking to encourage. Somewhat more restrictive are grants-in-aid, loan guarantees, direct loans, and contracting, which tend to exact more requirements in return for the subsidies they offer. On the outer border of this category are mandatory labeling and corrective fees and charges, which impose potential burdens on those who fail to comply. These fees are still in some sense voluntary, however, since the citizen is still permitted to engage in the penalized behavior but has to pay a fine or tax on it.

• Finally, in the "highly coercive" category are social and economic regulations, both of which impose formal limitations on activities considered undesirable.

Based on the implementation literature reviewed earlier, it seems reasonable to hypothesize that, other things being equal, the more coercive the tool, the more *effective* it is likely to be, and the more likely to yield *redistributive* results, as shown in Table 1-6. These consequences flow from the clearer authority these tools give governments to act, the limited leeway they allow private actors to deviate from specified program purposes, and the limited costs that governments incur in operating them since much of the burden is imposed on external actors. Because of this, these tools are also more likely to generate political support among those most eager to engage government in a particular form of social action.

These features may help to explain why the consumer and environmental movements of the 1970s in the United States insisted on command-and-control regulatory arrangements, even though most academic economists cautioned against the use of this tool. After years of political struggle against often-powerful entrenched interests, advocates of protection typically wanted tools that provided the maximum certainty that the goals they sought would actually be achieved. Less coercive tools, even when backed by sophisticated economic theories, were often not able to provide this assurance.

The problem, however, is that coercive instruments purchase these advantages at a relatively high price, as Table 1-6 also shows. For one thing, they often entail a loss of *efficiency,* for society at large if not for government. This has been a central theme of economic critiques of social regulation: that the apparent efficiency this tool enjoys from the point of view of government is misleading since it focuses exclusively on the government's costs, which are trivial, and overlooks the far more substantial costs such regulations impose on the private sector. Critics argue, in fact, that these social costs

TABLE 1-6 *Policy Tools Grouped by Degree of Coerciveness*

Degree of Coerciveness	Illustrative Tools	LIKELY IMPACTS				
		Effectiveness	Efficiency	Equity	Manageability	Legitimacy/ Political Support
Low	Tort liability Information Tax expenditures	Low	Moderate	Low	Moderate	High
Medium	Vouchers Insurance Grants-in-aid Government corporations Loan guarantees Direct loans Contracting Labeling requirements Corrective taxes	Moderate	High	Moderate	Moderate	Moderate
High	Economic regulation Social regulation	High	High/Low	High	Low	High/Low

are likely be higher than necessary under regulation because by replacing market decisions with administrative ones regulation surrenders the market's efficiencies. The solution, economists like Charles Schultze therefore have argued, is not improved regulatory management but a change in the basic tool being used: in particular, a shift to less coercive tools that utilize marketlike incentives and thus make "public use of private interest."[73]

Coercive tools can also be more difficult to *manage* since they impose on administrative agencies the difficult job of keeping abreast of literally thousands of decisions made by hundreds of private entities in widely disparate settings. As Schultze has put it, under social regulation "[s]ocial intervention becomes a race between the ingenuity of the regulatee and the loophole closing of the regulator, with a continuing expansion in the volume of regulations as the outcome."[74]

Finally, because they restrict human freedom, coercive tools are presumptively suspect in liberal political regimes and therefore are vulnerable to political attack. As the political movements leading to the enactment of these tools subside, as they frequently do, therefore, the agencies administering them often find themselves face-to-face with hostile vested interests determined to use the full panoply of legal protections available to them to rein in public authority. To avoid being totally hamstrung, agencies often find it prudent to reach some *modus vivendi* with the affected interests. The result is the well-known phenomenon of "agency capture" by those it is seeking to control.[75]

Directness

While the degree of coerciveness is by far the most common basis for differentiating policy tools in the literature, it is by no means the only possible basis. To the contrary, the implementation literature of the 1970s and 1980s points our attention to another dimension that may be equally, or more, important, as the discussion above has already suggested. This dimension has to do with the *nature of the delivery system* that a tool utilizes, and particularly its degree of *directness*.

Directness measures the extent to which the entity authorizing, financing, or inaugurating a collective activity is involved in carrying it out. Underlying this concept are two crucial observations: first, that any effort to cope with a public problem is really made up of a number of separate activities; and second, that these different activities need not be carried out by the same entity. Thus, for example, it is possible to distinguish between the financing of a public service and its delivery. Moreover, each of these can be handled either publicly or privately. This creates a minimum of four possible combinations, as shown in Table 1-7: (1) public finance and public delivery; (2) public finance and private delivery; (3) private finance and public delivery; and (4) private finance and private delivery. The first of these, depicted in Cell A in Table 1-7, represents the stereotypical view of how government operates: government raises revenues through taxes and uses them to support the delivery of services to citizens by a government agency. As we have seen, however, this turns out not to be the most common pattern at all, certainly not at the national level in the United States. For one thing, even when the public sector is involved in both finance and service delivery, it is often not the same level of government that performs both functions. Rather, the federal government may raise some or most of the revenues, but it then often shifts them to state or local governments to finance the actual delivery of the services. Thus, Cell A itself becomes subdivided into four subcells. Alternatively, the public sector—either national or local—can raise the revenues but then contract with the private sector to deliver the services (Cell B). What is more, the private entities involved can be either for-profit or nonprofit firms. Finally, any of these delivery mechanisms can be con-

TABLE 1-7 *Patterns of Public Problem
Solving*

| | FINANCE | |
Delivery	Public	Private
Public		
(1) National	A	C
(2) State/local		
Private		
(1) Nonprofit	B	D
(2) For-profit		

nected to a private system of finance. Thus, for example, a public agency can charge a user fee for the services it provides, in which case the finance is private but the delivery public (Cell C of Table 1-7). Alternatively, special tax advantages can be provided for private purchases of services such as day care (Cell D of Table 1-7). All of these are forms of *public* action in the sense that they engage governmental authority, but each utilizes this authority in a different way and for a different part of the process.

Even this does not exhaust the range of combinations that is possible, however, since raising revenues and providing services are hardly the only actions that public problem solving can involve. Some tools—such as regulations—do not involve services or finances at all, but rather restrictions. In others, the services themselves are financial (e.g., the provision of mortgage finance for housing purchase). Imposing charges, creating inducements, providing information, delivering benefits—all of these as well can be used to promote public purposes. As a result, an extraordinary range of possibilities exists for combining public and private institutions in public problem solving.

Given these possibilities, it should be clear that "directness" is a matter of degree and that different tools can vary greatly in the degree of directness they embody. Generally speaking, the more the various functions involved in the operation of a public activity are carried out by the same institution, the more direct the tool. Thus, a direct tool is one in which authorization, funding, and/or delivery are all carried out by essentially the same governmental entity. Indirect tools parcel these various functions out to various other parties—semiautonomous agencies, other levels of government, community groups, nonprofit organizations, commercial banks, hospitals, and others. The more extensively functions are performed by "third parties," the more organizationally distinct and autonomous these third parties are from the authorizing body, and the greater the discretion the third parties enjoy in the conduct of their functions, the more *indirect* the tool. Thus, for example, tax expenditures are typically more indirect than contracts since they leave more discretion in the hands of citizens; however, grants are more indirect than tax expenditures because they surrender authority to other sovereign units of government, and these typically have greater powers to resist. All three of these are more indirect than service provision by government agencies, however.[76]

Table 1-8 illustrates this point by ranking tools in terms of their relative degree of directness. Thus, at the low end of the directness continuum are tort liability and grants, while at the high end are direct government service provision, government corporations, and information campaigns that governments conduct themselves. In between are tax expenditures (which leave considerable choice to recipients but nevertheless are administered by the enacting government), contracts, and, in the American context, federal social regulations that make extensive use of state and local governments.

As the grouping of tools here suggests, there is some overlap between the degree of coerciveness and the degree of directness of a tool. This is so because the more coercive tools are difficult to implement through indirect delivery systems. However, this overlap is far from complete. For example, information campaigns, one of the least coercive tools, are typically operated directly while social regulation, the most coercive, often leave

BOX 1-3 **Directness**

Directness measures the extent to which the entity authorizing, financing, or inaugurating a public activity is involved in carrying it out. A direct tool is one in which authorization, funding, and execution are all carried out by essentially the same entity.

ample opportunity for involvement by lower levels of government. Clearly, these two tool dimensions tap different facets of tool operations.

In classical public administration, a distinction between direct and indirect tools makes little sense since it is taken for granted that a publicly authorized and funded program should be carried out by a duly constituted, and staffed, public agency. Yet, as we have seen, much of the growth of government action over the last half century, especially in the United States, has taken place through indirect tools—such as grants, loan guarantees, tax expenditures, vouchers, and indirect regulation. The result, as noted earlier, is an elaborate system of "third-party government" that vests a substantial portion of the discretionary authority over the spending of public funds and the operation of public programs in the hands of a variety of third-party partners. Indeed, many tools that operate directly in other countries take a more indirect form in the

TABLE 1-8 *Policy Tools Grouped by Degree of Directness*

Degree of Directness	Illustrative Tools	LIKELY IMPACTS				
		Effectiveness	Efficiency	Equity	Manageability	Legitimacy/ Political Support
Low	Tort liability Grants Loan guarantees Government-sponsored enterprises Vouchers	Low	High	Low	Low	High
Medium	Tax expenditures Contracting Social regulation Labeling requirements Corrective taxes/ charges	Low/Med.	Medium	Low	Low	High
High	Insurance Direct loans Economic regulation Public Information Government corporations Direct government	High	Medium	High	High	Low

American context. Thus, for example, many European countries rely on public enterprise to handle the natural monopolies that often exist in public utility industries (e.g.,
electricity, telephones), whereas the United States tends to leave these businesses in
private hands and subject them to economic regulation. The United States has also
used more indirect approaches in its social regulatory programs in such areas as the
environment, worker safety, and health. While establishing national standards, these
programs leave much of the responsibility for implementation in the hands of state
and local governments and those being regulated.

One reason for the popularity of third-party government appears to be the political
advantages that indirect tools enjoy. In particular, indirect tools provide important
opportunities to cut affected interests into a "piece of the action" when government
programs threaten to infringe on their fields. The more fragmented political power is
in a country and the more controversial the issue, therefore, the more likely it will be
that indirect devices are used. Thus, for example, in recent American experience:

- By using a cost-based reimbursement "voucher" whose proceeds flowed to existing
  hospitals, it was possible to defuse the medical community's opposition to the
  creation of the federal Medicare program in the 1960s;

- By relying on loan guarantees instead of direct loans, it was possible to neutralize
  commercial bank opposition to federal involvement in home mortgage lending in
  the 1930s; and

- By using grants and purchase-of-service contracts, it was possible to enlist research
  universities to support the expansion of federal involvement in scientific research,
  and private nonprofit organizations to support the expansion of federal involvement in social services for the poor.

Federal constitutional structures also contribute importantly to the widespread use
of indirect forms of action. For much of American history, for example, the federal
government's authority to act on a wide range of domestic policy issues has been
contested thanks to constitutional provisions limiting the federal role and a political
structure and system of representation firmly anchored at the state and local levels.[77]
Use of indirect tools—particularly the grant-in-aid—has thus often been a political
and constitutional prerequisite for any federal involvement. State and local officials
have frequently resisted federal involvement unless that involvement is channeled
through them, and a meaningful degree of discretion is left to them in the definition
of the policy substance. Interests opposed to federal involvement have often used their
influence at the state and local level to insist on a significant state and local role as a
way to retain some degree of influence over the implementation of policies with which
they disagree. Use of indirect tools thus becomes the basis for political compromise,
shifting the battle over the definition of policy from the enactment stage to the implementation stage where state and local officials, and the interests that are more powerful
at the state and local level, can play a more meaningful role. The use of indirect tools
for federal environmental and welfare policy is probably attributable in substantial part
to this factor.[78]

These political advantages of indirect tools are hardly unique to the American context, however. Reliance on indirect instruments of public action is increasingly common
in other countries as well, driven by historical traditions of "subsidiarity,"[79] by a growing
diversification of social and political power, by deepening doubts about the capabilities
of state action alone to cope with complex social and economic problems, and by a
resulting inability of governments to secure sufficient authority to act on their own.[80]

The political advantages of indirect tools are not their only benefits, however. At
least three other benefits are often claimed for them:

- First, indirect tools can inject a useful degree of competition into the provision of public services, breaking the monopoly of governmental agencies and thereby potentially improving service quality and "customer orientation."

- Second, indirect tools can provide access to talents and resources that are desperately needed to cope with complex public problems, but that public agencies may not command. These include technical talents (e.g., university researchers, private service providers, loan officers) as well as financial and physical resources (existing facilities, charitable contributions). Indirect tools therefore can extend the reach of public agencies, making it possible for them to avoid costly start-up problems and maximizing the energies that can be brought to bear on public problems.

- Finally, indirect tools offer a greater degree of flexibility, making it easier for government to experiment, to change course when needed, and thus to remain responsive to new needs. This is so because the authorizing government does not have to create the entire administrative structure to operate an initiative.

While indirect tools may have important political and operational advantages, however, they also carry with them offsetting liabilities. For one thing, as Table 1-8 also notes, they can be far less effective and far more difficult to manage. This certainly seems to be one of the central conclusions of the implementation literature of the 1970s and 1980s. In his 1979 study of the implementation of three human service programs in Massachusetts, for example, Stuart Chase found that the most serious implementation problem was the presence "of some player or players in the implementation process whom the program manager does not control but whose cooperation or assistance is required."[81] Jeffrey Pressman and Aaron Wildavsky similarly found that even clear specification of goals and general concurrence on desired outcomes are no guarantee of success when multiple actors are involved in executing a program. The sheer mechanics of securing agreement at each stage of the process can still inject debilitating delays. No wonder "more direct means for accomplishing . . . desired ends" is their recommended "first rule in program design."[82]

Experience with indirect tools of public action thus has ironically provided new reason to value bureaucracy. "The costs of bureaucracy—a preference for procedure over purpose or seeking the lowest common denominator—may emerge in a different light," Pressman and Wildavsky thus note, "when they are viewed as part of the price paid for predictability of agreement over time among diverse participants."[83] By internalizing transactions, minimizing the legalisms involved in complex contractual negotiations with external actors, and providing a more stable framework for bargaining, direct government offers distinct advantages for accomplishing complex tasks.[84]

These conclusions find considerable support, moreover, in the new economic theories of organization. According to these theories, the "principal-agent" problems that inevitably arise *within* organizations are even more severe in cross-organizational relationships. This is so because having all of the factors of production in a single entity creates certain advantages:[85]

- It permits a more creative reward structure to induce agents to pursue the principal's objectives.

- It helps convey the expectation that all involved should work to a common purpose.

- It may help diminish the losses associated with breakdowns and delays in bargaining.

When multiple organizations are involved in a given task, the chances increase that the interests and values of the principal and the agents will diverge. The more dispersed

the authority, therefore, and the less the coincidence of interests and perspectives between principals and agents, the greater the risk of goal displacement and principal-
agent difficulties. Not just the extent of indirectness but also the type of third-party
partner a tool engages thus can affect the extent to which public purposes are achieved.
Public-sector managers of human service programs thus have traditionally shown a
preference for nonprofit contractors over for-profit ones when service contracting has
been employed on the grounds that nonprofits are more likely to share the objectives
of the public sector. Where principals and agents lack a shared set of values or worldviews, the task of ensuring that the principal's objectives are being served grows more
complex and more problematic.

Not only does the directness of tools have implications for the overall effectiveness
of programs, it also may have particular implications for their ability to promote *equity
and redistribution goals.* This is especially the case where the partners brought into the
operation of a public program by a tool lack incentives to achieve these equity goals.
Yet, this is often the case with private businesses. As management theorist Regina
Herzlinger has pointed out, "when resources are given to providers who in turn have
the discretion to allocate the goods and services they produce . . . [the] providers will
try to attract consumers who will improve their measurable performance."[86] In the
process, however, redistributive goals may be sacrificed as producers engage in "creaming" to attract better-off clients. While public agencies themselves are hardly immune
from these pressures, the risks appear greater with indirect tools.

Finally, while enjoying important immediate political advantages, indirect tools also
suffer from certain longer-term political limitations. In particular, they weaken the
perceived link between citizens and government by channeling services financed by
public revenues to recipients through private intermediaries or other levels of government. In the process, the connection between the taxes citizens pay and the services
they receive can become dangerously attenuated.[87]

In short, despite their advantages, indirect tools are especially difficult to manage.
Far from easing the public management problem, as is often supposed, they significantly complicate it instead.

Automaticity

A third key dimension in terms of which policy tools can be differentiated is the level
of *automaticity* they embody. Automaticity measures the extent to which a tool utilizes
an existing administrative structure for its operations rather than creating its own
special administrative apparatus.

BOX 1-4 *Automaticity*

Automaticity measures the extent to which a tool
utilizes an existing administrative structure to produce
its effect rather than having to create its own special
administrative apparatus.

Tools that utilize the market, for example, are
highly automatic. This would include corrective fees
and charges or the "tradable permit" system authorized by the 1990 Clean Air Act Amendments.[88]
Vouchers are another example of a market-based
tool: by placing purchasing power in the hands of
program beneficiaries rather than the institutions
that serve them, vouchers equip these beneficiaries
to make use of the market rather than an administrative mechanism to select the
quantity and quality of services they will receive.

The market is not the only existing system that can be mobilized to carry out public
purposes, however. Others include the tax system, the private credit system, the court
system, and, to a lesser extent, the networks of local governments and private, nonprofit
agencies. Where these existing systems are operational, important options exist for
structuring public interventions in ways that build on them rather than having to

establish separate administrative structures. Therefore, a certain overlap exists between the automaticity dimension and the directness dimension of tools. However, not all automatic tools are indirect, and not all indirect tools are automatic. For example, tax expenditures are automatic but not wholly indirect, whereas contracting is indirect but far from wholly automatic.

Table 1-9 below arranges various tools of public action in terms of their reliance on automatic, nonadministered processes. As this table shows, tools embodying fees and charges, vouchers, or tax expenditures are relatively automatic, as is the use of the existing tort law system to control environmental damage or ensure workplace safety. By contrast, social regulation, direct service programs, and government information campaigns are at the low end of the automaticity spectrum. In between are tools such as grants and contracting, which have some automatic features but operate within essentially administered systems.

Like the other tool dimensions we have examined, there is reason to believe that the automaticity dimension has significant implications for the performance of programs. Indeed, in a 1972 book on the preconditions of public program success, economist Robert Levine identifies this dimension as the single most important determinant of public program success. Programs are most likely to fail, Levine argued, when they rely on "highly administered systems." Instead, more reliance should be placed on "market-like and bargaining systems that combine the workable features of decentralization, self-administration, personal economic or political motivation, and the gross application of public policy rather than systems administered in detail by public officials to private clienteles according to plans laid out in detail by public planners."[89]

Economist Charles Schultze reached a similar conclusion in his pioneering 1977 analysis of regulatory programs, criticizing prevailing regulatory approaches as inherently inefficient because they utilize command and control techniques rather than re-

TABLE 1-9 *Policy Tools Grouped by Degree of Automaticity*

Degree of Automaticity	Illustrative Tools	LIKELY IMPACTS				
		Effectiveness	Efficiency	Equity	Manageability	Political Support
Low	Economic regulation Social regulation Direct government Government corporations Information Direct loans Insurance	High	Low	High	Moderate/Low	High
Medium	Grants Contracting Loan guarantees Labeling requirements	Moderate	High	Moderate	Low	Moderate
High	Vouchers Tax expenditures Corrective taxes/ charges Tort liability	Low	High	Moderate/Low	High/Moderate	Moderate

lying on the automatic mechanisms of the market to promote public objectives. Instead of prescribing what antipollution devices polluters must install to clear the nation's rivers, for example, Schultze recommends making "public use of private interest" by imposing effluent charges that would give polluters an economic incentive to find the lowest-cost way to meet environmental goals.[90]

Because they make use of existing mechanisms, such as the market, automatic tools can also be expected to be more *manageable*. In a sense, they reduce the *amount* of public management that is necessary, substituting for it the control systems already built into these existing systems—the market, the tax system, the court system, or the private banking system.

For all their appeal, however, automatic tools have proved in practice to fall significantly short of their promise. For one thing, there is reason to question how *effective* they are. The great advantage of automatic tools is that they make it possible to enlist existing systems in the pursuit of new objectives. However, this advantage is also the source of serious problems since these systems typically have their own objectives and dynamics. There is always a question, therefore, whether the public objectives will redirect the existing system or the existing system will co-opt, and distort, the public objectives. After all, it is the failure of the existing systems that often necessitates public involvement in the first place. For example, the demands for environmental and safety regulation grew directly out of disappointments with the effectiveness of tort law and the court system to handle consumer and environmental problems.

The effectiveness of automatic tools thus depends on identifying the incentives that can turn existing systems to desired public purposes. In practice this has proved to be more difficult than often assumed. Economist Robert Levine, for example, acknowledged "the hard barrier of our lack of knowledge about what incentives work for officials of local government. . . ."[91] The incentive structures of for-profit businesses are presumably easier to fathom, but even here complications arise. Contracting, for example, is assumed to be a fairly automatic tool because of its reliance on the private market. However, this assumes that a competitive market actually exists for the goods and services needed to address public problems. In fact, however, this critical prerequisite is often lacking in government contracting since government is often in the position of purchasing goods and services that are not generally available on the open market (e.g., military aircraft) in markets where the number of suppliers is highly constricted. Complicating matters further is the fact that the desired outputs in public programs are often difficult to specify and then to achieve (e.g., getting the most disadvantaged welfare recipients into permanent jobs). As management specialist Regina Herzlinger has noted, this makes it extremely difficult to "structur[e] enforceable contracts with the private sector" and to exercise the control function that such contracts require.[92]

Similar problems have arisen with voucher programs. The effectiveness of vouchers depends critically on the responsiveness of markets to the kind of demand that voucher recipients will make and on the ability of voucher recipients to make wise decisions. Both of these are often problematic, however, making vouchers potentially a source of windfall profits for providers without making recipients significantly better off.

Perhaps because of these problems, automatic tools also have political problems. On the one hand, their reliance on existing structures lends them a certain political legitimacy. However, because they enlist institutions and processes that have somewhat different objectives, such tools can rarely attract the enthusiastic support of those pushing for a policy initiative. Environmental advocates thus have been reluctant to embrace the concept of tradable pollution permits for fear that this would legitimize the right to pollute and create "hot spots" of heavy pollution in less desirable neighborhoods.

Consumer advocates have similarly resisted the idea of weighing the value of a human life against the cost of protection in structuring approaches to workplace or consumer safety. Therefore, despite their claims to greater efficiency, automatic tools have often lacked a political constituency.

Finally, experience with automatic tools has raised some serious questions about how easy they are to manage. Seemingly automatic tools turn out to be far more cumbersome to administer than advocates assume. Tradable permitting schemes, for example, still require the establishment of initial threshold pollution levels, the estimation of pollution charges that are consistent with prevailing technology and industry incentive structures, the collection of detailed information on actual pollution levels, and the maintenance and operation of a market in pollution rights.[93] As with the other tool dimensions, therefore, this one too involves difficult tradeoffs in terms of the criteria outlined earlier.

Visibility

The fourth tool dimension that seems likely to be important is the degree of visibility a tool exhibits in the normal policy review processes, particularly the budget process. Obviously, this dimension is highly sensitive to the structure of these processes. Thus, for example, countries that do not utilize a capital budget, like the United States, tend to put direct lending programs at a competitive disadvantage by requiring that the full value of a loan show up on the operating budget as an expenditure the year in which the loan is made.

Until changes were made in 1990, this gave a real advantage to loan guarantee programs over direct lending programs since the value of loan guarantees shows up on the budget only if and when they go into default. Similarly, until the 1970s in the United States no official record was kept of tax expenditures, making them largely invisible in the annual budget process.[94] Not until the 1990s, moreover, were such tax expenditures considered in the normal budget decisionmaking process.

BOX 1-5 *Visibility*

Visibility measures the extent to which the resources devoted to a tool show up in the normal government budgeting and policy review processes.

While the visibility of tools may be affected by the accounting practices in place, however, there are still some general structural features of tools that affect their standing along this dimension. Table 1-10 thus offers a tentative grouping of tools in terms of their degree of visibility. As shown there, insurance and regulatory tools are still relatively invisible, whereas direct government, grants, contracts, and vouchers tend to be more visible. Loan guarantees and tax expenditures are examples of tools that were once largely invisible in normal budget processes in the United States but have become more visible in recent years as a result of accounting changes designed to bring them into better view. Similar changes have been under way for more than a decade to increase the visibility of social regulatory programs by requiring economic impact analyses before regulations go into effect.

Visibility has perhaps its greatest impact in the political realm. At a time of budgetary stringency, invisibility is a tremendous political asset. Invisible tools therefore are the easiest to pass. This may explain why regulation, loan guarantees, and tax subsidies grew so massively in the 1970s and 1980s. Although different in many respects, all of these tools shared a low level of visibility in the normal budgetary process. In the case of loan guarantees, for example, until passage of new credit budgeting procedures in 1990, only the projected losses from loan guarantee defaults were carried on government budgets, while the face value of the contingent liabilities were relegated to a special annex. A similar procedure is used with insurance programs. In the case of regulation, only the direct cost of the regulatory agency personnel show up in the government's budget, whereas the indirect costs imposed on businesses and households are largely invisible. Finally, in the case of tax expenditures, until the adoption of the Budget and Accounting Act in 1974, these were largely invisible as well in the budget process, and it was not until the early 1990s that lawmakers were required to take explicit account of such tax expenditures in making annual budget decisions.

This dimension may also explain why corrective fees and charges have made rather limited headway as vehicles for environmental control despite the advantages claimed for them as efficient mechanisms of public action. Unlike tax expenditures, which are essentially invisible, corrective taxes and fees are highly visible and therefore harder to enact.

The very feature that makes invisible tools so attractive politically, however, makes them problematic along other dimensions. Most obviously, the less visible the tool, the more difficult it is to hold accountable. This can have implications for the *efficiency* of programs embodying this tool. One of the central criticisms of regulatory programs, for example, is that by keeping their true costs hidden, they impose burdens on the economy that are far greater than are needed to accomplish their purpose. Similarly, tax expenditures are sometimes accused of delivering windfall gains to taxpayers who would engage in a particular activity even in the absence of the subsidy. Programs embodying tax subsidies therefore may be highly inefficient, paying unnecessarily for behavior that would have occurred anyway. This same concern applies to insurance programs. Far from preventing activities that entail risk—such as locating houses in flood plains—insurance programs may inadvertently encourage them. However, their

TABLE 1-10 *Policy Tools Grouped by Degree of Visibility*

Degree of Visibility	Illustrative Tools	LIKELY IMPACTS				
		Effectiveness	Efficiency	Equity	Manageability	Legitimacy/ Political Support
Low	Economic regulation Social regulation Labeling requirements Insurance Tort liability	N/A	Low	Low	Low	High
Medium	Contracting Information campaigns Loan guarantees Tax expenditures	N/A	Moderate	Moderate	Moderate	Moderate
High	Direct government Government corporations Grants-in-aid Direct loans Vouchers Corrective taxes/ charges	N/A	High	High	Low	Low

relative invisibility keeps the inefficiencies of these tools from being recognized and addressed.

Because of these accountability problems, those opposed to public spending tend to resist the use of invisible tools. On the other hand, those on the receiving end of public largesse naturally prefer to have their benefits delivered in the least visible form. What this means in practice is that the stronger the constituency, the less visible the tool it is likely to be able to use for any benefits it receives. This may explain why low-income welfare recipients receive their benefits through highly visible grants-in-aid, whereas middle-class homeowners receive theirs through far less visible tax expenditures.

The visibility of tools may also have implications for the extent to which they are used to pursue equity goals because of the legitimacy attached to equity goals in the political arena. Therefore, the more visible the tool a program uses, the more likely the program will be to serve redistributive goals. Conversely, the more special subgroups of the population, such as oil-well owners or large investors, are being targeted for benefits, the more attractive it will be to use less visible tools.

V. FROM ANALYTICS TO ACTION: RESOLVING THE PARADOX OF THIRD-PARTY GOVERNMENT

The four dimensions identified above hardly exhaust the bases for classifying different tools of public action and analyzing their effects. Further fruitful distinctions can be drawn, for example, between tools that deliver their benefits in the form of cash versus those that deliver them "in kind"[95]; and between those that operate through producers and those that deliver their benefits directly to consumers.[96] What is more, at this stage of research the relationships between tool dimensions and tool consequences are more in the nature of plausible hypotheses than proven facts.

Even with these caveats, however, it should be clear that the "new governance" approach, and the tools framework on which it rests, has considerable analytic power as a source of insights into the challenges of public problem solving in the era of third-party government. Perhaps most fundamentally, the discussion has pointed up a critical paradox that seems to characterize contemporary efforts to respond to public problems. That paradox, very simply, is this: *policymakers seem to be under increasing political pressures to select those tools of public action that are the most difficult to manage and the hardest to keep focused on their public objectives.*

More specifically, a variety of factors—the growing fragmentation of political power, the increased complexity of public problems, the recent skepticism of government, the preoccupation with efficiency as the major criterion for public action—have put a premium on tools that are indirect, invisible, and automatic. Such tools have the advantage of defusing political opposition to governmental action, recruiting new talents and resources to the tasks of public problem solving, and avoiding the enlargement of the public sector. At the same time, however, they have the disadvantage of vastly complicating the tasks of public management and risking the subversion of public purposes. In a sense, we seem caught in a vicious circle in which disappointment with public action yields forms of such action that seem most likely to further disappoint. Clearly, the future of collective efforts to respond to public problems will remain gloomy unless this paradox can be resolved.

For this to be possible, however, it will be necessary to move beyond slogans and address the three critical challenges associated with the rise of third-party government:

The Management Challenge

The first of these is the management challenge. Contrary to the hopeful assumptions of some, third-party government poses immense management challenges, perhaps far more immense than those posed by traditional public administration. With power dispersed and numerous semiautonomous entities involved in the operation of public programs, even straightforward tasks become difficult. Indirect tools require advanced planning of far more operational details than is the case with more direct tools. Matters that could be dealt with internally on an *ad hoc* basis in direct government have to be settled in advance through legally binding contracts under "third-party government." Similarly, incentives have to be devised sufficient to induce desired behavior but not so substantial as to yield windfall gains; concurrence has to be secured at numerous points in complex decision chains; and disparate organizations have to be forged into effective networks capable of integrated action. Each of these tasks requires not only extensive programmatic knowledge, but also considerable diplomatic skill as well as detailed knowledge of the operational parameters of the different tools and the internal dynamics of the entities that the tool engages. Also necessary is a sophisticated appreciation of the context in which the tool is being deployed and how this compares to the conditions required for the tool to function optimally.

The Accountability Challenge

Side-by-side with this management challenge is the accountability challenge that third-party government poses. As noted, many of the newer tools of public action vest substantial discretionary authority in entities other than those with ultimate responsibility for the results. What is more, these other entities have their own autonomous sources of authority that allow them to operate with considerable independence of the authorizing body: they include sovereign state and local governments, private commercial banks, independent nonprofit organizations, profit-seeking companies, and universities. hospitals with powerful governing boards. Each of these enters its relationship with governmental authorities on its own terms, with its own expectations, objectives, and bottom line. What is more, as we have seen, the choice of the instrument that structures these relationships is often dictated as much by political considerations as by the appropriateness of the instrument for the purpose at hand. Under these circumstances, classical notions of democratic accountability may need to be loosened and more pluralistic conceptions developed. However, this will require extensive education of all involved, new decisionmaking procedures, and new attitudes.

The Legitimacy Challenge

Finally, and perhaps most significantly, for all its political appeal third-party government may ultimately pose even more serious challenges to popular support of government than did the bureaucratic model before it. Fundamentally, third-party government threatens to fray the link between citizens and the services they receive in return for the taxes they pay. It does so by vesting much of the responsibility for delivering these services in the hands of institutions other than those that voted the programs and raised the revenues for them. Under these circumstances, it is not surprising that citizens might begin to wonder where their taxes are going and what they receive in return.

The purpose of this book is to address these challenges and thus help to resolve the paradox that now confronts public problem solving. To do so, it seeks to develop three bodies of knowledge that are critical to the "new governance" that is now needed:

- First, *tool knowledge,* that is, knowledge about the operating characteristics of the different tools, about the players they engage, and about how they structure the play;

- Second, *design knowledge,* that is, knowledge about how to match tools to the problems being addressed in light of the objectives being sought and the political circumstances that exist; and

- Third, *operating knowledge,* that is, knowledge about how best to operate the new instruments to achieve these objectives in the most effective fashion.

Structure of the Presentation

To do this, this book is divided into three broad sections:

Overview

In the first place, this introduction and a subsequent concluding chapter are designed to put the "new governance" approach into perspective, to identify its central features, and to explain how it relates to other approaches to public problem solving.

Tool Chapters

The heart of the book consists of a series of chapters focusing on particular tools of public action now in widespread use, both in the United States and around the world. Altogether, fifteen such tools are examined in depth here. As noted in Table 1-11 below, this includes direct tools such as direct government service provision, government corporations, direct loans, economic regulation, and information campaigns; as well as indirect tools such as grants, contracts, tax expenditures, loan guarantees, insurance, social regulation, vouchers, fees and charges, government-sponsored enterprises, and tort law.

TABLE 1-11 *Tools of Government Action Covered in This Book*

Direct Tools	Indirect Tools
Direct government	Social regulation
Government corporations	Contracting
Economic regulation	Loan guarantees
Public information	Grants
Direct loans	Tax expenditures Fees and charges Insurance Tort law Vouchers Government-sponsored enterprises

For each such tool, the discussion below offers a detailed analysis prepared by a leading authority and focusing on a common set of topics. These topics include:

- The *defining features* of the tool, how the tool compares to others in terms of the key tool dimensions identified above (coerciveness, directness, automaticity, and visibility), and what *major design features* and resulting variants of the tool exist;

- The *extent and pattern of tool use,* including recent trends, both in the United States and elsewhere;

- The *mechanics* of tool operations, that is, the tasks that the tool entails, the actors it engages, and the roles these actors are typically called on to play;

- The dynamics of *tool selection,* including the circumstances for which the tool is most appropriate and the political considerations that affect whether it is likely to be selected;

- The *major management challenges* the tool poses and the way they can be handled; and

- The overall *advantages and disadvantages* of the tool for various purposes.

The result is a more comprehensive and thorough body of information on the major tools of government action than has heretofore been available, presented in a readable format, and designed to be accessible to scholars and practitioners alike.

Crosscutting Chapters

In addition to the overview material and the individual tool chapters, this book also includes a set of chapters examining the crucial crosscutting issues that the proliferation of new tools of public action and the growth of third-party government have posed. These include:

- The special *management challenges* of indirect government;

- The problem of *cost accounting* in third-party arrangements, where fixed costs have to be allocated among multiple activities;

- The more general *accountability challenge* that indirect government poses and the ways it can be addressed;

- The *politics* of tool choice;

- The impact of third-party government on *democratic governance and citizen attachment* to the political system; and

- The *international experience* with alternative tools of public action.

Tools Workbooks

Finally, to supplement the discussion here, a series of *Workbooks* has been prepared on the major tools. These workbooks contain documentary materials that help illustrate how particular tools operate. Each focuses on a particular program embodying a tool and includes materials such as the following:

- The basic authorizing language for the program

- Key facets of the legislative history surrounding the program

- The regulations issued to implement the program

- Key program management documents (e.g., sample Requests for Proposals, proposal rating sheets)

- Study questions to direct attention to key decisions that had to be made in structuring the tool for use in the program

Access to this workbook material is available through the Internet at http://www.
jhu.edu/~ccss/toolsworkbooks.

VII. CONCLUSION

A new era of public problem solving has dawned in the United States and many other
parts of the world. Instead of relying exclusively on government to solve public problems, a host of other actors are being mobilized as well, sometimes on their own
initiative, but often in complex partnerships with the state. In this new setting, traditional notions of public and private responsibilities are being turned on their heads
and traditional conceptions of public administration rendered largely obsolete.

To cope with this new reality, a new paradigm, a new conceptualization, is needed,
one that acknowledges the complex networks of interaction that now characterize our
efforts to deal with public problems, that appreciates the strengths these networks can
mobilize, but that also recognizes the challenges they entail.

We have argued that what we have called the new governance provides such a conceptualization. The new governance focuses our attention on the wide array of tools
now being used to address public problems and on the diverse collection of institutions
being activated in the process. In doing so, it alerts us to the increased substitution of
complex networks of organizations for the rigid hierarchies of old to solve public problems and to the resulting need for enablement skills rather than simple management
skills to cope with the resulting interdependencies. Far from simplifying the tasks of
policy management, the new governance thus emphasizes the increased difficulties it
now entails.

The new governance thus is a realistic framework for public decisionmaking even
while it is an optimistic one. It celebrates the proliferation of tools of public action and
the resulting activation of new partners for "public work," while squarely acknowledging the challenges this creates. More than that, it offers concrete insights into the
operational requirements that these various tools impose. The result, we hope, will be
a better basis both for public understanding of the way the public sector works and for
improving the effectiveness with which we address public problems. That, at any rate,
is our goal.

NOTES

1. Robert A. Dahl and Charles E. Lindblom, *Politics, Economics, and Welfare: Planning and
Politico-Economic Systems Resolved into Basic Social Processes* (New York: Harper and Row, 1953),
6, 16.

2. World Bank, *World Development Report 1997: The State in a Changing World* (New York:
Oxford University Press, 1997), 1.

3. World Bank, *World Development Report 1997: The State in a Changing World* (1997), 1–3;
Marcel Masse, "Economic, Political, and Technological Pressures Shaping Public Sector Reform,"
Proceedings of the Canada-South East Asia Colloquium on Transforming the Public Sector (Ottawa,
Canada: Institute on Governance, 1993); Donald Kettl, "The Global Revolution in Public Man-
agement: Driving Themes and Missing Links," *Journal of Policy Analysis and Management* 16,
no. 3 (1997): 446–462; Tim Plumptre, "Public Sector Reform: An International Perspective,"
Proceedings of the Canada–South East Asia Colloquium: Transforming the Public Sector (Ottawa,
Canada: Institute on Governance, 1993); C. Pollitt, *Managerialism and the Public Service* (Oxford:
Basil Blackwell, 1990).

4. Shahid J. Burki and Guillermo E. Perry, *Beyond the Washington Consensus: Institutions
Matter,* World Bank Latin American and Caribbean Studies Viewpoints (Washington, D.C.:
World Bank, 1998).

5. Included here is the "new institutionalism" associated with the work of Oliver Williamson

and the public choice theories associated with the work of Gordon Tullock. See Oliver Williamson, *Markets and Hierarchies* (New York: Free Press, 1975); Gordon Tullock, *The Politics of Bureaucracy* (Washington, D.C.: Public Affairs Press, 1965). For excellent summaries of these theories and their application to public bureaucracy see Terry Moe, "The New Economics of Organization," *American Journal of Political Science* 28 (November 1984): 739–777; and Gerald Garvey, *Facing the Bureaucracy* (San Francisco: Jossey-Bass, 1993), 25–35.

6. David Osborne and Ted Gaebler, *Reinventing Government: How the Entrepreneurial Spirit Is Transforming the Public Sector* (Reading, MA: Addison-Wesley, 1992), 48.

7. H. Brinton Milward and Keith G. Provan, "Measuring Network Structure," *Public Administration* 76 (summer 1998): 387–407.

8. For an interesting analysis of the impact of America's "nonstate" tradition on the development of public administration in the United States, see Richard J. Stillman, *Preface to Public Administration: A Search for Themes and Direction,* 2d ed. (Burke, VA: Chatelaine Press, 1999).

9. Donald Kettl, *Sharing Power: Public Governance and Private Markets* (Washington, D.C.: The Brookings Institution, 1993), 4.

10. Lester M. Salamon, *Partners in Public Service: Government-Nonprofit Cooperation in the Modern Welfare State* (Baltimore: Johns Hopkins University Press, 1995), 88.

11. For a description of the Netherlands case, see Ralph Kramer, *Voluntary Agencies in the Welfare State* (Berkeley: University of California Press, 1981), 19–36.

12. For a comparison of the German and U.S. systems, see Lester M. Salamon and Helmut K. Anheier, "The Third Route: Government-Nonprofit Collaboration in Germany and the United States," *Private Action and the Public Good,* eds. Walter W. Powell and Elisabeth S. Clemens (New Haven: Yale University Press, 1998), 151–162.

13. Claire Ullman, "Partners in Reform: Nonprofit Organizations and the Welfare State in France," in *Private Action and the Public Good,* eds. Powell and Clemens (1998), 163–176.

14. Lester M. Salamon et al., *Global Civil Society: Dimensions of the Nonprofit Sector* (Baltimore: Johns Hopkins Institute for Policy Studies, 1999), 14.

15. See, for example, Jeffrey L. Pressman and Aaron B. Wildavsky, *Implementation* (Berkeley: University of California Press, 1973); D. Kettl, *Sharing Power* (1993), 4–5.

16. For a useful summary of this conventional wisdom, see Vincent Ostrom, *The Intellectual Crisis of Public Administration* (University: University of Alabama Press, 1973).

17. Barton and Chappell, *Public Administration: The Work of Government* (1985), quoted in Richard Stillman, *Preface to Public Administration* (1999), 150.

18. Erwin Hargrove, "The Missing Link: The Implementation Challenge in Policy Research," working paper (Washington, D.C.: Urban Institute Press, 1975). A considerable body of "implementation" literature has emerged in more recent years, but, as noted below, it has not systematically come to terms with the array of new tools of public action either. See note 28 below.

19. See, for example, Mohan Kaul, "The New Public Administration: Management Innovations in Government," *Public Administration and Development* 17, nos. 13–26 (1997); Andrew Massey, *Managing the Public Sector: A Comparative Analysis of the United Kingdom and the United States* (Aldershot, U.K.: Edward Elgar, 1993); Osborne and Gaebler, *Reinventing Government* (1992); Owen E. Hughes, "New Public Management," in *International Encyclopedia of Public Policy and Administration,* ed. Jay M. Shafritz (Boulder: Westview Press, 1998), 1489–1490.

20. Robert Dahl and Charles E. Lindblom, *Politics, Economics, and Welfare* (1953), 8.

21. Frederick C. Mosher, "The Changing Responsibilities and Tactics of the Federal Government," *Public Administration Review* 40 (November/December 1980): 541–548.

22. Lester M. Salamon, "The Rise of Third-Party Government," *Washington Post* (29 June 1980); and Lester M. Salamon, "Rethinking Public Management," *Public Policy* 29, no. 1 (summer 1981): 255–575.

23. See, for example, Christopher C. Hood, *The Tools of Government* (Chatham, NJ: Chatham House Publishers, 1983); Stephen H. Linder and B. Guy Peters, "From Social Theory to Policy Design," *Journal of Public Policy* 4, no. 3 (1984): 237–259; Lorraine M. McDonnell and Richard F. Elmore, "Getting the Job Done: Alternative Policy Instruments," *Educational Evaluation and Policy Analysis* 9, no. 2 (summer 1987): 133–152; Stephen H. Linder and B. Guy Peters, "Instruments of Government: Perceptions and Contexts," *Journal of Public Policy* 9, no. 1 (1989):

35–58; Donald Kettl, *Government by Proxy: (Mis?)Managing Federal Programs* (Washington, D.C.: Congressional Quarterly Press, 1988); Lester M. Salamon, ed., *Beyond Privatization: The Tools of Government Action* (Washington, D.C.: Urban Institute Press, 1989); Anne Schneider and Helen Ingram, "Behavioral Assumptions of Policy Tools," *Journal of Politics* 52, no. 2 (May 1990): 510–529; Marie-Louise Bemelmans-Videc, Ray C. Rist, and Evert Vedung, eds., *Carrots, Sticks and Sermons: Policy Instruments and Their Evaluation* (New Brunswick, NJ: Transaction Publishers, 1998). Beyond this, some individual tools have attracted considerable attention. For example, the tool of grants-in-aid has been thoroughly examined in a series of publications produced by the Advisory Committee on Intergovernmental Relations during the 1970s and early 1980s and in U.S. Office of Management and Budget, *Managing Federal Assistance in the 1980s* (Washington, D.C.: 1983). "Regulation" has been examined as a tool of public action in a number of studies, including Charles Schultze, *The Public Use of Private Interest* (Washington, D.C.: The Brookings Institution, 1977); and Neil Gunningham, Henry Grabosky, and Darren Sinclair. *Smart Regulation: Designing Environmental Policy* (Oxford: Oxford University Press, 1998).

24. Beverly Cigler, "A Sampling of Introductory Public Administration Texts," *Journal of Public Affairs Education* 6, no. 1 (January 2000): 48, 51. For evidence that some headway is being made, see David L. Weimer and Aidan R. Vining, *Policy Analysis: Concepts and Practice,* 3d ed. (Upper Saddle River, N.J.: Prentice-Hall, 1999), 196–252; and H. G. Frederickson, *The Spirit of Public Administration* (San Francisco: Jossey-Bass, 1997), 4–11, 78–96.

25. Salamon, *Beyond Privatization* (1989).

26. I am indebted to George Frederickson for his suggestion to use the term "governance" to depict what I earlier termed the "tools approach" to public problem solving. Frederickson uses the term "governance" to refer to a broader array of phenomena than is intended by the term here—namely, the processes of policy formation as well as implementation. The central idea of multiple stakeholders involved in the task of governing remains the same, however. As noted below, I have added the term "new" to the term "governance" to suggest a greater consciousness about the consequences of choices among tools and accompanying actors. See George Frederickson, *The Spirit of Public Administration* (1997), 78–96.

27. For a succinct summary of the classical theory see Ostrom, *The Intellectual Crisis in Public Administration* (1989), 20–41; Garvey, *Facing the Bureaucracy* (1993), 18–23. Similar concerns also lay behind the European development of administrative theory, as reflected in the work of Max Weber; Stillman, *Preface to Public Administration* (1999), 109–123.

28. For a vigorous defense of the American administrative state, see Charles Goodsell, *The Case for Bureaucracy: A Public Administration Polemic,* 3d ed. (Chatham, N.J.: Chatham House Publishers, 1994). For a discussion of the continuing vitality of "direct government" as a tool of government action, see Chapter 2 by Christopher Leman.

29. This line of argument also was evident in the public administration literature more generally. See, for example, Ostrom, *The Intellectual Crisis of American Public Administration* (1989).

30. See, for example, Pressman and Wildavsky, *Implementation* (1973); Hargrove, *The Missing Link* (July 1975); Donald S. Van Meter and Carl E. Van Horn, "The Policy Implementation Process: A Conceptual Framework," *Administration and Society* 6, no. 1 (February 1975), 447–474; Eugene Bardach, *The Implementation Game: What Happens after a Bill Becomes a Law* (Cambridge, Mass.: MIT Press, 1977); Walter Williams, *The Implementation Perspective: A Guide for Managing Social Service Delivery* (Berkeley: University of California Press, 1980); Robert T. Nakamura and Frank Smallwood, *The Politics of Policy Implementation* (New York: St. Martin's Press, 1980); Daniel Mazmanian and Paul Sabatier, *Implementation and Public Policy* (Glencoe, Ill.: Scott, Foresman, 1983).

31. Implementation studies have generated numerous lists of factors thought to influence program success but with limited progress in cumulating these findings into a more generalizable body of theory. One attempt to summarize this literature identifies no fewer than seventeen such factors that have so far been identified and need to be taken into account. Included here are such factors as the clarity of the law, the adequacy of the causal theory embodied in it, the multiplicity of decisions points, the characteristics of the implementing agencies, the presence of an implementation entrepreneur, and the adequacy of external review. Mazmanian and Sabatier, *Implementation and Public Policy* (1983). For a general discussion of the limited success of implemen-

tation studies in generating testable theory, see Helen Ingram, "Implementation: A Review and Suggested Framework," in *Public Administration: The State of the Discipline,* eds. Naomi B. Lynn and Aaron Wildavsky (Chatham, N.J.: Chatham House Publishers, 1990), 463; Calista, "Policy Implementation," in *Encyclopedia of Policy Studies,* ed. Stuart Nagel (New York: Marcel Dekker, 1994), 118.

32. Michael Howlett, "Policy Instruments, Policy Styles, and Policy Implementation: National Approaches to Theories of Instrument Choice," *Policy Studies Journal* 19, no. 2 (spring 1991): 1–21.

33. For a discussion of these theories, see Moe, "The New Economics of Organization" (1984), 762–768; Garvey, *Facing the Bureaucracy* (1993), 26–33.

34. E. S. Savas, *Privatization: The Key to Effective Government* (Chatham, N.J.: Chatham House Publishers, 1987); Stuart Butler, *Privatizing Federal Spending: A Strategy to Eliminate the Deficit* (New York: Universe Books, 1985).

35. S. J. Burki and G. E. Perry, *Beyond the Washington Consensus,* 125. Osborne and Gaebler, *Reinventing Government* (1998), 20. For a general discussion of the new public management agenda of which the reinventing government perspective is a part, see Kaul, "The New Public Administration" (1997), 13–26; Larry Terry, "Administrative Leadership, Neo-Managerialism, and the Public Management Movement" 58, no. 3 (May/June 1998): 194–2000; Hughes, "New Public Management," (1998), 1490; Chrisopher Pollitt, *Managerialism and the Public Services: Cuts or Cultural Change in the 1990s* (London: Blackwell, 1993).

36. Moe, "New Economics of Organization" (1984), 749–757; John W. Pratt and Richard J. Zeckhauser, "Principals and Agents: An Overview," in *Principals and Agents: The Strategy of Business,* eds. John W. Pratt and Richard J. Zeckhauser (Cambridge, Mass.: Harvard Business School Press, 1991 [1985]).

37. J. A. de Bruijn and E. F. ten Heuvelhof, "Instruments for Network Management," in *Managing Complex Networks: Strategies for the Public Sector,* eds. Walter J. M. Kickert, Erik-Hans Klijn, and Joop F. M. Koppenjan (London: Sage Publications, 1997), 122–123.

38. W. J. M. Kickert, E.-H. Klijn, and J. F. M. Koppenjan, "Introduction: A Management Perspective on Policy Networks," in *Managing Complex Networks,* eds. Walter J. M. Kickert, Erik-Hans Klijn, and Joop F. M. Koppenjan (1997), 33.

39. Ronald Moe, "Exploring the Limits of Privatization," *Public Administration Review* (November/December 1987): 453–460.

40. As Ronald Reagan put it in 1981, "We have let the state take away the things that were once ours to do voluntarily." For further discussion of this perspective as it applies to the non-profit sector, see Lester M. Salamon and Alan J. Abramson, "The Nonprofit Sector," in *The Reagan Experiment,* eds. John L. Palmer and Isabel V. Sawhill (Washington, D.C.: Urban Institute Press, 1982), 223–224.

41. For a discussion of the theoretical basis for government-nonprofit cooperation in these terms, see Lester M. Salamon, *Partners in Public Service* (1995), 33–49.

42. See, for example, James Austen, *The Collaboration Challenge: How Nonprofits and Businesses Succeed through Strategic Alliances* (San Francisco: Jossey-Bass, 2000); Reynold Levy, *Give and Take: A Candid Account of Corporate Philanthropy* (Cambridge, Mass.: Harvard Business School Press, 1999).

43. See, for example, Schultze, *The Public Use of Private Interest* (1977).

44. Kettl, *Sharing Power* (1993), 6. See also Robert W. Bailey, "Uses and Misuses of Privatization," in *Prospects for Privatization: Proceedings of the American Academy of Political Science,* ed. Steve Hanke, 36, no. 3 (1987), 150.

45. Burki and Perry, *Beyond the Washington Consensus: Institutions Matter* (1998).

46. World Bank, *World Development Report* (Washington, D.C.: World Bank Group, 1997), 1.

47. Dennis Rondinelli, "Privatization, Governance, and Public Management: The Challenges Ahead," *Business and the Contemporary World* 10, no. 2 (1998), 167.

48. Negotiation and persuasion operate within administrative agencies as well, of course. In the new governance, however, they are clearly the dominant form of management action.

49. Luther Gulick, "Notes on the Theory of Organization," in *Papers on the Science of Admin-*

istration, eds. Luther Gulick and Lyndall Urwick (New York: Institute for Public Administration, 1937), 13.

50. See, for example, Hughes, "New Public Management" (1998), 1489–1490; Christopher Pollitt, *Managerialism and the Public Service* (1993), 6–10.

51. W. J. M. Kickert and J. F. M. Koppenjan, "Public Management and Network Management: An Overview," in *Managing Complex Networks,* eds. Kickert et al. (1997), 50.

52. See, for example, Ruth Hoogland DeHoog, "Human Service Contracting: Environmental, Behavioral, and Organizational Conditions," *Administration and Society* 16 (1985), 427–454.

53. For a discussion of such civic initiatives, see Carmen Sirianni, *Civic Innovation in America: Community Empowerment, Public Policy, and the Movement for Civic Renewal* (Berkeley: University of California Press, 2001).

54. Edward Skloot, "Privatization, Competition, and the Future of Human Services," Unpublished paper prepared for delivery at the Council on Foundations Conference, New Orleans (21 April 1999).

55. Eugene Bardach and Robert A. Kagan, *Going by the Book: The Problem of Regulatory Unreasonableness: A Twentieth Century Fund Report* (Philadelphia: Temple University Press, 1982), 123–151. Peter May develops this point more fully in Chapter 5.

56. See, for example, Ruth Hoogland DeHoog, "Competition, Negotiation, or Cooperation: Three Models for Service Contracting," *Administration and Society* 22, no. 3 (November 1990): 317–340.

57. Michael Lipsky, *Street-Level Bureaucracy* (New York: Russell Sage Foundation, 1980).

58. This definition is quite similar to that suggested by Evert Vedung, who defines public policy instruments as "the set of techniques by which governmental authorities wield power in attempting to ensure support and effect or prevent social change." Evert Vedung, "Policy Instruments: Typologies and Theories," in *Carrots, Sticks, and Sermons,* eds. Bemelmans-Videc et al. (1998), 21.

59. This usage is close to that suggested by the "new institutionalism," particularly in economics. As economic historian Douglas North puts it, institutions are "regularities in repetitive interactions . . . customs and rules that provide a set of incentives and disincentives for individuals." Douglas North, "The New Institutional Economics," *Journal of Institutional and Theoretical Economics* 142 (1986): 231. For a broader discussion of the "new institutionalism," see Walter W. Powell and Paul J. DiMaggio, "Introduction," in *The New Institutionalism in Organizational Analysis,* eds. Walter W. Powell and Paul J. DiMaggio (Chicago: University of Chicago Press, 1991), 1–40.

60. For an argument that the difference between "block grants" and "categorical grants" is not sufficiently great to warrant treating them as different tools, see Paul E. Peterson, Barry G. Rabe, and Kenneth K. Wong, *When Federalism Works* (Washington, D.C.: The Brookings Institution, 1986), 21–23.

61. E. S. Savas, *Privatization: The Key to Effective Government,* 62; Osborne and Gaebler, *Reinventing Government,* 21; E. S. Kirschen et al., *Economic Policy in Our Time* (Amsterdam: North Holland Publishing, 1964); Gaebler and Osborne, *Reinventing Government* (1992). For a general discussion of the difficulties of comprehensive and authoritative lists of policy tools, see Linder and Peters, "The Design of Instruments for Public Policy: Groundwork for Empirical Research," in *Policy Theory and Policy Evaluation,* ed. Stuart Nagel (Westport, Conn.: Greenwood Press, 1990), 103–119.

62. Christopher Hood, *The Tools of Government* (1983).

63. McDonnell and Elmore, "Alternative Policy Instruments" (1987), 12.

64. Schneider and Ingram, "Behavioral Assumptions of Policy Tools" (1990), 514–521.

65. Evert Vedung, "Policy Instruments: Typologies and Theories," in *Carrots, Sticks, and Sermons,* eds. Bemelmans-Videc et al. (1998), 21–52. In the earlier version of this scheme, F. C. J. van der Doelen divided tools into three "families" based on the type of intervention the public sector uses: (1) the legal family, (2) the economic family, and (3) the communications family. See F. C. J. van der Doelen, *Instrumenten voor energiebesparing* (Enschede Netherlands: Universiteit Twente, 1993) cited in J. A. de Bruijn and E. F. ten Heuvelhof, "Instruments for Network Management," in *Managing Complex Networks,* eds. Kickert et al. (1997). On the general pop-

ularity of classifications using the degree of coercion as the central criterion, see Linder and
Peters, "The Design of Instruments for Public Policy," 114.

66. Hans DeBruijn and Hans A. M. Hufen, "The Traditional Approach to Policy Instruments,"
in *Public Policy Instruments: Evaluating the Tools of Public Administration*, eds. B. Guy Peters and
Frans K. M. van Nispen (Cheltenham, U.K.: Edward Elgar, 1998).

67. Theodore Lowi, "American Business, Public Policy, Case Studies, and Political Theory,"
World Politics 16 (1964): 677–715; Peterson, Rabe, and Wong, *When Federalism Works*, 15–20.

68. Pressman and Wildavsky, *Implementation* (1973), 143.

69. Howlett, "Policy Instruments, Policy Styles, and Policy Implementation," *Policy Studies
Journal* 19, no. 2 (1991): 1–21.

70. Anne Larson Schneider and Helen Ingram, *Policy Design for Democracy* (Lawrence: University Press of Kansas, 1997), 5–7, 129–135; Stephen Rathgeb Smith and Michael Lipsky, *Nonprofits for Hire: The Welfare State in the Age of Contracting* (Cambridge, Mass.: Harvard University
Press, 1993), 207–211.

71. Linder and Peters, "The Design of Instruments for Policy," 114; Vedung, "Policy Instruments: Typologies and Theories" (1998), 35–36.

72. For a detailed discussion of the types of market failures that serve as rationales for public
intervention, see Weimar and Viner, *Policy Analysis* (1999).

73. Charles Schultze, *Public Use of Private Interest* (1977). For a fuller discussion of these
market-oriented approaches, see Chapters 5 and 8.

74. Schultze, *Public Use of Private Interest* (1977), 57.

75. On the phenomenon of regulatory capture, see Merver Bernstein, *Regulating Business by
Independent Commission* (Princeton: Princeton University Press, 1955).

76. Differences in degree of directness also exist within tool categories. Thus, for example,
block grants are more indirect than categorical grants. Similarly, contracts for major military
systems are more indirect than contracts for the purchase of easily specified, off-the-shelf products since more discretion has to be left to the contractor in major systems acquisitions.

77. Daniel Elazar, *American Federalism: The View from the States* (New York: Thomas Y.
Crowell, 1973), 3.

78. On environmental policy, see Nancy Kubasek, *Environmental Law* (Englewood Cliffs, N.J.:
Prentice-Hall, 1990), 124–141. For a discussion of the role that Southern conservative opposition
played in the choice of a grant-in-aid with substantial state discretion for the nation's basic welfare
program, Aid to Dependent Children, see Lester M. Salamon, *Welfare: The Elusive Consensus*
(New York: Praeger, 1976).

79. Salamon and Anheier, "The Third Route: Government-Nonprofit Collaboration in Germany and the United States" (1998), 151–162.

80. See, for example, L. J. O'Toole, K. I. Hanf, and P. L. Hupe, "Managing Implementation
Processes in Networks," in *Managing Complex Networks*, eds. Kickert et al. (1998), 137.

81. Gordon Chase, "Implementing a Human Services Program: How Hard Will It Be?" *Public
Policy* 27 (fall 1979): 385–435.

82. Pressman and Wildavsky, *Implementation* (1973), 143.

83. Pressman and Wildavsky, *Implementation* (1973), 133.

84. Christopher Leman, "Direct Government: The Forgotten Fundamental," in *Beyond Privatization: The Tools of Government Action*, ed. Lester M. Salamon (1989), 3–38. For an update
of this analysis, see Chapter 2.

85. John W. Pratt and Richard J. Zeckhauser, "Principals and Agents: An Overview" (1991),
11. On the importance of coincidence of "worldviews" in potentially minimizing principal-agent
problems, see William G. Ouchi, "Markets, Bureaucracies, and Clans," *Administrative Science
Quarterly* 25 (March 1980): 129–140.

86. Regina Herzlinger, *A Managerial Analysis of Federal Income Redistribution Mechanisms:
The Government as a Factory, Insurance Company, and Bank* (Cambridge, MA: Ballinger, 1979).

87. Smith and Lipsky, *Nonprofits for Hire* (1993), 207–211; Schneider and Ingram, *Policy
Design for Democracy* (1997), 5–7, 129–135. For further elaboration of this point, see Chapter 20.

88. Under the tradable permit system, a target is set for the total amount of pollution permitted
in an air quality district, but companies are free to purchase rights to emit pollutants in excess

of their fair share from other businesses in the same district. For a more detailed discussion of tradable pollution permits and corrective fees and charges as tools of public action, see Chapter 8.

89. Robert A. Levine, *Public Planning: Failure and Redirection* (New York: Basic Books, 1972), 17, 23.

90. Schultze, *The Public Use of Private Interest* (1977).

91. Levine, *Public Planning* (1972), viii.

92. Herzlinger, *Managerial Analysis,* 111.

93. For an analysis of the administrative challenges entailed in the application of market-based tools to environmental protection, see National Academy of Public Administration, *The Environment Goes to Market: The Implementation of Economic Incentives for Pollution Control* (Washington, D.C.: National Academy of Public Administration, July 1994).

94 Until very recently, in fact, tax expenditures did not show up in the regular budget documents or figure prominently in budget debates. This changed in the early 1990s when budget agreements stipulated that both tax and spending decisions had to be taken into explicit account when budgetary decisions were made.

95. Most economists would argue, for example, that cash benefits are more efficient than in-kind benefits since they allow beneficiaries to utilize resources where they value them the most. However, in-kind tools such as vouchers and loan guarantees have substantial political advantages since they can often mobilize producer interests in support of particular programs and neutralize opponents who fear that recipients will squander benefits on purposes other than those intended.

96. Consumer-side subsidies such as vouchers and tax expenditures are thought to be more efficient because they allow consumers to shop for the best combination of service and cost. However, producer-side subsidies such as grants and contracts retain the political edge because they are more likely to stimulate producer-side political support.

Direct Government

Christopher K. Leman

When budgetary brinkmanship interrupted U.S. federal appropriations twice for a total of twenty-six days between November 1995 and January 1996, fewer than one-third of all federal employees were sent home. More than 1.9 million employees remained at their jobs as authorized by the 1884 Antideficiency Act, which provides that when appropriations have lapsed, the government cannot incur obligations or accept voluntary services "except for emergencies involving the safety of human life or the protection of property."[1]

Most of the federal employees sent home were those that had been conducting the government's business indirectly and whose absence certainly inconvenienced contractors, borrowers, grantees, state or local agencies, the regulated sector, and others reliant on indirect government. However, the direct government employees who remained on the job during these "shutdowns" had a right to feel that they were protecting human life and property.

Thanks to their efforts:

Disaster did not strike. The Federal Aviation Administration continued to guide air traffic and the Coast Guard to guide ships at sea. The National Aeronautics and Space Administration (NASA) continued to operate the space shuttle Atlantis (aloft when the November 1995 shutdown began). The Department of Veterans Affairs and the military hospitals continued in-patient and emergency medical care. Inspectors for the U.S. Department of Agriculture continued to test for diseased meat. The five power marketing administrations continued to distribute electricity.

The nation was not defenseless. The Department of Defense continued its vigilance and the Department of State its diplomacy. The Coast Guard continued to assist the Border Patrol in safeguarding the nation's borders and coastlines. The Federal Bureau of Investigation, Drug Enforcement Administration, Bureau of Alcohol, Tobacco, and Firearms, Customs Service, and Secret Service continued to combat smuggling, fraud, kidnapping, illegal sale of machine guns and explosives, terrorism, and assaults on public figures. The Bureau of Prisons and the military prisons did not release the thousands of convicts under their custody.

Government property and facilities remained secure. Many different agencies continued to maintain their portions of the one billion acres of federally owned land. The General Services Administration's Federal Telecommunications Service remained open (to operate the federal phone system), as did many other in-house communications and computing offices in the various agencies. The Government Printing Office (GPO) continued to publish the Congressional Record, the Federal Register, passports for the State Department, and postal cards for the U.S. Postal Service, and to operate Web sites giving free electronic access to government publications.

The national economy was maintained. Treasury Department agencies continued to service the monetary and banking system and the stock exchanges and maintained faith with the government's creditors by continuing to collect taxes. The Naval Observatory's atomic clock continued to keep the official time, and the National Institute of Standards and Technology continued to broadcast that time around the world. The National Weather Service continued many of its data-gathering and forecasting efforts (relied on by every private weather forecasting company). The Patent and Trademark Office continued to process protections for new inventions and trademarks. Social Security checks to retirees, survivors, and the disabled continued to be written, and the U.S. Postal Service continued to deliver them.

When the shutdowns did affect the direct federal provision of goods and services, these incidents were widely lamented. The Centers for Disease Control and Prevention suspended public health training and surveillance of disease and greatly cut back laboratory services provided to health departments and institutions. The Bureau of Labor Statistics delayed the issuance of the Consumer Price Index. The Bureau of Indian Affairs ceased processing federal royalty payments for over 25,000 Native Americans. The Minerals Management Service ceased the issuance of leases and permits for oil and gas development on the federally owned outer continental shelf. The Library of Congress locked its doors and closed its Web sites, including coverage of Congress—which was debating possible ways out of the budgetary impasse that caused the shutdown.

This episode is hard to square with the themes of failure and disappointment in much of the public and scholarly assessment of government in recent decades.[2] It better matches the upbeat evaluations of government performance prior to the 1960s, when the emphasis was on governmental success and effectiveness.[3] This chapter explores the intriguing possibility that the difference in tone between the two eras is no accident: the earlier discussion of successes focused on the direct government provision of goods and services, while the later discussion of failure focused on programs that embody the more indirect tools that government is increasingly using.

Government's indirect tools have attracted much attention recently because they are the most numerous and expensive being used, and they have far-reaching and controversial impacts. However, pessimistic lessons drawn from the indirect government experience miss the point that many direct government activities have been and continue to be more successful than those carried out indirectly. In its very success, of course, direct government has a built-in risk of going to excess; partly for that reason, any democracy will place limits on it. Yet, direct government remains a "forgotten fundamental" that bears reexamination.[4]

I. DEFINING THE TOOL OF DIRECT GOVERNMENT

This section defines the tool of direct government and relates it to other tools in terms of four basic features—*directness, automaticity, coerciveness,* and *visibility.* It then discusses important ways that direct government differs from the tools of indirect government, and yet it is interrelated with them in practice. The section concludes with a fourfold classification of the tasks of direct government based on the challenge of managing them.

Defining Features

Direct government is the delivery or withholding of a good or service by government employees. With this tool, government is quintessentially in a direct role in the same way as are the millions of families, religious groups, community organizations, charities, and small businesses that people depend on for the necessities of life and the pursuit of happiness. Indirect government turns to such human institutions as its mode of delivery, but direct government is more like them in itself having a direct relationship with the consumers of its goods and services.

Relation to Key Tool Features

Directness

By definition, direct provision of a good or service is done through a government agency rather than through a third party as in more indirect tools. In this sense, direct government represents the "command and control" approach that economist Charles Schultze has contrasted with nonadministered, marketlike mechanisms.[5]

An inescapable feature of direct government is the use of bureaucracy to mobilize resources and to carry out decisions. While bureaucracy has many drawbacks, it has the distinct advantage of internalizing transactions that must often be handled through complex contractual relationships in indirect government. Direct government thus can paradoxically be more flexible and responsive than indirect government since changes in operations can be handled internally, whereas complex legal relationships between government and its third-party partners must be amended in the case of indirect tools.[6] The highly formalized specification, bidding, and dispute resolution processes described by Steven Kelman in his chapter on contracting illustrates this point.

To be sure, every agency that directly delivers goods or services also makes some use of indirect means, if only in procuring office supplies, plane tickets, or consultant help. The classification of a program as direct government is not compromised when it relies on goods and services provided by others so long as the government agency remains centrally involved in the delivery of the good or service to the citizenry.[7] In fact, not all the people working in direct government need be government workers. Indeed, in the United States, faced with ceilings on the number of government employees, government agencies increasingly have relied on contract employees, who are on contract but receive their main supervision from the agencies themselves, and these contract employees are so closely integrated into the direct delivery of goods and services that they are best seen as a part of the direct tool rather than as a tool of indirect government.

A government agency can exercise the same functions both directly and indirectly, and in a complementary way, as when the National Institutes of Health directly operate the world's largest complex of biomedical research laboratories while also indirectly funding a larger research effort outside the federal government. The Government Printing Office does a great deal of printing and retail sales, but it also procures from the private sector about three-quarters of its printing and makes government documents available through universities and public libraries through the Federal Depository Library Program.

Direct government agencies can also carry out work under contract from other agencies and from nonprofit groups, businesses, or individuals. U.S. post offices (then a completely direct governmental agency) were an essential resource in registering millions of Americans for the newly formed Social Security program of the 1930s.[8] A large proportion of the income of the National Institute of Standards and Technology and the U.S. Geological Survey comes in the form of payments for goods and services from other federal agencies, state and local agencies, and corporations. Almost 10 percent of the workload of the Social Security Administration is on the behalf of other agencies. Under contract with the Department of Energy, the Forest Service manages 150,000 acres of timberlands on the Savannah River Reservation, acreage larger than some of its own national forests.

Automaticity

Automaticity measures the extent to which a tool utilizes an existing administrative structure (e.g., the market system or the tax system) to produce its effects rather than having to create its own special administrative apparatus. In this sense, direct government is perhaps the least automatic of all tools. Indeed, it is precisely its dependence on the instrumentalities of government that gives it its defining feature. In direct government programs, governmental agencies directly provide services, facilities, or products to citizens. To accomplish this, specialized agencies geared to this task must be created. This increases the amount of administration that is required, but it guarantees that the agencies and mechanisms enlisted for a particular task are specialized in it and therefore more likely to be equipped professionally to carry it out. Therefore, in no sense can the management of direct government be taken for granted. In indirect programs, by contrast, instrumentalities and processes designed for other purposes are enlisted to serve public purposes. This reduces the amount of governmental administration that is required but also means that the objectives of the public program and the skills, priorities, and standard operating procedures of the borrowed mechanism or instrumentalities may diverge.

Coerciveness

Coerciveness measures the extent to which a tool restricts or forces individual or group behavior as opposed to merely encouraging or discouraging it. Direct government is particularly suited to the exercise or threat of coercion. The use or threat of force is central to the national defense; it is also evident in the power of quarantine wielded by public health departments, in tax and tariff collection agencies' mandatory powers to force payment, in law enforcement agencies' maintenance of order, and in the work of prisons, jails, and mental institutions. If the courts allow, capital punishment can even end a person's life.

However, coerciveness is not inherent in direct government. Rather than use regulation to force action by some other level of government or by a business, nonprofit organization, or individual, a government agency can take that same action itself. Thus, rather than require employers or hospitals to offer free health care to eligible veterans, the U.S. government operates a network of medical centers to provide this free care directly. Similarly, many direct government programs, such as Social Security, involve the provision of subsidies or services.

Visibility

Direct government is generally quite visible to the public. The physical visibility of its installations and personnel is an important factor in its political viability. Because taxes are often the main source of funding for direct government, its costs can be found prominently displayed in public budget documents. The public can more easily associate these costs with results than is often the case with indirect government, where the budget indicates a transfer payment that is ultimately spent not by government but by a third party. Direct government (e.g., the Patent and Trademark Office, Federal Aviation Administration, Bureau of the Census, and the various land and water management agencies) sometimes generates fees and other revenue sources that are not as easy to spot in budgets and in the budgetary process.

Unlike some indirect tools such as regulation, whose main cost is borne not by government but by the private sector, the main cost of direct government is on budget. Citizens pay through taxes and other charges for what they are getting from direct government.

Direct government activities also often have an inherent physical visibility. U.S. military bases are located in many states. State and local police, and local firefighters, are ubiquitous. Dams, locks, and fish ladders operated by the Army Corps of Engineers, Bureau of Reclamation, and various municipal utilities are among the largest tourist attractions in their vicinities. In rural and scenic parts of the country, many citizens have contact with personnel of the Forest Service, National Park Service, Fish and Wildlife Service, and Bureau of Land Management—agencies whose visibility is enhanced by employee uniforms, vehicles, and distinctive buildings. The millions of acres managed by these agencies are prominently identified with signs and have stunning scenery and inexpensive recreational facilities enjoyed by the touring public. Visitors cannot pass through most national parks without needing to stop at a booth staffed by a ranger.

Still, direct government can have hidden elements, too. For example, government-subsidized competition (e.g., public campgrounds), or government-enforced monopolies (e.g., postal delivery) can impose hidden costs on the private sector. What is more, citizens are often hard put to understand which of the taxes they pay go to support direct government—and which indirect government.

Design Features and Major Variants

While all programs embodying the tool of direct government share the features identified above, there are also significant variations in the nature of the tool from program to program. Broadly speaking, it is possible to differentiate three types of direct government programs based on the function being performed.

1. *Production Activities.* First, direct government can be used to produce and deliver goods and services. Examples here would be public education systems, water supply systems, Social Security, the Veterans Administration hospitals, and the activities of the Forest Service and the Park Service.

2. *Police Functions.* A second type of direct government program involves the legitimate exercise of force, which is a classic function of direct government. Traditional police work, national defense, the operation of prisons, the operation of the criminal justice system, and tax collection all fall under this general heading.

3. *Facilitative Functions.* Finally, direct government is often used to perform a variety of facilitative functions required for other institutions to be able to perform their roles. Included here would be the maintenance of a court system to permit the enforcement of contracts among private parties, the management of the currency, the operation of the postal system, and economic management more generally.

The reason these different functions are important to differentiate is that they require somewhat different management styles and procedures. In his 1989 book, *Bureaucracy,*[9] for example, political scientist James Q. Wilson argues that the ability of central managers to control the behavior of their subordinates in a bureaucratic organization, and hence the degree of centralization appropriate for the management of the organization, depends on whether the organization is engaged in production tasks (similar to the production activities above), procedural tasks (similar to the facilitative tasks above), craft tasks (the police functions above would likely fall into this category), or coping tasks (some of the production activities as well as some of the police functions might fall into this category). As reflected in Table 2-1, the outputs and outcomes of production tasks are observable, suggesting that they can be centrally directed. By contrast, coping tasks are much more difficult to direct centrally since much more depends on the discretion exercised by "street-level bureaucrats."[10] The remaining two types of tasks—procedural and craft—fall in between these two extremes.

II. PATTERNS OF USE OF DIRECT GOVERNMENT

At the federal, state, and local levels in the United States, the direct delivery of goods and services represents a major share of governmental employment but a smaller share of public spending. The direct government role in almost all other countries is greater than it is in the United States.

United States

Aside from the direct Social Security and other payments it makes to individuals, direct government accounts for only 9 percent of the federal budget (see Table 2-2). However, direct government functions engage a larger proportion—as much as two-thirds—of the federal workforce. Continuing many direct government services during the government "shutdowns" was feasible because these services did not cost much in comparison with the indirect government programs that were suspended.

Direct governmental provision of goods and services is deeply rooted in American history. The U.S. Mint, Bureau of the Census, Customs Service, National Institute of Standards and Technology, and armed services derive their authority from specific mentions in the U.S. Constitution itself and have origins dating to the earliest years of

TABLE 2-1 **Management Tasks and the Observability of Outputs and Outcomes**

	Outcomes Observable	Outcomes Unclear
Outputs observable	Production tasks	Procedural tasks
Outputs unclear	Craft tasks	Coping tasks

TABLE 2-2 **Shares of U.S. Federal Budget Spent Directly or through Intermediaries**

	Share of Federal Budget, 1995 (Percent)
Direct domestic goods and services	4
Direct armed services	5
Payments to individuals	58
Grants to state and local governments	5
Contracts with nongovernmental entities	13
Interest on the national debt	15
Total	100

SOURCE: Table is based on data in Donald F. Kettl et al., *Civil Service Reform: Building a Government That Works* (Washington, D.C.: The Brookings Institution, 1996), 12.

the Republic. A century after founding and closing two national banks, early in the twentieth century Congress created a powerful new Federal Reserve Board and consolidated coinage and currency in the U.S. Mint and the Bureau of Engraving and Printing.

Since early in the nineteenth century, the U.S. Army has constructed many navigation, flood control, and water supply projects, most of which it still operates. Federal debates over internal improvements were not so much over whether the federal government should get involved, but how much and where. The army also conducted much of the exploration of the continent (starting with army captains Meriwether Lewis and William Clark); managed Yellowstone National Park for forty-four years before the 1916 creation of the National Park Service; and completed the Washington Monument when the nonprofit group that started it ran into difficulties. The U.S. Navy (via the Naval Observatory) keeps the official time.[11] The U.S. federal government generates 5 percent of the nation's electricity, and is a major water wholesaler.

Direct delivery of goods and services is even more common at the state and local levels. As a result, state governments have two-thirds more employees than the federal government, and local governments have four times more employees than the federal government.[12] The colonies and then the states mustered their own militias, which, although they fought alongside the U.S. Army, were commanded by state appointees. Since 1903, the army has had the authority during wartime to command state National Guard units, but state appointees continue to command them during peacetime.[13]

Prior to the twentieth century, regular agencies of the states also constructed roads, waterways, harbors, and other internal improvements.[14] Although most road construction is now conducted under contract, state and local agencies directly do a lot of road maintenance, installation of signs, and operation of traffic signals. State and local agencies remain the dominant, direct providers of law enforcement, justice and corrections, fire protection, libraries, schooling, public health services, and social services. In the late nineteeth century, the cities greatly increased public works and public services, a role that continues today.[15] In the United States, local governments are the leading retailers of water, and they treat most residential wastewater and dispose of most solid waste.

Visits to state parks and to local parks, respectively, exceed those to national parks and national forests combined. Most enrollment in colleges and universities is in institutions operated by state or local governments. Similarly, most elementary and secondary students attend public schools operated by local school districts. Some cities even own and operate utilities that supply electricity to residents and businesses. Several state corrections systems have more employees and prisoners than does the federal Bureau of Prisons. State and local governments also provide libraries, schools, and public health and social services. Some also operate transit systems, ports, and airports, although this is more commonly done by special district governments.

Other Countries

In many other countries, government directly delivers a wider range of goods and services than it does in the United States. Nationalized industries are more common in virtually every other country. At one time or another, many national or state government agencies have produced and marketed oil, gas, steel, or electricity, and operated television networks and telephone systems. The United States is the only major country whose telecommunications network is entirely run by the private sector.

The rise of the "welfare state" in much of western Europe led to a substantial expansion of direct government, especially in the Scandinavian counties. Much of the health care, education, social welfare protections, and social services available in these countries is provided by direct government agencies. In the United Kingdom, most health care is provided through the National Health Service, a government agency. Similarly, in France, a long tradition of centralization has left critical domestic functions (such as education and social care) in governmental hands, although a substantial decentralization took place during the 1980s that shifted responsibility for some of these functions from the central government to provincial governments, many of which in turn enlisted the aid of nonprofit groups.[16]

III. BASIC MECHANICS

Whatever the nature of the activity to be carried out, direct government involves a number of common tasks. Four of these in particular seem most critical: (1) developing an organizational structure and assigning responsibility within it; (2) formulating an organizational culture and sense of mission; (3) recruiting, socializing, and managing human resources; and (4) securing and accounting for financial resources. Let us examine each of these in turn.

Structuring and Delegating Formal Authority

Bureaucracy is an administrative system that, quite remarkably, allows central authorities to delegate complex or faraway tasks with reasonable confidence that those responsible will carry them out. A first task in the operation of direct government therefore is to fashion an administrative structure to make and enforce assignments. A key question here is the determination of where formal decisionmaking authority is to be located.[17] Agency executives usually have the ultimate authority, but they are wise to delegate part of it to others, and to design an administrative structure in which it can be used effectively and accountably. There is only so much that can be ordered from on high. Field-level personnel have the knowledge and time to give administrative meaning to broad policies. As Peter Drucker has observed, "decentralization strengthens top management. It makes it more effective and more capable of doing its own tasks. It results in greater authority for top management."[18] Rosabeth Moss Kanter urges: "To expand power, share it."[19]

Box 2-1 presents a range of alternative techniques for structuring authority in direct government agencies. One of these, for example, is to rely on formal rules and orders. A rule applies to all in an organization, while an order is usually tailored to a specific employee. (Unwritten rules and expectations are a part of the organizational culture, discussed in the next section.) Although rules have gotten a bad press, not all rules are bad; in fact, good rules are essential to effective management. As Charles Perrow observes: "Rules do a lot of things in organizations: they protect as well as restrict; coordinate as well as block; channel effort as well as limit it; permit universalism as well as provide sanctuary for the inept; maintain stability as well as retard change; permit diversity as well as restrict it."[20]

BOX 2-1 *Techniques for Structuring and Delegating Authority*

- Rules and guidelines (laws, regulations, directives, manuals, and so forth)
- Orders and commands
- Reporting requirements
- Inspections and management reviews
- Agreements with those to whom power is delegated
- Decentralized administrative structure (divisions, districts)
- Matrix (dual lines of authority)
- Self-managed teams

With craft tasks and coping tasks, however, rules can proliferate without ever capturing the reality at the street level.[21] Rules (e.g., in police handling of suspects' evidence) strict enough to make abuses impossible would also render administration ineffective for good purposes as well. In fact, rules may leave such room for discretion that they may be more important in lending legitimacy than in influencing what the agency does.[22] In Donald Warwick's study of the State Department, although the department's leadership has no real control over employees in the field, congressional pressure leads them to adopt many useless rules that make the department less accountable and more difficult to manage.[23]

There are orders, and then there are orders. As Warren Bennis observes, an order does not have to be, "Don't think, dummy—Do what you're told!" An order can be, "Think! I'm not going to tell you what to do."[24] The American business theorist Mary Parker Follett remarked: " . . . how can you expect people merely to obey orders and at the same time to take that degree of responsibility which they should take? Indeed, in my experience, the people who enjoy following orders blindly, without any thought on their own part, are those who like thus to get rid of responsibility."[25]

The degree and nature of decentralization depend greatly on the nature of the task assigned to government. Divisions organized by product line or purpose are often preferred to those organized by function or process.[26] Geographic districts are also highly useful. Divisions responsible for production and process tasks, respectively, may use a "matrix" structure that requires field units to be accountable to two different perspectives in the agency. Reports, inspections, and management reviews put field personnel on notice that their actions are being monitored. While field personnel are known to resist certain rules and orders, they will generally wish to avoid the need for upper-level managers to intervene and overrule their decisions.

Integrating around a Culture and Mission

A hard-won lesson of human history and the recent management literature is that, necessary though it is to delegate, central managers must work actively to ensure that those to whom power is delegated will use it responsibly and not for their own ends. This does not mean that agencies must be tightly controlled from the center, however. Indeed, a central theme of the management literature is that delegated power is best managed not solely by force, but significantly through cooperation. An unrealistically formalized picture has sometimes been drawn from misinterpretation of German social theorist Max Weber's 1919 picture of the "ideal type" of bureaucratic authority.[27] In fact, Weber feared the abuse of bureaucratic power that was not leavened by traditional and personal authority. American management theorist Chester Barnard realistically combined the formal and the informal sides of bureaucracy, stressing that an organization's goals can be achieved only if balanced with the needs and consent of its members.[28]

The delegation of formal authority into a decentralized administrative structure therefore will fail to produce results unless it is reinforced by an organizational culture, a common set of cognitive perceptions and personal values and motivations.[29] Especially in the ambiguous world of craft and coping tasks, rules and orders will be stretched beyond the breaking point unless the organization's culture recognizes them as a means to an end.

In his 1957 classic, *Leadership in Administration,* sociologist Philip Selznick argued that if an organization's mission captures employees' imagination and emotions, they will pursue it enthusiastically for self-fulfillment rather than grudgingly by being commanded from above.[30] The values and perceptions prevalent in an organization are important means to attract and keep able employees and to make their decisions predictable. Large organizations face a particular challenge in maintaining an integrated organizational culture.[31]

Effective management of a public agency requires employees' agreement on what Selznick called its "distinctive competence," the mission that best sums up why the agency exists and what it is trying to do. An agency's mission has to do with both the substance of its tasks and how they are to be carried out. Important components include common thinking on the history and mission of the organization, the importance and quality of its work, how to treat colleagues and the public, and how decisions should be made (including which of the written rules should most be heeded).

Examples of direct government agencies whose distinctive central mission contributes to a highly functional organizational culture include the National Park Service, Social Security Administration, Federal Aviation Administration, and U.S. Mint. Pursuing conflicting missions invites ineffectiveness.[32] In its border duties, the Immigration and Naturalization Service struggles with the conflicting tasks of preventing illicit immigration, while also welcoming immigrants who arrive legally.[33]

An agency with a strong organizational culture can usually rationalize within its mission some tasks that seem not closely related to its signature tasks. The Social Security Administration has not only sent out checks, but also conducted Selective Service registration, assisted the Medicare program and the Internal Revenue Service, and recorded vested rights in pension plans.[34] A Forest Service internal consensus survived for decades even as the larger society became more divided on whether the agency was allowing too much or not enough logging in the national forests. However, the once-strong organizational culture of the Forest Service seems to have weakened in recent years as a result of internal disagreement in the professional worldviews of the various specialists, such as forest engineers, biologists, and hydrologists.

Box 2-2 lists techniques for promoting organizational culture and integration. The existing culture will have its own inertia, and an entire literature of "organization design" suggests ways to tweak it with new settings and interactions.[35] Managers can choose from an impressive range of work groups, teams, quality circles, retreats, and other integrative techniques that place an employee in new contexts. Staff meetings, newsletters, and e-mails, the layout of an office, handling of employee suggestions, training—all are management choices and should be carefully thought out, or they can have unintentionally negative impacts on the organizational culture.

Knowledgeable and visible involvement of executives and managers can boost any of these techniques. The leader's example is watched constantly and can have positive or negative consequences. The late John Stanford, a U.S. Army general who successfully managed a Georgia county and then Seattle's school system, recalled that parents and teachers initially assumed he would be a "Patton-esque commander, inflexible and abrasive, more able to order than to listen, willing to sacrifice our city's children for a questionable cause. But I also knew how far from the mark that was. Thirty years of leading in the military had taught me that most leaders are the antithesis of those traits. Leading means inspiring, not commanding."[36] Exec-

---

BOX 2-2 *Techniques for Integration around a Culture and Mission*

- Sincere and demonstrated leadership commitment to core values and beliefs
- Meetings (work unit, multiunit, "town meetings")
- Team building (e.g., quality circles, "brainstorming," retreats, sports)
- Labor-management partnerships
- Training (external or in-house), mentoring, coaching, the "implicit curriculum"
- Work groups (e.g., task forces, committees, project- or problem-solving teams)
- Newsletters, memos, e-mails, videos, to convey goals, stories, slogans
- Environmental design (e.g., office layout to encourage personal contact)
- Quality management measures and incentives
- Questionnaires, suggestion systems

utives and managers will be wise to demonstrate dedication and collegiality, to insist that employees be inclusive with one another, and to implement employee-initiated changes.

Selznick offers the hopeful view that leaders can help an agency recognize and promote a new mission and de-emphasize an outmoded one. Wilson is more pessimistic about possible change, stressing the extent to which the existing tasks of field operators shape an agency's culture and limit what is possible. Certainly, time is a limitation. Rainey recounts an instance in which many Social Security Administration employees were unaware of a set of strategic objectives that the agency's director had sent to them a year earlier.[37] The strategic objectives became more real throughout the agency only after the director held meetings in each of the agency's regions.

Selecting, Motivating, and Sanctioning Personnel

The success of formal rules and orders and of informal culture and integrative techniques is greatly dependent on having employees with skills and incentives that are up to the organization's tasks. The successful manager is careful in selecting employees for each position, appraising their progress, and encouraging good performance and discouraging poor performance.

Around the world, much government employment is covered by civil service laws designed to replace favoritism, prejudice, and the spoils system with more objective standards for hiring, promotion, firing, and discipline. Laws or regulations typically place a limit on the maximum that can be paid to any public employee and require the classification of positions into different specialties, each with qualifications and a salary range.

Governmentwide civil service laws and regulations that were originally adopted to establish a merit system are increasingly seen as a barrier by managers in the field who want more discretion to hire the right person, and quickly; to offer a competitive compensation package and pay raises; and to discipline and demote for poor performance.[38] Tenure protections can protect "deadwood," leaving less room for needed new personnel, while reductions in force often fall on those most recently hired. The system makes it difficult for managers to offer much merit pay (raises are mostly automatic and seniority related) or to correct poor employee performance.

Government agencies have less flexibility than business and nonprofit employers to offer higher salaries or bonuses for scarce specialties and for the highest managerial levels. Also, by its nature, government cannot offer any share of equity or profits. However, Rainey's survey of the literature finds that "below the highest levels of the organizations, pay levels are often fairly comparable in the public and private sectors."[39] To its permanent employees, government offers fairly generous retirement and health benefits, more vacation days per year, and greater security than is typical in the private sector.

Many government employees place an inherent value on working for the public and do not place as high a priority on money as do private sector employees.[40] As James Q. Wilson observes: "Those who argue that behavior of an organization is nothing more than the sum of the behaviors of its rationally self-interested members cannot account for an army at war.... What does matter are the rewards a soldier receives from other soldiers."[41]

Personnel management measures that have been used with some success in the exercise of direct government are shown in Box 2-3. Managers who find their discretion limited in awarding merit pay or bonuses often make use of other forms of reward. When promotion is not an immediate option, exemplary employees can be rewarded by improved job assignments, facilities, and administrative support. Dual career ladders can reward advancement in one or more technical specialties, while still allowing advancement in general management positions.

Employees do not always welcome transfers, but transfers can enrich their experience and can reduce the tunnel vision of each organizational unit. Narrow job assignments have a certain logic, but are often insufferable to those assigned them. Job redesign can add responsibilities or training that introduce a specialist to issues beyond that specialty. To manage conflict between occupational subcultures, managers can create settings highlighting what each specialty uniquely brings to the table, encouraging dialogue and adjustment.

In general, public agency managers have fewer techniques available to correct poorly performing employees than they do to encourage good performance. Poor performance is not only a waste of scarce resources, but a detriment to morale and the culture of success. Significant improvement is possible if a supervisor meets regularly with poorly performing employees to warn of concerns and monitor agreed-upon targets for improvement. However, performance appraisal raises difficult issues for supervisor and subordinate alike, and in many agencies these appraisals are not carried out as required, or may be superficially done and the results ignored. Concern over seeming to play favorites or to have it "in" for someone deters some managers from singling out subordinates one way

BOX 2-3 *Techniques for Personnel Management*

- Regular discussion and appraisal of performance
- Merit pay, extra time off
- Merit-based promotions and other assignments
- Bonuses, awards, recognition ceremonies, mementos
- Transfers among organizational divisions and locations
- Dual career ladders
- Work enhancement (job redesign, job rotation)
- Rewards for group performance
- Voluntary buyouts, no-layoff policy

or the other. However, personnel decisions must be used as a management tool and can be wielded in a way that is seen as being fair.

Although civil service protections make it difficult to dismiss or demote an employee based on performance alone, demotion and firing are much easier for employee misconduct (ethical or legal violations). Managers retain significant discretion to wield milder correctives such as changed responsibilities, transfers, and diminished facilities and administrative support. However, the time required to make a poorly performing employee "shape up or ship out" can be substantial—one reason why public agency managers do not always deal with this problem effectively.

Securing and Accounting for Financial Resources

A budget is a plan for how an organization is to spend the funds provided to it.[42] Although budgeting is important in business organizations, it is only one of several financial and accounting tools used. For public agencies, budgeting is absolutely central because elected officials and the public are so deeply concerned about the disposition of public money, and because they and agency managers themselves have few alternative techniques for giving direction.

The literature of accounting distinguishes between *financial accounting,* which largely responds to external standards and requirements, and *management accounting,* which is designed primarily to communicate and enforce objectives throughout the organization. In their contrast of financial accounting with management accounting, Robert Anthony and Glenn Welsch emphasize that management accounting is a means to an end, rather than an end in itself, and that it makes greater use of nonmonetary information and more emphasis on the future and has less need for precision than does financial accounting.[43]

The distinctive needs of financial accounting and management accounting can conflict. Regulators, lenders, and investors have so increased their demand for financial accounting information that corporations have neglected nonfinancial management accounting data that would help in achieving their key tasks.[44] Financial accounting can be especially expansive in public agencies, which, lacking measures of investment return, face greater scrutiny from legislators and the public on whether each dollar was spent as was agreed to in the budget.

BOX 2-4 *Techniques for Budgeting and Accounting and for Measuring Performance*

- Line-item budgeting
- Multiyear budgeting
- Program budgeting
- Performance budgeting
- Activity-based costing
- Financial accounting
- Management accounting
- Management by objectives
- Program evaluations
- Benchmarking
- Organizational report cards

In passing the Single Audit Act (1984, 1986), Congress recognized that concerns about financial accounting had reached such extremes that state or local agencies, nonprofit organizations, and businesses receiving federal funds were suffering productivity problems from repeated audits. Interestingly, the Single Audit Act does not apply to federal agencies themselves, whose management can suffer equally from duplicative audits.

By various names (management by objectives, performance or program budgeting, benchmarking, organizational report cards), techniques are available to build management accounting information for public agencies.[45] The key question is how closely to link a management accounting system to the budget. The negotiation of a budget can produce agreement on substantive outputs and their costs—targets that can be monitored while in progress and upon completion to assess performance. However, the special requirements of financial accounting are such that there can be an advantage to having a separate and more intuitive management accounting system that focuses on such matters as performance targets, benchmarks, and activity costs.[46]

Managing the Whole

Each of the four classes of techniques just discussed is, alone, insufficient for managing a public agency. In practice, all four must be used in combination, and success in each category depends on success in the others. Obviously, adequate and properly accounted-for funds are a presupposition for much else in an organization. Wise personnel decisions bring the effective employees in and up, while unwise personnel decisions are a drag on productivity and a blow to morale. An irrational structure of authority will foster a dysfunctional organizational culture, and vice versa.

Less obviously, positive choices in each of the above types of management techniques are also interdependent on one another. Philip Selznick argued that the leadership task is a dual one that relates ends and means: promote consensus on an appealing mission, and design an authority structure to achieve the mission.[47] Instances in which a leader has successfully founded a new public agency or revitalized an existing one typically demonstrate a recognition of the interrelationships among the four classes of techniques.[48]

Astute, positive leadership creates its own momentum. Hal Rainey observes: "For all the politics that surrounds public managers, experienced officials and observers still report that the skills, integrity, experience and expert knowledge of a public administrator can give that administrator a positive form of power with members of the or-

tion. Their apparent success in securing cooperation from subordinates sometimes only
reflects their ratification of what those in the field would have done anyway.

IV. TOOL SELECTION

Rationale

Direct government has often been relied on because it is the only tool that is readily
available. In the past, tools of indirect government were at an early stage of development, while direct government bureaucracies were already functioning. For example,
in the nineteenth century, a wide variety of responsibilities for public works construction and land management fell to the Department of Army. Of course, in recent decades
the tools of indirect government are also well developed, so there is more choice among
tools for a particular task.

In fact, the rise of indirect government has occasioned major debate over which are
the "inherently governmental functions" that should not be exercised by a contractor
or other indirect party.[50] Because Congress and the courts have been unwilling to
venture much into this territory, it is unlikely to be settled with any finality. The most
useful guidance is the Office of Federal Procurement Policy's Letter 92–1, which states
that "a function that is so intimately related to the public interest as to mandate performance by Government employees" includes activities "that require either the exercise of discretion" or "the casting of value judgments" for government decisions. The
decisions most at issue are those that:

1. Bind the United States to take or not take some action by contract, policy, regulation, authorization, order, or otherwise.

2. Determine, protect, and advance its economic, political, territorial, property, or
   other interests by military or diplomatic action, civil or criminal judicial proceedings, contract management, or otherwise.

3. Significantly affect the life, liberty, or property of private persons.

4. Commission, appoint, direct, or control officers or employees of the United States.

5. Exert ultimate control over the acquisition, use, or disposition of the property,
   real, or personal, tangible or intangible, of the United States, including the collection, control, or disbursement of appropriated and other federal funds.

More generally, it is possible to identify a number of situations where a putative case
exists for using the tool of direct government as opposed to more indirect tools.[51] These
situations include the following:

- *Where the exercise of legitimate force is involved.* Direct government is particularly
  appropriate in situations where deprivation of someone's life, liberty, or property
  is being contemplated. Government is, after all, the institution to which we look
  in a democracy for the legitimate exercise of force. Policing and incarceration
  functions therefore are appropriately handled through direct government unless a
  compelling case can be made that indirect tools offer a clear advantage and, even
  then, only within limits.

- *Where performance cannot easily be left to chance.* A second circumstance where
  the use of direct government is appropriate is in situations where a function is so
  critical that its performance cannot responsibly be left to chance. Such situations

arise where public health and welfare are directly threatened. Firefighting therefore is often handled by direct government as are certain critical public health functions, such as disease control. Similarly, key infrastructure functions such as air traffic control, the provision of postal services, and the maintenance of the money supply are appropriately direct government functions. To be sure, opinions can differ about which of these are truly critical functions and whether indirect tools can provide as reliable a supply as direct ones, but the more critical the function, the stronger the case for direct government.

• *Where equity considerations are especially important.* Direct government also makes sense where redistribution is a principal goal of policy. The reason for this is that the indirect tools of government inevitably bring into the operation of public programs the outlooks and perspectives of external actors—private banks, universities, nonprofit agencies, industrial corporations—and these actors rarely have as deep a commitment to the equity goals of the public sector as do government agencies. This is not to say that direct government is fully successful in promoting redistributive objectives either. Political forces often undermine the commitment of direct government to equity goals as well. However, direct government probably still has a better chance of achieving redistributive objectives than most of the indirect alternatives.

• *Where no effective market exists to supply a good or service or is likely to in the foreseeable future.* A fourth circumstance in which direct government makes sense is where private providers are unavailable to supply a service and seem unlikely to develop for a considerable period of time. Public education very likely developed in this country as a consequence of this consideration. Similarly, modern space travel would likely have been delayed had a decision not been made to create a direct government agency (i.e., NASA) to orchestrate the process and assume much of the initial risk. The same was true of satellite communication and secondary market purchases of mortgage loans. Indeed, absorbing risk appears to be one of the classic functions of direct government: for large undertakings in which the risk is so massive that private interests are not able, or not willing, to absorb them, direct government provides a useful solution. The dilemma, however, is to decide when direct government has satisfactorily performed its role and can retire.

• *Where the maintenance of some governmental capability is essential.* Finally, even where indirect tools are entirely appropriate, there may be a case for a direct government role in order to preserve government's capability to hold contractors and other indirect government actors responsible for their performance. Thus, for example, the National Institutes of Health in the United States maintains both an in-house research program and a more extensive external grant-supported program in order to retain in-house capability to set priorities and evaluate the results of the external effort. Similar arguments are made with respect to defense contracting and federal laboratories in the nuclear energy field.

Political Considerations

While there are compelling substantive reasons for preferring direct government over indirect government in numerous circumstances, these reasons are often not sufficient to overwhelm the political obstacles that often exist to direct government. In the United States, at least, these obstacles are considerable. They include a traditional ideological hostility to governmental intervention in private affairs, a federal structure that vests considerable legal and political power in state and local governments, and a political apparatus that gives private interests exceptional opportunities to resist governmental intrusions into their turf. Therefore, if indirect tools are often chosen where the circumstances for their effective operation are lacking, direct tools are often avoided where they would be most appropriate.

Clearly, a tradeoff exists between the administrative advantages a direct agency gains in not having to rely on states, localities, nonprofit organizations, or businesses to deliver its goods and services, and the political loss it sustains in not having these entities to support it when elected officials decide how to allocate resources. Even George Washington ran afoul of this reality, thwarted by opposition to his dream of a national university, but the states eagerly supported federal aid to their agricultural colleges, beginning with the Morrill Land Grant Act of 1862, the federal government's first major grant program.

Indeed, it is not an accident that the federal budget is made up largely of grants, contracts, loans, and other indirect programs. These programs operate through state and local governments, nonprofit organizations, and businesses, which thus strongly support them. It is inconceivable that these interests would permit a similarly large federal role if it were exerted directly on or in competition with them. This reality gives a political advantage to indirect government, placing an inherent limitation on the size of direct government except in those societies lacking a substantial nonprofit and private sector and independent state and local governments that can stand up to the central government.

Lacking powerful constituencies like those that benefit so directly from the indirect tools of government, the agencies that directly offer goods and services nevertheless can be quite effective at mobilizing the support that is available. These programs can benefit from the support of veterans, retirees, farmers, vacationers, Indians, boaters, airlines, bankers, and so on. When there is no well-organized group available, an agency sometimes will "grow its own," as did the National Resources and Conservation Service in creating more than three thousand soil and water conservation districts that use the agency's technical assistance—and lobby on its behalf.[52]

Not all direct government programs have a constituency that is organizable. Certain public goods—weights and measures, maps and weather information, embassies and consulates, control of rare diseases, disposal of radioactive waste—are in such general demand that the federal government is given the task almost by acclamation. Benefits of such programs are widely diffused throughout society so that they lack strong advocates. However, public recognition of the need for this governmental role can also be widespread. Public surveys find the Centers for Disease Control—whose employees many Americans will never encounter—to be among the most highly rated of federal agencies.[53]

The political barriers to direct government are greatest when a proposed program faces well-organized opposition without enjoying well-organized support. The Smithsonian Institution, whose museums are free, has deferred to the long-standing opposition to its expansion outside the Washington, D.C., area from other museums, which generally have an admission charge.

To survive, a direct government agency will sometimes make a part of its program indirect to turn potential opponents into constituents. Thus, for example, the Smithsonian has developed traveling shows (with an admission charge, shared with the host museum) that visit museums across the country—allowing it to cooperate rather than compete. Similarly, in order to maintain federal ownership of their lands, agencies like the Forest Service, Bureau of Land Management, and Fish and Wildlife Service have allowed private companies to purchase timber, farming, grazing, or mineral rights, and although state and local governments have no direct authority over federal lands, a system of "intragovernmental federalism" prevails that represents their concerns within Congress and the executive branch.[54] Critics argue that the resulting compromises have displaced the original goals of the direct government programs, as is more frequently the case with indirect government.[55]

Direct government programs can benefit politically from their inherent visibility. The U.S. Postal Service receives the highest favorable ratings among federal agencies in polls of Americans, attributable in part to the daily contact they have with their mail carrier. The contact that many Americans have had with National Park Service rangers and the agency's association with the nation's most beautiful and historic places undoubtedly contributes to the fact that it is among the most highly rated of federal agencies in public surveys.[56]

A net public relations plus for direct government programs has been their portrayal in movies, television shows, and books. Television viewers of earlier eras felt they would have enjoyed knowing bus driver Ralph Kramden, Marshal Matt Dillon, Sergeant Joe Friday, Gomer Pyle U.S.M.C., Sheriff Andy Taylor of *Mayberry R.F.D.,* and Captain Kirk of the Starship [*Enterprise.*] Government has not fared as well in more recent TV seasons. A 1999 study of 1,234 episodes on ABC, CBS, NBC, and Fox found that "Few memorable characters appear as civil servants, and those who do make a lasting impression often fit the stereotype of the officious, indifferent or inefficient government bureaucrat," with some having notably unpleasant personality traits. Postal employees had to hope that viewers were laughing with rather than at them as they watched the boring Cliff on [*Cheers*] and the scheming Newman on [*Seinfeld.*] Recent TV drama series (e.g., *Hill Street Blues, ER, NYPD Blue, Homicide,* and *The X-Files*) feature competent and dedicated central characters, but the governmental system portrayed is fundamentally corrupt and dysfunctional.[57]

V. MANAGEMENT CHALLENGES AND POTENTIAL RESPONSES

One of the great ironies of direct government is that many of its most significant management challenges derive not from the nature of the tool, but from efforts to control and constrain it. Certainly, in the United States, fear of excessive government control or abuse of public authority has been a powerful political force, leading to successive waves of reform that have added to existing protections against potential misuse or abuse of public funds and authority but have also significantly complicated the management of public agencies. The extensive body of law that grew up around government contracting as detailed in Chapter 9 of this volume provides a compelling illustration of this phenomenon, but so do the extensive rules that govern the hiring and firing of public servants, the complex procedures for promulgating government regulations, and the use of personnel ceilings and hiring freezes to control government spending.

To correct some of the rigidities that earlier reforms built into the operation of direct government, reforms drawn from the business world have been introduced in recent decades. However, like their predecessors, many of these recent reforms have also produced inadvertent results, often complicating the management of direct government rather than easing it. This is apparent in the experience with two major management reforms that have been debated over the last two decades: privatization and entrepreneurial government. Reformers' efforts might better have been directed toward a reform that did not happen—of the civil service system.

Recent decades have seen debate over proposals to move certain governmental activities into the private sector. Congress agreed to charter the Patent and Trademark Office as a "performance-based organization" that would look a lot like a government corporation, but it refused to do so with the air traffic system of the Federal Aviation Administration. In 1996, the Canadian national government did actually sell its air traffic system to a company whose directors represent airlines, general aviation, unionized workers, and the public.[58]

Debates on privatizing air traffic control and the award of patents and trademarks have been conducted fairly dispassionately. Such was not the case with ideological debates over Reagan-era proposals—considered but never formally endorsed by the White House—to sell off some of the public lands.[59] The passions for and against selling public lands tended to drive out thoughtful analysis of incremental opportunities to improve management of these lands. Politically, wholesale privatization was a loser because timber companies, ranchers, miners, dam builders, and recreationists already have extensive access to these public resources. The national parks, national forests, and other public lands clearly are important symbols of national identity and pride, so it is not clear how much civic energy need be devoted to proposals for their wholesale privatization.

Yet on a more piecemeal basis, contracting out of public services is widespread on the public lands and in other sectors traditionally handled as direct government. Ironically, this effort has been driven not by ideological critics, but by the agencies themselves as they continue to pursue their missions within increasingly tight ceilings on total personnel. With the growth in the number of activities that an agency contracts out, it is fair to ask at what point should government insist on maintaining some irreducible minimum presence. In an extreme case, the Environmental Protection Agency's Superfund (a program to clean up hazardous waste sites) relied on contractors for advice on how much the program should rely on contractors.[60]

It is certainly intriguing that so-called virtual corporations can exist with almost no institutional core, doing their work through contracting. However, the main constituency that these corporations need to satisfy is their stockholders. It is difficult to conceive of a "virtual" government agency because any such agency would have a far more diverse constituency with plenty of external expectations. Complying with budget and accounting rules and responding to requests from Congress and others would require plenty of staff. The most basic argument against further thinning of the ranks is that government needs to maintain a certain reserve capacity of resources and skills that can be mobilized in an emergency. On short notice, there is really no alternative available.

Entrepreneurial Government

Rather than replace parts of the government with businesses and nonprofit organizations, another recent reform movement aims to make government more businesslike.[61] The Clinton–Gore administration gave particular visibility to proposals to "banish bureaucracy" through "entrepreneurial government."[62] To "steer rather than row," government is urged to contract out routine functions. It is urged to reduce rules and to adopt a well-focused mission for each agency, to become more customer driven, and to make better use of markets, pricing, investment thinking, competition inside government, and competition in the private sector. Managers must be liberated from processes and budgetary fine print and given incentives and accountability for the results. Agencies must develop strategic plans that identify and track measures of performance.

As pointed out in Chapter 1, entrepreneurial government furthers the existing trend toward the reliance on other organizations to carry out government functions, and thus compounds rather than solves the problem of governance. Direct government has been less vulnerable to this impact of entrepreneurial government because direct government continues to internalize many transactions that indirect government must handle as a partnership with one or more outside groups.

Proponents of entrepreneurial government fail to recognize the extent to which direct government's success in internalizing transactions throws doubt on their argument that government should delegate more tasks to other organizations. Contrary to the imagery of top-level "steering" and lower-level "rowing" (a distinction similar to the long-discredited view of a neat division between politics and administration), street-level bureaucrats often exercise discretion in ways that give meaning to policies that cannot be fully elaborated at the commanding heights.

Other elements of entrepreneurial government that have to do with the internal management of any organization are highly applicable to direct government, but they were already in use long ago. Managers in the most successful direct government programs enjoy a well-focused mission, enjoy significant discretion amid rules and budgets, take a customer approach (many prefer to think of the citizens as being their overseers or partners), and are held accountable by superiors based on regularly measured results.[63]

Performance measurement such as is required of federal agencies by the Government Performance and Results Act of 1993 faces the problems that some forms of data cost more to collect than their benefit to decisionmakers, and that some outcomes cannot be measured at all. In earlier decades, quantification that was done for Planning-Programming-Budgeting Systems (PPBS) and other management systems was found to disadvantage certain purposes whose outcomes could not easily be measured or related to spending and outputs.[64]

Elected officials' seemingly unlimited appetite for financial accounting (justifying expenditures afterward) may displace effort that also needs to go into management accounting (ensuring that funds will produce certain outcomes). Recent Forest Service difficulties in establishing the newly required performance-based budget categories are attributable in part to the fact that the House and Senate appropriations committees insisted that the agency provide "the same level of detailed information that had been provided under the old budget structure."[65]

Another drawback of the entrepreneurial government model is that bureaucrats will tend to assert their own vision of the public interest, reducing their accountability to existing laws and budget direction.[66] The most effective public agencies succeed in large part because their employees sincerely believe in the value of the agencies' missions. There is always the temptation to use agency resources to advocate the agency's cause with elected officials or the general public. When agency resources are used for self-promotion, society as a whole is denied a fair fight on whether the agency's mission is in fact worth pursuing.

In recognition of agency tendencies toward self-promotion, Congress in 1919 made it a criminal offense to use appropriated funds to lobby for or against legislation, or to urge others to do so.[67] Various prohibitions in appropriations acts make agency-funded lobbying also a civil offense, although more general prohibitions of this sort are needed, both at the federal and the state and local levels. When agency lobbying is a civil offense, prosecutors, courts, and commissions are more willing to act against it, and citizens have more leverage to encourage agency compliance.

Deregulating the Civil Service

Largely untouched by recent reform efforts is the federal civil service system—probably the greatest difficulty facing U.S. direct government. Civil service laws and regulations got their start more than a century ago in a wave of reform that saw merit as threatened by patronage and nepotism. Meanwhile, the system has evolved in ways that make it difficult to hire, retain, and reward the most qualified, and to sanction or fire those not performing well.[68] The system features slow hiring processes, hyper-specialized positions and qualifications, automatic promotions, across-the-board raises, lifetime tenure, and seniority rights. If experienced managers do find their way through this labyrinth (see Section III), their success in spite of it is certainly faint praise for the civil service system, which should actively be assisting their efforts.

State governments (such as Georgia and Florida) and other countries (such as New Zealand, Australia, and the United Kingdom) have ambitiously reworked their civil service rules. Reforms have been more limited at the U.S. federal level; in fact, the elimination of the Federal Personnel Manual probably did more harm than good because many agencies simply readopted it as their own, leaving its complexities even less subject to governmentwide improvement. The main progress has been by allowing agencies to opt out of existing rules by adopting their own system. The growing list of agencies exercising this option includes the Department of Defense, the intelligence agencies, the Federal Aviation Administration, the Department of Veterans Affairs, and NASA.

VI. OVERALL ASSESSMENT

How well does direct government stack up then as a tool of government? This section seeks to answer this question by assessing direct government according to the criteria of *effectiveness, efficiency, equity, innovation and responsiveness,* and *legitimacy.*

Effectiveness

Effectiveness is the ability to reach a desired objective. A direct government agency has a very good chance of delivering on a reasonable assignment because it can draw on its own employees and physical resources. Even with very effective management, indirect government programs such as those that regulate or dispense grants often cannot attain their desired result because the ultimate policy outcome is in the hands of others. As Charles Schultze observed:

> The single most important characteristic of the newer forms of social intervention is that their success depends on forms of affecting the skills, attitudes, consumption habits, or production patterns of hundreds of millions of individuals, millions of business firms, and thousands of local units of government. . . . The boundaries of the "public administration" problem have leapt far beyond the question of how to effectively organize and run a public institution and now encompass the far more vexing question of how to change some aspect of the behavior of a whole society.[69]

Some purposes are most effectively carried out when integrated into an overall management process and the culture of an agency in ways that are difficult to specify in laws and regulations. The Social Security Administration's process for resolution of disputes and appeals over disability determinations is considerably simpler and more conclusive than would have emerged if these decisions were to be made by the courts.[70] Environmental laws like the National Environmental Policy Act and the Endangered Species Act have been implemented more successfully by agencies of direct government (e.g., the Army Corps of Engineers, National Resources and Conservation Service, and Forest Service) than by agencies whose indirect nature requires more sharing of power.[71]

Research on indirect government shows that the need to gain the cooperation of other organizations introduces potentially impassable roadblocks, requiring time and compromise that can frustrate the original purposes of intervention. Indirect government greatly depends on the cooperation of other organizations and on entrepreneurs inside and outside of government who can piece together the bargains needed for action. The vertical integration that characterizes direct government encompasses many of the key participants into a single agency. By not depending as much on other organizations, direct government can internalize many transactions and reduce their cost. In doing so, it is achieving some of the same economies as when a corporation finds it cheaper to manage its own employees to produce a good or service than to obtain it by contracting with another business.[72]

Transaction costs with indirect government can be fairly dramatic. In his chapter on the tort system (under which government's role is mainly to referee private parties' lawsuits that are often concluded by jury decisions), Peter Schuck points out that for every dollar received as compensation to those who sued for asbestos damages, litigants on both sides spent 39 cents. In contrast, the Social Security program, which regularly mails entitlement checks directly to individuals based on their eligibility criteria, has transaction costs that are well under ten cents for each dollar that recipients receive. Most disputes over Social Security payments are handled administratively rather than in the courts.[73]

Once internalized in government, a transaction still requires negotiations among an agency's hierarchical levels, geographic and functional divisions, or professional specialties, but managers have more opportunity for informal influence, and more authority to exert formal control, than do their indirect government counterparts. Where networks of other organizations are important to success in the direct delivery of goods and services, the agency responsible may be better equipped than indirect government agencies to manage that network effectively.

The successes of indirect government have almost invariably been stories of remarkable individuals desperately building and holding together coalitions that, at least temporarily, turn a network into a successful program. Direct government has as much or more leadership to draw on than the tools of indirect government, but its success is not quite so dependent on extraordinary leadership. Direct government successes have hinged less on unique individuals than on an organization's subunits negotiating undramatically with one another according to established processes.

Since it is widely agreed that government suffers from a shortage of leaders and entrepreneurs, it is of no small consequence that direct government agencies are a partial organizational substitute for them. Direct government can be aimless, incompetent, or corrupt, but these problems are usually more possible to correct than when similar problems arise with indirect government, where managers have few resources to make improvements.

In recent years, the agencies that deliver goods and services directly have had particular difficulty with their computer and software procurement. There have been successes, as with the army's design and purchase of VIABLE, an integrated system for managing personnel, payroll, and supply records.[74] However, computer acquisition and management problems have arisen even in agencies like the Federal Aviation Administration, Forest Service, Internal Revenue Service, and National Weather Service that have been seen traditionally as well managed. Undoubtedly, contributing to the problem is the difficulty in retaining employees (such as in the computer field) who can earn much more in the private sector than government is allowed to pay them, but the greater problem seems to have been a shortfall in the quite affordable skill of managing multiple contractors.[75]

Experience at printing from its own plant seems to carry over to the GPO's skills at contracting, as vendors describe its specifications as "the best the Government produces."[76] Keeping their hand in a direct production activity may help GPO managers avoid the oft-lamented transformation of indirect government administrators from "doers" to paymasters and auditors.

Political systems vary in the extent to which elected officials, with their short-term incentives, provide direct government agencies the funds needed to invest in major capital construction or renovation. Roger Noll's chapter tells how countries like Brazil, Japan, and Australia have instituted government corporations in place of the ministerial agencies that were underinvesting in telephone services, leaving customers with poor service and sometimes a long wait for an account and even for a dial tone. Still, the governments of France and other countries continue to provide telephone service directly and seem to invest sufficiently in needed capital improvements. U.S. federal and local utilities that provide water and power also do not neglect capital investments, although short-term budget crises can intervene, as when during its fiscal crisis of the mid-1970s, New York City terribly neglected the maintenance of its bridges.

Efficiency

Cost-effectiveness is the ability to achieve a given level of benefit most efficiently, that is, at a minimum cost. (Another, more global conception of efficiency ventures a judgment about society's overall welfare and productivity from a given size or role of government.) Under the Office of Management and Budget's Circular A-76, federal agencies since 1955 have been required to consider purchasing from businesses or nonprofit organizations any goods and services that are not inherently governmental and that can be obtained more cheaply outside government. Agencies are not required to contract out an activity if they can demonstrate through a bidding process the ability to conduct it themselves at a lower cost than if they were to contract out the activity. In practice, federal agencies have not subjected most of their activities to A-76 review.

However, some cost comparisons for an activity that would otherwise be conducted within government have suggested a savings to the public from contracting out of the activity. This finding is consistent with independent research findings that, when a private sector comparison exists, government provision of goods or services has often been found to be less cost-effective.[77] However, the situation is changing as a result of 1996 guidance for the A-76 process to encourage agencies to try to underbid private competition. Although government agencies have lost many of these competitions, they have won their share as well. Underbidding well-known corporations, the Agriculture Department's Kansas City–based National Information Technology Center won the contract to build a $250 million Federal Aviation Administration data center, and the Interior Department's Denver-based Administrative Support Center won the contract to provide payroll services for the Social Security Administration.[78] In addition to printing U.S. currency, the Bureau of Engraving and Printing prints stamps for the U.S. Postal Service, and currency and stamps for some foreign governments, successfully bidding against corporations and other national postal services.

Cost-effectiveness in agencies like the National Institute of Standards and Technology, National Weather Service, and Bureau of the Census has been encouraged by constant contact with their commercial customers. The auctioning of minerals and timber from the public lands introduces into the land management agencies a sensitivity to markets. Among the arguably least cost-effective of federal agencies have been those enjoying a monopoly in supplying the government's internal services, such as building management by the General Services Administration.

As Steven Kelman argues in his chapter, research showing an efficiency advantage of business over direct government provision of goods or services has largely focused on activities in which the performance criteria are easy to specify and monitor. However, such comparisons are more difficult for the thankless and difficult "coping" or "procedural" tasks that government takes on because no business or other social institution is willing to tackle them. Some tasks virtually require that government lose money.[79]

There is no monetary profit for government in guaranteeing the rights to administrative process, public documents, open public meetings, and so on, but in a broader sense, individual citizens and society as a whole certainly benefit from government's provision of these rights. Such rights are less widespread in the private sector, in part because they are more difficult to enforce there (as with the continuing difficulty of federal regulators in enforcing the "right to know" regarding toxic materials in privately owned factories and dumps).

Where procedural rights are seen as imposing excess costs, it ironically has proved easier with direct government than with indirect government to limit these costs. Whereas contracting is notoriously litigious, the degree of litigation with direct government programs has been much less, and sometimes actually prohibited, as is the case with questions about eligibility for direct cash payments from the Social Security Administration.

Equity

Equity—the effort to overcome economic inequalities among people—is a higher priority in government than in many other organizations. Equity questions seem easier to judge than other criteria. As James Q. Wilson observes, "We cannot easily say whether the pupils were educated, the streets made safer, or some diseases prevented; but we can say whether every pupil got the same textbook, every citizen got the same police response, and every patient got the same vaccine."[80]

Some programs are established specifically to provide a decent minimum to clients whose needs are not adequately addressed by private sector companies or government corporations. As pointed out in Chapter 3, loans offered by direct government agencies like the Department of Veterans Affairs are more solicitous of disadvantaged borrowers than those offered by government corporations, which act more like banks in their lending policies. If the Government Printing Office had been a government corporation, it would not have so effectively moved to provide free over the World Wide Web the electronic versions of documents that GPO formerly sold only in paper versions; for its initiative, the agency between 1993 and 1997 suffered a 30 percent drop in orders and a 16 percent drop in revenues, with further reductions in prospect.[81]

To be sure, the political alliances that sustain an agency can lead it to distribute its efforts more evenly across the country than efficiency, or equity, would recommend.

The location of many U.S. military bases has more to do with political than military necessity. The National Resources and Conservation Service traditionally deployed its technical assistance efforts rather broadly across the country, despite the fact that the problem of soil erosion was never evenly distributed and has shifted over time; efforts by several presidents to retarget the program have been largely frustrated by congressional opposition.[82] On the other hand, some agencies can effectively be captured by a region. Western clienteles will not allow the Bureau of Reclamation to construct water projects in the East (which has most of the nation's water) and have hampered the Bureau of Land Management in its efforts to reach out to more national constituencies.[83]

Innovation and Responsiveness

Contrary to the stereotypes, public agencies have been remarkably innovative, and much of this innovation has come from those involved with direct government. U.S. Army doctor Walter Reed was instrumental in ending yellow fever epidemics. Federal employees have been responsible for life- and labor-saving inventions, popular images like Smokey the Bear and Rosie the Riveter, architectural masterpieces like the U.S. Capitol Building, and charming parkways and structures in the national parks and forests. As federal employees, John Philip Sousa and Woody Guthrie wrote some musical favorites, and Walker Evans and Dorothea Lange did pioneering photography.

The U.S. Coast and Geodetic Survey and the U.S. Geological Survey pioneered survey and mapping methods now used throughout the world. The Forest Service created the American forestry profession, and by the 1920s had introduced the country to both industrial forestry and the preservation of wilderness areas. Innovative water project designs by the Army Corps of Engineers and the Bureau of Reclamation continue to be influential models throughout the world, even as controversy over the environmental impacts of such projects within the United States has pushed these agencies to develop equally large-scale ways to mitigate or undo the damage.

Since 1790, the U.S. Census has been the world's most regular and sophisticated census. To analyze the 1890 results, the Census Bureau was the first user of a punch card machine invented by its former employee Herman Hollerith, and after the patents expired the bureau developed refinements that were then adopted by his company, which later became International Business Machines (IBM). Analysis of the 1950 census was done partly with the first UNIVAC computer, which the National Institute of Standards of Technology (then the National Bureau of Standards) purchased for the Bureau of the Census, and which the two agencies had helped design. Other early users of computers—well before private industry—included the Social Security Administration, Internal Revenue Service, and the military services.[84]

However, an agency that welcomes innovations to help in its mission can also be hostile to innovations that threaten its mission. Deep-seated dedication to a mission becomes a drawback when this mission needs to be changed.[85] Thus, the Forest Service has been hostile to discussion of alternatives to public land ownership. The Army Corps of Engineers and Bureau of Reclamation have resisted economic analyses questioning the need for the water projects these agencies design. The Social Security Administration has not welcomed discussion of alternatives to the social insurance paradigm.[86]

The pluralism of organizations involved with indirect government encourages some forms of experimentation not found as often with direct government. The welfare reform changes that Congress adopted during the 1990s stemmed significantly from innovations that emerged from state and local welfare programs.

Political responsiveness means accountability to various interests and adjustment to their desires. Contrary to the stereotype of bureaucracy as being insulated from popular pressures, the agencies that directly deliver goods or services are subject to all kinds of directions and restraints. As pointed out in Chapter 3, the Internal Revenue Service receives constant pressure from the public, Congress, and the president to give special weight to the needs and rights of taxpayers, and as a result it is not as aggressive a tax collector as it would be if it were a government corporation.

Depending on the observer, the publics that make claims on an agency may seem either legitimate and deserving, or selfish and corrupting.[87] National-level pressures can be criticized as being remote, in contrast to "participatory democracy" at the grassroots. However, local pressures can be criticized as narrow threats to a national mandate that is best expressed through national laws and elected officials. It is difficult to generalize whether either direct government or indirect government is more subject to capture by a constituency. Charles McKinley showed in a remarkably detailed study that the size and stability of direct government agencies provide an effective framework for bargaining with external interests (for managing a network, in today's language).[88] On the other hand, a study of Britain, France, and Italy found that government enterprises were relatively unresponsive to government leaders and to the market alike.[89]

While competition between agencies has often been criticized as a source of friction and waste, it can be a tool for responsiveness. Overlap between missions invites active political competition by each to be the most effective, innovative, and efficient. Two or more of the military services compete not just in recruiting, but in ground force strategy, and airplane and missile hardware. Three federal agencies construct water projects and five have historic preservation functions. There are four major federal law enforcement agencies. Five federal agencies manage more than 20 million public land acres each.

A fair criticism of direct government is that it has difficulty responding as needs arise that require rapid increase or rearrangement in public employees and facilities. Steven Kelman's chapter has some interesting history on how NASA consciously relied on contracting for the huge, rapid space buildup of the 1960s. A similar buildup entirely federally staffed would have been difficult during the 1960s, and even more so today amid strict ceilings on total federal employment, but under wartime circumstances, direct government was the tool of choice for rapid mobilization.[90] Perhaps the single most impressive mobilization was the Manhattan Project, which, as a direct project of the War Department, secretly produced the world's first atomic bomb.[91]

If direct government agencies do not respond well to needs that require major re-deployment of employees and changes, however, neither do the tools of indirect government, if the experience of research laboratories is indicative. The direct federal Agricultural Research Service has 107 laboratories and 400,000 acres of experimental farms that better reflect agricultural issues of the past than those that are most pressing today or in the future, but federally supported researchers at state agricultural colleges have also been slow to adapt to new needs.[92] National laboratories operated under contract to the Departments of Defense and Energy have more rapidly taken on some new missions, but they have been just as resistant to proposals to redeploy employees and facilities to other locations, or to close down any laboratories.

Legitimacy

One final criterion in terms of which the tool of direct government can usefully be assessed is its political legitimacy. This criterion has special salience in a democracy because of the fears that often exist about unbridled governmental power and the potential it creates for infringement of citizen rights. Indeed, the real concern about direct government is not its ineffectiveness, but its potential overzealousness, its propensity to take tasks to excess. Certainly, history is rife with atrocities that would not have been possible without direct government involvement. Twentieth-century examples include the Armenian massacres, the Holocaust, the killing fields of Cambodia, and systematic killings in Bosnia and Kosovo. The twenty-first century will doubtless offer its own examples.

Even in democratic societies, authorities that should have kept the peace have sometimes led the violence. In Tulsa in 1921, a white mob that killed up to three hundred African-American men, women, and children, rendered thousands more as either homeless or refugees and leveled their prosperous residential and business district, included some of the Oklahoma National Guard and many individuals who had been deputized by the local sheriff.[93] At Ludlow in 1913, when mining company guards deputized by the local sheriff killed four men and a boy, the unarmed miners welcomed the Colorado National Guard, but soon found it staffed with some of the same mining company guards who proceeded to compound the massacre.[94]

In our own time as well, the FBI wiretapped and attempted to discredit and blackmail Martin Luther King, Jr. and other people of conscience.[95] Although the Bill of Rights was added to the U.S. Constitution by the states as a check on the federal government, its subsequent use has been directed mainly at state and local abuses, many of which went unpunished before the federal courts quite tardily began to apply its protections. The Jim Crow system of racial discrimination emerged under state and local government, whose police and courts enforced it for generations.[96] Even when, in the 1950s, the U.S. Supreme Court began to declare these abuses unconstitutional, southern state and local politicians pledged "massive resistance" and withheld the use of state and local police to enforce the rulings. To integrate the Little Rock, Arkansas, schools in adherence to the U.S. Constitution, President Eisenhower had to call on the U.S. Army. Well after this period, the Mississippi Sovereignty Commission continued a rear-guard action of illegal harassment against civil rights advocates.[97]

Thus, direct government is a double-edged sword. While capable of tremendous good, it also is capable of great harm. Many of the restrictions that make direct government appear so cumbersome and unresponsive at times derive, in fact, from the effort to avoid these harms. Generally speaking, these restrictions have proved effective. While abuses of power can and do occur everywhere, in many countries they are most notable for their rarity.

Reflecting this positive record, although public surveys that have been conducted in the United States and in Europe find that half or more of the public believe that government cannot "basically be trusted,"[98] when surveys ask people about their own experiences with direct government, such as with police, social workers, schoolteachers, and parks and transportation workers, levels of satisfaction range from 66 percent to 70 or 75 percent.[99]

VII. CONCLUSION AND FUTURE DIRECTIONS

This chapter demonstrates that, in contrast to the well-documented failures of indirect government, the direct government provision of goods and services has in many cases achieved its assigned mission. This high rate of success is partially attributable to the fact that the U.S. government has been kept from attempting direct government tasks at which it would be likely to fail. In other countries, government has undertaken additional commercial activities, with at best uneven results.

However, a more important reason for the success of direct government is simply that it is designed to succeed. The direct government delivery of goods and services depends far less on others for follow-through than do the tools of indirect government. Direct government has its share of failures, but many are less inherent in the situation than are those of indirect government. Failures can be remedied, and often are. With some governmental tasks, the spirit of the laws is best realized when the laws are implemented flexibly and with various unofficial adjustments rather than through contractual changes that require complex legal negotiations. The agencies of direct government have often achieved a responsiveness that belies the image of immovable or oppressive bureaucracy.

Evidence for the success of direct government is actually good news for indirect government as well. Many federal indirect program dollars are going to states and localities, which are using them, as assigned, to deliver goods and services directly to clients. A successful direct state or local program may make up for some of the deficiencies of indirect government at higher levels.

The very success of the tool of direct government is the major problem with it. Its characteristic drawback has been not in falling short, but in carrying its assigned goals to excess, so that the tool becomes an end in itself. Just as bureaucracies are difficult to establish, they are also difficult to redirect or disband, and can take on a life of their own. A mission may persist far beyond the need for it, much as in the tale of *The Sorcerer's Apprentice,* who brought a broom to life but could not reverse the spell when the broom's work was done.

Potential excesses have given Americans an instinctive distrust of direct government, discouraging its growth. These barriers help control the excesses of direct government, an outcome much to be desired, but they also lead to a reliance on indirect government even where direct government would perform better. In accepting a greater role for indirect government, we have sometimes preferred an ineffective tool to one that is more likely to succeed, leaving the impression that government cannot be made to work when in fact it can.

When direct government can work but is not politically acceptable, while indirect government is politically acceptable but proves to be unworkable, the temptation too often is to dispense with the governmental role entirely and often to leave problems unsolved. Perhaps by clarifying the relative advantages of direct government and the situations in which it is most germane, it will be possible to escape this dilemma at least in part. One thing, however, seems clear: despite the era of "third-party government" in which we find ourselves, the tool of direct government continues to have an important role to play.

ACKNOWLEDGMENTS

For comments and suggestions on earlier drafts, the author thanks Herbert Kaufman, Carolyn E. Krall, Craig B. Leman, Nancy F. Leman, Jeffrey Michka, Harvey M. Sapolsky, James Q. Wilson, Lester M. Salamon, and the other authors for this volume. The author can be reached at 85 E. Roanoke Street, Seattle, WA 98102, cleman@oo.net.

VIII. SUGGESTED READING

Goodsell, Charles. *The Case for Bureaucracy: A Public Administration Polemic.* 3d ed. Chatham, N.J.: Chatham House, 1994.
Kettl, Donald F., and H. Brinton Milward. *The State of Public Management.* Baltimore: Johns Hopkins University Press, 1996.

Lynn, Naomi B., and Aaron Wildavsky, eds. *Public Administration: The State of the Discipline.* Chatham, N.J.: Chatham House, 1990.

Mashaw, Jerry L. *Bureaucratic Justice: Managing Social Security Disability Claims.* New Haven: Yale University Press, 1983.

Selznick, Philip. *Leadership in Administration: A Sociological Interpretation.* New York: Harper, 1957. Reprinted in 1984 by University of California Press.

Warwick, Donald P. *A Theory of Public Bureaucracy: Politics, Personality, and Organization in the State Department.* Cambridge, Mass.: Harvard University Press, 1975.

Williamson, Oliver E. *Markets and Hierarchies: Analysis and Antitrust Implications, A Study in the Economics of Internal Organization.* New York: Free Press, 1975.

Wilson, James Q. *Bureaucracy: What Government Agencies Do and Why They Do It.* New York: Basic Books, 1989.

NOTES

1. The Antideficiency Act, 31 U.S. Code Section 1341–1342.

2. Jeffrey L. Pressman, *Federal Programs and City Politics: The Dynamics of the Aid Process in Oakland* (Berkeley: University of California Press, 1975); Jeffrey Pressman and Aaron Wildavsky, *Implementation,* 3d ed. (Berkeley: University of California Press, 1979).

3. Edward K. Banfield, *Government Project* (New York: Free Press, 1951); Herbert Kaufman, *The Forest Ranger: A Study in Administrative Behavior* (Baltimore: Johns Hopkins University Press for Resources for the Future, 1960); Herman K. Somers, *Presidential Agency: The Office of War Mobilization and Reconversion* (Cambridge, Mass.: Harvard University Press, 1951).

4. Christopher K. Leman, "The Forgotten Fundamental: Successes and Excesses of Direct Government," in *Beyond Privatization: The Tools of Government Action,* ed. Lester Salamon (Washington, D.C.: Urban Institute Press, 1989).

5. Charles Schultze, *The Public Use of Private Interest* (Washington, D.C.: The Brookings Institution, 1977).

6. See also John Dunlop, "The Limits of Legal Compulsion," *The Conference Board Record* (March 1976).

7. Of course, governmentwide regulations on procurement and on the hiring and firing of personnel could, in theory, be directive enough that an otherwise direct government program would be the indirect tool of the agency that administers these regulations.

8. Charles McKinley and Robert W. Frase, *Launching Social Security: A Capture-and-Record Account. 1935–1937* (Madison: University of Wisconsin Press, 1970).

9. James Q. Wilson, *Bureaucracy: What Government Agencies Do and Why They Do It* (New York: Basic Books, 1989). See also John J. DiIulio et al., "The Public Administration of James Q. Wilson: A Symposium on Bureaucracy," *Public Administration Review* 51, no. 3 (May/June 1991): 193–201; John W. Ellwood, "Political Science," in *The State of Public Management,* eds. Donald F. Kettl and H. Brinton Milward (Baltimore: Johns Hopkins University Press, 1996).

10. Michael Lipsky, *Street-Level Bureaucracy: Dilemmas of the Individual in Public Services.* (New York: Russell Sage Foundation, 1980).

11. R. G. Hall and W. J. Klepczynski, "Time Service," *Naval Research Reviews* (October 1976).

12. U.S. Census Bureau, *Statistical Abstract of the United States: 1999,* table 534.

13. Samuel P. Huntington, *The Soldier and the State: The Theory and Politics of Civil-Military Relations* (Cambridge, Mass.: Harvard University Press, 1957).

14. Oscar and Mary Handlin, *Commonwealth* (Cambridge, Mass.: Harvard University Press, 1948); Louis K. Hartz, *Economic Policy and Democratic Thought: Pennsylvania 1776–1860* (Cambridge, Mass.: Harvard University Press, 1968).

15. Jon C. Teaford, *The Unheralded Triumph: City Government in America, 1870–1900* (Baltimore: Johns Hopkins University Press, 1984).

16. Lester M. Salamon et al., *Global Civil Society: Dimensions of the Nonprofit Sector* (Baltimore: The Johns Hopkins Center for Civil Society Studies, 1998).

17. For summaries of the literature, see Peter M. Blau, *On the Nature of Organizations* (New

York: Wiley, 1974); Claude S. George, Jr., *History of Management Thought,* 2d ed. (Englewood Cliffs, N.J.: Prentice-Hall, 1972); Howard E. McCurdy, *Public Administration: A Bibliographic Guide to the Literature* (New York: Marcel Dekker, 1986); Henry Mintzberg, *The Structuring of Organizations* (Englewood Cliffs, N.J.: Prentice-Hall, 1979); Hal G. Rainey, *Understanding and Managing Public Organizations* (San Francisco: Jossey-Bass, 1991); and Wilson, *Bureaucracy.*

18. Peter Drucker, *Management: Tasks, Responsibilities, Practices* (New York: Harper and Row, 1973), 301–302.

19. Rosabeth Moss Kanter, "Power Failure in Management Circuits," *Harvard Business Review* (July–August 1979): 65–75.

20. Charles Perrow, *Complex Organizations,* 29–30.

21. Michael Lipsky, *Street-Level Bureaucracy: Dilemmas of the Individual in Public Services* (New York: Russell Sage, 1980), 14.

22. John W. Meyer and Brian Rowan, "The Structure of Educational Organizations," chap. 4 in Marshall W. Meyer and Associates, *Environments and Organizations* (San Francisco: Jossey-Bass, 1978).

23. Donald P. Warwick, *A Theory of Public Bureaucracy: Politics, Personality, and Organization in the State Department* (Cambridge, Mass.: Harvard University Press, 1975). Warwick observes (p. 215): "So long as bureaucrats remain a handy scapegoat for public frustration, they are unlikely to relinquish the comforts of a layered structure bedecked with regulations."

24. Warren Bennis, "Foreword," in Douglas McGregor, *The Human Side of Enterprise,* 25th anniversary printing (New York: McGraw-Hill, 1985), vii.

25. Mary Parker Follett, "The Giving of Orders," originally published in Henry C. Metcalf, eds., *Scientific Foundations of Business Administration* (Baltimore: Williams and Wilkins, 1926). Reprinted in *Classics of Public Administration,* eds. Jay M. Shafritz and Albert C. Hyde (Chicago: Dorsey Press, 1987).

26. Thomas H. Hammond, "In Defence of Luther Gulick's 'Notes on the Theory of Organization,'" *Public Administration* 68 (summer 1990): 169.

27. Max Weber, "Bureaucracy," chap. 6 in *From Max Weber: Essays in Sociology,* eds. H. H. Gerth and C. Wright Mills (New York: Oxford University Press, 1945). Originally published in German in 1919.

28. Chester Barnard, *The Functions of the Executive* (Cambridge, Mass.: Harvard University Press, 1938). Perrow relates that as a telephone executive and Depression-era local director of emergency relief, Barnard exerted formal authority more freely than his theory would have predicted. Charles Perrow, *Complex Organizations: A Critical Essay* (Glenview, Ill.: Scott, Foresman, 1979), chap. 2.

29. Janet Weiss, "Psychology," in Kettl and Milward, *The State of Public Management,* 118–142.

30. Philip Selznick, *Leadership in Administration: A Sociological Interpretation* (New York: Harper and Row, 1957).

31. Mintzberg, *The Structuring of Organizations;* Jay R. Galbraith, *Organization Design* (Reading, Mass.: Addison-Wesley, 1977).

32. Peter Drucker, "The Deadly Sins of Public Administration," *Public Administration Review* (March/April 1980); Wilson, *Bureaucracy.*

33. John Crewdson, *The Tarnished Door: The New Immigrants and the Transformation of America* (New York: Times Books, 1983); Milton Morris, *Immigration: The Beleaguered Bureaucracy* (Washington, D.C.: The Brookings Institution, 1985).

34. Jack S. Futterman, "The Social Security Administration's Recent Reorganizations and Related Administrative Problems," National Commission on Social Security, *Social Security in America's Future* (March 1981), Appendix E.

35. Mintzberg, *The Structuring of Organizations;* Galbraith, *Organization Design.*

36. John Stanford with Robin Simons, *Victory in Our Schools* (New York: Bantam, 1999).

37. Rainey, *Understanding and Managing Public Organizations,* 257.

38. Donald Kettl, Patricia Ingraham, Ronald P. Sanders, and Constance Horner, *Civil Service Reform: Building a Government That Works* (Washington, D.C.: The Brookings Institution Press, 1996).

39. Rainey, *Understanding and Managing Public Organizations,* 131.

40. Rainey, *Understanding and Managing Public Organizations,* 131.

41. Wilson, *Bureaucracy,* 45–46.

42. Aaron B. Wildavsky, *Budgeting: A Comparative Theory of Budgetary Processes* (Boston: Little, Brown, 1975).

43. Robert Anthony and Glenn A. Welsch, *Fundamentals of Management Accounting* (Homewood, IL: Irwin, 1977).

44. H. Thomas Johnson and Robert S. Kaplan, *Relevance Lost: The Rise and Fall of Management Accounting* (Boston: Harvard Business School Press, 1987).

45. See William Gorham and David L. Weimer, *Organizational Report Cards* (Cambridge, Mass.: Harvard University Press, 1997), 3–5 for a useful discussion of distinctions among various types of performance measures.

46. On activity-based costing, see Jonathan Walters, "A Dollar's Worth of Government," *Governing* 9, no. 10 (July 1996): 45–46.

47. Selznick, *Leadership in Administration,* 37.

48. Eugene Lewis, *Public Entrepreneurship: Toward A Theory of Bureaucratic Political Power* (Bloomington: Indiana University Press, 1980); Jameson W. Doig and Erwin C. Hargrove, *Leadership and Innovation: A Biographical Perspective on Entrepreneurs in Government* (Baltimore: Johns Hopkins University Press, 1987); Rainey, *Understanding and Managing Public Organizations.*

49. Rainey, *Understanding and Managing Public Organizations,* 75.

50. General Accounting Office, *Government Contractors: Are Service Contractors Performing Inherently Governmental Functions?* GGD-92–11 (1991); Paul Light, *The True Size of Government* (Washington, D.C.: The Brookings Institution, 1999).

51. This section draws heavily on Lester M. Salamon, "The New Governance and the Tools of Public Action: An Introduction," in this volume.

52. Charles M. Hardin, *The Politics of Agriculture: Soil Conservation and the Struggle for Power in Rural America* (Glencoe, Ill.: Free Press, 1952).

53. Pew Research Center for People and the Press, *Deconstructing Distrust: How Americans View Government* (Washington, D.C., 1998), 16.

54. Christopher K. Leman and Robert H. Nelson, "The Rise of Managerial Federalism: An Assessment of Benefits and Costs," *Environmental Law* 12, no. 4 (summer 1982): 981–1029.

55. Grant McConnell, *Private Power and American Democracy* (New York: Knopf, 1966).

56. Pew Research Center, *Deconstructing Distrust,* 16.

57. S. Robert Lichter, Linda S. Lichter, and Dan Amundson, *Images of Government in TV Entertainment* (Washington, D.C.: Center for Media and Public Affairs, 1999). This study (p. 110) found that three-fourths of the television shows broadcast between 1955 and 1974 affirmed the basic integrity of the legal and political system, whereas three-fifths of those broadcast since that portray the legal and political system as fundamentally corrupt and dysfunctional.

58. Matthew L. Wald, "Canada's Private Control Towers," *New York Times* (23 October 1999), C1.

59. Christopher K. Leman, "The Revolution of the Saints: The Ideology of Privatization and Its Consequences for the Public Lands," in *Selling the Federal Forests,* ed. Adrien E. Gamache (Seattle: College of Forest Resources, University of Washington, 1984).

60. John J. DiIulio, Jr., Gerald Garvey, and Donald F. Kettl, *Improving Government Performance: An Owner's Manual* (Washington, D.C.: The Brookings Institution, 1993), 21–22, 34.

61. The proposed new management systems have in fact sometimes conflicted, based on the different business models they are drawn from. For example, Total Quality Management (inspired by the successes of the late W. Edward Deming in helping make Japanese corporations more competitive after World War II) emphasizes a team approach, placing it somewhat in conflict with systems such as management by objectives and performance-based pay that operate primarily through individual managers. See Jonathan Walters, "Fad Mad," *Governing* 9, no. 12 (September 1996): 48–52.

62. David Osborne and Ted Gaebler, *Reinventing Government: How the Entrepreneurial Spirit is Transforming the Public Sector* (New York: Penguin, 1992); David Osborne and Peter Plastrik,

Banishing Bureaucracy: The Five Strategies for Reinventing Government (Reading, MA: Addison-Welsey, 1997); Al Gore, *Common Sense Government: Works Better and Costs Less* (New York: Random House, 1995).

63. See Kettl, *Reinventing Government,* 24–29, on problematics of the customer orientation.

64. Wildavsky, *Budgeting,* chap. 18; Allen Schick, "A Death in the Bureaucracy: The Demise of Federal PPB," *Public Administration Review* (March/April 1973); Leonard Merewitz and Stephen Sosnick, *The Budget's New Clothes* (Markham, 1971); Ida Hoos, *Systems Analysis in Public Policy: A Critique* (Berkeley: University of California Press, 1972); Richard Rose, *Managing Presidential Objectives* (New York: Free Press, 1976); Thomas H. Hammond and Jack H. Knott, *A Zero-Based Look at Zero-Base Budgeting* (New Brunswick, N.J.: Transaction Books, 1980).

65. General Accounting Office, *Forest Service Management: Little Has Changed as a Result of the Fiscal Year 1995 Budget Reforms,* RCED-99–2 (Washington, D.C., 1998).

66. Ronald C. Moe, "The President's Role as Chief Manager," chap. 15 in *The Managerial Presidency,* 2d ed., ed. James P. Pfiffner (College Station: Texas A&M Press, 1999).

67. Louis Fisher, "Lobbying with Appropriated Monies Act," in *General Management Laws: A Selective Compendium,* Congressional Research Service, Library of Congress (1999); General Accounting Office, *H.R. 3078, The Federal Agency Anti-Lobbying Act,* T-OGC-96–18 (Washington, D.C., 1996). Criminal prosecution under the Lobbying with Appropriated Monies Act is up to the Justice Department, but in the law's more than eighty years, no one has ever been prosecuted under it.

68. Kettl, Ingraham, Sanders, and Horner, *Civil Service Reform,* 93. Note that quite aside from any civil service law, in the 1990 opinion *Rutan v. Republican Party of Illinois,* the U.S. Supreme Court struck down political tests in public hiring.

69. Schultze, *The Public Use of Private Interest,* 12.

70. Jerry L. Mashaw, *Bureaucratic Justice: Managing Social Security Disability Claims* (New Haven: Yale University Press, 1983).

71. Environmental Law Institute, *NEPA in Action: Environmental Offices in Nineteen Federal Agencies. A Report to the Council on Environmental Quality* (Washington, D.C., 1981); Serge Taylor, *Making Bureaucracies Think: The Environmental Impact Statement Strategy of Administrative Reform* (Stanford, CA: Stanford University Press, 1984); Steven Lewis Yaffee, *Prohibitive Policy: Implementing the Federal Endangered Species Act* (Cambridge, Mass.: MIT Press, 1982); J. N. Clarke and D. McCool, *Staking Out the Terrain: Power Differentials among Natural Resources Management Agencies,* 2d ed. (Albany: State University of New York Press, 1996).

72. Oliver E. Williamson, *Markets and Hierarchies: Analysis and Antitrust Implications, A Study in the Economics of Internal Organization* (New York: Free Press, 1975); Oliver E. Williamson, *The Economic Institutions of Capitalism: Firms, Markets, Relational Contracting* (New York: Free Press, 1985); Christopher K. Leman, "The Concepts of Public and Private and Their Applicability to North American Lands," in *Land Rites and Wrongs: The Management, Regulation and Use of Land in Canada and the United States,* eds. Elliot J. Feldman and Michael A. Goldberg (Cambridge, Mass.: Lincoln Institute of Land Policy, 1987).

73. Mashaw, *Bureaucratic Justice.*

74. Donald F. Kettl, *Government by Proxy: (Mis?)Managing Federal Programs* (Washington, D.C.: Congressional Quarterly Press, 1988), 43–45.

75. Kettl, Ingraham, Sanders, and Horner, *Civil Service Reform.*

76. Booz, Allen, and Hamilton, *Management Audit of the Government Printing Office,* Executive Summary, Submitted to the General Accounting Office (21 May 1998), ES-6.

77. Wilson, *Bureaucracy.*

78. Michael E. Serlin, "In the Ring: Agencies Are Fighting It Out with Each Other and Private Companies to Buy and Sell Services on the Open Market," *Government Executive* (September 1997): 14–22.

79. Laurence Lynn, *Managing the Public's Businesses: The Job of the Government Executive* (New York: Basic Books, 1981), 126.

80. Wilson, *Bureaucracy,* 132.

81. Booz, Allen, and Hamilton, *Management Audit of the Government Printing Office,* ES-5.

82. Christopher K. Leman, "Political Dilemmas in Evaluating and Budgeting Soil Conservation

Programs: The RCA Process," in *Soil Conservation Policy, Institutions, and Incentives,* eds. Harold Halcrow, Melvin Cotner, and Earl Heady (Ankeny, Ia.: Soil Conservation Society of America, 1982).

83. Sally K. Fairfax, "Coming of Age in the Bureau of Land Management: Range Management in Search of a Gospel," in National Research Council/National Academy of Sciences, *Developing Strategies for Rangeland Management* (Boulder: Westview Press, 1984), 1715–1759.

84. Joseph W. Duncan and William C. Shelton, *Revolution in U.S. Government Statistics 1926–1976* (U.S. Department of Commerce, 1978).

85. Selznick, *Leadership in Administration;* Wilson, *Bureaucracy,* 222–223.

86. Martha Derthick, *Policy Making for Social Security* (Washington, D.C.: The Brookings Institution, 1979).

87. McConnell, *Private Power and American Democracy;* James Q. Wilson, *Political Organizations* (New York: Basic Books, 1973).

88. Charles W. McKinley, *The Management of Land and Related Water Resources in Oregon: A Case Study in Administrative Federalism* (Washington, D.C.: Resources for the Future, 1965).

89. Stephen Young, "A Comparison of Industrial Experiences," in *Planning, Politics, and Public Policy: The British, French, and Italian Experience,* eds. Jack Hayward and Michael Watson (Cambridge: Cambridge University Press, 1975), 147.

90. Herman P. Somers, *Presidential Agency: The Office of War Mobilization and Reconversion* (Cambridge, Mass.: Harvard University Press, 1951).

91. Nuel Pharr Davis, *Lawrence and Oppenheimer* (New York: Simon and Schuster, 1968).

92. James T. Bonnen, "Historical Sources of U.S. Agricultural Productivity: Implications for R & D Policy and Social Science Research," *American Journal of Agricultural Economics* 65, no. 5 (December 1983); General Accounting Office, *Agricultural Research: Information on Research System and USDA's Priority Setting* RCED-96–92 (Washington, D.C., 1996), 46.

93. Oklahoma Commission to Study the Tulsa Race Riot of 1921, *Tulsa Race Riot* (28 February 2001).

94. The state guard and local deputies shot to death a boy and eight men (including three prisoners, one of whom, a strike leader, was first bludgeoned by the Guard commander) and set fire to the tents, killing another eleven children and two women. A report for the U.S. Commission on Industrial Relations found that by 20 April 1914, the Colorado National Guard "no longer offered even a pretense of fairness or impartiality, and its units in the field had degenerated into a force of professional gunmen and adventurers who were economically dependent on and subservient to the will of the coal operators." (George P. West, Report on the Colorado Strike [1915], excerpted in *American Violence: A Documentary History,* eds. Richard Hofstadter and Michael Wallace [New York: Knopf, 1970]).

95. Sanford Ungar, *FBI* (Boston: Little, Brown, 1976).

96. C. Vann Woodward, *The Strange Career of Jim Crow,* 2d ed. (New York: Oxford University Press, 1966).

97. Kevin Sack, "Opened Files Reveal Secret Shame of Mississippi," *New York Times* (17 March 1998). Founded in 1956 to "preserve the Mississippi way of life," that state's Sovereignty Commission (closed in 1977) spied on the personal lives of sixty thousand citizens and used intimidation and false imprisonment to discourage civil rights efforts. The commission gave Ku Klux Klan members information on three civil rights workers that these members later murdered. The Commission also tampered with juries in the first two trials of the man who, after its abuses were exposed, was convicted at a third trial of assassinating Medgar Evers.

98. Pew Research Center, *Deconstructing Distrust,* 53.

99. Charles T. Goodsell, *The Case for Bureaucracy: A Public Administration Polemic,* 3d ed. (Chatham, N.J.: Chatham House Publishers, 1994), 25–29.

CHAPTER THREE

Government Corporations and Government-Sponsored Enterprises

Thomas H. Stanton and Ronald C. Moe

George S. Anderson is the executive vice president of the Government National Mortgage Association (Ginnie Mae), a U.S. government corporation that provides financing for the secondary market for home mortgages. Ginnie Mae provides a U.S. government guarantee for mortgage-backed securities that help to fund U.S. government housing programs. Currently, over $540 billion of Ginnie Mae–guaranteed mortgage-backed securities are outstanding.

Despite this immense volume of business, Anderson operates Ginnie Mae with an in-house staff of only sixty-five people, plus contractor staff of about seven hundred people. Anderson is a civil servant, and federal laws and policies limit his ability to make management decisions about the financial activities of Ginnie Mae or the resources that Ginnie Mae can dedicate to its operations.

Ginnie Mae is authorized to be headed by a president, an executive level III position with a salary that in 1999 was capped at $125,900 annually. That position has been vacant for two years, however, and Anderson, a member of the U.S. Senior Executive Service, is responsible for heading Ginnie Mae.

On January 1, 1999, Franklin D. Raines became the chairman and CEO of the Federal National Mortgage Association (Fannie Mae), a private investor-owned U.S. government-sponsored enterprise (GSE) that also provides financing for the secondary market for home mortgages. Fannie Mae buys mortgages for its portfolio and guarantees mortgage-backed securities. Fannie Mae issues debt obligations and mortgage-backed securities backed by an implicit rather than explicit U.S. government guarantee.

At the end of 1999, Fannie Mae held $575 billion of mortgages in portfolio and guaranteed another $679 billion of mortgage-backed securities. Fannie Mae has a staff of about thirty-eight hundred people plus ample contractor support. Mr. Raines is accountable to the board of directors of the company and, through the board, to shareholders. In 1998, his predecessor as CEO earned a compensation of $3.1 million, plus new stock options valued at more than $4 million, and recognized additional options from earlier years valued at $4.7 million.

Ginnie Mae and Fannie Mae represent two organizational forms, the government corporation and the GSE, respectively, that government can use to help provide public services. The contrast between Ginnie Mae and Fannie Mae highlights the fact that even though government corporations and GSEs may perform similar functions, they are quite different types of institution. The extensive presence of such organizations in some sectors of the U.S. economy makes it important that policymakers understand the strengths and limitations and the appropriate application of these organizational forms as tools of government policy.

I. DEFINING THE TOOL

81

CH 3:
GOVERNMENT
CORPORATIONS
AND
GOVERNMENT-
SPONSORED
ENTERPRISES

Defining Features

Governments usually create government corporations and GSEs to carry out activities of a businesslike nature. Government corporations and GSEs occupy an organizational space between pure government departments and pure private market enterprises. So many structural variations are possible that precise definitions are hard to apply. Indeed, the political process tends to adopt variations rather than technically pure types of organization. Critical distinctions relate to (1) whether government or private parties own and control the organization, (2) whether the organization is chartered to serve a public purpose rather than merely private purposes, and (3) the nature of the subsidies that the government grants to the organization.

In the United States, the important legal distinction that separates government corporations and GSEs is the difference between an "agency" of government and a government "instrumentality." An agency, including the government corporation, is a part of government.[1] By contrast, an instrumentality such as a GSE is an organization that carries out public purposes under law, but is not a part of government.[2]

The Government Corporation

Definition

A government corporation is a government agency, owned and controlled by government, which is set up as a separate corporate entity legally distinct from the rest of the government of which it is a part. This form is often used for activities that are expected to be revenue producing and potentially self-sustaining; however, this need not be the case.

Different countries use organizational terminology differently. The problem of definition also is compounded by organizational confusion within a country such as the United States, where the term "government corporation" has been applied to entities such as the Corporation for National and Community Service solely to convey the impression of a businesslike operation that is somehow unencumbered by bureaucratic constraints.[3]

In some countries, government corporations may include some private ownership, even though government generally controls the corporation.[4] State and local governments may establish government corporations in sectors such as transportation (e.g., a port authority), energy (a publicly owned utility company), agriculture and industry (the Township and Village Enterprises of China), and especially the financial sector (e.g., the state-owned Landesbanken in Germany or state or local housing finance agencies in the United States).

The government corporation, because it is a separate legal entity that can sue and be sued in its own name, rather than in the name of the larger government, constitutes an organizational form that overlaps with but is distinct from the terms "public enterprise" and "state-owned enterprise." Unlike many public enterprises, government corporations always are parts of the government.

The government corporation also differs from the usual government agency, however. Policymakers form government corporations to permit them to have greater operating flexibility than might be appropriate for the usual government agency. Because government corporations often fund themselves on a financially self-sustaining basis, it is unnecessary to subject them to the appropriations and budget limitations that restrict the ordinary government department or agency. Rather, government corporations are supposed to be free to use a business-type budget, retain revenues, and make investments without regard to the annual limitations of the government budget process.

This type of flexibility is warranted because of the logic of the government corporation: if the corporation is financially self-sustaining, then it does not compete with other government agencies for scarce appropriated funds. Moreover, a limitation on permitted expenditures by a government corporation is likely to cause a reduction in revenues that could have been raised if the expenditures had been made. Thus, if one tried, for example, to reduce spending by the U.S. Postal Service by, say, 3 percent, then one likely outcome might be that revenues of the Postal Service would decline by a similar amount.

By contrast, the ordinary agency of government spends money but does not earn revenues to cover the costs of its operations. For such an agency, the budget and annual appropriation help to allocate scarce governmental resources among the broad range of constituencies and public purposes that compete in the political process for the authority to spend scarce tax dollars.

Depending on the language of their particular charter acts, government corporations also benefit from other rules that are more flexible than would apply to ordinary departments and agencies.[5] Some government corporations may be subject to more flexible civil service and classification rules, procurement rules, and procedural rules that otherwise might require open meetings, for example.[6] The result of these flexibilities is that the government corporation gains added capacity to carry out its public purposes.

So established, the government corporation can facilitate government provision of goods or services. Many examples of direct government, such as power production, management of a port or airport facility, or provision of postal services, can be performed either through a government corporation or through an ordinary (i.e., noncorporate) government agency.

Government corporations also differ from so-called performance-based organizations (PBOs). Although the government corporation is a legally distinct entity, the PBO generally is not. Also, the government corporation in the United States is generally revenue producing and potentially self-sustaining, whereas PBOs may rely on appropriations of public funds. In other countries, the term "government corporation" may include organizations that are not revenue producing and function much as PBOs are intended to function in the United States.[7]

The Government-Sponsored Enterprise

Definition

In the American context, the government-sponsored enterprise, compared with the wholly owned government corporation, is a government-chartered, privately owned, and privately controlled institution that, while lacking an express government guarantee, benefits from the perception that the government stands behind its financial obligations.[8] In return for statutory privileges, including tax benefits and regulatory exemptions, as well as reduced borrowing costs, the GSE is confined by its charter to serving specified market segments through a limited range of services.[9]

Thus, the Fannie Mae and Freddie Mac charter acts limit them to serving as secondary mortgage market companies. That means that the GSEs may purchase and sell and securitize mortgages, but may not originate the loans. Mortgage origination is left

83

CH 3:
GOVERNMENT
CORPORATIONS
AND
GOVERNMENT-
SPONSORED
ENTERPRISES

to the so-called primary lender, which deals directly with the borrower. The Fannie Mae and Freddie Mac charter acts also limit the companies to dealing in mortgages up to a size that is prescribed by statutory formula (in 2000 the mortgage size limit was $252,700) and require that mortgages that the GSEs purchase must have loan-to-value ratios of less than 80 percent unless, with some exceptions, the mortgages are covered by private mortgage insurance.

As discussed more fully below, despite the detailed language of many GSE charter acts, it is not easy to specify a meaningful public purpose for a GSE in today's efficient markets. The GSE must be profitable, which means that the public purpose must yield economic returns to shareholders comparable to other market returns to investors. On the other hand, the GSE should serve public purposes that are not already being well served by other institutions in the market.

In return for accepting a statutory charter limiting its activities, the GSE obtains special benefits. These generally include tax exemptions, regulatory exemptions, and the authority to borrow substantial funds with the perception of implied government backing. In concept, the form and extent of special benefits should relate somehow to the public purposes that the GSE is supposed to serve; in practice, the GSEs enjoy their greatest financial benefits in forms that policymakers tend not to understand.

Of special note is the ability of GSEs to borrow in the federal agency credit market by issuing obligations that have many of the attributes of U.S. Treasury obligations. However, while the full faith and credit of the government expressly backs U.S. Treasury obligations, GSE obligations are backed by an implied government guarantee. The implied nature of the government guarantee keeps GSEs out of the federal budget. Nonetheless, it is a very real guarantee, and few investors expect that the government would allow any GSE to fail. This expectation was reinforced when the government bailed out the failed Farm Credit System in the mid-1980s and legislated to require banks to provide financial support for a GSE-like entity, the Financing Corporation, in 1996.

GSEs benefit from a related substantial privilege that is not spelled out explicitly in their charter acts. This is the ability to run a highly leveraged financial business with much less permanent shareholder capital than is required of other firms that conduct similar businesses. Thus, in 1999, Fannie Mae had a ratio of stockholder equity to assets plus outstanding guarantees of 1.41 percent; the Freddie Mac ratio was 1.25 percent.[10] This is several times the leverage that U.S. or international regulators would permit for commercial banks or thrift institutions in a comparable line of business.

For the private owners of a GSE, high leverage is a boon: GSE profits can be distributed among far fewer shareholders than otherwise would hold stock in the GSE, and thus they can enjoy significantly higher returns on their equity investments than would be possible if the GSE were capitalized according to more prudent standards. By contrast, as discussed below, thin capitalization means that the government has far less protection from the financial risk that arises from the government's implicit guarantee of GSE obligations. The combination of high leverage and the ability to issue virtually unlimited amounts of debt in the federal agency debt market mean that GSEs can achieve significant competitive advantages in some markets.

This competitive advantage relates to one other benefit of a GSE charter: it is a unique charter that is unavailable to other competitors (except for other GSEs) that provide similar financial services. In other words, the distinct package of financial, regulatory, and tax benefits and charter obligations that the law provides for Sallie Mae is not available to any other competitor. In the case of Fannie Mae and Freddie Mac, the two largest financial institutions in the United States, the law allows them to share a virtual monopoly in a major segment of the secondary mortgage market.

The relationship of the government corporation to the GSE is nicely seen in the separation of Fannie Mae from Ginnie Mae in the United States in 1968. Driven by a change in budget rules, the government decided to sell to private investors the right to engage in the more profitable part of funding the secondary mortgage market. Fannie Mae was transformed into a GSE with a special-purpose charter that encompassed the more profitable financing functions; the government sold stock to private shareholders and changed the nature of its guarantee from an explicit full-faith-and-credit obligation to an implicit obligation. In creating the GSE, the government privatized ownership and control of Fannie Mae but retained ultimate financial liability for the company's obligations. In the process, Ginnie Mae was created as a wholly owned government corporation, located within the Department of Housing and Urban Development, and charged with carrying out those subsidized activities not profitable enough to interest private investors.

Relation to Key Tool Features

The nature of government corporations and government-sponsored enterprises can be understood by examining how they relate to the four dimensions that this book uses to analyze each tool: *coerciveness, directness, automaticity,* and *visibility.*

Coerciveness

Coerciveness measures the extent to which a tool restricts individual or group behavior as opposed to merely encouraging or discouraging it. The coerciveness of a government corporation or GSE depends partly on the (1) goods or services that it provides and (2) the extent that it exerts market power or monopoly power over its customers. As a general rule, the government corporation or GSE interacts with users of its services on a commercial basis: the U.S. Postal Service (a government corporation in all but name) or the National Railroad Passenger Corporation (Amtrak) treats their users as customers who buy their goods and services. As such they are not highly coercive. On the other hand, the U.S. Postal Service is a national monopoly for certain classes of mail, backed by laws that restrict competition from other firms and prohibit customers from using any other entity. In that sense, a government corporation can be very coercive.

GSEs are similar. On one hand, private mortgage lenders and mortgage insurance companies are free to deal with whomever they please in the mortgage market. On the other hand, the government has given the GSEs so much market power that a mortgage lender or mortgage insurance company would be foolhardy to disregard the forms and procedures that Fannie Mae and Freddie Mac prescribe. The coerciveness may be informal, but it is very real. A GSE that possesses less market power, the Farm Credit System, is more constrained in the amount of influence that it may exert over its customers and potential customers.

In short, both government corporations and GSEs may rank low in their degree of coerciveness, but both can rank medium or even high, depending on their market power.

Directness

Directness measures the extent to which the entity authorizing or inaugurating a program is involved in carrying it out. Government corporations tend to be direct government and thus relatively high on this dimension. Some government corporations, such as Ginnie Mae, are largely indistinguishable from the government departments in which they are located. The law vests Ginnie Mae's powers in the Secretary of Housing and Urban Development rather than in the president of Ginnie Mae or the corporation itself. In many respects, Ginnie Mae is as tightly integrated into the department as is any other part of HUD. By contrast, other government corporations, such as the Tennessee Valley Authority (TVA), may exhibit substantial autonomy from the rest of the executive branch of government.

GSEs are not direct government at all. Instead, they often grow into economically and politically powerful institutions that are capable of resisting government efforts to make them more accountable. A Treasury Department report on Fannie Mae and Freddie Mac, the two largest GSEs, describes this as a problem, reflecting what it calls "the tension between profit and public purpose."[11]

Indeed, GSEs can, and usually do, become virtually autonomous from the government that charters them. GSEs usually try to expand the extent of their autonomy from year to year, both through amendments to their charter legislation and through expansion of the scope of their business activities. Thus, GSEs are low on directness.

Automaticity

Automaticity measures the extent to which a tool utilizes an existing administrative structure to produce its effect rather than having to create its own special administrative apparatus. Government must establish a government corporation and provide it with the staffing and resources needed to carry out its mission. Thus, government corporations are low on the dimension of automaticity. Depending on the particular context, it may or may not be easy to establish a government corporation as a financially viable entity. Many of today's U.S. government corporations, including TVA, Ginnie Mae, the Export-Import Bank, and the Federal Deposit Insurance Corporation (FDIC), trace their origins to the New Deal. The major government corporation of that era was the Reconstruction Finance Corporation, a financial behemoth that helped to channel government loans and equity investments into virtually all sectors of the economy.

Government must also create GSEs by enacting enabling legislation, but the private sector carries out much of the implementation. To the extent that government benefits confer a strong market position on a GSE, the GSE can expand with an automaticity that can surprise the policymakers who created it. Thus, for example, Freddie Mac began with little effort. The Congress chartered Freddie Mac in 1970 at the behest of the savings and loan industry and provided for an infusion of capital from the Federal Home Loan Bank System, another GSE that the thrift industry already owned.

On the other hand, it has been hard to establish some GSEs. The government established the Farm Credit System (FCS) in 1916 to provide an accessible source of credit for farmers. Parts of the FCS failed shortly after its inception because of a depression in rural agriculture in the 1920s. After the Great Depression began, the government supported the rural economy with a massive infusion of direct loans and loan guarantees through the RFC and the Federal Farm Mortgage Corporation, a government corporation. The government provided a direct infusion of capital to the twelve Federal Land Banks of the FCS, and the FCS repaid the government's investment by 1947. The FCS failed again in 1985, and again the government provided funds to return the system to solvency.

Visibility

Visibility measures the extent to which the resources devoted to a tool show up in the normal budget process. Although government corporations are hardly invisible in the federal budget, many of them are much less visible than comparable agencies that are

85

CH 3:
GOVERNMENT
CORPORATIONS
AND
GOVERNMENT-
SPONSORED
ENTERPRISES

not in corporate form. One reason for this is that the federal budget entries for government corporations may include business-type financial reports rather than the year-by-year federal accounting that is required of other government agencies.

The Credit Reform Act of 1990 has made some government corporations more visible than before. Because of the Credit Reform Act, government corporations such as the Overseas Private Investment Corporation (OPIC) and the ExIm Bank now must budget and account for their direct loans and loan guarantees annually in a manner consistent with the budget submissions of noncorporate government agencies. While this requirement increases visibility, it also appears to contradict the logic of the Government Corporation Control Act and its requirement that government corporations submit business-type budgets. Even so, government corporations tend to score lower on visibility than do other government agencies. This can be because the government corporation benefits from strong stakeholders that have a stake in low visibility, as in the case of TVA, or because the corporation is hidden within the much larger budget of its host department, as in the case of Ginnie Mae.

GSEs are even less visible to the public policy process: their activities are completely off budget. Indeed, it was the need to remove the government's secondary mortgage market operations from the federal budget that prompted the Johnson administration to propose the creation of Fannie Mae as a GSE in 1968. The government does bear a massive contingent liability from the perception of an implicit government guarantee of GSE obligations, but this implicit guarantee also is off budget.

Even when a GSE fails, the bailout may be off budget. This occurred in 1987, when the government created a Farm Credit System Assistance Corporation to provide an infusion of over a billion dollars into the failed FCS. Both the Assistance Corporation and the infusion, later repaid by the FCS, were off budget.

Indeed, some policymakers have used the invisibility of the GSE structure to provide massive amounts of public funding for unpopular purposes. Anxious to avoid public opprobrium for the savings and loan debacle, the government created two GSE-like entities, the Financing Corporation and the Resolution Funding Corporation, to provide many billions of dollars to pay off depositors in failed savings and loan institutions. The government preferred this approach to direct federal funding because of its virtual invisibility in the policy process.[12]

Design Features and Major Variants: Major Types of Government Corporations

All government corporations are separate legal entities that are granted a degree of operating flexibility to carry out their public purposes. They differ from one another in the organizational capacity provided by their charters, their governance structures, and the extent that they mix the legal attributes of public and private institutions, including ownership.

Organizational Capacity

The capacity of a government corporation is determined by the terms of its legal charter.[13] Important elements of capacity include access to (1) financial resources, through the authority to collect revenues in return for the goods or services that it provides and to borrow money to pay for investments, (2) staff and contractor resources, and (3) good program design so that the corporation in fact can be financially self-sustaining.[14] Government corporations vary considerably in the extent to which they enjoy such legal authority. This is particularly the case for government corporations that operate as a part of a larger governmental unit. For example, Ginnie Mae, which is a part of HUD, lacks the authority to carry out necessary personnel and procurement actions without clearing them through the extensive department processes. Therefore, the preferred approach is to allow the government corporation to carry out its own operations, such as staffing and procurement, independently of many of the administrative rules that may apply to the larger department.

87

CH 3:
GOVERNMENT
CORPORATIONS
AND
GOVERNMENT-
SPONSORED
ENTERPRISES

Governance

The statutes for some government corporations specify that cabinet members shall sit as *ex officio* members of the governing board. A board of directors that is composed of the Secretaries of Labor, Commerce, and the Treasury, for example, governs the Pension Benefit Guaranty Corporation. This is intended to help assure a balance among the three major constituencies for the PBGC guaranty: workers, employers, and the taxpayer. In fact, such a system of *ex officio* membership tends not to work well; the cabinet members or other designated official directors tend to appoint lower-ranking officials to represent them who generally lack the mandate to make serious substantive decisions. The result can be quite detrimental to the corporation.

Another governance issue involves the question of whether the corporation should be governed by a single head or by a multimember board. In the United States, single-headed corporations include those whose work is considered to be primarily operational rather than laden with political content. Single-headed corporations include Ginnie Mae and the St. Lawrence Seaway Development Corporation. Government corporations headed by a board include most of the others, such as Amtrak, TVA, the U.S. Postal Service, and Federal Prison Industries.

In contrast to this mixed pattern, a major report of a panel of the National Academy of Public Administration strongly urges that a single administrator head government corporations. The report argues that in government a multimember board of directors is susceptible to being split by a variety of policy differences; in contrast to a shareholder-owned private corporation, the directors of a government corporation lack the legal obligation to shareholders that could help to promote consensus.[15]

Governmental Versus Private Attributes

U.S. legislation may confuse public and private attributes in government corporations. The Congress has created the Corporation for Public Broadcasting and the Legal Services Corporation, for example, and prescribed by law that they would be designated as private nonprofit corporations. This designation of private status is singularly inappropriate given that the president of the United States appoints all members of their corporate boards of directors and the Congress has appropriated literally billions of dollars to fund their operations.[16]

If Congress goes too far, the judiciary occasionally will set limits on the mixture of public and private attributes. Thus, the 1981 NAPA panel stated that it was a "misleading fiction" for government corporations such as Amtrak, the Legal Services Corporation or the Securities Investor Protection Corporation to be deemed by statute to be private corporations that were not agencies or instrumentalities of the United States. Since the panel wrote its report, the U.S. Supreme Court, in a case involving Amtrak, has affirmed that Amtrak indeed is a government corporation, and a part of the government for some constitutional purposes.[17]

In contrast, other countries may impose different types of distinctions between public and private aspects of government corporations. In civil law countries such as France, definitions become critical in determining the nature of the law that applies to government corporations. Government corporations operate differently if they are subject to public law rather than private corporation laws.

In many countries, and especially those whose laws are based on those of the United Kingdom, the government may sell ownership stakes in government corporations that range from minority private ownership to 100 percent private ownership. Yet, so long as government appoints its directors and managers, it is a government corporation for purposes of carrying out governmental functions. Even some partially privatized public enterprises in which private shareholders own a majority of the stock may remain under some government control. This may be accomplished through the device known as the "golden share" that permits government to exert control over affairs of the corporation.[18] No such leeway is permitted under U.S. budget rules.[19]

Major Types of GSEs

Significant differences also exist among GSEs, with respect to (1) ownership and governance structure, (2) whether they are created to be one single company or a group of companies, and (3) the mix of government and private attributes in their charters.

Ownership and Governance

GSEs are privately owned companies. They are governed by the terms of their charter acts and by the bylaws that they adopt, and sometimes they may require assistance from their regulator to help settle a point of corporation law that is not spelled out in their charter. There is no federal law of corporations to help resolve questions of shareholder rights, responsibilities of directors, and other matters, except as these may be inferred from general legal principles. This makes it important to spell out such matters in the GSE's enabling legislation. To address this issue, the charter act might provide that, to the extent consistent with federal law, shareholders in an investor-owned GSE shall have the rights relative to the GSE and its management that are accorded to shareholders under the Business Corporation Act of the District of Columbia.

Most GSE-enabling acts vest direction of the GSE in a board of directors, a majority of whom is elected by its shareholders. A minority of GSE directors is appointed by the president of the United States, or by a federal regulator, as the case may be. The Fannie Mae and Freddie Mac charter acts, for example, prescribe that shareholders elect thirteen out of eighteen members of the board of directors, and the president of the United States appoints the other five. The two charter acts further prescribe that, of the presidentially appointed directors, at least one shall be from the home-building industry, one from the mortgage lending industry, and one from the real estate industry.

While such presidential appointments add to the perception that the government stands behind the obligations of a GSE, such directors add virtually nothing to the government's ability to influence the activities of the GSE. The law of corporations is clear that all directors of a GSE, whether shareholder elected or not, owe a fiduciary responsibility to the company and its shareholders. The investor-owned GSEs reinforce this legal obligation by awarding generous stock options to all directors, including those appointed by the president of the United States, so that they gain a direct personal interest in increasing the annual profits of the GSE.

For most of the GSEs, the board of directors selects the chief executive officer of the company. The CEOs of the more profitable GSEs tend to be compensated generously, with stock options constituting a good part of the compensation package. Officers and employees of GSEs are part of the private sector; they are not government workers, and their compensation tends to be much more generous than anything that a government official might aspire to while in government. Today this is true even of CEOs of the GSEs that function as cooperatives.

GSEs may be organized as investor-owned companies or as cooperatives. The choice between these two forms of enterprise plays a major role in determining the behavior and life cycle of a GSE. Fannie Mae, Freddie Mac, Sallie Mae, and Farmer Mac all are investor-owned companies. Their shares (with some variations) trade on the New York Stock Exchange. Their directors and corporate officers are compensated with packages that include stock options and a consequent incentive to maximize profitability of the firm.

89

CH 3:
GOVERNMENT
CORPORATIONS
AND
GOVERNMENT-
SPONSORED
ENTERPRISES

Fannie Mae, Freddie Mac, and Sallie Mae are among the most profitable and most consistently profitable financial institutions in the United States. They seek to expand their franchise, for example, by expanding their market power into the primary market to provide services that otherwise would be provided by the lenders that are their customers and that originate loans to sell to the GSEs.

By contrast, the Farm Credit System and Federal Home Loan Bank System are co-operatives, owned and governed by people or firms that benefit from their services. The dynamics of a cooperative are quite different from those of the investor-owned firm.

Cooperative ownership means that a GSE will not compete with its member-owners. Thus, the Federal Home Loan Banks, owned by financial institutions, seek to enhance the profitability of its members rather than trying to displace them. While Fannie Mae and Freddie Mac (investor-owned GSEs) have deployed new technologies to help make substantial inroads into the profits of mortgage lenders, the Federal Home Loan Banks have remained somewhat behind. With the exception of one program first developed by the Federal Home Loan Bank of Chicago to fund home mortgages in a new and potentially profitable way, the primary purpose of the Federal Home Loan Banks con-tinues to be to channel inexpensive federal agency funds for the use of their members.

Corporate Structure

A second variation among GSEs relates to whether they are a single company, similar to Fannie Mae, Freddie Mac, and Sallie Mae, or whether they are multiple companies within a system such as the banks of the Federal Home Loan Bank System or the Farm Credit System. If the GSE is created as a single company, then it is difficult for effective competition to emerge, except possibly from another GSE. If the GSE is a system, then it is possible that competition can emerge among the institutions of the system, thereby enhancing the likelihood that the GSE will serve its public purposes more effectively, rather than trying to keep monopoly profits for itself.

Indeed, the Roosevelt administration attempted to go one step further in the direc-tion of multiple chartering. The 1934 National Housing Act contained provisions that allowed any incorporator willing to commit the necessary capital, and accept the bene-fits and limitations of the federal legislation, to obtain a charter for a so-called National Mortgage Association. This created a chartering process that would have been quite similar to the structure for chartering National Banks or federal thrift institutions. No incorporators applied for such charters,[20] and the Roosevelt administration then created Fannie Mae, at first as a wholly owned government corporation subsidiary of the Re-construction Finance Corporation. Given the benefits of competition, it would seem as if the option of granting multiple charters to GSEs through a government regulator is preferable to the alternatives.

Public-Private Mix

The third variation among GSEs relates to the mix of government and private attributes in their charters. As a general rule, it is risky to try to impose government control or to confer governmental powers and immunities on private companies. Freddie Mac was a classic case of this problem. From its inception in 1970 until a change in its charter in 1989, three federal officials who also were the three members of the Federal Home Loan Bank Board, the financial regulator of the savings and loan industry, governed Freddie Mac.

When the savings and loan debacle began, the Federal Home Loan Bank Board lacked the funds needed to close failing thrift institutions. The Bank Board used its governing position to engage Freddie Mac in a number of financially questionable transactions motivated by a desperate effort to feed what then was known as the "black hole" of institution failures. The confusion of governmental control and private ownership thus led to a confusion of public and private roles of the GSE. In 1989, the Congress abolished the Federal Home Loan Bank Board and created an eighteen-member board of directors for Freddie Mac patterned on Fannie Mae's board.

Until 1989, the Freddie Mac charter also contained other provisions that confused public and private characteristics. Although Freddie Mac was a privately owned company, its charter conferred upon the GSE, " . . . all immunities and priorities, including . . . all immunities and priorities under any such law or action, to which it would be entitled if it were the United States or if it were an unincorporated agency of the United States."

This provision thus exempted Freddie Mac from antitrust laws and also conferred sovereign immunity from suit and a priority in claims in bankruptcy, among other benefits. Fortunately, Congress repealed that provision in 1989 before Freddie Mac grew to a size where the need for the discipline of the antitrust laws became especially important.

II. PATTERNS OF TOOL USE

Current Extent: Government Corporations

U.S. Federal

Depending on definitional judgments,[21] some twenty-one federal government corporations were operational in the United States in 1999. These helped provide government services in areas such as transportation (Amtrak, St. Lawrence Seaway), communications (the U.S. Postal Service), electric power (TVA), credit (e.g., FHA, Ginnie Mae, OPIC and ExIm Bank), and insurance (e.g., FDIC, PBGC, and OPIC). Many of these are quite substantial operations. The U.S. Postal Service delivers more than 200 billion pieces of mail each year; the Federal Deposit Insurance Corporation provides federal backing for about $3 *trillion* of insured deposits at about nine thousand banks and thrift institutions; and the Pension Benefit Guaranty Corporation provides a government guarantee for the retirement incomes of about 43 million employees, about one-third of the U.S. workforce, in nearly forty thousand defined benefit pension plans. Table 3-1 lists U.S. federal government corporations, the year they were established, and their public purposes and primary activities.

Again depending on definitional distinctions, state and local governments in the United States have established literally thousands of government authorities and enterprises, especially in areas such as transportation, power production, and finance. Many of these are established in corporation form. They are supposed to be financially self-sustaining from revenues that they derive from operations. Often the states establish these organizations as a way to avoid constitutional limitations on borrowing. When they issue bonds to finance construction and other capital-intensive activities, these organizations may benefit from a federal government subsidy in the form of the federal tax exemption, and possibly a state and local exemption of income on these bonds from taxation. The result is to lower borrowing costs substantially, so long as the particular enterprise manages itself in a financially prudent way or otherwise maintains its credit rating. Table 3-2 provides an overview of major areas of government corporation activity at the state and local level, plus examples.[22]

91

CH 3:
GOVERNMENT
CORPORATIONS
AND
GOVERNMENT-
SPONSORED
ENTERPRISES

International

Especially in developing countries and the countries of central and eastern Europe and the former Soviet Union, public enterprises (that may or may not be government corporations in their organizational form) may play a major role in sectors of the economy such as transportation, power production, telecommunications, industry, and agriculture. The World Bank has conducted significant research into state-owned enterprises, largely in an effort to urge developing countries to privatize such enterprises.[23] However, that literature is permeated by economic perspectives, dwelling largely on the higher productivity of private firms compared with public enterprises, and tends not to parse organizational issues, such as whether a state-owned enterprise is a government corporation.

Many countries with developed economies use the government corporation as a tool to promote more efficient operations than might be possible through the usual government agency. The government of Japan, for example, created many government corporations after the Second World War. The eighty-one current government corporations include NHK (the Japan Broadcasting Corporation), the Japan External Trade Organization, and the Japan National Oil Company. The Japan Highway Public Corporation, the Government Housing Loan Corporation, and the Japan Finance Corporation for Small Business make investments in important economic sectors such as infrastructure on behalf of the Fiscal Investment and Loan Program (FILP). FILP is funded from postal savings and other money deposited with the government, and FILP investments are expected to be repaid with interest. Thus, in contrast to public highways that are funded by public revenues, FILP funds the Japan Highway Public Corporation to finance construction of toll roads so that the financing can be repaid.[24]

Finally, a number of countries, most notably the United Kingdom, have been active in attempting to sell off their government corporations and enterprises to private ownership. Between 1979 and 1995, the British government sold forty-one different government companies, including such giants as British Telecom, British Gas, British Petroleum, and British Airways.[25] The Japanese government has also begun to implement a policy of consolidating or privatizing government corporations.[26]

GSEs

The definition of GSE as a privately owned instrumentality of government that has access to an implicit but not explicit government guarantee of its obligations gives rise to a short list of some of the largest and most influential financial institutions in the United States, such as Fannie Mae and Freddie Mac. This is shown in Table 3-3.

By contrast, it is much more difficult to arrive at a list of such institutions internationally. European governments tend to provide explicit guarantees of the obligations of some companies, and this takes them out of the definition that applies in the United States.

For example, Credit Foncier de France is a privately owned but government-controlled corporation that since World War II has served as the government's vehicle for making subsidized housing loans. Credit Foncier made substantial real estate loans to promoters and developers during the 1980s and took substantial losses on those loans. In the 1990s, Credit Foncier foundered, and it obtained a $4–$5 billion line of credit from the government. The company's 1998 annual report states that the French government is introducing legislation that will permit multiple companies to obtain specialized property-lending charters that are modeled on those of Credit Foncier.[27] The result will be the creation of a system of private institutions that do not rely on government backing.

TABLE 3-1 *U.S. Government Corporations*

Government Corporation	Date Created	Primary Purpose	Primary Activities
Federal Deposit Insurance Corp.	1933	Secure bank and thrift deposits	Provide deposit insurance, regulation and examination
Tennessee Valley Authority	1933	Produce and market electric power	Generate, transmit, and sell electric energy
Export-Import Bank of the U.S.	1934	Promote U.S. exports and facilitate imports	Provide insurance, loans, and guarantees
Federal Housing Administration Fund	1934	Support the home mortgage market	Provide mortgage insurance
Federal Prison Industries, Inc.	1934	Employ and train inmates; assure safe and secure federal prison operations	Produce goods for sale to correctional institutions and federal departments
Federal Crop Insurance Corp.	1938	Promote agricultural stability	Provide crop insurance
Commodity Credit Corp.	1948	Support the agricultural commodity sector	Provide agricultural producer loans and export credit guarantees
St. Lawrence Seaway Development Corporation	1954	Provide a safe, efficient, and reliable waterway and promote distribution of goods between the Great Lakes and overseas markets	Operate and maintain that part of the seaway within U.S. waters
Government National Mortgage Association	1968	Facilitate funds for home mortgages	Guarantee mortgage-backed securities
Corporation for Public Broadcasting	1968	Facilitate the full development of public telecommunications systems and programming	Provide grants to support public television and radio
Overseas Private Investment Corporation	1969	Promote U.S. private investment in developing countries and emerging market economies	Provide insurance and financing for U.S. investments
National Railroad Passenger Corporation (Amtrak)	1971	Provide intercity and commuter rail passenger transportation in the United States	Provide direct passenger rail service

Origins and Recent Trends: Government Corporations 93

CH 3:
GOVERNMENT
CORPORATIONS
AND
GOVERNMENT-
SPONSORED
ENTERPRISES

U.S. Federal

John Thurston traces the government corporation, in English-speaking countries, back to the Savings Bank of Victoria in Australia in 1841. He states that Australia used the government proprietary corporation (i.e., one owned and controlled by government to carry out commercial-type activities) for the construction and operation of railroads, when private capital proved inadequate to meet public needs.[28] Yair Aharoni traces the origins of state-owned enterprises in many countries, including nineteenth-century ownership of German railroads by some of the Land (i.e., state) governments. However, Aharoni's description does not indicate that the corporate form was used.[29]

During and after World War I, governments established public corporations that were located outside the normal government structure and were independently fi-

TABLE 3-1 *(continued)*

Government Corporation	Date Created	Primary Purpose	Primary Activities
Rural Telephone Bank	1971	Provide supplemental financing for rural telecommunications companies	Provide loans
United States Postal Service	1971	Provide postal services	Provide postal services
Pension Benefit Guaranty Corporation	1974	Administer pension plan termination program	Provide a guaranty of private pension benefits
Legal Services Corporation	1974	Provide financial support for legal assistance in noncriminal matters	Fund and oversee poverty law programs to provide adequate legal counsel for those who cannot afford it
National Credit Union Administration Central Liquidity Facility	1978	Meet the liquidity needs of federal and state credit unions	Provide loans
Neighborhood Reinvestment Corporation	1978	Promote reinvestment in older neighborhoods by local financial institutions	Provide loans and grants to promote urban development
The Financing Corporation	1987	Serve as an off-budget financing vehicle to help pay for the savings and loan debacle	Issue debt obligations to fund the Federal Savings and Loan Corporation Resolution Fund
Resolution Funding Corporation	1989	Serve as an off-budget financing vehicle to help pay for the savings and loan debacle	Issue debt obligations to fund the Resolution Trust Corporation
Community Development Financial Institutions Fund	1994	Promote economic revitalization and community development	Provide investment assistance to appropriate financial institutions

SOURCE: Adapted from U.S. General Accounting Office, *Government Corporations: Profiles of Existing Government Corporations,* GAO/GGD-96–14, December 1995.

nanced and largely insulated from ministerial direction and control. These include the Port of London Authority and Central Electricity Board in the United Kingdom.[30]

John McDiarmid traces the first government corporation in the United States to the government's purchase of the Panama Railroad Company in 1904.[31] The Federal Land Banks, part of the Farm Credit System (FCS), began in 1916 with almost 100 percent of its capitalization provided by the U.S. government. Over the years the government sold its stock, and today the FCS is a completely privately owned GSE.

With the advent of World War I, the federal government created a number of government corporations, including the War Finance Corporation, which extended financial assistance to industries that were considered essential to the war effort. The government later terminated these corporations or absorbed their activities into the permanent executive branch agencies.

In 1932 the Hoover administration sought and obtained legislation to create perhaps the most significant of all government corporations in the United States, the Reconstruction Finance Corporation (RFC). Modeled on the successful War Finance Corporation, the RFC became a major part of the government's efforts to combat the Great Depression by lending money to individuals and businesses and replenishing the capital of private companies. In 1935, in the depths of the Depression, RFC financing activities represented 5.8 percent of the entire gross national product (GNP).[32]

The New Deal also saw the creation of a large number of other government corporations, including the Federal Deposit Insurance Corporation, the Tennessee Valley

TABLE 3-2 *Activities of State and Local Governmzent Corporations*

Sector	Primary Purposes	Activities	Examples
Economic Development	Encourage development of industry and business	Provide loans, tax abatements, lease-back arrangements, and other financing	Empire State Development Corporation; Kansas Development Finance Authority
Education	Support primary and secondary education facilities; provide loans and grants to postsecondary school students	Finance, construct, and manage school facilities; provide student loans and grants	Arkansas Student Loan Authority; Virginia State Education Assistance Authority
Energy and Natural Resources	Produce and market electricity, gas, and water	Finance, construct, and operate power, natural gas, and water plants	New York Power Authority; Washington Public Power Supply System
Environmental Protection	Support and operate solid, hazardous, and sewage waste and pollution control facilities	Finance, construct, and maintain sewage treatment plants, waste disposal facilities, and pollution control operations	Georgia Environmental Facilities Authority; Ohio Air Quality Development Authority
Health care	Support and manage health-care facilities	Finance, construct, and manage hospitals, nursing homes, clinics, elderly homes, and other health-care facilities	Alaska Medical Facility Authority; Washington Health Care Facilities Authority

Authority, the Commodity Credit Corporation, and the Export-Import Bank of the United States. All of these exist today.

95

CH 3:
GOVERNMENT
CORPORATIONS
AND
GOVERNMENT-
SPONSORED
ENTERPRISES

The late 1960s and 1970s saw another burst of creation of government corporations in the United States. This included the creation of the Overseas Private Investment Corporation (OPIC), Amtrak, and the Pension Benefit Guaranty Corporation, and the conversion of the Post Office Department into the United States Postal Service, a government corporation in all but name. Internationally, many countries turned to the state-owned enterprise as a means of trying to promote economic development.

In more recent years, and despite the impressive performance of many government corporations in countries such as the United States and Japan, the government corporation has fallen into disfavor as an organizational form. In the United States, proposals to reinvent government have involved recommendations to create so-called PBOs that would not necessarily be self-sustaining financially or even engaged in commercial-type activity. The Clinton administration has proposed dozens of PBOs, and Congress has created two so far, the Office of Student Financial Assistance of the U.S. Department of Education, and the Patent and Trademark Office of the U.S. Department of Commerce.

TABLE 3-2 *(continued)*

Sector	Primary Purposes	Activities	Examples
Housing	Build and manage housing and development projects or provide funding for housing and community development purposes	Administer public housing and private redevelopment projects; make loans and grants to individuals and businesses	Chicago Housing Authority; Indiana Housing Finance Authority
Ports	Support projects concerning rivers, lakes, oceans, and other waterways	Provide financing, construction, and maintenance of canals, ports, harbors, docks, wharves, and terminals	Port of Corpus Christi Authority; Chesapeake Port Authority
Public-Use Facilities	Support projects concerning facilities used by the public	Provide financing, leasing, construction, and maintenance of convention centers, sports stadiums, parking facilities, recreational facilities, public beaches, galleries, and museums	Louisiana Public Facilities Authority; Maryland Stadium Authority
Transportation	Support projects concerning transportation facilities	Provide financing, construction, and maintenance of highways, toll roads, tunnels and bridges, airports and heliports, and public mass transit systems	Fargo Municipal Airport Authority; New Jersey Turnpike Authority

SOURCE: Adapted from Jerry Mitchell, "The Policy Activities of Government Corporations," in *The American Experiment with Government Corporations*, 1999, pp. 17–18. With the permission of M. E. Sharpe, Inc.

Jerry Mitchell believes that the earliest state government corporation was the Port Authority of New York and New Jersey, established by interstate compact in 1921.[33] This model was followed by the creation of numerous state and local port authorities and by the New York Power Authority in 1928. Mitchell points to Franklin Roosevelt's favorable impression of government corporations from his experience as the governor of New York as a factor that led to his later enthusiasm as president for creating new national government corporations.

GSEs

International and United States

As an institutional form, the government-chartered private company to carry out public purposes has a far older lineage than the wholly owned government corporation. Indeed, in mercantilist times, the sovereign would charter private companies, such as the Bank of England or the East India Company, to carry out activities that the state could not carry out for itself.

The Bank of England became Alexander Hamilton's model for the first Bank of the United States, a central bank primarily privately owned, with a one-fifth government stake, and governed by a private board of directors. The bank was chartered for a period of twenty years, and it sunsetted in 1811. The government chartered the second Bank of the United States in 1816, again for a twenty-year period, and later chartered

TABLE 3-3 *Government-Sponsored Enterprises (GSEs) by Size and Function*

GSE	Year Established as a GSE	Public Purpose	Size at Year-End 1999
Farm Credit System	1916	Lend to agriculture	$89 billion
Federal Home Loan Bank System	1932	Lend to financial institutions to fund mortgages	$583 billion (assets)
Fannie Mae (Federal National Mortgage Association)	1968	Serve the secondary home mortgage market— fund mortgages	$575 billion (assets) plus $679 billion (mortgage-backed securities guaranteed)
Freddie Mac (Federal Home Loan Mortgage Corporation)	1970	Serve the secondary home mortgage market—fund mortgages	$387 billion (assets) plus $538 billion (mortgage-backed securities guaranteed)
Sallie Mae (Student Loan Marketing Association)	1972	Serve the secondary market for student loans— fund student loans	$44 billion (assets)
Farmer Mac (Federal Agricultural Mortgage Corporation)	1987	Fund agricultural mortgages	$2.6 billion (assets) plus $1.1 billion (mortgage-backed securities)

97

CH 3:
GOVERNMENT
CORPORATIONS
AND
GOVERNMENT-
SPONSORED
ENTERPRISES

other private companies, notably, transcontinental railroads and a system of national banks, to perform public functions. In 1913 the government created the Federal Reserve System to be the nation's new central bank.

Building on these antecedents and on U.S. studies of cooperative organizations in Europe, the federal government created the first actual GSE, the FCS, in 1916. The creation of the other GSEs followed in subsequent decades. The important point to note here is that in the United States, just as in many European countries, the system of government chartering of private institutions to carry out public purposes is a much older organizational form than the government corporation itself.[34]

As was true of the government corporation, the periods that were most conducive to creating GSEs in the United States were the Great Depression (the Federal Home Loan Bank System) and, more significantly, the late 1960s to early 1970s (Fannie Mae became a GSE; creation of Freddie Mac and Sallie Mae).

The period since the creation of Fannie Mae as a GSE in 1968 has been a profitable one for most GSEs. Benefiting from their access to subsidized federal credit, the GSEs have roughly doubled in their aggregate size every five years since 1970, from total debt obligations of $38.9 billion in 1970 to total debt obligations and mortgage-backed securities outstanding of $2.1 *trillion* in 1999. When adjusted for inflation, this represents a real rate of growth about four times that of the economy as a whole.[35]

This rapid expansion occurred because of the favorable charter privileges of the GSEs that allowed Fannie Mae and Freddie Mac to expand rapidly and eventually dominate much of the residential mortgage market, and that allowed Sallie Mae to become by far the largest holder of federal student loans.

By contrast, the Federal Home Loan Banks suffered a reverse when their owner-members, the savings and loan industry, failed by the thousands in the 1980s. Similarly, the Farm Credit System failed in the mid-1980s and was bailed out through a federal off-budget funding mechanism called the Farm Credit System Assistance Corporation.

GSEs today are at a turning point. The commercial banking industry, long resentful of Sallie Mae and its privileges, managed to persuade Congress in 1993 to impose a significant offset fee on the GSE's portfolio operations. Sallie Mae now has negotiated a long transition period for giving up its government sponsorship and becoming a completely private company.

Fannie Mae and Freddie Mac now serve a mature housing market. They have used new technologies to increase their market power over the primary market and also are exploring other ways to expand their financial base, for example, by providing so-called universal accounts to homeowners that use the home as a major source of collateral for expanded consumer lending. At some point they may follow Sallie Mae and give up their government sponsorship in return for giving up the restrictions imposed by their GSE charters.[36]

III. BASIC MECHANICS

The Government Corporation

The establishment of a government corporation involves a number of basic steps that generally include the following:

- Identify the public purposes to be served and the functions involved.

- Determine that these functions are financially self-sustaining or potentially self-sustaining.

- Determine how they will be paid for if some functions are not financially self-sustaining.

- Determine the organizational location for the government corporation or whether it will be an independent agency.

- Draft a sound corporation charter; establish the corporation as a wholly owned government corporation within the Government Corporation Control Act if this is a federal government corporation.

- Enact charter legislation to establish the corporation.[37]

- Obtain an initial appropriation to fund the first year of operations of the corporation (this initial funding may be structured as a loan or as an initial government investment in the corporation).

- Appoint a chief executive for the corporation and other officers as may be prescribed by the charter.

- Appoint other officials of the corporation.

- Begin operations.

Beginning operations is a step that varies considerably depending on the government corporation and its core mission. The mechanics of delivering mail or producing electricity or guaranteeing mortgage-backed securities differ considerably from each other. Thus, the U.S. Postal Service today has some 837,000 employees, the Tennessee Valley Authority has about 13,700 people, and the Government National Mortgage Association operates with fifty-six full-time staff.

Despite these differences, government corporations today need to be aware of the need to be nimble and information based in their activities. New technologies are changing virtually all sectors of the economy, and government corporations cannot afford to remain locked into outdated approaches to doing business.

The Government-Sponsored Enterprise

As a matter of legal drafting, some of the earlier GSE charters, and especially the Fannie Mae Charter Act of 1968, tend to offer better crafting than more recent charters. The Fannie Mae Charter Act, for example, has been filled with holes as Congress acquiesced to myriad technical amendments that have had the effect of expanding the discretion of the GSE and significantly reducing its accountability to the government.[38]

Along with the drafting of a GSE charter, policymakers will need to provide for government supervision of the safety and soundness of the GSE. Here the preferred model is that of the Farm Credit Administration, which received a range of powers, comparable to the powers of federal bank regulators, in the aftermath of the financial failure of the FCS during the mid-1980s.

There are two ways to create a GSE, depending on whether the GSE represents a conversion of an existing government corporation (the Fannie Mae example) or the creation of a completely new organization (e.g., Freddie Mac). The mechanics of establishing the GSE are similar in both cases:

- Identify the public purposes to be served and the functions involved.

- Determine that these functions are financially profitable.

- Determine that these functions cannot be performed more effectively without creating a company with special government privileges.

- Define and estimate the cost of special privileges (e.g., subsidized borrowing rights, tax preferences, regulatory exemptions) that will be granted to the GSE.

99

CH 3:
GOVERNMENT
CORPORATIONS
AND
GOVERNMENT-
SPONSORED
ENTERPRISES

- Determine whether the GSE shall be required to support some public-purpose activities that are not as profitable as its core business and determine how service to those public purposes will be enforced by the government.

- If some functions are not financially profitable, leave them with the government or create a tandem government program, financed through appropriations, to carry them out.

- Determine the congressional or legislative committees and executive branch agencies that will have oversight responsibility for the GSE (1) with respect to financial safety and soundness, and (2) continuing service to a significant public purpose.

- Obtain consensus as to an exit strategy so that the GSE can become a completely private company, without special ties to the government, after a fixed period of time.

- Draft a sound corporation charter; if no other exit strategy is available include a ten-year sunset provision in the charter and authority for the secretary of the Treasury, or other financially capable official, to oversee the transition from GSE status.

- Enact charter legislation to establish the corporation and to create a safety-and-soundness regulator with the powers and mandate of a federal bank regulator.

- Create an interim board of directors to sell stock in the GSE and issue debt obligations.

- Sell stock in the GSE, either to investors or to cooperative owners, as the case may be.

- When the stock is issued, hold an election for the first members of the board of directors.

- Appoint a chief executive for the GSE and other officers as may be appropriate.

- Appoint other officials of the corporation; if the GSE represents a successor organization to a government activity, some government employees may leave government service and join the GSE, as provided by the charter act.

- Begin operations.

The GSE is a complicated instrument of government policy. The public benefits and public costs of GSEs will hinge on drafting details that few policymakers are likely to appreciate. Fortunately, today there are officials at a new Office of GSE Policy at the Treasury Department, at the Congressional Budget Office, and at the Office of Management and Budget who are familiar with GSEs and their strengths and limitations. It is imperative, to avoid flawed legislation, that drafters of a charter of a proposed new GSE consult such officials before their bill becomes public.

IV. TOOL SELECTION

Rationale

The Government Corporation

President Harry Truman set forth criteria in 1948 for creating a government corporation, which remain valid today. A government corporation is likely to be an appropriate tool of government to carry out programs that are (1) of a business nature, (2) revenue producing and potentially self-sustaining; (3) involve a large number of business-type transactions with the public, and (4) require a greater flexibility than the customary type of appropriations budget ordinarily permits. Thus, government corporations may be created to engage in activities such as power production, operation of an international waterway, provision of financial guarantees, or operation of railway service that are considered to embody a public purpose.

It important to keep in mind Harold Seidman's admonition that a wholly owned government corporation is a government agency.[39] As a government agency, the government corporation possesses many special benefits—such as the freedom from the need to pay returns to investors, access to inexpensive funding through the Treasury, and freedom from the obligation to pay income taxes (and many times, an exemption from an obligation to make payments in lieu of taxes)—compared with the usual private company that provides similar goods or services on a for-profit basis. Private competitors are likely to resent competition from a government corporation that uses special government benefits to drive companies out of a market. Reflecting this, a panel of the National Academy of Public Administration urges, "Corporations expected to be profit making should be established in the private sector, and government corporations should be self-sustaining or potentially self-sustaining."[40]

Over time, markets are likely to change in ways that reduce the importance of some of the services that government corporations provide. Thus, the advent of giant cargo ships has helped to diminish the market share of the ports served by the St. Lawrence Seaway Development Corporation that operates a waterway that is too narrow for many of today's vessels. There is also evidence from a number of countries that evolving markets or nimble private companies are likely to undercut the ability of a government corporation to be financially self-sustaining in providing some kinds of services, such as power production or even provision of mail service.

In recognition of the difficulty of serving high-priority public purposes over the years, the Office of Management and Budget has called for periodic reauthorization of all government corporations. That way government can review the corporation's performance and also consider possible privatization.

The government corporation is generally not suitable for functions that the government carries out as sovereign, such as the enforcement of criminal laws or conscription for national defense or tax collection, in contrast to the provision of commercial or business-type services. Proposals of the sort that surfaced in the late 1990s to convert the Internal Revenue Service (IRS) into a government corporation thus seem inappropriate. The problem with this is that a government corporation would be motivated to increase its revenues through determined and thorough collection of taxes. This would have exacerbated rather than diminished the problem of aggressive IRS behavior that the Senate Finance Committee was trying to address at that time.

Also, as Seidman points out, a government corporation is likely to focus on financial returns, potentially to the detriment of other public purposes:

> Whatever the legislative intent, corporate bodies inevitably give priority to those programs which produce revenues and downgrade those which do not. [G]overnment corporations ultimately are judged by the bottom line and not by their contribution to political or social objectives such as regional development or improved inner-city housing.[41]

The Government-Sponsored Enterprise

With respect to GSEs, the major rationale is some market imperfection that limits the ability of the private sector to meet an important need without government assistance. Thus, the Office of Management and Budget has suggested the following rationale for GSEs:

GSEs were created because wholly private financial institutions were believed to be incapable of providing an adequate supply of loanable funds at all times and to all regions of the country for specified types of borrowers.[42]

101

CH 3:
GOVERNMENT
CORPORATIONS
AND
GOVERNMENT-
SPONSORED
ENTERPRISES

Thus, the Farm Credit System began in 1916 as a way to provide credit at a time before electricity or even automobiles were common in rural America, and farm communities often were remote from competitive sources of credit. By creating an alternative delivery system for credit in those communities, the FCS helped to overcome market imperfections and encourage the flow of credit.

The Federal Home Loan Bank System started in 1932 as a way to provide government-backed funds to finance the illiquid portfolios of thrift institutions in the Great Depression and the financial failure that it caused in the home mortgage market. Fannie Mae also began in the Great Depression, in 1938, as a wholly owned government corporation subsidiary of the Reconstruction Finance Corporation, to help fund mortgage loans insured by yet another new deal agency, the Federal Housing Administration.

Sallie Mae began in 1972 as part of an effort to provide government funding for the recently established federal student loan program. Student loans were small and costly to service in small numbers. Banks tended to offer student loans to their customers primarily as a way to build consumer loyalty for other financial products. Sallie Mae offered an opportunity to create a large-scale financial institution that could purchase large volumes of student loans and develop profitable economies of scale.

By contrast to these examples, market imperfections are much more difficult to find today. The most recent GSE, Farmer Mac, has had to return to Congress several times since its inception in 1987 to obtain adjustments to its charter so it can offer more profitable types of financial services. As late as 1999, Farmer Mac continued to make a large percentage of its earnings from financial investments unrelated to its statutory public purpose.

Political Considerations

Political considerations also play a major role in determining whether a particular government corporation or GSE will be created and in affecting the extent that the organization will operate prudently in the furtherance of valuable public purposes.

The Government Corporation

An influential constituency that has a stake in the effective performance of the public functions to be served by a government corporation is a natural prerequisite to the creation of such a corporation. Proposals were developed during the early 1990s to transform four agencies into government corporations: (1) the United States Patent and Trademark Office (PTO), (2) the Bonneville Power Administration (BPA), (3) the Federal Housing Administration (FHA), and (4) the Naval Petroleum and Oil Shale Reserves (NPOSR) of the U.S. Department of Energy.

The status of the four proposals several years later clearly reflects the power and interests of the relevant constituencies. Of the four, the proposal to create a U.S. Patent and Trademark Corporation came the closest to success. The issuance of patents and trademarks is a function of great concern to some of the largest corporations in the United States. Congress declined to turn the PTO into a government corporation, but in 1999 did enact legislation to give the agency the status of a PBO with increased personnel and procurement flexibilities.

Two of the proposals did not fare well in the legislative process. The proposed corporatization of Bonneville Power raised issues among powerful constituencies in the Northwest, including customers that today receive power at heavily subsidized prices and environmentalists. The Federal Housing Administration proposal faced opposition from private providers of mortgage insurance who may have seen increased FHA effectiveness as a way for the government to eat into their business. Enacting new legislation is more difficult than stopping it, and the opposition of mortgage insurers was more than sufficient to outweigh the support of mortgage bankers for the proposal.

Perhaps the most remarkable development was that regarding the Naval Petroleum Reserves. While earlier Congresses might have been receptive to a proposal to create a government corporation, either for long-term government management or as a transition to private ownership, the new Republican majority of the 104th Congress was predisposed toward privatization. The major Naval Petroleum Reserves oil field at Elk Hills was owned jointly by the U.S. government and by Chevron USA, with the U.S. government holding a majority interest. Chevron objected to the corporation proposal and urged the new Congress to enact legislation, now signed into law, to sell the government's stake in the Elk Hills field. The government sold the Elk Hills field in 1998, although Chevron was not the successful bidder.

These examples are interesting because they represented efforts to corporatize governmental functions without altering the agency's programmatic authority. They illustrate the general point: the creation of a government corporation depends critically on the influence of contending political constituencies. In favor of corporatization are constituencies that have a stake in enhancing the effective operation of business-type activities of government; against corporatization are private firms that see themselves disadvantaged from competition by a government corporation, plus various governmental constituencies that fear losing control over important activities if they are situated within a government corporation that has sufficient autonomy to carry out its activities but is not subject to the many controls that apply to conventional government agencies. Government corporations would seem to function best when their constituency is influential enough to obtain high performance of a public purpose, but not so powerful as to obviate the reasonable forms of accountability to larger concerns of public policy.

The Government-Sponsored Enterprise

Given the immense size of the contingent liability that they pose to the national government, GSEs raise these issues of political balance and constituency in potentially more serious ways.

If a constituency is strong enough to create a GSE, it will enjoy many advantages in the effort to maintain and expand the GSE and its political franchise. Especially as a GSE gains market power, it can use this market power to generate a political constituency among its customers to defend or expand on the status quo. Also, GSE profits can be used to garner support among academics and other supporters such as low-income groups that seek grants to support their activities.[43] Thus, market power leads to political power; political power in turn leads to favorable changes to the GSE's charter to help expand its market power.

For a GSE that commands sufficient subsidies to create market power, there seem to be few natural checks on the process of expansion. The larger GSEs now are displacing many of the private firms that were among their earlier supporters. In the political realm, however, the history of the United States does reveal a strong antipathy toward the provision of special privileges to a government-sponsored company, and especially to government-sponsored monopolies.[44] The tea American colonists threw into Boston Harbor was owned by the English East India Company, a government monopoly. Similarly, there was widespread support for Andrew Jackson's war on the Bank of the United States.

In the majority of such cases, the most vociferous opponents of government-sponsored companies are to be found among smaller competitors who feel themselves to be unfairly disadvantaged. The GSEs too are subject to such resentment. The Farm Credit System, for instance, finds itself kept in check by opposition from competing rural banks. It now appears as if a similar process of political discontent may be taking place with respect to Fannie Mae and Freddie Mac.[45]

Concern about the safety and soundness of GSEs and the imbalance between their public costs and public benefits also has developed in some parts of government. Since the savings and loan debacle and the failure of the Farm Credit System in the 1980s, the U.S. Treasury Department, Office of Management and Budget, Congressional Budget Office, and General Accounting Office all have manifested some concern about the government's inability to protect itself against the financial exposure created by a GSE.

V. MANAGEMENT CHALLENGES AND POTENTIAL RESPONSES

The Government Corporation

Governments generally are subject to powerful new forces that are changing their operating environments. Because they operate in a more commercial context, government corporations are affected to an even greater extent than other federal agencies. These forces are as follows:

1. Continuing controversy over the proper role of government, especially in providing services that might be provided by private companies (e.g., the Postal Service, Tennessee Valley Authority, ExIm Bank).

2. An increasingly efficient economy that obviates past market shortcomings that government corporations were created to serve (TVA, ExIm Bank).

3. New technologies that make obsolete some old ways of doing business (Federal Housing Administration, TVA, Postal Service).

To survive, some government corporations, and especially those that face private sector competition, will need to actively cope with these changes. Government corporations need to use the flexibility of their charter acts to make the multiyear investments and engage in personnel and staffing adjustments not usually available to the ordinary government agency, so that they can adapt to the new environment.

On the other hand, this operating flexibility or even autonomy raises another problem. Government corporations (e.g., TVA or the Washington Public Power Supply System, WPPSS, in the late 1960s and various state and local authorities from time to time) can get into trouble if they make unwise decisions that reflect a lack of accountability of government corporations to the governmental process.[46] The federal government today is beset by a mentality that too often seeks to impose draconian new controls in response to the perception of even minor improprieties. Government corporations, if they misuse the benefits of their operating autonomy, risk losing the flexibility that is essential to cope with today's changing environment.

The availability of a financial bottom line permits government to hold a government corporation more accountable than otherwise would be possible; to meet its annual goal of being financially self-sustaining (or of progressing each year toward financial self-sufficiency), the corporation must internalize conflicting goals of revenue generation and service to public purposes and must weigh them properly. The government has at least one clear measure, in the form of the financial bottom line, by which to measure the corporation's performance.

103

CH 3:
GOVERNMENT
CORPORATIONS
AND
GOVERNMENT-
SPONSORED
ENTERPRISES

This advantage is removed when lawmakers and executive branch officials try to conform government corporations to the inappropriate legal and budget requirements that apply to ordinary government agencies and that may seriously reduce the ability of government corporations to respond to their changing environments. The imposition of credit budgeting would seem to be such a restriction that, for government corporations that in fact are financially self-sustaining, adds nothing of quality to their financial accountability.

The problem of accountability also becomes more difficult when responsible government bodies lack the capacity to supervise activities and expenditures of government corporations. Seidman observes, for example, that budget examiners of the U.S. Office of Management and Budget and the staff of congressional appropriations committees generally are not trained to analyze the business-type financial statements that government corporations must submit each year.

OMB points out the importance of maintaining a balance between flexibility and accountability:

> The challenge involved in designing government corporations is to balance the need for autonomy and flexibility with the need for accountability and oversight. . . . [T]he goal should be to provide an operational structure that allows Federal entities to carry out their functions in the most effective and efficient manner, and in a way that maintains accountability to decision makers.[47]

The need to maintain this balance is important in the management, and not only in the design, of government corporations. In the United States, government corporations tend to manifest a sound financial discipline that often may be lacking in other government agencies. The credit agencies structured as bona fide government corporations to administer federal credit programs (Ginnie Mae, ExIm Bank, OPIC) are able to obtain unqualified audited financial statements each year. This transparency helps to protect them from making the types of mistakes that could undermine confidence in their operations.

Another major problem for government corporations relates to the tension between the demands of efficient production of goods or services and the demands imposed by the political process that government corporations serve other public purposes as well. Government corporations thus may face major obstacles when they seek to improve the effectiveness of their operations. This includes political pressure to maintain uneconomic Amtrak rail service to or through districts of influential members of Congress, and the constraints that widespread unionization may impose on the Postal Service when it deals with workforce, staffing, and technology issues.

Finally, a lack of accountability and fiscal discipline, especially but not solely in developing countries, can cause state subsidies to be squandered. In the United States, a government corporation may be able to defer recognition of substantial losses and thus avoid the application of financial discipline to contain those losses. This problem is exacerbated in countries that operate on the basis of less rigorous financial controls for government and private enterprises. In China, government enterprises have been able to operate for years on the basis of hidden government subsidies that help to obscure drastic financial deterioration.[48] The Chinese government is actively searching for ways to change the governance and perhaps also the ownership of economically unsound state-owned enterprises.[49]

One valuable model for effective government supervision of government corporations comes from Canada. The Crown Corporations Directorate of the Treasury Board of Canada is staffed by senior civil servants who brief the Treasury Board and Parliament on the activities, expenditures, and resource needs of all Canadian crown corporations. The staff of the Crown Corporations Directorate prepares reports from time to time on issues concerning crown corporations, such as governance structures and the responsibilities of directors.[50]

105

CH 3:
GOVERNMENT
CORPORATIONS
AND
GOVERNMENT-
SPONSORED
ENTERPRISES

The paradox for many developing countries is that, in contrast to Western economic development, they have built large state-owned enterprises to conduct economic activities rather than chartering the kinds of privately owned companies that substituted for a weak state in mercantilist Europe and the early United States.

The Government-Sponsored Enterprise

The government faces major challenges in attempting to regulate the public benefits and limit the potential public costs of GSE operations. The important issues that government faces in trying to oversee the GSE as a useful tool of public policy include:

1. Exercise by GSEs of an increasing dominance over the governmental process

2. Inability of the government to supervise GSE safety and soundness and the government's resulting financial exposure

3. Inability of the government, with notable exceptions, to induce GSEs to serve public purposes that conflict with the interests of shareholders

4. The lack of an exit strategy even if the GSE (a) becomes a government-sponsored monopoly that displaces other competitors in the marketplace or (b) fails to serve useful public purposes

Virtually all of these problems can be traced to the so-called iron triangle that tends to emerge when GSEs are created, embracing the congressional authorizing committee that creates the GSE, the constituencies that benefit from the GSE as a purchaser or provider of services, and the GSE itself.

Indeed, GSEs may find that they can gain greater benefit from manipulating the political process than from dealing with market forces. Thus, despite having lost their ability to serve a public purpose of significant value, the Federal Home Loan Banks have been able to turn to their congressional authorizing committees and to their federal regulator, the Federal Housing Finance Board, to permit their entry into lines of business that may be more attractive. This pattern of seeking active management of their political environment has been a hallmark of mercantilist-type companies and their successors in the United States, including the Banks of the United States and the transcontinental railroads.[51]

Accountability to Government

To deal with the issue of political accountability, government should create one or more highly capable sources of institutional strength, both in Congress and in the executive branch. In Congress, for example, it was the powerful and technically very capable House Ways and Means Committee that took the lead in 1989 to create a financial regulator of safety and soundness for Fannie Mae and Freddie Mac, the two largest GSEs.

Under the auspices of the Ways and Means Committee, the Treasury Department then was able to conduct studies of the safety and soundness of all the GSEs and to recommend improvements in oversight. The Ways and Means Committee is different from the congressional authorizing committees: it has not tried to create its own GSE and instead, as the committee of Congress that must raise revenues to pay for a financial bailout, it has a direct stake in assuring that the government properly oversees GSE safety and soundness.

Government creates GSEs to carry out public purposes and needs to regulate their service to high-priority public purposes and to supervise their financial safety and soundness. Effective regulation and supervision can help to increase the public benefits of a GSE and decrease its potential public costs. As the Office of Management and Budget states:

> GSEs should have a Federal overseer created in law, with a regulatory regime that establishes and monitors performance of their mission and ensures that the entity is operating in a sound manner that minimizes risk to the government while enabling it to accomplish its mission.[52]

This is easier said than done. The problem once again is the political strength of GSEs. As a technical matter, successes and failures of federal regulation of banks and other institutions with insured deposits have given us a good sense of the proper frame-work for supervision of safety and soundness.[53] Yet, many of the attributes of reasonable public supervision of financial soundness, such as an insistence on prudent capital standards or the systematic review of business activities by federal examiners, may be unattractive to the private owners of a GSE.

The 1991 *Report of the Secretary of the Treasury on Government-Sponsored Enterprises* stresses that federal supervision of GSE safety and soundness is fraught with the danger of regulatory capture:

> The problem of avoiding capture appears to be particularly acute in the case of regulation of GSEs. The principal GSEs are few in number; they have highly qualified staffs; they have strong support for their programs from special interest groups; and they have significant resources with which to influence political outcomes. A weak financial regulator would find GSE political power overwhelming and even the most powerful and respected government agencies would find regulating such entities a challenge.[54]

This means that regulation of GSEs is best placed within a large and capable financial regulator that has the capacity to withstand political assaults on its supervisory activities. Then-Treasury Undersecretary Robert Glauber recommended in 1991 that the regulation of GSEs be placed in the Treasury Department, the Federal Deposit Insurance Corporation, or the Board of Governors of the Federal Reserve System. Since then, the GSEs have grown substantially in size and influence. Today, the best recommendation would be to house oversight of all GSEs at the Treasury Department, in a distinct office comparable to the Office of the Comptroller of the Currency, which supervises national banks.[55]

Promotion of Public Purposes

As a general rule, government can use three approaches to try to assure that GSEs serve high-priority public purposes throughout their existence. First, the government could define the authorized activities of a GSE with some specificity, and then could adjust the statutory provisions over time. This approach is limited by (1) the government's inability to muster the political will to make a GSE give up any part of its existing charter act authority just because public priorities may change; (2) the lack of understanding among policymakers of the consequences of making particular changes in a GSE's enabling legislation; and (3) the tendency of Congress to enact small so-called technical amendments that the GSEs propose, again without policymakers understanding how the legislation will relax previous limitations that directed a GSE to serve particular public purposes in a particular way.

Second, the government can vest a government department or agency with the power to require service to particular public purposes, within the framework of the GSE's charter act. Thus, the law directs the secretary of Housing and Urban Development to establish goals for Fannie Mae and Freddie Mac to fund mortgages for underserved borrowers and communities. However, the law states that, when they fund mortgages for low- and moderate-income housing, the GSEs are supposed to receive a "reasonable economic return that may be less than the return earned on other activities." This limitation, plus the relative political weakness of the Department of Housing and Urban Development vis-à-vis the GSEs, has meant that the department's housing goals do not require the GSEs to do more to serve underserved borrowers (e.g., minorities or lower-income borrowers or communities) than do other mortgage market lenders already.[56]

107

CH 3:
GOVERNMENT
CORPORATIONS
AND
GOVERNMENT-
SPONSORED
ENTERPRISES

Third, and potentially most effective, the government can simply require that a GSE set aside a fixed percentage of its income to serve high-priority public purposes. In 1989, Congress amended the Federal Home Loan Bank Act to require that the Federal Home Loan Banks set aside 10 percent of their income each year in a fund to help reduce the costs of mortgages for underserved borrowers and communities. The Federal Housing Finance Board, the government regulator of the Federal Home Loan Banks, oversees this Affordable Housing Fund. The value of this approach is that it limits the ability of a GSE to use its political strength against a regulator to reduce the amount of its contribution to meeting the needs specified by law. The percentage of income is fixed by law and thus is easy for the government to administer.

An Exit Strategy for GSEs

Government needs to return to the practice of earlier years and place a specific sunset period, say ten or twenty years, in the charter of each GSE. The logic for this is clear and has been articulated by Sallie Mae in a document published after that GSE decided to give up its government sponsorship:

> In creating the various GSEs, Congress did not contemplate the need at some point to unwind or terminate their federal charters. However, Congress did not assume the perpetual existence (and continual expansion) of individual GSEs in the context of changing social and economic priorities. The missing element in the GSE concept is the notion of a life cycle for government sponsorship. GSEs are *created* to increase the flow of funds to socially desirable activities. If successful, they grow and *mature* as the market develops. At some point, the private sector may be able to meet the funding needs of the particular market segment. If so, a *sunset* may be appropriate.[57]

The Treasury Department takes the following position on sunsetting GSEs:

> The Treasury has for a number of years, in Democratic and Republican Administrations, believed that it is appropriate to wean a GSE from government sponsorship once the GSE becomes economically viable and successfully fulfills the purpose for which it was created with Federal sponsorship, or when the purpose for which it was created ceases to exist.[58]

Indeed, sunset provisions were a familiar part of early public-purpose charters. The two Banks of the United States, the lineal ancestors of today's GSEs in the United States, had twenty-year sunset provisions in their charters; it was the twenty-year sunset provision of the second Bank of the United States that precipitated President Andrew Jackson's "Bank War."

Here, too, political considerations are paramount. Sunset provisions in a GSE charter are only as strong as the political constituencies behind them. As the Congressional Budget Office noted in this regard:

> Of course, such options [to prepare for removal of government sponsorship] beg a question: why would the GSEs agree to those policies as a first step toward the withdrawal

of their subsidy? That admission simply acknowledges that once one agrees to share a canoe with a bear, it is hard to get him out without obtaining his agreement or getting wet. If the GSEs were to support privatization, they and the Congress could certainly carry it out without financial disruption.[59]

VI. OVERALL ASSESSMENT

How well then do government corporations and GSEs perform as tools of government? To answer this question, it is helpful to assess them against the criteria of effectiveness, efficiency, equity, and legitimacy used generally in this book.

The Government Corporation

Effectiveness

In the United States, government corporations appear to be generally very effective in carrying out appropriate public purposes. In good part, the financial discipline of many government corporations derives from their organizational structure and the way that it creates an incentive for corporation managers to tie their investments in revenue-producing activities to the revenues that actually will result.

The government corporation must achieve a balance: in contrast to other government agencies, it must focus on the financial bottom line while serving its public purposes. On the other hand, unlike a private company, such as an investor-owned GSE, the government corporation often is not free to achieve its bottom-line objectives by neglecting the less profitable parts of its statutory responsibilities.

Of course, financially self-sustaining operations do not always take place as planned. If government loses control of its government corporations, as in the case of the TVA and WPPSS nuclear programs, then serious losses can occur and serious diversion of scarce public resources can result. A lack of accountability is at the root of the failure of the government corporation as a useful tool in many developing countries.

Therefore, on balance, one could suggest that, for the United States, it might be worthwhile to turn more government commercial-type activities into government corporations, so long as they meet the criteria articulated by President Truman. This is true even if, as would be proper in some cases, the government corporation is a transitional stage on the way to privatization. Running some government activities through a government corporation, as in the case of NAPA's recommendations for the Naval Petroleum Reserves, can help to give government a good sense of the value of the corporation or its assets if privatization is sought.

By contrast, the government-owned corporation or enterprise is fraught with difficulty in many developing countries. Without the ability to impose financial or political accountability, many governments face the prospect of seeing their government corporations or enterprises continue to absorb scarce economic resources until they become mere caricatures of productive companies. Governments need to be especially wary before they link other public purposes, such as the provision of employment opportunities, and ultimately a social safety net, to the expansion of government-owned corporations and enterprises. As the Chinese have found, it can be difficult to disentangle these public purposes from the need to curtail wasteful activities of a state-owned firm.

Efficiency

Efficiency relates to the contribution that a government corporation makes to the quality of the market that it serves. In this dimension, the efficiency of a government corporation relates to its mission. Ginnie Mae helps to improve the market for federally insured mortgages without using significant government subsidies, and therefore might be considered to enhance economic efficiency. In contrast, a government corporation such as the Federal Crop Insurance Corporation is merely a vehicle for delivering a substantial government subsidy and, as such, is unlikely to enhance general market efficiency. The contributions to efficiency of a government corporation can change over time: TVA began as a leader in efficient power production, but today, as electric utilities have become more efficient in a deregulated environment, TVA would seem to lag behind other organizations. Thus, the efficiency of government corporations depends on the individual context; government corporations range from quite high (Ginnie Mae) to fairly low (TVA) in their contributions to economic efficiency.

Equity

Government corporations (unlike GSEs and other private companies) serve all parts of their charters without favoritism. Thus, Ginnie Mae is available to securitize and help fund mortgages for low-down-payment (i.e., financially more risky) FHA, VA, and RHS home loans in the same way that it deals with mortgages for other FHA, VA, and RHS home buyers. Similarly, Amtrak and the Postal Service provide extensive service within their geographic territories. The Post Office charges the same amount to send a first-class letter from New York to Alaska as it does to send a letter to Boston.

On the other hand, government corporations are appropriate only for financially self-sustaining activities. This means that cross-subsidies are limited by the propensity of private actors (e.g., private parcel express companies) to skim the cream from the customer base of a government corporation. Moreover, unless government is ready to appropriate a subsidy directly, the government corporation is not an appropriate means to deliver a subsidy that could call its financial self-sufficiency into question. The government corporation also is inappropriate for an outright grant program that does not raise revenues from its transactions, such as the Corporation for National and Community Service or the Legal Services Corporation.

Legitimacy

The government corporation sometimes faces attacks on its legitimacy because of management decisions such as efforts to pay employees higher-than-usual government salaries and to obtain other perks that other government officials consider exorbitant. Attacks on legitimacy also come from private firms that resent competition from a government corporation such as the Postal Service or Amtrak or TVA.

These attacks seem to have made the government corporation less popular as a tool of government than circumstances would warrant. The United States has changed significantly from the days when President Roosevelt in 1933 proudly described the TVA as "clothed with the power of government but possessed of the flexibility and initiative of private enterprise."

For many other countries as well, the government-owned corporation or enterprise has lost some of its attractiveness. Programs of privatization and divestment of state-owned firms have taken place in countries around the world, including the United Kingdom, Japan, New Zealand, Singapore, Chile, and the Republic of Korea.

109

CH 3:
GOVERNMENT
CORPORATIONS
AND
GOVERNMENT-
SPONSORED
ENTERPRISES

Effectiveness

The GSE is an effective tool of government when the objectives of shareholders and the government are aligned; otherwise, it is ineffective. This is true because, both for cooperative and investor-owned GSEs, the owners come first in the minds of managers.[60]

On the one hand, the GSE manifests many strengths compared with the government agency. Especially in the early part of the twentieth century, GSEs provided significant benefits to borrowers and the markets that they served. The Farm Credit System, for example, pioneered variable rate loans and the provision of credit at the point of sale of goods, such as seed or tractors, which needed to be financed. Fannie Mae as a government corporation helped to spur the creation of a title insurance industry to facilitate the transfer of title to homes.

As GSEs, Fannie Mae and Freddie Mac helped to promote the growth of the private mortgage insurance industry and the conventional (nongovernment guaranteed) mortgage market. Fannie Mae and Freddie Mac also helped to standardize mortgage forms and procedures during the early 1970s and thereby improved the functioning of the residential mortgage market. Following the lead of Ginnie Mae, a government corporation, Freddie Mac and then Fannie Mae helped to promote necessary legislation and a market in mortgage-backed securities. Finally, Sallie Mae and then Fannie Mae and Freddie Mac have been among leaders in their segments of the market in adopting new technology-based servicing, loan management, and loan underwriting systems.

On the other hand, GSE shareholders come first, and it can be difficult for government to influence the direction that a GSE takes or the extent that it serves its public purpose. To the extent that the GSE's managers or shareholders find this objectionable, the government can have a hard time trying to effect any change. The Department of Housing and Urban Development has had great difficulty, for example, trying to issue regulations that finally will require Fannie Mae and Freddie Mac to lead rather than lag other mortgage lenders in serving disadvantaged minorities and other underserved borrowers.

Efficiency

For GSEs also, efficiency can be understood in terms of their enhancement of the quality of the part of the market that they serve. GSEs made considerable contributions to economic efficiency in earlier years when their designated markets contained significant imperfections. In their first decades of operation, for example, the Federal Home Loan Banks were able to raise money in the money centers of the Northeast and channel the funds to growing mortgage markets in the Midwest, West, and South.

In the United States, the earlier financial market imperfections in agriculture, residential mortgages, and student loans have been largely overcome by a combination of (1) repeal of earlier legislation that prevented commercial banks and other lenders from serving a national market, (2) growing efficiency of the financial markets markets, and (3) selective government credit programs. Without market imperfections to overcome, a GSE is unlikely to flourish except if its charter contains immense federal subsidies that could be provided more efficiently through a credit program or other mechanism. The Congressional Budget Office published a study that found, for example, that in 1995 Fannie Mae and Freddie Mac received over $6 billion in federal subsidies, but passed on only about $4 billion to benefit the residential mortgage market.[61]

Equity

111

CH 3:
GOVERNMENT
CORPORATIONS
AND
GOVERNMENT-
SPONSORED
ENTERPRISES

In contrast to FHA, VA, and the Department of Education, Fannie Mae, Freddie Mac, and Sallie Mae move to the most profitable parts of their charters. They lag rather than lead in serving disadvantaged borrowers and those kinds of loans that may be more expensive to service properly. Thus, Sallie Mae holds primarily the highest-quality loans. Although Sallie Mae does not preclude purchases of loans of trade school students, the GSE tends to serve borrowers at better schools. Similarly, Fannie Mae and Freddie Mac lag the primary mortgage market in their service to disadvantaged minorities, low-income borrowers, and low-income communities.

When GSEs find that their charter is confining, they attempt to obtain legislation to relax the restrictions. Fannie Mae and Freddie Mac, for example, recently obtained legislation to remove the size limits on the multifamily mortgages that they may purchase; they thus gained the authority to fund apartment buildings, condominiums, and special housing for high-income people who generally do not need access to government-backed credit, at least on equitable grounds.

Legitimacy

GSEs spend considerable effort defending their legitimacy. Fannie Mae and Freddie Mac have established foundations that provide grants to academics and community groups. Fannie Mae has established so-called partnership offices in almost every state to work with local community and political leaders and the housing community and to dispense small amounts of money and small housing programs in those geographic areas. Fannie Mae and Freddie Mac spend heavily on image advertising on television and radio and in influential print media.

This wide-ranging effort helps the GSEs to respond to questions about the legitimacy of their continuing profitability based on a government-granted special charter that is not available to other competitors. As noted earlier, there is a deep-seated American resentment against large monopoly companies and especially government-chartered monopolies. This resentment traces from the Boston Tea Party and Andrew Jackson's "Bank War" to Populist unhappiness with the monopoly behavior of the railroads, and later to the breakup of AT&T, the telecommunications monopoly, during the 1980s. It remains to be seen how these issues of legitimacy play out in the political process surrounding the GSEs.

VII. FUTURE DIRECTIONS

The Government Corporation

The government corporation is a valuable tool of government that deserves more attention in efforts to redesign government programs in the United States. In contrast to fashionable approaches such as the PBO, which rely on devices such as performance contracts with senior agency officials, the government corporation achieves an organizational bottom line that helps the entire institution to balance the accomplishment of a public mission against financial soundness. The government corporation should be self-sustaining. However, to the extent that the government is able to appropriate funds to support activities such as student loan programs, the government corporation also might be a useful tool for such activities, even though they are not financially self-sustaining without the additional appropriations.

However, as the TVA example shows, the government needs to develop the capacity to hold government corporations accountable. The Canadian model of a special

"Crown Corporations Directorate" might be a useful device to try in the United States, located perhaps within the Office of Management and Budget. Also, given the remarkable efficiency of today's markets, a combination of corporatization and then privatization may be a useful step for a number of government commercial activities. For example, deregulation of the production and transmission of power in the United States may make some change imperative in the purchase and transmission of power by U.S. power administrations such as Bonneville, and corporatization might be a good first step.

The state-owned enterprise has been a conspicuous failure in many developing countries. The problem appears to be that government in many of these countries lacks the institutional capability to hold state-owned enterprises accountable, either financially or for the achievement of important public purposes.

The Government-Sponsored Enterprise

In the past, GSEs have served important public purposes. When market imperfections exist, a GSE can be a valuable tool of government. However, as the private economy develops into a robust and efficient allocator of resources, the shortcomings of the GSE become more pronounced. Efficient markets increase the potential public costs of GSEs and reduce their ability to provide public benefits. Thus, given the efficiency of today's financial markets, the creation of new GSEs in the United States is not likely to be helpful in serving public purposes.

This is so because there is a structural flaw in the model for the larger GSEs. This is the creation of a government-subsidized firm with benefits that other firms do not receive. Once the GSE uses its government benefits to gain an entrenched market position, government loses the ability to direct this tool to serve important public purposes. Even when its original charter act purposes become obsolete or unimportant, the government usually lacks the capacity to redirect the activities of a GSE. The GSE can become the "sorcerer's apprentice," quite useful at first, but later impossible to stop or redirect.

The government also can lose the ability to assure that GSEs will be held accountable for financial safety and soundness. Shareholders want a highly leveraged company because of the consequently higher returns they receive on their equity; congressional authorizing committees tend to see financial failure as a merely conjectural possibility, and thus place a low priority on assuring safety and soundness until financial problems actually emerge. With their generally low capitalization, rapid growth, and limited financial supervision, today's GSEs in the United States represent the most recent example of the precept that for financial institutions risk will migrate to the place where government is least equipped to deal with it.

VIII. SUGGESTED READING

Government Corporations

Mitchell, Jerry. *The American Experiment with Government Corporations.* Armonk, N.Y.: M. E. Sharpe, 1999.
Moe, Ronald C. *Managing the Public's Business: Federal Government Corporations.* Washington, D.C.: Committee on Governmental Affairs, United States Senate. S. Prt. 104–18. April 1995.
National Academy of Public Administration. Standing Panel on Executive Organization and Management (NAPA-EOM) Web site: http://www.napawash.org/EOM.

Government-Sponsored Enterprises

113

CH 3:
GOVERNMENT
CORPORATIONS
AND
GOVERNMENT-
SPONSORED
ENTERPRISES

Congressional Budget Office. *Controlling the Risks of Government-Sponsored Enterprises.* Washington, D.C., April 1991.
———. *The Public Costs and Public Benefits of Fannie Mae and Freddie Mac.* Washington, D.C., July 1996.
Stanton, Thomas H. *A State of Risk.* New York: HarperCollins, 1991.

NOTES

1. See *Cherry Cotton Mills v. U.S.,* 327 U.S. 536 (1945).

2. The law governing federal instrumentalities, including GSEs, derives largely from two cases involving the second Bank of the United States, *McCulloch v. Maryland,* 17 U.S. (4 Wheat.) 738 (1819); and *Osborn v. Bank of the United States,* 22 U.S. (9 Wheat.) 738 (1824). Instrumentalities can be divided into those that are for-profit and those that are nonprofit, chartered by government and managed by a board of directors that may be largely autonomous from the government that appoints them. To keep the discussion manageable, this chapter will cover investor-owned or cooperative instrumentalities of the national or state government but will not discuss nonprofit organizations, except in passing. In the United States, nonprofit instrumentalities include federally chartered organizations such as the American National Red Cross and state-chartered nonprofit corporations that carry out a variety of activities in furtherance of public purposes. In the United Kingdom, the nonprofit Student Loans Company administers the U.K. student loan program as an adjunct to the Department for Education and Employment.

3. For the U.S. national government, the Government Corporation Control Act, 31 U.S.C. chapter 91, provides a list of government corporations that are subject to the act.

4. See Ian Thynne, "The Incorporated Company as an Instrument of Government: A Quest for a Comparative Understanding," *Governance: An International Journal of Policy and Administration* 7, no. 1 (January 1994): 59–82; and Ian Thynne, "Basic Concepts and Issues," *Corporatization, Divestment and the Public-Private Mix: Selected Country Studies,* ed. Ian Thynne, *Asian Journal of Public Administration* (1995): 1–9.

5. Compare Ronald C. Moe, ed., *General Management Laws: A Selective Compendium,* Congressional Research Service, CRS Report RL 30267 (1999).

6. For a list of the applicability of some laws to U.S. government corporations, see U.S. General Accounting Office, *Government Corporations: Profiles of Existing Government Corporations,* GAO/GGD 96–14 (Washington, D.C., December 1995). In the United States, one important provision relates to the discretion of a corporation to determine the necessity for and character of its expenditures; this provision relieves government corporation from application of restrictions that the appropriations laws otherwise would apply to government agencies.

7. Model legislation to create PBOs, and discussion of their attributes, can be found on the Web site of the National Performance Review, http://www.npr.gov.

8. This definition is consistent with the definition Congress enacted in amendments to the Congressional Budget Act of 1974 (at 2 U.S.C. Section 622 (8)).

9. It is clear both from the statutory definition and from the pattern of institutions that exist in the United States at least that GSEs are essentially financial institutions. Similarly, the Hong Kong Mortgage Corporation is a government corporation, currently backed by an express government guarantee, which is preparing for eventual conversion into a privately owned GSE with attributes and mortgage market functions similar to Fannie Mae in the United States.

10. Office of Federal Housing Enterprise Oversight, *Report to Congress* (Washington, D.C., 15 June 2000), 109, 119.

11. U.S. Department of the Treasury, *Government Sponsorship of the Federal National Mortgage Association and the Federal Home Loan Mortgage Corporation* (Washington, D.C., 11 July 1996), 81.

12. Thomas H. Stanton, "Government Sponsored Enterprises: Another View," *Public Budgeting & Finance* (autumn 1989): 81–86.

13. For example, in the United States, it is the state level of government that authorizes creation of most corporations; thus, state law rather than federal law contains the many important legal provisions that affect the day-to-day governance and operations of a corporate organization, including a government corporation. As is discussed below, government corporations should include in their authorizing legislation a number of corporate law provisions that are needed for effective operation of a government corporation.

14. A dated but still valuable guide to important legal provisions that help to confer capacity upon a federal government corporation is Sidney D. Goldberg and Harold Seidman, *The Government Corporation: Elements of a Model Charter* (Washington, D.C., Public Administration Service, 1953).

15. National Academy of Public Administration, *Report on Government Corporations,* vol. 1 (Washington, D.C., August 1981).

16. See U.S. General Accounting Office, *Government Corporations: Profiles of Existing Government Corporations,* GAO/GGD 96–14 (Washington, D.C., December 1995); and Harold Seidman, "The Quasi World of the Federal Government," *The Brookings Review* 6, no. 3 (summer 1988): 23–27.

17. *Lebron v. National Railroad Passenger Corporation,* 513 U.S. 374 (1995).

18. See, for example, Ian Thynne, "The Incorporated Company as an Instrument of Government: A Quest for a Comparative Understanding," *Governance: An International Journal of Policy and Administration* 7, no. 1 (January 1994): 59–82.

19. U.S. federal budget rules prescribe that, if the government owns even a small fraction of a going organization, then all activities of that organization must be displayed as a part of the appendix to the federal budget. (See the President's Commission on Budget Concepts, 1967.) The consequence of this general rule, which does have limited exceptions, is that private parties do not own any part of wholly owned federal government corporations, and the federal government does not own a formal stake in any so-called mixed-ownership government corporations. The 1967 rule led the federal government to separate the operations of the Federal National Mortgage Association into two parts, as noted above.

20. For reasons discussed in Thomas H. Stanton, *A State of Risk* (New York: HarperCollins, 1991).

21. See U.S. General Accounting Office, *Government Corporations: Profiles of Existing Government Corporations,* GAO/GGD 96–14 (Washington, D.C., December 1995); and Ronald C. Moe, *Managing the Public's Business: Federal Government Corporations* (Washington, D.C.: Committee on Governmental Affairs, United States Senate, S. Prt. 104–118, April 1995).

22. Jerry Mitchell, *The American Experiment with Government Corporations* (Armonk, N.Y.: M. E. Sharpe, 1999); and Donald Axelrod, *Shadow Government: The Hidden World of Public Authorities* (New York: Wiley, 1992); provide many more examples of government corporations at the state and local level.

23. See, for example, World Bank, *Bureaucrats in Business: The Economics and Politics of Government Ownership* (New York: Oxford University Press, 1995).

24. Ministry of Finance—Financial Bureau, Government of Japan, *FILP Report '98* (Tokyo, via Ministry of Finance Web site, October 1998).

25. Peter Curwen, "The United Kingdom," *Corporatization, Divestment and the Public-Private Mix: Selected Country Studies,* ed. Ian Thynne, *Asian Journal of Public Administration* (1995): 10–35.

26. Institute of Administrative Management, Administrative Management and Reform in Japan: Summary of the 1998 Annual Report of Management and Coordination Agency (Tokyo: March 1999), 29–34.

27. English-language version, at pp. 12–13.

28. John Thurston, *Government Proprietary Corporations in the English-Speaking Countries* (Cambridge, Mass.: Harvard University Press, 1937).

29. Yair Aharoni, *The Evolution and Management of State-Owned Enterprises* (Cambridge, Mass.: Ballinger Publishing, 1986).

30. Harold Seidman, "Organizational Relationships and the Control of Public Enterprise,"

Organization and Administration of Public Enterprises: Selected Papers (New York: United Nations, 1968), 156–168.

115

CH 3:
GOVERNMENT
CORPORATIONS
AND
GOVERNMENT-
SPONSORED
ENTERPRISES

31. John McDiarmid, *Government Corporations and Federal Funds* (Chicago: University of Chicago Press, 1938).

32. Celestea Gentry, *Federal Credit Programs: An Overview of Current Programs and Their Beginnings in the Reconstruction Finance Corporation* (Washington, D.C.: U.S. Department of the Treasury, Office of Corporate Finance, 18 July 1980).

33. Jerry Mitchell, *The American Experiment with Government Corporations* (Armonk, N.Y.: M. E. Sharpe, 1999). The earliest state government enterprise (but not a government corporation) was the Erie Canal, constructed as a wholly owned government enterprise under authority of an 1817 special act of the New York state legislature. The Erie Canal was funded from earmarked revenues and tolls from canal operations but was not a corporation with a distinct legal and financial identity distinct from other parts of the New York state government.

34. This history is explored in Thomas H. Stanton, "Nonquantifiable Risks and Financial Institutions: The Mercantilist Legal Framework of Banks, Thrifts, and Government-Sponsored Enterprises," *Global Risk-Based Capital Regulations,* vol. 1, eds. Charles A. Stone and Anne Zissu (Burr Ridge, Ill.: Irwin Professional Publishing, 1994), 57–97; and Yair Aharoni, *The Evolution and Management of State-Owned Enterprises* (Cambridge, Mass.: Ballinger Publishing, 1986).

35. For a discussion of the mortgage-backed security activities of the GSEs, see Thomas H. Stanton, *A State of Risk* (New York: HarperCollins, 1991).

36. See U.S. Department of Housing and Urban Development, *Studies on Privatizing Fannie Mae and Freddie Mac* (Washington, D.C., 1996).

37. Useful guidance on the content of such charters can be found in the 1996 Government Enterprises and Government Sponsored Enterprises Standards Act, S. 2095. Although that legislation was not enacted, it does provide a useful template that can help indicate some of the more important features of a corporation charter. The bill can be found at the NAPA-Executive Organization and Management Panel Web page, http://www.napawash.org/EOM. The OMB Memorandum on Government Corporations (1995) also contains valuable discussion. Policymakers also should consult Harold Seidman's discussion of the nature of government corporations and some of the important issues to be considered in their establishment; Harold Seidman, *Politics, Position and Power: The Dynamics of Federal Organization,* 5th ed. (New York: Oxford University, 1998), 187–196.

Unfortunately, there does not appear to be a statutory template for state government corporations; policymakers would be well advised to review the charters of successful government corporations in states such as New York and then to adapt those charters to the particular legal requirements of the state where the government corporation is to be created.

38. S. 2095, the 1996 Government Enterprises and Government Sponsored Enterprises Standards Act, also provides a useful template for policymakers who intend to create a new government-sponsored enterprise.

39. Harold Seidman, *Politics, Position and Power, The Dynamics of Federal Organization,* 5th ed. (New York: Oxford University, 1998), 193.

40. National Academy of Public Administration. *Report on Government Corporations, Vol. 1* (Washington, D.C., August 1981), 18. The Office of Management and Budget Memorandum on Government Corporations generally follows the four Truman criteria but (at p. 2) adds a similar caveat that:

"A first-order question is whether the government should perform [the proposed] function at all. . . . The possibility should be considered of moving operations (in whole or in part) that can sell good or services on a self-sustaining basis into the private sector."

41. Harold Seidman, review comments on an earlier draft of this chapter, 1 March 2000. Dr. Seidman provides examples from the Tennessee Valley Authority and the U.S. Postal Service.

42. Memorandum on Government Corporations, 14.

43. Jim Leach, "Dissenting Views of Representative Jim Leach," in *Government-Sponsored Housing Enterprises Financial Safety and Soundness Act of 1991,* House Report 102–206 (Washington, D.C.: Committee on Banking, Finance and Urban Affairs, U.S. House of Representatives), 112–115, at p. 115, 17 September 1991.

44. James Willard Hurst, *The Legitimacy of the Business Corporation* (Charlottesville: University Press of Virginia, 1970).

45. Kathleen Day, "Fear of What Fannie May Do: Lenders Say the Federally Chartered Company Is Out to Steal Their Business," *Washington Post* 8 (August 1999): H01.

46. See, for example, U.S. General Accounting Office, *Tennessee Valley Authority: Financial Problems Raise Questions about Long-term Viability*, GAO/AIMD/RCED 95–134 (Washington, D.C., August 1995).

47. Office of Management and Budget, Executive Office of the President, *Memorandum for Heads of Executive Departments and Agencies: Government Corporations*, M-96–05 (Washington, D.C., 8 December 1995).

48. Nicholas Lardy, *China's Unfinished Economic Revolution* (Washington, D.C.: The Brookings Institution, 1998).

49. Chi Fulin, *Pressing Tasks of China's Economic Transition* (Beijing: Foreign Languages Press, 1996).

50. The Web site of the Crown Corporations Directorate can be accessed through the NAPA-EOM Web page.

51. Thomas H. Stanton, "Nonquantifiable Risks and Financial Institutions: The Mercantilist Legal Framework of Banks, Thrifts, and Government-Sponsored Enterprises," *Global Risk-Based Capital Regulations*, vol. 1, eds. Charles A. Stone and Anne Zissu (Burr Ridge, Ill.: Irwin Professional Publishing, 1994), 57–97.

52. Office of Management and Budget, Executive Office of the President, *Memorandum for Heads of Executive Departments and Agencies: Government Corporations*, M-96–05 (Washington, D.C., 8 December 1995), 14.

53. See Thomas H. Stanton, "Federal Supervision of Safety and Soundness of Government-Sponsored Enterprises," *Administrative Law Journal* 5, no. 2 (summer 1991): 395–484.

54. U.S. Department of the Treasury, *Report of the Secretary of the Treasury on Government-Sponsored Enterprises* (Washington, D.C.: Government Printing Office, April 1991), 8.

55. Compare S. 1621, the "Federal Enterprise Regulatory Act of 1991," drafted by the U.S. General Accounting Office at the request of members of the Senate Committee on Governmental Affairs and introduced on 1 August 1991, recommending creation of an independent board, modeled upon the FDIC structure, to regulate all GSEs.

56. U.S. General Accounting Office, *Federal Housing Enterprises: HUD's Mission Oversight Needs to Be Strengthened*, GAO/GGD 98–173 (Washington, D.C., July 1998).

57. Sallie Mae, *The Restructuring of Sallie Mae: Rationale and Feasibility* (Washington, D.C., March 1994), 13–14, emphasis in original.

58. Darcy Bradbury, deputy assistant secretary of the Treasury for Federal Finance. Statement before the Subcommittee on Postsecondary Education, Training and Lifelong Learning, Committee on Economic and Educational Opportunities, and the Subcommittee on National Economic Growth, Natural Resources and Regulatory Affairs, Committee on Government Reform and Oversight, U.S. House of Representatives. Washington, D.C., 3 May 1995. The Office of Management and Budget (1995, p. 14) takes a similar position.

59. Congressional Budget Office, *Controlling the Risks of Government-Sponsored Enterprises* (Washington, D.C., April 1991), 44.

60. As Sallie Mae's then chief executive officer told a Senate oversight subcommittee some years ago: "We are a private corporation and as such, with stockholders and bondholders, we have a fiduciary responsibility to those individuals. . . . We are not charged with subsidizing the guaranteed student loan program or subsidizing the students." Edward A. Fox (President and CEO of Sallie Mae). Statement before the Subcommittee on Education, Arts and Humanities, Committee on Labor and Human Resources, United States Senate, *Oversight of Student Loan Marketing Association (Sallie Mae)*, Hearing (Washington, D.C.: GPO, 12 August 1982), 135.

61. Ibid.

CHAPTER FOUR

Economic Regulation*

The Telecommunications Act of 1996 is the first major revision of telecommunications regulation since 1934, and most likely will provide the statutory framework for the infrastructure and services of the new digital information age. Before the act was passed, Congress held extensive hearings about the future of communications regulation. Numerous representatives of firms, trade associations, and consumer groups offered proposals. Part of the act deals with cable television, and one witness at these hearings was Richard H. Cutler, president of Satellite Cable Services, who spoke on behalf of the Small Cable Business Association. Mr. Cutler's company provided cable service to ten thousand households in fifty-seven small towns in South Dakota, the home state of the act's cosponsor, Senator Larry Pressler. The following are excerpts from Mr. Cutler's testimony.[1]

Mr. Cutler: "The 1984 Cable Act deregulated cable and made it possible for people like myself . . . to build cable TV in some of these small communities. In fact, Chairman Pressler continued to ask me why we cannot build a system in Humboldt, South Dakota. And Humboldt, South Dakota, was eventually built during this era of deregulation . . . .

The Cable Act of 1992 [which reregulated cable TV] and the subsequent FCC rulings have a devastating effect on many small operators. We mistakenly believed that because we were providing good service at reasonable rates, the bill would not apply to us. . . . And, by the way, the company that built [the Humboldt system] is Douglas Communications, a member of our group, . . . that is now having some financial trouble . . . .

Of our 350 members of the SCBA, we estimate approximately one-half of them are currently in trouble. . . . The people at the FCC do not seem to understand the unique issues of the small cable operator. . . .[W]e would particularly implore you to exempt from rate regulation immediately upon enactment of this legislation, the cable operators. . . . [A] couple of other sources of pressures on rates that I think you could address.

First, we need fair pole attachment rates. The competitors [to cable systems] are going to be the telephone companies and the utilities. And they control many of those power poles. And it is very important that . . . there will be a fair determination on pole rates. . . .

Also, it is very important that there be nondiscrimination in programming rates. Chairman Pressler and I have worked for the last ten years to try to eliminate the pricing differentials between the large and small cable operators. . . . [W]e cannot compete fairly if we are paying [an] additional price for programming. And now we have DBS [Direct Broadcast Satellite] and MMDS [Metropolitan Multichannel Distribution Service] in our backyard. These providers are buying the programming at lower rates. . . . They are selling into our backyard . . . .

If the rural phone companies are given an advantage over the rural cable companies, . . . we will not be able to compete."

---

*This chapter was prepared by Lester M. Salamon based on material supplied by Dr. Roger Noll.

When the Senators questioned the witnesses, the following colloquy ensued.[2]

Senator Gorton: "Mr. Cutler, I have just one question. . . . You want us to deregulate the prices you can charge your customers, but further regulate the prices that your suppliers can charge you?"

Mr. Cutler: "Well, you could take it that way."

Eleven months later the act was passed almost completely deregulating cable television, while requiring that local telephone companies supply pole attachments at reasonable rates. Immediately, monthly cable bills began to rise. Cable channel capacity was increasing, so consumers generally were receiving more channels as prices rose. Nevertheless, news media reported consumer complaints. The *Detroit News* carried a story about Maria Gilbert, a housewife from Grosse Pointe Farms (a wealthy Detroit suburb), who reported that her monthly bill had risen about 20 percent (or five dollars).[3] According to Ms. Gilbert: "Service is less than desirable. Between work and classes and everything, I don't watch it enough to get my money's worth." Bradley Stillman, telecommunications policy director of the Consumer Federation of America, agreed, observing: "The bottom line is these companies are monopolies and they're raising rates because they can."

I. DEFINING ECONOMIC REGULATION

The issues that arose during the hearings about cable television illustrate the challenges involved in implementing the tool of economic regulation. Briefly, economic regulation is a specialized bureaucratic process that combines aspects of both courts and legislatures to control prices, output, and/or the entry and exit of firms in an industry. Prominent examples of this tool are setting price ceilings and other operating requirements for utilities that historically have been monopolies, such as cable television, electricity, railroads, and telephones.

Defining Features

The defining features of economic regulation are sometimes difficult to grasp because in common parlance "regulation" is used in reference to a broader range of policies and policymaking processes. Defining economic regulation narrowly and more precisely allows policy analysts to distinguish between categories of government actions that have very different purposes and effects.

The first complication in defining the tool of economic regulation is that sometimes "regulation" refers to the rules and procedures of government agencies regarding the qualifications for participation in their programs. Examples are requirements for submitting proposals for government grants or contracts, and procedures for setting the fees that doctors and hospitals receive for patient care under the Medicare program. In this book, by contrast, the term "regulation" refers mainly to rules governing private activities, not the internal operation of government programs.[4] This distinction is important. Rules governing the implementation of a program are part of government management, not a tool of government action. As defined here, "regulation" refers to rules about economic activities in which the agency issuing these rules is not otherwise a participant.

A second complication in defining economic regulation is that it refers to the process for developing and enforcing rules as well as the rules themselves. A distinctive feature of regulation is that it is agency-made law. Two other means for promulgating legally binding rules are legislation and judicial decisions. Some statutes contain rules to govern private behavior as well as to establish government programs. An example is speed limits on street and highways, and the French law that the price of a plain baguette cannot exceed three francs. Judicial decisions apply constitutional, statutory, and common law to a particular conflict. Because courts usually follow precedent, that is, defer to past decisions on similar cases, novel court decisions sometimes become enduring rules to govern economic activity.

Regulation refers to rules written by appointed public officials to implement often vaguely worded statutes that delegate rule-making authority to an agency. With this delegation of lawmaking power comes complicated procedural requirements. Because bureaucrats lack the political legitimacy of elected officials and constitutional courts, they face procedural safeguards that are not applied to legislative or judicial processes.

A third complication is that regulation takes two rather different forms: economic regulation and social regulation. These types of regulation differ with respect to the purposes they serve and the methods that they use. *Economic regulation* controls the entry and exit of firms (*entry controls*), prices (*price controls*), and/or output (*production controls*). *Social regulation* deals with the effects of economic activity on the health, welfare, or social well-being of citizens. Examples of social regulation are rules to control pollution, discrimination, and the safety of workplaces and products.

The distinction between economic and social regulation is far from precise. Sometimes economic regulation is used for social purposes, and social regulation sometimes uses price, output, and entry controls. For example, in licensing broadcasters (entry control), the Federal Communications Commission (FCC) gives preference to applicants that do not own newspapers in the same city (to promote competition in news reporting and advertising, and so an economic regulation) and to applicants in which women and minorities have substantial ownership interests (to promote diversity in programs and employment, and so a social regulation). Likewise, in the 1980s, some state regulators set electricity prices so that utilities earned higher profits on investments in renewable energy resources and energy conservation than on investments in traditional generation technologies. The purpose of this policy was to create incentives to reduce fossil fuel consumption, air pollution, and nuclear waste.

Despite overlaps between economic and social regulation, their differences are salient enough to treat them as related but distinct tools of government. This chapter focuses on economic regulation, and the next chapter deals with social regulation.

Relation to Key Tool Features

In the introduction, Lester Salamon defines four key common features of tools: *coerciveness, directness, automaticity,* and *visibility.* Economic regulation ranks high in coerciveness, low in automaticity, and intermediate in directness and visibility.

Coerciveness

Coerciveness measures the extent to which a tool restricts individual or group behavior as opposed to merely encouraging or discouraging it. Economic regulation is highly coercive in that firms may not participate in regulated markets unless licensed to do so by the regulator, and can be fined or have their licenses canceled if they do not comply with the rules. Consumers can also be punished for violating regulatory rules, such as operating a broadcast station without a license or reselling electricity or telephone service to a neighbor. Coerciveness is one of the defining characteristics of both economic and social regulation.

Although regulation inherently is highly coercive, regulators usually have considerable discretion in deciding how much coercion will be used. For example, the Interstate Commerce Commission (ICC), prior to surface freight deregulation in 1980, specified precisely which products each license holder could ship in which direction between each pair of cities in the United States, and set the price of every service that every firm offered (a total of over 4 billion prices). Meanwhile, the FCC, operating under statutory language that was nearly identical to the ICC's, simply set an overall revenue ceiling for all long-distance services that were offered by the American Telephone and Telegraph Company (AT&T), and let the company decide how to price calls between any two cities at any particular time of day. Later, after competition was established in long-distance service, the FCC's price ceiling was above the prices actually charged, so that its price ceilings did not actually constrain the behavior of regulated firms.

Directness

Directness measures the extent to which the entity authorizing or inaugurating a program is involved in carrying it out. Economic regulation is direct in that regulatory agencies control entry, set prices, and fine anyone who violates their rules. However, economic regulation is indirect in that, within the limits established by regulatory rules, production and consumption decisions are made by participants in regulated markets, not by the government. The ultimate purpose of economic regulation is not to promulgate rules and issue licenses, but to change the terms of transactions between buyers and sellers. The most direct form of price and output control is through public enterprise, whereby government owns and operates the industry. An example is the postal system. A less direct method would be to use taxes and subsidies to achieve the same objectives by using economic incentives.

Automaticity

Automaticity refers to the extent to which a tool utilizes existing administrative structures (e.g., markets or taxes) rather than creating a new administrative apparatus. Economic regulation usually ranks low in terms of automaticity in that economic regulation substitutes administrative decisions about prices, entry, and output for the decisions that would be made in an unregulated market. Nevertheless, regulators sometimes rely on market mechanisms to achieve their policy objectives.

For example, the FCC and similar agencies in other nations use "spectrum auctions" to decide which firms can offer radio telephone service and other wireless telecommunications. In this case, regulators use an administrative process to decide how many firms will receive a license to enter the industry, and a market process to allocate these licenses among competing applicants. Another example is "benchmark" regulation, in which regulated prices are set equal to the prices that arise in another market, perhaps one that is unregulated and competitive. Finally, in a few cases, regulation is procompetitive and used only intermittently and temporarily to encourage competition rather than to substitute for a market process. Notwithstanding these exceptions, economic regulation almost always takes the form of a specialized, enduring bureaucratic process, not an automatic one.

Visibility

Visibility measures the extent to which a tool is visible in budget and policy processes, and hence is politically salient in the democratic process. Economic regulation has a mixed ranking on this dimension because it is highly visible to those who are most affected by it, but largely invisible to most citizens.

Regulatory agencies try to make their activities visible by publishing their findings, rules and enforcement decisions, and even operating hotlines and Web sites to provide information to ordinary citizens. Moreover, regulatory agencies are required to let anyone with a direct stake in their actions participate in their decision processes by submitting information and arguments and by examining and critiquing the submissions of others. Thus, regulation is among the government processes that are most open to widespread monitoring and participation by ordinary citizens.

Regulated firms and their largest customers take advantage of these opportunities to keep informed and to participate, and as a result regulation is highly visible to them. But despite the outreach policies of agencies, relatively few citizens pay attention to economic regulation because they have little personal motivation to do so. As taxpayers, citizens have little reason to be concerned about regulation because the budget of a regulatory agency is very small compared with many other programs. As consumers, citizens have a much larger stake because an agency's budget, which covers only the government's cost of operating it, is a tiny portion of the costs and benefits of its actions. The total cost of economic regulation includes expenditures of regulated firms and others for participating in regulatory proceedings and, as discussed elsewhere in this chapter, the loss in economic efficiency that is the inevitable result of substituting regulation for a market. Research has estimated that in several industries the total cost of economic regulation amounts to billions of dollars annually, which is between ten and one hundred times the budget of an agency. On the benefit side, in huge utility industries such as electricity and telephone service, if regulation only reduces prices by even 1 or 2 percent, its benefits include billions of dollars in saving to consumers.

As impressive as these total benefits and costs might be, they amount to only a few dollars per capita. Hence, consumers are likely to have many other more important things to worry about than whether telephone service will rise by a dollar a month. As a result, most citizens do not put forth the effort to become informed about economic regulation. The invisibility of economic regulation to most citizens creates real strains on democratic control of regulatory agencies.

Major Variants in Design Features

The prototype for the tool of economic regulation substitutes administrative control of prices, production, and entry in an industry for the outcomes that would arise in a market. The major variations from this prototype are to limit regulation to one or two of these three major activities, or to use economic regulation to promote unregulated competition rather than to substitute for it.

Price regulation without either production or entry controls is rare, but not unknown. In the United States, almost all cities regulate taxi fares, and most issue a limited number of licenses to operate taxis (entry control), while requiring that taxi firms provide service on a 24-hour-a-day basis (production control). The logic behind this system is that by limiting entry during lucrative daytime periods, regulators can compensate firms for operating late at night, when prices may be inadequate to recover costs because too few people need service. In a few cities, regulators set the price but license all taxis that satisfy minimum safety requirements. Two inconsistent explanations are offered for this policy: to protect consumers against price gouging, and to enable drivers to earn an adequate living without working long hours or driving too fast in order to maximize the number of fares in a day.

Entry control without price or production regulation is used in some types of retail trade, especially in Europe and Asia. To obtain a license an applicant must show that additional retail outlets are needed. Some countries also limit the maximum size of retail outlets, the merchandise that a licensee can sell (e.g., fish stores cannot sell meat, and noodle shops cannot sell cheese), and the days and hours of operation, which are production controls. In the United States, some state and local governments control the number of liquor stores and bars, but otherwise entry controls on retail trade are rare.

The most important example of entry control pertains to industries that use the electromagnetic spectrum, including broadcasting. Commercial radio began after World War I, and soon thereafter nearly all nations declared that the electromagnetic spectrum was a public resource to be allocated and governed by the state. Most nations reserved broadcasting for public enterprise, like the BBC in the United Kingdom, RAI in Italy, and Radio France. In the United States and a few other countries, broadcasting was left to the private sector, but government created a regulatory system to license broadcast entities.[5]

Production controls without either entry or price controls are rare but not unknown. An example of pure production control is rationing, which is common during national emergencies such as war or famine. During World War II, the United States adopted an extensive system of rationing to limit consumption in order to free production capacity to support the war effort. After setting a ceiling on national consumption of a product, the government distributed coupons to citizens, which then had to be surrendered to a retailer when buying the commodity. These coupons amounted to a second currency: a consumer needed the right amount of both coupons and money to buy the product.

Another example of production controls is marketing quotas in agriculture. For example, long ago the federal government set limits on sales of tobacco for every farmer who previously had grown tobacco in the United States. Because growers can sell their production limits to other farmers within the same county, this rule does not prevent entry or exit, and, although the government subsidized tobacco farmers, the price of tobacco was determined in the market rather that regulated.

Procompetitive regulation is an adjunct to, rather than a substitute for, market competition. The distinction between these two cases is important. Usually regulation is anticompetitive in that it is based on the belief that the normal market process, including entry by new competitors, will not lead to socially desirable prices and output. By contrast, procompetitive regulation does not attempt to control all transactions. Instead, it selectively intervenes when competition breaks down or before it emerges, then retreats when competition is robust.

For example, after long-distance competition emerged in the United States, the FCC relaxed regulation in three ways. First, the FCC eliminated the requirement that a firm could enter long distance only if it proved that the incumbent monopoly carrier (AT&T) had failed to provide a desirable service, and used licensing only to enforce technical standards and to keep the Commission informed about activities in the industry. Second, the FCC applied price regulation only to the dominant carrier, AT&T, and not to its smaller competitors. Third, regulated prices became a ceiling but not a floor, so that AT&T could match the prices of its competitors without FCC approval. By the early 1990s, literally hundreds of firms had entered long distance and the FCC's price rules had no effect, as competition forced AT&T to charge less than regulation allowed.

II. PATTERNS OF USE
OF ECONOMIC REGULATION

Historically, economic regulation has been applied to many different industries. In addition to traditional infrastructure industries such as telephones, electricity, and railroads, economic regulation sometimes is used to set prices for basic necessities, such as minimum prices for milk and maximum prices for bread and rental housing. In many nations staple agricultural crops are regulated extensively with respect to both price and production quantities. During the Communist era in Eastern Europe, private businesses operated in some retail industries, but bureaucratic overseers set the prices of their products and inputs, including the wages of their employees.

Economic Regulation in the United States

The United States has nearly two centuries of experience with economic regulation, beginning with state regulation of tariffs for toll roads and canals around 1800. Economic regulation migrated to the federal government in 1887 with the passage of the Interstate Commerce Act (ICA), which established the ICC to regulate the railroads. The ICC was very popular after its creation, and as a result the language of the ICA was copied almost verbatim when the government began to regulate long-distance telephone service in 1910. Federal economic regulation subsequently was imposed on interstate sales of power, many agricultural products, broadcasting, truck, water, air and bus transportation, oil and natural gas pipelines, the wellhead price of natural gas, and, finally, during the shortages of the 1970s, petroleum.

Many federal regulatory laws were enacted during the Great Depression as part of President Franklin Roosevelt's New Deal, including amendments to acts passed earlier to regulate telephones and broadcasting and new legislation to regulate agricultural commodities, airlines, trucks, water transport, insurance, banking, and natural gas. In addition, early New Deal legislation established planning boards for a wide variety of industries that were severely impacted by the Great Depression; however, for reasons discussed below, the Supreme Court declared these laws unconstitutional.

The states also expanded economic regulation from the early nineteenth century until the 1980s. The ICA gave the ICC the authority to regulate all rail transportation, but it also gave states the authority to regulate shipments that were completely within the same state. The Constitution reserves to the federal government the authority to regulate interstate commerce. In railroads and other infrastructure industries, the facilities that are used for intrastate service are also used for interstate service, so that economic regulation by one level of government can affect the quality and cost of service that is regulated by the other level. Hence, the right to regulate interstate commerce gives federal regulators the authority to override state regulation. Nevertheless, nearly all federal regulatory statutes delegate to the states some autonomy to regulate the intrastate portion of an industry, and nearly all states choose to regulate all infrastructure industries.

Local governments also participate in some aspects of regulation. Legally, local governments are extensions of state governments, so their authority to regulate is at the sufferance of states and subject to the same constitutional limitations as state regulation. However, states typically delegate to local governments the important function of regulating land use, such as through zoning and business licenses. This authority is sometimes used for regulatory purposes, such as to control the number or size of firms in a local industry.

Local governments also participate in controlling entry into utility businesses, like electricity and telephones. These industries need access to streets and private property for distribution networks. Local governments grant this access, usually in return for certain guarantees concerning services. A relatively recent example is cable television, in which local franchising authority is used to negotiate such things as the capacity of the cable system, the number of channels to be used for the free use by local government and civic groups, and the neighborhoods that will be offered service. Initially, these agreements specified the price of cable service, but the federal government successfully asserted jurisdiction over cable prices on the ground that broadcast services are part of interstate commerce. Eventually, this authority was used to deregulate cable prices and to prohibit state and local governments from reregulating.

During the 1970s, the growth of economic regulation was reversed. Nearly all economic regulation of transportation disappeared, and competition replaced regulation in elements of electricity, telecommunications, and natural gas; however, in many cases, "deregulation" led to a new set of regulations to guide the transition from monopoly to competition. Moreover, elements of these industries remain largely monopolized and subject to "transition" regulation years after the goal of deregulated competition was adopted. As a result, some economic regulatory agencies are larger, not smaller, in the deregulation era.

Economic Regulation in the Rest of the World

Until recently, most of the world relied on state-owned enterprises (SOEs) to provide core infrastructure services. The major exception was Canada. Although Canada had more SOEs than the United States, it utilized regulated private enterprise in some infrastructure industries, notably, telecommunications. SOEs are not unknown in the United States. Some of the largest electric power companies are owned by either the federal government (e.g., the Tennessee Valley Authority) or local governments (e.g., the Los Angeles Department of Water and Power). Nevertheless, until about 1990 the extent of private ownership of infrastructure industries was far greater in the United States than elsewhere.

In the nineteenth century, most infrastructure industries in the world began as private companies that were not regulated or that were regulated through local government franchising.[6] Nationalization began in Europe at roughly the same time that economic regulation was introduced in the United States. But Europeans did not initially extend nationalization to their colonies. A few former colonies nationalized some utility companies during the Great Depression, but most nationalizations in the colonies took place during the 1950s and 1960s. At this time most firms were foreign owned and provided limited service only in the large population centers. Nationalization was partly an expression of nationalism, especially in newly independent states, and partly an expression of discontent with the quality of service.

Unfortunately, in both advanced and developing countries, nationalization rarely caused service to improve and frequently made it worse. Nationalized entities suffered from politicization of employment and prices, so that they usually charged low prices, paid high wages, and employed more people than were needed to operate the firm effectively. As a result, when the United States entered the deregulation era, the rest of the world began a reprivatization wave, selling SOEs to the private sector.

Far from eliminating government involvement, privatization led to economic regulation as a substitute for government management. For example, when the United Kingdom privatized British Telecom, it also established a new regulator, the Office of Telecommunications, and when electric generation was privatized, the Office of Electricity Supply was established to regulate that industry. In Mexico, Telecommunications of Mexico (Telmex) was privatized in 1990, and in 1996 the Federal Commission for Telecommunications (Cofetel) was created to regulate it.

Even in countries that did not fully privatize, private firms were allowed to enter segments of the industry to compete with the former monopoly SOE. For example, Germany and Japan have sold a minority interest in their SOE telephone companies to private investors and have opened the industry to competitive entry by fully private companies, but subject to regulation.

In short, economic regulation is hardly disappearing as a tool of government. To the contrary, its use seems to be expanding around the world.

III. BASIC MECHANICS

As discussed in Section I, the prototypical economic regulatory program involves three basic activities: first, controlling which firms can operate in an industry; second, setting the prices of the regulated products; and third, constraining the output of regulated firms. For each of these, moreover, a set of rules must be established and applied. In the discussion that follows, we examine each of these activities in turn, focusing first on the promulgation of basic rules.

Promulgation and Application of Rules

The task of a regulatory agency is to implement the policies in its underlying statute. Usually the statute that establishes a regulatory policy defines the market that is to be regulated. Most statutes also require that regulated firms provide service to anyone who wants it. These laws also state the purposes of regulation, but typically they provide only vague directions about the goals of regulatory policy. For example, several regulatory statutes simply instruct an agency to pursue the "public interest, convenience and necessity." This inevitably leaves considerable discretion in the hands of the administrators.

To constrain this discretion, all regulatory agencies operate under statutes and court decisions that shape the procedures that agencies must follow in implementing their statutory mandate. The most important of these statutes, the Administrative Procedure Act, recognizes three types of proceedings: rulemaking, cases that apply the rules, and cases that enforce the rules.

Types of Proceedings

RULEMAKING. Rulemaking refers to adopting general regulations for all firms in an industry, such as a method for setting prices, requirements for a license, or an approach to establishing production controls. For example, in a proceeding called *Specialized Common Carriers,* the FCC abandoned its policy of reserving all long-distance services for a designated monopoly carrier (AT&T) and set forth conditions under which it would allow other carriers to enter the industry.

REGULATORY CASES. Regulatory case decisions deal with regulating a specific firm, such as responding to its license application or setting its prices. For example, in the states with the most sophisticated regulatory agencies, each year regulators separately review the investment decisions, costs, revenues, profits, and prices of each electricity and telephone company. At the FCC, the *MCI* decision allowed AT&T's first long-distance competitor into the market.

Rulemaking and case decisions have similar requirements, and regulators have a great deal of discretion in deciding which procedure to adopt in response to a new policy controversy. Most agencies are not legally required to issue general rules, but can mimic courts by establishing their policies in a series of case decisions rather than in a rule-making proceeding. Similarly, when regulating industries with numerous firms, agencies can set general rules regarding prices and output in rule-making proceedings and avoid individual case decisions. For example, before natural gas wells were deregulated in 1980, the Federal Power Commission used "field price regulation," setting the same price for all wells in the same geographic area on the basis of the average costs of a well.

ENFORCEMENT CASES. Enforcement cases, which are called adjudication, essentially are trials in which the regulator investigates whether someone has violated either the agency's underlying statute or one of its implementing regulations. The primary difference between regulatory and enforcement cases is that in the latter the agency is required by the courts to satisfy a higher standard of proof. The law treats license applications and license enforcement very differently. A citizen does not have a fundamental right to a license, but once a license is granted, a citizen does have the right to use the license unless the licensee can be proved to have violated the laws and regulations governing its use. As a result, denying a license is far easier than taking one away.

Basic Requirements for Regulatory Decisions

Agencies are required to follow certain substantive rules in regulating an industry. These requirements apply to both rulemaking and case decisions, and to decisions about entry and exit (licenses), prices, and production controls.

FEASIBILITY. As a legal matter, the requirements that regulators impose on regulated firms must be economically and technically feasible. Regulators cannot require that firms violate the laws of nature, produce products for which there is no demand, or set prices so low that costs cannot be recovered. In American law, the legal principle at work here is the "rational basis" standard: regulators bear the burden of proof that their decisions are not "arbitrary and capricious," and that a connection exists between the regulation and the problem it is intended to solve. Unless constitutional rights are involved, neither courts nor legislatures labor under such a constraint.

CONSTITUTIONALITY. In the United States, regulators face constraints that are derived from federal and state constitutions. In the early nineteenth century, the Supreme Court held that state regulation violated the constitutional provision that requires states to honor contracts,[7] and late in the nineteenth century the Court decided that some federal regulatory statutes violated the "delegation doctrine," under which only Congress can enact laws. These precedents have long since been overturned, although some legal scholars and political leaders still believe that the Court erred in reversing its views on delegation.

Perhaps the most important constitutional restriction on economic regulation is the prohibition against "takings." The Fifth Amendment to the U.S. Constitution states that the federal government cannot expropriate private property without due process of law and just compensation. The 14th Amendment applies the same rule to state and local governments. In the case of regulation, "due process" means that regulators must allow firms to present information and arguments before regulations are issued, must take this information into account in making decisions, and must let firms earn a reasonable return on investment unless the regulation pertains to a threat to public health and safety. Economic regulators can rule that a firm is not entitled to recover costs that are wasteful or are not incurred for providing regulated service, but regulators cannot set prices so low that a firm cannot recover costs that are reasonably incurred to provide regulated service. The latter is deemed a taking without just compensation.[8]

Some regulated monopolies claim that the takings doctrine applies if regulators allow competitors to enter a formerly regulated monopoly. New competition sometimes creates "stranded investments"—facilities that become unnecessary or obsolete because competitors take away their customers. Firms argue that regulation guarantees that their reasonable investments will be recovered, so that introducing competition that strands these investments is no different than setting a price that is below cost.

The idea that introducing competition is a taking has been rejected by U.S. regulators and, thus far, the courts, although the Supreme Court has not resolved the issue. However, this view is now the law in New Zealand. The British Privy Council, which acts as New Zealand's highest court, ruled that the incumbent telephone monopoly was entitled to recover its stranded costs through charges levied on competitors.

STATUTORY AUTHORIZATION. The legal constraints of statutes and executive orders (decrees) also limit the discretion of regulators. All agencies implement authorization acts that state the agency's policy objectives, legal powers, and spending authority, and can be sued if their actions lie outside the scope of their underlying statutory mandate. As discussed above, regulatory agencies are subject to special laws about their decisionmaking process, such as the Administrative Procedure Act, that generally do not apply to other bureaucratic decisions. Likewise, the chief executive, in carrying out the responsibility for implementing statutory policies, can issue directives about the organization and management of regulatory agencies as long as these directives are not in conflict with the statute that created the agency.

JUDICIAL REVIEW. In most nations, the decisions of regulatory agencies can be appealed to the courts. Among the possible grounds for appeals are the evidence cited by the agency does not provide a reasonable basis for the agency's conclusions; other material evidence was ignored by the agency; the agency violated its own procedures in gathering information and reaching a decision; the agency's decision conflicts with or is not authorized by the underlying statute on which the regulation is based; and the agency erred in denying some interested party the right to participate in its decision process.

IMPLICATIONS. Because the procedural requirements for regulatory decisions are complex and judicial review of the agency's procedures and decisions are likely to be thorough, the administrative requirements faced by regulators are an important distinctive factor that shapes regulatory policy. Together these constraints place a significant burden on regulators to issue regulations that can withstand legal challenges. This burden is apparent in all significant regulatory decisions. Typically, important decisions are very long, running hundreds of pages. By contrast, the police do not issue long documents explaining why someone was arrested, and agencies that make research grants do not write hundreds of pages explaining why some scholars receive a grant and others do not. Regulatory decisions usually contain extensive discussions of the statutory basis of the agency's decision, the information and arguments offered by all parties who participated in the decision, and the decision to favor one party's evidence over the evidence of another. Likewise, decisions often address constitutional issues, such as due process, delegation, and takings, in anticipation of court appeals.

While these constraints impose limits on regulators, they also strengthen regulation as a tool of government. Most scholars believe that a well-designed formal decision process is necessary for effective regulation because formal procedures give credibility and durability to regulatory decisions. Formal law enables regulated firms to rely on regulation not to be unreasonable, inconsistent, and unpredictable, which are necessary conditions for firms to be willing to make significant long-term investments.

Controlling Entry

One of the key activities about which rules must be promulgated and applied in economic regulation is the regulation of the entry and exit of firms into a regulated market, which is implemented by mandatory registration, usually called licensing. The details of licensing depend on whether the agency seeks to use licensing to prevent entry, to extract concessions from entrants about the nature of the service that they will provide, or simply to assure that entrants understand the rules and regulators know that a firm is providing service. Some license requirements, such as local businesses licenses, amount to nothing more than filing notice that a firm is entering a market and certifying that the firm understands and will abide by the rules. These licenses are automatically granted without a formal case review.

Other licensing processes are designed explicitly to restrict competition. This is the case, for example, where natural monopolies are thought to exist. In these cases, the term of a license is long, and licensing focuses on erecting barriers to entry. During the 1970s, some agencies used licensing to prevent all entry. For example, the CAB did not permit a single entrant in commercial trunk airlines for forty years, and in some cases never bothered to deny a license or even schedule a hearing in response to an application.

When licensing is based on a policy that views competition skeptically, the licensing procedure usually requires that an applicant prove that entry is desirable. This proof normally has two elements: qualification and need for service.

The qualification element refers to whether the applicant is capable of providing adequate service. Firms typically need to reveal their detailed investment plans to prove that they are technically feasible and that their officers and employees possess the necessary technical and business skills for successful provision of service. In addition, the applicants are required to demonstrate that the firm has sufficient financial resources to bear the costs of entering the industry.

The-need-for-service element requires the firm to prove that incumbent licensees cannot or will not provide the same service. Usually this requirement is not satisfied by showing that the entrant will have lower costs or a superior product, but by showing that some potential customers are not being and will not be served by incumbents.

Licensing that prohibits or strictly limits entry has become extremely rare. The deregulation movement that began in the mid-1970s largely succeeded in convincing political leaders that regulated firms should not be protected against competition. In the United States, the federal government became favorably inclined toward competitive entry in regulated industries before many states and passed several statutes that overrode state laws and regulations that prevented entry. For example, the Public Utility Regulatory Policy Act of 1980 required states to allow firms deploying renewable energy resources into electricity generation, and the Telecommunications Act of 1996 required states to allow competition in local telephone and cable television service.

The FCC's spectrum auctions are a licensing procedure that limits entry without eliminating competition or imposing price and production requirements. The FCC allocates the electromagnetic spectrum among alternative uses and has allocated less for wireless telecommunications than consumers want and firms are willing to supply in order to preserve frequency assignments for other purposes, such as high-definition television, emergency services, air traffic control, and national defense communication.

The FCC's spectrum allocation causes scarcity in wireless services, so that the lucky firms that obtain these licenses can receive far greater profits than would be possible if the market had no entry restrictions. Consequently, firms are willing to pay a great deal for these licenses. The spectrum auction is a licensing process that allows the government to capture the value of spectrum scarcity from license applicants.

In still other cases, the purpose of licensing is to extract service concessions from applicants. In these cases, licenses are not intended to prevent entry so much as to make certain that firms provide services that regulators most desire. These licenses typically have a shorter duration, giving regulators the opportunity to alter service demands. In these cases, licensing is closely related to production and price controls, and so is discussed in the sections dealing with the mechanics of these regulatory decisions.

Controlling Prices

The core of economic regulation is to control prices of monopolies on the basis of three sometimes conflicting objectives: to prevent abuse of monopoly power while enabling the firm to earn a sufficient profit to induce adequate investment; to facilitate competition among firms that compete with the regulated firm in some markets but that must buy services from the monopoly; and to assure "universal service," or reasonable access to some level of service for virtually everyone.

Historically, regulators had a simpler task. Their job was to set prices to recover the cost of a monopolist without allowing monopoly profits, assuming that the monopoly was natural. Most of the methods of price regulation were invented in this simpler era before potential competition and universal service became significant issues. As time has passed, scholars and government officials have come to believe that important segments of regulated industries are not, and maybe never were, natural monopolies, and that competition is likely to be more efficient than regulated monopoly. This evolution in the perceived role of economic regulation has placed severe strains on the traditional approach to price setting.

The obvious solution to the regulatory pricing problem is *cost-of-service regulation:* set prices to cover the firm's costs, including the profits that are necessary to induce adequate investment, but no more; and set the price of each service on the basis of the costs that can be attributed to that service. Although cost-of-service regulation appears to be a rather mechanical accounting exercise, in practice it can be very complex and controversial. One problem is that price regulation must be forward-looking, in that regulators set prices for the future, but the most reliable cost data pertain to the past. The other problem is determining whether a firm is well managed in that it minimizes long-term costs.

More specifically, cost-of-service price regulation involves six distinct tasks: calculating variable costs, estimating capital facilities costs, applying the "used and useful" test, determining the cost of financial capital, adjusting total costs for past mistakes, and adopting a pricing system to recover reasonable costs. In this section we examine this traditional approach to regulatory price controls. In a later section we then examine some of the newer incentive approaches now being tried in response to a number of significant challenges that have arisen to the traditional approach.

Calculating Variable Costs

Accounting practice separates the costs of a firm into "variable" and "capital" costs. At the heart of this separation is the economically meaningful concept of the durability of an input to the production process. Capital costs refer to inputs that, once acquired, are used in the production process for more than one year, such as land, buildings, and equipment. For example, the capital costs of a railroad are rights of way, track, terminals, locomotives, and rail cars. Variable costs are the costs of inputs that are acquired and fully utilized in less than a year. The main components of variable costs are wages and salaries of employees, taxes, and material inputs to production, such as coal for electric generation and electricity for operating a telephone system. If the costs of an input are incurred continuously, the annual cost is easy to measure. Thus, the process of estimating variables costs is a mechanical accounting exercise: inspect the books of the regulated firm to determine how much was spent on variable inputs during the year.

Estimating Capital Costs

The estimation of capital costs also has a mechanical accounting aspect, which is to examine the books to ascertain how much the firm has spent on the facilities that it owns. However, estimating the annual capital costs is far more complex. The complex part is determining how much of these costs are to be attributed to operations in a single year. The term that applies to this concept is *depreciation,* or the extent to which the useful service of an asset in some sense is "used up" in a given year. A firm's annual capital facilities cost is the total amount of depreciation of its capital investments during the year.

The *depreciation rate* is the annual percentage decline in the value of a capital asset, and the depreciation cost of a capital facility is the product of its depreciation rate times its value at the beginning of the year. The depreciation rate depends on an asset's physical life—how long it can be expected to operate before becoming useless junk— and on whether and when it will become functionally obsolete. Different capital facilities can have widely differing depreciation rates. Rights of way do not depreciate because they are not "used up" over time and have little chance of obsolescence, but computers have a useful life of only a few years because usually they are obsolete before they cease to function due to rapid technological progress in both hardware and software. As a result, the annualized capital cost of service is a complex and abstract concept.

The Used and Useful Test

The basic concept behind the "used and useful" test is to determine whether a regulated firm follows good business practices in acquiring inputs. This test addresses three questions: (1) Is the input actually used in producing regulated services, as opposed to lying idle or being used to produce something else? (2) Did the firm pay more for the input than would have been paid had it exercised reasonable diligence in finding a seller and negotiating a price? (3) Has the firm adopted the most efficient production technology to maximize the value of the regulated service to customers? A *cost disallowance* occurs if the regulator decides the answer to any of these questions is negative.

The used and useful test is applicable to all of a firm's variable and capital costs, but as a practical matter tends to be applied only to the most important elements of a firm's cost. One reason is that regulators are not likely to possess enough information to be effective in second-guessing a firm about choices of technology and day-to-day production decisions. In addition, because of the political implications, regulators do not question elements of contracts that the firm negotiates with a labor union.

Despite limitations to its application, cost disallowance is an important part of economic regulation. During the late 1970s and early 1980s, the electric utility industry was especially impacted by two forms of disallowance, one for capital investments and another for long-term fuel contracts for generators. During this period many electric utilities suffered enormous cost overruns for nuclear power plants, paying substantially more than the cost of alternative generation technologies. These cost overruns led some state regulators to disallow part of the costs of nuclear plants as not used and useful.

Likewise, during the late 1970s some natural gas pipelines and distribution utilities entered into "take or pay" contracts for acquiring natural gas, in which the utility was required to pay a high price for gas regardless of whether it actually could sell the gas to its customers. The belief underlying these contracts was that the price of oil would remain high and that environmental regulations would limit the use of coal. Hence, the demand for natural gas for electric generation facilities would soar, while limits on the availability of gas as a nonrenewable resource would translate soaring demand into high prices. These expectations proved to be false. Some regulators concluded that pipelines and distribution companies had exercised poor business judgment in signing take-or-pay contracts, and so disallowed part of their costs of acquiring gas.

An important element of the used and useful test is determining the appropriate production capacity of the regulated firm. This application of the test is actually a part of production control and therefore is discussed in that section.

Financial Cost of Capital

Once regulators have decided the amount of allowed costs of capital facilities that the firm has experienced in the year, they must further adjust this cost to reflect the fact that long-term capital investments must recover more than their original cost to induce investors to pay for them. The financial cost of capital of the firm reflects the amount that it must pay investors to make use of their funds to buy long-term capital assets. The financial cost of capital is the product of the current book value of the firm's capital investments multiplied by the minimum annual percentage return on investment—in regulatory parlance, the *allowed rate of return*—that the firm must pay investors to enable it to raise funds in capital markets. In many regulatory proceedings, the item that receives the most attention is estimating the financial cost of capital because it is enormously complex and has great financial significance.

The complexity of estimating the allowed rate of return arises in part from the fact that firms have many kinds of investors, including debt of varying duration and priority, as well as common and preferred stock. The regulator must estimate the minimum rate of return on each type of financial instrument that would enable the firm to use that instrument to raise capital. These rates reflect the risk of the asset—that is, the future unknown variability in the amount that the firm actually will pay, given that the firm may experience a major disallowance or shortfall in demand that reduces its profitability or perhaps forces it into bankruptcy. If the firm does face financial difficulty, owners of different financial instruments have different claims on the cash flow of the firm, so that the amount of risk of one asset depends on the fraction of the firm's financial obligations that are accounted for by instruments with a higher priority claim on the firm. Thus, the financial cost of capital from one instrument depends on the firm's *capital structure,* or the relative amounts of all types of debt and equity. Therefore, to estimate the minimum cost of capital to the firm, the regulator must determine the optimal capital structure as well as the rates of return that all instruments would require if the firm had that capital structure.

The financial significance of this part of the process arises from the fact that most regulated industries are extremely capital intensive. Total capital costs, including depreciation and allowed return on investment, can be two-thirds or more of the costs of a regulated firm, and typically the allowed rate of return is roughly double the depreciation rate, so that allowed return on investments commonly account for as much as half of total costs. Hence, even a seemingly tiny difference in the allowed rate of return—say, between 10.1 and 10.0 percent—can change the revenue requirement of a telephone or electric utility by hundreds of millions of dollars.

Adjusting for Past Mistakes

The starting place for determining the firm's total revenue requirement is the sum of allowed variable costs, allowed depreciation, and allowed return on investment. However, this figure may then be adjusted to account for past mistakes and "windfalls" on the sale of assets. If in the previous year the firm did not recover its allowed cost, the regulator must allow the firm to add the unrecovered costs to this year's revenue requirement. In some cases, regulators also will subtract excess return on investment if the firm's revenues exceed its allowed costs; however, in other cases, regulators are not legally entitled to recapture excess returns.

A windfall arises if an asset that is used in providing regulated service is sold for more than its depreciated book value at the time of sale. For example, if the company sells its corporate headquarters for more than its current book value, some regulatory agencies subtract these gains from the firm's revenue requirement for that year. Whether this actually occurs depends not only on whether the regulator's statutory authority permits this action, but also on whether the regulated firm is allowed to have unregulated subsidiaries. If a firm can engage in unregulated activity, the firm can avoid having windfalls subtracted from the revenue requirement by placing ownership of the facility in the name of the unregulated affiliate and charging rent to the regulated utility, subject to the possibility of a "used and useful" test of the amount of rent. Of course, this approach has a disadvantage in that the firm is no longer guaranteed its allowed rate of return on the investment in its headquarters. If rents in the area fall, so must the rent the affiliate charges the regulated service, whereas if the headquarters facility is owned by the regulated company, it is allowed to recover allowed returns on that investment as long as its costs were reasonable at the time the facility was acquired.

Adopting a Pricing System

Once the firm's revenue requirement is determined, regulators then are obligated to set prices so that the firm can recover those costs. If the firm were to produce only one product, this part of the process boils down to satisfying a simple equation: price times quantity sold equals the revenue requirement. By implication, the regulator must estimate sales volume for the coming year in order to set the price, but, of course, sales volume varies with the price, so the actual requirement is that the regulator must know the firm's demand curve. In practice, regulators almost never actually solve the pricing problem this way. Instead, they assume that sales next year will equal sales this year, or that the trend rate of growth in sales will continue. If regulated prices do not change much from year to year, this procedure does not introduce much error into the calculation.

Of course, no regulated firm sells exactly one service. Regulated firms typically provide many different services in many different geographic areas, which makes the pricing problem quite complex.[9] To deal with this complexity, a number of pricing strategies are available.

One common pricing principle is *product-specific cost recovery,* that is, each product should pay for itself. The attraction of this principle is efficiency. If each product pays for itself, the users of the product have demonstrated by their purchases that the value of the product to them exceeds the cost of producing it, and the producers have demonstrated that the benefits of producing that product exceed the benefits of producing alternative products.

Determining the cost of a product produced by a multiproduct firm is far from easy, however. One price benchmark is *stand-alone cost*, or the cost of producing that product and nothing else. If the industry has *economies of scope*—that is, the firm enjoys cost savings by producing the two products together, rather than separately; however, prices that recover stand-alone costs will generate revenues that exceed total costs, and so provide excess profits. Consequently, stand-alone costs are more compelling as an upper bound on prices, rather than a price formula.[10]

Another cost standard for setting prices is *incremental cost*. The incremental cost concept can be applied either to a unit of a product, called the *marginal cost*, or to the total production of one product, called *average incremental cost*.[11]

These cost standards have an important efficiency advantage in that customers of a service pay neither more nor less than the actual additional cost of providing it. As a result, every consumer is served who is willing to pay the cost of service, and consumers who are not served have a lower value on service than the cost of providing it.

An example of incremental cost methods is *peak-load pricing*. In this case, a regulated firm is regarded as producing two outputs: service when demand is likely to require all of the firm's capacity, and service when demand falls short of capacity. For example, in electricity, peak demand usually occurs either at night in the winter (when lighting demand is most intense) or during the day in the summer (when people are most likely to use air conditioners). The importance of this distinction is that the utility builds production capacity to satisfy peak period demand so that efficiency requires that peak-period usage should face prices that include all capacity costs. Off-peak use requires no additional capital expenditures and so should face prices that cover only the operating costs of the system. Notice that in this example the physical products in the two periods are identical: kilowatt hours of electricity. The notion of regarding them as separate products is derived from their different incremental costs.

Incremental cost standards have a disadvantage in that they do not permit a natural monopoly to recover its total costs. Except under unusual conditions, if the firm has economies of scale in a particular service, marginal cost is less than average incremental cost, and, if the production process has economies of scope, the sum of the incremental costs of the two products is less than their total cost. In these cases, incremental cost standards establish a reasonable lower bound for prices but are not satisfactory as a pricing formula.

Because stand-alone cost and incremental cost define the boundaries of prices, four other pricing methods are used to decide where prices should be within these bounds: *residual pricing, fully allocated costs, value of service,* and *nonlinear pricing.*

In *residual pricing*, regulators first divide services into two priority classes in terms of intrinsic social importance. For example, in telephony, some state regulators have defined residential local service and pay telephones to have high "social priority." The basis for setting prices for these services, if a cost standard is used at all, is some version of incremental cost. Regulators then subtract the expected revenue of the priority services from the expected total costs of the firm and use another method to set these prices so that the firm recovers all of its costs.

Fully allocated costs are a mechanical method for adjusting incremental costs so that the firm can cover all of its costs. The regulator first calculates either marginal or average incremental cost, uses these as provisional prices, and estimates the magnitude of the shortfall of revenues with respect to total costs. Next, the regulator increases the provisional prices in proportion to some measure of the relative importance of the services, for example, the relative quantities of service or the revenues they would generate.

Fully allocated cost methods have two basic problems. First, as with residual pricing, for some products the price determined by this method may exceed stand-alone costs and so induce inefficient entry even if the firm is a natural monopoly. Second, and more important, there is no objective basis for deciding which fully allocated cost method to adopt. In essence, fully allocated costs are nothing more than a procedure for assigning cost-recovery responsibilities across categories of customers without recourse to any well-articulated normative principle, and so are fundamentally arbitrary.

Value of service pricing builds on the idea that people who value a service more highly should pay more for it. Thus, value of service pricing is another name for price discrimination based on demand intensity. Value of service pricing was first used in railroad regulation, in which regulators set freights higher for products with a very high price per unit volume and weight. For example, shipping a pound of diamonds was much more expensive than shipping a pound of wheat. The logic behind this price difference was that because diamonds are expensive, a given freight charge would be a far smaller fraction of its final market price than would be the case for wheat. Hence, assigning more cost recovery responsibility to diamonds than to wheat has less effect on the final sales of the two products. An important aspect of value of service pricing is that it is not based on an equity principle, but has its roots in efficiency: set prices to minimize the effect on output. The idea is not that diamond customers are less deserving than wheat customers, but that freight prices will not have much effect on diamond sales but may have a big effect on wheat sales.

This idea is formalized in the theory of *Ramsey pricing,* named after economist Frank Ramsey. Ramsey prices are the solution to the following problem. Suppose that costs will not be recovered if every price is set equal to marginal cost or average incremental cost, so that at least some products must have prices that exceed marginal cost. The set of prices that cause the least amount of distortion in total sales while recovering total costs are Ramsey prices. These prices obey the *inverse-elasticity rule:* the markup of price over marginal cost for each product should be inversely proportional to the elasticity of demand for that product.[12] Thus, for a product with highly inelastic demand, the markup over incremental cost is high, whereas, for a product with highly elastic demand, the markup is low.[13]

Thus far, the discussion of pricing has assumed that every product will have a single price that applies to all amounts of sales to a particular customer. *Nonlinear pricing* refers to a price formula in which a customer faces a different price for different amounts of service. One common nonlinear price system is a *two-part tariff,* in which a customer pays a fee to be allowed to purchase the service, and then another fixed charge per unit of service obtained. An example is an electricity tariff that includes a fixed monthly charge plus another charge per kilowatt hour of electricity that is consumed.

Another illustration of nonlinear pricing is *block rates* in which monthly usage is divided into ranges (called blocks), and different prices per unit of usage are charged for consumption within each block. For example, an electricity customer may face a low price for the first few kilowatt-hours of use, and then another price for use beyond that level. *Declining block rates,* where price is lower as usage increases, is a form of volume discount that encourages usage by recovering all or most of the fixed costs of a utility from the first few units of usage, and typically is associated with circumstances in which the utility has economies of scale. *Increasing block rates* are the opposite and are associated with either "universal service" objectives (which make some minimum usage affordable to low-income consumers), services that use scarce natural resources (which therefore have a rising supply price), or services that cause environmental degradation.

The advantage of nonlinear pricing is that it permits marginal cost pricing while preventing losses or excess profits. The price structure can be calculated so that every customer faces a price equal to marginal cost for the last unit of usage, and therefore no usage is curtailed for which the social cost of service is less than the customer's valuation of that usage. All the costs of the natural monopoly that are not recovered from prices at marginal cost can then be collected in other parts of the price structure where usage is not affected. For example, if a customer is willing to pay $2 for the first unit of usage and $1 for the second (as is consistent with downward sloping demand), and if the utility's cost is $.50 plus $1 for each unit of use, pure marginal cost pricing will set the price at $1, sell two units of output, and inflict financial losses of $.50 on the utility. However, if the first unit is priced anywhere at $1.50 and the second at $1, the customer will still buy two units and the utility will recover all of its costs.

Controlling Production

In addition to controlling entry and regulating prices, economic regulation also often utilizes production controls. Such controls take two basic forms: controlling total output or capacity, and specifying technical conditions of production (i.e., setting standards).

Output Controls

The distinctive feature of economic regulation is that it focuses exclusively on price and output, not on other social consequences of economic activity.[14] Most output controls are part of the system of price regulation. In a few cases, regulators directly control only output, but their actions indirectly affect price as well.

If regulators control prices, firms may lack an incentive to satisfy all demand at the regulated price. To counteract this effect, regulations often impose a *common carrier requirement,* which requires firms promptly to provide service on a nondiscriminatory basis to anyone who is willing to pay the regulated price.

Another output control that often accompanies price regulation is a requirement to serve areas that firms would not normally serve because service is uneconomic. For example, to obtain a license to fly the most profitable routes between large cities, the CAB required that carriers agree to serve small cities. In basic telephone service, state regulators require that carriers serve low-income neighborhoods or areas with low population density where subscriber revenue was likely to be too low to recover all costs. In these cases, firms remain financially viable by charging higher prices in the more desirable places to offset losses in low-revenue areas.

Regulators combat the disincentive to provide high-cost service by imposing service requirements as part of licensing; however, as discussed above, these requirements must be economically feasible in that regulators must not impose output requirements that cause firms to be unprofitable. Feasibility is achieved by *cross-subsidization,* which means setting some prices above average cost to offset the losses on the services that are priced below average cost.

Still another type of output control that is associated with price regulation is to determine the capacity requirements of regulated firms. Recall that implementing the used and useful test requires that regulators decide the production capacity that is allowable in setting rates. Because regulation usually sets prices equal to average cost, a unit of capacity that is only used during periods of peak demand will generate far less revenue than a unit of capacity that is used all or most of the time, and so is not likely to recover its costs from just the revenues that it generates. Nevertheless, society can benefit if regulated firms have excess capacity most of the time for two reasons. First, many capital investments are "lumpy" in that capital facilities costs would be much higher if firms frequently tried to adjust capacity. Second, excess capacity serves as insurance against unexpected failures of some facilities.

The difficulty with allowing some excess capacity is that, however reasonable this argument is, its implementation is quite difficult. The initial problem is that it is not even clear whether price regulation increases or decreases the incentive of firms to invest in excess capacity since the used and useful test can expose regulated firms to charges of overinvesting and the risk that these investments will be disallowed years later.

The other problem with regulating capacity is the difficulty of determining the point at which the cost of additional capacity exceeds the cost of the service outages that this capacity would prevent. To make this calculation, regulators and firms must be able to provide reasonable estimates of future demand and the likely costs of waiting to install more capacity when demand growth will require it, which also requires a forecast of future technological developments that might radically shift either demand or costs. For example, what appeared to be excess capacity in the telephone network quickly dissipated when consumers began to make use of the Internet, and the restoration of growth in per capita income during the 1990s, after two decades of very slow growth, quickly eroded what had been thought to be excess capacity in electricity generation.

In some cases, output control is not paired with price regulation. If a market is both competitive and otherwise unregulated, requiring firms to expand output beyond what would arise in the market is not feasible. The reason is that competition will drive prices to average cost, leaving no excess profits to finance additional production at a price below cost. Hence, stand-alone output controls virtually always focus on curtailing some production to less than the market would produce, which implies that the effect of output control is to make firms more profitable than they would be under competition. However, this effect cannot be achieved without also imposing entry controls, since excess profits in a competitive market will attract firms to the industry. Thus, stand-alone output control also is typically implemented through a licensing process that is designed to limit or prevent entry.

Standards

A second form of production control involves the use of standards. Standards are most common in so-called *network industries,* that is, industries in which the products of different firms must be technically compatible to maximize the value of their products to consumers. For example, a lightbulb must fit into the socket of a lamp. Many regulated services are network industries. Telephones and computers must be compatible with the telecommunications network, electrical appliances must be compatible with the electricity system, railroad cars must fit on tracks, and in all three cases adjacent utilities must be compatible in order to transport calls, electricity, and freight between regions.

In most industries, private trade organizations set technical standards, under the watchful eye of antitrust authorities to prevent firms from using the standards process to create cartels, but in many regulated industries, standards are a part of economic regulation. Economic regulation involves standard setting because standards affect costs, costs affect prices, and prices affect demand and capacity requirements. For example, during the late 1980s and early 1990s, the FCC conducted a rule-making proceeding to set technical standards for high-definition televisions (HDTV) because different standards required different amounts of electromagnetic spectrum for a broadcast station, had different implications regarding the compatibility of HDTV and ordinary television, and different costs of station equipment and receivers.

As in determining excess capacity, standard setting raises especially difficult challenges because it involves forecasting future technological developments and the effect of these developments on demand before the technology is available to consumers. In the private sector, standards are voluntary, so that a firm that believes technology should develop in a different way is free to go it alone to prove that its technology is superior. However, under regulation, standards are mandatory, so that the market process is unlikely to correct a technical mistake. Regulators typically deal with this uncertainty by using negotiations that arise from a rule-making proceeding to seek broad consensus not only on what standard to adopt but when to deploy it. For example, in the HDTV proceeding, the FCC forced advocates of different approaches to develop a consensus standard. By seeking consensus, regulators make firms confront and resolve disputes about the evolution of technology and demand and minimize the danger that standards inadvertently will confer competitive advantage on one part of the industry at the expense of another. In addition, consensus provides political cover against future criticism if the standard proves to be seriously flawed or simply sits on the shelf unused.

Enforcement

In addition to regulating entry, price, and production, economic regulatory agencies must enforce their regulations. Enforcement differs from rulemaking and case decisions because the law gives defendants in an enforcement action greater protection against arbitrary or unreasonable decisions.

Some enforcement actions are against regulated firms for violating regulatory rules. The obvious violations—not charging the right price or not abiding by license requirements to provide nondiscriminatory service to everyone who requests it—do not occur very frequently. Most violations pertain to mistakes or even fraud in dealing with customers or competitors, and to failure to abide by the accounting rules of regulation.

Enforcement actions against regulated firms can be triggered by either complaints from their customers or periodic audits by the regulatory agency. Larger, more sophisticated agencies initiate comprehensive audits of the activities of regulated firms to determine whether the information that they submitted in either rule-making proceedings or case decisions was accurate, and spot-check the operation of regulated firms to determine whether the firm is complying with production controls and standards. If either citizens or the agency's staff has evidence that a violation has taken place, an enforcement action is undertaken. Some agencies are required to take their complaints to court, while other agencies can conduct hearings, determine whether a violation has occurred, and impose fines and suspend licenses. In the latter case, defendants can appeal the agency's decision to a court, but the court's role is limited to determining whether the agency followed proper procedures and reached a decision that is supported by the evidence.

An enforcement issue that received considerable attention during the 1990s is "slamming" by long-distance telephone companies. Local telephone companies automatically connect direct-dial long-distance calls from a particular number to a long-distance carrier on the basis of customer lists that are provided by long-distance carriers. If a long-distance carrier notifies a local-access company that a customer has signed up for its service, but the customer has not requested the switch, the long-distance carrier is guilty of slamming. Both federal and state regulators have rules against slamming, and they impose fines and even rescind licenses when slamming is widespread.

A second category of enforcement proceedings pertains to the violations of regulations by other than regulated companies. For the most part, these enforcement actions deal with unlicensed entry. For example, citizens are barred from broadcasting without receiving a license, and until legislation during the 1990s eased some of the restrictions, customers of telephone, electric, and gas utilities were prohibited from reselling their service to others. In most cases, citizens who violate regulatory rules can be punished only by the courts, not by the agency. In these cases, the agency gathers information about the violation, then asks the judiciary to prevent the violation and punish the violator.

IV. TOOL SELECTION

Because economic regulation is complex and is likely to create incentives for regulated firms to operate inefficiently, this tool should not be taken up casually. But what are the circumstances under which the use of this tool makes sense? The answer to this question is important not just for abstract theoretical reasons, but to provide guidance to political leaders, agency officials, and business executives about when and how regulation should be implemented.

The decision to apply economic regulation is, of course, a political one, which has given rise to two fundamentally different explanations for it. One explanation is derived from normative theory (welfare economics and distributive justice). This view implicitly assumes that political decisions are motivated by a desire to improve the efficiency of the economy and the equity of the distribution of wealth. The other explanation arises from theories of political and bureaucratic behavior. These theories typically assume that government decisions are strongly influenced by the self-interested motives of participants in the political process, including elected officials, civil servants, and special interests that are active in electoral, legislative, and regulatory processes. This section explains the normative rationale for economic regulation and then explores the political rationale.

Substantive Rationales: Market Failure

According to normative economic theory, the job of regulation is to correct market failures. The concept of market failure applies to either inefficiencies or inequities arising from unregulated private markets. An assumption of the market failure view is that the institutions of private property and exchange through markets are normatively respectable, so that the task of government is to make them work better, rather than to replace them.

Market failure can arise for four reasons:

- If a market is a natural monopoly
- If participants in the market are imperfectly informed about some important aspect of production, prices, or consumption
- If an economic activity creates an "externality," that is, an impact on parties who are not involved in the production or consumption of a product
- If the market produces inequities, for example, when a group of consumers, usually the poor or residents of rural communities, are denied adequate access to a product that is regarded as a necessity

The most common market failures that underpin economic regulation, and that will be discussed in detail here, are natural monopoly and inequity. Three other rationales for economic regulation are ruinous competition, imperfect consumer information, and financial (as opposed to environmental) externalities. These rationales are far more central to social regulation, and so will not be treated here except to define them.

Natural Monopoly

Perhaps the most persuasive rationale for economic regulation is to deal with natural monopolies. An industry is a natural monopoly if total industry output can be produced at lowest cost by a single firm, in which case competition may be unsustainable and inefficient. Natural monopoly differs from two other types of monopoly: when a firm owns valuable intellectual property (patents, copyrights, trade secrets) that legally entitles the owner to monopolize a product as a reward for innovation or creativity, or when monopolization is the result of an anticompetitive action, such as collusion among firms or actions by an incumbent firm that exclude competitors for reasons other than superior efficiency or intellectual property.

Economic regulation is not appropriate to deal with the latter two types of monopoly. An intellectual property monopoly is purposely created by government to induce innovation, so that economic regulation to prevent monopoly prices and profits would be counterproductive. Similarly, if a monopoly is neither natural nor legally protected by intellectual property rights, but nonetheless succeeds in charging high prices, thwarting efficient entry, and engaging in other monopolistic practices, the appropriate remedy is antitrust, not regulation.

The significance of the concept of natural monopoly is that it implies that competition is not feasible, so that government supervision of the industry is needed to make the industry perform well. Natural monopoly arises from economies of scale and can be extended by economies of scope. Both of these terms refer to attributes of the production costs of a product. Loosely speaking, economies of scale are present if increasing output causes less than a proportional increase in costs, and economies of scope are present if producing two products in the same production process is cheaper than producing each separately. If the production of a product exhibits economies of scale, costs are minimized if all production is undertaken by a single firm. If two products have economies of scope, then it is always cheaper to produce both products together than each separately.

Utilities such as electricity, natural gas, telephones, and water all have a common feature that exhibits strong economies of scale. In each case, service can be decomposed into two components: *access* and *usage*. Access consists of providing a physical conduit—a wire or a pipe—to deliver service to a customer, and usage is making use of the conduit to make calls or to acquire electricity, gas, or water. Thus, the cost of utility service is the sum of providing access and undertaking usage. The cost of usage services does not exhibit either economies or diseconomies of scale, but access may be different.

The physical process of building an access system is rather simple: dig a ditch or tunnel or erect poles and place wire or pipe in the hole or on the pole. Because wire or pipe to serve a large number of customers can use the same hole or poles, the cost of providing access can exhibit economies of scale. This is so because the cost to provide the first access to the first customer requires incurring the costs of both holes or poles and wire or pipe, but the cost of serving additional customers necessitates only the cost of wire or pipe. Hence, the average cost of access service declines as usage increases so that service exhibits economies of scale until the conduit capacity of the hole or poles is reached.

Whether economies of scale are sufficient to create a natural monopoly depends on the size of the market and the significance of the component of production that exhibits scale economies. In the preceding utility example, if the fixed component of the access charge is small or the number of customers is large, overall scale economies will be insignificant, or if the capacity of the most efficient system of holes and poles is small compared with the number of customers, multiple parallel conduits will be built, and so economies of scale no longer will be present.

The importance of economies of scope is that they can extend the domain of natural monopoly and thereby affect the regulator's decisions about the boundary of regulation. For example, if a firm enjoys economies of scale in one product, economies of scope can cause a second product to be part of a natural monopoly, too, even if the second product does not have economies of scale. The logic of the argument is that, first, efficiency demands that only one firm produce the first product and, second, efficiency demands producing the second product jointly with the first. Hence, the monopolist in the first product also should have a monopoly in the second.

Even if natural monopoly is present, regulation might not improve the performance of the industry. Natural monopoly does not necessarily imply that only one firm will survive in the market or that, in the absence of regulation, firms will charge high prices and earn excess profits. Instead, the industry may become an oligopoly in which firms engage in some price competition, or a monopoly that behaves as if the market were reasonably competitive. The latter occurs when a market is a *contestable* natural monopoly, which means that entry is easy and inexpensive so that if an incumbent tries to charge monopoly prices, another firm will enter at a lower price and capture all of the business.

Even if a natural monopoly is secure and so can set monopoly prices, economic regulation still may be undesirable because the cost of implementing it is too high compared with its likely benefits. Regulation has a direct cost, which is the resources that the regulator, the firm, and any other interest that participates in regulatory decisionmaking (including attempting to influence the political overseers of regulation) expend in the policymaking process. Regulation also has indirect costs. Economic regulation inevitably distorts the incentives of the regulated firm and its customers. By protecting the firm against competitive entry, regulation softens the incentives for the firm to operate efficiently. In addition, economic regulation in some way uses estimates of costs to set prices, which further weakens the incentives to operate efficiently by passing through higher costs through price increases. Moreover, because inevitably some prices are not closely tied to the cost of providing that service, regulation encourages consumers to overuse subsidized services and to underuse the services that generate the subsidies.

Because regulation has costs, regulators necessarily must be concerned about the appropriate scope of economic regulation: exactly where is regulation likely to have a beneficial effect on prices, and where is it likely to generate more costs than benefits? In practice, regulatory agencies, not political leaders and not the regulated industry, often initiate deregulation on the basis of their own assessment that the natural monopoly rationale either no longer applies or was flawed from the beginning. For example, the deregulation era in U.S. telecommunications began during the late 1960s with an assessment by the FCC that some parts of long distance—private networks and dedicated circuits—were not a natural monopoly. By 1977, the FCC had concluded that all long-distance services ought to be open to competition. During the 1980s, several other countries accepted this same model, as competition in long distance was introduced in Australia, Chile, Japan, New Zealand, and the United Kingdom. Then, in 1998, nearly one hundred countries signed the World Trade Organization Agreement on Telecommunications, which committed them to allow some competition in long distance. A similar process is now under way with respect to electricity generation.

Inequity

Goals related to distributive justice, or equity, form the second major substantive rationale for economic regulation, leading in some cases to regulating competitive industries. Equity objectives take several quite different forms, with very different implications for how regulation is promulgated and its effects on regulated markets. The basic equity rationales are as follows: (1) universal entitlement to some basic good or service, regardless of ability to pay; (2) some sources of income are undeserved and should be redistributed through regulation; and (3) other types of income are especially deserving and should be increased by regulation.

In traditional economic regulation, an important equity concern pertains to consumers and is expressed as the *universal service* objective. The underlying concept is that all citizens have an entitlement to minimum access at affordable prices to core services, such as water, electricity, and telephones. In industries other than core utilities, the term "universal service" is not used, but the concept is the same: every citizen is entitled access to core products at affordable prices. An example of the latter is the ceiling price of three francs (about fifty cents) for a baguette in Paris. An example of the former is "lifeline" telephone rates for low-income households.

Frequently, the universal service objective is not stated with sufficient precision to clarify the scope of products that it covers, nor are the obligations of regulators and firms to make certain that universal service is achieved. Hence, regulators have a twofold problem: identify exactly what service is to be universally provided and develop regulations to achieve this objective.

In regulated utility industries, the universal service rationale is the basis for several pricing policies. One is low-cost service to low-income households based on a means test. Another is rate averaging, which means charging all customers the same price regardless of the cost of serving them. The normative principle at work here is that fairness dictates that everyone should pay the same price for the same service. The first and second policies frequently are combined in that residential access to utilities is priced below cost so that all can afford it, but all are charged the same price. The third universal service policy, which is at odds with the second, is that prices should be lower in small towns and rural areas. The basis for this policy has several articulations: rural communities make less use of the system because they have fewer neighbors to call; rural communities are more dependent on telephones because people are separated by greater distances; and lower utility prices can slow the decline of rural areas, which are economically threatened.

The most important implication of these equity principles is that they lead to cross-subsidies within the price structure of a regulated company. Recall that regulators cannot cause a firm to earn less revenue than its legitimate production cost. Hence, if one service or customer is subsidized, the company must be compensated. In principle, these subsidies could be paid by government, as is the case in housing assistance and food stamp programs. In practice, universal service subsidies in regulated utility industries rarely are directly paid by government. Instead, they are financed by cross-subsidies.

Low-income assistance is the least controversial universal service policy. Opposition to it focuses more on the means for achieving it than on its existence. One problem is that low-income customers receive a subsidy for only some service. If they buy more, they face the same price for additional service as all customers and end up cross-subsidizing themselves. For example, in telephony, long-distance and local toll calls are heavily taxed to support all forms of universal service. A poor family that makes several toll calls each month pays as much subsidy for other universal service goals as it receives for local access.

The other two universal service objectives are far more significant financially than assistance for the poor. They are also much more controversial. The more important involves rural and small-town subsidization. States typically categorize customers according to the size of the community in which they live, and they set different prices for communities of different populations. The overall effect of this price structure is that small businesses in large cities pay far more than cost for their utility services, residential customers and large businesses in large cities pay roughly the cost of most services, and both business and residential customers in rural areas are heavily subsidized.

This pattern of subsidies raises important equity and efficiency issues. The equity issue is whether the location of service is a good indicator of deserving status. For example, big cities typically have a higher proportion of poor households than rural areas, yet it is the rural customers that get the subsidies. So far as efficiency is concerned, cross-subsidies are inefficient in that they distort consumption of utility services. Research demonstrates that in the United States changes in access prices have almost no effect on the number of households that are connected to a utility. However, usage of utility services is far more sensitive to price. Hence, the universal service subsidy system accomplishes very little in inducing more people to attach themselves to utility networks, but it substantially curtails usage by those who are attached.

These arguments have led most policy analysts and many regulators to conclude that subsidies should focus exclusively on those who cannot afford service and should be financed by as broad a tax as possible. Regulatory agencies cannot impose broadly based taxes, so the best that they can do is spread the cost of the subsidy as broadly as possible among regulated services.

Another equity argument for economic regulation is to eliminate undeserved excess profits from either natural monopoly or scarcity. *Monopoly rents* are simply the excess profits of a firm that enjoys an unregulated monopoly. *Scarcity rents* arise when the demand for a particular good increases, but more of it cannot be produced or the cost of producing more rises as production increases. Even in competitive markets, the price of a scarce good will exceed its production costs for at least some producers.

This was the happy situation that confronted J. R. Ewing, the antihero of the nighttime soap opera *Dallas*. J. R. owned near-useless land in west Texas on which oil was discovered. Oil is a nonrenewable resource, so the amount of it that can be produced is fixed. Moreover, some oil fields are cheaper to exploit than others, and west Texas, although not as inexpensive as Saudi Arabia, is a low-cost area. In the oil market, price is far above the cost of finding and extracting west Texas oil, causing oil companies to pay J. R. a fat royalty for the right to drill on his land. This process makes J. R. wealthy for reasons having nothing to do with his effort or skill, while hard-pressed consumers face gasoline prices that include J. R.'s royalty. A similar tale can be told about the lucky owners of paintings by Vincent van Gogh (who never sold a painting during his life) or land in Manhattan when New York became the nation's commercial center. Regardless of the heights to which their prices soar, neither the number of van Gogh paintings nor the amount of land in Manhattan can be increased, so owners of both receive scarcity rents.

These examples of scarcity illustrate the conceptual basis for several government interventions. The equity argument is that income earned due to the scarcity of a physical asset is not as deserving of respect as income earned from one's own effort and (scarce) skills. If so, scarcity rents in things (although not people) are legitimate targets for extraction by government through economic regulation.

For most of the twentieth century, the price of natural gas at the wellhead was regulated by the Federal Power Commission. The purpose of this regulation was to set wellhead prices that equaled the cost of exploiting gas reserves, rather than the market price that would reflect its scarcity value. Oil, too, was subjected to economic regulation by the Federal Energy Regulatory Commission (FERC) during the 1970s, when the Organization of Petroleum Exporting Countries (OPEC) successfully cartelized the world oil market, cut production, and forced prices to increase substantially. FERC could not control OPEC prices, but could regulate the price of domestic oil and retail petroleum products, which account for about half of U.S. consumption. By keeping domestic prices low, FERC prevented U.S. owners of oil reserves from capturing a huge financial windfall (like OPEC oil sheiks) and allowed U.S. consumers to pay prices for petroleum products that were roughly halfway between domestic and world oil prices.

Similar arguments have been used to justify rent control in New York and many other cities.[15]

The scarcity-rent rationale for economic regulation also raises serious efficiency and equity issues. Price regulation to extract scarcity rents usually creates shortages. In the case of natural gas, setting prices at the average cost of production from existing wells eliminated the financial incentive to exploit reserves where the cost of recovery was above the regulated price but below the price that would balance supply and demand. This result was inefficient, because some consumers were denied gas even though they were willing to pay more than the cost of producing it. Likewise, oil price regulation during the heyday of OPEC led to shortages that caused long waiting lines at gas stations, thereby substituting the loss of valuable time for the financial loss from higher prices. In similar fashion, high-income but longtime residents of Manhattan are charged lower rents than recently arrived moderate-income families. Indeed, the latter might pay high rents to the former in a sublease.

In addition, economic regulation to extract scarcity rent creates incentives for those regulated to engage in behavior that reduces the value of the regulated asset. In the case of housing, for example, as the gap between market value and rent widens, landlords have no incentive to maintain the quality of an apartment. Instead, their best business strategy is to let the quality of the apartment deteriorate to match the rent.

A third equity rationale involves circumstances in which favored suppliers would not earn an adequate income if the government did not intervene to elevate the prices that they receive. Examples of policies that serve this objective are the minimum wage and agricultural price supports and marketing orders. Many nations have agricultural price supports and minimum wages like those in the United States. In addition, in some countries retail shops are regulated for essentially the same reason as farm products. Almost all nations subscribe to the objective of "preserving the family farm," and many other countries also seek to "preserve the small shopkeeper."

Whereas other rationales for economic regulation seek to set prices so that the regulated firm roughly recovers its cost but receives nothing extra, this form of economic regulation tries to force price above cost. Consequently, the basic idea is for the government to manage a cartel for favored producers. One approach is to determine a "fair" price for the regulated product. In agriculture, the standard method is to calculate the "parity price." Parity refers to the ratio of the product's price to some other group of prices, such as all consumer goods or agricultural inputs, in some past period. If a product price is set at 100 percent of parity, the gross revenues from selling a unit of the product can buy the same amount of other goods today as it could in the past.

This form of regulation has the exact opposite effect of regulation to eliminate scarcity rents. Whereas the latter causes shortages, regulation that seeks to increase prices tends to create surpluses. If businesses in a competitive market perceive that prices will be above their costs, they will expand production up to the point at which diseconomies of scale push average cost up to price.

The best historical example of this effect is the persistent agricultural surpluses in the United States from the end of World War II until around 1970. During this period the government set prices for the most important agricultural products above the competitive market price and bought the excess production from farmers. Sometimes the excess production was given to poor countries or sold at a loss on the world market, but much of it simply rotted in government storage facilities.

Retail trade regulation in some countries is similar to regulation in agriculture, with Italy and Japan historically having been exceptionally protective of retailers until some reforms during the 1990s. Usually retail regulation is implemented locally, with regulators licensing a fixed number of shops for each type of product, specifying the maximum square feet for each type of retail shop, preventing shops of one type from selling products of another type (e.g., cheese shops cannot sell vegetables, and dress shops cannot sell shoes), and prohibiting firms from selling products below cost. The effect of these policies is large. Before reforms, Japan and Italy employed a much larger fraction of their labor forces in retail trade than other advanced, industrialized countries, and their consumers paid much higher retail prices.

Other Market-Failure Rationales

In addition to the natural monopoly and equity rationales for economic regulation, three other types of market failures also provide some justification, although these apply more forcefully to social regulation than to economic regulation.

The first of these is *ruinous competition,* which refers to a circumstance in which the competitive process is thought to cause widespread bankruptcy of efficient firms through excessive price cutting. For example, some industrialists and political leaders thought that ruinous competition was a contributing factor to the Great Depression of the 1930s and proposed that government set minimum prices in competitive industries to prevent it. This argument led to the regulation of trucking and airlines from the 1930s until they were deregulated during the late 1970s. One remaining vestige of this view is the regulation of taxi fares in nearly all major cities.

Economics research has generated overwhelming evidence against the ruinous competition rationale for regulation. The wave of economic deregulation that began during the 1970s was instigated in part by extensive research that revealed, first, that regulation of competitive markets caused prices to rise and production efficiency to fall; and, second, that pockets of these industries that had remained unregulated were vibrantly competitive and financially healthy.[16] For example, when the CAB regulated interstate airlines, three large states—California, Florida, and Texas—did not regulate service within their states, and all enjoyed better service and lower prices than were provided in similar regulated markets. Similarly, when the Interstate Commerce Commission regulated interstate trucking, shipments of agricultural commodities and self-shipment by manufacturers were exempted, and in both cases costs were lower than for regulated shipment.

A second additional rationale for economic regulation is the existence of *financial externalities.* Financial externalities arise when rational, informed behavior by customers of a financial institution causes the failure of a firm that actually is well managed and ought to be solvent. For example, for a bank to recover its costs, it must use some of its deposits to make loans. If all of its depositors decide to withdraw their deposits, the bank would not be able to pay them, even if the loans are all perfectly sound. Each customer may know that the bank is sound, but may fear that others may attempt to withdraw their funds, and so attempt to make a withdrawal before others cause the bank to become insolvent. If enough customers behave in this fashion, a sound bank may fail, thereby causing harm to both the bank and its customers. Economic regulation can ameliorate, if not solve, this problem by imposing rules that delay withdrawals, guarantee deposits, or establish minimum standards for cash reserves.

Finally, economic regulation may be justified when *imperfect information* exists. Imperfect information simply means that consumers or producers are not completely informed about some important feature of a transaction. For example, consumers may not buy a particular product very often and may have to devote considerable time and effort to finding several sellers and determining the price that each charges. If so, one seller may be able to sell the product at or near the monopoly price, even if the market otherwise appears to be competitive. In principle, regulation might improve the performance of the market by requiring that all sellers clearly post their prices or by imposing a ceiling price. For example, if a customer seeks to have a prescription filled for a brand-name drug, many states require that pharmacists inform customers about the availability and price of generic substitutes. Likewise, some states insist that gasoline stations post their prices on signs that are clearly visible to motorists as they drive by.

The Politics of Economic Regulation

In addition to these normative rationales for economic regulation, a variety of political factors also help explain the choice and evolution of this tool. The politics of regulation refer to two processes: the decision to create a new regulatory program (enactment) and the ongoing process of carrying out regulation (implementation). Enactment is primarily a story about the evolution of these laws as they are put into effect by administrative agencies operating in a political environment.

Enactment

That something other than the substantive rationales is responsible for the selection of economic regulation is apparent from the evidence presented above indicating that regulation is often the tool of choice in situations where the normative rationales do not seem to apply—that is, where natural monopolies do not exist and where dubious equity objectives are sought. How can we explain these outcomes? The answer, it appears, is that political factors that go beyond the normative rationales often encourage the choice of this tool.

In the first place, politicians have strong incentives to encourage the use of economic regulation to respond to voter fears during periods of intense concern about particular economic problems, such price increases in essential products like electricity or fuel, or severe economic crises. Many federal regulatory laws thus were enacted during the period of rapid urbanization and industrialization at the turn of the twentieth century when Populist fears of large corporations suffused American political debate. Subsequently, many federal regulatory statutes were enacted during the Great Depression of the 1930s, when public fears about economic policy were especially intense. During such periods, politicians feel compelled to "do something" in response to public outcries. Indeed, they often stimulate such outcries. The imposition of controls on powerful corporations is an attractive remedy in such circumstances: it shifts the blame to highly visible corporate giants and creates the impression of decisive action, regardless of whether the action meets the substantive rationales for this type of intervention.

Contributing to the political attractiveness of regulation as a tool of action, moreover, is a second attribute of this tool: its relative invisibility in the budgetary process. As noted earlier, economic regulation imposes its costs in subtle and indirect ways that do not show up on the ledgers of government agencies. Rather, the costs are shifted to private businesses, to consumers at large, or to the economy. The costs of this tool thus are conveniently hidden from popular view, which makes them far more palatable politically.

Third, the choice of economic regulation is in some sense culturally determined. American political culture, in particular, with its hostility to government, and hence to government enterprise, has built a veritable political wall around the most natural alternative to regulation—public ownership of key industries. As noted earlier, this alternative has been chosen much more commonly in other countries. Because of the powerful ideological norms against government ownership in this country, economic regulation, which leaves ownership in private hands and guarantees a rate of return sufficient to cover costs, has been the preferred response to apparent economic exploitation.

Finally, and perhaps most important, there is persuasive evidence that many economic regulatory programs were enacted not to protect the mass of consumer-voters from the effects of market failure, but to protect regulated firms from other firms seeking to compete with them at the expense of the general public. In other words, far from seeing regulation as an imposition on regulated firms, this line of argument sees it as a vehicle through which regulated firms secure protection from their competitors. Supporting this line of argument is the concept of *mobilization bias.* Mobilization bias refers to the fact that well-organized groups with a high stake in a policy issue are much more likely to mobilize themselves to participate in a political process to shape that policy than are more disinterested consumers, each of whom usually has too small a stake to become part of a political movement to pressure elected officials on these policies. Hence, traditional politics will tend to produce policies that favor regulated industries at the expense of their consumers. Whatever the arguments presented to consumer-voters, economic regulation will therefore make headway only when it also serves the interests of the industries most directly affected.[17]

Evidence for this line of argument can be found in the history of the first federal regulatory agency, the ICC. From the beginning the ICC functioned primarily to facilitate the formation of railroad cartels. Prior to the establishment of the ICC, trunk rail lines periodically engaged in price wars, but the ICC stopped this competition by adopting mandatory price floors and then delegating to regional rate-making committees of railroad executives the task of setting these prices.[18]

Even the regulatory laws of the Great Depression provide examples of cartelization by regulation. This was the case, for example, with airline and trucking regulation. Airline regulation raised prices and prevented the entry of any new airlines for over thirty years, and the same was true of trucking regulation. By the time airlines and trucks were deregulated in the late 1970s, scholars estimated that regulation raised prices between 25 and 40 percent. Similarly, natural gas was regulated in 1940, and the effect was to cut prices to consumers; however, the primary advocates of this policy were retail gas utilities, who wanted to lower prices for natural gas at the wellhead in order to compete more effectively with electric utilities.

The lesson from these examples is that no single explanation accounts for the enactment of all regulatory laws. Changes in regulatory policy have been initiated by industries that seek regulation, large firms that seek protection from monopoly suppliers, or populist movements that seek to curtail monopoly power—or that seek simply to get lower prices, even if that requires expropriating property in a competitive industry with no excess profits. In some cases, proponents of self-serving regulatory policies to establish a cartel drape their arguments in normative rhetoric, and possibly these arguments succeed in convincing some citizens and elected officials to favor ill-conceived regulatory policies. In any case, the politics of regulatory enactment are sufficiently complex that we cannot conclude that regulation is either always or never socially desirable.

Implementation

The second aspect of regulatory politics has to do with the shaping of regulatory policies after regulatory laws are in place. Mobilization bias and regulatory capture apply even more persuasively to implementation than to enactment. Even agencies that are created to control monopolies sometimes come to serve the interests of regulated firms at the expense of consumers and other firms that seek to enter regulated markets.

The feature of regulation that makes it vulnerable to capture is the narrowness and obscurity of many of its decisions. When a regulatory law is passed or significantly amended, at stake is the cumulative effect of many subsequent decisions by the regulatory agency about prices, output, and entry. These subsequent decisions about whether to let a firm enter a market or to set the price of a service are likely to be far less consequential than the passage of the act. As a result, regulatory decisions are likely to be completely invisible to the general public.

The procedures used in regulation seem to encourage openness and participation. Regulatory procedural rules accord standing to those affected by regulation and a burden on the regulator to show that it took into account the information and arguments of anyone who makes use of this standing to participate in a regulatory decision. However, procedural rules can accentuate mobilization bias. Participation in the regulatory process, like participation in electoral politics, is costly in time and money. Hence, those with large stakes in the outcome are more likely to find participating in a regulatory decision worthwhile. As the decisionmaking process becomes more costly, fewer potential participants are likely to find participation worthwhile, so that distortions due to mobilization bias may become larger.

The effect of procedures on mobilization bias is itself a political choice. Legislation can facilitate extensive participation by providing the agency with a large budget for its own analysis, and even for subsidizing participation by public-interest groups. In a sense, Congress can decide the degree to which an agency is likely to be captured by legislating its procedures and appropriating its budget. For this reason, the cuts in the budgets of many regulatory agencies during the early 1980s were widely viewed as an effort to shift regulatory policy in favor of regulated firms.

V. MANAGEMENT CHALLENGES AND RESPONSES

Given the complexity of economic regulation and the immense difficulties of keeping track of the technological and economic changes affecting regulated industries, it should come as no surprise that this tool has encountered a variety of very significant management challenges. Four of these challenges deserve particular attention here.

Overcoming the Perverse Effects of Cost-of-Service Regulation: Incentive Regulation

In the first place, as is apparent from the "basic mechanics" discussion above, cost-of-service regulation is very complex and intrusive, and so costly to the agency and the firm. In addition, cost-of-service pricing creates perverse incentives for regulated firms to increase their costs. Examples of inefficient yet profit-maximizing strategies under cost-of-service regulation are the following:

1. *Gold-plating:* engaging in unnecessary expenditures

2. *Excess capacity:* building more excess capacity than is needed to provide insurance against outages or to accommodate "lumpy" investments

3. *Excessive capital intensive investments (the Averch-Johnson Effect):* substituting capital investments for variable costs, such as by buying equipment that is extremely durable and so requires little repair and maintenance even if the capital costs are very large compared with the savings in variable costs

4. *Cross-subsidization* of services with elastic demand: reducing the price of a high-elasticity product, while offsetting the loss with a price increase for a product with low demand elasticity, causing output to expand substantially in the first market but to fall by a small amount in the latter, which increases total costs and hence total allowed profits

One promising approach for dealing with these problems is to replace cost-of-service regulation with *incentive regulation*. Incentive regulation refers to a mechanism for setting prices that weakens the connection between costs and prices in order to provide a sharper incentive to cut costs. The objective is to establish pricing rules that do not encourage inefficiency. Because the problems of cost-based pricing arise from using cost estimates to set prices, these methods seek to diminish the role of costs in setting prices.

Two forms of incentive regulation have been implemented extensively recently: *earnings sharing* and *price caps*.

Earnings Sharing

This method of price regulation starts with an estimate of the firm's total costs but uses more flexibility than cost-of-service regulation in controlling the firm's revenues and prices. Under this method, the firm agrees not to be reimbursed for all its costs should revenues fall short of allowed costs in return for being allowed to keep a share of the excess profits it earns if revenues exceed allowed costs. Typically, the process begins by calculating costs and prices exactly as in cost-of-service regulation. In addition, the agency and the firm negotiate an upper and lower bound on the realized rate of return on investment. For example, if the allowed return on investment is estimated to be 12 percent, the boundaries might be 8 and 16 percent. If a firm earns less than the lower bound (8 percent), it can raise prices to the level required to bring its earning to this level, and if the firm earns more than 16 percent, it must cut prices until profits fall to this level.

The earnings sharing rule is then applied to all outcomes between 8 and 16 percent. In this range, prices are adjusted by half the amount necessary to cause the firm to earn the allowed rate of return. Thus, if a firm can cut costs by more than the regulators expected in estimating its revenue requirement, it can keep half of the cost saving, but must pass the other half on in price reductions. The purpose, of course, is to overcome the perverse incentives of cost-of-service regulation to increase costs.

Price-Cap Regulation

Under price caps, regulators impose a formula for setting future prices that is unrelated to future costs. Firms then are free to pick any combination of prices that satisfies the formula. The price-cap formula is based on a previous set of prices that were determined by cost-of-service regulation. The price-cap formula, sometimes called "RPI minus X," is a price index that is based on expected changes in inflation (RPI means retail price index) and productivity (the X factor). Typically, the productivity factor is the average rate of cost reduction in the industry for several previous years. Price-cap regulation allows average prices to increase by the difference between the rate of inflation and this historical percentage rate of cost reduction.

Price caps have several very attractive features. First, as is apparent, the firm no longer has any incentive to pad costs. If it can reduce its costs, it can keep the entire gain forever. Second, a firm that faces a price-cap formula will adopt the profit-maximizing set of prices that cause the least distortion in sales among all combinations of prices that satisfy the formula. Third, price caps reduce the incentive to operate at a loss in some markets in order to incur more costs and therefore to have higher allowed overall profits. Although the mathematical proof of this statement is complicated, the reason for this effect is that the price-cap formula does not allow a firm fully to offset losses in one market with price increases in another.

Price caps cope with many of the perverse incentives of cost-of-service regulation, but they are not without problems. First, if regulators make even the slightest mistake in estimating the future rate of productivity growth of the firm, the price-cap formula eventually will need to be updated. For instance, if the firm's rate of productivity growth is slightly higher than expected, profits will steadily increase until the firm eventually earns monopoly profits, in which case the price-cap formula has no effect on prices. If the political process generated a demand to regulate the monopoly initially, most likely it will continue to generate the same pressure in the future when profits are again perceived to be excessive, or if the firm's rate of productivity growth is slightly lower than the rate assumed in the formula, the firm eventually will be unable to recover its costs, and it will be able to successfully sue regulators for a taking without compensation. In either case, regulators update the formula based on cost history, which then undermines the cost-minimizing incentive created by the price-cap formula.

Second, price-cap regulation does not easily accommodate the introduction of new products. The basic formula assumes some baseline price, output, and cost, but a new product has none of these. Hence, regulators must incorporate new products into the formula by making assumptions about all of these variables. The most common mechanism is to initialize the new service by setting its price through a cost-based method, usually average incremental cost. In industries with rapid technological progress and a large number of products, like telecommunications, accommodating new products can be a very serious regulatory problem.

Despite these shortcomings, however, incentive regulation is coming increasingly into use as a modern substitute for the more rigid process of cost-based price regulation. Most likely, some amalgam of the two approaches will prevail.

Preventing Anticompetitive Behavior

Not only can regulation produce perverse pricing results, but it can also be used by regulated firms to undermine competition. Three types of such anticompetitive practices have been quite prevalent: first, *abuse of process,* which involves deliberate use of the regulatory process to impose cost and delay on competitors; second, *anticompetitive pricing,* which involves setting prices below cost for the purpose of driving another firm from the market; and third, *anticompetitive leveraging,* which involves using monopoly power in one market to disadvantage competitors in another market.

Perhaps the most significant anticompetitive issue at present, however, arises in the context of the *interconnection problem.*[19] This problem arises in situations where competitors must deal with a regulated monopoly in order to offer their own services but then compete with the monopolist in another part of an industry. The interconnection problem arises when an incumbent firm uses anticompetitive tactics to harm entrants in these newly competitive sectors. Interconnection controversies can arise almost anywhere: in electricity generation when an integrated electric utility competes with companies that must use its transmission and distribution system; in long-distance telephone when a local-exchange monopolist competes with companies that must use its local networks to originate and terminate calls; and in local telephone service where an entrant must allow its customers and customers of the incumbent to call each other.

In advanced industrialized democracies, and even some developing countries, this interconnection problem is the most important regulatory issue at the dawn of the twenty-first century. The challenge to regulators is to develop interconnection regulations to protect against discrimination. As a result, deregulation in part of the industry actually can increase the scope of regulation by adding a whole host of interconnection issues to the agenda of the regulator.

Information Management

Another management problem facing regulatory agencies concerns access to objective information. In most regulatory settings, the principal source of information is the regulated industry itself, which submits huge quantities of data to justify its requests for price increases and other favorable regulatory decisions. To the extent that the regulatory agency has limited access to alternative sources of information, the regulated firm has a huge strategic advantage, for it can withhold information that might be damaging to its preferred outcome and make proposals that have the effect of setting the policy agenda for the regulator. The management challenge is to overcome this strategic advantage.

If an agency has ample resources, one solution is for its staff to undertake independent investigations and to submit their findings and recommendations. Another course of action is to encourage others to participate. The range of potential participants is broad—citizens groups, firms that sell to or buy from the regulated firm, and other government agencies that have expertise in the area. For example, the Antitrust Division of the Department of Justice, which litigated the antitrust case against AT&T and which reviews merger proposals in the industry, and the National Telecommunications and Information Administration in the Department of Commerce, which is responsible for executive branch telecommunications policy, frequently participate in FCC proceedings, and the 1996 Telecommunications Act instructs the FCC to give great weight to the Antitrust Division on issues concerning the state of competition in the industry.

Whereas some agencies have the authority and the budget to pay others to participate in their processes, the primary mechanism available for inducing participation in cases is publicity: to announce that a case is pending, to explain the issues, and explicitly to ask for information that is relevant to the agency's decision. The problem with this strategy is that in some cases the agency's legislative mandate dictates that it respond to cases initiated by regulated firms very quickly. This rule advantages regulated firms, for they may take as long as they want to prepare their case before initiating it, and then force others to reply within a matter of weeks.

Managing by Commission

A final management problem facing economic regulation results from the structure of regulatory agencies. Economic regulatory agencies are frequently led by multimember commissions that are required to be balanced in terms of their partisan composition and the members of which often have relatively long fixed terms of office. The advantage of this form of organization is that it stabilizes regulatory policy through changes in the partisan control of government and, therefore, to some degree, depoliticizes regulatory policies. However, multimember commissions face the problem of resolving differences among commissioners not just in making decisions, but in prioritizing cases and allocating staff among pending proceedings. Most agencies confer upon the chair of the commission the authority to control most staff resources, after assigning a small personal staff to each commissioner; however, this approach does not fully resolve the issue. Every case must garner a majority of commissioners in favor of a decision, and a chair who ignores the priorities of other commissioners is likely to face great difficulty in getting majority support.

The most common approach to this problem is to have a "chief of staff" who is a civil servant and who consults with the entire commission about priorities. Larger agencies sometimes have several such officials, being organized into functional bureaus, each with a bureau chief. Federal agencies often have bureaus for each regulated industry, plus a general counsel, a bureau for economic policy analysis, and a technical (or engineering) bureau. Whereas in some agencies the chair can appoint these officials, typically other commissioners are consulted. These officials usually are very influential, especially where the commissioners have strongly differing views about priorities.

Given the deregulation movement that has been under way in the United States and many other countries over the last two decades, it would be easy to conclude that economic regulation is a failed policy tool. But this conclusion would be wildly incorrect. This is evident if we evaluate economic regulation in terms of the basic criteria of efficiency, equity, legitimacy, and effectiveness.

Efficiency

With respect to *efficiency*, economic regulation does cause firms to be less efficient in the sense of operating at greater cost than would be the case if the industry were private and unregulated, but this assumes that the alternative to regulation is a competitive industry. Thus, economic regulation gets poor markets with respect to its effects on efficiency in markets such as air transportation, truck transportation, and natural gas extraction, which are now thought to be competitive.

In the utility sector until recently, however, the relevant alternative to regulation was thought to be not competition but monopoly, which in most of the world led to nationalization. During the period before deregulation in the United States and privatization elsewhere in the world, infrastructure industries generally were significantly more efficient under a regime of regulated private ownership than under nationalization,[20] and as regulators have moved away from regulating competitive markets, and away from cost-of-service rate-making to incentive regulation in the regulated markets that remain, economic regulation has become even more efficient.

Equity

With respect to *equity*, economic regulation certainly is controversial. The main equity accomplishment of economic regulation is to prevent monopoly utilities from extracting monopoly prices. Beyond this achievement, almost all economic regulatory agencies reallocate regulated services among customers through licensing requirements and cross-subsidies. Whereas low-income households and areas where service costs are so high as to be unaffordable receive some implicit subsidies, for the most part the mechanism regulators use for achieving equity objectives is very blunt, causing most of the subsidy to go to people who are not in financial need. Although in advanced economies almost everyone receives core utility services, the main reason for this happy result is that regulated firms have a financial incentive to extend service ubiquitously, not that universal service programs have much of an effect on the extent of service.

However, as with efficiency, the equity performance of economic regulation is improving. By introducing competition, regulators have been forced to eliminate many cross-subsidies and to replace them with explicit, need-based subsidies that are far more effective in reaching the target population.

Legitimacy

Economic regulation does not receive high marks in terms of its political legitimacy. Indeed, economic regulation has always been highly controversial precisely because it is agency-made law. The Constitution empowers elected officials to write statutes and courts to resolve disputes about their implementation and enforcement. Regulatory agencies write laws that are as binding as statutes, but those who write them are unelected bureaucrats who often act in obscurity. Both judges and legislatures, in recognition of the dubious legitimacy of such laws, have imposed complex procedural requirements on regulators to make regulation more transparent and to protect citizens from arbitrary decisions; however, these procedures can have the effect of advantaging well-organized industry interests at the expense of consumers, and so do not fully solve the legitimacy problem.

As with the other criteria, however, the legitimacy of economic regulation cannot be viewed in a vacuum. At least in the United States, economic regulation, for all its political questionableness, is still far more legitimate a tool of public action than the alternative of public ownership that is often used to deal with the problem of "natural monopoly" in many other countries. Indeed, it is this relative legitimacy of economic regulation over public ownership that probably helps account for the relative ubiquity of economic regulation in the United States.

Effectiveness

Quite apart from its relative political legitimacy, economic regulation, at least in core utility industries, is also an *effective* tool of government policy. At a relatively low cost to both government and regulated firms, economic regulation has been effective in allowing vibrant infrastructure industries to grow while constraining their prices and profits, and thereby making them affordable to almost all citizens in advanced economies. The movement in the rest of the world toward privatization with regulation reflects this reality.

The main reason that deregulation is spreading is thus not that economic regulation does not work, but that much of what used to be regarded as a natural monopoly is now increasingly viewed as potentially competitive, so that the entry controls associated with regulation have ended up thwarting competition. Competition is a superior alternative to economic regulation if the nature of production technology allows several reasonably efficient firms to operate in the same market. Basically, the best that economic regulation can hope to do with respect to the operating efficiency of regulated firms is to replicate the competitive outcome, but this makes no sense when competition itself is available.

VII. FUTURE DIRECTIONS

The future of economic regulation in the United States thus is secure, although probably at a much smaller scope than was the case in the middle of the twentieth century, or that is evident today. Until more information and experience are obtained, considerable uncertainty remains about the validity of natural monopoly as a rationale for regulation in some utility sectors, such as distribution and transmission in electricity and local nonmobile telephone service. Even if these sectors are no longer (or never were) natural monopolies, in advanced countries the incumbent former monopolist now serves all or nearly all businesses and residences through an integrated network so that it may take decades for competitors to gain enough of a foothold to make these services competitive.

Elsewhere in the world, economic regulation is a growth industry as nations privatize infrastructure industries and then regulate incumbents until competition emerges. Some nations have made the mistake of granting the privatized incumbents a long period of protection from competition and have created relatively weak regulators— agencies with little authority and insufficient resources to control the incumbent monopoly, but usually these mistakes are temporary. Exclusivity is rarely granted for more than a decade, and poor performance under weak regulation usually leads to reforms to strengthen regulation, in part by trying to make it more procompetitive.

The future of regulation throughout the world is likely to be more closely linked to antitrust policy, with regulators increasingly regarding their task as facilitating competition and, reluctantly, regulating where competition fails to emerge. Similarly, the preferred method of regulating prices is rapidly becoming incentive regulation. This approach requires regulatory agencies to be well staffed by professionals who can implement sophisticated rules regarding prices and interconnection among competitors, and to work closely with antitrust agencies. In short, like other tools of government, economic regulation involves its own procedures and requires its own distinctive skills, and these skills are becoming more sophisticated, not less.

VIII. SUGGESTED READING

Bernstein, Marver H. *Regulating Business by Independent Commission*. Princeton, N.J.: Princeton University Press, 1955. The classic work on the capture of regulatory agencies by regulated firms.

Ito, Takatoshi, and Anne O. Krueger, eds. *Deregulation and Interdependence in the Asia-Pacific Region*. Chicago: National Bureau of Economic Research and University of Chicago Press, 2000. Contains several essays about economic regulation in the newly industrializing nations of East Asia, including the relationship between regulation and free trade.

Levy, Brian, and Pablo T. Spiller, eds. *Regulations, Institutions, and Commitment: Comparative Studies of Telecommunications*. New York: Cambridge University Press, 1996. Focuses on the economic implications of political and organizational issues in regulating telecommunications, with case studies of Argentina, Chile, Jamaica, the Philippines, and the United Kingdom.

McCubbins, Mathew D., Roger G. Noll, and Barry R. Weingast. "Administrative Procedures as Instruments of Political Control." *Journal of Law, Economics, and Organization* 3, no. 2 (1987): 243–277. Discusses the effects of administrative procedures on policy and how the policy biases of agencies are created through procedural rules in legislation.

Noll, Roger G., ed. *Regulatory Policy and the Social Sciences*. Berkeley: University of California Press, 1985. Contains essays from anthropology, economics, law, political science, and sociology on the organization, procedures, and performance of regulatory agencies.

NOTES

1. United States Senate, *Hearing on Telecommunications Policy Reform,* Committee on Commerce, Science, and Transportation, 104th Cong., 1st sess., 21 March 1995, 54–56.

2. Ibid., 107.

3. Tim Kiska, "The High Costs of Cable," *Detroit News* (3 May 1996): E-1.

4. The term "regulation" is appropriate when one government entity regulates the activities of another. Examples are regulation of political campaigns by the Federal Election Commission and of local water systems by the federal government.

5. For more details on the political origins and economic consequences of broadcast regulation, see Roger G. Noll, Merton J. Peck, and John J. McGowan, *Economic Aspects of Television Regulation* (Washington, D.C.: The Brookings Institution, 1974).

6. For interesting discussions of the origins of some utility industries, see John E. Kingsbury, *The Telephone and Telegraph Exchange: Their Invention and Development* (Longman-Green, 1915); Rava Ramamurti, ed., *Privatizing Monopolies: Lessons from the Telecommunications and Transportation Sectors in Latin America* (Baltimore: Johns Hopkins University Press, 1996); and Gabriel Roth, *The Private Provision of Public Services in Developing Countries* (New York: Oxford University Press, 1987).

7. The Supreme Court ruled that a corporate charter was a contract between a state and a private business, and that enacting a regulatory statute amounted to a breech of contract by the state. States eventually avoided this decision by passing "reservation clause" amendments to their state constitutions, which reserved the right of the state to issue further regulations for state-chartered corporations. For details about the origins of economic regulation by the states, see

Mark Kanazawa and Roger G. Noll, "The Origins of State Railroad Regulation: The Illinois Constitution of 1870," in Claudia Goldin and Gary D. Libecap, eds., *The Regulated Economy: A Historical Approach to Political Economy* (Chicago: University of Chicago Press and National Bureau of Economic Research, 1994).

8. Some legal scholars argue that all regulation is a taking and that government should pay the costs of regulatory compliance. The basis for this argument is that regulation is a taking if it reduces the market value of firms that produce regulated products. Proponents of this view argue that if regulators were required to pay for the costs imposed by regulation, government would be forced to ask whether the social benefits of a regulation exceed its compliance costs.

9. The conceptual simplicity of cost-based pricing, but the complexity of its implementation is illustrated by an example. Suppose that a firm is a monopoly and produces two products. Let q_1 be the quantity supplied of the first product, q_2 be the quantity supplied of the second, $C(q_1,q_2)$ be the costs of producing these outputs (including return on investments), and p_1 and p_2 be the prices of the two products. The basic cost-of-service pricing rule is simply:

$$p_1q_1 + p_2q_2 = C(q_1,q_2). \tag{1}$$

Unfortunately, equation 1 tells us very little about which prices to set. For example, we can set the first price to zero and the second to total cost divided by q_2, or we can divide C by the sum of the two outputs, or we can decide that one product should be twice as pricey as the other, picking, say, p_1 and $2p_1$ so that equation 1 is satisfied. Thus, the requirement that prices should roughly recover costs is not very strict. Other considerations must enter into selecting one of the infinite number of prices that satisfy this requirement.

10. To see this algebraically, the stand-alone cost benchmark implies:

$$p_1q_1 = C(q_1,0) \text{ and } p_2q_2 = C(0,q_2). \tag{2}$$

But if the industry has economy of scope, then:

$$C(q_1,0) + C(0,q_2) > C(q_1,q_2). \tag{3}$$

11. Returning to the example, the marginal cost of the first product is

$$C(q_1,q_2) - C(q_1 - 1,q_2), \tag{4}$$

and the average incremental cost of the first product is

$$[C(q_1,q_2) - C(0,q_2)]/q_1. \tag{5}$$

12. The elasticity of demand is minus one times the ratio of the percentage change in output to the percentage change in price. (Because higher prices cause lower sales, the ratio is multiplied by minus one to make it a positive number.) Demand is *inelastic* if this ratio is less than one (price changes have a relatively small effect on sales) and is *elastic* if this ratio exceeds one (price changes lead to relatively large changes in sales).

13. Ramsey pricing principles frequently are used in regulatory proceedings, but they rarely are the sole basis for setting prices. Ramsey pricing imposes substantial informational demands on regulators because they must know the incremental cost and the elasticity of demand for every product. In the case of the ICC, which once regulated 4 billion prices, Ramsey pricing would have been impossibly difficult to implement compared with the simpler principle of setting prices so that the shipping costs of all commodities are roughly the same percentage of their market price. Second, political factors cause regulators not to give equal consideration to all regulated products. If regulators regard customers with low demand elasticities as the most deserving, due to either principled equity concerns or the practical political power of these customers, Ramsey prices will not be implemented.

14. Pure output controls are far more common in social regulation. Examples are nondiscrimination requirements for public accommodations (restaurants, hotels); control of outputs that are environmentally or ecologically harmful (banning lead in gasoline, limiting fish catches); and constraints to protect consumers (prescription requirements for pharmaceuticals, bans on hallucinogenic drugs). Here the focus is on output controls as part of economic regulation.

15. Under rent control, the occupant of a dwelling is protected against rent increases that

exceed ceilings that are imposed by city regulators. In some cities, the original occupant is entitled to sell or lease the right to a rent-controlled apartment. Thus, rent control does not necessarily reduce the rents that actual tenants pay, but instead simply transfers part of these rents from the landlord to the lucky person who was a tenant when controls were initiated.

16. For an excellent survey of research on the economic effects of regulation, see Paul L. Joskow and Nancy L. Rose, "The Effects of Economic Regulation," in *Handbook of Industrial Organization,* eds. Richard Schmalensee and Robert Willig (Amsterdam: North-Holland Publishing, 1989). For an account of how this research influenced Congress to deregulate several industries, see Martha Derthick and Paul J. Quirk, *The Politics of Deregulation* (Washington D.C.: The Brookings Institution, 1985).

17. The classic work on how agencies are formed to create a cartel is George J. Stigler, "The Theory of Economic Regulation," *Bell Journal of Economics and Management Science* 2, no. 1 (winter 1971): 3–21.

18. The hypothesis that the ICC was a mechanism for helping to stabilize railroad cartels was first put forth in two roughly simultaneous books: Gabriel Kolko, *Railroads and Regulation, 1877– 1916* (New York: W. W. Norton, 1965), and Paul W. MacAvoy, *The Economic Effects of Regulation: The Trunkline Railroad Cartels and the ICC before 1900* (Cambridge, Mass.: MIT Press, 1965). The definitive empirical study documenting that this hypothesis is correct is Robert H. Porter, "A Study of Cartel Stability: The Joint Executive Committee, 1880–86," *Bell Journal of Economics* 14 (1983): 301–314.

19. For extensive discussions of the interconnection problem in electricity, telephones, and transportation, see Paul L. Joskow and Roger G. Noll, "The Bell Doctrine: Applications in Telecommunications, Electricity, and Other Network Industries," *Stanford Law Review* 51, no. 5 (May 1999): 1249–1315.

20. For an extensive review of the evidence about the relative performance of private and public enterprises, see World Bank, *Bureaucrats in Business: The Economics and Politics of Government Ownership* (New York: Oxford University Press, 1995).

CHAPTER FIVE

Social Regulation

Peter J. May

February 1993 was not a good month for the family of Riley Detwiler, the Jack-in-the-Box fast-food chain, the suppliers of hamburger patties to Jack-in-the-Box, or the newly installed Clinton administration. Seventeen-month-old Riley died as a result of infection from a bacterial strain, *Escherichia coli* (*E. coli*) 0157:H7, linked to tainted and undercooked hamburger from a Jack-in-the-Box restaurant located in western Washington. He was one of four children who died after being infected with the *E. coli* strain. Another five hundred people became ill. Riley's death was particularly tragic because he had not even eaten the tainted hamburger. The bacterial strain was transmitted by a playmate who had done so. The media attention surrounding Riley's death, and the outbreak in general, brought the issue of food safety onto the crowded agenda of the new administration. Investigations of the outbreak found that federal inspectors had failed to identify tainted hamburgers that had been provided by a supplier to Jack-in-the-Box. State health inspectors had also failed to detect the fact that employees of Jack-in-the-Box were preparing hamburgers at a temperature below that required by state health department regulations.

The Jack-in-the-Box crisis is not an isolated case concerning contaminated food. In recent years, there have been large recalls of meats in the United States, a ban imposed by European countries on importing beef produced in Great Britain over fear of "mad cow" disease, and a ban on poultry from Belgium because of dioxin-contaminated feed. That these problems could arise in countries with well-developed systems for regulating food safety is all the more shocking to an unaware public. Indeed, meat processing is one of the most regulated industries in the United States. In 1998, the U.S. government spent $600 million for inspection of meat and poultry in sixty-two hundred processing facilities throughout the country. Some seventy-four hundred compliance officers from the federal Food Safety and Inspection Service inspected the processing, handling, and packaging of meat for compliance with U.S. Department of Agriculture (USDA) standards that specify requirements for plant sanitation, facilities, and operation.

Despite this extensive regulatory system, the Food Safety and Inspection Service of the USDA estimates that annually nearly 5 million cases of illness and more than four thousand deaths in the United States are associated with contaminated meat and poultry products. Largely in response to the sensation created by the *E. coli* scare, the Clinton administration initiated an overhaul of the way in which meats are inspected. This resulted in a new state-of-the-art, science-based inspection system for selected categories of meat processing. This new regulatory approach requires selected processors to identify potential sources of contamination within processing plants, to monitor those critical control points, and to institute additional controls that are aimed at preventing contamination. Rather than inspecting for specific actions by the affected producers, federal inspectors monitor for compliance with a plant's hazard control program and undertake studies of potential sources of contamination. The Jack-in-the-Box episode illustrates the need for social regulation, in addition to suggesting the challenges for the design and use of this tool. Social regulation compels actions on the part of individuals, firms, or lower levels of government in an effort to improve public welfare. Such regulation has been used as a tool of government to accomplish a number of public purposes. Many social regulations, like those addressing the processing of meat, are aimed at preventing harm to the public. Others, such as rules governing land use to provide open space or affordable housing, are aimed at providing public benefits. Establishing the boundaries of social regulation is difficult because this tool encompasses a variety of actions, policy domains, levels of government, and approaches to implementation. Indeed, the term "social regulation" is itself potentially misleading, as it is commonly used, to refer to a diversity of social, environmental, public health, and safety regulations. An objective of this chapter is to clarify the boundaries between social regulation and other tools of government.

The traditional conceptualization of social regulation calls attention to the use of the heavy hand of government—the "stick"—as a means of coercing compliance with rules. However, a notable trend in the recent development of regulations is the blending of deterrent measures with the use of incentives in order to stimulate, rather than compel, compliance. Also relevant is new thinking about the way in which regulations are developed and administered. This is illustrated by the new hazard control approach to meat inspection. This chapter discusses these newer approaches to the design and implementation of social regulation.

Prior reviews of social regulation as a tool of government emphasized the unreasonableness of many regulations.[1] These conclusions were primarily based on analyses undertaken during the 1980s that point to regulatory excesses. The reforms in regulatory processes in the United States introduced in recent years attempt to provide a sounder footing for the rules and standards that are the heart of regulations. Recent assessments of the costs and benefits of social regulation that are reviewed in this chapter provide a more positive assessment of the effectiveness of social regulation, although the issue of regulatory unreasonableness remains.

This chapter examines the key features of social regulation, the extent and patterns of use of this tool of government, variation in tool design and implementation, considerations for selecting this tool, management challenges that the tool poses, and the overall effects of the tool. The overarching theme of the chapter is that carefully crafted social regulation can be an effective tool of government in preventing harm and securing benefits.

I. DEFINING THE TOOL

As discussed in Chapter 4, the functions and concepts of regulation are generic. As a tool of government, regulation consists of rules that identify permissible and impermissible activity on the part of individuals, firms, or government agencies, along with accompanying sanctions or rewards, or both. The distinction between economic and social regulation is somewhat artificial. It is also increasingly blurred. Nonetheless, it is common to draw a distinction between the two based on the policy goals involved and the type of regulatory devices employed.

Social regulation is aimed at restricting behaviors that directly threaten public health, safety, welfare, or well-being. These include environmental pollution, unsafe working environments, unhealthy living conditions, and social exclusion. By contrast, economic regulation is aimed at ensuring competitive markets for goods and services and at avoiding consumer and other harms when such markets are not feasible. This is accomplished through regulating prices and/or conditions for firms entering specific markets. The lines become blurred when economic regulation is used to achieve social goals or when economic instruments are used as part of social regulation. Public utilities regulators allowing cross-subsidies to foster Internet access in schools illustrate the former (the latter is discussed more fully later in this chapter). The two types of regulation also differ in terms of who is typically affected. Social regulation addresses the behaviors of individuals, firms, or lower levels of government. Economic regulation addresses the behaviors of firms.

Defining Features

Any social regulation has four key elements: (1) rules that govern expected behaviors or outcomes, (2) standards that serve as benchmarks for compliance, (3) sanctions for noncompliance with the rules, and (4) an administrative apparatus that enforces the rules and administers sanctions. The rules entail specification of deadlines for taking action and/or standards of performance. Compliance is assessed with respect to either the date and process by which various actions are completed or adherence to the relevant standard, or both. To the extent that compliance must be coerced by means of threats of imposing sanctions, systems for monitoring compliance and for carrying out enforcement are necessary.

Although it is undergoing reform, the regulatory system for meat inspection in the United States typifies the way in which social regulation is employed as a tool of government. Compliance officers from the U.S. Food Safety and Inspection Service inspect the processing, handling, and packaging of meat for compliance with USDA standards concerning plant sanitation, facilities, and operation. A number of administrative actions can be undertaken when deficiencies occur repeatedly or when there is a failure to prevent shipping of adulterated meats. These include seizing the adulterated or misbranded meats, issuing letters of warning, withholding "marks of inspection" (i.e., the USDA label), and withdrawal of federal inspection—effectively closing down production. Extreme cases can be referred to the appropriate U.S. attorney for criminal prosecution.

Within the United States, the choice and form of social regulations are constrained by a variety of legal considerations that are addressed more fully in Chapter 4.[2] One issue is a prohibition stemming from the Fifth and Fourteenth Amendments of the U.S. Constitution against taking of private property without just compensation. There is a long history of challenges to environmental regulations on these grounds, most recently including a 1992 ruling by the Supreme Court in favor of a landowner over regulatory "taking" of a right to develop private property.[3] Subsequent cases and interpretations have suggested that regulations are constitutionally justifiable if they pass a test of "rough proportionality" that balances public benefits with restrictions of property rights.

Another issue concerns the power of regulatory agencies to develop regulations, given that the Constitution provides that only Congress can write laws. The basic authority of regulatory agencies to promulgate regulations was decided by the Supreme Court in 1936. In addition, the Administrative Procedures Act of 1946 sought to establish a procedure that insulates administrative agencies from challenges against delegated authority. Whether regulatory agencies overstep their authority remains a source of legal challenge to regulations. Indeed, this issue was the basis for a noteworthy appeals court panel decision in 1999 that found that the Environmental Protection Agency (EPA) overstepped its authority in drafting national air quality standards for ozone and particulate matter. A subsequent Supreme Court review overturned the appeals court's conclusion about the basic issue of delegation of authority.

Regulatory programs vary considerably in what they call for or prohibit. Some regulations simply require that individuals or firms provide information for others to act on. For example, among other requirements, the Emergency Planning and Community Right to Know Act (Title III of the Superfund Reauthorization Act of 1986) requires chemicals manufacturers and other facilities with toxic materials to list the chemicals they are manufacturing. Some regulations require specific processes to be followed. For example, the National Environmental Protection Act requires development of environmental impact statements for major real estate development projects. As illustrated by regulations governing the processing of meat, most regulations require particular actions. Some regulations prohibit particular actions, as illustrated by a variety of employment regulations that prohibit discrimination in employment.

Regulatory programs also differ in the timing of their intervention, especially as they concern potential harms from newly created products such as a new drug or chemical agent. Regulations governing new products or technologies by definition tend to be stricter than those governing existing products or technologies. This is because it is much easier to establish new requirements than it is to impose them retroactively. One choice is *ex ante* regulation for which the newly created product must be shown to be harmless before it is allowed to be publicly available. The other choice is *ex post* regulation for which a producer makes the newly created item publicly available with assurances of safety after more limited evaluation. Regulatory action is taken after the fact if harms occur. In principle, *ex ante* regulation provides a greater margin of safety, assuming that large-scale testing is undertaken; however, it is a costly process that incurs delays before potentially life-saving drugs or valuable products can be introduced. *Ex post* regulation shifts the burden to producers and the liability system, while allowing products to go to market more quickly. The choices made in the timing of regulation vary among items that are regulated over time and across countries.

Although we normally think of regulation as entailing rules established by government to restrict the behavior of private entities or citizens, social regulation also includes mandates from higher levels of government to lower levels.[4] Intergovernmental mandates either impose process requirements (e.g., requirements for state transportation planning as a condition for federal highway funds) or require specific regulatory actions to be taken by the lower-level governments (e.g., state monitoring of air quality). In either case, higher-level governments monitor compliance by lower-level governments and impose sanctions if the mandated actions are not undertaken.

Relation to Key Tool Features

As compared with other tools of government, social regulation is highly *coercive* and intrusive, surprisingly *indirect*, usually not very *automatic,* and relatively *invisible.*

Coerciveness

Coerciveness measures the extent to which a tool restricts individual or group behavior, as opposed to merely encouraging or discouraging it. The use of sanctions and enforcement in compelling compliance with rules makes social regulation inherently coercive. The fact that social regulation seeks to alter the behaviors of those who are regulated also suggests a high degree of intrusiveness. Consider regulations that are designed to limit the harmful effects of runoff from farms on water quality.[5] Farmers are required to undertake substantial changes in farm practices such as the storage of manure during winter months, limits on the time of year that liquid-manure fertilizers are applied to crops, and restrictions on cultivation of crops near streams and water sources. The regulations are intrusive because they restrict potentially remunerative farm practices and because compliance is expensive. They are coercive because they impose fines or other sanctions on farmers who fail to comply with the requirements.

Directness

Directness measures the extent to which the entity authorizing or inaugurating a program is involved in executing it. Social regulation requires direct intervention on the part of government at the stage of adoption in order to specify rules or to establish intergovernmental mandates. Yet, particularly as practiced in the United States, social regulation turns out to be a surprisingly indirect tool of government. This is because implementation is often delegated to other levels of government, relies on self-reporting by regulated entities, or makes use of third parties to help with enforcement. The implementation of regulations to ensure the safety of buildings in the United States illustrates various aspects of the indirectness of regulation.[6] Most states enact building codes that set forth construction requirements designed to prevent the collapse of buildings and loss of life. Authorizing statutes typically specify the roles of local governments, required actions for enforcing code provisions, and penalties for violations. The technical details of the construction standards are typically based on model building codes developed by one of three national private code organizations. Enforcement of building codes is usually delegated to cities and counties. Cities and counties, in turn, often rely on third parties such as structural engineers to help with inspection tasks for complex structures.

Automaticity

Automaticity measures the extent to which a tool uses an existing administrative structure to produce its effect, rather that having to create its own administrative apparatus. Very few social regulations are self-enforcing in the sense that compliance is automatically obtained. Right-of-way rules on highways are self-enforcing to the extent that motorists who drive in the wrong direction are likely to wind up in an accident. Obviously, adherence to speed limits is not automatic. Like compliance with most social regulations, driving within the limits needs to be either induced or compelled. Compliance is usually compelled by enforcement systems that impose penalties when noncompliance is detected. Voluntary compliance can be sought by educating affected entities as to the benefits of regulations or by providing technical and financial assistance to ease compliance.

Visibility

Visibility measures the extent to which the resources devoted to a tool show up in the normal budget process. Social regulations are relatively invisible tools of government. Although elaborate procedures are in place to open regulatory processes to public view, the technical nature of most regulations tends to work against carrying this out. In addition, the costs that regulations impose on regulated entities are often unknown. Most important from a political perspective, other than the relatively minor administrative costs of enforcement, the costs of regulation are invisible in government budgetary processes. This fact provides a powerful incentive for elected officials to impose what can be viewed, in a narrow budgetary sense, as requirements with relatively few costs. Reforms designed to make regulatory processes more transparent attempt to address this issue by providing a fuller accounting of the costs of regulation (these reforms are discussed later in this chapter).

Each of the defining features of social regulation—rules, standards, inducements, and enforcement—can be crafted in a variety of ways. The major distinction in the form of rules is between those that specify actions to be undertaken or avoided (substantive rules) and those that specify a process to be followed (procedural rules).[7] Substantive rules may either specify a desired action or prohibit certain actions. In practice, social regulations typically contain a mix of these different types of rules. Regulations also specify the situations to which the rules apply, as well as the conditions for exemptions from their application.

Consider provisions of the Meat Inspection Act introduced earlier. Among other substantive rules, any meat or meat food product that has passed inspection is required to be marked with the label "inspected and passed" before inspection is deemed complete. Other provisions prohibit slaughtering of animals, except as specified by the act, with a specific prohibition against the use of inhumane methods of slaughter. Procedural requirements typically specify reporting requirements or appeal procedures. For example, the Meat Inspection Act sets forth recordkeeping requirements concerning the disposition of animals.

Rules are often sufficiently complex that they require specification of standards for performance. Standards serve as the benchmarks for determining compliance with a given rule. Standards come in a variety of forms. They may be either design standards that specify the use of particular materials or means that must be used to achieve compliance (e.g., meat-labeling standards specifying size and placement of labels) or performance standards that specify levels of expected performance (e.g., ambient air quality levels to be achieved). A common practice is to make use of reference standards, developed by national code organizations, as benchmarks for desired performance.

Compliance with rules and standards is rarely automatic and, as such, needs to be induced. The traditional approach is to coerce compliance by means of threats of penalties for failing to adhere to rules or for failing to meet the designated standards. An alternative is to reward regulated entities for complying and to make it easier for regulated entities to comply. In practice, newer social regulations contain a mix of coercive, facilitative, and incentive features. These approaches reflect different assumptions about the regulatory problem. The

---

BOX 5-1 *Major Social Regulatory Laws of the United States: Original Dates of Enactment*

Environmental Quality
- Clean Air Act (1970)
- Clean Water Act (1972)
- Comprehensive Environmental Response, Compensation, and Liability Act (1980)
- Federal Fungicides, Insecticides, and Rodenticides Act (1947)
- National Environmental Policy Act (1970)
- Resource Conservation and Recovery Act (1976)
- Toxic Substances Control Act (1976)

Food and Drugs
- Federal Food, Drug, and Cosmetic Act (1938)
- Pure Food and Drug Act (1906)
- Meat Inspection Act (1907)
- Nutrition Labeling and Education Act (1990)

Health and Safety
- Consumer Product Safety Act (1972)
- Federal Hazardous Substances Act (1960)
- National Manufactured Housing Construction Safety Standards Act (1974)
- National Traffic and Motor Vehicle Safety Act (1966)
- Occupational Safety and Health Act (1970)

Social Policy
- Americans with Disabilities Act (1990)
- Fair Housing Act (1968)

Compiled from Kenneth J. Meier and E. Thomas Garman, *Regulation and Consumer Protection*, 2d ed. (Houston: Dame Publications Inc., 1995).

---

traditional enforcement approach assumed that compliance would not be readily achieved in the absence of coercion. The new approach assumes that compliance is more readily achievable. The key implication of this distinction is that compliance can be enhanced through other means than enforcement alone.

Penalties and inducements are components of the overall enforcement system, designed to bring about compliance. Enforcement systems seek to either compel compliance through frequent monitoring and the application of sanctions or produce voluntary compliance by demonstrating the benefits of compliance and providing incentives to comply.[8] Regardless of the enforcement approach, the design of an enforcement system entails choices, addressed later in this chapter, concerning effort devoted to educational activities, surveillance, technical assistance, inspection, and prosecution of violations.

II. PATTERNS OF TOOL USE

Social regulations are almost as old as government itself.[9] A rule specifying the consequences of faulty construction of buildings can be found in the Code of Hammurabi of ancient Babylon. More modern building code provisions include those of the Romans in the first century CE for regulating the safety of public buildings. The Plymouth colony enacted requirements in 1626 concerning roofing materials. Fire codes were enacted in many cities after the great London fire of 1666. Regulations concerning food quality date back to England's prohibition in 1263 of the adulteration of bread. Laws regulating pollution date back to a prohibition by King Edward in 1307 prohibiting the use of soft coal in kilns. The first national agency to address air pollution in the world was created in England in 1863 as the Alkali Inspectorate. Food safety legislation in the United States dates to the enactment in 1907 of the Meat Inspection Act. The legislation was a direct reaction to the hysteria that followed publication of *The Jungle*, Upton Sinclair's scathing indictment of Chicago's meat-packing industry.

Until the latter part of the nineteenth century, social regulations were typically prompted by attention-forcing events such as publication of *The Jungle*. It was not until the consumer and environmental movement of the 1970s that rapid expansion of social regulation took place in the United States. This was soon emulated in other industrialized countries. As a consequence, social regulations have become pervasive at all levels of government in the United States and other countries.

Current Extent of Social Regulations

The scope of social regulation is evident in the many aspects of the people whose lives it touches. Thus, in the United States, social regulations govern what we eat (food inspection, labeling, and content), where we live (land use and construction regulations), the care of children (regulation of child-care facilities), how we are educated (school attendance, curriculum, teacher certification requirements), the conditions under which we work (occupational safety and health regulation), the clothes we wear (labeling and product quality requirements), the safety of automobile travel (vehicle standards and driving regulations), the quality of the air we breathe and the water we drink (environmental regulations), the facilities in which we spend our waning days (nursing-home regulation), and how we are buried (the regulation of funeral homes). In addition, intergovernmental regulations affect many aspects of the way in which states and local governments go about their business.

Box 5-1 lists major regulatory laws in force in the United States. Although there is no single compilation of regulatory statutes in the United States, the pervasiveness of the use of the tool at the federal level is evident from a few statistics. More than four hundred public laws enacted since 1988 can be referenced by the keyword "regulation," which includes both economic and social regulations. During the 1970s, nearly twenty major regulatory laws were enacted in the United States. Among other provisions, these laws established major new regulatory agencies that in turn had the power to establish new regulations. The agencies include the Consumer Product Safety Commission, the Environmental Protection Agency, the Food and Drug Administration, the National Traffic Safety Administration, and the Occupation Safety and Health Administration.

Social regulation is also an important tool at the state and local levels of government. Regulations at the local level predate those at the state and federal levels. Major categories of state regulatory activity include state consumer protection laws ("lemon" laws), occupational licensing (certification and testing), educational standards and regulation, regulation of child care and nursing homes, building safety (state building codes), and health, safety, and environmental regulations that parallel similar federal regulations. Major categories of regulatory activity by local governments include zoning and land-use regulations, housing codes, and a variety of ordinances regulating such things as signs, noise levels, and traffic safety.

Intergovernmental regulation grew extensively as a tool of government in the United States during the 1970s with the enactment of twenty-two significant mandates. Until enactment of the Unfunded Mandates Reform Act in 1995, the use of intergovernmental mandates remained unabated during the 1980s and 1990s.[10] Box 5-2 lists major federal laws enacted between 1983 and 1990 that contain direct mandates to be carried out by state or local governments.

The development of social regulation in other countries has paralleled regulatory patterns in the United States. Indeed, there is a remarkable consistency of subjects of regulation among diverse countries. For example, shortly after enactment of the National Environmental Protection Act in the United States in 1970, similar regulatory provisions were adopted in most countries that are members of the Organization of Economic Cooperation and Development. Other similarities in regulatory topics have been noted in cross-national studies of pollution prevention, chemical regulation, hazardous waste cleanup, occupational health and safety, and environmental policy.[11] More recent concern about food safety led to the establishment of regulatory agencies in Canada, France, and Ireland and a food safety campaign across European Union member states.

In general, the United States tends to have a much more formal system of regulatory development and a more legalistic and formal style of regulatory enforcement than the style adhered to in other countries. Some cross-national studies, such as Gormley and Peters's examination of regulation of child care, and Day and Klein's study of nursing-home regulation, suggest that the differences in national styles of regulation are greater on paper than they are in practice.[12] Although the American approach to social regulation has distinctive elements,

BOX 5-2 *Major Intergovernmental Mandates (1983–1990)*

Environmental Quality

- Hazardous and Solid Waste Amendments of 1984
- Ocean Dumping Ban Act of 1988
- Safe Drinking Water Amendments of 1986
- Water Quality Act of 1987

Health and Safety

- Asbestos Emergency Response Act of 1986
- Highway Safety Amendment of 1984
- Safe Drinking Water Amendments of 1986

Social Policy

- Americans with Disabilities Act, 1990
- Age Discrimination in Employment Amendment of 1986
- Child Abuse Amendment of 1984
- Fair Housing Act Amendments of 1988
- Immigration Reform and Control Act of 1986
- Voting Accessibility for Elderly and Handicapped, 1984

Compiled from Paul Posner, *The Politics of Unfunded Mandates: Whither Federalism?* (Washington, D.C.: Georgetown University Press, 1998), 233–237.

it is important to recognize that there is a good deal of variation in regulatory approaches within the United States, as well as within other countries.

Recent Trends

The election of market-oriented governments in many Western countries during the mid-1980s heralded a backlash against social regulation. In the United States, the Reagan administration established a stringent (on paper at least) system of regulatory review that required more extensive cost-benefit tests of new regulations. This review process helped stem the growth of regulations, but it also introduced considerable delay and red tape. The review process carried forward until early in the Clinton administration when a new regulatory review process was established.[13] In response to concerns voiced by state and local officials about intergovernmental mandates, Congress enacted the Unfunded Mandates Reform Act in 1995. This put in place procedures for assessing the impacts of major federal mandates on other levels of government and on the private sector. Reviews of the early experience with these provisions suggest that they have had little impact on whether to adopt mandates, but they have had some impact in shaping mandate design.[14]

Along with reforms of the process of developing regulations, a number of countries have been rethinking approaches to social regulation. Noteworthy developments in the United States include adoption of marketlike mechanisms, such as emission trading programs for pollution reduction, and the use of negotiated rulemaking to develop rules. The United States, however, has not always been the leader in regulatory innovations. More useful models for new forms of regulation can be found in other countries. The Dutch, for example, have negotiated extensive accords with industries from different sectors of the economy to promote environmental sustainability. Policymakers in New Zealand completely revamped their approach to environmental management in 1991 by substituting a far-reaching intergovernmental cooperative planning mandate for the prior diverse set of highly prescriptive policies.[15]

III. BASIC MECHANICS

The administration of social regulation involves four basic steps: (1) establishment of rules that set forth expectations of behavior or outcomes, (2) development of standards for evaluating compliance with these rules, (3) establishment of penalties and rewards to induce compliance with rules, and (4) design and implementation of an enforcement system for monitoring and securing compliance. Each of these, in turn, entails a variety of actions.

Rules: Setting Expectations

Rules are the central component of social regulation in that they set forth expectations about behavior. The fact that rules are written down differentiates social regulation from unwritten codes of conduct such as norms of social interaction. "Good" rules can be defined, following Deborah Stone, with respect to their legitimacy, fairness, and predictability.[16] Legitimacy relates both to the source of the rule and to the appropriateness of the situations to which it applies. A number of legal considerations govern these aspects of regulatory rules and their development. In particular, rules must be based on clear statutory authority and must be developed in accordance with prescribed rulemaking processes. Stone notes that fairness is the most difficult aspect because there is a tradeoff between consistency (treating likes alike, eliminating arbitrariness) and flexibility (allowing sensitivity to special circumstances). Predictability is important in setting consistent expectations and is eased by having simple provisions rather than a complex formulation. Taken together, these comments suggest the attributes of a "good" rule, shown in Box 5-3.

Rulemaking Procedures

An elaborate process exists for regulatory rulemaking in the United States.[17] As spelled out in the Administrative Procedures Act of 1946 (as amended), this process is intended to protect citizens from arbitrary administrative action by ensuring openness and access to rulemaking. It does so by requiring a series of public notifications and reviews of pending rules, with opportunities for public comments either in formal hearings (formal rulemaking) or in less formal written comments (informal rulemaking).

More specifically, the rulemaking process involves a number of steps: (1) a prerule stage involving analysis of potential standards and a potential notice of advanced rulemaking, (2) a proposed rule stage involving publishing the proposed rule in the *Federal Register* for comment, (3) a public comment and evaluation stage followed by drafting and review of the final rule (or in some instances withdrawal), and (4) a final rule stage involving publication of the final rule in the *Federal Register* with commentary about responses to public review, followed by (5) implementation of the rule or standard.

BOX 5-3 *Attributes of Good Rules*

- Commonly viewed as necessary
- Appropriate to the situation being addressed
- Provide for consistent application with reasonable exemptions
- Sets forth predictable expectations
- Can be understood by affected entities

Informal rulemaking has the obvious advantage of being less costly and time consuming. Yet, even informal rulemaking can take years as illustrated by the rulemaking for the "hazard analysis and critical control point systems" rule developed by the Food Safety and Inspection Service. A proposed rule was published in the *Federal Register* in February 1995. The initial comment period for the rule during the spring of 1995 was for 120 days. It was extended for another 30 days and later reopened for another 95 days. During this time, seven informal hearings, three scientific conferences, a conference of federal and state officials, and scheduled public hearings were held. These forums and more than seventy-five hundred written comments led to revisions in the proposed rule and another series of hearings with publication of related proposed rules in December 1995. The proposed final rule for the new system, comprising eighty-five pages in the *Federal Register*, was published in July 1996. Supplemental development of technical standards and procedures for implementing the new regulatory system, including additional rulemaking, has continued into 2001.

A central issue for rulemaking is to balance the need for expertise with the desire for a fair and open process. Critics of rulemaking fail to achieve the desired openness while also being time consuming and cumbersome. As discussed later in this chapter, newer forms of rulemaking attempt to address these problems.

Standards: Setting Benchmarks

Rules are often sufficiently complex that they require specification of standards for performance. Standards serve as the benchmarks for determining compliance with a given rule. Examples of the different types of standards, introduced earlier, are shown in Box 5-4.

Establishing standards entails consideration of the desired approach (design versus performance standards) and consideration of the technical issues of what constitutes an appropriate standard. Technical expertise is essential for devising appropriate and defensible standards, which may entail detailed studies of health and environmental consequences of different threshold values. For example, development of the hazard analysis and critical control point (HACCP) system rules and standards by the Food Safety and Inspection Service required consideration of the microbial causes of food-borne illnesses along with the technical details of meat processing, storage, and transportation. The necessary expertise is either developed in-house by regulatory agencies (e.g., EPA, FDA) or through reliance on private consensus-based standard setting and testing organizations. The latter include the American Society of Testing and Materials (ASTM), the American National Standards Institute (ANSI), and the Underwriters Laboratory (UL).[18] Blue-ribbon panels or committees are sometimes engaged to provide both expertise and legitimacy for new rules or standards. The Food Safety and Inspection Service drew on results of a National Academy of Sciences study of food safety and engaged several expert panels in developing the HACCP system.

Legal expertise is also essential for development of rules as practiced at the national level in the United States. Legal advice is often necessary concerning appropriate rulemaking procedures, maintenance of records of contacts and information, and potential conflicts of interest. Legal expertise is also important for addressing challenges to rulemaking. One criticism of the formality of the rulemaking process in the United States is that it has resulted in a degree of legal formalism that is counterproductive in providing too-ready means for challenging regulations and their development.

A third form of expertise that is increasingly required in regulatory rulemaking is expertise in economic analyses. Such expertise is necessary for conducting the required cost-benefit analyses and impact assessments for regulations. As with technical expertise, regulatory agencies often turn to consultants or other experts to provide economic analyses. For example, the Economic Research Service of the USDA conducted an important cost-benefit analysis of the HACCP system for food safety.

Broader management skills are required for integrating technical, legal, and economic information; adhering to legislative intent; and managing the regulatory rulemaking process. Decisions must be made about the process itself with respect to the visibility of rule development, extent of involvement of expert panels, and the appropriate rulemaking procedures. Coordination is often required with other agencies and with other levels of government. The development of the HACCP system by the Food Safety and Inspection Service of the USDA required the cooperation of the FDA for related programs, the Department of Transportation for transportation of perishable foods, and states and localities for assessing intergovernmental impacts.

BOX 5-4 *Types of Regulatory Standards*

- **Design (specification standards)**—Specify the use of particular materials or means that must be used to achieve compliance. *Example:* Meat-labeling standards that specify the size in inches of the label to be attached to meat packages.

- **Performance standards**—Specify levels of expected performance. *Example:* Total daily maximum load (TDML) of phosphorus in a particular body of water.

- **Reference standards**—Design or performance standards developed by national or private standard-setting organizations. *Example:* Requirements that scales used for weighing meat fulfill standards for scales developed by the National Institute of Standards and Technology.

A key challenge for the design of a social regulation is to find the appropriate mix of penalties and rewards to induce compliance. Each can be crafted in a variety of ways.

Design of Penalties

The use of penalties presumes that regulated entities are motivated to comply because they fear the fines (or other sanctions) for failure to comply with regulations. More specifically, the presumption is that regulated entities engage in "calculated compliance" that weights the costs and benefits of compliance. Relevant costs include the expected costs of sanctions for not complying, while taking into account the likelihood of getting caught.[19] From this perspective, the appropriate penalty is one that is sufficient to alter the decision calculus in favor of compliance. For example, sanctions for failing to comply with meat inspection regulations vary from notifying plant managers about problems to seizing adulterated foods and withdrawing federal inspection. One of the key findings of research about sanctions is that compliance rates are relatively insensitive to the level of the penalty, but they are much more sensitive to the likelihood of detecting violations.[20] As such, the frequency of inspection may be a more important consideration than the level of penalty in compelling compliance.

The preceding discussion suggests that some regulated entities view fines and other civil penalties as a "cost of business." One approach to altering this calculus is to impose criminal sanctions that can be applied to flagrant violations of rules involving gross negligence or other efforts to subvert a regulation. For example, in fiscal year 1998, the Environmental Protection Agency referred 266 criminal cases to the Department of Justice, charging 350 criminal defendants.[21] In addition to serving as a specific deterrent for specific violations, criminal penalties serve as a general deterrent in putting regulated entities on notice that harsh penalties can be invoked.

Design of Rewards

The use of rewards, or incentives, assumes that regulated entities want to comply but that they either do not know how to comply or cannot afford to take the necessary actions. For example, the Food Safety and Inspection Service is undertaking the development of generic hazard analysis and critical control point models for regulation that individual producers can then adapt to their particular situation. This relieves the firms from the expense of developing the models and also provides consistency in the overall regulatory framework.

Incentives make use of positive rewards to induce compliance.[22] These include publicizing the fact that compliance has been obtained, prizes for "best practices" in achieving compliance, and greater flexibility for regulated entities with good compliance ratings. The "energy star" program of the Environmental Protection Agency has been a particularly successful program in motivating and publicizing voluntary adoption of energy-efficiency standards. Manufacturers of products that meet EPA energy-efficiency standards are able to advertise that fact and apply an "energy star" seal to the products. This certification is equivalent to a product endorsement, like a Good Housekeeping seal of approval, that has commercial value in meeting consumer demands for energy efficiency. The EPA also promotes "self-policing" efforts by lessening civil and eliminating criminal penalties for firms that voluntarily discover, report, and correct violations of environmental regulations.

Enforcement Systems: Obtaining Compliance

Enforcement systems are necessary to identify noncompliance and to invoke penalties or other measures for obtaining compliance. As illustrated by the meat inspection program, regulatory programs are generally thought of as having extensive enforcement systems involving an army of inspectors and swift retribution for noncompliance. However, such extensive enforcement is relatively rare. In most countries, and for most social regulations, enforcement typically rests heavily on voluntary reporting by regulated entities, as well as infrequent inspection. The details of the enforcement system—or, more precisely, the compliance system—are reflected in the enforcement strategy of regulatory agencies and the enforcement styles of inspectors.[23] Let us consider the key decisions involved in establishing an enforcement strategy.

Detecting Violations

The design of surveillance and inspection entails decisions about procedures for detecting violations and priorities for targeting inspections. Complaint-based systems for detection of violations are the most common form of surveillance. They have the virtue of simplicity, but they are also haphazard in coverage. Moreover, complaints can serve as vehicles for retaliation by disgruntled individuals or as a basis for retribution by employers against those who bring complaints. Refinements of complaint systems include toll-free numbers for registering complaints and mechanisms that allow for anonymous filing of complaints.

Given the inevitable gap between available inspection resources and needs, choices have to be made about priorities for inspection. The general advice of the enforcement literature is to target those regulated entities that historically have high rates of violations or that comprise a large percentage of the activity under regulation. This approach requires a historical basis for determining compliance patterns and profiles of regulated entities. Perhaps the best example of targeted inspection in the United States is the use of the "taxpayer compliance model" by the Internal Revenue Service to identify tax returns for audits based on past patterns of violations and revenue recovery.

Given that most regulations entail multiple components, a related problem is to determine which items to inspect. The typical advice is to inspect major items, but the identity of these may not be obvious and may differ among regulated entities. The new approach to regulation of meat inspection (the HACCP system) requires meat processors to identify major control points in their production process on which firms and inspectors should focus attention.

Invoking Sanctions

Regardless of the process and targeting of inspection, procedures need to be established for invoking sanctions. The available sanctions and other tools of compliance are usually specified as part of the authorization of a social regulation with details provided through rulemaking by the relevant regulatory agency. A number of steps are required to invoke civil or criminal penalties. Civil penalties are typically imposed through administrative law systems of regulatory agencies, involving administrative law judges and appeal procedures. Criminal penalties are imposed through referral for prosecution to the Department of Justice. Both entail procedures for notifying regulated entities about infractions, opportunities for appeal of that notification, documentation of evidence, determination by judges of violation, imposition by judges of appropriate penalties, and appeals procedures.

The realities of any regulation are provided by the day-to-day interaction of inspectors with regulated entities. Inspectors communicate the meaning of a given regulation and exercise discretion in deciding how to deal with particular violations of rules. Given these critical roles, an important management challenge is to foster a desired enforcement style among inspectors.

What constitutes the best enforcement style has been a matter of debate in the regulatory literature, but some general consensus has begun to emerge.[24] Inspectors who are too informal and unwilling to invoke threats are likely to be ineffective unless there is already a high degree of willingness to comply. They simply will not be taken seriously. Inspectors who are too rigid and bullying will be off-putting, if not overwhelming. If regulatees think their threats will not be backed by the relevant legal system, legalistic regulators will not accomplish their purpose.

Inspectors who employ a mix of flexibility and coercion are generally thought to be the most effective, although identifying the appropriate mix is problematic. John Scholz develops this logic in arguing that a "tit-for-tat" enforcement style is better suited for bringing about the desired learning and resultant compliance than is accommodation or legalism.[25] This means that an inspector first cooperates with regulatees on the presumption that they will cooperate and choose to comply voluntarily. If compliance is not obtained, the appropriate response on the part of the inspector is to threaten sanctions. As such, the enforcement style is adjusted to fit the circumstances and past patterns of interaction. Such flexibility in enforcement is difficult to bring about because regulatory officials generally desire consistent application of rules, and both regulated parties and regulatory advocates seek certainty.

Reporting Systems

Rounding out the design of enforcement systems is the development of reporting systems for tracking inspections, violations, and dispositions. Such reporting provides an essential basis for improving enforcement targeting. This requires establishing systems for recordkeeping and for reporting of enforcement outcomes. For example, the Food Safety and Inspection Service issues a quarterly inspection report that provides information about inspections and violations of provisions of the Meat Inspection Act. Publicizing enforcement information also serves an important educative function in showing that regulatory agencies are serious about enforcement, providing a general deterrent to noncompliance.

Allocating Staff

The central challenge that drives the above decisions about priority setting and targeting is the gap that often exists between needs and inspection staff resources. This gap also shapes decisions about the allocation of staff among different enforcement roles. These roles generally consist of surveillance and responding to complaints, ongoing inspection involving multiple potential inspection points, follow-up evaluation of noncompliance actions, and training and supervision. How these roles are handled also raises organizational issues concerning the degree to which enforcement functions are centralized in an effort to promote headquarters control or decentralized to fit agency regional office structures. Added to this mix are the potential complications of use of third parties for inspection and for oversight of self-reporting by regulated entities.

There is no single best model for resolving the key agency choices concerning the allocation and organization of enforcement personnel. Different approaches potentially apply depending on the enforcement situation. One approach is to emphasize surveillance (e.g., through random inspections) and high-profile enforcement actions to foster a climate of general deterrence, for which all the affected entities become concerned that they could be subject to enforcement action. This is appropriate if many different entities are being regulated, as it is impossible to conduct systematic inspection of each with any reasonable frequency. A different approach is to emphasize ongoing inspection and follow-up evaluation, with attention to improving self-reporting, so that regulated entities improve their ability to comply with regulations. This is appropriate if the ratio of inspection staff to regulated entities is sufficiently high to permit regular inspection, as is the case for the inspection of meat processing.

Considering Regulatory Federalism

One of the more complicated aspects of regulation in multitiered systems of government is the role assigned to different levels of government. Regulation of private entities is sometimes carried out by national-level agencies, as illustrated by the role of the Food Safety and Inspection Service in inspection of meat processing practices. Often, parallel state regulatory programs exist. In the case of food safety, states regulate meats not transported across state lines, whereas the federal government regulates meats involving interstate transportation. Most national regulations entail some form of involvement of other tiers of government. "Regulatory federalism" is a generic term that refers to the carrying out of regulations by different layers of government.

Many regulatory programs treat state, or local, governments as regulatory agents acting as administrative extensions of the federal government.[26] Typically, implementation and enforcement functions are delegated to states that are certified to carry out those functions and given some discretion in how they are carried out. States are required to have standards that are at least as stringent as federal standards. For example, the Clean Air Act delegates enforcement authority to states that develop acceptable plans for meeting federal air-quality standards. States are not required to undertake these functions, but they have strong incentives to do so in order to have greater control of the program, and are often able to obtain reimbursement of relevant administrative expenses. Federal regulatory agencies have the authority to revoke state delegated powers—a sanction that can be used to cajole states into strengthening their programs—and to enforce regulations directly on a case-by-case basis.

Other regulatory programs treat state, or local, governments as trustees for which there is wider latitude in designing and carrying out regulatory programs. The growth management planning mandates of a number of American states illustrate this form of intergovernmental mandate.[27] The various state mandates require cities and counties to develop comprehensive plans for managing growth but leave open the specific regulatory rules to be contained in those plans. The intergovernmental mandates specify issues to be addressed by the plans and deadlines for submitting them for state approval. State officials review the plans and can have the power to impose penalties, such as withholding tax revenues if plans are not brought into compliance with state requirements. This power is usually not invoked, however. Often the development of plans is facilitated through state-provided technical information and funding.

Variation in the Basic Mechanics

The specification of rules and standards for regulation of lower levels of government differs from that for regulation of private entities in several respects. Intergovernmental mandates usually specify deadlines and the format for developing regulatory programs by lower-level governments but pay limited attention to specification of what constitutes full compliance. For example, the growth management programs of states (discussed above) establish planning requirements for local governments, deadlines for developing plans, and, to varied degrees, the format of those plans. Missing from these mandates are detailed standards of what constitutes high-quality plans.

Sanctions include revoking all or part of the authority of the lower level, preempting their regulatory role for specific decisions, or withholding tax or other revenues. Inducements include financial inducements to undertake regulatory tasks (e.g., repayment of administrative costs), authority to tailor regulatory provisions to the local setting (usually with restrictions on that authority), and immunity provisions against private lawsuits for failing to take adequate regulatory actions. In general, harsh sanctions are unlikely to be invoked against states, or localities, for noncompliance with intergovernmental regulations, given the political costs involved.

Enforcement systems for intergovernmental regulations usually entail direct oversight of lower-level governments and less emphasis on complaint-based surveillance or on self-regulation than occurs in regulation of the private sector. Because of differing relationships with lower-level governments among regional offices of regulatory agencies, oversight is often uneven across different areas of the country.

IV. TOOL SELECTION

As with other tools of government, the decision to impose social regulation is an inherently political decision that reflects a balancing of values and perspectives. Decisions about whether to regulate go hand in hand with decisions about the design and implementation of social regulations. Given this, debates about the form of social regulation are often as contentious as those about whether to regulate.

Rationale: Overcoming Imperfections of the Legal System

As Eugene Bardach[28] notes, it is useful to think of social regulation as correcting failures of the legal system—mainly limitations of liability and tort law—to prevent harms or to promote positive ends (see Chapter 15). These, in turn, arise from failures of the market system. Consider the example of air pollution that arises from the failure of firms to internalize the costs of such pollution (an externality). In principle, an individual could sue a facility and attempt to prove a harm (tort) or show negligence (invoking liability) as the result of such pollution. In practice, however, the costs and time involved are too great for bringing suits concerning many facilities. Hence, regulation is an appropriate solution.[29]

Unlike economic regulation, for which there are relatively clear notions of what constitutes economic market failure as a basis for regulatory intervention, the failures that provide the rationale for social regulation are less well defined. These generally consist of failures of liability or tort systems, or both. Because this definition provides ample opportunity for regulatory intervention, the decision to impose social regulation is inherently political. This fact is well reflected in the history of social regulations, as discussed earlier.

Political and Legal Considerations

A variety of political and legal considerations affect decisions to use social regulation as a tool of government. Perhaps the overriding consideration is that elected officials often perceive regulation as an instrument with relatively few costs. This is because the major costs of regulation are not borne by government. As a consequence, they do not show up in budgetary processes. Yet, elected officials are wary of potential backlash from regulated entities that bear the burdens of regulation. This poses a tradeoff be-

tween the consequences of failing to regulate and the costs, in terms of potential backlash, imposed by a given regulation. This tradeoff has a variety of political and legal
implications.

Political Considerations

Proponents of regulation emphasize the harms that regulation will address. Opponents
emphasize the burdens it imposes. Often the specific regulatory issue is joined to
broader debates about the intrusiveness of government or the rights of individuals. For
example, seatbelt regulations were delayed for a number of years in the United States
because of debate concerning the rights of individuals to choose whether to buckle up,
free of governmental interference. More generally, fundamental beliefs in individual
freedoms and concern about governmental interference serve as political constraints
to regulation in the United States.

Debates over regulation often pit well-organized and well-funded potential regulated
entities against more diffuse potential beneficiaries of regulation.[30] The potential regulatees have strong incentives to fight, or otherwise water down proposed regulations,
whereas the broader beneficiary groups have lesser incentives to advocate for regulations. James Q. Wilson argues that political entrepreneurs must step forth and lead the
political debate. Alternatively, there must be sufficient moral outrage over abuses to
overcome resistance to regulation.

The history of social regulation in the United States is replete with cases involving
such moral outrage and political entrepreneurship.[31] Examples of scathing revelations
that led to major regulations include Upton Sinclair's indictment of the meat-packing
industry, Rachel Carson's indictment of the use of pesticides, and Ralph Nader's indictment of the automobile industry. Noteworthy political entrepreneurs who played
key roles in enacting social regulations in the United States include Senators Edward
Muskie (environmental regulation) and Warren Magnuson (health and safety regulation). Beyond these visible cases, the enactment of social regulations usually entails
intensive lobbying among affected interests to delay regulatory provisions, to create
exemptions, or to limit enforcement powers.

One concern relating to the politics of regulation is that regulated entities will manipulate the development of regulations or their enforcement in ways that undermine
regulatory intent. In the extreme, regulated entities will capture the process to codify
regulations that benefit their interests at the expense of society. This is a particular
concern with efforts to seek greater consultation with industry and other regulated
entities as part of the development of rules and standards.

Efforts have been made in the United States for more than twenty years to increase
the attention paid to the implicit economic costs of regulations. The particulars of the
processes have varied over time but generally involve requirements that federal agencies
assess the costs and benefits of available regulatory alternatives and issue only regulations that show positive net benefits. In principle, this will lead to beneficial regulations,
at least in terms of their economic efficiency. In practice, these analyses are fraught
with uncertainties and analytic challenges.[32]

Legal Considerations

Perhaps the most certain aspect of the development of rules and regulations in the
United States is that they will be subject to legal challenges from various sources. Indeed,
it is a common presumption that any given rule or standard will be subject to a variety
of challenges ranging from the technical basis for the standard to the adequacy of the
process of rulemaking. The consensus of legal scholars is that courts typically defer to
agency expertise, but the courts also pay close attention to the rulemaking process. As

summarized by Clarence Davies and Jan Mazurek[33] in their study of environmental regulations, an agency's final action will likely be rejected if it is shown to be "arbitrary or capricious" or if it lacks basis in fact. Rules are likely to be overturned if defects are found in the rulemaking process such as failure to respond adequately to public comments about draft rules. The likelihood of legal challenge is one of the exceptional aspects of the American system. In other countries with more consultative traditions of regulatory development, such challenges are far less common.

V. MANAGEMENT CHALLENGES

Social regulations have been criticized on a number of grounds that embody basic challenges to their design and implementation. In response, a number of reforms have been undertaken in the way in which social regulations are designed and administered. The United States has not always been in the lead in these reforms, particularly as they relate to intergovernmental and environmental regulations. Nonetheless, much has happened to make social regulations of the 1990s different from those of only a decade earlier.

Overcoming Restrictiveness: Economic Incentives

One major criticism of social regulations has been that they are too restrictive. The heart of this criticism relates to the traditional command-and-control approach to social regulation entailing specification of rules, standards, and enforcement mechanisms.[34] Critics make a number of points about the restrictiveness and inefficiencies of this approach. One is that the rules are overly rigid and often do not fit the circumstances. This argument suggests that regulated entities are better equipped to decide how to address a problem than are government regulators. Another criticism is that the administrative apparatus to monitor and enforce regulations is highly inefficient, undermining the intent of regulations. Critics argue that the restrictiveness of rules and inefficiencies of enforcement lead to delays, unnecessary burdens, and stifling of innovation. As a consequence of these criticisms, which burgeoned during the 1980s, regulatory reformers have sought alternatives to the traditional command-and-control approach.

One modest reform is to substitute use of performance standards, which specify performance to be achieved, for the conventional designation of design standards, which specify particular actions to be undertaken. This, in principle, allows regulated entities a variety of paths to meet regulatory goals without prespecifying particular actions. Although performance standards hold out the promise of innovation, experience has shown that regulated entities tend to adopt the dominant technology in place at the time of the regulation. There is little incentive for them to innovate. Indeed, they have considerable incentive to adopt known technologies that will not be challenged for failing to meet the regulatory requirements.

The missing ingredient is to alter the incentives of regulated entities to innovate or go beyond minimum standards, or both. Recognition of this gap has led to extensive advocacy for greater use of economic incentives as instruments of regulation.[35] In general, the idea is to use economic means to reflect the true costs of decisions to comply with a given regulation and to establish marketlike incentives for regulated entities to seek the best means for reaching regulatory goals. As shown in Box 5-5, there are a variety of economic instruments that can be incorporated into social regulations. Many of these are treated in Chapter 8 as a separate tool of government.

The simplest form of economic incentives is a charge or tax imposed on such harms as pollution. Such charges force polluters to face the true costs of pollution (through internalizing the external costs they impose on others), creating economic incentives to adjust their behaviors accordingly. The diverse set of examples of the use of charges includes economic incentives for recycling in localities in the United States, an extensive tax system to promote reduction of solid waste in Denmark, taxes on industrial and agricultural water pollution in the Netherlands, and a pollution charge system in Russia.[36]

BOX 5-5 *Economic Instruments for Social Regulation*

- **Property rights**—Assignment of property rights to overcome collective action problems. *Example:* Assignment of fishing rights for particular catch areas or time periods.

- **Charge or taxes**—Apply a fee or tax to a given level of harmful product or output. *Example:* Effluent charges and dumping fees.

- **Performance bonds**—Financial guarantee that work will be performed. *Example:* Bonds required of construction contractors as conditions for obtaining a license.

- **Deposit refund systems**—Cash or other guarantee that waste (or other good) will be handled according to specified rules. *Example:* Deposit systems to induce return of empty beverage containers.

- **Tradable permit systems**—Rationing system for emissions that creates incentives to seek low-cost means for reducing emissions. *Example:* Pollution reduction permit system created by California's South Coast Air Quality Management System.

More complicated forms of economic incentives include the creation of tradable permit systems for pollution control. Two steps are involved. One is establishing overall targets for pollution. The second is establishing permits that allow firms to pollute at given levels. By giving out fewer permits than existing pollution levels, a market can be fostered for the permits. Firms that find it costly to reduce pollution will seek to purchase permits, driving up their price. Firms that find the permits costly to obtain will seek to lower pollution and/or improve the technology for pollution reduction. One noteworthy example is the program for controlling sulfur dioxide emissions enacted as part of the Clean Air Act Amendments of 1990.

It is difficult to summarize the variety of uses of economic instruments in social regulation and to separate the claims from the realities of their use. Although they are becoming more common as instruments for pollution control, economic instruments are rarely used outside the environmental arena. Moreover, the use of economic instruments still entails much of the conventional regulatory apparatus. Overall targets (standards) need to be established along with meaningful units for taxes or pollution permits. An administrative apparatus needs to be created for operating the system of incentives and for policing violations of the rules (an enforcement system). Penalties need to be established for those violations. Clearly, economic incentives are important regulatory instruments, but they are only a partial substitute for regulations.

Reducing Conflicts: New Forms of Rulemaking and Industry Involvement

Particularly in the adversarial legal culture of the United States, the process of regulatory development is conflict ridden. As noted earlier, administrative and legal challenges to regulations are the norm, and not the exception. These conflicts stem from a variety of sources, the most basic of which is the belief that a given regulation is either unnecessary or unreasonable. Such challenges are exacerbated by the tight deadlines that agencies often face in trying to develop standards and administrative rules. Regulatory officials often find themselves in an intolerable situation, caught in a conflict between pressures from superiors to implement regulations and pressures from regulated entities to slow down the process.

New forms of regulatory rulemaking have recently been explored in an attempt to reduce these conflicts.[37] Common to these new forms is more direct involvement of industry in the development of standards and rules. Traditional rulemaking processes allow regulated entities and their industry organizations to comment on draft rules and standards, but that involvement is often overly formalized, piecemeal, time consuming, and expensive for all parties concerned. Efforts to involve industry more directly include greater use of advance notification about rules, informal consultations, and the use of negotiated rulemaking processes. One example of this approach is the Common Sense Initiative of the Environmental Protection Agency.[38] Beginning in 1994, the agency convened panels of stakeholders for six designated industrial sectors and charged the panels with identifying regulatory and other policy changes that would make the regulatory programs more effective. Davies and Mazurek[39] cite statistics showing that less then 10 percent of rules proposed by the major American regulatory agencies from 1994 to 1997 involved negotiated rulemaking, itself a time consuming process. In practice, informal consultations appear to be much more common.

Perhaps more promising in reducing conflicts are efforts to increase the flexibility of the rules with which regulated entities must comply. This is an important component of the "hazard analysis and critical control point" system for meat inspection. With this approach, meat processors are given flexibility in designing control systems to address potential hazards at critical points in meat processing. Another example is the excellence and leadership program, Project XL, of the Environmental Protection Agency.[40] Under this program, firms in selected industries with a good history of compliance with EPA regulations are able to propose site-specific ways of reducing regulatory burdens. These can be accepted as substitutes for existing rules, as long as the new ways achieve better results than are expected under the existing rules. To date, participation in this program has been limited.

Complexity: Permit Systems

It is far from straightforward to decide what rules and standards apply to complex facilities, much less to enforce them. As a consequence, regulators need a road map that is specific to their facility. The use of permits, which is common in environmental regulations, provides this. Permits specify allowable conditions for site-specific operations of a firm as they apply to particular harms. They are issued by regulatory agencies for a particular period of time (typically five years). The process for obtaining permits ranges from simple application forms to detailed reviews and public hearings. The latter provides an opportunity for those stakeholders that are most directly impacted by the activities of a particular facility to be involved in how it is regulated.

Permit systems do help reduce complexity, but the process of obtaining permits can be both time consuming and expensive for firms. Moreover, the conditions for permits often work against flexibility in operations that are necessary today in many manufacturing facilities. Recognition of these problems has led to regulatory innovations in permit systems at the federal and state levels. For example, the Environmental Protection Agency has experimented with using the permit process as a way of streamlining numerous independent, and sometimes conflicting, requirements that apply to individual facilities. A number of projects under the EPA's Project XL have involved innovative approaches to permitting.

Inconsistent Implementation: Discretion and Confidence

Regulatory officials often find it challenging to find the right balance between flexibility and consistency in the application of rules. The consequences of erring on the side of too much discretion for inspectors are inconsistencies in enforcement actions and, in extreme cases, corruption. The consequences of erring too much on the side of consistency are loss of the inspector's sense of professionalism and rigid enforcement, leading to overregulation. The appropriate use of discretion is fostered through such mechanisms as training programs, pairing of senior and junior inspectors, and regular review of inspectors' actions. Consistency is fostered by the establishment of agency enforcement manuals, centralization of enforcement functions, use of agency personnel (rather than third parties) for inspection, and multiple clearances for undertaking enforcement actions.

Effective compliance systems require confidence about regulatory agencies on the part of both regulated entities and citizens. Regulatees need to trust agency personnel and to have confidence in their actions. Compliance is less likely to be forthcoming if regulatees consider enforcement unfair.[41] For a regulatory agency to secure resources, citizens who benefit from regulations and elected officials who oversee the agency need to understand the benefits of agency actions. Establishing good public relations means more than putting out occasional press releases about enforcement actions. Informational materials explaining the functions of the agency and regular reporting on the status of enforcement actions are important. Another key component is to establish mechanisms for consumers to lodge inquiries or register complaints. For example, the Food Safety and Inspection Service maintains a toll-free hotline about meat and poultry food safety. This hotline received nearly 165,000 calls in 1998.

Inadequate Resources: Leveraging Enforcement Resources

Another challenge is deciding how to leverage limited agency resources for inspection. The most common way to do this is to shift the burden of inspection to regulated entities through procedural requirements that they conduct inspections and maintain records of those inspections. Ian Ayres and John Braithwaite[42] discuss variants of this under the label of "enforced self-regulation." Failure to conduct the inspections or to maintain the records constitutes procedural noncompliance that is itself subject to penalties. Under this approach to enforcement, regulatory agencies oversee reporting and conduct spot checks of compliance.

In some instances, industry associations take on major enforcement responsibilities that reduce the burdens on regulatory agencies even further. The diversity of roles range from industry associations serving in essence as regulatory enforcement agents to industry self-regulation.[43] One of the more commonly cited examples of the latter is the Responsible Care program of the American chemicals industry, under which industry members agree to adhere to a set of ethical and practice guidelines. A different role of industry is illustrated by a "voluntary compliance initiative" undertaken in 1998 by the Environmental Protection Agency in combination with the National Pork Producers Council. The council provides funding for certification of inspectors and participating pork producers have operations assessed for Clean Water Act violations by those inspectors.

Another mechanism for leveraging agency inspection resources is to involve third parties in the enforcement process.[44] This can take on a variety of forms. The most direct is hiring of consultants to undertake specialized inspection tasks. Greater leveraging of resources is obtained if a market for third-party inspection can be established. For example, an extensive market for energy conservation exists in the United States that was spurred by the development of energy-efficiency standards, the creation of rating systems for measuring compliance with those standards, and certification of third-party inspectors for carrying out voluntary inspection.

Cooperation among different levels of government can also facilitate regulatory implementation. However, such cooperation cannot simply be mandated. Rather, it must be based on incentives such as grants or technical assistance. As important, agencies responsible for implementing the policies must reflect a cooperative philosophy in their day-to-day dealings with lower levels of government. When partners have a history of mistrust and differing policy objectives, bringing about the necessary cooperation can be a noteworthy management challenge. The ability to be a facilitative partner depends on the level of agency commitment to intergovernmental program goals and the capacity to carry them out. To the extent that facilitative approaches are desired, increasing agency commitment alone may not be sufficient. Indeed, research findings suggest that a high level of commitment without a commensurate level of capacity leads to the adoption of more formal, legalistic implementation—the very process that states and localities recoil against.[45]

The dilemma for regulatory managers involved in intergovernmental programs lies in deciding how much freedom to allow state (or local) partners. Being restrictive helps gain uniformity in policy application but runs the risk of a backlash from the state or local governmental partners. Yet, being flexible runs the risk of lax actions on the part of states (or localities). Davies and Mazurek[46] illustrate the difficulty that the Environmental Protection Agency has had in finding this balance. After announcing a new National Environmental Performance Partnership System in 1995, the EPA found itself in a position of intervening in major cases of what EPA officials characterized as lax environmental enforcement by states. This backtracking led to a worsening of federal and state relationships instead of helping to foster the hoped-for cooperation.

VI. OVERALL ASSESSMENT

Two considerations that have been discussed throughout this chapter complicate making a summative assessment of social regulation as a tool of government: (1) the variability of different forms of social regulation with respect to the extent to which they compel or cajole compliance, and (2) the way in which the actions of regulatory agencies and inspectors shape the day-to-day realities of regulation. As a consequence, social regulation can lead to widely different experiences and outcomes. With this caveat in mind, the following discussion evaluates social regulation in terms of four criteria: (1) effectiveness and manageability, (2) economic efficiency, (3) equity, and (4) legitimacy.

Effectiveness and Manageability

No one would disagree that "unreasonable" and "overly burdensome" regulations are undesirable. But how can such regulations be identified, and how frequently do they occur? Anecdotes about excessive regulation abound, but systematic analyses are in short supply.

In general, the effectiveness of social regulations depends on three factors: (1) the reasonableness of what is required, (2) the ability and willingness of regulated entities to comply, and (3) the adequacy of resources for enforcement and for inducing compliance through facilitative actions. The first two aspects go together. Regulated entities are more willing to comply with regulations that they perceive as being reasonable. By definition, it is within their interest to comply with such regulations. Meat processors understand the need to reassure consumers about food safety. Because of this, the USDA inspection serves an important function for the industry. By contrast, businesses comply less wholeheartedly with debatably picky rules for occupational safety and health. So, too, the adequacy of enforcement resources clearly makes a difference in the frequency and quality of inspections, which have been shown to be important factors in motivating compliance. In addition, the amount of technical assistance and information provided to regulated entities can affect their ability and willingness to comply.

Davies and Mazurek[47] conclude from their review of the costs and impacts of environmental regulations in the United States that, since the 1970s, substantial improvements have been made in air and water quality. Although it is true that the decline in pollution levels cannot be causally linked to environmental regulations, the timing does, in fact, coincide with an era of expansion of environmental regulations. Whether the same ends could have been accomplished at less cost and burden is another question addressed in the following discussion.

Not all social regulations have been equally effective. One of the more heavily criticized programs in the United States has been regulation of occupational safety and health. W. Kip Viscusi[48] notes that the regulatory efforts made by the Occupational Safety and Health Administration (OSHA) during the early 1970s were widely regarded as having been ineffective. His analysis of subsequent efforts during the 1980s suggests "small but significant" effects in improving worker safety.

A number of management challenges were noted earlier in this chapter concerning the design and implementation of social regulations. Those regulations that address first-order, visible, and concentrated harms are more easily managed than those that address indirect and diffuse harms or benefits. Thus, it is easier to regulate emissions from industrial pollution than to regulate diffuse sites that have been contaminated with hazardous waste. Pollution levels can be directly measured and monitored, the responsible parties are relatively easy to identify, and incentive structures (e.g., emissions trading schemes) can be developed to promote pollution reduction and technological innovation. By contrast, hazardous waste sites present challenges for measuring pollution levels and cleanup, uncertainties about responsible parties, and limited potential for introducing marketlike mechanisms for compelling cleanup.

Efficiency

Efficiency considerations take two different forms. One is the overall efficiency of regulatory efforts (allocative efficiency), as measured by calculations of the net benefits of regulations. Studies that have addressed the aggregate costs and benefits of social and environmental regulation in the United States show that, on the whole, these regulations are justifiable. The second aspect of efficiency is the degree to which regulations produce regulatory outcomes at the least cost for governmental agencies and for regulated entities. The findings are more mixed about this aspect of efficiency, reflecting the widespread sense of regulated entities that many social and environmental regulations are overly burdensome.

The most extensive review of the aggregate costs and benefits of federal regulations in the United States is a 1997 report of the Office of Management and Budget.[49] The study draws attention to the difficulty of making estimates of costs, and especially of benefits, while also noting the limited value of national-level compilations of these figures. With these limitations in mind, the Office of Management and Budget concluded that the benefits of social and environmental regulation, amounting to $136 billion and $162 billion, respectively, in 1996 dollars, far exceed their costs, amounting to $54 billion and $144 billion, respectively.[50]

The degree to which regulations produce the least costly outcomes is also difficult to assess, but a variety of indicators suggest that many social regulations are indeed more costly or burdensome than they would be if they had been better designed and implemented. In their review of environmental regulations, Davies and Mazurek[51] cite several statistics that back up this basic observation. These investigators find wide disparities in the costs of reducing pollution, suggesting that at least some pollution reduction programs could be carried out at lower costs. They also cite large discrepancies in the costs of saving lives under different regulations, suggesting wide differences in regulatory effectiveness or standards.

Equity

In principle, social regulations can be designed to be as equitable as any tool of government. In practice, the variation with which they are implemented leads to potential inequities. The rules that specify the desired (or prohibited) actions for a given social regulation also specify the situations to which the rules apply. This, along with provisions for exemptions, suggest that on paper, at least, regulations can be designed to be equitable in terms of treating like situations in a similar manner and in making distinctions in special circumstances. Regulatory provisions that allow for appeal of enforcement provisions also help to foster equitable treatment, although there may be biases in the way in which appeals are addressed.

More slippage occurs during implementation when differences can arise in the way in which individual situations are handled. Inspectors differ in their willingness to provide exemptions for extenuating circumstances, such as the financial inability of regulatees to comply with rules. In addition, a variety of studies show that regional offices of regulatory agencies respond to competing pressures to be either tough or lax in different ways.[52] Some might argue that such adaptation of regulations to fit local circumstances is appropriate; others might see this as inequitable.

The potential for abuse stems from the discretion granted individual inspectors or other front-line personnel charged with implementing social regulations. Often this entails inconsistent application of rules, but it can include corruption. The potential for corruption is greater when there is little supervision, inspection tasks are complex, and inspectors are paid low wages. For example, some 13 percent of local governmental building officials responding to a national survey reported one or more incidents of corruption in building regulation during the 1980s.[53] In an effort to reduce the potential for corruption, social regulations often specify tough penalties for attempts to influence inspectors. Such penalties mean little if the potential for corruption is not addressed as part of the management of enforcement systems.

Legitimacy

As with laws in general, social regulations cannot be effective if they rest entirely on sanctions for noncompliance or rewards for compliance. Enforcement systems are generally too weak and reward systems too limited to bring about widespread compliance by these means. Regulated entities must be motivated to comply for intrinsic reasons stemming from their belief in the need for, and reasonableness of, the regulation. These are important aspects of the legitimacy of regulations.

A number of studies have documented the importance of trust in governmental agencies as a key aspect of perceptions of the legitimacy of governmental actions.[54] Given its reliance on coercion, social regulation as a tool of government places a premium on such trust. Restoring trust in governmental ability to protect citizens from food-borne illnesses was one of the key considerations of the Clinton administration in deciding to devise the new federal approach to regulation of food safety.

VII. FUTURE DIRECTIONS

Social regulation is one of the oldest means by which governments have sought to prevent harms or to secure benefits for society at large. The growth of social regulation during the 1970s and the subsequent backlash during the 1980s to the expanded role of government in devising what were considered by many as unreasonable requirements have been widely documented. Reviews of social regulation as a tool of government written during the late 1980s, as with Eugene Bardach's discussion,[55] reflect these concerns. A number of reforms have since been undertaken in the design and administration of social regulations. The United States has not always been in the lead in these reforms, particularly as they relate to intergovernmental and environmental regulations. Nonetheless, much happened during the 1990s to change social regulation from what it was only a decade earlier. The differences are more evolutionary than revolutionary, but they still are noteworthy.

One important change has been a philosophical one about the role of government in bringing about compliance with regulations. The traditional perspective has been that regulatory agencies should exercise a heavy hand—the "stick"—in bringing about compliance. This approach has been shown to be problematic because of a lack of necessary resources for compelling compliance and because of backlash over the inequitable use of the heavy hand of government. The alternative perspective is that of government as a facilitator in helping to bring about compliance with rules that are widely accepted as essential for society at large.

A second, related evolution has been with respect to the rules that are at the heart of regulations. The traditional approach had been specification of desired actions (or prohibited actions) and the ways of bringing those about. Compliance was measured by the degree to which those specific actions are undertaken. The alternative is to emphasize outcomes by devising rules that require deliberative processes or plans for reaching those outcomes, and/or by specifying desired performance levels. Proponents of procedural rules and performance standards argue that these foster innovation and permit lower-cost regulatory solutions.

A third development is a change in thinking about the way in which regulations are administered. The traditional approach, at least as an ideal, involved direct regulation by governmental entities that employ inspectors who carry out enforcement actions. The alternative approach recognizes the limitations of the traditional ideal and emphasizes the role of nongovernmental entities in bringing about compliance. This ranges from the use of third parties in carrying out inspection to self-regulation by professional associations or by industry sectors.

A fourth development is the way in which social regulations are developed. The overall goal is to devise more reasonable regulations. In the United States, there have been two approaches at the national level. One has been the institution of requirements that regulations must pass cost-benefit tests by showing net benefits that contribute to economic efficiency. Related to this has been the enactment of legislation designed to lessen the burdens of intergovernmental mandates on lower levels of government. The second approach to more reasonable regulations has been to devise new means for regulated entities to participate in the development of regulations. Procedures such as advance notice and negotiated rulemaking are intended to make rules more reasonable and accepted as a basis for improving their legitimacy and compliance with them.

The preceding developments relate to the design and structure of regulations. Equally important have been changes in the day-to-day administration of regulations. This is reflected in the actions of regulatory agencies and inspectors, whether directly employed by government or by other entities. Here the critical challenge has been to devise an enforcement style consistent with the shift toward regulations that emphasize flexibility and reasonableness. How to bring this about has been a key challenge.

It is easy from discussions like this to get the sense that recent years have brought about wholesale change in social regulation. In reality, many of these noteworthy developments occurred when new regulations were developed. Few of these changes affect the myriad of regulations already on the books, although regulatory agencies in the United States have been mandated to revisit existing regulations. As a consequence, the mix of regulatory tools ranges from traditional, coercive approaches to the newer, facilitative approaches. This diversity makes it difficult to generalize about social regulations or to establish tight boundaries between social regulation and other tools of government.

The overarching message of this chapter is not to extol the virtues of newer forms of regulation. These generally fare well in comparison with the past, but experience with them is too limited to praise them wholeheartedly. Rather, the central message is that with proper design, social regulation can be an effective tool of government in preventing harms and securing benefits. Much also rests on implementation that supports, rather than undermines, the intent of social regulation. Perhaps more than any other tool of government, the success of social regulation rests on finding the appropriate fit between the motivations of affected entities and the design and implementation of the tool. These tasks are not straightforward or simple, but a number of positive steps can be taken by those who craft and implement social regulation to enhance this fit. It is hoped that careful attention to the selection and design of tools encouraged by this book will help foster such steps.

ACKNOWLEDGMENTS

The author thanks Raymond Burby, Dan Fiorino, Lester Salamon, Michael Shapiro, Soeren Winter, and the authors of other chapters in this book for helpful comments on earlier drafts of this chapter.

VIII. SUGGESTED READING

Ayres, Ian, and John Braithwaite. *Responsive Regulation: Transcending the Deregulation Debate.* Oxford and New York: Oxford University Press, 1992.

Bardach, Eugene, and Robert Kagan. *Going by the Book: The Problem of Regulatory Unreasonableness.* Philadelphia: Temple University Press, 1982.

Gunningham, Neil, and Peter Grabosky with Darren Sinclair. *Smart Regulation: Designing Environmental Policy.* Oxford and New York: Oxford University Press, 1998.

Kagan, Robert A. "Regulatory Enforcement." In *Handbook of Regulation and Administrative Law,* edited by David H. Rosenbloom and Richard D. Schwartz, 383–422. New York: Marcel Dekker, 1994.

Kubasek, Nancy K., and Gary S. Silverman. *Environmental Law,* 3d ed. Upper Saddle River, N.J.: Prentice-Hall, 1999.

Scholz, John T. "Managing Regulatory Enforcement." In *Handbook of Regulation and Administrative Law,* edited by David H. Rosenbloom and Richard D. Schwartz, 423–463. New York: Marcel Dekker, 1994.

NOTES

1. See, among others, Eugene Bardach, "Social Regulation," in *Beyond Privatization: The Tools of Government Action,* ed. Lester M. Salamon (Washington, D.C.: Urban Institute Press, 1989), 197–229; and Donald Lemaine, "The Stick: Regulation as a Tool of Government," in *Carrots, Sticks and Sermons: Policy Instruments and Their Evaluation,* eds. Marie-Louise Bemelmans-Videc, Ray C. Rist, and Evert Vedung (New Brunswick, N.J.: Transaction Publishers, 1998), 59–76.

2. Also see Nancy K. Kubasek and Gary S. Silverman, *Environmental Law,* 3d ed. (Upper Saddle River, N.J.: Prentice-Hall, 1999), 25–39.

3. *Lucas v. State of South Carolina Coastal Council.* See Kubasek and Silverman, *Environmental Law,* 3d ed. 32–35.

4. More generally, see Donald F. Kettl, *The Regulation of American Federalism* (Baltimore: Johns Hopkins University Press, 1987); Paul Posner, *The Politics of Unfunded Mandates: Whither Federalism?* (Washington, D.C.: Georgetown University Press, 1998); and David M. Welborn, "Conjoint Federalism and Environmental Regulation in the United States," *Publius: The Journal of Federalism* 18, no. 1 (1988): 27–43.

5. See Peter J. May and Søren Winter, "Regulatory Enforcement and Compliance: Examining Danish Agro-Environmental Policy," *Journal of Policy Analysis and Management* 18, no. 4 (1999): 625–651.

6. See Peter J. May, "State Regulatory Roles: Choices in the Regulation of Building Safety," *State and Local Government Review* 29, no. 2 (1997): 70–80.

7. Also see Barry Mitnick, *The Political Economy of Regulation* (New York: Columbia University Press, 1980), 396–407.

8. For elaboration of this distinction, see Albert Reiss, Jr., "Selecting Strategies of Social Control over Organizational Life," in *Enforcing Regulation,* eds. Keith Hawkins and John Thomas (Boston: Kluwer-Nijhoff Publishing, 1984), 23–25; and Robert A. Kagan and John T. Scholz, "The 'Criminology of the Corporation' and Regulatory Enforcement Strategies," in *Enforcing Regulation,* eds. Keith Hawkins and John Thomas (Boston: Kluwer-Nijhoff Publishing, 1984), 67–95.

9. The history of regulations that follows is drawn from Vincent T. Covello and Jeryl Mumpower, "Risk Analysis and Risk Management: An Historical Perspective," *Risk Analysis* 5, no. 2 (1985): 103–120.

10. For discussion of these trends, see Timothy Conlan, *From New Federalism to Devolution, Twenty-five Years of Intergovernmental Reform* (Washington, D.C.: The Brookings Institution, 1998).

11. Comparative studies of nations' regulatory approaches include (1) a study of pollution prevention, Lennart J. Lundquist, *The Hare and the Tortoise: Clean Air Policies in the United States and Sweden* (Ann Arbor: University of Michigan Press, 1980); (2) a study of chemical regulation, Ronald Brickman, Sheila Jasnoff, and Thomas Ilgen, *Controlling Chemicals, The Politics of Regulation in Europe and the United States* (Ithaca, N.Y.: Cornell University Press, 1985); (3) a study of hazardous waste cleanup, Thomas Church and Robert Nakamura, "Beyond Superfund: Hazardous Waste Cleanup in Europe and the United States," *Georgetown International Environmental Law Review* 7, no. 1 (1994): 15–57; (4) a study of occupational health and safety, Steven Kelman, *Regulating America, Regulating Sweden* (Cambridge, Mass.: MIT Press, 1981); and (5) studies of environmental policy, more generally, Susan Rose-Ackerman, *Controlling Environmental Policy: The Limits of Public Law in Germany and the United States* (New Haven: Yale University Press, 1995), and David Vogel, *National Styles of Regulation, Environmental Policy in Great Britain and the United States* (Ithaca, N.Y. and London: Cornell University Press, 1986).

12. See William T. Gormley, Jr., and B. Guy Peters, "National Styles of Regulation: Child Care

in Three Countries," *Policy Sciences* 25, no. 3 (1992): 381–399; and Patricia Day and Rudolf Klein, "The Regulation of Nursing Homes: A Comparative Perspective," *The Milbank Quarterly* 65, no. 3 (1987): 303–347.

13. The Reagan administration regulatory review was established as E.O. 12291. The Clinton administration regulatory review was established as E.O. 12866. For background, see U.S. Office of Management and Budget, *More Benefits, Fewer Burdens: Creating a Regulatory System That Works for the American People* (Washington, D.C.: Office of Information and Regulatory Affairs, Office of Management and Budget, 1996).

14. See Theresa A. Gullo and Janet M. Kelly, "Federal Unfunded Mandate Reform: A First-Year Retrospective," *Public Administration Review* 58, no. 5 (1998): 379–387; Posner, *The Politics of Unfunded Mandates.*

15. For discussion of the New Zealand reforms, see Peter J. May et al., *Environmental Management and Governance: Intergovernmental Approaches to Hazards and Sustainability* (London and New York: Routledge, 1996).

16. Deborah Stone, *Policy Paradox, The Art of Political Decision Making,* 2d ed. (New York: W. W. Norton, 1997), 282–294.

17. For a discussion of rulemaking procedures, see Cornelius M. Kerwin, *Rulemaking: How Government Agencies Write Law and Make Policy,* 2d ed. (Washington, D.C.: Congressional Quarterly, 1999).

18. Ross Cheit cites more than twenty-five thousand standards in the United States that have been established by the top twenty nongovernmental standards organizations. See Ross Cheit, *Setting Safety Standards: Regulation in the Public and Private Sector* (Berkeley and Los Angeles: University of California Press, 1990), 7.

19. See Laura Langbein and Cornelius Kerwin, "Implementation, Negotiation and Compliance in Environmental and Safety Regulations," *Journal of Politics* 47, no. 3 (1985): 854–880; George Stigler, "The Optimum Enforcement of Law," *Journal of Political Economy* 70, no. 5 (1970): 526–536.

20. See Raymond J. Burby and Robert C. Paterson, "Improving Compliance with State Environmental Regulations," *Journal of Policy Analysis and Management* 12, no. 4 (1993): 753–772; Wayne B. Gray and John T. Scholz, "Analyzing the Equity and Efficiency of OSHA Enforcement," *Law and Policy* 13, no. 3 (1991): 185–214.

21. U.S. Environmental Protection Agency, Office of Enforcement and Compliance Assurance, *Enforcement and Compliance Assurance, FY98 Accomplishments Report* (Washington, D.C.: U.S. EPA, June 1999).

22. More generally, see Peter N. Grabosky, "Regulation by Reward: On the Use of Economic Incentives as Regulatory Instruments," *Law and Policy* 17, no. 3 (July 1995): 257–282; and Neil Gunningham and Peter Grabosky with Darren Sinclair, *Smart Regulation: Designing Environmental Policy* (Oxford and New York: Oxford University Press, 1998).

23. For elaboration of this distinction, see Peter J. May and Raymond J. Burby, "Making Sense out of Regulatory Enforcement," *Law and Policy* 20, no. 2 (1998): 157–182. For discussion of regulatory enforcement styles and strategies, also see William T. Gormley, Jr., "Regulatory Enforcement Styles," *Political Research Quarterly* 51, no. 2 (1998): 363–383, and Robert A. Kagan, "Regulatory Enforcement," in *Handbook of Regulation and Administrative Law,* eds. David H. Rosenbloom and Richard D. Schwartz (New York: Marcel Dekker, 1994), 383–422; and John T. Scholz, "Managing Regulatory Enforcement," in *Handbook of Regulation and Administrative Law,* eds. David H. Rosenbloom and Richard D. Schwartz (New York: Marcel Dekker, 1994), 423–463.

24. For a review of relevant literature, see May and Winter, "Regulatory Enforcement and Compliance."

25. John T. Scholz, "Cooperation, Deterrence, and the Ecology of Regulatory Enforcement," *Law and Society Review* 18, no. 2 (1984): 179–224; also see discussion of the "enforcement pyramid" in Ian Ayres and John Braithwaite, *Responsive Regulation, Transcending the Deregulation Debate* (Oxford and New York: Oxford University Press, 1992), 35–38.

26. For elaboration of this distinction in intergovernmental mandates, see Peter J. May et al.,

Environmental Management and Governance: Intergovernmental Approaches to Hazards and Sustainability (London and New York: Routledge, 1996).

27. See Raymond J. Burby and Peter J. May, *Making Governments Plan.*

28. Bardach, "Social Regulation," 198.

29. It is interesting to note that land use and environmental regulations came about because of the failures of the legal system (through nuisance law) to correct problems from industrial pollution. See Raymond J. Burby, "Baton Rouge: The Making and Breaking of a Petrochemical Paradise," in *Transforming New Orleans and Its Environs: Centuries of Change,* ed. Craig E. Colten (Pittsburgh: University of Pittsburgh Press, 2000): 160–177; also see, Covello and Mumpower, "Risk Analysis and Risk Management: An Historical Perspective."

30. James Q. Wilson, "The Politics of Regulation," in *The Politics of Regulation,* ed. J. Q. Wilson (New York: Basic Books, 1980), 357–394.

31. For one of many examples, see Christopher J. Bosso, *Pesticides and Politics, The Life Cycle of a Public Issue* (Pittsburgh: University of Pittsburgh Press, 1987).

32. See discussion of these issues by the U.S. Office of Management and Budget, Office of Information and Regulatory Affairs, *Report to Congress on the Costs and Benefits of Federal Regulations* (Washington, D.C., 1997).

33. J. Clarence Davies and Jan Mazurek, *Pollution Control in the United States, Evaluating the System* (Washington, D.C.: Resources for the Future, 1998), 165.

34. For a discussion of regulatory unreasonableness, see Eugene Bardach and Robert Kagan, *Going by the Book: The Problem of Regulatory Unreasonableness* (Philadelphia: Temple University Press, 1982). For a review of the criticisms of command-and-control approaches to regulation, see Gunningham and Grabosky, *Smart Regulation,* 38–50.

35. See, among other sources, Robert W. Hahn and Robert N. Stavins, "Incentive-Based Environmental Regulation: A New Era from an Old Idea?" *Ecology Law Quarterly* 18, no. 1 (1991): 1–42; National Academy of Public Administration, *The Environment Goes to Market* (Washington, D.C.: NAPA, 1994); and Gunningham and Grabosky, *Smart Regulation,* 69–83.

36. For international examples, see Mikael Skou Andersen, "Assessing the Effectiveness of Denmark's Waste Tax," *Environment* 40, no. 4 (1998): 11–15, 38–41; and Gjalt Huppes and Robert A. Kagan, "Market-Oriented Regulation of Environmental Problems in the Netherlands," *Law and Policy* 11, no. 2 (1989): 215–239.

37. More generally, see Edward P. Weber, *Pluralism by the Rules: Conflict and Cooperation in Environmental Regulation* (Washington, D.C.: Georgetown University Press, 1998).

38. See Daniel Fiorino, "Toward a New System of Environmental Regulation: The Case for an Industry Sector Approach," *Environmental Law* 26, no. 2 (1996): 457–488; and Michael E. Kraft and Denise Scheberle, "Environmental Federalism at Decade's End: New Approaches and Strategies," *Publius: The Journal of Federalism* 28, no. 1 (1998): 131–146.

39. Davies and Mazurek, *Pollution Control in the United States,* 157.

40. See Fiorino, "Toward a New System of Environmental Regulation," 457–488.

41. See Margaret Levi, *Of Rule and Revenue* (Berkeley and London: University of California Press, 1988), 48–70; and Tom R. Tyler, *Why People Obey the Law* (New Haven: Yale University Press, 1990).

42. Ian Ayres and John Braithwaite, *Responsive Regulation;* also see Gunningham and Grabosky, *Smart Regulation,* 93–134.

43. See Neil Gunningham and Joseph Rees, "Industry Self-Regulation: An Institutional Perspective," *Law and Policy* 19, no. 4 (1997): 363–414; and Peter N. Grabosky, "Using Non-Governmental Resources to Foster Regulatory Compliance," *Governance: An International Journal of Policy and Administration* 8, no. 4 (1995): 527–550. For discussion of the chemical industry's "responsible care" program, see Joseph Rees, "Development of Communitarian Regulation in the Chemical Industry," *Law and Policy* 19, no. 4 (1997): 477–528.

44. See Janet Gilboy, "Compelled Third-Party Participation in the Regulatory Process: Legal Duties, Culture, and Noncompliance," *Law and Policy* 20, no. 4 (1998): 135–155.

45. Peter J. May, "Mandate Design and Implementation: Enhancing Implementation Efforts and Shaping Regulatory Styles," *Journal of Policy Analysis and Management* 12, no. 4 (1993): 634–663; and Peter J. May, "Can Cooperation Be Mandated? Implementing Intergovernmental

Environmental Management in New South Wales and New Zealand," *Publius: The Journal of Federalism* 25, no. 1 (1995): 89–113.

46. Davies and Mazurek, *Pollution Control in the United States,* 41–43.

47. Davies and Mazurek, *Pollution Control in the United States.*

48. W. Kip Viscusi, *Fatal Tradeoffs, Public and Private Responsibilities for Risk* (New York: Oxford University Press, 1992), 206–222.

49. U.S. Office of Management and Budget, Office of Information and Regulatory Affairs, *Report to Congress on the Costs and Benefits of Federal Regulations* (Washington, D.C., 1997).

50. One of the key studies upon which the OMB report is based is more cautious in citing substantial net benefits for social regulations but potential net costs for environmental regulations; see Robert W. Hahn and John A. Hird, "The Costs and Benefits of Regulation: Review and Synthesis," *Yale Journal on Regulation* 8, no. 1 (1991): 233–280.

51. Davies and Mazurek, *Pollution Control in the United States.*

52. See William T. Gormley, Jr., "Food Fights: Regulatory Enforcement in a Federal System," *Public Administration Review* 52, no 3. (1992): 271–280; David M. Hedge, Donald C. Menzel, and Mark A. Krause, "The Intergovernmental Milieu and Street-Level Implementation," *Social Science Quarterly* 70, no. 2 (1989): 285–299; David M. Hedge., Donald C. Menzel, and George H. Williams, "Regulatory Attitudes and Behavior: The Case of Surface Mining Regulation," *Western Political Quarterly* 41, no. 2 (1988): 323–340; and Neal Shover, John Lynxwiler, Stephen Groce, and Donald Clelland, "Regional Variation in Law Enforcement: The Surface Mining Control and Reclamation Act of 1977," in *Enforcing Regulation,* eds. Keith Hawkins and John Thomas (Boston: Kluwer-Nijhoff Publishing, 1984), 121–145.

53. See Raymond J. Burby, Peter J. May, and Robert C. Paterson, "Improving Compliance with Regulations: Choices and Outcomes for Local Government," *Journal of the American Planning Association* 64, no. 3 (1998): 324–334.

54. See Levi, *Of Rule and Revenue,* 48–70; and Denise Scheberle, *Federalism and Environmental Policy: Trust and the Politics of Implementation* (Washington, D.C.: Georgetown University Press, 1997).

55. Bardach, "Social Regulation," 198.

CHAPTER SIX

Government Insurance

Ron J. Feldman

Homeowners in Grand Forks, North Dakota, decide each year if they will purchase insurance to cover damage from floods. The Red River runs through town, and homeowners know that it regularly rises above flood levels but does not normally cause property loss. This potential insurance transaction differs from the norm in one very important respect. In this case, the government is the insurer. Standard homeowners' policies in the United States traditionally have not covered damage caused by floods. The federal government created the National Flood Insurance Program (NFIP) in 1968 in response. However, rather than relying exclusively on government organizations and staff, the program makes extensive use of third parties. In a cooperative arrangement, participating property and casualty insurance companies write and service the flood insurance policy. The federal government covers underwriting losses and provides insurance only in communities that adopt floodplain management regulations.

New homeowner PattiJean Hooper opted to ignore the advice of her insurance agent and neighbors in Grand Forks to buy federal flood insurance in the beginning of 1997. She purchased a policy from the insurance agent because of commercials from the NFIP warning of spring flooding.[1] Others viewed the $250 flood insurance assessment as too expensive given the low probability that the Red River would flood her neighborhood. Of course, the Red River did flood in a disaster of record proportions. Ms. Hooper was so familiar with her policy by the time of the flood that she had moved many of her belongings to the second floor of her house (personal contents below grade level were not insured).

Despite the commercials, Ms. Hooper was among a distinct minority in Grand Forks covered by a flood insurance policy (only 10 percent of houses were covered).[2] Yet, those who did not buy flood insurance still received protection from loss. Both the state and federal governments provided various forms of disaster assistance worth several billion dollars. The government provided disaster assistance even though the reduction of after-the-fact payments to disaster victims is a primary objective of flood insurance.

Ms. Hooper's story captures many of the themes developed in this chapter. First, some risks, floods included, have attributes that make insurance provision by private firms less likely. In theory, the government has unique capabilities that allow it to offer insurance against those risks, although this promise has not always been realized in practice. Second, the primary goals of government insurance programs, despite the private market failure rationale, are often tangential to pure insurance. The government views flood insurance, for example, as a potentially cheaper method for supporting those living in flood plains. The government has effectively met some of its social goals through insurance programs. Third, controlling potential losses from government insurance requires proactive management and policies, particularly when the insured can take actions that increase their claims. For example, Ms. Hooper increased the amount of property covered under her policy and thus increased her potential claim when she moved her furniture above grade level. Fourth, some government insurance programs rely on the private sector, insurance agents in this case, to carry out their objectives, raising the pitfalls and opportunities presented by third-party government.

Finally, insurance programs are organizationally complex and pose a significant number of managerial and political challenges. Government insurance programs can take well-known steps through the pricing of insurance, restrictions on coverage, and sharing of losses to address some of these challenges. The flood insurance program, for example, tries to limit coverage to areas with flood mitigation efforts. However, many of these managerial tactics can make it more difficult for the insurance program to achieve its social goals. Generally, government insurance programs have not managed their potential exposure well over the last several decades. The premiums set by the federal flood insurance program, for example, are not designed to cover higher-than-average future losses even though the program is supposedly self-financing.

The rest of this chapter provides more details on the government's use of the insurance tool to provide services to citizens. Section I defines the tool, shows how it compares with others tools in relation to some key tool features, and spells out the major design features and resulting variations in its form. Section II examines the patterns of tool use on the international, U.S. federal, and U.S. state and local levels. Section III covers the basic mechanics of tool operations. Section IV discusses the issues of tool selection. Section V details the management challenges posed by the tool and methods for overcoming them. Section VI provides an overall assessment. Section VII offers concluding remarks and some thoughts on the future of government insurance. Section VIII provides suggestions for further reading.

I. DEFINING THE TOOL

Government insurance is a tool through which governments agree to compensate individuals or firms for losses from certain specified events. Eligible recipients are typically charged a fee, or premium, for participation in the insurance program, and participation is often mandatory. Government insurance programs can be operated directly by government agencies or indirectly with the aid of private insurers. In either case, government typically bears the financial responsibility for covering any claims that exceed the pool of resources assembled in the program.

Defining Features

Defining features of government insurance thus include the following:

- The risk of suffering a potential financial loss, usually of a relatively large amount, is shifted from a single household or firm to a central organization, for example, a government agency. (Those transferring the risk are called the insured, and the entity bearing the risk is called the insurer.)

- The potential loss is transferred through a technique called risk pooling and is described in more detail in Box 6-1.

- The insured pay a small, certain amount called premiums to the government insurance program. In return, the insurer agrees to pay up to a prespecified amount to the insured when the event causing the covered financial loss occurs and the insured submit a claim.

Government insurance shares the defining features above with private insurance. Government insurance is distinguished from insurance offered by private firms by two additional and related features:

- Because of certain unique powers of government, such as its ability to tax and compel participation in government programs, government insurance tends to be offered for risks against which private firms may be unwilling to insure.

- Whereas private firms offer insurance to earn profits, insurance is often used by government to achieve other economic or social goals such as raising the income of certain constituents.

BOX 6-1 *Risk Pooling*[1]

Shifting risk from one party to another (e.g., from a car driver to a car insurer) is fairly commonplace, but the notion of pooling risk can be confusing, so further explication may be helpful. Risk pooling involves a group of individuals or firms agreeing to split losses when a particular event, such as a car crash, occurs. Pools offer important benefits to the participants. In particular, the margin of error associated with the expected outcome—losses from auto accidents, for example—becomes smaller as the group sharing losses gets larger. Because of this law of large numbers, the chance that any one participant will suffer an extreme loss decreases after the participant enters into a risk pooling agreement. Estimates of car damage for the large pool are therefore less variable than estimates for a single individual. This feature allows poolers to determine how much each participant must pay into the pool each year to cover expected losses. As a result, risk pooling lets households or firms swap the potential of a huge loss for smaller payments on a regular basis.

To clarify this point, suppose two drivers, Click and Clack, each has an 80 percent chance of avoiding an accident over the next year. Each also has a 20 percent chance of getting into an accident causing $2,500 in damages over the same period. Click and Clack decide to form a risk pool whereby they agree to evenly split the losses from any accident that occurs to either of them. It is important to note that each of their risk of loss is uncorrelated. That is, the chance that Click gets into an accident is unrelated to the chance that Clack gets into an accident and vice versa.

Before the risk pool was created, Click and Clack each had a 20 percent chance of suffering a $2,500 loss. What is the chance of such a loss after the risk pool is created? Because they agreed to split losses evenly, both Click and Clack would need to suffer accidents in order to suffer a $2,500 loss. The chance of both having an accident is the chance of one having an accident (20 percent) times the chance of the other having an accident (20 percent). This is the same logic used to determine the likelihood of flipping a coin and receiving a heads two times in a row (50 percent × 50 percent). As such, there is a 4 percent chance that both men will suffer an accident (0.2 × 0.2). This is the power of risk pooling. Adding more individuals to the risk pool with uncorrelated losses makes it less likely that an extreme event will occur. In statistical terms, the standard deviation of the expected outcomes decreases. Because there is less variability in expected outcomes, the ability to estimate what will occur in the future, if past trends hold true, increases.

---

[1] This box and the example in it rely heavily on Scott Harrington and Gregory Niehaus, *Risk Management and Insurance* (Boston: McGraw-Hill, 1999), 49–55.

Like other tools, insurance can usefully be compared to other tools along four key dimensions: directness, coerciveness, automaticity, and visibility. Because government insurance programs take two quite different forms, however, how this tool ranks in terms of these dimensions varies depending on the particular form. Thus, governments essentially operate some of their insurance programs directly, collecting fees, managing the resulting resources, and settling claims. As we will see, in the United States the programs covering potential defaults of financial institutions generally operate in this fashion. Another group of government insurance programs operates more indirectly, however. Here government enlists private agents to carry out some of the basic tasks—collection, risk assessment, and claim settlement. This difference has obvious implications for how the insurance tool compares with other tools in terms of the four dimensions noted above, namely, *directness, automaticity, coerciveness,* and *visibility.*

Directness

Directness measures the extent to which the entity authorizing or inaugurating a program is involved in executing it. In directly run insurance programs, the authorizing government designs the program in some detail and retains the powers that determine the exposure of the government to loss. However, responsibility is often invested in government corporations rather than in standard government departments. (See Chapter 3 on government corporations.) In programs that rely on the private sector to sell the insurance, provide service to the policyholders, and determine how much money the government program owes policyholders when they make claims, however, the private sector retains discretion in carrying out their tasks. These types of government insurance programs, such as crop insurance in the United States, are fairly indirect and are akin to tools such as grants

Automaticity

Automaticity measures the extent to which a tool utilizes an existing administrative structure to produce its effects rather than having to create its own administrative apparatus. The automaticity of government insurance programs, like their degree of directness, varies with the type of program. The more direct programs require the establishment of a governmental apparatus to design and implement the tool. On the other hand, those that rely heavily on private insurance agents and insurance adjusters to deliver the governmental service have a higher level of automaticity similar to loan guarantees. The relative degree of automaticity probably reflects the state of the private insurance industry at the time the legislature created the government program. When there are no private sector firms offering similar insurance, the government creates its own systems. Flood insurance, in contrast, was conceptually similar to other forms of insurance offered to homeowners and therefore could be delivered through the same private agents who sell homeowners policies.

Coerciveness

Coerciveness measures the extent to which a tool restricts individual or group behavior as opposed to merely encouraging or discouraging it. Government insurance programs use both rewards and punishments and therefore rank in the midrange in terms of coerciveness. Like other tools, such as tax expenditures or grants, insurance programs often try to reward program users by providing them with financial gain. Government insurance programs often provide financial subsidies to the insured, but government insurance can also punish those deemed undeserving by reducing their financial benefit and even excluding them from participation. In addition, in some programs, such as deposit insurance, participation is mandatory.

Visibility

Visibility measures the extent to which the resources devoted to a tool show up in the normal budget process. Insurance is one of the least visible of policy tools, and public budgets have much to do with that situation. Although the contingent liability to which insurance programs expose the U.S. federal government reaches into the trillions of dollars, the federal budget does not report these potential claims on taxpayers until losses occur. Perhaps as a consequence of this, relatively few in the general public ever have more than a superficial understanding of government insurance programs, and few legislators focus on them either. Even the direct beneficiaries of the insurance programs may not understand how the programs operate. The low visibility arises not only from the peculiar budgetary treatment but also from the inherent complexity of government insurance and the often convoluted rules and programmatic forms that result from using this tool to achieve a variety of social goals. In this respect, insurance is similar to the tax expenditure tool.

Design Features and Major Variants

The creators and administrators of government insurance programs must address some fundamental questions when designing the programs. Which risks will be insured? How much loss protection will the insurer offer? How will losses be shared? Who will be eligible for insurance? What will the link be between premiums and future claims? Will risk pooling be achieved voluntarily or through compulsion? Who will be the contact between the insurance program and the customer? Will the program make use of private insurers for some functions? The answers to these questions help distinguish the final form the government insurance program takes.

Establishing the Risks to Insure

Government insurance programs often begin as a general desire to protect firms or households from an event that occurred recently, such as the demise of a large firm that had not put funds aside for its pensioners. However, policymakers or the managers of the government insurance program itself must soon enumerate the risks government insurance will cover in order to actually design the program. The identification of covered risks clearly depends on the desired goals of the insurance being offered as well as the exposure to loss the government is willing to assume. The U.S. federal flood insurance program provides coverage against a flood from a river but not from water damage caused by heavy rains. The U.S. federal crop insurance program will cover damage from weather but not from poor plowing. More specifically, the government crop insurance program will cover damage to wheat, for example, but not lettuce.

Establishing How Much Loss Protection to Offer

To maintain solvency, the government insurance program must cap the coverage supplied, although this cap can change over time. For example, in 1934 the U.S. deposit insurance program protected depositors from risk of loss on $2,500 in deposits after the failure of their bank. By 1980, the program covered $100,000 in deposits. The U.S. pension insurance program has a similar cap. The maximum pension payment the U.S. government pension insurance program covered in 1999 was $3,051 per month.

Creating a cap raises other questions of design and insurance program rules. The U.S. deposit insurance program provides useful illustrations. Does the $100,000 limit apply to the total amount of a depositor's accounts or should this limit be applied to each of the accounts? What kinds of coverage will joint or trust accounts receive? Will accounts held by foreign nationals in U.S. banks be covered? Sometimes questions of this type are answered in the general design of the government insurance program, whereas at other times the agency carrying out the writing of the insurance contract, discussed in Section III, must fill in these details.

Establishing If Losses Are Shared

All providers of insurance should require the insured to bear at least some potential for loss when an insured event, such as a car crash, occurs. Why? When the insured face a cost if they make an insurance claim, they have an incentive to remain vigilant and avoid actions that increase the chance of making a claim. The basic design of the insurance program often establishes the types of loss sharing that will occur.

Government insurance programs have several methods available to them for sharing losses with the insured. First, as described above, they can cap the total amount of loss that they cover. Second, the government program can require a copayment or deductible. These arrangements require the insured to make a payment before they receive coverage on their loss. Finally, the government insurance program can choose to split losses through a coinsurance arrangement. The insurer may decide to cover 75 percent of losses under such a scheme. Deposit insurance programs in other countries, such as the United Kingdom, Poland, and Chile, require depositors to bear some loss when they make a claim after their bank fails.[3] Government insurance programs in the United States generally make relatively little use of these loss-sharing arrangements.

Establishing Eligibility

Determining who is eligible for a government insurance program occurs, at least in part, through coverage decisions. A lettuce grower will not be eligible for insurance if the failure of a lettuce crop is not protected by the government crop insurance program, but there will still be many eligibility questions remaining, with the most important focusing on the restrictiveness of eligibility criteria. If the government insurance program does not place many restrictions on eligibility, it could end up covering a disproportionate number of firms or households who have a very high chance of making an insurance claim.

As a rule, government insurance programs do not significantly restrict eligibility. Congress requires the government insurance program to insure depositors of banks even when the bank has an extremely high chance of failure. The broader eligibility criteria built into government insurance programs often reflect the social goal of providing protection to those who would not receive coverage otherwise.

The Relation between Premiums and Cost

The essence of insurance is the transfer of a large potential loss in exchange for the payment of small, certain premiums. Implicit in this arrangement is the notion that premiums will bear some reasonable relation to expected claims. If premiums are set lower than expected claims, the insurer will have severe difficulty in honoring its commitments unless it has access to nonpremium income.

As noted, government insurance often seeks to achieve social goals through the insurance tool, and altering the relationship between premiums and future costs provides an important mechanism for doing so. The government can deliver subsidies to targeted groups by not charging the insured the amount needed to cover future claims. This undercharging represents a subsidy since no private firm would offer insurance at below-market premiums.

Government insurance programs vary quite a bit in the degree to which premiums cover their expected costs. Some government insurance programs, such as crop insurance, rely on a direct government payment to make up the difference between the subsidized premiums they charge and the claims they pay out. Other government insurance programs, such as U.S. flood insurance, try to charge some households an amount to cover claims while not charging others this so-called fair premium. Still other government insurance programs, such as the U.S. agency that protects private firms' overseas investments, claim to charge a premium that will fully cover expected losses.

Mandatory or Voluntary Risk Pooling

Government insurance programs have two main methods for pooling risk. The first is to attract a large group to participate in the insurance program voluntarily. Some government insurance programs that protect against natural disaster rely on voluntary participation. A second option mandates that every firm or person in a certain class, such as all depositors of banks in a country, receive coverage. This guarantees that a large number of firms or households participate in the insurance pool.

Liaison between Customer and Government Insurance Program

A final issue in program design concerns the means by which the government insurance program distributes the insurance and reviews claims made against it (adjustment). As will be discussed in more detail, some government insurance programs use the existing private insurance apparatus for distribution and adjustment, while others use government structures for these purposes.

Summary: Two Major Variants

Although insurance programs can mix and match these various features, there has been some clustering of programs around certain design features. Many of the programs that protect against losses from certain natural disasters rely on voluntary participation and tend to use private-sector entities to distribute the insurance and adjust claims. These government insurance programs also appear more likely to have explicit subsidies provided to them in order to encourage participation.

On the other hand, many of the insurance programs that protect against loss from the insolvency of financial institutions, such as a bank, rely on mandatory participation and tend to be more direct in their operations. These insurance programs also tend to have very broad eligibility rules. Over time, the premiums for these programs have been reformed to link them more closely to expected losses, although these efforts have had only marginal success in some cases.

II. PATTERN OF TOOL USE

Governments often provide insurance on a very large scale. Potential exposure is measured in the trillions of dollars for the United States alone. While their financial exposure is large, governments normally restrict their provision of insurance to a select group of risks. These include the risk that certain types of firms will go insolvent and the risk that certain natural or man-made disasters will damage property. National, rather than local, governments in the United States and abroad usually provide such coverage. Over the last ten to fifteen years, many of the programs reviewed here have suffered large losses and have been subject to one or more reforms designed to reduce potential losses.

This chapter focuses on government insurance programs that meet a core group of defining features. Simply calling a government program "insurance" does not imbue the program with enough of those defining features to make it insurance. For this reason, we have excluded social insurance programs, such as Social Security, from this chapter. Also excluded are financial guarantees and insurance purchased or provided for government employees.

Current Extent

Government insurance programs are quite large and have grown over the last several decades. The largest government insurance programs for most countries provide protection for those who have funds invested or deposited in financial institutions. A second type of government insurance program protects households and businesses against a variety of natural disasters. These insurance programs can also expose the sponsoring government to huge losses.

U.S. Federal

The U.S. federal government has had between 3 and 5.5 trillion dollars in total exposure as the result of providing insurance over the last few decades (see Figure 6-1 for the

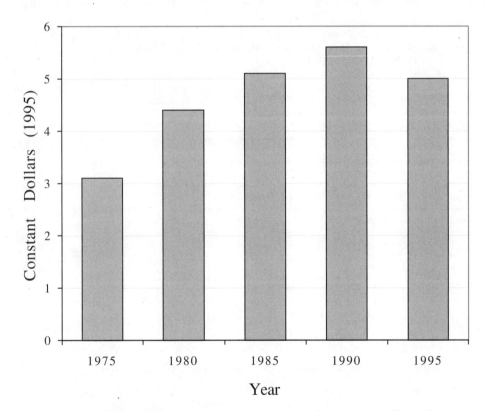

FIGURE 6-1 *U.S. federal government total insurance in force. Source: General Accounting Office.*

most recent, consistent trend data). The amount peaked in the early 1990s and dropped following the banking crisis of the 1990s.

Insurance against Firm Insolvency

There are two main types of firm insolvency insurance offered by the federal government in the United States. One type is insurance for depositors against the failure of their financial intermediaries, including commercial banks, firms that specialize in housing finance such as thrifts, and cooperative intermediaries such as credit unions. (All of these firms will be referred to as banks unless otherwise noted.) Under this government insurance program, depositors with $100,000 or less in deposits are guaranteed full recovery of their funds if their bank fails. The Federal Deposit Insurance Corporation (FDIC) is surely the most well known of the U.S. government insurance programs and has carried out these duties since 1934.

The second type is insurance for pensioners against the insolvency of the firm that had promised them pension benefits. The federal government entered the market for pension insurance in 1974. When a firm terminates a pension plan that has assets insufficient to cover its liabilities, the federal pension insurer becomes the plan's trustee, takes over plan assets, and pays the pension to plan participants.

These two programs are responsible for most of the trillions of dollars of government insurance exposure in the United States (see Table 6-1). For example, there are about 2 trillion dollars in insured deposits at approximately nine thousand commercial banks. (The number of insured deposits at thrift institutions is considerably smaller, with credit unions having even less.) The federal pension insurance program has exposure

TABLE 6-1 **Measures of Insurance Exposure of U.S. Federal Insurance Programs ($ Billions)**

		INSURANCE		
Year	Pension[a]	Deposit[b]	Crop[c]	Flood[d]
1999	N/A	2,868	32	519
1997	N/A	2,746	25	462
1995	37	2,664	24	350
1993	59.6	2,602	14	268
1991	34.5	2,734	11	223
1989	26.3	2,757	14	266
1987	20.7	2,655	N/A	166
1985	11.2	2,415	N/A	140

[a] Level of underfunding in PBGC-insured single-employer plans; not available post-1997.

[b] Insured deposits of commercial banks and thrifts (author's estimates from 1985 to 1988).

[c] U.S. total crop insurance liability.

[d] Insurance in force.

SOURCE: Federal Deposit Insurance Corporation Annual Reports; Pension Benefit Guaranty Corporation Pension Insurance Data Books; Risk Management Agency of the U.S. Department of Agriculture; and National Flood Insurance Program Monthly Statistics.

to participants in 45,000 covered pensions and is already paying monthly retirement benefits to 206,000 workers in 2,510 plans, with another 260,000 workers entitled to payments after their retirement.

Natural and Man-Made Disaster Insurance

The U.S. federal government provides two major insurance programs against natural disasters, both of which make extensive use of third-party, private firms in their operation. The first is crop insurance. Since 1933, this insurance has protected agricultural producers against losses from low yield and crop quality due to adverse weather and unavoidable damage from insects and disease. In a recent innovation the program also offers insurance against drops in producer income.

The second insurance program against natural disasters is the flood insurance program, described in the introduction to this chapter, which covers losses to property from floods. The federal government also offers protection from losses resulting from man-made actions, including political events that reduce the value of overseas investment as well as property damage caused by hostilities. Natural disaster insurance programs can be quite large in scope, although the total exposure is usually smaller than for government programs insuring against insolvency risk. The man-made disaster programs tend to be quite small.

There have been repeated efforts to broaden the role of the federal government in the indirect and direct provision of catastrophic insurance coverage. For example, legislation has been introduced to require the U.S. Treasury to bear some of the risk of loss from insurance policies covering earthquake and hurricane damage.[4]

U.S. State and Local

State governments in the United States provide another type of insurance against failure of a financial firm. Specifically, the states insure policyholders whose private insurance firm fails and cannot make good on their future claims. In addition, many states use the regulatory tools described in Chapters 4 and 5 to ensure that individuals with a high chance of loss receive coverage. For example, states can force private firms to cover the loss of "residual pools," which consist of applicants whom insurers would otherwise reject.[5]

International

Although it is difficult to generalize about government insurance programs in other countries, there is evidence to suggest that international government insurance exposure and activity generally mirrors that of the United States. The staff of the World Bank identified the growing contingent liabilities of governments from insurance and other programs as critical to evaluating any country's fiscal condition.[6] Recent surveys find that about seventy countries offer deposit insurance, with many having features akin to the U.S. program.[7] The European Union has even issued a directive to standardize features of government deposit insurance (e.g., coverage levels) across member countries. Pension insurance is also offered in many European countries as well as in Canada, Chile, and Japan. Likewise, these government pension insurance programs share some features and goals with the American pension insurance system.[8]

In addition to firm insolvency insurance, governments in other countries also provide protection against natural disasters. Governments in a number of developed and developing countries provide crop insurance.[9] Also, governments outside the United States protect homeowners' property against earthquakes, floods, and the like through the direct provision of insurance and through more indirect means. In an example of the latter, France requires homeowners' insurance policies to include comprehensive disaster protection. The private insurer can pass on some of the risk from this coverage to an insurance firm whose claims-paying ability is guaranteed by the French government.[10]

Exclusion of Credit Guarantees, Self-Insurance, and Social Insurance

Excluded from the discussion are three further types of programs: (1) loan guarantees, (2) government self-insurance, and (3) so-called social insurance programs. Loan guarantees are excluded because they do not use traditional risk pooling and other core insurance mechanisms. They are treated in another chapter of this book. Government programs that provide life and other forms of insurance to government's own employees as a benefit reflect the administration of government rather than a tool by which government meets a policy objective.

Social insurance is a more subtle case. Such programs protect citizens against the risk that they will run out of money due to insufficient savings, separation from the work force, or significant medical bills. In the United States, this would include programs such as Social Security, Unemployment Insurance, and various medical programs, including Medicare. Although they may have the term "insurance" in their name, these programs are dissimilar enough from insurance as defined in Section I to merit their exclusion from the chapter. While the programs do shift risk, they do so not through risk pooling but rather through taxation, a voucher, or a grant.

The lack of risk pooling is further reflected in the total disconnection between premiums and future costs. Participants in a social insurance program "receive payments based on their past earning from funds to which they have contributed," and the payments are based on a participant's "connection to the labor force."[11] Indeed, there is no attempt to segregate the insured by the probability of a given risk occurring. Payments into the Social Security fund do not relate to the chance that one will not have saved enough by old age. Rather, the government extends coverage to almost all individuals on essentially the same terms. Indeed, these programs are better thought of as benefit programs offered by the government instead of by an employer.[12]

If these programs are so different from insurance, why do they have insurance names and use some insurance-related nomenclature? The use of insurance terminology and structures in the social insurance programs often reflects a political belief that these terms protect the program from opponents. For example, "the notion of a trust fund was borrowed from private insurance to provide security for the receipts accumulated by the Social Security system."[13]

The exclusion of social insurance programs does not mean that all the insurance programs reviewed in this chapter make full use of risk pooling or ensure that premiums cover all future costs. Indeed, as noted, government insurance programs vary by those exact design features. However, the social insurance programs are so extreme in their absence of insurance features as to merit distinction and, ultimately, exclusion.

Recent Trends

Government insurance programs have grown over the last few decades in the United States, as shown in Figure 6-1. Internationally, the growth of these programs has begun to receive detailed analysis from bodies such as the World Bank in their overall evaluation of government activities and fiscal health. In particular, there has been fairly rapid growth for many insurance programs that were relatively small in terms of their total exposure thirty years ago (see Table 6-2 for the most recent, consistent data).

The growth in the size of government insurance programs was accompanied by an increase in actual and expected losses. In the case of financial solvency insurance in the

Inflation Adjusted Percent Change over Five-Year Period	INSURANCE			
	Deposit	Pension	Flood	Crop
1990–1995	− 12	− 18	28	42
1985–1990	1	19	22	40
1980–1985	18	10	13	44
1975–1980	14	100[a]	78	40
1970–1975	24	N/A	100[b]	0

[a] Pension insurance was created in 1974 and had a face value of $735 billion in 1995 dollars by 1980.

[b] Applicable data available only as of 1975 when face value was $36 billion in 1995 dollars.
SOURCE: Author's calculations from U.S. General Accounting Office, *Budgeting for Federal Insurance Programs*, September 1997, 38.

United States, for example, the insurance fund for thrifts suffered losses of $160 billion during the 1980s requiring a large infusion of taxpayer funds. The insurance fund for commercial banks suffered losses of about $30 billion during the commercial banking crisis from 1987 to 1992.[14] The liabilities of the pension insurance agency exceeded its assets by about $3 billion in the early 1990s, and estimates at that time put its future losses in the $35 billion range.[15] Analysts also raised serious concerns about the ability of the state insurance program to weather the early 1990s insolvency crisis in the insurance industry.[16] There have been similar types of insurance losses in other countries as well. The World Bank reports that there were well over 100 banking crises since the late 1970s throughout the developed and developing countries, with some of these countries offering explicit deposit insurance schemes.[17]

Other U.S. government insurance programs appeared at risk of suffering large losses as well. Evaluations of flood insurance during this same period found that its structure provided incentives to the insured to file larger claims and that financial resources were likely to be inadequate to meet expected losses.[18] Crop insurance losses were higher by several billion dollars than premiums from 1987 to 1994.[19] As noted more fully in the management challenges section below, these losses have led to renewed efforts to manage risk and limit future exposure.

III. BASIC MECHANICS

The task of operating a government insurance program involves eight major steps, as outlined below.

Writing the Insurance Contract/Rules

First, policymakers establish the general rules on risks to be covered, eligibility, forms of risk sharing, and so forth when designing each specific insurance program. These design features cannot remain general because insurance coverage is provided by means of legally enforceable agreements and rules. The insurance contract and program rules allow the insurer and the insured to understand what is expected of each other. Precise language allows the insurer to avoid covering losses it did not intend to absorb.

The process of turning the legislative language of policymakers into the specific language needed for implementation is not unique to government insurance programs. It typically involves legal staff and others from the government interpreting the intent of the legislature along with legal constraints established by the courts. A government insurance program will usually follow the administrative procedures that apply to all government agencies and issue the contractual language or program rules through a standardized process. This often requires the government insurance program to submit an interim rule for comment and issue a final rule consistent with the legislative and rulemaking process.

Pricing: Setting Insurance Premiums

Setting premium rates is perhaps the most important task facing the administrator of the government insurance program. On the most basic level, an insurance program cannot finance itself unless the assessments charged equal expected costs. Premiums set on this same basis for individual households and firms are referred to as "actuarially fair premiums." On a more profound level, pricing influences the behavior of the insured. A lower than appropriate premium provides incentives for the insured to take on too much risk. More precisely, the insured will continue to take actions that increase their expected losses if the additional costs of taking the risks, for example, in the form of premiums, are less than the additional benefits received from taking the actions.

Fair premiums are also needed to limit the amount of cross-subsidization that insurance can produce. Cross-subsidization results when those in the risk pool with a higher chance of making a claim pay a premium that is systematically below the fair amount, while those with lower claim probabilities pay more than the fair cost. Those paying more than their fair share have an incentive to exit the risk pool because they are not getting a good deal. The exit of the low-risk entities from the pool could leave a disproportionate number of higher risk but undercharged entities in the pool. This concentration of higher-risk households or firms will lead to higher than expected losses compared with the pool whose risk the insurer had originally accepted. As a result, the insurer will have to raise premiums to try to cover higher future losses as well as the cross-subsidies. The increase in premiums could cause even more overcharged entities to exit the pool, leading to a vicious circle and the potential collapse of the insurance program.

Traditionally, government insurance programs paid little attention to such risk factors and simply charged flat rate premiums, especially for firm insolvency programs, that is, premiums for the insured did not vary with their probability of making a claim. Even today, all the major U.S. insurance programs still rely to some degree on flat-rate premiums in order to subsidize the insured. In the most extreme case, state insurance programs do not charge premiums but try to raise revenue as needed. Some government insurance programs have taken steps toward more risk-based premiums.

The problem, of course, is this change could make the program less effective in meeting social goals. In addition, fair pricing requires sophisticated management systems and the collection of data on the occurrence of the event being insured such as the frequency of floods and the extent of property damage they cause in a given area. The government's crop and flood insurer, for example, must have data on crop yields and flood patterns that go back many years. In fact, these programs have such information, and these data can be broken down by the characteristics of the firm or house-hold to be insured to determine loss rates for broad categories (e.g., all wheat growers in a given county in Indiana). The government insurance program will then use a variety of analytical techniques on the loss data to forecast expected future losses. Techniques to estimate future loses vary by program and range from very complex statistical methods that try to isolate the effect of a given attribute on the probability of loss to simple extrapolations of historical averages.[20]

The government insurance program typically calculates initial premiums for general classes of the insured (e.g., wheat farmers) and then figures out how much to add or subtract for more unique characteristics of an applicant (e.g., use of irrigation). The insurer must use groups to set premiums because it would be cost prohibitive for the insurer to evaluate, sort, and monitor each member of the pool according to his or her individual expected cost. The insurer creates new pricing categories or groups until the cost of creating additional ones, due to rising administrative and informational ex-penses, for example, exceeds the benefits of charging highly individualized premiums.

The examples used so far relate to the insurance programs protecting against loss from natural disaster. In general, the firm insolvency insurance programs rely on similar techniques for estimating losses. However, financial insolvency insurance also has access to alternative estimating techniques, including models normally used to value financial instruments such as derivatives (e.g., option contracts). This increases the complexity of estimating the fair premium for these insurance programs.

The government, not its third-party contractors, almost always sets the prices for the insurance program. This situation may change because recent developments in the markets for insuring against catastrophes make it more likely that private entities could assume some of the risk of loss that the government now bears. In particular, financial engineers have created financial instruments, such as specialized types of bonds or derivatives, that allow investors in financial markets to assume some of the risk of loss from natural disasters.[21] If the government shifted some of the risk of loss to private investors, it would greatly increase the influence that the prices set in private markets would have on government programs.

Distribution: The Related Tasks of Selling, Servicing, and Marketing Insurance Policies

Some government insurance programs must sell their products, and there are several distribution systems and methods they can use to accomplish that goal. Government entities offering insurance on a voluntary basis tend to use the distribution systems already established by private insurance firms. The government crop and flood insur-ance programs rely on private insurance agents to distribute their product. These agents also sell other insurance, such as homeowners policies, offered by private firms. Gov-ernment insurance programs tend to reimburse these private distributors based on a fixed formula covering costs plus a market return. Although some government insur-ance programs request that the private agent target specific groups, such as farmers with relatively low incomes, the agents are generally given wide discretion in selling the insurance. Governments also tend to use private agents to provide ongoing service to policyholders, such as answering questions on policies in cases where the private agents sell the insurance.

Government insurance programs that rely on private-sector insurance agents have an increasing number of distribution alternatives. A number of private insurers that might have used agents in the past now offer their products through call centers and over the Internet. Insurers have also increased their distribution through banks and other institutions that sell financial products. The use of the private sales infrastructure allows the government to benefit from innovations in distribution practices.

A final distribution issue for government programs that use third parties concerns sales practices. As is the case with other tools utilizing third parties, government agencies administering insurance policies that rely on third parties must take care that the private agents do not violate industry and legal guidelines. This is particularly important in view of the existence of state insurance regulations that apply to the sale of government insurance through private agents.

Sales are less a concern for government insurance programs that mandate coverage of a specific class of firms or households. The FDIC, for example, does not have to sell banks deposit insurance because banks cannot reject insurance coverage. The government body administering the mandated program normally answers questions and provides other ongoing service to the policyholder.

The marketing of government insurance through advertising and other activities that increase the targeted audience's awareness of a product has close connections to sales and servicing. Government insurance programs such as flood insurance have carried out significant private-sector-style marketing campaigns to promote sales to households and business owners. The marketing campaigns for these insurance programs may have both government and private sponsorship, although the government controls the content of the marketing.[22] Most marketing by compulsory government insurance programs involves educational efforts about the protection provided. Written publications or legal documents notify the insured of their coverage and encourage those with losses to file claims.

Underwriting: Will Insurance Be Offered and in What Form?

The steps described so far concern generic policies that apply to entire groups. At some point, the insurer must apply its contract and pricing schedule to a particular firm or household. As has been the case so far, the underwriting process will vary with the level of compulsion of the program and the involvement of the private sector. Programs that use the private sector provide detailed guidance about how to apply the policies and procedures of the insurance program. Nonetheless, the underwriters must use some subjective judgment given their task, and the government would face steep costs trying to second-guess every decision of private agents.

Third parties administering government insurance programs exercise some discretion in assessing applicant eligibility. In contrast, insurance programs providing automatic coverage do not screen out candidates. Instead, these compulsory government insurance programs use regulation to try to force the insured to meet certain standards. Pension plans must comply with Department of Labor guidelines, for example. Both voluntary and mandatory programs gather information on the applicants to determine in which pricing category they fall. The information could be gathered from applications or from third-party vendors, such as credit bureaus, who may sell the relevant information.

In almost all cases, the government bears the vast majority of the risk of loss from underwriting decisions even when private firms make the underwriting decisions. Efforts in the U.S. crop insurance program to force private insurance firms to bear a larger share of the loss, for example, have not produced a measurable amount of risk bearing by the private firms.[23] This outcome could change if the government were able to make greater use of private capital markets to bear some of the risk of loss, an idea being considered by the U.S. deposit insurance program.[24]

An insurance program must manage a tremendous inflow and outflow of information and funds. These flows are managed via the "back office" functions of the government insurance program and include activities such as internal accounting, customer service, premium collection, and distribution of claims payments. The government insurance program will flounder if its back-office operations fail to process these flows proficiently. When private agents and firms service government insurance policies, they assume some of these administrative functions as well. Although critically important, these functions are not unique to government insurance and exist for any government or private organization that must manage a financial relationship with households and firms.

Investing Premiums

Government insurance programs must determine how they invest the funds they receive (assuming that premium income exceeds claims made to date). Programs on the federal level usually require investment of premium income in U.S. Treasury-type securities. This investment strategy emphasizes an important difference between public and private insurance. A private insurance firm could not credibly back its policies by investing assessments in its own bonds. The federal government can invest in its owned debt because of its ability to tax and thus raise funds to pay off insurance claims if they exceed collections in any given year.

In some cases, the government insurance program is not supported by taxes and instead must follow investment strategies more similar to those of private insurers. These strategies require the articulation of investment objectives and restrictions on the types of exposure allowed because of the risks the investment poses. Investments in fixed-income instruments such as bonds or in real estate create default risk (i.e., the chance the insurer will not receive its principal and interest in a timely and full manner). Insurers also face risk from changes in market interest rates. The investment strategy should additionally require cash management policies. The government insurance program must avoid a case where it must pay claims immediately while its funds are tied up in long-term investments.

Reviewing Claims (Adjustment)

The insurer has to determine the validity of claims made against it and the amount of money the insurer owes the insured party. This activity is called claims adjustment. The government insurance program can develop its own in-house adjustment force or rely on adjusters who also service private insurance contracts.

Government insurance programs that rely on private firms to carry out distribution and servicing also tend to use private firms to review and adjust claims. As a result, adjustment in natural disaster programs, in the United States at least, often follows the process used by private insurance firms. Adjusters first determine if the government program is responsible for making a payment for the claim. As noted, the contract should specify covered items. The adjuster will then determine if the insured actually suffered a loss. If a loss occurred, the adjuster will determine the payment the government insurance program must make, again based on prespecified criteria. The contract could specify that the insured receives a payment based on the current value of the property that suffered the loss as opposed to the replacement value. As this description suggests, the adjuster must routinely exercise judgment, thereby building discretion for the third party into the process.

In contrast, most government insurance programs that protect against loss from financial institution insolvency rely on their own adjustment staff. This likely reflects the difference in distribution methods and the more complicated adjustment policy for firm insolvency insurance. The amount that the government insurance program must pay depends heavily on the valuation of the assets held by the firm at insolvency. The government will pay less, for example, if a covered bank has valuable assets at the time of failure. The government insurance program can also reduce losses by recovering funds through lawsuits against firms such as those that have illegally raided their pension funds. Complex rules about how the insurer, the insolvent firm, and the other creditors of the firm split up assets after firm insolvency often complicate the adjustment process for the government insolvency insurer.

Monitoring and Response

A household or firm that receives government insurance can change its characteristics over time. The new characteristics of the insured could involve a change of status from eligible to ineligible. Therefore, the insurer must establish methods for monitoring insured entities over time. The monitoring regime is particularly important in the firm insolvency realm, where firms can quickly raise their probability of making a claim. Government insurance programs protecting against financial insolvency normally rely on the reports and investigations of a financial regulator to determine expected losses at a point in time. In addition, the government can require the insured to send information on a regular basis or purchase information on the insured from third-party vendors.

Managing Capital

A final task in operating an insurance program is to determine how much capital to hold. Capital is the difference between assets and liabilities, and it represents the resources that an insurer uses to pay claims if premium income and the return made on investing premiums are inadequate. Questions concerning capital are especially critical for private insurers. The more uncertain the costs of providing the insurance, the more capital the private insurer must raise from investors to ensure it can survive large claims, and the higher the premiums it will have to set to generate returns for investors. Despite the attention it receives, capital is not always as important for public programs because governments do not raise funds from private investors. The government insurer is not required to hold any funds if it can borrow money to pay claims.

IV. TOOL SELECTION

There are three major reasons why governments establish and manage insurance programs:[25] first, to overcome market failures; second, to achieve broader social goals such as the prevention of banking panics; and, third, to curry favor with influential interest groups through a tool that is largely invisible and yet has great symbolic value because of its self-financing character.

Certain conditions are needed to create the environment for private firms to operate viably in the insurance market. If some or all of these conditions are not present, a rationale may exist for government involvement to provide needed protection.

Correlated Losses

First, private risk pooling is most effective when the probability of one insured person suffering a loss is independent of, or uncorrelated with, the chance that others in the pool will suffer a loss at the same time. Adding firms or individuals to the risk pool who are likely to make a claim at the same time as those already in the pool can lead to catastrophic losses to the insurer. Simply put, an insurance pool with correlated losses serves to concentrate risk of loss rather than spreading it. To withstand such a huge potential loss, the insurer would have to hold a commensurately large amount of financial resources, but the cost of obtaining those resources could be so high as to price the insurance out of consumers' budgets (assuming the resources could be raised at all).

There are several types of risk that appear to have correlated losses. A natural disaster such as an earthquake or a hurricane can strike many of those who would seek protection against such calamities at the same. Crop failures due to extreme weather also tend to occur for many producers at the same time. Many farms over fairly large geographic areas may receive too much/too little rain. A downturn in the national or regional economy could lead many banks to fail at the same time.

National governments, in theory at least, have characteristics that may allow them to address such lack of independence. First, some national governments have the ability to borrow large amounts of funds that they can repay by means of taxes. The government therefore will remain solvent even if losses are correlated across the insured pool. Second, government can force all the potential insureds to participate in the insurance pool, thus potentially diversifying the timing of losses. For example, damage from floods could be correlated in a region, but the government insurance program could require homeowners nationwide to participate in the program.

Adverse Selection

A second type of market failure that can justify government intervention occurs when the insurer cannot distinguish between applicants who pose a higher risk of future claims and those posing a lower risk. In that case, the insurer could inadvertently accept the applicants who have the greatest chance of making a claim. The underlying cause of this "adverse selection" is that the insured have a better idea about their likelihood of making a claim than does the insurer. Because they are at an information disadvantage relative to the insured, the insurer could end up charging too little to cover future losses. Although the insurer could try to charge a very high premium or utilize audits and investigations to determine the riskiness of the insured, these options would likely end up making the insurance too expensive. Therefore, insurers will simply refuse to enter markets where adverse selection is pervasive.

In theory, government insurance has a unique ability to address the adverse selection problem. Most important, government insurance programs can force both high-risk and low-risk entities into the insurance pool. This helps to explain the high degree of compulsion in many government insurance programs.

Moral Hazard

Past experience will also not accurately forecast future claims if actions taken by the insured after they receive insurance increase expected losses. Examples of this moral hazard problem abound. A family may decide to build a house a little closer to a river despite the increased risk of flood damage, knowing that flood insurance will allow them to recoup their loss if a flood occurs. Generally speaking, the insurer will not be able to manage losses effectively unless losses result from chance rather than the actions of the insured.

The government has some unique compulsory powers for addressing the potential for moral hazard. For example, government can allow households to purchase flood insurance only if their community agrees to adopt and enforce a floodplain management ordinance. In a similar vein, the government can enforce a system of financial regulation and examinations to prevent banks from taking risks that could increase their probability of failure. Likewise, the government can establish a legal framework that requires safeguards for pension funds. In addition, the government can establish very steep penalties for those taking actions that lead to insurance claims.

Broader Goals

The ultimate rationale for government use of the insurance tool is usually not the provision of insurance for its own sake. Instead, insurance can potentially serve a larger societal goal. Deposit insurance offers an important example of a broader objective for government insurance. Banks cannot sell their assets quickly and pay off all depositors at the same time. Those depositors who wait to get their funds back therefore may be out of luck and thus have reason to "run" the bank and withdraw their funds. Runs on a single bank can turn into runs on the banking system as a whole. Banking panics have been costly events in the United States and other countries. One method for preventing panics is to provide depositors with sufficient insurance so that they will not lose their deposits when their bank fails. Because of some of the reasons discussed previously, such as correlated risks, private insurers may not be able to offer this form of protection.

Governments also justify insurance as being a cheaper method of providing government services than alternative tools. In the United States, the government provided after-the-fact assistance to families and firms who suffered losses from floods. The creation of federal flood insurance was supported as a more cost-efficient way for the government to provide assistance to those suffering losses from flood damage.[26] Flood insurance could reduce the government's costs by requiring payments from the insured. Flood insurance also came with a number of restrictions and rules that the government thought would lower the total costs from flooding. In particular, flood insurance encourages more prudent building codes in flood-prone areas as well as other mitigation techniques and efforts.

Finally, government insurance can address cases where rational decisions made by individuals could lead to outcomes inconsistent with society's best interests. For example, take wartime property insurance. The U.S. government believed that private owners of planes and ships would not commit their property to support the national defense without insurance against property and liability loss. Traditionally, private firms have not offered wartime property insurance at affordable rates because of the high probability of loss, lack of independence, and lack of data. As a result, the U.S. government now offers wartime property insurance.

Although the preceding discussion suggests that factors leading to the absence of private market insurance could justify government intervention, there is some evidence that even with less than ideal conditions, private firms would have been able to offer some of the insurance products currently offered by the government. For example, some scholars have argued that private solutions to the problem of banking panics have developed in the past and could develop again if government relinquished control over the market.[27] Likewise, analysts have argued that private firms have developed the resources to provide pension insurance.[28] As noted, advances that make it more likely that private markets can insure against catastrophic natural disasters have developed even while the government debates entry into the arena.

Moreover, even if a theoretical justification for government insurance exists, policymakers should seriously consider a second, more practical, test before choosing this tool. Specifically, can government managers actually utilize their advantages and effectively manage the mechanics to ensure that the insurance program meets financial and social objectives? For example, is the government insurance program allowed to use pricing, risk sharing, and limitations on the provision of insurance in order to keep costs under control? In addition, is the government prepared to apply the resources necessary to meet financial objectives? These resources include the specialized staff needed to operate the program effectively and the data necessary to determine expected losses. These practical questions are particularly important because governments use insurance as a vehicle to achieve other political objectives more often than as an efficient method for managing risks. Therefore, it is to these objectives and rationales that we must now turn.

Political Rationale

Quite apart from its economic rationale and contribution to larger public purposes, insurance programs have several attributes that make them popular for elected officials and beneficiaries. In particular, the costs and the subsidies of government insurance programs are nearly invisible, in part due to the budgetary treatment of the programs. The programs also have an attractive self-financing component to them. Finally, the indirect nature of some government programs can provide benefits to policymakers.

Low Visibility

The public budget and the budget process put a spotlight on the costs of many tools of government. In contrast, the public budget in many countries often provides misleadingly low figures on the costs of government insurance. Many public budgets account for government insurance on a "cash basis." As a result, the costs of the program show up in the budget when the government makes a payment to the firm or person submitting a claim. The premiums from the insured show up in the budget when paid. The net effect is to show government insurance as a moneymaker for the government even when future claims will swamp future premiums. Policymakers could find the invisible, even misleading, nature of the cash-basis treatment attractive, especially if they face limited ability to spend funds on budget due to deficits. In fact, analysts have cited the invisible budgetary treatment of insurance as encouraging policymakers to ignore growing costs in insurance programs. In response, they have proposed improving the budgetary information available to the public by requiring that the budgets show expected losses for insurance programs in the current period rather than when payments are made.[29]

Even if the budget did capture expected future costs, it is unlikely that it would highlight the subsidy that government insurance programs often offer. Insurance programs provide a subsidy through fairly indirect means. Specifically, charging the insured a lower than actuarially fair premium provides the insured with a subsidy. This mechanism allows policymakers to select important constituencies to receive insurance coverage from which they reap substantial benefits. In return, political officials could expect support from these constituencies. Because the fair premium is not routinely calculated by the government, the subsidy is essentially invisible.

Beyond this, the costs of government insurance are fairly diffuse and are often spread across all taxpayers. In contrast, the benefits of insurance programs tend to be narrowly focused, for example, on farmers with poor crop outcomes or on managers of a bank near insolvency. As a result, the general taxpayer has little incentive to monitor the program or hire an agent to monitor it; the costs of the monitoring will likely outweigh the costs to taxpayers of supporting the insurance program.

Self-Financing

The fact that the insured pay the government even a nominal amount for insurance provided by the government also makes this tool attractive to policymakers. The insured are not getting "something for nothing," even when the premiums do not cover true costs. Marketing material of the U.S. Flood Insurance program makes this point.

> Because the NFIP uses flood insurance premium dollars, not taxpayer dollars, to pay claims and operating expenses, all taxpayers benefit when flood victims have flood insurance. The NFIP reduces Federal disaster assistance outlays. . . . Since 1978, almost $8.3 billion in flood losses have been paid from premiums, thereby reducing the burden on the taxpayer.[30]

This helps to explain why policymakers may find government insurance superior to grants or other tools that provide a more direct subsidy, even though direct subsidies would allow the government better to target the population to receive the benefit, reduce the administrative costs of providing the benefit, and lower the government's potential exposure to loss (as well as increasing the satisfaction of the recipient).

Political Benefits of Indirect Government

Government insurance programs can also provide valuable benefits to other stakeholders in the political process. As noted, some insurance programs, such as crop insurance, make use of private insurance firms in distribution and adjustment, while the federal government retains most of the risk of the insurance. Private firms find this system lucrative and provide a natural base of support for the program and for policymakers who support the government insurance program. Local government officials also benefit from government insurance programs and support policymakers in favor of government insurance. For example, the flood insurance program provides subsidies to certain property owners in flood plains, encouraging development and related property tax revenue.

V. MANAGEMENT CHALLENGES AND POTENTIAL RESPONSES

Important challenges to government insurance solvency arise from the less than ideal economic environment in which governments provide insurance. While governments have some options for addressing the insurance environment, many of the responses are politically unpalatable and, thus, not made fully available to the government insurance program. There are also challenges to the government insurance program due to a lack of demand for government insurance and a lack of data. In addition, there are a number of important challenges and potential responses that arise from using third parties to help carry out government insurance programs. Finally, there are unique management challenges, such as staffing and responsiveness, that come from providing insurance in the public setting.

Providing Insurance in an Environment of Correlated Losses, Adverse Selection, and Moral Hazard

As noted in Section IV on tool selection, government insurance is often provided in situations where there are problems of correlated losses, adverse selection, and moral hazard. This makes the management of government insurance program even more difficult than the management of insurance more generally.

Correlated Losses

Virtually all the insurance programs offered by governments have the problem of correlated losses exposing the insurer to very large losses. While federal governments can often absorb such losses, the government insurance program would still have to charge something close to the fair premium if it plans to achieve a self-financing regime. It might be quite difficult to set the fair premium if losses occur in bunches.

Moral Hazard

Government insurance is often provided in cases where the problem of moral hazard has been acute. Insurers have always faced at least a little moral hazard and therefore have developed several methods for addressing it. First, the insurer can share losses through methods already discussed (e.g., caps, deductibles, coinsurance, and copayments). Second, the insurer can refuse to cover claims that occur as a result of certain actions. For example, a beneficiary cannot normally receive payment on a life insurance policy by murdering the insured party. Third, the insurer can monitor the actions of the insured party and charge premiums that vary with risk or exclude her from the insurance pool altogether if she engages in behavior that makes losses more likely. The insurer could, for example, sharply raise premiums immediately after a claim, giving the insured party an incentive to shun avoidable claims. The insurer could also offer the insured party credits that lower her rate if she takes loss-reducing actions (e.g., installing a smoke alarm).

Government insurance programs have all of these options plus the ability to enact regulatory and legal frameworks to limit behavior that could increase losses. However, the government has been reluctant to use many of the techniques described above to manage moral hazard because they can often hinder the achievement of social goals. The subsidy value of government insurance and hence the rationale for government involvement will decline if government raises premiums in response to increased risk-taking. Moreover, the ability of regulation to limit losses has been found lacking on several occasions. In particular, regulation has often proved to be an ineffective method for reducing risk taking because the insured household or firm can frequently circumvent it.[31]

In fact, governments have taken steps that make moral hazard a more severe problem. For example, government insurance has often been designed to cover 100 percent of losses. This leaves the insured little reason to avoid an insured event or engaging in potentially high-loss activities. An insolvent farmer may decide to engage in a high-risk but high-return planting strategy, figuring she can either reap the rewards or put the loss to the insurer. The government has allowed these high-risk parties to remain in the insurance pool, thereby exposing the government to the potential for significant loss.

In addition, government has provided protection to those who are not legally covered in programs ranging from deposit insurance to crop insurance. Extralegal coverage leads an even larger group of firms and households to engage in loss-increasing behavior. More important, the expansion of coverage makes it quite difficult for the government insurance program to reduce moral hazard in the future. Those who received extralegal coverage in the past could continue to believe they will receive such coverage in the future despite government pledges to the contrary.

That said, after potential for losses and actual losses rose during the 1970s and 1980s, policymakers did take steps to try to better manage moral hazard. Banks that received deposit insurance, for example, were subject in the early 1990s to more stringent financial regulation in order to limit their potential for failing. Indeed, during the 1990s, firms across the globe that received government insurance against insolvency were often required to maintain higher levels of financial resources.

Adverse Selection

The government insurance program can compel all firms or households of a certain type into an insurance pool to address the problem of adverse selection, but compulsion has its limits. As noted, the ability to force cross-subsidies runs into the problem that those paying too much for insurance will take steps to opt out of the pool and reduce their exposure to insurance assessments. Pension plan sponsors who have little risk of underfunding their plan will not want to subsidize sponsors who have higher risks. These low-risk sponsors could escape the insurance pool by establishing new forms of pensions that are not insured.

Another method for managing adverse selection involves restricting entry into the insurance pool. Government insurance programs, however, do not systematically exclude high-loss applicants, preferring instead less restrictive options. The government flood insurance program, for example, used to require applicants to wait five days after they applied before they could receive insurance coverage. This waiting period was increased to thirty days to prevent those with extremely high probabilities of loss, because communities upstream were being flooded out, from receiving coverage.

Lack of Demand

A second management challenge of government insurance has resulted from limited demand. Both crop and flood insurance depend to some degree on voluntary purchases and both have had participation rates below the desired level for several reasons. First, the lack of independence and adverse selection can lead to high prices, although both of these programs subsidize rates in order to stimulate demand. The high prices of insurance may be particularly problematic if those most likely to suffer a loss from an event have very limited income. Low-income families may be able to buy houses only in flood plains, and poor farmers may be able to afford only agricultural plots with highly variable production outcomes.

Second, those targeted for government insurance traditionally have received federal support even when they did not purchase insurance. Disaster assistance limited the incentive for agricultural producers to purchase insurance, which left the program with low demand. The government has tried to limit this effect by forbidding those who do not sign up for crop and flood insurance from receiving other forms of government help after a loss. These pledges are often not credible, however. The government recently provided *ex post* assistance for agricultural producers who had explicitly waived the right to such payments when they refused to purchase crop insurance.

Third, the methods individuals use to make decisions about the purchase of disaster insurance can deviate significantly from rational assessments of costs and benefits.[32] Individuals often convert the low chance of loss from disasters to a zero chance of loss. In addition, households will make a best guess at a potential loss and use that initial estimate as the base on which future adjustments will be made. Yet, that initial estimate can end up being extremely inaccurate. Governments can respond to this problem by advertising the actual risks of an insurable event. The flood insurance program has increased its participation rates over recent years and attributes part of the increase to its marketing efforts. The government can also require households to purchase the insurance.

Lack of Data

A third management challenge results from lack of data. The government insurance program is often the first entity to offer certain forms of insurance. As a result, information on the likelihood of an event occurring may not exist or the cost of producing such information may be quite high. Moreover, there will be no information on how the provision of insurance will make future results different from past results. Methods for mitigating potential losses include putting a restrictive cap on losses covered, ensuring that the number of policies offered grows at a slow rate, and adjusting the terms of the policy on a very frequent basis to respond to losses.

Challenges of Third-Party Provision

Reliance on private, third parties to distribute, service, and adjust government insurance programs has raised several significant managerial challenges (a more general discussion of the use of contractors is found in Chapter 9). The specific challenges discussed result, for the most part, from the discretion that third parties have in carrying out their duties on behalf of the insurance program and from the financial incentives the programs provide to the contractors. Both factors can lead the third parties to behave in a manner contrary to the programs' objectives.

A particularly controversial issue has been the appropriate reimbursement system for the private contractors. One concern involves the disincentives that reimbursement systems provide contractors in carrying out the social goals of the insurance program. The U.S. crop insurance program sets reimbursement rates based on premium income generated by the policy sold by the contractor. This reimbursement system gives private insurance agents the motive to sell large crop insurance policies and not sell smaller policies to lower-income farm producers. Yet, the program seeks to provide a safety net to such so-called limited resource producers.[33] Managers can address these types of concerns by writing contracts that reward contractors for behavior consistent with program goals.[34]

In addition, both the U.S. crop and flood insurance programs have faced criticism for paying too much to third parties, and the reimbursement rate for both programs has been lowered in the 1990s. In fact, observers of these programs have argued that distribution and servicing of the insurance could be cheaper if done directly by the government.[35] If the insurance program must pay for its costs from premium income, higher reimbursements to contractors means more expensive policies and thus less benefits for the insured. In some cases, management of the program cannot effectively address this concern because legislatures set the reimbursement amount in law. Private contractors can effectively mobilize lawmakers to oppose reductions in their reimbursements. In other cases, management of the insurance program can try to address these concerns by accumulating verifiable data on actual expenditures of third parties in a timely fashion and setting the reimbursements based on such data.

Ensuring that the discretion that third parties have in underwriting and adjusting insurance claims does not run counter to program objectives presents a second major challenge. The government insurance program traditionally bears the risk of loss from a claim. The contractor who provides insurance to a high-risk candidate or who provides an overly generous claims payment to the insured does not normally bear any cost for her decision nor does the private insurance agent servicing the policy have much reason to monitor the riskiness of the insured.

As a result, the private insurance firms working on behalf of the government insurance program have little reason to use their discretion to take steps that reduce the government's exposure. In fact, government auditors have accused private adjusters working for government insurance programs of allowing a significant amount of improper claims payments.

The government insurance programs can take several steps to address concerns about the discretion of the third parties. The programs can and often do require training and certification of the third-party firms in order to ensure that they understand the rules and procedures of the program. In addition, a thorough auditing and financial control system can influence how private parties use their discretion. Perhaps most important, the programs can require that the private contractors bear some of the loss from claims payments in order to better align their incentives with those of the government insurance program.[36] Managers must take care in structuring risk sharing so as to not dissuade third parties from serving high-risk applicants targeted by government.

Finally, management must address the potential for outright fraud in connection with using private firms to implement the insurance program. For example, the insurance program must take steps to prevent the person selling or adjusting the insurance policy from having a financial stake in the insured business that would benefit from a claim.

Providing Insurance in a Public-Sector Environment

There are at least two additional managerial challenges for those providing insurance in the environment of the public sector. The first relates to the responsiveness of elected officials, while the second relates to personnel.

Responsiveness

Insurance programs require frequent modifications to keep losses within desired ranges. Elected bodies with rules designed to foster debate and inclusion are often not capable of making the timely decisions required to keep the insurance program in fiscal shape. Elected officials could delegate the authority to make the necessary adjustments to the professional managers of the programs in order to address that concern. However, many of the adjustments a professional staff would make in terms of pricing and coverage could reduce the benefits of the programs to constituents. This can give elected officials the incentive to retain control of the major features of the insurance program, resulting in a sporadic adjustment to the program.

Personnel

Government insurance programs require personnel with analytical, back-office, and distribution skills. Private-sector insurance firms as well as other providers of financial services demand staff with similar expertise. Private-sector competitors offer higher compensation for staff with these skills given their for-profit status. This presents a challenge for recruitment and retention of key employees by government insurance programs. In some cases, government insurance programs have tried to address this problem by requesting that Congress exempt them from civil service restrictions. These sorts of exemptions have been easier to achieve when the administering agency of the government insurance program is a government corporation that is at least semi-independent from government personnel policies. A government insurance program can also try to address this concern by relying on the private sector to carry out certain tasks, although, as noted, this presents its own challenges.

VI. OVERALL ASSESSMENT

Insurance as a tool by which governments achieve their objectives is a mixed bag. It has achieved many of the social and larger economic goals of policymakers successfully and, in theory, can improve overall resource allocation. It also has a high degree of legitimacy. However, the tool poses managerial and political challenges that make it difficult to limit its use to situations where government action will be most effective, costs will remain within financial limits, and benefits will stay focused on the targeted population.

Effectiveness

On some quite visible levels, government insurance has been successful. Clearly, it has protected households and firms from the financial loss that would accompany certain events, such as a flood. Government insurance has also been quite effective in achieving the broad economic goals set out for it. Deposit insurance is a proven means to eliminate bank panics. Finally, government insurance has achieved some of its social goals. Insurance provides subsidies to agricultural producers.

However, government insurance certainly has not been an unmitigated success. Indeed, its effectiveness in achieving some of the goals discussed above must be put in context. Protecting the banking system or an individual household from harm does not represent a substantial victory if it merely reflects the transfer of a loss from a specific group of firms or households to the government. The government must, in turn, pay for these losses and must force the charge on all other groups in society.

Although policymakers rarely state resource allocation as a formal objective, many government insurance programs are at least implicitly justified by arguments suggesting that the private sector would not provide a particular type of insurance. This argument suggests that the failure of markets supports the use of the government insurance tool. In theory, some of the characteristics of government insurance programs discussed could address the market failure. However, many of the same government insurance programs have attributes that lead to the poor use of society's resources.

The underpricing of many government insurance programs could very well lead to excessive risk taking on the part of the insured. Too much risk taking means that resources are channeled to uses that are inferior. Crop insurance has encouraged the planting of crops in areas that simply cannot support them. The government may also provide insurance where private markets would otherwise develop. Not surprisingly, a number of analyses suggest that government insurance programs have led to losses to society from which no parties have benefited.[37] These losses could exceed the benefits of the programs. Economists at the World Bank and International Monetary Fund, for example, have found that countries offering deposit insurance are actually *more* likely to experience a mass of bank failures than countries that do not, other salient factors held constant.[38]

Effectiveness also concerns the degree to which the tool encourages accountability. As noted in Section IV, insurance programs often obscure the delivery of subsidies and other benefits rather than creating an environment conducive to enhanced accountability. It is difficult to hold elected officials accountable for insurance programs because of the time delay between costs and benefits, the lack of informative data on program performance, and the overall complexity of the programs among other attributes.

Efficiency

The ability of insurance to act as the lowest-cost method for achieving the goals of the government sponsoring the program remains an open question. This is true both in terms of an accounting definition of costs and a broader definition that counts the poor use of economic resources as a cost. In terms of accounting costs, government insurance programs generate savings if they replace disaster assistance efforts. However, governments have ended up providing both insurance and disaster relief, possibly obviating any potential savings.

In terms of resource allocation, we have noted that government insurance programs have produced mixed results. Government insurance has prevented events such as banking panics that have very high costs for society. At the same time, government insurance has also received considerable blame for encouraging catastrophic losses; a number of deposit insurance programs have suffered losses equal to a noteworthy portion of GDP in their country.[39] In addition, the regulation necessitated by government insurance is costly. Other well-regarded government actions, including making funds available from the central bank to the banking system, have proved effective in addressing catastrophic events and potentially at a lower cost than insurance.

Equity

A government can structure an insurance program to focus the benefits of the program on those viewed as most deserving under some well-articulated standard. For example, the government could restrict government insurance to those below a certain income, but government insurance programs, in fact, do not often have this type of feature. Much more common are limits on the amount of loss the insurer will cover, which ostensibly could lead to more protection for lower-income households. However, some of the limits established to protect "the little person" provide much greater protection than that goal would require. Deposit insurance provides $100,000 in coverage, although the most recent data found that median household deposits were $2,300.[40]

The often indirect method by which governments provide subsidies through insurance is inconsistent with efforts to target benefits to the deserving as traditionally defined. The subsidies provided through the insurance tool often end up going to the parties that have the highest chance of making a claim. This means that insurance may benefit farmers who take the greatest risks in planting crops. A third of all payments from the U.S. flood insurance program have gone to households who make repeated claims, even though repetitive loss structures make up a very small percent of the total program policies.[41]

Government insurance programs are fairly rare in the United States and probably abroad as well, although the scope of the few programs that exist is extremely large. This outcome largely reflects the very vibrant private insurance market in the United States and other developed countries as well as the intense regulation of the insurance industry, which often allows policymakers to achieve their policy objectives without direct production. Support for government insurance programs also reflects the focus of these programs on losses that private firms may not cover or at least not cover at a low price. The fact that many beneficiaries of government insurance pay something for the benefits they receive, even if it is far below the amount needed to sustain the program in the long run, is a powerful symbol and gives the programs more legitimacy than a grant program. In total, the limited use of the insurance tool, the potentially costly events they cover, and their appearance of self-funding provide a high degree of legitimacy to these programs.

VII. FUTURE DIRECTIONS

Risk pooling can provide substantial benefits by allowing firms and households to shed a potentially large cost in exchange for a series of certain fixed payments. A government insurance program theoretically can provide those benefits in certain cases where the private sector cannot. The government can also use the insurance tool to accomplish social goals not directly related to risk pooling. At the same time, achievement of both the risk pooling and social objectives can come at substantial financial and economic costs.

Balancing the costs and benefits of an insurance program is challenging. Part of the difficulty reflects the inherent complexity in running an insurance program. However, the limitations that have been placed on government insurance programs go a long way in explaining why their costs may exceed benefits at times. Policymakers do not always allow government insurance programs to use the techniques, including pricing, coverage restrictions, and loss sharing that are necessary to control their losses. Policymakers may believe that these techniques will hinder the achievement of social goals and other program features that policymakers find attractive. At times, policymakers have so hampered the ability of government insurance programs to achieve long-run solvency that even analysts who support the larger goal of an insurance program (e.g., reduction in banking panics) have called for careful examination of alternative tools.[42]

The conflicting nature of government insurance makes it difficult to forecast the future use of this tool. The recent history of increased exposure could lead governments to take steps that bring long-term stability to government insurance programs. If government insurance programs produce substantial losses in the future, policymakers may restrict their use even further. At the same time, policymakers clearly value the political and social benefits that insurance programs can create. These benefits could lead to new insurance programs or the easing of private-sector-type restrictions on existing programs.

VIII. SUGGESTED READING

Harrington, Scott, and Gregory Niehaus. *Risk Management and Insurance.* Boston: McGraw-Hill, 1999.

Kunreuther, Howard, and Richard Roth, eds. *Paying the Price: The Status and Role of Insurance against Natural Disasters in the United States.* Washington, D.C.: Joseph Henry Press, 1998.

U.S. Federal Deposit Insurance Corporation. *History of the Eighties: Lessons for the Future.* Washington, D.C., 1997.

U.S. General Accounting Office. *Budgeting for Federal Insurance Programs.* Washington, D.C., 1997.

U.S. Office of Management and Budget. "Underwriting Federal Credit and Insurance," in *Analytical Perspectives, Budget of the United States Government, Fiscal Year 2000,* 181–200. Washington, D.C.: Government Printing Office, 1999.

NOTES

1. This story is found on the National Flood Insurance Program's Web site at http://www.fema.gov/nfip/oped01.htm.

2. The Federal Emergency Management Agency reports that as of March 1997, 935 out of the 10,657 homes in Grand Forks were covered by flood insurance; in March 1998, 3,048 out of 10,657 homes were insured.

3. Asli Demirguc-Kunt and Harry Huizinga, "Market Discipline and Financial Safety Net Design," *World Bank Policy Research Working Paper* 2183 (1999): 6.

4. Mark Selinger, "Disaster Insurance Bill Survives House Banking Committee Consideration," *BNA Banking Daily* (12 November 1999).

5. Insurance Information Institute, "Insurance Issues Update: Residual Markets," March 1999.

6. Hana Polackova, "Government Contingent Liabilities: A Hidden Risk to Fiscal Stability," *World Bank Policy Research Working Paper* 1989 (1999).

7. Gillian Garcia, "Deposit Insurance: A Survey of Actual and Best Practices," *International Monetary Fund Working Paper* 99/54 (1999).

8. James H. Smallhout, *The Uncertain Retirement: Securing Pension Promises in the World of Risk* (Chicago: Irwin, 1996), 179–268.

9. Shantayanan Dervarajan and Jeffrey Hammer, "Risk Reduction and Public Expenditures," *World Bank Policy Research Working Paper* 1869 (1997): 19–20.

10. John Campbell, "Cataclysm," *St. Louis Federal Reserve Regional Review* (summer 1997): 11.

11. Alicia Munnell, "The Current Status of Our Social Welfare System," *New England Economic Review* (July/August 1987): 4–12.

12. Social insurance is defined by the National Academy of Social Insurance as a system sponsored by the government through which individuals (and/or their employers) contribute into a fund when working and receive benefits as an earned right when retired, disabled, unemployed or in need of health care. This definition is found on http://www.nasi.org/q&a.htm.

13. Munnell, "Current Status," 6.

14. United States Congressional Budget Office, *The Changing Business of Banking: A Study of Failed Banks from 1987 to 1992* (Washington, D.C., 1994), 1.

15. United States Congressional Budget Office, *Controlling Losses of the Pension Benefit Guaranty Corporation* (Washington, D.C., 1993).

16. United States Congressional Budget Office, *The Economic Impact of a Solvency Crisis in the Insurance Industry* (Washington, D.C., 1994), 47.

17. Gerard Caprio, Jr., and Daniela Klingebiel, "Bank Insolvencies: Cross-Country Experience," *World Bank Policy Research Working Paper* 1620 (1996), 3.

18. United States General Accounting Office, *Flood Insurance: Financial Resources May Not Be Sufficient to Meet Future Expected Losses* (Washington, D.C., 1994).

19. United States General Accounting Office, *Crop Insurance: Additional Actions Could Further Improve Program's Financial Condition* (Washington, D.C., 1995).

20. Details on estimation methods for federal insurance programs are found in United States General Accounting Office, *Budgeting for Federal Insurance Programs* (Washington, D.C., 1997), 152–217.

21. Kenneth A. Froot, "The Evolving Market for Catastrophic Event Risk," *NBER Working Paper* 7287 (1999).

22. Details on the marketing campaign of the U.S. Flood Insurance Program can be found at http://www.fema.gov/nfip/coverii.htm.

23. United States Department of Agriculture Office of Inspector General, *Report to the Secretary on Federal Crop Insurance Reform* No. 05801–2-At (April 1999).

24. Thanks to Art Murton for this point.

25. U.S. Office of Management and Budget, "Underwriting Federal Credit and Insurance," in *Analytical Perspectives, Budget of the United States Government, Fiscal Year 2000* (Washington, D.C.: Government Printing Office, 1999): 181–200 provides a somewhat similar set of criteria for determining when to select government insurance.

26. United States Federal Emergency Management Agency, National Flood Insurance Program, *Answers to Questions about the National Flood Insurance Program* (Washington, D.C., 1999), 1.

27. George Benston and George Kaufman, "Is the Banking and Payments System Fragile?" *Journal of Financial Services Research* 9 (December 1995): 209–240; and Charles Calomiris and Joseph Mason, "Contagion and Bank Failures during the Great Depression: The June 1932 Chicago Banking Panic," *American Economic Review* 87, no. 5 (1997): 863–883.

28. Carolyn Weaver, "Government Guarantees of Private Pension Benefits: Current Problems and Market-Based Solutions," in *Public Policy Toward Pensions,* eds. Sylvester Schieber and John Shoven (Cambridge, Mass.: MIT Press, 1997), 157.

29. For a discussion of the issue see F. Stevens Redburn, "Measuring Revenue Capacity, Effort and Spending: How Should the Government Measure Spending? The Uses of Accrual Accounting," *Public Administration Review* 53 (May/June 1993): 228–236.

30. National Flood Insurance Program, "FEMA Implements the Most Extensive Flood Insurance Reforms in 30 Years" (23 September 1999) located at http://www.fema.gov/nfip/reform.htm.

31. For a discussion of regulation, moral hazard, and government insurance, see Richard Ippolito, *The Economics of Pension Insurance* (Homewood, Ill.: Irwin, 1989) and Edward Kane, *The S & L Insurance Mess: How Did It Happen* (Washington, D.C.: Urban Institute Press, 1989).

32. Risa Palm, "Demand for Disaster Insurance: Residential Coverage," in *Paying the Price: The Status and Role of Insurance against Natural Disasters in the United States,* eds. Howard Kunreuther and Richard Roth (Washington, D.C.: Joseph Henry Press, 1998), 51–66.

33. United States Department of Agriculture Office of Inspector General, "Report," 27–29.

34. United States General Accounting Office, *Crop Insurance: Opportunities Exist to Reduce Government Costs for Private-Sector Delivery* (Washington, D.C., 1997).

35. Lawerence Dyckman, "Crop Insurance: Further Actions Could Strengthen Program's Financial Soundness," *U.S. General Accounting Office Testimony before the U.S. Senate Committee on Agriculture, Nutrition, and Forestry* (21 April 1999). Changes to the reimbursement policy of the flood insurance program can be found at http://www.fema.gov/nfip/reform.htm.

36. Points related to claims payments are discussed in United States General Accounting Office, *Crop Insurance: USDA Needs a Better Estimate of Improper Payments to Strengthen Controls over Claims* (Washington, D.C., 1999); and United States Department of Agriculture Office of Inspector General, "Report."

37. See Ippolito, *The Economics of Pension Insurance;* Barry Goodwin and Vincent Smith, *The Economics of Crop Insurance and Disaster Aid* (Washington, D.C.: AEI, 1994); and Anthony Santomero, "Deposit Insurance: Do We Need It and Why?" *Ekonomia* 1, no. 1 (1997): 1–19 for examples.

38. Asli Demirguc-Kunt and Enrica Detragiache, "The Determinants of Banking Crises: Evidence from Developing and Developed Countries," *IMF Staff Paper* 45 (1998); and Asli Demirguc-Kunt, "Does Deposit Insurance Increase Banking System Stability?: An Empirical Investigation" (unpublished manuscript).

39. Eugene White, "The Legacy of Deposit Insurance: The Growth, Spread, and Cost of Insuring Financial Intermediaries," *NBER Working Paper* 6063 (1997); and Caprio and Klingebiel, "Banking Insolvencies."

40. Arthur Kennickell, Myron, Kwast, and Martha Starr-McCluer, "Households' Deposit In-

surance Coverage: Evidence and Analysis of Potential Reforms," *Journal of Money Credit and Banking* 28, no. 3 (August 1996, pt. I): 313.

41. Stanley Czerwinski, "Flood Insurance: Information on Financial Aspects of the National Flood Insurance Program," *Testimony of the General Accounting Office before the House Subcommittee on Housing and Community Opportunity, Committee on Banking and Financial Services* (October 1999): 9.

42. Frederic Mishkin, "Moral Hazard and Reform of the Government Safety Net," forthcoming in the *Journal of Financial Services Research.*

CHAPTER SEVEN

Public Information

Janet A. Weiss

In 1945 the U.S. Forest Service (USFS) began distributing posters, radio messages, and newspaper and magazine ads featuring a bear dressed in a ranger's hat. Smokey, as the bear was called, became the centerpiece of a long-running campaign to educate the public, and children in particular, about fire safety in forests. In 1947 the ad agency, working with the Forest Service, developed the slogan "Remember, only you can prevent forest fires." A bear cub rescued from a forest fire on Capitan Mountain in New Mexico in 1950 was named Smokey, and he was installed with great ceremony in the National Zoo. Six million children signed up to be official Smokey Bear junior forest rangers.[1]

The Smokey Bear campaign is an example of a policy intervention addressed to an extremely difficult problem. Wildfires are destructive and expensive. The destruction of forests and animal habitat, loss of property and human life, the cost of firefighting, and the cost of fire insurance add up to hundreds of millions of dollars each year. In the central, southern, and eastern United States, nearly all wildfires are caused by people or equipment operated by people. As the Forest Service saw during the 1950s, it had two major alternatives. First, it could invest in fire suppression: equipment, airplanes, helicopters, pumps, and highly trained, mobile, brave, and flexible firefighters to stop fires once they start. Second, it could analyze why fires happen and develop programs to prevent them from starting or spreading. Both seemed important, but given how many fires were started by people, prevention had to address citizens. Can a federal agency change the behavior of millions of people who go into wooded areas each year with a wide variety of purposes, a wide variety of skills, some dangerous habits (smoking, lighting campfires, cooking stoves), and little supervision? Spread over millions of acres all over the country, the private nature of the risky behavior and its geographic dispersion meant that monitoring was impossible. Although it could prohibit fires under some circumstances, the USFS had few ways to enforce selective prohibitions on behavior in forests.

One answer was an information campaign making people aware of the consequences of their actions and teaching them to behave in ways that were safer. The Smokey Bear campaign demonstrates one of the ways that public policy can reach out to citizens, show them how their behavior is connected to policy outcomes that affect everyone, and teach them alternative skills and behavior that lead to outcomes that policymakers intend. It made people aware of the consequences of their own behavior, explaining skills and alternatives for safer handling of fire, and relying on them to use those skills and alternatives under appropriate circumstances. It is an example of information as a policy tool.

Scattered evidence suggests that the Smokey Bear campaign has influenced awareness and knowledge of fire prevention and safety behavior, which have then spilled over to changes in behavior. The managers of the program claimed that the savings in resource damage that may be credited to the program between 1947 and 1977 were $17 billion,

217

with especially good results in the South, where more than half of the wildfires caused by people occurred.[2]

I. DEFINING THE TOOL

Basic Features

Information is a tool for eliciting desired policy outcomes. Policymakers inform an audience of target actors about a policy issue or pattern of behavior to influence what people think, know, or believe when they engage in target behavior. People change what they do because public policy has changed what they think or has changed what they think about, without necessarily changing anything else about the situation.[3]

A wide variety of interventions may rely on information as the basic instrument. One general kind of intervention occurs when government officials gather (or already possess) information that they distribute to actors who need or want it so that they may produce the desired outcome. Examples of this top-down variety include public information campaigns (such as the Smokey Bear campaign of the USFS), technical assistance, dissemination of research findings, statistical systems, counseling, and, more ominously, propaganda and indoctrination. The National Institute of Mental Health gathered and distributed statistics on the length of time that patients lived in mental hospitals to show state officials that institutionalization was expensive and ineffective compared with community treatment.[4] The Environmental Protection Agency promoted environmentally responsible waste management by offering state and local governments considerable technical assistance and support in handling their responsibilities for waste management. Their activities included publishing a guide for local waste managers, issuing studies on ways to promote waste minimization, holding conferences on hazardous household waste, running training programs for recycling coordinators, offering model operator certification standards for waste-to-energy facilities and landfill operators.[5] These activities gave state and local officials the information, skills, and commitment to pursue effective waste-handling strategies in their communities.

A second general kind of information tool sets in motion a process of information collection or learning. Government officials may not themselves have the information required to produce the outcome, but they require or enable other actors to generate or share such information. In this second category, common examples include training, research, reporting and recordkeeping, auditing, evaluation, labeling, public disclosure, environmental impact statements, and public hearings. These interventions are typically less top-down in orientation than the first category. They require target actors to collect or report certain kinds of information that will be useful for the actors themselves, for government officials, or for consumers to act upon. For example, federal health officials sought to improve Americans' diets by mandating that food products have labels showing the nutritional value of food products. This policy is designed to change the behavior of food consumers by providing accurate, consistent information about the foods that people purchase at the grocery store. Food purchases themselves are not regulated. Consumers need not make the choices that federal health officials might prefer. However, the labels provide the consumer with the information they need to make healthy dietary choices.

All policies that use information as a tool are premised on the assumption that people respond to information. Therefore, to understand this policy tool, one has to understand the ways in which information influences behavior. The simplest assumption is that people are rational; they make decisions by adjusting automatically and continuously to information that bears on any consequences of their actions. Although there is some truth in this simple view, much of the time full information is not available to all individuals, and all individuals are not perfectly responsive to the information that is available. The use of information policies must be grounded in a realistic and sophisticated understanding of how and when information may influence behavior that is connected to policy outcomes. Without making unrealistic assumptions about rationality, information still may have powerful effects on people. In addition, information can mobilize third parties to exert influence on target actors to get them to change.

Information used as a policy instrument has to be distinguished from rationality in another important respect. Information used as a policy tool is not necessarily true, correct, or accurate. Using information as the active ingredient in public policy does not necessarily make the policy either rational or humane. To get results, information policies need not use good information. Just as commercial advertising, for example, can be persuasive regardless of whether its claims are true, information-based policies may work, regardless of whether their claims are well founded, nor do information interventions rely entirely on objective facts. In fact, nearly all policy-related information has both cognitive and normative content. In communicating what is and what may be, these policies may send strong signals about what should be. Some uses may be tilted toward more cognitive content, as, for example, in the labeling of chemicals used at work sites. Other uses may be tilted heavily toward normative messages, as in drug abuse prevention campaigns that convey strong moral disapproval (rather than information useful to current drug users or those trying to help them to refrain).[6] Hence, information should not be seen as an objective or technical intervention. Intervening with information carries values, at least implicitly, into the relationships between policymaker and citizens.

Relation to Common Tool Features

Directness

Information policies are marvelously versatile. They may be classic direct interventions, as when government officials inform citizens what they are supposed to do. For example, the Swedish government informed citizens that they should henceforth drive on the other side of the road, or the U.S. government informed citizens that they should evacuate their homes to escape catastrophic hurricanes.[7] Information policies may also be indirect. Thus, the Securities and Exchange Commission has maintained confidence and liquidity in the securities markets by requiring publicly traded companies to disclose extensive financial information to investors. The government plays little role in providing, auditing, or endorsing such information. Corporations compile the information, which is then audited by accounting firms and distributed to potential investors for their use in making decisions to buy and sell. The financial industries, auditing profession, and investors thus carry out the disclosure policy.[8] In another example, federal education policies to benefit disadvantaged children included a policy that all programs that received federal funds had to be evaluated to see whether students' academic performance improved. The evaluations were conducted by the local districts and customized to answer questions appropriate to local goals.[9] Because the information pertinent to policy questions may come from any quarter, public policies that use information as a tool may take both direct and indirect forms, depending on the demands of the problem at hand.

Automaticity

Automaticity measures the extent to which a tool utilizes an existing administrative structure (e.g., the market system or the tax system) to produce its effect rather than having to create its own special administrative apparatus. In some cases, the delivery of information to the target audience relies on channels created for other purposes such as the Internet, print, or broadcast media. In these cases, policymakers benefit from the availability of preexisting vehicles for distributing information, but they are also constrained by the limits of such channels for reaching the desired audience at the right time with the right message. However, information policies seldom work automatically. If the desired information was already being generated and conveyed to the appropriate audiences, then information would be unnecessary and ineffective. In fact, information interventions are often needed explicitly to counteract the information provided by other social and economic institutions. Information policies require the continuing engagement of government officials to decide what information to convey and to whom and how. The rapidly changing and competitive environment of information that bombards all citizens makes it essential for policymakers to attend carefully to information content and delivery. This enables any given information program to reach an audience with the right messages. Comparing the two major variants, those in which public policy elicits information from other levels of government, nonprofit organizations, or business, which is then communicated to other audiences, are somewhat less demanding of policymakers' time and attention than those in which government officials collect, organize, and communicate information themselves.

Visibility

Visibility measures the extent to which a tool is visible in the normal government budget and policy processes. The visibility of information interventions varies substantially. Although information seldom requires huge outlays that would invite close scrutiny in the budget process, information may become very visible through other channels. Public information campaigns are, almost by definition, highly public and visible efforts by government officials to attract attention to the public good in order to influence behavior. Information collected by federal agencies may attract substantial political controversy, as information collection has become defined as "paperwork burden."[10] Whether citizens distrust the intentions of government information collectors (as in some citizens' reluctance to respond to the decennial census) or whether the targets of information collection seek to protect themselves against disclosure (as in the resistance of some industries to the collection of information about workplace health and safety), the government's efforts to use information become embroiled in political controversy with surprising frequency.

Of course, much of the time information interventions are less visible. Technical assistance, for example, builds expertise and capacity in particular policy domains, but the government's role may easily escape the notice of anyone beyond those who receive the technical assistance directly.[11] Alcohol or cigarette warning labels are somewhere in the middle of the visibility continuum. They are visible to consumers of these products, but people do not necessarily associate the labels with government policy.

Coerciveness

The intrusiveness of information policies is the subject of vigorous disagreement. On one end of the spectrum, Evert Vedung and Frans van der Doelen claim that "information is the softest and most lenient instrument in the government tool-kit."[12] Such leniency derives from the discretionary nature of response to information interventions.

If households, firms, nonprofit organizations, or other governments receive policy-related information and choose how to respond, then the tool seems less coercive than tools that require specific behavior or punish contrary responses.[13] At the opposite end of the spectrum are scholars of large social systems, such as Charles Lindblom[14] and Jurgen Habermas.[15] In their view, government intervention in shaping the information available to citizens weakens and distorts the flow of ideas and discussion necessary for a free society. Using the power and resources of government to spread some ideas and perspectives (but not others) disempowers citizens, induces passivity, and enhances the power and status of government officials.[16] These effects can in no way be described as lenient or voluntary; indeed, they may be more intrusive in more enduring ways than other tools of public policy.

Both of these perspectives have validity. Information interventions have two faces, one celebrated and the other castigated.[17] No simple characterization does justice to the complex and powerful relationships between government and citizens created by information.

II. PATTERNS OF TOOL USE

Although governments around the world devote substantial energy and resources to information policies, few data are available to estimate their prevalence or trends in use over time. One partial glimpse of the extent of use of information as a policy strategy comes from the U.S. federal government. The Catalog of Federal Domestic Assistance (CFDA) lists policies and programs that benefit citizens. Benefits and services are provided through seven financial types of assistance and eight nonfinancial types of assistance. Of the fifteen categories, three are information interventions:

1. *Advisory services and counseling:* Programs that provide federal specialists to consult, advise, or counsel communities or individuals, to include conferences, workshops, or personal contacts. These may involve the use of published information, but only in a secondary capacity.

2. *Dissemination of technical information:* Programs that provide for the publication and distribution of information or data of a specialized, technical nature, frequently through clearinghouses or libraries. (This does not include conventional public information services designed for general public consumption.)

3. *Training:* Programs that provide instructional activities conducted directly by a federal agency for individuals not employed by the federal government.

Nearly all federal agencies make use of information interventions. Table 7-1 tracks spending (in constant 1998 dollars) for these information-based policies and programs between the years 1979 and 1999 by the cabinet departments and major independent agencies. The table shows that the United States has spent between $5 billion and $7.7 billion per year on these activities over the last twenty years. The table also shows that nearly every department and agency has invested consistently over the years in programs of this kind, suggesting the broad spectrum of policy problems that information policies address.

Table 7-2 shows how much has been spent over the years on the three types of information programs. This table shows that some of the programs use only one type of assistance (advisory services, dissemination of technical information, or training). Others use combinations of these types with other kinds of federal assistance. The first four rows of the table show the programs that rely strictly on the three information interventions, and the bottom four rows show the programs where information is combined with other forms of assistance. In the bottom half of the table, the fraction of spending on information cannot be separated from the spending on other activities. So the top half of the table represents the unambiguous cases of spending on information, and the bottom half shows a blend of information and other federal activities. From a low of $2.12 billion in FY 1984 to a high of $3.56 billion in FY 1999, these clean cases of information programs represent a small fraction of the federal budget but a significant and continuing activity across the federal government.

Of course, the CFDA data considerably understate the federal effort devoted to information. Investment in research and development is not included in these counts, because these programs are categorized in the CFDA as project grants, rather than any of these three information policies. Communications programs for the prevention of alcohol, health, or drug problems also are not included because these are usually classified as project grants. Statistical agencies are not included at all. Yet, national statistical systems are critical to policy in a wide range of areas, especially economic

TABLE 7-1 *Federal Spending on Information Programs by Department, 1979–1999**

	FY 1979		FY 1989		FY 1999	
	# Programs	Obligation	# Programs	Obligation	# Programs	Obligation
Agriculture	18	$1,837.4	17	$925.4	16	$1,009.7
Commerce	18	$861.2	16	$1,241.3	20	$1,901.3
Defense	3	$27.3	2	$21.2	2	$8.0
Education	0	—	1	$0.6	0	—
Energy	10	$16.0	6	$29.5	4	$10.3
Health and Human Services	9	$233.3	4	$29.8	3	$22.5
Housing and Urban Development	2	$5.2	3	$14.1	2	$17.5
Interior	25	$383.3	13	$90.0	17	$45.7
Justice	12	$133.1	14	$80.7	15	$113.4
Labor	18	$832.3	15	$856.2	14	$672.4
State	0	—	0	—	0	—
Transportation	5	$44.1	9	$82.0	10	$136.1
Treasury	3	$330.4	3	$369.4	3	$270.5
Veterans Affairs	3	$398.4	3	$223.0	3	$811.8
Environmental Protection Agency	0	—	2	$0.3	3	$36.0
Federal Emergency Management Agency	0	—	4	$8.6	5	$54.1
Small Business Administration	2	$44.4	5	$345.1	3	$1,175.3
Other Independent Agencies	48	$868.0	30	$688.9	30	$1,485.5
TOTAL	176	$6,014.6	147	$5,006.2	150	$7,770.0

*Obligations are in constant 1998 dollars, in millions.
SOURCE: Catalog of Federal Domestic Assistance, 1979, 1989, 1999.

policy and health policy.[18] So, the CFDA data are a very partial look at the federal effort devoted to policies that rely on information. Yet even this partial glimpse suggests a broad-based and extensive level of activity.

Table 7-3 shows a sampling of the U.S. laws and practices that require labeling and disclosure. These also cross many different policy areas: Truth in Lending, Truth in Savings, Environmental Impact Statements, Hazardous Materials Disclosure (OSHA), Toxic Release Inventory, Community Right to Know, Energy-Efficiency Labels, Nutrition Labels, Insecticide Labels, Tobacco Warning Labels, and Alcohol Warning Labels. Labeling and disclosure policies have added up to a substantial body of policy that relies on informing consumers, citizens, and employees about policy-related matters and expecting them to act in ways that advance policy objectives.[19]

Research on particular information strategies, such as public information campaigns, shows that campaigns have been used in many policy domains, including safety, public health, energy, environment, employment, civic participation, child rearing, family planning, and in countries all over the world.[20] A number of successful information campaigns have been conducted in poorer countries around the world, where governments have limited resources for more expensive interventions.[21] Other information

TABLE 7-2 *Federal Spending on Information Programs by Type of Program, 1979–1999**

	FY 1979		FY 1989		FY 1999	
	# Programs	Obligation	# Programs	Obligation	# Programs	Obligation
Information Programs						
Advisory Services and Counseling Only	17	$715.1	11	$758.4	16	$1,021.8
Dissemination of Technical Information Only	45	$1,188.1	45	$1,634.1	38	$2,097.5
Training Only	15	$88.0	12	$96.5	15	$109.6
Combinations of Information Programs[a]	31	$718.5	21	$565.7	13	$335.0
Programs That Combine Information and Other Tools						
Information Programs Combined with Grants or Payments	13	$807.5	18	$395.6	12	$338.2
Information Programs Combined with Direct Provision	29	$1,282.9	17	$220.0	16	$350.4
Information Programs Combined with Enforcement	14	$425.9	8	$332.5	15	$984.1
Information Programs Combined with Other Tools[b]	12	$788.5	15	$1,003.4	25	$2,533.5
TOTAL	176	$6,014.6	147	$5,006.2	150	$7,770.0

*Obligations are in constant 1998 dollars in millions.

[a]Programs that include any combination of Advisory Services, Dissemination, and Training elements.

[b]Programs that combine Advisory Services, Dissemination, or Training with Loans, Insurance, Sales or Uses of Property, or Federal Employment, or combine information programs with multiple other tools.

SOURCE: Catalog of Federal Domestic Assistance, 1979, 1989, 1999.

strategies have been quite prominent at the state and local levels. For example, many state and local governments have created "report cards" on the performance of schools, hospitals, and health-care providers, or discharges of pollutants by manufacturing facilities. The purpose of compiling and publishing such reports is to discourage undesirable behavior by service providers and to inform, empower, and encourage citizens to exert pressure at the street level for better performance.[22] Training for youth, for welfare recipients, and for dislocated workers has been another information strategy used heavily by state and county governments to reduce unemployment and dependency on welfare.[23]

Information is widely used as a strategy of intervention by all levels and kinds of government entities. However, the paucity of data makes it difficult to know whether its use is increasing or changing over time.

TABLE 7-3 *Major U.S. Disclosure and Labeling Requirements*

Title	Description	Date of Passage
Truth-in-Lending Act	Mandates disclosure of an extensive list of price and non-price information in consumer credit transactions	1968
Truth-in-Savings Act	Requires institutions to disclose account fees, terms, and annual percentage yield	1991 (effective 1995)
National Environmental Policy Act	Requires that environmental impact statements (EISs) be submitted to the Environmental Protection Agency	1969 (amended several times since 1969)
Energy Policy and Conservation Act	Attempts to improve efficiency of major home appliances through required energy labels and consumer education programs	1975
Fair Packaging and Labeling Act	Requires that information on various products (including food) be provided to consumers in a standard format	1966
Pure Food and Drug Act	Required sellers to give potential buyers accurate information about the weight and content of their packages	1906
Insecticide Act	Stated that labels could not bear "false or misleading" statements. Required that the proportion of each active ingredient be disclosed on label	1910
Nutritional Labeling and Education Act	Requires labels with specific nutrient content information, complete ingredient information, standards for nutrient content, and health claims	1990 (Deadline for implementation was May 1994)
Federal Insecticide, Fungicide, and Rodenticide Act (FIFRA)	Requires registration of pesticides for use in the United States and prescribes labeling and other regulatory requirements to prevent unreasonable adverse effects on health or the environment	1947
Freedom of Information Act	Provides that any person has a right of access to federal agency records, except to the extent that such records (or portions thereof) are protected from disclosure by certain exemptions or by special law-enforcement record exclusions	1966

The design and operation of an information tool require that policymakers carry out five essential tasks. First, they must define the target audience or subject of the policy intervention. Second, they must decide what information will be useful and convincing to that audience with respect to the policy intervention. Third, they must obtain this information. Fourth, they must deliver the information in a way that the audience will notice, believe, and act upon. Fifth, they must mobilize social and institutional contexts to support the desired use(s) of the information. Each of these tasks suggests a host of

TABLE 7-3 *(continued)*

Title	Description	Date of Passage
Electronic Freedom of Information Act Amendments	Addressed the subject of electronic records, as well as the subject areas of FOIA electronic reading rooms and agency backlogs of FOIA requests	1996
Tobacco Warning Label	Warning first required on tobacco products in 1965; "cigarette smoking may be hazardous to your health" Warning changed in 1969 to "the surgeon general has determined that cigarette smoking is dangerous to your health" By 1971, tobacco companies were required to disclose tar and nicotine content in ads In 1984, four different warnings, including risks to pregnant women and lung cancer (15 U.S.C. 1331–1341, 1982)	
Alcohol Beverage Labeling Act	Requires that the following two warnings be placed on all alcoholic beverage containers: "Women should not drink alcoholic beverages during pregnancy because of the risk of birth defects" and "Consumption of alcoholic beverages impairs your ability to drive a car or operate machinery and may cause health problems"	1988
Hazard Communication Standard (HCS)	Requires employers to establish hazard communication programs to transmit information on the hazards of chemicals to their employees by means of labels on containers, material safety data sheets, and training programs	Original rule was promulgated in 1983 and has been amended several times
Emergency Planning and Community Right-to-Know Act	Requires designated facilities to submit an inventory report of chemicals they are storing, using, or emitting to the LEPC, State Emergency Response Commission, and local fire department annually	1986
Toxic Release Inventory	Mandated the establishment of a database of companies that use and/or emit large amounts of certain chemicals into air or water	1986 (Database available in 1989)
Saccharin Study and Labeling Act	Required the following warning on products with saccharin: "Use of this product may be hazardous to your health. This product contains saccharin which has been determined to cause cancer in laboratory animals"	1977

issues for policymakers to consider. Each poses challenges and dilemmas, and each rests on assumptions about the ways in which knowledge is linked to action. In the discussion that follows, I refer to several important ways in which knowledge can be linked to action: rational information processing, providing feedback, framing, directing attention, mobilizing social identities, evoking social norms, and building social support. These are the underlying processes that permit information to be an effective policy tool.

Defining the Audience

Who is the target audience of policy intervention? Although this appears to be the simplest question, it is often far from simple. Policymakers must know whom they wish to influence in order to achieve the policy objective. Once the target audience is specified, the information policy can be tailored to that audience's needs and circumstances.

Several characteristics of the audience have important consequences for implementing information policies. The size and heterogeneity of the audience determine how easy it will be to reach them with any given strategy. Training, for example, is labor intensive and easier to execute for small homogeneous groups. When the audience is very large or geographically dispersed, training may be far too expensive or difficult; other strategies, such as public information campaigns, may work better.

The interest and receptivity of the audience to the information also may vary. Some audiences are in a position to benefit in a direct way from public information, such as employees at work sites where hazardous chemicals are used. These audiences are more interested in information, such as disclosure about the health risks associated with such chemicals, than people who see little connection with their own lives. Other audiences have little interest (or active hostility) to the issues about which policymakers wish to inform them.[24] When audiences are indifferent or resistant, policymakers need to work harder to find the avenues that will reach the audience. For example, information campaigns to prevent drunk driving may encounter denial from people who drink and then drive. However, the campaigns might find a more receptive audience in the companions of drinkers (people who might be designated drivers or those who might call a cab for someone who has been drinking), the hosts of parties where alcohol is served, or bartenders and restaurant employees. Each of these audiences has somewhat different agendas and interests to which policy must be sensitive. Similarly, acquired immune deficiency syndrome (AIDS) prevention information campaigns vary substantially when directed at gay men, intravenous drug users, prostitutes, or families of those infected with human immunodeficiency virus (HIV), because each of these groups has different levels of receptivity.[25]

Some audiences are already well informed about the subject of policy intervention. Others are not. The level of education and awareness in the audience prior to intervention is another major factor in designing an appropriate policy.

In some cases, policymakers seek to influence multiple audiences simultaneously. For example, information disclosure about the energy efficiency of home appliances was adopted to influence consumers so that people could make purchase decisions with more complete information about energy costs of refrigerators, water heaters, and other appliances. If consumers responded by taking the lifetime energy consumption of appliances into account, the policy goal of energy conservation was achieved. However, another important audience was the manufacturers of appliances. If the manufacturers knew that information about the energy efficiency of their products (and their competitors' products) would be provided to all potential purchasers, they might be motivated to put more energy-efficient products on the market. If more efficient products came to market as a result of the required disclosure, then the policy goal of the disclosure policy would be achieved through the influence on manufacturers as well as consumers. In such a case, the policy should be designed with the needs and interests of both audiences in mind.

If policy designers are not clear about their audience, or have too many diverse audiences in mind, they face overwhelming challenges in addressing all the remaining tasks.

Deciding What Information Will Be Useful

An information tool can only work when the information provided is relevant to the target behavior and is persuasive to those members of the audience whose actions are the focus of the policy. Note that the value of information must be judged in the context of the policy problem and the audience. The question is what information will be useful and convincing to these particular audiences with respect to the target behavior. In selecting information to use for intervention, policymakers need to take into account both general insights into human cognition and behavior and the particular context of the policy at hand. Let me begin with the general issues.

Information Processing

If people had limitless capacity to absorb and process incoming information and had endless motivation for continually updating their calculations about optimal behavior, the challenge of finding relevant and persuasive information would be less daunting. Policy implementation could focus on giving people complete, accurate, and relevant information about the desired behavior and its consequences, and people would adjust accordingly. Research in the cognitive sciences suggests that people do take in large quantities of information about the world and use that information in their reasoning and beliefs. However, the processes of human thinking are somewhat different from what a rational choice model implies, and this has major implications for the selection of information to use for policy purposes. Substantial empirical evidence shows that people are not vigilant information processors with boundless appetites for more and better evidence.[26] Once they do process information, the connections between incoming information and subsequent action are often circuitous.

One useful way to characterize human thinking is to recognize that people use both implicit and explicit cognition.[27] Explicit thinking is conscious and effortful; we are aware that we are thinking and can verbalize the content of that thinking. Implicit thinking is unconscious; it operates without effort and out of our awareness. In implicit cognition, we cannot describe what we are thinking. However, such preconscious cognitive work is neither emotional nor irrational. People learn without being aware that they have learned, or without being able to say what they have learned.

Recent research on such automatic or implicit thinking demonstrates that these forces influence an impressive range of everyday behavior.[28] People can detect systematic regularities in their environment and act in accordance with those regularities. However, when asked, they may not realize that they have been influenced by information because their processing was implicit rather than explicit.[29] In short, people have the capability to learn from information about the world even when they are not aware that they are learning and without an explicit purpose guiding their information processing. Therefore, information can be influential through both implicit and explicit cognitive channels. Much behavior that is of policy interest is habitual or routine. Even when people are not making deliberate, conscious calculations about what they do, they still may respond to information in the world around them and connect it to their subsequent behavior.

Although people exhibit systematic and predictable patterns of memory, perception, and inference, they cannot be counted on to act on new information in the ways that a purely rational model might predict.[30] The most important divergence from mathematical models is the human inclination to give great weight to prior knowledge and expectation, and to do this automatically and unthinkingly. Although people can and do process new information, they see that information through lenses created by prior knowledge. This has many adaptive functions, as it speeds information processing and offers clarity and guidance in the face of complexity and uncertainty. If people had to approach every decision without any preconceptions, the number of potential hypotheses that might explain a given situation would be overwhelming. It is advantageous to go into complex situations with some initial ideas and expectations, and to use these as a starting place for evaluating causal and probability relationships. However, it has disadvantages as well, in that people give insufficient weight and attention to information that is not aligned with their expectations and are not aware that they are doing so. For this reason, the prior knowledge of the audience plays a large role in their reactions to new information. More effort must be invested in changing prior understanding than in introducing completely new topics or ideas.

Framing

People not only bring their own preconceptions to their understanding, they also are very sensitive to the ways in which the information is organized and presented. The framing of information has significant effects on how people respond to it.[31] Concepts, categories, or knowledge structures are critical building blocks of thinking. These structures serve several fundamental purposes. First they partition the world into categories; as a result, people need to do less cognitive work. By chunking information, people are able to perceive, learn, and remember more efficiently.[32] Knowledge structures serve to organize and assimilate new information as it arrives. They make it easy to process information congruent with existing structures and make it more difficult to process disconfirming or incongruent data. They allow us to infer the details of particular situations (correctly or incorrectly) on the basis of abstract, general knowledge. They permit individuals to size up very complex, ambiguous, and contradictory information environments almost instantly and without any awareness of effortful processing.

The lesson for the implementation of information policies is that information processing (and subsequent behavior) can be influenced by which of several plausible knowledge structures are triggered in a given situation. Shifting the frame of reference or encouraging people to define the situation differently can produce shifts in information processing, with implications for the individual's preferred action.

People often have rather small appetites for seeking out new information, particularly with respect to either very familiar behavior or with respect to events or problems that are remote from their lives. Moreover, many policy problems are sufficiently complex and uncertain that even substantial information seeking would be unlikely to yield full information. The human inclination to rely on cognitive shortcuts creates an opportunity for information policies to exert influence. By introducing new information, policymakers may help people to elaborate and restructure what they already know. They can introduce new perspectives, interpretations, and evidence that can cast familiar decisions in a new light or can reveal the connections between apparently distant events and the here-and-now issues that people care about.

This added value becomes especially important when policymakers seek to use information policies to hold organizations accountable for performance. For example, warning labels about safe product use, environmental impact statements, or mandatory disclosure of the true costs of consumer credit transactions provide feedback about performance.[33] The citizens who receive this information often have their own direct experience with these firms, agencies, or organizations, but the information included in these interventions puts individual experience into a larger perspective and may reveal systematic patterns that would be very difficult for individuals to detect on their own. In this way, bottom-up accountability is enhanced by providing citizens with information relevant to their lives and concerns.

Tailoring Information to Particular Circumstances

In addition to these general ideas about how best to craft information messages to connect them to the desired behavior of an audience, research suggests several ways in which information needs to be customized to particular circumstances before it can be influential. In selecting information for purposes of intervention, policymakers can make better choices if they are well informed about the target audience and the situation. I have already discussed several important audience characteristics, especially prior knowledge. Important elements of the situation include the complexity of the information message, the credibility of the source of information, and the clarity of the link between the information provided and the outcome that policymakers hope to achieve. Conveying complex messages that audiences will understand and use is far more difficult than it may appear. For example, the Food and Drug Administration took years of research and many cycles of elaborate testing to address this question in the case of nutritional education.[34] The agency had to decide what nutritional information would be of value to consumers in helping them to select healthier diets and how to format the information in a way that consumers would understand it. The link between the information provided and the desired outcome was strengthened by placing the information on food product labels, drawing a closer connection between the situation in which consumers receive the nutrition message, and the food purchase decisions they make.[35]

Research also suggests that both the motivation and the ability to process new information are affected by the specific circumstances in which people are exposed to the information. When people are motivated and able to process information carefully, then their attitudes and behavior tend to be based on a thoughtful, attentive appraisal of relevant information.[36] However, many factors can disrupt this systematic, careful processing, leading people to rely much less on the informational content of messages they receive. Such factors include being distracted, overloaded, or stressed; finding the issue not personally involving, or irrelevant to personal circumstances; having little confidence in their ability to understand or judge the information provided; finding the message too intimidating or complex; or associating the message with an overly familiar or distasteful previous message.[37] Understanding these factors may help policymakers to craft information messages in ways that are more likely to be persuasive.

Obtaining the Information

Once policymakers have decided on the information they wish to provide to the audience(s), the information must be obtained. This is relatively straightforward when the government agency responsible for the information policy already possesses the information. It is another matter when the needed information does not yet exist, or is held by some other government or in the private or nonprofit sectors. If the information does not yet exist, the policy must include provisions for the information to be generated, collected, and delivered either to the government agency itself or directly to the intended audiences.

Obtaining information for policy use presents technical, organizational, and political challenges. The census, surveys, required reports as a condition of government funding, inspections, mandatory disclosure, and research are the major ways in which policymakers generate information for subsequent use in intervention. Some of the technical challenges commonly encountered include defining exactly what is to be measured and how, getting agreement on measures that can mean the same thing across diverse reporting units, and providing unambiguous guidance about the time frame for generating information. When the entities reporting data fail to use comparable measures, aggregate in comparable ways, or use the same time frame, then the information generated is neither valid nor reliable. Its value for policy purposes is thereby attenuated, both because it is less informative and it is vulnerable to attack by competing interests. Some of the organizational challenges involve convincing those who have the information to comply with the required data collection, finding ways to minimize the costs of imposing new information collection requirements on nongovernmental entities that cannot or will not afford to pay those costs, implementing procedures for monitoring and checking the accuracy or quality of data reported, and providing ways to aggregate and interpret the information. Some of the political challenges include coping with organized resistance to information collection from those who do not wish to disclose embarrassing or illegal behavior, or from those who seek to protect their privacy against government intrusion.

Many of these dynamics arise when policymakers collect information, especially from nongovernmental entities.[38] To ensure that they end up with the information they want, policymakers need to ensure that the data they collect are accurate, complete, and timely. Since those who control the information may have incentives to distort or conceal their reports, the collection of information nearly always needs some provision for monitoring to ensure that information is provided as intended. Monitoring, auditing, and checking of information collection may involve antagonizing those who provide the information, and hence may raise political opposition. In the United States, political values legitimize resistance to government information collection; this has led to extensive legal and budgetary restrictions on direct collection of information by government.[39] These political constraints may make it impossible to get the best possible information for the policy purpose and force policymakers to rely on information that is less costly to obtain but also less convincing to the audience.

Delivering the Information

Information cannot exert influence unless it reaches the intended audience. There are relatively few options for delivering information, but the choice among them has significant consequences. Policymakers may rely on direct contact with the target audience or may use an intermediary. Direct contact may be face to face, in groups, by mail, phone, or Internet. The intermediary may be the mass media (print or broadcast), information provided at the point of purchase or transaction, or some alternative institution, such as schools or the workplace. The selection of delivery channel may depend on the availability, cost, and effectiveness of the channel in reaching the intended audience. Some channels are obviously poor candidates for reaching desired audiences. Thus, making information available on the Internet may be an easy way to reach certain segments of the population, but not at all promising for reaching people with no access to computers or no familiarity with their use. Substantial evidence suggests that using multiple channels to deliver information is more effective than using only one.[40] With multiple channels, information that reaches people through one channel, such as television advertising, is reinforced by information that reaches people in the workplace or school.

Even if no intermediary is used, putting information in front of people does not guarantee that it will be seen, heard, or used. Government-sponsored information competes with information from entertainment, news, commercial advertising, newspapers, magazines, radio, mail, and, of course, the press of daily life. Somehow the information must be sufficiently compelling to attract attention to itself, to engage the notice of the reader, listener, or viewer. Information may need to be delivered to the audience in a way that is novel, creative, intense, graphic, fast paced, visually arresting, or suspenseful in order to engage the interest of the audience long enough to be noticed and remembered.[41]

Attention is a scarce resource, and can, in principle, be allocated to derive optimal advantage.[42] However, people seldom make such calculated choices about attention. Instead, attention is allocated by habit, rule, or simple sequencing.[43] People may be familiar with a problem but do not necessarily attend to all its dimensions or consequences when engaging in policy-relevant behavior. People need to be reminded of the connections between the information and the behavior. This is where information interventions enter the picture. Changes in behavior can be evoked by directing people's attention to some aspects of the problem rather than to others. Thus, environmental impact statements require attention to the environmental consequences of particular development proposals, adding to the consideration of economic factors that might otherwise guide construction decisions.[44]

Another path for getting people to notice and remember information is to connect information to social identity, especially to the concept of the "self." One notion of the self is the self-concept, that is, what each of us knows and believes about ourselves.[45] A second notion portrays the self as an active agent of mental life that knows, evaluates, compares, and act.[46] These ideas about the self can be used to mobilize particular kinds of action. People look at tasks to be done, set personal standards of performance, observe their own performance, and then evaluate their performance against their standards or goals. When individuals do not meet their own standards, they respond evaluatively, and these evaluations have consequences for subsequent behavior. The standards, however, are subject to change and influence, at least to some degree. Internal standards are influenced by social comparison, cues from the situation, and framing the task as relevant to values or domains important to the individual.[47]

Another critical dimension is the identity as a member of a social group (or groups). People take action to affirm their identity as group members when those identities are made more salient to them, or when their identities are threatened by external circumstances. Identity as members of a nation, a family, an occupation, a community, a race, a religion, or a political movement may inspire individuals to acts of conspicuous bravery as well as more ordinary adjustments in behavior.[48] People are deeply committed to the social groups they belong to, and their politics and actions are shaped by these affiliations.[49] Information policies can make use of these identities to mobilize individuals to actions consistent with their affirmed identity. Thus, for example, educational campaigns might link patriotism and national interests with requests to conserve energy, obey speed limits, or pay taxes, connecting policy-relevant behavior to a group identity that many people value.

Behavior of interest to policymakers is usually embedded in social contexts that guide and support it. Therefore, information interventions not only must provide information to individuals who can use it; they must recognize the social architecture of the contexts in which information leads to decisions and behavior. Information may be used to influence both individuals and other members of their social networks who can contribute to the desired behavioral impact. For example, a review of energy conservation programs finds that traditional mass-media campaigns to promote conservation have been less successful than programs that make use of social networks.[50] Door-to-door canvassing by local volunteers, neighborhood meetings, and cooperation with grassroots community groups made it much more likely that people listened to information about energy conservation and adopted appropriate measures at home. Similarly, mobilizing social support to help smokers quit may be more important than informing smokers themselves about the health risks of cigarettes.[51]

Individuals often care deeply about what other people think about their behavior and are influenced by the social meaning of their actions. An individual's own judgment of appropriate or desirable behavior often depends on cues from others, rather than on a strictly autonomous calculation of what to do. By communicating about the likely social consequences of particular acts, policymakers may make certain responses more likely.

Public policy can communicate information about what others are doing and thinking. Observational learning or modeling is a critical way in which people learn what to do and how to do it. As Albert Bandura says, "Through the years, modeling has always been acknowledged to be one of the most powerful means of transmitting values, attitudes, and patterns of thought and behavior."[52] People also get guidance from social comparisons about what to do, which is especially valuable in circumstances that are ambiguous or confusing.

Public policy can communicate information about the expectations that others have of the individual. This information helps to define the roles that people fulfill and to help them perform those roles in accord with the expectations of others. Acting in roles gives structure to situations and conveys to individuals a set of action alternatives consistent with their role.[53] However, under some circumstances the guidance offered by roles breaks down. Old roles may not offer guidance that applies to new situations. Multiple roles may impose contradictory demands, which confuse the actor about what to do next. In such situations, guidance about what particular roles demand (parent, employer, citizen, health-care provider, etc.), or which role demands are highest priority, can be helpful to individuals to guide action.

Public policy can communicate information about the approval or disapproval that others feel about the behavior. In physics, for every action there is a reaction. In social life, for every act there is an interact.[54] The more a person believes that important people in his or her life value the performance of a given behavior, the more likely that the person will engage in the behavior. Individuals conform with such norms in order to confirm belonging to a group. Experts in social influence have developed ways to invoke widely shared norms as techniques for engaging people in behavior that they would otherwise reject.[55] Information policies can connect the behavior of interest to a norm held by other people valued by the target individual.

Another mechanism by which information policies can influence behavior is by mobilizing social support or social pressure for the desired behavior. Policy-relevant behavior does not take place in a social vacuum. The direct influence of other people can make a significant difference. By stimulating family, friends, neighbors, professionals, or co-workers to reinforce the desired change, policy interventions increase their leverage on the problem. This mechanism is most likely to be influential when the target change imposes significant costs on the audience, so that the members of the audience require social support to behave as policymakers wish. For example, policies that promote social support are common in arenas such as weight loss, smoking prevention, drug and alcohol use, recovering from mental illness, or assimilating new immigrants.[56] The U.S. Department of Transportation used the slogan "Friends don't let friends drive drunk" in its advertising to discourage drunk driving. The effort here is to legitimize and mobilize the intervention of companions of the person who might drive under the influence of alcohol.[57] When the policy is aimed at organizations rather than individuals, similar dynamics may apply. Mandatory disclosure of a bank's pattern of mortgage lending can mobilize community groups to exert pressure on the bank to respond more equitably to community needs.

Social support and pressure become more important when the target behavior requires joint or coordinated efforts of social groups, rather than action by individuals. For example, research on armies in combat illustrates the importance of activating mutual support when asking soldiers to endure the dangers of war. Different armies use different policies and practices to foster that cohesion, including efforts to train and instill commitment to the well-being of the unit.[58]

When policy implementation makes use of social contexts, more opportunities for influence become available. Given that information interventions already use multiple pathways to influence, program managers can expand their effectiveness by engaging social and institutional forces.

IV. TOOL SELECTION

Substantive Considerations

Information policies are useful under a wide variety of circumstances:

- When the policy problem is caused by information asymmetry or information costs. Disclosure and warning policies are often used to correct problems of access to information by consumers, firms, nonprofit organizations, or others who are engaged in policy-relevant behavior. For example, the Truth in Lending Act mandates that lending institutions disclose prices and conditions that apply to a range of consumer credit transactions. These disclosures are intended to enhance the transparency of credit decisions and improve the efficiency of credit markets by ensuring that consumers are more informed about their options and purchases.[59]

- When the targets of public policy are very broadly dispersed but not organized. When policy outcomes require the cooperation of large numbers of people who are not organized into collectivities that make regulation efficient, information interventions may be especially useful. For example, the Smokey Bear campaign is directed at the safety behavior of individuals who hike, camp, or drive through national forests. This target audience is diverse, geographically dispersed through remote areas, and difficult to identify and influence through other institutions. Information campaigns are one way to exert influence under these challenging circumstances.

- When the interests of policymakers and those of target citizens are closely aligned so that voluntary compliance is a reasonable expectation. Information is especially useful when members of the target audience wish to engage in the desired behavior but are prevented from doing so by ignorance or lack of pertinent information. This is especially common in policies to reduce risks to health and safety. Policies to reduce the risks of pesticide use, for example, rely heavily on the provision of detailed information about proper use and safety precautions, in the expectation that consumers will use the product in accordance with label instructions.[60]

- When there is broad agreement about desired outcomes. In some policy areas, considerable consensus on outcomes exists. Few people object to receiving information explaining how to prevent their infants from dying of diarrheal disease by using oral rehydration therapy. In such cases, information interventions can capitalize on broad social support for the outcome and mobilize the energy and resources that citizens are already prepared to devote to the goal.

- When no legal or politically acceptable alternative tools are available for influencing behavior or when policy outcomes occur in partnerships or coalitions in which traditional authority-based tools are attenuated. Examples include behavior that takes place in private (such as sexual behavior) or in relationships that are deemed outside the domain of government action. In some countries this includes relationships between spouses or between parents and children, so that child abuse and domestic violence may be the focus of some information interventions. Information may also be aimed at getting people to stop smoking, drinking, misusing prescription drugs, or to eat healthier diets, because such personal risk taking is not considered to be an arena for other policy tools.

Information interventions are not well justified under other circumstances:

- When uniform compliance or response is desired or necessary to achieve the policy goal. Responses to information interventions are always variable, depending on the accessibility and receptivity of the audience to the information. If uniformity is valued, then information policies are unlikely to be the preferred option.

- When the policy problem is a shortage of resources. Information can help people make the best of the resources they have available, but this tool does not create new resources in a direct way.

- When no information is available that may help to alleviate the policy problem. This is most likely to occur when policy problems are grounded in conflicts of values or ideology, or tradeoffs among cherished values.

Political Considerations

As always, the policymaking process that leads to the selection of information as a tool is at least as much a political negotiation as it is an analytical exercise. Information interventions have substantial political advantages and disadvantages that have little to do with their prospects for successful achievement of policy goals.

Information interventions may have political appeal regardless whether they are well suited to policy goals. Politicians may find it appealing to use information, especially the more visible variants, when they are less interested in results than they are in the symbolism and visibility of policy. An example is some of the antidrug campaigns that offer no realistic prospect of reducing drug abuse, but symbolize governmental concern.[61] Information policies in this category may reflect self-serving efforts by policymakers to placate constituents by doing something without actually delivering any significant results. They may also convey reassurance or the intention to help in the future under circumstances when more direct action is too costly or controversial or when no one knows how to solve the problem more directly.

Information interventions are tempting to elected officials because they may be cheaper than alternatives. For example, the USFS has spent considerably less on Smokey Bear than on the engineering, surveillance, and containment techniques it uses to reduce the incidence and damage of forest fires. In developing countries especially, information interventions may be the only affordable option for policies affecting health, safety, and nutrition.[62] The Man Is Health campaign in Tanzania used radio broadcasts to advocate for construction of latrines; 700,000 latrines were built in response, all at private expense.

Political considerations also tempt policy designers to see problems as matters of individual choice rather than more systematic social or economic dynamics. Thus, public health information campaigns may "blame the victim" by emphasizing individual rather than structural changes to manage health issues. It is politically easier to blame individuals for eating improperly or getting too little exercise than to blame market forces and business decisions that employ people in stressful and risky jobs, aggressively promote unhealthy food, drink, and tobacco, and fail to provide affordable medical care.[63] It is politically easier to give communities and employees better information about toxic chemicals in their backyards and workplaces than to get companies to stop releasing toxic chemicals into the air and water.

Information interventions are politically attractive because they represent (or appear to represent) a commitment to educated choice and informed citizens. Information policies can provide resources to support civic education. For example, in the environmental domain, citizens require access to information before they can participate constructively in decisions with environmental consequences. The Toxic Release Inventory and environmental impact statements are designed to make such information available. Information policies can also smooth out some of the information inequality that gives better educated citizens more knowledge and access to knowledge than those who are less well educated. For example, public information campaigns to increase awareness of the health risks of asbestos were especially focused on blue-collar workers who had not learned about asbestos through other channels.[64]

Thus, information interventions are sometimes used even when they have little likelihood of working, because they have political benefits to government officials. In a variety of ways, information-based strategies can make government officials look good.

However, this advantage is double edged. Information carries political risk as dangerous, coercive, and tyrannical. The dangers of manipulation arise when government access to information is used by public officials "to legitimize favored courses of action and threaten or reassure people so as to encourage them to be supportive or to remain quiescent."[65] Although no single communication may appear coercive, the cumulative effect of state-sponsored information activities may be overpowering. Lindblom concludes that democracies, like authoritarian regimes, have embarked upon "capturing the minds of members of society in large part through kinds of communications that misrepresent and in other ways obstruct informed and thoughtful probing. . . . In the history of humankind there is nothing quite like this institutionalization of deliberate, planned, carefully calculated impairment."[66] To avoid undermining the basis of democratic control by citizens, government officials must tread carefully when attempting to influence what citizens know, pay attention to, and find most important.[67] Declines in the public's confidence in government information are particularly troubling, because they undermine the potential to use information for good purposes.[68] To preserve the credibility of government information, information interventions should be designed with sensitivity to the political risks by promoting informed and effective choice by citizens, with timely messages free of deception, with acknowledgment of multiple perspectives on issues, and with special efforts to help low-income citizens benefit from information.

V. MANAGEMENT CHALLENGES

The management challenges of public information fall generally into four categories: design of the policy, delivery of the information, follow-up mechanisms to support use, and the appropriate use of technology. I have mentioned a number of these in earlier sections, so here I highlight some of the key points.

The design issues include defining the audience(s), understanding the roles that information can play in influencing the policy-related behavior of these audiences, choosing which information to convey, collecting that information and ensuring its accuracy, informative quality, and completeness, and updating information when necessary to reflect changes in the problem and the audiences. To illustrate the management challenges posed by this list, consider the case of school performance reports. School performance reports may be required as a state or national strategy to improve the quality of particular schools and school districts. Which indicators of school quality should be included? This is not only a difficult technical issue, but it is vigorously contested by various groups with differing agendas for schooling. Should the information focus on measures of the outcomes of schooling (success in employment or higher education, mastery of knowledge or skills) or output measures (graduation rates, promotion to the next grade) or process measures (availability of a range of services, fair treatment of different children, class size, parent involvement)? Ideally, performance reports should include a range of different kinds of measures. Once these have been selected, the performance reports need to be comparable across different levels of schooling (elementary, middle, and high schools) and schools of differing size, structure, and emphasis. Perhaps the reports should emphasize how the schools compare with the state or national average, or perhaps comparisons should only be made with other schools with similar resources and student populations. School officials may need substantial guidance to translate their own records into the precise measures that are included in the reports. If each school has its own way of calculating graduation rates, then the reports of one school cannot be compared with the others. The veracity of the reports needs to be checked to ensure that schools report accurately. Delinquent reports need to be tracked down to ensure that the reports are complete. Schools that are short of staff and resources are especially likely to have difficulty in reporting fully and promptly. In short, the management of the performance report policy must contend with the diversity, conflict, complexity, and limited capacity of the schools providing information for the reports and find ways to ensure that the information collected serves the policy purposes.

Managers also need to address the process of delivering information to the audience. The delivery issues include finding channels for conveying information that will succeed in reaching the intended audiences (whether these are intermediaries or more direct channels) and creating a format for delivering information that is accessible and useful for audiences. To continue the example of the school report cards, the formatting of the report cards must permit parents, journalists, employers, taxpayers, real estate agents, home buyers, and other members of the public to make comparisons across schools. This requires that the format be simple enough to be understood, clear enough to permit comparisons with similar schools, but include enough information so that the audience can figure out which schools can be appropriately compared to which other schools. Using visual or graphic presentation in addition to text and numbers can enhance the likelihood that the information will be understood. The report cards also need to be delivered to the interested audiences through channels that are transparent and effective. This may mean the distribution of hard-copy reports to the press and to all parents of schoolchildren, oral presentations at meetings, or electronic distribution of reports, or some combination of methods.

The follow-up issues include overseeing the delivery of information, creating a capacity to reply to questions and inquiries generated by the information intervention (for example, with a toll-free number or Web site, or a technical assistance staff to facilitate understanding of organizational reporting), and designing strategies to support the use of information by members of the audience (training, technical assistance, evaluation). Follow-up is essential in the school report cards example when some schools fail to report fully or on time, or report data that are incorrect. Follow-up is also essential to ensure that data are collected and stored in a format that allows retrieval in the future. Parent or community groups may need help in interpreting the reports and understanding what they imply for raising school quality. Principals and teachers may need help in comparing their school's performance to other schools or to their own historical performance, and in translating the reports into a plan for improvement. Without this assistance, the value of the school reports for improving performance will be reduced substantially.

The technology issues include using computing and the Internet to make information widely available and to target delivery of information more efficiently, ensuring that data are complete, timely, and readily searchable, capitalizing on the interactive capabilities of technology to make information more useful and ensuring that technology is available to low-income communities and citizens with adequate support to allow them to use it. If the Internet is used as one channel for disseminating the school reports, the policy needs to address the successful transfer of reports from schools to a central location (usually the state education agency), where data can be made available. Once all of the reports are available centrally and standardized, verified, and posted, then access to the reports needs to be advertised and kept current. Members of the audience need to know where to find and how to obtain information in a usable form on a continuing basis. If the access to technology is limited among key parts of the audience (as is certainly the case in many school districts), then alternate delivery channels need to be developed to ensure that all parts of the audience have equal access.

Although it is just one example, the management challenges posed by a system of school report cards indicate that information interventions require considerable attention to management in both design and execution.

VI. EVALUATION

Perhaps because of political controversy about government collection and the use of information, the evaluation of information policies has been subject to considerable scrutiny and skepticism. In this section, I focus on research that addresses the effectiveness of three selected information policies: organizational reporting, public information campaigns, and labeling. Although I do not cover the full range of information policies, these three examples are widely used and illustrate the range of effects that policymakers can anticipate. After reviewing how and when these information interventions produce their intended effects, I turn to other criteria of evaluation: *equity, efficiency,* and *legitimacy.*

Organizational Reporting

Organizational reports used for public policy (like the school report cards discussed above) are designed to generate specific information within organizations and report it to designated audiences. These reports have the potential for two kinds of effects: those on the organizations that create the information and those on the audiences who receive it. Because the policy purpose of the reporting is usually clear to the staff of the organizations, the organizations may experience pressure to ensure that the data they report show the organization in a favorable light. This internal process is one possible pathway to improvements in the desired performance. The other pathway relies on the power of the audience(s) for the reports to exert influence over the organization, either directly or indirectly.

For example, civil rights monitoring has the potential to elicit change through both of these paths. The collection of data about racial disparities in education,[69] health care,[70] or mortgage lending[71] has resulted in adjustments by the school districts, hospitals, and banks to repair apparently discriminatory practices. As one report on mortgage lending concluded, "Lenders cannot take action if they do not realize that they are discriminating. Neither regulators nor fair housing groups have sufficient resources to investigate all lending institutions. Self-testing is one important strategy that lenders can use to monitor their performance and identify any problems that may exist."[72] Each time the report or survey is done, people within the reporting organizations must view their daily work through the frame of civil rights concerns, which may lead to adjustments in how they function.

Information from civil rights reports may also be used by groups outside the organization to lobby for change. Elected officials sympathetic to civil rights concerns, parents, patients, customers, and community groups have used data reported on the surveys to protest practices to which they objected. For example, comparative information about civil rights practices in public schools became a resource for coalition building on behalf of equal treatment for certain groups of children.[73]

In health care, organizational reports have proliferated in recent years, and in some cases have significantly improved the quality of care. For example, the New York State Department of Health has compiled and published data about New York hospitals' mortality rates for cardiac patients, beginning in 1990. As a whole, New York hospitals experienced steady declines in actual mortality rates from 1989 (the year before the report cards were released) through 1992, from 3.52 percent down to 2.78 percent by 1992, a decline of 21 percent. Using a risk-adjusted indicator of mortality, the rates declined even more significantly (by 40 percent).[74] Although some fraction of this striking improvement was due to a national trend in quality of care, much could not be attributed to these trends. During the period covered by the annual report cards (1989 to 1992), the observed mortality rate for cardiac patients in New York declined by 22 percent compared with a 9 percent decline for the rest of the United States.[75] Pennsylvania, like New York, introduced a cardiac surgery report card during this period; hospitals there also showed statistically significant improvements relative to the rest of the country.[76]

These desired policy results can be traced to the hospitals' responses to the organizational reports. A study of hospital chief executives in New York and California found that the reports were widely distributed among hospital staff. The administrators said that reports based on clinical data were rated more positively, understood better, and seen as more useful than reports based on administrative data.[77] Hospitals that received low-quality ratings for their obstetrical services in Missouri were more likely to launch changes in their policies and practices than hospitals that received higher ratings.[78] For example, Missouri hospitals with higher than average rates of Caesarean deliveries in 1993 had significantly decreased their use of Caesareans by 1994. When the cardiac surgery reports in New York revealed that surgeons who performed relatively few bypass operations annually had higher patient mortality rates than other surgeons, some hospitals moved to permit only high-volume surgeons to perform this procedure.[79]

Comparative reports on health maintenance organizations (HMOs) also seem to have led to some quality improvements. The Health Plan and Employer Data and Information Set (HEDIS) rating system judges HMOs on more than sixty quality indicators, including preventive practices, access to care, costs, and patient satisfaction. Faced with these and other publicly available ratings, some HMOs have changed their practices.[80] For example, Health Partners, a Minneapolis HMO, increased the percentage of children immunized against childhood disease from 54 to 89 percent in a four-year period. Health Partners' medical director attributed the improvement to the presence of the HEDIS ratings.[81] People had their attention directed to possible problems; they reconsidered their focus and frame for defining quality of care; they focused on improving their performance on those dimensions that would receive publicity.

Since 1988 the U.S. Environmental Protection Agency has required businesses that produce specified toxic chemicals to report the volume and disposition of any release into the environment, and these reports are publicly available. The Toxic Release Inventory (TRI) is the organizational report designed to help reduce the risks associated with these chemicals.[82] Evidence suggests that more than half of all reporting facilities made at least one operational change as a result of the public inventory.[83] Facilities with more hazardous emissions and located in more politically active communities have made more reductions in emissions than those with less active neighbors.[84] The more that government officials work to ensure that information is easily available, in multiple channels and in usable formats, the more successful they have been at reducing toxic releases.[85] A wide range of users have made use of the TRI, including federal regulators, state agencies, journalists, public-interest groups, ordinary citizens, as well as industry groups. Their use of this information has been facilitated by easy access to data through the Environmental Protection Agency's Web site[86] and through the Web sites of other interest groups that combine TRI data with other information on environmental conditions.[87] The combination of ready availability of data, an interested press, and active advocacy groups has put pressure on corporations to reduce their emissions, in some cases very substantially.[88]

The evidence thus far in health care, environmental protection, education, and civil rights suggests that the use of organizational reports by external actors (such as citizens, consumers, or patients) may be less important than the effect of reports on the actors internal to the organizations who produce the reports. Staff of the organizations are more directly motivated to use the reports as an opportunity to make improvements and avoid criticism or controversy.[89] The public users may become important users of the information, but their role in achieving policy goals seems to be less direct and predictable.

Public Information Campaigns

Public information campaigns, like the Smokey Bear campaign described earlier, attempt to change what people think and what people think about, usually with an eye to eventually shaping behavior. Like organizational reports, they may work along several pathways, including providing information, framing, directing attention, and evoking social norms. They have been used with a very wide range of audiences, from an entire nation to carefully targeted groups, across a very wide range of policy domains.[90]

The challenges of evaluating the effectiveness of information campaigns are severe; it is very difficult to isolate the contributions of information campaigns to complex behavior that is bombarded by many competing influences.[91] It is challenging to find appropriate samples to compare those exposed to a campaign to those who know nothing about the campaign's message. Individuals differ in how often they pay attention to mass-media channels in which they would be exposed to campaign messages.[92] These and many other factors make it difficult to judge whether campaigns have produced significant behavioral change.

The available evidence on effectiveness, imperfect as it may be, is mixed. Some campaigns do seem to have the intended effects on awareness of the issues, intensifying concern for the issues, reinforcing positive beliefs, and moving people toward action. Other campaigns have no discernible effects on the intended audience, whereas still others have counterproductive results, called boomerang effects. Fifty years of research have identified a number of factors that promote campaign effectiveness.[93]

When public information campaigns capture the attention of the right audience for the message, they are more likely to be effective. For example, the National Cancer Institute launched a campaign to increase consumption of fruit and vegetables, called the "5 A Day" program. The campaign designers selected a target audience of people who reported eating two to three servings of fruits and vegetables a day and were also trying to eat more. Focusing on this audience (rather than people who ate no vegetables at all or who had little interest in improving their diets) permitted the campaign to generate the most momentum for the available resources.[94] For another example, the U.S. Army's "Be All That You Can Be" recruiting campaign used a catchy slogan, sophisticated production values, and careful ad placement to attract the attention of better-educated potential recruits.[95] Many campaigns operate in only one channel (for example, television ads). However, research suggests that multiple channels are often more effective. For example, a community program to reduce the risk of cardiovascular disease used five types of media materials: television public service announcements, television shows (either thirty- or sixty-minute shows produced by the campaign), booklets and pamphlets containing information about risk factors, printed tip sheets offering brief health suggestions, and newspaper coverage, including a regular column by campaign writers.[96] The campaign found significant reductions in smoking, cholesterol, blood pressure, resting pulse, and overall risk for cardiovascular disease.[97]

Another predictor of effectiveness is whether campaigns deliver credible messages that audiences understand. Clarity of the message, credibility of the source, fit with prior knowledge, and the duration of exposure are all elements in how much impact the campaign will have on its audience. Campaigns promoting energy conservation illustrate these dynamics. For example, a field experiment in New York found that consumers were less likely to conserve electricity in response to a message from their utility company (Consolidated Edison) than in response to the identical message from the New York State Public Service Commission.[98] The credibility of the message source affected how the audience received the message. Efforts by the U.S. Department of Energy to convince homeowners to make energy-saving home improvements foundered when the messages used were too complex and technical; simpler messages had more impact.[99] A review of energy programs concluded that more effective appeals are characterized by vivid information, clear and simple language, personalized information (recommendations tailored to particular circumstances), credible sources, highly visible demonstrations of important arguments, and suggesting a range of actions to take.[100] For example, people who received a message that "the impact of air infiltration around doors, windows, and fixtures is equivalent to a hole the size of a basketball in your living room wall" were more likely to caulk and weatherstrip than those who received the correct formulas for heat-loss calculations.

Once the audience has seen the campaign and understood the message, the message must have an influence on the outcome of interest. Campaigns that use pathways customized to the audience's needs and interests and that use multiple pathways seem to work better.[101] For example, a rat control campaign in Bangladesh sent fliers and posters to farmers. The messages contained instrumental appeals (reporting the extent of damage to crops caused by rats) and religious appeals (Muslim texts advocating killing rats). The campaign orchestrated a collective strategy of working with neighboring farmers to eliminate rats rather than simply driving them from one farm to the next. However, many of these farmers were illiterate and therefore unlikely to respond to written appeals. So the campaign included another component that worked through children. In school, children received comic books and participated in essay contests about rats. The hope was that children would discuss these with their parents and that would amplify the direct campaign messages. Therefore, the campaign worked to inform, direct attention to, provide a point of view to, and mobilize a variety of kinds of social support for the desired activity. Significantly more farmers conducted rat control during the subsequent harvest season.[102] Another example comes from the long-running efforts to use information to prevent AIDS transmission. Research suggests that increasing knowledge about AIDS alone has an inconsistent impact on preventive behavior among gay men and heterosexual young people, and no impact on intravenous drug users or prostitutes.[103] Information campaigns were more successful in increasing safe sex practices when they not only informed people about AIDS, but also informed the audience about what other people think about AIDS. Young people in particular found it persuasive to learn that their potential sexual partners approved of safe sex practices, and helpful also to see examples of how to communicate successfully with a sexual partner about AIDS prevention. A more complete and realistic diagnosis of the reasons that people were not using safe sex practices led to campaigns addressed to the individual and interpersonal forces that lead to the desired behavior.

Of course, efforts to mobilize social norms as well as individual choice do not always work. The norms evoked by the campaign can only be effective if the audience is attached to the norm and sees the link between the norm and the target of the campaign. Many family planning campaigns, for example, emphasize the connection between the decision to have children and population pressure on the country, appealing to patriotism to limit childbearing. However, appeals to patriotism have not seemed to influence many couples' decisions to have children.[104] The link between the norm and the outcome was not convincing to the audience.

Many factors influence whether public information campaigns succeed in achieving the intended policy goals; I have here touched on only a few.[105] Much has been learned by applying the lessons of private advertising and psychological research to the public arena. However, much continues to depend on the fit between the policy problem and the campaign. Diagnoses of the relationship between the problem and the audience, of the variety of influences on the audience, and of the contexts in which the audience will receive and interpret the message contribute to the prospects for significant policy impact.

Labeling

Labeling and disclosure policies are designed to promote informed choices under conditions of some risk. The risk may be that of imperfect information, such as in the cost of consumer credit or the energy efficiency of home appliances, but usually the risk addressed is health and safety.[106] Labels help to mitigate the risks associated with products or activities that are legal but dangerous in some respects, such as alcohol, tobacco, household chemicals, or chain saws. Like organizational reports, they may have their intended effect in two ways, through decisions by consumers to alter their behavior with respect to the target product, or through decisions by manufacturers to alter products in ways that make them less risky. As with organizational reports and public information campaigns, the way in which information is selected and communicated to the audience turns out to have a major impact on the effectiveness of the labels, warnings, and disclosures.

Since 1980, the U.S. and Canadian governments have required major household appliances to carry a label indicating how much energy they require to operate. These labels provide consumers with the information to consider energy efficiency when making purchase decisions. The evidence suggests that the energy labels have had some impact on consumers' purchase decisions, but only a marginal one. Since the labels have been required, consumers have become much more aware of the labels; the public views the labels favorably as an energy policy strategy.[107] Those who are aware of the labels say that the label information affected their purchase.[108] However, the labels have not significantly influenced buying behavior, except for the relative handful of consumers who use extensive information search and compare alternatives without facing time pressure in making their purchase.[109]

Nearly everyone is aware of cigarette warning labels. Nearly 100 percent of individuals have heard that "cigarette smoking is dangerous to your health" and other text from the required warnings on cigarette packages. Because warning labels were introduced at the same time as other information interventions to educate the public about smoking, it is impossible to say whether the labels themselves have had much impact. Nevertheless, the vast majority of smokers do believe that smoking causes risks to health. United States' cigarette consumption, which had steadily increased up until the mid-1960s, stabilized after the introduction of antismoking campaigns, warning labels, and tax increases on tobacco, and has declined since the 1980s.[110]

Alcoholic beverage containers carry similar warning labels, as required by the Alcohol Beverage Labeling Act of 1988. A number of studies have examined the effects of the labels on drinkers and nondrinkers. Over time there has been a steady increase in awareness of the labels, although nondrinkers have had little exposure to the labels and are unsurprisingly less aware of their existence.[111] People do seem to remember the claims and find them believable.[112] However, the evidence suggests that the labels have relatively little impact on perceptions of heavy drinkers on the risks associated with drinking. In Australia, alcohol bottles are labeled not only with general health warnings, but also with information about the number of standard drinks in the container. This information has made it easier to judge how much alcohol drinkers consume. These labels seem to lead to improved accuracy among consumers in judging how much is safe to drink.[113]

Little research has examined changes in actual drinking. During the decade after the labels were introduced, alcohol consumption steadily declined. However, it is difficult to know what role (if any) the warning labels have played.[114] The best available evidence comes from one longitudinal study of twenty-one thousand African-American women that focused on drinking by pregnant women.[115] Controlling for patient characteristics and external factors (such as unemployment), this study found a decline in drinking during pregnancy that began in 1990, eight months after the implementation of the alcohol warning labels. This effect is consistent with attention to the warnings, because labeled bottles were just becoming widely available on store shelves. However, warning labels alone have not been sufficient to address all the risks of drinking in this vulnerable population.[116]

Nutrition labels have been required on all packaged food products since 1994 to help consumers make more informed food purchases and to discourage inaccurate or misleading health claims on food products. The labels include both positive and negative information about food elements associated with healthy diets (such as dietary fiber, serving size, and vitamins) and elements associated with disease and health risks (such as saturated fat, sodium, and cholesterol). Although many foods have been labeled by manufacturers for years, the mandatory labels are intended to standardize the formats and claims of nutritional content.[117]

A number of studies have investigated consumers' responses to the nutritional labels. Christine Moorman found that consumers got and understood more information after new labels were introduced; she suggests that the labels probably increased the frequency of comparative shopping because comparisons among similar products became cognitively easier to make.[118] Although consumers increased their use of information for both healthy and unhealthy products, they increased their use of information for unhealthy products much more.

Consumers' responses to the nutrition labels are affected by many factors. These include a consumer's prior knowledge of diet-disease relationships, health status, motivation to use nutrition information, level of skepticism about nutritional claims, ability to read the label, and shopping time constraints.[119] Certain groups of consumers are clearly less interested in nutrition information and therefore less influenced by the labels. These groups include households with low income, low levels of education, no children, low at-home food expenditures, and individuals without medical problems or medically restricted diets.[120]

Nutritional labels also work through influence on products. Food companies may reformulate their products to produce better profiles on the nutrition labels. Thus, shortly before the labels became a requirement, a number of cookie and cracker manufacturers changed their products to eliminate palm oil and lard, which contain high levels of saturated fats.[121] Manufacturers compete for market share with nutritionally aware consumers and seek to avoid unfavorable comparisons with other products.[122] This influence, which is nearly impossible to measure but clearly related to the policy goal, may occur regardless of whether consumers use label information at the point of sale.

Product labels informing customers of hazards and safety information are required on a variety of consumer goods and on substances that may be encountered in the workplace. As with health, energy, or nutrition labels, people who receive information about product risks are likely to respond to it in a variety of ways, according to their preferences for risk, alternatives, and social context. Like the other labels, product safety labels affect the behavior of users of the product only if the users notice, understand, and remember the information, and then adjust their decisions and behavior in accordance with the new information. Some market evidence suggests that these labels may affect purchases. Sales of soft drinks containing saccharin declined by 6 percent after a label warning of possible carcinogenic effects was introduced; sales of high-phosphate detergent declined by 12 percent after environmental risk information was added to packages.[123] Other evidence on product labels is less encouraging. People seem to be little influenced by information on safe use provided with pharmaceutical products, although they say that they read the mandatory package inserts.[124]

Consumers are more likely to notice and understand warning labels when they are noticeable (through attention to size, graphics, and format), placed in a context that makes sense for the target behavior (near the point of sale, near the point of use or consumption), believable, and not too long or complicated. Product labels offer new information but may do so in ways that overwhelm consumers with detail, contingency, and complexity.[125] Some users of household chemicals[126] and pesticides[127] have responded to complex labels with use that is *more* risky, suggesting that too much information leads to confusion or deliberate avoidance. The careful design of information to highlight the most important risks in clear and simple language (instead of "do not operate heavy machinery," use "do not drive your car") and provide explanations for taking safety precautions make it more likely that consumers read and understand the label information. Other label design components that seem effective in product use and misuse include: (1) a single, attention-getting word (e.g., "Warning!") as an indicator that the label contains important information; (2) a summary statement that identifies each relevant hazard; (3) a description of the outcomes of ignoring the hazard(s); and (4) descriptions of behaviors that may result in injury or damage and appropriate remedial or emergency treatment. Label formats also make significant differences in whether and how people respond. In Canada, a uniform system of pictograms has simplified the recognition of hazardous products. This is especially important when language, education, or age means that many labels cannot be read by illiterate adults or children.

As in the case of energy and nutrition labels, product safety labels may also achieve their policy goals through pressure on manufacturers to design safer products. One way for companies to avoid scaring consumers is to change the product. For example, Gillette reformulated Liquid Paper, Dow reformulated K2r spot remover, Kiwi Brands reformulated its shoe waterproofing spray, and other manufacturers have reduced the lead in their products, all to avoid warning consumers about carcinogenic ingredients.[128] Similarly, the 1997 decision by the European Union to require labels informing consumers that food products have been modified genetically has stifled the willingness of food companies, distributors, and retailers to market such products.[129]

Either through effects on product users or on manufacturers, well-designed warnings and labels do seem to reduce some risks and increase safe behavior.[130]

Additional Criteria for Evaluating Information Policies

Up to this point, I have focused on the effectiveness of information interventions under a variety of circumstances. I have devoted detailed attention to the effectiveness of information as a policy tool because many policy analysts assume that information is ineffective. I have discussed at length also because effectiveness is a first-order consideration in policy design. Assuming some threshold of effectiveness, other criteria for assessing information interventions become critical for understanding the use and impact of particular policies in practice.[131] In particular, the equity, efficiency, and legitimacy of information policies are important considerations in the policy process.

Equity

The criterion of equity raises concerns about the ways in which the benefits and costs of a policy tool are distributed among citizens. The distributive consequences of using particular policy interventions have both political and substantive impact. The implications of information policies for equity are not straightforward; in fact, they are quite paradoxical. One risk is that information interventions may exacerbate inequalities between those who already have a lot of information and those who do not. Citizens who are not literate, who have limited fluency in the native language of the country, who have limited education, who are too poor to afford newspapers, magazines, television, computers, or Internet access have less exposure to information from all sources, have fewer opportunities to benefit from the information, and find it more difficult to use information they do receive. These are the same groups who may find it most difficult to make use of information provided through public policy. Evidence shows that citizens from lower-income households have considerably more trouble than those in higher-income households in understanding and using information provided to the mass public, whether it relates to AIDS prevention, proper use of household chemicals, or the adequacy of the local public school.

The flip side of this argument is that information offers the opportunity for public policy to correct information gaps, empowering groups that traditionally have had little access to information relevant to their situation. In some cases, information intervention can narrow the advantage of the highly educated. Less well-educated citizens may make the greatest gains from information provided by government, especially when public policy uses channels and messages that are well suited to the needs of these populations.[132] With relatively little additional cost, information can be shared with groups who traditionally have been left out. For example, posting information about the annual performance of public schools on the Internet spreads information to many more parents than those savvy, well-connected, and persistent few who have always had access to performance information from school officials. Ensuring that the same information is available in alternate formats (in school newsletters, for example), in languages other than English, and that someone is available to answer questions about the performance indicators significantly broadens the group of parents who may be able to obtain, understand, and use the information.

Because information is a public good, it escapes some of the equity concerns that arise with other tools. However, getting and using information entails costs that vary across the population, and these must be addressed to enhance the equity of information policies.

Efficiency

The efficiency of information intervention sadly has been neglected in the policy literature. None of the major variants has been analyzed carefully to assess its cost-effectiveness under various circumstances. Although many claims about efficiency have been made, these are little more than guesses. The relatively low financial cost associated with some information policies tempts unwary analysts to conclude that they must be efficient. However, without better data on the full range of costs and benefits, it is difficult to see how this conclusion can be justified. This gap signals a major need for further research.

Legitimacy

In contrast, much ink has been spilled over the criterion of legitimacy of information policies. This has been a roaring debate in American political thought for nearly two hundred years. In 1848, Alexis de Tocqueville warned of the immense "tutelary power" of majoritarian government in the United States.[133] Tutelary power has always had the potential to undermine freedom and democracy by preventing citizens from asking too much or knowing what they want from government. This line of argument was picked up after World War II by those social scientists most appalled by the pernicious propaganda used by fascist regimes in Europe.[134] Concerns arose about the active manipulation of information by government on multiple fronts: threatening democratic processes by circularity of democratic control, by self-aggrandizement by government

officials, closing off opportunities for choice or autonomy, promoting passivity in political discussion, or as Paul Lazarsfeld and Robert Merton put it, "indirectly but effectively restrain[ing] the cogent development of a genuinely critical outlook."[135]

At the same time, other strains of American political thought have always celebrated
information, informed citizens, and education as bulwarks of democracy.[136] Information empowers various participants to enter into policy debates effectively, broadening
the networks of those whose voice is heard, who are represented in policymaking processes.[137] Education, training, and information may go beyond narrow, instrumental
effects on particular acts or decisions to influence a meaningful sense of community
membership, connection to other citizens, feelings of political efficacy, trust in political
institutions, and capacity to mobilize like-minded citizens to exercise power. These
positive effects seem to be amplified when policies are designed to encourage and
support involvement by diverse constituencies through provisions for interaction, discussion, and participation.

To inform, educate, and persuade is, from another point of view, to distract, deceive,
and manipulate. The very qualities that enhance legitimacy and strengthen democracy—sharing information with citizens who may act differently as a result—put legitimacy at risk by allowing government officials to evade accountability by discouraging debate and diverting criticism. Information interventions raise questions about
the legitimacy of the larger democratic system as well as about how citizens and governments deal with one another in particular instances. As Christopher Hood says,
"there is no such thing as an intrinsically innocent instrument of government."[138] However, the innocence of information policies evokes unusually intense contention. Policy
designers should not be lulled into accepting either the rosy or the paranoid view; both
have merit. There is a fine line to walk between informing people and systematically
deflecting popular demands on government that are the heart and soul of democracy.[139]

VII. FUTURE DIRECTIONS

Information interventions are quite common; yet, they get little attention in the policy
world. Some see them as too weak, and therefore just window dressing. Some see them
as too strong, and therefore antidemocratic. Policy designers must try to steer a course
between these extremes to design effective, efficient, and democratically wise public
policy.

Combinations of Tools

The analysis of the role of information in intervention reveals complementarity with
other forms of intervention, including most of the tools described in this volume.[140] As
the bottom half of Table 7-2 shows, many U.S. federal policies (representing billions
of dollars of annual spending) combine the use of information strategies with grants,
regulation, direct service delivery, and other tools. Information-based policies can show
people how to understand or interpret other policy interventions, encouraging people
to take advantage of services available to them or to comply with restrictions imposed
on them. They offer the possibility that people will learn new skills that will enable
them to participate more effectively in a range of public policy programs. They can
engage the norms and values that are implicated in behavior important for policy.
However, they do not always operate directly on that behavior—there is a more circuitous route from the policy intervention to the target behavior than is true, for
example, of a legal prescription or regulatory intervention. This more indirect path

makes it challenging to know, as a researcher or as a policymaker, precisely what effects can be attributed to the policy.

A Focus on Learning

Information and ideas as policy interventions are one way to stimulate and channel how and what people learn in organizations, professions, communities, or regions. However, learning is a process that is not easy to control or channel. You can design a learning environment, but once you set learning in motion, it is hard to be sure exactly where you will end up. In particular, learning will not always lead in a predictable way to producing intended results. Policy designers who want to ensure uniformity of compliance or response will need to look to other policy strategies.

The Role of Information Technology

New technologies for gathering, sorting, and distributing information have revolutionized government use of information through this century and are likely to present countless new opportunities in the coming century. As the advent of broadcast media made mass propaganda far more powerful, it also extended the empowering possibilities of providing much more information to many more people who, through higher levels of education, were better able to use it. Information technology has kicked off the same kind of revolutionary consequences for public policy use of information. In particular, the widespread availability of computers and Internet access makes it possible to gather, analyze, and send information in ways that would have been unimaginable in the recent past. Information technology also enables interactive exchange of information, so that citizens can customize the information they seek, at the same time that government officials can identify more efficiently those citizens whom they wish to influence. Many of the examples of information interventions discussed in this chapter have been made practical at reasonable cost thanks to the power of information technology.

The technical advances of coming years will enable future generations of information policies to become more sophisticated, customized, and widespread. However, the ease or difficulty of moving and classifying information is only partly a matter of technology. Technology is embedded within social and political institutions, and its users are embedded within social and political communities. The contexts in which information is created, interpreted, categorized, communicated, and understood have always been, and will remain, the most powerful determinants of the value of public information.

VIII. SUGGESTED READING

Gormley, William T., Jr., and David Weimer. *Organizational Report Cards*. Cambridge, Mass.: Harvard University Press, 1999.

Hadden, Susan G. *Read the Label: Reducing Risk by Providing Information*. Boulder: Westview Press, 1986.

Lindblom, Charles E. *Inquiry and Change*. New Haven: Yale University Press, 1990.

Rice, Ronald E., and C. K. Atkins. *Public Communication Campaigns*. 2d ed. Newbury Park, Calif.: Sage Publications, 1989.

Viscusi, W. Kip, and Richard Zeckhauser. "Hazard Communication: Warnings and Risk," *Annals of the American Academy of Political and Social Science* 545 (1996): 106–115.

Weiss, Janet A., and Mary Tschirhart. "Public Information Campaigns as Policy Instruments," *Journal of Policy Analysis and Management* 13 (1994): 82–119.

1. E. E. Morrison, *Guardian of the Forest: A History of the Smokey Bear Program* (New York: Vantage Press, 1976); Rice, R. E. "Smokey Bear," in *Public Communication Campaigns,* 2d ed., eds. R. E. Rice and C. K. Atkin (Beverly Hills, Calif.: Sage, 1989).

2. Rice, "Smokey Bear."

3. Persuasion (what people think) and agenda setting (what people think about) are the pillars of Bernard Cohen's analysis of the effects of mass media more generally. Bernard C. Cohen, *The Press and Foreign Policy* (Princeton: Princeton University Press, 1963).

4. Janet A. Weiss, "Ideas and Inducements in Mental Health Policy," *Journal of Policy Analysis and Management* 9 (1990): 178–200.

5. Boyce Thompson, "Managing Our Waste: A *Governing* Special Report." *Governing* 2 (September 1989): 5A–26A.

6. Pamela Shoemaker, ed., *Communication Campaigns about Drugs* (Hillsdale, N.J.: Erlbaum, 1989).

7. See Philip Kotler and Eduardo L. Roberto, *Social Marketing* (New York: Free Press, 1989).

8. Frank Easterbrook and Daniel Fischel, "Mandatory Disclosure and the Protection of Investors," *Virginia Law Review* 70 (1984): 669–715.

9. Milbrey McLaughlin, *Evaluation and Reform* (Cambridge, Mass.: Ballinger, 1976).

10. Janet A. Weiss, "The Powers of Problem Definition: The Case of Government Paperwork," *Policy Sciences* 22 (1989): 97–121.

11. "Technical Assistance in the U.S. Department of Health and Human Services: Report of the Technical Assistance and Training Liaison Work Group," U.S. Department of Health and Human Services, July 1997.

12. Evert Vedung and Frans C. J. van der Doelen, "The Sermon: Information Programs in the Public Policy Process: Choice, Effects, and Evaluation," in *Carrots, Sticks and Sermons: Policy Instruments and Their Evaluation,* eds. Marie-Louise Bemelmans-Videc, Ray C. Rist, and Evert Vedung (New Brunswick, N.J.: Transaction Publishers, 1998), 104.

13. Also see Hood's discussion of information as government "nodality." Christopher C. Hood, *The Tools of Government* (Chatham, N.J.: Chatham House, 1988).

14. Charles E. Lindblom, *Politics and Markets* (New York: Basic Books, 1977); Charles E. Lindblom, *Inquiry and Change: The Troubled Attempt to Understand and Shape Society* (New Haven: Yale University Press, 1990).

15. Jurgen Habermas, *The Theory of Communicative Action,* trans. by Thomas McCarthy (Boston: Beacon Press, 1984).

16. Mark Yudof, *When Government Speaks* (Berkeley: University of California Press, 1983); Jacques Ellul, *Propaganda: The Formation of Men's Attitudes,* trans. by Konrad Kellen and Jean Lerner (New York: Knopf, 1965); Benjamin Ginsberg, *The Captive Public: How Mass Opinion Promotes State Power* (New York: Basic Books, 1986).

17. Janet A. Weiss, "Policy Design for Democracy: A Look at Public Information Campaigns," in *Public Policy for Democracy,* eds. Helen Ingram and Steven Smith (Washington D.C.: The Brookings Institution, 1993), 99–118; Deborah Stone, *Policy Paradox* (New York: W. W. Norton, 1997), 303; Doris Graber, *Public Sector Communication* (Washington, D.C.: Congressional Quarterly Press, 1999).

18. William Alonso and Paul Starr, *The Politics of Numbers* (New York: Russell Sage Foundation, 1987).

19. See also Wesley Magat and Kip Viscusi, *Informational Approaches to Regulation* (Cambridge, Mass.: MIT Press, 1992); Susan G. Hadden, *Read the Label: Reducing Risk by Providing Information* (Boulder: Westview Press, 1986).

20. Janet A. Weiss and Mary Tschirhart, "Public Information Campaigns as Policy Instruments," *Journal of Policy Analysis and Management* 3, no. 1 (1994): 82–119; Robert Hornik, *Development Communication: Information, Agriculture, and Nutrition in the Third World* (New York: Longman, 1988); C. P. Cell, *Revolution at Work: Mobilization Campaigns in China* (New York: Academic Press, 1977).

21. Robert Hornik, *Development Communication.*

22. William Gormley and David Weimer, *Organizational Report Cards.*

23. Burt S. Barnow and Christopher King, eds., *Improving the Odds: Increasing the Effectiveness of Publicly Funded Training* (Washington, D.C.: Urban Institute Press, 2000).

24. Sharyn Sutton, George Balch, and Craig Lefebvre, "Strategic Questions for Consumer-Based Health Communications," *Public Health Reports* 110 (1995): 725–733.

25. Jeffrey Fisher and William Fisher, "Changing AIDS-Risk Behavior," *Psychological Bulletin* 111 (1992): 455–474.

26. Amartya Sen, "Rational Fools: A Critique of the Behavioral Foundations of Economic Theory," in *Beyond Self-Interest,* ed. Jane J. Mansbridge (Chicago: University of Chicago Press, 1990); Richard Thaler, *Quasi-Rational Economics* (New York: Russell Sage Foundation, 1991).

27. Keith J. Holyoak and Barbara A. Spellman, "Thinking," *Annual Review of Psychology* 44 (1993): 265–315.

28. C. Neil Macrae and Galen V. Bodenhausen, "Social Cognition: Thinking Categorically about Others," *Annual Review of Psychology* 51 (2000) 93–120; J. A. Bargh, "The Automaticity of Everyday Life," in *Advances in Social Cognition,* ed. Robert Wyer, vol. 10 (Mahwah, N.J.: Erlbaum, 1997), 1–61.

29. For example, people who were asked to predict the future motion of objects dropped from moving carriers often made bad predictions. When these same people were shown a graphical representation of the path they had predicted for the object, they could readily discriminate between those trajectories that were physically possible and those that were physically impossible. At some level they knew the rules of physics that applied but were unable to use the rules explicitly in making their predictions. Mary K. Kaiser et al., "Judgments of Natural and Anomalous Trajectories in the Presence and Absence of Motion," *Journal of Experimental Psychology: Learning, Memory, and Cognition* 11 (1985): 795–803; Dennis R. Proffitt et al., "Understanding Wheel Dynamics," *Cognitive Psychology* 22, no. 3 (1990): 342–373.

30. Johnson-Laird, P. "Deductive Reasoning," *Annual Review of Psychology* 50 (1999): 109–135.

31. Alexander Rothman and Peter Salovey, "Shaping Perceptions to Motivate Healthy Behavior: The Role of Message Framing," *Psychological Bulletin* 121 (1997): 3–19; Daniel Kahneman and Amos Tversky, "Choices, Values, and Frames," *American Psychologist* 39 (1984): 341–350.

32. Susan Fiske and Shelley Taylor, *Social Cognition* (Reading, Mass.: Addison-Wesley, 1990).

33. See, for example, William T. Gormley, Jr., and David L. Weimer, *Organizational Report Cards* (Cambridge, Mass.: Harvard University Press, 1990).

34. Julie A. Caswell and Daniel I. Padberg, "Toward a More Comprehensive Theory of Food Labels," *American Journal of Agricultural Economics* 74 (May 1992): 460–468.

35. William J. McGuire, "Theoretical Foundations of Campaigns," in *Public Communication Campaigns,* 2d ed., eds. R. Rice and C. Atkin (Newbury Park, Calif.: Sage, 1989); Cialdini, *Influence.*

36. Richard E. Petty and D. T. Wegener, "Attitude Change: Multiple Roles for Persuasion Variables," in *Handbook of Social Psychology,* 4th ed., eds. Daniel Gilbert et al., vol. 1 (1998): 323–390.

37. Wendy Wood, "Attitude Change: Persuasion and Social Influence," *Annual Review of Psychology* 51 (2000): 539–570.

38. Note, however, that it is often difficult to collect information from other governmental agencies, even at the same level of government. For examples of this difficulty in federal education policy, see Janet A. Weiss and Judith E. Gruber, "The Managed Irrelevance of Federal Education Statistics," in *The Politics of Numbers,* eds. William Alonso and Paul Starr (New York: Russell Sage Foundation, 1987).

39. Janet A. Weiss, "The Powers of Problem Definition: The Case of Government Paperwork," *Policy Sciences* 22 (1989): 97–121.

40. Caroline Schooler, Steven Chaffee, June Flora, and Connie Roser, "Health Campaign Channels: Tradeoffs among Reach, Specificity, and Impact," *Human Communication Research* 24 (1998): 410–432.

41. Lewis Donohew, Elizabeth Lorch, and Philip Palmgreen, "Applications of a Theoretic Model of Information Exposure to Health Interventions," *Human Communication Research* 24 (1998): 454–468.

42. James March and Herbert Simon, *Organizations* (New York: Wiley, 1958).

43. James March, *A Primer on Decision Making* (New York: Free Press, 1994).

44. Marc Landy, Marc Roberts, and Stephen Thomas, *The Environmental Protection Agency: Asking the Wrong Questions* (New York: Oxford University Press, 1990); Serge Taylor, *Making Bureaucracies Think* (Stanford, Calif.: Stanford University Press, 1984).

45. David H. Demo, "The Self-Concept over Time: Research Issues and Directions," *Annual Review of Sociology* 18 (1992): 303–326.

46. Albert Bandura, *Social Foundations of Thought and Action: A Social Cognitive Theory* (Englewood Cliffs, N.J.: Prentice-Hall, 1986).

47. Bandura, *Social Foundations of Thought and Action.*

48. Craig Calhoun, "Indirect Relationships and Imagined Communities: Large-Scale Social Integration and the Transformation of Everyday Life," in *Social Theory for a Changing Society* (New York: Russell Sage Foundation, 1991), 95–130.

49. Aaron Wildavsky, "Choosing Preferences by Constructing Institutions: A Cultural Theory of Preference Formation," *American Political Science Review* 81 (1987): 3–21.

50. Scott Coltrane, Dane Archer, and Elliot Aronson, "The Social Psychological Foundations of Successful Energy Conservation Programs," *Energy Policy* (April 1986): 133–148.

51. Clifford W. Scherer and Napoleon K. Juanillo, Jr., "Bridging Theory and Praxis: Reexamining Public Health Communication," in *Communication Yearbook/15*, ed. S. A. Deetz (Newbury Park, Calif.: Sage, 1992), 312–342.

52. Bandura, *Social Foundations of Thought and Action*, 47.

53. Robert Merton, "Structural Analysis in Sociology," in *Approaches to the Study of Social Structure*, ed. Peter Blau (New York: Free Press, 1975), 21–52.

54. Karl Weick, "Cognitive Processes in Organizations," in *Research in Organizational Behavior*, ed. Barry Staw, vol. 1 (Greenwich, Conn: JAI Press, 1979), 41–74; Karl Weick, *Sensemaking in Organizations* (Thousand Oaks, Calif.: Sage, 1995).

55. Robert B. Cialdini, *Influence: Science and Practice*, 3d ed. (New York: HarperCollins, 1993); Wendy Wood, "Attitude Change: Persuasion and Social Influence," *Annual Review of Psychology* 51 (2000): 539–570.

56. Terrance L. Albrecht and Mara B. Adelman, *Communicating Social Support* (Newbury Park, Calif.: Sage, 1987).

57. Weiss and Tschirhart, "Public Information Campaigns."

58. William D. Henderson, *Cohesion, the Human Element in Combat: Leadership and Societal Influence in the Armies of the Soviet Union, the United States, North Vietnam, and Israel* (Washington, D.C.: National Defense University Press, 1985).

59. Thomas Durkin and Gregory Elliehausen, "The Issue of Market Transparency: Truth-in-Lending Disclosure Requirements as Consumer Protections in the United States," in *Enhancing Consumer Choice*, ed. Robert Mayer (Columbia, Mo.: American Council on Consumer Interests, 1990), 255–265.

60. Hadden, *Read the Label*, chap. 7.

61. A. Forman, and S. Lachter, "The National Institute on Drug Abuse Cocaine Prevention Campaign," in *Communication Campaigns about Drugs*, ed. P. J. Shoemaker (Hillsdale, N.J.: Erlbaum, 1989).

62. Hornik, *Development Communication.*

63. Charles Salmon, ed., *Information Campaigns: Managing the Process of Social Change* (Newbury Park, Calif.: Sage, 1989); Lawrence Wallack, "Improving Health Promotion: Media Advocacy and Social Marketing Approaches," in *Mass Communication and Public Health*, eds. C. Atkin and L. Wallack (Newbury Park, Calif.: Sage, 1990).

64. V. S. Freimuth, and J. P. Van Nevel, "Reaching the Public: The Asbestos Awareness Campaign," *Journal of Communications* (spring 1981): 155–167.

65. Murray Edelman, *Constructing the Political Spectacle* (Chicago: University of Chicago Press, 1988) 104.

66. Charles E. Lindblom, *Inquiry and Change* (New Haven: Yale University Press, 1990), 114.

67. Yudof, *When Government Speaks.*

68. Covello discusses research on public confidence in information on environmental health risks, concluding that government communications often appear "unresponsive, dishonest, or

evasive." Vincent T. Covello, "Risk Communication: An Emerging Area of Health Communication Research," in *Communication Yearbook/15*, ed. S. A. Deetz (Newbury Park, Calif.: Sage, 1992), 359–373.

69. Janet A. Weiss and Judith E. Gruber, "Deterring Discrimination with Data," *Policy Sciences* 17 (1984): 82–119.

70. David Barton Smith, "Addressing Racial Inequities in Health Care: Civil Rights Monitoring and Report Cards," *Journal of Health Politics, Policy and Law* 23 (1998): 75–105.

71. Urban Institute, "What We Know about Mortgage Lending Discrimination in America," Report to the Department of Housing and Urban Development, September 1999. http://www.hud.gov/pressrel/newsconf/menu.html.

72. Urban Institute, "What We Know about Mortgage Lending Discrimination in America."

73. Weiss and Gruber, "Deterring Discrimination with Data."

74. Edward L. Hannan, Harold Kilburn, Jr., Michael Racz, Eileen S. Shields, and Mark R. Chassin, "Improving the Outcomes of Coronary Artery Bypass Surgery in New York State," *Journal of the American Medical Association* 271 (1994): 761–766; Mark R. Chassin, Edward L. Hannan, and Barbara A. DeBuono, "Benefits and Hazards of Reporting Medical Outcomes Publicly," *New England Journal of Medicine* 334, no. 6 (1996): 394–398.

75. Eric D. Peterson, Elizabeth DeLong, James G. Jollis, Lawrence H. Muhlbaier, and Daniel B. Mark, "The Effects of New York's Bypass Surgery Provider Profiling on Access to Care and Patient Outcomes in the Elderly," *Journal of the American College of Cardiology* 32, no. 4 (1998): 993–999.

76. William T. Gormley, Jr., and David L. Weimer, *Organizational Report Cards.*

77. P. S. Romano, J. A. Rainwater, and D. Antonius, "Grading the Graders: How Hospitals in California and New York Perceive and Interpret Their Report Cards," *Medical Care* 37 (1999): 295–305.

78. Daniel R. Longo, Garland Land, Wayne Schramm, Judy Fraas, Barbara Hoskins, and Vicky Howell, "Consumer Reports in Health Care: Do They Make a Difference in Patient Care?" *Journal of the American Medical Association* 278, no. 19 (1997): 1579–1784.

79. Edward L. Hannan, Albert L. Siu, Dinesh Kumar, Harold Kilburn, Jr., and Mark R. Chassin, "The Decline in Coronary Artery Bypass Graft Surgery Mortality in New York State: The Role of Surgeon Volume," *Journal of the American Medical Association* 273 (1995): 209–213.

80. Thomas Burton, "Operation That Rated Hospitals Was Success, but the Patience Died," *Wall Street Journal* (23 August 1999): 1.

81. John Morrissey, "HEDIS to Expand Performance Guidelines," *Modern Healthcare* (22 July 1996).

82. Archon Fung and Dara O'Rourke, "Reinventing Environmental Regulation from the Grassroots Up: Explaining and Expanding the Success of the Toxics Release Inventory," *Environmental Management* 25 (2000): 115–127.

83. U.S. General Accounting Office, *Toxic Chemicals: EPA's Toxic Release Inventory Is Useful but Can Be Improved* (June 1991).

84. James T. Hamilton, "Exercising Property Rights to Pollute: Do Cancer Risks and Politics Affect Plant Emission Reductions?" *Journal of Risk and Uncertainty* 18, no. 2 (August 1999): 105–124.

85. Chilik Yu, Laurence O'Toole, James Cooley, Gail Cowie, Susan Crow, Stephanie Herbert, "Policy Instruments for Reducing Toxic Releases," *Evaluation Review* 22 (1998): 571–589.

86. For the data organized by facility, see http://www.epa.gov/opptintr/tri; for the data organized by industry sector, see http://www.epa.gov/oeca/sfi.

87. See, for example, the Environmental Defense Fund's Scorecard at http://www.score card.org.

88. Mary Graham, "Regulation by Shaming," *Atlantic Monthly* (April 2000): 36–40; Fung and O'Rourke, "Reinventing Environmental Regulation."

89. Martin Marshall, Paul Shekelle, Sheila Leatherman, and Robert Brook, "The Public Release of Performance Data: What Do We Expect to Gain?" *Journal of the American Medical Association* 283, no. 14 (12 April 2000): 1866–1874.

90. Weiss and Tschirhart, "Public Information Campaigns."

91. Philip Kotler and Eduardo Roberto, *Social Marketing: Strategies for Changing Public Behavior* (New York: Free Press, 1989).

92. John Zaller, "The Myth of Massive Media Impact Revived: New Support for a Discredited Idea," in *Political Persuasion and Attitude Change,* eds. Diana Mutz, Paul Sniderman, and Richard Brody (Ann Arbor: University of Michigan Press, 1996), 17–78.

93. For reviews of some of this work, see Everett M. Rogers and J. Douglas Storey, "Communication Campaigns," in *Handbook of Communication Science,* eds. C. R. Berger and S. H. Chaffee (Beverly Hills, Calif.: Sage, 1987), 817–846; Donald F. Roberts and Nathan Maccoby, "Effects of Mass Communication," in *The Handbook of Social Psychology,* 3d ed., eds. G. Lindzey and E. Aronson (New York: Random House, 1985); Charles Salmon, ed., *Information Campaigns: Managing the Process of Social Change* (Newbury Park, Calif.: Sage, 1989); William J. McGuire, "Theoretical Foundations of Campaigns," in *Public Communication Campaigns,* 2d ed., eds. R. Rice and C. Atkin (Newbury Park, Calif.: Sage, 1989).

94. Sharyn Sutton, George Balch, and Craig Lefebvre, "Strategic Questions for Consumer-Based Health Communications," *Public Health Reports* 110 (1995): 725–733.

95. L. Shyles and J. E. Hocking, "The Army's 'Be All That You Can Be' Campaign," *Armed Forces and Society* 16 (1990): 369–383.

96. Carol Schooler, Steven Chaffee, June Flora, and Connie Roser, "Health Campaign Channels: Tradeoffs among Reach, Specificity, and Impact," *Human Communication Research* 24 (1998): 410–432.

97. June A. Flora, Nathan Maccoby, and John W. Farquhar, "Communication Campaigns to Prevent Cardiovascular Disease," in *Public Communication Campaigns,* 2d ed., eds. R. Rice and C. Atkin (Newbury Park, Calif.: Sage, 1989).

98. C. S. Craig and J. M. McCann, "Assessing Communication Effects on Energy Conservation," *Journal of Consumer Research* 5 (1978): 82–88.

99. B. Farquhar-Pilgrim and F. F. Shoemaker, "Campaigns to Affect Energy Behavior," in *Public Communication Campaigns,* eds. R. Rice and W. Paisley (Beverly Hills, Calif.: Sage, 1981).

100. Scott Coltrane, Dane Archer, and Elliot Aronson, "The Social Psychological Foundations of Successful Energy Conservation Programs," *Energy Policy* (April 1986): 133–148.

101. Weiss and Tschirhart, "Public Information Campaigns."

102. R. Adhikarya, "The Strategic Extension Campaigns on Rat Control in Bangladesh," in *Public Communication Campaigns,* 2d ed., eds. R. E. Rice and C. K. Atkin (Newbury Park, Calif.: Sage, 1989).

103. Jeffrey Fisher and William Fisher, "Changing AIDS-Risk Behavior," *Psychological Bulletin* 111 (1992): 455–474.

104. Rogers and Storey, "Communication Campaigns."

105. For an extended discussion, see Weiss and Tschirhart, "Public Information Campaigns."

106. Susan G. Hadden, *Read the Label: Reducing Risk by Providing Information* (Boulder: Westview Press, 1986); Wesley A. Magat and W. Kip Viscusi, *Informational Approaches to Regulation* (Cambridge, Mass.: MIT Press, 1992).

107. John D. Claxton, J. R. Brent Ritchie, and Gordon H. G. McDougall, "Evaluating Acceptability and Effectiveness of Consumer Energy Conservation Programs," *Journal of Economic Psychology* 4, nos. 1–2 (1983): 71–83.

108. Robert Dyer and Thomas Maronick, "An Evaluation of Consumer Awareness and Use of Energy Labels in the Purchase of Major Appliances: A Longitudinal Analysis," *Journal of Public Policy and Marketing* 7 (1988): 83–97.

109. Dyer and Maronick, "An Evaluation of Consumer Awareness."

110. Kip Viscusi and Richard Zeckhauser, "Hazard Communication: Warnings and Risk," *Annals of the American Academy of Political and Social Science* 545 (1996): 106–115; Kenneth Warner, "The Effects of the Anti-Smoking Campaign on Cigarette Consumption," *American Journal of Public Health* 67 (1977): 645–650.

111 Michael E. Hilton, "An Overview of Recent Findings on Alcohol Beverage Labels," *Journal of Public Policy and Marketing* 12 (1993): 1–9.

112. David P. MacKinnon, Mary Ann Pentz, and Alan W. Stacy, "The Alcohol Warning Label and Adolescents," *American Journal of Public Health* 83 (1993): 585–587.

113. Tim Stockwell, "Influencing the Labeling of Alcoholic Beverage Containers: Informing the Public," *Addiction* 88 (1993): 53S–60S.

114. Hae-Kyong Bang, "Analyzing the Impact of the Liquor Industry's Lifting of the Ban on Broadcast Advertising," *Journal of Public Policy and Marketing* 17 (1998): 132–138.

115. Janet Hankin, James Sloan, and Robert Sokol, "The Modest Impact of the Alcohol Beverage Warning Label on Drinking during Pregnancy among a Sample of African-American Women," *Journal of Public Policy and Marketing* 17 (1998), 61–69.

116. Craig Andrews and Richard Netemeyer, "Alcohol Warning Label Effects," in *Marketing and Consumer Research in the Public Interest*, ed. Ronald Paul Hill (Thousand Oaks, Calif.: Sage, 1996).

117. David Kessler, "Building a Better Food Label," *FDA Consumer* 25 (September 1991): 10–13.

118. Christine Moorman, "A Quasi-Experiment to Assess the Consumer and Informational Determinants of Nutrition Information Processing Activities: The Case of the Nutrition Labeling and Education Act," *Journal of Public Policy and Marketing* 15 (1996): 28–44.

119. Julie Caswell and Daniel Padberg, "Toward a More Comprehensive Theory of Food Labels," *American Journal of Agricultural Economics* 74 (1992): 460–468.

120. Alan D. Mathios, "Socioeconomic Factors, Nutrition and Food Choices," *Journal of Public Policy and Marketing* 15 (1996): 45–54; Scott Burton and Abhijit Biswas, "Preliminary Assessment of Changes in Labels Required by the Nutrition Labeling and Education Act of 1990," *Journal of Consumer Affairs* 27 (1993): 127–144; M. W. Kreuter, L. K. Brennan, D. P. Scharff, and S. N. Lukwago, "Do Nutrition Label Readers Eat Healthier Diets? Behavioral Correlates of Adults' Use of Food Labels," *American Journal of Preventive Medicine* 13 (1997): 277–283.

121. Caswell and Padberg, "Toward a More Comprehensive Theory of Food Labels."

122. Julie Caswell and Eliza Mojduszka, "Using Informational Labeling to Influence the Market for Quality in Food Products," *American Journal of Agricultural Economics* 78 (1996): 1248–1253.

123. J. Edward Russo and France Leclerc, "Characteristics of Successful Product Information Programs," *Journal of Social Issues* 47 (1991): 73–92.

124. Jeffrey Stoltman and Fred Morgan, "Product Safety, Information, and Behavior," *American Behavioral Scientist* 38 (1995): 633–645.

125. Hadden, *Read the Label*, 1986.

126. Magat and Viscusi, *Informational Approaches to Regulation* (Cambridge, Mass.: MIT Press, 1992).

127. Hadden, *Read the Label*, 1986.

128. W. Kip Viscusi, *Product-Risk Labeling* (Washington, D.C.: American Enterprise Institute Press, 1993); Graham, "Regulation by Shaming."

129. Scott Kilman, "Food Fright: Biotech Scare Sweeps Europe and Companies Wonder If U.S. Is Next," *Wall Street Journal* (7 October 1999), A1.

130. Eli Cox, M. S. Wogalter, S. L. Stokes, and E. Murff, "Do Product Warnings Increase Safe Behavior? A Meta-Analysis," *Journal of Public Policy and Marketing* 16 (1997): 195–204.

131. Deborah Stone, *Policy Paradox: The Art of Political Decision Making* (New York: W. W. Norton, 1997).

132. Examples are discussed in Janet A. Weiss, "Policy Design for Democracy: A Look at Public Information Campaigns," 1993.

133. Alexis de Tocqueville, "The Power Exercised by the Majority in America over Thought," *Democracy in America* (New York: Harper Perennial, 1969), 254.

134. For example, Ellul, *Propaganda*.

135. Paul Lazarsfeld and Robert Merton, "Mass Communication, Popular Taste, and Organized Social Action," in *The Communication of Ideas*, ed. L. Bryson (New York: Harper and Row, 1948).

136. Robert Reich, ed., *The Power of Public Ideas* (Cambridge, Mass.: Ballinger, 1988); John Dryzek, *Discursive Democracy* (New York: Cambridge University Press, 1990).

137. Judith E. Innes, "Information in Communicative Planning," *Journal of the American Planning Association* 64 (1998): 52–63.

138. Christopher Hood, *The Tools of Government* (1988), 140.

139. Suggestions about how to do this in the case of public information campaigns can be found in Weiss, "Policy Design for Democracy: A Look at Public Information Campaigns," 1993.

140. Janet A. Weiss, "Theoretical Foundations of Policy Intervention" in *Public Management Reform and Innovation,* eds. H. George Frederickson and Jocelyn Johnston (Tuscaloosa: University of Alabama Press, 1999).

CHAPTER EIGHT

Corrective Taxes, Charges, and Tradable Permits

Joseph J. Cordes

Like many other cities and towns, Seattle faced a problem of what to do about its trash. The city was rapidly exhausting the capacity of its own landfill and needed to find a new place to dispose of its garbage. Another county was willing to take Seattle's trash, but only if Seattle was willing to pay.[1] Seattle's response was to start charging its residents for garbage disposal based on the amount of trash brought to the curb. Seattle charged $16.10 for each large trash can set out per week. To encourage recycling, paper and glass that was separated for recycling was hauled away free of charge, and the charge for hauling away yard waste was set at $4.25 per month.

Seattle households responded in several ways. As intended, voluntary recycling increased, and there was a significant decline in the total amount of tonnage that needed to be buried. An unintended—and not entirely desirable—effect was also that residents began doing what has been described as the "Seattle stomp," which involved compressing garbage into the smallest volume possible to make it fit into a single can.

In a completely different venue, the environmental compliance managers of two different electric power companies turned on their computers to look at the auction board for sulfur oxide emissions allowances. The Clean Air Act of 1990 allowed each utility to emit no more than a certain amount of sulfur oxide into the air, but the act also permitted a company that was able to keep its emissions below its allowed limit to sell its "unused allowance" to another company that could then use these extra allowances to exceed its own limit.

According to the auction board that flashed on their computer screens, the "going price" for the right to emit a pound of sulfur oxide was $90 per ton. The engineers for one company, which we shall call New Electric Power, estimated that it would cost $80 for each extra ton of sulfur oxide emission that New Electric cut back. New Electric Power thus could earn a profit of $10 on each right to emit a ton of sulfur oxide that it could sell in the open market. The other company, which we shall call Smokestack Power and Light, estimated it would cost $100 per ton to cut back its sulfur oxide emissions. Smokestack could save $10 on each right to emit a ton of sulfur oxide beyond the legal limit that it could buy in the market. Thus, New Electric Power offered to sell the right to emit five thousand tons of sulfur oxide at a price of $90 per ton, which was quickly snapped up by Smokestack.

The transaction was a win-win situation for all concerned. The utility that sold emission allowances garnered a profit of $50,000, and the utility that bought this allowance enjoyed a cost saving of $50,000. Society also reaped benefits of $100,000 by shifting more of the responsibility for emissions reduction away from a company where it would cost $100 for each ton of sulfur oxide emission that was cut back to a company where the cost of reducing sulfur oxide pollution was only $80 per ton.

These vignettes differ in their specifics, but there is a common thread. Each illustrates the use of Adam Smith's famous "invisible hand" of the marketplace instead of direct social regulation to change socially harmful behavior.

In the trash disposal example, Seattle could have attempted to deal with its trash disposal problem by refusing to pick up more than a certain number of trash cans per household each week, or by requiring that glass and bottles be recycled. Instead, the city provided its citizens with financial incentives to cut back on the amount of waste, but the example also illustrates a potential pitfall of relying on the market. The waste disposal fee also encouraged people to change their behavior—by compacting garbage as densely as possible—in a way that was not entirely intended.

The case of the buying and selling of emissions permits illustrates the use of market incentives to achieve an existing regulatory goal more flexibly and cost effectively. With permit trading, government regulators did not need to know which electric utility was able to cut back emissions more cheaply. All that was needed was to allow utilities to trade with each other in rights to pollute. The market price for such permits then automatically "sorted out" which company was "better" at achieving the overall regulatory goal at a considerable saving in the amount of total social resources devoted to achieving improved air quality.

I. DEFINITION AND BASIC FEATURES

Defining Features

Corrective charges and tradable permits are a class of policy tools that involve using prices and other market mechanisms to create financial incentives for individuals to change their behavior in ways that reduce social harms or secure benefits for society at large.

As noted in Chapter 5, social regulation is one means of effectuating certain socially desired change in behavior. A defining feature of social regulation as a policy tool is its reliance on command and control and other administrative procedures to compel changes in behavior. If society seeks to curtail the harmful consumption of tobacco and alcohol, laws can be enacted that make it illegal to purchase tobacco or alcohol. Businesses can be legally prohibited from emitting more than a certain amount of pollution into the air and water, or a city could attempt to solve its trash disposal problem by refusing to pick up more than a certain amount of trash set out each week at curbside.

An alternative to social regulation is to use financial penalties or rewards to change behavior. If society disapproves of smoking or drinking, it can make these activities more expensive and leave it up to individuals to decide whether engaging in the harmful activity is worth the cost. If society wants to encourage people to do more recycling, it can make it more expensive to dispose of garbage that is not recycled. Businesses can be allowed to emit harmful substances into the air and water if they are willing to pay someone for the privilege of doing so.

Relation to Key Tool Features

As discussed in the introductory chapter, corrective taxes, charges, and permit trading may be usefully classified in terms of whether these tools are coercive, direct, visible, and automatic.

Coerciveness

Coerciveness measures the extent to which a tool restricts individual or group behavior as opposed to merely encouraging or discouraging it. Corrective taxes, charges, and permit trading are policy tools that rank moderately low in terms of coerciveness. On the one hand, the use of these tools ultimately relies on the legal authority of the state to change behavior. For example, smokers would not voluntarily pay tobacco taxes, and a market in pollution permits would not exist but for the existence of prior environmental regulation. However, unlike social regulation, which mandates changes in behavior through relatively coercive prohibitions and controls, corrective taxes and charges, and permit trading schemes, rely on relatively noncoercive financial disincentives to discourage harmful activities by making them costly, or to reward socially beneficial behavior.

257

CH 8:
CORRECTIVE
TAXES,
CHARGES,
AND
TRADABLE
PERMITS

Directness

Directness measures the extent to which the entity authorizing or inaugurating a program is involved in carrying it out. Because corrective taxes, charges, and tradable permits rely on largely decentralized market choices made by individuals and businesses in response to financial penalties or rewards, this class of policy tools is also less direct than the tool of social regulation, although somewhat more direct than subsidies. When the government taxes cigarettes, it does not explicitly instruct smokers to smoke less: smokers can smoke as much as they wish, provided that they are willing to pay the price. However, the government does directly impose a cost, and the resulting higher price of cigarettes creates a financial incentive to cut back on smoking.

Similarly, in assessing taxes or fees on pollution or waste disposal, the government does directly operate a tax or fee system, but it does not dictate how much pollution a business ultimately emits, or how much trash a business or household brings to the curbside. Nonetheless, polluters will have a financial incentive to cut back on pollution in order to reduce their tax bill, and people and businesses will be more apt to think twice about disposing "excessive amounts" of trash if doing so is not free. In the case of trading of pollution permits, a government bureaucrat is directly involved in setting the overall regulatory target that needs to be met, but the permit trading scheme essentially leaves it up to individual companies to decide how each will choose to comply with this overall target.

Visibility

Visibility measures the extent to which the resources devoted to a tool show up in the normal budget process. Taxes and charges and permit schemes are rather visible policy tools. Taxes and charges typically need to be explicitly approved and authorized by the appropriate legislative body, and in many cases are subject to periodic review. Also, unlike regulatory standards that can obscure the full cost of complying with social regulations because these costs are borne by private parties, corrective taxes make such costs visible in the budget and political process.[2] Moreover, any decision to alter the financial incentives created by taxes and charges requires changing the rate and/or the base of the tax or charge, which almost always engenders considerable and highly visible political debate.

Allowing polluters to trade rights to pollute is also an action that must be explicitly authorized as part of broader legislation regulating industrial and other uses of the environment. For example, as discussed in more detail below, the current system of pollution trading in the United States was established under Title IV of the Clean Air Act Amendments of 1990 (CAAA).

Automaticity

Automaticity measures the extent to which a tool utilizes an existing administrative structure to produce its effect rather than having to create its own special administrative apparatus. Corrective taxes, charges, and permit trading rank moderately high in terms of being automatic. For such systems to work, structures to collect fees and special taxes must often be created. However, a smoker does not need to know the social costs of smoking in order for cigarette taxes to affect his or her behavior. Every time he or she buys a pack of cigarettes, society is implicitly reminding him or her that it disapproves of smoking by taxing it. Similarly, a business or home that faces an appropriate charge for disposal of its waste does not need to know the cost of waste disposal to the community. Finally, the market for pollution permits automatically creates incentives for businesses to find environmentally smarter ways of producing goods and services. Thus, this class of tools stands midway between vouchers and direct government in the degree of automaticity it exhibits.

Design Features and Major Variants

Corrective taxes, charges, and permit trading schemes share broad tool features in common. However, they also differ from each other in a number of important ways. In this section we zero in on some of these differences.

Corrective Taxes

Designing corrective taxes or fees requires attention to issues that are common to the design of all taxes. One must decide on *what to tax* (the tax base), *how much to tax* (the tax rate), and *how to tax* (the administrative mechanism for collecting the tax).

As is discussed more in the basic mechanics section of this chapter, choosing the base of a corrective tax often involves an added dimension because the underlying objective of the tax is to elicit a desired change in behavior, rather than to raise revenue *per se*. The case of alcohol and gasoline taxes is an example. In the case of alcohol, the intent is to curb abusive drinking, rather than drinking *per se* (unless one is a member of the Women's Christian Temperance Union). In principle, the goal would be to tax only drinking that is abusive. In practice, such a tax would be almost impossible to design or administer, so one is left with taxing general alcohol consumption.[3]

A similar issue arises in the case of gasoline taxes. The objective might be to encourage automobile makers to develop cars that not only used less fuel but also cleaner fuel. However, a tax that accomplished this purpose would be more complicated than a tax on purchases of gasoline by the gallon.[4] Such a levy, if set at a high enough level, would encourage automobile makers to make more fuel-efficient cars, and would also encourage people to substitute mass transit for driving. There would, however, be no financial incentive for automobile makers to make cars that burned more "environmentally friendly" fuel, or for drivers to substitute such cleaner fuel for regular fuel, unless "dirty" fuel (such as leaded fuel) were taxed more heavily than other fuel, as is done in the German Federal Republic.[5]

There may also be a potential conflict between the objectives of raising tax revenue and of using taxes and fees to regulate behavior. For example, if the objective is to maximize the amount of revenue collected from a tax or charge, one may seek to tax activities whose demand or supply is not sensitive to price, but using taxes as instruments to influence behavior presupposes that the behavior to be influenced will be at least somewhat sensitive to price. Taxes that are good sources of revenue are also often levied on bases that are easy to administer and monitor. However, a tax that is easy to administer may not create the financial incentives needed to change behavior in the way desired.

Finally, for a corrective tax to work, an administrative mechanism must be established to collect and enforce it. A major design issue here is whether to rely on an existing administrative mechanism (e.g., existing sales tax collection processes), or to create new mechanisms and procedures. The former offers obvious efficiency advantages but may subject the tax to procedures that are not well targeted to the program's objectives.

259

CH 8:
CORRECTIVE
TAXES,
CHARGES,
AND
TRADABLE
PERMITS

Corrective Fees

The issues that need to be addressed in designing fees, such as charges for waste disposal, are broadly similar to those that arise in designing corrective taxes. Decisions need to be made about what to charge for, how much to charge, and how to collect and administer the charge.

As in the case of taxes, the choice of the base of a fee or charge has an important effect on its outcome as a policy tool. For example, the case of waste disposal fees in Seattle described in the introductory vignette illustrates how the choice of the base of a charge can have unintended as well as intended consequences. In that case, by gearing the charge to the volume, rather than the weight, of the waste, local authorities created an incentive for residents to pack more waste into each container.

A potentially important difference between corrective taxes and corrective fees and charges is that the latter are more likely to be raised and administered independently of the existing tax system, which can have both disadvantages and advantages. On the one hand, when a corrective fee or charge is administered outside the tax system, existing and often proven structures for raising tax revenue cannot be used to administer the collection of the fee and monitor compliance. On the other hand, the need to create a new administrative structure may also help free the administration and collection of corrective fees from legal and/or political constraints that are associated with taxes. In addition, fees and charges often receive different budgetary treatment than do taxes.[6] For example, it is more likely that the revenue raised from a corrective fee or charge will be dedicated to specific uses than the revenue raised from a corrective tax.

Permit Trading

Issues raised in the design of permit trading schemes are quite different from those raised in the design of corrective taxes and fees. One important difference is that permit trading has not been viewed as a policy tool for reducing the overall level of any behavior. The main policy tool that serves this purpose is social regulation. Thus, in the introductory vignette, the permit trading scheme did not define how much sulfur oxide each utility was allowed to emit; that was determined by the Clean Air Act Amendments of 1990, a regulatory program.

Moreover, although permit trading could be used in principle to raise government revenue, permit trading has yet to be used for this purpose and seems unlikely to be in the future, for reasons discussed more fully below. In the vignette, for example, the proceeds from permit sales were kept by the utility that was able to sell emissions allowances.

The defining feature of permit trading as a policy tool is that the intent is to rely on market forces of demand and supply to allocate the burden for complying with a mandated reduction in a given behavior, such as pollutant emissions. In designing the tool, the government thus needs to create an administrative framework that allows the emergence of markets that are "well behaved" in two dimensions. The market for permits must have properties that are typically associated with well-functioning private markets, such as adequate information about buyers, sellers, and prices, and an adequate volume of trades. In addition, the volume of trading that results must result in an overall allocation of allowances that is consistent with the overall level of behavior that is mandated by law.

The exact mechanics of creating such a framework are discussed in more detail below, but several elements are involved in creating the needed framework. One is the ability to specify clear standards for expected performance both by individual parties and for the "system as whole," as well to monitor compliance with these standards. Another is to provide or to facilitate institutional arrangements that make it easy for buyers and sellers to arrange trades. A third is to ensure that permit markets function competitively and fairly.

II. PATTERNS OF TOOL USE

Corrective Taxes and Charges in the United States

Corrective taxes and charges in the United States are levied in various forms by all levels of government. It is difficult, if not impossible, to provide a single empirical measure of how widely these tools are used to implement policy. On the one hand, corrective fees and charges are a relatively modest source of government revenue at all levels of government. Yet, the amount of revenue raised from a corrective tax or charge may not reveal its importance as a policy tool. A corrective tax, for example, could be quite effective as a tool for reducing harmful behavior while raising relatively little revenue precisely because it succeeded in reducing the amount of the taxed activity.

Nonetheless, the revenue raised from corrective taxes and charges provides some information about patterns of tool use because, as discussed below, support for many corrective taxes and charges is often driven by a desire to raise revenue. Moreover (as in the case of alcohol and tobacco taxes), changes in the amount of revenue raised from corrective taxes and charges sometimes signal changes in patterns of reliance on this tool of policy.

An alternative gauge of the extent of use of corrective taxes and charges is the extent to which the tax or charge actually provides measurable incentives for people or businesses to change their behavior. The rate at which certain activities are taxed clearly provides some indication of the size of the incentive, but ultimately the effect of a corrective tax depends on what is taxed as well as on the tax rate.

Alcohol and Tobacco Taxes

Taxes on alcohol and tobacco are among the oldest and most widely used corrective taxes, not only in the United States, but also abroad. Smoking and drinking are taxed at both the federal and the state and local levels in the United States. In 1997, combined federal and state tobacco taxes ranged from a low of 21 percent of the price of a pack of cigarettes to a high of 49 percent.[7] Most recently, New York State increased its tax on cigarettes to $1.11, which is currently the highest in the nation.[8] In fiscal year 1996, federal alcohol taxes amounted to roughly $2.00 per fifth of 80-proof distilled spirits, $0.30 per six-pack of beer, and $1.75 per bottle of wine.[9]

Taxes on tobacco and alcohol, which in 1950 comprised almost 10 percent of all federal tax collections, had steadily declined in importance as a revenue source over a forty-year period, and in 1989 accounted for only 1 percent of all federal taxes.[10] During this same period, federal cigarette taxes as a percentage of cigarette prices fell from 38 to 11 percent. This decline was caused in part by the growth in income and payroll taxes, but it also reflected a certain "benign neglect" by Congress, which chose not to adjust alcohol and tobacco tax rates to keep pace with inflation. Thus, according to a 1990 Congressional Budget Office study, between 1950 and 1989, the tax rates on

261

CH 8:
Corrective
Taxes,
Charges,
and
Tradable
Permits

cigarettes and on distilled spirits declined in inflation-adjusted terms by one-third.[11] This trend was reversed in 1989, largely because the budgetary environment created a favorable political climate for increasing these taxes.

Aside from these budgetary politics, which created strong incentives for Congress to find ways of raising revenue that did not involve increasing income taxes, support for increasing taxes on tobacco and alcohol also fit a newfound enthusiasm for placing more reliance on the "marketplace" as a means of addressing a host of social problems. There were growing concerns about the costs to society both of smoking and abusive consumption of alcohol in the 1980s. Policymakers were seeking ways of reducing these social costs by reducing the consumption of tobacco and alcohol. The idea of using taxes to restrict the consumption of certain goods by making them more expensive was not new. Sumptuary taxes—taxes on goods or activities that society found to be "morally objectionable"—had been levied both in the United States and elsewhere for several centuries.[12] What was different, however, was a shift in emphasis on consciously viewing alcohol and tobacco taxes as an instrument for achieving certain behavioral objectives—such as preventing youths from becoming smokers, or reducing death on the highways.

Since the round of increases in federal cigarette taxes enacted in the early 1990s, and scheduled to take effect in 2000 and thereafter, there have been several attempts to increase federal cigarette taxes even more, driven in part by a desire to raise more tax revenue in ways that could be portrayed as reducing other social harms.

Alcohol and tobacco taxes comprise a larger share of revenues at the state than at the federal level, and in many cases state taxes on tobacco and alcohol are higher than are their federal counterparts. In part, this reflects an implicit political understanding to reserve sales and excise taxes as a revenue source for (mainly) state governments.

Environmental Taxes and Fees

At the federal level, raising revenue from taxes and charges levied on activities that have an environmental impact is still a relatively modest undertaking. A January 1999 Joint Committee on Taxation (JCT) publication lists a total of three taxes (excluding the gasoline tax) that are levied on tax bases that arguably bear at least some relation to environmentally harmful activities: the Leaking Underground Storage Tank (LUST) Trust Fund excise tax, the gas guzzler excise tax, and the excise tax on ozone-depleting chemicals.[13]

Taken together, federal environmental taxes raise less than $100 million in revenue in 1999. Although the amount of revenue raised is at best a very imperfect indicator of tool use, the fact that federal environmental taxes raise such a small amount of revenue in a $7 trillion economy suggests that presently they play a very modest role as a tool of federal environmental policy.

These taxes also exemplify the somewhat different uses of environmental taxes and charges.[14] The LUST Trust Fund tax is levied at a rate of 0.1 cent per gallon on gasoline and other motor fuels, with the proceeds of the tax earmarked to defray any costs of cleanup associated with leaks from underground storage tanks. The tax provides no financial incentive for changes in the design of such tanks, or other measures, that would reduce the incidence of leaks, and hence its underlying purpose is not to change behavior. Rather, the tax is intended to spread the costs of a government program to those who occasion such costs.

In contrast, both the gas guzzler tax and the excise tax on ozone-depleting chemicals are intended to change behavior. The gas guzzler tax imposes a financial penalty on automobiles whose fuel economy rating falls below a certain threshold. It is assessed at rates starting at $1,000 per vehicle for vehicles whose fuel economy rating is less than 22.5 miles per gallon, but at least 21.5 miles per gallon, and rises to $7,700 per vehicle for vehicles with a fuel economy rating of less than 12.5 miles per gallon.

Similarly, the tax on ozone-depleting chemicals was crafted in response to an international agreement—the Montreal protocols—that restricted the production and consumption of ozone-depleting chemicals. The tax identifies a list of eight chemicals to be taxed that correspond to those chemicals identified for control under the Montreal protocol. The tax applies not only to domestic production but also to imports of these chemicals, as well as to imports of goods that use these chemicals in production. Tax liability in 2000 is determined by multiplying the production of each chemical by $7.60 per pound, and then again by an ozone-depleting factor that measures the amount of environmental harm done by each chemical.[15]

As of this writing, however, despite a flurry of interest in environmental taxes in the early 1990s, no new federal environmental taxes have emerged on the scene. There was a proposal to include a fairly substantial set of energy taxes in President Clinton's 1993 budget proposal, but these taxes were quickly removed from the overall package in response to considerable political opposition.

At the state and local levels, there is a fairly widespread use of various environmental taxes, fees, and charges at the state and local levels. In 1995, according to Bohm and Kelsay (1999), 44 states levied a hazardous waste generator fee, 43 levied a hazardous waste disposal fee, 38 levied an underground storage tank fee, 36 levied hazardous waste disposal fees, 28 levied waste tire fees, 14 levied a motor fuels fee, 7 levied a low-level radioactive waste generator fee, 6 levied a coastal/inland spill fee, and 4 levied a water quality fee. These taxes and charges represent a mix of "benefit taxes" whose primary purpose is to generate tax revenue to fund environmental cleanup, and true corrective taxes and fees that are consciously intended to change behavior.

Gasoline Taxes

Federal and state gasoline taxes present an interesting separate case. Initially, these taxes were proposed as a kind of rough user charge to help pay for transportation infrastructure and not as a corrective tax. With the onset of the energy crisis of the 1970s, they came to be used, in a rough way, to encourage greater efficiency in the consumption of gasoline. In the late 1980s, there was some discussion of raising gasoline taxes as way of reducing airborne pollution, but it was recognized that taxing gasoline *per se* was a rather blunt instrument for reducing pollution emitted by automobiles because these taxes operated only by reducing consumption of gasoline.[16] Thus, at present, although most observers would acknowledge that gasoline taxes could play a role as an instrument of environmental policy, these taxes are not consciously used for this purpose in the United States. They are seen first and foremost as a highway user charge, second as a tool for dealing with energy security, and only then as a possible form of environmental charge.

Tradable Permits

The use of tradable permits as tools to supplement environmental regulation is quite recent. Although the idea of using permit trading schemes to cut the costs of environmental regulation had been proposed by academic economists as early as the 1970s, the possibility of actually adopting such a scheme became a reality in 1990 when the Bush administration proposed to implement permit trading in Title IV of the CAAA.[17] Despite initial opposition (see below), the Administration's approach was adopted by

263

CH 8:
CORRECTIVE
TAXES,
CHARGES,
AND
TRADABLE
PERMITS

Congress, and Title IV of the CAAA mandated the first large-scale use of tradable emissions permits as a tool of environmental regulation.

The first trade of permits between two private companies took place in 1992 with the sale of 10,000 allowances by Wisconsin Power and Light to the Tennessee Valley Authority at a price of $265 per allowance. The second was the sale of 25,000 allowances by the Alcoa Corporation to Ohio Edison at a price of $300 per allowance. Since then, the pace of sales has accelerated.

Paul Joskow et al. report that between March of 1993 and March of 1997 permits, allowing the annual emission of over 12 million tons of sulfur dioxide (SO_2) were traded in these markets. Over 11 million tons of this total represents private trades. The total volume of trades represents roughly 10 percent of the total allowances distributed annually to polluters.

Taxes, Fees, and Permits in International Perspective

As in the United States, taxes on tobacco, alcohol, and gasoline are nearly ubiquitous in other countries and have their origins as sumptuary taxes or as convenient ways of raising revenue.[18] However, a number of European countries have made more conscious use of gasoline taxes as a corrective tax to discourage the consumption of gasoline and to reduce driving and emissions. European cigarette taxes also make up a much larger share of the price of cigarettes than in the United States.[19]

European countries also rely more on incentive-based user charges and fees for other purposes. In part, this may stem from the fact that, as noted by Stephen Farber (1998), the "polluter pays principle" has become a popular guiding principle in European environmental policy. Under this rubric, polluters must either bear the cost of measures undertaken to reduce pollution or bear the costs of environmental damage. By itself, the concept of polluter pays does not necessarily translate into the explicit use of corrective fees and charges to change behavior, but environmental taxes and fees that are designed to change behavior, as well as to distribute the costs of pollution to polluters, are more prevalent in European countries than they are in the United States.

In contrast, other countries have not yet explicitly linked permit trading schemes to major environmental legislation as has been done in the United States. In part, this may reflect the fact that, especially in Europe, the process of environmental regulation seems to involve a greater degree of administrative give and take between government and the regulated.

III. BASIC MECHANICS

Corrective Taxes and Fees

The general mechanics of levying corrective taxes and/or fees are basically similar to those that arise in implementing any tax or fee. Mechanisms have to be put in place to ensure that the appropriate activities or transactions are taxed, that the tax is collected, that the tax is levied on the right entity, and that steps are taken to monitor and enforce compliance.

Determining the Base of the Tax or Charge

The first step in the process is deciding what is to be taxed and then ensuring that the tax is levied correctly. This can be a relatively simple matter when the harm that is to be prevented or reduced is directly associated with the consumption or production of a particular good or service. For example, since the harm of smoking is directly associated with the number of cigarettes that are smoked, cigarette consumption is an appropriate tax base.

In the case of other corrective taxes, however, choosing the appropriate tax base is more complicated. As Farber notes, in practice, selecting the base of a corrective tax or fee typically involves some compromise between the objective of the regulation and ease of administration.[20] For example, in the case of a good whose production causes the emission of pollution as a byproduct, one would, in principle, seek to tax the emission of the pollutant directly, instead of imposing a tax on each unit of the good that is produced. This is necessary in order to provide the producer with a financial incentive to seek ways of reducing the amount of pollution that is emitted per each unit of production. In practice, it may be hard to administer such a tax, and, instead, one may be left with the simple expedient of taxing the good. This reduces the harm to the environment by curtailing production and consumption of the good, but does so in a second-best fashion.

Determining the Tax Rate or Charge

Once the base of the tax or fee has been identified, the rate of tax or the amount of the fee can be set. Because the rate of a corrective tax or fee will reflect objectives of social policy, this requires more information than is typically required to choose a tax rate or charge when the policy objective is simply to raise revenue.

Just as there are practical problems in choosing the base of a tax or fee, problems are also likely to be encountered in setting the rate of tax or the fee. Economists would argue that the rate of a corrective tax or fee should be commensurate with the social costs that arise from the activity one is seeking to regulate. This approach to setting the tax presumes, however, that there is some "optimal" amount of harm that society should be prepared to accept, which can be controversial.

Moreover, even if there is broad agreement that the policy goal should be attaining a socially optimal level of harm, information about the relevant external costs of an activity may be sparse. For example, suppose that the policy rationale for taxing cigarettes is to make sure the smokers bear the full social costs of their actions. Then choosing the "proper" rate of corrective taxation requires information about the social costs of smoking that would not be borne by smokers if tobacco products were not taxed. Such estimates are available, but there is enough uncertainty about their magnitude that they provide at best only a rough guide to setting the tax rate.[21]

A more modest objective is to reduce a socially harmful activity by some legislatively desired amount. To do so, one needs to choose a tax or fee that raises the price of the regulated activity by "enough" to produce the desired cutback.

In either case, choosing the tax rate requires that one have some additional information about the good that is to be taxed. To implement the economists' approach, one would need to have an estimate of the dollar magnitude of the harm caused by the activity. To set a tax high enough to achieve some desired cutback in production, one would need information on how sensitive the activity was to changes in its price. As is illustrated by the case of the tax on ozone-depleting chemicals discussed below, information of this sort can be quite sketchy.

Collecting the Tax or Fee

Arrangements must also be made to collect the tax or fee. As a general matter, tax administrators seek to minimize the number of taxpayers because it simplifies collecting and monitoring compliance with the tax. As a practical matter, this consideration argues in favor of collecting corrective taxes from sellers rather than buyers. Corrective fees and charges can also be collected from sellers, but in many cases can also be levied directly on consumers, especially when the collection of the fee can be easily linked to provision of a service—such as trash collection—that can be easily monitored.

Fortunately, there is little or no conflict between collecting a tax or fee from the side of the market that is easier to administer and police and making sure that the tax or fee provides the desired financial incentive for changes in behavior. The purpose of levying corrective taxes or charging corrective fees is to make certain socially harmful goods or activities more costly. What ultimately matters is how the tax or fee affects the market price of the taxed good or activity, and tax incidence analysis shows that the economic effects of taxes are ultimately determined by the market forces of supply and demand and not by who is required to remit the actual tax or payment to the government.[22] Hence, policymakers are free to levy the tax on the side of the market— sellers or buyers—that is easiest to administer.

Compliance and Enforcement

Procedures must also be developed to monitor and ensure compliance with corrective taxes and fees. Monitoring typically takes the form of auditing the financial records of those charged with collecting and remitting a tax or charge to make sure that proper amounts of tax are assessed and levied.

The ease of monitoring will depend not only on the number of entities that are subject to monitoring, but also on the informational complexities involved in measuring the range of activities that are subject to tax. It is, for example, easier to monitor compliance with a tax when the base is linked to existing financial, accounting, and production records, such as the volume of goods produced and sold, than it is to monitor compliance with a tax base—for example, volume of pollution discharged into the atmosphere—requiring that new forms of recordkeeping be established.

In addition, those who must pay a tax or fee can legally *avoid* the tax or charge by substituting untaxed for taxed activities, and those who are subject to taxes or fees will seek to exploit any legally available opportunity of making such substitutions. Thus, the implementation of a corrective tax or fee will require that procedures be developed for determining when an activity is or is not subject to a corrective tax or charge, as well as for resolving legitimate disputes that can arise when there are differences of opinion about whether a particular good or activity is taxable.

Taxes and fees also create financial incentives for illegal *evasion*. Thus, the use of corrective taxes and fees as a policy tool requires either the use of existing legal structures (or the creation of new ones) to determine when evasion has occurred, as well as to assess civil or criminal penalties for illegal conduct. Since such mechanisms are often already in place in existing tax systems, this becomes an argument for using taxes rather than specialized fees for such corrective purposes.

Illustration: Designing a Tax on Ozone-Depleting Chemicals

The U.S. tax on ozone-depleting chemicals is a good illustration of several of the issues and tradeoffs that must be resolved in the design of a corrective tax.[23] The goal was to develop a tax that would provide the appropriate incentives to reduce the use of ozone-depleting chemicals, but that could also be feasibly administered.

As noted by Thomas Barthold (1994), crafting an effective, yet also administratively workable, tax required that several issues be resolved. One issue was that of *what should be taxed*. In this case, an international consensus had been reached in the form of the Montreal Protocol, which the Bush administration had endorsed, to reduce the emis-

265

CH 8:
CORRECTIVE
TAXES,
CHARGES,
AND
TRADABLE
PERMITS

sions of chlorofluorocarbons (CFCs) into the environment, because these chemicals were believed to play a major role in destroying stratospheric ozone. The broad policy goal was to levy a tax that would lead to reduced emissions of these harmful chemicals.[24]

In principle, corrective taxes should impose taxes on activities that are commensurate with the social harm done by those activities. Yet (as in the case of alcohol consumption discussed above), it was recognized that the production of chlorofluorocarbons *per se* did not destroy stratospheric ozone, but rather the release of these chemicals into the atmosphere during the production process. As Barthold notes, more typically it was the use of these chemicals as refrigerants in refrigerators and automobile air condi-tioners and in the production of electronic circuit boards that was the main source of environmental harm, and even more specifically it was not necessarily the use of CFC in automobile air conditioners that was a problem, but rather the use of CFCs in improperly installed and/or maintained automobile air conditioners. By this logic, the most effective tax would have been one that was placed on leaks of CFCs from autos.

However, a tax that honed in only on those CFCs that harmed the ozone layer was not even remotely administratively workable. The "ideal" tax would need to be levied on millions of drivers with faulty automobile air-conditioning systems. Alternatively, one might consider taxing more heavily at the production level refrigerants that were destined for use in automobiles when compared with those destined for use in homes on the theory that refrigerants destined for use in cars were more likely to leak into the atmosphere, but there was no administratively workable way of making such a distinction.

At the same time, there were less than a dozen manufacturers of ozone-depleting chemicals, and only a few more importers of these chemicals from abroad. To the extent that one believed that all ozone-depleting chemicals ultimately found their way into the atmosphere in one way or another, a case could be made for imposing a tax on domestic producers of these chemicals as well as on importers, and such a tax could be administered relatively easily.

The treatment of imports raised a further issue. Did foreign environmental regulation and/or taxes increase the cost of imported ozone-depleting products by an amount comparable to the tax imposed on domestic production of these goods? If the answer was "yes," then domestic users would not have an incentive to avoid the U.S. tax by substituting imported for domestically produced ozone-depleting chemicals and goods using these chemicals.

There was no reason, however, to assume that foreign-produced ozone-depleting products were subject to comparable taxes or regulations. Hence, imports needed to be taxed in order to ensure that American users of ozone-depleting products did not simply substitute cheaper foreign imports for American products.

In addition to determining the most administratively workable base of the tax, it was necessary to choose the proper tax rate. As mentioned above, some effort was made to assign differential tax rates to different types of ozone-depleting chemicals based on scientific studies of the ozone-depleting potential of each chemical and its longevity in the upper atmosphere. Thus, in a crude way, the tax was designed to exact more of a financial penalty from those ozone-depleting chemicals that caused more physical harm. Yet, as Barthold notes, there is no necessary link between physical and economic harm. In other words, there is no evidence that in 2000 the base tax rate of $7.60 corresponds to the environmental damage done by these chemicals. Moreover, there is some evidence that the initial tax rates that were chosen in 1989 were set at least in part with an eye to raising a needed amount of revenue.

Permit Trading

267

CH 8:
CORRECTIVE
TAXES,
CHARGES,
AND
TRADABLE
PERMITS

The mechanics of using permit trading as a policy tool include some issues that are common to regulation. These are the need to clearly specify standards of performance and to monitor and enforce compliance. In addition, other issues need to be addressed when permit trading is used to implement such standards.

Setting Standards of Performance

The rationale for allowing permit trading is to permit an overall regulatory target—for example, reduction in total emissions of M thousand pounds—to be achieved in the most economically flexible manner. Regulators must, however, be able to ascertain that this overall goal is achieved, which requires the ability to monitor compliance with the regulation at each source. This, in turn, means that one must be able to set clearly defined limits on allowable emissions at each source. Title IV of the Clean Air Act Amendments of 1990, for example, initially sought to reduce the 1980 level of emissions of SO_2 by 10 million tons per year (about a 50 percent reduction) by the year 2000. To achieve this objective, individual companies were assigned an initial limit on the amount of SO_2 that they could emit that was consistent with this overall target. This target was administratively defined in terms of emissions allowances that were "given" to each company—for example, Metropolitan Power and Light was given allowances that would permit it to emit, say, 100,000 tons of SO_2 during the year 1996. The major innovation that accompanied the introduction of permit trading was to give each company considerable flexibility in complying with the law.

Enforcing Standards of Performance

In addition to specifying standards of performance, sanctions need to be established for noncompliance. In the case of the Clean Air Act of 1990, compliance was encouraged by imposing a fine of $2,000 per each ton of emissions that exceeded any year's allowances, and by requiring violators to offset excess emissions in one year by an equal amount of lower emissions in the subsequent year.

Relating Emissions to Permits

Permit trading requires an additional layer of monitoring to keep track of the trades that take place.[25] In the case of Title IV of the CAAA, such tracking is accomplished by a computerized tracking system administered by the Environmental Protection Agency. The system has the following elements. Initially, each affected unit is given an individual allowance account (a "unit account") in the EPA computer system. A unit could either be an entire company with a single plant, or one of several plants owned by the same company. The allocations of each unit for each year between 1995 through 2025 are placed in these accounts. At the end of each year, each unit has enough allowances of the appropriate vintages to cover its allowed emissions for that year. For example, at the end of 2000, if Metropolitan Power and Light were assigned an overall emissions allowance of 100,000 pounds of SO_2, then Metropolitan Power and Light would need to have 100,000 allowances in its account to emit SO_2 either for the year 2000, or previous years. (In other words, a company could bank or acquire options in a current year for use in future years, but not "borrow" allowances from future years for use in the current year.)

Creating an Orderly Market for Permits

Another issue in the implementation of permit trading schemes is the creation of an orderly market to facilitate trades. This was a matter of some concern when permit trading was first launched. Thus, Title IV of the CAAA mandated that the EPA hold a series of auctions that were intended to "jump-start" the market. These auctions were held once a year and covered only two or three vintages at a time. The auction was held by withholding just under 3 percent of allowances and then selling these allowances in spot and seven-year advance auctions. Because the purpose of the auctions was to reveal information about the market price of permits, and not to raise revenue, the auctions were set up to be revenue neutral in the sense that auction revenues were not kept by the government, but instead were returned to utilities in proportion to their shares of the allowances that were initially withheld.

In 1993 and 1994, allowances sold in EPA auctions accounted for over a half and a quarter, respectively, of all allowances traded. Since then, as noted by Joskow et al. (1998), trading of pollution permits has taken place in two very different arenas. The majority of emissions trades has occurred in the private marketplace and has involved bilateral transactions either directly between two different utilities, or between a single utility and private market makers who have found it profitable to serve as brokers between utilities seeking to buy and to sell permits.

The second way that allowances have been traded has been through a set of annual auctions that have been held by the government. The share of publicly traded allowances among overall trades dropped further to about 10 percent of allowances in 1994, and in 1997 accounted for about 5 percent of all allowances traded. Joskow et al. note that the initial auctions helped establish visible market values that served the basic goal of getting the market started and helped stimulate the creation of private market trading activity of all kinds. Yet, one clear lesson from the Title IV experience is that the private market was capable of responding quite rapidly to the potential gains from trade that were created by the permit trading scheme. As noted by Robert Stavins (1998), the experience shows that " . . . the private sector (was able to) fulfill brokerage needs, (provide) price information and (match) trading partners, despite claims to the contrary when the program was enacted. Entrepreneurs . . . stepped in to make available a variety of services, including private brokerage, electronic bid/ask bulletin boards, and allowance price forecasts."

IV. TOOL SELECTION

The basic rationale for using financial incentives as a tool of policy is that under the right circumstances such devices can be at least as effective as direct social regulation while offering some additional benefits that come from giving more flexibility in deciding how to comply with regulations to those that are regulated.

Advantages—Corrective Charges and Taxes

Flexibility and Efficiency

One of the main advantages of relying on corrective taxes or fees instead of direct controls is that there are a variety of situations in which relying on market prices "economizes" on the information that is needed to alter behavior. Waste disposal offers one example.

Suppose that a municipality decides that it wishes to reduce the volume of garbage by, say, 25 percent. It can try to achieve this objective by implementing a set of regulations that directs what people can and cannot take to the curbside. These regulations would then need to be enforced, and it might well turn out that the regulations would either prohibit—or fail to include on the approved list—ways in which households on their own might find ways of cutting back on household waste. Suppose, however, that there were demand studies that showed that increasing the price of garbage collection by 100 percent per pound was likely to get households to cut back on the amount of waste brought to the curbside by 25 percent. Then, one might expect that doubling the fee charged for garbage collection would also achieve the desired cutback. In this case, however, it would be left up to households to decide how they would cut back, and there would be no need to implement and enforce a potentially complicated set of regulations. All that one would need to do would be to raise the fee and let the market do the rest.

269

CH 8:
CORRECTIVE
TAXES,
CHARGES,
AND
TRADABLE
PERMITS

Another example is the case that economists have made for using either corrective pollution taxes or permit trading to achieve legislatively mandated levels of environmental quality.[26] The claim is that price incentives can help lower the costs of controlling pollution whenever multiple sources contribute to the overall level of pollution, and regulators do not care how the required total reduction in pollution is distributed among the multiple sources. In such cases, it is desirable to distribute the total reduction in pollution so that the added cost of reducing emissions by an extra unit is the same at each source, which means that emissions from sources with relatively low incremental costs of controlling pollution would need to be cut proportionately more than emissions from sources with relatively high incremental costs of pollution control.

In principle, one could achieve this outcome by means of direct regulation. However, from a practical standpoint, this would require regulators not only to have information about "high-cost" and "low-cost" sources of pollution, but also to translate this knowledge into a set of differentiated targets for pollution reduction among the sources. Aside from the rather substantial information requirements of such a regulatory scheme, it would face formidable political obstacles, since it would require some sources to cut back more pollution than others. Thus, it is not surprising that traditional "command and control" forms of environmental regulation do not distribute reductions in emissions in this manner. Instead, regulations typically require proportionate reductions at all sources.

Alternatively, instead of mandating the same proportional reductions of pollution at each source, a legislated target for overall pollution reduction could be set, and polluters could then be required to pay the same tax on each unit of effluent discharged into the environment. Each polluter would have a financial incentive to reduce pollution up to the point where the added cost of abating an additional unit just equaled the tax. Because all polluters would face the same tax, the added cost of reducing an additional unit would be the same at all sources. Producers who could control environmental emissions relatively cheaply would cut back pollution proportionately more than businesses with relatively high costs of pollution control.

Several studies have compared the costs of limiting pollution through across-the-board reductions in emissions at all sources, regardless of relative cost, with the cost of achieving the same total change in emissions more flexibly. These studies show that substantial costs could be saved by moving away from the across-the-board approach. For example, studies that compared the cost of limiting emissions using direct controls with the least-cost solution have found cost savings as high as 50 percent.[27]

The "Double Dividend"

Proponents of corrective taxes also contend that this policy tool offers a "double dividend" because it allows government tax revenue to be raised in a way that is less costly to society while also serving some broader social purpose. Taxing particular goods or activities generally causes less of the taxed good or activity to be produced and consumed. If there is no social purpose in restricting output of the taxed goods, consumers and producers suffer a loss in economic well-being. This excess burden is a real cost of collecting taxes over and above the taxes paid. In principle, the excess burden of taxation can be reduced, perhaps even eliminated, by taxing activities whose consumption or production imposes social costs that are not reflected in market prices. Because there are social gains from restricting such activities, taxing them may actually improve economic well-being, or at least reduce it less than if more socially desirable activities are taxed. Many of the objects of social regulation—such as pollution, smoking, and abusive drinking—are widely believed to impose external social costs that are not widely reflected in the prices of those goods and services. This translates easily into the perception that one can "do well" (i.e., raise additional needed revenue), while "doing good" (i.e., reducing the costs of environmental pollution) by taxing certain socially undesirable activities.

Complements Other Regulatory Tools

In some other cases, corrective taxes, fees, or permit trading schemes can serve as an additional policy tool to reinforce direct social regulation. Smoking and drinking are good examples. Society wishes to prevent smoking and drinking among teens. There are laws that prohibit the sale of tobacco and alcohol to minors, but these laws are imperfectly enforced. One way of providing an additional, and relatively easily enforced, signal to minors that smoking and drinking are prohibited is to make these activities more expensive by taxing them.

Disadvantages—Corrective Charges and Taxes

There are, however, also potentially serious disadvantages to relying on price incentives.

Uncertainty

Often there is little or no information about how people are likely to react to price incentives, while it may be relatively easy to observe and monitor the behavior that one is seeking to regulate. In such cases, implementing direct regulations may be the surest way of achieving the desired policy goal.

Similar issues arise when using environmental taxes or fees in place of direct regulations.

Regulators must live with a greater uncertainty about the level of pollution control when they tax the polluters than when the polluters are regulated directly. If, for example, the tax rate is set too low because there is uncertainty about how businesses will respond to an emissions tax, pollution will be reduced by less than the legislatively desired amount. If the tax is set too high, pollution would be cut by more than the legislatively mandated amount. In principle, one could deal with this uncertainty by adjusting the tax until the desired policy goal was attained, and the market would give the regulator the information needed to make such adjustments.[28] However, fine-tuning environmental tax rates may be easier said than done. If pollution tax rates cannot be changed over time, or can be changed only infrequently, the choice between pollution taxes and direct controls involves comparing the more economically costly but also more certain control offered by direct regulation with the less costly but also less certain control offered by environmental charges. Thus, relying on corrective taxes rather than direct controls to achieve legislatively mandated standards might be an attractive option only if the certainty of control is less important than the costs of control. However, in cases where it is imperative to limit emissions to a given amount regardless of the cost, the uncertainty associated with corrective charges becomes a more serious limitation.

The Financial Burden

271

CH 8:
CORRECTIVE
TAXES,
CHARGES,
AND
TRADABLE
PERMITS

From the perspective of those who are regulated, taxes and fees pose an additional financial disadvantage when compared with direct regulation. Typically, a direct environmental regulation takes the form of requiring the business to emit no more than some mandated level, which requires an outlay to cut back emissions. However, if the cutback is achieved by means of a tax or fee, the business bears not only the cost of cutting back emissions, but also the cost of paying the tax or fee on the remaining charges. Several studies done in the 1980s showed that taxing pollution at rates high enough to create true incentives for abatement would easily increase revenues—and the associated financial burden—from environmental taxes severalfold.[29] Moreover, these increased taxes would not be evenly distributed among industries and products. For example, in the case of taxes on stationary sources of air pollution, perhaps 75 percent of the added tax burden would fall on seven industries. Robert Crandall (1983) has suggested that these impacts could be softened by taxing emissions only above some minimum threshold. In principle, this approach would provide financial incentives for abatement beyond this threshold level while reducing the burden (and the revenue collected) from prospective taxes on pollution. It would, however, also increase the costs of administering and complying with such taxes. This problem, however, may not be as significant in the case of fees and charges on waste disposal, mainly because the level of the fee or charge that would be required to provide the desired incentives would not impose a large tax burden.

Advantages—Permit Trading

Allowing polluters to trade pollution permits with each other has many of the advantages of taxing pollution, while avoiding some of the disadvantages. As described above, the essential feature of tradable permit schemes is that regulators set a desired level of overall environmental emissions, issue permits to pollute to individual polluters, and then allow permits to be bought and sold. Under this arrangement, polluters with relatively high costs of controlling pollution would find it worthwhile to buy additional rights to pollute from polluters with relative low costs of control. Polluters with relatively low costs of controlling pollution would find the costs of cutting back on pollution to be less than the income they could receive by selling rights to pollute.

Because the total amount of permits is fixed to equal the legislatively mandated level of pollution, the trading of pollution permits does not affect the total amount of pollution reduction. It does, however, redistribute total abatement among pollution sources with the high and low costs of control. As long as trades can be arranged with little or no transactions costs, pollution permits would be traded until each producer faced the same marginal cost of abatement. Thus, like taxes, tradable permits can lower the cost of achieving legislatively mandated levels of environmental quality. Unlike taxes, however, tradable permits would produce a certain level of pollution control. In addition, tradable permits do not impose the same financial burdens on regulated industries. Indeed, when compared with the alternative of direct regulation, all parties involved actually realize a financial gain from the ability to trade rights to pollute with each other.

Disadvantages—Permit Trading

As noted by Stavins, one of the reasons for the relative success of the SO_2 trading experiment is that the cost of achieving the overall policy goal differed widely among sources.[30] A flexible market-based approach makes particular sense in such circumstances, but there are other instances in which such differences, and hence the potential gains from permit trading, may not be as great. In this case, the added benefit from relying on a more decentralized approach may not be worth the added complexities of creating such a system.

Another potentially important limitation on the use of permit trading schemes is the implicit presumption that "more pollution than allowed" at one source can be offset by a physically equal amount of "less pollution than allowed" at another source. Making this assumption effectively assumes that the social harms to be avoided are at least roughly commensurate at each source. Yet, this may not always be true scientifically. In such cases, permit trading can lead to localized "hot spots" with relatively high levels of pollution because of high costs of abatement.

Political Considerations

Despite the (almost uniform) support of economists for a greater reliance on market-based approaches to changing socially harmful behavior, the political acceptance of this policy tool has been uneven. There has, of late, been considerable political support for increasing taxes on smoking and fees on hazardous waste. In contrast, there are formidable obstacles to the enactment of significant environmental taxes, and the acceptance of pollution permit schemes has been rather limited.

Clearly, one political attraction of corrective taxes or fees is that they raise tax revenue. In 1989, Congress was caught between Scylla and Charybdis of a large and (at the time) growing budget deficit, and a president who had issued a "read my lips, no new taxes" pledge in the campaign. The president's stand made Congress especially receptive to policies that arguably could be described as serving a "larger social purpose" than simply raising government revenue. Similar factors led to support for the excise tax on ozone-depleting chemicals, which, as noted by a staff member of the Joint Committee on Taxation, emerged from an "almost serendipitous" consensus.

> The budget proposed auctioning the rights to produce such chemicals, although administration officials indicated privately that a tax on the producer's side would be as acceptable as an auction of the rights to produce. At the same time, a Congressional budget resolution mandated the House Committee on Ways and Means and the Senate Committee on Finance to raise revenue from sources within their jurisdictions, which would include taxes, but not auctions. At least one member of each tax-writing committee had already introduced legislation to tax ozone-depleting chemicals. Consequently a tax on ozone-depleting chemicals represented a sorely-needed revenue source which had sponsorship from within the tax-writing committees and had the endorsement of the President who otherwise proclaimed he was opposed to new taxes. The result of this confluence was that the tax was included as part of the budget reconciliation process with little opposition.[31]

The same argument—that one could "do good while doing well for the Federal treasury"—was repeated again in President Clinton's 1993 proposed budget, which included a fairly sizable hike in federal tobacco taxes that were described as "no regrets taxes."

The revenue that is collected from taxes and fees, however, reflects a tax that must be paid by someone, and this tool feature generates political opposition, especially to taxes or fees that are perceived as being "too high." The fact that any administratively workable tax or fee typically must be levied on all consumption or production, not just consumption or production in excess of some legally mandated amount, means that

implementing social regulations through corrective taxes and fees can actually be financially more costly to the regulated than direct regulation. The relative uncertainty
of achieving desired targets can also be considered to be a political liability of certain
tax and fee schemes.

The above criticisms, however, do not apply with the same force to permit trading
schemes, which at least on paper seem to be a win-win situation for all concerned. Yet,
there was considerable opposition to the inclusion of permit trading in the CAAA.

Stavins notes that political opposition to permit trading came from several quarters.
One was symbolic: environmental groups that supported stricter regulations portrayed
such programs as giving businesses a "license to pollute." These groups were also concerned that giving firms emissions permits would seem to confer a property right—a
right to emit—that would be difficult to curtail through the political process in the
future.

Roger Noll (2000) also provides a fascinating account of how the political support
for emissions trading has ebbed and flowed as a result of changes in the relative benefits
and costs of using different tools of environmental regulation.[32] Noll argues that initially
there was a tacit regulatory bargain between established industries and environmentalists that favored adopting direct regulation over market-based incentives. This bargain basically rested on implementing environmental regulations by enacting fairly
Draconian "new source performance standards" that tended to favor established facilities over new ones. Thus, environmental regulations had the effect of protecting
established facilities from competition by new entrants. From the environmentalists'
perspective, this arrangement also made social regulation more palatable because it
avoided imposing standards on established businesses that could have had the effect of
bankrupting many companies and increasing unemployment in regulated industries.

Noll argues, however, that the passage of time, changes in demand, international
trade, and the advance of technology reduced the benefits of this bargain to both sides.
Established industries found themselves in a situation where they needed to modernize
their increasingly obsolete facilities in order to meet import competition, and suddenly
they too came up against the new performance standards that had previously been their
source of protection. Supporters of environmental regulation found it harder to enact
additional emission controls because of the increased opposition now coming from
established industry. Thus, both the regulated and supporters of regulation found it in
their interest to explore more flexible forms of regulation that placed more reliance on
permit trading as a mechanism for reducing compliance costs.

Despite the increased openness to making environmental regulations more flexible
by introducing permit trading schemes, Noll goes on to observe that the pace of adopting this reform has been slow because the basic thrust of recent policy was not just to
substitute an arguably more flexible for a less flexible policy tool, but to combine this
with increasing the level of regulation. Noll argues persuasively that bundling a regulatory reform with increased regulatory stringency is likely to cause the reform to fail,
or be less complete. One reason is that the initial system of relatively inefficient direct
regulation exists not because of some political accident, but instead reflects a kind of
political equilibrium that gives more weight to certain interests. The other is that the
inevitable result of making products, workplaces, or the environment more healthy and
safe is to subject some actors to regulation who have hitherto been able to avoid it,
even though the new, more stringent system is structured to have lower compliance
costs than the existing system. The upshot is that those who have a reason to oppose
the new regulation also have a reason to oppose the reform that is tied to the new
regulation.

273

CH 8:
CORRECTIVE
TAXES,
CHARGES,
AND
TRADABLE
PERMITS

V. MANAGEMENT CHALLENGES AND POTENTIAL RESPONSE

As noted in another chapter, relying more on economic incentives as tools of social policy is one response to the criticism that social regulation, with its command-and-control approach, can be overly restrictive as a policy tool. However, shifting toward more decentralized, market-based approaches to regulation poses its own set of challenges because implementing and managing these policy tools either requires creating new institutions or adapting existing government institutions that have purposes other than regulating behavior. More generally, policymakers also need to ensure that market-based approaches actually provide meaningful financial incentives for private parties to change their behavior. These management challenges are outlined more fully below.

Establishing Appropriate Administrative Structures

Although they are often considered relatively automatic, corrective fees and taxes have their own administrative complexities, as we have seen. Already established mechanisms for collecting government revenue can be used to administer corrective taxes, but these institutions need to be adapted to reflect the fact that such taxes are levied to change socially harmful behavior as well as to raise revenue. For example, managing large-scale environmental taxes requires expertise about both the design and administration of taxes that is to be found in tax agencies, and about the administration and management of environmental regulations that is to be found in environmental agencies. Imposing environmental taxes on "new" bases, such as emissions, may also require creating new mechanisms for monitoring tax compliance that differ from conventional ways of auditing financial and production records.

In some cases, fees and charges can be collected under existing arrangements, but as in the case of corrective taxes, these existing arrangements need to be modified. Implementing charges that are designed to foster recycling and reduce the amount of trash brought to the curb might "simply" require replacing an existing flat monthly charge for trash service with a more elaborate schedule of fees to reflect the amount and type of trash left for pickup. Additional complexity, however, would be introduced into the process of preparing and collecting bills, and new systems of monitoring would be needed. For example, if the amount of the charge varied with the number of trash cans left for pickup and the amount of trash that was presorted for recycling, the agency charged with implementing the fee would have to develop an administratively workable way of keeping track of the amount and type of trash left at curbside by each customer.

In other cases, there may be no existing arrangements that can be easily adapted to collecting a new fee or charge. For example, a community that previously provided waste disposal as a "free" public service would need to create a new system for imposing and then collecting charges for waste disposal that varied with the amount and type of trash collected.

Creating Incentives

Another management challenge is to balance the need for taxing activities that are easy to monitor and administer with providing private parties with the right incentives. In the case of the Seattle waste disposal program, levying a charge that varied with the number of (standardized) garbage cans set out for pickup had the intended effect of reducing the overall volume of waste that needed to be disposed, but the behavior that could be easily "monitored" was not the actual amount of waste brought to the curb in terms of weight, but rather its bulk, measured in terms of whether the waste could fit into a standard-size garbage can. The result was a price incentive that encouraged people not only to bring less waste to the curb, but also to pack their waste more densely, which may not have been entirely compatible with the overall objective of reducing the total amount of waste to be disposed.

275

CH 8:
CORRECTIVE
TAXES,
CHARGES,
AND
TRADABLE
PERMITS

Monitoring

In the case of permit trading, one might think that the key management challenge would be to create and maintain a well-functioning market for permits. Yet, the experience with permit trading in the United States demonstrates that such a market can be developed and sustained with a minimum of active government involvement, provided that there is adequate monitoring of the performance of private parties and tracking of the volume of trades that take place.

Creating such a monitoring and tracking system, however, is a major management challenge in itself. Adequate and timely monitoring of compliance with regulatory targets requires that technologies for measuring the physical amount of emissions must either exist or be developed, and sophisticated information systems for keeping track of the buying and selling of permits must also be created. Clearly, both the measurement and information technologies that are needed to implement a successful permit trading system have benefited greatly from the rapid diffusion of computers and management information systems in government and industry.

Coordination

A further management challenge to permit trading arises from the need to coordinate the use of this policy tool with other features of the regulatory landscape. For example, some opponents of permit trading were concerned that utilities, which were the prime object of regulation, would not have an incentive to participate in permit trading because state regulatory commissions would not allow them to reap the rewards from lower costs of compliance. In fact, there is some evidence that this factor may have reduced the amount of permit trading.[33]

VI. OVERALL ASSESSMENT

Have corrective taxes, fees, and permit trading proved to be useful tools of policy? As we have seen, these tools rank fairly high in terms of efficiency. More at issue, however, is their effectiveness—whether corrective taxes, fees, and permits are capable of changing behavior as intended. Also of concern is their legitimacy and their contribution to equity. In this section, we assess each of these types of tools in terms of these criteria.

Corrective Taxes and Fees

Effectiveness

So far as corrective taxes and fees are concerned, as noted earlier, one of the major challenges is to find a tax rate that is sufficient to deter the behavior that public policy is trying to discourage. Where the behavior brings unique or especially large satisfaction or rewards to consumers or firms, the tax rate may need to be virtually confiscatory in order to deter the behavior. Therefore, one of the great concerns about corrective taxes and charges is that they may prove ineffective in precisely the circumstances where they are most needed.

Fortunately, empirical studies to date have tended to refute this concern, at least in part. Such studies consistently find that people and businesses do respond to corrective taxes and fees by curtailing a range of socially costly activities. There is considerable evidence that smoking is fairly sensitive to price and thus can be curtailed by taxing cigarettes. Estimates of this sensitivity indicate, for example, that the average combined federal-state cigarette tax rate, which raises the price of cigarettes by roughly 25 percent, reduces consumption of cigarettes by between 10 and 25 percent.[34] It also appears that cigarette consumption by young smokers is especially price sensitive. Indeed, recently the World Bank has offered a strong endorsement of using cigarette taxes to curb smoking worldwide.[35]

Other studies have also found that cigarette taxes affect cigarette consumption in a way that is similar to increasing smokers' perceptions of the risks of smoking. Kip Viscusi (1997), for example, has shown that the average national excise tax on smoking has the same discouraging effect on smoking as would a perception by smokers that there was a 27 percent chance that smoking causes lung cancer.

Alcohol taxes also appear to be effective tools for curbing abusive drinking. There is broad evidence that alcohol consumption is sensitive to price, and one major study has found that higher beer taxes contribute to reduced highway fatalities from drunk driving accidents.[36] As in the case of cigarette taxes, there is also evidence that younger consumers, who are more apt to be abusive drinkers, are more sensitive to price, and hence more sensitive to alcohol taxes than older drinkers.

Charges for waste disposal also have performed as expected. When Seattle began charging $16.10 per month for each can picked up weekly, and coupled this charge with an offer to haul away for free paper, glass, and metal that had been preseparated for recycling, total tonnage that needed to be buried fell by 22 percent, and voluntary recycling rose from 22 percent of waste to 36 percent—a rate that was almost three times the national average. When Charlottesville, Virginia, decided to charge $.80 per 32-gallon bag or can of residential garbage collected at curbside, the volume of garbage presented for collection was estimated to decline by 37 percent, after controlling for other factors. (The weight of Charlottesville garbage, however, fell by a smaller amount—14 percent—in part because Charlottesville residents began practicing their own version of the Seattle stomp.[37])

Whether similar results will obtain in other settings where the behavior to be affected involves greater economic stakes is an open question. Polluters may, for example, willingly pay a fee or charge rather than reduce their emissions unless the fee or charge is set exceedingly high.

Nevertheless, the evidence to date is more encouraging about the effectiveness of corrective charges than skeptics have assumed.

Equity

On balance, the use of corrective taxes and fees as policy tools also meets generally accepted notions of fairness, provided that the rate of the tax or fee bears some relation to the harm that the fee or tax is intended to correct. Thus, even though a tax on smoking may be regressive with respect to income because it hits the poor harder than the rich, it nonetheless can be regarded as fair to the extent that the tax bears some relation to the external costs borne by smokers. Similarly, with respect to environmental taxes and other charges such as waste disposal fees, the charge is fair as long as the tax or fee is related to the environmental damage to be prevented or ameliorated.

Legitimacy

277

CH 8:
CORRECTIVE
TAXES,
CHARGES,
AND
TRADABLE
PERMITS

Corrective taxes also perform well in terms of legitimacy. This is so for two somewhat different reasons. Taxing activities with social costs is seen as a legitimate expression of society's *moral* disapproval of certain activities. As noted above, taxes on alcohol and tobacco have their origins as sumptuary taxes—taxes imposed for moral or religious reasons on "sinful activities."[38] Similarly, taxes on polluters have been justified on the grounds that it is "only fair" that the polluter pay.

A somewhat different rationale for corrective taxes and charges is that they provide a means of making sure that people pay for "external costs" that their activities impose on the rest of society. While this justification may seem similar to the sumptuary tax rationale, there is an important difference. If corrective taxes are seen as legitimate for *economic* rather than for *moral* reasons, the magnitude of the tax should, in principle, bear some relationship to the economic costs of the social harm that the tax is intended to correct. For example, there is some evidence that current federal and state tobacco taxes fully reflect the costs of smoking that are not borne by American smokers. If one accepts this evidence, the case for taxing cigarettes even more heavily is weaker if the policy objective is to reduce smoking to a socially "optimal" level than it is if the policy objective is to curtail smoking as much as possible because it is wrong to smoke.[39]

Permit Trading

Efficiency

Trading of environmental permits also scores high in terms of efficiency. By increasing flexibility permit trading has lowered the costs of complying with environmental regulations. Several different estimates suggest that allowing permit trading may have cut the costs of complying with the CAAA by between 30 and 50 percent.

Effectiveness

Perhaps just as important, the flexibility built into the permit trading system has produced some surprises in terms of effectiveness. One was the rapid expansion in the nationwide use of relatively cheap, low-sulfur coal that became possible because of significant declines in rail rates. While no one claims that allowing permit trading caused rail rates to decline, there is a general agreement that the flexibility introduced by permit trading made it possible for utilities to take advantage of this development.

Another unexpected outcome was that many utilities found it economically advantageous to exceed the required cutbacks required under Phase I of the CAAA in order to be able to bank allowances for future use in Phase II, which began in January 2000. As noted by Douglas Bohi and Dallas Burtraw,[40] banking of allowances was a "win-win" outcome for the environment and for industry. "Overcompliance" with emissions targets set for Phase I provided environmental and public health benefits sooner than would otherwise have occurred. In exchange, industry was able to cut its cost of compliance and ease into the more stringent emissions set in Phase II.

Equity

Allowing permit trading may seem to transfer income from high-cost companies (who will buy permits) to low-cost companies (who will sell permits), but this disguises the fact that both buyers and sellers are made better off by being allowed to trade, compared with the alternative of direct controls. A potentially more serious concern that blends concerns of fairness along with those of economic efficiency is that permit schemes that are implemented by distributing emissions allowances free of charge to existing businesses favors existing firms and can be a barrier to new entrants.

Legitimacy

As noted above, counterbalancing these advantages, permit trading does have the disadvantage of appearing to give polluters a "license to pollute." As such, it lacks some legitimacy. The concept of allowing more pollution at one site to be balanced by less pollution at another can also be controversial. As noted by Stavins, such ethical objections to the use of market incentives to control pollution have diminished in recent years, but have not disappeared entirely.[41]

VII. FUTURE DIRECTIONS

The acceptance of using market incentives to regulate socially harmful behavior has grown, although skeptics remain. The skepticism seems greatest when proposals to expand the range and scope of existing regulations are under discussion. If "past is prologue," this observation implies that the political climate for using market incentives as a regulatory policy tool is likely to be most favorable after the initial political battle for regulating private behavior has been fought and won.

Nonetheless, the future seems bright for the use of corrective taxes, fees, and tradeable permit schemes. Making more use of market incentives to modify socially harmful behavior has garnered significant support, based in no small part on the demonstrated success of these policy tools.

There is evidence that using market incentives to change socially harmful behavior can be effective and offers fairly significant economic benefits compared with more direct means of control. In the case of corrective taxes and fees, the past record shows that people and businesses respond in predictable ways to financial incentives, and the prospect of raising revenue from taxing activities that are widely regarded to be "social bads" can be politically attractive. The first large-scale experiment with permit trading also has achieved results that are largely consistent with the expectations of its proponents, and this success should contribute to more acceptance of this tool in the future.

This is important because past political opposition to the adoption of such market-based regulatory tools has been motivated in part by a real concern about the practical feasibility of achieving policy goals with such decentralized approaches. Continuing improvements in measurement and information technologies are likely to diminish the force of this concern even further. In the case of corrective environmental taxes and charges, improved measurement technologies should make it easier over time to tax socially harmful activities more directly—for example, by taxing emissions instead of having to tax more easily observed activities such as production or sales. Better measurement and information technologies also make it easier to implement permit trading schemes. More generally, as the costs of acquiring and processing information continue to fall, the workability of such flexible, market-based approaches seems likely to rise, thereby helping to expand the prospects for such market-based tools for influencing behavior.

VIII. SUGGESTED READING

279

CH 8:
CORRECTIVE
TAXES,
CHARGES,
AND
TRADABLE
PERMITS

Corrective Taxes and Fees

Barthold, Thomas. "Issues in the Design of Environmental Excise Taxes," *Journal of Economic Perspectives* 8, no. 1 (1994): 133–151.

Cook, Phillip, and Michael Moore. "Alcohol," National Bureau of Economic Research, Working Paper W6905 (1999).

Farber, Stephen. "Environmental Taxes and Fees," in *Handbook on Taxation,* eds. W. Bartley Hildreth and James A. Richardson. New York: Marcel Dekker, 1999.

World Bank. *Curbing the Epidemic: Governments and the Economics of Tobacco Control.* Washington, D.C.: World Bank, 1999.

Permit Trading

Bohi, Douglas, and Dallas Burtraw. "SO_2 Allowance Trading: How Experience and Expectations Measure Up," Resources for the Future, Discussion Paper 97–24 (1997).

Joskow, Paul L., Richard Schmalensee, and Elizabeth Bailey. "The Market for Sulfur Dioxide Emissions," *American Economic Review* 88, no. 4 (1998): 669–685.

Noll, Roger. *The Economics and Politics of the Slowdown in Regulatory Reform.* Washington, D.C.: AEI-Brookings Joint Center for Regulatory Studies, 2000.

Schmalensee, Richard, Paul L. Joskow, A. Denny Ellerman, Juan Pablo Montero, and Elizabeth Bailey. "An Interim Evaluation of Sulfur Dioxide Emissions Trading," *Journal of Economic Perspectives* 12, no. 3 (1998): 53–68.

Stavins, Robert N. "What Can We Learn from the Grand Policy Experiment? Lessons from SO_2 Allowance Trading," *Journal of Economic Perspectives* 12, no. 3 (1998): 69–88.

ACKNOWLEDGMENTS

I am grateful to Thomas Barthold, Bruce Davie, and Lester Salamon for helpful comments on earlier drafts of this chapter.

NOTES

1. This vignette is based on the description of the Seattle program found in *The Economics of Public Issues, eds.* Roger L. Miller, Daniel K. Benjamin, and Douglass C. North (Reading, Mass.: Addison-Wesley, 1999), 164–171.

2. See Paul Portney, "Economics and the Clean Air Act," *Journal of Economic Perspectives* 4, no. 4 (1990), 173–81, who notes that only a small fraction of the cost of environmental regulations are reflected in government outlays, with the bulk of such costs borne by private companies.

3. See Thomas Pogue and Larry Sgontz, "Taxing to Control Social Costs," *American Economic Review* 79, no. 1 (March 1989), 235–243.

4. For a discussion, see Congressional Budget Office, *Federal Taxation of Tobacco, Alcoholic Beverages, and Motor Fuels* (Washington, D.C.: Congressional Budget Office, 1990), 56–65.

5. Bundesministerium der Finanzen (German Finance Ministry), *Unsere Steuern von A bis Z* (Our Taxes from A to Z), p. 122, at http://www.bundesfinanzministerium.de.

6. Congressional Budget Offices, *The Growth of Federal User Charges* (Washington, D.C.: Congressional Budget Office, 1993), 3–14.

7. Action on Smoking and Health, *Cigarette Facts, Including International, Historical, and State Tables,* 17 January 1999, at http://ash.org/cigtaxfacts.html. In 1997 the federal tax on cigarettes was increased to $0.34 per pack in 2000–2001, and $0.39 in subsequent years, while in fiscal year

1996, state cigarette taxes averaged $0.317 per pack, ranging from a low of $0.25 in Virginia to a high of $0.815 in Washington State. See Kip Viscusi, "Tobacco Taxes," in *Encyclopedia of Taxation and Tax Policy,* eds. Joseph J. Cordes, Robert D. Ebel, Jane G. Gravelle (Washington, D.C.: The Urban Institute Press, 1999), 406–408.

8. "Big Tax Hike on Cigarettes Hurts Small N.Y. Stores," *Washington Post* (16 July 2000), A11.

9. Thomas F. Pogue, "Alcohol Beverage Taxes, Federal," in Cordes et al. (1999), 6–7.

10. Congressional Budget Office (1990), 103–108.

11. Congressional Budget Office (1990), 11.

12. Bruce Davie, "Sumptuary Taxation," in *The Encyclopedia of Taxation and Tax Policy,* eds. Joseph J. Cordes, Robert D. Ebel, and Jane G. Gravelle (Washington, D.C.: The Urban Institute Press, 1999).

13. Joint Committee on Taxation, U.S. Congress, *Schedule of Present Federal Excise Taxes* (Washington, D.C.: U.S. Government Printing Office, 29 March 1999), 17–22.

14. This section, and the discussion of federal environmental taxes, generally draws heavily on Thomas Barthold, "Issues in the Design of Environmental Taxes," *Journal of Economic Perspectives* 8, no. 10. (1994), 133–151.

15. Thus, for example, the chemical CFC-11 is assigned an ozone-depleting factor of 1.0, while Halon-1211, 1301, and 2402 are assigned factors of 3.0, 10.0, and 6.0, respectively. Other chemicals, such as CFC-113 and 115, and methyl chloroform are assigned factors of less than 1.0. The result is that the ozone-depletion excise tax per pound of CFC-12 equals $7.60 per pound, the taxes that apply to Halon-1211, 1301, and 2402 are three, ten, and six times that amount, respectively, and the excise taxes on CFC-113, 115, and methyl chloroform are less than $7.60. The base rate of the ozone-depleting chemicals tax is scheduled to increase by $0.45 per pound per year. See Barthold (1994) and Joint Committee on Taxation (2000).

16. Congressional Budget Office (1990), 58–59.

17. Paul Joskow, Richard Schmalensee, and Elizabeth M. Bailey, "The Market for Sulfur Dioxide Emissions," *The American Economic Review* 88, no. 4. (1998): 669–685.

18. See Davie (1999).

19. Cigarette taxes range from a low of 70 percent of the price of a pack of cigarettes in Sweden to a high of 85 percent in the United Kingdom. See Action on Smoking and Health (1999).

20. Stephen Farber, "Environmental Taxes and Fees," in *Handbook on Taxation,* eds. W. Bartley Hildreth and James A. Richardson (New York: Marcel Dekker, 1999).

21. See, for example, World Bank, *Curbing the Epidemic: Governments and the Economics of Tobacco Control* (Washington, D.C.: World Bank, 1999); and Philip J. Cook and Michael J. Moore, "Alcohol," National Bureau of Economic Research, Working Paper W6905 (January 1999).

22. See Joseph J. Cordes and Harry S. Watson, "The Theory and Practice of Tax Incidence Analysis," in *Handbook of Public Finance,* eds. Fred Thompson and Mark T. Green (New York: Marcel Dekker, 1998), 93–135.

23. This discussion draws extensively on Barthold (1994), 138–142.

24. One reason for considering taxes as a means of reducing the production of CFCs was to prevent producers of these chemicals from earning "excess profits" as a result of legally being required to restrict supply. I am grateful to Bruce Davie for raising this point.

25. This section draws extensively on the descriptions of permit trading provided in Douglas Bohi and Dallas Burtraw, "SO_2 Allowance Trading: How Experience and Expectations Measure Up," Discussion Paper 97–24, Resources for the Future, February 1997; Joskow et al. (1998); Richard Schmalensee, Paul L. Joskow, A. Denny Ellerman, Juan Pablo Montero, and Elizabeth Bailey, "An Interim Evaluation of Sulfur Dioxide Emissions Trading," *Journal of Economic Perspectives* 12, no. 3 (summer 1998): 53–58; and Robert N. Stavins, "What Can We Learn from the Grand Policy Experiment? Lessons from SO_2 Allowance Trading," *Journal of Economic Perspectives* 12, no. 3 (summer 1998): 69–88.

26. This section draws heavily from Joseph J. Cordes, Eric M. Nicholson, and Frank J. Sammartino, "Raising Revenue by Taxing Activities with Social Costs," *National Tax Journal* 43 (1990): 343–356.

281

CH 8:
CORRECTIVE
TAXES,
CHARGES,
AND
TRADABLE
PERMITS

27. Michael Maloney and Bruce Yandle, "Bubbles and Efficiency," *Regulation* (May/June 1980): 49–52.

28. This argument is made in William J. Baumol and Wallace Oates, *The Theory of Environmental Policy* (Cambridge: Cambridge University Press, 1988).

29. Robert J. Crandall, *Controlling Industrial Pollution* (Washington, D.C.: The Brookings Institution, 1983); and David Terkla, "The Efficiency Value of Effluent Tax Revenues," *Journal of Environmental Economics and Management* 11 (1984): 107–123.

30. Robert N. Stavins (1998).

31. Barthold (1994), 137.

32. This section summarizes points made in Roger G. Noll, *The Economics and Politics of the Slowdown in Regulatory Reform* (Washington, D.C.: AEI-Brookings Joint Center on Regulation, 1999), at http://www.aei.brookings.org/publications/.

33. Stavins (1998), 81.

34. Viscusi (1999). See also Kip Viscusi, "Cigarette Taxation and the Social Consequences of Smoking," in *Tax Policy and the Economy*, ed. James M. Poterba (Cambridge, Mass.: MIT Press, 1995).

35. World Bank (1997).

36. Cook and Moore (1999); and Christopher Ruhm, "Alcohol Policies and Highway Vehicle Fatalities," National Bureau of Economic Research, Working Paper W5195 (July 1995).

37. Miller, Benjamin, and North (1999), 164–171.

38. See Davie (1999), 343.

39. The socially optimal level would be the amount of smoking that results when the price of a pack of cigarettes (inclusive of cigarette taxes) just equals the costs that a smoker imposes on the rest of society by smoking that pack.

40. Bohi and Burtraw (1997).

41. Stavins (1998), and as cited in Michael J. Sandel, "It's Immoral to Buy the Right to Pollute," *New York Times* (15 December 1997), A29.

CHAPTER NINE

Contracting

Steven J. Kelman

Students applying for the federal government's student loan program might reasonably assume that they will come in contact, at some point, with the Office of Student Financial Assistance in the U.S. Department of Education, the federal agency with responsibility for this program. But nothing could be further from the truth. In fact, virtually every contact these students will have will be with a private organization serving as a contractor for the federal government.

The application form, for example, has been developed by an outside contractor, and the forms themselves are printed and mailed by contractors.[1] A contractor enters the data from the filled-in forms and sends the data electronically to another contractor, which used a computer program to determine student eligibility with the aid of government-established formulas. The contractor then sends the eligibility information to the university the student has applied to. Even the servicing of the loan is handled by a contractor, and, if the student defaults, the government will have to enlist another contractor to collect.

This example illustrates an important point: none of the tools of government discussed in this book is more ubiquitous than contracting. People working in the Department of Veterans Affairs need not concern themselves with tax incentives; those in a state highway department can ignore vouchers; employees of a local school district never run into loan guarantees. There are even important government missions that use few or no regulatory tools to achieve their missions (diplomacy and war fighting, for example). However, every public agency and every private organization of any size contracts for some of the goods and services needed to achieve its purposes. Therefore, almost everyone working in the public sector will come into contact, at least to some extent, with the tool of contracting.

I. DEFINING THE TOOL

Contracting, as a tool of government, is a business arrangement between a government agency and a private entity in which the private entity promises, in exchange for money, to deliver certain products or services to the government agency or to others on the government's behalf. The private entity may be either a for-profit business or a nonprofit organization.

Defining Features

Implicit in this definition are a number of key features that characterize contracting as a tool. First, contracting involves a choice by government not to produce a product or service itself but to buy it from the outside. Thus, rather than produce weapons itself as it has sometimes done in the past through government-run arsenals, the Department of Defense chooses to buy weapons from contractors.[2] Governments buy an enormous range of products and services, from personal computers, office supplies, and lawn-mowing services to child protective services, huge database software programs, and fighter planes.

The second basic feature of a contract is that it is a "business arrangement" analogous to business arrangements that occur in the private sector. Unlike some other tools of government, such as tax incentives or vouchers, contracting is used widely outside government. For example, Coca-Cola uses contracting as a tool when it deals with advertising agencies, information technology providers, or corn syrup vendors. By far, the vast majority of contracting occurs among business firms. Experience from private-sector contracting may be relevant to government contracting, both in thinking about the appropriate boundaries for in-house production versus contracting and in thinking about how best to structure a business relationship.

Another significant feature of contracting is the distinction between contracting for procurement of products and services used directly by the government agency and contracting for the delivery of government-funded services by third parties to external recipients. The latter is often called "purchase-of-service" (POS) contracting. This chapter focuses primarily on procurement contracting, and the following chapter focuses on POS contracting.

Relation to Key Tool Features

Contracting may be compared to other tools described in this book along the four dimensions identified in the introductory chapter: *directness, automaticity, coercion,* and *visibility.*

Directness

Directness measures the extent to which the entity authorizing or inaugurating a program is involved in executing it. On the directness scale, compared with other tools, contracting is ranked in the medium category. In one sense, contracting is less direct, since it leaves production in private hands. However, in a number of important ways, contracting may be a more direct tool of government action than many other tools. First, in a contract the government is free to be as explicit as it chooses in the requirements it imposes on the contractor. It may be more directive than the most directive project grant in imposing requirements on a contractor, or it may leave as much discretion to the contractor as is left in the least directive block grant. Generally, the government imposes more requirements on contractors than it does on private parties whose behavior it seeks to change through other economic incentive tools such as tax expenditures, vouchers, or loan guarantees.

Second, although contracting uses economic incentives to induce behavior that otherwise would not have occurred, it is more direct than most other economic incentive tools because in a contract the third-party behavior that is being sought is clearly brought forth in response to the tool. By contrast, tools that simply subsidize or encourage certain behaviors by private parties, such as tax expenditures or loan guarantees, spend resources paying for behavior that might have taken place anyway.

Third, contracting, except for POS contracting, is more direct than some other tools because generally the authorizing government contracts for *inputs* into final services that government, not the contractor, delivers. Contractors produce weapons, not national defense; computer systems used at border checkpoints, not border control; evaluations of policy effectiveness, not policy choices.

Automaticity

Automaticity measures the extent to which a tool utilizes an existing administrative structure to produce its effect rather than having to create its own administrative apparatus. On the automaticity scale, contracting is ranked in the medium category. If there are suppliers who sell their products or services to the commercial marketplace independent of government requirements, contracting can effectively use the existing market structure. Government often uses existing commercial arrangements already widely used by businesses, and it uses marketplace competition to select suppliers.

However, contracting is less automatic when there is no nongovernmental market for what the government is buying, as with contracting for weapons, fingerprint identification systems, or most human services. Also, the selection of a contractor is far less automatic than the selection of a provider of services offered through other third-party tools such as vouchers or loan guarantees (e.g., Section 8 housing vouchers or student loans). When vouchers or loan guarantees are used, any private firm meeting certain minimum requirements may participate, whereas in competitive contracts there are winners and losers. A bank cannot lose the opportunity to provide student loans as long as it meets certain requirements, whereas a federal agency contracting for credit cards for government users will choose one credit card vendor over another. Thus, contracting relies on extensive administrative regulations for choosing and overseeing contractors, which departs from a pure market model.

Coerciveness

Coerciveness measures the extent to which a tool restricts individual or group behavior as opposed to merely encouraging or discouraging it. On this scale as well, contracting ranks in the medium category compared with other tools. Contracts are more restrictive than tools such as public information, grants, and vouchers, but are less restrictive than tools such as corrective taxes and regulations.

Contracts involve a voluntary incursion of obligations in exchange for compensation. No private firm or organization is coerced into executing a contact with a government agency. However, the potential contractor may feel some degree of coercion if it has become dependent on government contracts for its survival.

Government coercion may be used in the administration of contracts if it becomes necessary to terminate an existing contract. In addition, certain contractor behaviors, such as submitting false claims or defective products, may be subject to civil and/or criminal penalties that go beyond common-law contractual remedies for breach of contract in private contractual relationships.

Visibility

Visibility measures the extent to which the resources devoted to a tool show up in the normal budget process. Compared with the other tools discussed in this book, contracting falls into the relatively high visibility category. Most contract expenditures are treated as regular budget outlays, even though they are often not specifically identified as contracts. Thus, contracting is more visible in the budget and accounting processes than tools such as regulation, loan guarantees, insurance, and tax expenditures.

In addition, the contracting process in the United States is generally quite transparent or visible at the federal, state, and local levels. In many instances, laws or regulations require that special efforts be made to announce broadly the intention of a government agency to purchase products or services through a contract so that the maximum number of eligible bidders are informed. The rules or guidelines for the selection of a contractor are generally also codified in public documents.

Thus, for example, information about federal government contracts is published daily in *Commerce Business Daily*. This publication lists notices of proposed government procurement actions, contract awards, and other procurement information. All federal procurement offices are required to announce proposed procurement actions over $25,000 and contract awards over $25,000 that are likely to result in any subcontracts. Each edition contains approximately five hundred to one thousand notices.

Design Features and Major Variants

Three goals have consistently figured in debates about how the processes for government contracting should be designed. The first goal of the design of contracting is to get a good deal for the government. A "good deal" means that the government gets good prices and good performance from the firms with which it does business.

The second goal of the design of contracting is to prevent corruption and promote integrity on the part of government officials, especially in regard to awarding contracts and accepting work performed under a contract.

The third goal in the design of contracting is fairness to people interacting with the contracting system. Being fair means treating similar cases alike and different cases differently. Fairness requires that all qualified contractors have equal access to bidding for the business of "their" government. Decisions should be impartial and related to efficiency and effectiveness. Contracting can also help achieve more general "socio-economic" goals, such as promotion of small and/or minority business, wage protection for contractor employees, and jobs for American workers, the handicapped, or veterans.

Given these overall goals, a number of design issues confront legislators and contracting practitioners. How these issues are addressed shapes the different variants of the contracting tool.

Source Selection

First, key decisions have to be made about how the government agency selects the contractor. The continuum of design options ranges from *sole-source procurement,* where the government negotiates with only one contractor, through various kinds of *limited competition* in which the government solicits bids from a prequalified list of firms or invites some limited group of firms to bid on an *ad hoc* basis, to *full and open competition* in which any firm is entitled to bid and have its bid fairly evaluated.

Within a competitive regime, the government may choose the bidder (1) who complies with all contract requirements and bids the lowest price or (2) who provides the best tradeoff between price and various quality-related factors, traditionally called in the U.S. federal government "best value" source selection.[3] Some observers of contracting refer only to low-price procurements as "competitive," but, in fact, there are a number of possible source selection alternatives that are all fully competitive. Additional information about source selection is presented in the basic mechanics section of this chapter.

Pricing

A second issue concerns how the government compensates the contractor. There are two basic options: *cost reimbursement* and *fixed price.* In fixed-price contracts, the agency pays the contractor a specific sum of money for well-defined products or services. This arrangement may be used for either sole-source contracts or competitive contracts. The price may be adjusted through a negotiated change order if the agency needs to change the nature or quantity of the services or products required. In cost-reimbursement contracts the agency pays the contractor for all legitimate direct and indirect costs attributable to the contract. This payment arrangement is used primarily when the uncertainty about what the product or service will actually cost the contractor is so great that the contractor is unwilling to commit to a fixed price.

An important design feature of each of the pricing alternatives is contract incentives. Contracts may include special provisions that allow additional compensation for the contractor if certain conditions are met. Additional information about these pricing options and their variations is presented in the basic mechanics section of this chapter.

Discretion for Government Officials

A third design issue concerns how much discretion should be delegated to government officials. Discretion—the degree to which government officials may make decisions based on their own best judgment, rather than on rules—is an issue throughout the contracting process, from decisions about what to buy, to contractor selection, to contract administration. Here the continuum of design options goes from establishing rules governing all aspects of contracting to allowing contracting officials to make all decisions about source selection or contract administration. Along the continuum, full and open competition allows less discretion than limited competition, and low-bid source selection allows less discretion than best-value selection.

Oversight

A fourth issue in contracting concerns the amount of oversight of contractors. Oversight means monitoring of the actions of contractors. In theory, oversight could range over a continuum from total reliance on any representation a contractor makes or on any product or service submitted in fulfillment of the contract's requirements to a government inspector checking everything the contractor does.[4] However, neither extreme is practical.

Oversight may include anything from inspection or testing of incoming products to the examination of bills that have been submitted to the measurement of contractor performance against contractual service standards. Special laws applying to government contractors such as civil or criminal penalties for submitting false bills to the government are another form of oversight of contracting. Most oversight occurs after a contract is awarded.[5]

Type of Contract Vehicle

Contracts also vary in terms of the contract vehicle used. If the purchase is a one-time event, a basic contract is used. If there will be multiple purchases over time, a special variation such as a *task order contract* or a *delivery order contract* could be used. A task or delivery order contract may be a *requirements contract* or an *indefinite delivery/ indefinite quantity contract,* depending on whether the government will buy all its needs from one contractor. These variations are discussed in more detail later in this chapter.

Type of Performance Commitment

Contracts also vary with respect to the commitment required from the contractor. There are basically two variations. A *completion contract* obligates the contractor to achieve specific results or produce specific products. A *best-efforts contract* only requires the contractor to exert its best efforts to achieve the designated goal. These two variations are also discussed in greater detail later.

Primary Purpose

Finally, contracts vary in terms of their primary purpose. Generally, one may distinguish between *incidental-support* and *mission-critical* contracting. Incidental-support contracting provides assistance to government employees undertaking an agency's substantive mission—for example, running the cafeteria in a government building. Mission-critical contracting involves using third parties to deliver, or to play a significant role in delivering, the final actions of government—for example, running an information technology logistics system that makes sure that tanks and airplanes stay operational. Often, contracting for mission-critical products or services raises more complex issues because the products or services being delivered are less easy to describe or define.

II. PATTERNS OF TOOL USE

Unlike some other tools discussed in this book, contracting has been around since the beginning of the Republic.[6] Contractors have also helped to realize significant public purposes—not simply to obtain incidental items such as office supplies—since the contracting tool was first used. In the early years of the Republic, mail delivery, which served the important public policy goal of helping create an American nationality, was contracted out.[7] Much weapons production has also always been contracted out, although through the end of the nineteenth century, significant weapons production occurred in government arsenals. The use of contracting has increased apace with the growth of government, and, like much of the growth of government, has especially spurted in times of war.

Table 9-1 shows trends in nominal dollars spent on U.S. federal government contracting in recent years.[8] Tables 9-2 and 9-3 show similar data for U.S. state/local governments and for selected foreign governments (both central and local government spending).[9] The money the U.S. federal government spends on contracts is about 15 percent of the federal budget and about 40 percent of the discretionary budget; U.S.

TABLE 9-1 *Trends in U.S. Federal Procurement*

| | | DOLLARS FOR | | |
Fiscal Year	Total Dollars	Services (Excluding Construction)	Computer Hardware	Information Technology Services
1990	171	86	3.2	3.9
1991	184	93	3.7	4.7
1992	174	96	3.9	5.9
1993	173	97	4.1	6.5
1994	171	100	4.3	6.9
1995	173	101	4.7	8.1
1996	169	102	5.4	8.0
1997	170	99	5.4	8.5
1998	177	103	5.6	10.3

Note: All figures are in billions of dollars. Figures in column 2 exclude foreign military sales.
SOURCE: Federal Procurement Data System.

TABLE 9-2 *Trends in U.S. State and Local Procurement*

Fiscal Year	Total Dollars	Procurement Spending as a Percentage of Total Spending
1989	960	39
1990	1,047	39
1991	1,094	39
1992	1,119	38
1993	1,147	37
1994	1,221	38
1995	1,310	38
1996	1,392	39
1997	1,511	40
1998	1,594	40
1999	1,750	41

Note: All figures are in billions of nominal dollars.
SOURCE: U.S. Department of Commerce, Bureau of Economic Analysis.

state and local procurement is a higher percentage of that spending. Another, quite dramatic way to think of the significance of contracting is the estimate that the federal government's contractor workforce was about 5.6 million, compared with a federal in-house civilian workforce of about 2 million.[10]

As can be seen from Table 9-1, the dollar value of U.S. federal government procurement remained stable in nominal dollars and declined in real dollars during the 1990s, a period of tight budgets in the context of efforts to reduce the federal deficit. This may seem surprising given the view that contracting is increasing. The stable overall federal procurement numbers reflect a decline in weapons spending during this period. However, spending on contracted services, as opposed to all contracts, increased by over 20 percent during this period. This reflects the growing importance of the service economy. Even for services, federal procurement spending increased by only about 2 percent a year in nominal dollars, suggesting no real growth. Even more dramatic was a near tripling in spending for information technology services, reflecting the increased importance of computerization. Even computer hardware spending went up by about 60 percent, despite declining unit prices.

Internationally, procurement as a percentage of government spending has also tended to remain stable during the 1990s. By contrast, U.S. state and local procurement has increased quite dramatically in real dollars and has even increased somewhat as a proportion of total state and local spending, probably reflecting the growth of outsourcing for local services.

| Country | CENTRAL GOVERNMENT | | LOCAL GOVERNMENT | |
| | PERCENTAGE OF BUDGET SPENT ON PURCHASES OF GOODS AND SERVICES | | | |
	Year	Percentage	Year	Percentage
Brazil	1990	6	1990	28
	1993	5	1993	28
France	1990	9	1990	19
	1997	8	1997	21
Ghana	1990	18	1990	n.a.
	1993	17	1993	n.a.
India	1990	13	1990	10
	1997	12	1995	9
Mexico	1990	7	1990	n.a.
	1996	9	1996	n.a.
Sweden	1990	8	1990	16
	1997	9	1997	16
United Kingdom	1990	18	1990	21
	1995	21	1995	22
Zimbabwe	1990	19	1990	49
	1993	20	1991	49

SOURCE: Adapted from International Monetary Fund, *Government Finance Statistics Yearbook,* vol. 22 (1998).

The discussion in the balance of this chapter focuses primarily on contracting by the U.S. federal government. State and local policies vary significantly among jurisdictions; however, at the relatively general level presented here, most jurisdictions have approaches similar to those of the federal government. International policies vary even more widely. At a general level, policies in most western European countries are fairly similar to those of the U.S. federal government, although contracting is generally less regulated.

III. BASIC MECHANICS OF TOOL OPERATION

Once the decision to contract to buy something has been made, contracting involves (1) *structuring the business arrangement,* (2) *source selection,* and (3) *contract administration.* Some decisions on the mechanics of contracting are set *systemwide,* through laws, regulations, and organizational arrangements. Others involve decisions about the design of an individual contract, made by the contracting authority on a procurement-by-procurement basis within the discretion allowed by the laws and regulations.

Government procurement in the United States at all levels occurs in an environment significantly structured by statute and regulation. The same is the case for state and local governments. Local governments typically follow procurement laws established at the state level.

In recent years, contracting mechanics have become an issue in international trade negotiations. The American government has argued that a lack of transparency in source selection, such as limits on the eligibility to bid, lack of clear evaluation criteria, and failure to require explanation of source selection decisions, limits the ability of firms in one country to compete for government contracts in other countries and thus constitutes a barrier against international trade, analogous to tariff protection. An Agreement on Government Procurement was negotiated in 1979 in connection with the so-called Tokyo Round of international trade negotiations, and a new agreement was concluded in 1994. The 1994 agreement has been signed by most wealthy countries, including the United States, Canada, the members of the European Community, and Japan, but among poorer nations by only China. Procurement provisions were also included in the 1992 North American Free Trade Agreement (NAFTA) among the United States, Canada, and Mexico protecting the rights of companies in each country to bid on procurements in the other countries.

All phases of the contracting process involve an interaction within the government between users, who are buying products and services, and contracting officials, who are experts on the contracting process. In 1998, the federal government employed over twenty-seven thousand contracting officials, about two-thirds of them in the Defense Department, down from a high of thirty-one thousand in 1990. Previously, the federal government employed a significant number of purchasing agents who processed small, routine transactions, such as ordering a chair for an office, but changes in procurement procedures such as the introduction of the use of credit cards has virtually eliminated this group of employees over the last decade.[11] Contracting officials are responsible for assuring compliance with procurement regulations and, increasingly, for helping structure the overall business arrangement. Other contracting officials play a significant role in contract administration after the contract is signed. Government lawyers and budget staff are also involved in the contracting process.

Step One: Structuring the Business Arrangement

Within the systemwide decisions about the mechanics of the procurement system, there is an enormous range of options for structuring a contracting business relationship. Sometimes the choice of contracting strategy is strongly influenced by the nature of the product or service the government is buying. The government cannot buy new fighter planes the same way it buys paper clips.

The most important questions regarding structuring a business arrangement are (1) What kind of contract vehicle will be used? (2) How will the requirement be specified? (3) Will the government buy "off-the-shelf" commercial products and services? (4) What performance commitment will the government demand? (5) How will the contract be priced? (6) Will the contract include incentives? and (7) How will any "socioeconomic" requirements be furthered?

Selecting the Contract Vehicle

As noted earlier, the basic business decision the government needs to make about contract vehicle is whether it wishes to make a one-time purchase or establish a "task" or "delivery order" contract. A one-time purchase would be the construction of one specific government office building, the purchase of 100,000 gallons of airplane fuel, or the operation of a government data center for the next five years. A "delivery order contract" would be to establish with a contractor a price list for a range of office supplies and allow the government agency to purchase supplies off that list on an as-needed basis. A "task order contract" would be to establish a master contract—with either hourly labor rates or fixed prices for certain kinds of tasks established in advance—with a software development contractor for writing customized computer security software the agency needs for five years, with specific assignments to be developed over the life of the contract.

Task or delivery order contracts may be either *requirements contracts* or *indefinite delivery/indefinite quantity (IDIQ) contracts.* Requirements contracts commit the government to buy *all* its needs over a specified period of time from the contractor who has been selected—for example, all its office supplies from one contractor. IDIQs allow, but do not require, the government to order from the contract.

Government officials typically prefer task or delivery order contracts to one-time purchases for two reasons: quantity discounts and the ease of use. The government can often get dramatically lower prices by buying in quantity. For example, the cost for overnight delivery of a three-pound package for the entire federal government is under $4 compared with $25 at retail.

Perhaps the biggest reason for the popularity of task or delivery order contracts is that they are faster and less complicated than running a new competition every time a product or service is needed. Electronic commerce, which allows easy ordering over the Internet and quick delivery, has made these contract vehicles even more attractive.

However, those concerned with maximizing competition among vendors traditionally have been concerned that delivery order contracts would be insufficiently competitive if the government were allowed to modify or add to the products that could be ordered. Such objections dramatically limited the utility of delivery order contracts, particularly in rapidly changing markets. The same critics objected to task order contracts for services since the specific work was not specified at the time of contract award.

These objections dissipated during the 1990s, and the use of these contract vehicles has spread rapidly. Such contracts typically specify a list or a category of products or services that may be allowed to change over time within a broad scope. Virtually all these contracts are IDIQ contracts rather than requirements contracts. In 1994 Congress established a preference for awards to multiple contractors when task or delivery order contracts are awarded, with an informal, streamlined competition among the winners for individual task or delivery orders.[12] This approach is now standard in the award of contracts for computers. Agencies award several contracts, have contractors post prices on the Internet, and allow competition among awardees to drive prices down and keep service up.

Recently, there has been an explosive growth of the use of task order contracting for information technology services using the multiple-award approach. In the federal government such contracts are rapidly supplanting the traditional one-time purchases. Agencies award contracts with a very broad scope of possible work ("information security," "electronic commerce," or even "systems development") to multiple contractors and conduct simplified competitions, often taking only a few weeks, for individual task orders.

Specifying the Requirement

The second step in structuring the business arrangement is specifying the "requirement." "Requirement" means what the government is purchasing. The contractor must meet the requirement or either explain why government action made meeting it impossible or get the government to change the requirement after contract award.

A requirement may specify the results the government wants or simply specify an overall direction in which the government wants the contractor to go. Thus, two different ways to specify a requirement to improve the fuel consumption of a military aircraft might be to

1. Work to improve as much as possible the fuel consumption of a C-17 aircraft

2. Improve the fuel consumption of a C-17 aircraft by 25 percent

One would think the government would prefer the second kind of requirement because of the vagueness of the first kind. In fact, solicitations of the first sort are extremely common. The government may not know at the time of the solicitation what results it seeks—perhaps because the work is at the cutting edge of current knowledge—and wishes to wait until it learns more in the course of the contractor's work to specify expected results. Unfortunately, sometimes the solicitation does not specify results only because it would require more effort.

If the requirement is expressed in terms of results, two alternative ways of specifying the results are possible:

1. In *design* terms (e.g., the grass at a military base shall be cut at least once a week between 15 April and 15 September, and once a month between 16 September and 14 April, using mowers meeting Underwriter's Laboratory Standard L1447–1988 for electric lawn mowers)

2. In *performance* terms (e.g., the grass at a military base shall be kept at an even height of no more than 1/2 inch)

Traditionally, government has made extensive use of design specifications for everything from military components to food for army mess halls. The Defense Department had literally thousands of military specifications ("milspecs") as well as manufacturing standards ("milstandards").

The prevailing view is that performance specifications are generally superior because what the government ultimately cares about is performance, and performance specifications allow contractors to use their own ingenuity to efficiently deliver the desired result. In 1994 the U.S. Department of Defense announced a policy that special approval would be needed any time a weapons system wanted to use a milspec. Advocates of design specifications, particularly in the military arena, argue that such specifications have met the test of time, particularly in terms of good performance over the life of the item. They worry that the government will not enforce contracts if items built to performance specifications fail to meet the contract's durability or reliability requirements.

"Off-the-Shelf" Commercial Products and Services

A choice government frequently faces is between buying available "commercial off-the-shelf" items (COTS) and having the product or service developed specifically for government use. Items developed specifically for government are generally called "developmental" or "government-unique" items.

The most common reason for the government to buy developmental products or services is that the required levels of performance are not available with COTS. Most milspecs require levels of performance or reliability far greater than those typically found among commercial variants of the product in question. For example, the army might require that laptops for use in the field be able to withstand significantly greater extremes of heat, cold, or vibration than those used in homes or offices. Other examples include especially high reliability requirements for equipment used for air traffic control or security requirements for data transmission involving individual income tax returns.

Sometimes the government must contract for developmental items because the product or service the government needs is not produced commercially. The classic example is weapons systems. There is no commercial version of an Abrams tank or an F-16 airplane.

However, often in the past, the government specified items in ways that could not be provided by off-the-shelf products because of convenience or inertia. For example, ketchup and peanut butter were ordered in large metal boxes that could be conveniently stored and then dished out in smaller portions on mess hall tables. Or, when a contract was recompeted, the requirement from the previous contract was simply slapped on as the new requirement, perpetuating government-unique requirements that had been developed earlier. In other cases, the government did not want to make the small changes in its business processes required to use an off-the-shelf software package such as word processing.

Traditionally, the government was not sufficiently aware of the large price penalty paid for the short production runs of government-unique items compared with COTS. The development costs of COTS can be spread out over large number of sales, whereas similar costs for items being sold only to the government can be spread out over much smaller runs. Furthermore, for very small runs, the cost of configuring machinery for specialized products can also be significant. During the 1980s, the Defense Department paid $600 for coffee pots, not because of contractor profiteering, but because of the actual high costs of producing a limited run of pots that could survive the extreme conditions possible in military aircraft flight.[13]

Developmental items are also often high risk. It is hard to predict the extent to which they will achieve performance goals. Examples would be developing a laser beam that can shoot enemy missiles down or developing expert system software to detect bank deposits that are likely to involve money criminals are laundering.

Some items manufactured to government specifications are bought repeatedly after initial development, such as night goggles, so follow-on buys have few cost or performance risks. However, many of the most significant developmental items, such as weapons systems and custom information technology systems, score high on cost and performance risks.

In recent years, government has begun paying far more attention to tradeoffs between performance and cost or risk. The military has made a wholesale move toward buying food and clothing off-the-shelf. Using COTS has become far more common in information technology, for both computer hardware and software.

Type of Performance Commitment

What is a contractor agreeing to do when signing a contract? In a "completion contract," the government expects the contractor to achieve certain results. Contracts for COTS are always completion contracts. In a "best-efforts contract," the government merely expects the contractor to put forward its best efforts. In a best-efforts contract, the contractor will have met the obligations even if the efforts produce nothing, unless it can be shown that the contractor did not exert its best efforts. Contracts for scientific research are virtually always best-efforts contracts. Contracts to "improve fuel consumption as much as possible" or "work on a new logistics system" are best-efforts contracts.

Obviously, all things being equal, the government is better off with a completion contract rather than a best-efforts contract. However, all things are not equal. The big factor driving toward best-efforts contracts is risk. Sometimes it is possible to specify performance precisely, but hard to know in advance whether it will be possible to achieve the performance the government wishes. For example, it is possible to specify a desired performance result for a new military aircraft (e.g., how quickly it can safely change altitude), but the result has never been obtained before, and the risk of not attaining it is great. In such an environment, contractors generally will not be willing to commit themselves to a completion contract in which they promise to attain the specified results on a fixed budget.

Unfortunately, sometimes the government chooses a best-efforts contract as an easy way out, rather than spending the additional time and effort involved in developing performance standards. The temptation is particularly great to do this with recurring requirements. If the initial contract for delivering child-care service was a best-efforts contract, the recompetition may simply recycle the old statement of work, even though the accumulated experience would allow the development of performance standards needed for a completion contract.

Pricing Contracts

The basic alternatives in contract pricing are *cost-reimbursement contracts* of various sorts and *fixed-price contracts.* Cost-reimbursement contracts allow the contractor to be paid for all legitimate direct costs (labor and materials) and indirect costs (overhead and other costs not attributable to an individual contract but apportioned among individual contracts), plus a profit. Sometimes, costs are reimbursed only up to a specified maximum. The argument for cost-reimbursement contracts is the same as for best-efforts contracts—the cost risks are too great for contractors to commit themselves to fixed prices. Cost-reimbursement contracts are virtually always best-efforts contracts. Cost-reimbursement contracts are much more expensive to administer than fixed-priced contracts.

In a fixed-price contract, the government agrees to pay a specified sum of money for a specific requirement. The fixed price may be for the entire product or service, or it may be per transaction. Completion contracts are typically fixed-priced contracts.[14]

In cost-reimbursement contracts, contractor profit levels are regulated. The simplest form of cost-reimbursement contract is called *cost-plus-fixed fee,* where the fixed fee represents the contractor's profit. The idea of having a fixed fee added onto the contractor's costs is designed to prevent a situation where the contractor makes a higher profit the higher the costs. Cost-plus-a-percentage-of-costs contracts are illegal in U.S. federal government contracting. Cost-reimbursement contracts may also include incentive features to encourage the contractor to economize on costs.

Fixed-priced contracts may be awarded either competitively or sole source. The most important examples of sole source fixed-price contracts are production contracts for new weapons systems, awarded on a sole-source basis as a follow-on to competitively awarded contracts for the initial development of the system.

In appearance, competitively awarded fixed-priced contracts are very straightforward. The government sets out its requirement. Contractors bid a fixed price to perform it. The price is established by competition. In contrast to a cost-reimbursement contract, the government cares nothing about the contractor's costs or how much profit it makes, since competition has assured that the government gets a good price. Under such an arrangement, if the contractor is able to perform the work for significantly below the fixed price, it reaps a large profit. If it overruns, it loses money.

In reality, things are often not so simple. The government may change its mind about exactly what it wants and add features or services not part of the original requirement, or the contractor may perform according to the requirement, but the government does not get the performance it sought. Then a "change order" must be negotiated, either on a fixed-price or cost-reimbursement basis. In general, a contractor has an incentive in a fixed-price contract to interpret the original requirement as narrowly as possible and to receive as many change orders (for which it is paid extra) as possible. This creates the danger of creating an adversarial relationship between the government and the contractor over the exact scope of the original requirement. Change orders add to the cost of the contract, and they are negotiated in a sole-source environment with the contractor, depriving the government of the benefits of competition. Finally, if the contractor loses money on a fixed-price contract, it may try to get some money back by submitting claims for additional payment, typically alleging that something the government did interfered with the contractor's ability to deliver at the fixed price—for example, that the government delayed getting the work started and during that period of time wages for contractor employees rose.

Sole-source fixed-priced contracts have many similarities to cost-reimbursement contracts because, to assure itself that it is not overpaying, the government frequently bases the fixed price on the government's best judgment about the contractor's prospective costs.

In the process of negotiating the fixed price for a sole-source contract, the contractor is required to submit a "cost buildup" as part of its proposal, and the government uses this as a basis, together with regulatory guidelines for the profit rate the contractor is allowed to earn, to negotiate the price. The cost buildup is an estimate of the labor categories and hours, as well as material and indirect costs that are required.[15]

For sole-source fixed-price contracts, the government does not check on actual costs as it does in cost-reimbursement contracts. This difference means that the U.S. federal government normally requires, as established in the Truth in Negotiations Act (1962), that the contractor certify, under civil or even criminal penalties, that prospective cost information submitted is accurate.[16] The government often audits this information after contract award.

Contract Incentives

Recognizing the problems that best-efforts and cost-reimbursement contracts create for the government, there has long been an interest in providing incentives for contractors to improve performance in a best-efforts environment and to keep costs under control in a cost-reimbursement environment.

The most common form of such incentive contract has been the *cost plus award fee contract*. The government establishes a number of criteria that may involve cost control or various aspects of delivering results (e.g., keeping to schedule, design innovativeness, economizing on use of fuel), according to which it will judge the contractor on a regular basis during contract performance. It also establishes an award-fee pool, a sum of money available to give the contractor, over and above cost reimbursement and a fixed fee, for various levels of achievement according to the award fee criteria. The contractor is then awarded some percentage of this award-fee pool, from 0 to 100 percent, depending on the contractor's performance under the various award-fee criteria.

In most U.S. federal government award-fee contracts, the base fee on the contract is quite modest, and most of the contractor's profit comes from the award fee. This creates pressures for grade inflation in award fees; award fees at 80 to 90 percent of the available pool are typical.

One kind of incentive contracting that specifically targets cost reduction is an *incentive fee* contract. In incentive fee contracting, a baseline cost estimate is established, and the contractor is given some agreed-upon percentage of the savings for reimbursable costs under the baseline and penalized for costs over the baseline.

Recently, there has been growing interest in new forms of incentive contracting. In the reconstruction of the Santa Monica Freeway after the 1994 Los Angeles earthquake, contractors were paid a bonus for each day they completed the work under the maximum number of days they had bid to complete it; some state highway departments are using versions of this incentive arrangement for other kinds of highway construction.[17] A number of states and foreign jurisdictions have successfully used *share-in-savings contracting*, where the contractor is paid a percentage of the savings its efforts generate. For example, the California income tax system was successfully modernized in an arrangement where the contractor was paid a proportion of the administrative savings, reduced interest payments on late refunds, and increased enforcement revenues their efforts generated. If the contractor failed, it would not have been paid at all.[18] The air force has experimented with *award term contracting*, where the incentive for an outstanding contractor is to have the length of the contract extended.

Promoting "Socioeconomic" Goals

"Socioeconomic" goals are promoted through two broad techniques. One is to provide preference in source selection to bidders with certain characteristics, such as small or minority businesses. This may involve price preferences such as percentages added onto the bids of non-American or nonminority business suppliers, or it may involve set-asides (limiting bidding on certain contracts to certain kinds of businesses or products, such as recycled paper). The other method is to establish contract provisions that bind a contractor to implement certain policies that go beyond legal requirements imposed on businesses in general, such as payment of "prevailing" wages or special efforts to hire veterans.

Step Two: Source Selection

Source selection is the process by which the government solicits and evaluates bids and selects a winning contractor. Source selection is based on a solicitation the government issues, generally called a "request for proposals" (RFP).[19] The solicitation includes the essential features of the government's strategy for structuring the business arrangement, such as specifications, pricing arrangements, and incentive features. It also explains how the government will evaluate bids.

Who May Bid

As early as 1792 for postal delivery contracts and 1809 for other U.S. federal government contracts, legislation has embraced the principle of widespread advertisement and competitive bidding for public contracts.[20] The Competition in Contracting Act (CICA), the basic competition statute currently governing federal procurement, establishes the principle of "full and open competition," the idea that any firm be allowed to bid on a government contract. CICA provides a number of exceptions, such as the "unusual and compelling urgency" of the procurement or the presence of only one source who can do the job, that may be used to justify limiting those who may bid. Depending on the dollar value of the procurement, a decision to use other than full and open competition must be approved at an organizational level varying from the contracting officer to the senior contracting official at the agency. Such approvals are required for any limitations on who may bid, although they are almost always used in cases where the government seeks to buy "sole source." By contrast, in many other countries, bidding has been traditionally limited to "prequalified" sources, those determined in advance to be eligible to bid for government work. In some local jurisdictions in the United States, it is easier to get permission to do sole-source contracting.

The international Agreement on Government Procurement represents an effort to get as close as American negotiators were able to reach to spreading CICA principles globally by assuring greater access to bidding and more transparent procedures. "Any conditions for participation in tendering procedures," the agreement states, "shall be published in adequate time to enable interested suppliers to initiate and, to the extent that it is compatible with efficient operation of the procurement process, complete the qualification procedures" and that "any conditions for participation in tendering procedures shall be limited to those which are essential to ensure the firm's capability to fulfill the contract in question."

As part of promoting competition, governments have requirements for how solici-

tations must be disseminated. In the U.S. federal government, announcements of solicitations for contracts valued at more than $25,000 must be placed in a daily publi-
cation issued by the Department of Commerce, the *Commerce Business Daily*. Since
1997 it has been available on the Internet. Today, most agencies also make the solicitations themselves available to interested bidders on the Internet. A central location for
publication of announcements about solicitations for the entire federal government is
intended to reduce the costs of doing business with the government by giving firms,
particularly small businesses, one convenient location to learn about government contracting opportunities. In addition, there are statutory minimum periods of time that
agencies must keep an announcement of the availability of a solicitation "on the street,"
as well as minimum times agencies must give interested bidders to respond to the
solicitation. In recent years, minimum times have been decreased for situations where
the federal government is buying commercial items.

Evaluation Criteria

Evaluation criteria for competitively negotiated procurements include both (1) *what
the government values,* or "evaluation factors," and (2) *how much the government values
them,* or "evaluation weights." One source selection approach is to choose the bidder
who complies with the specifications, terms, and conditions in the solicitation and
offers the lowest price ("low bid"). A second approach is to make tradeoffs between
price and quality/performance risk ("best value").

Low-Bid Source Selection

The simplest version of the low-bid source selection method is to use sealed bids.
Bidders are invited to submit, under seal, a statement formally accepting all the requirements and conditions of the solicitation, along with a price to do the work. Bids
are formally and publicly opened. The low bidder wins, provided the firm has accepted
all the requirements and terms and provided it is determined that it meets a set of
minimal requirements for financial solvency and performance capability, such as not
currently being debarred from contracting with the government.

Whenever the government wants to receive and evaluate proposals from bidders,
and not simply receive a declaration of responsiveness and a price bid, it engages in
"competitively negotiated procurement." In this type of procurement, the government
receives proposals, which may be quite detailed, but also may communicate with bidders to better understand what they are bidding and/or to improve the deal they are
offering the government.[21]

One selection method for competitively negotiated procurements is, like for sealed
bids, to award to the lowest bidder. However, in contrast to sealed bidding, the government evaluates proposals to determine whether a bidder has met all the technical
or capability requirements (rather than simply accepting a statement from the bidder),
may negotiate with bidders after the receipt of proposals, and may set a higher bar in
terms of performance on previous contracts that the contractor must meet. In the U.S.
federal government, this is called a "low-price, technically acceptable" decision rule.

The decision rule "award to the low bidder" after an open competition has been a
classic way to award government contracts. This solution was brilliant, and even its
critics—of whom I am one—have sought to smooth its many sharp edges rather than
abandon it entirely. Competition brings the advantages of the market mechanism for
reducing price, increasing quality, and encouraging innovation. It promotes fairness by
offering all seeking to sell to the government an opportunity to participate. Awarding
to the low bidder promotes economy in the fulfillment of government requirements,

provides a transparent arrangement that assures bidders they have been treated impartially, and reduces the opportunity for corruption. Not many principles of tool design kill so many birds with one stone.

However, award to the low bidder creates a number of problems. Low-bid awards too often go to contractors who, intentionally or through ignorance, underestimate the cost or difficulty of the government's requirements, which increases the risk of contract nonperformance. Contractors often win through a conscious strategy to "buy in and get well," bidding unrealistically low initial prices and hoping to make money through contract modifications after award. Low-bid selection also becomes more difficult the vaguer the government's specifications. More generally, low-bid selection places very high demands on the government's ability to get its exact specifications right, since there is no reason for a contractor to propose a level of performance even slightly above that specified in the solicitation, even if it could achieve those results at minimal cost. Furthermore, it is difficult in a sealed-bid environment to exclude those with poor records of past performance and to reward those with good records. Finally, low-bid source selection is very risky for best-efforts contracting since it is likely to result in the government getting poor-quality personnel who have little prospect of achieving the government's goals.

Best-Value Source Selection

Traditionally, in the U.S. federal government, and still in many state and local jurisdictions, accepting sealed bids and awarding the contract to the low bidder was the preferred evaluation method. The worry was that methods allowing tradeoffs would be too subjective, give too much discretion to government officials, and be insufficiently transparent. However, in recent years, especially in the U.S. federal government, low-bid awards, for the reasons stated above, have lost favor. Instead, in making a source selection, the government trades off price and various quality-related factors.

CICA requires that a solicitation must include all evaluation factors. The three most common evaluation factors in best-value source selections are price, technical capability, and past performance. CICA requires that price be a factor in every evaluation. In many best-value source selections the award goes to the lowest bidder because the government may still decide that the firm that has bid the lowest price offers the best value, all things considered.

The starting point for the evaluation of a bidder's technical capability is the bidder's "technical approach" or "understanding of the requirement," a part of the proposal where the bidder explains how they intend to do the work. This is particularly important for best-efforts contracts where the agency wishes to know about the bidder's approach in order to judge how promising it looks. Although less important than for best-efforts contracts, the government is also interested in learning about the bidder's technical approach for completion contracts in order to evaluate the contractor's risk of failure and how well they are likely to handle change orders. Beyond that, in a best-value procurement, the government may state that it values a performance level beyond the mandatory minimum requirements stated in the solicitation and invite bidders to propose a higher performance level.

The second broad class of nonprice evaluation criteria is what Ralph Nash calls "capability factors," that is, those related to a bidder's ability to perform and interest in performing.[22] For many years, such factors played only a small part in U.S. federal government procurement because they were seen as too subjective and threatening to the integrity of the system by creating "favoritism" to incumbent bidders. During the 1990s, however, the past performance of bidders has become a major evaluation factor and is required by regulation (FAR 15.304(c)(3)). The idea is to provide an incentive for good performance by rewarding or punishing bidders for the quality of their performance when they bid on future contracts.

CICA also requires that a solicitation include the relative weights of all evaluation factors (e.g., "technical excellence and price are the most important, followed by past performance, with the percentage of the work to be subcontracted to small businesses and the qualifications of key personnel least important and approximately equal in importance"). The Agreement on Government Procurement requires that the solicitation include "the criteria for awarding the contract, including any factors other than price that are to be considered in the evaluation of tenders and the cost elements to be included in evaluating tender prices."

CICA never required factors to be weighted numerically, and the Defense Department has for a long time frowned on such a practice as too constricting. However, until the 1990s, many agencies specified exact point scores for different factors and subfactors, sometimes down to several decimal places. This practice has now virtually disappeared from U.S. federal government procurement, although it is seen in some state and local jurisdictions.

To take a very simple example of how the system works, the government may wish to buy over the next year one hundred thousand 75-watt lightbulbs meeting American National Standards Institute Standard C78.1385–1998 to be delivered in lots as small as fifty to a list of army bases around the Southeast within a week of ordering. The government is willing to pay a premium for the option of twenty-four-hour delivery, and bidders must provide evidence based on feedback from other customers of their ability to deliver quality lightbulbs on time throughout the Southeast. The evaluation criteria, in relative order, are price, compliance with the technical criteria, past performance, and pricing of the twenty-four-hour delivery option. The government will make a tradeoff across scores on these factors.

Proposal Evaluation

In response to a solicitation, the government receives written proposals from interested bidders. To assure the integrity and fairness goals of the system, two basic principles of proposal evaluation are (1) grading proposals based solely on published evaluation factors and their weights and (2) transparency, achieved through the explanation and documentation of decisions. These two factors drove proposals to become longer and longer and to be made in writing only. Bidders want to get as much material in the proposals as possible, and a written file makes documentation easier.

Agencies typically reserve the right to make an award based on initial written proposals. However, in most cases, agencies choose to enter into negotiations with the best bidders to resolve problems or uncertainties in the proposal, as well as to try to get a better deal for the government. This is done by establishing a "competitive range," those bidders who are finalists.

The government establishes, for significant procurements, a source selection team to grade proposals. These teams consist of contracting people and program people who will be working on the activity supported by the contract. Depending on the complexity of the proposals, the team may be divided up into separate teams evaluating technical, past performance, and cost criteria. Other government officials are not allowed to intervene in the activities of a source selection team once it has begun working. Since proposal evaluation was traditionally a long and tedious process, it has often been difficult to get the best program people to serve on source selection teams. Depending on the size of the procurement and the agency, the final source selection decision is made by a "source selection authority," at a level above the evaluation team.

After the government's selection is announced, federal law requires that unsuccessful bidders be "debriefed" to explain why they did not win. The requirement for explanation and justification is another feature of the transparency of the system. A comparable feature appears in the Agreement on Government Procurement: an unsuccessful bidder shall be provided "pertinent information concerning the reasons why its tender was not selected and on the characteristics and relative advantages of the tender selected as well as the name of the winning tenderer."

Transparency and group decisionmaking are important ways to reduce the danger of corruption, particularly in best-value source selections that give government officials greater discretion. It is relatively easy to corrupt even rule-bound officials if the grounds for decision can be kept secret. It is relatively difficult to corrupt officials with discretion if decisionmaking standards and the grounds for choice based on those standards are transparent and if many people are involved in the decision.

Bid Protests

Probably no procurement system in the world allows as rich a set of opportunities for judicial or quasi-judicial protests by disappointed bidders as does the U.S. federal system. The theory behind the protest system is to provide for enforcement of the rules the system has established. The basic bid protest forum is a quasi-judicial one, the General Accounting Office (GAO). Protesters must prove that the government has failed to follow procurement regulations. Although its procedures have become somewhat more formalized over the years, it is still a relatively informal protest forum, generally using only written briefs by the parties and seldom using depositions of witnesses or extensive document discovery. Protesters win about 15 percent of cases filed at the GAO. Generally, the GAO is rather deferential to government decisions, finding for the protester only in cases of grave and clear violations of procurement regulations. Historically, some other protest bodies have rereviewed the government's entire decisionmaking process to see if they agreed with the decision the government made.

One of the most important new features of the 1994 Agreement on Government Procurement was new provisions bringing bid protests to foreign countries, many of which have not traditionally included them in their contracting systems.

Step Three: Contract Administration

If a contract is to be worth more than the paper it is written on, the government must administer it after award. Contract administration involves several activities: (1) monitoring costs (for cost-reimbursement contracts), (2) monitoring performance, (3) contract modifications, (4) settling claims, and (5) contract termination or closeout.

A relative lack of attention to contract administration has been a serious problem with the contracting tool. Frequently, government has been unwilling to hold contractors' feet to the fire when they do not perform as they promised in the contract. Frequently, contractors have been allowed to deliver goods or services that fail to meet contract requirements and/or that generate excessive costs in cost-reimbursement work.[23] The phrase "shoddy," in fact, comes from a kind of low-quality cloth contractors used for Union uniforms delivered early during the Civil War.[24] Although corruption involving contract award has been endemic at the U.S. state and local levels, as well as internationally, at the federal level corruption problems have occurred mostly with contract administration, especially corruption involving item inspection.

The problems of monitoring costs and item inspection, especially for military weapons and parts, have been the subject of legislation at the U.S. federal level. The basic solution has been more oversight, not more automaticity. As with source selection, the result has been a highly regulated system. However, while source selection rules mainly regulate the government, contract administration rules mainly regulate contractors. For the U.S. federal government, the basic underlying statute is the False Claims Act, passed in 1863 to deal with Civil War contracting abuses and tightened in 1986 by lowering standards of proof. This act prohibits the submission of false bills or of products or services not meeting contractual requirements.

In cost-reimbursement contracts, the government also typically specifies kinds of costs, called "allowable costs," the government will pay. For example, contractor costs for certain kinds of entertainment, or for lobbying, are prohibited. Frequently, there are political debates over whether certain contractor costs are allowable—for example, salaries paid top contractor executives or the costs incurred in fighting unionization efforts at contractor facilities. Allowability rules are typically established by statute or regulation, so the agency need not worry about them in structuring any particular cost-reimbursement contract. The government also often establishes cost-accounting rules for the allocation of indirect costs to cost-reimbursement contracts.[25]

The Department of Defense has established a major organizational apparatus for oversight of defense contractors. The Defense Contract Audit Agency (DCAA) monitors bills submitted under cost-reimbursement contracts and audits compliance with cost-accounting standards, as well as the accuracy of cost data submitted during source selection. The Defense Contract Management Agency (DCMA) monitors compliance with contract performance requirements. Major defense contractors have full-time DCAA and DCMA inspectors actually resident in their plants. In addition to DCAA, private parties, often whistle-blowers working or formerly employed by a contractor, may bring private legal actions for contractor violations of the False Claims Act and receive a bounty of between 10 and 30 percent of recoveries if successful. The efforts of these private individuals thus complement those of government inspectors and auditors.

Government oversight subjects government contractors to requirements (such as maintaining special accounting systems for compliance with contracts) and legal liability (such as under the False Claims Act) that do not exist for firms that do not do business with the government. This serves as a disincentive for firms to do business with the government in the first place, especially if only a small part of their sales would be with the government. Critics argue that this is a serious problem that government-unique oversight requirements create.[26]

Monitoring Costs

The DCAA monitors bills submitted to the Defense Department, and to many civilian agencies,[27] and they compare them against time cards and bills for purchased materials. In recent years, and in the context of personnel cutbacks and contractor complaints about excessive auditing that cost more money than it saves, the Defense Department has made efforts to concentrate auditing efforts on contractors with a poor history of honesty.

All in all, although phony or padded bills were once a big problem in government contracting, the federal government now does a good job of making sure that it does not get many bills for work not performed or materials not bought.

Monitoring Performance

The DCMA often makes the final decision about whether to accept products a contractor delivers to the government. The Office of Operational Test and Evaluation makes similar decisions for new weapons systems and is independent of both the program and contracting organizations.

Inspection procedures work best and are most well established for physical products.

Contracts often establish test procedures that items must meet before they are accepted. Over the years the government often went overboard establishing onerous inspection procedures for commercial off-the-shelf items such as computers. Traditionally, a good deal of the effort of DCMA went into inspecting items for compliance with milspecs and inspecting defense plants for compliance with milstandards.

Monitoring performance under service contracts is usually more difficult and problematic. These problems are particularly acute for best-efforts contracts. Auditors can check whether individuals who have submitted a time card have been at their desk but have real difficulty determining whether a person who has been at his desk for an hour has worked efficiently or productively. Therefore, the government has often required the submission of detailed contractor reports explaining what they have been doing, often on a weekly or even daily basis. Frequently, such reports provide an occasion for government micromanagement of the approaches the contractor is using to do the work. When contractor personnel are working at a government site, within the physical reach of government program officials, these officials also often micromanage how the contractor approaches the work.

When the government contracts for services using performance specifications, performance can be monitored by examining the results the contractor has achieved. U.S. federal guidelines for performance-based service contracting (appearing in FAR, Part 37) stress the importance of quality-assurance plans as part of these contracts to detail the frequency and methodology of results monitoring. However, service contracting monitoring involving performance-based quality assurance plans rather than through the micromanagement of inputs requires a technical retraining and cultural reorientation of those responsible for monitoring that still has a long way to go.

An additional way to monitor the performance of contractors is through the award-fee determination process. Award-fee contracts include formal award-fee determination boards to evaluate the contractor against the award-fee criteria. The award-fee determination provides an opportunity during the administration of best-efforts contracts for the government to monitor results and not just inputs. Likewise, with the increased attention to contractor past performance in source selection, there has been a growth in the use of "report cards" for contractors during contract administration. These are intended as input into later proposal evaluations, but some agencies are beginning to use them for contract administration. They give government and contractor a regular chance to sit down and discuss how a contract is going. However, the federal government establishes significant "due process" protections regarding report cards for contractors, giving them an opportunity, for example, to enter material into the report card explaining or contesting negative comments and to appeal negative grades to a level above the government official who gave the original rating (FAR 42.1503). This produces a tendency toward grade inflation.

Contract Modifications

Contract modifications ("change orders") are a fact of life of contract administration. Situations change, requirements change, and technological capabilities frequently change during a contract. The government often learns things after contract award that it did not know before the award that could cause it to seek changes. Often, the initiative for contract modifications comes from the government.

The modification process takes place after contract award and thus, typically, in a sole-source environment. Thus, there is no competition based on price or technical approach, creating more of a risk that the government will overpay for change orders. This in turn creates an incentive for contractors to propose change orders, even unnecessary ones. Change orders are also problematic if a contract is modified to soften up the performance requirements of the original contract because the contractor is having trouble meeting them. In addition, some contractors intentionally adopt a "buy-in" strategy, bidding low prices and superior technology in the competitive environment of source selection, hoping to "get well" later in the sole-source environment of change orders. Since change-order price negotiations are conducted in a sole-source environment, they often require contractor submission of certified cost data.[28]

Another concern with contract modifications is that frequent requirements change ("scope creep") can make it more difficult to accomplish the intended results. Critics of many large government information technology projects, such as modernization of the air traffic control system, have argued that constant changes in requirements made it very difficult for designers to know what they were supposed to be doing and allowed success to be a constantly receding target. Many suggest that agencies need to be more disciplined about the change-order process for large information technology projects by allowing an "open season" for modification requests only at specified times during contract performance.

Contract Claims and Disputes

Contract claims appear when the contractor or the government asks for money that one party believes is owed them by the other. Most claims are made by the contractor against the government. For fixed-price completion contracts, contractors may make claims to receive additional payment to perform the work specified in the original contract. One source of such claims is the allegation that government-imposed delays increased contractor costs. In addition, in fixed-price situations, the contractor may allege that the government has demanded additional work beyond the scope of the contract. Contractors may also make a claim when the government refuses to accept and pay for products or services the contractor delivers. For cost-reimbursement, best-efforts contracts—where contractors are paid for delays or changes—such claims seldom arise. The most common contractor claims in this environment involve disallowance of costs and are made at the end of contract performance. Finally, the government may make claims against a contractor for a price reduction due to the submission of incorrect or incomplete cost or pricing data at the time of contract award or for various kinds of reimbursement in the event a contract is terminated for default.

Contractor claims are initially handled by the agency to which they are submitted. If informal efforts to resolve the claim fail, the government will issue what the U.S. federal government calls a "final determination of the contracting officer" regarding the claim.

If the contractor is unwilling to accept the agency's decision, the claim becomes a dispute. In the U.S. federal government, contract disputes are regulated by the Contract Disputes Act of 1978, which establishes the right to have a dispute that cannot be resolved with the procuring agency heard either by an independent quasi-judicial agency "board of contract appeals" or by the U.S. Court of Federal Claims at the choice of the plaintiff. Appeals may go as far as the Supreme Court.

Most claims are resolved at the agency level. As far back as 1980, only two years after passage of the Contract Disputes Act, the U.S. Office of Federal Procurement Policy stated that "it is the Government's policy . . . to try to resolve all claims by mutual agreement at the contracting officer's level, without litigation."[29] During the 1990s, this preference became more pronounced with increasing efforts to have disputes dealt with through alternate dispute resolution (typically mediation, occasionally arbitration).

Claims create an environment of animosity between government and contractor that can undermine the cooperation needed for contract success. The biggest sources of disagreement arise when the contractor blames government action (e.g., frequent

changes in program management and direction) for the contractor's failure to deliver
on time or otherwise perform, or when the contractor submits a claim for work it states
is beyond the scope of the contract but that the government thought was included.
Occasionally, claims, like contract modifications, may form an explicit part of a "buy
in low and get well later" contractor strategy.

Contract Closeout or Termination

When cost-reimbursement contracts are completed, the government must close out
the contract by making final determinations of whether the government owes the contractor more money than has been paid during contract performance or whether, by
contrast, the contractor owes the government money. Typically, what is still at stake is
a final determination of contractor indirect costs. Sometimes, final closeouts do not
occur for several years after a contract is actually completed.

Typically, contracts run their course. Sometimes, however, the government terminates them before they are completed. The most dramatic form of termination is called
"termination for default," where the government cancels a ·contract because the contractor failed to perform. In the U.S. federal government, for a terminated fixed-price
contract, the contractor will not be paid for any work the government deems unacceptable. If the contractor has received advance payments for undelivered or unacceptable items, those payments must be returned to the government. If the government
pays a higher price when it reprocures the items covered under the terminated contract,
the contractor must pay the government so-called excess reprocurement costs. Finally,
a contract terminated for default will hurt the contractor's past performance ratings
on future government work for which it also bids.

It is virtually impossible to prove a case for terminating a contractor for default
in a best-efforts contract. Terminations for default almost never occur for cost-
reimbursement contracts.

The decision to terminate a poorly performing contractor for default is a business
decision for the government. Sometimes the government puts up with poorly performing contractors because of the time it takes to reprocure or, unfortunately, because of
the prospect of bitter litigation where the government may not have fully documented
the problems with the contractor. The FAR (49.402–3(f)) specifically tells contracting
officials when considering terminations for default to look at factors such as "the ex-
cuses for the failure," "the availability of the supplies or services from other sources,"
and "the urgency of the need for the supplies or services and the period of time required
to obtain them from other sources, as compared with the time delivery could be obtained from the delinquent contractor."

Due to the drastic nature of termination for default, the rules offer significant due
process protection to contractors. Terminations for default must be preceded by a "cure
notice" formally explaining the problems and giving the contractor ten days to show
they are, or will be, remedied. Terminations for default are frequently challenged in
court, and the government must be able to show that its actions did not materially
contribute to the contractor's performance problems.

An alternate form of termination, which is essentially unknown in private contracts,
is the unilateral ability of the federal government to terminate a contract "for convenience"—that is, simply because the government decides it does not need the products
or services anymore.[30] According to John Cibinic and Ralph Nash, "The concept of
termination for convenience of the government was developed principally as a means
to end the massive procurement efforts that accompanied major wars."[31] Termination
for convenience clauses began appearing in many government contracts during World
War I. They became mandatory in the Defense Department in 1950 and in civilian
agencies in 1967.[32]

Contractors are treated considerably more generously when contracts are terminated for convenience than when they are terminated for default. They are reimbursed for work undertaken up to the time of termination, including costs of labor, purchased materials and parts, indirect costs, and costs of "the preparations made for the terminated portions of the contract" (FAR 49.201). Contractors may not be reimbursed, however, for "anticipatory profits," that is, the profits they would have earned on work performed after contractor termination.

A dramatic example of the sums of money at stake in the distinction between a termination for default and a termination for convenience was the protracted litigation over the U.S. Navy's cancellation of the A-12 attack aircraft in 1991. The plane had been contracted for under a competitive fixed-price contract, even though it required significant development efforts. The navy believed the contractor, McDonnell Douglas, was not performing and terminated the contract for default, demanding a $1.3 billion refund of advance payments that had been made to the contractor. In 1998 the U.S. Court of Federal Claims ruled that the government had failed to prove the case for termination for default and declared the termination a "termination for convenience." The decision awarded the contractor a payment of $1.2 billion in termination costs, plus interest.[33]

Because of the loss of anticipated profits a termination for convenience produces, contractors sometimes challenge terminations for convenience in court. Courts have given the government relatively wide latitude in these situations, with the major exception that the government must demonstrate that there has been some "change in circumstances" that justifies the termination (such as the end of a war).[34] Sometimes, when the government fears it might lose a legal challenge to a termination for default but wishes to get rid of a contractor, it chooses to terminate for convenience, a far more generous solution for the contractor.

IV. TOOL SELECTION

Principal-Agent Theory and the Make-Buy Decision

The most common alternative to contracting is direct provision. In industry, this choice is generally called the "make-buy decision." An entire body of theory, called "principal-agent theory," is available to guide such decisions. The theory provides guidance on how somebody who wishes to accomplish a purpose (the "principal") with the help of others who are to serve on his or her behalf (the "agents") can best structure a relationship to maximize the chances that the goals the principal seeks are achieved.

Two common forms of relationship between principals and agents are contractual relationships, where agents agree to do certain specific things for the principal, and an employment relationship, where agents agree to subject themselves to a principal's general direction. Principal-agent theory is helpful in thinking about the make-buy decision because it suggests when it is likely to be better to structure principal-agent relationships as contracts ("buy") and when as employment relationships ("make").

Principal-agent theory typically assumes that agents do not share the principal's goals and thus will not accomplish them well if left to their own devices. This is referred to as "shirking." To increase the chances that agents will perform the way principals want, the principals must provide incentives and/or invest in monitoring of agents' performance. Using this insight, John Donahue[35] argues that contracting as a tool is more appropriate, compared with direct provision in the following three circumstances:

1. *The more precisely a task or result can be specified in advance.* Examples of precisely specified tasks or results include entering data from a paper form onto a computer

with a specified level of accuracy, providing ten thousand telephones of a certain make and model, or keeping a data center up and running 99.5 percent of the time during normal business hours.

If the government poorly specifies what it wants, a contractor may "shirk" by providing what appears to the government as poor performance but that literally meets the conditions of the contract. A contract specifying only that a student loan collection agency "call" a delinquent borrower three times would be fulfilled by leaving three messages on the borrower's answering machine or simply informing the borrower that their loan was delinquent and then going on to the next call. A contract that asks only that a contractor put in its best efforts to solve a certain problem cannot hold the contractor to solving any problem.

Poor advance specification of a contractor's job often necessitates change orders, typically when it is realized that what the government literally required will not accomplish the government's purposes. Change orders creates problems, however, as discussed earlier. Poor or incomplete specification of tasks or results provides an incentive for contractor "buy-in." Bidders may use a strategy of "bid what they ask for, not what they want," whereby the contractor intentionally bids to the government's specifications without informing the government that meeting those specifications will not solve the government's problem and expecting that, after award, contract modifications under favorable terms will be possible.

In situations where it is difficult to specify performance, there are advantages to using employees rather than contractors. The reason is that since employees agree to accept general direction from their employer, nothing needs to be renegotiated or modified if the government wishes to change the performance it seeks. Employees have no ability to exploit the government in such situations that is analogous to the ability contractors have in connection with contract modifications.

A commonly used alternative is a cost-reimbursement best-efforts contract. Since contract specifications and requirements are far more vague, the government may change directions to the contractor similarly to the way it can with its own employees. It does not need to worry about negotiating contract modifications. However, it may be more difficult to monitor contractor effort for cost-reimbursement best-efforts contracts than to monitor the effort of employees on similar kinds of tasks.

2. *The more performance can be evaluated after the fact.* The easier it is to monitor performance, the fewer the dangers of contractor "shirking." If monitoring performance is difficult, an advantage of using employees to do the work is that it is generally easier to supervise them closely than to supervise contractors.

    Contractor performance may be evaluated by looking at the results of the contractor's efforts or by monitoring the contractor's efforts in a level-of-effort environment, either by direct observation or through other means. When the government specifies no specific performance results at all or when it does specify results but contracts only for best efforts, monitoring contractor performance is extremely difficult. The government can do a decent job monitoring bills to detect padded invoices, but, even with the activity reports it often requires, the government has a near impossible time distinguishing between failure despite best efforts and failure due to shirking.[36]

3. *The more competition there is among potential providers.* One frequently expressed fear about contracting is that competition will dry up after the initial award. Losing bidders may exit the new market, and the government will become hostage to monopoly exploitation by the initial winner after the first round of bidding. The

more there is a significant market for a product or service outside government, the less the danger the government will be held hostage. If the market is mostly a government one, the greater the number of agencies or jurisdictions that buy the product or service (say, garbage collection versus repair of sophisticated military hardware), the less the danger. If the government wants only local providers as contractors, such as contracting for social services from local nonprofits, competition is likely to be minimal as well. Finally, the degree of competition is related to how significant the start-up costs would be for a new contractor.

Other Issues in the Make-Buy Decision

In addition to considerations growing out of principal-agent theory, a number of issues for the use of contracting grow out of management theory and practice. Contracting, compared to direct provision, is more appropriate in the following four situations:

1. *The less the activity is core to the agency's mission.* Much of the growth of outsourcing within the private sector over the last decade has resulted from the conclusion by corporate executives that a company should focus energy and management attention on the organization's "core competencies" and not get diverted to peripheral production not central to the organization.[37] A similar argument may be made for the public sector: the more an activity belongs to an agency's core policymaking, regulatory, enforcement, and key service delivery functions, the more it should be provided in-house; the more it does not, the more it should be contracted out. At the extreme, certain activities are regarded as "inherently governmental" because they involve making policy decisions or rely on the government's monopoly of the legitimate use of violence, and therefore are inappropriate for contracting no matter what the other advantages of contracting might be. This argument would apply to contracting out diplomacy or IRS tax enforcement, and could, in my view, convincingly be applied to contracting out the operation of prisons or welfare benefit determination decisions.

2. *The more the government faces surges and ebbs in demand for the product or service.* If a military base needs to remove toxic wastes in its soil, it could hire waste remediation experts as civil servants. However, when the job was done, the government would have some number of civil servants on board and no ready work for them. The same would be the case if the government used in-house experts to reengineer a benefits processing system rather than hiring contractors to help. As a general matter, it is easier not to renew a contract for work for which the demand is likely to ebb and flow over time than it is to fire civil servants. By contrast, for ongoing, relatively stable operations—say, motor vehicle registration and licensing—this argument does not apply.

3. *The more private contractors have an easier time hiring people with skills the government needs.* Generally, government employment packages are relatively generous to less-skilled employees and less so to higher-paid people. It is difficult to hire top-quality experts in information technology, financial management, manufacturing management, management consulting, or electrical engineering with government employment packages, especially when private firms offer stock options. The more the government needs people with those skills to deliver products or services, the more contracting becomes the tool of choice.

4. *The more there are economies of scale in production.* Problems with poorer prices due to lack of economies of scale would obviously arise if each government agency

tried to manufacture its own computers. Less obvious and more important, organizations employing a larger number of people in a specialty have advantages in attracting a good workforce. A frontline cafeteria supervisor employed by a government agency (or by General Motors) who wishes to advance but to stay inside the organization only has available the opportunities in that agency's cafeterias. A counterpart in a nationwide food-service firm has an enormously larger number of managerial opportunities available throughout the entire company.

Balancing Considerations in the Choice between Contracting and Direct Provision

To say that contracting becomes *relatively* less attractive than direct provision as a tool the less the conditions suggested by principal-agent theory discussed earlier are present does not imply that it is *absolutely* less attractive. This is partly because of the other considerations, such as core competencies or the ability to hire good people, just discussed, that affect the advantages of contracting versus direct provision. However, principal-agent problems do not exist only between contractors as agents and the government, but also between government employees as agents and the government. In general, the more that principal-agent problems exist for the contracting tool, the more they are likely to exist for direct government provision as well—with the taxpayer as principal and the government employees as agents. In situations where it is difficult to monitor the performance of contractors, it is likely to be difficult to monitor the performance of employees as well. William Niskanen[38] argues that the basic problem with government bureaucracies is that the difficulties legislators have monitoring the resource levels an agency needs to perform its tasks creates significant problems with "shirking" and excessive agency resource consumption. One source of principal-agent problems, the lack of competition for providing the product or service, is endemic to direct government provision.

Therefore, principal-agent problems are not an argument for direct provision over contracting unless it can be shown that they are likely to be fewer than with contracting. This indeed may sometimes be the case. The ability to give general orders to employees when exact performance results cannot be specified is an example of the advantages of in-house provision. Another reason is that it is easier to appeal to public spirit and support for an agency's mission with government employees than it is with contractors. If successful, such an appeal makes it possible to overcome the conflict of interest that is the basis of the principal-agent problem. However, in some circumstances it may be easier to control principal-agent problems involving contractors. If there is an ongoing competitive market for contractors, it will be easier to replace contractors than employees. There is also a greater acceptance of the use of performance requirements for contractors than for government employees.

The academic phrase, "principal-agent problem," is seen in the world of practice as the problem of "control." Fears are frequently expressed in public organizations that contracting out leads to a loss of the "control" managers have over performance of a function. The analysis above applies to the fear of "losing control." Thus, counterintuitively for some observers, government managers may have more control over contractors than over employees.

The most intractable principal-agent challenges arise when the government contracts for major weapons system development and production.[39] The basic problem is that the government is trying to develop new technology beyond the current state of the art for a limited market. Problems of high risk with best-efforts arrangements, difficulty in performance monitoring, and limited competition intersect. The extensive literature on the economics of defense contracting suggests that every "solution" creates problems of its own. Efforts to use fixed-price completion contracts generally have failed spectacularly, with contractors who fail to achieve performance goals seeking relief in the form of reduced requirements and/or financial bailout. Best-efforts development contracts create principal-agent problems. Once production begins, the Defense Department generally buys the weapon from the contractor who has developed it, putting the government in a sole-source situation. A common suggestion has been to establish competition for production, but this creates its own problems. High fixed costs for limited production runs may mean that the benefits of competition do not outweigh the costs of a duplicate infrastructure. In addition, the prospect of supranormal profits for a successfully developed weapons system may be a good incentive for the successful development of the weapon. Probably the strongest arguments for buying weapons rather than developing and producing them are the greater ability of private firms to hire good scientists and engineers, along with the virtues of competitive pressures among firms that encourage good technical ideas.

In this environment, the largest improvements in contracting for weapons may come from trying to make progress in areas outside the domain of these problems. Thus, for example, in recent years the Defense Department has brought down the costs of some weapons by changing the specifications to allow the greater use of commercial components and subsystems. More stable funding for weapons buys, through multiyear contracting, also lowers production costs. Both of these changes may improve contracting for weapons systems while skirting principal-agent problems involved in developing new weapons.

Contracting Versus Tools Other Than Direct Provision

In many situations where government uses economic incentive tools such as tax incentives, loans, loan guarantees, or vouchers, contracting would appear to be a superior, although seldom used, alternative. Consider the case of low-income housing, for example. The norms—and hence the politics—of contracting make it far easier to impose specific performance requirements for contracted housing units as opposed to those induced by other tools. Using the contracting tool may also make it easier to achieve residential integration or neighborhood service goals that are very difficult to achieve through vouchers, and more difficult through tax incentive or loan tools.

The competitive environment of contracting also creates a greater assurance that government is not "overpaying" to achieve the level of housing sought. Firms will bid a minimum inducement they need to achieve the government's goals, compared with the much greater risk of "overpaying" per unit of benefit with administratively, or politically, determined levels of tax breaks or loan guarantees. In addition, particularly in the case of vouchers, there is the probability that some of the low-income units might have been produced even without government funds.

Political Considerations in Tool Choice and Design

Lots of money and jobs are at stake in decisions about government procurement. It should not be surprising that decisions about procurement involve political controversy. These controversies involve both decisions about whether to make or buy in the first place and most of the issues of tool design discussed in this chapter, especially those about oversight of contractors and the use of contracting to achieve broader goals.

In the U.S. federal government today, corruption, the central historic political question involving the politics of contracting, has basically disappeared from the agenda, although this is by no means the case in other countries or even in a number of American local jurisdictions. However, interest group politics remains a potent source of pressure shaping the use of this tool.

Among those with stakes in the outcomes, trade associations representing government contractors, unions representing government employees, and, often, organizations representing values or interests that could be promoted through government contracting, are well organized.

1. *Trade Associations and Individual Firms.* Trade associations representing government contractors generally take stands on all of the politically controversial issues involving procurement. However, individual firms may be important political actors on their own in these issues, either because they are important political actors in one jurisdiction or congressional district or because they have operations in many locations. Individual firms, rather than trade associations, are most likely to have the potential to become involved in source selection decisions or in supporting money for a program where they already have received the contract.

Obviously, trade associations will favor the use of contracting over direct provision by government and will politically support high levels of funding for programs using contracting. This phenomenon first received widespread attention during the 1930s when pacifist and isolationist critics argued that a crucial force behind American entry into World War I was lobbying by munitions manufacturers—the "merchants of death"—who wanted more government money spent on weapons contracts. This worry reappeared during the 1960s with criticisms of the "military-industrial complex," a phrase first appearing in President Eisenhower's farewell address to the nation in 1961. In the political campaign to save the B-1 bomber during the 1970s, defense firms pioneered techniques to increase the number of members of Congress whom they could approach based on district connections by developing lists of subcontractors sorted by congressional district. Previously, lobbying efforts generally had been concentrated on members in districts where the company had its headquarters or where the factories producing the weapon platform itself were located.[40] Critics of privatizing prison management worry that private prison firms will lobby for strict sentences in order to increase the prison population.

If a program is provided directly by the government, government employee unions might lobby on its behalf, but generally this is unlikely to happen because the unions represent government employees in general and will not usually want to lobby for one program over another. Furthermore, even if these unions did lobby on behalf of an individual program, at the federal level union membership is concentrated in the Washington area, unlike membership in contractor associations.

It is assumed by the general public that firms also actively seek to influence source selection decisions on individual contracts through lobbying or campaign contributions to elected officials either in the executive or legislative branch. This may well occur in some state or local jurisdictions, as well as internationally. In the U.S. federal government, despite the widespread perception to the contrary, intervention by elected officials in individual source selection decisions is highly unusual. Contractors, particularly smaller, less experienced ones, do frequently contact their local member of Congress to seek help in winning a procurement. Members will then write the agency and request that it explain its source selection decision or exhort the agency to give the constituent every legal consideration if the decision has not yet been made. Federal procurement officials virtually never receive anything that could be called "political pressure" to award a contract to one bidder, however.

In terms of the design of source selection, trade associations representing higher-end information technology and professional services firms generally have supported "best value" contracting rather than automatic award to low bidders, as well as changes to make source selection procedures less rule bound. Small-business groups, more distrustful of government and hence of granting greater discretion to government officials, generally have opposed the relaxation of the rules.

2. *Unions.* As of 1998, 38 percent of all U.S. government employees were unionized, compared with only 10 percent of private-sector employees.[41] Almost 44 percent of local government workers are union members. The largest federal union is the American Federation of Government Employees (AFGE), with about 600,000 members; the largest state/local union is the American Federation of State, County, and Municipal Employees (AFSCME), with about 1.3 million members.[42] Gradually, the center of gravity of trade unionism is moving more and more toward the public sector and away from traditional industry, a trend even more dramatic when one takes into account that unions in the construction industry are becoming increasingly concentrated among construction firms specializing in government contracting.

Federal unions may not bargain over wages, although public employee unions in twenty-four states may do so.[43] Thus, a significant focus of union efforts becomes political activity in support of the values and interests of public-sector employees. Opposition to outsourcing public employee jobs is an important issue on the agenda of public employee unionism. This includes the issue of outsourcing teacher jobs, either through government contracts with private providers of schooling or through vouchers that allow students individually to choose private as well as public schools.

3. *Organizations supporting use of the contracting tool to achieve general social goals.* Contracting also attracts the political attention of a wide variety of groups eager to mobilize the power of federal procurement to advance their goals. For example, organizations of racial minorities or women seek to direct contracting dollars to minority- or women-owned businesses, respectively, while groups facing significant foreign competition seek to limit government purchases to domestically produced goods. Indeed, organized groups supporting virtually any general public goal are potential lobbyists for use of the contracting tool to further that goal.

4. *Elected Officials and Other Political Participants in Contracting Policy.* Although many political scientists and most journalists assume that the politics of any area are dominated by organized groups, participants with "good government" concerns play an important role in the politics of contracting. The redesign of contracting to cope with corruption and to promote "economy and efficiency" in spending government money represented a victory for the ideas of the Progressive Era over the force of organized interests. The media gets episodically interested in contracting, mainly in connection with corruption scandals. At the U.S. federal level, good government elected officials tend to be overrepresented on congressional committees making general procurement policy (Governmental Affairs in the Senate, Government Reform in the House). Efforts to deregulate the procurement system during the 1990s emanated from Vice President Al Gore's "reinventing government" program.

Paul Light argues[44] that increased contracting allows public officials to state they are "shrinking" the number of public employees while still meeting the public's demand for services. What may happen in a number of circumstances is that elected officials insist on government employee headcount reductions and that agencies then, on their own, decide to meet needs through contracting.

For activities currently performed in-house but recommended for contracting out, one compromise solution common both in the United States and western Europe is "public-private competition." The public employees compete for the work with private contractors, using a source selection process analogous to the one used to select contractors in situations where contracting will definitely be used. While the approach is popular among elected officials, unions are reluctant about the competition, and trade associations generally complain that the government may be biased in its evaluation, seldom reflecting all the government's indirect costs in its cost comparisons.

V. MANAGEMENT CHALLENGES

The most important management challenges for government contracting today include (1) establishing performance standards and monitoring contractor performance, (2) streamlining the system, and (3) the use of "socioeconomic" requirements in contracting.

Establishing Performance Standards and Monitoring Contractor Performance

Improving the quantity and quality of performance monitoring of contractors is the most serious management challenge faced in the use of the contracting tool, particularly in cases where the requirement is expressed merely as a direction, not a result, and more broadly in cases of best-efforts contracting. There may be no other single change in the mechanics of the contracting tool that could produce a greater positive impact on the results the tool delivers than improvements in performance standards and performance monitoring.

Interest in performance-based contracting is growing, particularly for services, at both state/local and federal levels. The development of performance standards has been slow and uneven, partly because it is often hard to do, and partly because this is a new way of doing business for the government. The first step in defining performance standards is to ask how the government would know if the contract were successful. Once standards for success are defined, the next step is operationalizing the standards into performance metrics and then monitoring performance.[45]

The weapons system test and evaluation organization in the Defense Department is probably the best organizational infrastructure for performance monitoring among all government units that use contracting for mission-critical purposes. The problem is not that weapons system performance is unmonitored, but that the government is often unwilling to hold the contractor's feet to the fire for unmet performance commitments. The program office running a weapons program is committed to the program's success and realizes that failure may produce cutbacks or cancellation. For example, as Don Kettl reports, when the Sergeant York antiaircraft guns during the 1980s failed the initial performance tests, "instead of canceling the weapon because it failed the tests, the army canceled the tests."[46] Sometimes, contracts are modified to extend delivery dates or relax performance demands. (The Sergeant York program was eventually canceled.)

Performance monitoring infrastructure is generally poorly developed for services, a special problem given the growing role of service contracting. To the extent that any real monitoring of services occurs at all, it generally takes the form of input monitoring. The resulting second-guessing and micromanagement of contractor activities has often been unhelpful or even counterproductive.

It is sometimes argued that the more the government contracts out an activity, the more it loses the ability to monitor performance. The government loses the employees who have the knowledge and competence necessary to monitor contractor performance. However, this worry may be more apparent than real. The skills needed to monitor performance are not the same as those needed to do the work. When the government had many employees to monitor contractors, the employees did not typically monitor performance but rather micromanaged contractor activities. If the government does not have the expertise to monitor performance, it can, ironically, contract with "independent verification and validation" firms that specialize in performance monitoring. The government also can use nonprofit and for-profit firms to help establish performance requirements where the agency lacks the technical knowledge to do so. Overall, policy direction can be provided by senior officials who either have come up through the ranks of the organization as a whole or who are brought in from the outside.

Streamlining the System

Another management challenge for contracting is to achieve its goals without burdening the system with excessive red tape and paperwork that dramatically slow procurement lead times, discourage contractors from seeking government business, and turn contracting officials into clerks rather than business advisers. In a history of U.S. federal government contracting published in 1992, just before the streamlining efforts of the 1990s began, James F. Nagle wrote that "a system that began with no written guidance now finds itself bound in paper from end to end.[47] Streamlining is not simply about the government's convenience, but about signaling government employees about the sense of urgency they should have in meeting the goals the contracting tool is supposed to support.

Over the last decade, the U.S. federal government and some state and local jurisdictions have attempted to streamline the system. In the U.S. federal government, these efforts began under the auspices of the reinventing government" effort directed by Gore beginning in 1993. Influenced by the business management doctrine of the 1980s, the government began to reduce the high level of regulation by increasing the discretion for government officials and by reducing the oversight of contractors. In this context, a number of parts of the Federal Acquisition Regulation were modified. In 1994 a set of "core guiding principles" was added to Part 1 of the regulations stating that "[t]he role of each member of the Acquisition Team is to exercise personal initiative and sound business judgment in providing the best value product or service to meet the customer's needs." The principles also stated that "in exercising initiative, Government members of the Acquisition Team may assume if a specific strategy, practice, policy or procedure is in the best interests of the Government and is not addressed in the FAR, nor prohibited by law (statute or case law), Executive order or other regulation, that the strategy, practice, policy or procedure is . . . permissible." The idea was to reverse the traditional presumption that "if the regulation doesn't allow it, it's prohibited."

Socioeconomic Requirements

Most levels of government in the United States have had various kinds of contracting preference programs for minority- and women-owned contractors involving set-asides and/or price preferences. The basic argument for the use of contracting to deal with social problems is that it places the immense buying power of government in support of a worthy goal. The basic counterarguments are that it raises the price government pays and discourages the development of a culture within contracting organizations focused on getting the government a good deal. In addition, the promotion of social goals by imposing special obligations on contractors, such as hiring handicapped workers, creates a disincentive for firms to do business with the government. Such provisions may discourage the entry of new competitors into the government marketplace.

The main threat to these social programs in recent years has been a series of Supreme Court decisions (*Richmond v. J. A. Croson Company*[48] for local and *Adarand Constructors v. Pena* in 1995[49] for federal contracting) that established a standard of "strict scrutiny" requiring the program to respond to specific patterns of discrimination and be "narrowly tailored" to achieve its goals with a minimum of intrusion. In response, the Clinton administration tried to preserve as much as possible of the existing procurement affirmative action structure while limiting its application to industries where historical discrimination in federal contracting could be demonstrated.

VI. OVERALL ASSESSMENT

As one of the most pervasive policy tools in use in this era of third-party government, how, then, does contracting measure up overall? To respond to this question, we will assess contracting on the basis of four general measures: effectiveness, efficiency, equity, and legitimacy.

Effectiveness

Contracting is clearly, and uncontroversially, a far more effective way to contribute to the production of government action than direct provision for a very wide range of everyday activities of government. Nobody believes the government should make its own computers, cars, or office supplies rather than buying them by contract. This tool makes it possible for government to tap the strengths and capabilities of the private business and nonprofit sectors in the service of public purposes.

However, as suggested earlier, this tool is far from perfect. There are clearly many contracts that do not work well—particularly for major weapons systems and for complex information technology projects. Contracting is least effective where vigorous competition does not exist among suppliers and where the specification of performance is difficult—two situations (particularly the latter) that are all too common in fields where government typically operates. Therefore, while contracting is an effective tool, it is hardly effective universally.

Efficiency

Contracting has been and will continue to be a highly efficient tool of government in circumstances in which the market is competitive and the parties to the contract operate with integrity. Although the news media love to expose dramatic examples of fraud and abuse in the contracting system and identify outrageous prices government agencies allegedly pay for commonplace items, there are actually billions of dollars spent every year by governments for goods and services that are reasonably and competitively, often very competitively, priced. There are situations where the federal government gets better prices than does any company in America. The keys to efficient contracting are leveraging the government's large buying power to obtain discounts and assuring the effective administration of the contract from execution to closeout.

Equity

A third goal of contracting is fairness to people interacting with the contracting system. When properly administered, the contracting process can provide equal access to all qualified contractors who want to bid for the business of their government. The tool can also be used to promote broader socioeconomic goals, as discussed in greater detail in the preceding section of this chapter. However, when used for such purposes, the policymakers should be aware of the potential negative consequences for other legitimate public policy goals such as the efficient use of public funds.

Legitimacy

Contracting is almost universally viewed as a highly legitimate tool for accomplishing public purposes. Its legitimacy flows in part from the extensive use of contracting outside government, the long history of government contracting, and the competitive, entrepreneurial market economy it supports. The primary challenge to its legitimacy is the exposure to fraud and abuse by both the private contractor and the public agent.

VII. FUTURE DIRECTIONS

Contracting has been a tool of government action for a longer period of time than most of the other tools in this book. In contrast to tools such as vouchers or tax incentives, no one would argue that the tool should not be used at all. The trend has been to rely increasingly on contracting as a tool.

The concentration of expertise in the private defense and information technology industries that drove the development of defense contracting starting with World War II and information technology contracting starting during the 1950s marked a definitive change in the center of gravity toward contracting and away from direct provision as a tool of government action. Contracting is far from always successful as a tool of government action, mainly because of principal-agent problems that become increasingly severe as the ability appropriately to specify the government's requirements and/or monitor performance decreases. However, in the situations where contracting is problematical as a tool, similar principal-agent problems are likely to arise with direct government provision, so it is not at all clear that even where contracting is problematical, it is a worse alternative than others.

Not surprisingly, the actual choices government has made between contracting and direct provision do not exactly track theories for when the tool is most or least appropriate. Critics who believe the government uses contracting too much can point to instances of contractors performing work that would seem "inherently governmental." In the Environmental Protection Agency's toxic waste cleanup program, for example, "Contractors were involved not only in the actual business of cleanup, but . . . helped EPA respond to congressional inquiries, analyze legislation, and draft regulations and standards. . . . Contractors researched Freedom of Information Act requests received by the agency. They drafted memos, international agreements, and congressional testimony for top EPA officials. . . . They even wrote the Superfund program's annual report to Congress."[50] At the same time, often because of historical traditions of direct provision that become politically difficult to overturn, Defense Department employees deliver many commercial services from payroll processing to development and operation of logistics information systems, which appear to be ideal for contracting. However, I do not believe a strong case exists that the overall balance between direct provision and contracting is badly out of whack.

Therefore, contracting seems likely to persist and expand as a tool of government action. Our challenge is to design and operate it in a way that allows it to achieve the objectives of which it is capable.

VIII. SUGGESTED READING

Cibinic, John, Jr., and Ralph C. Nash, Jr. *Administration of Government Contracts,* 3d ed. Washington, D.C.: George Washington University Press, 1995.

Donahue, John. *The Privatization Decision.* New York: Basic Books, 1989.

Gansler, Jacques S. *Defense Conversion: Transforming the Arsenal of Democracy.* Cambridge, Mass.: MIT Press, 1995.

Kelman, Steven. J. *Procurement and Public Management: The Fear of Discretion and the Quality of Government Performance.* Washington, D.C.: AEI Press, 1990.

Kettl, Donald F. *Government by Proxy.* Washington, D.C.: CQ Press, 1988.

Nagle, James F. *A History of Government Contracting.* Washington, D.C.: George Washington University Press, 1992.

Nash, Ralph C. *Formation of Government Contracts.* Washington, D.C.: George Washington University Press, 1998.

NOTES

1. The term "contractor," which is the one used in government contract law, will be used in this chapter to describe firms doing business with the government.

2. (In this chapter, the word "contractor," taken from public contracting law, will be used to describe the private entity contracting with the government, a usage that is somewhat different from that common commercially, where the phrase "contractor" generally is limited to the construction industry.)

3. In 1997, when the source selection rules of the Federal Acquisition Regulation were rewritten, it was stated that achieving the best value was the goal of all source selection methods; what had traditionally been called "best value" source selection was renamed the "tradeoff method." (FAR 15.101, 15.302).

4. For forceful presentation of this critique of government oversight requirements see Jacques S. Gansler, *Defense Conversion: Transforming the Arsenal of Democracy* (Cambridge, Mass.: MIT Press, 1995); and Center for Strategic and International Studies, *Integrating Commercial and Military Technologies for National Strength* (Washington, D.C.: CSIS, 1992).

5. An exception is oversight of the accuracy of representations, for example, about the contractor's costs that may be made during the bidding process.

6. James F. Nagle, *A History of Government Contracting* (Washington, D.C.: George Washington University Press, 1992), chap. 1.

7. For an interesting discussion, see Richard R. John, *Spreading the News: The American Postal System from Franklin to Morse* (Cambridge, Mass.: Harvard University Press, 1995).

8. I would like to acknowledge the assistance of Grafton Bigelow of the General Service Administration's Federal Procurement Data Center and of Lauren Uher of the Office of Federal Procurement Policy in providing these data.

9. I am grateful to Geoff Lubien, Data Resources Inc., for generous assistance in locating and interpreting the state and local procurement data. I would like to thank Greg Dorchak for calculating figures for international procurement from International Monetary Fund data.

10. This estimate was made by Paul C. Light, *The True Size of Government* (Washington, D.C.: The Brookings Institution Press, 1999), chap. 2.

11. I am grateful to Richard Loeb of the Office of Federal Procurement Policy for help gathering these numbers.

12. In the Federal Acquisition Streamlining Act—see below.

13. See Steven Kelman, "The Grace Commission: How Much Waste in Government?" *The Public Interest* 78 (winter 1985).

14. Completion contracts might also be cost-reimbursement contracts with a ceiling payment. In such a case, however, there would be no incentive for the contractor to spend less than the ceiling. However, one may remedy this problem using a fixed-price incentive fee contract. (See below.)

15. Rules about unallowable costs and accounting for indirect costs apply, as they do for cost-reimbursement contracts. (See below.)

16. For many years, contractors were often required to submit the same certified cost data for many competitive contracts, especially in the Department of Defense. Since developing this cost data required cost systems adapted to government requirements, this practice deterred many commercial firms from competing for Defense Department work. The debate about this issue has been part of the larger debate about the impact of government oversight on the willingness of commercial firms to do business with the federal government. (See above.) During the 1990s, there were changes in law and regulation to discourage requests for cost data when the government buys commercial items.

17. See John Scanlon, "An Innovative Procurement Effort Where Valuing Time Dramatically Speeds Up Acquisition and Deliveries of Results: Responding to a Crisis—A Federal/State Partnership," a case written for the Council for Excellence in Government conference Real Acquisition Reform: Managing Risk in the New Environment (1995).

18. John Scanlon, "Problem Solving Partnerships and Joint Ventures to Share Risks and Benefits in Developing Large System Technology Projects," a case written for the Council for Excellence in Government conference Real Acquisition Reform: Managing Risk in the New Environment (1995).

19. Again, in U.S. federal contracting law, "solicitation" and "request for proposals" are terms that are not used to refer to sealed bids, which are called "invitations to bid." The generic term will be used here for all kinds of source selection procedures.

20. Nagle, *History of Government Contracting*, chap. 2.

21. Sole-source procurements are also initiated by RFPs and elicit a proposal from the contractor. The government may negotiate to get a better price or, if the contract is of a best-efforts type, about the contractor's technical approach.

22. Ralph C. Nash, *Formation of Government Contracts* (Washington, D.C.: George Washington University Press, 1998), 720.

23. See, for example, the discussion in Nagle, *History of Government Contracting*, 205–211.

24. James M. McPherson, *Battle Cry of Freedom* (New York: Ballantine Books, 1988), 324.

25. Cost-accounting rules are discussed at greater length in Chapter 17 in this volume.

26. See Gansler, *Defense Conversion: Transforming the Arsenal of Democracy*, 1995; and Center for Strategic and International Studies, *Integrating Commercial and Military Technologies for National Strength*, 1992.

27. Civilian agencies that do not use DCAA often use their own Inspector-General offices for this function.

28. This can create a problem for commercial firms that were not required to submit cost data when the underlying contract was awarded. See note 26 above.

29. Quoted in John Cibinic, Jr., and Ralph C. Nash, Jr., *Administration of Government Contracts* (Washington, D.C.: George Washington University Press, 3d ed., 1995), 1283.

30. Private contracts frequently give this right, with appropriate notice, to *both* parties. Federal government contractors have no right to terminate their contract with the government "for convenience."

31. Cibinic and Nash, *Administration of Government Contracts*, 1073.

32. Ibid., 1074.

33. "A-12 Contractors Awarded $12B in Damages for Pentagon's Improper Default Termination," *Federal Contracts Report* 69 (23 February 1998). That decision was reversed on appeal; as of this writing, almost a decade later, the case is in mediation.

34. Ibid., 1079–1082.

35. John Donahue, *The Privatization Decision* (New York: Basic Books, 1989), chaps. 3, 5.

36. Kenneth J. Arrow, "The Economics of Agency," in *Principals and Agents,* eds. John W. Pratt and Richard J. Zeckhauser (Boston: Harvard Business School Press, 1985), 37.

37. C. K. Prahalad and Gary Hamel, "The Core Competence of the Corporation," *Harvard Business Review* 68 (May 1990): 79–91.

38. William Niskanen, *Bureaucracy and Representative Government* (Chicago: Aldine, 1971).

39. For more on this subject, see William P. Rogerson, "Economic Incentives and the Defense Procurement Process," *Journal of Economic Perspectives* 8, no. 4 (autumn 1994): 65–90; and William P. Rogerson, "Profit Regulation of Defense Contractors and Prizes for Innovation," *Journal of Political Economy* 97, no. 6 (December 1989): 1284–1305.

40. Nick Kotz, *Wild Blue Yonder: Money, Politics, and the B-1 Bomber* (New York: Pantheon Books, 1988), 127–129.

41. U.S. Bureau of Labor Statistics, "Labor Force Statistics from the Current Population Survey: Union Member Summary" (Washington, D.C.: Department of Labor, 25 January 1999), 2.

42. AFGE figures come from U.S. Office of Personnel Management, *Union Recognition in the Federal Government* (Washington, D.C.: Office of Personnel Management, 1997).

43. This information was provided by AFSCME.

44. Light, *True Size of Government.*

45. For advice on developing performance-based contracts, see Office of Federal Procurement Policy, *A Guide to Best Practices for Performance-Based Service Contracting* (Washington, D.C.: Office of Management and Budget, 1996); and Robert D. Behn and Peter A. Kant, "Strategies for Avoiding the Pitfalls of Performance Contracting," *Public Productivity and Management Review* 22 (June 1999), 470–489.

46. Donald F. Kettl, *Government by Proxy* (Washington, D.C.: CQ Press, 1988), 28.

47. Nagle, *A History of Government Contracting,* 466.

48. 488 U.S. 469.

49. 515 U.S. 200.

50. Donald F. Kettl, *Sharing Power: Public Governance and Private Markets* (Washington, D.C.: The Brookings Institution, 1993), 111–112.

CHAPTER TEN

Purchase-of-Service Contracting

Ruth Hoogland DeHoog and Lester M. Salamon

Helen Ziegfried was still a 1960s flower child when she decided she wanted to become a social worker and help disadvantaged women with children overcome their poverty. Therefore, she was overjoyed when, armed with her newly minted master of social work degree, she landed a job with the New York City Department of Social Welfare as a caseworker in the Aid to Families with Dependent Children Program during the late 1960s. Her enthusiasm soon turned to dismay, however, as she began to move through the ranks of her agency and discovered that most of the personnel in this large social welfare agency had almost no contact with the clients the agency is funded to serve. Rather, following a long-standing pattern in this agency, as social service spending increased during the late 1960s and early 1970s, it was channeled increasingly into contracts with the city's extensive network of private, nonprofit agencies. Ziegfried, trained as a professional social worker to minister to the needs of the disadvantaged, therefore found herself instead functioning as a contract manager for a host of complex social service contracts with a wide array of private agencies over whom she had at best imperfect control and about whose work she frequently had grossly inadequate information.

With the passage of the Personal Responsibility and Welfare Reform Act of 1996, moreover, Ziegfried's work underwent further changes. Now not only social service funding but also some of the funding for basic income assistance was also to be used to purchase services. However, given the stress on work and performance in the new welfare program, new pressures were brought to bear on agency officials to show numerical results. Furthermore, new for-profit providers entered the competition for service contracts, raising additional questions about the standards that should govern contract awards and the tasks involved in contract administration. For Ziegfried, this has produced additional tensions between her social work norms and skills and the demands she faces as the manager of a series of multimillion-dollar contracts with a complex array of for-profit and nonprofit providers—work for which she feels singularly ill prepared.

Ziegfried's plight reflects the pervasive impact that the tool of "purchase-of-service contracting," a distinctive form of government procurement, has had on the work of public employees, and indeed on the entire human service delivery system in the United States and, increasingly, in other countries around the world. In this chapter, we examine the nature of this tool, discuss the extent of its use, review the basic mechanics through which it operates, explore the reasons for its use, and assess the extent to which it lives up to its promise.

I. DEFINING THE TOOL

Purchase-of-service (POS) contracting has long been a central feature of America's human service delivery system, but it expanded massively during the 1960s and 1970s, especially in the Northeast and Midwest, where a longstanding tradition of government-nonprofit cooperation to address social and economic problems has long existed. If anything, however, reliance on such contracting has expanded even more extensively in recent years, embracing for-profit as well as nonprofit firms.

Defining Features

Purchase-of-service contracting essentially involves an agreement under which a government agency enlists a private organization to deliver a service to an eligible group of "clients" in exchange for money. Services covered by POS contracting include family counseling, employment training, senior citizen day-care programs, foster-care services, youth mentoring programs, substance abuse counseling, housing assistance, and migrant-worker health assessments. Thus, POS contracting differs from the procurement contracting discussed in Chapter 9 in that it involves government purchase of services for third parties rather than for the government's own use.

Typically, human services are purchased by state, city, or county governments and delivered by nonprofit agencies, although intergovernmental agreements and contracts with other public agencies or for-profit businesses are increasingly important in certain fields. Although some of these contracts are made with individuals (e.g., foster-care parents, specialized medical professionals, in-home chore service providers), our attention in this chapter focuses on contracts extended to nonprofit and for-profit agencies, which provide the bulk of these kinds of services.

Human service contracting has several features that distinguish it from other types of contracting, such as purchases for government's own use (e.g., building maintenance, computer service contracts, employee training programs) or contracts for so-called hard public services (e.g., refuse collection, street sweeping, drivers' and motor vehicle license renewal).[1] First, these services are often directed at assisting or changing the behavior and circumstances of disadvantaged populations (e.g., the homeless, mentally ill, children). Therefore, the services are often complex and involve many uncontrollable factors and produce uncertain outcomes. As a result, the measurement of performance and success is problematic, or at least not readily agreed upon, even by professionals. Therefore, it is more difficult to reward and punish contractors because so many factors may be outside their control.

Second, these services are usually highly labor intensive, involving personal care in group homes, job training centers, senior activity programs, credit counseling programs, substance abuse counseling, adult day care, child care, and services for the disabled. Thus, the costs may be difficult to reduce or control, and the exercise of discretion by the service providers is a critical element of the process itself.

Third, because of the populations served, the difficulties in defining performance, and the degree of service discretion involved, the purchasing agency must invest significant time and expense to review and monitor the service delivery process. While other public services or goods may include some automatic mechanisms to indicate service problems (e.g., citizen complaints about their garbage collection), these mechanisms are often unreliable or absent in the production of human services, where clients have limited opportunities or resources to voice their needs or complaints.

Human service contracting also differs from other contracting with respect to the purchasing process. First, a high degree of competition among private suppliers for service contracts is often not desirable or useful, as it might be in the hard services. Service coordination, continuity, and cooperation among several agencies are often seen as important elements of the system of care, and these require something other than one-shot purchases of goods or services. Thus, the formal competitive process of purchasing goods and services is not strictly followed in many POS arrangements. Human service contracts typically are negotiated, not competitively bid, as they are for many other public services. The relationships established between the contractors and the government are critical, producing what Oliver Williamson has referred to as "relational contracting."[2] As a result, some argue that a cooperative, rather than a competitive, approach may be more appropriate in many of these services.[3]

In addition, the nature of the eligible contractors typically has differed in human service contracting. In particular, nonprofit, as opposed to for-profit, organizations are more commonly central, although this has been changing recently. Although observers suggest that the differences in practices between for-profits and nonprofits are becoming smaller, their legal status, governance systems, and financial practices still vary significantly. Nonprofit organizations have a long history of providing human services in situations where profits are not possible. Their incentive structures are generally oriented toward the services produced, not toward profit maximization for owners or shareholders. In short, human service contracting is an important area of contracting and privatization; yet, its unique characteristics mean that generalizations drawn from other services do not necessarily apply.

Relation to Key Tool Features

Compared with other tools of public action examined in this volume, POS contracting tends to be relatively *indirect, automatic, noncoercive,* and *visible.*

Directness

Directness measures the extent to which the entity authorizing or inaugurating a program is involved in carrying it out. POS contracting is a fundamentally indirect tool of public action, relying on nongovernmental actors to deliver publicly financed services to eligible citizens on the government's behalf. Because it involves a specific service contract, usually with a single provider for a set period of time, however, human service contracting may be viewed as being somewhat more direct than some other indirect tools, such as vouchers or loans, which leave far more choice to consumers. Generally, the client is not involved in POS contracting, although in some human services the client may be given a choice of using a contractor or direct government services.

Automaticity

Automaticity measures the extent to which a tool utilizes an existing administrative structure to produce its effect rather than having to create its own special administrative apparatus. Because it relies on marketlike relationships, POS contracting is also a relatively automatic tool. At the same time, the market for human services is not well developed, and little competition may be present. In addition, the service providers may not be completely responsive to the service specifications and may not produce good-quality services. Even then, the renewal of contracts with low-performing contractors may be necessary because of the lack of other options, either in the public agency or among private agencies. As a consequence, POS contracting often turns out to be far less automatic than it appears.

Coerciveness

Coerciveness measures the extent to which a tool restricts individual or group behavior as opposed to merely encouraging or discouraging it. Like other forms of contracting, POS contracting essentially offers a reward in the form of a money payment for the provision of a service by a private vendor to a designated client. As such, it is a generally noncoercive tool. At the same time, from the point of view of contractors, POS contracting can often appear quite coercive because of contract specifications about clients to be served, procedures to be followed, other conditions to be met, and reports to be filed. Certainly, POS contracting is more coercive than grants, since service contracts hold the contractor to account for serving the government's objectives, whereas grants are far more responsive to the recipients' objectives.

Visibility

The final general tool feature in terms of which POS contracting can be compared with other tools is the degree of visibility it exhibits. Visibility can take many different forms, including visibility in the budget process, visibility in the political process more generally, and visibility to the users of the services. Programs embodying contracting are typically on-budget expenditures and therefore highly visible in the normal budget process. Furthermore, contracts are often publicly announced and may even require approval by local elected officials. At the same time, like other tools of indirect government, the fact that services are financed by government but delivered by private agencies may cause some confusion in the minds of the general public and users of the services about what is the real nature of this tool. Therefore, users may not be aware that the services they are receiving are actually being financed by government, creating a disjunction that can threaten political support for the programs, a point that is explored in more detail in other chapters of this volume on accountability and democratic control.

Major Variants

While POS contracts share a number of common features, they can also take a number of different forms, depending on the services being purchased (e.g., easily defined "hard" services such as transportation as opposed to "softer" services such as family counseling), the types of agents used (nonprofits, for-profits, individuals, or public agencies), and the clients being served (e.g., low income, elderly, handicapped). These features will determine the degree of specificity of the contract language, the extent of formalization of the contracting process and arrangements, and the accountability standards to which contractors are held.

Reflecting these various dimensions, three broad forms of POS contracting can be identified. The first is *competitive contracting*, in which formal requests for proposals are issued and competitive proposals received from potential providers. The second is *negotiated contracting*, in which a limited number of potential providers is invited to submit expressions of interest in providing a range of services, and the government agency chooses one or a handful with which to enter into more concrete negotiations about the contours of the services to be provided and the reimbursement to be paid. Finally, a more fully *cooperative contracting* approach can be used where a strong relationship has developed between a public agency and a reputable provider and the public agency wishes to work with the provider to ensure a supply of critically needed services into the future.

Historically, the *competitive* model has been the most commonly discussed approach and is the one typically assumed in the literature. However, the *negotiated* and *cooperative* approaches have gained widespread usage as the contracting system has matured.

One other dimension along which POS contracting can vary involves the scope of the contract. Historically, service contracts were awarded for separate, discrete services. Increasingly, however, public agencies are entering into "umbrella" or "master" contracts with private agencies in order to deal more effectively with the array of services often required to achieve a particular policy objective, such as enabling welfare recipients to achieve financial independence. Under this arrangement, public agencies award large, general contracts to agencies that in turn have broad responsibility for selecting, training, and monitoring subcontractor agencies. This allows for a more streamlined process in awarding contracts and starting services than is often possible when the government must secure multiple contractors through separate proposal processes. The private agencies may also be able to avoid some of the legal constraints that public officials operate under in soliciting and advertising contracts.

II. PATTERNS AND EXTENT OF USAGE

Patterns of Tool Use

Purchase-of-service contracting has a long history in the United States. As early as the late nineteenth century, local governments in the United States were contracting with private, nonprofit agencies to conduct adoptions and provide social services to needy families. Two-thirds of the amounts spent on relief of poverty in New York City by the early 1890s, for example, took this form.[4]

This practice, however, spread widely once the federal government began funding community development, health, and other human services during the 1960s. For example, between 1963 and 1972, federal funding to state governments for social services leaped from $194 million to almost $1.7 billion before leveling off to approximately $2.5 billion for the next decade.[5] Thanks to the Social Security Act Amendments of 1967, which authorized state and local governments to contract with private agencies for the delivery of the resulting services, much of this increase translated into purchases of services from other public and private agencies. The upshot was an explosion in government support for nonprofit organizations and a considerable expansion of the nation's nonprofit sector as a consequence. Despite budget cutbacks during the 1980s, moreover, contracting with nonprofit agencies continued to expand, stimulated by conservative ideological preferences for private over public provision of public services. In addition, for-profit firms were increasingly encouraged to enter into POS arrangements with government agencies and a substantial for-profit human service industry began to emerge in such fields as home health, nursing home care, and behavioral health.

These trends have been reinforced by the welfare reform law enacted in 1996. Under the Personal Responsibility and Welfare Reform Act of 1996, an integrated and wide array of social services is provided by nonprofit and for-profit service agencies to reduce the welfare caseload and assist families in becoming self-sufficient. The funds formerly used for direct welfare payments may now be used for a range of support services, such as transportation, child day care, and job training, many of them purchased from private vendors. Additionally, in many areas today, child support enforcement and disbursement are being completely turned over by the states to private, for-profit agencies that promise improved collections and efficiency for state government coffers.

The consequence of these changes is that POS contracting has become an immense industry in the United States. While data on its full scale are difficult to secure, a rough estimate would include approximately 50 percent of all federal spending in the major social welfare budget functions of social services (for families, children, adults, and communities), employment and training programs (primarily Job Corps and JTPA), and community development. By fiscal year (FY) 1997, the total expenditures for these three fields combined equaled $38.3 billion.[6] With welfare cash assistance payments now being converted to services under Temporary Assistance to Needy Families (TANF), income assistance funding now also goes to private organizations. Several large for-profit firms (e.g., Lockheed Martin, Maximus) as well as small local businesses have developed proposals and expertise to obtain these contracts in such states as Texas, Wisconsin, and Florida. Although some of these firms have been viewed with suspicion and fear by existing nonprofit agencies and social work professionals, many elected officials have welcomed their more businesslike approaches to getting people jobs and training.

International Experience

Purchase-of-service contracting is also increasingly widespread outside the United States. Indeed, the practice of governmental reliance on private agencies to deliver a wide array of human services is even more deeply entrenched abroad, particularly in western Europe, than it is in the United States, although this reliance has often been handled through grants rather than through contracts. Thus, the Netherlands has organized much of its human service delivery around the concept of "pillarization," under which human services in such fields as education, health, day care, elderly care, and counseling are delivered through private agencies organized along religious or ideological lines but financed largely by government.[7] In Germany, the Catholic doctrine of subsidiarity similarly produced a widespread pattern of reliance on "free welfare associations" to deliver much of the government-financed human services.[8] Reflecting this, recent work on the scope, structure, and financing of the nonprofit sector in western Europe has revealed a huge nonprofit sector financed largely (60 to 70 percent) by government in such countries as Ireland, the Netherlands, Germany, Belgium, and even France.[9]

In recent years, moreover, the grant-based funding of nonprofit agencies for the delivery of human services in western Europe increasingly has given way to a contract-based system in which tenders are issued and bids accepted and reviewed. Such POS contracting systems have been especially evident in the United Kingdom and in Australia and New Zealand, but the spread of this tool is evident elsewhere as well.

III. BASIC MECHANICS

Purchase-of-service contracting involves a number of critical steps. Many of these duplicate steps involved in other forms of contracting, but several are peculiar to service contracting in particular. While these steps provide the framework for the contracting process, some of them may be absent or reordered in the different contracting designs mentioned above.

Service Planning and Contract Initiation

The first step in the contracting process is determining whether the service can and should be purchased. As one student of contracting has noted:

> [O]ne of the most serious deficiencies in planning for contracting is that program officers frequently fail to consider first the elements essential to a decision on whether or not to contract. They do not evaluate their goals, the resources (personnel and funds) required, their in-house capability vs. that of contractors, a cost analysis (in-house vs. contractor), timing, and legal parameters. Only if consideration of these and other factors leads program officers to decide that contracts are necessary and cost-effective should the process itself begin.[10]

This contracting decision need not be an all-or-nothing one. Some portion of a service could still be produced in-house, and another part could be done by an outside agency. Sometimes this is purely a pragmatic decision to ensure service access or coverage; other times it is a way to compare costs and quality of services between two different sets of employees and agencies. In addition, if a service is contracted out, an award can be made to a single agency or multiple agencies, occasionally allowing for a choice of suppliers or locations for clients. Certain parts of the administrative process, not just the direct client service activity, might also be contracted out to a different agency. For example, contract monitoring and evaluation have been performed by research agencies, university centers, or outside consultants. As noted earlier, master or umbrella contracts can be written to cover a package of different services. Then the contractor agency subcontracts some of the services to other agencies and is responsible for most of the contract administration.

Solicitation of Bids

The second basic phase in POS contracting is the solicitation of bids. This involves two important steps.

Preparing the Solicitation

First, a solicitation and specification package, a Request for Proposal (RFP) or solicitation of bids, must be prepared. Ideally, this should take the form of a tight, clear, and complete specification of service performance standards, penalties, and perhaps incentives. These service components typically are written by the program staff who know the services and performance they desire. The program staff typically also confers with the government's contract staff who must ensure that the language and procedures comply with various federal, state, or agency rules and regulations. The document will outline not only the service specifications and evaluation criteria, but also include information about agency eligibility or preaward requirements.

Advertising the Solicitation

Once the solicitation has been formulated, it must then be brought to the attention of potential provider agencies. This can be done by advertising the RFP in the appropriate media outlets and providing firms and agencies with information in preproposal conferences. A more informal "heads-up" notification of eligible agencies in the area or a mailing to these agencies prior to (or instead of) publication of a formal RFP in a newspaper, government document, or professional publication can also be useful. The skill and attention the government agency brings to the task of preparing and disseminating the contract announcement are as important as the ones they bring to writing the service specifications. Indeed, where only one or two inexperienced agencies are able or willing to compete for the award, the government agency may provide a higher level of technical assistance, usually one-on-one, in preparing the service plan, budget, and proposal. Where many agencies are interested, a preproposal conference to provide all agencies the same information may be scheduled if time and other resources permit.

Proposal Review and Awards

The agency's review of submitted proposals may be done by a panel of judges, or by a single official, sometimes in consultation with other officials. Usually, these individuals are involved in the program area, not in the purchasing unit. The reviewers are obligated to use the evaluation criteria in the RFP, but they will also use their own judgment to determine how well the proposal fits the specifications. Some proposals may be disqualified because the offering agency is not eligible (e.g., a private, for-profit agency), or is deemed incapable of carrying out the service (e.g., insufficient financial stability), or the proposal is not responsive to the specifications of the announcement. While the proposal is the primary source of information on which the reviewers can rely in forming their judgment, on-site visits or additional financial or service information in the form of interviews and/or documents can also be requested.

Award decisions are a critical point in the contract process. Public officials must be aware of the potential threats to the fairness of the process—primarily corruption, collusion, fraud, favoritism, and conflict of interest. Certain safeguards (e.g., disclosure of conflict of interest by public officials, accounting requirements) are often mandated by federal, state, or local laws, but vigilance is still necessary to ensure a clean process that strictly adheres to all relevant regulations, statutes, and ordinances. Legal challenges to the award decision are not only costly and time consuming, but they can also delay implementation of a needed service.

Once the award is announced, implementation often does not begin immediately. Certain administrative or service issues may still need to be resolved. Only then is a contract drawn up and signed by the various officials acting on behalf of the government and the contractor. This may turn into a lengthy negotiation over contract specifications and performance measures, if any, when new services or requirements are involved.

Contract Management and Monitoring

Once a contract is signed, the service planning and implementation processes begin. The contract itself can be a single-year or multiyear award, depending on the program's regulations, state law, and/or bureaucratic decision rules. Approving a contract, however, may not mean the services are immediately provided. The contractor may need to hire and train employees, find subcontractors, and arrange for appropriate facilities. All of this may delay the start-up of services.

Since the government unit is ultimately accountable for the cost and quality of contracted services, monitoring and evaluation must also be carried out. Public officials can employ several accountability methods to review contract compliance and service performance, including regular site visits, monthly or quarterly reports, random checks of the files, financial documentation of costs, and client complaint mechanisms. However, some of these require additional training and other staff resources. Due to the costs, agencies usually do not engage in a full-scale summative evaluation of contracted services and prefer to encourage continuous improvements in services as they review the implementation process.

Contract Renewal or Termination

At the end of a contract period, decisions must then be made about whether to renew or terminate a contract. This can be a difficult decision, although the general rule of thumb tends to be to renew contracts since the transaction costs are far less than seeking out new service agencies. Terminating a contract midyear is highly unlikely for the same reasons. However, at least three different situations may lead the government to decide not to renew a contract: (1) the current contractor's service performance and contract compliance are significantly below expectations, and the agency does not seem capable of making improvements; (2) the funding for the service is cut; or (3) the service priorities are shifted in another direction. Even when one of these situations occurs (e.g., when there is clear evidence of mismanagement), strong political pressure may be placed on the government to continue the contract with the current provider. This makes the initial RFP specification and award decision all the more important and may help to explain why experienced government officials often reduce their risks by choosing to negotiate contracts with established, experienced agencies.

IV. TOOL SELECTION

Some of the arguments both for and against contracting have had an ideological twist to them. Therefore, when selecting the contracting option, administrators should be aware of both the advantages and disadvantages of service contracting, as well as the underlying assumptions about the process.

Rationale

The contracting tool has been promoted by many advocates on grounds that it promotes efficiency and effectiveness by taking advantage of a market-type mechanism.[11] Competition in the proposal process is believed to ensure low-cost and responsive services because potential contractors will pare their costs and improve their services to get and keep contracts. Proponents assume that "big government" and "bad bureaucracy" are circumvented by contracting out for human services to small, flexible, and nonbureaucratic agencies that are more in tune with their clients' needs and more efficient in their operations. Some argue that government may have a higher level of control over the services and performance than would be possible under vouchers, or grants, primarily due to contract requirements, compliance monitoring, and renewal decisions.

Another argument for contracting is that it affords government agencies greater flexibility than direct service provision to change priorities, operations, and funding levels when necessary by changing the contract specifications and service providers. In addition, private organizations may have the professional expertise, client access, or facilities that are simply unavailable to the public agency. Related to this advantage is the avoidance of certain legal, personnel, and administrative requirements on government that might limit discretion, cost savings, program success, and the flexible use of employee skills. For example, in job placement service contracts for welfare recipients, private businesses can readily offer incentive pay or commissions based on placements of clients, which are impossible or difficult to implement in government agencies. A for-profit employment agency that already has established contacts with many large companies may then be more successful in finding jobs for low-income clients. Beyond this, many observers believe that private agencies can more quickly adapt to new systems, services, client needs, and administrative requirements than can more entrenched public agencies. For example, they have an ability to hire (and fire) short-term or specialized expertise.

Contracting is also believed to encourage agencies to cooperate and to overcome the suspicion often attached to government programs by enlisting nonprofit agencies with solid reputations in the relevant communities. As a result, it can improve the prospects for generating higher levels of client participation and satisfaction. For example, private agencies may have better access to target populations and may literally "speak their language." Contracting also makes it possible to take advantage of innovative service methods or expertise that nonprofit service providers often develop.

Decisions on whether to use the contracting tool therefore depend on considerations such as the following:

- Whether competition and choice among agencies are present in the service environment

- Whether reputable agencies are available with specialized expertise, good administrative staff, and trusting relationships with clients and/or community

- Whether the government has enough information/expertise to understand the service, agencies, and client populations

- Whether the government and contract agencies have sufficient resources to operate the contracting process effectively

- Whether any legal or administrative prohibitions about this tool exist

Contracting is likely to be an appropriate option in situations where state laws do not prohibit it, where some degree of competition or choice exists among reputable and trusted agencies, where the government has a sufficient amount of information, and where sufficient resources are likely to be committed for the entire process. Even where some of these conditions are not present, however, the cooperative or negotiation models of contracting may still be considered appropriate even though the competition model may not be.

Political Considerations

Quite apart from these substantive reasons, the use of contracting for the provision of human services has also been driven by essentially political reasons. For one thing, in the United States contracting has provided a way to sidestep long-standing conservative opposition to government involvement in social welfare and human service provision. By enlisting private agencies, government has been able to extend the provision of human services without enlarging government bureaucracies or conjuring up the image of direct government intrusion into sensitive human service areas, such as adoption or day care. Indeed, some of the earliest service contracting was designed to ensure that adoption placements remained responsive to the religious backgrounds of the natural parents. This was achieved by contracting the adoption placements out to religiously affiliated, private social service agencies. The fact that private charitable organizations often had influential community leaders on their governing boards no doubt helped legitimize this process and contributed to securing a role for these agencies in the expanding human service "business" that government involvement helped to produce.

A slightly different political dynamic was at work in the choice of contracting to handle the antipoverty program funds in the United States during the early 1960s. Here, the fear was that control by local governments dominated by racist or otherwise insensitive political leaders would keep impoverished communities disempowered. By channeling funds to community-based nonprofit agencies, POS contracting would break the monopoly of the local powers that be.[12]

These political considerations were further augmented during the 1980s and 1990s by the rise of conservative and neoliberal ideological forces that viewed contracting as part of a broader strategy to "privatize" public services. Far from a mechanism that would facilitate the expansion of government human service activity, however, contracting came to be viewed in this line of thinking as a way to reduce public spending and limit the government's role.[13]

Although political support for contracting has been quite significant, this tool has generated its share of opposition as well. Perhaps most significant has been the opposition from public employees and the unions representing them. Public employees complain that private contractors achieve economies in the provision of human services primarily by squeezing the already depressed wages of service workers and by eliminating jobs and/or substituting drugs for the more labor-intensive personal treatment of clients.[14] Public employees therefore are highly motivated to rally support for their jobs against contracting-out efforts and can often put enough pressure on elected officials to stop such arrangements.

More recently, political opposition to contracting has arisen from service users seeking greater control over the services made available to them, and conservative political forces that see in service contracting a powerful political force aligning politicians, private service agencies, and government bureaucrats in favor of expanded government spending. To break these service alliances, conservatives have tended to favor voucher approaches instead of provider-side subsidies through service contracts. This approach has also been favored by religious conservatives on the grounds that prohibitions on government support for religion kept churches out of the human service contracting business, whereas vouchers provided directly to clients could be used to pay for services that religious institutions provide.

V. MANAGEMENT CHALLENGES AND POTENTIAL RESPONSES

Despite its many substantive and political advantages, service contracting also poses a number of challenges both for government agencies and for service suppliers.

Challenges for Public Agencies

Government agencies face a number of problems and issues in contracting out services.

Loss of Control

Reliance on contracting may put the government in a vulnerable position where essential services are concerned and lead to some loss of control over the services they purchase. If the government has shed its experienced employees or sold its capital assets (e.g., its buses for senior transportation services) and no other agency exists to provide the service, no options may be immediately available if the contractor fails to comply with the contract or if it goes out of business. Disruption in service delivery or discontinuity in service quality may result from either a change in providers or a government takeover of a service. Perhaps a less serious, but also important, problem is that in many smaller communities the lack of competition among service providers may mean that the government has no choice of contractors and no bargaining leverage in negotiations—it has to take what is offered by the available agency, and it cannot easily change priorities or service methods.

Excessive Costs

The costs of contracting, while expected to be equal to or lower than direct provision, often are not. Experienced service providers may have an information advantage over the government when new services are contracted out. In these cases, the expected benefits due to competition may not be realized. Another disadvantage to extensive contracting are the transaction costs incurred in operating the process—advertising contracts, providing technical assistance for proposal writing, monitoring agencies and services off-site, and training both public and contract employees in contract compliance and government regulations. These administrative costs may actually increase the overall costs of services well beyond those provided through traditional government agencies, even though the direct costs of the service contracts may appear lower. On the other hand, some nonprofit agencies have found that their contracts do not fully cover their administrative costs, such that they end up subsidizing some of the services themselves.

Lack of Sufficient Providers

For some specialized services and in smaller communities, the number of eligible provider agencies may be so small or nonexistent that the expected competition among providers does not occur. The few existing agencies may have experience working with only certain types of populations and may be slow to reorient their staff or expand their expertise. Since public social services, mental health, and public health agencies have long had a monopoly over services for low-income people in many locales, for example, few other agencies developed the kind of expertise and capacity to work with these groups. In some cases, the barriers to entering the market are sizable and the possible benefits so few that new agencies may not emerge to respond to the demand. If contracting is used, the more collaborative or negotiated model may be needed, and additional time and effort in technical assistance may be necessary.

Limited Capabilities of Provider Agencies

Not only the numbers but also the managerial competence of provider agencies poses problems for government in POS contracting. This is particularly the case where nonprofit agencies are the providers. While nonprofits have certainly improved their management and fiscal capacities in recent years, many local nonprofits are run by highly committed, but inadequately trained, executives. They may have strong political and public support in their communities and may have excellent professional reputations. Their expertise in producing desired services and serving certain client groups offers strong inducements for state and local governments to contract with them. Nonetheless, smaller and newer agencies may struggle with the sometimes complex administrative and accountability requirements imposed by the government. Often they have not been able to afford the professional managers and staff (e.g., grant writers, financial managers, program evaluators) to develop complete proposals, ensure service compliance, and manage the reporting requirements.

Role Ambiguities

Beyond these specific difficulties, contracting also raises a number of broader concerns. The blurring of the traditional boundaries between public and private sectors can create confusion about responsibility, ownership, and funding sources not only for those who work "in the system," but also for citizens and clients. Clients may be unclear about who is really responsible for service decisions and therefore about where to direct their service complaints or questions. Clients may not know, for example, that the county social welfare agency should be contacted to express concerns about an unsatisfactory service delivered by a private nonprofit organization. On the other hand, a nonprofit organization may receive the credit for a well-funded and successful service that is actually financed through government funding. This lack of understanding about the contracting system may undermine public support for government funding, challenge the legitimacy of public agencies, and mislead the public about the funding base of nonprofit agencies. As two recent observers have noted:

> In essence, contracting with nonprofit agencies diffuses responsibility for public services. To be sure, public services are not always responsive to citizen complaints, but at the very least the locus of responsibility is clearer. . . . [Contracting] shifts the risk and responsibility of

service delivery to the private agency and creates the nonprofit contract agency as a buffer between the citizenry and the state.[15]

Because of this, some scholars have argued that some activities, particularly those involving the legal use of coercive force, are uniquely governmental functions that should not be extended to other parties, even under a contract that preserves client, inmate, or citizens' civil rights.[16] This applies to POS contracting in corrections, group homes for the mentally ill, and juvenile detention. In some states, child protective services cannot be contracted out but must be produced by public employees because of the serious and coercive nature of the decision to remove a child from a parent's home.

Organizational Complexity

The contracting system also creates a variety of organizational problems. The organizational model of hierarchy, chain of command, and employee supervision found in direct government services has been replaced with a network model in which multiple organizations of different types, sizes, and missions often collide and conflict as much as they cooperate to serve human needs. Therefore, service contracting does not avoid the problems of bureaucracy, communication, and coordination; these management problems are often exacerbated with multiple contracts, services, and agencies. At times, public administrators are caught between trying to comply with the arm's-length approach of the competitive model of contracting and pursuing the more supportive cooperative approaches. Government administrators need to be skilled in handling the contracting procedures in a fair, open, and professional manner. At the same time, they must also be able to encourage qualified agencies to participate in the process by providing extra technical assistance, tailoring contracts to individual needs, helping agencies start a new contract operation during implementation, and encouraging performance improvements.

Challenges for Provider Agencies

Contractor agencies, for their part, face an additional set of challenges that result from the bureaucratic red tape, uneven client referrals or enrollments, slow processing of contract reimbursement payments, and extensive reporting requirements that often accompany POS contracting. They also complain of either lack of referrals or too many or improper referrals of cases, which can affect their performance measures. Many of these difficulties result from improper training of public employees, inadequate communication between the public and private agencies, turfism displayed in interagency competition, poor estimation by the government about the number of eligible clients, and improper coordination practices. The consequences for the contractor include cash-flow problems, inability to estimate costs accurately, and the difficulty of using staff and other resources efficiently and effectively. In more serious situations, agencies may find that they cannot pay their employees enough to keep them, or must incur short-term debt to meet their payrolls.

Inappropriate or Inadequate Monitoring

One source of these problems with human services contracting is that the monitoring and evaluation responsibility is often poorly performed. Government officials tend to take on a regulatory role in monitoring services, checking paperwork and financial procedures to see that agencies are in compliance with their contracts. The focus on the proper inputs and outputs means that client outcomes are often overlooked. Certainly, some human services by their very nature are difficult to monitor, measure, and evaluate. Especially when a service is new or a contractor is inexperienced in some areas, government monitors naturally avoid dealing with the more troublesome issues of service quality, effectiveness, and outcomes.

Often, however, government administrators responsible for the services are not equipped professionally or organizationally to perform these monitoring and oversight tasks. They may have multiple responsibilities in addition to monitoring off-site locations of contractors, and they may be understaffed, underfunded, inexperienced, or inadequately trained for the job. They may have had little experience performing the service itself and may not know how to recognize problems or workable solutions. Under these circumstances, most nonprofit agencies simply focus on monthly or quarterly activity reports on such straightforward measures as the number of clients served, client referrals, or service costs, especially since contract reimbursement and renewal decisions are often related to these reports. In the process, however, agencies may have an incentive to obscure or misrepresent service or fiscal problems. Only where careful, detailed, and consistent monitoring, evaluations, and site visits are implemented can the government agency really understand service performance and outcomes.

Provider Priorities and Pressures

The management issues faced by the government have become closely intertwined with those of the agencies they hire.[17] Each contractor has its own set of norms, goals, client groups, and philosophies that may conflict with those of the government giving them money and soliciting their help. In addition, contractors themselves have multiple funding sources that are often tied to complex funding streams that may pass through several levels before arriving at the agencies. Agencies may receive grants, contracts, and donations that are given in various amounts with many different strings and paperwork requirements attached. For example, funds may come from many sources: public (federal, state, county, city, school boards) and private (foundations, other nonprofits, universities, for-profit companies).[18] Agencies may be required by their funders to coordinate services with other agencies, or cooperate in planning programs for clients. Therefore, the interpersonal, management, and financial skills of the recipient agencies must be quite well developed to handle the competing demands coming from different directions.

This degree of complexity on the nonprofit side would be a demanding task under any circumstances. What makes it even more difficult is that, due to funding constraints, service demands, and the proliferation of agencies, nonprofits often compete against one another for resources in many communities and regions. While agencies naturally find it to their advantage to specialize and distinguish themselves from one another, they find it harder to do so when their grants and contracts are short term and new funding sources must be found. Competition for contracts and grants, although viewed as healthy by promarket advocates, introduces problems of turfism and survival when resources are not abundant. This can create a barrier to human service coordination and integration. In addition, to be competitive, agencies are under pressure to understate their indirect costs and low-ball the total cost or the per unit reimbursement rate. This then necessitates subsidizing the underfunded service from other sources, or running the operation on a shoestring without sufficient administrative support.

Improving Contracting Procedures

To overcome these problems and produce better services for clients, a variety of innovations have been introduced in POS contracting.

New contracting models have been developed to provide services when the conditions appropriate for the competitive model are not present or desirable.[19] One of these, the *cooperative approach,* is used for services for which the government has little experience or in cases where the government is highly dependent on a single agency. The other, the *negotiation model,* is used where long-standing relations have been forged between the government agency and a provider.

Which contracting model to use thus comes to depend on three factors:

- The characteristics of the external service environment—especially the number of eligible service suppliers

- The level of the government agency's key resources (e.g., personnel, funds, time, and expertise) that are available for this process

- The degree of uncertainty about funding, future events, service technologies, and causal relationships between service outputs and desired client outcomes

In general, when there are several potential service suppliers, sufficient resources are available for the full competition process, and the level of uncertainty is low, the standard *competitive approach* is appropriate. An example of this model is used in many states to provide in-home chore services for senior citizens or disabled people. The service is a standard one, and several private firms (both nonprofit and for-profit) usually bid on these contracts. Both the price and quality of the proposal are considered in the award decision. Some of the details of the service and the reporting requirements might still have to be worked out through a negotiation between the two sides after the award decision is made, but the major administrative work involved usually occurs in the front end of the process. However, if an agreement cannot be reached, the next ranked provider can be contacted.

The *negotiated contracting process* is a more informal method of recruiting contractors and awarding contracts. A full-scale search or solicitation of all available suppliers is not used; rather, the government contacts (usually informally) only a small number of previous contractors and other reputable agencies that have similar services or clients. They are asked to write a proposal for a service that may not have a detailed description or a complete set of evaluation criteria. The prospective contractors must include the most essential service and reporting elements, but they have a wider latitude to design alternative service delivery methods than under the competitive process. When the government selects the preferred agency, serious negotiations begin between the two sides to work out the many details of reimbursement, service design, client referrals, evaluation methods, and so forth.

Negotiated contracts are probably far more common than competitive ones since many result from renewals of contracts that may have been awarded initially through a competitive process. For example, a typical negotiated service contract might be a transportation program for the elderly. Once a contractor invests in the vehicles for the service, it is unlikely that the government would want to seek out another contractor. What would be negotiated at the contract renewal point might be price (or cost reimbursement), service call-up protocols, hours of service, reporting requirements, or client complaint methods. At times, this negotiated approach may be used for new services; however, this makes little sense when only one or two agencies are known to be available or interested in the contract, and a full RFP process would involve extensive time and effort.

The *cooperative contracting process,* sometimes called the "partnership model," may be used not only for renewals, when a strong, trusting relationship has been established between the government agency and a provider, but also under conditions of uncertainty and resource scarcity. When the government agency has not performed a service itself, and may not have much knowledge about the service or clients, it may wish to work closely with one agency that has the appropriate resources and experience. In this relationship, the government and the contractor are relatively equal partners. The system is quite unbureaucratic and involves a high degree of discretion by the program managers, who work closely with the contractor agency to design a contract and service delivery system that meets the clients' needs. Often, the provider has already performed a needs assessment, may have other sources of funding for the service, and has both client trust and employee expertise. The contract is often designed to be quite unspecific, due to the uncertainty, and may not include any performance standards. It is expected by both sides to the agreement that the contract will be the beginning of a long-term relationship, not merely a single-year service, and that modifications to the agreement and services will be necessary along the way as more information and feedback are obtained.

These cooperative relationships can be found in many human services, sometimes as a result of many years of cooperation with a single agency and sometimes due to a new opportunity or service. This model provides for a flexible contracting system that is adaptive to change and uncertainty without the constraints of artificial deadlines, unrealistic contract provisions, or complex procedures. The system makes full use of the service deliverers' knowledge of the service and clients and recognizes that contractors often have better information and more professional expertise than the government does. It does not punish service providers for failing to meet the required details of administration, but works with them in a process to ensure compliance over the long run.

While this model encourages cooperation, learning, and ongoing problem solving, it may be open to charges of cozy insider relationships. Outsiders may legitimately argue that new agencies are prevented from competing for contracts, or that government officials may be encouraged to overlook substandard performance because of the ongoing relationships. Thus, administrators must be careful to engage all possible agencies when starting the dialogue and to encourage the contractors to improve their performance according to objective standards.

One recent example of how this approach can work occurred in a populous North Carolina county and involved job preparation services for welfare clients. A large local foundation offered to provide funds for Goodwill Industries' efforts to move low-income people off welfare into employment if the county would pay for the training services component. When Goodwill officials came to the county's Department of Social Services with this funding already committed, the county clearly had no need for a lengthy competitive contracting process. It negotiated certain service and reporting requirements, but the experienced Goodwill officials took the lead in determining the client outreach and training methods.

Performance Contracting

A second response to some of the management problems with POS contracting has been to make greater use of *performance contracts*. Such contracts focus more attention on the results or client outcomes of contracts while giving contractors more leeway on the process. The general assumption is that, free of process constraints, agencies will have the incentive to find the most effective approach.[20] For example, in a job training and preemployment counseling program, performance can be measured in terms of job placements, with requirements for minimum pay levels and minimum duration. These kinds of contracts are quite problematic in the human services because of the difficulties of accounting for human behavior and economic factors outside the control of the contractors. Performance contracting may also induce agencies to select participants most likely to succeed ("creaming"), or orient their programs simply to what is being measured. Other problems result from agencies' self-reporting of performance, especially when their records and clients may not be regularly scrutinized for accuracy or independently evaluated for performance. The greatest responsibility for implementing performance contracting lies with the government—it must have the resources to create the measures, the data collection systems, and the enforcement mechanisms. It also must have the common sense and political will to work with the service suppliers and, if necessary, refuse to renew contracts for nonperformance. Despite the complexities introduced by performance contracting, this approach promises greater accountability for service outcomes and also encourages both government agencies and their contractors to focus on this crucial issue.

Improving Contracting Relationships

In addition to changes in the basic structure of contracting, improvements are also needed in the management skills and interorganizational knowledge on the part of both government officials and their contract partners. Thus, the government side needs to improve its understanding of nonprofits and how their goals, resource constraints, and voluntary character make them different from public agencies. This includes greater awareness of the diversity of agency types; the unique cultures, histories, service mixes, and missions of different organizations; and the degree of dependence agencies have on government funding.

Government managers of contracted services should also rethink their roles and their training vis-à-vis contractors. They should more explicitly understand their role as boundary spanners—reaching out more effectively to a wide network of nonprofit and for-profit agencies through information exchange, cooperative planning, and service feedback. Their training should include negotiating, conflict resolution, contract writing, communication, technical assistance, monitoring and evaluation skills, as well as an understanding of the nonprofit sector's unique characteristics and constraints. They should be more aware of the advantages and disadvantages of using the three primary models of contracting—competition, negotiation, and cooperative partnership. In sum, they have to learn how to cope with the uncertainties and risks involved in POS contracting, as well as how to reduce them.

On the other hand, nonprofits need to improve their understanding of bureaucracy, government, and politics. They also need to improve their skills in proposal writing, cost estimation, contract negotiation, financial management and reporting, administrative coordination and oversight, and program evaluation.

Several approaches have been used, either explicitly or implicitly, to improve the communication and understanding among the three sectors in service contracting. These include joint training programs and workshops, joint management contracts, strategic planning efforts, personnel exchanges, and explicit hiring strategies to obtain staff members with experience in the other sector. Graduate education that broadens, rather than narrows, one's professional outlook would also be advisable—for example, public administration or policy programs encouraging their students to enroll in social work and nonprofit courses, and vice versa.[21] Contract managers in both sectors should seek out other methods that will prepare their employees to work with their counterparts in other agencies.

VI. OVERALL ASSESSMENT

As we have discussed, POS contracting has some unique challenges due to the complex human problems it seeks to address. When state and local governments decide to purchase services, they surrender a degree of control over the results. In addition, they cannot necessarily use the same procedures and obtain the same results as when purchasing other types of services, such as landscaping, refuse collection, or vehicle maintenance.

Contracting for human services has proved in many fields to be a flexible and effective method by which to deliver services through reputable agencies that have programmatic and service expertise. More recently, contracting has placed greater emphasis on measuring performance and evaluating outcomes, not merely as a way to reward good performance, but also to improve the quality of services. However, the presence of numerous intervening factors has made it difficult to show that this tool is more effective than direct government services.

To what extent the goal of improved efficiency is met through contracting for services is also unclear. Nonprofits and private firms offer uncertain efficiency advantages, since some cost reductions may be obtained through loosened personnel constraints, lower wage and benefit structures, and less-experienced employees.

Service contracting offers the possibility of increased equity and responsiveness in the distribution of services to clients. It may allow more opportunity to tailor services and programs to targeted client groups by agencies that have a better relationship with clients, in more convenient geographic locations. As a result, clients may have more successful outcomes. Additionally, having trusted agencies offer the service in a familiar setting may avoid some negative perceptions about unresponsive government bureaucracies.

Related to this, the contracting tool is viewed by many as having a high level of political legitimacy. It may engender greater support for certain programs for disadvantaged populations that have an otherwise weak base of support among elected officials by mobilizing public and nonprofit organizations in support of them.

At the same time, POS contracting has a number of drawbacks, as we have seen. The rationale for contracting rests heavily on the idea that "competition" for contracts encourages the design of better programs and services, and potentially greater emphasis on service evaluation and outcomes measurement. In reality, however, too few agencies are often available to deliver particular services, limiting government's choices and potentially increasing political influence over renewals. In addition, contracting often encounters management problems and issues of the sort discussed in the previous section, such as intrusive monitoring and oversight; lack of service coordination; late reimbursement payments; multiple reporting requirements; communication difficulties; and lengthy and complicated procedures for proposals, awards, renewals, and negotiations.

VII. FUTURE DIRECTIONS

In summary, contracting has become a permanent part of the social service delivery system and seems likely to continue to offer advantages for government, nonprofits, and clients. We have learned a great deal about how to improve this tool and make it work fairly well. Creative and responsible public administrators acting with a certain degree of discretion within a well-designed system may be the key to the smooth operation of POS contracting. A new emphasis on performance contracting and service outcomes may also be able to encourage a more appropriate emphasis on clients rather than on the proper paperwork processes.

Nonetheless, some unanswered, or unanswerable, questions must continue to be addressed about the appropriate balance between public and private service delivery, as well as between public desires for accountability, efficiency, and cost controls, on the one hand, and private agencies' need for independence, creativity, and stability, on the other.

Through POS contracting, the public and nonprofit sectors have become increasingly interdependent. Government agencies are increasingly dependent on private agencies to serve low-income or dependent clients. Nonprofit and for-profit human service agencies cannot respond to human needs without public financing and support. As a result, they are heavily dependent on the government's administrative procedures and staff capacity to produce a clearly understood process of contract decisionmaking— clearly articulated RFPs; a predictable schedule for proposal reviews, negotiations, and implementation; prompt payments; consistency in service monitoring and reviews; timely renewals; and a reduction in bureaucratic requirements.

In becoming highly interdependent, each side of the contracting equation—the buyer (government) and the seller (nonprofit agencies)—have had to address additional fundamental questions about their basic functions and roles. For government, the questions include: To what extent should government give up its service delivery role in exchange for merely a management role? At what point does it become a "hollow state?" What responsibilities cannot be shed to private agencies? What constitutional questions (e.g., separation of church and state) are involved in nonprofit social service provision?

Additional issues arise for nonprofit agencies in their reliance on contracts for funding their operations.[22] These basic questions include: How dependent should a nonprofit agency be on government funding? To what extent does the lure of public funding persuade nonprofits to alter their missions, goals, and accountability mechanisms? Does an agency exchange its voluntary character for a professional management culture when accepting public funds? How committed are nonprofits to lobbying administrators and legislators to continue the funding of key programs? To what extent does goal displacement occur when agencies seek contracts and ward off competitors?

While consensus on these issues may not be possible, continued discussion and research have already produced numerous improvements and provide the best hope for additional improvements in the future.

VIII. SUGGESTED READING

American Federation of State, County, and Municipal Employees. *Passing the Bucks: The Contracting Out of Public Services.* Washington, D.C.: AFSCME, 1983.

DeHoog, Ruth H. *Contracting Out for Human Services: Political, Economic, and Organizational Perspectives.* Albany: State University of New York Press, 1984.

Demone, Harold W., Jr., and Margaret Gibelman, eds. *Services for Sale: Purchasing Health and Human Services.* New Brunswick, N.J.: Rutgers University Press, 1989.

Gidron, Benjamin, Ralph M. Kramer, and Lester M. Salamon, eds. *Government and the Third Sector: Emerging Relationships in the Welfare State.* San Francisco: Jossey-Bass, 1992.

Gronbjerg, Kirsten A. *Understanding Nonprofit Funding: Managing Revenues in Social Services and Community Development Organizations.* San Francisco: Jossey-Bass, 1993.

Rehfuss, John A. *Contracting Out in Government: A Guide to Working with Outside Contractors to Supply Public Services.* San Francisco: Jossey-Bass, 1989.

Smith, Steven Rathgeb, and Michael Lipsky. *Nonprofits for Hire: The Welfare State in the Age of Contracting.* Cambridge, Mass.: Harvard University Press, 1993.

NOTES

1. For an update of local government services, see, for example, Gilbert B. Siegel, "Where Are We on Local Government Service Contracting? *Public Productivity and Management Review* 22 (March 1999): 365–389.

2. Oliver E. Williamson, *The Economics of Capitalism: Firms, Markets, Relational Contracting* (New York: Free Press, 1984); it should be noted that defense contracting has often been used as an example of relational contracting as much as the human services have.

3. See DeHoog, "Competition, Negotiation, or Cooperation?" *Administration and Society* 22 (November 1990): 317–340; and Peter M. Kettner and Lawrence L. Martin, "Making Decisions about Purchase of Service Contracting," *Public Welfare* 44 (1986): 30–37.

4. Amos Warner, *American Charities* (New York: Thomas Y. Crowell, 1894).

5. Martha Derthick, *Uncontrollable Spending for Social Services Grants* (Washington, D.C.: The Brookings Institution, 1975), 8.

6. Alan J. Abramson, Lester M. Salamon, and C. Eugene Steuerle, "The Nonprofit Sector and the Federal Budget," in *Nonprofits and Government,* eds. Elizabeth T. Boris and C. Eugene Steuerle (Washington, D.C.: Urban Institute Press, 1999), 99–139. Unfortunately, state and local governments do not record service contracts for clients separately from those professional services they obtain for their own use or to replace public employees, nor do we have exact figures to differentiate between grants and contracts.

7. Ralph Kramer, *Voluntary Agencies in the Welfare State* (Berkeley: University of California Press, 1981), 19–36.

8. Lester M. Salamon and Helmut K. Anheier, "The Third Route: Social Service Provision in the United States and Germany," in *Public Goods and Private Action,* eds. Walter Powell and Elizabeth Clemens (New Haven: Yale University Press, 1998), 151–162.

9. Lester M. Salamon et al., *Global Civil Society: Dimensions of the Nonprofit Sector* (Baltimore: Johns Hopkins Center for Civil Society Studies, 1999).

10. M. Collett, "The Federal Contracting Process," *Bureaucrat* 10, no. 2 (1981): 18–19.

11. There are many books and articles about the advantages of contracting, although not many that focus on human services explicitly. For a summary of this tool's advantages, see E. S. Savas, *Privatization: The Key to Better Government* (Chatham, N.J.: Chatham House, 1987).

12. Peter Marris and Martin Rein, *Dilemmas of Social Reform: Poverty and Community Action in the United States,* 2d ed. (Chicago: Aldine, 1973).

13. Savas, 1987.

14. American Federation of State, County, and Municipal Employees, *Passing the Bucks: The Contracting Out of Public Services* (Washington, D.C.: AFSCME, 1983).

15. Lisa A. Dicke and J. Steven Ott, "Public Agency Accountability in Human Services Contracting," *Public Productivity and Management Review* 22 (June 1999): 502–516.

16. Ronald Moe, "Exploring the Limits of Privatization," *Public Administration Review* 47 (November/December 1987): 453–460.

17. Steven Rathgeb Smith and Michael Lipsky, *Nonprofits for Hire: The Welfare State in the Age of Contracting* (Cambridge, Mass.: Harvard University Press, 1993), 119.

18. See Kirsten A. Gronbjerg, *Understanding Nonprofit Funding: Managing Revenues in Social Services and Community Development Organizations* (San Francisco: Jossey-Bass, 1993).

19. DeHoog, 1990.

20. See Robert D. Behn and Peter A. Kant, "Strategies for Avoiding the Pitfalls of Performance Contracting," *Public Productivity and Management Review* 22 (June 1999): 470–489.

21. Salamon, "Nonprofit Management Education," in *Nonprofit Management Education: U.S. and World Perspectives,* eds. Michael O'Neill and Kathleen Fletcher (Westport, Conn.: Praeger, 1998).

22. Smith and Lipsky, 1993.

CHAPTER ELEVEN

Grants

David R. Beam and Timothy J. Conlan

Janice Gillono, a member of the Village of Skokie, Illinois, police department with many years' experience, was appointed in the Fall semester 1999 as a School Resource Officer at the campus of the Niles West High School. This newly created position allows her to work with administrators and teachers in addressing such problems as trespassing, truancy, disorderly conduct, and drug and alcohol abuse at the school and among its students—all important issues in themselves, and potential precursors of more serious offenses as well. After the April 20, 1999, Columbine High School massacre in Colorado, and many other similar incidents of violence, every parent and school and law enforcement official has special reason to want to improve security in such educational environments.

Historically and presently, of course, most law enforcement and most public education is supported out of local governments' "own source" fiscal resources. However, Officer Gillono's salary is paid in large part by the U.S. Department of Justice (DOJ) under its Community Oriented Policing Services (or "COPS") program.[1] This program is one of a pervasive system of grants-in-aid under which federal tax dollars are put to work by states and communities throughout the country. Additional financial support for the School Resource Officer comes from a variety of other public and private sources.

Responsibility for securing this aid rested chiefly with Dane Smith, a civilian working as the police department's budget coordinator. This was not the first time that Smith and Skokie had competed for, and ultimately obtained, federal funds to augment its police services. An earlier COPS grant had allowed the creation of a small police substation at a large outdoor shopping mall, where some 60 percent of the Village's arrests—mostly for shoplifting—were made. While these funds expired after three years, once the substation was established it proved useful and has continued to be maintained. Other grant funds had supported Skokie's creation of a new bike patrol unit.

DOJ's COPS grants are allocated on a competitive basis among applying jurisdictions. However, Skokie was one of many successful applicants. Indeed, a simple listing of COPS grant awards to other communities in Illinois alone fills thirty-four pages of one-line entries, in small print.[2]

These grant awards were part of a far broader national initiative aimed at putting a total of 100,000 new officers on the nation's streets, fulfilling a pledge President Clinton made during his November 1992 election campaign. They reflected a portion of a broader anti-crime strategy adopted by Congress with the Violent Crime Control and Law Enforcement Act of 1994 (the "Crime Act"). That statute authorized $8.8 billion over six years for various new local law enforcement initiatives, building on an earlier national effort, the Law Enforcement Assistance Administration, established by the Safe Streets Act in 1968. Prior to that time, local police services had been almost exclusively financed by local governments. Federal grant outlays for the administration of justice were zero in 1965, but rose to $795 million by 1976. They declined again, to just $69 million in 1984, but rose steadily thereafter. With the 1994 Crime Act, the national government was once again very importantly involved in trying to augment and reform local government policing practices, with total grant outlays estimated at over $6 billion in six major program areas for fiscal year (FY) 2001.[3]

Features common to many federal grant-in-aid programs are illustrated by the COPS grants to Skokie and other jurisdictions:

- First, they are often awarded on a competitive basis—jurisdictions must apply and be selected as worthy by federal administrators.

- Second, they are often "categorical" in character (i.e., they can only be used for specified purposes).

- Third, they are intended to be both "stimulative" and temporary. They encourage a new service, but then expire, leaving local governments to continue the once-aided functions on their own.

- Fourth, they emanate from but one of a number of rather similar programs. Indeed, there are a half-dozen separately specified types of COPS grants, each serving a particular aim and having distinct application or administrative requirements.

- Fifth, the program is strikingly ambitious. Although federal aid dollars for local crime prevention are quite small compared with state and local outlays, COPS grants are intended to help reform the manner in which police services are provided.

- Sixth, these grants show how closely federal funds (and also the federal rules that accompany them) are interwoven with day-to-day local government operations, even in functions as historically "local" as police protection, and even in communities of quite modest size and of relatively great financial strength.

- Seventh, Skokie's school resource officer initiative shows a high degree of intergovernmental collaboration, not only by encouraging the city to work with a separate local jurisdiction—the school district—but also by obtaining funds from at least six distinct federal, local, and philanthropic sources.

- Eighth, federal COPS assistance built on preexisting activities of many recipient jurisdictions, in that the "community policing" concept was gaining support across the nation well before federal support was made available. However, the program has the aim of speeding this process of diffusion and providing technical guidance. Along with fiscal resources, it also offers a way for federal officials to "claim credit" for doing more about excessive crime rates.

I. DEFINING THE TOOL: GRANTS

Defining Features

Conceptually, grants are payments from a donor government to a recipient organization (typically public or nonprofit) or an individual. More specifically, they are a gift that has the aim of either "stimulating" or "supporting" some sort of service or activity by the recipient, whether it be a new activity or an ongoing one. Through this device, a governmental agency (the "grantor") participates in the provision of a service, while leaving to another entity (the "grantee") the task of actual performance. Responsibility for providing the service thus is shared by multiple levels of government or by governments and private nonprofit entities. Grants are also offered by many private philanthropic organizations, although such foundation grants are not considered in this chapter.

Grants thus differ from "direct" government activities, on the one hand, and from the many other types of indirect action (contracts, loans, social regulation, etc.), on the other. Unfortunately, existing official definitions are not entirely sharp and clear. In addition, despite efforts toward standardization, terminology differs somewhat from agency to agency. Similarly, there is no definitive understanding of what constitutes a separate "program," leading to further uncertainty about the total number of grant programs.[4]

For purposes here, what must be stressed is that grants form a structured but still comparatively loose relationship between the grantor and grantee. Unlike loans, they need not be paid back to the grantor. Neither is the grant recipient obligated to provide a particular product to the donor government (as is the case with contracts). Furthermore, perhaps reflecting this, grants are generally directed toward other levels of government, nonprofit organizations, universities, or individuals, rather than private for-profit businesses.

Grants can take a variety of forms. Cash payments are most common now. However, early in American history, when land constituted the chief resource of value available to the national government, various "land grants"—to states, corporations, and individuals—were the most important type of federal grant.[5] Grants also may be made of equipment or some other in-kind resource, such as commodities distributed for school lunch programs. Since the adoption of the national income tax in 1913, however, cash grants have become by far the most common.

Relation to Key Tool Features

Compared with other policy instruments, grants are quite indirect, relatively noncoercive, and moderately visible. All but a few large grant programs are discretionary, although they gain a measure of automaticity by virtue of their reliance on the existing administrative structures of grantee organizations.

Directness

Grants are perhaps the principal "indirect" tool of governmental action. Indeed, the very idea of "indirect" government in many ways grew up around recognition of the increasing importance of federal grants, especially during the 1960s and early 1970s, when the federal government shifted decisively from areas in which it acted for the most part via the provision of services by its own employees or through national regulations to the indirect administration of policies through the states and localities. Although this was a major change, it also built on a long history of federal aid to state and local governments in fields varying from education through welfare to highway construction.

Most important for our purposes, grants leave a considerable amount of the available discretion over the operation of programs financed by a donor government in the hands of the recipient organization. When the recipient is a sovereign government itself, as is the case with the American states, the ability to restrict the recipient's behavior is all the more constrained. Much of the debate over federal grants hinges on this issue of the degree to which the donor agency should attempt to control the use that the recipient makes of the grant resources, and the ways in which this is done.

Automaticity

Automaticity measures the extent to which a tool utilizes an existing administrative structure (e.g., the market system or the tax system) to produce its effect rather than having to create its own special administrative apparatus. From the point of view of the granting government, grants rank fairly high in terms of automaticity since they essentially involve relying on the administrative systems of other entities to carry out particular functions (e.g., provision of education, social services, highway construction, policing). Rather than create a federal police presence in Skokie, for example, the COPS program was able to support one already in existence there. In addition, at the local level grant resources are often used not to provide direct services but to purchase services from other vendors, either through regranting the funds to lower levels of government or utilizing a contract to purchase services from a private nonprofit or for-profit vendor.

343 CH 11: GRANTS

Coerciveness

Coerciveness measures the extent to which a tool restricts individual or group behavior as opposed to merely encouraging or discouraging it. Generally speaking, grants are noncoercive in this sense. They are intended to encourage a recipient to take a certain action, not to restrict the action. What is more, acceptance of grants is wholly voluntary, at least in principle.

However, grants must also be judged as more "coercive" now than they once were. For one thing, the restrictions attached to many grants have expanded. In addition, while up until the 1960s many localities (if not all states) could choose to "go it alone" without accepting federal grants and their accompanying rules, that no longer seems possible or desirable almost anywhere. Certain very large grant programs (such as Medicaid and welfare funds) are essentially impossible to reject, and the rules attached often seem coercive to the states that receive them. Finally, grants have become increasingly entangled with federal social mandates, an issue explored in more detail below.

Visibility

Grant programs tend to be fairly visible. Grant funds are regularly recorded on budget. Large programs often get press attention; major new initiatives are heralded; and the receipt of funds is often publicized. On the other hand, many programs (perhaps most particularly the numerous smaller ones) are almost completely invisible to the public at large, and most individual citizens would find it impossible to say the extent to which national, state, and local revenues were included in the support of their local roads, schools, libraries, police, or other departments and agencies. Grants are certainly *not* visible in the same way that such direct federal operations as are a U.S. post office, Amtrak train, national park, or military installation.

Design Features and Major Variants

Given their numbers and diversity, there is no such thing as a "typical" grant. While all grants are similar in broad outline, they vary greatly in specific characteristics and in many details of their administration. Nevertheless, it is possible to distinguish them along three basic dimensions—scope or breadth of purpose, method of allocation, and degree of federal regulation and control.

Scope of Purpose

In terms of their scope of purpose, three types of grants exist. First are *categorical grants;* that is, grants that must be used for particular—very often, quite narrow—objectives as specified by the donor and agreed to by the recipient. In the United States, most federal grant programs are of this kind.

Second are so-called *block grants,* which provide assistance for fairly broadly defined functions (e.g., community development, social services) and leave the recipient more discretion in determining the precise use of the funds. Many current block grants in the United States were formed through the consolidation or merger of several closely related categorical grant programs. Their creation was a major thrust of the "New Federalism" initiatives of the Nixon and Reagan administrations of the 1970s and 1980s.[6]

The final type of grant, more common outside the United States, is *general purpose assistance* from one level of government to another. This type of grant has essentially no restrictions on the use of funds. The main such program in the United States, General Revenue Sharing ("GRS"), provided $6.1 billion in assistance annually as of 1980. However, it proved temporary: enacted in 1972 in part out of the expectation of ongoing federal surpluses in the mid-1960s, it was eliminated for states in 1980 and for local governments in 1986 partly on the basis that there "was no longer any revenue to share."[7] But while it existed, GRS allocated funds to essentially all state and local jurisdictions with essentially no limitations on appropriate expenditures.

Method of Allocation

In addition to scope of purpose, grants can be distinguished by their method of allocation and duration. Here, the basic distinction is between "formula" and "project" grants. This is the fundamental division made in the United States *Catalog of Federal Domestic Assistance*[8] (CFDA), which is the most comprehensive listing of grants for American governments, organizations, and individuals.

BOX 11-1 *Definition of Formula and Project Grants*

A. *Formula Grants*—Allocations of money to States or their subdivisions in accordance with a distribution formula prescribed by law or administrative regulation for activities of a continuing nature not confined to a specific project.

B. *Project Grants*—The funding, for fixed or known periods, of specific projects or the delivery of specific services or products without liability for damages for failure to perform. Project grants include fellowships, scholarships, research grants, training grants, traineeships, experimental and demonstration grants, evaluation grants, planning grants, technical assistance grants, survey grants, construction grants, and unsolicited contractual agreements.

Source: U.S. General Services Administration, *1999 Catalog of Federal Domestic Assistance* (Washington, DC: U.S. Government Printing Office, June 1999), XIII.

As Box 11-1 notes, the recipients of a "formula" grant are automatically entitled to receive predetermined amounts of funds allocated according to statistical calculations that typically employ rough proxy measures of programmatic need. Some formula grants (e.g., Medicaid, the single most costly program) are awarded on the basis of an "open-ended" matching formula. That is, the federal government matches state expenditures without any upper limit. These grants are "entitlements" to the states and "uncontrollables" from the national vantage point in that the level of funding depends on state actions, not the independent decisions of the Congressional appropriations committees. In other formula grants, the total funding is fixed, but the allocation among recipient jurisdictions is based on a formula specified in the law (e.g., in proportion to the number of pupils the state has in federally impacted schools as a share of all such pupils in all states).

In contrast to formula grants, "project" grants—like the COPS grants—are awarded through a competitive application process and must be used to support a particular activity for a limited period of time—generally one year, although such grants often may be renewable.

In the United States, most federal grant dollars are expended through formula grants. However, most of the grant programs are "project" grants, which tend to be smaller in size. This makes some sense since formula distribution is reasonable only when there are adequate funds for distribution to the universe of eligible recipients. Where less funds are available, or the recipients very numerous (as with municipal or county governments), project grants are the natural choice. Thus, highway and welfare grants to states are based on a formula, while COPS grants are allocated on a project basis among applying localities.

Degree of Federal or Donor Control

Finally, grant programs can vary widely in the degree of control over their use exerted by the grantor, and donors have a variety of techniques at their disposal for assuring that recipients perform as promised or intended.[9] Many of these techniques grew directly out of previous abuses. For example, the proceeds of early federal land grants to states were sometimes squandered or unaccounted for by the recipient states, so over time a range of increasingly sophisticated control mechanisms was adopted.[10]

Today, typical federal grants to state and local governments require an *application,* describing the intended beneficiaries, detailed plans, and scheduled operations. After receipt of funds, recipients are typically required to undergo annual financial *audits* and file annual *reports.* Some grants also require *matching contributions* or impose *maintenance of effort requirements* in an attempt to assure that recipients do not use federal funds merely to supplant state or local spending for the same objectives. In recent years, federal grants also increasingly have been encumbered by a range of *crosscutting* requirements that apply to all or most federal aid programs. Such requirements range from environmental standards to bans on racial, sex, age, and handicapped discrimination to requirements that federal aid recipients pay workers the prevailing union wage.[11]

Federal research grants also use many of these same techniques to regulate and delimit recipients' use of grant funds. Like project grants to states, localities, and nonprofit organizations, most federal research grants require a detailed initial application—which may be subjected to blind, peer review screening—as well as a variety of reporting and auditing requirements. In addition, research grants increasingly have also been subjected to a variety of crosscutting restrictions, including limits on human subject research, nondiscrimination requirements, and drug-free workplace certification.

Other Design Features

The formula/project, categorical/block, and degree of control dimensions are the keys in defining the major types of grants. However, programs also differ along a number of other dimensions. These include, for example, variations in recipients—that is, whether states, local governments, Indian tribes, nonprofit organizations, research institutions, or others, are eligible to receive funds. Even grants to governments have room for variation. In many cases, grants to states are "passed through" to localities and these pass-through requirements can be specified or left to state discretion. Different procedures may also be provided for federal grants to states and those for local governments. These and other design features are considered in some of the discussion that follows.

II. PATTERNS OF GRANT USE

Current Extent

U.S. grants are among the most widely used policy tools of America's federal government. If the fifty states, other nations, and private foundations are included, they are among the most prominent of all tools of policy.

The U.S. Office of Management and Budget identified 928 funded grant programs among the 1,412 federal assistance programs of all types listed in the *1999 Catalog of Federal Domestic Assistance*.[12] Of these, 591 (or 63 percent) are grant programs for state and local governments. But there also are a large number of grants—over 300—that offer direct support to nonprofit groups or individuals for such purposes as specialized research (for example, from the National Science Foundation or National Institutes of Health) or for fellowships or training.

Federal grants to state and local governments are important financially, accounting for some 17 percent of all federal outlays and about 25 percent of state and local governmental expenditures.[13] They are awarded by most federal departments, although some much more heavily than others. By the criteria of both number of programs and dollar volume of awards, the Department of Health and Human Services (with 155 separate programs and recent yearly obligations of $155 billion) is the number one grant-awarding agency, as Table 11-1 indicates. Also relatively high by both criteria is the Department of Education. In terms of functional fields, grants are most heavily used in health; income security; education, training, and employment; social services; and transportation.[14]

As these data suggest, while the number of grants is imposingly large, the dollar volume of most grants is relatively small. Most of the funds are concentrated in a handful of very large programs, with Medicaid—which provided an estimated $104.8 billion, or about 39 percent of all grant aid to State and local governments, in FY 1998—the largest of all.[15] Altogether, the top ten grants account for fully two-thirds (66 percent) of grant obligations, and the top twenty account for more than three-quarters, as Table 11-2 indicates.

The U.S. Federal grant system thus consists of three parts: (a) Medicaid (39 percent of the fiscal total); (b) a few other fairly large grants (another 39 percent), and (c) an additional 571 programs that collectively account for only 22 percent of grant obligations. The consequence is that the grant system looks quite different when viewed fiscally (where only a few programs seem to "really matter") or administratively and politically (where each program clearly merits separate recognition and consideration).

To these programs for states and localities may be added the numerous grants awarded by the federal government to universities (private as well as public) and individual researchers.

Nonfederal Grants

In addition to the Federal grants are the even more numerous grants from states to their localities. State grants consist of two basic types, often not readily distinguished: "pass-throughs" of dollars that originated in the federal treasury, and grants supported by funds raised from states' own resources. Combining both sources, state aid to local governments exceeds federal aid to states and localities. In 1996, for example, states provided $248 billion in aid to local governments, compared with federal grants totaling $228 billion that year.[16] Although precise data are not available, historic patterns suggest that about 30 percent of the $248 billion in state aid was pass-through federal funding. The remaining 70 percent came from state own-source tax revenues.[17]

In some design aspects, state grants mirror critical features of federal grants, but they differ in important ways too. For example, approximately 8 percent of state aid is provided as general support payments.[18] The remainder is conditional aid for specific purposes, including education (62.3 percent), welfare (12.4 percent), and highways (4.2 percent).[19] Furthermore, a portion of state assistance is provided in the form of shared tax revenues rather than grants *per se*. In such cases, a dedicated portion of some state-collected tax is turned over to local governments, based on a specific legislative formula. Much of the states' general support for local governments is of this kind.[20]

Moreover, the most recent data available indicate that about one-half (48 percent) of state aid to localities is distributed on an "equalization" basis, through formulas based on such factors as population, tax capacity, fiscal need, and property tax rates.[21] However, in this, as in many other areas of state and local finance, state practices are characterized by great diversity. One comprehensive grant study found that the amount of state aid distributed by an equalization formula ranged from as much as 77 percent (in Maine) to as little as 6 percent (in Nebraska).[22]

Grant making by philanthropic organizations is also widespread. By one count, there are at least 38,500 grant-offering foundations in the United States. While some of these

TABLE 11-1 *Federal Grants-in-Aid to State and Local Governments, by Department, Ranked by Number of Grants, 1998**

Department or Agency	Number of Grants	% of All Grants	Obligations ($ in millions)	% of All Obligations
Health and Human Services[a]	155	26.2	155,275	58.09
Education	100	16.9	21,474	8.03
Interior	58	9.8	1,788	0.67
Agriculture	55	9.3	18,784	7.03
Commerce	39	6.6	622	0.23
Justice	38	6.4	4,410	1.65
Environmental Protection Agency	36	6.1	3,100	1.16
Housing and Urban Development	33	5.6	23,733	8.88
Transportation	19	3.2	29,331	10.97
Labor[a]	19	3.2	7,447	2.79
Federal Emergency Management Agency	11	1.9	273	0.10
National Foundation on the Arts and the Humanities	8	1.4	228	0.09
Veterans Affairs	6	1.0	341	0.13
Appalachian Regional Commission	5	.8	253	0.09
Energy	4	.7	163	0.06
Defense	4	.7	73	0.03
Equal Employment Opportunity Commission	1	.2	27	0.01
Total[a]	**591**	**100.0**	**$267,322**	**100.00**

*Excludes grants with no reported obligations.

[a]Excludes an estimated $20.3 billion in unemployment benefits to individuals (not to states) included in the Catalog in Attachments A and B.

SOURCE: *December Update to the 1998 Catalog of Federal Domestic Assistance* (December 1998) and OMB, Budget Analysis and Systems Division, The Number of Federal Grant Programs to State and Local Governments: 1980–1998, 21 June 1999.

TABLE 11-2 *The Twenty Largest Grant Programs to State and Local Governments, 1998*

Program	1998[a] Obligation ($ billions)	Percent of Total
1. Medicaid	104.8	39
2. Highway Planning and Construction	21.9	8
3. Temporary Assistance for Needy Families	16.7	6
4. Section 8 Rental Certificate Program	8.1	3
5. Title I Grants to Local Educational Agencies	7.4	3
6. National School Lunch Program	5.9	2
7. Head Start	4.3	2
8. State Children's Insurance Program	4.2	2
9. Child Support Enforcement	4.1	2
10. WIC	3.9	1
11. Special Education Grants to States	3.8	1
12. Foster Care—Title IV-E	3.5	1
13. Community Development Block Grants— Entitlement Grants	2.9	1
14. Public and Indian Housing	2.9	1
15. Federal Transit Formula Grants	2.7	1
16. State Administration for Unemployment Insurance[b]	2.5	1
17. Federal Transit Capital Investment Grants	2.3	1
18. Social Services Block Grant	2.3	1
19. Rehabilitation Services—Vocational Rehabilitation Grants to States	2.2	1
20. Public Housing Comprehensive Grant Program	2.2	1
Subtotal	$208.8	78
Remaining 571 programs	$58.5	22
Total, CFDA obligations, 591 programs	$267.3	100

[a]Estimated obligations from the December Update to the 1998 Catalog of Federal Domestic Assistance (CFDA), December 1998, except as noted.

[b]Obligations from the FY 2000 Budget, February 1999.
SOURCE: OMB, Budget Analysis and Systems Division, The Number of Federal Grant Programs to State and Local Governments: 1980–1998, 21 June 1999.

are large and well known, the majority are small, lack staff, and award only a few local grants each year.[23] Total dollars awarded annually have been estimated at $19.5 billion as of 1998[24]—an important but still modest amount when compared with the large sums dispensed in Washington and state capitals.

Grants are used in other nations around the world as well. However, there are significant differences between the American grant system and those of most other countries.[25]

One striking contrast is the far greater extent to which the U.S. federal government relies on "specific purpose" categorical aid programs, rather than more flexible subsidies. Elsewhere, grant systems are designed more to offset "vertical imbalances" between the revenue available to the national government and those for "lower-level" units, such as provinces and cities, and to help alleviate "horizontal imbalances" in the revenue available to areas with differing degrees of economic advancement.

Furthermore, an increasing trend toward greater use of broad-purpose, flexible grants is evident in numerous countries, including Finland, France, and Japan.[26] In Japan, for example, about 63 percent of municipal income comes from central government grants, with most of this in the form "general purpose" aid allowing for a great degree of local discretion. In Sweden, since 1992 specific grants have been heavily reduced in number and replaced by a single general block grant. Norway also has shifted from specific to general grants in the last decade.

Recent Trends in the United States

Among the most prominent trends in U.S. federal grants over the last two decades have been renewed growth in both fiscal and numerical terms following a brief slowdown; a shift toward grants involving payments to individuals; the erosion of the more flexible funding forms; and the growth of grant-related regulatory mandates.

Grant Growth

As noted earlier, grants-in-aid have been a favored tool of government in the United States since at least the mid-nineteenth century. At the federal level, land grants gave way to cash grants with the adoption of the federal income tax in 1913. The number and dollar amount of grants grew greatly during the twentieth century, with major "bursts" of activity associated especially with the New Deal of the 1930s, the establishment of the interstate highway program in 1956, and the Great Society and War on Poverty of the 1960s. By most measures, federal grant outlays then grew sharply until the late 1970s, and declined in the 1980s—with the chief cuts coming early in the decade, during the first Reagan administration. Political debate and even some scholarly pronouncements of the time suggested that the "era of big government"—or high levels of federal activity—was over. However, grant growth resumed thereafter, as Figure 11-1 shows. While grants declined in real (constant 1992 dollar) terms from 1980 to 1990, they rose from $144.7 billion in 1990 to an estimated $238 billion in FY 2000, a $93 billion increase. Moreover, the rate of increase during the 1990s—an average of about 5.1 percent per year—has exceeded that of prior periods.[27] Similarly, FY 2000 grants as a percentage of total federal outlays, domestic programs, and gross domestic product match or exceed their levels of a decade ago.[28] The number of grants has also increased since 1982, after sharp reductions in the early Reagan years, rising from 303 funded programs then to 591 programs in 1998, as Figure 11-2 shows.

More Payments to Individuals

Nearly all of the recent fiscal growth has been in grant programs involving payments to individuals, a category that includes programs such as Medicaid, welfare aid, child nutrition, and housing assistance. These have increased 250 percent since 1980. In contrast, grants for physical capital (or "infrastructure") have increased only 12 percent,

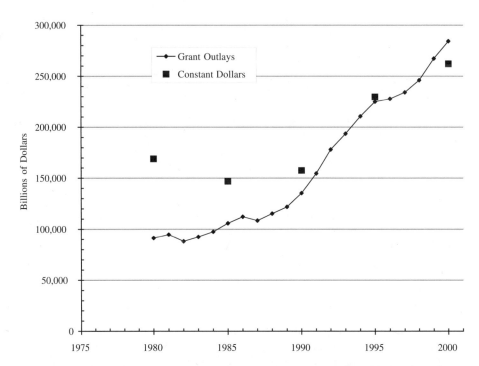

FIGURE 11-1 *Federal grants to state and local governments, 1980–2000. The value
for 2000 is an estimate. Source: Data from Executive Office of the
President,* Analytical Perspectives, Budget of the United States
Government, Fiscal Year 2000 *(Washington, D.C.: U.S. Government
Printing Office, 1999), p. 236.*

while grants for other purposes have actually declined 23 percent during this same
period. Payments to individuals thus account for almost two-thirds of all grants since
1995, compared with less than one-third during the period 1960–1980.[29]

This shift in grant composition did not represent a deliberate policy choice on the
part of Congress and various administrations. Rather, it reflected the fact that many
programs involving payments to individuals are relatively uncontrollable under current
law. Programs such as Medicaid are legal entitlements that obligate the government to
make payments to any person or institution that meets established eligibility requirements. The recent change in welfare—from the open-ended structure of Aid to Families
with Dependent Children (AFDC) to the capped block grant structure of Temporary
Assistance to Needy Families (TANF)—had the purpose and effect of limiting some
such "automatic" increases.

Some observers have made much of the relative growth of aid to individuals, suggesting that the American federal system is moving toward a more appropriate balance,
with the national government focusing on "redistributive" functions and states and
localities on "developmental" or "distributive" ones.[30] However, the very large number
of existing grants with "distributive" purposes, as well as the recent "closing of the open
end" on welfare grants—rather than the replacement of the system with a uniform
national program, as had been sought during the Nixon administration—run counter
to this trend.

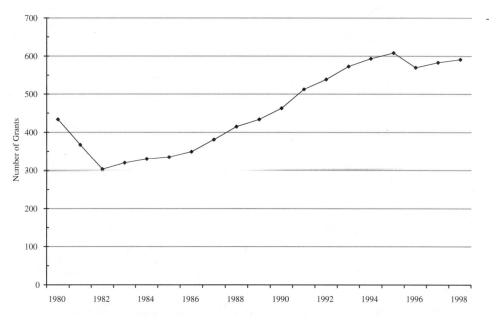

FIGURE 11-2 *Changing number of federal grants, 1980–1998. The values for 1996 and 1997 are estimates. Source: OMB, Budget Analysis and Systems Division, The Number of Federal Grant Programs to State and Local Governments: 1980–1998, 21 June 1999.*

The Erosion of Flexible Funding

A third important trend in U.S. grant programs has been the consistent tendency of Congress to restrict and "recategorize" broad-based funding soon after such discretion is granted to state and local recipients. Block grants are the most common form of broad-based assistance. They figured prominently in the "New Federalism" programs of Presidents Nixon and Reagan. Nixon won enactment of the community development (CDBG) and employment training (CETA) block grants in the early 1970s, while Reagan consolidated more than fifty separate categorical programs and three existing block grants into nine new block grants with the 1981 Omnibus Budget Reconciliation Act (OBRA).[31] Many more consolidations were proposed by the Republican majority in the 104th Congress,[32] and several, including a new child care block grant and TANF—the new "welfare reform" program—were adopted, although TANF may be a clock grant in name only since no prior programs were consolidated.

Although the number of block grants has increased considerably over time, the proportion of federal aid provided in the form of block grants and other broad-based assistance has not. As Table 11-3 illustrates, it rose sharply in the mid-1970s as General Revenue Sharing and several Nixon-era block grants were phased in. Broad-based funding diminished under President Carter, only to rise once more in response to the flurry of block grants adopted in Ronald Reagan's first term. Thereafter, flexible funding declined steadily until the late 1990s, even though the number of block grants rose gradually from 1984 to 1993. This was due in large part to the elimination of the $6 billion General Revenue Sharing program in the mid-1980s. In addition, the faster increase in expenditures through narrow-purpose categorical aids diminished the relative importance of broad-based funding. These figures would be even more dramatic, moreover, were it not for the inclusion of spending on TANF—the largest single block

TABLE 11-3 *Number and Relative Scale of Block Grants Identified by the Advisory Commission on Intergovernmental Relations (ACIR): Selected Fiscal Years, 1975–1997*

	1975	1978	1981	1984	1987	1989	1991	1993	1997
Number of block grants	5	5	6	12	13	14	14	15	24
Broad based spending as a percent of all grant spending	9.2	14.7	10.6	13.3	12.1	10.4	10.8	10.6	17.5
General purpose spending as a percent of all grant spending	14.1	12.3	7.2	7.0	1.9	1.9	1.4	1.1	.1
Total % flexible spending	23.3	27.0	17.8	20.3	14.0	12.3	12.2	11.7	17.6

SOURCE: Advisory Commission on Intergovernmental Relations (ACIR), *Characteristics of Federal Grant-in-Aid Programs to State and Local Governments: Grants Funded FY 1995* (M-195, June 1995, p. 3); and David B. Walker, *The Rebirth of Federalism*, 2d ed., New York: Chatham House, 2000, pp. 7, 10.

grant program—in the block grant totals. While this program does indeed offer states more discretion in some respects, it also imposes tough requirements and demanding deadlines in others, and many doubt that it truly fits the classic "block grant" definition.

Growing Grant Mandates

The reduced role of flexible forms of grant aid is consistent with another trend, the growth of intergovernmental mandating. Until the 1960s, virtually all grant-related regulations were program specific. That is, they were requirements designed to assure that each individual program's funds were properly planned for, budgeted, and accounted. During the 1960s and 1970s, however, the federal government added a significant number of new and more intrusive types of intergovernmental regulations. Some of these could be applied independent of federal aid, although they sometimes accompanied grant programs. But two new types operate exclusively through grants: first, *crosscutting requirements*, which apply to many or all federal grants simultaneously; and, second, *crossover sanctions*, in which the penalties imposed for noncompliance with one grant can "cross over" and sanction a different, typically much larger grant.

By one count, eighteen of these new intergovernmental regulations had been applied to federal grants by 1980.[33] Despite protests and avowed presidential disapproval, such mandates continued to grow even more sharply thereafter, with crossover sanctions and four crosscutting requirements adopted during the 1980s alone.[34]

Because of this continued growth, federal mandates became the principal focus of "intergovernmental reform" efforts by states and localities in the early 1990s. These led to the adoption of the Unfunded Mandate Reform Act (UMRA) in 1995.[35] However, to date, UMRA is having only modest effects on the growth of new federal mandates on state and local governments.[36]

Research Grant Trends

Federal and foundation funding of scholars and universities also rose dramatically after World War II, so much so that it revolutionized the academic enterprise in research intensive fields, altering the structure and finances of institutions and the behavioral patterns of individual scholars.[37] Research grants have been one of the most important components of this external funding stream, although most available statistics do not distinguish between funding provided as grants and that provided as contracts. Consequently, it is possible to gauge the overall trends in research funding but not the precise role that grants, per se, have played.

Overall, federal outlays for research and development grew most rapidly from 1955 to 1965, jumping from less than $10 billion to almost $50 billion in real terms. During this period, federal R&D outlays increased from 2 percent to 12 percent of total federal outlays.[38]

While federal research and development spending as a whole has declined in real terms since 1985, real R&D outlays to universities continued to climb substantially during this period. Over half (55 percent) of the estimated $15.2 billion in federal support for academic R&D in 1998 was directed to the life sciences (mainly medical research) with another 16 percent for engineering and 10 percent for the physical sciences.[39]

These levels of federal funding have affected the behavior and institutional structures of academic institutions. Don Price wrote as early as 1965 that "no major university today could carry on its research program without federal money,"[40] and the same remains true now. In 1998, the NSF estimated that federal funds supported almost 60 percent of academic research, with another 7.2 percent from states and 6.9 percent from foundations.[41]

In response, universities have created special administrative units to oversee and promote sponsored research, categories of externally supported research faculty have been created, and sponsored research has become an important component in many university tenure decisions. In addition, research universities have created research centers and institutes as alternatives to traditional academic departments in their efforts to attract sponsored research.[42] Such entities have proved to be especially useful because they can be tailored to suit the narrowly focused programs that many donors prefer.

III. BASIC MECHANICS OF GRANT-IN-AID OPERATIONS

In its most basic elements, the operation of a grant program has three principal phases:

- The legislative creation and establishment of the program
- The selection of appropriate recipients and awarding or allocation of funds
- The monitoring and assessment of how grant program recipients have performed, both during the process and after its completion

These, in short terms, might be described as the *authorization, allocation,* and *assessment* phases of a grant program. However, what must be emphasized is that each of these phases—and most particularly the first, the authorization and design phase—involves dozens, even hundreds, of decisions and variants. Certainly there is no simple "cookie cutter" for federal grant operations in the United States: the more than 900 programs vary enormously in detail. True, some progress toward grant "standardization and simplification" has been made through OMB management circulars and other intergovernmental process improvements, and it is often the case that grants devised by the same authorizing committee have a certain "family resemblance," resulting largely from repeating agreed-upon approaches over and over. Still, the areas of difference remain enormous.

The most important choices about a grant program are made at the time it is authorized in law. As detailed in a listing prepared by the Administrative Conference of the United States and reproduced in Box 11-2, these include decisions about the administering agency, allowable purposes of expenditure, the identification of appropriate recipients, and the basis of allocation of funds among these recipients.[43]

Administering Organization

Essentially all federal departments and agencies now offer grants to state and local governments. As Table 11-1 showed, DHHS is the leader in terms of both the number of programs and the size of grant obligations, with some 155 separately distinguishable programs.

Responsibility for grant giving is typically directed to the head of a particular agency, who then delegates it further. Still, in this as so many other areas of legislative drafting, critics point out that there is too much variation coming "from a lack of a standard model."[44] In the case of the COPS program, a new DOJ unit, the Office of Community Oriented Policing Services, was created by Attorney General Janet Reno in October 1994, less than a month after the VCCA was signed into law.

The identification of the administering agency can be quite important since this agency typically has substantial discretion in determining how a grant program actually operates. This is particularly true with "project" grants, where the administering department defines the award criteria and ultimately chooses the winning applicants. Even in formula grant programs, however, the administering agency can enforce the program guidelines strictly or loosely. What is more, even with categorical programs the legislation creating the program often leaves significant ambiguity about the exact purposes to be served, or at least about the range of activities that can be construed as serving the purpose. The administering agency therefore often has considerable discretion in deciding these ambiguous issues.

BOX 11-2 *Outline of a Typical Grant Statute*

Sec. 1. Short Title
Sec. 2. Table of Contents
Sec. 3. Findings and Purposes
Sec. 4. Definitions
Sec. 5. Establishment of Administering Office
Sec. 6. Authorization of Appropriations
Sec. 7. Authorization of Assistance
Sec. 8. Allotment Formula
Sec. 9. State Plan Provisions
Sec. 10. Discretionary Grant Provisions
Sec. 11. Conditions of Assistance
Sec. 12. Accountability, Audit, Monitoring Provisions
Sec. 13. Sanctions and Incentives
Sec. 14. Rulemaking Power
Sec. 15. Administrative and Judicial Review Provisions

Source: Administrative Conference of the United States, Office of the Chairman, *Drafting Federal Grant Statutes: Studies in Administrative Law and Procedure 90–1* (1990), 57–58.

Description of Supported Activities

The great bulk of grant programs serve relatively narrow purposes, and thus specify rather closely those particular kinds of activities that the donor organization wishes to support. In the case of DOJ's COPS grants, the general objectives of the program are to "increase police presence, to improve cooperative efforts between law enforcement agencies and members of the community, to expand community policing efforts through the use of technology and other innovative strategies, to address crime and disorder problems, and to otherwise enhance public safety." However, appropriate uses and restrictions also are specified in far more detail.[45]

In contrast, in a "block grant" program, the description of appropriate aims should be broader and more encompassing. As a point of comparison, the funds made available by DOJ under the Local Law Enforcement Block Grants Act of 1986 can be used for one or more of seven program-purpose areas, ranging from the hiring and training of new law enforcement officers to the establishment of drug courts and the development of crime prevention programs.[46] Here there are relatively few restrictions, with a principal one being that federal funds may not be used for acquiring armored vehicles, fixed-wing aircraft, yachts, and limousines.[47]

Eligibility

The eligibility of various classes of recipients for grants is also typically specified clearly in statute, although this too is "good advice, often not followed."[48]

In general, in the case of project grants, localities and other possible recipients compete for a share of grant funds. For example, with the COPS grants, eligible recipients include units of local government, states, Indian tribal governments, other public and private entities, and multijurisdictional or regional consortia composed of such units. Broadly inclusive language of this kind is commonplace.

In the case of formula grants, states are typically the recipients, but specific kinds of localities are identified in some of the few relatively large federal-local formula grant programs. Under the 1974 CDBG program, the central cities of Metropolitan Statistical Areas, other metropolitan cities of over 50,000 population, and urban counties with at least 200,000 residents are eligible to receive grants on an "entitlement" or formula basis.[49] The Local Law Enforcement Block Grant Program distributes funds by formula to units of local government in proportion to their Part I violent crimes when compared with all other local governments in its state.[50]

Of course, localities may receive funds directed to states on a "pass-through" basis as well. That is, states often use some or all of the federal funds that they receive to make grants to other units or service providers. And, in many cases, grants are made to states specifically with this intention in mind. For example, localities not eligible for the CDBG's "entitlement" formula grants can apply for a separate fiscal pot of funds awarded to states specifically to meet the needs of such smaller jurisdictions.[51]

Beneficiary eligibility can be distinguished for applicant eligibility: those who are served versus those who receive and provide. For example, under Medicaid, states apply for and administer the grants (or in some cases hire this function out to a private organization), but funds are actually given to health-care providers for services to certain classes of financially needy individuals.

Distribution of Funds

Another crucial issue in the design of grant programs is the determination of how grant funds are to be distributed. As stressed previously, this varies greatly depending on whether the program is a formula or project grant. For the former, this important question is settled through a statutory (or, in some cases, administratively established) statistical equation. Commonly, there is a minimum amount per participating jurisdiction, plus another portion allocated on the basis of one or more proxies of "need." The latter is often some kind of population-based count, like the number of school children, the number of elderly, or another indicator of a recipient state's demographic profile.

As an example, the DOJ has a $63 million formula grant aimed at encouraging states to establish substance abuse treatment programs for incarcerated prisoners.[52] Each participating state receives a base amount of 0.4 percent of the total funds available, while funds remaining are allocated in proportion to the share that each state's prison population bears to that of all states together.[53] Under this method, grant amounts awarded in 1999 ranged from $6,399,016 in California down to just $265,833 in North Dakota.[54]

Some formulas, like this one, are quite simple, but others are fairly complex.[55] For example, the 1974 Community Development Block Grant program distributes funds to eligible "entitlement" cities under a dual set of calculations.[56] One formula is based on three factors: population (weighted 25 percent in the formula), poverty (50 percent), and overcrowded housing (25 percent). When various jurisdictions and constituencies proved to be unhappy with the allocation of funds provided under that formula, a second formula was added to the law that distributed funds according to relative local economic growth rates (20 percent), poverty (30 percent), and age of local housing stock (50 percent).[57] Needless to say, disputes over funding formulas are among the most intense issues in the design of grant programs.

In the case of project grants, which are awarded by federal departments on a competitive basis, a variety of kinds of considerations can be included as relevant criteria. In comparison with formula grants, however, a much greater degree of discretion is left in the hands of the administering agency both in selecting recipients and determining the amount they receive.

Conditions of Assistance

Grant programs also typically specify a large number of additional conditions of assistance, which may vary from program to program. These may include application provisions; preapplication coordination processes; application deadlines and information on the time for approval or disapproval, as well as any possible method of appeal; requirements for matching funds and other financial obligations; the duration and phasing of assistance; and opportunities for renewal.

Allocation: Application, Selection, and Awarding of Funds

Once a grant program is enacted, steps must be taken to get the funds out to the recipients. This process varies considerably between formula and project grants, but the basic steps are common.

Regulations

In the first place, the responsible agency must establish the rules it will use to operate the program and issue a set of "regulations" spelling these out. The regulations detail the administrative processes and criteria the agency will use to award funds, the purposes for which the funds are available, how the agency interprets any ambiguous language in the legislation establishing the program, and the monitoring and review process the agency will use to determine performance. As with all program regulations, grant program regulations are published in the *Federal Register* and comments invited from any interested parties before final regulations are promulgated.

Marketing

In addition to issuing regulations, grant program administrators must market their programs to potential recipients. This involves letting recipients know of the availability of assistance and of the procedures the agency will use to distribute the funds. The issuance of regulations is part of this marketing process, but agencies also use other means as well, such as newsletters, official announcements in the daily *Federal Register*, speeches and presentations at conferences organized by potential recipient organizations, special agency publications (e.g., the National Institute of Health's Guide or Grants and Contracts), and increasingly on agency Web sites. As part of this process, the administering agency typically issues a formal Request for Proposals (RFP) reviewing the purposes of the program, the eligible recipients of assistance, the activities eligible for aid, the criteria that will be used to make awards, the deadlines for receipt of proposals, the exact format of the proposal, and, in the case of project grants, the weights that will be assigned to various criteria in making awards. These RFPs, too, must be published in the *Federal Register,* although no comment period is required.

Application

From the recipient's point of view, the grant process begins with identifying possible sources of funds and submitting one or more applications. In addition to the *Catalog of Federal Domestic Assistance,* official announcements for most new programs appear in the daily *Federal Register,* which, too, is searchable online.[58]

After identifying a funding source, potential applicants are urged to communicate with the program's official information contact to obtain an application kit and associated materials.[59] For many programs, the appropriate form is the standard Application for Federal Assistance (SF 424).[60] Completed applications must describe the applicant organization, the project purpose and areas to be served, indicate a budget and funding level requested, and demonstrate community support. For most programs, there are specific deadlines in a regular grant application review cycle.

Applications for programs often must be submitted to a state "single point of contact" for coordination and review.[61] Specified under Executive Order 12372, this process for "Intergovernmental Review of Federal Programs" was initiated in 1982, replacing a prior procedure under OMB Circular A-95.[62] Both provided mechanisms to assure that grant applications from various sources are properly coordinated, so that applying jurisdictions or agencies are aware of similar or possibly conflicting proposals.

The grant application process is generally fairly complex, even for formula grants where funding is assured. Recipient entities must generally specify the uses to which they plan to put the grant funds, designate a "single agency" that will have responsibility for the operation of the program, and provide a variety of "certifications" concerning their adherence to various conditions that might attach to the funds or to federal grants in general (e.g., nondiscrimination provisions, "prevailing wage" requirements, handicapped access stipulations).

In the case of project grants, applications are often even more complex since the applicant must spell out a sufficiently interesting approach to the problem being addressed by the program to win the competition for a grant award and must "sell" itself to the administering agency as a capable partner committed to the goals of the program and able to carry it out effectively. This requires effective "grantsmanship" (i.e., reading between the lines of the program regulations and "psyching out" the priorities and preferences of the program administrators). It also often requires the mobilization of political pressure.

For example, DOJ's Office of Juvenile Justice and Delinquency Prevention offers what are commonly known as "Drug-Free Community Grants."[63] The program is focused on community coalitions that collaborate in efforts at reducing substance abuse among youth and adults. Applicants must provide a five-year strategic plan; show that they have worked effectively for a period of at least six months, and demonstrate a substantial community volunteer effort.[64]

Application Review and Award Process

To review applications, the administering agency must then develop a review process. The review can either be done in regional offices or centrally, depending on the size of the program and the degree of discretion involved. Typically, review teams include program, budget, and legal staffs, all of whom must be trained in the details of the program. Review teams assess the proposals against an agreed-upon set of criteria, each of which carries a predetermined weight. Inevitably, however, a certain degree of discretion and subjectivity enters these judgments. In the case of project grants, agency staff then decide which proposals to accept, and what the level of funding will be for each. Once this has been decided, negotiations then commence with the grantee organizations to fit the proposed activities to the available funds and to settle any outstanding issues. An award letter and contract are then drawn up and signed by the relevant agency official and the representative of the donee organization.

Although grant award decisions for most programs are handled by agency officials, applications for grant funds for scientific research purposes are generally examined first by temporary boards of "extramural" professional specialists through a "peer review" process. The purpose of this process, as described by the National Institutes of Health (NIH), is to rate the scientific and technical merit of the proposed research or research training. Recently, NIH has revised its process to include explicit ratings on the topic's significance, the appropriateness of the approach, the degree of innovation, the background of the investigator, and the quality of the environment in which the work will be undertaken.[65]

Post-Award Management and Assessment

Program Implementation

Once grant awards are made, most of the responsibility for program implementation shifts to the recipient organization, usually with a fair degree of discretion. In the federal welfare program (Aid to Families with Dependent Children, now Temporary Assistance to Needy Families), for example, basic decisions about which families are eligible for assistance, what the "need standard" is, and what level of assistance will actually be provided are left to state discretion. Similarly, with the "federal" highway program, while the federal government specifies certain road standards, state highway departments decide what routes will be used, who will build the roads, and in what priority. They also let and oversee the contracts with the private companies that do most of the construction. Similarly, with the federal Social Service Block Grant Program, states decide how much of the funds to keep and how much to pass on to local jurisdictions, and these jurisdictions then decide what services to support and whether the services will be delivered by government employees or contracted out to nonprofit or for-profit organizations.

Monitoring and Evaluation

Once a grant award has been made, the donor organization performs a largely monitoring and evaluation function. Its ability to do so, however, is often limited because of a lack of resources for true evaluation studies and the limited reporting requirements often written into grant laws and contracts. Indeed, the movement toward block grants has been accompanied by a reduction in reporting requirements so that agencies often find themselves in the dark about what is being done with the funds they award. Another technique donor agencies can use are field visits, but in the U.S. federal government restrictions on agency travel have also limited the extent to which this route is open as well. Grant recipients generally are required to maintain financial records and potentially submit to a financial audit. For many federal programs, the record-keeping standards are described in OMB Circular A-102. Audit provisions are included in Circular A-133 for state and local governments and nonprofit institutions.[66]

Provisions of these kinds are necessary to help assure that funds are not misspent. But assuring basic financial propriety is, of course, often not enough. For this reason, some agencies engage in programmatic monitoring or conduct evaluations of program results, and, in some cases, they may turn to external assistance for this purpose. For example, the Office of the Assistant Secretary for Planning and Evaluation in DHHS made $2,250,000 in funds available to encourage studies on welfare reform outcomes and issues related to the TANF block grant reauthorization for fiscal year 2000.[67]

In the case of COPS grants, the Department of Justice requires quarterly and final financial reports, as well as programmatic progress reports. A fiscal audit of all grantees that expend over $300,000 per year is required under OMB Circular A-133, while smaller recipients must retain records for possible review for at least three years following the conclusion of federal assistance.[68] In addition, the agency has a number of processes designed to assure that their grant recipients are meeting the program's aims. In 1999, these included visits with some 900 grantees, including all those serving populations of over 150,000 and all the smaller jurisdictions receiving at least $1 million in funding. The activities of a number of other smaller recipients also were reviewed with site visits.[69]

IV. TOOL SELECTION: THEORY AND PRACTICE

Rationale for the Use of Grants

There are three prominent theoretical rationales for the use of grants, rooted in constitutional, administrative, and economic considerations, respectively. Unfortunately, each of these has modest explanatory value in accounting for the scope or structure of the current grant system, at least in the United States. What is more, the three are in important ways contradictory, and none seems to have been fully persuasive to legislators. Instead, many aspects of the current federal grant system in the United States are explained in large part by political factors.[70]

Constitutional Considerations

Grants have long been judged to be the most appropriate tool available to the federal government for handling a broad range of domestic functions, especially those functions that traditionally had been performed by states, localities, universities, and nonprofit organizations. The basic reason for this preference lies in America's constitutional structure.

The U.S. Constitution, as traditionally understood, limited the areas that could be addressed by the national government to certain, relatively few, enumerated subjects. States enjoyed co-equal sovereignty in their separate (and initially far larger) sphere. This narrow scope of direct federal legislative action was seemingly further assured by the Tenth Amendment, which reserves powers not authorized to the Congress to the states or to the people.

This historic legal structure established some of the key features of the American governmental system. For example, we have a federal postal service because that function is clearly provided for in Article I, Section 8 of the Constitution. Less obviously, perhaps, federal authority is extended to crimes that have some arguable relationship to the federal government's clearly stated constitutional powers. Mail fraud therefore is a federal crime, and kidnapping is included, too, because it can involve the crossing of state lines. However, murder is not, as it is considered an offense against the people of a state, rather than the nation at large.

In practice, however, changing standards of Constitutional interpretation have greatly expanded some aspects of federal power. Supreme Court decisions during the 1920s and 1930s held that the federal government possesses the authority to tax and spend for the general welfare, in addition to its more clearly enumerated powers, and limited the ability of citizens to challenge activities of these kinds.[71] This is the legal basis on which the system of federal grants is based, extending federal authority to provide grants even in areas in which more direct federal involvement in service delivery would seem constitutionally inappropriate.

Furthermore, over time, the national government came to have clear fiscal superiority, the result in part of the creation of a national income tax system, the extreme economic emergency of the Great Depression, and the necessity of financing participation in global conflicts. This gave it the monetary resources needed to develop an imposing array of grant programs.

Thus, the grant came to be seen as the perfect vehicle for involving the federal government in such domestic activities as transportation, social welfare, health, education, and many other fields formerly left largely to the states, counties, and cities, while leaving the recipient governments a considerable degree of responsibility, freedom, and discretion in operating the programs. These same characteristics also made the grant the tool of choice for dealings between the federal government and private universities to advance scientific knowledge, as universities were as jealous of their independence from federal authority as were state and local officials.

A broad range of governmental functions are therefore now jointly funded through grants. For example, while there are what are known as national or "U.S." highways, as well as state highways and county roads and municipal streets, in practice financial support for all of these systems is from mixed federal and state revenue sources. Rules governing the use of these roads are also mixed. Thus, for example, states license drivers and establish traffic laws (even on "U.S." highways), but a "national" speed limit and a minimum drinking age of twenty-one were pressed onto the states as a condition of receiving their federal highway construction funds.

Relationships between states and their localities are quite different. Under "Dillon's Rule," as it is called, localities are the creatures of the state legislature. For this reason, issues about the state-local allocation of fiscal responsibilities, and systems of state aid to localities, present questions of an entirely different legal and political character from those involving relationships between the federal government and the states. Similarly, state regulation of local governments—for example, specifying the number of days local schools must be open, or the character of subjects to be taught—does not raise issues of state "interference" in local affairs the way the same actions by any national agency would. While grants are used by states, they did not need to become the principal instrument by which state governments influence local governmental activities, since states clearly possessed direct legislative powers.

The U.S. Constitution has, then, strongly encouraged the use of grants-in-aid as an alternative to either the direct provision of federal services or the outright regulation of states and localities. Grants became the tool of choice because they helped square the Constitutional circle of extending the federal role while respecting the autonomy and prerogatives of subnational jurisdictions.

Administrative Rationales

Intergovernmental grants have also been justified on the basis of administrative efficiency. Not only would direct federal provision of certain services be dubious legally, it would also be administratively cumbersome and duplicative, particularly in a large country like the United States. Since the country already possesses an extensive network of state agencies, municipalities, counties and townships, as well as special districts for education and many other particular services, it makes sense to take advantage of these numerous jurisdictions rather than to establish a host of separate units or offices for various federal domestic activities.

Reflecting this, most communities have "branch" national offices only for the postal service, and perhaps the Social Security Administration, military recruitment, the Agriculture department, or some locally important transportation functions, like airports or river navigation. Instead, most federal programs are operated by states and localities. Consequently, overall, state and local employees outnumber federal employees by a ratio of about five to one.[72] In many cases, states similarly utilize their localities, such as counties and townships, as delivery agents for state services.

The upshot is a system that some have termed "cooperative federalism."[73] From this perspective, the grant device provides a way for federal, state, and local officials to work together to attain such shared objectives as improved highways, more adequate welfare aid, better education, and so forth. Furthermore, advocates of this view can point to examples of such intergovernmental cooperation dating back to the Founding era itself. Indeed, some experts argue that federal–state–local "cooperation" in the provision of services—which grants-in-aid embody—has always been the norm.[74]

The historical accuracy of this interpretation can certainly be challenged, but this view has offered a good rationale for federal interventions that were both politically popular and, at least in some cases, pragmatically necessary. What it does *not* do, however, is specify those circumstances in which grants-in-aid are or are not appropriate. Rather, it invites interventions in any field in which political consent can be obtained.[75]

Economic Theory

In contrast, what is known as the theory of fiscal federalism offers a clear and explicit rationale both for the creation of federal (and state) grants to "lower" governmental units in certain circumstances and for the form that such grants should take.

In this view, the national government possesses the strongest and "fairest" revenue source: a broad-based, progressive income tax. In contrast, states and localities—because of their more limited scope, their historic reliance on sales and property taxation, and the interjurisdictional mobility of capital and individuals—often are unable to raise taxes to a level sufficient to their needs, and thus experience revenue shortfalls or serious fiscal pressures.

The same jurisdictional factors that limit their ability to raise revenue also discourage states from spending as much as they should on many service functions. This problem is likely to appear wherever there are benefit "spillovers" from a service—that is, wherever a portion of the benefits of a service (like pollution control measures or education) are realized by nonresidents. Why tax oneself to help those who live elsewhere?

The resulting "fiscal mismatch" between revenues and needs could, in principle, be remedied by a properly designed system of grants-in-aid, utilizing grants of two types. The need for general revenue would best be met by broad-based general support grants to the most impoverished jurisdictions, and the problem of benefit spillovers or "externalities" could be addressed by categorical matching grants that are designed to encourage outlays of an optimal level in the specific fields where such spillovers occur. As a U.S. Treasury Department study put it:[76]

> If 20 percent of the benefits of local police services provided by a city is realized by commuters and visitors to the city from throughout the State, a State matching grant paying 20 percent of the city's total outlays for those services would ensure an appropriate level of provision. The effect of the matching grant is to reduce the net cost of the services to the city to 80 percent of their nominal cost. As this is the proportion of the benefits realized by city residents, the decision of their government on the allocation of resources to the services could, therefore, be presumed to be optimal.

This theory is wholly unconcerned with issues of constitutional law or administrative simplicity, as the foregoing example shows. What is more, it assumes that it is possible to measure quite exactly who benefits how much from a particular public service.

This theory of fiscal federalism provides a strong theoretical rationale for intergovernmental grants, but only so long as these grants are carefully designed to offset the effects of benefit "spillovers" or equalize fiscal capacity among different jurisdictions.[77] In practice, however, grants are very seldom established as this theory prescribes, at least in the United States. First, general support grants no longer exist, and have never played a major role in the United States. Second, categorical grants exist in fields in which there are no spillover effects, and they often lack the features (such as precisely set matching levels and open-ended funding) that true "optimizing" grants would possess.[78] In addition, the distribution of funds through specific grants or the grant system as a whole is generally difficult to justify on any clear economic or programmatic grounds.

The result is that while the theory of fiscal federalism may present an interesting analytical ideal, it does not describe the motivation for creating most grant programs or accurately characterize the features of their design. As Howard Chernick points out,

> there is a substantial divergence between the economic principles of fiscal federalism and the actual structure of our grant-in-aid system. . . . [T]he actual structure [is] quite different than that predicted by the spillover model.[79]

Or, as Charles Schultze, a noted economist and the former head of President Carter's Council of Economic Advisors, has commented: "The paradigm of grants as price subsidies to an independent decisionmaking unit designed to change the incentives it faces is not very useful for analyzing most of the existing social grants."[80]

Political Considerations

At least as compelling as these constitutional, administrative, and economic arguments for the use of grants are a set of political considerations that have made them a particularly attractive instrument for public action, especially in the United States. In fact, the political advantages of grants have been so strong that they have led to the use of the grant tool even where the substantive rationale for it is highly questionable.

Political power in the United States has long been greatly decentralized. American political parties, business and professional associations, and national political representation all were rooted at the state level. Few national initiatives, at least in the domestic sphere, could proceed very far without substantial state-level support. By the same token, however, those opposed to federal involvement in a particular policy sphere had ample opportunities to mobilize resistance at the state and local level.

The great advantage of the grant as a tool of policy is the opportunity it provides to co-opt some of the potential opposition to national initiatives by cutting states into a significant part of the action involved in implementing federal programs, thus giving them a substantial degree of discretion over the results. Consequently, those opposed to federal involvement can take some solace in the prospect of being able to influence how federal resources are actually used. Grants thus provide the basis for a political compromise between those in favor, and those opposed, to federal action.

In field after field, therefore, the price of extending federal involvement has been the acceptance of the grant as the principal tool of federal action. For example, the use of the grant instrument was pivotal in overcoming Southern resistance to federal welfare aid during the 1930s: instead of establishing a direct program of federal income support to widows with dependent children, the federal government established a grant program that provided matching aid to state governments for this purpose, but left to the states the decision on whether to offer the program to their own residents, and if so, on what terms. Similarly, federal support for education was conditioned initially on using a grant tool that left most of the discretion in the hands of state and local school boards.

The "pluralistic" character of political power in America also supports the use of the grant tool. Relatively narrow categorical grant programs, each meeting the specific aims of particular constituencies, provide an excellent way to respond to the multiple sets of interests on the American political scene (including organized lobbies, administrators, and legislators), each concerned with a different issue—highways, agriculture, welfare, health, law enforcement, and so forth. The extensive network of small categorical grants allows federal officials to "claim credit" for addressing particular problems, and it gives assurance to both them and clientele groups that particular needs are being addressed.[81]

Even when they were weak or lacking initially, political constituencies for particular grant programs generally develop over time. These consist of interest groups with a stake in the programs that the grants support, as well as administrators at the federal, state, and local levels who are involved in the operation of the programs and their counterparts in the legislature. Indeed, so entrenched do these interests become that some scholars have described the resulting pattern of intergovernmental relations as "picket-fence federalism," with coalitions of federal, state, and often local bureaucrats, in alliance with outside interest groups, managing particular programs and defending their independence from the crosscutting pressures of general purpose politicians. This political constellation helps to explain the persistence of categorical grants over broader purpose grants despite the frequent calls for grant reform. Such organized interests much prefer the specificity of purpose that these programs provide to the far more diffuse objectives of block grants, since the latter provide far less assurance that their favored activities will secure support.

Politics is also of central importance in the distribution of grant funds. From the standpoint of economic principle, one might suppose that national grants-in-aid would be allocated only to the states or localities with the least fiscal resources. Indeed, as noted above, fiscal equalization grants of this kind—payments to the poorer provinces only—exist in Canada and in some other federal nations. In practice, however, all American states receive significant grant resources. The reason is that having a large number of recipients wins a program broader political support.[82]

Consequently, the correlation between measures of need (whether fiscal or social) and grant receipts is very weak.[83] All states generally participate in all fiscally important programs, with overall allocations roughly in proportion to their populations. This might be said to reflect the "House" principle of representation on the basis of population. Often, because of minimum funding requirements and other formula provisions, smaller population states benefit a bit disproportionately, which might be said to reflect the "Senate" principle of jurisdictional equality.

Even at the level of individual programs, there is a tendency to disperse funds broadly. This often reflects an effort by legislators and administrators to gain passage of a new program or to assure a continuing coalition of political support for an existing one. The fiscal implications of major statutory changes are often assessed carefully on a state-by-state or interjurisdictional basis, with all involved politically hoping to receive some reasonable return. This is true even for programs that, in theory, are to be closely targeted to need.[84]

V. MANAGEMENT CHALLENGES AND POTENTIAL RESPONSES

Because grants are so common, in one sense grant administration is a well-established process. At the same time, since at least the 1940s both the grant system as a whole and many individual grants have been subjected to repeated criticism and efforts at managerial reform.[85] Numerous suggestions for improved grant administration have been advanced by the U.S. General Accounting Office and the U.S. Office of Management and Budget; the former U.S. Advisory Commission on Intergovernmental Relations; state and local governments; intergovernmental researchers and scholars of federalism; individual federal departments, and through various official management reform initiatives—among them most recently the Clinton–Gore "National Performance Review" (NPR).

Systemic Concerns: Reducing Duplication and Confusion

Clearly, the major concern, dating back even to the 1950s, is that there are simply too many small, often similar, but differently operated and narrowly defined categorical grant programs. The conclusion expressed by the comprehensive Clinton–Gore "National Performance Review" study, *Creating a Government That Works Better and Costs Less,* echoes themes that have been repeated many, many times previously. It emphasized that:[86]

> Washington provides about 16 percent of the money that states and localities spend. . . . Much of Washington's domestic agenda—$226 billion to be precise—consists of programs actually run by states, cities, and counties. But the federal government doesn't always distribute its money . . . wisely.
>
> For starters, Washington allocates federal money through an array of more than 600 different grant programs. Many are small: 445 of them distribute less than $50 million a year nationwide; some 275 distribute less than $10 million. Through grants, Congress funds some 150 education and training programs, 100 social service programs, and more than 80 health-care programs.
>
> Considered individually, many categorical grant programs make sense. But together, they often work against the very purposes for which they were established. When a department operates a small grant program, it produces more bureaucracy, not more services. Thousands of public employees—at all levels of government—spend millions of hours writing regulations, writing and reviewing grant applications, filling out forms, checking on each other, and avoiding oversight. In this way, professionals and bureaucrats siphon money from the programs' intended customers: students, the poor, urban residents, and others. State and local governments find their money fragmented into hundreds of tiny pots, each with different—often contradictory—rules, procedures, and program requirements. . . . The rules and regulations behind federal grant programs were designed with the best of intentions—to ensure that funds flow for the purposes Congress intended. Instead, they often ensure that programs don't work as well as they could—or don't work at all. Virtually every expert with whom we spoke agreed that this system is fundamentally broken. . . . Everyone wants dramatic change—state and local officials, federal managers, [and] congressional staff."

In the view of such critics, the narrow operational lines from Washington to the localities make the grant system much like a "picket fence," placing too much emphasis on "vertical" relations among governmental specialists at each level and with too little concern for "horizontal" linkages that are necessary to both sound overall policy and effective administration. Grant legislators, administrators, and associated interests have been described as forming excessively influential "iron triangles" and "vertical functional autocracies" that confound the efforts of generalist administrators—governors, mayors, and the public—to establish sound priorities and assure administrative accountability and efficiency.

In the face of these difficulties and objections, three kinds of reform proposals have commonly been made: (1) grant consolidation; (2) grant simplification, standardization, and coordination; and (3) a "tradeoff" of functional responsibilities.

Grant Consolidation

First, block grants have often been proposed as a way to consolidate several similar grants into one. Advocates of block grants argue that the excessive number of narrow categorical grants leads to a distortion of local priorities and produces considerable confusion and duplication in management. Broad-based and general-purpose aids hold out the possibility of both greater simplicity, better responsiveness to local priorities, and better "targeting" of resources by need.

For these reasons, their greater use has been recommended by most official study groups over five decades. For example, the U.S. Advisory Commission on Intergovernmental Relations urged that consolidated block grants be used as the preferred instrument of federal assistance when the following conditions pertain:

1. A cluster of functionally related categorical programs has been in existence for some time.

2. The broad functional area to be covered is a major component of the recipients' traditional range of services.

3. Heavy support is intended for those recipient services, which the Congress determines to also have national significance.

4. No more than mild fiscal stimulation of recipient outlays is sought.

5. A modest degree of innovative undertakings is anticipated.

6. Program needs are widely shared, both geographically and jurisdictionally.

7. A high degree of consensus as to general purposes exists among the Congress, the federal administering agency, and recipients.[87]

Yet, despite these and many similar official recommendations and related presidential initiatives, to reduce the number of categorical aids, the block grants device has proved hard to adopt, even more difficult to maintain, and has not at any rate reduced the number of separate grants overall.[88]

The reason is implicit in what has been discussed already. For all their faults categorical grants do seem to promise the possibility of greater accountability to the donor agency, since their purpose is so clearly specified. What is more, they offer an opportunity to respond to the particular interests of particular constituencies. Elimination of categorical grants has therefore typically been resisted by Congress and most beneficiary interests.

Grant Simplification

A second response to the complexity of the grant system has been an effort at simplifying and standardizing administrative procedures and obtaining better coordination among separate categorical programs and different grant-administering agencies. During the era of the categorical grant "explosion" of the mid 1960s, this was a principal goal. While the infusion of federal funds was often welcomed by state and local officials, the differences in procedures and the requirements imposed by so many federal grantor agencies were not. Standardized procedures and sources of information, urged on especially by the U.S. Office of Management and Budget, have helped to overcome these difficulties to some extent. Individual departments also have taken important steps to benefit their own grantees.

The newest initiative of this kind is the Federal Financial Assistance Management Improvement Act of 1999.[89] Agencies have been instructed to work with OMB to develop uniform administrative rules and common application and reporting systems, and also to identify statutory impediments to grant simplification. Grant recipients have been asked to suggest those aspects of the grant "life cycle" that are most in need of streamlining, and to indicate those programs that are the most burdensome.[90]

Recently, a major thrust has been to make more information available through the Internet, another goal of the act. For example, the Department of Health and Human Services provides much grants-related information—including sources of funding, administrative procedures, policy statements, and cost principles and procedures—through its "GrantsNet."[91] Federal agencies also are moving toward electronic submission of grants. Many are now using a comprehensive electronic grant administration system known as "The Federal Commons," which provides a common interface for grantee users.[92] The Commons is a project of the Inter-Agency Electronic Grants Committee.[93] Similarly, the National Science Foundation is looking toward the complete implementation of a paperless proposal and award system, known as FastLane.[94]

Tradeoff Proposals

The third approach to dealing with the systemic problems of the grant system has been to propose a "tradeoff" of governmental functions between Washington and the states by eliminating grants in some areas, while assuming fuller federal fiscal or administrative responsibility in others. Under this strategy, the federal government might (for example) assume the entire financial cost of assuring equitable systems of income support and medical insurance for the poor by taking over welfare and Medicaid and administering them uniformly, just as it does Social Security and Medicare for the elderly. At the same time, Washington would discontinue its grants in the many areas where it plays a less important fiscal role, such as education, employment training, local police protection, and so forth. But, although the logic of increasing clarity regarding "who is in charge of what" seems strong, there is enormous resistance to eliminating almost any federal programmatic activity and also to centralizing almost any federal activity. As a consequence, while this approach has been suggested frequently, it has never advanced far legislatively.[95]

Inefficient Allocation of Funds

In addition to the fragmented structure of the grant system, a second systemic problem with grants as currently structured in the United States has to do with the way they distribute resources. According to the economic theory of grants, donor monies should be directed chiefly to those jurisdictions in the most severe financial or programmatic distress, so that, like Robin Hood, the federal tax and policy system would be used to "rob the rich" to help "pay the poor." Indeed, it is often believed to work in roughly that way. But in reality, as noted previously, grant funds are often allocated on the basis of a formula and, typically, political considerations seem to dictate that all states, or a very broad range of localities, be awarded funds. Overall, the consequence is that the general distribution of grant funds does not help much to even up the financial or programmatic well-being of different parts of the country.

By most standards, money is spread around too widely and without sufficient concern for "targeting" to the most needy jurisdictions. A variety of studies have shown
that grants generally are not targeted to states under the greatest fiscal stress.[96] Indeed,
the overall distribution of grants has been found to be rather close to an equal per
capita amount across all the states.[97]

What these aggregate studies conclude also is true of particular programs. Grant
formulas usually fail to consider the economic well-being of recipients. Only 15 percent
include both a programmatic and fiscal need measures, according to a careful GAO
analysis.[98] The consequence is that funds have often been judged to be poorly directed.
For example, the Maternal and Child Health Block Grant provided more aid to states
with lower concentrations of low-birthrate babies than to those with higher concen
trations. Similarly, more aid was given to some states with lower health-care costs than
to those with higher costs.[99]

In the case of "project" grants, the frequently voiced concern is that the allocation
of grants is sometimes unduly influenced by overt political considerations. That is,
politicians and administrators may seek to assure the continuation and expansion of
their programs by distributing funds widely enough to assure majority support in
Congress, and by providing additional benefits to powerful members of authorizing or
appropriations committees and subcommittees.

One criticism of the COPS grants is that a significant proportion of funds have not
gone to areas most in need of crime-fighting assistance. Of the officers hired in the
program's first two years, more than half were in cities with below-average crime rates,
or those that were so small that they did not even report crime data.[100] Indeed, DOJ is
not required to direct federal resources to those jurisdictions with the greatest need for
assistance. By law, 50 percent of funds must go to police agencies serving populations
of less than 150,000 people, and in practice units with less than 10,000 population
received nearly 50 percent of all grant awards.[101]

Individual Program Concerns

If reducing the number of separately authorized categorical programs and rationalizing
the flow of funds have been the dominant managerial issues facing the grant system,
they certainly have not been the only issues. Other concerns have arisen frequently
concerning:

- Difficulty in assuring that funds are disbursed and spent in a timely manner

- Problems with grant funds being spent for inappropriate purposes

- The failure of grants to accomplish their intended purpose—or, at least, difficulty
  in knowing whether the aims of programs have been accomplished

In part, these are administrative problems, relating to inadequate oversight. But they
also are related to inherent weaknesses in the grant device itself, which has obvious
sources of tension built in between grantor and grantee.

At its best, a grant provides a mechanism for sharing financial and administrative
responsibility in pursuit of common objectives. Very often, however, there are competing pressures and conflicts of interest. Grant recipients may be perfectly content to
receive funds under any guise that they can turn to their own purpose, whether these
be tax relief or some other local priority, and Washington, while having some interest
in assuring that funds are spent properly, is very dependent on state and local political
and administrative support to operate its programs at all. Federal officials generally
lack the capacity to monitor the expenditure of funds and delivery of services closely,

and they also know that they are much more likely to be judged by the intentions of a program than by its actual results.

Furthermore, the multiplicity of governmental and nongovernmental layers and actors, loosely bound together simply by the gift and receipt of funds, together with relatively modest methods for supervision, auditing, and evaluation, makes it uncertain—and difficult to determine—if the intentions of the donors are accomplished. Lengthy programmatic chains—which often involve a federal agency in Washington; a federal regional or field office; a state agency; a local recipient; and perhaps also a separate beneficiary organization or contractor—create many opportunities for poor communication and opportunities for poor use, or misuse, of funds.

The potential difficulties are compounded when grant statutes are not very carefully crafted, which is very often the case. As a study by the U.S. Administrative Conference noted:[102]

> Too often . . . administrators [of grant programs] are constrained by poorly crafted statutes. Many of these laws are simply unclear. . . . Other statutes create and regulate the environment of grant programs whose actual environments are little understood. When good drafters lack grant expertise, or grant experts lack drafting skill and experience, the result may be a program that is difficult to manage efficiently or equitably according to the administrator's desires and the legislator's expectations.

Delays in Spending Funds

One manifestation of these tensions is the difficulty that often arises in making sure that grant gets spent. Establishing a program legislatively is one thing, but actually implementing it is another, as numerous studies have stressed.[103]

The much-publicized "urban empowerment zone" program has run into such difficulty in New York and elsewhere. Initiated by the federal government in 1994, the program promised qualifying areas $100 million each over ten years for loans, grants, and job training programs. Applying cities and states had to contribute $100 million of their own funds. But, according to a *New York Times* article,[104]

> [N]early halfway into the five-year program, just over $26 million of the city's share has been spent on projects, plus $9 million in administrative costs. The process is so slow that city officials . . . have spent no money for the zone this fiscal year, which began [about 11 months ago]. . . .

The administrative and political complexity, and the jurisdictional rivalry, common to grant programs, contributed to this delay. The *Times* added:[105]

> The pool of money has been frozen largely because each proposal requires the approval of officials in three levels of government, whose views often differ. And memories of [waste in] past urban renewal programs . . . have resulted in what some say is almost paralyzing caution this time. . . .

In the case of COPS grants, too, critics contended that the pace of hiring was far too slow, despite DOJ's efforts to expedite the process. Two years after its enactment, they noted, less than a third of the promised 100,000 officers had actually been placed into service on the nation's streets.[106]

Improper Expenditure of Funds

Even in the more usual case—when funds are spent on schedule—it is difficult to assure that they are spent for the intended national purpose. In some cases, as with anything involving money, there is actual fraud or abuse. And in some situations, administrative practices may be so inefficient as to attract notoriety. Serious abuses are always hard to prevent, but they are even more difficult when a grant is employed, rather than direct delivery of services, because responsibility is divided among so many levels and units of government, each largely independent.

For example, one recently released GAO study of Medicaid reimbursements to schools captured headlines nationwide.[107] Schools are eligible to receive federal reimbursements for the cost of providing health-care services to their students. However, the GAO found that some schools misdirected funds. "Schools, under the advice of private billing companies, charged Medicaid for groups of services, not all of which actually were provided to students. . . . Schools also billed for activities that are not covered by Medicaid and didn't provide adequate documentation to justify other billings."[108] Because states retain a portion of these reimbursements, they had a financial incentive to ignore questionable billing practices.

Even under the best of circumstances, grant funds tend to be highly "fungible." That is, grants received for one purpose can fairly readily be used to support some other objective.[109] Indeed, a U.S. General Accounting Office review of numerous econometric studies concluded that about 60 percent of every federal grant dollar "substitutes" for funds that states or localities otherwise would have spent from their own resources. Despite the specific purposes for which they are designed, a major effect of federal grants seems to be simply to "free up" the recipient's funds for other programmatic purposes or for tax reductions.[110] This is hard to justify to those who believe that federal programs truly represent some kind of "national priority" concerns, or that Washington should be able to account accurately for the manner in which resources it raises are ultimately spent.

Requiring a financial match on the part of grant recipients and imposing "maintenance of effort" (MOE) requirements on recipients can mitigate these substitution effects. But most grants, including a majority of the eighty-seven largest grant programs, lack these design features.[111]

In the case of COPS grants, some critics have objected that a significant proportion of funds have been used to hire civilian employees, to pay overtime, or for the purchase of office equipment.[112] These only indirectly help to increase the numbers of "cops on the beat."

While the COPS program does include a maintenance of effort provision, and DOJ expects recipients to be able to show that they have increased the number of officers employed, in practice DOJ monitoring was quite limited, especially in the program's early years. Lack of sufficient staff and an emphasis on getting the new grant program into operation meant that site visits or even telephone monitoring were not undertaken systematically. Rather than conduct proactive investigations, DOJ's three-person legal staff only reviewed cases referred to it by grant advisors or grantees.[113]

Failure to Achieve Objectives

That money is spent, and even spent for its intended purpose, does not of course mean that appropriate national or local objectives are actually accomplished. To better ascertain actual results, the field of policy evaluation was developed, and many new organizations specializing in the evaluation of public-sector programs were created both within and outside government, especially in the wake of the many new Great Society/ War on Poverty social programs of the 1960s. The result has been much more careful consideration of the effectiveness of various grant interventions.

Still, evaluations are by no means complete or comprehensive, and it remains the case that "most federal agencies don't know if their programs are working effectively," to quote the title of a GAO review of employment training programs.[114] It found that[115]

Federal agencies closely monitor the billions of dollars they spend on employment training for the poor. . . . Most agencies, however, neither collect information on participant outcomes nor study program effectiveness—both of which are needed to know how well programs are helping participants enter or reenter the workforce. As a result, agencies cannot be sure how successful the programs have been in preparing people to obtain jobs. Even when participants were hired, agencies did not know whether the employment resulted from program participation or whether participants could have found the same kind of jobs without federal assistance.

Studies that do exist often have equivocal conclusions. For example, a detailed study of the Job Training Partnership Act (JTPA)found that some participant groups, notably adult women, experienced significant wage increases as a result of JTPA training. But other groups, and especially teenagers, experienced no gains or even had reduced earnings following participation.[116]

Overall, it is fair to say that definitive conclusions on the actual programmatic results of grants in general are hard to come by, and even assessments of individual programs, or particular sets of programs, are often lacking, weak, uncertain, or open to controversy.

VI. OVERALL ASSESSMENT

Grants, defined here as a kind of "gift," represent a compromise between more direct or stringent methods of addressing public problems and simply allowing subnational jurisdictions and organizations to "go it alone," relying exclusively on their own resources. As such, they are relatively easy to justify from a constitutional, administrative, economic, and political standpoint. Indeed, it is difficult to imagine how the United States could have faced the challenges of urbanization and industrialization that have been so important over the last century without the development of this tool.

But the grant "gift," however commonplace and useful, is not without its difficulties. Delivering a service directly, through a lengthy bureaucratic chain, with boss supervising boss supervising subordinate, is hard enough, as every observer of large-scale organizations knows. However, the opportunity for shortcomings expands when numerous organizations are linked to each other through essentially voluntary grant relationships. And it is magnified, too, when the number of programs proliferates greatly, as has been the case in the United States. Under these circumstances, the prospects for inefficiency and management challenges certainly seem substantial.

The consequence is that, in the eyes of most expert observers, the grant-in-aid seems to have quite a mixed record of performance. More specifically, when measured against the four standard criteria of legitimacy, effectiveness, equity, and accountability, grants seem to rank highly only on the first. Their performance on the remainder has been less positive, however.

Legitimacy

From the beginning, grants were widely regarded as the most appropriate way for the federal government to support or expand public services in areas of traditional state and local responsibility because they essentially put the federal government in the position of "cooperating" with, rather than displacing, those governments in the provision of services. Even then, there were constitutional and political challenges, but these have now largely been settled. Today, grant programs can be proposed and adopted in essentially any functional field, and for essentially any legitimate public purpose. While advocacy of the grant device was for some time favored especially by political liberals, use of the grant device has provided a way to reconcile liberal purposes with conservative means; and conservatives have long since found that grants can be used to advance their social or economic agenda as well.[117]

Recent controversies concerning legitimacy have focused less on grant spending than on the evermore stringent requirements that have been attached to grant programs. By the 1980s and early 1990s, opposition to the growth of "unfunded federal mandates" had become the primary complaint of state and local governments. Although modest procedures to restrict the practice were enacted into law in 1995, federal (and state) mandates continue to be regularly enacted.[118]

Still, compared with several alternative instruments—such as the expansion of direct federal provision of services or the imposition of direct federal regulations on state and local governments—grants continue to rank relatively high on the scale of political legitimacy. Either of these alternatives would be much more easily condemned as expanding federal "bureaucracy" and intervention too aggressively.

Effectiveness

Far more questionable, however, is the effectiveness of the grant tool. To be sure, judgments about effectiveness are heavily affected by assumptions about what the real objectives of a program are, and these can differ for different players in the system. From certain points of view, many grant programs have been remarkably effective. The federal-state highway grant program, for example, has built an enviable network of interstate highways that now crosses the entire country at numerous points. The Medicaid program provides health-care coverage for millions of indigent children and nursing home care for millions of indigent seniors. The Head Start Program provides preschool educational opportunities for millions of deprived children. Beyond these individual program accomplishments, moreover, the grant tool has contributed importantly to the maturation of state administrative systems. The typical grant-in-aid requirement that states identify a "single state agency" to administer each federal grant program, and the accompanying requirements for audits and financial records, have helped to upgrade state administrative structures in a wide assortment of fields.

At the same time, program evaluations and implementation studies in the 1960s and 1970s have raised important doubts about how effective many grant programs really are, at least with respect to the federal objectives of the programs. Title I school aid may succeed in providing extra resources to hard-pressed local public schools, but not in overcoming the disadvantages of their neediest students. Urban renewal funding may have allowed city governments to clear away urban blight and revitalize urban cores, but not to improve the living conditions of the inner city poor. In short, the grant tool seems prone to "goal displacement," as the goals of the implementing entities come to have at least equal weight to those of the funding donor. While a great deal of uncertainty still clouds judgments in this area, it would seem that grants merit an overall moderate rating in terms of effectiveness.

Efficiency

By almost all accounts, moreover, the current federal grant system is also not an efficient mechanism for the accomplishment of either federal or state/local objectives. The "leakage" of funds to other purposes, while hard to calculate precisely, is thought to be very substantial. The very large number of very small programs, many in closely related areas, suggests significant duplication of effort. Although some improvements in grants management have been made over the years, grants should be more carefully designed than typically has been the case if they are to be more efficient.

Equity

On the fourth criterion, equity, the grant system has long ranked poorly. As we have seen, funds from most programs are distributed broadly, rather than targeted to those jurisdictions of greatest need or those in the greatest financial distress. While the system as a whole has increased the monetary resources available to state and local governments, it is hard to argue that the resulting benefits have been fairly or rationally distributed.

Equity criteria have been difficult to satisfy, in part, because they fly in the face of the political coalition building that is useful to establish or maintain programs. "Highly targeted" grant programs aimed at just a few jurisdictions have difficulty obtaining sufficient support from constituents, organized interests, and members of Congress to gain enactment and ensure survival. Indeed, a wide dispersal of funds is often necessary to secure the adoption of a program in the first place.

Debates over equity of distribution have been familiar in the realm of academic research grants as well. When funds have been too highly targeted to a handful of elite research institutions, other institutions have complained and lobbied for their "fair share." Supportive members of Congress have responded by seeking to earmark research funds to institutions within their home state.

Accountability

Finally, both individual programs and the grant system have long posed issues of accountability. It is clear that most citizens do not and could not understand the complexities of intergovernmental funding. Grants cloud the chain of accountability. They introduce additional complexity, with multiple actors, complex motives, and strong incentives for finger pointing if things go wrong. While such consequences can result from all tools of third party government, the flexibility associated with grants poses greater problems of accountability than the more restrictive alternatives such as contracts.

Categorical grants are intended to enhance accountability by more narrowly restricting funding purposes. Even when this goal is realized in one particular program, however, responsibility in the system as a whole remains greatly diffused by the large number of grants and the corresponding number of semiautonomous actors.

VII. FUTURE DIRECTIONS

Grants-in-aid were the earliest and long the most important tool of indirect or third-party government. They grew in number and dollar volume because a sharp increase in federal operations (direct provision of services) was deemed impracticable or improper, and because state and local governments were considered—for constitutional reasons—to be largely beyond the scope of direct federal regulation, which grew so importantly in the private business sphere.

At this point in time, grants to state and local governments are more numerous, and grant expenditures higher, than at any other point in history. Their growth resumed after an important but brief hiatus during the early Reagan years. The most numerous and costly form of grant is the specific-purpose or "categorical" program. These currently number nearly six hundred. There is a much smaller number of broad-based "block" grants—around twenty, although the number is not now officially counted because of definitional uncertainties. There is no longer a general support grant to states and localities of the type initiated in the early 1970s, although such grants exist in many other nations and figure prominently in public finance theory. As a consequence, "flexible" spending is down, even though the number of block grants has risen somewhat.

Taking these developments together, it is clear that there was no significant "devolution" of the grant system (or other federal responsibilities) during the 1980s and 1990s, as many have claimed.[119] Nor can it be claimed that "the era of 'big government' is over," where grants (or related intergovernmental mandates) are concerned. Neither has there been any meaningful "rationalization" of the grant system. In fiscal terms, there has been some movement from federal "grants to governments" toward "grants to individuals." However, there has been no movement toward federal assumption of responsibility for such functions, in areas such as medical assistance and welfare, as has often been proposed.[120] Indeed, the "closing of the open end" of the welfare block grant went in exactly the opposite direction.[121]

More of the Same

Given that the last twenty years included considerable presidential and Congressional effort at reducing and streamlining the federal domestic role—and on reducing the number of grant programs in particular—one could easily conclude that "more of the same" is the most probable forecast. There is every reason to believe that the American grant system ten years from now will not look much different in broad outline from what it does now. Many of the recent trends identified earlier seem likely to continue: the number of separate categorical grants will probably rise, grant outlays for individuals will take an ever-increasing share, regulatory "mandating" via the grant device will grow, and there will be no really substantial "devolution" of federal power and authority to localities and states. While the future state of the economy is, of course, nearly as unpredictable as that of the political system, for now the nation seems on a sound financial footing, and the deficit pressure that might have encouraged a serious reconsideration of federal, state, and local responsibilities has now dissipated.

Recurring Cycles of Growth and Reform

However, if grants remain a major feature of the policy system, so, too, very likely will grant reform, at least episodically. The current grant system continues to depart markedly from the prescriptions of every major rationalizing theory. The composition of the grant system as a whole has long raised important questions regarding fragmentation, duplication, and inconsistency. It is generally agreed that there are too many grants, especially too many very small grants, both overall and in many specific functional areas. Little care is typically devoted to grant design, with legislators and agencies often following models already extant in their field of concern. Individual programs have raised issues of implementation, efficiency, and evaluation. The fungibility of funds suggests that only a fraction of federal expenditures is used to augment the intended services. Grants often are not distributed according to programmatic or financial need, with "political" considerations affecting both formulas and project awards. There is little consistent reporting on program results, and grant programs are but rarely terminated.

In the past, serious recommendations have been advanced to deal with all of these issues. Significant reform proposals were occasionally adopted, most notably during the early 1970s and the early 1980s. While each succeeded for a time in simplifying the system and reducing the number of separate aid programs, none has made a lasting impact. After each round of reform, the number of new programs has crept up again, new restrictions have been added, and old management initiatives have faded into the background.

Yet the cycle of growth and reform has now been repeated many times, and is likely to continue into the future. With each rebound of complexity, support for simplicity returns. Grant "reform" should be an ongoing political and administrative concern, and efforts to "rationalize" the grant system should continue to be advanced.

Shift from Grants to Other Tools for Domestic Policy Purposes

Although grants are more numerous than ever, and grant spending is at a historic high, there also appears to be a notable shift away from the grant-in-aid as the preferred instrument of federal policy, even in dealing with state and local governments or fields historically or predominantly addressed by them. In recent years, some of this policy activity has moved toward other policy tools, most specifically regulation and tax incentives. Both of these have the advantage of seeming to involve even less federal financial expenditure, and tax incentives in particular appear to require less federal administrative "interference." Grants are no longer the most fashionable policy tool, the newest or most acceptable way, as they were especially during the 1950s and early 1960s. Other policy instruments have become more important.

For example, during the 1980s, federal regulatory mandates on state and local governments seemingly grew more rapidly than grant expenditures or programs.[122] At the same time—and despite the contrary mandate of the Tax Reform Act of 1986—legislators seemed increasingly enamored with the use of special tax provisions to accomplish selected goals.

The consequence is that it can no longer be taken for granted that federal officials will automatically turn to the grant-in-aid mechanism to pursue their domestic social policy objectives, as was the case during the 1950s and 1960s. The U.S. Department of Housing and Urban Development's recent empowerment zone/enterprise community initiative, which combines $2.5 billion in tax benefits with $1.5 billion in grant aids, succeeding the community action grants and model cities grants of the 1960s, are indicative of this trend.[123]

Similarly, President Clinton's May 1999 proposals for education reform emphasized the aid "stick" more than the aid "carrot," calling for federal grant dollars to be used as a lever to win acceptance of nationally favored strategies, rather than proffering assistance to those districts that comply voluntarily. In order to "do a far, far better job of spending the $15 billion in federal aid we send to our schools every year," he argued, "states and school districts that choose to accept federal aid must take responsibility for turning around failing schools, or shutting them down." The president also called for "report cards" to parents on school performance and school drug use and violence; strong and fair discipline codes; an end to the practice of "social promotion" from one grade to the next; higher educational standards for teachers in subject matters they teach, and subject matter and skills tests for all new teachers—among a variety of new national requirements.[124] This very strong regulatory thrust departed widely from the guarantee included in the 1958 National Defense Education Act, which prohibited "any direction, supervision or control over the curriculum, program of instruction, administration, or personnel of any educational institution or school system."[125]

The president's package was advanced in competition with a Republican-backed plan that relied heavily on tax breaks—Individual Retirement Account (IRA)-like accounts to pay private elementary and secondary school tuition—that was making its way through the Senate.[126] In an earlier era, Republicans might have opposed grant assistance, or sought relatively string-free educational improvement block grants, rather than turned to the use of tax incentives.

As these examples suggest, to many political leaders in both parties, grants are no longer the only way to do business, and indeed often are not the most attractive one. No one could claim that the "grant era" is over, but the era in which grants clearly were the paramount tool of federal domestic social policy is probably over.

VIII. SUGGESTED READING

Conlan, Timothy J. *From New Federalism to Devolution: Twenty-five Years of Intergovernmental Reform.* Washington, D.C.: Brookings Institution Press, 1998.

U.S. Advisory Commission on Intergovernmental Relations. *Categorical Grants: Their Role and Design,* Report A-52. Washington, D.C.: U.S. Government Printing Office, 1978.

U.S. Department of Health and Human Services. "GrantsNet." Available online at http://www.hhs.gov/progorg/grantsnet/.

U.S. General Accounting Office. *Grant Programs: Design Features Shape Flexibility, Accountability, and Performance Information,* GGD-98–137. Washington, D.C.: General Accounting Office, 1998.

U.S. General Services Administration. *Catalog of Federal Domestic Assistance* Washington, D.C.: U.S. Government Printing Office, published annually with one update. Available online at http://www.cfda.gov.

Walker, David B. *The Rebirth of Federalism,* 2d ed. New York: Chatham House, 2000.

NOTES

1. http://www.usdoj.gov/cops/index.html//3/15/99.

2. Listings of COPS grant awards are available at http://www.usdoj.gov/cops/foia/foia_err.htm.

3. Office of Management and Budget, *Budget of the United States Government FY 2000: Historical Tables,* pp. 206–210.

4. U.S. Office of Management and Budget, Circular A-11. Available online at http://www.whitehouse.gov/OMB/circulars/A11/All.html.

5. W. Brooke Graves, *American Intergovernmental Relations: Their Origins, Historical Development, and Current Status* (New York: Charles Scribner's Sons, 1964), chap. 14.

6. See Timothy J. Conlan, *From New Federalism to Devolution: Twenty-five Years of Intergovernmental Reform* (Washington, D.C.: Brookings Institution Press, 1998), chapters 3 and 8; and U.S. General Accounting Office, *Block Grants: Characteristics, Experience, and Lessons Learned.* HEHS-95–74. (Washington, D.C., 1995).

7. On the intellectual origins and creation of General Revenue Sharing, see Samuel H. Beer, "The Adoption of General Revenue Sharing: A Case Study in Public Sector Politics," *Public Policy* 24 (spring 1976); and Paul Dommel, *The Politics of Revenue Sharing* (Bloomington: Indiana University Press, 1974). On the demise of GRS, see Bruce Wallin, *From Revenue Sharing to Deficit Sharing: General Revenue Sharing and Cities* (Washington, D.C.: Georgetown University Press, 1998).

8. U.S. General Services Administration, *Catalog of Federal Domestic Assistance,* issued annually with an update. Available in print, CD-ROM, and diskette, and on the World Wide Web at http://www.cfda.gov/.

9. See David B. Walker, *The Rebirth of Federalism,* 2d ed. (Chatham, N.J.: Chatham House, 2000), 241–250; and U.S. General Accounting Office, *Grant Programs: Design Features Shape*

Flexibility, Accountability, and Performance Information, GGD-98–137 (Washington, D.C.: General Accounting Office, 1998).

10. Graves, *American Intergovernmental Relations,* chap. XIV.

11. U.S. Advisory Commission on Intergovernmental Relations, *Regulatory Federalism: Policy, Process, Impact, and Reform,* A-95 (Washington, D.C.: 1984).

12. 1999 CDFA, p. III. *Assistance* is defined in the Catalog as a program or activity that involves "the transfer of money, property, services, or anything of value, the principal purpose of which is to accomplish a public purpose of support or stimulation authorized by Federal statute. [It] includes, but is not limited to, grants, loans, loan guarantees, scholarships, mortgage loans, insurance, and other types of financial assistance, including cooperative agreements; property, technical assistance, counseling, statistical, and other expert information; and service activities of regulatory agencies. It does not include the provision of conventional public information services." CFDA, p. VII.

13. Executive Office of the President, *Analytical Perspectives, Budget of the United States Government, Fiscal Year 2000* (Washington, D.C.: U.S. Government Printing Office, 1999), Table 9–2, p. 236.

14. U.S. Congressional Budget Office, An Analysis of the President's Budgetary Proposals for Fiscal Year 2000, (Washington, D.C.: Congressional Budget Office, April 1999), 16. Available online at http://www.cbo.gov/showdoc.cfm?index = 1209&sequence = 0&from = 1.

15. OMB, Budget Analysis and Systems Division, *The Number of Federal Grant Programs to State and Local Governments: 1980–1998* (21 June 1999), 4.

16. Council of State Governments, *Book of the States* (Lexington, Ky.: Council of State Governments, 1999), 288, 432.

17. Walker, *The Rebirth of Federalism,* 227.

18. Council of State Governments, *Book of the States* (Lexington, Ky.: Council of State Governments, 1999), 432.

19. Walker, *The Rebirth of Federalism,* 228. These data are for 1996.

20. J. Richard Aronson and John L. Hilley, *Financing State and Local Governments,* 4th ed. (Washington, D.C.: The Brookings Institution, 1986), 79.

21. U.S. Department of the Treasury, *Federal-State-Local Fiscal Relations: Report to the President and Congress* (Washington, D.C.: Department of Treasury, September 1985), 129.

22. Ibid., 132.

23. Jane C. Geever and Patricia McNeill, *The Foundation Center's Guide to Proposal Writing,* rev. ed. (New York: The Foundation Center, 1997), x.

24. *Foundation Yearbook: Facts and Figures on Private and Community Foundations* (New York: The Foundation Center, 2000), 4.

25. For a more detailed discussion, see Ehtisham Ahmad, ed., *Financing Decentralized Expenditures: An International Comparison of Grants (Studies in Fiscal Federalism and State Local Finance Series)* (Aldershot, Hants, U.K.: Edward Elgar Publishers, 1997).

26. Organisation for Economic Co-Operation and Development, *Managing across Levels of Government* (Paris: OECD, 1997). Available online at http://www.oecd.org/puma/mgmtres/malg/malg97/toc.htm.

27. Executive Office of the President, Analytical Perspectives, FY 1999, pp. 236–7.

28. Ibid., Table 9–2, p. 236.

29. Ibid.

30. See Paul Peterson, *The Price of Federalism* (Washington, D.C.: The Brookings Institution, 1995), p. 10.

31. See Conlan, *From New Federalism to Devolution.*

32. House leaders had initially urged the merger of some 336 separate categorical programs into eight new block grants. See Conlan, p. 236.

33. ACIR, *Regulatory Federalism: Policy, Process, Impact, and Reform,* A-95 (Washington, D.C.: ACIR, 1984), appendix table 1.

34. ACIR, *Federal Regulation of State and Local Governments: The Mixed Record of the 1980s,* A-126 (Washington, D.C.: ACIR, 1993), 47.

35. Timothy J. Conlan, James D. Riggle, and Donna E. Schwartz, "Deregulating Federalism? The Politics of Mandate Reform in the 104th Congress," *Publius* 25 (summer 1995): 23–39.

36. See Paul L. Posner, *The Politics of Federal Mandates* (Washington, D.C.: Georgetown University Press, 1998).

37. Don K. Price, *The Scientific Estate* (New York: Oxford University Press, 1965).

38. Office of Management and Budget, *Historical Tables.*

39. Ibid., 32.

40. Price, *The Scientific Estate,* 37.

41. NSF, *National Patterns,* 32.

42. Gerald J. Stahler and William R. Tash, "Centers and Institutes in the Research University," *Journal of Higher Education* 65 (September/October 1994): 540.

43. For further detail on the administration of federal grants, see Administrative Conference of the United States, Office of the Chairman, *Drafting Federal Grant Statutes: Studies in Administrative Law and Procedure 90–1* (1990). See especially Malcolm S. Mason, "A Guide to Federal Grant Statute Drafting," pp. 1–154. See also U.S. Office of Management and Budget's information on grants management, available online at http://www.whitehouse.gov/OMB/grants/index.html, and OMB's Management Circular A-102 and Circular A-110. Available online at http://www.whitehouse.gov/OMB/circulars/a102/a102.html and http://www.whitehouse.gov/OMB/circulars/a110/a110.html.

44. Mason, "Guide," 72.

45. For a description of acceptable uses, see U.S. General Services Administration, *1999 Catalog of Federal Domestic Assistance* (Washington, D.C.: U.S. Government Printing Office, June 1999), program number 16.710.

46. Local Law Enforcement Block Grants Act of 1996, H.R. 728; Omnibus Fiscal Year 1997 Appropriations Act, Public Law 104–208.

47. See Catalog of Federal Domestic Assistance program number 16.592.

48. Mason, "Guide," 83.

49. Community Development Block Grants/Entitlement Grants, CFDA 14.218.

50. CFDA 16.592.

51. Community Development Block Grants/State's Program, CFDA 14.228.

52. CFDA 16.593, "Residential Substance Abuse Treatment for State Prisoners."

53. U.S. Department of Justice, Office of Justice Programs, Corrections Program Office, "Residential Substance Abuse Treatment for State Prisoners, FY 1999 Program Guidance and Application Kit." Available online at http://www.ojp.usdoj.gov/cpo/applicationkits.htm, 8 March 2000.

54. U.S. Department of Justice, Office of Juvenile Programs, Corrections Program Office, "Residential Substance Abuse for State Prisoners: FY 1999 Program Guidance and Application Kit," p. 14. Available online at http://www.ojp.usdoj.gov/cpo/applicationkits.htm, 3 March 2000.

55. A detailed review of grant formulas appeared in U.S. General Accounting Office, *Grant Formulas: A Catalog of Federal Aid to States and Localities,* GAO/HRD-87–28, March 1987.

56. Housing and Community Development Act of 1974, Title I, as amended, Public Law 93–383. For a policy related discussion of the politics and local impact of different formulas, see Michael J. Rich, *Federal Policymaking and the Poor: National Goals, Local Choices, and Distributional Outcomes* (Princeton, N.J.: Princeton University Press, 1993).

57. According to the Catalog of Federal Domestic Assistance, the specific definition of these formula factors for funding allocations is as follows: (1) total resident population from the 1996 Census of Population and Housing; (2) number of persons with incomes below the poverty level from the source 1990 Census; (3) number of housing units with 1.01 or more persons per room from the source 1990 Census; (4) age of housing; number of year-round housing units built in 1939 or earlier from the source 1990 Census; (5) growth lag; the lag in population growth as computed from population in 1960 to current population estimate from the source 1960 Census and P25, Census Report. See 1999 CFDA, 14.218: Community Development Block Grants/Entitlement Grants, http://aspe.os.dhhs.gov/cfda/p14218.htm.

58. The *Federal Register* is available at http://www.access.gpo.gov/su_docs/aces/aces140.html.

59. For a brief summary, see "Developing and Writing Grant Proposals" in the Catalog of Federal Domestic Assistance, http://www.cfda.gov/public/cat-writing.htm.

60. This application form is available online at http://www.whitehouse.gov/omb/grants/.

61. A listing of State Single Points of Contact (SPOCs) is available online http://www.white house.gov/omb/grants/spoc.html.

62. "Intergovernmental Review of Federal Programs," E.O. 12372, 14 July 1982. Available online at http://www.nara.gov/fedreg/eos/e12372.html.

63. CFDA 16.729, "Drug-Free Communities Support Program Grants." The program was established by the Drug-Free Communities Act of 1997.

64. Ibid.

65. National Institutes of Health, "Review Criteria for and Rating of Unsolicited Research Grant and Other Applications," *NIH Guide* 26, no. 22 (27 June 1997). Available online at http://grants.nih.gov/grants/guide/1997/97.06.27/notice-review-criter9.html.

66. OMB Circular A-133, revised 24 June 1997. Available online at http://www.white house.gov/OMB/circulars/a133/a133.html.

67. See *Federal Register* 65, no. 39 (28 February 2000), pp. 10498–10502. Available online at http://aspe.hhs.gov/adminhom/hsp00gnt.htm (1 March 2000).

68. *Catalog of Federal Domestic Assistance,* program 16.710, "Post-Assistance Requirements." Available at http://www.cfda.gov/public/viewprog.asp?progid=559 (1 March 2000).

69. http://www.usdoj.gov/cops/gpa/comp_monitor/default.htm (1 March 2000).

70. For a more extensive discussion, see David R. Beam, Timothy J. Conlan, and David B. Walker, "Federalism: The Challenge of Conflicting Theories and Contemporary Practice," in *Political Science: The State of the Discipline,* ed. Ada Finifter (Washington, D.C.: American Political Science Association, 1983), 247–279.

71. See *United States v. Butler,* 297 U.S. 1 (1936), and *Helvering v. Davis,* 301 U.S. 619 (1937).

72. OMB, *Budget of the United States: Analytical Perspectives,* chap. 10.

73. The classic statement of this view include Morton Grodzins, "The Federal System," in *Goals for Americans* (Englewood Cliffs, N.J.: Prentice-Hall, 1960), 265–282; and Daniel J. Elazar, *The American Partnership: Intergovernmental Cooperation in the Nineteenth Century United States* (Chicago: The University of Chicago Press, 1962).

74. The classic statement of this view include Morton Grodzins, "The Federal System," in *Goals for Americans* (Englewood Cliffs, N.J.: Prentice-Hall, 1960), 265–282; and Daniel J. Elazar, *The American Partnership: Intergovernmental Cooperation in the Nineteenth Century United States* (Chicago: The University of Chicago Press, 1962).

75. See John Kincaid, "From Cooperative to Coercive Federalism," *The Annals of the American Academy of Political and Social Science,* 504 (May 1991): 139–152.

76. Office of State and Local Finance, Department of the Treasury, Federal-State-Local Fiscal Relations: Report to the President and Congress (Washington, D.C.: U.S. Government Printing Office, September 1985), 15.

77. See, for example, Wallace E. Oates, *Fiscal Federalism* (New York: Harcourt, Brace, Jova-novich, 1972), chap. 3.

78. See David R. Beam, "Economic Theory as Policy Prescription: Pessimistic Findings on 'Optimizing' Grants," in *Why Policies Succeed or Fail,* eds. Helen M. Ingram and Dean Mann (Newbury Park, Calif.: Sage, 1980), 137–162.

79. Howard Chernick, "Economic Principles, Economic Pressures, and the Evolution of Federalism," Paper prepared for a conference on "The New Federalism and the Emerging Role of the States," Institute of Government and Public Affairs, University of Illinois at Chicago, (19–20 September 1996), 4, 6

80. Charles L. Schultze, "Sorting Out the Social Grant Programs: An Economist's Criteria," *The American Economic Review* 64 (May 1974): 182–183.

81. For more on the political appeal of categorical grants, see David R. Mayhew, *Congress: The Electoral Connection* (New Haven: Yale University Press, 1973).

82. Thomas J. Anton, *American Federalism and Public Policy* (New York: Random House, 1989).

83. Department of the Treasury, *Federal-State-Local Fiscal Relations,* 197–202; Peterson, *The Price of Federalism,* chap. 6; and Margaret T. Wrightson and Timothy J. Conlan, "Targeting Aid to the Poor: What Have We Learned About Allocating Intergovernmental Grants?" *Policy Studies Journal* (fall 1990).

84. Michael J. Rich, *Federal Policymaking and the Poor: National Goals, Local Choices, and Distributional Outcomes* (Princeton, N.J.: Princeton University Press, 1993).

85. For a brief overview of some early key grant reform initiatives, see Conlan, *New Federalism,* 23–24.

86. Al Gore, *Creating a Government That Works Better and Costs Less: Report of the National Performance Review* (Washington, D.C.: U.S. Government Printing Office, September 1993), 35–36.

87. U.S. Advisory Commission on Intergovernmental Relations, *The Intergovernmental Grant System: Summary and Concluding Observations,* A-62 (Washington, D.C.: U.S. Government Printing Office, 1978), 24.

88. Paul L. Posner and Margaret T. Wrightson, "Block Grants: A Perennial, but Unstable, Tool of Government," *Publius* 26 (summer 1996): 87–108.

89. Federal Financial Assistance Management Improvement Act, PL 106–107, 20 November 1999.

90. See Department of Health and Human Services, "Opportunity to Comment—Simplification of Federal Grant Programs." Available online at http://www.hhs.gov/progorg/grantsnet/grants-1.htm. 8 August 2000.

91. U.S. Department of Health and Human Services, "GrantsNet." Available online at http://www.hhs.gov/progorg/grantsnet/.

92. See "The Federal Commons" at http://www.fedcommons.gov/.

93. See http://ec.fed.gov/gcharter.htm.

94. Office of the Director, National Science Foundation, "Important Notice: Working toward a Paperless Proposal and Award System," Notice No. 123, 3 September 1998. Available online at http://www.nsf.gov/pubs/1998/iin123/iin123.txt.

95. For a discussion and the most recent proposals of this kind, see Rivlin, *Reviving the American Dream,* chap. 7–9.

96. U.S. General Accounting Office, *Federal Grants: Design Improvements Could Help Federal Resources Go Further,* Report GAO/AIMD-97–7 (Washington, D.C.: U.S. General Accounting Office, December 1996), 23.

97. Chernick, "Economic Principles," 7.

98. U.S. GAO, *Federal Grants,* 26.

99. Ibid., 25.

100. Robert J. Waste, *Independent Cities: Rethinking U.S. Urban Policy* (New York: Oxford University Press, 1998), 87.

101. U.S. General Accounting Office, *Community Policing: Issues Related to the Design, Operation, and Management of the Grant Program,* GAO/GGD-97–167, 2–3, 6.

102. U.S. Administrative Conference, *Drafting Federal Grant Statutes,* v.

103. The classic studies are Martha Derthick, *New Towns In-Town* (Washington, D.C.: Urban Institute Press, 1972); and Jeffrey Pressman and Aaron Wildavksy, *Implementation* (Berkeley: University of California Press, 1972).

104. Amy Waldman, "Thin Support and Red Tape Mire Development Zone in New York City," *The New York Times* (24 May 1999).

105. Ibid.

106. Waste, *Independent Cities,* 87.

107. Karen Gullo, "Audit: Schools Lose Millions in Aid," *Associated Press* (5 April 2000). Available online at http://news.excite.com/news/ap/000405/02/news-medicaid-schools. The GAO study itself is "Medicaid in Schools: Improper Review Demands Improved HCFA Oversight," HEHS/OSI-00–69 (5 April 2000).

108. Ibid.

109. One study found that this was especially true of closed-ended unconditional grants, such as revenue sharing and, to a lesser extent, block grants. See Edward M. Gramlich, "Intergovernmental Grants: A Review of the Empirical Literature," in *The Political Economy of Fiscal Federalism,* ed. Wallace E. Oates (Lexington, Mass.: Lexington Books, 1977), 227–234.

110. U.S. GAO, *Federal Grants,* 1.

111. Ibid., 3.

112. Waste, *Independent Cities,* 87.

113. U.S. GAO, *Community Policing,* 7–8.

114. U.S. GAO, *Multiple Employment Training Programs: Most Federal Agencies Do Not Know If Their Programs Are Working Effectively,* GAO/HEHS 94–88 (Washington, D.C.: U.S. Government Accounting Office, GAO, 2 March 1994).

115. Ibid.

116. Abt Associates, Inc., *The National JTPA Study: Title II-A Impacts on Earnings and Employment at 18 Months* (Cambridge, Mass.: Abt Associates, 1993).

117. Examples of the latter include grants to encourage teenage chastity and to encourage states to stiffen criminal penalties.

118. Posner, *The Politics of Federal Mandates.*

119. See Conlan, *From New Federalism to Devolution,* chap. 12. See also John Kincaid, "De Facto Devolution and Urban Defunding: The Priority of Persons Over Places," *Journal of Urban Affairs* 21, no. 2 (1999): 135–167.

120. Alice M. Rivlin, *Reviving the American Dream.*

121. Sanford F. Schram and Samuel H. Beer, eds., *Welfare Reform: A Race to the Bottom?* (Washington, D.C.: Woodrow Wilson Center Press, 1999).

122. ACIR, *Federal Regulation,* p. 68.

123. See Department of Housing and Urban Development, "Empowerment Zone/Enterprise Community Initiative." Available online at http://www.hud.gov/cpd/ezec/ezcinit.html.

124. Office of the Press Secretary, The White House, "Remarks of the President on Education," 19 May 1999.

125. Summary of Major Provisions of the National Defense Education Act of 1958. Available online at http://ishi.lib.berkeley.edu/cshe/ndea.html.

126. Associated Press, "Panel Okays Private School Tax Breaks," 19 May 1999, 2:20 PM.

CHAPTER TWELVE

Loans and Loan Guarantees

Thomas H. Stanton

William Apgar directs the federal government's major home mortgage agency, the Federal Housing Administration (FHA). However, Apgar does not build any housing, nor does his agency usually make loans for people to buy housing. Rather, he supervises people who process requests to provide federal mortgage insurance for loans that approximately twelve thousand commercial banks and other private mortgage lenders extend so that Americans can finance their homes.

Apgar is the most senior of some thirty-four hundred officials who work for the FHA, which is a part of the U.S. Department of Housing and Urban Development (HUD). Other people staff the housing finance agencies that help to fund homes on behalf of state and some of the larger local governments in the United States. All of these people work through private lenders that originate, service, and otherwise administer this little-understood tool of government action. The FHA alone currently has over $400 billion dollars of mortgage insurance—a form of federal loan guarantee—outstanding for single-family homes in the United States today.

This chapter introduces the reader to loans and loan guarantees, the two major forms of government credit program. FHA single-family mortgage insurance, a loan guarantee program, is the largest credit program of the U.S. government.

I. DEFINING THE TOOL

Defining Features

The government provides credit through loans or loan guarantees as a way to encourage funding for borrowers or activities that are considered important, either politically or economically.

The Direct Loan

The government makes a direct loan when it borrows from the Treasury to lend money directly to borrowers. After making the loans, the government then services the loan, (i.e., collects scheduled repayments from the borrowers) and forecloses or otherwise attempts to collect on the loan if a borrower cannot make scheduled payments.

The Loan Guarantee

When the government guarantees a loan, a private lender, such as a commercial bank or mortgage lender, makes the loan to the borrower. The government enters into a contractual agreement to make full or partial payment to the lender in case the borrower defaults on the guaranteed loan. The private lender originates the loan, secures the government guarantee, and services the loan according to government regulations or minimum standards.

381

Loans and loan guarantees differ in the extent to which they embody some of the key features in terms of which tools can be compared: (1) *coerciveness,* (2) *directness,* (3) *automaticity,* and (4) *visibility.*

Coerciveness

Coerciveness measures the extent to which a tool restricts individual or group behavior as opposed to merely encouraging or discouraging it. It highlights an important feature of federal credit programs: there is a dichotomy between the extension of credit to a borrower and the effort to collect on loans and avoid defaults. When the government provides direct loans or loan guarantees, all parties to the transaction welcome this action. Sometimes a borrower may object to the amount of paperwork and personal disclosure that is required, but this would seem to be the limit of coerciveness in the origination of the loan.

By contrast, the effort to assure timely and full repayment of federal credit can involve sanctions that the government or its agents must apply. For a direct loan program, the government may apply sanctions, such as an offset against an income tax refund, against a defaulted borrower. Or the government may suspend a school from eligibility to participate in both the federal direct and guaranteed student loan programs.

For a guaranteed loan program, the government may apply sanctions against lenders who fail to underwrite or service loans properly, or if a lender makes a claim against a federal guarantee and puts the defaulted loan back to the government, then the government may apply sanctions directly against the borrower. In terms of a comparison with other tools of government, federal credit programs today can be considered to involve a medium amount of coerciveness to repay loans, depending on the particular loan program.

Directness

Directness measures the extent to which the entity authorizing or inaugurating a program is involved in executing it. The direct loan and the guaranteed loan differ from one another in the extent to which they use third parties to make loans, service them, and collect on defaults. As tools of government, direct loans tend to be more "direct" than guaranteed loans.

Thus, under the rural housing direct loan program, the U.S. Department of Agriculture extends federal credit through local offices and services those loans through a centralized automated servicing center located in St. Louis, Missouri. If a rural borrower defaults on a direct loan, first the servicing center and then the local office will attempt to work with the borrower to reinstate timely loan payments. If this is not a promising alternative, the local office will attempt to mitigate loss on the loan and ultimately may institute foreclosure proceedings on the borrower's home.

By contrast, a guaranteed loan program such as the Section 7(a) business loan program of the U.S. Small Business Administration (SBA) operates largely through private lenders. In the SBA preferred lenders program, the SBA authorizes the private lender to attach a government guarantee to a specified volume of business loans that conform to SBA eligibility requirements. The private lender originates the small business loan, applies the federal guarantee, and services the loan according to SBA standards. If a borrower becomes delinquent, the lender works to bring the loan current and, if unsuccessful, attempts to mitigate the loss and ultimately to foreclose if necessary. The lender then makes a claim on the SBA guarantee for the lender's fraction of the loss on the defaulted loan.

383

CH 12:
LOANS
AND
LOAN
GUARANTEES

While guaranteed loan programs rely on lenders as intermediaries, some direct loan programs may use other kinds of intermediaries. For example, the Federal Direct Student Loan program of the U.S. Department of Education uses schools to originate loans for their students. The department recognizes that servicing is best done through experienced private sector contractors, rather than by officials of the department, and has hired a large contractor to service its direct student loans. If loans become delinquent, the department uses contractors to collect on the loans and to mitigate losses.

One sign of the greater directness of direct loans, compared with loan guarantees, is the quality of information available to the federal credit agency. Government managers tend to have much more complete and timely information about direct loans than about loan guarantees. For guaranteed loan programs, important financial information resides with the private lender that made the loan; lenders often do not transmit this information to the government unless a loan becomes troubled and the lender is preparing to file a claim on the government guarantee. The availability of high-quality information is critical for both direct loan and loan guarantee programs if government is to protect its financial position and assure that the program carries out its mission.

Thus, in terms of directness, guaranteed loan programs are "low" on the dimension of directness. By contrast, direct loan programs range between "high" on directness (e.g., the rural housing loan program) and "medium" (the direct student loan program).

Automaticity

Automaticity measures the extent to which a tool utilizes an existing administrative structure to produce its effects rather than having to create its own administrative apparatus. On this dimension, loan guarantees tend to be more automatic than direct loans, in the sense that government can use an existing private financial services system to provide guaranteed loans to borrowers. By contrast, as in the case of direct loan programs of the U.S. Department of Agriculture, the government may need to create a delivery system to originate and service its direct loans.

The element of automaticity shows why credit, including both direct loans and loan guarantees, can be tricky for government to provide effectively. Automaticity also shows the tension in credit programs between the initial provision of credit to borrowers, which can be very automatic, and the much greater effort that may be required to collect on loans once they have been made or guaranteed.

With respect to loan origination, guaranteed loans rank high in automaticity; many direct loan programs rank low. By contrast, the collecting on loans and avoidance of defaults on direct loans or loan guarantees is far less automatic and can involve considerable effort for a federal credit agency. Given the substantial effort that the federal government has had to make in recent years to collect on defaulted direct and guaranteed loans, credit programs are justifiably scored as "low" on the dimension of automaticity in this respect.

Visibility

Visibility measures the extent to which the resources devoted to the tool show up in the normal budget process. Prior to the 1990 Credit Reform Act, federal direct loan programs were highly visible in the budget, but loan guarantees were virtually invisible. The government budget treated direct loans as if they were cash outlays with the full loan amount recorded as an expenditure in the year that the loan was disbursed. The government then treated loan repayments as budget receipts in the year that the government received them. By contrast, loan guarantees were not treated as outlays when they were issued; rather, they showed up in the budget only in cases of default when the government actually paid off a lender. This disparate budget treatment created a clear budgetary advantage for loan guarantees over direct loan programs.

The Credit Reform Act of 1990 changed this situation considerably and made both direct loans and loan guarantees highly visible in the budget process of the U.S. government. A major purpose of credit reform was to place credit programs on a comparable footing with other government programs. Credit budgeting requires a calculation of the so-called credit subsidy (i.e., the budgetary outlays that will be required to fund new loans or loan guarantees that the government provides each fiscal year).

Credit reform recognizes that a loan's true cost is not captured by its cash flows in any one year; the true cost is the net value of its cash flows to the government over the life of the loan. This value is the loan's "subsidy cost," which is the net present value of a loan's expected cash inflows and outflows over the life of the loan. Budgeting for loan programs with this present value-based accounting system represented a significant departure for the otherwise cash-based federal budget.

To budget under credit reform, a government agency estimates the cash flows it will pay out or receive over the life of all direct loans or loan guarantees that it originates in a given budget year. The agency then discounts these to provide a single estimate of all future cash flows. Major elements of this calculation include the present value of (1) the cost of estimated future loan defaults or claims against a government loan guarantee, and (2) any preferential interest rates on the loans. These costs are offset by up-front or periodic fees that the program may charge.

For example, if the estimated present value of a direct loan's cash outflows equals $100 and the present value of its inflows equals $90, its subsidy cost is $10, and its subsidy rate is 10 percent. If an agency proposed to make $2,000 of these loans, it would seek an appropriation of 10 percent of the desired face value, or $200. The credit subsidy does not include the costs of administering a credit program; those costs are budgeted separately each year.[1]

Credit reform has meant that credit programs today have visibility in the U.S. government budget comparable to other tools such as direct government and tax expenditures. The annual budget request for each federal credit agency includes an estimate of the funds that will be required to cover the credit subsidy for new loans provided or guaranteed for the next fiscal year under each of the agency's separate credit programs.

One interesting contrast exists between government credit programs and insurance programs. Although both of these tools of government may involve the provision of financial support to individuals or companies, credit reform has increased the visibility of credit programs, while insurance programs remain largely beyond the purview of federal budget decisions.

Design Features and Major Variants

A well-designed government credit program will balance the tension between doing good (i.e., serving worthy constituencies) and doing well (i.e., assuring that loans are rigorously underwritten and originated, serviced, and foreclosed on). Many important design features relate to this issue.

Defining Eligible Borrowers

The most critical element in the effective design of a credit program relates to appropriate targeting: The loan or guarantee is most beneficial economically if it is directed at borrowers in a band between those who are not creditworthy enough to be able to handle their government loan, and those who are so creditworthy as to have full access to private loans without needing a government subsidy. A failure to target credit properly can cause harm either from denial of credit to creditworthy borrowers or from the provision of too much credit to people who cannot handle it.

385

CH 12:
LOANS
AND
LOAN
GUARANTEES

A notable example comes from the Federal Housing Administration. For many years, into the 1960s, FHA applied financially conservative underwriting standards and applied outright forms of redlining, i.e., denial of access to credit, to groups of eligible borrowers in center cities.[2] Then during the mid-1960s, FHA reversed course and began to insure large numbers of financially unsound center city mortgages that soon defaulted and contributed to "widespread speculation, default and foreclosure, the abandonment of homes, and the spread of neighborhood blight . . ."[3] It took many years for FHA to develop underwriting criteria that reflect an appropriate balance of objectives in targeting the program.

Determining the Amount of Subsidy to Provide

Government credit programs vary widely in the amount of subsidy that they provide to borrowers. Government provides credit subsidies in various forms: by paying some of the interest, by providing grace periods before the borrower must begin making interest payments, by charging lower fees than are needed to keep the program financially self-sustaining, or by offering tax exemptions on interest receipts, as is done, for example, with the bonds of state housing finance agencies.

When the subsidy rates on such programs or program subgroups run over 30 percent, as is sometimes the case, loan programs essentially come to resemble grants. Indeed, credit programs are attractive tools for policymakers who want to serve constituents who may not be considered eligible for outright grants. Extension of credit can be justified on grounds that the loan will be repaid on a businesslike basis. In fact, low quality of information for many federal credit programs can make it hard to determine the actual extent to which they contain a subsidy.

The Credit Reform Act of 1990 plays a major role in directing the attention of policymakers to the amount of subsidy that a program provides. During the 1970s and early 1980s, for example, the Congress did not need to budget for loan guarantee programs, even if they included some significant chance of default. In those years, the federal government extended credit to failing companies, including Lockheed Aircraft and Chrysler, and to New York City.[4] Such programs would be harder to enact today because lawmakers would need to obtain an estimate of the credit subsidy involved and then find appropriated funds to pay for the estimated subsidy.

Deciding Whether Loans Will Be Backed by Collateral

If loans are intended to help a borrower to purchase or refinance real property, they generally will be secured loans. Secured loan programs include the residential loan programs of the FHA, Veterans Administration (VA), Rural Housing Service, and SBA, for example. By contrast, a consumer-type loan, such as a student loan, tends not to be backed by collateral.

For a lender in the private sector, loan collateral is a valuable way to reduce financial risk. For some government loan programs, the issue can be more difficult. The government may find that foreclosure, for example, on a farmer's property or on the home of someone who recently obtained an SBA disaster home loan, sometimes carries unacceptable political costs even when the borrower is in complete default on the loan. The preferred design option is to avoid requiring collateral unless the ability to foreclose or to encourage a preforeclosure sale actually can help to improve the government's financial position.

Government can share the risk of default with private parties such as lenders or, in the case of student loans, participating schools. Government can share risk by guaranteeing only a portion of a loan. Risk sharing is an important way to augment government credit management with the services of private parties who share the risk of financial loss and therefore may have an incentive to manage the risk to assure timely repayment of the loan. Through risk sharing, the private lender or other private party can gain a stake in managing the origination and servicing of loans as if their own money were at stake. If lenders have little or no stake in the financial risk of government loans, then their incentives can become distorted.[5]

It may be difficult to calibrate an appropriate amount of risk sharing for some programs. OMB Circular A-129, in its standards for proposed new credit programs, attempts to address this issue. The circular states that, "Private lenders who extend Government guaranteed credit [should] bear at least 20 percent of the loss from any default."[6] However, for some programs, a 20 percent risk share may be outweighed by the returns to lenders from the program so that a year or so after origination they no longer have a significant financial stake in the loans that they hold and service. On the other hand, a 20 percent risk share may be enough to deter lenders from making some loans, especially to borrowers who are perceived as being insufficiently creditworthy.

The guaranteed student loan program currently requires lenders to share 5 percent of the financial risk; program supporters fear that any greater amount of risk sharing might deter lenders from originating loans to some disadvantaged students, especially those who attend vocational schools, who may be considered to be most in need of financial assistance. The government of Canada has adopted such an approach. Instead of providing an open-ended entitlement to student loans, as in the United States, the Canadian government pays lenders 5 percent on each loan that they make to cover the cost of future defaults. If the lenders keep defaults below this amount, they benefit; if defaults are higher, the lender bears the additional costs.[7]

Direct loan programs also can use risk sharing as a means of improving the alignment of incentives between a loan program and the private firms who may help to service the loans. State finance agencies, for example, may pay servicers each month a percentage of the money (i.e., the cash flows) that they collect from borrowers in repayments. The servicer thus has an incentive to service loans well so that the stream of repayments, and the associated servicing income, remains at high levels.

Loan Terms

Loan terms include elements such as the fees and interest rates associated with loans, the size of loans, and their maturities and conditions of default. All of these factors tend to vary across federal loan programs; the federal government has not yet standardized the definition of conditions for a loan default, for example.

Some of the most successful federal programs have involved extensions of credit for new types of loans. FHA single-family mortgage insurance involved the creation of the thirty-year self-amortizing mortgage to allow borrowers to obtain long-term funding for their homes. The thirty-year FHA mortgage replaced the earlier form of financing through a balloon mortgage that the homeowner was required to refinance every few years. The successful experience of FHA mortgage insurance over several decades permitted the development of a private mortgage insurance industry to take similar kinds of risks with thirty-year level-payment mortgages. The Export-Import Bank similarly tends to lead the private market by providing longer term financing for exports to particular countries.

Addressing Elements of Financial Risk

387

CH 12:
LOANS
AND
LOAN
GUARANTEES

There are a number of ways to address financial risks in a credit program, and these vary according to the particular type of loan or borrower. For example, limiting the maximum loan-to-value requirements can help to assure that borrowers have a significant equity stake in their homes and thus that they will make every effort to pay their mortgage loans on time.

With its emphasis on up front disclosure of the likely costs of credit, the Credit Reform Act has increased the financial accountability of credit programs. The new budget treatment has created an incentive for policymakers to avoid program elements that could cause high default rates. The government has become more successful at imposing limits on the financial risks posed by lenders and other program intermedi aries, notably schools in the student loan programs.

II. PATTERNS OF TOOL USE

U.S. National Government

The U.S. government extends credit for a broad range of purposes, from overseas activities to the needs of people caught in a disaster. The federal government today has over $200 billion of direct loans and almost a trillion dollars of loan guarantees outstanding. Outstanding federal direct loans and guarantees amount to about 10 percent of the total indebtedness of U.S. households and nonfinancial businesses.

Volume of Loans and Guarantees

Table 12-1 lists the major credit programs of the U.S. government and the volume of credit outstanding for each. As noted there, the largest programs provide credit for housing (FHA, VA, and rural housing), education (direct and guaranteed student loans), and agriculture (Farm Service Agency and rural programs), plus a variety of business purposes (SBA and some export programs).

Figure 12-1 shows the volume of federal direct loans and loan guarantees outstanding in recent decades. Over the last twenty to thirty years the volume of federal loan guarantees has grown significantly, while the volume of direct loans outstanding has remained at a more constant level.

Historical Overview

The practice of extending credit for public purposes has a long history in the United States, dating back to the seventeenth century and the New England colonies.[8] After the establishment of the United States, state and local governments, and eventually the federal government, extended loans to support a number of infrastructure improvements, such as canals and railroads.[9]

With the entry of the United States into World War I, the government created the War Finance Corporation (WFC), a wholly owned government corporation. By war's end, the WFC had lent money to support a wide variety of enterprises, including public utilities, power plants, mining and chemical firms, and railroads. During the economic downturn of 1920–1922, the Congress transformed the WFC into a peacetime emergency finance corporation authorized to make loans to support exporters and individuals in the depressed agricultural sector. The government had established the WFC to be a temporary measure and disestablished it by 1929.[10]

In 1932 the government established a new Reconstruction Finance Corporation

TABLE 12-1 *Federal Credit Programs**

Program	Outstanding 1999
DIRECT LOANS	
Federal Student Loan Programs	65
Farm Service Agency (Excl. CCC), Rural Development, Rural Housing	45
Rural Electrification Admin and Rural Telephone Bank	29
Housing and Urban Development	14
Agency For International Development	11
Public Law 480	11
Export-Import Bank	12
Commodity Credit Corporation	7
Federal Communications Commission	8
Disaster Assistance	7
Other Direct Loans	22
Subtotal: Direct Loans	234
LOAN GUARANTEES	
FHA Mutual Mortgage Insurance Fund	411
VA Mortgage	221
Federal Family Education Loan Program	127
FHA General/Special Risk Insurance Fund	93
Small Business	39
Export-Import Bank	25
International Assistance	19
Farm Service Agency and Rural Housing	17
Other Loan Guarantees	23
Subtotal: Loan Guarantees	976
TOTAL FEDERAL CREDIT	1,210

*Outstanding loans and loan guarantees, in billions of dollars.
SOURCE: Office of Management and Budget, Executive Office of the President, *Analytical Perspectives, Budget of the United States Government, Fiscal Year 2001* (February 2000), Table 8-1, p. 208.

based on the successful model of the WFC. From 1932 through the end of World War II, the RFC disbursed more than $2.7 billion in direct loans, including loans to financial institutions, mortgage loans and loans for agriculture, railroads, mining, exports, and other businesses, as well as $1.2 billion for stock subscriptions in banks, insurance companies, and other financial institutions.[11]

With the failure of thousands of banks, savings and loan institutions, and other

389

CH 12:
LOANS
AND
LOAN
GUARANTEES

Dollars in billions

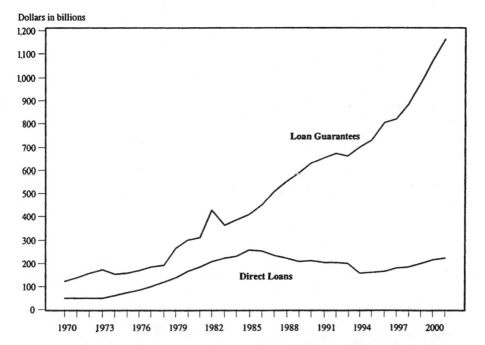

FIGURE 12-1 *Face value of federal credit outstanding. Source:* Budget of the United
States Government, Fiscal Year 2001, Analytical Perspectives, *Chapter
8, "Underwriting Federal Credit and Insurance," p. 207, Chart 8-1.*

private sources of credit, the Roosevelt Administration also created many other new
credit programs. These included the single-family mortgage insurance program of the
FHA, a variety of federal agencies to provide credit to agriculture and rural communities, and to businesses. Many of today's federal credit programs, including those of
the FHA, SBA, and the Export-Import Bank of the United States, trace back to this
period.

Many of these programs were remarkably successful. They helped provide funds to
banks and borrowers that found themselves in temporary straits because of the Great
Depression, and generally helped to revive confidence in the financial markets by placing the financial strength of the federal government behind otherwise illiquid private
obligations.

Over the last twenty to thirty years the volume of federal loan guarantees has grown
significantly, while the volume of direct loans outstanding has remained at a more
constant level. First, starting in the late 1960s, the government greatly expanded federal
loan guarantees. The federal government responded to urban unrest with new FHA
mortgage insurance programs, both for single-family homes and for apartment buildings. Many of these programs involved heavily subsidized interest rates as a way of
helping to lower housing costs for low-income homebuyers and renters. The government also created the guaranteed student loan program in 1965 and greatly expanded
its coverage in subsequent years.

Credit programs of the Farmers Home Administration (the FmHA, now succeeded
by the Rural Services Agency) multiplied sixfold in outstanding volume between 1973
and 1984, to $61 billion. This resulted from more generous loan terms and also from
an expansion of types of loan program that the agency offered. In good part, the
expansion of FmHA programs after 1981 represented a way for the government to bail

out private lenders, including rural banks and the Farm Credit System, that were hard hit by an agricultural downturn.

Starting with the Reagan administration, the federal government made a serious effort to curtail domestic budget resources. For federal credit programs, budget constraints caused a shift in the form of the federal program, from direct loans to loan guarantees, rather than a constriction in the actual volume of credit outstanding.

This was possible because of the distorted budget treatment of direct and guaranteed loans before credit reform. The volume of outstanding loan guarantees rose, while the volume of direct loans declined. The volume of outstanding loan guarantees continued to increase even after the Credit Reform Act was implemented, and this too reflects the effects of budget scoring rules. Congressional policymakers discovered that they could reduce the subsidy component of a direct loan or loan guarantee program and use the savings to provide a greater volume of loans for constituents.

U.S. State and Local Governments

By contrast to the virtually unlimited credit capacity of the federal government, state and local governments have much less financial capacity to issue debt obligations or to pledge their credit to issue loan guarantees. Unlike the federal government, states and localities are generally limited by their constitutions from engaging in deficit spending; this limits state and local governments in the amount of credit that they can extend on the basis of the strength of their governmental credit.

Bond issues back the most common forms of state credit programs. The federal government may provide some support to this form of credit program by providing a subsidy through a federal tax exemption for debt obligations issued by state or local governments or their instrumentalities. State and local authorities include power authorities, development finance authorities, housing finance agencies, student loan finance agencies and health-care facilities authorities, for example.[12]

One interesting state lending vehicle is the state bond bank. By pooling the credit standing of participating local governments, plus some form of credit enhancement that the state government might provide, the bond bank permits localities to borrow at lower cost or on more favorable terms than they could otherwise. At least seventeen states now have some bond bank programs to help serve their localities.

Another type of credit program is the state revolving loan fund. Revolving loan funds provide credit to businesses or localities to help finance long-term economic development or environmental projects such as local wastewater or drinking water facilities. A revolving fund begins with seed capital, usually a federal grant or long-term loan, and lends money for designated public purposes on favorable financial terms. As borrowers repay their loans, they replenish the revolving fund so that loans can be provided to new borrowers or to fund new activities.[13]

International Experience

Many national governments outside the United States provide credit for a variety of public purposes. German state (i.e., "Land") governments own so-called Landesbanken, which are authorized to fund a variety of activities, including providing real estate, trade, and commercial loans. In housing, the Japanese government plays a major role in funding home mortgages through the wholly owned Government Housing Loan Corporation (GHLC). The GHLC provides perhaps 40 percent of the country's mortgage credit, in the form of heavily subsidized loans, which during the late 1990s offered borrowers mortgage interest rates of around 3 percent. In 1999, the GHLC had about 7.2 trillion Yen ($50 billion) of home loans outstanding.[14]

391

CH 12:
LOANS
AND
LOAN
GUARANTEES

The French government also has had a tradition of providing subsidized credit for income-eligible homeowners. However, the French have been turning away from government provision of mortgage credit. The French had used a quasi-governmental mortgage bank, the Credit Foncier de France, as its instrument for providing mortgage credit.[15] In 1998 the French government bailed out the Credit Foncier de France and took steps to create the legal framework for a system of private mortgage credit banks that would be authorized to issue mortgage-backed bonds to fund mortgages.

In the area of nationwide credit support for student loans, the government of the United Kingdom utilizes the Student Loans Company Ltd., a nonprofit adjunct to the U.K. Department for Education and Employment, to extend credit to students. The United Kingdom provides a system of income-contingent repayment on student loans. Students defer making loan payments while they are in school, and then make their loan repayments through the U.K. Inland Revenue, the tax authority. By contrast, a recent survey of developing countries conducted for the International Finance Corporation found that, with a handful of exceptions, "there were no government student loan companies, and banks were not generally in the habit of lending to students either . . ."[16]

Developing countries do, however, provide government loans either directly or through state-owned banks to support favored sectors of the economy and especially state-owned enterprises. Many times these countries have been harmed when their loan programs turned into open-ended subsidies for money-losing enterprises. The net result, most notably in China, has been that a government directs massive amounts of valuable resources into activities that can prove to be immensely wasteful.[17] In many countries, government loan managers lack an incentive to recognize defaults and losses on loans, especially to powerful economic institutions and firms managed by influential political figures.

Credit programs also have a long history internationally. The Roman Republic established a credit bank in 352 BCE, to provide direct loans and loan guarantees on preferential terms to help provide relief for poor debtors. The bank apparently met with little success.[18] At the time of King George III, the British government enacted legislation to provide loans for infrastructure improvements, to relieve economic distress of private firms, and to support public and private organizations that were expected to provide expanded job opportunities to the unemployed. Special acts of Parliament in 1784 and 1799 authorized government loans to fund the completion of projects by two local canal companies, and subsequent acts expanded this practice of offering government loans.[19]

One interesting and multifaceted model comes from post–World War II Germany. In 1948, the new West German government and West German state (i.e., "Land") governments established the Kreditanstalt fuer Wiederaufbau (KfW, literally, the "Reconstruction Finance Corporation"). KfW's first task was to provide credit and equity financing in support of the reconstruction of the postwar West German economy. Although unrecognized in current KfW literature, it would seem as if the model of the U.S. Reconstruction Finance Corporation might have played a role in the design of KfW.

KfW accomplished its task of financing West German reconstruction and then turned to new financing activities on behalf of the West German government. KfW today helps to provide project financing for the energy, steel, and coal sectors and infrastructure investments, and to provide loans and equity investments for small- and medium-sized businesses. Similar to the role of ExIm Bank in the United States, KfW also provides financing for German exports and the European aircraft industry (Airbus). The government corporation seeks to make a profit, but not to maximize profits each year on its operations.

III. BASIC MECHANICS

The basic mechanics of a federal direct loan and a guaranteed loan, respectively, involve a series of steps, from development of the loan program to final repayment or collection on a loan, and the writing off of losses.

Start-Up

All government loan programs involve a preliminary phase of developing regulations, contractual agreements, and loan documents that reflect the provisions of the law that authorizes the program. Both direct and guaranteed loan programs require that forms and procedures be developed to screen borrowers according to the statutory standards for eligibility in the program. For a loan guarantee program, the program agency also must establish procedures for certifying and decertifying lenders as to eligibility to participate in the program. Other certifications also may be needed. For example, the Department of Education must determine the eligibility of schools to participate in student assistance programs, including loans.

Marketing

Especially at the beginning of a loan or guarantee program the government may need to help develop a market for the program. Lenders, other institutions, such as schools, and borrowers must be persuaded to participate. The SBA, for example, continues its efforts to increase lender participation in its programs.

Market development was a major issue for federally guaranteed student loans. The Congress enacted the student loan program in the late 1960s to provide a 100 percent guarantee against the risk of default. However, most banks found these loans small and expensive to service. Thus, for many years lenders remained reluctant to participate heavily in the guaranteed student loan program. Eventually, some of the larger private lenders and state governments created specialized student loan businesses to purchase the loans from the originating banks. These specialized student loan businesses began to realize economies of scale from holding and servicing student loans that were unprofitable for lenders that held only small numbers of loans. At that point the program was ready to take off.

Origination

Origination is the process of actually extending a loan. It involves a contractual agreement between the lender and the borrower as to the terms of the loan. Origination requires underwriting the loan (i.e., determining whether the borrower is capable of repaying the loan in a timely manner and assessing the value of any collateral used to secure the loan). For example, federal business loans and home loans tend to require a lien against the borrower's property as collateral.

If a loan is a federal direct loan, the originator may be a federal agency, such as the SBA when it provides direct loans to disaster victims, or an intermediary such as a school that originates student loans. If a loan is federally guaranteed, a private lender will originate the loan pursuant to a contractual agreement with a federal agency to guarantee repayment of the loan by the borrower. Lenders that originate federally guaranteed loans include commercial banks, savings and loan institutions, and also other types of lenders, such as mortgage bankers for FHA-insured mortgages and VA and RHS-guaranteed home loans, or finance companies for some business loans.

393

CH 12:
LOANS
AND
LOAN
GUARANTEES

The process of loan origination highlights important operational differences between direct loans and loan guarantees. In a direct loan program, government officials maintain control over the process of determining borrower eligibility and deciding whether to make the loan. By contrast, for guaranteed loans government delegates much of the control over origination to the lender and the lender decides whether to make a particular government-guaranteed loan.

This creates an opening for the problem that economists call "moral hazard." The government's guarantee distorts the usual economic behavior of a private lender. Enough fee and interest income may accrue from a guaranteed loan in the first year or two that the lender becomes indifferent to the risk of later default. By originating loans that defaulted in high numbers, some lenders, notably in the failed FHA programs of the late 1960s, cumulatively caused the government billions of dollars of taxpayer losses, plunged borrowers into debt and bankruptcy, and harmed the very communities that the programs were intended to help. By contrast, there have been instances where lenders have been too conservative and have been reluctant to extend credit to borrowers the government was trying to reach.

Many government loan guarantee programs try to address problems of moral hazard by monitoring the default rates of loans that lenders originate for government programs. New budget scoring systems also may prove helpful in measuring lender performance.[20]

Disbursement

Disbursement is the actual transfer of funds from the government or the lender, as the case may be, to the borrower. Disbursement on a residential mortgage loan tends to occur all at once, at settlement when the borrower purchases or refinances the home. Disbursement on other types of loan may occur in stages. For instance, students may receive disbursements of student loan funds at the beginning of each semester.

Servicing

Once the loan is disbursed, the borrower has the money and must begin to repay the loan according to its terms. During this phase, the loan must be serviced. Servicing is the process of (1) arranging to receive timely payments from the borrower, and (2) receiving and accounting for the funds as borrowers remit them. Some loans provide for a grace period before repayment is due. Students do not begin repayment of their U.S. government loans until six months after graduation, for example.

Lenders service the government guaranteed loans that they hold, and government agencies are responsible for servicing direct loans. Given the pressure to downsize government and the growth of new servicing technologies that increase efficiencies and economies of scale, federal agencies increasingly contract with private firms to service their direct loans. Loan asset sales also can help to outsource the servicing function for federal direct loans and nonperforming guaranteed loans that the government has acquired from lenders.

If a borrower is late in making a scheduled payment, the loan becomes delinquent. If the borrower does not come back into current payment status, there comes a point, defined differently for different federal credit programs, when the borrower is deemed to be in default on the loan agreement. Delinquencies and defaults require action, in the collections stage of the credit cycle, to reinstate the borrower into current status, to work out or restructure the loan, or to pursue other remedies, such as foreclosure.

In servicing, loan guarantee programs again tend to manifest the problem of moral hazard: because the government guarantees some or all of the loan, the lender tends to be less careful in servicing a government-guaranteed loan than in managing its own unguaranteed loans. The problem of moral hazard also can arise for direct loans if government contracts out the servicing: unless the servicing contract is performance based, so that the contractor has a financial stake in servicing each loan well, government may find that the contractor has little incentive to do an effective job.

Some federal loans, notably student loans, are backed only by the borrower's contractual obligation to repay the loan. Other loans, such as FHA or VA mortgage loans, are backed by collateral. In other words, they are secured loans. If the borrower defaults on the loan, the government or its agent or the lender, as the case may be, has the legal right to seize the property that is the loan collateral and sell it to help reduce the amount that is lost on the default.

Loan Sales and Securitization

Especially with new technologies that create economies of scale in loan management, lenders have an incentive to package their loans and sell them, either to larger institutions or in so-called securitization transactions. This also helps to encourage lenders to participate in a program because they know the loan paper can be converted to cash. Government often has created special institutions to provide so-called secondary market services (i.e., to purchase loans from lenders or otherwise provide funding for the loans that they originate).

Ginnie Mae, the Government National Mortgage Association, is a major secondary market institution that helps lenders to securitize government-guaranteed home mortgages. In a Ginnie Mae securitization, a lender originates or otherwise assembles a large number of government-guaranteed loans (i.e., FHA or VA or rural housing loans), places them in a trust structure, and issues mortgage-backed securities that allow investors to buy a share in the cash flows from the mortgages in the trust. Ginnie Mae facilitates this process by providing a guarantee to holders of the mortgage-backed securities that they will receive timely payment of the principal and interest due each month on the mortgages. Because Ginnie Mae guarantees these mortgage-backed securities with the full-faith-and-credit of the U.S. government, investors eagerly purchase such securities. Without the Ginnie Mae guarantee, lenders would not find as ready a market for their mortgages.

Government has also encouraged development of other secondary market institutions to support guaranteed loan programs. In the student loan market, for example, state agencies or nonprofit organizations may issue bonds, often tax exempt, to fund pools of student loans that they purchase from the originating lenders. Other major secondary market institutions are government-sponsored enterprises, discussed in another chapter.

Government Loan Asset Sales

The U.S. government increasingly uses loan asset sales as a way to receive value from loans that it holds, including direct loans and defaulted guaranteed loans that it has repurchased from lenders. The U.K. Student Loans Company also has conducted size-able sales of direct loans from its portfolio.

395

CH 12:
LOANS
AND
LOAN
GUARANTEES

Building on the largely successful asset sales experience of the Resolution Trust Corporation (RTC) in the late 1980s and early 1990s, HUD sold billions of dollars of nonperforming loans that it had been unable to collect on.[21] The SBA also has begun a series of loan asset sales as a way to reduce the workload burdens on the staff of that downsized agency. Federal experience from several agencies indicates that government can structure incentives so that the private sector will collect on nonperforming loans without treating the borrowers unfairly.

Prepayment, Repayment, or Collection

When a borrower repays the loan, the loan process is formally at an end. Prepayments occur when the borrower pays ahead of time, for example, because of a desire to refinance a home. If a borrower fails to make timely payment, the government or private lender, as the case may be, makes efforts to collect on the loan.

The federal government may use its own staff to collect on direct loans or else will contract with private firms to collect from borrowers. The U.S. Department of Education, for example, has created an especially sophisticated relationship with contractor collection companies to obtain high performance both in collecting on delinquent or defaulted loans and in fair treatment of borrowers.

In some cases, a federal government agency also is responsible for collecting on defaulted guaranteed loans. Until recently, for example, lenders that participate in the SBA Section 7(a) business loan program were permitted to put their defaulted federally guaranteed loans back to the SBA for collection and workout. Increasingly, the federal government requires lenders to deal with the defaulted guaranteed loans that they hold. In such cases, the lender may close out the loan, for example, through foreclosure or a forced sale on the home or business property that a borrower has pledged as collateral for the loan. The lender then collects from the federal government the amount of the federal guarantee on that loan that could not be recovered from the borrower.

A number of federal programs, such as the HUD multifamily mortgage insurance program, have found that their delinquent or defaulted borrowers will remain current on all private obligations; they stiff only Uncle Sam.[22] Increasingly, government credit agencies are trying to deal with this problem. Through the application of laws such as the Debt Collection Improvements Act of 1996, the federal government has begun to exert considerable effort to collect on the debts of individual borrowers who have defaulted on their federal direct or guaranteed loans.

Federal agencies apply a number of techniques to induce defaulted borrowers to make good on their obligations. A number of federal credit agencies have joined in a cooperative arrangement, known as CAIVRS, or the Credit Alert Interactive Voice Response System, to help screen applicants for new federal loans. The originators of federal direct and guaranteed loans run a computer search of the borrower against the database of past defaulted borrowers; CAIVRS signals if there is a match, so that the borrower is requested to repay the past obligation before becoming eligible for new federal credit.

Other tools include a federal income tax offset that allows federal credit agencies to attach income tax refunds of a defaulted borrower and offset the proceeds against the borrower's outstanding credit obligation to the federal government. Agencies such as the ExIm Bank and U.S. Agency for International Development also may benefit from the sovereign power of the U.S. government, to the extent that foreign governments are reluctant to default on their loans to the U.S. government for fear of being denied access to aid or credit in the future.

Write-Off and Recognition of Losses

When a loan is uncollectable and the government or its agent has no further remedies available to help mitigate the loss, then the loan must be written off. This is a process of explicit accounting for the fact that, unlike a performing loan, the written-off loan has no further value. Loans become uncollectable for a variety of reasons, including the bankruptcy of a borrower or a policy decision, such as the recent international agreement to write off uncollectable debt owed by the poorest third-world countries.

It can be very hard for a government agency to write off its losses from uncollectable loans. There is no incentive for a government official to take the formal accounting step and recognize the financial loss. In some programs serious disincentives may exist, for example, if field offices maintain their staffing levels by alleging that staff are needed to manage large numbers of troubled loans. In that context, a pattern of prompt write-offs of uncollectable loans could result in pressure to downsize.

The inability to recognize losses is yet another example of the precept that bad news travels slowly. Government agencies will correct this problem only when they develop accounts that are based on accurate monitoring of the cash flows to and from all loans and loan guarantees.

At some point, the failure to recognize financial losses can become catastrophic. The Chinese government has experienced the costs of postponing the recognition of losses until they become intolerably large. China has been reluctant to close down state-owned enterprises that are in default on immense debts. The enterprises have used their lease on life to make large-scale mistakes, such as massive overproduction of unsalable goods and services, whose costs will burden the Chinese economy for years to come.[23]

IV. TOOL SELECTION

Rationale for Credit Programs

As a general rule, government credit programs seek to provide credit to borrowers who somehow are considered to lack access to private loans on reasonable terms. The Office of Management and Budget (OMB) has published Circular A-129, *Policies for Federal Credit Programs and Non-Tax Receivables,* suggesting three reasons why a government credit program may be proposed to supplement and subsidize private sources of financing:

- To correct a capital market imperfection
- To subsidize borrowers or other beneficiaries
- To encourage certain activities[24]

Market Imperfections

Credit programs are most effective when they overcome what economists call a market imperfection. A market imperfection can be defined in practical terms as some flaw in the market that deprives creditworthy borrowers of access to credit on appropriate terms. When a government program overcomes the imperfection, the program can provide loans to creditworthy borrowers without running the risk of intolerable levels of defaults.

397

CH 12:
LOANS
AND
LOAN
GUARANTEES

When private credit markets are in disarray, most notably during the Great Depression, federal credit programs can serve a large number of potentially creditworthy borrowers who are not well served by private lenders. In good times, market imperfections are harder to find. Many market imperfections were caused by restrictive legislation that, for example, confined banks and other lenders in the geographic markets that they could serve. Today, the Congress has undone many of those laws and thereby removed the market impediments.

Other examples of credit market imperfections include discrimination, e.g., in the residential mortgage market. In 1998, 12 percent of FHA loans for home purchases went to African-American homebuyers, and 13 percent to Hispanic homebuyers. This was over three times the proportion of such borrowers served by nongovernment loans. FHA also served a significantly larger proportion of low- and moderate-income people and neighborhoods than did the nongovernment loan.[25] Also, in the federal direct and guaranteed student loan programs, the government is providing credit to student borrowers who may not yet have established enough evidence of creditworthiness to be able to qualify for private credit on comparable terms.

If there is no market imperfection, the government program may have difficulty trying to serve enough creditworthy borrowers that have not already been served by private lenders. The remaining borrowers in a program as a group may not be sufficiently creditworthy to avoid a significant risk of default. Also, if borrowers are considered to be financially disadvantaged, the government may be reluctant to impose fees on their loans to compensate for the amount of financial risk that is involved. The result is likely to be a potentially high level of subsidy that is required to support such a program.

Providing a Subsidy

Government may decide to target credit on preferential terms to borrowers or activities that are considered to merit a subsidy, even if no market imperfection may be apparent. The Export-Import Bank of the United States (ExIm Bank), for example, may provide loans on subsidized terms to help offset the prospect that foreign governments will subsidize their own companies in export markets and thereby deprive U.S. firms of sales in those markets. If other countries distort competition by subsidizing their exports, then the United States is ready to provide its own countervailing support.

With some exceptions, it is not clear that government makes a wise decision when it ties a subsidy to the extension of credit. The financial markets today are unbundling financial services because of the greater efficiency that can come from applying each type of service to its own best purposes. Similarly, the government needs to recognize that the person or firm or other entity that needs access to credit may not need access to a subsidy, and vice versa. In particular, if people or firms are not creditworthy, they may need grant-type assistance or special counseling or other subsidies, but they will not be promising candidates for a loan.

Government Credit as a Pioneer

Government often functions best as a pioneer in the credit markets. The FHA pioneered the thirty-year level payment mortgage; over time, private mortgage insurers followed FHA's lead and offered similar products. By extending credit to disadvantaged but creditworthy borrowers, possibly accompanied by some form of financial counseling, the government also can show private lenders that those borrowers are profitable credit risks.

The Micro and Small Enterprise Development program of the U.S. Agency for International Development is attempting to create such a demonstration effect in developing countries. By sharing risk with local lenders, the program seeks to expand the access to credit of creditworthy but neglected groups such as women entrepreneurs. These are ideal types of credit programs so long as government is willing to pay the price of success and eventually turn over a large number of its creditworthy constituent borrowers to the private sector.

Political Considerations

Developing a Constituency

Although there are counterexamples, credit programs can be hard to start and hard to end. The issue is one of constituency; in the beginning of a program, constituencies may not welcome a federal program that might disrupt their current way of doing business. Yet, once a program matures it tends to have developed a determined constituency whose well-being may be threatened by termination or even by reforms.

Some constituencies may be small; it is their influence that counts. Elisabeth Rhyne conducted interviews in the early 1980s with respect to SBA business loans and found that, "All of the interviewees placed the [congressional small business] committees first, the banks second, and small business third in level of commitment to the program."[26]

As Rhyne concluded, "It is my hypothesis that one of the reasons that [the SBA business loan program] continues to survive is that it meets certain needs of the Congressmen and Senators on the House and Senate Small Business Committees who oversee the programs."[27]

The Choice between Direct Loans and Loan Guarantees

The choice between direct loans and loan guarantees involves political considerations. Private financial institutions are a powerful constituency that favors loan guarantees because the loan guarantee avoids the threat of direct government participation in the credit business, because of the fees and interest income that a lender can earn from a federally guaranteed loan, and because of the opportunities federal loans provide to nurture a borrower relationship (e.g., of a student who later may take out a consumer loan or home mortgage from the bank). Lenders have welcomed the increase in volume of outstanding federal loan guarantees and also, for some programs, may welcome the growth in borrowing at less subsidized interest rates. By contrast, lenders tend to view direct loans, except to the least creditworthy borrowers, as a competitive threat from the federal government.

Constituencies as a Source of Inertia

Lenders not only can provide a strong base of support for a program; they also may become a powerful source of inertia to maintain the features of a loan guarantee program in familiar ways. In one of its early efforts to address problems of high defaults in the guaranteed student loan program, the Department of Education developed regulations to set minimum standards of performance for lenders that service federal student loans. For years, lenders objected to these rules, known as the due diligence regulations, largely because they set formalistic standards that differed significantly from the performance-based approaches that banks took in servicing their own non-federal loans.

Today the department is trying to free itself from these rules because of the need to reduce defaults through higher quality servicing based on performance and measurable outcomes. Now that participating lenders have developed the requisite data processing systems to conform to the due diligence regulations, many of them resist the idea that the department again will change the rules.

399

CH 12:
LOANS
AND
LOAN
GUARANTEES

Program Expansion

Once a program constituency emerges, the Congress may enact laws to permit an expansion in the outstanding loan volume. Often the Congress will expand a targeted program to include groups of borrowers who may be quite different from those that the program originally served. In the student loan program, the Congress relaxed earlier limitations and permitted students to take out federal loans even if they could not show financial need. This expanded the program to serve middle class borrowers, and not merely those most in need.

The government expanded FHA single-family and multifamily mortgage programs during the 1960s to serve central cities. In that case, FHA programs already served the middle class and suburban areas; it was only afterward that the Congress enacted subsidized programs such as the Section 235 homeownership and Section 236 rental housing programs to make housing available to low-income renters and homebuyers. Those programs combined FHA mortgage insurance with substantial interest rate subsidies that were intended to make the housing more affordable.

Credit Budget Politics

The Credit Reform Act of 1990 has created a budget framework that affects many legislative decisions about credit programs. Perhaps most important, credit reform subjects virtually all credit programs, including guarantees as well as direct loans, to annual budget constraints. When faced with budget constraints, the Congress often decides to reduce the amount of subsidy that a loan program provides, so that a fixed amount of appropriated funds can serve more constituents.

The Congress has a variety of options in this regard. For example, in 1992 the Congress enacted legislation to permit students to take out unsubsidized student loans, regardless of their financial need. While the government makes the interest payments for students in school under the subsidized student loan program, the student must make those interest payments for the unsubsidized loans. More recently, the Congressional Budget Office (CBO) suggested that the terms of SBA business loans might be adjusted to eliminate the amount of federal subsidy involved. The CBO suggested that the Congress could achieve this by increasing the amount of risk sharing with private lenders and by increasing the loan-related fees that borrowers would pay the government for their SBA loans.

V. MANAGEMENT CHALLENGES AND POTENTIAL RESPONSES

The most critical elements in effective management of a credit program relate to the mandate, capacity, and accountability of the agency or department that is responsible for administering the program. A critical problem that many programs face is the erosion of creditworthy borrowers through a process of adverse selection. Consider each of these four factors in turn.

Balancing Risks and Mission

In program management too, the basic challenge for a credit program is to maintain balance between doing good and doing well, that is, between extending credit to those creditworthy borrowers who need it and assuring that the program does not incur unacceptable losses. Some credit programs have mastered this tension between program goals and financial soundness; others have foundered because of their incapacity to deal with it.

An agency that does not actively manage the tension can face mounting difficulties. The problem with credit programs is that financially imprudent lending tends to become apparent only after a period of years; this gives an unwary agency considerable time to expand the volume of unsound loans or loan guarantees outstanding, so that accumulated losses can become substantial.

Achieving a proper balance may require an agency to try to manage its political environment. Credit programs often involve powerful constituencies that have interests that conflict with the management of a program in a cost-effective manner. Thus, the Congress is eager to provide funds so that the SBA can provide credit to victims of disaster, but the Congress seems less willing to appropriate funds to help the SBA to improve its ability to service those loans properly.

The Congress also may be reluctant to provide an agency with the resources or mandate to foreclose upon influential borrowers or to supervise lenders effectively, or to take other steps that protect the agency's financial position. This was especially true in earlier years. The 1970s and 1980s saw the publication of numerous reports and disclosures about high levels of defaults in many federal programs. Following the publicity surrounding the damage caused by such defaults, and especially since the enactment of the Credit Reform Act of 1990 and the need to budget and account for loan defaults, the Congress has provided federal credit agencies with increased program authority to reduce the volume of loans that lenders or others originate to borrowers with a high likelihood of defaulting.

Programs that the government manages through wholly owned government corporations tend to be especially capable of striking a good balance between doing well and doing good. As discussed in the chapter on government corporations and government sponsored enterprises, government corporations are supposed to be financially self-sustaining (except to the extent that the Congress from time to time may appropriate funds to subsidize uneconomic activities). Similarly, some state finance authorities, and especially some that are structured to be nonprofit corporations, may achieve a workable balance between their activities and their available resources.

Capacity

A second management challenge relates to the availability of staff and systems to manage credit programs. A credit program requires staff and information-based systems to monitor the default rates of government-guaranteed loans originated or serviced by participating lenders, for example, and to apply appropriate corrective measures to deal with poor performers.

Many federal agencies are feeling the effects of years of hiring freezes and mandatory staff reductions. The U.S. General Accounting Office (GAO) reported in 1993 that Ginnie Mae had only about seventy staff to oversee hundreds of billions of dollars of mortgage-backed securities, and urged that OMB and HUD, the department in which Ginnie Mae resides, take steps to grant Ginnie Mae a modest staff increase. By 1999, the volume of outstanding Ginnie Mae securities had risen to $540 billion, while staffing had dropped to fifty-six people. Thanks to the robust U.S. economy in the six years following the GAO report, Ginnie Mae was able to get by with its diminished staffing capacity. The paradox is that policymakers undoubtedly will allocate more resources to the agency if it suffers a spate of issuer defaults, as happened in the late 1980s just before Ginnie Mae received its last boost in staffing.

401

CH 12:
LOANS
AND
LOAN
GUARANTEES

Capacity also includes staff quality and training. Past hiring freezes mean that many federal agencies lack the necessary infusion of young professional talent who can help to apply new technologies and work processes to the administration of credit programs. Also, skilled financial and technical professionals find ample opportunities in today's prosperous private credit markets, and public service has lost some of its luster.

These problems of capacity, subsumed under the term "hollow government," have significant implications for the design and management of federal credit programs. On the one hand, if agencies are short of in-house staff, then they must privatize many functions, just to obtain the needed personnel. On the other hand, government cannot run services with contractors alone; government also needs capacity to assure that the relationship between the agency and its contractors is properly structured and managed. When a contractor fails, as happened to the Department of Education in the student loan consolidation program, it is the department that takes the heat.

Effective agency leadership can help to resolve such issues. The Rural Housing Service of the Department of Agriculture, for example, engaged in a multiyear program to centralize servicing of rural housing direct loans in St. Louis to add new technological capability to field offices to help with loan origination and servicing, and to relocate and downsize staff to accommodate the changes. The Rural Housing Service obtained a multiyear commitment from the Office of Management and Budget of the funds needed for the new technology and staff training. All parties lived up to their commitments, and the new office is now operating on the basis of state-of-the-art servicing technologies.

Capacity also affects the ability of government to hold third parties accountable for their performance. The final stages of the credit cycle, to the extent that they involve defaults and the need to work out troubled loans, can be very expensive and difficult for the government to resolve. In part, the problem may involve a politically powerful constituency that resists a federal agency's enforcement of its rights under a loan agreement. Federal credit agencies such as HUD increasingly have used asset sales as a way to reduce the immense burden on staff that can result from a backlog of troubled loans.

Keeping Third Parties Accountable

To carry our credit programs through third parties, government must assure that its financial partners remain accountable for achieving program goals. After taking losses in many programs, the federal government is devoting increased resources to monitoring the performance of lenders who originate and service guaranteed loans. For federal single-family housing programs, Ginnie Mae has been a leader in developing lender-monitoring systems, both for its own use and for use of the VA home loan program.

During the late 1980s a number of issuers of mortgage-backed securities defaulted on their obligations so that Ginnie Mae took billions of dollars of losses from its guarantees. The agency moved promptly to build a management information system, to track issuers of its mortgage-backed securities and the lenders who originated the mortgages in those pools. Ginnie Mae uses an automated financial data system to monitor delinquency and default rates of issuers and originators and mortgage pools that fall outside of expected parameters. Ginnie Mae officials believe that the system, now known as GPADS (the Government Portfolio Database Analysis System), has been extremely cost effective. The payoff is measured in terms of the government's capacity to act before rather than after loan origination and servicing practices create unacceptable financial losses.

The effectiveness of such monitoring systems can depend on the legal authority that the Congress has made available to an agency that seeks to apply sanctions or to take other actions with respect to a third party whose actions are associated with high levels of defaulted loans. For the Department of Education, the Congress has provided authority to take action against schools that participate in the federal direct or guaranteed student loan program and whose students default in high numbers on their federal loans.

Thanks to new legislation that permits easier enforcement than in earlier years, the Department of Education has been able to report substantial progress in reducing default rates of schools that participate in the federal guaranteed student loan program. Using the particular definition in the law that permits the department to terminate schools with unacceptable default rates, overall defaults dropped from 21.4 percent on loans going into repayment in FY 1989 to 9.4 percent on loans going into repayment in FY 1996. This is a reduction of more than 50 percent.

Despite their increased attention to accountability, government credit agencies may neglect one important source of market discipline: they tend not to report their delinquent or defaulted business borrowers to private credit bureaus. Sometimes this reluctance comes at the behest of a congressional committee. The problem has been partially cured in the Debt Collection Improvements Act of 1996 and the statutory requirement that the status of defaulted individual (but not business) borrowers be reported to credit bureaus.

Federal credit agencies need the capacity to obtain accurate financial information and act promptly in response. Perhaps the greatest problem of accountability for federal credit programs relates to the unreliability of many data sources, especially for guaranteed loan programs. The good news for credit programs is that new management information systems permit increasing accuracy in credit administration and the generation of program information. Moreover, federal credit agencies have shown an increasing ability to learn from one another's promising practices.[28]

Under leadership from the Deputy Director for Management of OMB and a special Senior Advisor for Federal Credit and Cash Management, federal credit agencies are cooperating in a Federal Credit Policy Working Group that allows managers to exchange information in a supportive environment. Federal housing credit agencies, for example, are cooperating to create a joint federal housing data warehouse. Other federal agencies, including HUD and SBA, with support from the Federal Deposit Insurance Corporation, are sharing knowledge about the proper way to design and manage loan asset sales programs.

Adverse Selection

The problem of adverse selection relates to the ability of private firms such as lenders or mortgage insurers to keep the most profitable loans and to direct less profitable—and generally less creditworthy—borrowers to apply for government direct or guaranteed loans.

Federal credit programs contain structural elements that foster adverse selection. First, many credit programs by their terms offer credit only to those borrowers who have been turned down for similar credit by the private market. Second, government credit often is priced at a standard price, regardless of the creditworthiness of the borrower. This creates an incentive for private firms to offer a better price to more creditworthy borrowers than these borrowers can obtain from the government. As more creditworthy borrowers leave government programs, those programs find themselves with a higher proportion of less creditworthy borrowers than before.

An actuarial study of the FHA single-family program has pointed out that private

403

CH 12:
LOANS
AND
LOAN
GUARANTEES

lenders are applying new scoring-based technologies to find creditworthy borrowers. This could cause increased adverse selection: "That is, without modifying its underwriting rules, FHA might end up with lower average quality loans."[29]

The problem of adverse selection was difficult for FHA even before the application of those new technologies. In 1986, FHA mortgages were 1.9 times more likely than conventional mortgages to become ninety days past due. By mid-1998, the ratio had jumped to 4.4 times higher for FHA compared with conventional mortgages. Credit quality of VA mortgages compared with conventional mortgages also declined by similar amounts.

One can expect the application of scoring-based technologies to affect the credit quality of loans made or guaranteed by other government programs as well. Business loan programs of the SBA and some rural loan programs would seem to be good candidates for increased adverse selection, as the private sector increases the application of scoring-based systems to serve creditworthy borrowers who otherwise would apply for government loans.[30]

At some point, to diminish the potential impact of adverse selection, policymakers may want to explore options for changing the form of some credit programs. One idea along these lines was contained in OMB's FY 1996 passback concerning the FHA single-family mortgage insurance program. OMB proposed that FHA replace its traditional single-family mortgage insurance with a program of credit enhancements. In other words, FHA would provide grant funds to compensate private lenders for the additional default risk on the low-downpayment mortgages that FHA traditionally has supported.[31]

This proposal met with opposition from the mortgage banking industry, which includes many lenders that now have specialized in making FHA and VA loans under the current loan guarantee structure, and the idea was not included in the final version of the administration's FY 1996 budget. Nonetheless, it provides a useful model of how the transformation of a tool, here from a loan guarantee to a grant, can improve the ability of government to manage and budget for credit programs in today's environment. The proposal's demise also provides an illustration of the fact that stakeholder issues may prevent policymakers from adapting programs until the status quo for some of them becomes untenable.

VI. OVERALL ASSESSMENT

To what extent, then, do loan and loan guarantees constitute useful tools of public action? To answer this question, it is useful to examine these tools in relation to four important criteria: *effectiveness, efficiency, equity,* and *legitimacy*.

Effectiveness and Manageability

Credit programs have been especially effective when government acts as a pioneer to demonstrate that new forms of lending can be successful. A list of such programs might include the FHA thirty-year level payment single-family mortgage, government guaranteed student loans, and the microenterprise loan program of the U.S. Agency for International Development. These programs have used the financial strength of the government to experiment with new types of loans, loans on more favorable terms, or loans to underserved borrowers that the private markets were too cautious to make on their own. Credit programs such as SBA disaster loan programs also have been effective in helping creditworthy borrowers to recover from temporary financial setbacks.

By contrast, loan and loan guarantee programs have been less successful when they represent a way to convey a subsidy without demonstrating that the loans can be profitable. Failed FHA loans to center cities and high default rates on loans to students at proprietary schools, for example, only added to the reluctance of private lenders to provide such credit.[32]

Also, government has found it hard to manage many direct loan and loan guarantee programs. Constant changes in the credit markets have made it difficult for programs to maintain their balance between the mandate to provide credit to intended constituencies and the need to protect their programs against unacceptable levels of default and financial loss.

At the same time, new technologies, and especially the application of flexible data management systems, promise to make credit programs much easier to manage than ever before. The new systems will permit loan administration to occur on almost a real-time basis. Electronic data interchange between lenders and federal guarantee programs, and between government loan officers and centralized loan administration centers, promises to improve the manageability of many programs. Customer service also will increase, as round-the-clock toll-free numbers substitute for face-to-face meetings between borrowers and the people who service their loans.

The open question for many credit programs is whether stakeholders, including federal employees as well as private third parties, are willing to negotiate constructive outcomes so that credit agencies have the mandate and capacity to run their programs well. During the early 1990s, the Clinton Administration proposed to transform the FHA into a more effective government corporation called the Federal Housing Corporation.[33] This proposal met with opposition from private mortgage insurance companies who often view the government as a taxpayer-subsidized competitor and who did not favor any increase in the effectiveness of that competitor. The rapid demise of that idea stands as a warning that negotiations to increase the capacity of federal credit agencies often may not be easy. Internationally, the experience of many countries, especially but not solely in the developing world, has been that they may lack the institutional capacity or the mandate to require repayment of loans that governments make to politically powerful people or institutions.

Efficiency

Government credit programs, especially after the Great Depression, had considerable scope for improving the efficiency of economic markets. Some credit programs, such as those that help to demonstrate the creditworthiness of some borrowers who have been neglected by the private markets, continue to play such a role. Yet, dramatic increases in efficiency of private financial markets have rendered some programs obsolete. When the markets work well, government has less to contribute. This again is true both for direct loans and loan guarantees.

There is another problem with government credit: it encourages indebtedness. In other words, by easing access to mortgage credit, a federal program encourages not merely housing, but also the indebtedness that is fundamental to the tool. There is reason to believe, for example, that federal school loans have helped to facilitate the massive increase in debt that many of today's students must bear.

Equity

Almost by its nature, credit is an inequitable tool. Consider vertical equity first (i.e., equity across income classes). The most creditworthy borrowers—who tend least to need many types of credit—are the most attractive candidates to receive loans. The private sector has become quite adept at serving creditworthy borrowers. This means that many of the people whom the private sector deems not to be creditworthy, in fact, may be people who cannot repay their loans and who therefore are unsuitable recipients of significant amounts of government credit. Government is limited to serving a sometimes narrow band of borrowers who do not receive appropriate access to private credit, but who are likely to be able to repay their government loans.

405

CH 12:
LOANS
AND
LOAN
GUARANTEES

Thus, a report of the Economic Research Service of the U.S. Department of Agriculture warns that high debt loads can limit the utility of federal credit as a way to encourage beginning farmers to purchase commercial farms.[34] Helen Dunlap, then HUD Deputy Assistant Secretary for Multifamily Housing, has made a similar point about the need for government to provide what she calls "equity" (i.e., carefully structured investments) to support rental housing for poor people, and not merely large amounts of federal credit.[35]

The GAO published a study, albeit on the basis of limited data, that reported that grant assistance was effective at reducing the college dropout rate of minority students and low-income students; assistance through federal student loans, by contrast, had no appreciable effect on dropout rates.[36] Whether a larger study would support this conclusion, the point remains: credit is not a remedy for the financial problems of those poor or otherwise disadvantaged people who have difficulty repaying their loans.

The experience of other countries in student loan programs bears out the problem of targeting credit in an equitable manner. In developing countries, issues of targeting include the problem of providing a government subsidy to members of a country's elite that do not need it, as well as the opposite problem, of imposing such stringent economic requirements that the most needy students do not qualify.[37]

In the United States, it is the middle class that seems to have been the largest beneficiary of credit programs, to finance suburban homes and student loans, for example. There appears to be a stratification of some loan markets. With exceptions, the private sector serves the most creditworthy borrowers, often without government assistance. Loan guarantee programs provide loans or serve borrowers with somewhat less credit strength, and direct loan programs, for example, for rural borrowers or disaster loans, tend to make loans that are of lower credit strength than guaranteed loans.

Horizontal equity raises the question of whether similar people or firms receive similar benefit from a program. For some programs, it would seem that some well-situated firms have tended to benefit disproportionately from particular agricultural or business loan programs. The ExIm Bank, for example, is working hard to expand its service to other firms so that it can offset its image as "Boeing's Bank."

Where the private market continues to exhibit shortcomings, federal credit programs can play a significant role. The home mortgage market of the United States, for example, continues to exhibit some discrimination, with respect to race and neighborhood. Here, FHA, VA, and the Rural Housing Service all help to improve horizontal equity, by serving greater proportions of racial minorities and disadvantaged communities than are served by lenders through conventional (i.e., nongovernment guaranteed) loans.

Legitimacy

Policymakers tend to favor credit programs over other tools such as grants because of the expectation that the recipients will repay their government loans. This gives government credit the attractive appearance of a businesslike activity.

When particular credit programs develop a substantial constituency, they can become very popular. For example, the single-family home loan programs of the FHA and VA are considered to have helped to finance the American dream in the suburbs after World War II.

Such success stories are harder to find today. Ginnie Mae, one of the most successful federal financial guarantee programs, is virtually ignored today, by the Congress and the media, and even by some parts of the mortgage industry that it has supported for many decades. In recent years, even well-managed credit programs such as those of the ExIm Bank and OPIC have had their legitimacy questioned, with charges that they represent "corporate welfare." Their very success suggests to some commentators, notably at think tanks with a conservative orientation, that their credit functions are best served by the private credit markets, without government intervention.

Perhaps the most popular federal credit programs today are the SBA disaster home loan and disaster business loan programs. In some sense, these programs are reminiscent of the Great Depression: they serve people and firms who previously were creditworthy but who have suddenly come upon hardship. In terms of legitimacy in the Congress and among the public, these would seem to be credit "worthy" people, in the sense of the legitimacy of their claim to receive government credit assistance.

When credit programs fail, they cause substantial defaults that hurt borrowers and that taxpayers must pay for. The Congress and the media are quick to pounce on such shortcomings. In 1970, for example, the House Banking Committee held an investigation and charged that the FHA "may be well on its way toward insuring itself into a national housing scandal."[38]

Shortly thereafter, the government first suspended and then terminated many of the criticized programs. Too often, housing credit programs seem to undergo cycles of enthusiasm as lenders and borrowers try out new programs, followed by disillusionment when they fail. On all of these issues of legitimacy, the particular context and performance of a credit program appear to be more significant than whether it provides direct loans or loan guarantees.

VII. FUTURE DIRECTIONS

Lester Salamon has written of tools of government that, "the key is to fit the tool to the nature of the task."[39] In the United States in today's economy, the available tasks for government credit are more diminished than ever before. This makes credit a tricky tool to apply, at least in this country.

Design of a high-quality credit program requires attention both to the quality of the institution that administers the program and also the financial soundness of the program itself. Perhaps most important, a well-designed credit agency or program, such as the WFC after World War I or a number of New Deal programs, will benefit from an exit strategy so that the program might end on a note of success rather than failure.

Despite some shortcomings in design and management of credit programs, they remain the source of over a trillion dollars of credit for people, firms, and other entities in the United States. The essential task for policymakers and program stakeholders today is to improve the design and management of credit programs and institutions and learn from past experience so that they can avoid incurring the kinds of substantial public costs that have toppled some programs in the past. When policymakers focus on this tool, they need to understand its particular demands and characteristics as a way to assure that credit programs continue to provide their public benefits for many years to come.

VIII. SUGGESTED READING

407

CH 12:
LOANS
AND
LOAN
GUARANTEES

Federal Publications

Federal Credit Policy Working Group, Office of Management and Budget, *Federal Credit Reform Tutorial.* A copy of this introduction to credit reform for credit managers, including case studies and an interactive teaching tool, is available at http://www.financenet.gov/financenet/fed/fcpwg/fcpwgtutorial.

Office of Management and Budget (for the current Fiscal Year), *Budget of the United States Government, [Fiscal Year]: Analytical Perspectives,* chap. 8, "Underwriting Federal Credit and Insurance." A copy of the Analytical Perspectives for FY 2001, including the credit and insurance chapter, is available at http://www.access.gpo.gov/usbudget/fy2001/pdf/spec.pdf. See also http://www.access.gpo.gov/usbudget/fy2001/pdf/credit.pdf.

Academic Studies

Stanton, Thomas H. Improving the Design and Administration of Federal Credit Programs." *The Financier: Analyses of Capital and Money Market Transactions* 3, no. 2 (May 1996): 7–21. A copy of this article is available at http://www.the-financier.com/finance/form.htm.

———. "Managing Federal Credit Programs in the Information Age: Opportunities and Risks." *The Financier: Analyses of Capital and Money Market Transactions* 5, no. 2 & 3 (summer/autumn 1998): 24–39. A copy of this article is available at http://www.the-financier.com/finance/form.htm.

———. "Credit Scoring and Loan Scoring as Tools for Improved Management of Federal Credit Programs." PwC Endowment for the Business of Government (1999). A copy of this report is available at http://www.endowment.pwcglobal.com.

Vandell, Kerry D. "FHA Restructuring Proposals: Alternatives and Implications." *Housing Policy Debate* 6, no. 2 (1995): 291–393.

NOTES

1. See "Primer on Credit Reform," published by the Federal Credit Policy Working Group, Office of Management and Budget, Federal Credit Reform Tutorial, at http://www.financenet.gov/financenet/fed/fcpwg/fcpwgtutorial.

2. Calvin Bradford, "Financing Home Ownership: The Federal Role in Neighborhood Decline," *Urban Affairs Quarterly* 14, no. 3 (March 1979): 313–335.

3. Hilbert Fefferman, "The Redlining of Neighborhoods by Mortgage Lending Institutions and What Can Be Done About It," *Redlining: A Special Report by FNMA* (Washington, D.C.: Federal National Mortgage Association, 1976), 27. Failed loan programs for farmers and some students show a similar effect of harming the borrowers that were the nominal beneficiaries of the credit program. See examples in Thomas H. Stanton, "Improving the Design and Administration of Federal Credit Programs," *The Financier: Analyses of Capital and Money Market Transactions* 3, no. 2 (May 1996): 7–21.

4. U.S. General Accounting Office, *Guidelines for Rescuing Large Failing Firms and Municipalities,* GAO/GGD–84–34 (March 29, 1984).

5. As one study observes: "Although the [guaranteed student loan] program makes heavy use of the nation's private credit system, the private banks in the program act not as sellers in a market system but as administrative agents in a centralized bureaucracy." Michael S. McPherson and Morton Owen Schapiro, *Keeping College Affordable* (Washington, D.C.: The Brookings Institution, 1991), 159–160. Since that statement was written, the student loan program has increased risk sharing with lenders, but only modestly.

6. Office of Management and Budget, Executive Office of the President, *Policies for Federal Credit Programs and Non-Tax Receivables,* Circular A-129 (Washington, D.C., 1993), 30.

7. Personal communication from Arthur Hauptman, consultant to the World Bank (May 2000).

8. Roy A. Foulke, *The Sinews of American Commerce* (New York: Dun & Bradstreet, 1941), 57.

9. Carter Goodrich, *Government Promotion of American Canals and Railroads 1800–1890* (New York: Columbia University, 1960), 13; Foulke, *The Sinews,* 211–212.

10. Woodbury Willoughby, *The Capital Issues Committee and War Finance Corporation* (Baltimore: Johns Hopkins, 1934), 48; James Stuart Olson, *Herbert Hoover and the Reconstruction Finance Corporation 1931–1933* (Ames: Iowa State University, 1977), 12.

11. R. J. Saulnier, Harold G. Halcrow, and Neil H. Jacoby, *Federal Lending and Loan Insurance* (Princeton, N.J.: Princeton University Press, 1958), 14–15, 58.

12. Jerry Mitchell, *The American Experiment With Government Corporations* (Armonk, N.Y.: M.E. Sharpe, 1999), 17; Donald Axelrod, *Shadow Government: The Hidden World of Public Authorities* (New York: Wiley, 1992).

13. James J. Mikesell and George B. Wallace, *Are Revolving Loan Funds a Better Way to Finance Rural Development?* Economic Research Service, U.S. Department of Agriculture. Agriculture Information Bulletin No. 724–05, October 1996; and John Petersen, *A Primer on State Bond Banks in the United States,* First Conference on Capital Market Development at the Subnational Level: Local Strategies to Access Financial Markets, Santander, Spain, 15 October 1998.

14. Government Housing Loan Corporation Web site at http://www.mof.go.jp/zaito/zaito99/kikan99_e/kikan99_10_e.htm.

15. Douglas B. Diamond, Jr. and Michael J. Lea, *Housing Finance in Developed Countries: An International Comparison of Efficiency,* Special Issue, *Journal of Housing Research* 3, no. 1 (1992).

16. James Tooley, *The Global Education Industry: Lessons from Private Education in Developing Countries* (Washington, D.C.: International Finance Corporation, 1999), 111.

17. See Nicholas Lardy, *China's Unfinished Economic Revolution* (Washington, D.C.: The Brookings Institution, 1998).

18. Frank Frost Abbott, *A History and Description of Roman Political Institutions,* 3d ed. (New York: Biblio and Tannen, 1963), 49.

19. George Heberton Evans, Jr., *British Corporation Finance 1775–1850: A Study of Preference Shares* (Baltimore: Johns Hopkins, 1936).

20. Thomas H. Stanton, "Credit Scoring and Loan Scoring: Tools for Improved Management of Federal Credit Programs" (Arlington, VA: PricewaterhouseCoopers Endowment, 1999).

21. Financial Management Service, U.S. Department of the Treasury, October 1–3, 1996, Workshop on Promising Practices: Transcribed Proceedings, IX-1. Transcripts of the three-day workshop are available at http://www.financenet.gov/financenet/fed/fcpwg/reports.htm; Thomas H. Stanton, "Managing Federal Credit Programs in the Information Age: Opportunities and Risks, *The Financier: Analyses of Capital and Money Market Transactions,* 5, nos. 2 & 3, (summer/autumn 1998): 24–39.

22. Financial Management Service, 1996, IX-4.

23. Lardy, *China's Unfinished,* 1998.

24. Office of Management and Budget (1993), 29.

25. *Inside Mortgage Finance,* "HMDA Data Show Denial Rates Edged Lower for All Racial Groups in Soaring Mortgage Market of 1998," (6 August 1999). Because of variations in the quality of reporting, HMDA data (required to be reported under the Home Mortgage Disclosure Act) can be taken only as rough approximations of the underlying statistics.

26. Elisabeth Holmes Rhyne, *Small Business, Banks, and SBA Loan Guarantees* (New York: Quorum, 1986), 26.

27. Rhyne, *Small Business,* 25.

28. Financial Management Service, U.S. Department of the Treasury, 1–3 October 1996.

29. Price Waterhouse, An Actuarial Review for Fiscal Year 1997 of the Federal Housing Administration's Mutual Mortgage Insurance Fund: Final Report (Washington, D.C., 19 February 1998), 7.

30. See, generally, Stanton, "Credit Scoring," 1999.

31. Office of Management and Budget, Executive Office of the President, "FY 1996 Passback:

Department of Housing and Urban Development" (Washington, D.C., 21 November 1994), 21–22.

409

CH 12:
LOANS
AND
LOAN
GUARANTEES

32. Economists have long observed that federal credit is a tool that works best to help overcome a market imperfection, but that it often is not an effective means of providing support for borrowers that have a significant risk of defaulting on their loans. Thus, economists summarized the track record of New Deal credit programs as follows:

First, it is fairly well established that the federal government had an exceptionally favorable record in those programs in which it refinanced debts that were in default during the economic depression of the thirties. The outstanding examples are the home mortgage refunding operations of the Home Owners' Loan Corporation and the farm mortgage refinancing carried out by the Land Bank Commissioner, both in the thirties. [T]he explanation for the favorable credit experience is that the borrowers for the most part were only temporarily embarrassed and economic recovery rather quickly put them back on their feet.

A second conclusion, equally well established, seems to be that the federal government has had an unfavorable credit experience when it has attempted to supply credit, sometimes during depression but even during periods of general economic prosperity, to business firms and farm enterprises unable—because of their newness, or owing to some weakness in financing position or management—to find financing on reasonable terms through private lenders. Large parts of the Reconstruction Finance Corporation's activities and certain of the programs in the agricultural field fall within this category.

R. J. Saulnier, Harold G. Halcrow, and Neil H. Jacoby, *Federal Lending and Loan Insurance* (Princeton, N.J.: Princeton University Press, 1958), 83.

33. See Kerry D. Vandell, "FHA Restructuring Proposals: Alternatives and Implications," *Housing Policy Debate* 6, no. 2 (1995): 291–393, for an excellent discussion of this and other proposals for increasing the capacity of FHA.

34. Charles Dodson, "Is More Credit the Best Way to Assist Beginning Low-Equity Farmers?" Economic Research Service, U.S. Department of Agriculture, Agriculture Information Bulletin No. 724–04 (August 1996).

35. Financial Management Service (1996), IX–20.

36. U.S. General Accounting Office, *Higher Education: Restructuring Student Aid Could Reduce Low-Income Student Dropout Rate,* GAO/HEHS 95–48 (Washington, D.C., March 1995).

37. Jamil Salmi, "Student Loans in an International Perspective: The World Bank Experience," draft working paper (Washington, D.C.: World Bank, 1999).

38. Quoted U.S. Department of Housing and Urban Development, *Housing in the Seventies,* Report of the National Housing Policy Review (Washington, D.C.: GPO, 1974), 83.

39. Lester M. Salamon, ed., with Michael S. Lund, *Beyond Privatization: The Tools of Government Action* (Washington, D.C.: Urban Institute Press, 1989), 18.

CHAPTER THIRTEEN

Tax Expenditures

Christopher Howard

On January 19, 1999, President Clinton delivered his annual State of the Union address to Congress and the nation. His talk that night was filled with policy proposals affecting nearly every function of government. At the top of his list were a series of initiatives designed to cope with a major demographic trend, the graying of America.[1]

> I was born in 1946, the first year of the baby boom. I can tell you that one of the greatest concerns of our generation is our absolute determination not to let our growing old place an intolerable burden on our children and their ability to raise our grandchildren. Our economic success and our fiscal discipline now give us an opportunity to lift that burden from their shoulders, and we should take it.

In addition to shoring up Social Security and Medicare, Clinton pledged to tackle the thorny problem of long-term care for the elderly. As the number and life expectancy of Americans had increased, so too had expenses for nursing home care. A year's stay at a nursing home could easily cost $20,000–30,000, and private insurance coverage was too expensive for most people to afford. Many of the elderly thus faced a difficult choice: they could spend down their life's savings to pay for a nursing home bed, then enroll in the means-tested Medicaid program, or they could move in with their adult children, which would often cause financial and emotional strain within the extended family. Recognizing that long-term care was a pressing issue for millions of Americans, Clinton proposed a $1,000 annual tax credit for the ailing elderly and those family members who cared for them. He argued that the nation's growing prosperity made such a move easily affordable.

A generation earlier, President Lyndon Baines Johnson also tried to harness a strong economy to benefit the nation's elderly. His approach was fundamentally different from Clinton's. The new (1965) Medicaid program created under Johnson was targeted at the elderly poor and paid for virtually all of their nursing home costs. Clinton's tax credit proposal was aimed more at the middle classes, broadly defined. Partly because the number of potential tax credit recipients was greater, the value per person was far less. The other obvious difference concerns the policy tool each president favored. Johnson created new forms of direct spending (Medicare, Medicaid) that would be administered by new bureaucracies. Clinton proposed new tax expenditures that relied on an existing bureaucracy, namely, the Treasury Department and the Internal Revenue Service (IRS).

The same pattern can be seen with respect to other policy domains. Whereas Johnson helped to enact Head Start and the Elementary and Secondary Education Act, Clinton advocated a variety of tax credits and tax deductions for child care and higher education. When Johnson wanted to reduce unemployment in the nation's cities, he created the Job Corps. Clinton, by contrast, proposed extending a package of tax credits and loan guarantees to private companies that moved some of their operations to distressed neighborhoods.

Clinton's speech that night reflected a more general trend in policymaking. During the 1990s, when elected officials wanted to tackle problems as diverse as boosting the incomes of the working poor, encouraging the use of alcohol fuels, making health insurance and college tuition more affordable, lengthening investors' time horizons, and lowering unemployment, they reached again and again for the tax expenditure tool.[2] It would be misleading to suggest that the Clinton administration somehow discovered tax expenditures. President Bush used this tool for his health care and urban policies, and President Carter did likewise with respect to energy and the environment. Indeed, tax credits and tax deductions have existed for most of the twentieth century. Nevertheless, they have become far more prominent in recent policy debates, and their current size and scope demand attention.

Increased reliance on a policy tool, however, does not always reflect a thorough understanding of that tool. Tax deductions and tax credits, part of a larger category called tax expenditures, have become more important in recent years despite repeated criticisms by policy experts in and out of government. Tax expenditures are frequently cited as classic examples of good politics but bad policy: easily enacted, largely hidden from view, seldom cut back, transferring billions of dollars to powerful but undeserving constituencies. These criticisms are justified in many cases, not proved in other cases, and sometimes just wrong. Under certain conditions, tax expenditures may be a reasonable choice, and some of the problems with this tool can be ameliorated. The purpose of this chapter is to help readers understand better how tax expenditures work, how they might work better, and why they are such a popular tool.

I. DEFINING TAX EXPENDITURES

A tax expenditure is a provision in tax law that usually encourages certain behavior by individuals or corporations by deferring, reducing, or eliminating their tax obligation. By using this tool, the government pursues its objectives, not by spending the tax dollars it collects, but rather by allowing individuals or corporations to keep and spend dollars they would otherwise owe the government. As legally defined, tax expenditures are "those revenue losses attributable to provisions of the federal tax laws which allow a special exclusion, exemption, or deduction from gross income or which provide a special credit, a preferential rate of tax or a deferral of tax liability."[3]

Defining Features

The definition of tax expenditures involves a number of key issues. The first of these concerns which tax laws are covered. The legislative history of the 1974 Budget Act, which formally defined tax expenditures and mandated publication of an annual tax expenditure budget, made it clear that the concept applied only to corporate and individual *income* taxes. Since then, the Treasury Department has produced a list of tax expenditures linked to estate and gift taxes, and some analysts have suggested ways of extending the concept to payroll and excise taxes, but the overwhelming focus in policy debates has been on income taxes.[4] Familiar examples include the home mortgage interest deduction and the dependent and child care tax credit.[5]

A second and equally fundamental issue involves identifying the "special" deviations from the "normal" tax system that constitute tax expenditures. Since 1974, the official estimates of tax expenditures in the United States have excluded the standard deduction, personal exemptions for taxpayers and their dependents, and graduated individual income tax rates. These are all considered part of the normal tax system.[6] What else is contained in the normal tax system is ambiguous enough that the U.S. government publishes two similar but not identical lists of tax expenditures—one by the Treasury Department and the other by the Joint Committee on Taxation (JCT) in Congress. Moreover, the two agencies use different economic assumptions to estimate the cost of these tax expenditures.[7]

Such differences are even greater internationally, making cross-national comparisons of tax expenditures especially difficult. Canada, France, and the United Kingdom count special exemptions to their value added taxes, which apply to items such as groceries and prescription drugs, as tax expenditures. Comparable provisions help offset some American states' sales taxes, but do not apply at the national level. Some European countries count various forms of family allowances as part of their tax baseline, and some countries do not. A few compute the imputed rental income from home ownership as a tax expenditure, but most do not. When these differences are combined with countries' competing methods for calculating depreciation allowances and the tax benefits for pensions, it is understandable why the Organisation for Economic Co-operation and Development (OECD) has chosen to publish individual country profiles and refrain from explicit comparisons among countries.[8]

Relation to Key Tool Features

Tax expenditures can usefully be compared to other tools of government action in terms of key characteristics: *coerciveness, directness, automaticity,* and *visibility.*

Coerciveness

Coerciveness measures the extent to which a tool restricts individual or group behavior as opposed to merely encouraging or discouraging it. Tax expenditures appeal to many policymakers because they appear to entail little coercion. The national government wants to encourage manufacturers to modernize, so it enables companies to accelerate depreciation of machinery and equipment. Companies are not compelled to upgrade their equipment, but if they do the government may help underwrite the costs. Likewise, the government does not require employers to offer health insurance and retirement pensions to their workers, but those who do may be able to deduct those costs as business expenses when computing their taxable income.

The phrases "may help underwrite" and "may be able to deduct" are important to understand, for the government often attaches quite specific, and quite complicated, eligibility rules to tax expenditures. This is essential if government officials want to reward specific kinds of behavior. Employers who do not like the government's rules stipulating, for instance, which employees should get pensions and health insurance within their firm, do not have to modify their behavior unless they want to claim the related tax benefits. Tax expenditures thus entice individuals and corporations to behave in socially desirable ways, but they do not compel such behavior.[9]

Nevertheless, not all tax expenditures operate as incentives.[10] While the majority of Social Security retirement pensions are excluded from income taxation, this tax expenditure does not entice more people to enroll in Social Security; individuals are compelled to participate in Social Security, and the tax expenditure helps to preserve the value of their pensions. Similar tax treatment is extended to recipients of disability insurance, survivors' insurance, workers' compensation, and a variety of veterans' benefits. Individuals with extraordinarily high out-of-pocket medical expenses can gain some relief through the tax code, and clearly the government is not trying to encourage this behavior.

Directness measures the extent to which the entity authorizing or inaugurating a program is involved in carrying it out. Tax expenditures are highly indirect. For the most part, the government uses tax expenditures to encourage individuals and corporations to buy homes, health insurance policies, heavy equipment, and the like from other individuals and corporations. The combination of public financing and private delivery marks these tax expenditures as classic examples of "third party government," much like loan guarantees.[11] This means that government officials can make only educated guesses about how much tax expenditures will cost and who will receive them, because the decision to claim benefits rests with taxpayers and their tax advisors. The indirectness of tax expenditures contributes to their uncontrollability. It also makes third-party providers a key political constituency.

In a minority of cases, the government uses the tax code to subsidize goods it provides directly, as with Social Security and the other benefit programs described above. Two other programs that fall into this category are the Earned Income Tax Credit (EITC), which is a direct cash transfer to the working poor, and the child tax credit; neither are connected to the purchase of a specific good or service. These tax expenditures are closer to direct government because benefits are publicly financed and publicly delivered. The decision to claim these benefits still rests with individual taxpayers who must complete the required tax forms, however.

Automaticity

Automaticity measures the extent to which a tool utilizes an existing administrative structure to produce its effect rather than having to create its own special administrative apparatus. Tax expenditures are in theory highly automatic. From an administrative perspective, new tax expenditures can be grafted onto the existing income tax system; they rely on existing government bureaucracies (primarily the IRS) and existing procedures for collecting taxes. This feature makes tax expenditures attractive to many policymakers, who believe that aid can be given quickly and without costly government red tape. From a budgetary perspective, the benefits of tax expenditures flow automatically. Tax expenditures function like budgetary entitlements, and occasionally they are referred to as tax entitlements. Spending on tax expenditures is not subject to the annual appropriations process in Congress, and spending on individual provisions is not capped. Once the tax laws have defined eligibility rules and methods for calculating benefits, tax expenditures are available to all who qualify.[12] This feature of the tool draws mixed reviews, depending on whether one favors or opposes special budgetary treatment for certain programs and policy objectives.

Visibility

Visibility measures the extent to which the resources devoted to the tool show up in the normal budget process. The visibility of tax expenditures has changed significantly over time, a reminder that policy attributes are not inherent or fixed.[13] One turning point occurred in the late 1960s and early 1970s. Before this point, no comprehensive list of tax expenditures existed. New programs were seldom subjected to broad or informed deliberation, and existing programs were rarely subjected to a rigorous evaluation.[14] Occasionally, the government investigated the extent of fraud surrounding an individual tax expenditure, but otherwise this tool was largely invisible. After 1974, tax expenditures were formally incorporated in budget documents and the budget process. New tax expenditures started to attract more attention from the media and members of Congress. Calls for periodic review and sunset laws were voiced occasionally. Even so, the visibility of tax expenditures was nothing like that of direct government, grants, or regulations. Congressional hearings and votes on individual programs were still rare, as were program evaluations.

A further turning point occurred in 1990, with enactment of the Budget Enforcement Act (BEA). Designed to hold the federal deficit in check, the BEA imposed pay-as-you-go rules on all new entitlements, including those delivered indirectly through the tax code. Put simply, any new or expanded tax expenditure had to be offset by a tax increase or spending cut.[15] The act's potential to make tax expenditures more visible was partially undermined by its initial design: it did little to cap the growth of existing, unmodified tax expenditures (or existing direct expenditures, for that matter). In addition, subsequent improvement in the economy—the rapid decline in the deficit and subsequent projections of record surpluses for years to come—made creating or expanding tax expenditures less of a zero-sum game, and thus somewhat less visible. Although such comparisons are subjective, it seems reasonable to conclude that tax expenditures are now more visible than loan guarantees and insurance and considerably less visible than regulations, grants, and direct government. This holds true whether one considers government officials, the media, or the general public to be the relevant viewing audience.

Major Variants

Tax expenditures are not so much a single policy tool as a family of closely related tools. Policymakers need to be aware of certain options when designing a tax expenditure.

1. *Taxable income versus tax liability.* Perhaps the most basic distinction is between tax expenditures that reduce taxable income and those that reduce tax liability. To reduce taxable income, policymakers create deductions, exemptions, or special exclusions. In some cases, it does not matter much which route is taken. However, in the case of deductions from the individual income tax, it does matter. Policymakers must decide whether to allow them to stand alone or be grouped with several itemized deductions, such as for home mortgage interest and charitable contributions. Itemized deductions are valuable only if the sum total is greater than the standard deduction, which as mentioned before is considered part of the baseline tax system. Itemized deductions tend to benefit more affluent taxpayers, who can afford to engage in enough tax-favored activities to exceed the standard deduction.

   To reduce tax liability, policymakers also have several options. They can establish lower tax rates, as is done with capital gains on assets held over a year. They can defer the tax liability until a later year, as is done with the investment income on company-based retirement pensions. They can create tax credits that are deducted from tax liability rather than taxable income; the new child credit is a good example. Whereas a tax deferral functions like a loan, a tax credit functions like an outlay. Finally, they can create a refundable tax credit, which not only reduces the taxes that certain taxpayers owe, but actually generates a cash rebate from the treasury. The EITC, and to a lesser extent the child tax credit, are the only existing examples of this option.[16]

   To see how the specific design of a tax expenditure matters, suppose that the national government wanted to use tax expenditures to increase the number of people with medical insurance.[17] Consider the case of a fictional self-employed worker earning $30,000 and paying 20 percent in income taxes. Without any tax expenditures, her income tax liability is $6,000. Now imagine that she purchases a health insurance plan for $3,000. If 50 percent of the premiums count as a *tax deduction,* then her taxable income would be reduced by $1,500 to $28,500. Her new tax liability would be $5,700 ($28,500 × 20 percent) and she would save $300 in taxes. On the other hand, if 50 percent of the premiums can be applied directly as a *tax credit,* then her tax liability would drop from $6,000 to $4,500 and she would save $1,500. A 50 percent tax credit would generate a much larger subsidy than a 50 percent tax deduction, which in this case could mean the difference between purchasing or not purchasing health insurance.

2. *Targeting of benefits.* Regardless of which type of tax expenditure is chosen, policymakers must decide how precisely to target the program. The more narrowly programs are targeted, the less likely they are to waste benefits, but the more difficult they are to determine eligibility. For example, state and local governments may want to give companies tax incentives for creating jobs. If they make the program available to all, then fast-growing companies that would have hired new workers anyway will be getting unnecessary subsidies. So policymakers might choose to target firms growing faster than the national average. Because at any given time some industries are growing faster than others, perhaps the program should be targeted at firms that exceed their industry average; adding ten new jobs at carpet mill might be more significant than twenty new jobs at a software firm. If public officials want to attract "good" jobs, perhaps they should limit the incentive to all new employees earning at least 150 percent of the minimum wage and remaining with the firm for at least six months. Or maybe it is important that new jobs be located in certain areas, such as poor rural counties or inner cities.

   In practice, the targeting of tax expenditures varies tremendously. At one end of the spectrum we find the deduction for personal property taxes. The only restriction there is that the tax be based on the value of the property (rather than, say, the weight of a vehicle). The instructions require but a brief paragraph in the Instructions for Schedule A, Itemized Deductions. At the other end of the spectrum are the rules governing company-based retirement pensions. Policymakers have attached literally hundreds of conditions to this tax expenditure, partly to ensure that pensions are widely available within the company and not limited to senior officials (i.e., nondiscrimination rules), and partly to ensure that pension funds are managed wisely. The resulting basic Form 5500, schedules, and accompanying instructions for employers are longer and more complex than virtually the entire individual income tax code. They require a veritable army of accountants, actuaries, tax lawyers, and benefits specialists to complete.

3. *Longevity.* The final variant in design is longevity. Individual tax expenditures usually remain permanent features of the tax code until someone makes a deliberate effort to terminate them, which seldom happens. John Witte identified twenty tax expenditures that had been created between 1909 and 1978 and never been modified, much less terminated.[18] Whenever sunset provisions or similar measures have been discussed for existing tax expenditures, business interests have countered that major investment and production decisions require a high level of predictability. They may not buy new machinery if they are constantly worrying whether the relevant tax expenditure will expire in a year. Similar arguments have been advanced concerning the tax benefits for retirement pensions and home ownership, which have long time horizons.

A handful of tax expenditures are temporary rather than permanent, and thus need periodic reauthorization. In 1998, for example, Congress extended for one year a tax credit for qualified corporate research expenses and two tax credits designed to increase employment among former welfare recipients and other categories of disadvantaged workers.[19] Occasionally, the status of a tax expenditure changes. The EITC started out as a temporary tax expenditure in 1975 and was made permanent in 1978. The Tax Reform Act of 1986 eliminated a few permanent measures, such as the deductibility of state and local sales taxes. By and large though, tax expenditures start out permanent and remain that way. They may well be modified, but they will endure.

II. PATTERNS OF TOOL USE

Tax expenditures are used to carry out almost all of the basic functions of government. Table 13-1 provides some overall estimates of the size of tax expenditures by budget function. It should be noted that technical objections exist to adding tax expenditures together (see Box 13-1). Leaving those objections aside, we can see that the overall volume is huge. For fiscal year 2000, tax expenditures are estimated to cost the national government the outlay equivalent of $745 billion. The total budget for direct expenditures, by comparison, is an estimated $1,790 billion, or roughly 2.5 times the size of the tax expenditure budget.

The use of tax expenditures varies by function. In some areas, such as defense, agriculture, and the administration of justice, they are used relatively little or not at all. Tax expenditures are much more significant in health ($113 billion) and income security ($149 billion). In international affairs, energy, and education/training/employment/social services, the cost of tax expenditures surpasses that of direct expenditures. And in one notable instance, commerce and housing, indirect spending through the tax code positively dwarfs what is done through traditional spending channels ($264 billion compared with $6 billion in direct expenditures).

What really stands out about tax expenditures is how many of them parallel functions commonly associated with the modern welfare state.[20] If we add tax expenditures for health, income security, Social Security, education, training, employment, social services, and housing (not commerce), we arrive at a figure of $480 billion, or almost two-thirds of all tax expenditures. This represents about 45 percent of direct expenditures on these functions through programs such as Medicare, Medicaid, Social Security, and Food Stamps. Clearly, one cannot have a meaningful discussion of U.S. social policy without including tax expenditures.

Who Benefits?

The data presented in Table 13-1 help to challenge one common misperception about tax expenditures. For decades, special exceptions to the tax code have been portrayed as the province of corporate interests and affluent individuals. In an oft-cited example from the 1950s, movie mogul Louis B. Mayer managed to secure an amendment to the tax laws that, while appearing neutral, applied only to him.[21] More recently, discussions of "corporate welfare" have made headlines.[22] As Republicans have pushed to cut means-tested programs for the poor and balance the budget, a number of Democrats have called attention to the billions of dollars in subsidies received by major U.S. corporations, often concealed from public view and imbedded in the tax code. Two of the more prominent critics have been the Clinton Administration's first Labor Secretary, Robert Reich, who framed the issue in terms of equity and fairness, and the Progressive Policy Institute, which deemed these subsidies an inefficient use of scarce resources.[23]

Budget Function	Tax Expenditures	Direct Expenditures
National defense	2.5	291.0
International affairs	19.3	17.0
General science, space, technology	3.4	19.0
Energy	2.7	− 2.0
Natural resources and the environment	1.8	24.0
Agriculture	1.1	32.0
Commerce and housing	264.3	6.0
Transportation	2.6	47.0
Community and regional development	1.8	11.0
Education, training, employment, and social services	76.6	63.0
Health	113.3	154.0
Medicare	0	203.0
Income security	149.4	251.0
Social Security	24.5	407.0
Veterans benefits and services	3.3	47.0
Administration of justice	0	27.0
General government	0	15.0
General purpose fiscal assistance	76.9	0
Interest	1.0	220.0
Other	0	− 42.0
TOTAL	744.5	1,790.0

Note: Negative spending means that receipts exceed outlays. General purpose fiscal assistance consists primarily of the exclusion of interest on public purpose bonds and the deductibility of state and local taxes other than on owner-occupied homes.

*Estimated outlays for FY 2000 in billions of dollars.
SOURCE: U.S. Office of Management and Budget, *Analytical Perspectives, Budget of the United States Government, Fiscal Year 2001* (Washington, D.C.: Government Printing Office, 2000). Accessed via http://www.access.gpo.gov/usbudget/fy2001/pdf/spec.pdf; U.S. Office of Management and Budget, *A Citizen's Guide to the Federal Budget* (Washington, D.C.: Government Printing Office, 2000). Accessed via http://www.access.gpo.gov/usbudget/fy2001/pdf/guide.pdf.

This characterization of tax expenditures is not so much wrong as misleading. It is true that at the national level, business interests benefit from a wide variety of tax expenditures. There are general provisions underwriting corporate investment in new plant and equipment; there are specific provisions aimed at timber growers, oil and gas producers, and life insurance companies.[24] Compared with other OECD nations, the United States appears to target tax incentives to specific industries much more often. They are a key reason why "the American tax code [is] by far the most complicated and particularistic in the world."[25] These are not, however, the largest items in the tax expenditure budget. The annual cost of most of these provisions is less than $1 billion, which in the realm of the U.S. tax system amounts to a rounding error. If we add all the tax expenditures for commerce, energy, and agriculture in FY 2000, we get around $150 billion. That is a sizable sum, but it is far less than the sum of tax expenditures with social policy objectives.

This point becomes more evident when we look in more detail at the most significant tax expenditures at the national level. The twelve largest tax expenditures accounted for over $550 billion, or three-quarters of all such expenditures in FY 2000. As shown in Table 13-2, their size ranges from $20 billion to over $100 billion. To put these figures in some perspective, consider that the deductibility of charitable contributions, the tenth-largest item on this list, will cost as much as *all* direct expenditures for science,

---

BOX 13-1 *Calculating Tax Expenditures: A Caveat*

Many of the comparisons made between major categories of tax expenditures, and between tax expenditures and direct expenditures, rely on aggregate figures. The Treasury list of tax expenditures includes some 130 individual items, and for ease of presentation I have combined them in the text. Nevertheless, the addition of individual tax expenditures is problematic. Both the Treasury and the congressional Joint Committee on Taxation (JCT) routinely attach language to their estimates that caution against the addition and subtraction of tax expenditures. The main reasons reflect the interdependent nature of many parts of the tax code and the uncertainty of behavioral responses to changes in the code. Deductions for charitable contributions offer a concrete illustration of these problems. Currently, a corporation that sponsors a show on public television can enter the amount as a charitable contribution on its tax returns. If the tax laws governing such contributions were somehow tightened, the company might instead enter the amount as a business expense (advertising), and the total revenue loss to the national treasury could be virtually unchanged. By the same token, if such laws governing individual contributions were tightened, some individuals might find it more advantageous to take the standard deduction, and itemized deductions for home mortgage interest and state and local taxes therefore might diminish.

In practice, adding and subtracting tax expenditures is quite common, even among tax experts.[1] One justification for doing so is that the sums are so enormous that they could contain significant errors and still permit some meaningful observations. For aggregate comparisons like those based on Table 13-2, a ballpark figure may be sufficient. It is also likely that some of the errors in totaling tax expenditures cancel each other out. Another justification is that all such estimates of government spending are imprecise. If the national government reduced benefits for Social Security, more of the elderly might apply for Supplemental Security Income and Food Stamps; if the national government canceled a weapons program, additional monies for the affected defense contractors and communities would likely be found. And yet we accept addition and subtraction of direct spending items in the budget. If these reasons are unpersuasive, perhaps it would help to know that Stanley Surrey, the father of the tax expenditure concept, did not hesitate to sum up these provisions.[2]

---

[1] Graetz, *Decline (and Fall?) of the Income Tax*, 235; Witte, *Politics and Development of the Federal Income Tax*, 288–298; Steinmo, *Taxation and Democracy*, 143; GAO, *Tax Expenditures Deserve More Scrutiny*, 33–38; Christopher Bergin, "Spending through the Tax Code: The Top Ten Tax Expenditures," *Tax Notes* 82, no. 8 (1999): 1100.

[2] Stanley S. Surrey and Paul R. McDaniel, *Tax Expenditures* (Cambridge, Mass.: Harvard University Press, 1985), 33–36, 51–53.

space, and technology that year. Accelerated depreciation of machinery and equipment (#9) will cost more than *all* direct expenditures for natural resources and the environment. The home mortgage interest deduction (#3) will cost more than *all* direct expenditures for veterans benefits, or transportation. The only parts of the traditional budget larger than the major tax expenditures are Social Security, national defense, interest on the debt, Medicare, and Medicaid.[26]

While retirement pensions ($104 billion) and medical benefits ($96 billion) have long been among the most expensive tax expenditures, they have seldom been cited as examples of corporate welfare, and with good reason. These parts of the tax code appear to provide for legitimate social needs rather than enhance corporate profits. Two other provisions benefit home owners, and a related provision (not shown) concerning the deductibility of state and local property taxes on owner-occupied homes ($22 billion) would rank number thirteen on the list. Although one could argue that the favorable treatment of capital gains is an indirect benefit to financial institutions and other corporate interests, it is individual taxpayers who benefit directly. Similarly, it would be difficult to see Machiavellian intrigue behind tax deductions for charitable contributions or interest on public purpose bonds. About the only item on this list that clearly fits with the stereotypical image of tax expenditures is the accelerated depreciation of machinery and equipment, which is not even one-half the size of the subsidies for retirement pensions, health insurance, or home mortgage interest. These figures could be way off, and the basic message would remain the same: tax expenditures do much, much more than favor certain industries, or business more generally.

TABLE 13-2 *Major Tax Expenditures**

Provision	FY 2000	FY 2001–2005
Net exclusion of employer pension contributions and earnings	$104.1	$602.3
Exclusion of employer contributions for medical insurance premiums and medical care	96.0	583.4
Home mortgage interest deduction	58.8	331.2
Capital gains (except agriculture, timber, iron ore, and coal)	54.1	295.6
Deductibility of state and local taxes (other than on owner-occupied homes)	40.2	238.7
Step-up basis of capital gains at death	36.1	203.9
Exclusion of interest on public purpose bonds	32.9	169.6
Earned income tax credit (including refund)	30.9	167.8
Accelerated depreciation of machinery and equipment	27.7	174.1
Deductibility of charitable contributions	27.0	154.2
Child tax credit (including refund)	25.7	138.7
Capital gains exclusion on home sales	23.2	126.7
TOTAL	556.7	3,186.2

Note: The child tax credit is distinct from the child and dependent care tax credit, although eligibility for one is linked to the other.

*Estimated budget outlay equivalent in billions of dollars.

SOURCE: U.S. Office of Management and Budget, *Budget of the United States Government, Fiscal Year 2001* (2000). Accessed via http://www.access.gpo.gov/usbudget/fy2001.

International Comparisons

Because of differences in how countries define and measure tax expenditures, it is hard to say precisely the U.S. experience with this tool compares to that elsewhere. Based on OECD data and his own calculations, Greve compared the prevalence of tax expenditures in eleven countries circa 1990. The United States appears about average, although the variation among countries is often quite large. Tax expenditures equaled 6 percent of GDP in the United States, about the same as Canada, Italy, and Sweden (5 percent), but significantly less than in Finland (14 percent) or Denmark (16 percent). As a percent of total public-sector expenditure, tax expenditures in the United States (16 percent) ranked above Germany (3 percent), Sweden (7 percent), Canada (10 percent), and Italy (11 percent) and behind the United Kingdom (22 percent), Ireland (23 percent), Denmark (26 percent), and Finland (37 percent).[27]

Other similarities can be observed at lower levels of aggregation. In most affluent democracies, for example, tax expenditures benefiting specific industries seldom if ever outweigh tax expenditures with social welfare objectives. Favorable treatment of retirement pensions is among the largest tax expenditures in Australia, Austria, Belgium, Canada, the United Kingdom, and the United States. Accelerated depreciation of machinery and equipment is among the largest business subsidies in many countries. One unsurprising difference is that tax expenditures for medical care are more important in the United States than abroad.[28] This finding is rooted in the absence of national health insurance and the heavy reliance on employment-based health insurance in the United States. Similarly, tax expenditures for charitable donations appear to be more significant in the United States than abroad, in part because of the greater role of the voluntary sector in meeting social needs.[29]

State and Local Comparisons

The equation of tax expenditures with corporate welfare is more credible at the level of the American states. Unfortunately, definitive statements are not possible because no master list of state tax expenditures exists. According to the National Association of State Budget Officers, only twelve states produce a tax expenditure report, and they differ in how they define tax expenditures.[30] What is clear is that state and local governments routinely offer tax incentives to attract and keep businesses within their jurisdiction. Some of these provisions apply broadly, as in tax exemptions for manufacturers' inventories, research and development, and new job creation. Others are targeted at specific industries or firms, such as a new auto assembly plant or microchip facility; these measures tend to be combined with loans, loan guarantees, or below-market sales of land to attract new employers. The Council of State Governments publishes a useful compendium of these tax expenditures, noting what kinds of incentives are available in each state but not how much is spent on each.[31]

Origins and Recent Trends

The first tax expenditure budget published in 1969 included several dozen items, evidence that tax incentives predated the formal acceptance of the tax expenditure concept. In fact, special exceptions to the tax code have been created throughout the twentieth century. Deductions for home mortgage interest, real estate taxes, state and local taxes, and casualty losses, and the exclusion of interest from public purpose bonds were all part of the first individual income tax passed in 1913. The charitable deduction dates from 1917, and lower tax rates for capital gains began in 1921. According to Witte, twenty-seven new tax expenditures were created between 1909 and 1919, eighteen between 1920 and 1945, twenty-four between 1946 and 1969, and twenty-two between 1970 and 1982—an average of more than one new tax expenditure per year. Although the rate of growth appears to have accelerated since 1970, it is important to remember that virtually all of the major tax expenditures listed in Table 13-2 were already in place by then.[32] The only new tax expenditures of any magnitude in the last few decades have been the EITC (1975) and the child tax credit (1997).

Measured in any number of ways, U.S. tax expenditures have grown considerably over the last few decades. Compared with the late 1960s, the number of individual tax expenditures has more than doubled. In 1967, the first year that government statistics are available, the total cost of tax expenditures was roughly $35 billion.[33] Expressed in constant dollars, the cost in 1967 was closer to $170 billion. The comparable figure for 2000 is over $630 billion, meaning that the real cost has more than tripled. The revenue loss attributable to tax expenditures in 1967 equaled almost 40 percent of total income taxes collected by the national government that year; by 2000, this figure is expected to be 55 percent. What this means, of course, is that tax rates are higher to support the current level of government activity than if tax expenditures were abolished. Expressed as a fraction of GDP, tax expenditures grew from 3.65 to 6.60 percent between 1967 and 2000. Most of the growth has been due to programs with long histories. A recent GAO study found that "almost 85 percent of 1993 tax expenditure revenue losses are attributable to tax expenditures listed before 1950, and almost 50 percent of these revenue losses stem from tax expenditures enacted before 1920."[34]

The reasons why tax expenditures have grown are complex. In some cases, such as the EITC, Congress and the president have deliberately expanded eligibility and increased benefits. The more common, and perhaps more troubling, pattern is for tax expenditures to grow accidentally or without explicit choice. When policymakers allowed the real value of the standard deduction to fall during the 1950s and 1960s, they effectively increased the number and value of itemized deductions for home mortgage interest and charitable contributions. When policymakers raised income tax rates on the rich in 1990 and 1993, few noticed that they had also increased the value of many tax expenditures claimed by the rich, since a tax deduction is worth more when the marginal tax rate is 40 percent than when it is 35 percent.

As is true of other entitlements, economic and demographic forces—such as inflation in the goods being subsidized, or the aging of the baby boom cohort—have served as important engines of expansion. As health care grows more expensive, so do health insurance premiums and thus the tax deductions for employers' health-care costs. As more people age and become eligible for Social Security, more people claim the tax exemptions for Social Security benefits. These forces are so strong that some tax expenditures (e.g., corporate retirement pensions, home mortgage interest) have expanded *despite* legislated changes that restricted eligibility.[35]

Growth has been the norm but not the rule. Tax expenditures are occasionally cut back or eliminated. The most important examples in recent years were contained in the Tax Reform Act of 1986. The act repealed the investment tax credit for businesses as well as deductions for long-term capital gains, two-earner married couples, state sales taxes, and interest on nonmortgage consumer debt. It restricted existing tax expenditures for accelerated depreciation, home mortgage interest, contributions to Individual Retirement Accounts (IRAs), and to employer pensions. These changes enabled policymakers to lower income tax rates without adding to the deficit. Lower tax rates, however, meant lower revenue losses for several measures that were unchanged— deductibility of state and local income taxes, real estate taxes, charitable contributions, and employer-provided medical benefits.[36] The Congressional Budget Office has estimated that the combined effect of these direct and indirect cuts would lower the total cost of tax expenditures by over $200 billion in FY 1991.[37] Those estimates later proved too optimistic, for policymakers ever since 1986 have reversed course and favored new and expanded tax expenditures.

III. BASIC MECHANICS

The policy process for tax expenditures is intimately tied to tax policy more generally. As such, it involves three basic steps.

Step 1: Enactment

The journey begins in Congress, where by law all revenue measures must originate. When tax expenditures are enacted or modified, most of the activity is confined to the Senate Finance Committee and the House Ways and Means Committee, which have exclusive jurisdiction over tax matters in their respective chambers. These committees receive technical support from staff at the JCT and the Congressional Budget Office. Because legislative committees tend to be organized by policy domain (e.g., agriculture, commerce, veterans affairs), and because other tools cut across policies, congressional jurisdiction over other tools is more widely dispersed. Likewise, while grants and regulations are administered by dozens of executive agencies, tax expenditures are essentially the sole responsibility of the Treasury Department and its Internal Revenue Service. One justification for this pattern is that taxation is a highly specialized field, requiring advanced training in accounting, actuarial science, and tax law. It is portrayed as a job best left to a relatively small group of experts in the legislature and executive.

Historically, Congress has been the most common source of new and modified tax expenditures.[38] Proposals to create or modify tax expenditures must go through the Ways and Means and Finance committees and be passed in identical form by both houses of Congress and signed into law by the president. Rarely if ever are tax expenditures considered as stand-alone bills. They are bundled in larger revenue or tax reform bills, in which they are usually but a small component. In theory, new tax expenditures, like all new entitlements, must be revenue neutral, a requirement that originated with the 1990 Budget Enforcement Act. In practice, legislators have started to bend these rules; the elimination of the deficit and appearance of budget surpluses have made strict fiscal discipline less imperative.

Step 2: Regulations and Forms

Once tax expenditures have been enacted, the action shifts to the bureaucratic arena. The Treasury and IRS must issue specific regulations, tax forms, and accompanying instructions, and somehow make these changes known to taxpayers.[39] Although less visible to the general public and the media, these steps are crucial in determining who gets what, and when.

It is important to note that while the tax bureaucracies often respond to tax legislation, they also issue tax regulations that are internally generated. The latter are referred to as interpretive regulations and "are issued under the general authority of section 7805 [of the Internal Revenue Code] that requires promulgation of 'all needful rules and regulations for the enforcement' of the code."[40] The idea for these regulations may come from a single Treasury official, IRS field agents, tax professionals, or taxpayers.

Action on interpretive regulations cannot begin without formal approval from senior officials within the IRS and the Treasury.

Whether issuing legislative or interpretive regulations, the IRS and Treasury follow essentially the same process: issue a notice of proposed rulemaking in the *Federal Register,* obtain public input, issue final regulations, and then make the necessary changes to tax forms and instructions. In several respects this process parallels that for social and economic regulations. Depending on the subject, the whole process can take anywhere from several weeks to several years. Years are needed not only when the legislated change is complicated, but also when the change has implications for other provisions of the tax code. Considering the large number of extant tax expenditures, the odds are good that any new change will have ripple effects elsewhere in the code. If quick action is needed, the IRS may issue temporary regulations along with the initial notice of proposed rulemaking, and make temporary changes to the relevant tax forms. These temporary regulations have the force of law and are in effect until they are withdrawn or replaced by final regulations. By law, temporary regulations expire after three years.

The process of drafting proposed, temporary, and final regulations is delegated to a team of IRS and Treasury bureaucrats, the core of which are tax attorneys. According to Stratton, these teams reflect the competing orientations of the two agencies: "The Treasury attorney-advisers tend to be recent recruits from the private sector, who bring 'a fresh perspective from the outside. . . .' The IRS attorneys bring technical expertise from having worked on the same issue for a number of years, and from exposure to what the agents are seeing in the field in appeals" (1997: 544–545).[41] Public comment is mandatory for legislative, but not interpretive regulations. The IRS must give at least thirty days, and in practice usually allows ninety days, for individuals, corporations, and tax professionals to comment on proposed legislative regulations. The Internet is starting to be used for this purpose as well; as of May 2000, the IRS Web site invited comment on proposed changes to the W-2 forms used by employers. In many cases a public hearing is held after the comment period ends, so that government officials and interested parties can discuss the strengths and weaknesses of the regulations in question.

This is not, however, the only avenue for public involvement. If the drafting team is unsure of what form the proposed regulations should take, and concerned that poor design could wreak havoc among taxpayers, team members may engage in a set of informal discussions with outside parties such as associations representing tax lawyers, accountants, and specific industries. Such contacts must be approved in advance by the IRS assistant chief counsel, and at no point are members of the drafting team supposed to indicate which rules they are inclined to adopt. As the IRS Regulations Handbook (sec 581.2) notes, "Great care should be taken not to provide information that could affect market behavior or provide participants with unfair advantage relative to the general public." Despite these guidelines, charges of favoritism toward specific groups are sometimes levied.

The drafting team must also seek support from within their agencies. Before issuing proposed, temporary, or final regulations, they circulate drafts to other parts of the IRS and Treasury and ask for comments. Before proposed regulations can take effect, they must be endorsed by the IRS Commissioner. Final regulations, also known as Treasury Decisions, require the signatures of both the IRS Commissioner and the Secretary of the Treasury. These regulations are then translated into new or modified tax forms and instructions.

How do taxpayers become aware of these changes? The IRS highlights the most important changes in a "What's New" section of the instructions accompanying the annual form that is mailed to taxpayers. One drawback of this method is that word of new or modified tax expenditures often arrives too late to influence taxpayers' behavior, as tax forms and instructions are mailed shortly after the tax year has ended. To compensate, the IRS has developed an impressive electronic Web site that is constantly updated. In 1999, Americans downloaded almost 90 million tax forms and instructions from this Web site.[42]

Not everyone, however, wants to pay close attention to the tax code or can make sense of these changes. Tax professionals in the private sector are the other major channel through which new tax laws reach the public. They are paid to keep a close eye on tax matters that work their way through Congress and the revenue agencies, and to guide their clients in finding the best ways to maximize tax credits, deferrals, and deductions.

In addition to tax regulations, the IRS issues *revenue rulings* and *revenue procedures.* These do not have the force of law and generally apply to a smaller category of problems than do proposed or final regulations. While revenue rulings offer guidance to taxpayers about the substance of the tax code, revenue procedures describe the internal operation of the IRS. Both are published in the *Internal Revenue Bulletin.* The IRS also issues *letter rulings,* which are replies to inquiries made by individual taxpayers about the tax treatment of some proposed activity. The IRS will not rule on all matters, however, and does charge taxpayers a fee to issue such rulings. If the IRS believes that the individual question has wide applicability, it may issue a more general revenue ruling. Finally, the IRS issues *technical advice memoranda,* which deal with completed transactions and are usually requested on behalf of tax exempt organizations and employee pension plans.

Step 3: Compliance

Once tax forms have been published, it is up to taxpayers to determine which tax expenditures they are eligible for, and the value of each. Taxpayers do so while completing their annual income tax returns, and the United States is unusual among OECD countries in relying on its citizens to assess their own tax liability. In the United Kingdom and Japan, by contrast, taxpayers do not file returns at all because the government has withheld the exact amounts needed from their paychecks.[43] Mandatory withholding is also used in the United States, and is the single most important means the IRS has for collecting revenues.[44] By the same token, unreported personal income, especially among the self-employed, is the largest source of tax evasion in the United States.[45]

Completing the relevant tax forms can be a time-consuming and confusing exercise, which is why many taxpayers seek outside help. One source is the IRS itself, which devoted over 15,000 staff years to taxpayer assistance in 1999, a 20 percent jump from 1997. Over 8,000 employees were assigned to IRS telephone help lines. This is not always a satisfactory approach, as the IRS phone lines are sometimes busy and the quality of tax advice is improving but imperfect.[46] Alternatively, taxpayers turn to family, friends, or, more likely, paid professionals. A 1997 poll found that 51 percent of individuals paid someone else to figure their taxes, and 14 percent found someone else to do it for free. An Associated Press poll conducted the following year found that 56 percent of respondents were paying for tax help.[47] For corporations, reliance on paid tax professionals is routine.

Although precise numbers are hard to come by, it seems fair to say that tax preparation is a major industry in the United States. H&R Block, which handles millions of individual returns each year, generated $1.3 billion dollars in revenue (and $314 million in pretax profit) from its tax preparation business in 1999.[48] Major accounting firms such as Arthur Andersen, Deloitte & Touche, Ernst & Young, and Pricewaterhouse-Coopers specialize in corporate clients. In 1998, the U.S. Commerce Department predicted that accounting, auditing, and bookkeeping services would continue their double-digit growth rate. Employment was forecast to grow to 625,000—primarily well-paid, white-collar workers.[49] This is one reason that major tax bills are often dubbed the latest "accountant and tax lawyer protection act" by the media; the more complicated and changeable the tax code, the more their services are needed.

In addition to the professional costs, taxpayers incur personal costs in completing their tax forms. A middle- or upper-income couple with children and a home could expect to spend 11.5 hours doing the work necessary to complete the standard 1040 income tax form, 4.5 hours to complete Schedule A (itemized deductions), a little over 1 hour to complete Schedule B (interest and dividend income), and about 2 hours to complete Form 2441 (child and dependent care expenses).[50] The couple's time has value. The basic corporate income tax form requires almost 200 hours of work, with any one of dozens of forms and schedules adding to that total, depending on the business. Should the firm offer a qualified pension plan, it can expect to spend over 100 hours completing Form 5500, and anywhere from 1.5 to 35 hours each on the ten possible schedules attached to this form.

One estimate calculated by Joel Slemrod, a noted public finance expert at the University of Michigan, put the individual cost of compliance with the federal income tax at $50 billion per year in the mid-1990s. Of this figure, $8 billion went to professional tax help and $42 billion represented the value of time spent keeping accurate records of income, deductions, and losses and completing tax forms. For their part, corporations spent a total of $20 billion, with Fortune 500 companies each spending an average of $2 million per year.[51] Add in $5 billion to run the IRS, and the total cost of compliance was $75 billion.[52] In other words, it cost about ten cents to raise each dollar of income taxes in the United States. Much, although by no means all, of these costs are attributable to the prevalence of tax expenditures in the tax code.

Taxpayers have the option to mail their completed returns to one of several IRS processing centers around the country, file electronically, or in some cases via phone. The due date is April 15. Taxpayers must then wait to see if their calculations and documentation have been accepted, which can take from a few weeks to a few months. The more tax expenditures claimed, the greater the chance of a computational error or an interpretation of eligibility rules that differs from the government's. If the IRS challenges the tax return, taxpayers receive written notice and can choose to accept or contest the government's calculation of taxes owed or refund due. If taxpayers believe the government is in error, a series of appeals is possible beginning with an informal hearing with the IRS. If that hearing proves unsatisfactory, the issue moves to a specialized tax court, and then to the regular federal court system.[53]

Each year the IRS also selects a small fraction of taxpayers for a formal audit, or what is now called an examination.[54] The burden of proof falls squarely on the shoulders of taxpayers, who must document their income, deductions, and losses to the satisfaction of local IRS officials. An audit can be conducted exclusively through the mail. More common is an office audit, in which the taxpayer travels to the nearest district office to make his or her case. About a quarter of all audits are field audits in which IRS agents come to the taxpayer, almost always a business. Many taxpayers prefer to be accompanied by a paid tax professional during these events, or may skip it entirely and leave the work to an accountant or tax lawyer.

The reasons why a tax return is selected for audit are opaque, and deliberately so. A special computer program, whose design is a closely guarded secret, assigns a score to all individual and some corporate tax returns. The higher the score, the more likely an audit. Large claims of losses or tax deductions appear to be two of the criteria used in this scoring system. The IRS may also call for an audit when officials find major discrepancies between tax returns and other tax information gathered from W-2 and 1099 forms. Taxpayers who claim a certain deduction or credit that has been flagged for special scrutiny because of past compliance problems may also find themselves audited. Finally, the IRS may collect data from newspapers and other public records if it suspects that taxable income or taxes owed have been underreported.

The odds of being "examined" (i.e., audited) by the IRS are quite low. The overall audit rate for individuals in 1999 was 0.9 percent, and the rate for corporations was 1.5 percent. Both rates have declined substantially in recent years; companies, for example, were half as likely to be audited in 1999 as they were in 1992.[55] Over this same period, corporations with annual earnings over $250 million saw their audit rate drop from 55 to 35 percent.[56] One reason for the decline is that the number of IRS revenue officers declined by over 20 percent between 1988 and 1999. Another reason is that Congress added some restrictions on the IRS in 1998 as part of a larger effort to rein in the agency and protect taxpayers' rights.[57] The IRS has also been pressured to devote more of its shrinking personnel to helping taxpayers complete their forms rather than auditing taxpayers later. Conceivably, some of the decline may be justified to the extent that taxpayers know that the IRS has better information about their finances and are thus less inclined to be creative with their tax returns. Nevertheless, the decline in the audit rate worries revenue officials, who fear that it will lead to lower compliance by taxpayers.

For individuals, the odds of an audit actually diminish as income goes up. Individual taxpayers earning less than $25,000 in 1999 were audited at a rate of 1.36 percent, while individuals earning over $100,000 were audited at a rate of 1.15 percent.[58] The chief culprit here is the EITC, which is targeted at low-income workers. Prompted by evidence that some taxpayers were receiving too large a benefit, and by pressure from Congress, the IRS has been taking a hard look at those who claim the EITC on their returns.

An audit may result in no additional taxes owed, or occasionally even a refund. Sometimes, however, the IRS finds that the taxpayer owes more. As with more routine changes to tax returns, taxpayers can appeal the results of their IRS audit, first within the agency and then through the courts. In short, it can take years—and the work of countless public revenue officials and private-sector tax professionals—before everyone eligible for a tax expenditure benefit actually receives it.

IV. TOOL SELECTION

Policymakers offer several rationales for employing tax expenditures.[59] The most common technical rationales are summarized below, roughly in order from most to least cited in policy debates. To the extent that policymakers invoke explicit comparisons, it is usually between tax expenditures and cash grants or direct government.

More Choice Means Greater Efficiency

According to proponents, the lack of coercion characteristic of tax expenditures is one of its most appealing features. In defending a new tax credit, Senator Pete Domenici (R-NM) once said that "my natural inclination is to let people do the problem solving rather than government."[60] It is better to offer a tax incentive and let businesses decide which equipment to buy, rather than issue regulations telling them what to buy. It is better to offer a tax incentive and let individuals choose which charity to support, rather than allow the government to pick which charities to subsidize directly. Greater choice leads to more efficient economic outcomes.

Benefits Are Delivered Swiftly and Cheaply

Tax expenditures also win support on grounds that they rely on existing bureaucracies and established tax collecting routines and do not require additional government bureaucracies. Add another line to a relevant tax form, a page or two of instructions, and the program is up and running. There is no need to create a new bureaucracy or new program, as might be the case with a new grant-in-aid. Thus, tax expenditures may be more efficient not only because they promote choice, but also because they keep administrative costs low.

Occasional Market Failures Are Corrected

The Treasury Department, usually antagonistic to tax expenditures (see below), has occasionally defended their creation or expansion to correct for market failure. During the early 1960s, Treasury officials supported enactment of an investment tax credit for business based on a concern that firms were devoting too few resources to enhance their future productivity.[61] In issuing a comprehensive study of the tax system in 1984, Treasury defended the existing deduction for charitable contributions by stating that "services of this kind may not be provided at optimal levels if left to the marketplace."[62] Treasury favored expansion of existing tax incentives for retirement savings in that same report. The reason—to increase the pool of funds available for capital formation, which it deemed inadequate.

Demand for Direct Tools Is Diminished

In some cases policymakers may support tax expenditures strategically so that more direct forms of government action are not undertaken. This rationale is particularly appealing to political conservatives. The idea is not simply to deny liberals a credit-claiming opportunity, but to prevent what appears to be bad policy from being enacted. One clear example comes from health care. The tax expenditure for company-based health insurance has been protected and allowed to expand partly to prevent the introduction of national health insurance. If policymakers can ensure that health insurance is widely available to workers as a fringe benefit, they are in a better position to reject calls for sweeping change.[63]

Social Stigma Is Reduced

Tax expenditures may have higher participation rates, and thus be more effective, because they allow individuals to claim benefits anonymously.[64] The implicit comparison is usually to cash grants. For instance, David Ellwood has written in defense of the EITC: "People are helped without any need of a stigmatizing, invasive, and often degrading welfare system."[65] This might explain why the working poor are more likely to claim the EITC than Food Stamps. This advantage need not be restricted to low-income citizens. One can imagine that some homeowners might hesitate to receive housing assistance if they had to visit a local housing agency each month and produce a valid lease and proof of mortgage payment. Instead, homeowners attach a copy of an annual statement supplied by their mortgage company when they submit their annual tax returns, and then mail the whole package to an IRS facility that may be hundreds of miles away.

Political Considerations

It would be naive to assume that the choice of tax expenditures is animated solely by these technical criteria. Policymakers, especially elected officials, are also attracted to tax expenditures for reasons related to ideology and reelection. What is striking is how often policymakers clash on the need for other tools of government and yet agree on the need for tax expenditures.

Not surprisingly, political conservatives and moderates who embrace limited government favor tax expenditures. They like the use of incentives and oppose the creation of new government bureaucracies. To many of them, tax expenditures are synonymous with tax cuts, which in the current political and economic climate have great appeal. Conservatives want taxpayers to keep more of their income, and they want to prevent liberals from using the projected budgetary surplus to launch new spending initiatives. Ideally, a number of conservatives would prefer across-the-board tax cuts rather than tax expenditures targeted at specific groups or industries. They do not want the government picking winners and losers, even if indirectly via the tax code. However, at the end of the day, a tax cut for select groups or businesses is better than no tax cut at all.

For political liberals, tax expenditures pose something of a conundrum. Many liberals are unsatisfied with the performance of this tool. Liberals tend to gravitate toward direct government, regulations, and grants, in part because they believe that individual autonomy can be enhanced by the more direct forms of government action, and in part because they are troubled by the degree to which the wealthy benefit from tax expenditures (see below).[66] In the name of political expediency, liberals may support tax expenditures as the most feasible approach to activist government. Because the Democratic party has been unable to sustain unified control of government in the last few decades, and liberals have been unable to exert clear control over the Democratic party, it has become more common to see liberals defend tax expenditures as "the only game in town."[67] If the choice is between doing something through the tax code or doing nothing, most liberals prefer to do something. Like many conservatives, liberals often embrace tax expenditures as a second-best solution.

Consequently, tax expenditures can be portrayed simultaneously as an extension and a retraction of government power. This feature alone helps explain why this tool can generate enthusiasm among a broad range of politicians. It also helps explain why moderate Democrats like President Clinton have been among the most ardent supporters. They want the government to address the same types of social problems that have concerned the Democratic party ever since the 1930s, but with a new set of tools. Their desire to "reinvent" government, by making it more efficient and less intrusive, is entirely consistent with their support for new and expanded tax expenditures.

The reelection motive shows up most clearly in the congressional tax committees. With jurisdiction over all tax matters, these members face the unpleasant task of continually extracting revenues from individuals and corporations. Tax expenditures offer members of these committees a welcome opportunity to distribute benefits to appreciative constituencies.[68] Economist and former tax official T. S. Adams observed in 1928 that "modern taxation . . . in its most characteristic aspect is a group contest in which powerful interests vigorously endeavor to rid themselves of present and proposed tax burdens."[69] Media accounts routinely refer to "Christmas tree" tax bills decorated with gifts for special interests.[70] The Select Revenue Measures Subcommittee of the

Ways and Means Committee has been nicknamed "Santa's Workshop."[71] In perhaps the baldest appraisal, a study by the public watchdog group Common Cause claimed that "seekers of special tax breaks make a quick congressional shopping trip to the tax-writing committees where tax expenditures are designed."[72]

An opposing view holds that interest groups are less important, although not irrelevant. Witte notes that some tax expenditures originated in administrative rulings from the IRS and were more a product of technical problem solving than interest group pressure. He also notes that many tax expenditures have grown without much demand from organized groups to broaden eligibility or increase benefits. I have suggested elsewhere that interest group pressure is less evident in the origins of tax expenditures than in their subsequent development, and more evident in relatively small provisions targeted at specific industries. Party politics and individual policy entrepreneurs may be as important as interest groups in this process.[73]

Both sides would agree that organized groups representing third-party providers are often more evident than those representing the ultimate beneficiaries. The National Association of Home Builders and National Association of Realtors are two of the main defenders of the tax expenditures for housing; no comparable National Association of Home Owners exists. Organizations like the Independent Sector and the American Red Cross, rather than organized groups of donors, keep a close eye on the tax treatment of charitable deductions. A whole host of financial institutions—banks, insurance companies, mutual funds—monitor the tax treatment of corporate retirement pensions. This pattern makes sense for at least two reasons: third-party providers believe that favorable tax treatment is essential to their survival, and they can afford to develop the expertise necessary to participate in policy debates over taxation. The upshot is that even if the tax expenditure tool failed to win support based on its technical performance, it would still attract a wide range of powerful advocates.

V. MANAGEMENT CHALLENGES

These political considerations are important to keep in mind, for in many ways tax expenditures are not as simple to administer as advocates claim. The management challenges may not be as visible as with other tools of government, but they do exist. The nature of these challenges differs for tax officials, legislators, and taxpayers.

Major Challenges

One of the distinctive features of tax expenditures is that the main administrative agencies responsible for their operation want to get rid of them. The Treasury Department and IRS have consistently opposed the creation and expansion of tax expenditures, and with good reason. Tax expenditures make their job more difficult.

The frequent use of this tool creates three related management problems for tax officials.[74] The first is that revenue officials are constantly required to update the tax code. Between 1986 and 1998, 61 pieces of legislation produced 6500 separate amendments to the U.S. tax code. Notable examples included the Tax Reform Act of 1986 (1850 changes) and the Taxpayer Relief Act of 1997 (over 800 sections modified, almost 100 new sections added). Some sections of the code have been changed multiple times; the EITC, for example, was modified on thirteen separate occasions between 1976 and 1997.[75] Consequently, IRS agents may be unsure which rules apply at any given time, may spend many hours trying to stay current with the tax law, and still make mistakes.

This is one reason that taxpayers who call the IRS for tax advice prior to submitting their tax returns may receive bad or misleading advice.

A second problem is that tax expenditures conflict with the main mission of revenue agencies, which is raising revenue. Treasury and IRS officials have made it clear that they favor a relatively "clean" tax code with few exceptions, few rates, and some progressivity. Such a code would require fewer people to administer, simplify their training, and create less room for error.

The third problem is that tax expenditures force Treasury officials and IRS agents to make judgments about retirement policy, housing policy, health policy, agricultural policy—virtually every single function of government that involves direct expenditures also involves tax expenditures. However much detail the initial legislative statute contains, revenue officials must still exercise some discretion in translating congressional intent into specific changes in the tax code and tax forms. When tax returns are submitted, revenue officials must decide whether the taxpayer is eligible, and if so for how much of a subsidy. Revenue officials do not always have the expertise to make these judgments, which is one reason that they usually recommend converting tax expenditures to direct expenditures and transferring responsibility to the appropriate agency (e.g., Social Security Administration, Commerce Department).

The management challenges facing Congress and the president are somewhat different. Tax expenditures make it even more difficult for them to address policy problems in a systematic, coordinated manner. The problems of fashioning a national health policy are compounded by the fragmentation of programs in different congressional committees and different bureaucracies. Direct expenditures for health are directed at the elderly, the poor, and veterans; comparable tax expenditures are directed at workers in unionized industries and white-collar occupations. Nowhere do officials sit down and decide what the right mix of tools should be for health. Canada, by contrast, reformed its budget process in the late 1970s by grouping all tax and direct expenditures in ten policy "envelopes." Policymakers in each envelope had a fixed sum of monies to allocate, and it was up to them to decide the right combination.[76] This reform required officials to make the kinds of trade-offs that critics of tax expenditures in the United States often demand. Less sweeping changes might include revenue loss limits on broad categories of tax expenditures.

The challenges facing taxpayers are different but no less significant. Given the difficulties discussed in Section III, it is not surprising that in a 1998 poll for *Time*/CNN, 67 percent of respondents said that the federal income tax code was too complex. In a different poll that year, income taxes were identified as the single most hated tax.[77] Since 1998, the Internal Revenue Service has maintained a Taxpayer Advocate Service to handle individual and corporate complaints. Each year, it is required to report to Congress on the major problems voiced by taxpayers and tax professionals, what the agency is doing about them, and what more it will do in the future. In the first two annual reports (1998 and 1999), the overall complexity of the tax code emerged as the number one complaint, ahead of whatever problems taxpayers had with rude, overbearing, or incompetent IRS agents.[78] As Box 13-2 indicates, the frustration can be palpable. It is also what leads so many taxpayers to seek help from accountants, actuaries, and lawyers.

Even those who pay for help, however, often find their returns challenged. For many years *Money* magazine has distributed a set of tax data to several dozen tax professionals around the country and invited them to calculate the fictional taxpayer's return. Every year the overwhelming result is lack of a majority opinion, much less consensus, among paid tax preparers. In some years no two returns were alike. This is not meant as an indictment of accountants and tax lawyers. The U.S. tax code requires 5.5 million words and some 17,000 pages and, as mentioned above, changes constantly.[79] Rather, the test demonstrates how complex the tax code is even to trained professionals and how much judgment is involved in complying with tax laws.

Responses to Challenges

Technically, it is not hard to imagine ways of addressing these challenges. The most dramatic step would be for Congress and the president to strip the tax code of all tax expenditures and use most or all of the additional revenues to lower tax rates. While such a move is a defining feature of some flat tax proposals, it could also be accomplished with a system of progressive tax rates. Alternatively, one could retain a handful of the most popular tax expenditures—in effect, enacting something like the Treasury's tax reform plan from the mid-1980s[80]—and still produce a radically simpler tax code. A less drastic step would involve some sort of moratorium on changes to the tax code, so that taxpayers, tax professionals, and tax officials could work under a consistent set of rules. Admittedly, none of these reforms scores high on the political feasibility scale.

On a less grand scale, a variety of tax experts have made specific suggestions for simplifying the tax code, which almost always involve changes to tax expenditures. One suggestion is to standardize eligibility criteria, particularly the income ranges over which tax benefits are phased in and out. Similarly, policymakers could standardize the definitions of "qualifying child" and "family member" in various tax expenditures targeted at low- and moderate-income taxpayers.[81] They could combine related tax expenditures into a single provision; they could replace some tax expenditures with increases to the standard deduction or personal exemptions. In most of these cases, however, the ability to target benefits precisely would be sacrificed to achieve greater simplicity. Beginning

---

BOX 13-2 *Complexity: The View from the Trenches*

In critiquing the tax code's treatment of retirement pensions, a representative of the New York Bar Association wrote to the IRS: "The penalty provisions of ERISA [the Employee Retirement Income Security Act of 1974] . . . are complex and they often impact on taxpayers who are tripped into noncompliance because of the complexity of substantive and procedural requirements under which qualified plans must operate. . . . There is a long way to go, and meanwhile the plans of small businesses are unfairly impacted because of the discretion that resides in the revenue agents, and the inability of small plans to pay for the representation that would be needed to challenge arguably arbitrary positions."[1]

Consider as well the experience of a nonprofit community development corporation in South Bend, Indiana that wanted to claim the low-income housing tax credit. The corporation's executive director, Jeffrey Gibney, recalled saying, " 'I hate this [expletive]!' I kept yelling to my co-worker, who was driving. . . . I threw the tax credit handbook into the back of the car several times. I said, 'It's just too complex for a small group like ours.' . . . But Gibney kept retrieving the handbook and studying how to use the tax credits because, he said, he had no other source of funds for housing projects. . . . When Gibney closed on his first project—the rehabilitation of 15 apartments—14 lawyers sat around the table. Legal and accounting fees and other nonconstruction costs consumed 40 percent of the project's total budget."[2]

---

[1] Quoted in the *FY 1999 National Taxpayer Advocate's Annual Report to Congress.* Accessed via http://www.irs.ustreas.gov/ind_info/rpt99-1.html.
[2] Rochelle L. Stanfield, "Big Money in Low Rents," *National Journal* 26, no. 19 (1994): 1068.

in the mid-1980s, some OECD nations (e.g., United Kingdom, Netherlands) tried to diminish the complexity of their tax codes by requiring compliance cost estimates for all new tax legislation, and the United States could do likewise.[82]

One recent development deserves special mention. Policymakers have increasingly used the tax code to help moderate- and low-income taxpayers get out (and stay out) of poverty, defray the costs of raising children, pay for health insurance, afford college, and save for retirement. These same taxpayers may experience considerable difficulty in learning about these programs, completing the necessary tax forms, and paying for professional tax help. At a minimum, some organization needs to publicize these programs well. To be fair, telling taxpayers how to pay less in taxes runs counter to the basic mission of the IRS. This is not to say that the IRS cannot do the job, only that it may need help. In fact, the IRS has worked in recent years with traditional social service bureaucracies, homeless shelters, and other local organizations to foster public awareness of the EITC. This approach was pioneered by the nonprofit Center on Budget and Policy Priorities, and indications are that it has been quite successful.[83] Few organizations can match the center's combination of tax expertise, contacts at the state and local level, and foundation support, so this model may be difficult to replicate, but it may be worth a try.

VI. OVERALL ASSESSMENT

A quarter century ago, former Treasury official and Harvard law professor Stanley Surrey lamented that "tax expenditures tumble into the law without supporting studies, being propelled instead by cliches, debating points, and scraps of data and tables that are passed off as serious evidence."[84] While more studies have been conducted in recent years, to a large degree this pattern still holds. What evidence there is suggests strongly that tax expenditures often violate basic standards of efficiency, effectiveness, equity, and legitimacy. The results are not uniformly negative, but the general direction is clear.

Efficiency

Much of the case for tax expenditures hinges on their greater efficiency. Critics of this tool argue that when tax expenditures change economic behavior, they do so in socially undesirable ways. Tax expenditures distort economic choices, diverting resources to uses that are less profitable in the market but yield compensating tax benefits. "When economic activity is targeted to satisfy the tax law rather than the market, our national income falls, and we are all poorer in the long run."[85] The tax incentives for housing, for instance, have long been accused of encouraging individuals, especially in the higher tax brackets, to overinvest in home ownership. These tax expenditures help drive up housing prices and drain the pool of mortgage credit, creating affordability problems for less affluent households. They divert resources from other investments, like stocks, thereby reducing the pool of funds available to enhance productivity and wages.[86] Tax subsidies for employer-provided medical benefits "reduce the marginal cost to the employee of each extra dollar's worth of health insurance and thereby induce employment groups to buy cost unconscious open-ended comprehensive insurance."[87] The General Accounting Office found that tax incentives for oil exploration and credit unions were similarly inefficient.[88]

Claims of greater administrative efficiency are easily overstated. Some legislated changes to tax expenditures entail substantial modifications to the tax code, which can take years for the IRS to translate into tax forms and tax-collecting procedures. In many cases administrative costs are not so much reduced as shifted away from government. As discussed in Section V, individuals and corporations spend tens of billions of dollars and millions of hours trying to comply with the nation's tax laws, and no small part of this cost is due to the proliferation of tax expenditures. As a general rule, the more precisely tax expenditures are targeted, the higher the administrative costs facing tax-payers.[89] Moreover, some direct government programs operate very efficiently. Administrative costs for Social Security, for instance, are less than 1 percent of benefits.

Effectiveness

One of the chief criticisms of tax expenditures is that they confer windfall benefits, rewarding taxpayers for actions they would have taken anyway.[90] Thus, tax expenditures may not have much effect on behavior. Some of the best evidence comes from state and local tax incentives for business. Studies have repeatedly shown that such incentives have little impact on firms' location and investment decisions, especially those targeted at specific firms or industries. One reason is that state and local taxes constitute a small fraction (less than 2–3 percent) of an average firm's cost of doing business. A related reason is that business tax burdens vary little across the states. Rather than being at-tuned to taxes, businesses choose where to locate and invest based on such factors as the quality of the local labor force, the quality of public services, proximity to customers and suppliers, and proximity to major transportation routes. While tax incentives may represent the most visible gesture state and local officials can make, and firms will undoubtedly insist on such concessions, there is little reason to believe that this practice does more than pad firms' bottom line.[91] Other studies have shown that the majority of firms claiming the national government's Targeted Jobs Tax Credit would have hired the same workers if the credit did not exist.[92]

Tax expenditures may be ineffective because of lack of coordination with comparable direct spending programs. One of the worst examples is agriculture, in which direct expenditures and tax expenditures appear to be in direct conflict. While the government is directly promoting family farmers and local ownership, it is indirectly subsidizing larger corporate competitors.[93] Less egregious examples are always possible because of institutional fragmentation in Washington. Some health programs are administered by the Treasury Department, and some by the Department of Health and Human Services. Some benefits programs for retirees are administered by the Treasury and others by the Social Security Administration. Some programs to promote the oil and gas industry are controlled by the congressional tax committees, and others by the resources com-mittees.

On the other hand, research suggests that the EITC has been effective in boosting the wages of low-income workers and keeping them out of poverty.[94] And, although the evidence is somewhat mixed, favorable tax treatment does seem to increase the level of charitable giving by individuals and corporations. The effects are stronger among the most affluent taxpayers with the highest marginal tax rates.[95]

Perhaps the most generous verdict on this count is the Scottish plea, "not proven." Most of the empirical studies demonstrating problems with effectiveness have been devoted to a handful of small tax expenditures.[96] We know very little about possible windfall benefits to employers who offer fringe benefits to their workers, or about the major tax subsidies for housing, which is where most of the money goes. Of course, this defense contains an admission that the effectiveness of tax expenditures has not been proved in most cases, either. Acquiring the knowledge needed to assess the effectiveness of tax expenditures will be difficult. Largely for reasons of privacy, it is hard to know which individuals and which firms are using which tax expenditures, and thus hard to monitor the effect of this tool.

Equity

Two widely accepted criteria of an ideal tax system are horizontal and vertical equity, and tax expenditures usually violate both. Horizontal equity means that taxpayers with comparable incomes have comparable tax liabilities. Under the current tax code, an individual earning $30,000 and paying off a home mortgage owes less income tax than an individual earning $30,000 and paying rent. That is an inequity. A manufacturer with $100 million in income may pay less tax than a retail chain with the same income, simply because of the tax benefits of investing in new plant and equipment. That, too, is an inequity. One of the main reasons the Tax Reform Act of 1986 is held in such high esteem by specialists in public finance is that, by closing and restricting a variety of tax expenditures, it restored some horizontal equity to the tax code.

Nevertheless, a decrease in horizontal equity might be justified based on taxpayers' differing abilities to pay. Imagine three taxpayers, each earning $30,000. Taxpayer A lacks health insurance and incurs $10,000 in medical bills. Taxpayer B lacks renters' insurance and loses $5,000 worth of household items in a fire. Taxpayer C meets none of these misfortunes. The current tax code allows Taxpayer A to deduct catastrophic medical expenses and Taxpayer B to deduct casualty losses, so both pay less in taxes than Taxpayer C. The preferential treatment of A and B does violate horizontal equity; it may also constitute good public policy.[97]

Vertical equity means that tax burdens should be based on ability to pay, usually understood as progressively higher marginal tax rates. Tax expenditures violate this standard with their pronounced skew in favor of more affluent taxpayers. Michael Harrington once remarked that a "tax system is a welfare system for the rich,"[98] and he was partly right. The benefits of tax expenditures do flow primarily to the more affluent members of society. However, many of them are not rich; they are solidly middle- and upper-middle income.

Table 13-3 shows the distribution of selected tax expenditures by the income of individual taxpayers. These figures are taken directly from recent JCT *Estimates* with the income categories combined in a few places for ease of presentation. It seems fair to refer to taxpayers with incomes between $30,000 and $50,000 as middle class (the median income for a family of four is near the middle of this range), those with less than $10,000 as poor, and those above $100,000 as rich. With the notable exception of the EITC, all of these tax expenditures benefit primarily individuals with average and above-average incomes. The poor are repeatedly excluded, and even those earning between $10,000 and $30,000 seldom participate in any meaningful way. In several cases—home mortgage interest (53.6 percent), real estate taxes (53.9 percent), charitable contributions (62.0 percent), and state and local taxes (71.7 percent)—the rich receive the majority of the benefits.[99] For the sake of comparison, the next-to-last line of Table 13-3 indicates what percent of all tax returns are accounted for by each income class. These figures demonstrate once again the skew in favor of more affluent taxpayers. Those earning less than $30,000 submitted almost one-half of all tax returns, and yet they seldom received anywhere close to one-half of the benefits of tax expenditures.

This table admittedly captures only a piece of the total picture, as many of the largest tax expenditures are missing. Because of data limitations and the indirect nature of this tool, it is technically difficult to estimate the distribution of most tax expenditures. The Employee Benefits Research Institute did so for employer-provided retirement pensions in 1992 and arrived at figures quite consistent with those in Table 13-3: less than 10 percent of the tax benefits went to individuals earning under $30,000, 28 percent went to those earning between $30,000 and $50,000, 43 percent to those earning between $50,000 and $100,000, and 20 percent to those earning over $100,000.[100] Sheils and Hogan have estimated that the average tax benefit for employer medical care in 1998 was $2357 for families with income over $100,000, $847 for families earning between $30,000 and $40,000; and $71 for families earning less than $15,000. Families earning over $100,000 received almost one-quarter of the total benefits, and families earning over $50,000 received over two-thirds of the total benefits.[101] Clearly, this "hidden welfare state" of tax expenditures benefits middle- and upper-income taxpayers far more than the poor.

The clear upward skew is not too surprising given that the tax code is subsidizing activities such as home ownership that are inherently easier for the affluent to engage in, that fringe benefits are often unavailable in small firms employing many low-wage workers, and that firms offering such benefits often make them proportional to salaries.[102] In addition, the general pattern of distributing benefits to the affluent is not surprising given that progressive income tax rates make the value of avoiding taxation greater for those in the upper tax brackets. As the last line in Table 13-3 indicates, individuals with above-average incomes pay the lion's share (90 percent) of income taxes in the United States. Because of the standard deduction, personal exemptions, and the EITC, many low-income individuals owe no income tax, which makes it hard for them to benefit from tax expenditures. William Gale, an economist at the Brookings Institution, has calculated that refundable tax credits are the only feasible means of delivering tax benefits to a family of four earning less than $28,000.[103] Currently, only the EITC offers any sizable refund. Thus, although tax expenditures may be distributed according to amounts of taxes paid, they are not distributed proportional to need, which is essential to vertical equity.[104]

TABLE 13-3 *Distribution of Selected Tax Expenditures, 1998*

		PERCENT OF BENEFITS BY INCOME OF TAXPAYERS				
Provision	Total Cost	<$10K	$10–30K	$30–50K	$50–100K	>$100K
Home mortgage interest	$47.0B	0.0%	1.3%	7.5%	37.7%	53.6%
State and local taxes	30.5	0.0	0.3	3.5	24.5	71.7
Earned Income Tax Credit	29.0	19.8	73.6	6.4	0.2	0.0
Untaxed Social Security and railroad retirement benefits	24.5	0.1	26.1	46.6	26.1	1.8
Charitable contributions	23.6	0.0	1.8	6.6	29.7	62.0
Real estate taxes	17.4	0.0	1.5	7.6	37.0	53.9
Child tax credit	17.0	0.0	13.4	29.8	48.9	7.8
Extraordinary medical expenses	3.7	0.0	5.9	20.2	43.2	30.7
Percent of tax returns in each income class		14.8	34.0	21.4	22.0	7.9
Percent of total income taxes paid by each income class		−0.1	0.1	9.6	27.7	62.4

SOURCE: U.S. Congress, Joint Committee on Taxation, *Estimates of Federal Tax Expenditures for Fiscal Years 1999–2003.*

Technically, problems of vertical inequity can be ameliorated. Caps can be imposed, either on the income of recipients (as in the EITC) or on the value of the good being subsidized (as is done loosely with the home mortgage interest deduction). The Alternative Minimum Tax, one of the most complicated sections of the entire tax code, is designed in part to limit corporations' and wealthy individuals' use of tax expenditures.[105] Itemized deductions are already phased out for high-income taxpayers, and the income levels could be lowered or the phase-out rate accelerated. Congress could, as some analysts have suggested, convert tax deductions to tax credits, preferably refundable credits, again like the EITC. Such credits are equally valuable to all taxpayers, whereas the value of tax deductions varies with an individual's or firm's tax bracket. As has been noted with respect to tax deductions for charitable giving, there is something odd afoot when the price of virtuous behavior is lower for the rich than everyone else. A tax credit would reduce those inequities.

The main obstacles here are not technical but political. Restricting the flow of tax benefits to the rich and upper-middle class might create motivated and well-funded enemies, something no elected official desires. The last major assault on tax expenditures, culminating in the Tax Reform Act of 1986, was successful in part because policymakers agreed not to make any major changes in the distribution of tax burdens.[106] Moreover, opinion polls have consistently shown that the public has little interest in more income redistribution.[107] These surveys point up the subjective nature of vertical equity: critics of tax expenditures appear to favor a more progressive income tax than do ordinary citizens, but both endorse the idea that higher tax rates should be applied to higher incomes. It is thus not clear how much less regressive tax expenditures would need to become to pass some standard of vertical equity, since no clear standard exists.

Legitimacy

Critics have long claimed that this tool lacks political legitimacy for reasons already mentioned in this chapter.[108] Even with the changes instituted by the 1974 Budget Act, tax expenditures lack the visibility of direct expenditures. Information about the size and scope of tax expenditures is buried in an appendix to the budget. Information about the distribution of benefits for many programs is unknown. This information is disseminated by media outlets that specialize in tax matters, but not in ways that are likely to reach the general public.

Tax expenditures may lack accountability as well. Rather than confront other spending priorities, tax expenditures are decided earlier as Congress establishes overall revenue goals. Tax expenditures are not reviewed on a regular basis, much less made to endure the rigors of the annual appropriations process. They are, with few exceptions, permanent features of the tax code. They grow without explicit decisions to increase spending. They are evaluated far less often than appropriations or traditional entitlements.

Critics fear that the proliferation of tax expenditures contributes to a loss of trust in government. Citizens become more infuriated with public bureaucracy as they try to navigate through a maze of tax forms and instructions. They cannot understand how such high tax rates produce so little revenue, and they assume that the answer is government waste, fraud, and abuse. Citizens look for ways to "beat" the tax system because they are convinced that only "suckers" comply fully. They support flat tax proposals, even those that would increase their tax liability, as long as those dreaded loopholes are eliminated. They become more convinced that the government is run for the benefit of powerful special interests.

Readers might well conclude that tax expenditures are always and everywhere a bad choice. Such a verdict would be understandable but too sweeping. In some cases the problems cited above may be evidence of poor design rather than some structural flaw. If policymakers wish to promote home ownership through the tax code, they could find a better vehicle than tax deductions. Deductions are more effective in helping people buy more expensive homes than in helping people buy homes at all. A tax credit, preferably refundable, would be more effective for it could target resources at those individuals who cannot yet afford to buy a home.[109]

Defenders of tax expenditures can also concede some problems and ask if alternative tools truly perform better. Windfall benefits are not unique to tax expenditures. One might argue that Medicaid pays doctors and hospitals to treat poor patients who would have received free care otherwise. Low visibility is not unique to tax expenditures, either. Over 60 percent of voters in the historic 1994 elections had not heard of the Contract with America despite a high-profile campaign waged by congressional Republicans.[110] Most Americans do not know the names of both their senators, cannot guess within 10 percent what fraction of the budget is devoted to Social Security or defense, and do not understand what Superfund does.[111] All of the recent proposals to create or modify tax expenditures suggest that elected officials are well aware of this tool. With respect to accountability, most of the charges leveled against tax expenditures apply equally to entitlements like Social Security and Medicare. And the supposed links between the tax system and lower trust in government are largely speculative. If tax expenditures have a legitimacy problem, it may not be substantially different from other major tools of government.

Many of the criticisms just mentioned apply to tax expenditures that are designed to change individual or corporate behavior. However, not all tax expenditures are tax incentives. As mentioned in Section I, some tax expenditures are designed to reduce or eliminate the income taxation of direct benefit programs. Their main objective is to prevent economic distress among retirees, veterans, the disabled, and those with high medical expenses. They tend to pose fewer problems of vertical equity than other tax expenditures. Because these tax expenditures look like tools of direct government, rather than third party government, we need to worry less about windfall benefits. Interestingly, tax expenditures tied to grants or direct government have seldom been criticized and may represent a reasonable use for this tool.

One specific program deserves mention. The EITC is in several respects a model tax expenditure. It is targeted at workers with below average incomes (thus enhancing vertical equity), but not at workers in specific occupations or industries (thus preserving horizontal equity). It is refundable, so workers who owe no income tax can still benefit. Unlike various jobs tax credits that have been tried, it does not confer windfall benefits on employers; the tax benefits flow directly to workers. Several studies have found that the EITC has been effective in reducing poverty and increasing labor force participation. These same studies suggest that some of the major problems with the program, especially the number of people who claim to be eligible but are not, are a result of poor design. If policymakers would simplify the definitions of income and family used, and stop changing them every year or two, a good program would perform even better.[112]

VII. CONCLUSIONS

In their characteristic form, tax expenditures generally fail to live up to their advance billing. Tax expenditures either do manage to change behavior, but in undesirable ways, leading individuals and firms to overconsume certain goods and underinvest in others. Or tax expenditures fail to change behavior and reward taxpayers for activities they would have engaged in anyway (i.e., windfall benefits). In either case, tax expenditures distort the horizontal equity of the tax code and reduce the amount of vertical equity. They may lower administrative costs to the government but impose sizable administrative burdens on taxpayers. The main exceptions to these generalizations are tax expenditures linked to other benefit programs like Social Security and veterans' benefits, and the EITC. Admittedly, these generalizations are based on limited data, but what evidence we have tends to discourage rather than encourage use of this tool. Whether the disadvantages of tax expenditures are any greater than those of other policy tools is a judgment that readers will have to make based on this entire volume and their own experiences.

This verdict points to a more restricted use of tax expenditures than is currently the case, or a more careful design of those that remain, but realistically the odds of major retrenchment are quite small. Too many individuals and firms have too much at stake: homeowners expect that when they sell, future buyers will be eligible for tax breaks and thus able to afford the sellers' price; employees expect that when they retire, their pension will have a certain value that reflects in part favorable tax treatment. Literally millions of third-party providers (doctors, builders, construction unions, realtors, pension fund managers, equipment manufacturers, stockbrokers) count on the tax code to foster demand for their goods and services. Policymakers are thus highly constrained by commitments made years earlier. Divided government and waning support among elected officials for more direct tools of government action make tax expenditures politically attractive.

One is reminded of the old saying, "give a boy a hammer and soon everything will look like a nail." Tax expenditures have been increasingly touted as the best tool for addressing problems as varied as long-term care for the elderly, business investment in R&D, and the cost of higher education. Their positive effects are frequently invoked but seldom proved. Going forward, policymakers would be wise to subject any future proposals for creating or expanding tax expenditures to close scrutiny. They should expect advocates of tax expenditures to demonstrate that their proposal will not exhibit the problems discussed in this chapter, and that this policy tool is preferable to alternative tools. If this test is administered fairly, tax expenditures may not be chosen as quickly or as often as they have in recent years.

VIII. SUGGESTED READING

Howard, Christopher. *The Hidden Welfare State: Tax Expenditures and Social Policy in the United States.* Princeton, NJ: Princeton University Press, 1997.

Organisation for Economic Co-operation and Development (OECD). *Tax Expenditures: Recent Experiences.* Paris: OECD, 1996.

Surrey, Stanley S., and Paul R. McDaniel. *Tax Expenditures.* Cambridge, Mass.: Harvard University Press, 1985.

U.S. Congress. Joint Committee on Taxation (JCT). *Estimates of Federal Tax Expenditures.* Washington, D.C.: Government Printing Office, most recent year.

U.S. General Accounting Office (GAO). *Tax Expenditures Deserve More Scrutiny.* Washington, D.C.: Government Printing Office, 1994.

U.S. Office of Management and Budget (OMB). *Analytical Perspectives, Budget of the United States Government.* Washington, D.C.: Government Printing Office, most recent year.

I would like to thank Michael Cassidy for his research assistance on this project. Lester Salamon provided valuable suggestions concerning the substance and organization of my argument.

NOTES

1. The State of the Union address was accessed via the Web site of the White House Office of the Press Secretary at http://www.whitehouse.gov/WH/New/html/19990119–2656.html.

2. Christopher Howard, *The Hidden Welfare State: Tax Expenditures and Social Policy in the United States* (Princeton, N.J.: Princeton University Press, 1997), 156–159; Ben Wildavsky, "Taking Credit," *National Journal* 29, no. 13 (1997): 610–612; Bruce F. Davie, "Tax Expenditures: the Basics," in *Evaluating Tax Expenditures: Tools and Techniques for Assessing Outcomes,* eds. Lois-ellin Datta and Patrick G. Grasso (San Francisco: Jossey-Bass, 1998), 9–23; Heidi Glenn, "List of Tax Expenditures Not Shrinking, JCT Report Shows," *Tax Notes* 82, no. 1 (1999): 7–9.

3. Public Law 344, 93rd Congress, 2d sess. (12 July 1974), section 3 (3).

4. Davie, "Tax Expenditures: The Basics."

5. Payroll taxes for Social Security, disability insurance, and Medicare could also be heavily affected by tax expenditures. Sheils and Hogan estimate that in 1998, the favorable treatment of company-based health benefits resulted in a revenue loss to the national government of $65.9 billion in income taxes and $36.0 billion in payroll taxes. John Sheils and Paul Hogan, "Cost of Tax-Exempt Health Benefits in 1998," *Health Affairs* 18, no. 2 (1999): 176–181.

6. U.S. Congress, Joint Committee on Taxation (JCT), *Estimates of Federal Tax Expenditures for Fiscal Years 1999–2003* (Washington, D.C.: Government Printing Office, 1998). According to the JCT, "personal exemptions and the standard deduction are treated as part of the normal income tax law because one may consider these amounts as approximating the level of income below which it would be difficult for an individual or family to obtain minimal amounts of food, clothing, and shelter." Interestingly, the JCT does count lower tax rates on corporate income as a tax expenditure. In its view, such rates are unrelated to a firm's ability to pay and offered instead as a subsidy to small business.

7. For instance, the JCT recently estimated that the tax expenditure for employer-provided health benefits would cost a total of $327 billion between 1999 and 2003. The Treasury estimated that the same provision would cost a total of $438 billion (Glenn, "List of Tax Expenditures Not Shrinking," 7). See JCT, *Estimates of Federal Tax Expenditures* for a good discussion of the differences between its list and the Treasury's.

8. Organisation for Economic Co-operation and Development (OECD), *Tax Expenditures: Recent Experiences* (Paris: OECD, 1996).

9. By contrast, excise and effluent taxes are used to discourage socially undesirable behaviors such as smoking, alcohol consumption, and pollution. See chap. 8.

10. Stanley S. Surrey, "Tax Incentives as a Device for Implementing Government Policy: A Comparison with Direct Government Expenditures," *Harvard Law Review* 83, no. 4 (1970): 705–738.

11. Frederick C. Mosher, "The Changing Responsibilities and Tactics of the Federal Government," *Public Administration Review* 40, no. 6 (1980): 541–548; Lester M. Salamon, "Rethinking Public Management: Third-Party Government and the Changing Forms of Government Action," *Public Policy* 29, no. 3 (1981): 255–275.

12. A rare exception is the low-income housing tax credit, which is a fixed sum allocated to the states based on population and largely administered by state housing agencies.

13. Howard, *The Hidden Welfare State,* especially chap. 9.

14. One exception was the investment tax credit passed in 1962.

15. Carol Matlack, "Zap! You're Taxed," *National Journal* 22, no. 5 (1990): 267–269.

16. The child tax credit is currently refundable only for taxpayers with three or more children. It will generate an estimated total refund of $550 million in FY 2000, compared to over $25 billion for the EITC.

17. This example is based closely on one from Sherry Glied, *An Assessment of Strategies for Expanding Health Insurance Coverage* (Menlo Park, Calif.: Henry J. Kaiser Family Foundation, 1997).

18. John F. Witte, *The Politics and Development of the Federal Income Tax* (Madison: University of Wisconsin Press, 1985), 312–313.

19. Glenn, "List of Tax Expenditures Not Shrinking," 7–9.

20. Howard, *Hidden Welfare State,* especially chap. 1.

21. Joseph A. Pechman, "Tax Reform: Theory and Practice," *Journal of Economic Perspectives* 1, no. 1 (1987): 11–28.

22. Aaron Zitner, "Tax Code Gives Companies a Lift," *Boston Globe* (8 July 1996), 1; Greg Leroy, "The Terrible Ten: Corporate Candy Store Deals of 1998," *The Progressive* 63, no. 5 (1999): 27–30.

23. Robert B. Reich, "Balanced Budget Easier If Corporate Welfare Ended," *USA Today* (22 December 1995), A12; Robert J. Shapiro and Chris J. Soares, *Cut and Invest to Grow: How to Expand Public Investment While Cutting the Deficit,* Policy Report No. 26 (Washington, D.C.: Progressive Policy Institute, 1997). The Progressive Policy Institute is the research arm of the Democratic Leadership Council, representing centrist and conservative elements within the Democratic Party. See also Jane G. Gravelle, *Corporate Tax Welfare* (Washington, D.C.: Congressional Research Service, 1997). Although Democrats generally took the lead on this issue, Rep. John Kasich (R-OH) and Sen. John McCain (R-AZ) were also prominent critics of corporate welfare.

24. Moreover, tax legislation frequently includes transition rules, first cousin to tax expenditures, that enable specific companies to save millions of dollars as new laws are phased in [see, for example, Jeffrey H. Birnbaum and Alan S. Murray, *Showdown at Gucci Gulch: Lawmakers, Lobbyists, and the Unlikely Triumph of Tax Reform* (New York: Vintage, 1987), 146–147].

25. Sven Steinmo, *Taxation and Democracy: Swedish, British, and American Approaches to Financing the Modern State* (New Haven: Yale University Press, 1993), 144.

26. U.S. Office of Management and Budget (OMB), *A Citizen's Guide to the Federal Budget: Budget of the United States Government Fiscal Year 2000* (Washington, D.C.: Government Printing Office, 1999). Accessed via http://www.gpo.gov/usbudget/fy2000/guidetoc.html.

27. Bent Greve, "The Hidden Welfare State, Tax Expenditure, and Social Policy," *Scandinavian Journal of Social Welfare* 3, no. 4 (1994): 203–211.

28. Jon Kvist and Adrian Sinfield, *Comparing Tax Routes to Welfare in Denmark and the United Kingdom* (Copenhagen: Danish National Institute of Social Research, 1996); OECD, *Tax Expenditures.*

29. Charles T. Clotfelter, *Federal Tax Policy and Charitable Giving* (Chicago: University of Chicago Press, 1985).

30. National Association of State Budget Officers (NASBO), "State Tax Expenditure Reports," *NASBO Information Brief* 2, no. 3 (1994); National Association of State Budget Officers (NASBO), *Budget Processes in the States* (Washington, D.C.: NASBO, 1997). Accessed via http://www.nasbo.org/pubs/budpro/frame.htm.

31. Keon S. Chi, *The States and Business Incentives: An Inventory of Tax and Financial Incentive Programs* (Lexington, KY: Council of State Governments, 1989).

32. Witte, *Politics and Development of the Federal Income Tax,* chap. 15; see also U.S., Congress, Senate, Committee on the Budget, *Tax Expenditures: Compendium of Background Material on Individual Provisions,* 102d Congress, 2d sess., 1992, S. Rept. 102–119.

33. The 1967 figure is based on revenue losses rather than budget outlay equivalents, which were not calculated until the early 1980s. To make the comparisons fair, I use revenue loss figures for 2000 as well.

34. U.S. General Accounting Office (GAO), *Tax Expenditures Deserve More Scrutiny* (Washington, D.C.: Government Printing Office, 1994), 32.

35. Howard, *Hidden Welfare State.*

36. Similarly, tax rate reductions passed in 1988 in the United Kingdom led to a significant reduction in the value of tax expenditures (Kvist and Sinfield, *Comparing Tax Routes to Welfare,* 24).

37. U.S. Congressional Budget Office, *The Effects of Tax Reform on Tax Expenditures* (Washington, D.C.: Government Printing Office, 1988).

38. Witte, *Politics and Development of the Federal Income Tax,* 321–324.

39. Roy Blough, *The Federal Taxing Process* (New York: Prentice-Hall, 1952); Paul R. Mc-Daniel, "Tax Expenditures as Tools of Government Action," in *Beyond Privatization: The Tools of Government Action,* ed. Lester M. Salamon (Washington, D.C.: Urban Institute Press, 1989), 167–196; William H. Hoffman, Jr., James E. Smith, and Eugene Willis, eds., *West's Federal Taxation: Individual Income Taxes* (Minneapolis/St. Paul: West Publishing, 1997); Sheryl Stratton, "How Regulations Are Made: A Look at the Reg Writing Process," *Tax Notes* 74, no. 5 (1997): 544–550; John L. Mikesell, "Tax Administration: The Link between Tax Law and Tax Collections," in *Handbook of Public Finance,* eds. Fred Thompson and Mark T. Green (New York: Marcel Dekker, 1998), 173–198.

40. Stratton, "How Regulations Are Made," 544.

41. Ibid., 544–545.

42. Transactional Records Access Clearinghouse (TRAC), *New Findings.* Accessed via http://trac.syr.edu:80/tracirs/findings/aboutIRS/keyFindings.html. TRAC, affiliated with Syracuse University, is a clearinghouse of information concerning the nation's major law enforcement agencies.

43. Joel Slemrod and Jon Bakija, *Taxing Ourselves: A Citizen's Guide to the Great Debate Over Tax Reform* (Cambridge, Mass.: MIT Press, 1996), 245–246; B. Guy Peters, *The Politics of Taxation: A Comparative Perspective* (Cambridge: Blackwell, 1991), 252–253.

44. The Tax Reform Act of 1986 required taxpayers for the first time to list the Social Security numbers of any claimed dependents over the age of two. Quite mysteriously, taxpayers claimed 7 million fewer dependents in 1987 than in 1986, and 75,000 families lost four or more dependents that year. This is the sort of deception that reporting requirements are designed to prevent. Michael J. Graetz, *The Decline (and Fall?) of the Income Tax* (New York: W. W. Norton, 1997), 96.

45. Transactional Records Access Clearinghouse (TRAC), *The IRS and Its Responsibilities* (Syracuse, N.Y.: TRAC, 2000). Accessed via http://trac.syr.edu:80/tracirs/findings/aboutIRS/irs Responsibilities.html; Slemrod and Bakija, *Taxing Ourselves,* 146–152.

46. TRAC, *New Findings.*

47. Kevin Coleman, *Tax Issues: National Public Opinion* (Washington, D.C.: Congressional Research Service, 1998); U.S., Congress, House, Committee on Ways and Means, *Hearing on the Impact of Complexity in the Tax Code on Individual Taxpayers and Small Business,* 106th Congress, 1st sess., 1999.

48. H & R Block, Inc., 1999 Annual Report. Accessed via http://www.hrblock.com/pdf/ir400.pdf.

49. Rick Telberg, "Forecast '98: U.S. Firms Poised for Sizzling Growth," *Accounting Today* 12, no. 1 (1998): 1, 38.

50. All figures are taken from the instructions accompanying each form and include time for recordkeeping, learning about the law, preparing the form, copying the form, and sending it to the IRS. Some observers believe these figures are too low.

51. To give readers a sense of how complicated and time-consuming this process can be, consider that the 1993 tax return from the Mobil Corporation was 6,300 pages long, weighed over seventy-five pounds, and cost the company $10 million to produce. Graetz, *Decline (and Fall?) of the Income Tax,* 85.

52. Joel Slemrod, "Which Is the Simplest Tax System of Them All?" in *Economic Effects of Fundamental Tax Reform,* eds. Henry J. Aaron and William G. Gale (Washington, D.C.: The Brookings Institution, 1996), 359–368; Slemrod and Bakija, *Taxing Ourselves,* 130–133.

53. For more concerning the courts, see Stanley S. Surrey and Paul R. McDaniel, *Tax Expenditures* (Cambridge, Mass.: Harvard University Press, 1985).

54. The discussion of auditing is based on Mikesell, "Tax Administration"; Walter Shapiro, "GOP Assault on IRS Was a Turning Point," *USA Today* (3 May 2000), 12A; TRAC, *New Findings;* U.S. Internal Revenue Service, *Examination of Returns, Appeal Rights, and Claims for Refund,*

Publication 556 (February 1999); Fred O. Williams, "Facing the IRS: How to Act, What to Do If the IRS Audits You," *Buffalo News* (23 May 2000), D1.

55. The audit rate for individuals in the 1960s was closer to 4 percent (Slemrod and Bakija, *Taxing Ourselves,* 152).

56. The rate of decline for more serious enforcement measures—levying taxpayers' assets, issuing liens on property, seizing assets, and referring taxpayers for criminal prosecution—have been even greater than for audits.

57. A subsequent investigation by the General Accounting Office found that many of the charges leveled against the IRS during congressional hearings in 1998 were groundless (Shapiro, "GOP Assault on IRS Was a Turning Point").

58. This means that individuals earning between $25,000 and $100,000 must have been audited at rates below 0.9 percent.

59. Howard, *Hidden Welfare State;* McDaniel, "Tax Expenditures as Tools," 170–172; Surrey and McDaniel, *Tax Expenditures.*

60. Quoted in Joel Havemann, "Tax Expenditures—Spending Money without Expenditures," *National Journal* 9, no. 50 (1977): 1909.

61. Donald Lubick and Gerard Brannon, "Stanley S. Surrey and the Quality of Tax Policy Argument," *National Tax Journal* 38, no. 3 (1985): 251–259.

62. U.S. Department of the Treasury, *Tax Reform for Fairness, Simplicity, and Economic Growth* (Washington, D.C.: Government Printing Office, 1984), 81.

63. Howard, *Hidden Welfare State,* 190–191.

64. Jeffrey P. Owens, "Tax Expenditures and Direct Expenditures as Tools of Government Action," in *Comparative Tax Studies,* ed. Sijbren Cnossen (Amsterdam: North-Holland, 1983), 171–197.

65. David T. Ellwood, *Poor Support: Poverty in the American Family* (New York: Basic Books, 1988), 115.

66. Robert Kuttner, "The Limits of Markets," *The American Prospect* 31 (March–April 1997): 28–36.

67. Rep. Pete Stark (D-CA), referring to the Targeted Jobs Tax Credit. Cited in Howard, *Hidden Welfare State,* 166.

68. R. Douglas Arnold, *The Logic of Congressional Action* (New Haven: Yale University Press, 1990), chap. 8.

69. T. S. Adams, "Ideals and Idealism in Taxation," *American Economic Review* 18, no. 1 (1928): 1.

70. Leonard Silk, "Tax Writers' 'Christmas Tree'," *New York Times* (26 June 1981), D2.

71. Elizabeth Drew, *Politics and Money: The New Road to Corruption* (New York: Macmillan, 1983), 66.

72. Jo Ann Klimschot, *The Untouchables: A Common Cause Study of the Federal Tax Expenditure Budget* (Washington, D.C.: Common Cause, 1981), ii.

73. Witte, *Politics and Development of the Federal Income Tax,* chap. 13; Howard, *Hidden Welfare State.*

74. Surrey and McDaniel, *Tax Expenditures;* McDaniel, "Tax Expenditures as Tools"; Howard, *Hidden Welfare State.*

75. U.S. Congress, House, Committee on Ways and Means, *Impact of Complexity of the Tax Code on Individual Taxpayers and Small Businesses: Hearings,* 105th Cong., 2d sess., 1998; U.S. Congress, Senate, Committee on Finance, *Complexity of the Individual Income Tax: Hearings,* 106th Cong., 1st sess., 1999.

76. Howard, *Hidden Welfare State,* 180.

77. Coleman, *Tax Issues: National Public Opinion.*

78. The complexity of the Earned Income Tax Credit, which has been subject to numerous changes, emerged as the third most pressing problem on this list. Almost one million taxpayers called the IRS for help with the EITC in 1999.

79. U.S., Senate, Committee on Finance, *Complexity of the Individual Income Tax.*

80. Birnbaum and Murray, *Showdown at Gucci Gulch,* 51–64.

81. U.S., House, Committee on Ways and Means, *The Impact of Complexity in the Tax Code on Individual Taxpayers and Small Businesses.*

82. Slemrod and Bakija, *Taxing Ourselves,* 141–142.

83. Christopher Howard, "Happy Returns: How the Working Poor Got Tax Relief," *The American Prospect* 17 (Spring 1994): 46–53.

84. Stanley S. Surrey, *Pathways to Tax Reform: The Concept of Tax Expenditures* (Cambridge, Mass.: Harvard University Press), 6.

85. Joseph J. Minarik, *Making America's Budget Policy: From the 1980s to the 1990s* (Armonk, N.Y.: M. E. Sharpe, 1990), 106.

86. Rolf Goetze, "Housing, Inflation, and Taxes," *New York Times* (18 March 1981), A27; Slemod and Bakija, *Taxing Ourselves,* 182–183.

87. Alain Enthoven, "Health Tax Policy Mismatch," *Health Affairs* 4, no. 4 (1985). 5–14; see also Slemrod and Bakija, *Taxing Ourselves,* 188.

88. GAO, *Tax Expenditures Deserve More Scrutiny,* 24.

89. McDaniel, "Tax Expenditures as Tools"; Howard, *Hidden Welfare State.*

90. This has been termed a problem of inefficiency by some (McDaniel, "Tax Expenditures as Tools") and of ineffectiveness by others (GAO, *Tax Expenditures Deserve More Scrutiny*).

91. Such practices may also be highly inefficient; some of the states that managed to lure a major auto plant did so at a cost of over $100,000 per new hire. The cheaper alternative would have been to pay the same employee $50,000 to stay home. For good reviews of this literature, see Robert G. Lynch, *Do State and Local Tax Incentives Work?* (Washington, D.C.: Economic Policy Institute, 1996). Accessed via http://epn.org/epi/epilync.html; and David Brunori, "Principles of Tax Policy and Targeted Tax Incentives," *State and Local Government Review* 29 (1997): 50–61.

92. Howard, *Hidden Welfare State,* chap. 8. For evidence of windfall benefits in qualified mortgage bonds, see GAO, *Tax Expenditures Deserve More Scrutiny,* 25–26.

93. Ibid., 185–186.

94. Robert Greenstein and Isaac Shapiro, *New Research Findings on the Effects of the Earned Income Tax Credit* (Washington, D.C.: Center on Budget and Policy Priorities, 1998).

95. Clotfelter, *Federal Tax Policy and Charitable Giving,* especially chap. 2; Charles T. Clotfelter, "The Impact of Tax Reform on Charitable Giving: A 1989 Perspective," in *Do Taxes Matter?,* ed. Joel Slemrod (Cambridge, Mass.: MIT Press, 1991), 203–235; Slemrod and Bakija, *Taxing Ourselves,* 188–190.

96. GAO, *Tax Expenditures Deserve More Scrutiny;* Lois-Ellin Datta and Patrick G. Grasso, eds., *Evaluating Tax Expenditures: Tools and Techniques for Assessing Outcomes* (San Francisco: Jossey-Bass, 1998).

97. I thank Kenneth Wertz of PricewaterhouseCoopers for suggesting this point.

98. Quoted in Steinmo, *Taxation and Democracy,* 157.

99. Again for reasons of data availability, it is impossible to offer similar numbers at the state level. One partial remedy to this problem may be supplied by the State Fiscal Analysis Initiative, which started in 1993. Financed by several foundations, the SFAI is designed to "strengthen the contributions of state-level nonprofit organizations to policy debates by enhancing their ability to provide reliable budget and tax analysis." It involves twenty-two states, the Center on Budget and Policy Priorities, and the Center for the Study of the States. For more information, see Karen M. Paget, *The State Fiscal Analysis Initiative* (Washington, D.C.: Center on Budget and Policy Priorities, 1997) and the Web site http://www.cbpp.org/sfai.htm. Nor does the 1996 OECD study cited in this chapter included distributional data for individual countries.

100. Cited in Howard, *Hidden Welfare State,* 32.

101. Sheils and Hogan, "Cost of Tax-Exempt Health Benefits in 1998." An earlier estimate by Eugene Steuerle provided a similar portrait. He calculated that the cash value of the tax expenditure for employer-provided medical benefits was $270 for the lowest income quintile and $1,560 for the highest quintile [cited in Barbara L. Wolfe, "Reform of Health Care for the Nonelderly Poor," in *Confronting Poverty: Prescriptions for Change,* eds. Sheldon H. Danziger, Gary D. Sandefur, and Daniel H. Weinberg (Cambridge, Mass.: Harvard University Press, 1994), 254].

102. Similar patterns have been observed in the tax benefits accorded company pensions in

the United Kingdom and Germany. Adrian Sinfield, "Social Protection Versus Tax Benefits," presented at the Symposium of the European Institute of Social Security, Helsinki, Finland (4–5 September 1997).

103. William Gale, "Tax Credits: Social Policy in Bad Disguise," *Christian Science Monitor* (16 February 1999): 11.

104. It seems reasonable to assume that these inequities were even worse in the past, if only because of changes in marginal tax rates. The rates in the top income brackets were 85–90 percent in the 1950s and around 70 percent in the 1970s. Currently, the top income tax rate is closer to 40 percent.

105. I thank Bruce Davie for bringing this point to my attention.

106. Graetz, *Decline (and Fall?) of the Income Tax,* 135–136. See also Timothy J. Conlan, Margaret T. Wrightson, and David Beam, *Taxing Choices: The Politics of Tax Reform* (Washington, D.C.: Congressional Quarterly, 1990); Birnbaum and Murray, *Showdown at Gucci Gulch.*

107. Benjamin I. Page and Robert Y. Shapiro, *The Rational Public: Fifty Years of Trends in Americans' Policy Preferences* (Chicago: University of Chicago Press, 1992), 127–129.

108. Surrey and McDaniel, *Tax Expenditures;* McDaniel, "Tax Expenditures as Tools"; GAO, *Tax Expenditures Deserve More Scrutiny;* Herman B. Leonard, *Checks Unbalanced: The Quiet Side of Public Spending* (New York: Basic Books, 1986).

109. McDaniel, "Tax Expenditures as Tools."

110. Darrell M. West and Burdett A. Loomis, *The Sound of Money: How Political Interests Get What They Want* (New York: W. W. Norton, 1998), chap. 5.

111. Michael X. Delli Carpini and Scott Keeter, *What Americans Know About Politics and Why It Matters* (New Haven: Yale University Press, 1996), chap. 2.

112. Greenstein and Shapiro, *New Research Findings on the Effects of the Earned Income Tax Credit.*

CHAPTER FOURTEEN

Vouchers

C. Eugene Steuerle and Eric C. Twombly

Deborah Johnson is a former welfare recipient who lived with her two small children in a public housing complex on Chicago's west side. Long frustrated by the crime, drugs, and gangs that afflict this complex, Deborah was initially overjoyed when she learned that the Chicago Housing Authority had decided to demolish the complex and make residents eligible instead for "Section 8 housing vouchers" that would give them financial assistance to rent housing anywhere in the metropolitan area.

However, it soon became clear that this new program was not as simple as it sounded. In the first place, the number of vouchers available was less than the number of housing units being demolished in her previous complex. Because she had recently completed a job training program, found a job, and gone off welfare, Deborah discovered that she had a lower priority number than women who were still on welfare. In addition, there were not enough housing units available in the Chicago metropolitan area that the Housing Authority would certify as eligible for housing voucher support at rental rates that she could really afford given the scale of the subsidy available. Beyond that, she faced the challenge of establishing new transportation arrangements for her new job and new day care arrangements for her two small children. The Chicago Housing Authority was committed to helping Deborah and the 850 other former residents of the public housing complex with these challenges, but with only five full-time staff dedicated to this task, the obstacles were enormous. What sounded like a straightforward opportunity to "enter the market" for housing just like any other consumer thus turned out to be a tortuous ordeal for Deborah and her family. In the end, it proved to be an ordeal well worth the effort, but there were many times along the way that Deborah had serious doubts.

The experience of Deborah Johnson with the Section 8 housing voucher program in Chicago is illustrative of the dilemmas involved in the implementation of voucher programs more generally. Vouchers are sometimes thought to be the theoretical domain of conservatives and free marketeers, but, in fact, they have long been part of the tool chest of policymakers of all political persuasions. Certainly, the growing prominence of vouchers in the United States is hinged to the pervasive tenets of privatization and devolution,[1] but even the GI Bill, which provided college assistance to World War II veterans, was at its core a voucher program. Within the context of devolving programmatic and fiscal responsibilities for providing public goods, vouchers can usefully be viewed not as an ideological goal, but as another policy tool, and like other tools of government, vouchers are highly effective in some cases, but inappropriate in others. Stated differently, a voucher is simply a means of subsidy or payment, not an end in itself.[2]

The purpose of this chapter is to provide an overview of vouchers as a tool of government action. We define and review the basic features of vouchers, demonstrating that they can be constructed in a wide variety of ways. We also explore the patterns of voucher usage, and how vouchers work to meet policy goals. From a managerial perspective, we discuss various design options, and suggest key management challenges. We conclude the chapter with an overarching assessment of vouchers as a key component in the government's policy tool chest.

I. DEFINING THE TOOL

Defining Features

Fundamentally, a voucher "is a subsidy that grants limited purchasing power to an individual to choose among a restricted set of goods and services."[3] The most commonly cited feature of a voucher is the choice that it provides to the beneficiaries of a government program. With a food voucher, for instance, a beneficiary can buy most types of food in a grocery store. With a housing voucher, the beneficiary might be able to choose among a variety of rental apartments. Vouchers thus differ from grants and contracts in that they vest more control in the hands of the ultimate beneficiaries of public programs rather than the suppliers of goods and services. They are therefore often referred to as "consumer-side subsidies" rather than "producer-side subsidies." The choice provided to the beneficiary is far from complete, however. By its very nature, a voucher also restricts what can be bought: the food voucher cannot be spent on clothing. Vouchers are also not open-ended; the amount of purchasing power a voucher provides is limited.[4]

Relationship to Key Tool Features

To clarify the nature of vouchers further, it is useful to compare them to other tools in terms of the four dimensions used generally throughout this book: their *directness, automaticity, coerciveness,* and *visibility.*

Directness

Directness measures the extent to which the entity authorizing or inaugurating a program is involved in carrying it out.[5] Following this definition, vouchers generally display a minimal degree of *directness* when compared with other policy tools, although variation exists across programs. Indeed, it is their highly indirect quality that gives vouchers their special character and appeal. Not only do vouchers shift control over the provision of public services from governmental agencies to private providers, but also they shift it from the providers to the consumers. While government sets eligibility and payment levels, it seldom directly provides the goods or services. Indeed, a primary goal of vouchers is to avoid direct government provision and also to break the monopolies often held by private providers.

Voucher recipients acquire purchasing power for a set of subsidized goods and services, and those goods and services are usually privately provided. Of course, the actual reimbursement of providers may come from clients or government. For instance, under certain child-care programs, recipients are directly supplied with vouchers to redeem with eligible providers. In contrast, the financial exchanges used in many employment and training programs do not pass through clients' hands directly. Instead, government directly reimburses providers even though clients have some choice about where they receive services. Thus, while government remains involved in the administration of the programs, voucher programs involve the relinquishing of significant decisionmaking control to voucher recipients.

Automaticity

Automaticity measures the extent to which a policy tool uses existing administrative structures to produce its effect rather than having to create its own special administrative apparatus.[6] Although generalization is difficult, vouchers provide a *high level of automaticity* relative to many other policy tools. This is so because vouchers essentially rely on the existing private market to supply the goods and services being subsidized and essentially provide beneficiaries a "chit" to use for purchases in this market.

While they rely more heavily on the market than many other policy tools, however, voucher programs are almost always accompanied by some degree of government administration. The amount of administration and regulation varies across voucher programs. Some voucher programs, such as higher education vouchers, largely work through the administrative structures of colleges and universities. Other vouchers programs, such as child-care vouchers, which often are granted at the discretion of local caseworkers, as well as those for employment and training and housing, necessitate more government administration than other mechanisms. Although vouchers are typically designed to involve less regulation than direct government provision of services and goods, they are certainly more regulated than cash subsidies—after all, the set of goods and services that can be bought is proscribed. Nevertheless, because of their likely use of private providers, voucher programs do not usually expand existing public bureaucracies by very much.

Coerciveness

Coerciveness measures the extent to which a tool restricts individual or group behavior as opposed to merely encouraging or discouraging it. Vouchers are *moderately coercive* with respect to the consumption of goods and services because vouchers both prescribe and proscribe.[7] On the one hand, voucher recipients must have some measure of choice regarding goods, services, or producers. This is the side of vouchers that is usually given attention by its promoters. Thus, individuals may use higher education vouchers at a myriad of accredited educational institutions. Those receiving vouchers for subsidized child care may use them at a wide array of center-based and family care providers.

However, a voucher also restricts the types of public goods and services that may be purchased—a side often given less attention. Indeed, elected officials make normative decisions regarding which items voucher recipients should consume. For example, a recipient cannot use a voucher for employment and training services to purchase groceries. One voucher program currently provides for grocery items available in only one cafeteria. Despite this restrictiveness, many voucher programs provide consumers with a considerable amount of choice. Under some state plans, clients may use vouchers to purchase child care from nearly any provider, even if the provider is unlicensed.

In some cases, such as food stamps, the voucher can closely resemble a cash subsidy. This occurs most generally when the voucher amount is less than what would have been spent on the item anyway. In such cases, there are really no net additional proscriptions because of the voucher; it simply changes the source of payment, thus freeing up resources to be spent elsewhere.

Interestingly, a voucher is neither open-ended nor universal in its design. Instead, a voucher is typically capped or set at a particular value. Up to the capped amount, a voucher plan may be designed to have copayment rates, deductibles, or ceilings on total allowable costs. In addition, only certain individuals with specific characteristics or needs can receive vouchers. Public officials set eligibility standards to determine which individuals qualify for vouchers; there are few, if any, subsidies for which all people are eligible. In this way, vouchers are used as a policy tool to target benefits at select populations.

Visibility

Visibility measures the extent to which the resources devoted to a tool show up in the normal budget process. Vouchers usually have *a high degree of visibility* in the budget and policy processes, when compared with other policy tools. All voucher programs operate through legislative action and therefore produce some degree of debate and potential controversy about their legitimacy. Some voucher programs are even capped in total value, although this is not universal. (For example, Food Stamps is an open-ended entitlement program whose costs expand automatically when the number of eligible individuals applying for benefits increases.) For all vouchers, increases in benefits over time require going back through the discretionary budget process to set new limits and budgets each year. Especially visible are those vouchers whose expanded use may threaten some established constituency, as people turn to new providers or different ways of spending their subsidy.

By high visibility, of course, we do not mean that there are always fights over what will be provided. Sometimes voucher programs are summarily renewed in the budget process, and without much fanfare. For several years during the 1990s, the number of Section 8 housing vouchers remained unchanged, and were reappropriated annually with a limited degree of public debate regarding their efficiency or effectiveness. Yet when advocates pushed for the expansion of Section 8 vouchers during the fiscal year 2000 budget hearings, the visibility of the program increased markedly. This, in turn, heightened expectations regarding the ability of housing vouchers to meet their prescribed policy objectives.

Design Features and Major Variants

Although voucher programs share certain common features, such as their consumer-side character and their restriction to certain eligible populations and specified goods or services, they also potentially differ along certain dimensions. In particular, public administrators face at least four key issues in designing voucher programs.

Eligibility

First, eligibility determinations must be made. Existing programs vary significantly with respect to which individuals may receive vouchers. Some eligibility decisions are income conditioned. To receive Food Stamps or housing vouchers, clients must fall below a minimum income standard. However, other vouchers are based on nonincome criteria. The Ultra Low-Flush Toilet Voucher program, which provides area residents with vouchers for new low-flush toilets or rebates from the San Diego Water Authority if they turn in their high-water-usage toilets, is both geographically based and open to all income levels. That is, a resident from outside of San Diego water district is not eligible to receive the voucher, and the voucher recipient need not be poor. Other voucher plans that are designed without regard to income levels include some employee retraining programs, and the widely discussed Goods for Guns program in Pittsburgh, which provides grocery and department store certificates as vouchers in exchange for handguns and other firearms.[8]

Degree of Choice

Second, administrators must decide on the degree of choice within the voucher program. Policymakers formally restrict what may be purchased and sometimes from which producers. Indeed, vouchers are often intended to restrict the ability of consumers—especially welfare recipients—to buy items thought to be less needed or desirable by the public or their elected officials.

For a number of reasons, curbing recipients' purchasing autonomy is an integral part of any voucher program. Restrictions built into voucher programs might be justified on the grounds of economic efficiency, although this cannot be taken for granted. Vouchers are a balancing act between the needs of recipients and the concerns of taxpayers. In order to take into consideration both those who subsidized and those doing the subsidizing, program designers attempt to find the most direct means to achieve their programmatic goal.[9]

In the same regard, restrictions are also a way to get the necessary goods and services to different members of a household, even when the payment is made through one member. If voucher recipients can only purchase goods that can be shared, such as housing, or goods they cannot easily restrict to themselves, such as medical care and, to some extent, food, then they will not be tempted to horde benefits. Thus, restrictions on choice are intended to insure the well-being of all intended beneficiaries.

While most policymakers agree that a level of restriction is required, the challenge is to decide how much is appropriate. Depending on the program, the choice of goods or services can fall almost anywhere on a continuum: from highly restricted to much less so. Policymakers must also decide how much freedom recipients will have in picking the producers of those goods or services. For example, in the field of government-subsidized child care, under the Child Care and Development Fund (CCDF), parents may use certificates for state-licensed child-care providers or for informal service providers, including relatives and neighbors.[10] In contrast, under the recently enacted Workforce Investment Act (WIA) authorizing the nation's major employment and training programs, program recipients use voucher-like "Individual Training Accounts," which limit choice to a list of qualified service providers.[11]

Incentive Structures

A third administrative decision is how to design voucher programs to alter consumer behavior. If well planned, vouchers offer the opportunity to address incentive structures in very direct ways, although certain drawbacks typically exist. One common design is for a voucher to provide a 100 percent subsidy for initial purchases, but no subsidy beyond a certain point.[12] This may have the disadvantage of leading some consumers to purchase more than is deemed efficient from either their own or society's perspective.

Another programmatic option is to provide a partial subsidy (although here we quickly merge into other policy tools, for instance, a simple tax subsidy, that often are not labeled vouchers). Either way, a voucher will not be open-ended for the individual recipient—that is, provide an unlimited subsidy for any amount of the good or service that is purchased.

Depending on the goals of the program and the consumer/provider reaction to various price subsidies, of course, it is not always optimal for a subsidy to cover the full cost of the item.[13] That is, the optimal rate of subsidy may be less than 100 percent, so that the subsidized person bears some of the cost. Beyond some level of consumption, moreover, the subsidy rate can fall to zero so that the individual pays the full freight. From a benefit-cost perspective, this is often the optimal design and one of the potential reasons why a voucher mechanism is chosen. Vouchers therefore are especially useful where the goal is to provide some minimum level of well-being, where the response rates of consumers and providers cannot be well predicted for budgetary purposes, or where the consumer experiences declining returns from additional consumption of the item.

Degree of Oversight

Government oversight of voucher implementation also varies significantly among programs. For example, the CCDF mandates only a minimal level of oversight; informal childcare providers are not required to be licensed with the states, although many stated urge providers to certify that they comply with safety standards. For employment and training providers to receive funds under WIA, however, they are required to meet and maintain eligibility criteria established by each state. They must also be certified under the Higher Education Act, the National Apprenticeship Act, or an "alternative procedure" developed by the state. In addition, all providers must submit annual performance-based information on the outcomes achieved by their students, and exceed minimum levels of performance set forth by states and localities.[14]

II. PATTERNS OF USE

Current Extent

Vouchers have been used in public programs for many years. In the area of housing assistance, Section 8 certificates have been used for about twenty-five years to promote access to better residential areas for low-income Americans. In addition, the Pell grant program, which provides financial support to low- and moderate-income college students, has existed since the early 1970s; Pell grants can be applied to tuition costs at a wide array of accredited academic institutions chosen by the consumer.[15]

However, the privatization of social services in the United States has brought vouchers to the forefront in policy arenas where they once had limited impact, including government-subsidized child care and employment and training services.[16] Indeed, a plethora of publicly subsidized goods and services are currently supplied through vouchers. Vouchers are used to provide food subsidies, K-12 and higher education, and housing services, to name but a few.

As noted in Table 14-1, the five major federal vouchers programs in the areas of child care, higher education, work force development, food, and nutrition receive annual appropriations that range from $1 billion to nearly $28 billion. In many fields, vouchers now outdistance most other forms of assistance. For example, the amount

TABLE 14-1 *Major Federal Voucher Programs with Annual Appropriation of at Least $1 Billion, Fiscal Year 2000*

Voucher Program	*Program Area*	*Appropriation Level (in billions)*
Child Care and Development Fund Block Grant	Child Care	$1.2
Federal Pell Grants	Education	$7.9
Food Stamp Program	Food and Nutrition	$21.2
Women, Infants, and Children (WIC) Program	Food and Nutrition	$4.0

SOURCE: *Budget of the United States Government: Fiscal Year 2001*, Appendix. (Washington, DC: U.S. Government Printing Office, 2000.) Smaller federal workforce development and nutrition voucher plans include the Title III-A Employment and Training for Dislocated Workers; the Title III Dislocated Workers Career Management Grants; the Trade Adjustment Assistance program; and WIC Farmer's Market Nutrition Program. Each program has annual funding levels of less than $1 billion.

spent on food stamps, at $21.2 billion, exceeds the amount spent on Temporary Assistance for Needy Families (TANF), at $16.7 billion, by nearly 25 percent.

While the federal government administers several voucher programs, even more activity occurs at the state and local levels. For example, many states have instituted voucher components as part of their initiatives to move welfare recipients into the labor market. Michigan developed a packet of vouchers that state officials have deemed a "tool chest," to improve the employment chances of people leaving public assistance. Recipients can use their vouchers to obtain public health services, job training, and family and child-care services. Using a mix of federal and state funds, Massachusetts instituted a voucher program to cover the full amount of child care costs for TANF families at licensed and exempt child-care centers. Designed to promote labor market attachment among those leaving the welfare rolls, the child-care assistance is available through vouchers to TANF families for one year.

Localities also have been at the forefront in the use of vouchers. Instead of supplying direct cash transfers, local governments in Pittsburgh, New Orleans, and Santa Rosa, California, have used vouchers to reimburse individuals who have relinquished their firearms in gun "buy-back" programs; recipients then may use the vouchers for goods at local department and grocery stores. Often, but not always, the localities' efforts are tied to state and national efforts. In the case of many welfare programs, for instance, financing comes mainly from higher levels of government, but administration is left to the localities.

Vouchers are also commonly used beyond the United States. Food stamps are common among industrial countries. Educational vouchers for primary and secondary education are used in some European countries, without significant controversy. Accor Corporate Services is a business operating worldwide, but primarily in Europe, that claims to have issued 38 billion vouchers to over 10 million people. Although many are business based, such as child care and transportation vouchers, even these are often tax motivated. Many other of the vouchers they service, however, are also for government clients.

Recent Trends

Vouchers continue to grow in importance and use. For low-income individuals who do not work, there has been a movement away from cash assistance, as in Aid to Families with Dependent Children or TANF, even while housing vouchers and child-care vouchers have expanded. For example, the number of TANF recipients declined by roughly 49 percent between August 1996, which marked the passage of the federal welfare reform legislation, and December 1999.[17] Conversely, despite the fact that the growth of Section 8 vouchers was frozen from 1995 through 1998, 50,000 housing vouchers were created in 1999.[18] For fiscal year 2000, Congress expanded the tenant-based component of the Section 8 program even further by authorizing an additional 100,000 vouchers. Child-care vouchers have grown especially in the last few years because of the enactment of welfare reform in various states and at the national level. This reform emphasized getting people off the roles but did not reduce federal assistance. Hence, with more federal dollars available to fewer people and with no expansion of direct cash assistance, child-care vouchers became a primary vehicle for providing assistance.

Vouchers are also an important and growing component of Medicare. Since the passage of The Tax Equity and Fiscal Responsibility Act of 1982, Medicare participants have been allowed the option of enrolling in and receiving care through health maintenance organizations, which accepted government-subsidized vouchers.[19] While this remains a controversial area, some recent health-care proposals would significantly expand the use of health vouchers either as a way to subsidize the nonelderly or as a mechanism to replace more traditional health insurance.

Some local school districts have experimented with vouchers to provide local children with new primary and secondary educational opportunities. Indeed, several cities, such as Cleveland, Milwaukee, and Cambridge, Massachusetts, have instituted school choice programs that are predicated on the provision of school vouchers to parents.

III. BASIC MECHANICS

Although voucher programs are often assumed to be self-executing, in fact they involve a host of administrative tasks. Eight of these in particular seem especially worthy of attention.

Specifying the Product or Service

The first step in the implementation of a voucher program is to define what is to be subsidized and to devise means to ensure that program resources are used only for these items. For instance, food stamps include many types of purchases, but they might not include dog food purchased at the grocery or food purchased in restaurants. To ensure against this, systems have to be developed to make sure that only sanctioned items are purchased with the voucher. For example, grocery stores and food chains use UPC labels and product scanners in checkout lines to identify which goods are eligible to be purchased with food stamps and which are not. The voucher recipient then is required to pay cash for ineligible items.

Determining Eligibility

Second, policy officials must define and certify eligible recipients. If the voucher is meant to be part of a welfare system, limitations might be placed on individuals by income or assets. Under any circumstances, a screening mechanism must be established to review applicants against the criteria established for the program and certify those who are eligible. Some vouchers, such as housing vouchers, involve queues. Here the federal government provides a limited number of vouchers to local housing authorities, which in turn set up a system to decide who gets them and who does not. Typically, there is a list of income and other criteria specified by the federal government, but then state and local governments define who moves to the top of the queue according to date of application or distinguishing needs, such as some major health impairment.

Distribution

Third, program administrators must determine and implement payment and distribution methods. Often the agency that has the responsibility of determining eligibility is simultaneously saddled with the distribution of the vouchers. Must the clients report to the agency? Will the voucher be sent through the mail? As noted before, vouchers may also be supplied directly to the producer rather than to the consumer, as in the case of some vouchers for higher education. While these vouchers may be spent at many colleges and universities, often it is the educational institution that coordinates these systems with other systems of grants and loans, which may be public or private.

Very recently, food stamps have been converted in some states to "smart cards" that operate like credit cards. Not only might this prove to be administratively efficient, but it also is likely to reduce the ability of food stamp recipients to "sell" food stamps to others in exchange for money.

Eligibility Recertification

Fourth, officials must establish communication systems between the distribution and eligibility processes. It is quite common for vouchers to be sent out on a regular basis, which, in theory, requires a continual check on whether each client is still eligible. However, in practice some voucher systems fail to achieve this goal. For example, many welfare programs—whether they use vouchers or not—are based on a monthly accounting period for determining income eligibility, but the clients are required only to report "changes." The default administrative determination is then the oft-incorrect supposition that no new report from the client implies a lack of change in income in the preceding month.

Recruiting/Certifying Suppliers

Fifth, program officials may need to inform, certify, and, in some programs, recruit legitimate suppliers. Depending on the design of the voucher program, some administrative apparatus may be required simultaneously to address supplier concerns. In the case of housing vouchers, for example, owners of rental housing must meet criteria associated with the voucher. For example, housing units must meet minimum size requirements, as well as health and safety standards. Moreover, to avoid price gouging by landlords and ensure the affordability of eligible housing for voucher recipients, program administrators must compute fair market rent values for a given locality and ensure that suppliers are providing units that do not exceed them. Similarly, in the case of food stamps, some suppliers, such as restaurants, may be excluded for administrative reasons even if they supply the eligible products. In the case of Medicare, a whole new system was required to deal with the types of insurance companies and associated health maintenance organizations that operate with a fixed payment voucher in lieu of traditional Medicare payments.

The regulation of suppliers also must be kept in balance because excessive restrictions may lead some producers to drop out of the voucher system. For example, some rental housing owners have cited too much regulation as one reason for pulling their housing out of the housing voucher system. By the same token, additional suppliers may need to be recruited not only so that clients have someplace to spend their money, but also to promote adequate competition. For instance, an educational voucher for primary education may not give parents many alternatives if there is only one school in their area.

Ensuring Adequate Consumer Knowledge

Sixth, some kind of information system, including marketing and counseling, is often required with voucher programs. Such systems can help address one of the common complaints about vouchers: that they put less-educated consumers at a disadvantage both in claiming their fair share of available vouchers and in using them efficiently in the market due to lack of information about the available suppliers and their products. Health care and primary and secondary education, for instance, are highly complex products in which information is held by professional suppliers (doctors and teachers).

In some cases, warnings must be issued to avoid the inappropriate use of vouchers. Information systems may be highly active, as when caseworkers determine who can use child-care vouchers; or relatively passive, as in the case of occasional notices sent to clients about changes in program rules.

Monitoring and Enforcement

Seventh, program administrators must design and implement systems of enforcement, monitoring, and evaluation. Occasional audits of both consumers and producers provide information on the efficiency of the voucher system. Error rates need to be determined. Researchers, both internal and external to the authorizing government agency, must be used to determine programmatic effectiveness and to convert information from statistical samples into population estimates related to the overall program.

Coordination

Finally, coordination with other programs is usually necessary and may require explicit budgeting of resources if it is to take place. For example, food stamps must be coordinated with other welfare payments such as cash payments under TANF. Some families are better served if they can engage in "one-stop shopping" for various benefits for which they may be eligible, including vouchers. Educational vouchers must be coordinated with other educational grants, subsidies, and rules (e.g., schools receiving vouchers must still meet a host of other state regulations on schools). Coordination can be both formal and informal. To determine the monthly allowance of food stamp or housing voucher assistance, for example, it is necessary to maintain records for other programs, as income from one source reduces eligibility for benefits from another source. Meanwhile, caseworkers trying to help clients receiving vouchers and other forms of public assistance will often guide them to training programs, educational opportunities, job banks, and special programs run by nonprofit agencies in the same area.

IV. TOOL SELECTION

Discussions of the appropriateness of vouchers typically center on the economic goals of efficiency and equity. However, the selection of vouchers vis-à-vis other policy tools takes place in a broader political environment. Indeed, the selection of goals and the ability of a voucher tool to meet them tend to vary significantly from one program to another. While it is ideal for policymakers to choose the government tool that maximizes social welfare, political factors almost always prove crucial in the final tool selection. In this section, the inherent advantages associated with vouchers are juxtaposed with the political considerations that often accompany their selection.

Rationale: Choice, Efficiency, and Equity

Choice

"Choice" is often the buzzword used to explain the potential advantages of vouchers.[20] Some have argued that a crucial benefit of the voucher form stems from the fact that it gives beneficiaries of government programs greater choice over the goods or services they obtain. Indeed, choice may increase the value of goods and services to beneficiaries because voucher recipients can select providers that best match their own preferences. In addition, the availability of choice under voucher plans may also result in efficiency gains due to greater competition among suppliers and the ability of public officials to control program costs.

The ability of consumers to choose among providers theoretically creates a more competitive environment. Under some voucher plans, most notably in social services, competition may rise on two levels. First, in service regimes that provide many choices to consumers, suppliers will compete for direct voucher funds from clients even if government ultimately reimburses producers. In this case, the focus of producers must shift from government as a primary funder to the many individual voucher recipients. Second, in service areas in which vouchers incrementally replace existing contractual arrangements, competition may increase for the declining number of government service contracts. The result of increased competition is a series of incentives for providers to supply high-quality services at the lowest possible cost in order to maintain or expand their market share. In the human service field, for example, this suggests that nonprofit, for-profit, and public providers are competing in new ways, as each strives to adjust to changing programmatic and fiscal realities. However, the implementation of new government tools may also cause these organizations to form service coalitions in which the pooling of resources can produce lower-cost, high-quality care. The use of vouchers may also cause new providers to enter markets, thus changing the mix of available types and quantities of services.

Increased competition among producers is not ensured by the introduction of voucher programs into existing markets, however. Indeed, providers that operate in markets where vouchers are supplanting contract revenue may be more vulnerable to organizational dissolution. In such circumstances the introduction of vouchers can reduce the universe of providers. In addition, when vouchers are introduced where there is limited competition or an inadequate supply of goods and services, they can have the unintended consequence of increasing the price for the goods or services being subsidized, which runs counter to the theoretical support for voucher usage.

Beyond this, the notion that vouchers promote *some* degree of competition among suppliers assumes that consumers are able to choose competently among goods, services, and providers. In the policy debate over vouchers, however, this remains a highly contentious assumption. For example, many opponents of school vouchers openly question whether parents are capable of choosing the best educational settings for their children. These critics provide several reasons for being concerned about recipients' abilities to make educated choices. Some feel that market information is not easily accessible; not all consumers have the luxury of comparison shopping. Another concern is that some services cannot be properly assessed until after they have been acquired and, by then, it is too late to make a different choice. Finally, others worry about instances of "asymmetrical information," in which producers have more knowledge about their products than do consumers and, therefore, can misinform or mislead them.

What this suggests is that vouchers are easier to implement for products that are easier to assess (e.g., food), or where information on quality is readily available, or where beneficiaries have the strongest incentives to invest the time and effort to acquire the information they need to make wise use of their vouchers. Many argue these conditions are not often met in the education field, which is what has made this field such a controversial arena for vouchers. Where these conditions are not met, vouchers typically have to be accompanied by information campaigns or regulations, which can defeat the market-based arguments for the use of vouchers in the first place. Not all consumers need to be informed for competition to yield better products, of course. To give a private sector analogy, consumers with knowledge about automobiles may increase demand for efficiency among all automobile producers. Then even those with less knowledge can benefit. Similarly, it is argued that educational vouchers, whether for higher education or primary and secondary education, can increase the quality of all schools.

The debate surrounding recipient decisionmaking is most heated for policy areas, such as education and health care, in which services are provided by professionals, such as teachers and doctors, who claim expertise and inevitably are given broad powers to make decisions for consumers (prescribing homework or drug treatment).[21] However, the controversy may also be attributed to the perceived capabilities of recipients. For example, without help from intermediaries, decisions for children might be entrusted to adults who may or may not make choices that are in the children's best interest. Mentally impaired clients may not be able by themselves to make informed decisions regarding services such as vocational rehabilitation.[22]

Efficiency

Voucher programs are also often defended in terms of their contribution to efficiency. Efficiency gains that result from voucher use may be measured in terms of cost, such as lower cost per output unit or reduced costs for the same amount of output. For example, greater efficiency in education might lead to greater levels of learning for the same cost or an identical level of learning at a lower cost. Because vouchers are often capped or set at a given amount, vouchers partially represent a key method for government to control program costs. When contrasted with open-ended subsidy programs, which may suffer from cost escalation without legislative action, voucher programs become quite appealing to law makers. For example, a substantial amount of the expected, long-term growth in the Medicare program stems from the open-ended manner in which the program was designed more than thirty years ago.[23]

Efficiency gains from vouchers derive largely from competition in the marketplace—the ability of different producers to offer alternative products to consumers and to compete in providing the most value per dollar spent. When there is no competition, and money can only be spent on one item, efficiency gains will be dissipated. The case of public housing being converted to vouchers provides a good example. Because there is no competitive supply and consumers are not given choices, public housing is often assessed as worth about 70 cents for every dollar spent by government. That is, clients would prefer 70 cents in cash to the $1 spent by government for the public housing, although clients will take the inefficient housing over nothing at all. Essentially, 30 cents is wasted because decisionmaking is so restricted. However, for a voucher to improve efficiency, that is, for the value of the housing to approach what the consumer would pay with the dollar subsidy, there needs to be more competition and additional choices for consumers. If the vouchers are so restrictive that almost no suppliers want to enter the market, or if the supply of eligible housing is extremely limited, then gains from the introduction of vouchers are limited.

Some voucher programs are also believed to decrease overhead and administrative expenses when compared with the direct public provision of goods and services. This argument is particularly prevalent in the school choice debate; for instance, some argue that direct public provision of education results in a ratio of nonteaching to teaching staff that is too high. School choice advocates claim that promoting competition in K-12 education markets through vouchers will force schools to reduce costly and potentially wasteful expenditures.

However, not every voucher plan reduces program costs. The availability of vouchers often causes demand, and therefore prices, to rise as more eligible consumers secure benefits. As a consequence, all consumers may end up being worse off if the supply cannot increase fast enough to meet the increased demand. This problem is particularly evident in subsidized child-care programs, in which vouchers are used by individuals who would have received child care irrespective of the government subsidy.[24] The use of vouchers in this area even allows relatives and friends of clients to be paid for services that would otherwise have been provided without direct public cost.

Equity

A third rationale for vouchers is the claim that they promote equity. While efficiency arguments are quite persuasive, the public—perhaps more than researchers and analysts—is often driven by concerns of fairness.[25] Each efficiency argument, moreover, can usually be recast as an issue of equity. For example, educational vouchers are often said to lead to improved (more efficient) schooling opportunities. From an equity standpoint, however, it is also argued that wealthy Americans can easily select where their children will receive their education by either sending them to a private school or moving to different school districts. However, vouchers make such options available to all, or at least to many more. Opponents of voucher plans counter that the economic benefits of choice may not be equitably transferred to individuals who require the greatest assistance, because of adverse selection, asymmetrical program information, or consumers' limited ability to choose. For instance, in the employment and training field, critics of vouchers have argued that clients may either misjudge their aptitude or the availability of jobs when choosing how to apply vouchers to gain employment skills.

Equity issues arise in a myriad of ways in voucher plans, and the notion of equity typically strikes a strong chord in the American policy process. For instance, in the subsidized child-care arena, some have argued that to reimburse formal service providers, but not relatives and friends, is clearly unfair. Thus, under many voucher plans, consumer choice has been dramatically expanded to include formal and informal child-care providers. What this suggests, however, is that vouchers work best where they can offset and not reinforce existing inequities of knowledge and resources, and where informal systems are not in place that could absorb a disproportionate share of program resources with no change in the availability of services.

Political Considerations

While the economic goals of choice, efficiency, and equity are important in assessing the attractiveness of vouchers, so too are political considerations. In many policy environments, vouchers are firmly enmeshed as a key method of financing and delivering public goods. For example, the use of vouchers was made mandatory by the 1990 Child Care Development Block Grant (CCDBG). All states are required to provide vouchers to eligible individuals as an option for child care. As a result, the use of vouchers for government-subsidized child care is now a standard service delivery mechanism, and often extends to care provided by relatives. Moreover, the continued use of vouchers in some program areas such as food and nutrition typically occurs without much public discourse.

However, in other policy arenas—most notably K-12 education and health care in the United States—the proposed use of vouchers, even on marginal scales, evokes tremendous and highly public disagreement. Such factors as political symbolism and interest group politicking help to explain the conflict that surrounds voucher proposals in various policy areas, and ultimately their choice as an implementation tool.

Part of the political attractiveness of vouchers results from the symbolism that surrounds their use, in particular the symbolism of "choice." Americans embrace the right to choose because it engenders notions of democracy and freedom.[26] Choice is also seductive because it evokes market-based ideals of efficiency and consumer-oriented equity, even though in practice vouchers do not automatically provide more choice.[27]

Beyond these symbolic politics, however, often lie more concrete interests. Indeed, the ideal of choice has made for interesting bedfellows in K-12 education and housing arenas. Some proponents favor market-based solutions and promote vouchers in these areas because the resulting competition among suppliers will spark increased quality and lower production costs. In essence, their arguments focus on the goal of efficiency. On the other hand, some advocates for the poor who might not normally look to market-based solutions may nonetheless see vouchers as an opportunity for the most disadvantaged members of society to reap quality public benefits that often elude them. For instance, a housing voucher has the theoretical ability to allow poor residents to leave dangerous neighborhoods for more stable environments.

Although symbolism is an important component in problem definition and agenda setting, the viability of the voucher, and its ultimate selection as a policy tool, depends more heavily on how interest groups calculate their gains and losses.[28] In fact, interest groups have been vital in expanding or restricting voucher use. Even though the poor, who tend to have modest political organization, constitute the core constituency of the Food Stamp program, the key to its continuation has been its support from key congressional leaders and the powerful American Farm Bureau Federation.[29] More recently, when the politics of food stamps was redefined as an issue of welfare reform and anti-immigration, advocates for the poor banded with other members of the Food Stamp coalition to defeat restrictive legislation.[30]

The reason for this is that many producer groups prefer tools of government action that most directly tie benefits to their particular outputs. Conversely, the least preferred form of public assistance among many producers is cash transfers to consumers because cash subsidies do not constrain consumer choices to particular goods and services and therefore cannot easily appeal to the producers of these goods and services. Depending on the extent to which strong interest groups are involved in their design, voucher programs strike an important middle ground among potential forms of public subsidies. Producers retain some control over which goods and services are purchased by subsidized individuals, while beneficiaries are provided with some degree of choice among producers of those products. As a result, vouchers are often a politically palatable form of government intervention.

School voucher proponents, however, have been largely unsuccessful in passing their initiatives in the United States (but not Europe), due in part to the political vitality of the National Education Association, The American Federation of Teachers, and school board associations,[31] all of which fear the negative consequences vouchers might have for public education. In the face of strong opposition by these interest groups and multiple defeats in both the courts and at the ballot box,[32] school choice advocates have turned to an alternative model of educational choice in the form of charter schools. Charters are perceived by some to be a safer compromise than educational vouchers, in part because they do not directly involve public funding of parochial schools. However, of potentially greater importance, they raise fewer political objections because they are portrayed as an *adaptation*—rather than a *rejection*—of an existing program with broad institutional support.[33] In many charter schools, many established rules (e.g., teacher salary and tenure, courses to be offered, support of athletics) are carried over from the public schools to the charter schools.

Coalition support for voucher programs also relates to the strength of the program's constituency. There is some evidence that constituency organization is correlated with program continuation. For instance, the Pell Grant program has built a relatively strong constituency within the higher education community.[34] Groups such as state colleges and universities, whether public or private, have consistently defended the program since its inception in 1973. However, the use of vouchers is not simply defined by the institutional support of advocates or proponents. The selection of vouchers as a government tool can also reflect the level of public attention given to a particular issue area. The Workforce Investment Act of 1998, which authorizes voucher-like Individual Training Accounts, passed through Congress with widespread bipartisan support, and, more importantly, without much public fanfare.

V. MANAGEMENT CHALLENGES AND POTENTIAL RESPONSES

One of the great political appeals of vouchers is their automaticity, their reliance on the presumably automatic mechanisms of the market, and their reduced need/or governmental administration. However, as we have seen, the management of vouchers is more complicated than often believed. Indeed, critics of voucher programs suggest that their implementation provides fertile ground for price gouging and consumer fraud in markets that are characterized by insufficient competition or lax governmental oversight. More specifically, at least five types of management challenges often accompany the operation of voucher programs.

Ensuring Competition among Suppliers

A first management challenge of voucher programs is to ensure a sufficient degree of competition among providers. Where supply is limited or competition nonexistent, vouchers can inadvertently cause increased prices for the subsidized good or service. Before implementing a voucher plan, public administrators must determine whether the program will help provide greater competition among suppliers, and then must monitor competitive conditions. For example, housing vouchers can yield a more competitive supply of housing than public housing contracts (not only initially, but years after the housing has been built). However, education vouchers may or may not provide greater competition, depending on factors including the size and demography of the market. Indeed, higher education may have a national market, while primary and secondary schools may have a regional market. If there is only one school in a market, which is the case in many rural locations, vouchers may fail to stimulate competition. Even here, vouchers may provide some enhancement to the market if they are transferable or can be used to bargain for other inputs.[35]

The degree to which vouchers encourage competition depends largely on the ability of consumers to access goods and services. Certain voucher programs include restrictions that do not allow recipients to shop for goods or services outside specific geographic areas. For example, some housing vouchers must be used in specific locations. Other times, recipients are unable to reach the goods and services due to personal constraints. Recipients with familial ties (such as care-taking responsibilities) may need to attend the college nearest to their home, despite having a voucher for higher education that allows them to choose from a variety of schools.

Overcoming Information Asymmetries

A second key management challenge of vouchers is to ensure that beneficiaries can make effective choices to maximize the benefits provided by the voucher. As noted above, some consumers have limited personal ability to choose effectively among several producers, or may suffer from a lack of information regarding the availability or quality of producers. For example, recipients of Section 8 vouchers may not have an accurate or complete list of vacant housing units that will accept their certificates.

Public officials often use two strategies to mitigate the effects of limited competition and asymmetrical information. First, administrators can establish regulatory frameworks to reduce or minimize potential disparities in program outcomes. Of course, too much regulation causes vouchers to act much like the direct public provision of goods and services. However, at least some government regulation is always required in voucher programs. Second, public officials may establish methods of informing consumers to help them make wise choices. For example, administrators can restrict potentially misleading advertising or produce consumer reports that guide voucher recipients in their decisionmaking.

Systems used to distribute information vary in quality.[36] Some inconsistencies are due to the size of the information dissemination effort. Administrators working with small-scale systems may find it difficult to provide enough information to influence decisions, while those dealing with large-scale systems run the risk of inundating consumers with too much information. Finally, maintaining information systems is a costly endeavor.

Managing Access

The fact that funding for vouchers is rarely sufficient to cover all of those who meet the established eligibility criteria creates a third set of issues for administrators. Excess demand for vouchers may create waiting lists or queues, which may increase the program's vulnerability to market distortions. Indeed, for fear of altering their eligibility and having to reenter a queue, recipients may be reluctant to move to obtain better jobs, more education, or support from relatives. Waiting lists decrease efficiency and equity gains by operating on a first-come/first-served, or lottery, basis. Moreover, waiting lists tend to encourage corruption, from small-scale brokering of inside information about how to be placed on a waiting list to larger-scale bribes—rampant at one point in the District of Columbia system for housing vouchers and public housing.[37]

Evaluating Performance

A fourth challenge in the operation of voucher programs is to identify valid performance measures. When voucher programs are promoted as a way to foster competition, additional measurement problems result. This is because voucher programs may produce competitive environments that lower costs or improve quality for all individuals, not just those receiving the voucher. Thus, testing program effectiveness by comparing recipient and nonrecipient outcomes may drastically understate the impact of the voucher.

To date, the government oversight of voucher implementation has varied significantly among programs. For example, the CCDF mandates only a minimal level of oversight; informal child-care providers are not required to be licensed with the states, although many states urge providers to certify that they comply with safety standards. For employment and training providers to receive funds under WIA, however, they are required to meet and maintain eligibility criteria established by each state. They must also be certified under the Higher Education Act, the National Apprenticeship Act, or an "alternative procedure" developed by the state. In addition, all providers must submit annual performance-based information on the outcomes achieved by their students, and exceed minimum levels of performance set forth by states and localities.[38]

Coordination with Other Subsidy Programs

Program administrators must also decide how best to coordinate multiple income-related programs, both those using vouchers and those that do not. As noted, vouchers are used to deliver a wide range of social services and are increasingly prevalent in human service areas where they once had a limited impact. Although an individual voucher may meet efficiency and equity goals, each additional voucher program (e.g., education, child care, employment, and training) complicates coordination tasks with respect to the amount of available consumer choice, proscription of goods, eligibility levels, administrative duplication and transaction costs, and effective marginal tax rates faced by individuals.[39]

Public officials may decide that a less cumbersome option is to create "bundled vouchers" under structured choice programs, which combine various social services into singular voucher plans. Some states have experimented with structured choice plans as a component of welfare reform. For instance, Michigan has adopted the "Tool Chest" program in which clients can select different social services that may be of greatest assistance as they transition from welfare to work. However, the consolidation of voucher programs may generate considerable political ramifications on two related fronts. First, existing interest groups may be less inclined to support programs that do not provide them with direct benefits. Second, the history of block grants demonstrates that program consolidation at times can reduce government support. Nevertheless, as the voucher becomes an increasingly prominent service delivery mechanism, public administrators must consider structured choice as a key design option in voucher implementation.

Adverse Selection as a Management Challenge

Finally, vouchers are often vulnerable to the problem of "adverse selection." Under adverse selection, those who join a group—whether it be a group health insurance policy or an educational establishment—will have an incentive to avoid subsidizing other people in the same system. For example, healthy individuals who purchase insurance together can increase the value of a fixed dollar voucher by excluding unhealthy individuals whose own vouchers will not cover their full health-care costs.[40] Similarly, a school that avoids accepting physically or learning disabled children can buy more for its needy students if it receives the same subsidy or tuition for everyone. Although the issue is not unique to vouchers, the setting of the subsidy at the individual level means it must be given special attention.

Public officials may be compelled to modify voucher programs to avoid undesirable selection effects. One approach is to add a layer of additional subsidy to try to duplicate the cross-subsidization that might occur if everyone were automatically placed in the same school system or given the same health insurance policy. For example, one method to restrict adverse selection in health care is to create subsidies that vary by different levels of health risk. Another approach for limiting the effects of adverse selection is to ensure that providers of goods and services do not exclude voucher recipients. For example, a health insurance pool or an educational program may be required to accept all applicants or at least give an equal likelihood of acceptance.

Dealing with adverse selection is by far one of the most difficult challenges facing policymakers. While a special issue for health care and educational vouchers, it can crop up elsewhere, as in housing. Overregulation can prevent many of the market gains from consumer choice from occurring, while underregulation can allow so much adverse selection that the basic distributional goals of the voucher program are not met. Balance is required, but it is seldom without a good deal of tension.

VI. OVERALL ASSESSMENT

Vouchers have emerged as an important vehicle to achieve public goals because they can—under optimal circumstances—produce significant efficiency and equity gains. Government may use vouchers to target goods and services to certain groups of recipients while exercising some control over consumer behavior by proscribing what may be purchased. Consumers may use vouchers to better match their preferences for goods and services than if they used other, more intrusive policy tools. Voucher programs may also be designed to generate greater competition among producers, which in turn may drive some inefficient suppliers from the market.

Vouchers are also highly effective as a budget device. Generally speaking, the limits or caps placed on how much can be spent by each recipient forces reconsideration each year of voucher programs. Although not a certainty, voucher programs are unlikely to entail run-away expenditures, and usually they will go through a visible, if sometimes contentious, budgetary process each year.

However, opponents of vouchers question the overall effectiveness of voucher programs. Indeed, critics of school choice argue that many parents are ill-equipped to make rational and informed decisions about their children's education, even if school performance data and public information are provided to them. The inability of parents to choose effectively among myriad schools with varying levels of performance may circumvent the theoretical efficiency gains of voucher programs. These critics of vouchers also suggest that voucher programs are inequitable. Because most school voucher plans do not provide vouchers to all students and do not cover the full cost of tuition at other educational institutions, opponents argue that vouchers may exacerbate the problems of primary and secondary education, particularly in low-income, urban areas. The implementation of school voucher plans might allow better schools to "cream" the best students from poor schools, leaving a group of poor students in urban neighborhood schools that face decreased funding because of falling enrollment. Critics of voucher plans claim that this scenario is hardly equitable.

These problems, however, are not inherent in vouchers *per se*. They may arise in particular circumstances and in specific settings. Vouchers may encourage competition in some geographical areas with many suppliers but not in others with few suppliers; they may be used ineffectively in consumer markets with little information but effectively where consumers are or can be better informed.

In a practical sense, vouchers require more regulation than some supporters care to admit and offer more gains in efficiency and equity than some opponents acknowledge. However, vouchers come in all shapes and sizes, as well, so an assessment of one type of design may not be appropriate for another. Part of the effectiveness of vouchers is their versatility and malleability. Therefore, it is usually more appropriate to evaluate a particular voucher design than to make a generic assessment.

The final decision on whether to implement a voucher instead of an alternative policy tool often hinges on its political support and the influence of the groups that support or reject its use. Supporters and opponents of voucher use do not confine their advocacy activities to the legislative process. When stymied or threatened by the expansion of school choice initiatives, for instance, several groups pressed their case for or against school vouchers through the judicial system. This suggests that the growing prominence of vouchers as a policy alternative has brought with it a rising level of political activity and advocacy—a natural process in democratic societies. Thus, while a voucher is a neutral policy tool that may produce significant efficiency and equity gains under the right conditions and circumstances, it has also acquired significant political and ideological baggage as a consequence of often intense political arguments. However, this

only demonstrates a consistent theme of this book: tool choices are not simply technical choices; they entail conflicts of values and interests as well.

463

CH 14:
VOUCHERS

VII. FUTURE DIRECTIONS

Policymakers and researchers across the ideological spectrum have embraced the expansion of vouchers to provide public goods and services. Although they must compete with direct government delivery, contracting of government services, competitive public suppliers, cash payments, and loans, among alternative delivery mechanisms vouchers are now the delivery mechanism of choice in a growing number of policy areas. Yet this chapter also demonstrates that vouchers can contain a substantial number of restrictions that can ultimately inhibit efficiency or equity gains. Indeed, vouchers may be used effectively to solve certain public problems, but may be highly inappropriate when applied to others. Moreover, despite the widening application of vouchers across policy areas, and their ability to be formed in a wide variety of ways, the very range of the possibilities presents difficult challenges for public administrators, suggesting that much attention must be given to their structural design.

Only by recognizing appropriate situations for voucher use and carefully addressing key management challenges can policymakers use vouchers to maximize efficiency and equity gains. And while it is not always easy to measure the success of vouchers vis-à-vis other government tools—especially when they induce gains in programs embodying these other tools as well—they represent a powerful component in the government's tool chest. Their expansion in recent years attests to their usefulness, but also increases our responsibility to learn better how to structure and manage them.

VIII. SUGGESTED READING

Chubb, John, and Terry Moe. *Politics, Markets, and America's Schools.* Washington, D.C.: The Brookings Institution, 1990.
Henig, Jeffrey R. *Rethinking School Choice.* Princeton, N.J.: Princeton University Press, 1994.
Lowry, I. *Rent Control and Housing Assistance: The U.S. Experience.* Washington, D.C.: Urban Institute Press, 1996.
Osborne, David, and Ted Gaebler. *Reinventing Government: How the Entrepreneurial Spirit is Transforming the Public Sector.* Reading, MA: Addison-Wesley Publishing Company, 1992.
Steuerle, C. Eugene, Van Doorn Ooms, George Peterson, and Robert D. Reischauer, eds. *Vouchers and the Provision of Public Services.* Washington, D.C.: The Brookings Institution, Committee for Economic Development, and Urban Institute Press, 2000.
Turner, Margery A., and K. Williams. *Housing Mobility: Realizing the Promise.* Washington, D.C.: Urban Institute Press, 1998.

NOTES

1. Eric C. Twombly and Elizabeth T. Boris, *The Use of Vouchers in the Provision of Human Services and Potential Implications for Nonprofit Organizations,* Paper presented at the Independent Sector Spring Research Forum, Alexandria, Virginia, (26 March 1999).

2. C. Eugene Steuerle, "Common Issues for Voucher Programs," in *Vouchers and the Provision of Public Services,* eds. C. Eugene Steuerle, Van Doorn Ooms, George Peterson, and Robert D. Reischauer (Washington, D.C.: The Brookings Institution, Committee for Economic Development, and Urban Institute Press, 2000).

3. Steuerle, "Common Issues for Voucher Programs," in *Vouchers and the Provision of Public Services,* 4.

4. One of the current controversies surrounding Medicare is whether it should be converted more into a program in which vouchers or voucher-like payments are provided for the purchase of insurance. Although traditional Medicare does provide a wide choice of doctors, it operates as a single insurer, and it is fairly open-ended as to how much healthcare will be provided over time. The voucher concept, which has already been implemented in part, allows more options to consumers with respect to the "type" of insurance policy chosen, but at the same time it allows the government to try to set limits on the cost of that insurance by setting the maximum voucher payment.

5. Lester M. Salamon, "The New Governance and the Tools of Public Action: An Introduction," in *The Tools of Government: A Guide to the New Governance,* ed. Lester M. Salamon (New York: Oxford University Press, 2001).

6. Ibid.

7. Steuerle, "Common Issues for Voucher Programs," in *Vouchers and the Provision of Public Services,* 5.

8. Posner et al., "A Survey of Voucher Use: Variations and Common Elements," in *Vouchers and the Provision of Public Services.*

9. Steuerle, "Common Issues for Voucher Programs," in *Vouchers and the Provision of Public Services.*

10. Besharov and Samari, 2000.

11. Barnow, 2000.

12. See Steuerle, "Common Issues for Voucher Programs," in *Vouchers and the Provision of Public Services,* 3–39. This structure is less applicable to other items, such as higher education.

13. Bradford and Shaviro, "The Economics of Vouchers," in *Vouchers and the Provision of Public Services.*

14. Employment and Training Administration, 1998.

15. Arthur M. Hauptman, "Vouchers and American Higher Education," in *Vouchers and the Provision of Public Services,* eds. C. Eugene Steuerle, Van Doorn Ooms, George Peterson, and Robert D. Reischauer (Washington, D.C.: The Brookings Institution, Committee for Economic Development, and Urban Institute Press, 2000).

16. Twombly and Boris, *The Use of Vouchers in the Provision of Human Services and Potential Implications for Nonprofit Organizations.*

17. U.S. Department of Health and Human Services. *Caseload Comparison Since The Signing of the Welfare Law: August 1996 vs. December 1999* (Washington, D.C.: The Administration for Children and Families, August 2000). Accessed at http://www.acf.dhhs.gov/news/stats/aug-dec.htm.

18. U.S. Department of Housing and Urban Development, *Opting In: Renewing America's Commitment to Affordable Housing* (Washington, D.C., April 1999). Accessed at http://www.hud.gov/pressrel/optingin.html.

19. Reischauer, "Medicare Vouchers," in *Vouchers and the Provision of Public Services.*

20. See Steuerle, "Common Issues for Voucher Programs," in *Vouchers and the Provision of Public Services,* 3–39.

21. An important distinction can still be made. In the case of primary and secondary education, voucher proponents argue that demand is too constrained because parents and children can contribute more to determining conditions under which education is received. Proponents for vouchers in health field assert that demand is too unconstrained; they argue that individuals have little or no understanding of the marginal cost of insurance because existing tax subsidies and expenditure programs encourage purchases from government or employers. In one case, demanders know too little about benefits, in the other, about costs.

22. Barnow, "Vouchers for Federal Targeted Training Programs," in *Vouchers and the Provision of Public Services.*

23. For a discussion of how automatic growth leads to an uneven level playing field for deciding national priorities, see C. Eugene Steuerle, Edward M. Gramlich, Hugh Heclo, and Demetra

Smith Nightingale, *The Government We Deserve: Responsive Democracy and Changing Expectations* (Washington, D.C.: Urban Institute Press, 1998).

24. Besharov and Samari, "Child Care Vouchers and Cash Payments," in *Vouchers and the Provision of Public Services.*

25. Steuerle, "Common Issues for Voucher Programs," in *Vouchers and the Provision of Public Services,* 3–39.

26. Burdett Loomis, "The Politics of Vouchers," in *Vouchers and the Provision of Public Services,* eds. C. Eugene Steuerle, Van Doorn Ooms, George Peterson, and Robert D. Reischauer (Washington, D.C.: The Brookings Institution, Committee for Economic Development, and Urban Institute Press, 2000).

27. See Loomis, "The Politics of Vouchers," in *Vouchers and the Provision of Public Services* (Washington, D.C.: The Brookings Institution, Committee for Economic Development, and Urban Institute Press, 2000).

28. For a more detailed discussion, see Loomis, "The Politics of Vouchers," in *Vouchers and the Provision of Public Services.*

29. Robert A. Moffitt, "Lessons from the Food Stamp Program," in *Vouchers and the Provision of Public Services,* eds. C. Eugene Steuerle, Van Doorn Ooms, George Peterson, and Robert D. Reischauer (Washington, D.C.: The Brookings Institution, Committee for Economic Development, and Urban Institute Press, 2000).

30. S. Kirchhoff, "House Clears Agriculture Bill Restoring Food Stamps to Legal Immigrants," *CQ Weekly* (6 June 1998).

31. Jeffrey R. Henig, *Rethinking School Choice* (Princeton, N.J.: Princeton University Press, 1994).

32. Jeffery R. Henig, Joseph J. Cordes, and Eric C. Twombly, "Human Service Nonprofits in an Era of Privatization: Toward a Theory of Political and Economic Response," Paper presented at the Annual Conference of the Urban Affairs Association, Louisville, KY, 15 April 1999.

33. Frank Kemerer and S. Sugerman, *School Choice: Politics, Policy and Law* (Washington, D.C.: The Brookings Institution, 1999).

34. Loomis, "The Politics of Vouchers," in *Vouchers and the Provision of Public Services.*

35. Other education inputs may include books and computer learning.

36. One set of advocates for educational vouchers want to set up a "Parent Information Center" to help parents pick the best school for their children. See John Chubb and Terry Moe, *Politics, Markets, and America's Schools* (Washington, D.C.: The Brookings Institution, 1990).

37. Cynthia Loose, "5 D.C. Housing Employees Charged; Only 10 of 400 New Rent Vouchers Issued Since 1990 Didn't Involve Bribery, Probe Finds," *The Washington Post* (13 April 1994).

38. Employment and Training Administration, *Implementing the Workforce Investment Act of 1998: A White Paper* (Washington, D.C.: Government Printing Office, 1998).

39. Robert Lerman and C. Eugene Steuerle, "Structured Choice Versus Fragmented Choice: The Bundling of Vouchers," in *Vouchers and the Provision of Public Services,* eds. C. Eugene Steuerle, Van Doorn Ooms, George Peterson, and Robert D. Reischauer (Washington, D.C.: The Brookings Institution, Committee for Economic Development, and Urban Institute Press, 2000).

40. Marilyn Moon, L. Nichos, K. Liu, G. Kenney, Margaret Sulvetta, S. Zuckerman, and C. Kintz, *Searching for Savings in Medicare* (Washington, D.C.: Urban Institute, 1995); K. Davis, "Medicare Reform: Assuring Health and Economic Security for Beneficiaries," Testimony before the Committee on the Budget of the United States Senate, 23 January 1997.

CHAPTER FIFTEEN

Tort Liability

Peter H. Schuck

Jim and Pamela Johnson purchased a new Subaru station wagon from a dealer. While driving on the highway, the vehicle suddenly spun out of control, crashed into a concrete barrier, and was wrecked. In addition to this property damage, the Johnsons were seriously injured by the crash and have suffered large medical expenses. Their wage income has been severely reduced because of their long period of hospitalization and convalescence, and they have been obliged to hire someone to help them with household chores. Private and social insurance cover much but not all of their medical expenses, only a small amount of their wage losses, and none of the chore services that they require. In addition, they have suffered emotional trauma that their health insurance does not cover.

Their lawyer has informed them that they may have strong claims in the tort system, in which courts may order those who negligently cause personal injuries and property damage to others to compensate the victims for their losses. The lawyer notes that a federal agency, the National Highway Traffic Safety Administration, regulates many safety features of automobile design and may help them to show that their vehicle was defective. She urges them to demand compensation from the Subaru dealer, the manufacturer, and perhaps the state government agency that is responsible for maintaining the highway. If their demands are not satisfied informally, the lawyer says, they can then consider whether to file suit in court.

I. DEFINING THE TOOL

Tort liability, as a tool of government, is the establishing of a right of persons or other entities to seek compensation or injunctive relief through the judicial system for harm that they have experienced caused by the negligence or other wrongful conduct of other persons or entities. This right is ordinarily established in court-recognized common law but may also be created by statutory law or by administrative regulation.

Tort law thus is an alternative to administrative regulation and other tools as a mechanism for preventing harm. Where regulation establishes legal prohibitions or restrictions on certain actions in advance of the harmful conduct and then imposes penalties for failure to comply, tort law relies on court actions brought by injured parties to seek remedies for harms that they have suffered. Four factors determine the nature of the legal rights and obligations that tort law defines and enforces: goals, liability rules, defenses, and choice of law rules.

Goals

Considerable controversy exists over the goals that tort liability should serve and how those goals should be weighted. According to most tort scholars, the dominant—and for some, the only—legitimate purpose of tort law was traditionally thought to be "corrective justice." This seeks to restore the *status quo ante* by using compensation to repair wrongfully inflicted losses and annul wrongfully obtained gains.

Increasingly, however, more practical or functional goals have augmented and even supplanted this corrective justice conception of tort law. In this view, tort law's principal goals are to deter excessive risk creation, to distribute injury losses more broadly, and to do so more efficiently. These goals, which are discussed in more detail in Section IV, may lead some functionalists to want to limit tort law or replace it with other mechanisms such as regulation and social insurance.[1]

Liability Rules

Tort law prescribes a body of substantive legal doctrine (i.e., rules or principles) to govern behavior. These rules or principles define the legally enforceable duties that an individual (or other entity) owes to others and the circumstances in which she may violate those duties (the "standard of care"). For example, tort law prescribes the legal duties that a physician owes to her patient and the standard of care that she must satisfy in order to avoid liability for injuries to the patient caused by her acts or omissions. The standard of care is usefully understood in terms of the risks of injury that the physician is permitted to create in the course of treating her patient. Ordinarily—and in the case of health care—tort law defines this standard of care as "reasonable behavior or care under all of the relevant circumstances." A failure to meet this standard of care is called "negligence" or "fault" or, in the specific case of medical treatment, "medical malpractice." Alternative standards of care are discussed below. In order to establish a defendant's tort liability, the plaintiff must prove that the defendant owed her a legally defined "duty of care," that the defendant breached this duty by violating the applicable legal standard (usually negligence), and that the defendant's breach of duty caused harm to the plaintiff of a kind that tort law recognizes as compensable.

Defenses

Even if the plaintiff can establish duty, breach, causation, and damage, tort principles may provide the defendant with a defense. If the defendant can prove that a particular defense applies, the defense usually frees the defendant of any liability. Examples of such complete defenses include assumption of the risk (i.e., the plaintiff knowingly and voluntarily consented to the risk), statute of limitations (i.e., the plaintiff did not bring suit within the requisite period of years), and immunity (i.e., the law bars liability for certain types of actors). The plaintiff's own negligence ("contributory negligence") traditionally was a complete defense, but this rule has been replaced by various versions of "comparative negligence" or "comparative fault" under which the plaintiff's negligence does not bar her recovery completely but instead reduces it according to the parties' relative fault.

Choice of Law Rules

Tort liability is largely adjudicated by state judges applying state law to disputes. State tort law mainly takes the form of common law principles, although there are an increasing number of statutes or regulations that affect tort adjudication. Judges in the state where the suit is filed (the "forum state") ordinarily apply its own procedural, substantive, and remedial law to the dispute. If, however, the accident and wrongful conduct occurred in another state, the judge will consult the forum state's "choice of law" rules, which determine which state's law will govern which issues in inter-state disputes of this kind. These choice of law rules may dictate that the judge apply the law of the other state (*lex delicti*) rather than the forum state's law (*lex fori*) to some or all of the issues in the case.

Relation to Key Tool Features

Tort law differs significantly from other tools of public policy along the dimensions of coerciveness, directness, automaticity, and visibility. Because tort law is perhaps the most fragmented, decentralized, and privately initiated and administered policy instrument of all, it scores relatively low on most of these dimensions.

Coerciveness

Coerciveness measures the extent to which a tool restricts individual or group behavior as opposed to merely encouraging or discouraging it. Tort liability is a relatively non-coercive policy instrument because it relies on what tort theorist Guido Calabresi calls market deterrence.[2] That is, tort law simply places a price on conduct that creates unreasonable risks of harm to other people, allowing individuals to decide for themselves whether and how they wish to act in light of those prices. In other words, tort law leaves one free to injure others so long as one is prepared to pay the price that tort liability imposes for such injuries. Indeed, the possibility that potential defendants are, or will become, insolvent and thus "judgment proof" to their victims may free them of even the obligation to pay that price. Tort law thus gives people a "license to injure" in much the same way that a system of tradeable pollution rights gives a "license to pollute" to companies that hold them. On the spectra of coerciveness and substantive prescriptiveness, Calabresi has observed, it lies somewhere between criminal law and administrative regulation at one end, and contracts at the other. The generality of tort standards (e.g., "reasonableness") and their close linkage to ordinary behavior and community standards also serve to blunt and soften their coerciveness.

Directness

Directness measures the extent to which the entity authorizing or inaugurating a program is involved in carrying it out. Tort law is a relatively indirect policy instrument because its motive and implementing force comes from litigants and their attorneys, not from government agents. In this respect, it resembles other third-party tools such as grants and vouchers through which government services are delivered primarily by third parties. The only public official who directly expounds and administers tort law is the judge, who is conventionally supposed to adopt a passive, arbitral role in which she simply reacts to disputes that private parties bring before her, rather than being herself an active initiator of proceedings.

Automaticity

Automaticity measures the extent to which a tool utilizes an existing administrative structure to produce its effect rather than having to create its own special administrative apparatus. Tort law is among the most automatic of policy instruments because it relies almost entirely on existing, indeed ancient, institutions—the court system, the jury, and the litigation bar—rather than having to create new ones. Until a case reaches trial, which the vast majority never do, the litigation process is administered almost entirely by the lawyers, with only an occasional intervention by the court.

This account of tort law's high level of automaticity, however, must be qualified in two respects. First, a new jury must of course be selected and impaneled for every new trial, although most tort cases are settled before that point is reached. Second, in environmental and product-related tort litigation, the court must sometimes design new institutions in order to conduct the litigation effectively. Legal scholar Judith Resnik has called such practices "managerial judging."[3] These improvisations might include court-appointed special masters; techniques for consolidating large numbers of claims, often in far-flung jurisdictions; "global settlement" mechanisms; special case management systems; novel procedures; distribution plans; and the like.

Visibility

Visibility measures the degree to which the resources devoted to the tool show up in the normal budget process. Despite the heated politics of tort reform and the controversiality of some high-profile cases, tort law is generally a very low-visibility policy tool. Only two kinds of tort system costs appear on public budgets: the court infrastructure, of which tort litigation accounts for only a part, and the liability costs borne by public agencies that must pay settlements or judgments in tort cases. For large municipalities, these liability costs can be very high; New York City's bill exceeds $300 million a year. Although other tort system costs may be large—how large is a matter of considerable debate—they are diffused throughout an immense economy in the form of factor prices, insurance premia, and behavioral effects that are difficult to observe and pinpoint, much less quantify.

Key Design Issues

In order to use tort law as a tool of public policy, a policy designer must address and resolve a number of discrete issues, most of which reflect the decidedly court-centered and thus legalistic character of tort law and the nature of the kind of remedies that it affords. Seven of these issues are considered here.

Standing

In order for one to maintain a tort action, one must possess "standing." The standing requirement is a quasi-constitutional doctrine holding that courts are only empowered to decide genuine "cases or controversies." This in turn is interpreted to mean that the plaintiff must show that she has suffered or is about to suffer a personal, legally cognizable injury at the hands of the defendant, an injury not common to the general public. If a plaintiff lacks standing, her claim will be dismissed at the outset without the court reaching the merits.

In the usual common law tort case, the plaintiff alleges that the defendant caused a discrete personal injury to her of a kind for which the law requires compensation; this allegation will suffice to give the plaintiff the necessary standing to sue. The mere fact that conduct is wrongful, however, does not mean that anyone who is adversely affected by it thereby has the standing to challenge it in court, much less to recover damages for their injuries. Although legislatures intend most statutory or administrative prescriptions to be enforced by public officials, not in private tort litigation, the court may interpret the statute to (1) confer standing (or a "private cause of action," in legal parlance) on a class of victims of which the plaintiff is a member, and (2) authorize the court to award money damages. Courts often hesitate to imply a private cause of action in the absence of express statutory language creating one. Indeed, the U.S. Supreme Court has established a presumption against finding private causes of action by implication from federal regulatory statutes. Congress can create private tort remedies for regulatory violations if it wishes, but the statute must do so explicitly and must also satisfy the constitutional "cases or controversies" constraint.

A legislature that establishes a private tort remedy must also decide which court or courts will have jurisdiction to adjudicate such disputes—both in the first instance (usually a trial court) and on appeal. Congress may decide to confer exclusive jurisdiction on the federal courts or may confer concurrent jurisdiction on the federal and state courts (as it has done with certain civil rights laws). Similarly, state legislatures must choose among different courts in their court systems in deciding where to lodge jurisdiction; they are not empowered to compel federal courts to take jurisdiction over state law disputes.

Although most tort litigation is brought in state courts and turns on state law, many tort cases are instead filed in federal court. The U.S. Constitution permits federal courts to hear disputes in which the plaintiff and defendant are from different states. Even in these so-called "diversity" cases, however, the federal court is required to apply the state tort law and choice-of-law rules of the state in which it sits. However, it must follow federal procedural rules.

Substantive Rules

After providing for a private cause of action in tort and for courts that may adjudicate it, the most fundamental policy choice to be made, of course, is prescribing the substantive standards of tort liability that the courts will apply. Although negligence is by far the most common standard of care, a standard of "strict liability" (i.e., liability without fault) governs certain types of activities, such as the use of explosives or the sale of defective products, and policymakers can apply it to still others. An activity subject to a strict liability standard creates liability merely by causing harm, even if the actor causing it was exercising reasonable care (i.e., was not negligent). In addition to the negligence and strict liability standards, liability may depend on the actor's "intention" to harm, which usually extends beyond malice, ill-will, and an affirmative desire to injure to include as well the knowledge that the action is highly risky to others.

Procedural Rules

Many of the legal procedures that govern tort adjudication are statutorily prescribed, but others are developed by judges. Procedural rules specify how claims must be presented to the court, which party bears the burden of producing evidence and persuading the judge or jury, and which standard of proof must be satisfied. In tort cases, "a preponderance of the evidence," also described as "more likely than not," is required, not the criminal law's "beyond a reasonable doubt."

Procedural rules also prescribe how jurisdiction over a party must be obtained, what kinds of notice must be provided, how discovery (i.e., disclosure of information possessed by a party or witness) is conducted, how other parties may be brought into the lawsuit, the powers that judges may lawfully exercise, motion practice (i.e., the rules governing requests for judicial orders), how decisions may be appealed, and so forth. Another set of rules, quasi-procedural in nature, govern the admissibility of evidence.

One procedure that has assumed special significance in certain types of tort litigation is the class action, which can enable a large number of similar claims to be litigated together in a consolidated form. Typically, a statute authorizes the use of the class action procedure but only if the court finds that the claims satisfy certain requirements—for example, that the claims are numerous and are legally or factually similar to one another; that the class action is a superior way of resolving the claims than litigating them individually; that the class would be adequately represented; and so forth—in which case the court certifies the litigation as a class action and allows it to proceed in that form.

Although the class action is often a procedural form that serves the interests of plaintiffs, defendants, or both, and although it is widely used in antitrust, securities, and consumer protection litigation, the courts frequently reject its use in tort cases, where the claims may raise different factual and legal issues and therefore may lack the requisite similarity. The availability of class actions in tort cases, especially in toxic tort cases such as asbestos or tobacco litigation, is currently a hotly contested issue in Congress and the courts.

Remedies

Once a defendant's tort liability is established, essentially two kinds of remedies (i.e., forms of relief) may be available. The most common remedy by far is money damages, which in turn can be subdivided into compensatory and punitive damages. Compensatory damages are designed to restore the plaintiff to the *status quo ante* insofar as money can do so. The categories of compensable damage may include physical injury, lost wages, medical expenses, other out-of-pocket costs, loss of profit opportunity, emotional distress, pain and suffering, hedonic loss, damage to intimate relationships ("consortium"), reputational loss, loss of privacy, and so forth. Punitive damages may be assessed against a defendant if the plaintiff can establish that the defendant's conduct was so egregious and socially abhorrent that an additional penalty is appropriate. Tort reform statutes in many states, however, now impose a variety of limits on the availability of punitive damages.

Because the accidents to which tort law ordinarily applies tend to be relatively sudden, unintentional, and isolated events, the only meaningful relief is post-accident money damages. Where the wrongful conduct is of a continuing nature, however, plaintiffs may seek injunctive relief—a judicial order requiring the defendant to act, or refrain from acting, in a particular way, on pain of being held in contempt and other sanctions. Injunctions are most common in "nuisance" actions, which often seek to remedy pollution or other conduct interfering with a plaintiff's use and enjoyment of her own property.

Policymakers who wish to expand on or modify these remedies can choose among many other possible variants. State tort reform statutes, for example, commonly impose caps on total damage recoveries or on particular subsets such as nonpecuniary damages, and often limit punitive damage awards by imposing caps, more demanding standards, special procedures, or requirements that some portion of the damages go to an entity other than the plaintiff. Environmental statutes often prescribe the kinds of injunctions courts may issue. Statutes may authorize courts to order more unconventional remedies such as a recall of unsafe products, notification of potential victims, or the award of medical monitoring costs to minimize future harm. In class actions, courts may require defendants to pay into a fund that is then distributed under court-ordered criteria and procedures. They may also fashion other forms of relief such as "fluid recoveries," requiring the defendant to act in ways intended to benefit class members more indirectly, such as a reduction in its future prices or creation of a research institute.

Temporal Issues

A policymaker using tort law as a tool must decide how the passage of time should affect liability. Two such temporal issues are especially important: Should the liability standard be retroactive or prospective only? What will be the statute of limitations? Liability rules elaborated by common law judges are presumptively retroactive; the judicial conceit is that because the court is simply "discovering" law that was there all the time, it is not unfair to apply the rule to the parties in the case before the court. Occasionally, however, a court may acknowledge that it is adopting a new rule that in fairness should not be applied to parties who acted on the reasonable assumption that the law was otherwise. Legislatures do not purport to be discovering pre-existing law; instead, they view themselves as institutionally free, subject only to constitutional limitations, to enact altogether new, retroactive rules without any notice beyond that of the legislative process itself. Even so, legislatures often opt for prospectivity, providing that certain provisions will not apply retroactively or will not become effective until some future date.

Statutes of limitations provide that a plaintiff must file her action within a certain period or her claim will be barred. Such provisions are designed to minimize the risk that courts will have to adjudicate, and defendants will have to defend against, stale claims on the basis of evidence that becomes less reliable or available with the passage of time. Here, the policymaker must decide on the specific limitations period that will apply to particular kinds of claims, the date from which this period will begin to "run," and the circumstances that will "toll" the statute (i.e., stop its running). These issues are particularly difficult in connection with long-lived products, or with environmental or product-related torts where many decades may elapse between one's exposure to a danger and the manifestation or discovery of the injury that may prompt one to consult a lawyer and file suit.

Counsel Fees

The engine driving tort litigation is the profit motive of plaintiffs' lawyers. Under the "American rule," each party—the winner as well as the loser—bears its own counsel fees and costs unless a statute provides for fee shifting between the parties. Under the contingent fee system, a lawyer may contract with a plaintiff to advance most or all of the litigation costs, receive a fraction (typically one-third) of whatever is recovered from the defendant, and receive nothing if the plaintiff loses. In class actions, the court must approve the plaintiffs' lawyers' fees, regardless of their contingent fee arrangements. Defendants generally must pay for their own lawyers unless their defense costs are covered by liability insurance. These practices contrast with the "British rule" under which losing plaintiffs must ordinarily bear defendants' fees and costs.

Policymakers can vary these rules in order to encourage or discourage litigation of a particular kind by altering the incentives of lawyers and parties. Wishing to encourage certain civil rights and environmental claims, for example, Congress has changed the default American rule for such cases and authorized courts to require defendants to pay the litigation costs of prevailing plaintiffs, with prevailing defined in various ways. By the same token, legislatures wishing to discourage the litigation of certain kinds of claims may make them less lucrative to lawyers by limiting the fees that clients are permitted to pay.

II. PATTERNS OF TOOL USE

In recent decades, the volume of tort litigation has become a major political issue at all levels of government. Many critics of the tort system—especially product manufacturers, health-care providers, and insurers—complain of a litigation explosion fueled by innovative judges, runaway juries, and profit-seeking plaintiffs' lawyers, while defenders of the system deny these claims on empirical grounds. It is true that America has always been a litigious society, even during the colonial period when communities were closer knit and less diverse. Depending on how one counts filed cases, however, the United States is by no means the most litigious nation per capita; if the statistics include summary debt collections, Germany, Austria, and Israel are more litigious, although rivaled by the most litigious U.S. states such as New Jersey and Virginia.

The major categories of tort cases involve claims relating to product liability, automobile accidents, workplace injuries, medical malpractice, and mass exposures. At the same time, the vast majority of payments received by those who suffer such personal injuries are handled not through the tort system but through other compensation mechanisms such as health or other personal insurance. Each year, one injury in ten results in some attempt to bring a liability claim, either by negotiating directly with the injurer or his insurer or by seeking legal representation in a claim or lawsuit. The use of the torts system, however, is much more common for the victims of automobile accidents than for other injuries.[4]

More than 95 percent of tort cases overall are filed in state courts, with the remainder (mostly product liability cases) filed in federal court. Unfortunately, the data available on these systems are quite different.

State Courts

No nationwide figures are collected on the caseload in state courts, nor do the data that are collected always distinguish among different kinds of civil cases, much less detail the kinds of tort claims filed. Instead, numbers and trends must be extrapolated from more detailed studies of smaller groups of states, usually those with the highest caseloads.[5] Thus, according to one survey, in 1993 approximately 360,000 tort cases were filed in courts of general jurisdiction in twenty-two states. A study of ten states found filings of approximately 160,000 auto accident and 130,000 non-auto tort cases. A study of seventy-five largest counties found that tort cases constituted about two-thirds of the civil cases that went to trial (fewer than 5 percent of the cases filed reach trial); of those, almost half were automobile cases and another 11 percent were medical malpractice cases.

As for trends, the number of tort cases filed grew 29 percent in the states that counted tort filings separately during the 1984–1996 period, with the increase in recent years concentrated in automobile cases and a smaller increase in medical malpractice cases.

Federal Courts[6]

Plaintiffs may file their tort claims in federal court if the defendant is a citizen of a different state and the value of the plaintiff's claim exceeds $50,000. In 1999, approximately 250,000 actions were filed in the federal trial courts; almost 40,000 of these (15 percent of the total) were tort cases, defined as those claiming personal injury or personal property damage. Of these tort cases, over 90 percent were divided fairly evenly between two categories: product liability claims (over 40 percent of these were asbestos related) and miscellaneous personal injury claims (about 8 percent of these were medical malpractice claims). The remaining tort cases consisted of property damage claims.

Compared with the trend in state court tort filings, the number of federal court tort filings—46,783 in 1998, a decline from 57,787 in 1997—has followed an irregular, volatile pattern that largely reflects a growing concentration of high-profile mass product liability and environmental cases such as asbestos and breast implants, which center on a relatively small number of products and industries. Indeed, more than 80 percent of the decline in tort filings between 1997 and 1998 was caused by an almost 30 percent decline in product liability cases, a decline that masked an even sharper *increase* (about 60 percent) in asbestos cases. In addition, many other federal court cases, particularly some in the large category of civil rights claims (41,853 filed in 1998), resemble tort cases in important respects but are not counted as such in the statistics.

Marc Galanter, perhaps the leading expert on changes in the volume of tort litigation over time, adds another dimension to litigation statistics by emphasizing how few tort actions are brought compared with the number of apparently negligently injured victims who could have sued but did not. In only about 10 percent of all accidental injuries, he notes, do victims even complain to the party whom they think was responsible—the share rises to 44 percent for auto accidents—and only a fraction of these complainants take the next step and file a tort complaint in court.[7] The National Center for State Courts, the authoritative source for state litigation statistics, summarized the situation based on data through 1996: "[t]here is no evidence of a tort litigation 'explosion'. . . . There was a dramatic increase in tort filings between 1982 and 1986, which intensified fears that there was indeed a tort litigation explosion. Through the mid-1980s, most states passed some form of tort litigation reform. Since 1986 . . . tort filings have been relatively steady. . . . Despite an increase in 1996, the total volume of tort cases in the 16 states still has not returned to the record high set in 1990. . . . If Michigan [which experienced a dramatic spike in 1996 just before the effective date of a new statutory cap on product liability awards] is excluded from the trend line, tort filings in the remaining 15 states increased 52 percent (rather than 69 percent) over the past 21 years." And the most recent and detailed study, which examined tort litigation in a single county in Ohio, essentially confirms the absence of any tort litigation explosion during the twelve-year period preceding Ohio's enactment in 1996 of a "tort reform" statute.[8] Although concerns about a tort "explosion" may be overstated, however, tort claims have nevertheless grown in both number and complexity over recent decades.

III. BASIC MECHANICS

As noted in the earlier discussion of tort law's indirectness and automaticity, the tort system is driven almost entirely by lawyers and operates under the supervision and administration of judges. Most of its basic institutions and procedures have been in place for many centuries in some form, even as many of its substantive rules have changed. Most disputes are resolved informally, and approximately 95 percent of the tort cases that are filed are settled before trial with little or no judicial involvement; the attorneys serve as third parties through which this tool delivers its benefits to citizens. More specifically, the tort system's operation can be summarized succinctly in the following series of steps.

1. *Complaint.* A party who believes that another has caused her legally compensable harm may file a complaint with a court with subject matter jurisdiction (i.e., the power to adjudicate that kind of dispute) and serve the defendant with a copy.

2. *Further pleadings.* This triggers a sequence of formal pleadings and responses by both parties designed to identify and narrow the factual and legal issues in dispute.

3. *Discovery.* Both parties may engage in extensive "discovery"—examining documents in the custody of others, deposing and physically examining witnesses, obtaining admissions of fact, and so forth—in order to acquire factual information that they can use as evidence to support their claims or defenses. Discovery is orchestrated by the lawyers; the court is only called in to resolve disagreements.

4. *Dispositive motions.* After discovery, one or both parties may file a motion asking the judge to enter judgment in their favor on the theory that no genuine, material

issues of fact are in dispute and the judge can therefore decide the case purely as a matter of law, without any necessity for a trial. The party who loses this motion may appeal the court's ruling to a higher court. Otherwise, the case continues; the judge sets a trial date and attempts through a series of orders to further narrow and structure the factual, legal, and evidentiary issues for trial.

5. *Pretrial settlements or jury selection.* Throughout the process, but particularly at this point and thereafter, the judge urges the parties to negotiate a settlement of the dispute and may even actively participate—herself and/or through a special master—in settlement discussions. If no settlement is reached before the trial date and the parties do not agree to have a bench trial (i.e., by the judge without a jury), the lawyers proceed to select a jury.[9] They do so through an often time-consuming, largely lawyer-administered "voir dire" process, which tends as a practical matter to produce many jurors who are relatively ignorant and unsophisticated about the kinds of technical issues increasingly arising in tort cases. Much of the cumbersome and costly apparatus of the trial, including many of the rules of procedure and evidence, are necessary only because of the risk that juries will be improperly influenced by the lawyers. In principle, the jury simply applies to the factual evidence the legal principles that the judge instructs it to follow. Because many tort law standards are open-ended (e.g., "reasonable care"), jurors inevitably enjoy some leeway or discretion that enables them to introduce their own values and attitudes toward the parties and the law.

6. *Dismissal or submission to jury.* At various points during the trial, the lawyers may ask the judge to take the case away from the jury and enter judgment as a matter of law. If the judge denies these motions and decides to send the case to the jury, the judge instructs the jury on the legal principles that the jury must apply to the factual evidence and sends it off to deliberate until it reaches a verdict (or the judge declares a mistrial).

7. *Verdict.* Ordinarily, juries render a "general" verdict that simply finds for the plaintiff or the defendant without providing any reasons or making any explicit findings of fact. In a particularly complex case, the judge may ask the jury to render a "special" verdict with specific findings of fact in response to factual questions that the judge puts to it. Accordingly, its verdict—unlike the judge's rulings on issues of law—carries little or no precedential or informational value other than the fact of the verdict itself.

8. *Post-trial motions and appeal.* After a verdict, the disappointed lawyer can move for judgment notwithstanding the verdict, for a new trial, or to reduce or increase the damages awarded by the jury. If the judge denies these motions, disappointed parties may appeal to a higher court (if appeal is permitted) that ordinarily renders its decision, often in a written opinion, on the basis of written briefs and an oral argument by the appellate lawyers.

9. *Execution of judgment.* Once all appeals have been exhausted and a final judgment is entered, a losing defendant must pay the damages awarded against it. If payment is not forthcoming, the plaintiff must initiate a process designed to execute the judgment by securing the defendant's assets and liquidating them in order to effectuate payment. In many cases, however, this process is unavailing—the defendant may be insolvent or its assets otherwise unreachable—and the plaintiff cannot recover fully or at all.

10. *Subsequent cases.* Another feature of the system that bears on the use of tort liability as a policy tool should be mentioned. Many legal and factual issues that have been

litigated to a verdict in a tort case must sometimes be litigated over and over again in subsequent tort cases. To considerably simplify the complex doctrine of "collateral estoppel" or "issue preclusion," even a defendant who prevails at trial is ordinarily subject to having to defend similar or even identical claims against new plaintiffs if they did not have an opportunity to be heard in the earlier case. If a plaintiff prevails at trial against a defendant, future plaintiffs can prevail on the basis of that earlier verdict only if the two claims and the defendant are the same, and the defendant had a full opportunity to litigate the issues and theories raised by the new plaintiffs.

IV. TOOL CHOICE

Rationale and Conditions

Tort law offers a way to promote health and safety without the necessity for cumbersome, often overly intrusive regulatory structures or government subsidy programs. Compared with other tools of public action, the fundamental promise of tort law is its ability to create incentives for care on the part of potential injurers without the administrative overlays required of many other tools. For tort law to fulfill this promise, however, a number of conditions must be satisfied.

First, the victim must be able in fact to establish that the injurer has caused the harm in question through conduct that the law condemns as negligent. When this cannot be done with reasonable reliability, tort law is unlikely to be an effective deterrent of harmful conduct since injurers will be motivated to continue their conduct with little fear of financial penalty.

Second, victims must possess both standing and sufficient incentive to sue the injurer. In many situations, however, particular victims are not individually harmed enough by the injurer's conduct to warrant the cost of suing, which makes tort law an unattractive remedy. One response to this shortcoming is to permit third parties (attorneys) to file "class actions" on behalf of a larger group of injured individuals. The courts, however, have generally not been sympathetic to class actions in cases of personal injuries where the legal and factual claims of each individual in the class are likely to be different. A major motivation for enacting regulatory programs involving official enforcement of health and safety standards in lieu of, or in addition to, tort law has been the inadequacy of enforcement through individual tort cases.

Third, the liability that will be imposed on negligent injurers must be large and certain enough to deter the harmful conduct without overdeterring socially valuable (although still risky) conduct. Since using tort law to reduce the risk of harm itself entails some costs and risks—the costs of taking precautions and the risk of discouraging socially valuable (although risky) conduct through the threat of liability—society's goal is not to deter all accidents but to deter only those that can be avoided at reasonable cost and thus are worth preventing. Tort law's goal, in short, is *optimal* deterrence. *A priori*, at least, overdeterrence is no more desirable than underdeterrence. Whether optimal deterrence requires injurers to bear the costs of all accidents they cause (a "strict liability" standard) or just the cost of the accidents that they negligently cause (a "negligence" or "fault" standard) is a central issue in tort law. The key choice in resolving this issue is which party, the injurer or the victim, should bear the costs of those accidents that would be unreasonably costly to prevent—accidents that in an economic sense are "not worth preventing." Advocates of strict liability contend that tort law should require injurers to pay for such accidents; advocates of negligence liability argue that the victim should not be compensated in such cases. For example, advocates of strict liability contend that a product manufacturer should be liable for all accidents that its product causes even if preventing such accidents necessitated installing a safety device that would cost more than the cost of the accidents the device would prevent (i.e., the device's safety benefits). In contrast, negligence advocates want the manufacturer to be liable only if the cost of the device was less than its safety benefits.

Political Considerations

Given these considerations, it is clear that the range of harms for which tort law provides effective protection is far from complete. Indeed, because it demands that the injurer take the initiative and bear the initial costs of seeking to establish the culpability for each harm, tort liability is not a very reliable instrument of protection against many kinds of environmental pollution and unsafe products. Nevertheless, many consumer groups will fiercely oppose any regulatory safety program that eliminates tort remedies against violators in favor of purely administrative or criminal remedies. From this perspective, tort law has at least three political advantages.

Automaticity

The fact that tort law relies on an existing and longstanding system not requiring the creation of a new regulatory structure is an important political advantage. One can promote whatever substantive rule one favors through litigation brought by a single lawyer with a single client and located in a jurisdiction thought to be congenial to that rule. No political coalitions need be formed, and the process of legal change through litigation may be sufficiently opaque and fragmented that political opponents of the change may not even notice it for awhile, much less mobilize to overturn or restrict it.

Individualism

The tort system embodies cherished American values: individual initiative and individual treatment. The common law system of adjudication by which tort law evolves is one in which private litigants, through their lawyers, directly animate and shape legal and policy change. This lawmaking function, moreover, usually occurs without the intercession of any public official except the judge, who tends to be more passive arbiter than active initiator. The jury in a tort case attempts to tailor its judgment to the unique circumstances of the parties and the particular facts underlying the dispute, which gives tort law a flexibility and contextuality that are seldom found in administrative regulation.

Tort law thus constitutes a symbol or shibboleth that in some ways becomes more compelling as American society grows more complex, corporate, and collectivized. The iconic images of tort adjudication vividly evoke the resonant ethos of individualism: the little guy battling the huge, bureaucratic system; the citizen's right to a day in court; the lawyer as the client's dedicated champion; the forum in which principle, not politics, provides the rules of decision; and the blindfolded figure of Justice before whom all are equally entitled to dispensation. Even when tort law employs the pragmatic technique of interest balancing, its justifications invariably speak the idealistic, antihierarchical, language of individual rights.

Morality and Ideology

Tort law also gains political advantage from its embodiment of public morality. This is institutionalized in its reliance on the jury as the ultimate decisionmaker. The jury consists of ordinary citizens engaged in the vital public functions of civic education, law application (which often amounts to lawmaking), and democratic accountability. Jurors learn about law and government through their jury service, but the learning also goes in the other direction, as jurors infuse their experience and values into law and government. These functions are so central to democratic governance that civil juries, along with grand and criminal juries, are guaranteed by both federal and state constitutions.

Through its reliance on juries, tort law tracks society's basic beliefs about right and wrong conduct. This is not to say, of course, that morality and law are or should be the same (the legal positivists long ago challenged that identity), but only that law, to be effective, cannot diverge too far from morality. Tort adjudication thus operates to affirm and reinforce society's essential norms. The strength of these norms may help to explain the remarkable tenacity of the negligence standard as the basic principle underlying legal responsibility in tort despite persistent criticisms of fault on functional, libertarian, and other grounds.

The Politics of Tort Reform

These political advantages of tort law as an instrument of public action are exploited by groups that favor the status quo in tort law. These groups, led by the plaintiffs' bar organized in the national Association of Trial Lawyers of America (ATLA) and its state chapters, and supported by many consumer groups, advocate broad rules of tort liability, a large role for the jury, greater jury discretion, and a continuation of the states' primacy in tort law. ATLA and its allies oppose proposals, known as "tort reform," that would restrict liability for medical malpractice, product liability, and other types of claims, limit compensatory and punitive damages, control lawyers' fees, and otherwise impede plaintiffs' recoveries.

On the other side are product manufacturers, state and local governments, insurance companies, and other defendant groups that oppose what they view as an excessive expansion of tort liability since the 1960s. Often working together under the umbrella of the American Tort Reform Association (ATRA), these groups challenge many features of the current tort system. In 1999, for example, ATRA succeeded in obtaining federal legislation limiting their exposure to Y2K liability. It has spearheaded a long-pending proposal in Congress to impose federal restrictions on the autonomy of state tort law.

ATLA is very well connected to state legislators, many of whom are ATLA members, and to the Democratic Party at all levels, to which it is a major financial donor. By the same token, ATRA's coalition of manufacturer, health care, insurer, and other corporate interests lobbies and advertises heavily to promote a more restrictive tort law. Because ATRA is a more diverse coalition, however, it is subject to more conflicting interests internally than is ATLA.

When the policy instrument under consideration is new or expanded regulation, however, the same defendant groups that ordinarily criticize tort law may shift ground, arguing that tort law, with all its flaws, is better than the proposed regulation. By the same token, consumer groups usually allied with ATLA on tort policy issues may strongly advocate administrative regulation. A difference, however, is that consumer groups almost never view regulation as a substitute for tort law; they prefer to have both operating.

In these political struggles, the individualistic ideology and populist imagery associated with the tort system constitutes a formidable resource for those interests, mainly ATLA and consumer groups, that favor the tort system in its current form. This means a tort law that is defined largely by common law rather than statutes and by state law

rather than federal law, which encourages free-wheeling litigation and claims aggregation practices orchestrated by a plaintiff's bar searching for deeper pockets, which
preserves broad jury discretion in the award of damages, and which leaves judges free
to enlarge the boundaries of liability. These attributes, however, carry political disadvantages. Spurred by heavy advertising by insurers and defendant groups and by media
coverage of tort system excesses, the public has become increasingly aware and resentful
of the system's darker side: inflated insurance costs, higher product prices, restricted
availability of risky but valued activities, and social litigiousness.

V. MANAGEMENT CHALLENGES AND RESPONSES

Because the tort system is so radically decentralized and diffuse, management issues
are defined and confronted by different state and local court systems and perhaps even
more directly by individual judges seeking to control their dockets. Beyond these localized issues, three more general management challenges can be identified—tort law's
integration with administrative regulation, burgeoning caseloads of more complex disputes, and high transaction costs.

Management Challenges

Integration with Administrative Regulation

With the rise of the administrative state, which prescribes through statute and regulation a vast number of safety and other standards aimed at reducing the incidence and
cost of accidents, the courts must somehow integrate these standards with the common
law principles developed by the tort system. When the legislature is explicit and clear
about how it wants the two systems to relate to one another, no special problems exist
other than the normal risk that the legislature has resolved this question unwisely.
Often, however, the legislature either does not address the integration question at all
or does so ambiguously. In such a case, a court adjudicating a tort claim that arguably
implicates the scheme of administrative regulation must decide how, if at all, it should
take account of the regulation, beginning with the issue of whether, in light of the
regulation, the plaintiff even has standing to assert a private tort claim in the courts.

Courts integrate the regulatory and tort systems in a number of ways, depending on
how they perceive the regulation's nature, language, intent, and compatibility with the
common law system and principles. There are many possible solutions. For example,
the court may decide any of the following: that the regulation was intended to "occupy
the field," leaving the plaintiff with no private tort remedy; that it does not alter the
common law, leaving the plaintiff free to proceed; or that the regulation alters the
common law standard of conduct to which the defendant will be held. The court may
also have some leeway in deciding how to treat the fact that the defendant either
complied with, or violated, the regulatory standard. It may rule that compliance pre-
cludes tort liability, is relevant to but not determinative of its tort liability, or is irrelevant to tort liability. Alternatively, it may rule that violating the regulatory standard
constitutes negligence *per se,* that the violation provides some evidence of negligence
for the jury to consider, or that the violation is irrelevant to the negligence issue.

Other integration issues may also arise, particularly when the regulatory program is
a relatively comprehensive one. The statute, for example, may require would-be plaintiffs to file a notice of injury with the agency, "exhaust their administrative remedies,"
or even obtain the agency's permission before filing a tort action in court. All of these

requirements are designed to permit the agency to consider providing the relief that the plaintiff seeks without the necessity for court action that might interfere with the administrative scheme.

More Complex Disputes

As indicated in Section II, the volume of mass product liability and environmental tort disputes is growing. The growth in this category of cases reflects the vast number of claims, sometimes in the millions, filed as a result of exposure to asbestos, silicone gel breast implants, fen-phen, tobacco, pharmaceutical drugs, weapons, radiation, and other products or processes.[10] Such cases often involve many complex factual and legal issues about general and specific causation, epidemiological proof, the state of scientific knowledge, criteria for allocating liability and damages among multiple parties on both sides of the case, defenses based on the behavior of individual plaintiffs, choice of law, bankruptcy, evidence, and many others. The cases generate lengthy and contentious pleadings, discovery, settlement negotiations, and, if necessary, trials and appeals, which, of course, entails enormous costs and uncertainties to all concerned. Since this litigation must compete for scarce judicial resources with a rapidly expanding criminal caseload (largely due to tougher antidrug laws) that demand a higher priority, courts have to send these civil cases to the back of the queue.

High Transaction Costs

Even without caseload increases, tort litigation, especially in complex cases, is notoriously expensive in terms of money and time to shift the cost of an accident to the wrongdoer. In the most well-known study of the transaction costs of asbestos litigation, RAND researchers found that the litigants in these cases spent 39 cents for every dollar that was paid to successful plaintiffs, with most of that going to lawyers on both sides. By way of crude comparison, the Social Security Administration's administrative costs account for well under 10 percent of benefits payouts. The high transaction costs of tort litigation have many unfortunate effects. They severely limit claimants' access to the system, an impediment that contingency fee arrangements does not fully overcome. They distort the terms of settlement in the 95 percent of filed cases that settle. They inflate insurance costs, which increases consumer prices and restricts access to insurance; this in turn discourages many socially valuable but risky activities. They give lawyers on both sides a socially perverse stake in retaining the existing tort system with all its inefficiencies and inequities, most of which redound to lawyers' benefit.

Responses to Challenges

With the important exception of "tort reform" statutes, which tend to address these problems in a blunderbuss fashion by using fairly crude rules designed to limit the extent of both tort liability and damages, and the limited exception of no-fault schemes, discussed below, policymakers have largely left it to the courts to devise solutions to these tort system problems. The courts have responded with a variety of approaches calculated to render their caseloads more manageable and reduce transaction costs to litigants. Many of these changes are procedural or evidentiary in nature, others would limit the fees that plaintiffs' lawyers can receive or the damages that plaintiffs can recover, while still others would alter the substantive liability rules themselves. Six of these approaches deserve particular mention.

Courts have used a number of procedural mechanisms to reduce their caseloads, manage them more efficiently, and lower transaction costs. They have consolidated similar claims for purposes of discovery or trial, extended these consolidation methods to claims filed in other jurisdictions, and expanded the use of class actions. They have tried to reduce the number of individual trials—and encourage settlements—by developing statistical profiles of claims, using representative plaintiffs, and holding summary trials. They have appointed special masters and other auxiliary court personnel to resolve subsidiary conflicts and use alternative dispute resolution methods. They have more actively orchestrated settlements, including "global" ones discussed below, that necessitate claims administration on a mass scale. In a variety of other ways, they have become active case managers.[11]

Contract Instead of Tort

Pressures on the court-based tort system can also be reduced by relying more heavily on the allocations of risks built into contracts rather than on tort law principles such as negligence in order to determine which party must bear the loss. Making, interpreting, and enforcing a contract through which the parties resolve in advance possible disputes over who should bear particular losses has many advantages over tort law. It is much easier, cheaper, faster, and more accurate for courts to do this than to attempt to resolve such disputes retrospectively by applying tort principles, which are very general and whose application to specific facts, especially by juries, is difficult to predict. Insuring against contractually defined risks is also much more efficient than insuring against potential tort liability to victims unknown. Thus, allocating risks of loss through contract both reduces the costs of transactions and creates efficient incentives to anticipate risks of significant magnitude. Finally, the notion that people should be bound by their promises is a fundamental norm in all societies.

Although this autonomy of contract still enjoys wide respect, the courts have limited it in recent decades in areas as disparate as the workplace, health care, recreational activity, and housing. Courts often refuse to enforce provisions of preprinted contracts that allocate accident risks, insisting on adjudicating liability according to tort principles. They usually justify this refusal, which they increasingly extend even to some contracts that were in fact negotiated. Courts do so on the ambiguous, conclusory ground that such provisions "offend public policy," often because they think that the parties possess unequal bargaining power. In this and other areas, tort law has reshaped contract law.

Immunities

The scope of tort liability and caseloads can also be shaped by limiting or extending various exemptions and immunities. Traditionally, for example, charitable institutions were generally immune from tort liability. Most suits between spouses and between parents and children were barred. Governments and government officials also enjoyed broad protection from tort liability, loosely referred to as "sovereign immunity."

In each of these cases, courts and legislatures recently have narrowed the scope of the immunities. At the federal level, for example, the Federal Tort Claims Act waives the sovereign immunity of the United States, but this waiver is subject to a number of exceptions and limitations—for discretionary decisions and many intentional torts, for example—that continue to protect the federal government from liability for many of its torts. The Eleventh Amendment to the U.S. Constitution also generally immunizes the states from being sued for money damages without their consent in federal court.

Individual states are also generally immune from suits brought against them in their own courts, although all have waived this immunity to some degree. Sometimes, plaintiffs can circumvent federal or state sovereign immunity by suing individual officials rather than the government itself, but those officials are often able to claim an absolute or qualified (good-faith) immunity nonetheless, and there are a variety of other special limitations on suits against governments and/or their officials.

Within these limitations, however, the government may be subject to liability for the torts of private third parties to whom it has contractually delegated its managerial responsibilities. In a recent case involving the private management of a state prison, the U.S. Supreme Court held that the government could not avoid possible liability for civil rights violations committed by employees of a private company managing the prison.

Collateral Sources

Another technique for reducing tort litigation is to alter the common law "collateral source rule." Under that rule, a plaintiff's recovery from the defendant is not reduced by reason of payments and other benefits that the plaintiff has received or will receive from other ("collateral") sources such as insurance, free in-kind services, and the like. The rationales for this common law rule were that plaintiff has already paid for these benefits in some sense, and that the defendant should not receive a windfall and a reduction in deterrence pressure simply because the plaintiff has done so. However, with the growth of social and private insurance, particularly for medical costs, many state legislatures have modified or replaced this rule with rules that reduce the defendant's liability by some or all of the plaintiff's collateral benefits. This change seeks to prevent plaintiffs from receiving more than they lost, to reduce claimants' incentives to sue, and to limit defendants' liabilities.

The collateral source rule underscores the importance of the interplay between social insurance and tort liability. Many analysts who compare tort law in the United States with that in other developed countries believe that the broad scope of American tort law has much to do with the relatively limited (as they see it) social insurance benefits provided in the United States, and that tort law in other countries is comparatively unimportant precisely because the welfare states there are more comprehensive. The most striking example is New Zealand, where the tort system was largely abolished during the early 1970s in favor of a social insurance scheme covering virtually all accidents. If these analysts are correct, tort law is an alternative not only to regulation but also to certain forms of social insurance system; as social insurance expands, tort law decreases.

Administrative Claims Facilities

Another technique to reduce pressures on the tort system is the creation of administrative claim facilities, usually as part of a "global" settlement of mass tort claims negotiated by defendants, their insurers, and plaintiffs' lawyers. The goal is to process these claims more efficiently and fairly than the tort system might do by specifying injury and compensation categories to be used for assessing claims administratively. Such systems resemble no-fault compensation laws in that they facilitate, or even dispense altogether with, the requirement of tort law that claimants prove causation, liability, and other elements of their claims rigorously and on an individual basis. Significantly, almost all of these non-tort arrangements, like other no-fault schemes, permit the claimant to opt out and return to the tort system under certain circumstances.[12]

The desire to reduce the scope of tort law has also led some governments to create schemes for compensating victims of certain kinds of accidents without requiring them to prove the injurer's wrongdoing.[13] The most important area in which such no-fault compensation has replaced the tort system is workplace accidents. In every state and the federal government, workers compensation statutes govern such accidents. Workers compensation effects a tradeoff. An injured worker's sole remedy against her employer is to file a claim with the employer's workers compensation insurance carrier, whose decision on the claim is then subject to appeal to an administrative board and ultimately to the courts. In order to receive an award, the injured worker need not prove the employer's negligence but must only show that the accident occurred in the course of her employment. On the other hand, her award is limited to scheduled amounts for pecuniary losses (e.g., wages, medical expenses, therapy) for a specified number of weeks; she is barred from recovering for the intangible losses (e.g., pain-and-suffering, loss of life's enjoyments, emotional distress) that she could have sought had she sued in tort. The worker may still be able to bring a tort action against a nonemployer such as the manufacturer of the machine that injured her.

Many states have also applied no-fault compensation schemes to property damage and personal injuries sustained in automobile accidents. Almost all of these statutes, however, do not really supplant the tort system; instead, they preserve the right to sue in tort once plaintiff's losses exceed a specified threshold, which tends to be quite low. Indeed, some commentators contend that automobile no-fault schemes actually encourage tort litigation by supplying plaintiffs with some immediate no-fault payments that they can then use to finance their tort actions. Politicians' interest in these schemes, moreover, essentially ended in the 1970s. Few if any states have adopted them since then, and although Congress recently has considered a variant of the idea, it seems unlikely to gain the necessary political support.

Some narrowly targeted no-fault laws have been adopted. Congress, for example, has enacted no-fault compensation schemes for certain vaccine-related childhood diseases, for certain swine flu-related illnesses, and for nuclear power plant accidents, and a few states have enacted schemes relating to certain perinatal malpractice claims. In each instance, however, victims may under certain circumstances reject the statutory no-fault alternative and instead proceed to sue in the tort system. Pending legislative proposals in Congress would assign asbestos-related claims to an administrative compensation program, analogous to workers compensation, that would resolve these claims more quickly on a no-fault basis with monetary awards derived from predetermined, administrative categories. Without waiting for such legislative relief, some judges in complex tort cases have adopted elements of this administrative, no-fault approach in their orders approving global settlements.[14]

VI. OVERALL ASSESSMENT

The tort system can usefully be assessed in terms of the criteria of effectiveness, equity, and legitimacy. In fact, however, these criteria are closely interrelated, even at an analytical level. The system's effectiveness, after all, depends in part on whether people perceive it to be fair, and vice-versa, while its legitimacy, which is wholly a matter of public perception, depends on whether people view it as being both effective and fair. A useful assessment, moreover, must be comparative (i.e., it must answer the question "compared to what?") and contextual (i.e., it must be context specific). Finally, one must acknowledge in all candor that, as noted earlier, there is little normative consensus on the precise mix and weighting of the values that the tort law should serve, and many of the empirical questions that are relevant to an assessment are unanswered and perhaps even unanswerable.

This is particularly true of optimal deterrence, which many tort law scholars view as its paramount goal. A number of factors make it very difficult to measure the deterrent effect of legal rules, including tort law. However, there are strong reasons to doubt that tort law's marginal deterrence of risky behavior is generally great.[15]

Tort law's doctrines and institutions constitute a major obstacle to optimal deterrence. Most tort law standards are radically indeterminate; they define legal duties in terms of reasonableness, foreseeability, and similarly ambiguous concepts. Few bright-line rules exist; even when they are available, the courts often reject them. For example, complying with a relevant and specific regulatory standard does not prove one's reasonableness; the jury remains free to reject that standard and make up its own. Juries then apply these vague principles to particular facts, yet juries are not required or even encouraged to explain, much less justify, their decisions. Judges, who possess a strong institutional interest in zealously protecting the secrecy of jury deliberations, have only weak controls over jury verdicts, which they seldom exercise. Indeed, judges ordinarily instruct juries to render only a general verdict with no explicit findings of fact, reinforcing their "black box" character. As a result, jury decisions, as distinguished from judges' rulings on questions of law, have no precedential significance even in similar cases.

Deterrence also founders on the reality that people's knowledge about tort law is very limited. If they think about risk at all, their own self-regard and desire to avoid pain and loss already supply an incentive to be careful. Most accidents caused by risky behavior are due to inattention, forgetfulness, and other momentary lapses of judgment rather than to the kind of rational decision to create risks that potential tort liability could affect. Even those injured in circumstances in which they might have a tort viable claim seldom decide to pursue it, and if they do they may have difficulty finding a lawyer willing to take their case even on a contingency. As Section I explained, a plaintiff is obliged to prove a great deal—legal duty, breach of duty, causation, damages, and negation of certain defenses—before the court will shift her loss to the defendant. Given the costs of suing, even successful tort plaintiffs, especially the most seriously injured, are usually undercompensated. To the extent that risky actors know all this, potential liability is less likely to deter them.

Liability insurance, which is pervasive in contemporary society, further mutes the deterrent threat of liability. Indeed, tort law is profoundly shaped by the existence of insurance on both a first-party and a third-party basis.[16] In first-party insurance, a person who is subject to a risk of injury purchases insurance to cover some or all of that risk, as when one buys a health insurance policy. First-party coverage, whether provided privately or socially, is usually on a no-fault basis; the insurer indemnifies the insured simply because the insured event occurred and without regard to how it occurred. In third-party (or "liability") insurance, a person who fears that she may injure others purchases insurance to cover some or all of that liability risk, as when a driver buys an auto accident liability policy. Here, the insurer pays only if the insured has incurred a legal liability to compensate a third party whom the insured has injured.

The tort system, absent a contract between the plaintiff and the defendant about who shall bear the risk of the injury, is in effect a system of mandatory third-party liability insurance. It is mandatory because one generally cannot opt out of the tort system even if one wants to do so; courts resist enforcing contracts that immunize an injurer from liability for negligence. It is a third-party insurance system in the sense that the insurer is insuring a risk that its insured imposes on a third party who has no contractual relationship with either of them. In effect, then, every health-care consumer must purchase, in addition to her physician's services, an insurance policy that gives her a right to sue the physician for malpractice in the tort system in the event of injury. The cost of this policy, reflected in the physician's fee, is equal to the premium that the physician must pay for medical malpractice insurance (or put aside for self-insurance) to cover the liability risk that the physician incurs by treating her.

From a public policy perspective, this mandatory third-party insurance feature of tort law is problematic. As a means of compensating injury victims, third-party insurance tends to be less efficient and arguably less equitable to low-income and low-risk individuals than first-party insurance, yet they have no way to opt out of the tort system and find a tradeoff between cost and risk that they might prefer. For many kinds of accidents, any desired level of compensation can probably be better achieved by substituting first-party insurance for tort law, while desired levels of deterrence may be achievable—this is less certain—by substituting regulatory or other non-tort strategies or at least integrating them better into the tort system.

Some risk decisions are made in contexts in which liability signals are fairly clear and salient, and these contexts account for much tort litigation. Many health-care providers, employers, and product manufacturers, for example, tend to be "high-attention decisionmakers," as legal scholar Howard Latin calls them. They possess the opportunity, information, and incentive to think rationally and in advance about the kind and level of risks they are prepared to create and about the tradeoffs such choices involve.[17] At the margin, then, these actors should be more readily deterrable by tort law than, say, automobile drivers. Since high-attention decisionmakers usually carry liability insurance, however, the optimality of the deterrence may turn on how risk-sensitive are their insurance premiums. It appears, however, that the risk rating of premiums is often quite crude. Much medical malpractice insurance, for example, is rated only by specialty and location. The workers compensation insurance that employers must purchase is often rated only by industry and size of workforce. Product liability insurance is difficult to rate because manufacturers possess little advance information of the kind insurers need with respect to potential consumers-victims and how safely they will use products. Unless and until insurers risk-rate their premiums in a more refined fashion, the cost of liability insurance will affect high-attention decisionmakers' risk choices only to a limited extent. For this reason, generating better risk information about specific actors—for example, publishing individual providers' incidence of malpractice on the Internet in a meaningful, nonmisleading format—should be an important policy priority in the future.

Fortunately, many non-tort deterrents exist. In addition to the self-regard discussed above, they include education, criminal and regulatory law, risk-rated insurance, reputational concerns, social norms of behavior, and a natural concern for others. One suspects that tort law deterrence operates only at the margin beyond whatever deterrent effects these mechanisms already create.

Tort law is even less effective in performing its loss distribution or compensatory function. Indeed, many of the conditions discussed above that weaken tort deterrence do so precisely because they limit victims' ability or propensity to sue and obtain full compensation. An even more fundamental barrier to compensation, however, is rooted in the very normative essence of tort law, which is corrective justice. Tort law is designed to effect compensation not to all victims but only to those (except where a strict liability standard applies) who are *wrongfully* injured by others; it is a system for determining when a loss suffered by A should instead be borne by B. However, most injured people are not injured by those who are violating tort law; instead, they are victims of their own carelessness, of conduct by others that the law does not condemn, or of simple misfortune for which no one else bears legal or perhaps even moral responsibility. Many tort victims, moreover, fail to seek redress informally, much less retain a lawyer to bring suit. Tort law offers no remedy for such people, nor would it do so even if all of the other barriers to recovery were eliminated, for then it would cease to be tort law.

Fortunately, there are better ways than tort law to compensate accident victims in many circumstances.[18] The most important alternatives are third-party no-fault insurance, and first-party insurance provided either privately or socially. As noted in Section I, first-party insurance is generally on a no-fault basis. Indeed, most transfers to injured people today occur not through tort litigation but through workers compensation (a third-party no-fault system) and first-party insurance covering disability, health care, wage loss, business interruption, property damage, and other such risks. The spread of first-party insurance coverage has prompted many state legislatures to restrict the scope of tort liability by requiring that tort awards be reduced by the amount of plaintiffs' collateral sources, of which first-party insurance payments are the most important.

Tort law also ill-serves its participatory ambitions. As many studies have demonstrated, plaintiffs generally play a very minor role in the prosecution of their cases, which are dominated by their lawyers and involve little genuine consultation. Indeed, the level of lawyer-client communication is quite limited, particularly in mass tort cases and class actions in which the lawyers' separation from particular clients is more or less structural. For similar reasons, the moral and ideological functions of tort law are more theoretical than actual. The opportunity to have one's "day in court" means little (or at least something quite different) when the cost of getting there is often prohibitively expensive and when 95 percent of cases that are brought are settled informally. Still, the contingency fee system does provide accident victims greater access to the courts than in other countries, and the David-and-Goliath metaphor propagated by tort lawyers and other populists is vindicated just often enough to retain some credibility. However fanciful in reality, this image continues to exert a powerful hold on the public imagination.

The assessor of tort law, then, is left with a kind of paradox. Those who study the tort system most systematically and rigorously generally find it both ineffective and inequitable—even, or especially, when compared with alternative mechanisms for reducing or optimizing the costs of accidents. At the same time, efforts to eliminate the tort system, or even to reform it in fundamental ways (which recent tort reform statutes in the states do not do), almost invariably fail. The persistent rejection of proposals since the 1970s to extend no-fault to new areas, or even to adopt genuine no-fault plans for automobile accidents rather than the tort system add-on plans that now exist in many states, is perhaps the clearest example. This failure has a number of explanations. The most plausible ones include the decisive political influence of the plaintiff's lawyers and others with strong stakes in preserving the status quo, the genuine normative and empirical uncertainties surrounding the leading policy alternatives such as no-fault and mandated first-party insurance (social or private), and a strong public belief in the ideology of the adversary system and the "day in court."

A fair assessment must conclude, then, that the many serious criticisms of the tort system have not yet succeeded in dislodging it or in destroying its legitimacy in the eyes of the public. Accordingly, tort law will continue as an alternative public policy tool, along with regulation, social insurance, contract, information, voluntary standards, and others.

Tort law already exists. It can be used without the need to enact a program, establish a bureaucracy, or appropriate public funds. From a political perspective, this is no small virtue, especially in an era whose public philosophy is less government. When one adds to this the fact that—with the important exception of the judge—tort law is largely privately administered and trumpets the values of individualism, accountability, public participation, and morality, one can easily understand its enduring popularity.

From certain policy perspectives, tort law has other characteristics that many will consider virtues. Decentralized and antibureaucratic, its decisions can achieve a level of responsiveness to context, factual particularity, and competing values that is less easily achieved by administrative regulation and other more rigid, rule-based systems. Vouchsafing decisions to judges and juries minimizes the possibility that interest group politics will determine outcomes.

From other policy perspectives, however, these virtues are vices. Grounding tort law in decentralized state law systems frustrates efforts to impose common national standards and impedes the operation of a national common market. Tort law's antibureaucratic character in effect shields its judges and juries from discipline and accountability, and its case-by-case and fact-specific contextuality can render its decisions unpredictable and unsystematic. It enables private litigants to make public policy without undergoing the rigors and democratic safeguards of the political process. Its focus on justice in the individual case is likely to blind it to the larger consequences of its decisions.

Taking all of these factors into account, one can identify certain conditions under which (other things being equal) tort law may be an effective policy tool for deterring certain conduct and compensating its victims. These conditions include the following:

1. Potential injurers are well informed about the relevant risks they create.

2. Potential victims are not and cannot at low cost become well informed about such risks.

3. Potential injurers and victims cannot cheaply enter into risk-allocation contracts.

4. The conduct in question is discrete and causes harm along well-defined, readily proved pathways.

5. Victims do not share causal responsibility for their injuries.

6. Victims are likely to learn about and pursue valid claims in a timely fashion.

7. Injurers are identifiable, sueable, and solvent.

8. Voluntary standards of care either do not exist or are inadequate to protect victims.

9. First-party insurance is not an efficient alternative.

Policymakers confronted with a social problem and an array of possible tools must systematically compare them before making a choice.[19] The future of tort law will in large part be determined by the future of three of its principal alternatives: contract, administrative regulation, and social and private insurance. The key question is whether the domains in which their authority governs the allocation of risk and the compensation of injuries will expand or will instead shrink. The more courts respect and enforce contracts, the less they will permit tort law to modify risk allocations to which the parties have already agreed. The more government regulates risks through explicit, bureaucratically enforced standards of conduct, the less courts will be inclined (and perhaps permitted) to allow juries in tort cases to devise and apply their own. The more the victims of accidents and other misfortunes are compensated through social insurance and first-party insurance mechanisms, the less that tort law will have to do.

VIII. SUGGESTED READING

Calabresi, Guido. *The Costs of Accidents.* New Haven: Yale University Press, 1970.

Komesar, Neil K. *Imperfect Alternatives: Choosing Institutions in Law, Economics, and Public Policy.* Chicago: University of Chicago Press, 1994.

O'Connell, Jeffrey, and Peter A. Bell. *Accidental Justice: The Dilemmas of Tort Law.* New Haven: Yale University Press, 1997.

Schuck, Peter H. *Agent Orange on Trial: Mass Toxic Disasters in the Courts.* Enlarged ed. Cambridge, Mass.: Harvard University Press, 1987.

Sugarman, Stephen D. *Doing Away with Personal Injury Law.* New York: Quorum Books, 1989.

NOTES

1. See, for example, Stephen D. Sugarman, *Doing Away with Personal Injury Law* (New York: Quorum Books, 1989).

2. Guido Calabresi, *The Costs of Accidents* (New Haven: Yale University Press, 1970).

3. Judith Resnik, "Managerial Judging," *Harvard Law Review* 96 (1982): 374.

4. Deborah R. Hensler et al., *Compensation for Accidental Injuries in the United States* (Santa Monica, Calif.: RAND Institute for Civil Justice, 1991), 175.

5. The statistics used for this subsection are drawn from Marc Galanter, "Real World Torts: An Antidote to Anecdote," *Maryland Law Review* 55 (1996): 1093; and from "State Courts Caseload Statistics—1998," National Center for State Courts, 137.

6. The statistics in this subsection are drawn from Marc Galanter, "Real World Torts," and from "Federal Judicial Caseload Statistics—March 31, 1999," Administrative Office of the United States Courts, 37.

7. Marc Galanter, "Real World Torts," 1093.

8. Deborah Jones Merritt and Kathryn Ann Barry, "Is the Tort System in Crisis? New Empirical Evidence," *Ohio State Law Journal* 60 (1999): 315.

9. The importance of juries in tort law can scarcely be exaggerated. See, for example, Robert E. Litan, ed., *Verdict: Assessing the Civil Jury System* (Washington, D.C.: The Brookings Institution, 1993); Neil Vidmar, "The Performance of the American Civil Jury: An Empirical Perspective," *Arizona Law Review* 40 (1998): 849–899.

10. See generally, Peter H. Schuck, *Agent Orange on Trial: Mass Toxic Disasters in the Courts* enlarged ed. (Cambridge, Mass.: Harvard University Press, 1987).

11. Peter H. Schuck, *The Limits of Law: Essays on Democratic Governance* (Boulder: Westview Press, 2000), 353–354.

12. Schuck, *The Limits of Law,* 345–391.

13. See, for example, Stephen D. Sugarman, *Doing Away with Personal Injury Law* (New York: Quorum Books, 1989); Jeffrey O'Connell and Peter A. Bell, *Accidental Justice: The Dilemmas of Tort Law* (New Haven: Yale University Press, 1997).

14. Schuck, *The Limits of Law,* 355–357, 371–372.

15. Sugarman, *Doing Away with Personal Injury Law;* O'Connell and Bell, *Accidental Justice.*

16. Kenneth S. Abraham, *Distributing Risk: Insurance, Legal Theory, and Public Policy* (New Haven: Yale University Press, 1986).

17. Howard Latin, "Good Warnings, Bad Products, and Cognitive Limitations," *U.C.L.A. Law Review* 41 (1994).

18. See, for example, Sugarman, *Doing Away with Personal Injury Law;* O'Connell and Bell, *Accidental Justice.*

19. Schuck, *The Limits of Law,* 419–455; Neil K. Komesar, *Imperfect Alternatives: Choosing Institutions in Law, Economics, and Public Policy* (Chicago: University of Chicago Press, 1994).

CHAPTER SIXTEEN

Managing Indirect Government

Donald F. Kettl

On December 10, 1999, federal agents arrested Wen Ho Lee and capped their three-year investigation of leaked national nuclear secrets. Lee was a twenty-year employee at the Los Alamos nuclear laboratory and had been working at the secret "X Division." Somewhere along the way, intelligence analysts suspected that the Chinese government had captured the secrets of the W-88 warhead, America's most advanced nuclear device. The analysts believed that the Chinese had obtained the design from Los Alamos, and Lee was their chief suspect.

After Lee's arrest, the general impression was of a federal employee who had gone bad—or who, at the least, had been sloppy with matters of utmost national security. In fact, Lee was not a federal employee, even though he was working on the federal government's most sensitive nuclear secrets. He was an employee of the Los Alamos National Laboratory, which the University of California-Berkeley operated under contract to the U.S. Department of Energy (DOE). In short, Lee was part of indirect government and the case, even if just a matter of mishandling classified ultrasecret computer files, was a problem of managing indirect government.

It was also a case that demonstrates how tightly indirect government has become woven into government operations. Since its beginning, Los Alamos has been a "GOCO": a government-owned, contractor-operated facility. Indeed, the entire Manhattan Project, which developed the first nuclear bombs, and the fifty years of nuclear weapons production that followed, built on the same model. The government—first the Atomic Energy Commission, and then the DOE—ran few of these facilities itself. From the production of nuclear materials in Hanford, Washington, or Savannah, South Carolina, to the machining of plutonium warhead triggers at Rocky Flats, Colorado, GOCOs have been the keystone of the nation's nuclear strategy. Rather than produce the weapons itself, the federal government has always relied on private contractors.

So extensive is the government's nuclear contract network, in fact, that DOE is little more than a loose holding company for its contractors. Paul Light, for example, has estimated that there are thirty-five contractor employees for every DOE worker.[1] DOE does other things as well, including setting national energy policy and monitoring energy supplies. Its nuclear functions, however, dominate its budget as well as its workforce, both in government and in the contractors. It is no exaggeration to argue that the effectiveness of the nation's nuclear weapons program—and ultimately the nation's defense—depends on how well DOE manages the indirect government that produces and maintains the weapons.

I. THE HIERARCHY PROBLEM

As the other chapters in this book make clear, indirect government has proliferated, from subtle incentives contained in the tax code through the implementation of welfare reform. Moreover, this is as true for state and local governments as it is for the federal government. Quite simply, the management of government is not one basic process but two: the production of government goods and services by government itself—a shrinking part of governmental activity; and the production of goods and services on behalf of government by others acting on its behalf, through one of the government's many indirect tools.

The spread of indirect government has been of both great and small importance to elected officials. Policymakers have often embraced it in a belief, often unsupported, that nongovernmental actors can deliver public services more efficiently than government agencies ever can. On the other hand, policymakers have often shown little interest in and less knowledge about the management implications of the indirect systems they have created. When Lee's case made national headlines, Congress's reaction was to restructure DOE's security apparatus, without charting how changes in DOE's headquarters would percolate out to the contractors.

Policymakers have often approached indirect government as a self-executing system. They frequently begin with a reverential view of market competition and an assumption that such competition is superior to government monopoly. They assume that leaving things to the market will produce superior services. And they assume that the management of government services through indirect mechanisms will happen spontaneously and with little need for government oversight. In fact, of course, no private-sector manager would assume that the company's contractors would deliver quality goods on time at a fair price. Private-sector experience teaches that outsourcing—the private corollary to indirect government—requires close management and careful oversight. The same is true of government.

Private-sector experience also teaches that managing such indirect strategies is different from managing goods and services produced by an organization's own bureaucracy. Even if the goods and services might be identical, the process that produces them is different and requires a different approach. Most complex organizations—public and private—are organized internally by hierarchy and controlled through authority. Decisions at the top trickle down the chain of command. Officials at each level have power because of the authority inherent in their positions. That does not necessarily mean that officials act most effectively by exercising that authority. However, the basic structure and process—as well as the ultimate fallback in case motivation-based approaches fail—are based on authority and hierarchy.

In indirect relationships, whether in government or the private sector, the basic approaches do not function on the basis of hierarchical authority. Top managers, for example, cannot order contractors to perform certain activities. They can negotiate, create incentives, or threaten nonrenewal of the contract, but they cannot command. The relationship within an organization traditionally builds on authority; the relationship between one organization and another organization, on the other hand, builds on market-based exchanges. The management and control systems follow. Bargaining and incentive systems replace command and control. The basic administrative problem of indirect government thus is developing effective management mechanisms to replace command and control. This holds as much for loose relationships, such as incentives in tax policy or loan programs, as it does for more formal ones, such as contracting out.

In most of these relationships, the centerpiece of the relationship is now a contract. That is, of course, the case for contracting out. However, the government uses written agreements, embodied in contracts and contract-like devices, in other policy tools as well. The federal government has increasingly negotiated written agreements with the states on issues ranging from waivers of welfare program requirements to environmental regulation. Direct and guaranteed loan programs rely on contracts as well:

borrowers promise to repay debts at specified rates, and they are liable in court should they fail to comply. Negotiated exchange relationships replace hierarchical authority.[2]

The management of indirect tools thus links with principal-agent theory. In that theory, relationships are exchanges: incentives and inducements in exchange for desired behavior. Elected officials create policy and establish relationships with agents—administrative agencies—to carry it out. Within bureaucracies, top-level officials likewise create relationships between themselves (as principals) and subordinates (as agents) who agree to carry out decisions in return for inducements (principally salary). Relationships between government agencies (as principals) and contractors (as agents) thus, in one sense, are simply variants of this basic pattern. However, differences in the basic relationship create different kinds of principal-agent relationships. Within an organization, agents not only agree to carry out a task. They also agree that, in doing so, they will subject themselves to the organization's basic rules and authority. Between organizations, the relationship is looser and more purely market based.

The point here is not that one system is inherently better than another. Rather, it is that they are different: managing authority-based relationships requires one approach; managing indirect relationships requires a different one. The dominant model, in both thinking and practice, is hierarchical authority. As government has increased its reliance on indirect tools, the thinking of policymakers has not adapted to the realities of indirect tools. Moreover, because government has frequently not developed instruments for managing indirect tools as fast as it has come to rely on them, managing indirect government is often harder than managing direct tools. In fact, government faces three major challenges in managing indirect government: using its hierarchical bureaucracy to manage nonhierarchical tools; dealing with multiple actors who often have widely different incentives and motivations; and reconciling government's bottom line—political accountability—with the diverse, sometimes conflicting, financial bottom lines of its partners. When, as is the case in Medicaid, the chain of implementation involves both intergovernmental and public-private-nonprofit partnerships, the challenges multiply.

Government's performance is only as good as its ability to manage its tools and to hold its tool users accountable. As the Lee case demonstrates, the federal government's programs are only as strong as its indirect partners. A weak link anywhere along the service chain, even if the weak link is far outside government's halls, undermines the effectiveness of public programs. Government thus must ensure that its service delivery partners have the capacity required to make shared service delivery work well. Moreover, government itself must develop the capacity to manage these indirect tools. If government (at all levels—federal, state, and local) retreats back to traditional hierarchical management strategies, it will not build the necessary leverage over its indirect partners. That can only undermine the effectiveness of public programs and diminish the government's ability to preserve important norms like responsiveness and equity.

The capacity problem spills over into the accountability problem that Paul L. Posner discusses in Chapter 18. Traditionally, accountability has been viewed as a problem of control. In nonhierarchical governmental programs, however, control is not an option. Accountability in indirect government hinges much more on obtaining good information. That, in turn, requires creating new mechanisms to generate, assess, and manage this information.

Networks and Public Management

How should we think about managing indirect government? *Network-based* approaches fit far better than traditional hierarchy-based approaches.[3] The fundamental relationships among those managing indirect tools sometimes can be very formal (like con-tracts, grounded in civil law) or very fuzzy (like tax incentives, in which the government creates opportunities for anyone wishing to use them). The relationships, moreover, tend to be between individuals within a government bureaucracy and others (acting either as individuals or on behalf of a private or nonprofit organization) outside it.

In short, the relationships are more like webs than hierarchies. Because the relation-ships cross organizational boundaries, few government agencies can any longer fully encompass any important problems. Government managers cannot "control" indirect programs because they cannot exercise control over those who implement them. As more government programs rely on indirect tools, managers must shift their manage-ment techniques to gain leverage over the networks that produce the goods and services. Managers, in short, do not manage programs or agencies. Rather, they manage *net-works*.

As Harvard Business School professor Nitin Nohira points out, every organization's environment is a network of other organizations. To do what they do, organizations interact with other organizations in their environment. Public policy implementation thus is a government agency's action embedded in a web of organizations, and a pro-gram imbedded in a web of other programs. The perspective of any one organization therefore misses important elements of the process. The actions of network participants can best be understood by understanding their place in these networks of relationships. Most organizational analysis—and the broader public understanding of government bureaucracies—begins by trying to understand where an official or program sits within the bureaucracy. Network theory argues that a manager's or program's place within broader networks is most important. It is one thing to look at how DOE sets energy policy. It is quite another to understand the connection between DOE and the Uni-versity of California as its contractor, and between the university and the Los Alamos lab as subcontractor.[4]

Nohira argues that networks shape action—and actions shape networks. How things work depends on how networks' components fit together. This, of course, is a challenging job for government managers. They have to learn the points of leverage in networks, change their behavior to manage those points of leverage, develop the processes needed to make that work, and change the organizational culture from a traditional control per-spective to one that accommodates indirect methods. It can be an even more challenging task for policymakers, who often worry little about program implementation. The fact that managers must work through networks limits their autonomy, increases their need to find cooperative strategies, and exposes them to greater political risk as they can exercise less control over what their nongovernmental partners do.

The Management Challenge

What does this mean for managing indirect government? Because indirect government is different from direct government, government managers relying on indirect govern-ment cannot control the front lines of service delivery by reaching down inside their own agencies. Indeed, they cannot control the front lines at all. Rather, they must find tools to influence the behavior of frontline service providers who work in other orga-nizations. Sometimes they must shape incentives to influence the choices of individual consumers. To ensure accountability, policymakers hold managers responsible for these programs. The managers, in turn, must develop new tools to ensure the effectiveness of their programs. They are responsible for ensuring high-quality results in programs that they do not directly control.

Moreover, government managers face additional challenges. Compared with private-sector managers, public-sector managers are responsible not only for what gets done but for how it gets done as well. Elected officials expect that public programs achieve their goals (effectiveness). They also expect that the programs achieve their goals at the lowest possible cost (efficiency). They expect that citizens will be treated fairly (equity) and that all citizens will have the same opportunity to receive services (equality). They expect that the process will be open and transparent, and they expect that those who manage the service-delivery system will listen carefully to citizens' views (responsiveness). In the end, they expect that policy results will match their programmatic desires (accountability).

This is a very tall order. Indeed, as economist Arthur M. Okun recognized, American government constantly wrestles with "the big tradeoff" among competing values. The institutional arrangements government creates to manage the tradeoff "represent uneasy compromises rather than fundamental inconsistencies."[5] It is always tempting to try to solve these problems by retreating to the hierarchical tradition. However, American government long since has made the decision to rely heavily on indirect government. Government has come to rely heavily on the flexibility and added capacity that indirect government brings. Moreover, indirect government is as much a political as an administrative strategy. It draws private and nonprofit organizations, as well as individual citizens, into the very fabric of governance. That spreads the benefits of public programs. It creates nongovernmental jobs in the government's partners. It turns the arguments about separating public and private functions on their heads—network-based partnerships blur the lines between the public and private roles.

The solution therefore lies in better equipping government to manage its indirect tools. Managing American government is a messy process at best. Managing indirect government is messier yet, precisely because indirect government incorporates more varied and complex social values into the process. Managing this system requires a three-part balance among process, people, and performance, and it requires building the capacity to do so.

II. PROCESS

The vending machine model of government services may be a caricature, but it nevertheless captures the way many people think about government management—and a lot about the way that managers actually manage and policymakers envision policy. It is easy to envision a government agency as a sophisticated mechanism that translates inputs (tax dollars) into outputs (goods and services). Policymakers put money in the top, expect agency managers to construct the machine's insides to produce the desired service, and then they wait for services to emerge. They do not worry much about what the insides of the machine look like any more than most consumers think about how a soft-drink machine actually takes coins and gives them cans. What matters is that inputs produce the desired outputs.

For policymakers, this approach works quite well. They do not really need to worry about the internal mechanisms by which government agencies work so long as they do work—that they produce the desired outputs in the desired way. That, in turn, reinforces hierarchy as the basic model. It defines the workings of the machine and line-item budgeting as the basic control mechanism. It also defines what resources go in the top and what activity ought to come out the bottom. This two-step process provides a valuable guide. It defines who is responsible for what, and it matches resources with their actions. Because indirect tools tend to operate through nonhierarchical networks, however, government managers must solve two problems. They must find effective mechanisms for shaping policy implementation, and they must find ways to link these newer mechanisms to the more traditional ones on which policymakers rely.

Two mechanisms are of special help: managing contracts and tracking the flow of money. Contracts help structure the networks of policy implementation. Following the money provides a guide to who actually does what. It helps managers escape the often-fictional view of the vending machine to get a detailed view of how government programs are implemented. Controlling the flow of money, moreover, provides a way of enforcing accountability for the quality of program implementation. Together, these mechanisms provide the basic framework for managing indirect government.

Managing Programs by Structuring Contracts

Contract-based relationships apply formally to many forms of indirect government. Contracting out (including procurement of goods and purchase-of-service contracting) as well as many insurance and loan programs build on formal, written agreements. The shift from direct government to contract-based tools is not only a change in tactics. It is also a fundamental change in legal mechanisms: from the administrative law of delegated authority, which has been based since 1946 in the Administrative Procedure Act and its revisions, to the civil law of contracts, which grows out of English common law.[6]

Private-sector companies, of course, have long managed their suppliers. Governments likewise have successfully relied on contractors for everything from building highways and nuclear weapons to policy advice and external auditing. To operate effectively through contracts, government needs to be a "smart buyer" of the goods and services it is purchasing.[7] This, in turn, is a three-part process. First, government needs to identify the good or service it wants to buy. No auto company, for example, would contract with a supplier to deliver windshields without specifying their size, strength, and other characteristics. Specifying goals has always been problematic in government contracts. Indeed, problems of goal conflict lie at the core of many indirect government strategies, as Posner argues in his chapter. Public goods and services often are not off-the-shelf items for which generally accepted standards already exist. That often means that the government-as-buyer and contractor-as-supplier must negotiate what the finished product ought to look like. Kelman's study of government computer procurement has found that public managers believe that private suppliers are likely to overpromise on what they can deliver. Moreover, unanticipated problems often pop up in many government contracts. That requires the government and the contractor to renegotiate the deal. That, in turn, makes it harder to hold vendors strictly responsible for their performance or to control costs.[8] The further the procurement moves away from off-the-shelf items, the more likely these problems become.

Second, government needs to sustain a strong and competitive market for the goods and services it buys. An underlying argument for indirect tools is that market competition makes the private sector more efficient. However, if limited markets minimize competition, this assumption crumbles. Indeed, private monopolies are no more efficient than public ones. For much of what the government buys, this is no problem. The federal government, for example, has issued procurement credit cards to many of its managers, which allow them to buy items at discount-price office supply stores and similar facilities. The General Services Administration has created a massive online shopping facility for common items.

The more government's service system moves from buying off-the-shelf items or inducing people to do more of what they are already doing, the harder it is to apply the standard private-sector model. For example, when the government launched the

Manhattan Project during World War II, not only were there no existing suppliers—no one was even sure if the atomic bomb would work. When state and local governments began contracting out for the management and delivery of welfare reform in the 1990s, competition among potential service providers was limited. In fact, many of the markets in which the government arranges for goods and services are "monopsonies," in which the government is the sole buyer of the service. When the private market does not provide real competition—or if it does not naturally produce the goods and services government wants to buy or encourage—the case for private-sector efficiency erodes and the government's job multiplies. It must stimulate the market to produce goods and services that otherwise would not be produced. Then it must guard itself against market failures that can drive up costs, reduce efficiencies, and benefit some citizens more than others. Other indirect government tools, especially tax and loan programs, uncover more problems. Indirect government often depends on the assumption that government can use the private market for public purposes. The further the government's intended results move away from the existing state of the market, the more difficult the government's problems become.

The government's own management systems can also get in the way of achieving its goals. The procurement rules, for example, make it difficult for public procurement managers to use their discretion to strengthen competition. Government's typical requirement to accept the low bid, without taking into account vendors' performance record, makes it even harder to sustain quality services at the consistently lowest prices. The federal government's procurement reforms in the late 1990s began to change that by allowing manages to take past performance more into account. However, government's rule-bound procurement system, created to ensure uniform treatment and prevent favoritism in contract awards, makes it hard to establish and maintain strong and competitive markets. The rules embody important political norms but also complicate management.[9]

Finally, government needs to assess the quality of the goods it buys. Private-sector managers would never dream of paying invoices without first determining that what they thought they were buying was what they actually received. The government faces the same challenge. Government's job is often harder, however. The goals of public programs frequently shift along the implementation trail. In fact, many public programs seek to ensure that service recipients have some power over the way a program works. Moreover, in government programs, shifting goals make it that much harder to assess contractors' performance. In the government, moreover, there is no bottom line and performance measures are rudimentary at best. Complaints can arrive from many different sources, from congressional oversight to citizen protests. The chain of accountability, especially in indirect government, is much more complex than either in the private sector or in public direct service delivery. This combination makes it harder to measure results or assess responsibility for problems—and it separates government's indirect tools from the private-sector management model so often invoked.

Throughout indirect government, however, the legal skeleton is the nation's system of civil law. It is the basic relationships among parties to contracts as well as the procedures for handling disputes. Some indirect tools, like loan programs, require written agreements by lenders and borrowers. Government corporations live in a quasi-world between the public and private sectors, with the legal requirements of each sector typically applying. These agreements hinge on important elements of civil law, especially contracts and torts. Many indirect tools thus work through multiple legal layers: fundamental precepts of civil law; the government's own procedures and requirements, which multiply if several levels of government are involved; and a program's own goals and requirements. Simply asserting that the law provides the ultimate guide for accountability of public programs does not help managers. They frequently face the challenge of discovering which legal frameworks apply and how to apply them. Indeed, as many former Soviet-bloc nations tried to sell off public industries and services, they discovered that the lack of a civil law tradition—what a contact is, how to structure it, how to resolve disputes in executing contracts—severely hampered the privatization effort.

Even in indirect tools not based on formal contracts, the legal structure shapes the tools' management. Regulatory tools flow directly out of the Administrative Procedure Act and its system of formal and informal rulemaking. The act fixes the procedures that federal managers must follow in issuing regulations and regulatory decisions. Tax expenditures sit in the rich   and huge   legal tradition surrounding the tax code. In short, even if contract law does not apply to all indirect tools, assessing the legal framework affecting each tool provides important clues to how it is managed and how disputes are resolved.

Managing Programs by Tracking Money

Indirect government, by breaking the chain of authority, disrupts the authority-driven approach to government management. The flow of funds, however, remains the basic tool for ensuring effectiveness and accountability. In indirect government, it is often deceptively hard to determine who actually is responsible for doing what. As John J. Lordan points out (see Chapter 17), financial accounting maps who spends how much money on which activities and provides a way to gauge accountability. Policymakers can thus shape outputs and outcomes by seeking leverage through the money flow. Moreover, by charting who actually does what, it promotes accountability by identifying who is responsible for which pieces of the system. It moves many of the key processes into civil court and mixes public and private mechanisms for responsibility.

Financial accounting in government has long been an analytical backwater. It has received little attention from mainstream scholars in public management and has been relegated instead to the "nuts-and-bolts" category. As indirect government has risen in importance, however, financial management and accountability have become more important as well. In a system that confounds traditional bureaucratic lines of authority and defies a clear mapping of responsibility, the money trail provides one of the few ways of determining just who is doing what to whom, when, and how. It is also one of the most powerful sources of leverage in a system where traditional authority-based tools frequently fall short.

St. Louis's "Job Link" program demonstrates the important role that good financial accounting plays in promoting high performance in indirect programs. Job Link focuses on helping public-assistance recipients make the transition from public assistance to work. It is a regional program that focuses on helping workers find jobs along an 18-mile light-rail line connecting East St. Louis with the airport. The local community college oversees the program and a local community organization, Better Family Life, carries it out. Better Family Life recruits workers, gives them training, places them in jobs, and then supports them for up to two years. As program director Carolyn D. Seward explains, "We tell clients, 'Success isn't just graduating from the program, it's also getting involved in your church, your children's school, the neighborhood crime watch. If you're living in the inner city, you're part of the solution or part of the problem.' "

In its first year, the program placed more than one hundred workers in jobs. Employers applaud their new workers and the training they receive. The concessions manager at the airport said, "Whatever they are doing at Better Family Life, they should pass it on" to other programs training workers. To make the program work, the St. Louis Regional Jobs Initiative agreed in advance to pay Better Family Life $500,000 for training and placing two hundred workers—at the rate of $2,500 per trainee, but only for workers still on the job after a year. The program's managers set five milestones, with portions of the $2,500 fee paid at each step: after the first week's training; at placement in a job; after four months of employment; after seven months on the job; and then after a full year's employment. The community college official overseeing the contract said, "We don't get paid unless we produce the product."[10] This approach places heavy emphasis on tracking the performance of each trainee.

Following the money thus provides the basic foundation for assessing a program's performance. Determining who actually spends the money, and what they spend it on, is the first step to determining in the end what results the public money buys. That, in turn, demands a strong monitoring and accounting system. The Job Link program promoted "outcome-based funding." It demonstrates that there is no accountability without matching performance against the milestones, and it is impossible to do either without determining who spends the money for what.

Doing so, of course, is not a trivial problem. Job Link is a complex network involving both governmental and nongovernmental organizations: government money passes through a management contractor—the community college—to frontline, nongovernmental managers. Other public programs rely on partnerships that are even more complex. Medicaid, for example, is a federal program administered by fifty different states, each of which adds its own twist (and often its own money) to the program. Private and nonprofit partners actually deliver the health care, while other third-party companies process the claims. The same is true in many other federal grant programs. Regulatory partnerships, like the Environmental Protection Agency's (EPA's) emerging partnerships with the states, likewise raise staggering problems simply of charting the partnership, let alone following the money.

On the other hand, the money trail can help map the relationships and provide information on just who is doing what. It is, at once, a goal-defining system, telling a partner where to aim; a performance-tracking system, assessing the partner's success in meeting the goals; a financial control system, linking payments to results; and an accountability system, telling policymakers what results they get for their money. By following the money, managers, elected officials, and citizens can get basic information about who is doing what. That does not tell them how well the programs' managers are doing. To get that information requires far more detailed monitoring and evaluation systems. At their core, however, all of these systems begin with tracking the money. In the complicated government/nongovernmental networks that manage many government tools, the money trail is perhaps the one reliable guide to who actually does what.

III. PEOPLE

Just as the hierarchically organized, authority-driven model dominates theory and process, it also powerfully shapes the government's personnel system. A century-old tradition, dating from the early Progressive era, created a civil service system with clear rules. The system uses tests and other objective measures to select and promote people on the basis of what they know, instead of whom they know. This has helped insulate the system from political interference and secure a strong base of technical expertise in government at all levels of the intergovernmental system.

However, the old system has proved a poor match for the challenges of managing twenty-first century government—especially indirect governmental tools. The current system, created to manage direct tools, is now a jury-rigged patchwork that seeks to bridge the gap between the system's original goals and the demands that public pro-grams increasingly make on it. The strains and creaks in the personnel systems at all levels of government have made it increasingly difficult to get the right people with the right skills into the right jobs to manage government's growing reliance on indirect tools. It has proved poor in recruiting the managers needed for indirect government, training them in the requirements of managing indirect tools, and creating the incen-tives for high-performing governmental careers.

People Problems

Three problems, in particular, plague the government's people systems. First, the civil service tradition recruits and promotes individuals largely because of their substantive knowledge. Government seeks first-rate accountants, chemists, engineers, environmen-tal policy analysts, clerks, and computer programmers. As their careers evolve, however, technical experts become supervisors and managers. The difficulty of this transfor-mation is legendary. American government has notoriously had problems helping tech-nicians make the transition into administration and management, especially because government invests so little money in training. People who are first-rate engineers do not always have the people skills to become first-rate managers.

Second, managing indirect government requires skills that the traditional civil service system tends to either undervalue or ignore. Managing indirect government requires great skill in managing networks, but the existing civil service system was created to manage hierarchies. Government managers might enter the EPA focused on a career in environmental policy and trained in engineering. They might well intend to spend their time developing new strategies for reducing pollution. However, EPA conducts most of its activity through intergovernmental partnerships (with states that do much of the frontline regulatory work) and contracts (with private companies doing most of the cleanup and remediation work). It is one thing to plan a career cleaning up the environment; it is another to end up with a career managing other people who actually do the work. That not only frequently causes motivation problems. It also creates challenges for the government in preparing managers for new tasks that the managers themselves did not anticipate.

Third, the traditional civil service system's very strength—its clear structure and rules—makes it hard for government to adapt to the fast-changing world of indirect government. Several federal agencies—the Internal Revenue Service, the Federal Avi-ation Administration, the Defense Department, and the National Weather Service—made multibillion-dollar mistakes because they failed to manage computer procure-ment contracts well.[11] In California, the attorney general probed the role of organized crime in a casino owned, but not managed well, by the U.S. Justice Department Mar-shals Service. In each case, the government lacked the capacity to specify what it wanted to buy, write good contracts, and monitor the contractors' performance.

Ad hoc efforts have been made to cope with these problems. In fact, the federal government's civil service system now covers just 56 percent of the federal government's workers. The merit-based testing-and-placement program provides the pipeline for only 15 percent of the federal government's new employees. More government agencies are hiring more employees through positions exempt from civil service recruiting, short-term positions, and other tactics to circumvent civil service requirements.[12] As a result, it has become a nonsystem that neither preserves the goals of nonpartisan com-petence for which it was originally created nor provides the skill set required to manage government's tools.

In a constant struggle to find—and keep—people with the skills to do government's work, government managers have devised exceptions and new routes of entry to government service. Vice President Gore's "reinventing government" campaign led officials of the federal government's central personnel agency, the Office of Personnel Management (OPM), to dump the personnel rules into a dumpster and proclaim the death of the dreaded SF-171 standard resume form. OPM devolved authority down to the departments and agencies. Like rumors of Mark Twain's death, however, the end of these federal rules was greatly exaggerated. Many federal agencies simply readopted the old federal rules as their own, rather than try to create a whole new version. Some states have experimented with even more radical reforms, including Georgia's effort to virtually abolish the civil service system for new hires, but much more needs to be done.

The Indirect Government Skill Set

Managing indirect tools is fundamentally a people problem. The very complexity of networked relationships puts greater emphasis on the bridge-building, boundary-spanning skills of managers. The problems surrounding the Los Alamos labs are as much people based (given DOE's problems in getting the right people with the right skills to oversee the research program) as contracting based (given the complexity of the relationships). The fundamental irony of privatization and its other third-party variants is that they require very, very strong public management to make them work well. Moreover, they require a skill set—writing and negotiating good written agreements, tracking the money, auditing results, and assessing performance—on which governments often place relatively little emphasis.

The required skill set is not one that government actively nurtures, or, for that matter, is it a skill set that most of the nation's schools of public affairs develop. Most programs focus either on policy analysis (the microeconomics of decisions), public management (the leadership of top officials), or public administration (most typically, the running of traditional organizations and direct programs). All of these skills are useful in managing indirect government, but they are far from adequate.

The skill set for managing indirect government is different from the collection of tools that most government civil service systems emphasize, or most public policy or public administration programs teach. Effective managers of indirect programs need five skills in particular:

1. *Goal setting.* All government managers need to understand the goals of the programs they run. In indirect programs, this is even more important. Government managers need to craft contracts, tax incentives, regulations, or other tools to achieve the public purpose. Moreover, they need to understand how to communicate those goals effectively to government's partners so that they work to achieve that purpose. The ability to distill a measure of clarity from political ambiguity, build consensus for those goals, and fine-tune tools to achieve the goals are critical skills.

2. *Negotiation.* Government managers cannot display these skills by relying on the authority exercised through their agency's hierarchy. They must find the right collection of inducements to nudge their partners to common ground. Effective managers of indirect programs must become good negotiators able to find common ground with their partners, while ensuring that legislated goals remain paramount. In some tools, like contracts, government managers must be able to reduce this common ground to legally enforceable language.

3. *Communication.* Managing indirect government thus requires government managers to negotiate a two-way street: sending signals to partners about public goals,

and collecting feedback about partners' performance. Unlike pure market mechanisms, where the balance of supply and demand creates a self-regulating system, government-driven partnerships require more tending. The government has deployed indirect tools most often for fuzzy goals, ranging from tax expenditures encouraging investments to contracts for delivering social services. Feedback is important both for assessing the results of the tools and for fine-tuning goals. Managers must learn to manage these feedback systems to measure their programs' performance.

4. *Financial management.* Both tracking activity and measuring performance require careful accounting of financial activity. The money trail provides crucial information about who is doing what, when. Effective managers follow the money: financial management shapes partners' incentives and gives government managers leverage over partners' activities. It is also a central element to the feedback system.

5. *Bridge building.* Operating the tools of indirect government also requires government managers to gain a keen understanding of their partners' perspectives. Different organizations usually have different organizational cultures. Nonprofit social service organizations often have client-oriented perspectives. Private-sector contractors and regulatees have corporate missions and the goal of maximizing their profits. Effective government managers understand the cultures of their partners and seek to build bridges to find common ground.

Thus, effective management of indirect programs requires sensitive and effective government managers. Existing training programs, however, tend not to recognize the importance of indirect tools or the skills their managers need. American civil service systems, designed to recruit and promote technical specialists, frequently fail to cultivate the crosscutting skills that the effective managers of indirect tools need.

IV. PERFORMANCE

At its core, managing indirect government requires managing programs the government does not itself directly deliver through mechanisms it does not directly control. That translates into the central performance issue for indirect government: Ensuring high-quality government performance requires finding ways to manage public-private-nonprofit networks.

Reinventing Government and the Performance Puzzle

This dilemma sits squarely at the core of the Clinton administration's "reinventing government" efforts. In March 1993, the administration launched a major effort led by Vice President Al Gore and christened the "National Performance Review" (NPR). The administration pledged "a government that works better and costs less."[13] Its first round focused on downsizing the federal workforce, improving customer service, reforming the procurement process, and launching hundreds of lower-profile activities in individual agencies. The second round, begun after the Republicans took over Congress in 1995, focused more on deciding what government ought to do than on how it ought to do it. Clinton and the congressional Republicans, after bruising battles that shut down the government twice, fought to a standstill and never resolved the core question of government's role—except to conclude that Americans seemed fundamentally to like the government they had.

With Phase III in 1998, however, the administration changed course. In clear recognition of the network-based world of federal policy, Vice President Gore changed the NPR to the "National Partnership for Reinventing Government." To signal his reinvention of reinvention, Gore gave the NPR a new slogan, "America@Its Best." The NPR devised five new strategies: transform "high-impact agencies" into more productive government operations; use outcome measurement to improve federal management; build partnerships and develop strategies to prevent problems; give employees more freedom to do their jobs while holding them accountable for achieving outcomes; and develop one-stop information and service. The NPR promised a stronger focus on an information-age government and even better customer service. Meanwhile, it expanded its focus to far broader goals, such as building a "safe and healthy America," "safe communities," a "strong economy," and the "best-managed government ever."[14]

The reinventers recognized far more directly that the results Americans care most about—safer streets, healthier communities, a stronger economy—were goals that the federal government pursued only indirectly. The federal government's leverage over the economy, especially in the short term, is weak at best. Indeed, as the economy became more globalized and the budget more trapped in uncontrollable spending, the leverage of elected officials over policy has shrunk. Local governments police the streets. Civil society broadly shares responsibility for health and safety. Thus, in seeking a more politically relevant performance agenda, the NPR distanced itself from results it could control. The NPR struggled with a tough dilemma: early phases that produced administrative results but little political impact, or more ambitious goals with clear political stakes but indirect federal leverage.

Buried within the NPR's policy dilemma, however, was a potentially powerful performance tool. In 1993, Congress passed the Government Performance and Results Act (GPRA), which required all federal agencies to identify their goals and measure their success in achieving them. Starting in fiscal year 1999, agencies in addition began submitting to the Office of Management and Budget a strategic performance plan that identified the objectives of each program and which indicators the agency would use in measuring both outputs and outcomes. By 31 March 2000, agencies must present the president and Congress with a program performance report on how successfully they had met their performance goals. The emergence of GPRA thus offers the federal government a valuable tool for catching up with the demands of managing indirect government: It provides managers with a way of focusing on what goals they seek and how well their programs achieve them, regardless of who actually does the work.[15] GPRA was designed to strengthen the ex post oversight that stands at the core of the federal government's oversight of most tools, as Posner contends in his chapter.

In fact, other governments have pursued output-based management for fifteen years. New Zealand government ministers have, since the late 1980s, written contracts with chief executives in their agencies. These contracts specify how much output (inspections conducted or citizens served) the government is buying and how much the government will pay for the products. The performance of chief executives is measured by their ability to deliver outputs at cost and on time.[16] The New Zealand reforms, in fact, have turned indirect government on its head: They use contracting, typically applied to government's relations with external suppliers, to structure the government's internal relationships and expectations.

GPRA is at once more ambitious and more sweeping. As in New Zealand, it requires government managers to define strategic goals and set output measures. However, unlike New Zealand, government managers not only have to measure outputs—what they do—but also outcomes—what broader impacts the programs have. For example, it is one thing for the Occupational Safety and Health Administration to conduct safety inspections of factories (outputs). It is another to ask how the inspections improve the safety of the workplace (outcomes). Output measurement is challenging; outcome measurement is even more difficult. Moreover, the New Zealand government manages most public programs directly, so that chief executives have a clearer line of authority to frontline service providers and an easier job tracking activity. GPRA is thus triply ambitious. It seeks to undertake a far more sweeping reform, in much less time, in a substantially more indirect system.[17] Not surprisingly, in its first five years few federal agencies fully rose to GPRA's challenges, and it remains to be seen whether GPRA will achieve the potential for which its advocates have planned. The objective, however, is quite laudable.

Many states likewise have established performance management systems. Virginia, Missouri, and Washington, for example, have integrated performance systems into their governance. In South Carolina, top officials use performance reports to hold agency heads accountable for their results. Benchmarks have proliferated throughout Oregon. Arizona has created program-based strategic plans. Kansas and California have established performance audits of individual agencies.[18]

These performance-based initiatives have surfaced three issues: redefining intergovernmental relationships through performance, creating strong financial accounting, and building effective personnel systems.

1. *Performance partnerships.* Some federal agencies have redesigned intergovernmental programs in performance terms. The EPA, for example, has encouraged the states to experiment with performance-based systems like the National Environmental Performance Partnership System (NEPPS). Developed in 1995, NEPPS allows states more flexibility in meeting national goals in exchange for closer state measurement of environmental results. NEPPS also encouraged states to create new partnerships: across different programs attacking similar problems; and across different "media-based" regulations—designed to reduce air, water, and soil pollution—dealing with related pollution sources. For example, the Delaware state government used the NEPPS flexibility to bring the state health and agriculture agencies into an environmental protection team because they share responsibility for drinking water, radon, and pesticide programs. New Jersey experimented with linking its state programs with EPA-funded programs, although some state officials worried that this connection might open the way to federal snooping into the way state officials managed the programs. Both states, moreover, used the NEPPS flexibility to improve their ability to focus on environmental justice as they framed their regulatory strategies.[19]

   Other states are following a well-worn slogan: "Don't litigate, mediate." Public officials are experimenting with alternative dispute resolution techniques to seek common ground among disputing parties. Government officials bring the parties face-to-face, arrange careful discussions of the issues, and seek a problem-solving consensus. Almost every state has experimented with one form or another of this technique. In Alabama, businesses can call anonymously to seek guidance on regulatory questions. Companies reporting their own noncompliance often receive a lower fine or, sometimes, no fine at all. On the other hand, companies that try to duck the process can have fines multiplied. In Wyoming, state law requires the Department of Environmental Quality to try to work with companies before launching litigation. As one exhaustive study concluded, "While EDR [environmental dispute resolution] is not a universal solution for all environmental conflicts, the experience of many states suggests that EDR is useful in bringing together stakeholders with different interests to resolve complex, multi-issue, environmental disputes."[20]

2. *Visioning the partnership.* The dramatic change in the Federal Emergency Management Agency (FEMA) demonstrates how careful attention to financial accounting and information management can improve performance.[21] FEMA is the federal government's emergency response agency—when hurricanes, floods, and tornadoes hit, state and local officials call on FEMA for aid. FEMA sends out teams, but one Virginia county official said that the team's arrival in his area after a 1995 flood was itself a disaster. Indeed, its poor performance after Hurricane Andrew destroyed large parts of southeast Florida in 1992 cemented the agency's reputation as one of the federal government's worst-run agencies.

James Lee Witt, however, took the reins in 1993 and launched a major redesign of FEMA's management systems. By 1997, Witt had turned FEMA around, getting checks into the hands of disaster victims within days. Witt turned FEMA around with a strong brand of personal leadership. He began his first day on the job by standing in Washington's headquarters lobby and shaking hands with employees as they came to work. He built a fast-track claim process and upgraded the information systems that process forms. Even Florida officials, enraged by FEMA's handling of Hurricane Andrew, had little but praise following storms in 1998. Senator Bob Graham (D-FL) hailed FEMA's response as "a 180-degree turnaround" from the Hurricane Andrew disaster.

The kernel of Witt's success was his redefinition of FEMA's function. Instead of seeing its role as providing services when disaster occurs, FEMA officials recrafted their role as a partner in a far broader intergovernmental and public-private effort. FEMA sketched out a "life cycle" of disaster management that saw disasters and their costs as a product, in part, of preparation, planning, and mitigation that needed to begin far in advance of disasters and continue long after to prevent their recurrence.[22] Instead of waiting for a hurricane to hit and dealing with the aftermath, for example, FEMA officials worked closely with state and local officials to improve evacuation plans. They built partnerships with the construction industry to design and build houses that are more hurricane resistant. FEMA, in short, moved from a limited form of direct service delivery to a complex network-based approach that stretched from the federal government into state and local governments and the private sector.

3. *Effective people systems.* No matter how good the government's financial management system, however, results depend ultimately on the skill of managers—both inside government in managing the partnerships, and outside government in actually delivering services. The USDA's Food and Nutrition Service (FNS), for example, faces daunting problems. It is responsible for the government's food-assistance programs. Moreover, FNS does not itself provide food assistance; state and local governments perform that job. FNS must ensure that surplus food, food stamps, reduced-cost school lunches, and supplemental food grants reach eligible families. It must also ensure that no waste, fraud, or abuse occurs in the process, and in recent years it has had to do so with a 40 percent reduction in its workforce. Ellen Haas, USDA's undersecretary for the nutrition programs, has tackled these problems by focusing on partnerships. She has stretched her smaller federal workforce by building stronger links with state and local government partners and she has helped prepare federal employees for this new role. Observers have widely applauded the partnership approach she has constructed.[23]

Indirect government, at its core, represents the pragmatic solution to two puzzles. First, especially since World War II, the ambition of American public policy greatly exceeded Americans' eagerness for a larger government. The expansion of indirect government provided a way for government to deliver more programs without creating new government bureaucracies. Government's partners did what, in other times and many other nations, government itself would have done.

Second, many of the postwar programs sought complex goals that required matching broad national objectives to widely varying local conditions. It was one thing to declare war on poverty. It was another to fight it in campaigns diverging widely from the inner cities to small towns and rural areas. No single approach could possibly fit all problems. A remarkable range of innovative indirect strategies and tactics followed. If that made results harder to judge and processes harder to control, it also fundamentally transformed governance and made governmental tools almost infinitely adjustable.

Indirect government thus has manifest advantages. It also poses a tough challenge, however: Its administrative realities do not match the nation's administrative traditions and systems. The result is a performance deficit, a mismatch between government's expectations and capacity. Government's processes are designed to promote hierarchical control through authority-based systems. The traditional budgeting and personnel systems remain deeply rooted in this tradition. In budgeting, policymakers define goals and allocate resources, and then both goals and resources are broken down into smaller pieces as they move down the chain of command. The personnel system, on the other hand, works from the bottom up, with testing and promotion processes devised to direct workers toward progressively more challenging jobs. Neither process, however, develops the tools or skills needed to manage indirect government effectively, because both processes grow out of a basic framework that fits indirect government poorly.

Some parts of government have conquered this problem. FEMA redefined its mission from a hierarchically based, direct service delivery approach to a network-based, indirect tools approach. After the *Challenger* disaster, NASA downsized its core staff of governmental employees, turned over more responsibility to contractors in exchange for stronger performance reporting, and transformed its procurement system to its famous "faster, better, cheaper" approach. The failure of several Mars missions caused critics to question the strategy, but it reflected an important underlying reality: NASA could not hope to manage its operations without expanding and strengthening its indirect tools, especially contracting.

Lessons for Managing Indirect Government

The basic lesson, thus, is simple. Managing indirect government requires strong and sustained capacity. That capacity is fundamentally different from what is required to manage more traditional direct tools. It requires refining old tools and, more important, developing new ones. As managers reinvent their systems, it also requires preserving the enduring values of American democracy—concern for broad values such as equity, responsiveness to citizens, and accountability to elected officials. Experience in both the United States and around the world teaches that a strong system for managing indirect government builds on five basic principles.

1. *Government as a smart buyer.* The basic principle is that indirect government is different from directly administered governmental services—and that it requires different management strategies and tactics. If direct service delivery puts a

premium on control through authority, indirect service delivery puts a premium on leverage through market and voluntary mechanisms. In short, it increases government's need to find ways of aligning the goals and behaviors of its partners with its own policy goals. At its core, of course, this is no different from the basic management challenge facing many private-sector companies. Many private-sector organizations have flattened their hierarchies, contracted out all but their core functions, and developed just-in-time delivery systems for parts and supplies. They have become more "horizontal" than "vertical" to increase their flexibility and effectiveness.[24] That means, in turn, that government's success in managing indirect government depends on caring passionately about what its programs accomplish and much less about how it accomplishes its work.[25] This role of government as planner, arranger, and measurer is very different from its role in direct service delivery.

The case is easiest to make for programs contracted out, in which the government is in a direct fee-for-service relationship with its nongovernmental suppliers. In these, the government operates through a formal contract and thus creates a direct principal-agent relationship. The contract defines the output, structures the relationship, and shapes the government's oversight role. Other indirect tools, from grants and insurance to loan guarantees and tax incentives, raise distinctly different issues. All, however, frame the government's basic role as a relationship between its job in shaping services and others' role in providing them. Thus, its role is at its core that of a smart buyer: deciding what government wants to do and working through its partners to ensure that what needs to occur actually happens.

Nowhere have such partnerships proliferated more than in environmental protection.[26] Indeed, as one recent study has pointed out, "Many aspects of national policy are, in practice, becoming customized by state, locality, industry, or facility." Governments at all levels have sought to devise pragmatic strategies for tackling the special problems they each face. At the same time, they have struggled to build linkages among related programs—for example, air and water pollution control programs that are managed by different parts of the same agency (or different levels of government) but that nevertheless affect the same community. Tackling the problems of urban sprawl requires even more complex partnerships between the public and private sectors; among the levels of government; among different government agencies; and among various government programs.[27] The rise of interdependent programs and networked managers has led governments at all levels to seek pragmatic strategies for linking related programs—and to work to ensure that important problems do not fall between the many cracks of America's intergovernmental system.[28]

2. *Improving government's people processes.* Because the current civil service system at the federal level and in most of the states so poorly equips government to manage such strategies, restructuring the government's personnel system is thus a prime imperative. In fact, civil service reform has been a central part of the reform process in every nation that has launched major government reform except the United States. In the United States, opposition from both public employee unions (worried about protecting their members' jobs) and congressional committees (anxious to protect their jurisdictions) have made it difficult even to get started. In the states, only scattered and modest reforms have emerged.

That has increased the gap between government's changing strategies and its people power to manage them. Indeed, the government's people problem is multilayered: retaining the right people to manage indirect programs, training people for progressively more challenging positions, aligning the civil service system better with the jobs to be done, and building a more flexible workforce to help government adapt better to a rapidly changing job market and to constantly shifting policy and management strategies. These are huge challenges. There are few political incentives for tackling the job and strong opposition even to trying. That suggests that the management gap, between government's policy tools and its capacity to manage them, will not close any time soon.

3. *Strengthening training for present and future government managers.* Although that diagnosis might sound hopeless, the American experience also suggests two medium-term resolutions. First, the government could invest more in the training of its key officials. Many countries that launched major reinventions—notably Australia and New Zealand—also invested substantially in the training of government officials. The investment of American government in employee training is notoriously low, although there is little research to suggest just how low. Employees frequently need retraining throughout their careers to keep up to date with new technical issues and, especially, to manage the transition from technical specialist to group administrator and, ultimately, agency manager. Training, moreover, often provides mutual reinforcement (as managers discover others struggle with the same issues) and a signal that the manager's work is valued (as managers learn that top officials believe they are important enough to invest in). The more turbulent the environment and the more complex the partnerships, the more important training becomes.

Second, public policy and public administration programs could adjust their curricula to meet the demands of managing indirect government. Few programs offer courses in negotiation or managing networks. Evaluation courses frequently focus on long-term studies rather than on action-oriented output and outcome assessment. Governmental accounting is rarely taught. And, in general, students frequently see these management issues as less sexy than policy analysis. In fact, of course, there are relatively few jobs for policy analysts and even fewer positions for recent graduates to make policy. Moreover, more graduates of these programs are taking positions with government's private and nonprofit partners. Aligning the curriculum with the management imperatives of the indirect government system would enhance the job prospects of the programs' graduates—and improve the management of all parts of the indirect service network.

4. *A commitment to public values.* With the rise of indirect government, more nongovernmental institutions are responsible for delivering public programs. An important but often overlooked fact is that this is not just a production function—delivering goods and services in exchange for a fee. It is also a value-transfer function. The what of government services as well as the how of their delivery are shaped by—and in turn define—basic social norms. The more government's indirect tools put nongovernmental partners in the important middle position between policymakers and citizens, the more the partners' behavior defines these values.

Managing indirect government relies on building values as well as instrumental efficiency into the networks' central nervous systems. Contracts, for example, need to include standards for responsiveness to citizens, without at the same time becoming overprescriptive. Assessments of loan programs need to include judgments about equity as well as the impact these programs have on lending markets. That, of course, raises a broader question about how to induce private and nonprofit organizations to incorporate public-sector norms. In turn, that is a problem of both organizational culture and management oversight. As nongovernmental organizations become more responsible for direct connections with citizens, however, the problem is inescapable.

One intriguing possibility, discussed more in the abstract than in practice, is rotation of government employees through nongovernmental partners. If government managers understand the nature of the partnership better, they are more likely to manage the partnership more effectively. By extension, if they spend some time during their careers working with government's partners, they might well spread public-service values.[29]

5. *Political leadership.* In the end, managing indirect government is much more than managing projects and tools. It is about creating public values, as Mark H. Moore has forcefully argued.[30] Indirect government arose in American governance not as a conscious embrace of a sweeping strategy but as a slow, incremental spread of disparate policy tools for pragmatic reasons. In the process, many agencies' administrative tools have been transformed radically, and many top managers and elected officials have little sense of the management systems over which they sit. How the systems are managed will create value; the only real question is which values they will create. That is why political leadership lies at the very core of the problem of managing indirect government. Indirect government is not so much a tactical toolbox as a strategic approach to governance. If it is to work effectively, it requires strategic leadership by top officials in addition to tactical administration by managers.[31]

VI. CONCLUSION

Indirect government has expanded faster than our thinking about how to make it work well—and much faster than our understanding of the administrative tools on which government relies for leverage. It is a truly revolutionary collection of strategies and tactics, and the odds that the American administrative system will unwind back to direct service delivery are slim. Building capacity to manage the indirect system therefore will become an even stronger imperative, from leadership by top government officials to a reinvention of management theory by academics. Government's performance hinges on cracking these nuts.

VII. SUGGESTED READING

Cooper, Phillip J., and Chester A. Newland, eds. *Handbook of Public Law and Administration.* San Francisco: Jossey-Bass, 1997.

Ingraham, Patricia W. *The Foundation of Merit: Public Service in American Democracy.* Baltimore: Johns Hopkins University Press, 1995.

Kelman, Steven. *Procurement and Public Management: The Fear of Discretion and the Quality of Government Performance.* Washington, D.C.: AEI Press, 1990.

Kettl, Donald F. *Sharing Power: Public Governance and Private Markets.* Washington, D.C.: The Brookings Institution, 1986.

Kickert, Walter J. M., Erik-Hans Klijn, and Joop F. M. Koppenjan, eds. *Managing Complex Networks: Strategies for the Public Sector,* Thousand Oaks, Calif.: Sage, 1997.

1. Paul C. Light, *The True Size of Government* (Washington, D.C.: The Brookings Institution, 1999).

2. Charles E. Lindblom explored the tradeoff of exchange and hierarchy in *Politics and Markets: The World's Political-Economic Systems* (New York: Basic Books, 1977).

3. See, for example, Walter J. M. Kickert, Erik-Hans Klijn, and Joop F. M. Koppenjan, eds., *Managing Complex Networks: Strategies for the Public Sector* (Thousand Oaks, Calif.: Sage, 1997); H. Brinton Milward and Keith G. Provan, "Principles for Controlling Agents: The Political Economy of Network Structure," *Journal of Public Administration Research and Theory* 8 (April 1998): 203–221; Provan and Milward, "A Preliminary Theory of Interorganizational Network Effectiveness: A Comparative Study of Four Community Mental Health Systems," *Administrative Science Quarterly* 40 (March 1995): 1–33; Nitin Nohira and Robert G. Eccles, eds., *Networks and Organizations: Structure, Form, and Action* (Boston: Harvard Business School Press, 1992); and Donald Chisholm, *Coordination Without Hierarchy: Informal Structures in Multiorganizational Systems* (Berkeley: University of California Press, 1989).

4. Nitin Nohira, "Is a Network Perspective a Useful Way of Studying Organizations?" in *Networks and Organizations*, eds. Nohira and Eccles, 4–8.

5. Arthur M. Okun, *Equality and Efficiency: The Big Tradeoff* (Washington, D.C.: The Brookings Institution, 1975).

6. On the administrative procedure act, see David H. Rosenbloom, *Framing Legislative Centered Public Administration: Congress's 1946 Response to the Administrative State* (Tuscaloosa: University of Alabama Press, forthcoming); Louis Fisher, *Conflicts between Congress and the President* (Princeton, N.J.: Princeton University Press, 1985), especially pp. 99–139; and Theodore J. Lowi, *The End of Liberalism: The Second Republic of the United States,* 2d ed. (New York: W. W. Norton, 1979). On contracting, see Steven Kelman, *Procurement and Public Management: The Fear of Discretion and the Quality of Government Performance* (Washington, D.C.: AEI Press, 1990); and Donald F. Kettl, *Sharing Power: Public Governance and Private Markets* (Washington, D.C.: The Brookings Institution, 1986). More generally, see Phillip J. Cooper and Chester A. Newland, eds., *Handbook of Public Law and Administration* (San Francisco: Jossey-Bass, 1997).

7. See Kettl, *Sharing Power,* especially chap. 8.

8. Kelman, *Procurement and Public Management,* 86–87.

9. Ibid., especially pp. 88–89.

10. This discussion draws on Michael deCourcy Hinds, "A Tale of Two Cities: The Jobs Initiative in Milwaukee and St. Louis," *Advocasey* 1 (spring 1999): 32–36.

11. See General Accounting Office, *High-Risk Series: An Overview* HR-95–1 (February 1995), 11–13, 54–59.

12. See Patricia W. Ingraham, *The Foundation of Merit: Public Service in American Democracy* (Baltimore: Johns Hopkins University Press, 1995), 34; and General Accounting Office, *Recruitment and Retention: Inadequate Federal Pay Cited as Primary Problem by Agency Officials,* GGD-90–117 (Washington, D.C.: September 1990), 3.

13. Al Gore, *From Red Tape to Results: Creating a Government That Works Better and Costs Less* (Washington, D.C.: GPO, 1993).

14. For a summary and analysis, see Donald F. Kettl, "The Three Faces of Reinvention," in *Setting National Priorities: The 2000 Election and Beyond,* eds. Robert D. Reischauer and Henry J. Aaron (Washington, D.C.: The Brookings Institution, 1999), 421–447.

15. For a broader discussion of these issues, see Philip G. Joyce, "Using Performance Measures for Budgeting: A New Beat, or Is It the Same Old Tune?" *New Directions for Evaluation* 75 (Fall 1997): 45–61.

16. Allen Schick, *The Spirit of Reform: Managing the New Zealand State Sector in a Time of Change* (Wellington: New Zealand State Services Commission, 1996); Colin James, *The State Ten Years On from the Reforms* (Wellington: State Services Commission, 1998); Graham Scott, Ian Ball, and Tony Dale, "New Zealand's Public Management Reform: Implications for the United States," *Journal of Policy Analysis and Management* 16 (1997): 357–381; Jonathan Boston and June Pallot, "Linking Strategy and Performance: Developments in the New Zealand Public Sec-

tor," *Journal of Policy Analysis and Management* 16 (1997): 382–404; Jonathan Boston, John Martin, June Pallot, and Pat Walsh, *Public Management: The New Zealand Model* (Auckland: Oxford University Press, 1996).

17. For an assessment, see General Accounting Office, *Performance Budgeting: Initial Experiences Under the Results Act in Linking Plans with Budgets,* AIMD/GGD-99–67 (Washington, D.C.: April 1999).

18. See report on "Managing for Results," *Governing* 12 (February 1999): 25–27.

19. U.S. Environmental Protection Agency, Office of State and Local Relations, *Region 9 Review of PPS* (EPA, 30 June 1999). http://www.epa.gov/regional/pps/region9.htm.

20. Rosemary O'Leary, Tracy Yandle, and Tamilyn Moore, "The State of the States in Environmental Dispute Resolution," *Ohio State Journal on Dispute Resolution* 14 (1999): 515–613, especially p. 613.

21. See "Mastering Disaster," *Government Executive* 31 (February 1999): 56–58.

22. See http://www.fema.gov/library/spln_7.htm.

23. See "Hunger Pains," *Government Executive* 31 (February 1999), 59–61.

24. Frank Ostroff, *The Horizontal Organization: What the Organization of the Future Actually Looks Like and How It Delivers Value to Customers* (New York: Oxford University Press, 1999).

25. See Donald F. Kettl, Patricia W. Ingraham, Ronald P. Sanders, and Constance Horner, *Civil Service Reform: Building a Government That Works* (Washington, D.C.: The Brookings Institution, 1996).

26. See National Academy of Public Administration, *Resolving the Paradox of Environmental Protection: An Agenda for EPA, Congress, and the States* (Washington, D.C.: NAPA, 1997); and *Setting Priorities, Getting Results: A New Direction for EPA* (Washington, D.C.: NAPA, 1995).

27. Bruce Katz and Jennifer Bradley, "Divided We Sprawl," *The Atlantic Monthly* 284 (December 1999), 26 ff.

28. Mary Graham, *The Morning after Earth Day: Practical Environmental Politics* (Washington, D.C.: Governance Institute/The Brookings Institution, 1999), 11.

29. See Donald F. Kettl, Patricia W. Ingraham, Ronald P. Sanders, and Constance Horner, *Civil Service Reform: Building a Government That Works* (Washington, D.C.: The Brookings Institution, 1996).

30. See Mark H. Moore, *Creating Public Value: Strategic Management in Government* (Cambridge, Mass.: Harvard University Press, 1995), especially p. 28.

31. See Kettl and others, *Civil Service Reform,* 4–5.

CHAPTER SEVENTEEN

Financial Accountability in Indirect Government

John J. Lordan

In March of 1952, the Honorable George V. Allen, the American Ambassador and Envoy Plenipotentiary to Yugoslavia, filed a routine claim for $399.06 in travel expenses for travel from his post in Belgrade to Trieste, Rome, and ultimately home to the United States. Over the next two years, Ms. Florence Reed, a U.S. General Accounting Office (GAO) employee who had final approval authority over the Ambassador's claim, pursued him around the world with paperwork questioning the travel route he took, the amount of time he spent at stops in Belgrade, Trieste, Florence, Naples, and New York; the business he conducted in those locations; and the amount he actually spent in each. In the end, Allen—by then Assistant Secretary of State—gave in and refunded $160.54 to the Treasury.

I. FINANCIAL ACCOUNTABILITY

Ambassador Allen's story illustrates the lengths that democratic governments will go to in order to assure an accurate accounting of public funds, even when the funds have been expended in pursuit of high-level matters of national and international importance. As such, it recalls British General Wellington's reply to his Foreign Office about a report of a petty cash shortage in one of his battalions. "This reprehensible carelessness," he is said to have remarked, "may be related to the pressure of circumstance, since we are at war with France, a fact which may come as a bit of a surprise to you gentlemen in [the Foreign Office]." In more balanced form, this concern for financial accountability is fundamental to democratic government, and affects all the tools of government.

Financial accountability problems are most evident in direct government where every element of spending is heavily regulated: hiring is controlled by complex civil service rules, salaries spelled out in rigid "schedules," fringe benefits specified in set packages, travel expenses subject to precise limits, etc. Regular reports comparing actual expenditures to budget are submitted to higher authority, and routine audits of those reports are carried out. Indeed, one of the motivations for utilizing indirect tools has been the desire to avoid some of the stringent fiscal accountability requirements of direct government.

Although less obvious, however, the financial strictures associated with indirect tools of government are sometimes just as complex. This chapter discusses the financial accountability measures applied to the various tools of indirect government, focusing particularly on grant program requirements and on efforts to standardize and simplify those requirements across a multiplicity of programs. Particular attention is directed to accounting for program costs in a multiprogram organization and the important, and sometimes controversial, issue of allocating indirect costs to individual grant awards. (An accompanying *Workbook* summarizes the widely used U.S. government

511

accounting principles applicable to various categories of grant and contract recipients, and illustrates how indirect cost rates are developed and applied.)

Basis of Financial Accountability

The financial accountability challenges in most government programs are very different from those associated with private transactions. In the private marketplace, financial accountability is provided by simple pricing mechanisms. If a buyer chooses to pay the asked-for price of a good or service, all accountability requirements are met by receipt of the good or service at the specified price. The buyer need not ask about costs, marginal costs, overhead, profits, rates of return, or any other business consideration that went into pricing by the seller. In fact, in most commercial activity the terms cost and price are used to signify two sides of the same transaction. That is, the "cost" of a sandwich is the "price" on the menu. One orders it or not depending on one's assessment of its value or utility. To the restaurant owner, however, cost and price have more precise meanings. The owner's cost is made up of the prices paid for the materials, labor, and overhead required to put the sandwich on the plate before the customer. These costs, while a matter of indifference to the customer, are of keen interest to the owner. The owner must know the cost of production in order to establish a price that will cover it and provide an expected profit. This simple formulation has been endlessly refined in microeconomic theory, but the basic balance between cost and price is present in even the most complex price theory models.

With this in mind, consider the case of Brian Jones, an official of the U.S. Department of Education, who is expected to find a supplier to provide specialized educational services to disadvantaged youths; or of Angelo Donelli, of the U.S. Department of Transportation, who is charged with creating a new road between two distant cities without knowing much about the terrain between them or the economic benefits that will flow from connecting them. How do these government officials know the price of what they want? How do they provide accountability to their superiors and to taxpayers for what they have decided to do with public funds? How can they be sure they are paying the right amount?

If these officials were able to use the direct government model, Jones would have developed a curriculum, acquired space, hired teachers, and rounded up the appropriate number of students. Donelli would have obtained rights of way, purchased grading equipment, hired engineers and road builders, and begun digging. The cost of either undertaking would be indeterminate at the outset, the quality of the outcome uncertain, and the only constraint on cost would be the available budgetary resources. Accountability would be owed at some point to whatever governmental body had authorized the projects and ultimately to the taxpayers of those jurisdictions.

However, Jones and Donelli do not have the option of direct action. Since the objective of the training program is to reach youths who are widely dispersed geographically and to have the training tailored to the needs of local labor markets, central planning and operation were judged to be inappropriate, and an indirect tool of government was chosen instead. Similarly, an entire network of roads connecting many cities and towns was envisioned for Donelli's program, dictating a more indirect structure for road construction as well.

As a consequence, the financial accountability issues facing Jones and Donelli become more complex. Since the government will not be spending money for teachers or road builders as it might have done in the direct government model, other organizations—contractors, grantees, or cooperating parties—will have to be drawn into participation; and agreements will need to be written specifying terms and promising payment. However, what amount of payment? What prices will be set to achieve these public purposes? And how will financial accountability be achieved?

513

CH 17:
FINANCIAL
ACCOUNT-
ABILITY
IN INDIRECT
GOVERNMENT

Like countless other officials, what Jones and Donelli have to settle for is a procedure for achieving accountability, not through prices (which, in the absence of an established market, do not exist), but through costs. That is, the essential contractual arrangement between their government agency and contractors, other governments, and nonprofit organizations is that their agency (the buyer) agrees to cover the cost of the goods or services to be provided—up to a specified limit. In that sense, the buying agency is making a budget allocation decision rather than a pricing decision. The agency says, in effect, "undertake this work, subject to our administrative requirements, and we will reimburse your costs." This puts the sellers (contractors, state or local officials, non-profit officials, etc.) in essentially the same position as providers of direct government services, that is, they must now hire teachers or roadbuilders and take such other steps as are necessary to carry out the program objective within the resources provided by the buyer.

However, there is an important difference between these "sellers" and officials carrying out direct government programs. The sellers have accepted, along with the money, the burden of cost accountability to the buyer (on top of whatever accountability rules exist within their own organization). No pricing mechanism stands as evidence of accountability to the buyer. The sellers will have to demonstrate at some point to Jones and Donelli, or to cost accountants and auditors in their agencies, that their "costs" were legitimate, necessary, allocable, and allowable. As the Jones and Donelli cases demonstrate, the basis of accountability in many government programs that operate through indirect tools is "cost," an unsatisfactory alternative to price. This focus on cost can result in inordinate attention to accounting and auditing, sometimes to the detriment of program management.

Cost-Based Accountability

The concept of cost-based accountability is relatively simple in a single-purpose, single-sponsor organization. A freestanding training institute, for example, supported by a special tax levy or by a single government grant or contract, should be able to demonstrate that all its recorded costs went for the single purpose of training its students. Teachers' salaries, the cost of supplies, operation and maintenance of its building, etc. can be added up and reported as the cost of training whatever number of students have passed through the program. However, there are some complexities even in this simple case: certain "costs" are not paid in cash (depreciation, interest owed but not yet due, and so forth). Other things paid for are not yet "costs" in the current period (purchases of materials held in inventory, equipment rental paid in advance, etc.). Accounting for these costs requires more than checkbook summaries. To be accountable for these costs, administrators have to assign the right costs to the right periods. This is specialized, but not difficult, work for accountants.

Cost-based accountability becomes far more complicated, however, when the organization is not a freestanding single-purpose one, and when funding of different programs comes from different sources. To continue the education example, suppose the organization is a university carrying out missions of education, research, and public service, and supported by tuition, research grants, and fees for medical services. The university is accountable to students and their families (and to various governmental bodies, if it is a public university) for setting tuition "prices" at some reasonable level. If it operates hospitals or medical clinics, it is accountable to patients, insurers, and governmental agencies for setting medical "prices" appropriately, and for adequately documenting the services provided. And, since it receives grants for some of its research work, it is an agent of indirect government and therefore has "cost-based account-ability" to one or more grantmaking agencies. This indirect government function takes place right in the middle of the university's interrelated functions and financing sources (see Box 17-1). That is, a portion of the research undertaken by the university is research that might have been carried out directly in a government laboratory. How-ever, at least in the United States, policymakers have long since concluded that the best way to produce the fundamental knowledge sought for the country is to support in-dividual faculty scientists who can interact with colleagues and advanced students in the traditionally open university environment.[1] Of course, not all the grant revenue of the university represents indirect government. Some may derive from private firms wishing to support emerging technologies or determine the efficacy of drugs or other intellectual property they own or control, or from private foundations or associations. These sponsors, too, may impose their own cost-based accountability requirements.

BOX 17-1 *Typical University Revenues and Expenditures*

State University
Revenue
Tuition
Room and board charges
State appropriations
Grants
Patient fees
Endowment income
Gifts

Expense
Salaries
Materials and supplies
Overhead
Heat, light, power
Depreciation
Interest
Administration

Cost-based accountability in this complicated mix of programs and funding sources requires so-phisticated systems for recording, assigning, allo-cating, and reporting costs. The cost accounting challenge presented by Box 17-1 is to identify the expenses (and parts of expenses) that can be prop-erly assigned to those individual grants that require cost-based accountability. Proper accounting also will require agreement with sponsoring agencies or other supporters on the definition of individual ele-ments of cost, and it is subject to policy consider-ations as to whether certain kinds of costs should be allowed in the calculation at all. For example, all might agree that salary costs of those who work on a particular grant should be covered by grant funds. However, should it be all of an individual's salary, or does that individual do other things as well (e.g., work on other grant projects, work on nongrant projects, carry out general administrative duties, and so forth)? Thus, even something as sim-ple as salary charges requires some ground rules, and the rule not surprisingly is proportional as-signment, that is, if an individual works half-time on a project, one-half the salary is assigned to the project. Examples of costs made unallowable for policy reasons are entertainment, bad debt write-offs, and fines and penalties.

Cost Accounting Principles

Cost accounting is a specialized field within the overall context of generally accepted accounting principles. All accounting systems (even simple checkbooks) provide his-torical information on what has happened within an organization during a specified period. They show information on the organization's revenues and expenditures, and serve three purposes: management control, reporting to outside parties, and special analyses.[2] Our concern here is primarily with reporting to outside parties. Some of this outside disclosure is provided through general purpose financial statements. These are the traditional balance sheets and operating statements contained in annual reports.

They reflect the overall financial health and stability of a corporation, unit of government, nonprofit organization, or other entity.

515

CH 17:
FINANCIAL
ACCOUNT-
ABILITY
IN INDIRECT
GOVERNMENT

The same accounting system that collects the information reflected in an organization's general purpose financial statements is used in subsidiary records called *cost accounting systems*. These systems attempt to attribute the costs of labor, materials, and overhead (inputs) to specific goods or services produced by the organization (outputs). Manufacturers use elaborate cost accounting systems to determine the exact unit cost of each of many products produced in the same factory, and often to determine the costs of each component of those products. Law firms and other professional organizations use these systems to determine appropriate billing rates for the different kinds of services they provide.

Accountability for programs of indirect government is usually provided on the basis of *full cost*. The term cost by itself is a measure of the amount of resources used for a particular purpose. In accounting terms this purpose is called a *cost objective*. The total amount of resources used for a cost objective is its full cost. Since cost objectives often are individual programs, full costs also are called *program costs*. The full cost objective is the sum of its direct costs plus a fair share of the organization's indirect (or overhead) costs.[3] Direct costs are those that can be identified with a single cost object. For example, the salaries and fringe benefits of an individual who works exclusively on one program are direct costs of that program. Indirect costs are costs incurred jointly for two or more cost objectives, and a fair share of these indirect costs must be allocated to each cost objective to determine its full cost.

There are well-established cost accounting principles for attributing direct costs to products and services, and for allocating indirect costs to them as well.[4] Accountants working in industry are more likely to be well schooled and experienced in cost accounting than their counterparts in government, education, or nonprofit organizations, but the basic principles of cost accounting apply to all these organizations. The principles may be arcane, but they are not conceptually difficult to master.

Cost Accounting Rules

As noted earlier, accountability for almost all programs of indirect government that operate through grants and contracts is cost based. Theoretically, cost-based accountability could be achieved with a single regulation calling for program reports to be prepared in accordance with generally accepted cost accounting principles. Accountants on both ends of an indirect government transaction would presumably understand those principles and be able to understand such reports. The reports could be audited on a regular basis and confirmation provided that they were prepared consistent with the regulation.

In fact, in an earlier era that is more or less how business was conducted. For example, cost reimbursement contracts for military hardware were a longstanding practice in the United States even before World War I. Because of uncertainty about how much a newly designed tank or warship might cost, contractors could not be induced to produce them at a specified price. The cost reimbursement contract—where costs were guaranteed and a reasonable profit on top of cost provided for—proved to be the answer. These contracts relieved the contractor of the risk of loss and, not incidentally, protected military procurement officials from the embarrassment of excessive profits being earned on such work. In the absence of government regulations, "costs" under these contracts were indeed determined by accountants, consistent with the accounting literature of the day, and accountability was provided on that basis.

Inevitably, abuses occurred. With profits tied to costs, contractors had no incentive to hold down costs; and, in fact, had incentives to inflate them. There also arose questions about the appropriateness of certain kinds of costs being charged to the government—entertainment, finders' fees, commissions, fines, "unreasonable" salaries, and so forth. Less egregious, but equally troublesome, were differences in judgement about whether a cost belonged to this cost object or that, or whether certain indirect costs should be allocated one way or another.

Regulations followed, and by World War II, the U.S. Department of Defense (DOD) had developed a so-called "Green Book" of detailed cost accounting rules that were codified later in the *Armed Services Procurement Regulations,* and more recently in the *Federal Acquisition Regulation.* The first set of cost accounting rules for nonindustrial participants in federal programs emerged in the United States in 1947. This "Blue Book" issued by DOD was entitled "Explanation of Principles for Determination of Costs under Government Research and Development Contracts with Educational Institutions."[5]

As Beam and Conlan show,[6] grant programs in the United States grew gradually after World War II, took off dramatically in the Great Society era of President Johnson in the 1960s, and became a permanent part of indirect government with greatly expanded funding under President Nixon in the 1970s. With the proliferation of programs funded through so many federal agencies, and benefiting so many states, cities, counties, towns, regional governments, special districts, colleges, universities, hospitals, private voluntary organizations, and other nonprofit organizations, there reached a point where administrative complexity threatened to bring program operation to a screeching halt. Each grant program had been authorized by separate legislation, each was funded through its own agency, and each sought to impose a different set of administrative requirements on recipients. Many of these requirements for such things as personnel, purchasing, property management, etc. had their origins in federal agency procedures and were not well suited to the organizations that received the grants. Most of the cost accounting rules imposed on these programs had their origin in DOD rules for defense contractors, but again each agency's rules were somewhat different.

At the peak of this confusion, the U.S. government was undergoing a reorganization of its central management functions. A new Office of Management and Budget (OMB) had been created out of the old Bureau of the Budget and charged with the responsibility of bringing greater order to government operations, including the many grant programs. Partly in response to the Intergovernmental Cooperation Act of 1968, OMB began developing guidelines on how federal agencies were to administer grant programs. The guidelines were in the form of OMB Circulars. The two most comprehensive of these were Circular A-102, "Uniform Administrative Requirements for Grants-in-Aid to State and Local Governments"; and Circular A-110, "Grants and Agreements with Institutions of Higher Education, Hospitals and Other Non-Profit Organizations: Uniform Administrative Requirements." These circulars, in turn, included fifteen attachments that addressed specific areas of grant administration. The circulars prescribed standards for the management of grant-supported activities, and applied not only to grantees but also to subgrantees that might have funds passed through from other levels of government or other nonprofit organizations. Federal agencies were instructed to issue regulations codifying these circulars but were otherwise precluded under the circular from imposing additional standards on recipients other than those required by law, without OMB approval.[7]

Accompanying these grant administration circulars were a more detailed set of OMB guidelines dealing with cost-based accountability. These included:

1. Circular A-21, "Cost Principles for Educational Institutions"

2. Circular A-87, "Cost Principles for State, Local and Indian Tribal Governments"

3. Circular A-122, "Cost Principles for Nonprofit Organizations"

517

CH 17:
FINANCIAL
ACCOUNT-
ABILITY
IN INDIRECT
GOVERNMENT

Each of these circulars sought to tailor the general rules of cost accounting to a particular type of organization that was likely to be carrying out one or more indirect government programs. Thus, Circular A-21 provided a range of alternatives for documenting salary costs in recognition of the extreme sensitivity of college and university faculty to anything like time-and-effort reporting that might be seen as infringing on their academic freedom. Similarly, Circular A-87 had to take into account the fact that costs incurred in one agency of a state or local government could legitimately be considered a cost of a program carried out by another, and Circular A-122 recognized and placed accounting value on volunteer services that often make up a considerable part of the workforce of nonprofit organizations.

Indirect Costs

By and large, the cost-based accountability rules set forth in the circulars discussed above have stood the test of time, but they have not been without controversy. By far their most controversial and least-understood feature has been the allocation of overhead, or "indirect," costs.

As discussed earlier, indirect costs are costs that cannot be immediately identified with a particular cost objective or program, except in single-purpose organizations operating under single funding sources. These costs by nature are general costs of operating an organization and, if the organization is carrying out several programs, the indirect costs must be "allocated" in some way to each of the programs. The allocation method called for in the OMB circulars is to develop an indirect cost rate by dividing estimated indirect costs by estimated direct costs (all or selected). The resulting rate, after negotiation with a designated or "cognizant" federal agency, is then applied to the direct cost of individual grants to arrive at the total cost. Under Circular A-21, indirect costs are referred to as "facility and administrative" (F&A) costs, a term of art that more accurately reflects their nature. The base of direct costs over which these F&A costs are allocated is "modified total direct costs." Modified direct costs are all direct costs except those that would distort the allocation, such as major equipment purchases or large subcontracts, things that are big cost items but do not result in increased spending on facilities or administration. As shown in Figure 17-1, the cost of a sample grant project funded at $200,000 is made up of $100,000 of regular direct costs, $40,000 of excluded direct costs, and $60,000 of F&A costs. The F&A rate is 60 percent and is applied only to the modified total direct costs of $100,000.

As one observer has pointed out,[8] this kind of description of the cost allocation process in indirect government, while essentially accurate, slides over the main point of contention between research universities and the government because it suggests a kind of precision in the rate-setting process that is impossible to achieve. At the heart of the process, Rosenzweig argues, is an ambiguity caused by the fact that universities produce more than one "product," that is, the same people who do research on grants and contracts also teach students, some of whom participate in the research. It is far from clear where teaching ends and research begins, and the same is true, of course, for the institutional underpinnings of both activities. For example, the same building, with its attendant operational maintenance costs, may be used for research, graduate

Sample Project

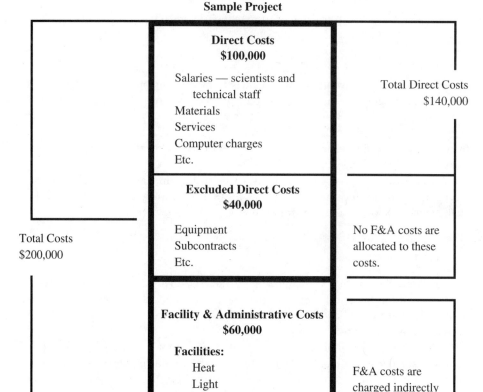

FIGURE 17-1 *University research costs. In this illustration, a total grant of $200,000 is made up of $140,000 in direct laboratory costs and $60,000 of facility and administrative—or indirect—costs. The F&A rate is 60 percent ($60,000/$100,000), applied to direct costs with certain exclusions. F&A costs represent 30 percent of the total grant ($60,000/$200,000).*

teaching, undergraduate teaching, and administration. Determining where one leaves off and another begins is far from an exact science.

Despite the technical nature of these calculations and negotiations—or perhaps because of it—indirect costs are often the subject of controversy. Grant-making agencies, legislators, and the general public (and sometimes even individuals employed by recipient organizations themselves) fail to see the connection between these costs and the programs they are concerned with. The general disdain that many hold for "overhead," considering them to be what Adam Smith unfortunately called "nonproductive costs," contributes to the large measure of policy concern that persists on the subject. Over a five-year period in the early 1990s in the United States there were three presidential proposals, six provisions in draft appropriations bills, six other legislative initiatives, and language in any number of committee reports calling for reductions or limits on the indirect costs of university-based research programs.

519

CH 17:
FINANCIAL
ACCOUNT-
ABILITY
IN INDIRECT
GOVERNMENT

Much of this political hostility stemmed from reports of "scandalous" costs that sometimes found their way into the indirect cost rates. For example, in 1991 the U.S. Congress held hearings on the indirect cost practices of one of the country's most prestigious research institutions, Stanford University. The hearings confirmed earlier press reports of indirect cost pools that included charges for entertainment, liquor, and flowers; depreciation on a yacht that had been donated to the university; on silverware used in the president's residence, and even on an antique commode as well as numerous other highly questionable items. While these costs had little impact on Stanford's negotiated indirect cost rate, their mere inclusion in the calculation brought into question the legitimacy of the whole rate-setting process. The repercussions of the scandal echoed through rate negotiations in all research universities for many years thereafter.

Audits

Cost-based accountability in indirect government programs brings with it the inevitable requirement for audits. These audits go far beyond the near-universal requirement that organizations have audited annual financial statements. Annual audits do provide an element of accountability to outside parties (shareholders, taxpayers, bond holders, and so forth), but by themselves they provide little accountability for individual grant or contract programs. Funding agencies want assurance that the costs charged to their programs were (1) an accurate reflection of the books and records of the organization, (2) reasonable and proper, and (3) consistent with the cost accounting regulations attached to the grants or contracts. Again, for a single-purpose organization with a single funding source, these needs can be met by a simple and straightforward audit. Audits become more complex in multipurpose organizations funded by several different agencies.

As discussed earlier, as the tools of indirect government came to assume a larger share of total government activity in the United States, more and more programs came to rely on general purpose units of state and local government, large research universities, and numerous multipurpose nonprofit organizations. This gave several federal agencies, state agencies, counties, cities, and towns a legitimate interest in auditing cost reports from organizations carrying out programs funded by them. The results were often chaotic. For example, the San Diego Human Services Department was visited by twenty-six groups of auditors in a single year.

In time the federal government recognized this problem and did something about it. As with administrative requirements and cost accounting rules, the job of streamlining the audit process fell to OMB. With assistance from the U.S. General Accounting Office, the auditing arm of the U.S. Congress, and with strong support from state and local government interest groups, OMB developed a "single audit concept." This was intended initially as a rationalization of the federal auditing process, and was done by naming one federal agency to do all the federal auditing at a single state or city agency, university, or nonprofit organization. OMB published lists of so-called "cognizant agencies," and called on other agencies to make any special audit needs known to the cognizant agency so that those needs could be incorporated into the audit process.

Later, state and local government auditors, and independent public accountants (who were routinely doing financial statement audits of almost all grant recipients), got into the act, advising greater reliance by the federal government on their work. As a consequence, there emerged a more full-blown concept of a single audit in OMB Circulars A-128 (1981), "Audits of State and Local Governments"; and A-133 (1987), "Audits of Institutions of Higher Education and Other Non-profit Institutions." These circulars brought together requirements for a traditional annual audit of financial statements and the additional "compliance auditing" required by federal grantmaking agencies. Compliance auditing required auditors to test whether federal requirements for competitive procurement, nondiscrimination, and a whole host of other federal requirements had been met. It also required testing to see whether federal cost principles had been complied with. These kinds of tests had not been made previously by non-federal auditors. The work was to be done, not by federal auditors, but by "independent auditors," who might be public accounting firms or state and local government auditors. The federal role was defined as one of oversight and follow-up, rather than direct auditing. In a sense, the circulars thus extended the concept of indirect government beyond the administration of public programs to the auditing of them as well. The U.S. Congress registered its approval of this new approach to securing comprehensive audit coverage by passing P.L.98–502, the Single Audit Act of 1984, and P.L.104–156, the Single Audit Act Amendments of 1996. These laws require a detailed examination of a recipient's system of internal control, a testing of the degree of compliance with such system, and a verification of the reliability of the financial reports being produced by the system.

It remains to be seen whether federal agencies will be content with the types of reports they receive under the Single Audit approach. These reports offer an auditor's opinion on the reliability of systems of internal control and on overall compliance with grant terms and conditions. They do not reflect grant-by-grant examinations of detailed financial transactions. Current indications are that the Single Audit Act is working well, but the same forces that led to the development of cost-based accountability could emerge to reinstitute a new wave of federal audits of grant recipients. That is, a scandal or a series of scandals that might have been avoided by more direct federal scrutiny could undo what has emerged as a fairly rational process of financial oversight.

Alternatives to Cost-Based Accountability

For all its recent development, cost-based accountability does not provide the incentives for efficiency, cost consciousness, or innovation that fixed prices provide in market-based transactions. Nonetheless, as discussed earlier in this chapter, practical considerations have led to the application of cost-based accountability in almost all programs of indirect government that operate through grants and contracts. This reliance on costs parallels the early reliance in government procurement on cost reimbursement contracting. However, in most procurement programs, managers have tried to emulate the private marketplace by moving gradually away from cost reimbursement to some form of:

- Incentive contract, where extra profit can be earned by lowering costs

- Reset pricing, where payment is decided on after part of the work has been done and some costs known

- Firm fixed-price contracts, where prices are negotiated on the basis of reliably estimated costs

- Competitive contracting, where several qualified bidders offer their best price, and the contract goes to the low bidder

This spectrum from cost-based to market-price accountability takes place even in procurement involving very complex products and technologies. No similar progression has been made in pricing grant transactions.

521

CH 17:
FINANCIAL
ACCOUNT-
ABILITY
IN INDIRECT
GOVERNMENT

The closest that grant programs have come to real simplification of cost-based accountability was general revenue sharing, which Donald Haider has pointed out was the simplest of all grant programs.[9] The program lasted from 1972 to 1986 and distributed anywhere from $4.5 billion to $6 billion a year in federal assistance to some thirty-nine thousand general purpose state and local governments based on a formula that used population, per capita income, and tax effort. Although the program included standards for civil rights, financial statement audits, public hearings, and use-reporting, these were minimal; and the Treasury Department's Office of Revenue Sharing, which administered the program, was able to function with only a handful of staff.

The political popularity of general revenue sharing, which literally shared the wealth with tens of thousands of jurisdictions and their political leaders, paved the way for special revenue sharing and block grants that followed. While not as popular with Congress as with state and local officials, these programs established broader categories of federal aid and therefore made easier the accounting and financial reporting that was required. However, none of these programs abandoned the concept of cost-based accountability.

One alternative, suggested by this author over twenty years ago, was to move toward "fixed-price grants."[10] The concept here was that as programs matured and experience built up, it should be possible to award a fixed amount at the beginning of a grant period and agree on a set of program accomplishments. Those accomplishments would be monitored, but there would be no need for cost-based financial reports. Obviously, the time for fixed-price grants had not come, but by not progressing from cost-based accountability to some form of market-based pricing, grant programs have been deprived of the efficiencies that accompanied that progress in procurement programs. The progression away from cost reimbursement toward increasingly competitive types of contracts imposes a discipline on costs by providing positive and negative incentives to the contractor. If contractors reduce costs, profits will increase; if they let costs rise, losses will result. These incentives led to efficiencies in production, greater cost consciousness, and technical innovation. The result is lower costs to the public. There is also a saving in administrative costs, since competitive contracts do not require as extensive cost accounting records, detailed financial reporting, on-site inspections, or after-the-fact audits.

Under current arrangements with grant and contract programs, however, the same programs are carried on year after year—and sometimes decade after decade—without any effort to provide the incentives that fixed prices have yielded in procurement programs. Of course, not all grant programs would lend themselves to fixed-price accountability, but surely some would. In fact, the National Institutes of Health have recently begun experimenting with "modular grants" for university-based research. These grants are for a fixed amount and allow considerable flexibility in shifting the components of cost that make up the total. It remains to be seen, however, how widespread modular grants will become, and whether they will truly shift the focus away from cost-based accountability.

II. CONCLUSION

This chapter has outlined the need for financial accountability in indirect government, explored the principles of market-based accountability, and pointed out that indirect government programs that operate through grants rely almost exclusively on cost-based accountability. This leads inevitably to an expensive and time-consuming focus on cost accounting, and on compliance with cost accounting regulations. The effort expended on accounting, reporting, and auditing financial records might be better spent on program management, innovation, and oversight. Moreover, reliance on cost-based accountability has prevented market forces from producing the cost reductions and innovation that serve the private economy so well.

The history of indirect government programs that operate through grants is that they have not moved along the spectrum of increasingly market-based pricing that characterizes well-managed procurement programs. It is likely that this focus on cost deprives program participants and taxpayers of the efficiencies that follow reliance on market-based pricing. While some experimental efforts are now underway, it may be that bolder experiments and further study would yield real economic advantages from moving away from traditional cost-based accountability.

NOTES

1. D. K. Price, *The Scientific Estate* (Cambridge, Mass.: Harvard University Press, 1965), 176–182.

2. Robert N. Anthony and David W. Young, *Management Control in Nonprofit Organizations* (Englewood Cliffs, N.J.: Irwin/McGraw-Hill, 1999), 7–8.

3. Anthony and Young, 8.

4. See, for example, Michael W. Maher, and Edward B. Deakin, *Cost Accounting* (Burr Ridge, Ill.: Richard D. Irwin, 1994); John G. Burch, *Cost and Management Accounting: A Modern Approach* (St. Paul, Minn.: West Publishing Company, 1994); and National Association of Accountants (now Institute of Management Accountants), *Statements on Management Accounting* (Englewood Cliffs, N.J.: Prentice-Hall, 1990).

5. Carol Van Alstyne and Sharon L. Coldren, "The Costs to Colleges and Universities of Implementing Federally Mandated Social Programs," American Council on Education, 1975.

6. David Beam and Timothy Conlan, "Grants," chap. 11, this volume.

7. Grants Management Advisory Service, *Federal Grants Management Handbook* (October 1998), 1.

8. Robert M. Rosenzweig, *The Political University* (Baltimore and London: Johns Hopkins University Press, 1998), 71.

9. Donald Haider, "Grants-in-Aid," in *Beyond Privatization: The Tools of Government*, ed. Lester M. Salamon (Washington, D.C.: Urban Institute Press, 1989), 108–109.

10. John J. Lordan, "Cooperation in Federal Auditing," *The Internal Auditor* (April 1979): 92.

CHAPTER EIGHTEEN

Accountability Challenges of Third-Party Government

Paul L. Posner

The case of guaranteed student loans illustrates the daunting performance and accountability challenges posed by third-party governance, yet it also illustrates that these challenges are not insurmountable when policymakers act with insight to address complex tool design and accountability issues. In this chapter, I describe some of these challenges and the efforts being made to cope with them.

Clearly, few issues are more central to the process of governance. The last sixty years have marked an unprecedented expansion of the role of government, particularly the federal government, in our nation's domestic life. During this same period, public confidence in the capacity of government to deliver on those expectations has eroded. One reason for this may be our increasing reliance on indirect governmental tools. Despite the growth of such tools, our understanding of how to think about accountability for them remains underdeveloped. Most scholarly treatments of accountability do not address issues associated with third-party governance.[1] As one analyst put it,[2]

> We do not know how best to maximize the quantity and quality of governmental product when the point of finance is split and often two or even three levels removed from the point of final output.

BOX 18-1 *Guaranteed Student Loan Program*

The federal government has offered guarantees for student loans from private banks for some years. By the early 1990s, over 20 percent of these loans were in default for over three years, necessitating expensive federal payments to the lending institutions holding these loans. Apparently, the 100 percent federal guarantee caused banks to be less than vigilant in their management of these loans. In addition, guarantees were extended to students in a wide range of proprietary trade schools that often failed to provide their students with the education necessary to find viable jobs to pay back the loans.

Perceptive federal policymakers took action in the 1990s to correct these problems and default rates dropped below 10 percent by the end of the decade. First, banks were given a financial stake to screen and monitor loans by being held responsible for a portion of defaulted loans. State guarantee agencies were provided grants to help prevent defaults and the Department of Education was given new authority to take back and manage defaulted loan portfolios from the states. More effective screening of proprietary schools was instituted as well, with thresholds established based on prior default records experienced by their students. Numerous schools have been terminated from the program as a result. New incentives and sanctions were applied directly to defaulting students, including an offset of federal tax refunds and a garnishment of wages. Finally, the Department of Education instituted a direct loan program during this period as well. This set a competitive incentive in place for banks to demonstrate to universities the efficacy of their loans over the new instruments available.

Third parties provide important advantages to the federal government—they enhance the legitimacy of the federal presence, share the costs, provide critical skills and authorities not available to the federal government, and help adapt federal programs to unique local conditions and needs. However, they also complicate the projection of national goals and raise unique accountability challenges. This chapter seeks to examine what we have learned about these unique challenges. To do so, it first examines what we mean by accountability, then identifies the sources of the accountability problems of third-party government, and finally considers some strategies for addressing these challenges.

I. DEFINING ACCOUNTABILITY

Accountability is a multifaceted concept fraught with ambiguity. Traditionally, accountability controls were envisioned as a way to prevent the arbitrary exercise of power by leaders. Clearly the touchstone in any democratic society, this concept has been recast more broadly for the modern administrative state to encompass the activities that help government programs meet expectations for performance held by their various publics.[3]

There are thus two important questions that should be addressed when discussing accountability—accountability for what and to whom. Accountability has its origins as a financial concept, derived from the Latin, "to compute." In this early application, it was associated with the proper accounting and legal expenditure of public funds. Although many would subscribe to this definition, they would not stop there. A federal program manager would likely expand the definition to include oversight mechanisms necessary to ensure that the goals set forth in statutes and regulations are in fact being achieved. A federal budget official might add procedures to ensure that federal funds are spent in the most efficient manner possible. An interest group advocate might add that what is most important is that the broad outcomes are being promoted in the most effective and equitable manner. A state official responsible for implementing the program would work to promote accountability of the program to the state's political community and would want to ensure that federal programs support, not distort, state priorities. All stages of the policymaking process, thus, are implicated in accountability for public programs.

Determining the locus for accountability—accountability to whom—will largely determine which political interests will frame the debate over the program as well as its objectives. Building on principal agent theory, there are a variety of principals and agents with a stake in government performance in a pluralistic democratic system.[4] Federal programs are accountable not only to a multitude of elected officials, but also to a plethora of interested groups, clientele, media, and other actors participating in the programs' policy issue network.[5] As Barbara Romzek observes, most public-sector employees face "multiple legitimate masters" to whom they must answer.[6] Norton Long's classic formulation of federal bureaucracies is relevant here: goals are necessarily ambiguous and conflicted because the political system is fragmented and conflicted.[7]

II. THE ACCOUNTABILITY CHALLENGE OF THIRD-PARTY GOVERNMENT

As challenging as accountability for government bureaucracies is, the issues and dilemmas are even more daunting for programs using third-party tools. Agencies that deliver services directly with their own employees have certain accountability advantages:

transactions are internalized within hierarchies that are more cohesive and responsive to central leadership.[8] Obvious challenges are presented when the federal government must use independent actors it does not fully control to achieve its goals, especially since, as Don Kettl has noted, transferring who does the work does not relieve the federal government of responsibility for the performance.[9]

525

CH 18:
ACCOUNT-
ABILITY
CHALLENGES
OF THIRD-
PARTY
GOVERNMENT

Sources of Accountability Challenges

The major challenge posed by third-party government stems from the diffuse political authority embedded in third-party relationships. Third-party providers have independent bases of political power and potentially conflicting goals and interests. Fundamentally, tool relationships are consequently best characterized as bargaining relationships in which the third-party partners often have the upper hand in both policy formulation and implementation. This is particularly true in view of the fact that at the outset of third-party relationships, federal managers are focused on gaining the participation of third parties to build support for the program throughout the nation. As Helen Ingram notes, participation is initially more critical to program survival than promoting compliance with goals, with the hope that goal congruence and compliance can emerge over time.[10]

This solicitation of third parties' support may reflect the relative weakness of national political support for many programs reliant on third parties at their inception. Philip Moneypenny argued many years ago that the federal government resorts to grants when program advocates cannot muster sufficient political support to sustain fully federal financed and operated activities.[11] Schneider and Ingram similarly argue that the federal government chooses more direct tools of policy intervention when delivering benefits to advantaged groups and utilizes indirect tools when delivering benefits to deviant or powerless interests.[12]

Specific features empower third parties with leverage in these relationships, and these have wide-ranging implications for accountability for third-party programs.

Political Resources

In the first place, third-party providers, whether they be states, nonprofits, universities, or defense contractors, have influence that affects both the setting of goals and the implementation of these goals as well. Richard Nathan has argued that any successful federal program must have the support of a horizontal coalition of program advocates and beneficiaries as well as a vertical coalition of providers.[13] Part of the influence of providers is attributable to their control over program resources and their ability to passively or actively withdraw from program participation.

In addition to this exit option, providers enjoy an influential voice in the policy-making process. James Wilson has argued that groups gaining or losing concentrated and narrow public benefits will enjoy disproportionate leverage over those groups with broader and less intense interests.[14] Providers are likely to enjoy disproportionate influence, since they are often well organized and financed and pursue a set of narrow and intensely felt interests. Providers such as states and large contractors, moreover, are able to mobilize support within congressional delegations due to the concentration of economic and political resources in specific states. Consequently, states can have a significant influence in setting program goals for grant programs, as well as in reformulating those goals during implementation.

Voluntary Participation

For most tools, the participation of third parties and beneficiaries alike is voluntary. Whether it be a grant, a loan, or a tax credit, third parties can, at least in theory, take it or leave it. Even for regulatory tools, some programs give third parties leverage by permitting them the choice of participating in the program as an enforcer of regulations meeting minimum federal standards—what has come to be known as the partial pre-emption strategy.[15] For some programs and tools, like procurement and project grants for research, voluntaristic participation may in fact confer an advantage to the federal government, for it ensures that only providers with sufficient interest participate. However, many federal programs have more universalistic ambitions. In fact, the rationale for many programs is to nationalize programs that are already underway in a number of communities and states and provide a minimum floor of benefits throughout the nation. It is here that providers have the greatest leverage to, in effect, engage in bargaining over the program's design and implementation features and affect outcomes through their own unilateral decisions.

Nathan shows how stricter federal eligibility requirements for Comprehensive Employment and Training Act (CETA) public service jobs in 1978 caused many local governments to withdraw from participation, an action that ultimately undermined the support for the program and prompted its termination. The goals of other programs can be undermined when subsidies and incentives fail to prompt third parties to provide sufficient levels of benefits or services. For instance, open-ended grants with variable matching rates for Medicaid and the old Aid to Families with Dependent Children program have been deployed to entice the states to achieve more uniform levels of public assistance and medical care throughout the country. However, even though poorer states such as Mississippi receive a much higher federal share of costs than do wealthier states such as Connecticut, these differential matching rates have largely failed to prevent significant disparities in benefit levels across these states.[16]

It might be objected that although tools may legally not require participation, it is very difficult for most providers to turn down the offer to participate in federal programs. This is no doubt the case; it is big news when a state turns down a major federal grant. However, this proves the point—most programs have to provide sufficiently rich packages of incentives to induce participation by providers. From an accountability and management perspective, we need to be concerned about what tradeoffs have to be made in the design and implementation process to gain this full participation. For instance, recently the federal interest subsidy for the guaranteed student loan program had to be increased when the nation's banks threatened to stop participating in the program. Although successful in finally obtaining the banks' involvement, federal subsidy costs increased to finance this extra incentive.

Monopolies

Complicating matters is the fact that providers often have monopolies over the means of program production, which gives them further leverage in bargaining with the federal government in program formulation and implementation. States and local governments, for example, are the only vehicle for program implementation. This makes it hard to invoke the ultimate weapon in the accountability arsenal of federal grant overseers to penalize noncompliance—the cutoff of federal aid—since such actions would ultimately hurt beneficiaries themselves. One Urban Institute study found that federal sanctions on state welfare programs were announced in twenty-four cases, but withdrawn in twenty-three.[17] Similarly, regulatory agencies have been shown to be reluctant to impose sanctions on critical industries, such as automobile manufacturers, that would jeopardize production and jobs.[18]

In other tools, federal program actions help spur the development of provider monopolies. In the area of contracts, competition can be limited when a single provider has a monopoly on expertise or production resources that are critical for the program. Certain defense contractors, for instance, enjoy leverage owing to their past production of particular weapons systems, which can put them in an indispensable position for subsequent competitions. In the regulatory arena, professional associations are given licensing authority by states, giving them monopolistic powers to regulate entry and define performance.[19] Federal recognition of accrediting associations for certifying higher education institutions, medical networks for determining rules for organ transplants, and the financial accounting standards board as the authority regulating financial reporting for corporations constitute other examples where monopolistic authority is, in effect, delegated to associations of third parties. In fairness, there are cases where federal tools are deployed to introduce new provider networks and competition to formerly closed systems, and these are discussed in a later section of this chapter.

527

CH 18:
ACCOUNT-
ABILITY
CHALLENGES
OF THIRD-
PARTY
GOVERNMENT

Information Asymmetries

Principal-agent theory tells us that agents enjoy influence by virtue of their inside knowledge about their own behaviors and motivations.[20] Third parties gain important leverage in bargaining with federal principals as a result. First, they have inside knowledge about their own prospective responses to federal program incentives and sanctions—a key advantage in bargaining. For instance, it is critically important for policymakers to know whether a new tax expenditure for higher education tuition or day care will, in fact, stimulate behavior changes by inducing more parents to send their children to college, and by prompting universities to raise their tuition. Similarly, in designing a grant, it would be important to know whether an increase in program funds will prompt increased spending by the states or a substitution of federal for state funds. For the most part, prospective information about responses to these kinds of program interventions is only known by recipients and providers, and even they may not be entirely sure how they will behave.

Equally critical is knowledge of the impacts of reducing or terminating subsidies or regulatory programs. Providers generally oppose such actions by proclaiming that their subsidized behavior would stop, with great harm to the national community. However, it is often unclear what their actual responses might be. For instance, when over eighty categorical federal grants were cut by 25 percent and consolidated in 1981, dire predictions from states and local providers rained down on Washington decisionmakers. However, field research confirmed that states largely replaced most of the cuts in health and social services programs in the following several years—a response that surprised officialdom in Washington.[21] Similarly, proposed cuts in federal insurance for foreign investment in high-risk nations has prompted an outcry by defenders of the Overseas Private Investment Corporation (OPIC), who warn of a pullback in investment by American corporations. Some, however, suggest that corporations will continue their overseas investments, pointing to the growth of an international private insurance market and to corporate investment in nations such as China that have been off limits for OPIC subsidies.[22]

Information on the retrospective performance of third parties is also difficult to ascertain. Agents have incentives to intentionally hide unfavorable information from principals. Although monitoring and reporting can help disclose key data, audits and field monitoring are often necessary to validate information on performance. This can be expensive for federal agencies, particularly where thousands of providers are involved. Data are often recorded in different categories, serving the needs of providers but complicating the ability of federal agencies to obtain uniform perspectives on performance.

Complex Implementation Chains

One of the leading misconceptions that federal officials make is that individual programs can be managed and evaluated in isolation from other federal, state, local, or private initiatives. In fact, the performance of any one program is influenced by a rich environment of collateral tools and programs at federal, state, local, and nongovernmental levels. Whether it be child care, early childhood education, or substance abuse, most major domestic problems have numerous federal categorical grants directed at them with little evidence of coordination or rationalization.[23] Even when resources from a variety of federal, state, and local funds are combined to fund common services, other problems arise, making it difficult to track the activities supported by specific federal programs. As one observer puts it:[24]

> The state gathers all of the requests for funds from the other state agencies, local governments, subdivisions, and private agencies and eventually funds the requests from the various pots of federal and state monies. There is no segregation of federal funds ... the state pool of money is made up of state and federal monies from a variety of sources.

Complicating matters further, there is often a variety of other federal tools addressing similar problems as well. For instance, a General Accounting Office (GAO) evaluation of the low-income housing tax credit found that the credit was accompanied by other grants, rental vouchers, loans, and insurance for most of the subsidized units.[25] Tax expenditures comprise a significant share of federal activity in other major program areas as well. For instance, tax expenditures comprise over 30 percent of total federal spending for health care (excluding Medicare) and nearly 60 percent for business subsidies. What is important is not that different tools are used but that they generally are not developed as part of a concerted strategy. Rather they emerge *ad hoc,* often from different congressional committees and agencies with differing agendas and interests. There has been little effort to harmonize or coordinate these disparate initiatives.[26]

Adding to the complexity, federal programs are delivered through long implementation chains that are often difficult to understand, let alone influence. Grants that reach the states, for instance, are only the first stop in a lengthy and complex delivery network featuring a variety of tools and agents. For example, child-care block grants provided to states are subsequently subgranted to counties. The counties, in turn, often contract directly with private providers for actual services as well as issue vouchers directly to families to purchase child-care services.[27] Accountability can become diffused and confused in such an environment, which really constitutes fourth- or fifth-party governance.

These practices prompt some to argue that only a "bottoms-up" view of implementation can provide a valid picture of program delivery.[28] Indeed, to some the complexities of implementation appear to be impenetrable to systematic understanding.[29]

Consequences of Accountability Challenges

These accountability challenges of third-party tools generate a unique set of performance problems that potentially undermine the effectiveness and efficiency of national programs while at the same time limiting accountability options available to resolve these issues. Of particular interest here are the accountability problems that arise from the perspectives of the national government, although third-party perspectives on these relationships are also important, as discussed later. It is important to recognize that these problems vary somewhat depending on the third-party tool being used and the specific design features embodied in the particular version of the tool. Broadly speaking, however, five generic problems can be identified.

Goal Diversion

529

CH 18:
ACCOUNT-
ABILITY
CHALLENGES
OF THIRD-
PARTY
GOVERNMENT

Perhaps the major accountability problem posed for the national government by third-party government is goal diversion. Independent implementers can use federal program resources to pursue goals and objectives that differ from those envisioned for the federal program. The implementation literature has long taught us that national policy goals can become recast or even unwound as third parties redefine programs in the crucible of their own backyards.[30] Paul Peterson argues that state and local governments are particularly likely to undermine the achievement of federal goals for redistributive programs where they have strong economic incentives to avoid becoming magnets for lower-income people.[31] Studies of environmental programs show that goal conflicts vary considerably among states, with differences in capacity and interest key variables predicting differential state conformance with environmental goals.[32]

Goal conflict can be expressed in several ways. In some cases, third parties avoid or sidestep federal policies. Western states, for instance, addressed the federal 55-mile-per-hour speed limit mandate by handing out warnings to violators, not tickets, sending a clear signal that exceeding the limit was tolerated. In the early 1990s, states used artful reimbursement strategies under the open-ended Medicaid program to bill all sorts of extra costs to the federal government.[33] In other cases, third parties actively resist federal goals, either by court actions or by taking their case to the Congress. For instance, former Governor Allen of Virginia forestalled an Environmental Protection Agency (EPA) mandate to conduct stricter vehicle emissions tests by appealing to a newly conservative Congress. California lobbied to prevent a federal welfare fund cutoff due to its failure to implement an effective child support collection system.[34]

At times, goals are compromised to bring about goal congruence, essentially by defining down deviance. Federal regulatory programs have been observed to be vulnerable to considerable goal slippage, as regulated entities seek to reopen the initial decision through active co-optation of federal regulators or passive resistance. In one model, the politics of speculative augmentation, federal policymakers are initially prompted to enact bold policy that subsequently is temporized and modified as the costs of reform become more salient and third parties become more sensitized to these costs.[35] As I discuss later, goal congruence also occurs over time as the preferences of third parties become nationalized as a result of participating in federal programs.

Fiscal Windfalls

A second type of accountability problem takes the form of provider use of federal subsidies for their own spending priorities. Whether it be tax expenditures to hire welfare recipients or grants to educate disadvantaged children, federal subsidies often do not succeed in changing behavior and causing additional services to be provided. Instead, they are used to supplant funds that the recipient would have spent anyway. A recent meta-analysis of econometric studies of grants found that for every dollar of federal aid to state and local governments, about 60 cents was used to supplant state and local funds that would otherwise have been provided for the aided activity.[36] In effect, substitution transforms categorical grant programs into a form of revenue sharing.

Tax expenditures are highly vulnerable to substitution as well. Tax expenditures to encourage the hiring of former welfare recipients have been found largely to subsidize employers who would have hired these people anyway. Tax exemption of mortgage bonds for lower-income first-time homebuyers have been found to aid people who could have qualified for conventional mortgages. Tuition tax credits have been claimed to be designed primarily to help parents who would have sent their children to college anyway, thereby providing little additional boost for college enrollments. Since universities will likely raise their tuition rates in response, they and not the parents would ultimately reap the windfall of this new tax credit.[37]

Moral Hazards

Third, tools that indemnify third parties for risks may undermine program purposes by encouraging third parties or recipients to engage in behavior that exacerbates the risks and undermines program goals.[38] Federal insurance and loan guarantee programs such as pension insurance, deposit insurance, and flood insurance are particularly vulnerable to this problem as the chapter on insurance has shown. Federalizing these risks by shifting the costs to the nation's taxpayers, however necessary from a social or political standpoint, nonetheless removes financial incentives to discipline economic decisions.

For instance, federal pension insurance enacted in 1974 provided employees assurance about the reliability of promised private pension programs. However, absent effective federal regulatory controls and incentives, it potentially can give employers and employee bargaining groups alike incentives to underfund benefits to free up funds for other urgent uses, such as wage increases or capital investment, with the knowledge that the government would bail out the pension plan in the end. Pension insurance also can distort investment choices by giving employers incentives to undertake risky investment strategies with plan assets, comforted in the knowledge that they will reap all the gains while the government will bear all the losses.[39] Similarly, as Chapter 6 noted, the design and management of federal deposit insurance played a major role in the financial crisis affecting the nation's savings and loans in the 1980s and early 1990s.[40]

Although the savings and loan crisis is perhaps the most notable example of the counterproductive consequences of federal subsidies, other kinds of subsidies also induce a form of moral hazard where well-intentioned subsidies induce effects that prompt offsetting reductions in program investment elsewhere in the economy. For instance, the 1997 federal grant to states to expand the numbers of lower income children with health insurance may very well prompt some employers to drop coverage for children newly eligible for this program. Similarly, research has shown that increases in the size of Pell grants are offset by a decline in institutional aid offered by universities to eligible students.[41]

Perverse Fiscal Incentives

Closely related to moral hazard, third parties may not have sufficient incentives to promote efficient programs when they have no responsibility for raising the funds that they spend. The potential incentive consequences were perhaps best captured by Adam Smith when discussing private corporations:[42]

> The directors of such companies, however, being the managers rather of other peoples' money than of their own, it cannot well be expected, that they should watch over it with the same anxious vigilance with which the partners in a private copartnery frequently watch over their own . . . Negligence and profusion, therefore, must always prevail, more or less, in the management of the affairs of such a company.

When federal grant recipients have little or no fiscal stake in a program, an essential disciplinary constraint on efficiency is removed. Federally funded programs with little or no cost sharing do not tend to benefit from the levels of political or management oversight normally provided by state, local, or private parties for their own funds. Federal categorical grants to states, for instance, received less real attention by state legislatures than state-funded programs, reflecting both the lack of financial payoff and relatively limited discretion available for narrowly drawn categorical programs. Although limited oversight by state-elected officials may not be welcomed by some program advocates, such programs can become isolated within states, cut off from vital political, legal, and financial resources that may be critical for successful program outcomes.

531

CH 18:
ACCOUNT-
ABILITY
CHALLENGES
OF THIRD-
PARTY
GOVERNMENT

Depending on their design, grants or other subsidies have the potential to discourage initiatives by third parties to reduce costs and enhance efficiency. Savings from program or management reforms generally accrue to the federal government alone. For instance, a recent GAO study of the Food Stamp Program found that while states' management commitment was critical to reducing overpayments, states faced a disincentive because savings accrued entirely to the federal government since food stamp benefits are entirely federally financed.[43] Of course, many factors affect performance and efficiency besides federal incentives, but one study of local libraries found that efficiency, as measured by circulation and other outputs, was inversely related to libraries' dependence on intergovernmental grants.[44]

Federally funded grants for mass transit and flood control have been accused of supporting unproductive and inefficient projects due to the absence of meaningful local cost-sharing requirements. Mass transit projects with little ridership were financed with 80 percent federal grants even though the benefits largely accrued to the residents of those cities. Critics argue that the relatively minor local cost share did not prompt the kind of review and screening that might have either prevented these projects from being started or perhaps prompted their modification to better address local needs. For flood control, projects were often started at the behest of congressional delegations with little or no cost sharing by local taxpayers. When the local cost sharing requirement was increased in 1986, the projects underwent more local scrutiny, and the projects selected were more often defensible on economic grounds.

Loan and loan guarantee programs can also suffer when lenders have no shared costs and face no risks from lending decisions. As noted earlier in this chapter, banks faced insufficient incentives to screen recipients of federally guaranteed student loans or institute timely collections because they faced no financial risk from the transaction. Similarly, lenders who hold and service Housing and Urban Development (HUD)-insured multifamily mortgage loans bear little or no financial risk of default, and it is no surprise that they become "passive" in their oversight of borrowers.[45] Office of Management and Budget (OMB) guidance on loans suggests that financial institutions participating in federal guaranteed loan programs should bear at least 20 percent of the loss from any default.

Similar fiscal incentive issues have surfaced with the contracting tool. Cost plus contracts that reimburse costs plus profit appeared to be the standard for many years. However, such contracts failed to provide savings incentives during performance. The fixed price contract does provide incentives—contractors are responsible for delivering prescribed outputs at a fixed cost and they reap the full benefit if they deliver at lower cost but also must absorb any costs exceeding the fixed price. Potentially, this device offers powerful incentives to monitor program efficiency. However, contractors will not bid on fixed price contracts where products or costs are uncertain, and reportedly federal agency officials are reluctant to force contractors to absorb excess costs over the agreed price when this threatens the solvency or competitiveness of major suppliers.[46]

Attraction of Opportunistic Partners

Finally, third-party subsidies can encourage the emergence of third parties whose primary goal is to profit from the subsidy rather than address the program's goals.

Examples here include the rise of proprietary trade schools formed to obtain student loans and the exploitation of Medicaid by providers obtaining reimbursement for services not actually provided or medically necessary. In the case of proprietary schools, many were attracted to the field by the income that could be earned from subsidized students, but then provided training that did not prepare these students for the job market. Developers of low-income housing are enticed by rich subsidies as well, which may be the only way to prompt development of these units. Yet, their commitment to maintain and sustain these units over the long term is highly uncertain.

At the root of this problem are subsidies that entice participation without sufficient risk—or cost sharing or screening to ensure commitment to the program. Tools such as formula grants and tax expenditures provide rich subsidies to ensure universal participation, but typically involve little or no cost sharing or risk sharing. Accordingly, such tools are likely, at least at the outset, to include third parties with only a weak commitment to the goals of the program.

Rent seeking is a closely related phenomenon where governmental tools confer substantial incomes to third parties. The "rents" that providers gain represent income conferred not by markets but by their status as providers of government programs. Examples here include payments to hospitals under Medicare, farmers under food stamps, or housing developers under numerous federal housing subsidies.

Whether these incomes are excessive or essential to stimulate sufficient supply of the aided benefit is a focus of considerable debate. For instance, under the "risk contract program," Medicare pays health maintenance organizations (HMOs) a fixed amount for each beneficiary enrolled. This amount is now based on the experience of the fee-for-service Medicare program adjusted for the relatively healthier status of seniors choosing the HMO option. While GAO and others have argued that managed care companies are receiving windfall profits from the contract formula, HMOs have been dropping out of the program when the federal agency seeks to reduce this alleged profit, claiming that their costs are not sufficiently reimbursed.[47] Debates over the alleged profits of government contractors similarly reflect the challenges facing principals in reviewing the claims submitted by their agents for these kinds of programs.

Even when provider incomes are kept within appropriate bounds, goal displacement nonetheless can occur as the income provided by the tool can become more politically salient than the ostensible programmatic objectives. While goal displacement occurs within bureaucracies as well, the use of third parties increases the stakes associated with the income effects of public programs by multiplying the stakeholders whose economic interests are bound to the programs. As a program evolves, the incomes provided to third parties can become a progressively more important influence on program decisions, eclipsing in some cases the underlying program goals themselves. The dependence of third parties on public subsidies can become an important constraint on public decisions in both overseeing program compliance and in choosing more promising providers or projects. Thus, for instance, the political choices associated with federal weapons or space projects become influenced not only by national security and scientific goals but by the major stakes involved for large contractors and thousands of their employees and stockholders.

III. STRATEGIES FOR RESPONDING TO ACCOUNTABILITY CHALLENGES

The foregoing suggests that the performance problems associated with third-party government are significant and vexing indeed. Yet, these problems, while endemic to these relationships, are by no means immutable. Most programs, in fact, incorporate various features to head off the kinds of policy fiascoes that analysts seem prone to highlight. As deLeon says, "things" do get implemented and carried out on a regular basis, although sometimes it takes programs a number of years to finally get it right.[48]

Major Accountability Approaches

Overall, accountability strategies attempt to achieve program objectives by pursuing two tasks: enhancing the capacities of third-party implementers and/or assuring a more appropriate alignment of third-party interests with national policy goals. When interests are aligned, public goods may still be underproduced when third parties lack sufficient capacity or awareness of their joint interests. The function of federal leadership here is to lower the costs of cooperation through such approaches as fiscal, technical, or information assistance.[49] In the more obvious cases where interests or goals are in conflict, strategies can center on either changing internal preferences within the provider community or shifting provider networks themselves. A broad array of devices can be deployed to bring about what is essentially a reframing of the policy agendas and attentions of networks of third parties to support national goals.[50]

These tasks are pursued through specific oversight and accountability strategies that go well beyond the traditional audit and reporting commonly believed to constitute accountability. Rather, strategies to address third-party performance problems embrace such fundamental program formulation and design issues as initial tool selection, tool design, provider selection, network transformation, oversight, and information feedback mechanisms. These strategies are interdependent—a potential problem prompted by a poor match between the tool and a program goal can complicate subsequent oversight but can also be ameliorated by appropriate provider selection and administrative oversight approaches.

Tool Selection

Some performance and management problems are built in at the outset by a mismatch of tools with goals and problems. Some instruments are better suited to certain policy tasks than others. As Lester Salamon has observed, each tool has a distinct political economy—a bundle of incentives, sanctions, rules, and processes that tend to have reasonably predictable performance and accountability consequences.[51] As Salamon also notes, however, in the policymaking process, tools are first and foremost strategies of political mobilization, and only secondarily analytic categories against which to evaluate the appropriateness of public policy proposals. It is not surprising, then, that tools are selected because they happen to fit with a particular mood or political perspective, not necessarily because they are the right instrument for the job at hand.

Block grants, for instance, have become a tool used to legitimize new federal initiatives during a conservative political era. While championing devolution during the policy formulation stage, many federal policymakers grow frustrated over time when they learn that the limitations placed on federal oversight and rules by this tool subsequently limit their ability to deliver on national policy goals and promises. The introduction of categorical requirements and the nationalization of reporting mechanisms often follow several years in the wake of initial passage.[52]

A number of other mismatches with real performance consequences have also been noted. John Donahue, for instance, concludes that contracting is often overextended to cover duties that are difficult to specify in advance and inherently judgmental and governmental in nature.[53] Paul Light has noted some leading areas where federal agencies have used contracts for inherently governmental functions due to restrictions on

533

CH 18:
ACCOUNT-
ABILITY
CHALLENGES
OF THIRD-
PARTY
GOVERNMENT

the hiring of federal employees.[54] Tax expenditures have also come under criticism when advertised as a way to provide benefits to low or moderate income taxpayers who get little or no gain from these provisions due to their zero or low initial income tax liability.[55] Partly due to the favorable and "businesslike" connotation attached to credit compared with more explicit subsidies, loans, and loan guarantees have also been used in areas where other tools, such as grants, are perhaps more appropriate.

Table 18-1 offers an approach for guiding the selection of tools to match generic policy purposes. This table shows how federal tool choices can be sorted against two dimensions: the universality of participation desired for the program and the federal tolerance for performance differences among third parties. The table suggests tool choices should flow from overarching policy decisions regarding the tolerance for policy differences across third parties and the scope of participation desired from the universe of third parties. Thus, regulation would be appropriate when the federal government wants both universal participation or applicability and has low tolerance for performance variations. Loans, on the other hand, would be appropriate when federal tolerance for diversity in outcomes is high and selective participation is appropriate.

Tools can fall into several of these categories, depending on their design. Thus, for instance, for the grant tool, a categorical formula grant could be characterized as calling for universal participation and relatively low tolerance for state or local differences from federal standards, thus falling into the upper left-hand quadrant of Table 18-1. A discretionary basic research grant, on the other hand, would be characterized by selective participation and could provide for high flexibility for researchers to pursue promising discoveries, thus falling into the bottom right-hand quadrant of Table 18-1.

This kind of framework can help us diagnose mismatches between tool choices and policy purposes. For instance, when looking at the criteria reflected in Table 18-1, we can see that loans are an instrument to use when we want recipients to self-select based on their prospective capacity to pay the loan off when it comes due. However, federal loans have sometimes been selected when national leaders have more universalistic participation in mind, including participation by lower income recipients without the wherewithal to pay back loans received. Thus, loans to farmers come to resemble grants because during farming recessions farmer defaults are greeted by forbearance and the issuance of new credit, not collections. From this perspective, loans can also prove to be an ineffective tool to reach the universe of lower-income students needing access to higher education.

Most programs ideally call for a synergistic combination of tools to promote effective performance, and problems can occur when policymakers are not alert to this dimension. For instance, the savings and loan crisis was in part prompted by broadening the scope of bank lending activities at the same time that federal regulatory oversight was

TABLE 18-1 *Criteria for Tool Selection*

Participation Policy	FEDERAL TOLERANCE FOR DIVERSITY	
	Low	High
Universal	Regulation	Tax expenditures
Selective	Contract	Loan

curbed. The implicit moral hazard associated with a more liberalized deposit insurance program required a combination of strong oversight and public accountability. The federal crop insurance program was undermined over many years when farmers realized they could wait for federal disaster grant payments during natural disasters in lieu of paying insurance premiums; this was reversed in the mid-1990s when Congress required insurance participation as a condition for disaster payments.

535

CH 18:
ACCOUNT-
ABILITY
CHALLENGES
OF THIRD-
PARTY
GOVERNMENT

Tool Design

The appropriate design of tools can also fend off management and performance problems. Linder and Peters observed that improper design condemns some programs to be "crippled at birth," a malady that the best public bureaucracies cannot overcome.[56] By design, I mean the combination of incentives, sanctions, and rules built into the program at the outset. Design can compensate for potential performance problems posed by individual tools. For instance, the moral hazard potential associated with insurance can at least be tempered with risk-sharing requirements such as coinsurance requirements, risk-adjusted premiums, and expanded capital requirements. Similarly, the fiscal windfall potential of grants can be addressed with effective maintenance of effort and matching requirements.

Tool incentives and sanctions can be conceived of as programmatic, participative, and managerial. *Programmatic features* are intended to promote the effectiveness of the program in achieving its program objectives. For instance, sanctions penalizing welfare recipients for not working and states for failing to meet thresholds of work participation for their welfare clients have a programmatic thrust to reinforce the underlying goals of the Temporary Assistance for Needy Families block grant itself. Programmatic decisions concerning which activities and recipients are eligible for funding can have a significant bearing on some of the performance problems discussed above. For instance, fiscal substitution may be prompted when federal subsidies are extended for services and goods that have low externalities, that is, services that local governments or taxpayers already have ample incentives to provide on their own without federal aid. Thus, if policymakers were concerned about protecting against substitution, care could be taken to concentrate federal subsidies on new or emerging activities with high externalities that nonfederal providers are least likely to undertake on their own. Similarly, targeting subsidies to lower income taxpayers, businesses or governments may also yield lower substitution because these recipients are less likely to have the capacity to fund activities from their own resources prior to the federal subsidy. Some tax expenditures are already targeted in this way, such as the child-care credit, which has an income ceiling.

Participative features define, mandate, or entice participation in the program in the first place. Although participation is mandated for coercive tools like regulations, for most tools participation is voluntary and must be induced by a package of financial incentives and appeals to broader values. As Ingram has noted, participation is the first and foremost political task for federal program survival, with compliance and goal congruence the goals only over the longer term. Universal participation is also the rationale for many programs whose primary purpose in fact is to ensure a minimum level of services, protection, or rights throughout the nation.

Managerial features are those provisions intended to boost responsibility and stewardship of the program by third parties. Grants and contracts include a plethora of financial accounting, reporting, and inspection requirements levied on third parties that attempt to enforce compliance and accountability for specific federal objectives, but other strategies are also pursued that seek to instill responsibility for proper stewardship for both federal funds and goals on the part of third parties. Matching, risk sharing, and maintenance of effort can help ensure the kind of fiscal interest necessary to prompt ownership and responsibility on the part of recipients. Research on grants, for instance, suggests that if nonfederal matching rates are high enough and if they require new cash, as opposed to inkind, investment, these requirements can provide the kind of fiscal stake to prompt managerial interest in federally assisted programs by third parties, all other things being equal.[57] Similarly, risk sharing, risk-adjusted premiums, and expanded capital requirements are among the incentives that can help overcome moral hazard in insurance by fostering greater fiscal responsibility for fiscal consequences of decisions by recipients. Funding incentives rewarding or penalizing third parties based on performance are another example of managerial features that can help prompt ownership and efficient management or programs. Thus, several federal grant programs are beginning to offer performance incentives to motivate more improved performance. States now can receive bonus payments if they reduce their food stamp error rates, and this seems to have prompted increased commitment in the states.[58]

Many of the management and performance problems discussed earlier can, in fact, be attributed to incipient conflicts between participative, managerial, and programmatic incentives. Although managerial incentives promise to foster the kind of stewardship that could mitigate or prevent the unique third-party performance problems discussed above, these provisions are often overshadowed and negated by the universality imperative when such provisions threaten to impede full participation in the program. Notwithstanding the benefits to be gained from greater risk and cost sharing, these provisions are often viewed as working too well to screen out partners and clientele deemed vital to the goals of the program. Thus, for instance, matching provisions might prompt some jurisdictions to opt out of federal grant programs and thereby jeopardize the goals of providing uniform service levels across the country. After all, the original rationale for most federal programs is to inspire a greater level of program activity than third parties had been providing in the absence of federal tools. Reflecting this, there has been a trend in recent years to lower or eliminate matching for federal grants. Half of all grants had no matching requirement at all in 1995 and those that did were too weak to provide the kinds of efficiency incentives necessary. Thus, in some ways, the performance problems characteristic of third-party government are, in fact, often designed into programs at the outset.

Provider Selection

The selection of third parties who can be depended on to be active and responsible supporters of the program is critical to program success. Philip Pettit argues that the selection of supportive providers can avoid the need for onerous and conflictual sanctions on performance.[59]

Some tools, such as contracts and discretionary project grants, permit the federal government to select its providers using criteria that help ensure the selection of providers committed to the program goals. The consideration of past performance and the desire of providers to maintain long-term relationships can provide the information to guide the selection process and promote incentives for program compliance.[60] As noted above, the Department of Education is now screening prospective trade schools more rigorously before they qualify for student loans. HUD's housing programs require a long-term commitment from developers to maintain housing units for low-income families as a condition for obtaining these subsidies in the first place. Regulatory tools sometimes use an analogous strategy to gain upfront control over third parties—licensing of participants using criteria-promoting policy goals. The Agriculture Department, for instance, requires states to inspect and certify all food vendors for participation in the Food Stamp Program to screen out providers likely to commit fraudulent transactions.

ACCOUNT-
ABILITY
CHALLENGES
OF THIRD-
PARTY
GOVERNMENT

The competition against specific criteria helps screen in providers who have the greatest potential to meet effectiveness and efficiency goals. Prospective performance can be at least partly judged based on past performance, reputation, organizational and personnel capacity, skills and resources, and other indicators. Notwithstanding these advantages, we know these approaches are not an ironclad guarantee of quality—contractors' bids have a tendency to be deliberately undercosted and overpromised, contractors and grantees with sunk costs in a project have an inside track in obtaining follow-up assistance, and agencies sometimes are not good judges of quality. Competition presumes the existence of a vigorous market of suppliers, which often is not the case, particularly when projects require unique expertise or capacity. As Don Kettl argues, market imperfections make it more difficult for the federal government to become a "smart buyer."[61] Government, not the market, must define the product, determine reasonable prices, and set standards of quality in the absence of the signals that competitive markets provide. The principal agent issues become correspondingly more consequential, as government principals must rely on agents who have exclusive knowledge of their own qualifications as well as price-quality tradeoffs, technical feasibility, and other key issues defining the contractual relationship. Defining appropriate incentives and standards, monitoring performance, and leveraging contractors' performance, become far more complex where competition is limited or nonexistent.

Other tools do not provide for the screening and preselection of providers. Whether it be grants, tax expenditures, regulations, and most loans, many programs are obligated to deal with all eligible providers and accept the provider world as it is. Lacking a strong screening mechanism, these tools often seek to shift the priorities and values of established provider networks from within—obviously not an easy task and one that may be achieved only over the longer term.

Federal programs build support within state and local governments, for instance, by establishing what researchers call a "picket fence" of program specialists and advocates within these governments disposed by professional training and values to support the federal program. Reinforced by federal personnel qualifications, single state agency requirements, and detailed citizen participation provisions, programs form coalitions between federal and state or local specialists across governmental and sectoral boundaries, often in opposition to the interests of these officials' nominal central government superiors.[62] Peterson and others have articulated a maturation model where third parties grow over time to adopt the goals of federal policy, due in part to the growth of like-minded professional networks and groups representing program clientele.[63] Program design can nurture these networks by prescribing qualifications for personnel working on aided programs and by institutionalizing roles and rights for beneficiary groups at the provider level. For instance, federal programs often define requirements for advisory boards to be appointed by providers, with exacting criteria for membership.

Having energized like-minded bureaucrats, these programs also seek to activate recipients or clientele by granting such groups appeal rights and court access. Such provisions, called "fire alarm oversight" by two observers, essentially can generate new interest groups within state or local government that can ultimately work to transform state or local priorities.[64] Studies suggest that such initiatives have succeeded in internalizing federal program priorities and interests within these governments over several decades. Although such programs were initially sources of intergovernmental conflict, over time states grew to become senior fiscal partners, replacing federal cuts in many cases in the 1980s.[65] There appears to be some evidence that comparable internalization occurs over time with federal regulatory goals. Corporations make investments in compliance and gain an interest in championing program goals that could give them an edge over new entrants or other competitors.[66]

In the past, the federal government has also created entirely new types of providers to deliver services when it felt that existing delivery networks were not responsive to federal programs. The Community Action Agencies and the Head Start program both were premised on the need to create alternative service delivery networks to compete with established state and local systems. Although these networks have now become institutionalized within state and local governments, other federal initiatives to change the structure of third-party delivery systems have had a more mixed record. Federal planning requirements in the 1960s and 1970s, for instance, sought to promote regional planning and coordination of services throughout metropolitan areas. Notwithstanding some limited progress, for the most part federally inspired regional planning bodies did not take root as important drivers of priorities or policy.

Federally inspired networks cannot only become the agents of the federal government for service delivery, but also help to reframe the debate within established third-party networks by introducing new interests and forcing these networks to reckon with new actors and interests. For instance, transportation planning at the state and local levels has changed in recent years partly due to linkages articulated by federal regulation between compliance with federal clean air goals and transportation initiatives. Not only can noncompliance with environmental standards prompt a cutoff of federal highway funds, but EPA rules force states to address land use and transportation plans in their clean air attainment plans. Federal and state environmental networks are now relevant to state transportation networks as a result of the federally enforced linkage.

One potentially transformational initiative receiving considerable attention is the use of vouchers to deliver public services. Such an approach could very well transform service delivery systems by breaking apart monopolistic providers within local areas and placing more leverage in the hands of clientele. Several major federal programs, such as HUD's Section 8 housing program and the new Child Care Development Block Grant, have encouraged the widespread use of vouchers. Existing provider networks are beginning to experience significant new competition and pressures as a result.[67]

Administrative Oversight

Oversight can also clearly make a difference to program performance and management. The process, capacity, skill, and interest of administrators has a clear impact and can overcome potential problems inherited from tool selection and design stages. One study of federal education grants, for instance, showed that strong congressional interest and aggressive oversight by the federal agency was able to transform the federal compensatory education grant program into a stimulant of greater state compensatory education spending, notwithstanding program design features that would have been expected to promote fiscal substitution.[68]

Federal oversight and accountability can be characterized as being ex ante or ex post, or some combination of the two. Generally, ex ante accountability concentrates oversight and control at the front end of the relationship. The burden of proof is on the third party to show how they will comply with federal requirements. Goals are negotiated interactively and federal expectations are documented in specific, often measurable terms. Typically, recipient plans and proposals are reviewed extensively at the front end and approved prior to the flow of funds. Federal agencies can use this prior approval to enhance their leverage in at least two distinct ways—first by selecting providers evidencing strong commitments to federal goals, and second by establishing terms and conditions promoting program outputs or outcomes. In Salamon's framework, the ex ante approach is similar to the direct model featuring active administrative control over program performance at the front end of the relationship.[69]

539

CH 18:
ACCOUNT-
ABILITY
CHALLENGES
OF THIRD-
PARTY
GOVERNMENT

For most tools, the federal government relies on ex post oversight strategies. Tools such as formula grants, tax expenditures, loans, and loan guarantees and most regulatory initiatives have only limited front end administrative controls in setting goals or reviewing providers. There is a presumption of compliance, and compliance is certified without rigorous up front examination. Bargaining occurs, as was noted earlier, but at a distance and through complex signaling and political processes. Changes to plans and budgets are generally adjusted at the third-party level without approval of each transaction from federal agencies—begging for forgiveness, not permission, is the hallmark of the ex post approach. Compliance is generally validated following the completion of performance through ex post audit. Monitoring during performance generally occurs on an exception basis when, for instance, complaints are brought to the federal agencies. The burden of proof shifts to federal agencies to demonstrate noncompliance or other performance issues. Federal influence can be limited at this stage due to the difficulties in recovering funds already spent. For these kinds of programs, program design and provider network commitment become more critical as strategies to promote accountability for federal goals.

Table 18-2 illustrates the differences between these two approaches. The distinctions drawn are for heuristic purposes, and many programs reflect a mix of the two. For instance, many categorical grant programs call on federal agencies to approve plans submitted by grantees and require approval for significant deviation in planned budgetary allocations during the performance period. Procurement represents the purest form of ex ante oversight, and block grants and tax expenditures reflect the ex post approach most faithfully.

Notwithstanding the advantages accruing to the federal government from the ex ante approach, there are compelling reasons for reliance on the more passive oversight strategy implied by the ex post approach. Christopher Hood suggests generally that the larger the clientele, the more government will switch from active to passive oversight strategies as a way to reduce bureaucratic burdens.[70] Differences in the federal role and the specificity and prescriptiveness of federal goals may also explain the reliance on ex ante versus ex post approaches.

As a general proposition, government oversight of implementation is constrained by the limited resources available to check on the thousands of providers often participating in public programs. For instance, individual contract officers at federal EPA and the Labor Department on average each handle twenty-six thousand contract actions a

TABLE 18-2 *Characteristic Oversight Features*

	Ex ante	Ex post
Goal setting	Negotiation	Statute
Provider selection	Competition	Formulaic
Front-end compliance	Prior approval	Certification
Performance monitoring	Transactional approval	Exception based
Validation	Periodic monitoring	Post audit

year.[71] Even for federal regulatory programs with a strong federal role and objectives it is acknowledged that federal agencies must rely on voluntary compliance and certifications by regulated entities in large part.[72]

Ironically, perennial constraints on the size of the federal workforce, reinforced by budgetary ceilings on federal personnel, have both contributed to the federal reliance on third parties as well as limited the scope of its ex post oversight.[73] Moreover, long-standing human capital problems within the federal workforce can serve to limit oversight capacity as well. Don Kettl's chapter discusses the unique skills challenges prompted by third-party governance, as managers must bridge gaps between organizations and weave together the networks producing services. The GAO has noted that these complex public management roles in overseeing the work of contractors and grantees are proving to be increasingly challenging to the federal workforce.[74] In programs such as the Environmental Protection Agency's Superfund and the Department of Energy's nuclear waste, federal officials themselves expressed concerns over their capacity to review the reasonableness and accuracy of cost estimates and performance reports from contractors and grantees.[75] The GAO also observes that staff are not well deployed in some agencies to monitor the wide range of third parties whose performance is critical to agency objectives. For instance, HUD has experienced widespread problems in monitoring real estate contractors, appraisers, lenders, local housing authorities, and landlords; for instance, HUD conducted on-site monitoring of only four of the thirty-seven hundred lenders participating in the department's home improvement loan insurance program in 1997.[76]

Perhaps to compensate for inherent resource constraints, the federal government has sought to delegate oversight for many tools to third parties as well. The audit of grants, for instance, now must be arranged by grant recipients themselves, either using their own auditors or contracting with accounting firms. Federal audit staffs play a role in following up on these reports and doing selected studies of their own. Many federal regulatory programs have reached out to engage states as regulatory partners, often in partial preemption programs under which the states receive partial federal funding and permission to exceed federal standards in certain cases. Even tax expenditures have come to use state agencies to select projects in certain cases, most notably the low-income housing tax credit and private activity bonds, where states allocate limited tax expenditures among developers and other entities within the state. The so-called direct federal loan programs actually use private collection agencies to process delinquent loans, whereas the guaranteed student loan program uses state guarantee agencies as key players. The Medicare program uses a diverse array of nonfederal entities to provide accountability for the program. Private insurance contractors are engaged to process and approve claims and separate contract staffs review claims paid for potential fraud.

Although a delegated, ex post oversight process may cover salient instances of third-party noncompliance, it would be unrealistic to expect this process to ensure that programs are responsibly and efficiently managed. Federal agencies' staffing and political constraints prevent them from becoming on-site auditors and overseers at third-party offices. This suggests that instilling appropriate third-party responsibility at the outset through the design of effective incentives is essential to good stewardship and accountability.

Tracking Money and Outcomes

Notwithstanding the devolution of active oversight, the federal government retains responsibility for obtaining information on program spending and performance. Even for such programs as block grants, third-party programs must provide national data to compete in annual congressional appropriations processes. However, obtaining national information on third-party environments is often fraught with political contro-versy. Third parties maintain data on spending and program outputs in categories meaningful to their own accountability stakeholders, and it is accordingly difficult for federal officials to establish uniform information needed to gain national perspectives on program implementation.

541

CH 18:
ACCOUNT-
ABILITY
CHALLENGES
OF THIRD-
PARTY
GOVERNMENT

At the very least, principals want financial information revealing the activities for which the funds were spent. This permits members of Congress to take credit for supporting discrete services and provides some accountability for how funds were spent. Tracking how federal dollars were spent appears straightforward enough, but this too becomes complex in third-party environments. The more that federal programs have broader goals in areas where third parties have significant investment, the more it will be difficult to isolate and track spending for federal initiatives separately. Federal funds and programs tend to be commingled with state and local funds and results are reported for an integrated set of initiatives—a result that many would applaud as an efficient outcome. In fact, at some point, federal funds become "fungible." In these cases, it is impossible to definitively establish and track the specific uses of federal funds for particular clientele, services, or activities.[77]

Fungibility has real consequences for the enforceability of specific federal fiscal pro-hibitions and restrictions. Federal restrictions on the use of funds for such items as administration or construction can easily be evaded by third parties who can simply shift their own funds to support the prohibited activity and use the federal money for activities previously financed with nonfederal funds. The real "impact" of federal funds in this case would be to free up nonfederal funds to support the prohibited activity. This kind of "multipocket budgeting" enables third parties to juggle federal and non-federal funding sources to escape real accountability.[78]

A more promising approach to accountability in fungible funding environments is the performance results perspective. Widespread reform initiatives to shift the focus of accountability from inputs and processes to outputs and outcomes have taken root around the world. In the United States, such initiatives were piloted by localities and states, then given new life at the federal level by the 1993 Government Performance and Results Act (GPRA). Federal agencies are required to prepare performance plans delineating objectives and indicators that address the outcomes of their programs. This outcome approach to accountability is potentially promising for third-party programs because it cuts across all entities working toward common performance objectives, encouraging them to view themselves as a single results-oriented partnership. It also carries a promise to deregulate third-party transactions, giving third parties more flex-ibility in deciding how to spend federal money and manage these programs in return for heightened focus on achieving results. Performance-based accountability has been introduced in grants under the rubric of performance partnerships, in procurement as performance contracting, and in regulation as performance-based standards.

As promising as these initiatives appear, they raise some critical accountability issues of their own which are just now being revealed as the federal experience with GPRA unfolds. As Don Kettl has noted, outcome reporting, although capturing a unified perspective, does not permit each participating public or private entity to identify its unique contributions to the overall program results.[79] New Zealand's performance management system clarifies accountability by holding public managers accountable for discrete outputs directly connected with government programs, not the broader outcomes or results to which these contribute. Donahue has observed that even output-based accountability in the procurement area breaks down when the bond between payment and ultimate results is severed.[80] In some respects, performance-based agree-ments exacerbate principal-agent problems. Inputs and level of effort are more easily assessed and tracked by principals. By contrast, the link between a given level of funding and prospective or actual performance is often more uncertain and difficult for principals to ascertain independent of agents' representations.

For instance, it is relatively easy to track the number of children served in a feeding program—agency projections can be compared with past levels achieved and actual numbers of children served can be validated by independent audit and evaluation. However, it is far more difficult for principals to assess agency claims that the feeding program will improve health outcomes by a specific amount. Absent definitive models on the linkage between the feeding program and health outcomes, which are usually lacking, principals must either accept agents' claims or search for some reasonable alternative model for this linkage. Actual health outcomes can be ascertained eventually, but it is difficult to audit or evaluate the production function linking the specific program intervention, for instance, numbers of children fed, to the outcome. Moreover, it often takes years for the outcomes of public interventions to be realized and measured. Of course, the dilemma is that accountability for outputs alone may not provide sufficient incentives for third parties to reach for the broader outcomes and results the public expects from public programs.

Performance-based agreements also presuppose a level of agreement on objectives that is often more apparent than real. Vague or conflicting objectives do not provide a firm basis for performance accountability at any level. Under these conditions, it becomes difficult for federal agencies to hold states or contractors accountable for performance shortfalls. Performance partnerships in the area of grants may be the most difficult to implement where they arguably can have the greatest impact on public services—in major programs—because agreement on objectives and measures may be most difficult to achieve here. Donahue similarly argues that contracts work best for the government when tasks are discrete and measurable, but when tasks are vague and ambiguous too much discretion and leverage are provided to contractors to define or redefine public objectives.[81]

A recent GAO report on EPA's performance partnership initiative for grant and regulatory programs illustrates the challenges. In 1998, nearly all states negotiated agreements with EPA giving them greater flexibility over spending federal funds and running operations in return for more specific accountability for achieving specific environmental goals. GAO noted some real advantages in improved communication between EPA and the states and providing greater flexibility for states to shift resources to meet unique state conditions. However, it also identified obstacles, including disagreements over performance levels and types of measures and difficulties in linking state activities to environmental results.[82]

Moreover, the outcome approach raises sensitive political questions about who defines the outcomes. The assertion of outcome goals for entire program areas by federal agencies challenges prevailing federalism norms, particularly for areas such as education, where the federal funds comprise only a minor share of the entire intergovernmental effort. If not done in full partnership with third parties, such initiatives can generate fears of excessive centralization of policy leadership in many domestic policy areas.[83]

IV. RELATING ACCOUNTABILITY MECHANISMS TO TOOLS AND PURPOSES

This chapter has defined some key performance issues and accountability challenges facing third-party tools in general. It goes without saying, however, that the challenge are not uniform across all tools and types of third parties. Nor can or should a single accountability strategy apply to all tools and third-party relationships. Indeed, we know that even for a single tool such as federal grants, different accountability schemes are appropriate for categorical versus block grants to reflect the differential federal roles contemplated under each.

Among the factors likely to determine the appropriate choice or tools and accountability strategies are the nature of the federal role intended by policymakers, the nature of the tool itself, the congruence between federal and third-party goals, the fiscal role undergirding the tool, and the relative weight placed on universal participation. Considerable additional research is needed to understand the systematic relationship between some of these key dimensions and performance outcomes, but several suggestive propositions can be offered here.

First, the foregoing section on conflicting accountability expectations suggests that the nature of the federal role should be crucial in determining the type of tool that is appropriate, the performance challenges that exist, and the accountability strategies to be followed. Three broad models can be posited, as shown in Table 18-3.

- Federal—programs where specific federal goals define performance expectations and implementation. Here the federal government would be expected to set specific and prescriptive goals and uses coercive and centralizing tools such as contracts and regulation. Third parties are placed in classic agent roles. To the extent possible, federal agencies would exercise up front control over provider selection and will maximize opportunities for front end review and approval of third-party plans and actions.

- Partnerships—programs where goals are set through bargaining relationships between the federal government and third parties. Where the federal role is defined in partnership terms, programs would be expected to define goals in broader terms and use such tools as categorical grants or partial preemption regulatory mechanisms that permit some third-party discretion and flexibility within federally set parameters. Under this scenario, federal agencies most likely would have little control over selecting third-party providers and must use established networks, but would seek to influence values and priorities of established providers through fire alarm and picket fence mobilization strategies. Oversight would be ex post for the most part and may be performance based as well, with indicators and measures jointly agreed to by federal and third-party officials.

TABLE 18-3 *Different Accountability Models*

| | NATURE OF FEDERAL ROLE | | |
	Federal	*Partnership*	*Third Party*
Goals	Federal prescriptive	Bargained	Third party
Third-party role	Agent	Partner	Independent
Tool choice	Contract/Regulation	Categorical grant	Block grant Tax expenditure
Provider selection	Competition/Create new networks	All eligible/Influence focus of networks	All eligible
Oversight	Ex ante	Ex post with federal agency reviews	Ex post with delegation to providers

543

CH 18:
ACCOUNT-
ABILITY
CHALLENGES
OF THIRD-
PARTY
GOVERNMENT

- Third party—programs where goals are set primarily by third parties themselves and the federal role is defined as supporting third parties to implement their own goals. Principal accountability for these programs is to constituencies at the third-party level who assume roles as truly independent actors. Typically, block grants or tax expenditures best lend themselves to this purpose. Federal agencies under this scenario would take providers as they find them, with oversight constrained to ex post reviews of funds and performance, most likely delegated to third-party institutions, such as state or local auditors or legislative oversight hearings.

These models define theoretical constructs, and actual programs and tools will probably constitute a mixture of these types.

These models might suggest an evaluative framework that could define mismatches between overall federal roles, program goals, and the tools and accountability arrangements supporting those arrangements. Thus, for instance, a mismatch could be identified when a federal program with specific and compelling national performance goals uses tools such as tax expenditures and strategies such as ex post oversight more suited for less centralized federal roles.

The nature of the tool itself can also condition subsequent performance in important ways. As discussed above, tools relying on more direct federal administrative reviews and approvals ex ante are likely to enjoy greater leverage over third-party behavior than tools relying more on ex post reviews. This is particularly the case for such tools as contracts and discretionary grants that can choose their providers based on some performance-related criteria. Tools relying on ex post reviews must usually take providers as they find them and seek to influence behavior through a mix of incentives and sanctions with more uncertain results. As Salamon has observed, tools relying on automatic as opposed to administered processes tend to be more vulnerable to the fiscal windfall and goal diversion problems discussed above.[84] Of course, this dimension is somewhat correlated with the federal role factor discussed just above, since the choice of more direct tools relying on ex ante administration is likely to be most appropriate where the federal role is highly centralized at the outset and program goals are fairly discrete and specific.

The congruence between federal and third-party values and interests is another important dimension affecting performance from these third-party programs. Kettl posits congruence as the critical variable affecting successful implementation in third-party programs.[85] Goal diversion and fiscal windfalls are but two manifestations of this problem, and federal agencies often have little leverage in the short term except to tolerate conflict or actually to modify federal goals to become more congruent with third-party capacities or interests. Congruence should not be expected to exist at the outset of the program, for there would be little rationale for a national program if third parties already had the capacity and interest required. Ellmore has suggested that areas with low congruence should adopt more coercive tools such as mandates since the gap between federal goals and behavior is relatively high.[86] Other research has suggested, however, that coercive tools are perhaps least likely to be adopted when conflicts between values of federal and third parties are highest, since third parties will use their political influence to thwart these approaches. Ironically, as goals and interests converge, coercive tools become more politically feasible as third-party providers acquire an interest in collaborating with federal officials to promote common goals and punish deviants.[87] Research has indeed shown that many federal programs over time succeed in bringing about congruence through the gradual internalization of national program norms and values by third parties.[88]

The fiscal role played by the federal subsidy can also be expected to have important implications for performance. Some federal subsidies are provided for services characterized by high externalities, that is, where benefits accrue largely to publics outside particular state or local communities. Accordingly, these communities are likely to have little incentive to provide significant investments of their own funds in these areas, thereby limiting the potential for fiscal substitution and windfalls when federal subsidies enter the picture. Conversely, when federal subsidies are provided for services that third parties already have ample incentive to invest in on their own, that is, services with low externalities where benefits largely accrue to taxpayers within those communities, different consequences can be expected. These types of subsidies are more vulnerable to fiscal substitution, as third parties would be more tempted to replace their own funds with the subsidy. Moreover, it is more difficult to track the specific uses of federal dollars as their relative contribution to total program financing drops, giving rise to fungibility.[89]

545

CH 18:
ACCOUNT-
ABILITY
CHALLENGES
OF THIRD-
PARTY
GOVERNMENT

The relative weight given to obtaining universal participation is also a factor that can have important consequences for the management of third-party programs. As discussed above, tools and programs seeking universal participation generally deprive federal programs of the leverage of selecting third-party providers up front and they also tend to be loathe to sanction providers once problems are discovered. Moreover, the participation imperative can limit the use of risk sharing, cost sharing, and other managerial provisions designed to foster responsibility within third parties.

V. MULTIPLE ACCOUNTABILITY PERSPECTIVES

The federal perspective is the primary view we have taken so far in this chapter, as the tools of governance reviewed here ostensibly have been established to serve national purposes on behalf of national policy communities. In this view, actions by third parties that modify or subvert federal program objectives are viewed as a problem to be solved. Diversity in implementation is a cause for concern, not celebration.

Central to the accountability challenge of third-party government, however, is the multiplicity of legitimate perspectives it brings to the designation of program goals and purposes. By inviting third parties into the design and implementation of these programs, an expectation is often created, intentionally or not, that some level of program accountability to nonfederal perspectives is legitimate as well. The consequence is an ambivalent accountability where programs are influenced by interests and values prevailing at many levels throughout the system.

Those who champion national policy goals and interests might well take a different view of third-party accountability if they realized that third-party roles are often essential to legitimize federal programs in the first place. Rather than a zero sum game where extensive third-party chains are viewed as a threat, third parties could be viewed as an enabler for an expanded federal role. In this view, most powerfully argued by Robert Stoker, third parties actually expand federal power to act on issues outside the realm of national authority in a federal, mixed market system.[90] Indeed, given the nation's historic resistance to large national bureaucracies, it is difficult to imagine gaining support for such programs as special education, interstate highways, or substance abuse if legions of federal civil servants were deployed to fan out throughout the nation to deliver them. From a functional perspective, the federal government simply does not have access to the policy levers needed to pursue many emerging national goals. The new national interest in education, for instance, must be pursued by tools engaging an educational system that is largely controlled by state and local governments. Federal air pollution standards rely on the inspection of motor vehicles to reduce emissions, which involves tools to engage the support of state motor vehicles laws and bureaus in enforcing periodic inspections. In fact, many federal programs require states to enact enabling legislation, recognizing the federal need to leverage or capture the substantial legal authorities of states in the pursuit of national policy goals. And private contractors often supply the necessary expertise that is not available or would be too expensive to acquire inside federal agencies. From this perspective, the goal diversion and fiscal windfalls accruing from these tools might be viewed as the price to be paid for expanding the federal role and the capacity to govern in new arenas. As Ingram has said, the federal government gains the opportunity to bargain with third-party entities.[91]

In addition to legitimizing and enabling a national presence, third-party tools of government are often justified as a way to decentralize federal initiatives and align them better with local values and interests. Flexibility in implementation permits third parties to experiment with innovative approaches and test out alternative program models when national leaders have limited foresight or political cohesion. The welfare reform block grant, for instance, followed several years of state experimentation with work programs that served as models for the time when Congress and the president achieved sufficient political consensus to enact a new framework. Accordingly, these tools invite third-party agents to adapt federal programs to the goals and needs of their own clientele and constituencies.

The paradox here is that, although engaging third parties helps decentralize federal programs, it simultaneously limits the responsiveness of third parties to their own constituencies. In effect, a convergence may occur between federal and local interests, but to no one's satisfaction—federal programs come to be more decentralized, but the priorities of nonfederal agents are themselves "federalized." This centralization of third-party priorities occurs across a range of tools—federal grants and mandates have centralizing effects on state and local priorities[92]; tax expenditures have collective and negative consequences for economic efficiency by distorting private economic decisions best left to the market[93]; large contractors become dependent on federal procurement to the point where they lose their competitive edge, which is the source of the efficiency they potentially bring to government.[94]

Yet another perspective on accountability in third-party governance is offered by network theory. This theory critiques conventional models of public management where implementation is assessed by how well it brings about the achievement of government goals. Instead of a governmental steering model, policy networks spanning organizational, governmental, and public-private boundaries are viewed as the drivers of public goal setting and implementation. In this view, the ex ante goals or policies of one of the participants, that is, government, is not the yardstick for accountability. Rather, goals emerge from the interaction of actors in the network. Implementation and performance are evaluated based on the capacity to cooperate and solve problems within networks. The focus is not on goal achievement but on whether conditions encourage the formation and sustainability of positive interactions across the network. Criteria for network management include creating win-win situations that make nonparticipation less attractive, limiting interaction costs, promoting transparency, and securing commitment to joint undertakings.

The government's role is not to impose unilateral goals—these would not be effective if they are perceived as being illegitimate by networks. Rather, its role is to work with networks to define goals and to gain cooperation for full implementation. It is acknowledged that government can also serve as a network manager and facilitator, creating or sustaining conditions for full and open participation.[95]

Network theory provides significant insights about the conditions for legitimate public action. It usefully suggests that policy networks of like-minded actors are a meaningful unit of analysis. It also reminds us that effective and workable networks are not an act of nature, but require sustenance and nurturing by network participants and government alike. In essence, networks help define the capacity to act publicly in an era where public action can no longer be contained within vertical hierarchies but necessarily engages horizontal relationships across institutional and sectoral boundaries.

Nonetheless, networks have their own externalities that government is presumably expected to address. Constraining governments to act solely within the boundaries of established networks needlessly limits the scope of public policy to those actions endorsed by what might become highly insular and insulated networks.[96] Government, thus, still has a special role—one that might very well be achieved through existing networks, or as we have said above, through a variety of other strategies, including the empowerment of new networks.

VI. CONCLUSIONS

Early in this chapter, I defined accountability to mean addressing the public's expectations for governmental performance. The foregoing suggests this is not easily done in any setting, but particularly in third-party environments. Much remains to be known about how best to promote performance and accountability in these relationships, but we do know that fostering accountability for federal goals is a major challenge complicated by underlying conflicts in goals and expectations in our system. Goals are frequently vague and conflicted, third parties have much to say about what the goals are and how they are applied, agencies have little leverage over selecting or deselecting providers, and oversight is often deliberately constrained. Perhaps part of the problem is a lack of knowledge about how to make these relationships work to promote performance levels most of us expect.

Yet, perhaps a larger part of the accountability dilemma has to do with the traditional focus of accountability provisions discussed at the outset of this chapter—to preclude the exercise of arbitrary power by leaders. It turns out that this has more to do with third-party relationships than we care to admit. As much as we would like these relationships to promote performance, for national goals, we use third parties because they promote other values, including decentralization, diversity, and innovation, and most importantly they respond to a rampant mistrust of government, particularly central government, that has characterized our political culture through its history.

In a fundamental way, third-party governance reflects the ambivalence most Americans feel toward government. We want effective government services but do not trust traditional bureaucratic and central government to do the job alone. Some would lament the limits placed on federal influence to implement national goals. However, given the very real political, cultural, and administrative limits on central power in our system, those who champion national policy goals and interests need to acknowledge the point raised earlier that third-party roles are often essential to legitimize federal programs in the first place.[97] From a political perspective, the involvement of third parties has probably served to enhance the legitimacy and political acceptability of the growth of the federal role in domestic policy over the last fifty years.

Recognizing the inevitability of third-party government for our system, the question becomes not whether to use third parties but how to do so in a way that promotes the high but potentially conflicting expectations held by federal and third-party actors for these programs. Much research needs to be done to enable policymakers and administrators to make more informed choices of tools, design options, and oversight

547

CH 18:
ACCOUNT-
ABILITY
CHALLENGES
OF THIRD-
PARTY
GOVERNMENT

mechanisms. The stakes are indeed high. Prompted by a healthy suspicion of government and contemporary ambivalence, do third-party governance tools at the same time lay the groundwork for even more frustration and disaffection with government by promising more than we can deliver through these mechanisms? And by pursuing both national programs and local control, it would be ironic indeed if we ended up with ineffective national programs and the nationalization of local third parties conscripted or enticed to serve as the new implementers of national policy.

VII. SUGGESTED READING

Donahue, John. *The Privatization Decision: Public Ends, Private Means.* New York: Basic Books, 1989.

Hood, Christopher. *The Tools of Government.* Chatham, N.J.: Chatham House Publishers, 1983.

Kearns, Kevin P. *Managing for Accountability: Preserving the Public Trust in Public and Nonprofit Organizations.* San Francisco: Jossey-Bass Publishers, 1996.

Kettl, Donald. *Government by Proxy.* Washington, D.C.: The Brookings Institution, 1989.

Kickert, Walter J. M., Erik-Hans Klign, and Joop F. M. Koppenjan, eds. *Managing Complex Networks: Strategies for the Public Sector.* Thousand Oaks, Calif.: Sage Publications, 1997.

Stoker, Robert P. *Reluctant Partners: Implementing Federal Policy.* Pittsburgh: University of Pittsburgh Press, 1991.

NOTES

1. Peter J. Robertson and Muhittin Acar, "Concentrated Hopes, Diffused Responsibilities: Accountability in Public-Private Partnerships," Paper presented at the American Society for Public Administration's 60th National Conference, Orlando, Florida, 10–14 April 1999.

2. Edward K. Hamilton, "On Nonconstitutional Management of a Constitutional Problem," *Daedalus,* 107 (winter 1978): 123.

3. Harvey Mansfield reflects the classic definition by arguing that accountability involves showing that an agent has done what he has been told to do, whether well or badly. See "Accountability and Congressional Oversight," in *Improving the Accountability and Performance of Government,* eds. B. R. Smith and J. Carroll (Washington, D.C.: The Brookings Institution, 1982).

4. Kenneth J. Arrow, "The Economics of Agency," in *Principals and Agents: The Structure of Business Decisions* eds. John W. Pratt and Richard J. Zeckerhauser (Boston: Harvard Business School Press, 1991), 37–54.

5. Hugh Heclo, "Issue Networks and the Executive Establishment," in *The New American Political System,* ed. Anthony King (Washington, D.C.: AEI Press, 1978).

6. Barbara S. Romzek, "Enhancing Accountability," in *Handbook of Public Administration,* 2d ed., ed. James L. Perry (San Francisco: Jossey-Bass, 1996) 97–114.

7. Norton Long, "Power and Administration," *Public Administration Review* 9 (autumn 1949): 257–264.

8. Christopher K. Leman, "The Forgotten Fundamental: Successes and Excesses of Direct Government," in *Beyond Privatization: The Tools of Government Action,* ed. Lester M. Salamon (Washington, D.C.: Urban Institute Press, 1989), 53–92.

9. Donald Kettl, *Performance and Accountability* (Washington, D.C.: National Academy of Public Administration, 1989), 49.

10. Helen Ingram, "Policy Implementation through Bargaining: The Case of Federal Grants-in-Aid," *Public Policy* 25 (fall 1977): 499–526.

11. Philip Moneypenny, "Federal Grants-in-Aid to State Governments: A Political Analysis," *National Tax Journal* 13 (March 1960): 1–16.

12. Anne L. Schneider and Helen Ingram, *Policy Design for Democracy* (Lawrence: University Press of Kansas, 1997).

549

CH 18:
ACCOUNT-
ABILITY
CHALLENGES
OF THIRD-
PARTY
GOVERNMENT

13. Richard Nathan, "State and Local Governments under Federal Grants: Toward a Predictive Theory," *Political Science Quarterly* 98, no. 1 (spring 1983): 47–57.

14. James Q. Wilson, *The Politics of Regulation* (New York: Basic Books, 1980).

15. Paul L. Posner, *The Politics of Unfunded Mandates* (Washington, D.C.: Georgetown University Press, 1998), chap. 1.

16. Donald J. Boyd, "Medicaid Devolution: A Fiscal Perspective," in *Medicaid and Devolution: A View From the States,* eds. Frank J. Thompson and John J. Dilulio, Jr. (Washington, D.C.: The Brookings Institution, 1998), 56–105.

17. Marc Bendick, Jr., *Quality Control in a Federal-State Public Assistance Program* (Washington, D.C.: Urban Institute Press, 1979), 7.

18. Steven E. Rhoads, *The Economists View of the World* (New York: Cambridge University Press, 1985), 53.

19. Grant McConnell, *Private Power and American Democracy.*

20. Arrow, "The Economics of Agency," 37–54.

21. Richard Nathan and Frederick Doolittle, *Reagan and the States* (Princeton, N.J.: Princeton University Press, 1987).

22. U.S. General Accounting Office, *Overseas Private Investment Corporation.*

23. U.S. General Accounting Office, *Managing for Results: Using the Results Act to Address Mission Fragmentation and Program Overlap* (Washington, D.C.: GAO, 1997).

24. Joel F. Handler, *Down From Bureaucracy* (Princeton, N.J.: Princeton University Press, 1996), 29.

25. U.S. General Accounting Office, *Tax Credits: Opportunities to Improve Oversight of Low Income Housing,* GAO/GGD/RCED-97–55 (Washington, D.C.: GAO, 1997).

26. U.S. General Accounting Office, *The Results Act: Assessment of the Governmentwide Performance Plan for Fiscal Year 1999* GAO/AIMD/GGD (Washington, D.C.: GAO, 1998).

27. Paul L. Posner et al., "Vouchers: A Survey of Their Use," in *Vouchers and the Provision of Public Services,* eds. Eugene Steurle, Robert Reischauer, and Van Dorn Ooms (Washington, D.C.: The Brookings Institution, 2000), 503–541.

28. Richard Ellmore, "Backward Mapping: Implementation Research and Policy," *Political Science Quarterly* 94, no. 4 (winter 1979): 601–616.

29. Peter deLeon, "The Missing Link Revisited: Contemporary Implementation Research," Paper delivered before the 1997 annual meeting of the American Political Science Association, Washington, D.C.

30. Jeffrey Pressman and Aaron Wildavsky, *Implementation,* 3d ed. (Berkeley: University of California Press, 1984); Martha Derthik, *New Towns In-Town* (Washington, D.C.: Urban Institute Press, 1972).

31. Paul E. Peterson, *The Price of Federalism* (Washington, D.C.: The Brookings Institution, 1995).

32. James P. Lester, "Federalism and State Environmental Policy," in *Environmental Politics and Policy,* 2d ed., ed. James P. Lester (Durham, N.C.: Duke University Press, 1995), 39–62.

33. U.S. General Accounting Office, *Medicaid: States Use Illusory Approaches to Shift Program Costs to the Federal Government,* GAO/HEHS-94–133 (Washington, D.C.: GAO, 1994).

34. Judith Havemann, "California Faces Loss of Funds," *Washington Post* (13 May 1999), A25.

35. Charles O. Jones, *Clean Air: The Policy and Politics of Pollution Control* (Pittsburgh: University of Pittsburgh Press, 1975). Anthony Downs has referred to this process as the issue attention cycle in "Up and Down with Ecology—The Issue Attention Cycle," *Public Interest* (summer 1972).

36. U.S. General Accounting Office, *Federal Grants: Design Improvements Could Help Federal Resources Go Further,* GAO/AIMD-97–7 (Washington, D.C.: GAO, 1996).

37. Lawrence E. Gladieux and Robert Reischauer, "Higher Tuition, More Grade Inflation," *Washington Post* (4 September 1996).

38. Y. Kotowitz, "Moral Hazard," in *Allocation, Information, and Markets* eds. John Eatwell, Murray Milgate, and Peter Newman (New York: W. W. Norton, 1992), 207–213.

39. Congressional Budget Office, *Controlling Losses of the Pension Benefit Guaranty Corporation* (Washington, D.C.: CBO, January 1995).

40. Congressional Budget Office, *The Economic Effects of the Savings and Loan Crisis* (Washington, D.C.: CBO, 1992).

41. Jon H. Oberg, "Testing Federal Student-Aid Fungibility in Two Competing Versions of Federalism," *Publius* 27, no. 1 (winter 1997): 115–134.

42. Adam Smith, *An Inquiry Into the Nature and the Causes of the Wealth of Nations,* ed. E. Cannan (New York: Modern Library, 1937), 700.

43. U.S. General Accounting Office, *Food Assistance: Reducing Food Stamp Benefit Overpayments and Trafficking,* GAO/RCED-95–198 (Washington, D.C.: GAO, 1995).

44. Richard Silkman and Dennis Young, "X-Efficiency, State Formula Grants, and Public Library Systems," Harriman College for Urban and Policy Sciences (Stony Brook-State University of New York at Stonybrook, 1981).

45. Thomas Stanton, "Improving the Design and Administration of Federal Credit Programs," *The Financier: ACMT* 3, no. 2 (May 1996): 7–21.

46. John Donahue, *The Privatization Decision,* (New York: Basic Books, 1989), 108.

47. Robert D. Reischauer, Stuart Butler, and Judith R. Lave, eds., *Medicare: Preparing for the Challenges of the 21st Century* (Washington, D.C.: National Academy of Social Insurance, 1998).

48. Peter deLeon, "The Missing Link Revisited: Contemporary Implementation Research."

49. Evert Vedung and Frans C. J. van der Doelen, "The Sermon: Information Programs in the Public Policy Process—Choice, Effects, and Evaluation," in *Carrots, Sticks and Sermons: Policy Instruments and Their Evaluation,* eds. Marie-Louise, Bemelmans-Videc, Ray C. Rist, and Evert Vedung (New Brunswick, N.J.: Transaction Publishers, 1998), 103–128.

50. Frank Baumgartner and Bryan Jones, *Agendas and Instability in American Politics* (Chicago: University of Chicago Press, 1993).

51. Lester Salamon, *Beyond Privatization: The Tools of Government* (Washington, D.C.: Urban Institute Press, 1989), 28.

52. Paul L. Posner and Margaret Wrightson, "Block Grants: A Perennial But Unstable Tool of Government," *Publius* 26, no. 3 (summer 1996).

53. Donahue, *Beyond Privatization.*

54. Paul C. Light, *The True Size of Government* (Washington, D.C.: The Brookings Institution Press, 1999), 138–174.

55. Christopher Howard, *The Hidden Welfare State* (Princeton, N.J.: Princeton University Press, 1997).

56. Stephen H. Linder and B. Guy Peters, "A Design Perspective on Policy Implementation: The Fallacies of Misplaced Prescription," *Policy Sciences Review* 6, no. 3: 459–475.

57. U.S. General Accounting Office, *Proposed Changes in Federal Matching and Maintenance of Effort Requirements* GAO/GGD-81–7 (Washington, D.C.: GAO, 1980).

58. U.S. General Accounting Office, *Food Assistance.*

59. Philip Pettit, "Institutional Design and Rational Choice," in *The Theory of Institutional Design,* ed. Robert E. Goodin (New York: Cambridge University Press, 1996), 79.

60. Steven Kelman, "Deregulating Federal Procurement: Nothing to Fear but Discretion Itself?," in *Deregulating the Public Service,* ed. John J. Dilulio, Jr. (Washington, D.C.: The Brookings Institution, 1994), 102–128.

61. Donald Kettl, *Sharing Power: Public Governance and Private Markets* (Washington, D.C.: The Brookings Institution, 1993).

62. See Deil Wright, *Understanding Intergovernmental Relations* (Monterey, Calif.: Brooks/Cole Publishing, 1982).

63. Paul E. Peterson, Barry G. Rabe, and Kenneth K. Wong, *When Federalism Works* (Washington, D.C.: The Brookings Institution, 1986).

64. Matthew D. McCubbins and Thomas Schwartz, "Congressional Oversight Overlooked: Police Patrols and Fire Alarms," *American Journal of Political Science* 28 (February 1984): 165–179.

65. See Peterson, Rabe, and Wong, *Making Federalism Work.* Posner and Wrightson, "Block Grants."

66. See George Stigler, "The Economics of Information," *Journal of Political Economy* 69 (June 1961): 213–225.

551

CH 18:
ACCOUNT-
ABILITY
CHALLENGES
OF THIRD-
PARTY
GOVERNMENT

67. Posner et al., "A Survey of Voucher Use: Variations and Common Elements," 503–540.

68. John Chubb, "The Political Economy of Federalism," *American Political Science Review* 79 (1985): 994–1015.

69. Salamon (ed.), *Beyond Privatization,* 44–46.

70. Christopher Hood, *The Tools of Government* (Chatham, N.J.: Chatham House Publishers, 1983), 138.

71. Light, *The True Size of Government,* 187.

72. Peter May, "Social Regulation: Preventing Harm and Securing Benefits," Draft paper prepared for Tools of Government project, Johns Hopkins University, 1999.

73. Light, *The True Size of Government.*

74. U.S. General Accounting Office, *Major Management Challenges and Program Risks: A Governmentwide Perspective,* GAO/OCG-99–1 (Washington, D.C.: GAO, January 1999).

75. U.S. General Accounting Office, *High-Risk Series: An Update,* GAO/HR-99–1 (Washington, D.C.: GAO, January 1999).

76. U.S. General Accounting Office, *Major Management Challenges and Program Risks: Department of Housing and Urban Development,* GAOOCG-99–8 (Washington, D.C.: GAO, January 1999), 28.

77. U.S. General Accounting Office, *Block Grants: Issues in Designing Accountability Provisions* GAO/GGD (Washington, D.C.: GAO, 1998).

78. Allen Schick, "Contemporary Problems in Financial Control," in *Current Issues in Public Administration,* 2d ed., ed. Frederick S. Lane (New York: St. Martin's Press, 1982), 361–371.

79. Donald F. Kettl, *Reinventing Government: A Fifth-Year Report Card* (Washington, D.C.: The Brookings Institution, 1998), 49.

80. Donahue, *The Privatization Decision,* 41.

81. Ibid.

82. U.S. General Accounting Office, *Environmental Protection: Collaborative EPA-State Effort Needed to Improve New Performance Partnership System* GAO/RCED-99–171, 1999.

83. See Beryl A. Radin, "The Government Performance and Results Act and the Tradition of Federal Management Reform: Square Pegs in Round Holes?," Paper prepared for the National Public Management Conference, Texas A&M University, December 3–4, 1999.

84. Salamon, *Beyond Privatization,* 46.

85. Donald Kettl, *Government by Proxy* (Washington, D.C.: Congressional Quarterly Press, 1988), 16.

86. Richard Ellmore, "Instruments and Strategy in Public Policy," *Policy Studies Review* 7, no. 1 (autumn 1987): 174–186.

87. Paul L. Posner, *The Politics of Unfunded Federal Mandates* (Washington, D.C.: Georgetown University Press, 1998).

88. Peterson, Rabe, and Wong, *Making Federalism Work.*

89. Paul L. Posner, "Federal Grant Design: What Washington Should Know and Why It Should Know It," Paper presented at the Annual Meeting of the American Political Science Association, Boston, 3–6 September 1998.

90. Robert Stoker, *Reluctant Partners* (Pittsburgh: University of Pittsburgh Press, 1991).

91. Ingram, "Policy Implementation through Bargaining."

92. Posner, *The Politics of Unfunded Mandates.*

93. Howard, *The Hidden Welfare State.*

94. Donahue, *The Privatization Decision.*

95. Network concepts presented in Walter J. M. Kickert, Erik-Hans Klijm, and Joop F. M. Kooppenjan, *Managing Complex Networks* (Thousand Oaks, Calif.: Sage Publications, 1997).

96. Stephen H. Linder and B. Guy Peters, "Relativism, Contingency, and the Definition of Success in Implementation Research," in *Policy Studies Review* 7, no. 1 (autumn 1987) 116–127.

97. Stoker, *Reluctant Partners,* 100.

CHAPTER NINETEEN

The Politics of Tool Choice

B. Guy Peters

The analysis and selection of policy instruments have been portrayed as a rational, linear, technical exercise—especially in the existing economics literature on the topic (Weimer and Vining, 1998). Instruments are, in this view, assumed to manifest certain objective characteristics that are apparent to all involved in the process. The nature of the tools and their characteristics are also assumed to be uncontroversial among the actors involved in the policymaking process. Finally, it has often been assumed that each policy problem at hand can be characterized in a relatively unambiguous manner (but see Ringeling, 1998; Peters, 1998) so that the link of instrument and problem can be made. This set of simplifying assumptions can provide a powerful way of understanding public policy since it reduces instrument selection to the technical exercise of selecting the instrument that is most appropriate for the nature of the policy problem.

The argument of this chapter is that the above characterization of instrument choice grossly oversimplifies the process of instrument choice because it ignores the important political factors involved. Theodore Lowi (1964; 1972) perhaps first made the now familiar argument that "policy causes politics." That is, the usual linear conceptualization that has politics and political preferences producing decisions about public policy may, in reality, function in reverse. Different varieties of policy (Lowi's regulative, distributive, and redistributive categories, for example) may themselves exert a major influence on the degree and type of political action manifested during their formulation and implementation.[1]

The same class of argument can be applied to the selection and assessment of policy tools (see Salamon, 1981). Policy instruments are not politically neutral, and the selection of one instrument or another for a policy intervention will generate political activity, and have political consequences. More importantly, political factors and political mobilization affect the initial selection of instruments and the ultimate implementation of policy. Attempting, therefore, to assess policy outcomes without also considering the means to be employed to achieve those ends as well as the politics shaping tool choices is likely to result in potentially faulty policy decisions.

Although analytically distinct, there are often genuine difficulties in separating political evaluations of the instruments being used for implementation from substantive evaluation of the policies with which they are linked. For example, economic regulation is unpopular in some political circles, but is that because of the instrument itself or because of the presumed economic consequences of this mode of government intervention?[2] Likewise, are tax expenditures opposed (as well as supported) politically because they tend to be less visible instruments, and thus shroud the true impact of the public sector (see Pear, 1997; Stevenson, 1997), or because their distributive consequences tend to favor the middle and upper economic classes (Howard, 1997)? Or both?

There is insufficient space to develop the topic fully, but we should also be cognizant of the need to "frame," or politically construct, policy instruments (Schon and Rein,

1994; Schneider and Ingram, 1993). Policy problems and policy instruments do not appear in the political system already conceptualized and defined; the political process is in part a locus of conflicts over the most appropriate definition of problems, usually at the agenda-setting stage (Baumgartner and Jones, 1993). Likewise, instruments themselves can be conceptualized differently; to some analysts a tax expenditure may be a means for the affluent to avoid paying their proper share of taxes, while to another it is simply an efficient, self-administering means of reaching policy goals.[3]

The different possible constructions will, in turn, engender different forms of political debate and also make different forms of political coalitions possible. Perhaps most important in these politics is the alternative instrument(s) against which any one tool is compared. For example, if loan guarantees (Stanton, Chapter 12 in this volume) are being considered as the mechanism for assisting students in higher education, the coalitions formed are likely to be different if the political process stresses direct grants as the principal alternative when compared with tax expenditures for parents. The former option might, for example, produce more vigorous involvement by colleges and universities than would the latter.

It is simple enough to say that instruments have their own politics, but that is only the very first stage in specifying how these politics are actually played out, and how politics are linked to different categories of instruments. Therefore, the bulk of this chapter will attempt to make this linkage, and to make it in both a practical and a theoretical manner. In so doing I will demonstrate how a variety of different conceptions of politics can be utilized to illuminate instrument choice, and also to understand political responses to instruments as they are implemented in individual programs. Understanding the source and nature of the political response to instruments can, in turn, assist the political or bureaucratic analyst who must make difficult recommendations about how government should intervene.

I. FRAMEWORK FOR ANALYSIS

To clarify our argument that instrument selection and evaluation are inherently political, we require a framework through which to elaborate that influence. One such framework is available in the comparative politics literature that identifies a set of five factors that influence the policy choices of political regimes: ideas, institutions, interests, individuals, and the international environment. These five "i's" in essence constitute a checklist of concepts that require consideration when thinking about instrument selection from a political perspective.

Interests

Perhaps the conventional manner of thinking about politics is to think of it as the pursuit of interests, whether individual or collective. The current craze of rational choice as an approach to political science (Tsebelis, 1990; Scharpf, 1997) is premised on the assumption that individuals do maximize their personal utilities through political action. Similarly, somewhat older modes of political analysis such as interest group theory, class analysis, and elite theory are all premised on more collective representations of interests as the primary mechanism motivating politics. For both the individual and the collective versions of interests-based theory, the basic logic is that politics is driven by the real or perceived interests of actors, and the desire of the actors involved to utilize the political process to achieve their own ends.

The interest-based approach is hardly a revelation for anyone familiar with politics, but its application to the analysis of tool choice remains insufficiently developed. As the introduction to this volume has shown, the fact is that tool choices affect whose ox will be gored, or whose nest will be feathered, by a particular policy. To be sure, it may be difficult to separate reactions to the substantive goals of the policy from reactions to the instruments selected to achieve those goals. However, there are clear instances in which political interests are directed as much toward instrument choice as they are toward the substance of the decisions. Indeed, Lester Salamon (1981) has argued that political factors often dominate other considerations in the choice of tool, creating a "public management paradox" in which the policy instruments that are the hardest to implement (those that are indirect) are the most likely to be adopted (because they enlist third-party producer groups in their operation). How, for example, does government cope with the problem of substandard or faulty medical care? Not surprisingly, trial lawyers as an interest group would prefer to retain the existing tort law mechanism of malpractice, while many in the medical profession might prefer going to mechanisms more similar to those found in European countries in which compensation boards determine awards, or where a *res ipsa* doctrine awards compensation on a more or less fixed schedule.[4] Likewise, the banking industry is a strong advocate of loan guarantees instead of direct government lending, and drug companies prefer labeling requirements to regulation.

The linkage of instruments and interests is often not as direct and obvious as we might think, given the importance of interests in explaining tool choice. Interest-based politics about policy instruments often revolves around second- or third-order consequences of the instruments in question. That is, instruments generally are designed to produce certain outcomes for a particular target group in society (see Ingram and Schneider, 1991). Whether it is successful or not in achieving those intentions, the instrument may deliver important benefits to other social and economic groups that will also mobilize them politically. For example, food stamps are intended to reduce food costs for poor people. By channeling the aid in a way that limits its use to food purchases in grocery stores, however, the choice of this tool enlists the support of farmers and grocers. There are numerous cases in which support from these second- and third-order beneficiaries are crucial to the political success of a program, and may perpetuate it even when the program does not reach the intended beneficiaries, and those beneficiaries are less than supportive.[5]

As well as organized interests outside government, politicians have tangible interests in the selection of instruments. In an era in which much of the public is highly skeptical of government and tends to favor government being as little involved in social and economic life as possible, the selection of less-intrusive instruments may have a strong appeal for politicians. Some scholars have argued more generally that instruments that are less invasive may be preferred to those that are more intrusive, but that argument appears more valid now than in the past.[6] Whether temporally specific or not, politicians in this argument are assumed to have an interest in selecting the least visible tool possible, consistent with delivering the policy as required.

The choice between different types of instruments may also split special interests that otherwise might be thought to be allies. For example, the Clinton health plan proposed in 1993 called for health care to be provided through a complex array of networks comprising doctors, hospitals, and other sources of medical care.[7] As well as tax funding, a good deal of the financial support for the program was to come from employers. This proposed instrument split the business community, with larger businesses who assumed they could pass the costs along to consumers supporting the plan much longer than small business who perceived themselves to be more economically vulnerable. In this case our usual broad classifications of interests appear to have been inadequate to capture the politics of instrument choice.

Although we generally conceptualize tool selection occurring at the policy formulation stage of policymaking, their politics often become apparent at the implementation stage. For example, if there is ample room for discretion in the distribution of program benefits at the implementation stage then the programs can be managed in ways to appease interests, especially if those interests are defined geographically. The distribution of military contracts in the United States has been a clear example of using the implementation process to build political coalitions. Likewise, the tendency to create "pork barrel" programs enables politicians to serve their constituencies and enhance their chances for reelection (Fiorina, 1992). Indeed, as Salamon has argued in the introduction to this volume, it is precisely the opportunity it affords to advantage particular groups in the implementation process that makes the choice of tools so politically charged.

In summary, examining the interests involved in the choice of a policy instrument is a good place to start an analysis of public policy. Politics can often resolve into a simple question of identifying the interests being advantaged or disadvantaged by the selection of a policy instrument. The stark reality of interests may be dressed up in the fancier clothing of ideas and the public interest, but beginning by asking *qui bono* is frequently productive of at least a partial explanation.

Ideas

Not only interests but also ideas and ideologies influence tool choices. The argument that ideas have an independent influence on public policy has become more popular during the last decade (Reich, 1990; Hall, 1993; Thelen, Longstreth, and Steinmo, 1992). Intellectually, this has been a reaction against the interest-based theories that have dominated the social sciences for the last several decades (March and Olsen, 1984; Green and Shapiro, 1994). Also at work, however, has been the attempt to fashion a conceptual challenge to the dominant "liberal" (in American terms) consensus that dominated policy from the New Deal until the mid-1970s. An important part of the resulting "conservative" assault on the American version of the welfare state has been a call for a shift in the instruments of public action from direct to indirect ones and from coercive to permissive ones. Hence, block grants and contracting have been preferred over direct government and economic incentives and disincentives over regulation.

The conservative assault has occurred in the context of a long-standing American hostility to government, and especially direct government intervention in social and economic life. Policy instruments that would in other national contexts be quite legitimate are suspect in the United States (especially at the federal level). Thus, American government has intervened in the economy through regulation rather than direct public ownership, and has a version of the welfare state based more on insurance than on universalistic subsidies. These examples could be proliferated, but the basic point is that the antistate mentality of Americans going back to the historical roots of the country has a pervasive impact on instrument choice.

Even if there are no *Weltanschauungs* guiding American political rhetoric that have motivated politics in much of the rest of the world, there may be more specific and operational ideas about what constitutes good policy, and good policy instruments. In some instances these ideas will approach some of the more comprehensive political ideologies by having an emphasis on the distributional consequences of policies and instruments. As already noted, an instrument that has a differentially negative impact on the poorer segments of society may be deemed unacceptable to many people on the basis of their political values rather than on the capacity of the instrument to achieve the goals it is designed to achieve.

Another way to say ideas when thinking about policy is to say "symbol." To the extent that a program can be attached to a positive symbol, then it is more likely to be successful politically. The ability of indirect instruments to attach themselves to ideas such as "freedom" is thus certainly an advantage over more intrusive mechanisms that do not permit individuals any real choice. Critics of a program using indirect instruments can, on the other hand, attack it using other symbols such as "fairness" or "equality" that might seem to be better served by direct intervention.[8] The power of these symbols and the effectiveness with which they are advocated can often determine which tool is chosen.

Ideas about good policy, and instruments, arise from several sources. In addition to broad ideological thinking, professional education inculcates certain ideas, and these are perpetuated by professional associations and other specialized bodies.

The public service itself is a profession with ideas about the best instruments to achieve policy goals. Reflecting this, members of the policy community (academic and practitioner) have clear ideas about instruments, and often are committed to particular modes of intervention (Linder and Peters, 1998). Not surprisingly, the public service tends, everything else being equal, to favor instruments that require more direct provision by the public sector. This view may, of course, have more than a negligible element of self-interest involved, given that the more direct instruments involve more public employment (see Blais, Blake, and Dion, 1998). The self-interested elements of this position manifest themselves especially clearly when it is being espoused by public-sector unions, for instance, teachers' unions opposing vouchers.

The "networks" or "communities" that exist within and around each policy area (Kickert, Klijn, and Koopenjan, 1997; Marsh and Rhodes, 1992) also often provide a set of ideas motivating the selection of tools. Although these structures have been conceptualized in a number of different ways, the concept of the "epistemic community" (Haas, 1989; Adler, 1992; Zito, 1999) most clearly identifies the role of ideas in policy discourse. In this view, policy communities are defined by their acceptance of a collective set of beliefs about policy, including such issues as cause and effect, common standards of measurement, and also by extension a set of agreed ideas about policy instruments. In the epistemic community conception of policymaking, policy change results primarily through learning and argument about the ideas that motivate policy choices (Sabatier, 1988; Howlett and Ramesh, 1993), rather than from the conflict of interests.

In American political debate the constitution represents something of an ideology so that arguments concerning the constitutionality of a policy have elements similar to ideological arguments in other political traditions. These constitutional arguments also extend to the selection of instruments. Perhaps the most powerful example of this is the emphasis placed on federalism in the American constitution and the resulting tendency to utilize grants-in-aid to states to implement domestic policies. Constitutional arguments also can be utilized, as is true for other modes of arguing on the basis of ideas, to disguise interests; the constitutional principle of separation of church and state can be used as a device for arguing against vouchers for parochial schools, for example, by groups (*inter alia* parents and teachers) that have something to lose if public money is diverted away from public education.

In summary, ideas do motivate decisions about policy instruments, although the connections between the tool choices and the presumed "cause" may be less clear than it was for the interest-based explanation. This is because tool advocates often prefer to dress their interest-based advocacy of instruments in terms of powerful and noble ideas.[9] Still, there does appear to be some independent impact on instrument choice of the way that people—both mass and elite—think about policy, and about politics more generally.

Individuals

Not only ideas and interests but also individuals can exert an impact on the choice of policy instruments. This is perhaps the weakest of the five alternative modes of explanation I will discuss, given that individuals appear to be less committed to policy instruments than they are to particular desired policy consequences. What is more, determining to what extent a decision about an instrument is a function of individuals, rather than their interests or the ideas that motivate them, is difficult if not impossible. Still, individuals do play a role in pressing for, or resisting, particular forms of policy interventions. Thus, for example, Dr. Martin Luther King cared perhaps as much about the instruments used in the struggle for equality as he did about actually attaining that goal.[10]

More generally, the tools of fashioning the appropriate tool to win approval for a policy innovation may be one of the principal functions of what has come to be referred to as the "policy entrepreneur" (Kingdon, 1996; Roberts, 1992; Hargrove, 1994). Although descriptions of the political process, even those written by political scientists, often make it appear as if issues move rather effortlessly from one stage to the next, in practice there is a good deal more political activity required if advocates are to be successful.[11] Each stage of the process requires leadership and a commitment to the policy, and even to a particular variation of the policy, if success is to be achieved in the end. There are too many powerful forces that can divert the movement or end it entirely, so that there have to be individuals involved to do the shepherding.

From what has been said it should be clear that the choice and design of instruments can be a critical part of this process, often determining whether a program can muster the support it needs. Selecting the instrument thus becomes a critical part of the role of the policy entrepreneur. The policy entrepreneur thus becomes the "tool broker," as Salamon puts it in the introduction to this book, adapting the tool to be used so as to achieve the optimum balance between effectiveness and political feasibility.

Institutions

A fourth political factor affecting the choice of policy instruments is institutional in character. According to this line of argument, which has recently gained intellectual currency (see Peters, 1998a), political choices are tempered and shaped by the institutions within which one operates. In other words, institutions have preferences about the tools of policy being used (see Atkinson and Nigol, 1989). For example, legislatures (and especially committees in the American system) may have preferences for the instruments with which they are familiar; they know what to expect with familiar instruments and believe that those instruments are capable of achieving a variety of policy goals. They may also have preferences for instruments over which they have greater control. So, some resistance to block grants arises as a reaction to a feared loss of control on the part of Congress over the purposes for which federal funds are used (Salamon, 1981; Kettl, 1988; Beam and Conlan, Chapter 11 in this volume).

That institutions have their own preferred ways of addressing policy issues may result from the history of the institution and the patterns of success and failure that have structured its learning experiences about the utility of policy instruments (see Olsen and Peters, 1997). Also at work can be the professional training of the individuals who comprise the organization, and the tendency of organizations to replicate their own membership. Finally, tool preferences may also result from the self-interest of the institution, and the desire to perpetuate ways of doing business that benefit it and its clients.

Complicating the institutional approach is the fact that, in the United States especially, a number of institutions interact to make policy choices. We are all familiar with the constitutional arguments about separation of powers, but the interaction of institutions goes beyond the three major institutions (see Weaver and Rockman, 1993). For deciding the details of policy, bureaucratic institutions also have a significant role to play. Further, the "logics of appropriateness" of the numerous organizations within the federal bureaucracy may conflict with one another, forming the basis for the very familiar bureaucratic politics in the policy process.

The politics of policy instruments also extends to differences in priorities and perspectives among different levels of government. Again, some of the issues arising among levels of government revolve around the degree of control associated with the particular tool being considered. In the United States grants-in-aid to state and local governments are preferred by the states as the instrument for federal involvement. They especially prefer block grants that transfer much of the control over policy to the states (see Beam chapter below). This political debate could be conceptualized in terms of the ideas involved (federalism as a constitutional idea, for example), in terms of the interests involved, but perhaps is best understood as a question of institutional power.

In summary, institutions are political actors, just as are individuals. They can use the policy process to achieve their collective goals, as well as those of the interests and individuals with which they are associated. Although we must be careful not to assign them too much of a life of their own, we would also miss a great deal of political reality if we did not take into account the distinctive role of institutions. In particular, institutions help to explain the persistence of certain instruments (even at times in the face of apparent failure) and why instrument choices tend to be similar across a wide range of policy problems.

International Environment

The final political factor that may explain the choice of policy tools is the international environment. With the rapid expansion of telecommunications, political ideologies increasingly flow across international borders, bringing with them new approaches to solving public problems and hence new tools of action. Thus, for example, Reaganism and Thatcherism gained considerable currency internationally as approaches to public policy bringing with them a dedication to privatization and market-type approaches to the solution of public problems that extended far beyond the borders of these countries. These approaches were encouraged as well by World Bank "structural adjustment" policies, which rewarded governments that adopted essentially pro-market policy measures and tools. The international environment may also influence tool choices more concretely. For example, there is reason to believe that globalization may be making instruments that target firms less attractive, and instruments that target individuals more attractive. That is, if capital is indeed more mobile, then any instrument that extracts resources or imposes burdens on a firm may result in the firm simply leaving for a more friendly locale, or so it is argued. This is then an international version of the game played by the American states in attracting and retaining industry. Whether real or not, the perception of the mobility of firms and capital has limited the range of policy instruments used by governments.

Although the usual interpretation of the international environment is that it weakens domestic policy instruments, especially those with an economic basis, and generally reduces the latitude of national governments, the contrary argument can also be made. The external environment also becomes a means of strengthening the hands of national governments and furnishes them tools that might not be palatable in normal domestic politics. For example, the Maastricht Treaty empowered the governments of Italy and Belgium, among others, to impose fiscal controls that might not otherwise have been possible in those rather divided political systems (Mann, 1997; Della Cannanea, 1996, especially chapter 1). Further, the ability to externalize the blame for any hardships imposed in meeting these criteria minimizes the blame potentially heaped on the politicians. NAFTA does not appear to have as yet created these benefits for North American politicians, but it may yet do so. The World Trade Organization (WTO), on the other hand, has been a substantial boon to the powers of American leaders attempting to control the effects of trade on the American economy; the WTO in essence has provided the president a whole new set of instruments that could be invoked to regulate international trade.

Similarly, international negotiations and agreements made it possible to support an electronics industry that otherwise might have been ruined by international competition ("Aeronatique: l'offensive americaine," 1999). This might not have been possible through conventional domestic policy instruments given American aversion to industrial policy. However, by negotiating international regulatory agreements it was possible to provide help less expensively than using domestic subsidies.

II. LINKING POLITICS AND INSTRUMENTS

The above discussion has suggested a framework for analyzing the politics involved in the choice of policy tools, but it has only begun to make the linkage between specific tools and the political characteristics that may influence their selection. The extant literature on this topic is rather meager, however, and the attempt to make that linkage can only propose hypotheses rather than provide definitive conclusions. The question, however, can be addressed in two ways. One is to think about the general characteristics used to describe tools (see Salamon, this volume). The other is to think about whether particular types of tools are more subject to one form of explanation than another. Both of these approaches provide some purchase on the issue, but neither offers a complete picture of the complex patterns of influence of political considerations on the tools.

Dimensions of Instruments

The introduction to this volume pointed to several crucial dimensions of policy tools. These dimensions are useful not only for understanding the nature of instruments, but even more so for understanding the selection of those instruments.

Visibility

One crucial political dimension of a tool is its visibility, or the extent to which the cost of the instrument being used is apparent to the public, whether that is the public in general or the more attentive public. In his earlier work on instruments, Salamon (1981,

p. 271) argues that more powerful political interests will be successful in having their benefits delivered through less visible means. The low visibility makes those benefits less obvious to potential competitors, and to taxpayers, and hence means that there will be less overt opposition to retaining the program. A similar argument may explain why governments make social benefits visible, whereas benefits for the middle class are less visible, for example, in the form of tax expenditures (Howard, 1997).

The more contentious a policy arena, the more difficult it may be to keep benefits invisible. In environmental policy, for example, industry and environmentalists often disagree fundamentally over the desirable nature of policy and have generated a visible and often confrontational policy regime that makes use of highly visible policy tools.

Finally, for political actors, the selection of visible tools may be desirable rather than undesirable. If the benefits of a program are highly concentrated then it may be wise to keep them less visible, but if those benefits are widely dispersed then making the benefits visible to the recipients may be beneficial. In the present era of substantial public skepticism about government programs, however, there are strong political incentives for keeping costs invisible, which may explain the popularity of tools such as tax expenditures and loan guarantees.

Directness

A second important dimension of policy tools is their directness, or the extent to which they operate directly on their intended targets. Salamon (1981) considered the impacts of this dimension on both the implementation capacity of instruments and their political attractiveness, noting that indirect tools have the great political advantage of attracting support from provider groups. To be sure, direct tools can offset this by establishing direct ties between citizens and the public sector.

Where these ties are positive, they can build legitimacy for government and strengthen the institutions delivering the service. The good news for the public sector is that the interactions of government officials and the public appear on average to be as good as are those of representatives of private-sector firms with their clients (Goodsell, 1981). At the same time, there is not much evidence that these interactions have actually done much to enhance government legitimacy. Greater directness in policy instruments therefore may not do much for building political support for direct tools. On the other hand, private-sector service providers such as banks and not-for-profit social service agencies have a great deal to gain from employing indirect policy instruments.

Finally, ideas in the form of political ideologies also may have some influence over the selection of more or less direct policy tools. Varone (1999) has argued that parties of the political left are more likely to adopt direct policy instruments, whereas those on the political right tend to opt for more indirect tools. This is so because indirect tools tend to disguise government involvement and leave a wider arena for individual choice, both of which are attractive to the political right.

Automaticity

Some policy tools tend to rely on existing processes, whereas others require new administrative arrangements and extensive administration. This dimension is in some ways like the direct and indirect dimension already discussed. Automaticity has, however, the additional element that any form of decision may be avoided in an automatic program, whereas an indirect program may still require a decision by the provider in the private sector—the bank must decide if the prospective student will receive the loan.

The political effects of automaticity are similar to those of directness. More automatic

programs may save on administrative costs, but also miss the opportunity to build
political coalitions, in this case either with recipients or with the intermediate institutions that might deliver the service. On the other hand, however, automatic programs
also tend to be less visible, and they therefore have some of the political advantages of
hiding a program from scrutiny. Further, in an era of great distrust of institutions, the
ability of citizens to implement the programs themselves may be seen as an advantage.

Individual Tools and Politics

The alternative way of approaching the issue of linking tools and politics is to ask
whether particular tools are more amenable to one form of explanation than are others.
Interests are always looming as the *eminence grise* of explanations, but there are also a
variety of other linkages of politics and tools. It is difficult to provide a complete
tabulation of all these linkages, given the numerous explicit and implicit ways in which
each of the five explanations may affect the selection of a policy tool. However, several
of the more important linkages can be identified.

Direct Government and Institutions

One of the clearest political linkages is between the direct provision of government
services and the nature of government institutions. For government to provide a service
directly requires the use of public bureaucracies, and those bureaucracies in turn have
the opportunity to shape the choice of tool. This opportunity for shaping tool choice
may be even more evident in the management of the tool than in its initial selection.
We know well, for example, that "street-level bureaucrats" are crucial in defining the
actual meaning of a program through their involvement in implementation (Lipsky,
1980; Brehm and Gates, 1999).

Social Regulation and Ideas

More than other policy tools, social regulation is dependent on ideas for its adoption
and for its effectiveness. Most of the programs identified as social regulation, such as
environmental and consumer safety regulations, have developed out of the spread of
policy ideas and their subsequent political manifestation as social movements (Tarrow,
1999). Although this tool is in some ways analogous to economic regulation, there is
a more central role for ideas in defining the nature of the tool and its targets. These
ideas have been crucial in contending with, and to some extent overcoming, prevailing
ideas of economic liberalism in American policy.

It is also important to note here the extent to which the idea of regulation has become
institutionalized in organizations such as the Environmental Protection Agency or the
Consumer Products Safety Commission. These organizations have tended to lock themselves into the set of ideas that were operational at the time of their formation, so that
they tend to perpetuate those ideas, and may socialize new members of the organization
into an institutional culture, creating a "logic of appropriateness" within the structure
(March and Olsen, 1989). Such institutionalization can be challenged by new ideas,
however, as the growth of economic-based instruments seems to be doing recently in
the regulatory realm.

The recent widespread interest in the tool of vouchers may also reflect the influence
of political ideas on tool choice. While there is a good deal of economic analysis that
can justify or undermine the use of vouchers, there is also a strong ideological logic in
the advocacy of this instrument related to the use of market-based approaches that
maximize individual choice as contrasted to collective choice through government.

Interests and Tax Expenditures

Interests also are more closely linked with some instruments than with others. Perhaps the clearest linkage is between interests and tax expenditures. As noted above, a dominant interest may have a strong reason to press for adopting a policy tool such as tax expenditures that disguises the true impact of the policy from the majority of the population. This lack of visibility not only enables the interest to achieve its policy goals without as much opposition as might be encountered, but also makes the winners and losers from the policy more ambiguous than they might be otherwise.

Individuals and Regulation

The more bureaucratic discretion there is in a policy instrument, the more opportunity there is for individuals to shape the ultimate nature of the policy well after the initial choice of tool is made (see Lipsky, 1980). Thus, automatic instruments, such as most tax expenditures, that involve little or no discretion have little opportunity for individual influence over the outcomes.[12]

In some instances, for example, regulation, it has been argued that in the American policy system there is insufficient discretion for enforcement personnel. This can be problematic since there is some evidence that rigidity and a legalistic emphasis on strict adherence to rules tends to be less productive than negotiation and bargaining in producing compliance by potential violators (Lundquist, 1985; Bardach and Kagan, 1982; May, Chapter 5 in this volume).

The Problem of Strategy

We have to this point been discussing politics primarily in terms of the ways in which instrument choices could be explained. We could, however, stand that analytic question on its head and ask about the implications of the above explanatory concepts for the selection of political strategies. That is, assuming that political and/or bureaucratic leaders want to reach certain policy goals, the choice of the instrument becomes part of the "package" that must be sold if they are to be successful. Given that, these modes of explanation become versions of strategies.

For example, one strategy available to policy entrepreneurs is to identify the interests that may be affected by a program, and to find means of involving, or co-opting, them into accepting the proposal. As noted, the immediate beneficiaries are not the only likely targets, and providers (public and private) may be equally good places to begin the process. Indeed, for social programs these providers will be higher status and, ceteris paribus, better political allies than would the recipients. The role of the entrepreneur therefore may be one of building coalitions through the strategic selection of a policy tool. That coalition may be across a range of interested parties that may otherwise have little in common.[13]

The pork-barrel strategy for managing policy instruments assumes a rather different approach for coalition building and enhancing political feasibility. Under this strategy, the best instrument is the one that gives everybody something in the course of implementing a program. This approach works best when the principal interests to be appeased are geographical rather than functional, as is the case in building a coalition among Congressmen.[14] Intergovernmental grants and procurement appear particularly well suited for this political strategy, as has been demonstrated a number of times in military contracting and in the distribution of federal highway funds, *inter alia.*

An institutional strategy guiding instrument selection would rely more on the capacity of organizations, public as well as private, to determine the instruments being used for policy. So, the strategy of the instrument advocate/entrepreneur would be to select the instrument that engages the institution most likely to administer the program in a way consistent with program purposes. That is, given that institutions have predictable predispositions, the choice of instrument must take account of the predisposition of the implementing institutions it engages. This strategy assumes, of course, that the instrument choices are rather malleable and that the institution in question would indeed want to take the policy on board—in some cases a policy can be more of a poisoned chalice than an opportunity.

Politics As One Criterion: Problems of Choice

This chapter has emphasized the importance of politics in understanding instrument choice. Politics is, however, but one of a number of criteria that must be utilized when making a decision about instrumentation for a program. The problem for choice, therefore, is balancing political criteria with other equally important criteria such as the effectiveness of the instrument, its reliability (or certainty in producing the outcomes desired), and the relative costs of producing the outcomes with different types of instruments. All of these are important for the full evaluation of an instrument in any potential setting (Bemelmans-Videc, Rist, and Vedung, 1998).

Although nominally grounded on different conceptual and practical bases, the other criteria being applied may also be politicized. For example, during a period in which the costs of government are politically sensitive, lower cost programs may be more palatable to the public than are more expensive methods of reaching the same goals. This is true almost regardless of the relative effectiveness of the two instruments being considered. Indeed, given that decisions about policy instruments inevitably are made in a political arena, it may be difficult to avoid politicizing tool choices and making all criteria in practice political criteria.

The politicization of instrument choice is both a positive and a negative characteristic of decisionmaking in the public sector. On the one hand, politicization reflects reality and ensures that instruments are selected in conformity with the prevailing political values. It basically ensures the political feasibility of the instruments. On the other hand, there are numerous additional concerns about instruments that should perhaps be considered "objectively" rather than purely politically. While there is a hint of politically naive assumptions about objectivity in some discussions of instruments, there also can be excessively cynical assumptions about the inevitable dominance of political criteria in the policy process.

The practical challenge for the political analysis of policy instruments, therefore, is to balance manifestly political concerns with other concerns—economic, ethical, effectiveness—in making decisions about instruments. Further, there is a need to balance the several alternative conceptualizations of cause-and-effect relationships available for the design of policy and the selection of instruments. Each instrument involves a set of assumptions about individual and/or institutional behavior, and these assumptions further are assumed to provide the means for changing outcomes for the economy and society. Selecting an instrument to "solve" a public problem therefore is no simple technical exercise, but rather a complex balancing of values that are inherent in the political process.

NOTES

1. Despite the numerous, and often well-taken, critiques of the particulars of Lowi's framework, the basic point of the reciprocal influence of policy and politics remains valid, especially as we think about the selection of policy instruments.

2. In this instance, one would expect the latter because this is one of the least intrusive instruments that might be selected for influencing the economy, and the actors most concerned about regulation tend to be opposed to government intervention. Further, the history of regulation has been that the affected interests are often able to "capture" the regulators and thus produce a style of regulation that is beneficial to the regulated.

3. This constructionist view is especially common in European policy analysis. See Bressers, Pullen, and Schuddeboom (1990).

4. *Res ipsa locquitur,* or the facts speak for themselves. In some medical systems, if an individual sustains an injury or is mistreated in a public hospital there is no need to prove negligence or incompetence—the facts of injury are sufficient to merit compensation.

5. A French housing program (HLM) that provides assistance for low-income renters tends to be supported more by landlords and by the local governments that administer the program than by the renters (Garin, 1999) for whom it is a less than optimal program. One wonders whether the principal supporters of the U.S. Tax code are not lawyers and accountants?

6. This view has been particularly associated with the school of Canadian instruments scholars such as Woodside, Phidd, and Doern (see Linder and Peters, 1998 for a discussion of various national schools of thought).

7. This instrument did not fit neatly into the classificatory schemes usually used in this area. In Hood's (1986) terms it is at once an instrument that would have marshaled a great deal of treasure yet the fundamental political sticking point politically was the elaborate organizational format. See Peters, 1996.

8. That is, direct delivery may produce more equality of treatment than would indirect instruments. An example would be public education contrasted with voucher programs.

9. This reasoning obviously runs the risk of being, in a Popperian sense, nonfalsifiable, given that it is difficult to demonstrate that interests were not indeed the root causes of the behavior.

10. That is, he cared very much that the methods used conformed to his philosophy of non-violence.

11. The "stages" model implied here has been subject to a number of critiques, although still remains the principal form of description and analysis in political science.

12. There is some individual role in the decision to use an available tax expenditure and in how it is used (does the individual attempt to evade taxes illegally?).

13. Charles Lindblom referred to this style of coalition building as partisan analysis. The idea is that the entrepreneur attempts to "sell" a program that he or she wants in terms of the values and interests of the potential partners.

14. Also, this is more of an elite strategy, so that the participants are less likely to be unaware of the distribution of costs and benefits.

CHAPTER TWENTY

Policy Tools and Democracy

Steven Rathgeb Smith and Helen Ingram

To avoid the strictures of the Endangered Species Act, which can shut down development, a cooperative governance experiment is going on in Southern California. California developers, environmental groups, and state and local officials are cooperating in environmental restoration plans. State and county parks and wildlife officials meet with developers and environmentalists to anticipate problems with sensitive species before they occur. Developers receive permits to build on part of their land in exchange for the dedication of some lands for habitat and funding of restoration work. Environmental groups, including the Nature Conservancy, have agreed to supervise and provide volunteers for restoration activities.

This kind of locally based, cooperative governance has implications for democracy. Environmental restoration gains in terms of public support as developer opposition to species protection is lessened. At the same time, democratic accountability may be compromised as environmental groups receive funding for collaboration in restoration activities they are supposed to monitor. Further, the absence of public controversy about growth in environmentally sensitive areas may undermine the possibility of a broader public debate about growth/environment tradeoffs.

Since the earliest days of the Republic, Americans have been skeptical of their government. Throughout the nineteenth century and into the twentieth century, we resisted the growth of the federal government. While the New Deal represented a watershed in terms of the role of the federal government in American life, many of the New Deal initiatives were temporary. It was not until the 1960s when a major, enduring expansion of government occurred. During the 1960s and thereafter, the federal government, as well as state and local governments, assumed new responsibilities in many policy fields, including social policy, the environment, consumer protection, and education.

Contrary to popular belief though, the growth of the federal government has not been primarily through direct government. Instead, it has been through a variety of more indirect means: contracting with private nonprofit and for-profit organizations, tax credits, vouchers, regulation, and loans, to name just a few. To a large extent, the debate on the merits of these policy tools has focused on efficiency and effectiveness considerations. If we contract with private organizations, does the federal government save money? Are tax credits to support low-income housing a good use of the taxpayer's money? Are faith-based social services supported with government funds more effective than other types of social service agencies?

In this chapter, we argue that the ongoing discussion about the many and varied indirect policy tools pays too little attention to the impact of these policy tools on citizen participation, democracy, and citizenship. We contend that these impacts should be closely scrutinized by policymakers because fundamental values are at stake.

We argue, then, that the choice of policy tools can fundamentally affect the governance of American public policies, including the opportunities for citizens to be involved in public affairs, the accountability of publicly funded programs to the citizenry, the access of citizens to public services, and the rules and procedures regulating publicly funded programs. Further, differences exist among policy tools in their effect on citizen involvement in the policy process.

To make this argument, we initially discuss the inadequacy of conventional policy analysis in assessing the linkage between policy tools and democracy. We then identify the fundamental features and characteristics of democracy that might be affected by different policy tools. The heart of the chapter is then devoted to an assessment of the relationship between some of the basic dimensions of policy tools—including *directness, visibility, automaticity,* and *coerciveness*—and various aspects of democracy. We conclude by offering strategies for policymakers and citizens to consider to ensure that the choice of policy tools does not have a negative effect on democracy and on the capacity of public managers to be responsive to citizen concerns.

I. TOOL CHOICES AND DEMOCRACY: A BLIND SPOT

In the last twenty-five years, the role of government and the relationship between citizens and their government have undergone dramatic change. Beginning in the 1960s, the left and the right attacked the bureaucracy, particularly the federal bureaucracy, for different failures related to democracy.[1] The left attacked the bureaucracy due to concerns about the deprivation of individual rights and inequities in the provision of government services. The right shared similar concerns but was also concerned about governmental inefficiency and the stifling of grass roots problem-solving initiative. Across the political spectrum, it was argued that conventional approaches to governmental accountability and ideas of democracy did not work because bureaucrats possessed broad discretion that made it difficult for either elected representatives or citizens to hold bureaucrats accountable.

These attacks on the bureaucracy prompted a rethinking of government, public management, and the tools of government and a receptivity to new approaches to solving public problems. This shift in thinking about the design of governance has yet to produce a parallel shift in policy analysis and evaluation, however. Although it has long been recognized that the means of public policies are at least as important as their ends, and that policies have ancillary effects that extend far beyond the putative goals, conventional frameworks of policy analysis continue to focus on effectiveness and efficiency and downplay or overlook the impact that the choice of tool might have for democracy and citizen involvement. For example, most contemporary studies of welfare reform concentrate on the numbers of welfare mothers who have found gainful employment and the percentages of households removed from the welfare roles. Relatively few studies have focused on the impact of experience with third-party welfare bureaucracy on citizen propensity to participate politically.[2] Most studies of the Comprehensive Environmental Response, Compensation, and Liability Act of 1980 (Superfund) have concentrated on the high cost and slow process of site identification, assessment, ranking, listing, remediation design, and clean up as well as the difficulties in locating hazardous waste treatment and disposal sites.[3] Far less attention has gone into the effects of Superfund on grass roots initiative in solving problems and citizen perceptions of the role of government and of citizen responsibilities.[4] The relative scarcity of studies of the impacts of tool choice on citizenship and democracy is all the more serious at a time when the landscape of governance is undergoing as fundamental a change as it is today.

II. DIMENSIONS OF DEMOCRACY,
CITIZENSHIP, AND CIVIC PARTICIPATION

567

CH 20:
POLICY
TOOLS AND
DEMOCRACY

To understand the impact that tool choices can have on citizenship and democracy, it is necessary to begin with a clear notion of the basic dimensions of these phenomena. American democracy is an unfinished, open-ended project. As John Dryzek has argued, governance is in large part a striving to expand the *franchise, scope,* and *authenticity* of democracy.[5] *Franchise* refers to the number of active participants in any political setting. *Scope* concerns the domains under public control. *Authenticity* is the degree to which democratic control is substantive, informed, and competently engaged. Citizenship is an identity or role that supports democracy. According to Mark Landy, citizenship is reducible neither to narrow utilitarian calculus nor to abstract ethical rumination. The ideal citizen is one who can synthesize questions of individual self-interest and public interest. Citizenship involves not only rights and privileges but willingness to make sacrifices. Civic participation must be closely related to the requisites of deliberation. Deliberation suggests balanced engagement in a discursive process in which learning and discovery take place.[6] It is important that in the pursuit of stronger democracy and more robust citizenship and participation, one value not be sacrificed in pursuit of another. For instance, broadened franchise and participation are not worthwhile if it comes at the expense of authentic, informed deliberation.

The long-standing emphasis on a sharp dichotomy between politics and administration in classic public administration has led to a general neglect of the extent to which administration, including the selection of tools, affects democracy, citizenship, and civic participation. Insofar as democracy, citizenship, and participation have been matters of concern in administration, it has generally been in relation to curbing the excesses of centralized bureaucracy. Especially during times in which patterns of governance are undergoing fundamental change, it is important to examine carefully whether expansion or contraction of democracy is taking place.

Expansion of the Franchise

Identification of citizens with government is critical to franchise. For the better part of our nation's history, fundamental attachment of the country's population was primarily to localities, states, and regions. As political historian Laura Jenson has effectively demonstrated, beginning shortly after the Revolutionary War, the allocation of veterans benefits through direct policy tools bound generations of men and their families to the national government.[7] The attachment of citizens to the nation grew enormously during the New Deal when direct involvement of the vast majority of workers in social security and other beneficial social programs dramatically heightened the salience and importance of national citizenship.

The choice of indirect policy tools that decrease the level and visibility of government as a source of values may well affect franchise. Moreover, policy tools that make the hand of government virtually invisible to the recipients of beneficial policy (e.g., grants-in-aid), while keeping it quite visible to those affected by restrictive policies (e.g., regulation), may cause an alienation from the central government.

Scope of Democracy

The scope of democracy is limited by the inability of disadvantaged citizens to participate fully in American life. As T. H. Marshall and others have argued, federal redistributive policies that guarantee civil, political, and social rights to all citizens so that they might participate equally in all spheres of society are critical.[8] As Salamon (Chapter 18 in this volume) has indicated, some tools are much more effective at redistribution than others. The choice of policy tools that are ineffective at redistribution or that are biased in favor of some and not others will have a negative impact on the scope of democracy. For example, research conducted by Suzanne Mettler supports the hypothesis that men of color and women were treated very differently from white males in the policy tools chosen by the New Deal, and that these differences persisted.[9] A kind of dual citizenship was created: Social Security and the Fair Labor Standards Act applied mainly to white men in nonagricultural employment and were administered directly by the federal government, but Aid to Families with Dependent Children and Unemployment Insurance applied to women and minorities were administered indirectly through the states. The choice of third-party government tools deprived men of color and women of equal treatment and also deprived them of the social and economic status requisite to effective citizenship.

Authenticity of Democracy

Informed consent is basic to democratic governance. Paul Posner (Chapter 18 in this volume) has indicated the extent to which the choice of tool can affect accountability, that is, the ability of the citizen to hold government responsible for policy performance or even to know what policies and programs are being pursued. From a democratic authenticity standpoint, the preferable policy tools are those that generate and deliver sufficient and balanced information. Experience with policy should be a learning process in which both administrators and citizens become better informed. Yet, some policy tools obscure action and generate information imbalances.

In an era in which large numbers of citizens are disengaged and alienated from government, policy tools that promote citizen participation and involvement are generally thought to be beneficial to the authenticity of democracy. However, mobilization alone is not sufficient. Informed engagement must reflect the real consequences of policy on the public. Policy tools can mobilize only a portion of the affected population and reflect only narrow interests. The result is that on the surface policies would seem to command a good deal of public support, and yet latent opinion may exist that simply has not been stimulated by the policy tools being employed.

Citizenship and Democracy

Engagement in authentic discourse requires citizens with a capacity for empathy and regard for others. Such citizens must also be positively oriented toward civic activism and willing to devote time and energy to public life. The extent to which people adopt and take seriously the role of actively engaged citizens can clearly be affected by the tools and policies pursued by government. The direct, highly visible benefits afforded veterans of World War II through the GI Bill resulted in significantly higher levels of participation in civic and political associations by recipients when compared with other veterans. Part of the explanation lies in the way in which policy altered civic roles and identities. This occurred through offering people a direct, visible, and highly positive experience of government and public provision, endowing recipients with a greater sense of membership in the polity.[10]

Once citizens are positively oriented toward government and other citizens, they are more inclined toward contributing toward the building of social capital. As articulated by Robert Putnam, social capital refers to networks and relationships characterized by trust and cooperation. Putnam argues that communities with higher levels of social capital are more likely to have citizens satisfied with their government and more effective public services.[11] In addition, Lisbeth Schorr in her important book, *Common Purpose,* calls attention to the link between the quality of life in communities and the outcomes of social policy initiatives.[12] Communities with active citizen participation in policy initiatives such as fighting crime or drug abuse are more likely to be effective. More recently, scholars such as Ronald Ferguson and Xavier de Souza Briggs have argued that community development needs to be reconceptualized to emphasize the citizen involvement and the building of cooperative social networks, if community development projects are to be successful.[13] This viewpoint has also been persuasively argued by policymakers and scholars working in the international development field in developing countries.[14]

III. CHARACTERISTICS OF TOOLS AND IMPLICATIONS FOR DEMOCRACY

The choice of policy tools is fundamental to the relationship of government and citizenry, and the rise of third-party government introduces sometimes surprising changes. As the discussion of different dimensions of tools will illustrate, a tool may have positive impacts on one aspect of democracy, perhaps franchise or support building, but it may have negative effects on another, such as equity and democratic authenticity. Further, policy tools must be considered in context. Previously adopted policy tools in a policy area set up expectations that subsequent tool choices may reinforce or change. Moreover, policy tools often occur in combination, and it is the entire political economy set in motion by the cluster of tools that must be taken into account.

Despite these caveats, it is possible to identify certain characteristic relationships between particular classes of tools and some of the key dimensions of democracy identified above. To see this, let us look at the consequences for democracy of the four basic characteristics of tools used throughout this book: *directness, visibility, automaticity,* and *coerciveness.*

Direct Policy Tools, Equity, and Public Support

Direct policy tools have the advantage of directly linking citizens with their government, and New Deal social programs such as Social Security and veterans programs such as the GI Bill have been highly popular and effective in positively associating those citizens who benefited with government. However, some constituencies have been underserved by such programs, and changes in the political context, including more negative attitudes toward bureaucracy, makes adoption of new programs with large-scale, direct provision of benefits unlikely. Further, the contemporary hostility toward government undermines support for some existing, directly administered programs.

Direct policy tools are the conventional mechanism through which to correct for inequalities. Direct delivery mechanisms are often chosen in redistributive policies that serve poor, insular minorities in such areas as civil rights and poverty. As Lester Salamon observes in the first chapter, redistributive goals often are sacrificed in complex delivery systems. At the same time, direct tools may not build the support, or franchise necessary for democratic policy. As James Q. Wilson has noted, direct government is perceived to have a "bureaucracy problem" characterized by problems of efficiency and responsiveness.[15] While made up of perhaps equal proportions of reality and myth, there can be no question that the case against bureaucracy has shaped public and political perceptions on the proper role of government. Bureaucracies have been charged with pursuing organizational agendas that maximize budgets and numbers of employees but not necessarily the public interest. Often very narrowly constructed public employee or clientele groups have benefited, while disadvantaged groups were ignored. Centralized bureaucracies can be inflexible when faced with varying local conditions and are slow to innovate. These bureaucracy problems make it very difficult to mobilize citizen support for redistributive public programs. For the most part, the public is not engaged in supporting these programs or holding them accountable.

Public support for programs employing direct policy tools that deliver benefits and bring equity to dependent populations is usually narrow, often limited to government service employees. These programs often do not enjoy widespread political clout due in part to the growing skepticism of government programs in the United States as well as the powerlessness of those they serve. Public hospitals offer a good example. At one time they were the key health-care delivery organizations in many communities, especially in the rural South and large urban areas. However, these hospitals have experienced a wave of closures throughout the country as government curtailed its direct commitment to health care, especially health care for the poor.

Indirect Tools, Participation, and Support

The growth of third-party government raises many concerns pertaining to citizen participation in public policy. Direct government has established norms and conventions on the extent to which citizens can participate in policymaking. For instance, if the local municipal Office of Economic Development is not doing its job, a citizen can complain to his or her city councilor or the mayor. The Office of Economic Development, in turn, is obligated to be responsive to citizens, although in practice public agencies may fall well short of responsiveness.[16] Or, if a citizen is dissatisfied with the municipal parks department, he or she can take his or her grievances to the department. If this person does not receive satisfaction, direct contact with the city council may be pursued, but what happens when the municipal parks department contracts out the operation of the city zoo to the nonprofit Friends of the Zoo. The zoo will now be governed by a private board of directors. Citizens will not have the same standing in relationship to this private nonprofit, greatly complicating the process by which citizens might participate in the governance and oversight of the zoo. Likewise, the city council will not be in the same position to exercise oversight, although to be sure contracts to operate the zoo can be written to encourage or require specific practices and procedures.

In short, indirect policy tools frequently do not have obvious and/or conventional means for citizens to be involved in policy governance and management. Indirect policy tools rely extensively on private, nonprofit, and for-profit organizations as well as quasi-governmental authorities such as public development authorities. Consequently, the governance of public services shifts at least in part to private agencies whose accountability structures and relationship to the citizenry are much different from those of government agencies. This indirectness requires rethinking traditional approaches to citizen involvement and participation in public policy.

At the heart of this problem is the lack of an easily definable public role since indirect policy tools blur the boundaries between the public and private, obscuring the role of the public sector in addressing specific public problems. Consider the consequences of the increased public policy reliance on the relatively indirect policy tools, contracting, and vouchers. In the last twenty-five years governments have increasingly relied on nongovernmental agencies to provide services, either directly through government contracts and grants or indirectly by providing vouchers to individuals who then use the voucher to purchase a service such as schooling or housing.[17] The growth of contracting and vouchers has important implications for citizen attitudes toward government. First, it can alter the very character of direct government services. For example, in situations of extensive contracting, government agencies may be consigned to provide services to the most difficult clients, while other services are contracted out to private agencies. This issue is also apparent in the debate about school vouchers, with many educators expressing concern that vouchers will facilitate an exodus of the most able students from public schools, leaving these schools with a disadvantaged student body, further undermining the quality and reputation of the public schools.

Second, contracting and vouchers diverts attention and resources from the public sector; thus, citizens do not necessarily connect the public services they receive from private nonprofit contractors to government, even though they are supported by public funds. The long-term result is to restructure the relationship between citizens and government. Citizens increasingly interact with private entities rather than government even when they are the beneficiaries of government funding. Government's reputation may suffer because it appears that the private sector, rather than government, is successfully addressing public problems.[18]

The current welfare-to-work programs offer an instructive example of these problems. Many state and local governments contract out welfare-to-work programs to private nonprofit and for-profit entities. These programs are often held to specific performance targets, but the structure of the contracts limits the ability of agency staff, board members, volunteers, and clients to be involved in the accountability process. Moreover, contracting allows governments to shift the risk of program failure to the private agencies, even as government retains control of performance assessment and funding. Welfare-to-work becomes a private agency problem rather than a governmental responsibility. For example, many nonprofit welfare-to-work programs receive most of their revenue from the government, but most citizens may not realize that these agencies have a significant public role. Further, even if the citizen knows that an agency receives public funds, the agency may not have established procedures to involve this person in the governance of the agency. Indeed, some agencies may make it very difficult for the person to be involved.

The privatization of governance is an even greater concern with the rise of many third-party organizations such as managed care firms, which contract with government to manage entire welfare or child welfare departments. These firms—which subcontract with local service agencies—have little incentive to involve a broad spectrum of the local community in governance, especially since many managed care firms are part of large for-profit chains. Moreover, managed care firms make the relationship between government and the citizenry even more indirect, thus creating even further obstacles for citizens to involve themselves in the policy process.

Contracting, vouchers, and other indirect policy tools do enlist new constituencies in the politics of public services. In some policy areas, political support may actually evolve to be both deep and broad. As contracting for services with private organizations has continued to expand throughout the country, for example, contract agencies— whether for-profit or nonprofit—have become a client of government policy, with a keen stake in government funding and regulatory policy. In response, service providers often organize politically, both individually and collectively. For instance, at the state level, statewide associations exist for the providers of an array of services, including home care, child care, residential child welfare, drug and alcohol treatment, and food banks, to name just a few. These associations advocate for the providers politically, help members address issues of mutual concern, and serve as an entirely new constituency for public funding.[19]

However, the new constituencies for contracted services extend beyond just the provider associations; they also include the board members and staff of the individual providers. Contracting enlists these individuals in the support of contracting. Since many service providers also have connections to their communities or are considered to be community assets, contracting also creates support for public funding in local communities.

Similarly, the Low Income Housing Tax Credit (LIHTC) created in the mid-1980s has a legion of supporters on Capitol Hill and at the state and local level. The design of the program requires the participation of private investors, lawyers, consultants, community organizations, and state and local government, to name just a few. Not surprisingly, the program expanded substantially in the last fifteen years, despite the efforts of leading members of Congress to cut it back.[20]

Vouchers also create new supporters. For example, the Section 8 housing voucher program has become an important income source for landlords and housing developers. Political support for Section 8 remains very high, although congressional appropriations have not nearly satisfied the demand. Based on the experience of housing vouchers, one would also predict that as vouchers for public and private education become more common, private educational institutions will become important constituencies for them.

While the use of indirect policy tools can create networks and mobilize political support, however, this mobilization does not translate easily into accountability over the implementation of the policy tools. A couple of examples illustrate this point. Contracting for child welfare residential services attracts the keen interest and support of private nonprofit and for-profit child welfare agencies. Associations representing these providers lobby for public contract funds and work with state administrators to craft appropriate regulations, but for the most part these contract agencies resist performance measurement and evaluation. Their primary advocacy goals focus on rate increases and favorable regulations rather than program effectiveness. To be sure, many of these agencies provide good services, but it is nonetheless true that child welfare services remain a deeply troubled area of public policy across the country. In most states, private (usually nonprofit) contract agencies are heavily involved in providing these services.

Performance evaluation and judicious analysis often get shunted to the sidelines in these policy debates. The politics of advocacy groups is in part rooted in the formation of these groups, which occurs in response to new government programs. Advocacy groups today need to frame their issue to appeal to the media and their own supporters and fundraising imperatives.[21] For example, statewide associations of home-care providers who receive government contracts need to focus on obtaining higher rates and favorable regulations for their members. Even though the staff are also interested in broader health-care concerns, including health care for the uninsured, it is difficult for the staff to advocate aggressively for these other issues. Association staff are usually tiny and resources scarce, leaving little time for involvement in nonpriority concerns. The national association of home-care providers have more resources, but the orientation of the association remains the same due to the expectations of the members.

Advocacy also means winning on terms agreeable to the associations and individual organizations. For instance, nonprofit and for-profit low-income housing organizations vie for influence in trying to obtain contracts or favorable regulations. Winning means success as defined by the organization. This is not to imply that these wins may not be good public policy. For example, low-income housing organizations are a very positive force in many disadvantaged communities. However, the politics of low-income housing means that it is very difficult for policymakers to address issues such as efficiency, responsiveness, and accountability.

Indirect Policy Tools and Fragmentation

Forty years ago, most public services were delivered in large government agencies. Citizens had relatively few choices and within a particular community services in a particular policy area, such as welfare or mental health, tended to be quite centralized. Indirect policy tools have opened up the possibility of providing public services through a much more diverse set of public and private agencies. The diversity of the service system is nothing short of amazing compared with forty years ago. However, the flip-side of diversity is fragmentation. Service agencies now occupy relatively small market niches serving a relatively targeted clientele. Thus, a recipient of assistance under the new federal welfare program may need to go to several different public and private agencies to receive assistance: one agency for the income maintenance benefits; another agency for training; and another agency for child care. The list can be quite long.

Policy fragmentation can make collaboration in support of important policy goals such as improving community health care or reducing drug abuse in a neighborhood quite challenging since it requires the joint action of many different agencies with quite varied missions and organizational goals. It can also make the participation of lay people in local affairs more difficult since many policy arenas are dominated by the many service agencies receiving direct and indirect assistance from government.

What has been lost in the growth of third-party government is the dominant, central public bureaucracy in a particular policy area, such as child welfare or public housing. This has made citizen organizing more difficult. To underscore this point, many unions have tried to organize new service agencies receiving public funds, such as nursing homes and home health agencies. However, the fragmented nature of the industries at the local level greatly complicates union organizing by raising the expense of organizing and dispersing services into many local private nonprofit and for-profit agencies.

Visibility/Invisibility and Democratic Participation

The proliferation of policy tools such as grants-in-aid, contracting for services, vouchers, tax credits, and loan guarantees in the last twenty-five years was fueled by a widespread desire to develop alternatives to the national state. These new tools would be closer to the people, more accessible, and less alienating. In practice it has not worked out as envisioned, in part because of the lack of visibility of many of these policy tools.

The visibility/invisibility of a policy tool is a key factor affecting its operation (Salamon, this volume). Insight into the specific impact of the visibility/invisibility of a policy tool on democracy and citizen participation is suggested by the work of Theodore J. Lowi[22] and James Q. Wilson.[23] Although their work differs in important ways, both scholars argue that the perception of costs and benefits faced by the citizenry is the critical determinant of which citizens and groups organize around a particular policy issue. For instance, Wilson uses the concept of distributed and concentrated costs and benefits. In the case of domestic sugar policy, the cost of high sugar prices is widely distributed and largely hidden in the overall price of sugar; consumers do not perceive that our domestic sugar policies are excessively costly or onerous. The result is a lack of protest or even interest in sugar policy on the part of most citizens. However, sugar producers reap enormous benefits from America's sugar policies so they are very involved in this issue, which remains largely debated outside of public view (since few citizens really care). In the same tradition, Wilensky suggested that America's smaller welfare state relative to Europe's was due to the heavy reliance of America on highly visible taxes such as the property tax rather than less visible taxes such as value added taxes characteristic of Europe. In America, people resist or protest higher taxes to support the welfare state because the specific taxes used are much more visible.[24]

Importantly, the issue of *perceived* costs and benefits also exists for policy tools. As noted, tax credits for low-income housing are a central means of financing low-income housing. These credits are quite complicated in terms of their implementation so most citizens are unaware of how they are used. However, these credits are enormously valuable to various nonprofit and for-profit housing developers, private investors, and third-party intermediaries. As a result, the politics of tax credits is similar to sugar politics: well-mobilized groups and providers with a direct material stake in the issue and a relatively disinterested public. Likewise, the policy debate on tax-exempt bonds has been almost completely dominated by state and local government finance agencies and large nonprofit institutions with a direct stake in the expansion of tax-exempt bond financing.

While the politics of particular policy tools may vary, as a general rule, citizens have tended to be relatively uninvolved in the politics of low-visibility policy tools such as tax-exempt bonds and tax credits. Other more highly visible policy tools such as vouchers tend to have more distributed costs and benefits. Consequently, the politics of vouchers have not been dominated by producer groups, but instead tend to be fought out at a broader ideological level among parties and various interest groups.

One other lesson to be drawn from the work of Wilson and Lowi is that the perceived role of government in connection with a policy tool may be very important in determining a citizen's broader view of government. The LIHTC is arguably an innovative approach to financing low-income housing that has been relatively free from major scandals and is administered by the Internal Revenue Service at the federal level and at the state level by state Housing Finance Commissions or Departments. However, this solid accomplishment of government may go unrecognized by the average citizen since the government is not directly and visibly building housing. Thus, a citizen's overall attitude toward government—and willingness to be engaged in political issues—may be affected in the long run. The lack of visibility of policy tools can exacerbate the problem of information asymmetry. Many government programs—whether direct or indirect—may not offer citizens the opportunity to be fully informed about the program. Thus, citizens may feel alienated and lack incentive to become engaged in the policymaking process on these programs.

Indirect policy tools such as tax credits, contracting with nonprofit and for-profit agencies, vouchers, and tax-exempt bonds can be difficult for many lay people to understand, even people who have some familiarity with a particular policy tool or area. Further, these indirect tools tend to hide the government's role and often require extra effort for citizens to obtain adequate information. Even when citizens realize that government is involved in a tax credit or contracting program, citizens may be unable to obtain the necessary information to be informed. This can be very discouraging and lead to disengagement and apathy on the part of citizens.

Two examples illustrate the above point. Typically, community development corporations (CDCs) receive tax credits to build low-income housing, but tax credit financing is very complicated, with many players in the nonprofit, public, and for-profit sectors. Even board members of CDCs find it very challenging to stay well informed on this issue. The complexity of tax credit financing creates obstacles to the goal of engaging local community members in the work of CDCs; instead, the boards of CDCs are often dominated by people from the housing and finance sectors.[25]

The other example is government contracting with a for-profit job training organization. Some community members may be upset that this agency is not providing quality service to the community. However, the agency is not obligated to disclose performance information to the community or even give community members standing in terms of access to their staff and board. Thus, the community will lack the necessary information to be in a position to challenge the agency on its programs.

The operation of many policy tools is so complex that, except for insiders, the role of government is masked. Citizens are often at a disadvantage in dealing with government programs because they lack sufficient information to judge the performance of these programs. Even when evaluations are done, moreover, they are often not disseminated broadly to local citizen and community groups. Thus, citizens lack the necessary information to critically evaluate programs that can profoundly affect their lives. This in turn can depress citizen involvement in the monitoring and oversight of these contract service agencies.

This information asymmetry problem has, in fact, spurred broad efforts to provide more information to citizens on the performance of public and private service organizations, including formal organizational report cards providing detailed information and outcome data on practices and procedures of key organizations such as hospitals.[26] And many cities, such as Portland, Oregon, have actively engaged citizens in evaluating the quality of municipal services.

Whether visibility and mobilization occur among the broad public or within only narrow constituencies has enormous import for democracy. Citizenship involves responsibility and commitment to the public welfare rather than simply the receipt of benefits and the assertion of rights. Democracy is not well served when governance is merely a contest among highly organized separate interests.[27] Hugh Heclo argues that we now have "hyperdemocracy" with almost too many groups and organizations involved in public policy. Every issue is highly politicized, with a variety of contending groups. Part of the reason for this widespread mobilization is changes in the media and technology that facilitate the engagement of new groups, including associations with scant resources, in the policy process. However, greater political mobilization also occurs in the context of an adversarial debate between advocacy groups where the public is disengaged. The contentiousness of these debates can ultimately produce citizen alienation and cynicism.[28]

Heclo's observations are directly relevant to our understanding of the linkage between policy tools and democracy. The expansion and proliferation of different policy tools encourages the formation of advocacy groups for these tools or programs. They are very mobilized in support of these programs; yet, the citizenry is largely disengaged. Further, these advocacy groups are interested in more public support for their programs; they are much less interested in programmatic accountability or the accountability of their groups to elected officials or the citizenry.

However, it is very important to emphasize that the visibility of a policy tool is related to the *perception* of its costs and benefits. Consequently, to the extent that this perception changes citizen participation and the overall constellation of groups involved in an issue will also change. The LIHTC was initially a "sleeper" of a program, but as the potential benefits became more apparent, many more groups and individuals became involved. Welfare reform—a program implemented largely through contracting with private nonprofit and for-profit agencies—has attracted a host of groups and individuals as advocates for various sides of the issue, in part because various interests were able to portray the issue as a broad-based one affecting welfare recipients, service providers, and government agencies.

Automaticity

The allure of some indirect policy tools is their apparent automaticity: low-income housing tax credits depend on the private investment market; contracting is based at least in part on the belief in the merits of market competition; and vouchers reflect a faith in consumer choice in the marketplace rather than decisions by government bureaucracies. Nongovernmental incentive systems and concerns replace those of government. Whether such incentive systems serve the interests of widening the franchise and scope of democracy and deepening its authenticity by providing public forums for deliberation and adequate information is incidental to the efficiency gains claimed from private or market processes. Moreover, automatic policy tools often are far less automatic in practice than theory would suggest, and the mechanisms necessary for their administration may have positive or negative impacts on democracy, depending on the context.

In order for contracting to work, for example, government needs to create an administrative apparatus to administer the funds and criteria to allocate them in a fair, equitable fashion. After the disbursement of funds, government also needs to create a monitoring system in order to ensure proper accountability. The overall effect is to create numerous opportunities for groups and organizations—although perhaps still not the lay public—to influence the contracting process.

As a generalization, though, indirect policy tools with characteristics of automaticity, however imperfect, do tend to make it very difficult for lay people to be engaged in the policy process since the existing systems they rely on, such as the private banking system or nonprofit service providers, are not subject to the same types of accountability requirements as direct government. To be sure, government can impose regulations on these private entities to enhance accountability, but it is often a very complicated process. For instance, the Community Reinvestment Act (CRA) requires banks to lend in disadvantaged neighborhoods. Over time, advocates for poor communities have used the CRA as an opportunity to intervene in the process of bank oversight, including bank applications for expansion and renewal. The process of bank certification has become less automatic, giving advocates for poor communities an opportunity to influence bank behavior. Indeed, the CRA has proved to be a surprisingly effective tool in pushing banks to do more lending in disadvantaged communities.

Coerciveness and Citizen Identity

As Lester Salamon observes in the introductory chapter, coercive policy tools are problematic for democracy in that the greater coerciveness a policy tool entails, the greater the infringement on individual liberty. Yet, authentic democracy involves willingness to sacrifice for the collective welfare as well as the assertion of rights. Democracy is reinforced when policy tools, such as social regulation, include clear prohibitions on actions, such as the release of highly toxic substances affecting public health, which are imposed equally on all polluters.[29]

Relatively coercive regulatory tools, according to Lowi,[30] have the highest probability of being democratic because they elicit general debate among contending coalitions of interests in legislative bodies as a whole. Broad principles are debated rather than particular favors to individual constituencies, as is the case in distributive policies. Moreover, the debate about regulatory tools engenders greater issue salience and broader public participation. However, coercion exercised against powerful interests can be politically very unpopular and introduce problems of insufficient public support.

The tendency is for legislatures to escape blame by passing general rules, while leaving detailed decisions, such as specifying targets, to regulatory agencies. Such general legislation leaves substantial discretion in the hands of regulatory agencies. Whether the implementation of regulatory tools is open, democratic, and participatory is problematic. An old and still-relevant literature suggests that regulatory agencies are often captured by regulated interests, especially at certain points in the life cycle of a regulatory agency.[31] At a minimum, regulatory agencies are dependent on the regulated for important information and general cooperation. Such relationships do not mean that regulation is responsive only to regulated interests. The institutional context is quite important here.[32] Regulatory tools wielded by strong, committed agencies, backed by supportive constituencies and overseen by legislative or other elected official watchdogs can succeed through fair and open rule-making processes. Environmental regulations at the state and federal levels provide convincing examples of effective and responsive regulation.[33]

Even in areas where relatively coercive regulatory tools are effective, regulation faces increasing criticism for being "command and control," which is imposing inflexible standards and mechanisms for compliance, insensitive to differences in local conditions or possible efficiencies that might be captured if the regulated were given more latitude. Many policy analysts, particularly economists, argue that greater use of market incentives (less coercion) requires less administration (greater automaticity) and allows and encourages regulated industries to discover and choose less costly ways to reduce pollution. Market incentives have been added onto and substituted for regulations in a number of areas. The 1990 Clean Air Act, for example, authorized emissions trading to reduce acid rain. At the local level, dozens of specific, relatively coercive regulations have been replaced in areas such as the Los Angeles basin with a less coercive market in air pollution credits.

Without question, regulated industries prefer economic incentives over regulations, and such incentives may be as effective in reducing air pollution, although this latter conclusion is less certain. However, pollution trading credits raise equity concerns. While uniform standards require reductions everywhere, trading credits may concentrate pollution in poor or minority neighborhoods within regional control areas. Moreover, less coercive market incentives may inadvertently send the wrong messages and lessons about values, citizenship, and democracy. Critics observe that relatively voluntary market incentives fail to stigmatize pollution and thus undercut the moral basis for environmental action. Using economic incentives may reinforce self-interested behavior that is damaging to the conception of citizenship as involving other-regarding norms such as obligation, duty, and sacrifice.[34] When policy tools aim to change target groups' behavior by inviting a market calculus, the action becomes individual, and people are encouraged to think like consumers. Such a stance is at odds with what Steven Kelman calls "public spirit"—the disposition to take serious account of the good of others and not just oneself in public life.[35]

Quite different kinds of problems arise when coercive tools are directed toward groups that are uninvolved and marginal in politics. One of the puzzles in the political participation literature is why some voters, who would seem to have an enormous stake in government programs because they are regularly targeted by various policies, are passive, quiescent, and often alienated from government.[36] Along with a paucity of resources, the messages some citizens receive in their experience with the tools chosen to deliver government programs to them explains their failure to participate. Some people experience government mainly through the enforcement of negative sanctions. The messages received by some groups related to democracy is that their plight is their own fault and that they deserve only punishment. If government pays any attention to such groups, it is likely to be unpleasant, and it is best to stay as far away from government as possible.

While there may be strong policy reasons for employing coercive tools to discourage certain practices, including drug use, the impact on how large numbers of certain categories of people perceive the role of government is dramatic. Consider that as many as a third of the black teenage population seems likely to spend at least some time in jail. Mandatory sentencing of drug offenders means that male African-Americans are especially likely to experience extreme coercion on the part of government. While drug use is about the same for whites and blacks, arrest rates are several times higher for blacks. Moreover, penalties are far stiffer for use of the drug of choice among blacks than it is for other drugs more favored by the dominant culture.[37] Of course, incarceration blocks direct political participation, communication from prisons is highly restricted, and even after release from jail the opportunity for political participation is low. Parole policies that prevent fraternization among ex-convicts discourage whatever political mobilization might take place to change conditions. For deviant populations, the experience with coercive tools provides every reason to avoid rather than engage in politics.[38]

Other groups, more positively constructed as dependents, are more likely to receive benefits, but means tests and other medium coercive eligibility restrictions adopted by many state welfare departments send messages that encourage passivity, resignation, and noninvolvement to citizen recipients.[39] One study of some Phoenix welfare mothers, whose comments in focus groups were recorded, illustrates messages sent and how orientations toward government were affected.[40] Slow and unreliable service, and seemingly capricious decisions, led welfare clients to believe that agency officials regarded them as unimportant, dishonest, and unworthy. For example, one welfare mother said:

> They're telling me 'you have 30 to 45 days to get your case done.' I told her I have rent to pay. I need my necessities. They can't understand that. They shrug their shoulders and say, 'well you still have 30 to 45 days, and they have other clients.' I understand that, but I complied and I did my part like you wanted me to. I was pre-approved. All you need to do . . . They're the ones who have the computer. You just put it in and send it. But they want to prolong it." Another woman added: "They act like it's coming out of their pocket. They act like when they get their check, they are going to each of their clients' houses and say, 'ok, here's your fifty, here's your fifty,' And they ain't giving me a dime.

These comments echo many heard by Joe Soss, who interviewed welfare clients in a mid-sized Midwestern city.[41] He found that only 8 percent of recipients believe that government listens to people like them. Such attitudes substantially affect willingness of target groups to participate in politics. Those who would seem to have the most to gain from participation in the design of the welfare system are least likely to become engaged. Moreover, the different messages received from tools by different racial and gender groups fuels the cleavages within American society and lowers the possibility of the citizens' empathy, which is crucial to authentic democracy.

IV. REDESIGNING POLICY TOOLS TO SERVE DEMOCRACY AND ENGAGE PARTICIPATION

A larger lesson of this examination of the implications of different policy tools for democracy is that the devil is in the details. Especially as delivery systems become less direct and more complex, increasing opportunities for ancillary positive and negative impacts on democratic governance exist. There are no certain strategies for choosing tools that promote democracy, since so much depends on particular contexts, and so little previous analysis has been done on the impact of policy design and choice of tools on citizenship and democracy.

A second lesson to be drawn from our discussion is that policy analysis and public management in the future must go beyond their traditional concerns with efficiency and effectiveness to attend much more carefully to the consequences of policy on citizenship and the formation of civic capital. To be sure, attempts to democratize public management and public policy have a long history. However, recent changes in public management and policy point the way to promising strategies for policy tool design and selection that are sensitive to the civic impact of policy tools.

Greater Openness and Transparency

Changes have been made to make administrative procedures more open, accessible, equitable, and democratic. Advance notice must be given of proposed rules changes, and the public must be given the opportunity to comment. Advisory committees with public members have been established to guide regulators and government administrators. The Freedom of Information Act (FOI) has been used by a number of citizen groups and individuals to force agencies to release information that otherwise would have been kept confidential. FOI requests have over time made government more transparent and more willing to make documents public. The National Environmental Policy Act of 1970 is a particularly notable reform in that it requires affected agencies to prepare documents in which they consider all reasonable alternatives to their proposed actions along with associated environmental impacts. Draft and final Environmental Impact Statement (EIS) are circulated to involved federal and state agencies and to the public for comment. As a result of this EIS process, the number of public meetings held by federal agencies prior to taking actions has expanded exponentially in recent decades.

Such administrative reforms have certainly made federal bureaucracies more responsive and accountable, although it is important not to exaggerate the extent to which they have created open, equitable forums. Administrative decisionmaking continues to be dominated by people with expertise. Moreover, public meetings often are poorly attended and dominated by a few vocal interests, and new procedures sometimes encourage endless disputation and procedural delays that benefit one or more parties. Disappointed losers often bring tactical suits in federal court on the basis of procedural irregularities. On balance, however, administrative reforms have moved federal bureaucracies in the right direction.

The Emergency Planning and Community Right-to-Know Act of 1986 introduced an interesting model for lowering the transaction costs of obtaining information critical to citizen education, mobilization, and participation. Under the legislation, industries must make public the amounts and location of releases of a large number of potentially damaging toxic substances. This act does have flaws, including its bias toward participants with high levels of expertise and the imperfect corporate compliance with it. Nevertheless, right-to-know has spurred citizen protests and community action. In this case, government is providing the public with critical information and fostering the creation of a sense of community with common stakes among all residents affected by exposure to dangerous substances.

Promoting Inclusive Decisionmaking

Another positive development is the shift by many federal agencies from the role of direct manager to the role of umpire of complex intergovernmental and public/private relationships, convening public meetings among affected partners to promote discourse in formulating and implementing shared goals. Grants are now sometimes designed so that local communities have a clear role in setting goals and allocating resources along with a clear obligation to deliberate. John Hird recently proposed such conditions on grants to clean up toxic waste sites.[42] In particular, he recommended the creation of a statewide citizens' committee to allocate funds. This committee would include ordinary citizens, some from communities with hazardous waste sites, as well as those concerned with other issues such as air and water pollution. This inclusive membership would make it much more likely that those pushing for expensive complete remediation at a very high cost would be challenged by others who would choose a lower level of clean up and spread the rest of the resources around other worthy environmental purposes. The result would be to reinforce the practices of empathy and discourse while encouraging more efficient and equitable allocation of money than through Superfund, which has been highly criticized.

Structurally, government has also moved to create various hybrid types of organizations—for example, community coalitions, public-private partnerships, and task forces—that involve the citizenry more directly in the assessment of community needs and the formulation of a response strategy. Empowerment zones, community coalitions to prevent substance abuse, and citywide initiatives such as the Atlanta Project to address the problems of the disadvantaged in Atlanta are just a few of the many examples of these new structural innovations that involve citizens in a new fashion in public service delivery and accountability.

Of course, some of these initiatives have not achieved their initial goals and aims. However, a record of experience now exists for many of these new types of community-based initiatives to allow for more specific and targeted advice for policymakers. We are now in a much better position to know what works and how to involve citizens in the decisionmaking process regarding the implementation of policy tools such as contracting and tax credits.

On other fronts, regulatory programs such as the Endangered Species Act can be supplemented with other environmental mediation programs that anticipate problems and put cooperative mechanisms in place to avoid command/control regulations. Ecosystem management, espoused by former Secretary Bruce Babbitt in the Department of Interior, envisions a holistic approach in which the needs of both people and wildlife are taken into account in a process that begins before species are listed. All the major stakeholders, including developers and environmentalists, are brought together to plan for habitat restoration and maintenance, and the government acts as the monitor of the binding agreements arrived at through mediated negotiations. Such experiences build communities at the same time as they avoid divisive conflict. Cortner and Moote write of the Trout Creek case where the issue was 250,000 acres of high desert grasslands, home to an endangered species of trout, and used for grazing by local ranchers in Oregon.[43] Environmentalists wanted the fish protected and threatened to sue the Bureau of Land Management. The Trout Creek Mountain Working Group, made up of a diverse group of neighbors and attended by agency officials, was able to agree to a three-year voluntary program of rest from grazing in the area. Throughout the rest period, the group met regularly and was able to settle on a pattern of grazing that protected the fish. The painstaking debate on ecological improvements had the side effect of greatly strengthening community ties.

Another example is illustrated by tax credits, often criticized as generally serving narrow interests and teaching the wrong lessons. Under carefully designed legislation, tax credits might be a tool to encourage civic engagement. For instance, the awarding of the LIHTC might be made conditional on the successful demonstration of community need reached through a deliberative process of community input.

Community Service

Guaranteed loan programs can also be designed to teach civic responsibility and empathy and to encourage civic engagement. Federally guaranteed student loans as presently operated encourage the accumulation of debt among younger citizens. In order to pay off student loans, young people often feel they must get lucrative jobs, even though the positions they choose lack public service opportunities. Further, because students pay back their loans to banks with interest, they are discouraged from feeling any particular obligation to society for their education. Experience suggests that altruism and public spiritedness are likely to become a habit in people early or not at all. Many nations outside the United States require several years of public service of young citizens, which may or may not be connected with publicly supporting their education. Service would be a much better way to repay, or pay in advance, for college loans. Service learning can also be built into school curricula through conditions for federal and state educational grants. A critical component of a liberal education needs to be the practice of citizenship through experiences with, and gaining empathy for, those who live in quite different social and economic circumstances than the typical college student.

V. TOOL DESIGN AS A DEVELOPMENTAL ACTIVITY

After reviewing the implementation of federal social programs of the 1960s and 1970s, Jeffrey Pressman argued that federal policy in urban areas needed to be conceptualized as a developmental strategy. He even suggested that federal urban aid be made conditional on certain institutional changes promoting greater democracy at the local level.[44]

Likewise, we believe that tool design should be attuned to its democratic implications. While devolution, decentralization, contracting, and other third-party, indirect tools of government have provided citizens with new possibilities to exercise choice and voice, they also create new problems and unanticipated consequences for democracy. The role of government is changing and must change further as direct service delivery gives way to cooperative management involving voluntary associations and public/private partnerships. Policy tools need to be redesigned to better serve democratic values. Government needs to be able to strategically intervene in the complex political economies surrounding policy delivery systems to encourage better access to information, to correct for power imbalances among stakeholders, and to create arenas and spheres for public discourse. Government must act as a conveyer of public dialogue, and protector of access, fairness, and balance in the implementation of third-party policy tools.

Public policy analysis and public management must emphasize different kinds of studies and training. Civic governance, democracy, participation, and citizenship must take their place along with efficiency, effectiveness, efficacy, and legitimacy as issues demanding attention. We need to know much more than we presently do about how different policy tools in various combinations affect civic capital in disparate contexts. Policy tools must be identified and/or invented that not only achieve program goals effectively and efficiently but also facilitate the growth of civic capital and the practice of citizenship.

VI. SUGGESTED READING

Cortner, Hanna J., and Margaret Moote. *The Politics of Ecosystems Management.* Washington, D.C.: Island Press, 1999.

Ingram, Helen, and Steven Rathgeb Smith, eds. *Public Policy for Democracy.* Washington, D.C.: The Brookings Institution, 1993.

Mettler, Suzanne. *Dividing Citizens: Gender and Federalism in New Deal Public Policy.* Ithaca, N.Y.: Cornell University Press, 1998.

Schneider, Anne Larson, and Helen Ingram. *Policy Design for Democracy.* Lawrence: University of Kansas Press, 1997.

Smith, Steven Rathgeb, and Michael Lipsky. *Nonprofits for Hire: The Welfare State in the Age of Contracting.* Cambridge, Mass.: Harvard University Press, 1993.

NOTES

1. Steven Rathgeb Smith and Deborah Stone, "The Unexpected Consequences of Privatization," in *Remaking the Welfare State,* ed. Michael K. Brown (Philadelphia: Temple University Press), 232–252; James Q. Wilson, "The Bureaucracy Problem," *The Public Interest* 6 (winter 1967).

2. Suzanne Mettler, *Dividing Citizens: Gender and Federalism in New Deal Public Policy* (Ithaca, N.Y.: Cornell University Press, 1998); Joe Soss, "Lessons in Welfare: Policy Design, Political Learning, and Political Action," *American Political Science Review* 93, no. 2 (June 1999): 363–380.

3. Daniel A. Mazmanian and David Morell, *Beyond Superfailure: America's Toxics Policy for the 1990s* (Boulder: Westview Press, 1992); U.S. Congress, Office of Technology Assessment, *Are We Cleaning Up?: 10 Superfund Case Studies* (Washington, D.C.: Government Printing Office, 1988); U.S. Congress, Office of Technology Assessment, *Coming Clean: Superfund Problems Can Be Solved* (Washington, D.C.: Government Printing Office, 1989).

4. Marc K. Landy, Marc J. Roberts, and Stephen R. Thomas. *The Environmental Protection Agency: Asking the Wrong Questions* (New York: Oxford University Press, 1990); John Hird, *Superfund* (Baltimore: Johns Hopkins University Press, 1994).

5. John S. Dryzek, *Democracy in Capitalist Times: Ideals, Limits, and Struggles* (New York: Oxford University Press, 1996).

6. Marc K. Landy, "Public Policy and Citizenship," in *Public Policy for Democracy,* eds. Helen M. Ingram and Steven Rathgeb Smith (Washington, D.C.: The Brookings Institution, 1993), 19–44.

7. Laura Jenson, "The Early American Origins of Entitlements," *Studies in American Political Development* 10 (fall 1996): 360–404.

8. Steven Rathgeb Smith, "The New Politics of Contracting: Citizenship and the Nonprofit Role," in *Public Policy for Democracy,* eds. Helen Ingram and Steven Rathgeb Smith (Washington, D.C.: The Brookings Institution, 1993), 163–197; T. H. Marshall, "Citizenship and Social Class," in *Class, Citizenship and Social Development: Essays* (New York: Doubleday, 1964), 71–134.

9. Mettler, *Dividing Citizens,* 1998.

10. Suzanne Mettler, "Bringing the State Back into Civic Engagement: World War II Veterans, the G.I. Bill, and American Citizenship," Unpublished paper, Department of Political Science, Syracuse University, Eggers 100, Syracuse, N.Y., 12344 (2000). smettler@maxwell.syr.edu.

11. Robert Putman, *Making Democracy Work* (Princeton, N.J.: Princeton University Press,

1993); Robert D. Putnam, *Bowling Alone: The Collapse and Revival of American Community* (New York: Simon and Schuster, 2000).

12. Lisbeth B. Schorr, *Common Purpose: Strengthening Families and Neighborhoods to Rebuild America* (New York: Anchor, 1997).

13. Ronald F. Ferguson and Sara Stoutland, "Recovering the Community Development Field," in *Urban Problems and Community Development,* eds. Ronald F. Ferguson and William T. Dickens (Washington, D.C.: The Brookings Institution, 1999), 33–75.

14. See Michael Woolcock, "Managing Risk, Shocks, and Opportunities in Developing Economies: The Role of Social Capital." Available at http://www.worldbank.org/poverty/scapital/library.htm.

15. Wilson, "The Bureaucracy Problem."

16. Michael Lipsky, *Street-Level Bureaucracy: Dilemmas of the Individual in Public Services* (New York: Russell Sage Foundation, 1980); James Q. Wilson, *Bureaucracy* (New York: Basic, 1989).

17. Lester M. Salamon, "Rethinking Public Management: Third Party Government and the Changing Forms of Government Action," *Public Policy* 29, no. 3 (summer 1981): 255–275; Lester M. Salamon and Michael S. Lund, "The Tools Approach: Basic Analytics," in *Beyond Privatization,* ed. Lester M. Salamon (Washington, D.C.: The Urban Institute, 1989), 23–50; Steven Rathgeb Smith and Michael Lipsky, *Nonprofits for Hire: The Welfare State in the Age of Contracting* (Cambridge, Mass.: Harvard University Press, 1993); Ruth Hoogland DeHoog, *Contracting Out for Human Services: Economic, Political and Organizational Perspectives* (Albany: State University of New York Press, 1984); DeHoog, this volume.

18. Steven Rathgeb Smith, "Government Financing of Nonprofit Activity," in *Nonprofits and Government: Collaboration and Conflict,* eds. Elizabeth T. Boris and C. Eugene Steuerle (Washington, D.C.: Urban Institute Press), 177–210.

19. Smith and Lipsky, *Nonprofits for Hire,* chap. 9; Claire F. Ullman, "Partners in Reform: Nonprofit Organizations and the Welfare State in France," in *Private Action and the Public Good,* eds. Walter W. Powell and Elisabeth S. Clemens (New Haven: Yale University Press, 1998), 163–176.

20. Steven Rathgeb Smith, "Government Financing of Nonprofit Activity."

21. Heclo Hugh, "Hyperdemocracy," *The Wilson Quarterly* 23, no. 1 (winter 1999): 62–71.

22. See Theodore J. Lowi, "American Business, Public Policy, Case Studies, and Political Theory," *World Politics* 16 (1964): 677–715; Theodore J. Lowi, "Four Systems of Policy, Politics, and Choice," *Public Administration Review* 32, no. 11 (1972): 298–310.

23. James Q. Wilson, *American Government* (Lexington, Mass.: D.C. Heath, 1979).

24. Harold L. Wilensky, *The Welfare State and Equality* (Berkeley: University of California Press, 1975).

25. The complexity of an issue can be disempowering and limit the discussion of an issue to professionals knowledgeable of the issue. For fuller discussion of complexity as an issue characteristic and its impact on political participation, see Roger W. Cobb and Charles D. Elder, *Participation in American Politics: The Dynamics of Agenda-Building* (Baltimore: Johns Hopkins University Press, 1972), especially pp. 98–99.

26. Gormley and Weimer, *Organizational Report Cards;* Steven Cohen and Ronald Brand, *Total Quality Management in Government* (San Francisco: Jossey-Bass, 1993); Christine W. Letts, Willian P. Ryan, and Allen Grossman, *High Performance Nonprofit Organizations: Managing Upstream for Greater Impact* (New York: John Wiley and Sons, 1999).

27. Lowi, "The Four Systems of Policy," 298–310.

28. Heclo, "Hyperdemocracy," 62–71. Theda Skocpol has also observed that despite the dramatic growth of interest groups, these groups lack an active membership that is engaged in the political process.

29. See Marc Landy, "Public Policy and Citizenship," in *Public Policy for Democracy,* ed. Helen M. Ingram and Steven Rathgeb Smith (Washington, D.C.: The Brookings Institution, 1993), 19–44.

30. Lowi, "American Business," 677–715.

31. Marver Bernstein, *Regulating Business by Independent Commission* (Princeton, N.J.:

Princeton University Press, 1955); James M. Landis, *The Administrative Process* (New Haven: Yale University Press, 1938).

32. Gary Mucciaroni, *Reversals of Fortune: Public Policy and Private Interests* (Washington, D.C.: The Brookings Institution, 1995).

33. Michael Kraft, *Environmental Policy and Politics* (New York: HarperCollins, 1996); Daniel A. Mazmanian and Paul A. Sabatier, *Implementation and Public Policy* (Glenview, Ill.: Scott, Foresman, 1983), May, this volume.

34. Steven Kelman, *What Price Incentives?* (Boston: Auburn House Publishing, 1981).

35. Steven Kelman, "Public Choice and Public Spirit," *The Public Interest* 87 (spring 1987): 80–94.

36. Sidney Verba, Kay Lehman Schlozman, and Henry Brady, *Civic Voluntarism in American Politics* (Cambridge, Mass.: Harvard University Press, 1995).

37. Kenneth Meier, *The Politics of Sin* (Armonk, N.Y.: M.E. Sharpe, 1994).

38. Anne Larson Schneider and Helen Ingram, *Policy Design for Democracy* (Lawrence: University of Kansas Press, 1997).

39. Soss, "Lessons In Welfare," 1999.

40. Yvone Luna, "Social Construction of Welfare Mothers: Political Messages and Recipient Response," Annual Meeting of the Western Political Science Association, March 2000, San Jose, California.

41. Soss, "Lessons In Welfare," 1999.

42. John Hird, *Superfund* (Baltimore: Johns Hopkins University Press, 1994).

43. Hanna J. Cortner and Margaret Moote, *The Politics of Ecosystems Management* (Washington, D.C.: Island Press, 1999).

44. Jeffrey L. Pressman, *Federal Programs and City Politics: The Dynamics of the Aid Process in Oakland* (Berkeley: University of California Press, 1975).

CHAPTER TWENTY-ONE

European Experience with Tools of Government

Arthur B. Ringeling

In this chapter I try to give a picture of international experiences with tools of government, focusing particularly on the countries of western Europe. Even this is a heavy burden though. Significant differences exist in societal and political-administrative structures and culture in western Europe. Focusing on western Europe is at least somewhat feasible, however, and also offers me a better opportunity to state my message. That message is that governmental tools are highly political. Peters and Salomon have already made that clear before in this volume. Focusing on western European countries can illustrate this time and again. Tools are anything but neutral means to given ends as instrumentalists are inclined to consider them.

For Europeans it is important to make this statement because they are so familiar with Machiavelli's insight that the ends justify the means. This message contradicts his view. Because of their political characteristics, political movements have a preference for one goal or the other.[1] For readers from the United States, too, the message is important, educated as they are in pragmatism and the rationalistic policymaking that results from it. Not only are policy instruments highly political, they are in part also the components of the ideologies of political movements. Given these qualities, debates over government tools have been an important part of the political and societal development of western European countries in the twentieth century. The western European experience thus confirms a central tenet of this book: writing about government tools is, in a certain sense, writing about political and administrative history.

To do this, it is necessary to begin by examining the nature of the state in the European context. From that starting point we can describe different tool patterns that historically developed on this continent. Against this backdrop we can then examine the impact of the new public management[2] on the patterns of tool use in Europe. Next we will try to explain the resulting patterns of tool use that can be distinguished in Europe. We will conclude with a number of remarks about the tools framework in comparative perspective.

I. WHAT KIND OF STATE?

Governments exist to realize certain policy objectives, and the tools they employ naturally vary with the objectives they are pursuing. However, there are different kinds of states. Some governments are more activist than others. Others want to play a more modest role in the development of society. Given this variety of governmental ambitions, governmental toolboxes must also differ.

Richard Stillman, for example, distinguishes among four concepts of the state in the debate about public administration in the United States: no state, bold state, pre-state, and pro-state.[3] The concept of no state stands for a minimalist view of what the role of the public sector should be. The bold state view represents an activist conception of

585

the role of the state in societal development. The pre-state or halfway state represents a moderate view of the role of the state, whereas the pro-state concept stands for the state as a professional technocracy.

Although Stillman limits his analysis to the United States, and although foreigners sometimes assume that all European countries exhibit the bold state concept, all four conceptions can be found in the developments that took place in western Europe in the last century.

Perhaps the best example of the no state tradition in the European context can be found in the United Kingdom, at least up until the 1920s of the last century, when social democrats took over government for the first time. At this point, societal conflicts began to be fought out in the companies and on the streets. Employers and unions opposed each other vehemently. Adversarial politics led to adversarial relationships in society as a whole. Class conflict was more visible and more openly fought out under these circumstances than in other countries in Europe. The Labour party, closely connected to the unions, used its control of the government to strengthen the position of the laborers. Regulation was, like in most countries, one of the instruments, but nationalization of big industries was another logical consequence of societal struggle.

After World War II, a system of social security and health service was created. Lord Beveridge was the intellectual author of this policy. In his thinking, the welfare state was a government affair. The provisions of social security were governmental efforts. By implementing this conception, the United Kingdom became more and more what Esping-Andersen called a "social-democratic" state.[4] However, the influence of Beveridge's philosophy was not limited to the United Kingdom. Most of western Europe adopted his ideas. The institutionalization differed, however, from country to country.

To some extent developments in France were comparable, but in that country, the no-state concept was absent. The dominant view was that the state had to take the lead in societal developments, a view once referred to as the "public management of society."[5] Governance was based on professional-technocratic expertise. Special schools were created in order to build up the necessary knowledge and professional people: the "*grandes ecoles.*" With that, France has as well traits of the bold state as of the pro-state conception. The important parties in France, from left to right, shared the conception of the centrality of the state. Their disputes concerned what the strong state should do and in what way, not the conception of the strong state itself. Not surprisingly, the tool of direct government fit most comfortably with their conception.

There is a third tradition in western Europe in which state and society are intensively intertwined. In these countries the welfare state is not a state affair alone, but societal organizations also play an important role in its realization. The countries concerned were examples of the (neo)-corporatist state. That model can be found in Belgium and Germany. The Netherlands can also be classified under this model despite the fact that it adopted to a high degree the ideas of Beveridge of universal social rights as a basis for a generous welfare regime, but the implementation of that philosophy was to an important extent left to semipublic and private organizations, which delivered most of the state-financed services.

In Stillman's terms the Netherlands can be called a pre-state. Governmental organizations and societal organizations share the burden of implementing tasks that are considered relevant by the state. In a number of western European countries as well, activities that are characteristic for the modern welfare state are implemented by private organizations, often called organizations of private initiative and also semipublic organizations (also named *quango's* or *para-statel* organizations). This is not a development of recent years, but one that is deeply imbedded in the tradition of important political movements. Principles such as "subsidiarity" and "sovereignty in one's own domain" were essential features of Catholic and Protestant politics in the last century. Despite the fact that nowadays around 60 percent of net national income goes through the hands of government, the Dutch state was always relatively small, but the public sector is very large when we take into account all those organizations executing public tasks.

587

CH 21:
EUROPEAN
EXPERIENCE
WITH
TOOLS OF
GOVERNMENT

This tradition can also be found in other parts of western Europe as Putnam shows.[6] It embraces countries that have a less clear dividing line between forms of public and private organization. In the Anglo-Saxon world organizations are either private or public. In different European countries, by contrast, the status of numerous societal organizations is hybrid. They are in part private, in particular with regard to their origin and legal status, but they fulfill at the same time public functions.[7]

II. FROM TYPE OF STATE TO TYPE OF TOOL

These different conceptions of the state in turn necessitated different types of tools.

Direct Government

All the different types of states made use of the tool of *direct government,* but the extent to which they did so differed. The countries following the bold state and the pro-state conceptions relied more strongly on direct government than the countries that adhered to the no-state and the pre-state conception, and the pro-state countries also made more use of regulation, economic as well as social.

Grants

Countries with a pre-state conception, by contrast, made use of a number of tools other than direct government. For example, to make the implementation of public tasks by organizations stemming from private initiative possible, financial ties had to be established between governmental organizations and private organizations. In the Netherlands from 1918 on, the Christian-Democrats invented the *grant* as a tool to finance public and private schools. The grants were given on the basis of an elaborate financial system with numerous criteria with regard to the number of pupils in a class, the number and quality of the educational staff, and the school facilities. This tool became a model in many other policy fields, such as public health, public housing, and welfare. Vast financial streams were developed between the public and the private sectors as a consequence.

These financial streams were not limited to relationships between government and semipublic organizations. During the twentieth century, and in particular after World War II, European governments subsidized industry and agriculture intensively. Subsidizing industry started after 1945 as an attempt to build the national economies after their virtual disappearance as a result of World War II. Premiums and tax reductions were given to business and industrial organizations for the investments they made. Until the end of the 1980s, subsidization was an important instrument to stimulate the national economies and promote economic innovation. Grants, loan guarantees, and tax expenditures were more popular than economic regulation and the prevention of cartels. To the extent that economic regulation existed, it was not pursued intensively, although this picture changed when the market regulations of the European Union became more important. In a later stage, goals with regard to the environment, energy consumption, education, and employment were added. This was referred to as "governance with the means."

Public Enterprises

A third tool of government, particularly evident in regimes of the social-democratic type, is *public enterprises*. The United Kingdom and France are the classic examples in this respect. The clashes between employers and laborers had been most heavy in these countries. When social democratic parties took over political power, they had to break the power of the employers. A way to do this was to bring the crucial production means of society under the control of the state.

Expectations of nationalization were high. By placing workers in a position of greater responsibility, nationalization was expected to produce a more equal distribution of wealth and income. It was thought that the economy would be stimulated as a result of the elimination of the wastes of competition, and third, it was presumed that as a result of higher productivity, production would be cheaper, resulting in lower prices.[8] Complementary to this change in ownership of enterprises was a planned economy, a subject handled later.

Public enterprises were thus a product of political ideology. The European situation differs from the American one in this respect.[9] In the latter country public enterprises were a rare phenomenon, but not so in western Europe. Important industries, in particular those industries where union influence was strong, like the coalmines, the steelworks, and the shipyards, were nationalized.

That was not all. Unlike the Liberals and Christian-Democrats, social democrats were not great admirers of private initiative or of the organizations stemming from private initiative. In the field of social policy, private initiative made people dependent on the generosity of the possessing class. This meant in their view soup and old clothes instead of a right to the necessary means of existence. Strong public organizations regulated by law, that is, the tool of direct government, was their alternative.

III. HORIZONTAL TOOLS

During the 1970s and the 1980s government tools became more horizontal than they were before. The distinction between vertical and horizontal tools has been proposed by De Bruijn and ten Heuvelhof.[10] By vertical tools they refer to more classic tools like the ones discussed above. In their view these instruments are often of a top-down character, reactive and imperative. Perhaps they fulfilled functions toward individuals in rather simple situations. However, confronted with complex situations they fall short.

Horizontal tools take into account the barriers that governments meet when they try to govern. These barriers include societal pluralism and diversity, the closeness and autonomy of the actors being governed, and the interdependence of societal actors, public as well as private. For this reason horizontal instruments that are not based on a view of government as an actor situated above other actors and as a central point of governance are necessary. Evidence of the use of such horizontal tools was already apparent in the rich European tradition of indicative planning. It has mushroomed in more recent years, however, in the spread of a second generation of multilateral instruments such as contracts and covenants, market-conforming instruments, and communicative instruments. In this section we look first at this planning tradition and then at a number of the horizontal instruments De Bruijn and ten Heuvelhof mention:

1. Communication

2. Networking and other forms of interacting

3. Public-private partnership

4. Voluntary agreements

5. Covenants

589

CH 21:
EUROPEAN
EXPERIENCE
WITH
TOOLS OF
GOVERNMENT

Planning

Planning was an important government process developed during the twentieth century. Social Democrats stood at its crib. In their view planning was an alternative for what they considered to be the shortcomings of the market. It was, in the first place, a vehicle for policymaking, for creating new societal conditions and relationships, but planning became much more than that. It became a way to orchestrate the implementation of public policy. In a number of European countries, public policy was implemented not only by public bodies, but also by semipublic and private organizations. The planning process was used to organize communication between governmental and societal organizations in a number of policy fields, like social, economic, educational, and environmental. The results of the discussions about policy then had consequences for the relationships between public and private organizations in implementing the plans.

The planning movement gained momentum after World War II. The European countries involved were severely damaged as a result of the war activities. There was a shortage in housing, roads, building materials, food, employment, and social provisions. The governments in the region had the task of rebuilding their countries. Planning fulfilled a useful function for their efforts. The idea of replacing the market at least partially by the planning device had great appeal. This was particularly the case in France. The leading role of the state in societal and economic development was institutionalized in long-range economic plans. However, planning also played a role in the domains of housing, spatial development, highway, and water policies.

The domain of planning expanded during the 1970s. In building up the welfare state, planning turned out to be an important process in a number of European countries. Education, social security, social work, public health, and, during the economic recession of the 1970s, employment became the new subjects of planning. Planning more and more became social planning. New planning bureaus with people from disciplines other than economics or engineering emerged.

To be sure, the style of planning that evolved in western Europe differed markedly from the style that emerged in the big companies or in the Soviet Union. Most significantly, perhaps, it was not only a state affair. It was also a way of communication between the public sector and the broader society. In France the consultation of industry and business was part of the planning process. In neocorporatist countries planning was a means of communication between governmental organizations and semipublic organizations and organizations resulting from private initiative. This was easy to understand because the latter, as made clear before, were implementing such an important portion of governmental policy. The Social-Economic Council in the Netherlands was an organization composed of representatives of employer organizations, labor unions, and what were called Crown members. Together they discussed social and economic policy, whether asked or not by the cabinet.

With the change in domain, the style of planning also changed. The blueprint planning of the engineers and the modeling of the economists were replaced by a planning style in which the process was as important as the results of that process. "New planning," it was called. Habermas, the German social philosopher, coined the term "communicative planning."[11] The 1980s, however, put the popularity of this type of horizontal planning under severe pressure.

Communication

It is a short step from this "new planning" to what is increasingly being called "horizontal tools," of which communication and public information is one of the major types. Information and public relations were heavily discussed government tools after the experiences with the propaganda of Nazi Germany and the former Soviet bloc. However, since the 1970s, these horizontal instruments seem to be fully back in the public toolbox. Some observers are inclined to talk about "government by speech," having in mind the extent to which these tools have been elaborated in the United States. The second half of the twentieth century shows a steady growth of organizations specialized in communication, public relations, and public affairs. These organizations worked for public as well as private organizations.

The greater emphasis on communication has resulted in more horizontal ways of policymaking. The Dutch consensus model spread itself over a variety of policy areas.[12] The domain of politicians narrowed as a result of interaction between public and private organizations. Horizontal communication became an important trait of policy processes in the Netherlands and other countries in western Europe. More and more not only politicians communicated, but governmental organizations and public officials as well. They consulted with private and semipublic organizations frequently. Public participation became organized and even regulated in a number of special laws. Participation was mandated not only in policymaking, but also in policy implementation. The distinction turned out to be fuzzy anyway. During the 1990s, all kinds of interactive policy processes were added to the repertoire.

Networking

Not only communications but more explicit networking has also grown in importance as governmental organizations have become aware of their dependencies when they try to realize certain policy objectives. Public policy is seldom the job of one organization. Other organizations are often needed to realize certain policies.[13] In order to do so, many kinds of consultative and advisory bodies were created. This was particularly the case when public, semipublic, and private organizations interacted. The policy areas mentioned before such as education, housing, health, and social welfare illustrate this, but the same is true for economic policy. Not only in the Netherlands, but also in other European countries, consultations between public and private actors happen regularly, whether a governmental committee exists for the specific policy domain or not.

On the European level, an extensive committee system has been developed. On almost every policy subject, committees composed of representatives of member states and interests groups have been created. These committees are an important working field for the lobbyists. This way of institutionalization of policymaking in the European arena is referred to as "comitology."[14]

Equally notable has been the ability of the Dutch government to intervene in the results of wage agreements between employers' organizations and labor unions. The government can limit pay raises as a part of its social-economic and financial policy. It also has the ability to make the results of wage agreements obligatory for all the enterprises in a certain industry. Business, industry, and unions use their networks with

591

CH 21:
EUROPEAN
EXPERIENCE
WITH
TOOLS OF
GOVERNMENT

government to discover the margins of what is acceptable and what is not. In other European countries these competencies are unthinkable.

Networking not only refers to the strategies that actors use to pay attention to other actors involved and to build up coalitions.[15] To a certain degree networking has been institutionalized, for instance, in the form of participation procedures and interactive policymaking. This kind of approach is used in a number of west European countries at different levels of government as well.

Public-Private Partnership

Public-private partnership also got another meaning during the 1980s. It was common in the past that public and private organizations collaborated. However, the tradition was mostly restricted to cooperation with organizations that were referred to earlier in this chapter as semipublic. During the 1980s new alignments came into focus as collaboration increased between government and private enterprises. Shopping malls, theatres, other cultural activities, and even public tunnels have been the focus of combined efforts. This was quite different from the decades before, when interaction between local government and project developers, and thus the mixture of public and business organizations, was considered suspect.

Voluntary Agreements and Covenants

Voluntary agreements have a long history in western Europe. In the Nordic countries it is common for actors involved in a certain policy field to try to reach an agreement with regard to policy proposals. When such an agreement is reached, government regulation will, as a rule, not take place. There is doubt, however, about the effectiveness of these voluntary agreements.[16] For partners from the private sector it is too easy to avoid government regulation while implementing the agreement only half-heartedly. Furthermore, the extent to which the industries in a certain sector are bound by the negotiation results reached by their sector organization turned out to be a problem.[17]

To correct some of these shortcomings of voluntary agreements, a slightly different tool, the "covenant," has come into widespread use in different policy sectors, especially environmental policy.[18] Covenants go one step further than voluntary agreements by giving the agreement the juridical form of a contract between the government and its negotiating partners. The partners typically prefer such a covenant above regulation. This gives the government and the contract partners rights and duties, while regulation in the same field mostly contains duties, and the instrument is more flexible than regulation, which can be changed only by long and painful procedures.

Summary

The distinction between vertical and horizontal instruments is less clear than De Bruijn and ten Heuvelhof presume. Instruments can be used in different ways, more horizontally or more vertically. Regulation is, in their view, considered a vertical instrument, but it can be used in strongly horizontal ways by giving certain actors rights and possibilities instead of prescribing their behavior. Participation procedures can be used in a formal sense, giving actors the possibility to voice their opinion without fundamentally changing the intended decision, or they can be used in a way to stimulate new solutions from societal groups and citizens. Most of the tools De Bruijn and ten Heuvelhof mention are not new either. They have been used in the west European setting for a long time, as this section has demonstrated. At the same time, following the period of construction of the welfare state, which brought a number of semipublic organizations stemming from private initiative more and more under the control of the state,[19] the government toolbox has become more horizontal in recent decades.

However, not all horizontal tools work as well as expected. The expectations that were connected to the introduction of horizontal tools have only partly been met. Their advantages compared to more traditional government tools to an important extent still have to be proven.[20]

IV. MARKET-ORIENTED APPROACHES

In the 1980s the west European toolbox changed considerably, not that regulation or planning disappeared as governmental tools. However, their prominence became relatively less important. The market mechanism got a higher priority for the distribution of goods and services. This development started in the United States and the United Kingdom at the end of the 1970s. Both Mrs. Thatcher and President Reagan were strong opponents of active state intervention, Reagan saying that, "Government was not the solution, but the problem," a statement Mrs. Thatcher could have made also. The 1980s became the era of shrinking government, deregulation, and privatization. The market had to play a more important role in the delivery of goods and services in society. As a result of these political views, the instruments used in the relationships between the public and the private sector changed.

Although the era of third-party government actually began much earlier, in the Anglo-Saxon world the 1980s accelerated the transition through its vehement antigovernment politics. This swing of the pendulum was also evident in western Europe, but it went less far. To some extent the administrative theory that underlay this movement came a decade later. Osborne and Gaebler[21] are generally considered the persons who put the philosophy into words. Their position was, according to them, less antigovernmental than an attempt to improve the functioning of government. On the other side of the Atlantic, in western Europe, their message was also heard. Steering rather than rowing, empowering rather than serving, funding outcomes not inputs, injecting competition into service delivery, earning rather than spending, and so on. This all in an attempt to reinvent government.

For a number of west European countries the New Public Management advice was hardly revolutionary, as was true as well in the United States.[22] Rowing was already done by the vast semipublic private sector implementing governmental tasks. These organizations, to a certain extent, competed with each other after they lost their religious or ideological foundation. People were in a position to choose between originally Protestant, Catholic, or neutral schools and opted for the best or the closest, irrespective of their denomination. The choice of a hospital became more a matter of the physician or the availability of beds. Certain industries, heavily dominated by the state, like gas exploration, the spirits, or the tobacco industry became profit centers by themselves. Competition and profit making were already there.

However, in this period a number of governmental organizations were privatized or became more independent than before. Moreover, outsourcing and the purchase of service contracting to commercial organizations could be observed more frequently, but opposition to these tools was, and still is, great, in particular from the labor unions. Examples are the public utilities and national airline companies in France and Italy. Consultancy firms, however, became a frequent visitor in the public sector, not the least to apply more business-like methods to governmental organizations.

Deregulation also became an item on the political agenda of the countries of Europe.

593

CH 21:
EUROPEAN
EXPERIENCE
WITH
TOOLS OF
GOVERNMENT

The content, however, was slightly different from that in the United States, where deregulation was designed to restore market competition. In Europe, by contrast, regulation was in part replaced by self-regulation of certain industrial and service sectors, which did not lead to a decline of regulation but to a change in the nature of regulation from public to private. In addition, the west European countries experienced growing interventions from the transnational level, in particular the European Union, issuing directives and regulations that had to be implemented by its member states. As a result, a lot of measures that the member states had taken in the past in order to protect certain industries were nullified. In addition, the Union became active in other policy domains such as monetary policy, environmental policy, and even social policy, and the instruments the Union chose were mostly regulatory. While deregulating domestically, therefore, the member states were thus obliged to make European regulations a part of their national legal systems. When the Netherlands implemented a European environmental policy directive through a covenant, Brussels thus reacted negatively. The implementation of European law had to be done by national law, not by what was considered a contract between private partners. The Netherlands obeyed, but by putting into law an older covenant and not the last one in order to prevent a conflict with its contract partners.

It can be argued that the European Union leads to a greater uniformity not only of national policies of the member states, but also of the instruments they choose. As a result, differences in governance styles among European countries will diminish to some extent.[23] However, at the same time the framework will be broadened, so that it can offer enough leeway for the further development of a growing number of countries with different stages of development and their own governing traditions.[24]

V. POSSIBLE EXPLANATIONS

What explains the selection of tools in the western European context sketched in the preceding sections? Four possible types of explanation seem possible: pragmatic, juridical, ideological, and political-administrative.[25]

Pragmatic

In the pragmatic view, the tools that work best are selected. The choice of instruments in this view is a question of optimization, selecting the best instruments given the policy goals. Policy debates often concentrate on this question. Market-based instruments work better than regulation in the environmental field is a frequently heard statement that fits the orthodox view.[26] Or it is better to use voluntary agreements than top-down regulation if environmental policy is to be successful. The discussion is centered on the effects of instruments from the point of view of policy intentions. Policymakers should choose those instruments that serve their purposes best. That is the core of the rational approach to instrument choice. Policy design is a result of what works and what does not.[27]

There are, however, problems in treating the instrumentation question as an optimizing problem. For one thing, this approach presumes that instruments have inherent characteristics that cause them to work out in a specific way. Regulation would lead to certain effects, economic instruments to others, but it has turned out that the consequences of instruments are not so easy to specify. Majone, for example, found that regulation and economic instruments do not have predictable consequences, at least in the environment field. Some countries have reasonable results while working with permits and effluent standards, while others do not. It turns out to be difficult to determine to what extent environmental effects are caused by one instrument or another.[28]

One reason for this may be that in practice instruments can never be found in a pure form. So, even if we suppose to have knowledge about the characteristics of policy instruments, their actual state is influenced by the fact that they always come in a mix.[29] This is not to say that optimizing considerations are not, or should not be, a part of the decisionmaking, but other considerations are also at work.

This is evident in the experience of European states in implementing the European Union measures. The intention of the European Union was to harmonize market conditions, and to some extent it succeeded in that aim. However, not all countries chose the same policy or the same instruments. So there must have been other considerations than those derived from the direct relationship between the given European policy goals and the tools they chose that played a role.[30]

Legal Traditions

One of those considerations is the legal tradition in place that determines which instruments are legally allowed.[31] Of course, laws can be changed, but the system of law is less flexible. So we will concentrate on that.

From the outset it must be emphasized that differences in legal traditions exist in western Europe. The most often-mentioned difference is that between the Roman law tradition and the common law tradition, the first to be found on the continent, the second in the Anglo-Saxon world. In the first tradition, the emphasis is put on the formal system of laws. Separate regulations are codified in law books. In the second, case law and judicial judgments take a more important place. This difference is well known and not without consequences for the tools at the disposal of the legislature and the executive branches of government. As a consequence, the continental countries applied regulation in a more formal sense and new efforts to inject a degree of regulatory flexibility have made more limited progress.

Political Ideology

From what I have described in the sections before, it may be clear that political ideology is also an important factor in the choice of government tools. Different political movements have different preferences with regard to the way government intervenes in societal relationships. In the following, I focus on the preferences of the Christian-Democratic, Social-Democratic, and Liberal movements.

The Christian-Democratic Movement, influential especially in western European countries such as Germany, Belgium, the Netherlands, Italy, and to a lesser extent France, focused on, among other things, the relationship between the state and societal organizations. In their view it was not necessary that the state execute certain tasks. In fact, it was better if it did not. Services could also be delivered by other societal organizations, in particular organizations with a certain religious character. The discussion around the turn of the nineteenth century was related to the financing of schools founded by religious groups. The principal decision in the Netherlands in 1918 was to finance public and private schools in the same way. That decision, often referred to as the Pacification, became the model for a lot of other policy fields, such as public housing, health, and social welfare. The Dutch system of pillarization was the result.[32]

The system of pillarization could only exist as long as the financing of private groups and organizations was secure. It was the Christian-Democratic movement that designed instruments to channel public funds to private organizations. The system was then

595

CH 21:
EUROPEAN
EXPERIENCE
WITH
TOOLS OF
GOVERNMENT

further enlarged during the rise of the welfare state. For sociologists like Van Doorn, this development provided reason to consider the Netherlands a welfare society instead of a welfare state.[33]

Nineteenth-century Liberals had a different set of tool preferences. For them, the major priority was to curtail the power of the absolute sovereign. Paradoxically, in their view, the best vehicle to do this was regulation. Rule making made clear what was permitted for government to do and what not to do. So the liberals laid the foundation of the democratic "*Rechtsstaat,*" as the Germans called it. The emphasis on regulation, on the establishment of human and constitutional rights, was a logical consequence of that reasoning.

The Social-Democratic approach to tool choice differed yet. Although initially hostile toward the state as an instrument of oppression used by the possessing ruling class, Social-Democratic perceptions changed during the twentieth century, as suffrage was extended. The state first was accepted as a temporary instrument for realizing socialist ideals. The change became total and the temporary character was dropped when general suffrage was realized and on the level of local government socialist policy brought forth results. The state became an instrument for governance of societal relationships, in particular between employers and laborers.

With the acceptance of the state, the instrument of direct government was accepted also. Similarly, with the acceptance of the system of law, regulation was used in an increasingly new way. In the past the emphasis lay on the *codification* of existing insights and practices and on how unjust in the eyes of social democrats were these practices. Now the regulatory tool was used in a way to change existing relationships, to create new, more just practices.

Political-Administrative Setting

The choices of tools countries make can also be explained in terms of their particular political-administrative setting. The political-administrative setting explains both the process of policy formulation and the results of that process, including the choice of instruments. The question of which actor will be involved and in which way differs from instrument to instrument.

This insight is hardly new. There are in the history of public administration all kinds of studies that illustrate the relationship between political-administrative setting on one side and the choice and application of instruments on the other side.[34] Also, economists have come to this insight, but few of them have understood the consequence of it. The preference politicians have for subsidies can be explained, for example, by the special tie they can build up with that part of industry to which the subsidy is targeted. So, there are reasons to choose particular instruments other than from the point of view of an optimal relationship between goals and means, the political position of the policymakers being one of them.

Governance Models and Instrument Choice

A final factor affecting instrument choice is the "governance model" a country exhibits. Particular countries seem to have preferences for certain approaches to governance. In our view this has to do with the political-administrative structure and culture of the country. These governance approaches in turn have implications for the instruments chosen.[35] Four such governance models in particular can be distinguished:

1. Command and control

2. Governance on main policy lines

3. Selective governance

4. Facilitative governance[36]

In the *command and control model,* the national government is the central player. It defines the problem and the solutions and does so in a rather autonomous way. So, central government orders other actors, public as well as private, to implement policy. A government that particularly uses direct regulation as the main instrument for environmental policy exemplifies this model. Standards are set in national regulations. Other actors have to abide by these standards. In a lot of countries this has been the usual model and, to some extent, it still is.

In the *main policy lines model,* central governments are still the important players. However, they design only the main lines of policy, giving other actors the opportunity to specify the details. In this model there is a greater reliance on the self-governance capacity of other actors. This model is characterized by the setting of framework laws and obligatory framework goals that other policy actors can fill in according to the circumstances. The grant-in-aid is the tool most consistent with this approach.

In the *selective governance model,* central government intervenes only on certain crucial points. These crucial points change the course of things, but other actors have to apply the instruments that are offered in the selective intervention. Subsidies are a good example of this kind of governance. No other actor is obliged to make use of subsidies. The same is true for other economic instruments. Covenants can be a part of the strategy followed in this model, but can also fit in other strategies.

In the *facilitative model,* the basic question for central governments is how to enable the self-governing capacities of other actors. Essential for a facilitative strategy is that central governments understand the problems that other actors are confronting very well. Only then can they supply them with the necessary instruments.

Is there a relationship between these governing models and the instruments governing bodies select? Do some instruments not fit better in a certain model than others? A plausible case can be made, for example, that horizontal instruments fit better in governance models that rely to a greater extent on the self-governance of the governed body, and vertical instruments are presumed to fit better in the command and control model or in governance on main lines.

However, there are counterarguments. The first is that instruments mostly come in a mix, as suggested earlier. Policies toward certain problems always contain a lot of different instruments.

The second argument is that instruments of a certain type can have a very different content. Here again, regulation can serve as an example. Not all regulation has the command and control structure. A lot of laws, especially laws with the threat of negative sanctions, have that structure, but there is also a lot of regulation that attributes certain rights and enables other actors or organizations to realize a specific policy.

The third and most important argument is that all instruments are used within national contexts with their own traditions, preferences, and power relations. Instruments change in nature and effects as a result of these conditions.

The implementation of European environmental policy mentioned before displays these differences in governance models. In Germany, a country where citizens are most worried about environmental issues, government took decisions on packaging policy that were opposed by industry. Politicians could do so because they could be rather sure of their grass roots support. In France, consultations with leaders of industry made policymakers understand that the German system was not a feasible road to follow. So France opted for a policy that was very close to the already existing incineration system. The Netherlands, to give a third example, changed its governance model over time.

During the 1970s and the beginning of the 1980s the command and control style dominated. It did not result in much. Government then developed an approach that was much more consistent with the governance model that dominated that country in a variety of other policy sectors: a more consensual style, permitting industries to find their own solutions by implementing a covenant that they had reached with the public authorities.

From our research we learn that there is no absolute link between the governance models a specific government follows and the instruments it adopts. Certain tools do not typically belong to one governance model and are excluded in another. At the same time, however, governance models tell us something about the arena, the relationships between different actors, which policy choices are feasible and which are not, and which instrument options are most likely. They can help us to understand why certain possibilities were taken into consideration in the policy processes studied and other possibilities were not. They also give us insights into why certain instruments are chosen in a political-administrative setting and others not.

Policy instruments, we can conclude from this type of explanation, have a political character. They are not neutral means that will be chosen or applied just for the reason that they work best. So, Machiavelli was wrong in stating that the goals would justify the means. Instruments can also be considered as goals in themselves—desirable to use, in particular when they are compared with other instruments.[37] Effectiveness is not the only reason to choose them. In the political history of Europe these longstanding preferences can be connected with the most important political movements. Governments use some instruments more than other instruments because of ideological reasoning deeply rooted in political life.

VI. THE TOOLS FRAMEWORK IN A COMPARATIVE CONTEXT

A number of conclusions flow from the discussion above.

First, the instrumental view on government tools, or what is called in this chapter, the pragmatic view, has not only value, but also serious shortcomings. The choices facing policymakers are limited due to a variety of reasons. Perhaps instruments are intended to be used as tools, but they are more than a tool alone. They are political weapons and marching banners alike. They are normative in nature irrespective of whether one follows a political strategy or, for that manner, the philosophy of "new public management."

Second, government instruments have to do with giving shape to society and with the role the state plays in a society. People differ in their preferences on these matters as well. That is what politics is about. For that reason also governmental tools are highly disputed.

Third, it is a misunderstanding to hold that it is characteristic for Europe to have a strong state and a dominance of direct governance. There are different traditions in this part of the world, the bold-state not being the dominant pattern. Countries in western Europe differ in the way the welfare state is institutionalized. Indirect government can be seen all over Europe, some countries having more experience with this phenomenon than others as a result of the different state traditions on this continent. Indirect government is not a new phenomenon in this region. It is imbedded in longstanding political (neocorporatist) ideology, to be found in particular among the Christian-Democrats.

Fourth, the different types of state also lead to differences among the toolboxes of

597

CH 21:
EUROPEAN
EXPERIENCE
WITH
TOOLS OF
GOVERNMENT

the countries involved. In the more social-democratic welfare states, bureaucracies were paired with public enterprises. In the more (neo)-corporatist welfare states government policy was implemented by private as well as public organizations. More horizontal tools are found to a greater extent in countries where more emphasis has been placed on consensus building, where public and semipublic organizations were active on the public domain and where a central position for the state was absent.

Fifth, new public management, or the market model, did have its impact in Europe. It fitted in the context of the 1980s that was less political than decades before. However, apart from the United Kingdom, the pendulum swung less far in Europe than in the United States. To a certain extent, the new insights this movement prophesized were embedded in already existing practices. Goods and services were in some countries already delivered by other organizations than state organizations. In the Nordic countries, however, the role of the state had to be reconsidered.

At the same time, my sixth conclusion, the European Union grew in importance for the policies of the member states, but its influence on instrumentation was limited because the European nations are responsible for the implementation of what is decided in Brussels. The policies of the member states became more and more the same, in order to obey the European decisionmaking. Their toolboxes, however, were harmonized less. Instrument choices are the result of political ideology, of different governance visions, of legal traditions, and have to fit in certain political-administrative settings.

Seventh and final, the toolbox is not constant. It changes over time as a result of the invention of new tools, national and international developments, and the interventions of the supranational institutions.

NOTES

1. A. B. Ringeling, *De Instrumenten van Het Beleid (The Instruments of Government Policy)* (Alphen aan den Rijn: Oratie Erasmus University Rotterdam and Samsom, 1983); also in B. Guy Peters, F. K. M. Van Nispen, eds., *Public Policy Instruments* (Cheltenham, U.K. and Northampton, Mass.: Edward Elgar, 1998), 204–217.

2. C. Hood and M. Jackson, *Administrative Argument* (Aldershot, U.K.: Dartmouth, 1991); C. Pollitt, *Managerialism and the Public Services* (Oxford: Basil Blackwell, 1993).

3. R. J. Stillman, *Preface to Public Administration* (New York: St. Martin's Press, 1991).

4. G. Esping-Andersen, *The Three Worlds of Welfare Capitalism* (Cambridge: Polity Press in association with Basil Blackwell, 1990).

5. A. P. J. van der Eijde, *Public Management of Society in France* (forthcoming, 2001).

6. R. D. Putnam, *Making Democracy Work* (Princeton, N.J.: Princeton University Press, 1993).

7. H. K. Anheier and W. Seibel, eds., *The Third Sector: Comparative Studies of Nonprofit Organizations* (Berlin and New York: De Gruyter, 1990); L. M. Salamon, *America's Non-Profit Sector: A Primer* (New York: The Foundation Center, 1992).

8. J. Redwood, *Public Enterprise in Crisis* (Oxford: Blackwell, 1980).

9. A. H. Walsh, *The Public's Business* (Cambridge, Mass.: MIT Press, 1978).

10. J. A. Bruijn and E. F. ten Heuvelhof, *Sturingsinstrumenten Voor de Overheid (Governance Instruments for the Government)* (Leiden: Stenfert Kroese, 1991).

11. J. Habermas, *Theorie des Kommunikativen Handelns (Theory of Communicative Acting)* (Frankfurt am Main: Suhrkamp, 1981).

12. A. Lijphart, *The Politics of Accommodation* (Berkeley: University of California Press, 1968); J. Visser and A. Hemerijck, *A Dutch Miracle* (Amsterdam: Amsterdam University Press, 1997).

13. A. Amundsen, *Joint Management of Energy and Environment in Industry* (Frederikstad: Oestfold Research Foundation, 1999).

14. S. S. Andersen and K. A. Eliassen, eds., *Making Policy in Europe* (London: Sage, 1993); H.

Wallace and W. Wallace, *Policy-Making in the European Union* (Oxford: Oxford University Press, 1996).

599

CH 21:
EUROPEAN
EXPERIENCE
WITH
TOOLS OF
GOVERNMENT

15. Bressers, "The Choice of Policy Instruments in Policy Networks," in *Public Policy Instruments,* eds. B. Guy Peters and F. K. M. Van Nispen (Cheltenham, U.K. and Northampton, Mass.: Edward Elgar, 1998), 85–105.

16. C. Gebers, *New Instruments for Sustainability: The New Contribution of Voluntary Agreements to Environmental Policy* (Darmstadt: Oko-Institut, 1998).

17. J. D. Liefferink, ed., *European Environmental Policy* (Manchester: Manchester University Press, 1997).

18. P. J. Klok, *Convenanten als Instrument van Milieubeleid (Covenants as Instruments of Environmental Policy)* (Enschede, the Netherlands: Universiteit Twente, 1989).

19. A. de Swaan, "De Verstatelijking van Verzorgingsarrangementen (Provision Arrangements in the Realm of the State)," *De Gids* (1976): 35–47.

20. B. Dente, ed., *Environmental Policy in Search for New Instruments* (Dordrecht: Kluwer Academic Publishers, 1995).

21. D. Osborne and T. Gaebler, *Reinventing Government* (Reading, Mass.: Addison-Wesley, 1992).

22. W. J. M. Kickert et al., *Aansturing van Verzelfstandigde Overheidsdiensten (Governance of Autonomous Government Services)* (Alphen aan den Rijn: Samsom, 1998).

23. K. Hanf and B. Soetendorp, eds., *Adapting to European Integration* (London: Longman, 1998).

24. S. S. Andersen and K. A. Eliassen, eds., *Making Policy in Europe* (London: Sage, 1993), 262.

25. A. B. Ringeling, *Instruments in Four,* Paper presented at the annual meeting of the Southern Political Science Association, Atlanta, Georgia, 1998.

26. Majone, *Evidence, Argument and Persuasion in the Policy Process* (New Haven and London: Yale University Press, 1989).

27. For an earlier critique of this view see L. M. Salamon, ed., *Beyond Privatization: The Tools of Government Action* (Washington, D.C.: Urban Institute Press, 1989).

28. G. Majone et al., *Regulating Europe* (London and New York: Routledge, 1996).

29. See also Salamon, "The New Governance and the Tools of Public Action: An Introduction," in this volume.

30. W. A. Hafkamp, M. Hozee, and A. B. Ringeling, eds., *The Effectiveness of Instruments for Environmental Policies in the Field of Industry* (Rotterdam: Erasmus University Rotterdam, 1999).

31. T. Koopmans, *Vergelijkend Publiekrecht (Comparative Public Law)* (Deventer, the Netherlands: Kluwer, 1978).

32. A. Lijphart, *The Politics of Accommodation* (Berkeley: University of California Press, 1968).

33. J. A. A. van Doorn and C. J. M. Schuyt, ed., *De Stagnerende Verzorgingsstaat (Stagnating Welfare State)* (Meppel/Amsterdam: Boom, 1978).

34. J. J. Ligteringen, *The Feasibility of Dutch Environmental Policy Instruments* (Enschede, the Netherlands: Twente University Press, 1999).

35. Another term often used for this phenomenon is "policy styles" [J. Richardson, *Policy Styles in Western Europe* (Boston: Allen & Unwin, 1982)]. We prefer the term "governance models," because policy styles refers mostly to a cultural phenomenon, whereas governance models not only imply cultural, but also structural elements of a particular political-administrative setting.

36. See also B. Guy Peters, *The Future of Governing: Four Emerging Models* (University of Kansas Press, 1996) for a somewhat different distinction.

37. L. M. Salamon, ed., *Beyond Privatization: The Tools of Government Action* (Washington, D.C.: Urban Institute Press, 1989).

CHAPTER TWENTY-TWO

The Tools Approach and the New Governance: Conclusion and Implications

Lester M. Salamon

A number of conclusions emerge from the discussion above about how public problems will be addressed in the years ahead, and consequently about the knowledge and skills that will be needed. Five of these conclusions in particular seem especially deserving of attention here.

A NEW PARADIGM

In the first place, it seems clear that a new paradigm truly is needed to comprehend the realities of public management and public problem solving in the current era. The traditional image of the hierarchic government agency acting on behalf of the electorate no longer characterizes much of what government does, at least in the United States. "Reinvented government," and to a lesser extent "privatization," bring us closer to contemporary realities, challenging the notion of a governmental monopoly on the resolution of public problems and highlighting the extent to which other actors are also increasingly involved. But neither of these quite suffices to capture the full dimensions of what is going on—the latter because of a tendency to exaggerate the extent to which the market can replace the state, and the former by ignoring or downplaying the special challenges that the new collaborative approaches to public problem solving entail.

To fill this gap, a new approach is therefore, needed. We have outlined the components of such an approach and suggested "the new governance" as an appropriate name for it since this term calls our attention to the two critical features that this approach embodies:

- First, a clear recognition that the task of public problem solving has become a *team sport* that has spilled well beyond the borders of government agencies and now engages a far more extensive network of social actors—public as well as private, for-profit as well as nonprofit—whose participation must often be coaxed and coached, not commandeered and controlled.

- Second, the realization that the resulting complex systems of public action are not self-executing, that they pose immense management and organizational challenges, but challenges that differ from those characteristic of direct government, and that consequently they must be approached in a new way.

To bring these collaborative systems and the challenges they pose into better focus, and to provide a better handle on their character, the new governance suggests a shift in the "unit of analysis" in policy work from government agencies and individual programs to the generic "tools" that are utilized to address public problems. Underlying this shift is a realization that the collaborative systems increasingly being relied on are hardly "free-form," that they do not consist simply of a set of "pick-up games" organized on the spur of the moment among otherwise disconnected players who are free to define all the rules *de novo,* but rather that they are structured through a more or less finite set of repertoires, which we have referred to as *the tools of government action,* and that define the actors involved in various types of undertakings, the roles they will play, and the relationships they will have to each other. American football, with its repertoires of preset plays, rather than the far more fluid game of soccer, may therefore serve as the appropriate metaphor for this new approach.

As we have seen, the range of tools that is now available to address public problems has proliferated massively, vastly complicating the task of comprehending, let alone managing, public action. Each of the multitude of instruments engages its own set of actors, utilizes its own operating procedures, has its own internal dynamics, and consequently imparts its own "spin" to the performance of public programs. "Privatization," for all its political appeal, is too general a euphemism to capture the diversity of these different arrangements or the peculiarities and specificities that accompany their use.

A central characteristic of many of the most widely used tools, moreover, is their indirection, their sharing of key aspects of discretionary authority between government agencies and a host of third-party partners. Under these circumstances, the traditional concerns of public administration with the internal operations of public agencies have become, if not irrelevant, at least far less germane. Instead, the task of public problem solving has come to resemble the management of diplomatic relationships among sovereign states. "Network management" rather than either public management or market dynamics comes closest to describing the central realities involved. This form of management involves mutual adaptation through bargaining and interaction rather than the command-and-control characteristic of public administration or the independent action characteristic of markets.

The new governance thus requires a new field of knowledge focused on the operating features of the different tools of public action and the optimal conditions for their use. Efforts to understand the tasks of public problem solving in this new era must therefore begin not only with a clear understanding of the problem to be solved, but also with an appreciation of the characteristics of the available repertoire of tools and how they structure the play.

TOOL CHOICES AS POLITICAL CHOICES

A second key implication to flow from this analysis is that the new governance is more than simply a management concept. Nor does "network management" exhaust its full meaning. Whereas network analysis focuses on the interactions of organizations "within a given framework of inter-organizational relationships,"[1] the new governance focuses as well on the initial structuring of these relationships. More specifically, it sees tool choices as *political,* and not just technical, choices, in the best sense of this term, that is, they involve decisions about values. This is so because tool choices affect the interests and perspectives that are likely to be served by particular programs. They do so in part by specifying the nature of the activity that a program involves (e.g., the degree of coercion employed). But they do so also by determining the set of actors who get to take part in the crucial implementation phase that programs also undergo.

The new governance and its tools perspective thus builds on the central insight that emerged from the implementation literature of the last two decades: namely, that policy rarely springs full-blown from the mind of legislatures. Rather, legislatures are often of mixed minds about the goals of policies, and critical matters of definition and emphasis consequently are left to later stages of the process. By structuring who plays what roles in these later stages, and with what degree of discretion, tool choices consequently shape which of several possible interpretations of a program's goals and objectives have the best chance of being translated into reality. The basic choice of tool, and the particular configuration of the "design features" of the tool, represent "bets" on the part of different constituencies about how a program will work, and about whose values and perspectives will be given the best chance of being effectuated. Interests affected by a particular program thus fight for the use of tools that give them, or those they trust, the most effective seat at the table during this critical implementation process.

Not only immediate political interests but also broader ideological predispositions shape the selection of tools. Tools often take on an ideological coloration that makes them attractive on *a priori* grounds regardless of their fit with the problem to be solved. Thus, for example, promarket enthusiasts favor vouchers and corrective fees as the optimum solution to most problems because these tools make maximum use of essentially market processes. By contrast, those more skeptical of market processes tend to lean toward direct government and regulation. Because these predispositions attract greater or lesser support in particular national contexts, patterns of tool choice also vary by country as well.

This political dimension of the choice of tools explains why these choices are so hotly contested and why most current policy debates end up being as much debates over the appropriate tool of public action to use as debates over whether public involvement is appropriate in the first place. In the process, considerations of manageability often take a backseat to considerations of political "saleability" in the design of public programs. The problem, however, is that these two sets of considerations are often not in harmony. On the contrary, at least in the American context, they seem most often to be at odds. Manageability tends to require operational simplicity, direct lines of responsibility, and a minimum of separate decision points. The generation of political support, at least in the United States, however, tends to require the sharing of responsibilities, the multiplication of decision points, and a resulting operational complexity. Too often, therefore, we choose tools of action that complicate rather than ease the prospects for effective public action. By identifying these tradeoffs and bringing them into clearer view, the new governance holds some promise of improving policy design, or at least of alerting those responsible for public action to the difficulties they must overcome.

THE DILEMMAS OF "THIRD-PARTY GOVERNMENT"

This brings us then to a third key implication of the present discussion: that collaborative or "reinvented" government may not offer the panacea that many of its advocates claim for it. To be certain, the indirect tools of action that are a particular hallmark of this approach bring enormous advantages with them:

- They make it possible to bring a wider array of societal resources to bear on the resolution of public problems than is possible with exclusively governmental approaches.

- They thus overcome many of the limitations of resources and public support that often plague the public sector.

- In addition, they offer an added measure of legitimacy to public action by engaging a number of other institutions in public work and thereby extending public action without expanding the size of the governmental bureaucracy.

- They secure the support of many of these involved parties in the promotion of policy initiatives and thus help break down resistance that might otherwise exist.

The problem is that these advantages are purchased at a high price in terms of a number of equally, or more, consequential disadvantages.

The Management Challenge

In the first place, as we have seen, contrary to the easy assumptions of the reinventing government and privatization schools, "third-party government" poses immense management challenges, perhaps far more immense than those posed by traditional public administration. With power dispersed and numerous semiautonomous entities involved in the operation of public programs, even straightforward tasks become difficult. As we argued earlier, indirect tools paradoxically require advance planning of far more operational details than is the case with more direct tools. Matters that could be dealt with internally on an *ad hoc* basis in direct government have to be settled in advance through legally binding contracts under "third-party government." Similarly, incentives have to be devised sufficient to induce desired behavior but not so substantial as to yield windfall gains; concurrence has to be secured at numerous points in complex decision chains; and disparate organizations have to be forged into effective networks capable of integrated action. All of this requires new processes and new skills that differ considerably from those characteristic of traditional government management.

Consequently, much more than generic management skills are needed in the world of the new governance. Also required is specialized knowledge about the operational dynamics of particular tools. Moreover, to the extent that generic management knowledge is useful, it is different from the knowledge now conveyed in most public administration training. In addition to knowledge about the internal dynamics of public agencies, what is needed increasingly is an understanding of the incentive structures of government's third-party partners, how to manage complex networks, how to negotiate with largely autonomous partners in interdependent systems, how to structure incentive systems to overcome the moral hazards of principal-agent relationships, and how to create a sense of shared responsibility for hard-to-measure outcomes. There is, in short, what Kettl terms an "indirect government skill set" that goes beyond what has been conveyed traditionally in public administration training. The goal setting, negotiation, communication, financial management, and bridge-building skills that Kettl identifies form a crucial part of this. But so too are the "activation," "orchestration," and "modulation" skills identified in the introductory chapter.

In short, the "new governance" requires a new public administration the outlines of which are only barely visible in current curricula and teaching materials in the field.

The Accountability Challenge

In addition to the management challenge it poses, "third-party government" also poses a serious accountability challenge. As the previous chapters have shown, many of the newer tools of public action vest substantial discretionary authority in entities other than those with ultimate responsibility for the results. What is more, these other entities have their own autonomous sources of authority that allows them to operate with considerable independence of the authorizing body: they are sovereign state and local governments, private commercial banks, independent nonprofit organizations, profit-seeking companies, universities and hospitals with powerful governing boards, and many more.

As "network theory" suggests, each of these entities enters its relationship with governmental authorities on its own terms, with its own expectations, objectives, and bottom line. What is more, as we have seen, the choice of instrument that structures the relationship is often dictated as much by political considerations as by the appropriateness of the fit between the instrument and the circumstances to which it is being applied. Organizational theorists caution, for example, against using contracting in situations where suppliers are limited in number and consequently can gain an undue advantage over the contracting entity.[2] Yet, this is precisely the circumstance that governments frequently face given the nature of the goods and services they are purchasing and the structure of the markets in which they operate. Similarly, principal-agent theory argues for utilizing "agents" whose purposes line up most "naturally" with those of the "principal" initiating the relationship.[3] Political realities, however, frequently dictate involving agents whose interests diverge substantially from those of the principal and who have the ability not only to disguise what they are doing with the discretion they enjoy in ways that principal-agent theory predicts, but also to defy the principal once this disparity is discovered. The upshot, as Posner has pointed out above, is to increase the chances of goal diversion, fiscal windfalls, moral hazards, insufficient fiscal incentives, and weakly committed or opportunistic partners.

Under these circumstances, the traditional notions of accountability embodied in administrative law, with their emphasis on controlling the discretion exercised by governmental agencies,[4] do not quite suffice. This is so for the obvious reason that governmental agencies are no longer in control of the programs they administer. What is needed, therefore, is both a different standard of accountability and a different frame of reference, including, very often, a different time frame. One of the more hopeful studies of accountability under federal grant-in-aid programs discovered, for example, that initial efforts to enforce accountability to federal objectives through rigorous and detailed guidelines ultimately provoked more resistance than cooperation. Over time, however, as program professionals came to occupy strategic positions at both federal and local levels federal vs. state conflict declined in salience and a compromise set of goals was worked out among the professionals running the program at both levels. In other words, instead of holding state officials to federal requirements, accountability came to be defined in terms of a joint federal-state professional understanding.[5]

This example highlights a point emphasized by Paul Posner: that third-party government and the indirect tools of government it utilizes fundamentally change the meaning of accountability in government programs. Instead of thinking of accountability as responsibility to the unit of government that authorizes the program, third-party government institutionalizes and legitimizes multiple perspectives on the goals and purposes of programs. Under these circumstances, the diversion of national goals in a nationally financed grant or contract program may not be a problem to be solved after all. Rather, it may simply be the price that has to be paid to give the authorizing government a seat at the table in the first place. In a sense, the use of indirect tools denies the authorizing government the authority to enforce its goals on other actors. Rather, it gives such governments at best a "hunting license" to enter into a bargaining relationship with these other actors.

This has profound implications, however, for the practice of administrative law. The central focus of administrative law has long been on controlling the exercise of discretion by administrative agencies. To do so, administrative law relies on essentially procedural controls such as the notice and comment requirements and prohibitions on ex parte contacts elaborated in the Administrative Procedures Act and associated case law. The aim of these procedures is to force administrative discretion into the open and ensure fair access to its exercise.[6] However, this requires that such discretion actually be exercised by the governmental agencies.

With the tools of third-party government, however, this basic requirement is violated. Through these tools, as we have seen, significant shares of the discretionary authority over the operation of public programs is vested in the third parties that actually implement the programs. In a sense, therefore, third-party government offers an institutional, rather than a procedural, solution to the problem of administrative discretion: rather than seeking to control the exercise of discretion *within* administrative agencies, it splinters the discretion and parcels portions out to the variety of third-party partners who come to share with government administrators the authority to shape program operations. This has the result, however, of placing significant portions of the discretionary authority over the operation of public programs beyond the reach of classic administrative law. Indeed, to operate most effectively, third-party tools require that program managers have wide latitude to bargain with their third-party partners, in direct opposition to the prohibitions on ex parte contacts stipulated in administrative law. Perhaps, it is for this reason that legal scholars such as Martin Shapiro have begun referring to a "new discretion."[7] Devices such as "negotiated rule-making," "cooperative regulation," "negotiated contracting," and "cooperative contracting" are the tangible manifestations of this new approach.[8] How to square these new approaches with the more traditional procedural safeguards of administrative law, however, is still far from settled, leaving administrators and courts alike significantly adrift.[9]

The Legitimacy Challenge

Finally, these developments pose even more profound challenges for democratic theory, and potentially for the popular support of government. In a sense, third-party government substitutes the indirect tools of public action for the traditional mechanisms of democratic control posited in classical public administration. Those mechanisms presumed that elected officials, acting in accord with the will of the people as expressed in elections, set policy directions and then hold administrators to account through the hierarchic controls of administrative agencies. Central to this approach was a willingness to concentrate public action in hierarchic agencies that could be held to account for the performance of public programs.

By contrast, indirect tools of government shred those hierarchic controls, leaving agency administrators, and the elected officials who lean on them, ill-equipped to ensure the results they want. In a sense, the public seems to have voted with its feet against this classic model. Frustrated by the perceived ponderousness and impersonality of large-scale bureaucratic agencies, it has turned instead to far more decentralized approaches, trading the clarity of control for the hoped-for responsiveness and efficiency of more indirect means, and hoping to gain in the process more direct opportunities for involvement in civic affairs.

Whether indirect government delivers on its promise, however, is far from assured. As noted in previous chapters, numerous opportunities arise for affected parties to use the authority they gain over public resources to implement their own partial views of what public policy should involve. In addition, third-party tools turn out to be tricky to administer and put into effect. Multiple clearance points have to be negotiated and numerous perspectives reconciled before action can occur. Beyond this, the link between the taxes citizens pay and the services they receive is attenuated in third-party government since third parties end up delivering many of the services that government finances. In the process, third-party government may delegitimize government in the very act of enabling it to operate in new spheres. Not surprisingly, this poses additional challenges in sustaining popular support for the governmental enterprise.

All of this points up the fourth significant conclusion that flows from this work: that a significant knowledge gap remains to be closed to claim the promise that the new governance offers. Essentially, the new governance is a call for a more realistic, less Pollyannaish, approach to the opportunities that public problem solving faces in the era of third-party government. To take full advantage of these opportunities, however, important work remains. More specifically, three crucial bodies of knowledge must be further developed, disseminated, and applied.

Tool Knowledge

In the first place, the new governance requires far more detailed knowledge about the distinctive tools of public action now being used to respond to public problems. As we have seen, these tools have not only proliferated in number but also grown increasingly complex. Yet, research and teaching about the tools of public action has hardly kept pace. Most public administration training remains focused on the tool of direct government and the operation of public agencies. Some tools, such as regulation and grants, have attracted considerable attention, but others have barely been examined in any depth.

The chapters in this volume go a considerable distance toward closing this gap, but much remains to be done. To improve the operation of public programs, far more research is needed on the distinctive features of the various tools of public action and on their characteristic consequences. Greater understanding is needed as well of the consequences of mixing and matching tool features, of selecting a particular tool, and then adding to it design features that negate or counteract some of its central characteristics (e.g., adding refundable features to tax expenditures to make them valuable to lower-income citizens). Those involved in addressing public problems need to acquire expertise not only about the operation of public agencies and the substantive fields of policy in which they will work, but also about the tools of action through which public action proceeds. Each of these tools has its own distinctive features, skill requirements, operating procedures, and set of institutional relationships. Developing such "tool knowledge" and conveying it to those involved in the implementation of public action, whether in public or private agencies, therefore remains one of the principal priorities that the new governance faces.

Design Knowledge

Important as tool knowledge is to the new governance, however, it is far from sufficient. Tools do not, after all, operate in isolation. They are context specific. This is what differentiates the "new governance" from the more ideological approaches to public-sector reform that have surfaced in recent years under such labels as "privatization," "deregulation," or "devolution." The new governance does not begin with the assumption that any particular tool is "*the* key to better government," as the title of a recent book on privatization puts it.[10] Rather, it argues that the choice of tool depends heavily on the problem it is intended to solve and the context within which it operates. Contracting makes most sense, for example, where products can be specified with reasonable precision and markets are reasonably competitive. Where these conditions do not obtain, however, contracting can backfire.

At the same time, the new governance acknowledges that decisions about the most appropriate tool cannot be decided automatically by mathematical formula even once the context is clear. Important values are also at stake, as we have seen, and multiple values at that. The use of contracting thus may serve the goal of efficiency, but this is only one of the goals that public action might usefully promote. Effective program design in the era of the new governance therefore requires information not only about the available tools and the context in which they will be applied, but also about the ranking of objectives to be served. Therefore, tool design requires a blend of technical and political judgment.

Finally, tool decisions need not be either-or decisions. Rather, different tools can be combined to produce joint effects. Such packaging makes it possible to blend the advantages and disadvantages of different tools into a more palatable policy stew. Frans C. J. van der Doelen has argued, for example, that such packaging can optimize the two competing objectives of any policy—legitimacy and effectiveness—by consciously combining stimulative features that contribute to legitimacy with restrictive ones that contribute to effectiveness. As he puts it:[11]

> Stimulative policy instruments (information, subsidies, contracts) legitimate a policy
> whereas repressive policy instruments (propaganda, levies, and orders or prohibitions)
> effectuate it. By combining stimulative and repressive forms of control models, in other
> words by giving and taking, the authorities enhance the feasibility and effectiveness of a
> policy.

Such blending of instruments perhaps has made the greatest headway in the environmental area, where a wide assortment of different approaches is now in evidence, including self-regulation, co-regulation, environmental audits, environmental management systems, eco-labeling, new product liability rules, fees, tradable permits, community right-to-know-legislation, and good neighbor agreements.[12] Major environmental laws, such as the Clean Air Act Amendments of 1990 in the United States, have consequently come to embrace a virtual "suite" of interventions—traditional command-and-control regulations, technology-based standards, performance standards, market-based permitting schemes, and many more. Similar medleys of tools are also increasingly evident in other fields as well. Thus, for example, the legislation creating the Empowerment Zones for urban regeneration in the United States in the early 1990s made provision for grants, loans, loan guarantees, bond financing, and tax expenditures and left it to local policymakers to decide how to blend these components to achieve the program's objectives in the particular contexts of their local areas. By the same token, the law creating the pension insurance and regulation system in the United States contains a rich combination of insurance, regulation, tax expenditure, and information tools.

Although instruments are increasingly being combined in inventive blends, the blending is still largely *ad hoc,* with too little attention given to how tools might be optimally combined into truly integrated systems, and with little systematic understanding of the relative advantages of different combinations in different social, economic, or institutional contexts.[13] For this, much more systematic research and analysis are needed. It is precisely such complex "design knowledge" that the new governance seeks to encourage.

Operating Knowledge

Finally, even the most expertly designed "suite" of tools will fail if those entrusted to operate them do not understand the tasks that are involved. As we have argued, management under the "new governance" is a different enterprise from that embodied in traditional public administration. Instead of *management skills,* what is increasingly required are *enablement skills,* the ability to bring multiple stakeholders with partially independent sources of power and influence to the table to share resources for a common end in a situation of extensive interdependence. Where traditional public management emphasizes "command and control" among entities arrayed hierarchically in a bureaucracy, enablement emphasizes bargaining and negotiation among semiautonomous entities arrayed horizontally in a network.

More specifically, as noted earlier, indirect government puts a premium on three skills that may be useful in direct government as well, but in a far more muted way.

- First, *activation skills*—the ability to mobilize and activate the complex partnerships that public action increasingly requires

- Second, *orchestration skills*—the ability to blend the partners involved in complex public action networks into effectively functioning systems rather than warring fiefdoms

- Third, *modulation skills*—the ability to find the right combination of rewards and punishments to elicit the necessary cooperation among the interdependent players of a complex policy network without providing windfall benefits to one or another actor for doing what they would have done anyway

At the operational level, this requires capability in the sorts of functions that Kettl identifies: goal setting, negotiation, communication, financial management, and bridge building.

Fortunately, some headway has been made in identifying these skills and developing the procedures for conveying them to others. For the new governance to achieve the breakthrough that is required, however, vastly more effort will need to be devoted to this task. This will require rethinking significant components of public administration and public policy training. It may also require a far greater integration among the three major fields of management training that have surfaced in recent years: business management, public management, and nonprofit management. Since the solution of public problems increasingly involves the joint action of these various institutions, greater attention needs to be paid to equipping leaders in all three to understand and interact with their counterparts in the others.[14]

RETHINKING THE ROLE OF GOVERNMENT

Finally, the foregoing discussion has important implications for the role of government in the twenty-first century. Contrary to the "privatization" theories that have been much in evidence in recent years, the new governance does not question the critical need for government in addressing public problems in the years ahead. To the contrary, this role may become more important than ever. The growing complexity and integration of social, economic, and political life virtually guarantees this, as does the need for a keeper of the rules of engagement among various institutions and sectors.

The nature of the government role may differ, however, from what either the traditional public administration or the "reinventing government" paradigms assume. On the one hand, government in the twenty-first century seems unlikely to return to the role of dominant supplier of public services suggested in the classical model. The breadth of the problems government has been called on to address and the services it has been called on to provide coupled with prevailing antibureaucracy sentiments makes this practically, as well as politically, impossible. Government needs its third-party partners both to legitimize and to execute the responsibilities it has taken on. On the other hand, however, government seems equally unlikely to perform the "steering" function attributed to it in the reinventing government paradigm. Despite its monopoly on the legitimate use of force, government simply lacks the authority and independence to enforce its will on other actors the way this concept implies. The relationships established in the world of third-party government are interdependent relationships, not hierarchic ones. This puts limits on the extent to which one party can "steer," while the other merely "rows."

What, then, is the role that government should play in the new governance? And how important is it? The answer is that government must serve as the "balance wheel" of the new systems of collaborative problem solving that will increasingly exist. Its function, as we have suggested, is to activate the needed partnerships and to make sure that public values, broadly conceived, are effectively represented in the collaborative systems that result. This means playing a role in the initial design of public action to ensure that safeguards are built into the operation of indirect tools to protect the public interest and ensure a public voice. It means engaging actively in the bargaining process that ensues after the initial design to protect against the hijacking of public authority for limited public or private ends. It means ensuring that values such as equity, participation, and the common good are effectively represented in these deliberations in addition to the values of efficiency and effectiveness.

This conception of the role of government in the era of third-party government comes close to the image of "the new public service" recently articulated by Robert Denhart and Janet Vinzant.[15] In this conception, the role of public management is not to deliver services but to promote community, to help citizens articulate shared interests, to bring the proper players to the table and broker agreements among them, and to function as "proxy citizens."

If anything, the proliferation of tools of government action, many of them vesting significant shares of discretionary authority over the operation of public programs in third-party actors, has made this public role far more important than ever before. At the same time, it has made it far more difficult. Public officials must now deal with citizens through extended chains of indirection. Their ability to guarantee the performance of public efforts is constrained by tools of action that leave them in a bargaining relationship with a complex array of public and private actors.

To perform effectively in this role, public managers must be able not simply to follow rules, but to engage in complex multiparty negotiations. To do so, they must know far more about the operating realities of the instruments on which their programs rely, and how these instruments can best be utilized to serve public purposes. In short, they must be equipped with the knowledge that the new governance—and this volume—seeks to foster.

CONCLUSION

The last fifty years have witnessed a remarkable revolution in the basic technology of public action in the tools or instruments used to address public problems. The array of potential policy instruments, and the diversity of design options for each, now makes it possible to find an instrument that fits almost any circumstance and to bring a wide assortment of social actors into the business of responding to public needs in the process.

Regrettably, however, our knowledge of the operating characteristics and programmatic consequences of these different instruments, and the public's awareness of the transformation of the public sector that they have produced, have lagged behind badly.

As a consequence, both the practice of public management and the building of citizen confidence have suffered.

The "new governance" is a call to correct this imbalance—to shift the unit of analysis in policy work, to cumulate a body of knowledge explicitly focused on the tools of action used to address public problems, to call attention to the quite different management skills and accountability requirements that many of these tools entail, and thereby to improve the design and management of public problem solving and the citizenry's comprehension of what public action now involves.

This volume was conceived as a start on these tasks. However, it is only a start. Much additional work lies ahead. Hopefully, the material presented here will provide a useful foundation on which to build.

NOTES

1. W. J. M. Kickert and J. F. M. Koppenjam, "Public Management and Network Management: An Overview," in *Managing Complex Networks* eds. Kickert et al. (1997), 47.

2. T. M. Moe, "The New Economics of Organization," (1984), 761.

3. John W. Pratt and Richard J. Zeckhauser, "Principals and Agents: An Overview," in *Principals and Agents: The Structure of Business,* eds. John W. Pratt and Richard J. Zeckhauser (Cambridge, Mass.: Harvard Business School Press, 1985), 14–15.

4. For a discussion of the classic approach to accountability in administrative law see Peter H. Schuck, *Foundations of Administrative Law* (New York: Oxford University Press, 1994), 7–8.

5. Paul Peterson, Barry G. Rabe, and Kenneth K. Wong, *When Federalism Works* (Washington, D.C.: The Brookings Institution, 1986). For a more general analysis of collaboration as a process of mutual adaptation among interdependent organizations see Barbara Gray, *Collaborating: Finding Common Ground for Multiparty Problems* (San Francisco: Jossey-Bass, 1989).

6. See, for example, Martin Shapiro, "APA: Past, Present, and Future," *Virginia Law Review* 72, no. 447 (1986); and Cornelius M. Kerwin, *Rulemaking: How Government Agencies Write Law and Make Policy,* 2d ed. (Washington, D.C.: Congressional Quarterly Press, 1999).

7. Martin Shapiro, "Administrative Discretion: The Next Stage," *The Yale Law Journal* 91 (1994): 1487–1522, reprinted in Peter Schuck, *Foundations of Administrative Law* (1994), 373–374.

8. On the negotiated and cooperative models of contracting see Ruth Hoogland DeHoog, "Competition, Negotiation, or Cooperation: Three Models for Service Contracting," *Administration and Society* 22, no. 3 (November 1990): 317–340.

9. For a discussion of the legal ambiguities surrounding the degree of accountability of third-party agents in public programs see Daniel Guttman, "Public Purpose and Private Service: The Twentieth-Century Culture of Contracting Out and the Evolving Law of Diffused Sovereignty," *Administrative Law Review* 52, no. 3 (summer 2000): 910–923.

10. The reference here is to E. S. Savas, *Privatization: The Key to Better Government* (Chatham, N.J.: Chatham House Publishers, 1987).

11. Frans C. J. van der Doelen, "The 'Give and Take' Packaging of Policy Instruments: Optimizing Legitimacy and Effectiveness," in *Carrots, Sticks, and Sermons,* eds. Bemelmans-Videc et al. (1998), 134.

12. N. J. Gunningham, H. Grabosky, and D. Sinclair, *Smart Regulation* (New York: Oxford University Press, 1998), 13.

13. Gunningham et al., *Smart Regulation* (1998), 12–13.

14. For further elaboration on this point see: Lester M. Salamon, "Nonprofit Management Education: A Field Whose Time Has Passed?" in *Nonprofit Management Education: U.S. and World Perspectives.* Eds. Michael O'Neill and Kathleen Fletcher (Westport, Conn.: Praeger, 1998), 137–45.

15. Robert Denhart and Janet Vinzant, "The New Public Service," *Public Administration Review* 60, no. 6 (2000), 553–557.

Abraham, Kenneth S. *Distributing Risk: Insurance, Legal Theory, and Public Policy.* New Haven: Yale University Press, 1986.

Adams, T. S. "Ideals and Idealism in Taxation." *American Economic Review* 18, no. 1 (1928): 1–8.

Adhikarya, Ronny. "The Strategic Extension Campaigns on Rat Control in Bangladesh." In *Public Communication Campaigns.* 2d ed. Edited by R. E. Rice and C. K. Atkin. Newbury Park, Calif.: Sage, 1989.

Adler, Emanuel. "The Emergence of Cooperation: National Epistemic Communities and the International Evolution of the Idea of Arms Control." *International Organization* 46 (1992): 101–146.

"Aeronatique: l'offensive americaine." *Le Figaro* (4 May 1999).

Aharoni, Yair. *The Evolution and Management of State-Owned Enterprises.* Cambridge, Mass.: Ballinger Publishing, 1986.

Albrecht, Terrance L., and Mara B. Adelman. *Communicating Social Support.* Newbury Park, Calif.: Sage Publications, 1987.

Alexander, Jennifer. "The Impact of Devolution on Nonprofits: A Multiphase Study of Social Service Organizations." *Nonprofit Management and Leadership* 10 (fall 1999): 57–70.

Amundsen, A. *Joint Management of Energy and Environment in Industry.* Frederikstad: Oestfold Research Foundation, 1999.

Andersen, Svein S., and Kjell A. Eliassen, eds. *Making Policy in Europe: The Europeification of National Policy-Making.* London and Thousand Oaks, Calif.: Sage Publications, 1993.

Anderson, Mikael Skou. "Assessing the Effectiveness of Denmark's Waste Tax." *Environment* 40, no. 4 (1998): 11–15, 38–41.

Anderson, Mikael Skou, and Duncan Liefferink, eds. *European Environmental Policy: The Pioneers.* Manchester: Manchester University Press, 1997.

Andrews, J. Craig. "The Effectiveness of Alcohol Warning Labels: A Review and Extension." *American Behavioral Scientist* 38, no. 4 (1995): 622–632.

Andrews, J. Craig, and Richard Netemayer. "Alcohol Warning Label Effects." In *Marketing and Consumer Research in the Public Interest,* edited by R. P. Hill, pp. 153–175. Thousand Oaks, Calif.: Sage, 1996.

Anheier, Helmut K., and Wolfgang Seibel, eds. *The Third Sector: Comparative Studies of Nonprofit Organizations.* Berlin and New York: Walter de Gruyter, 1990.

Anthony, Robert, and Glenn A. Welsch. *Fundamentals of Management Accounting.* Homewood, Ill.: Irwin, 1977.

Arnold, R. Douglas. *The Logic of Congressional Action.* New Haven: Yale University Press, 1990.

Arrow, Kenneth J. "The Economics of Agency." In *Principals and Agents,* edited by John W. Pratt and Richard J. Zeckhauser, pp. 37–50. Boston: Harvard Business School Press, 1985.

Atkin, Charles K., and Vicki Freimuth. "Formative Evaluation Research in Campaign Design." In *Public Communication Campaigns.* 2d ed. Edited by R. Rice and C. Atkin, pp. 131–150. Newbury Park, Calif.: Sage, 1989.

Atkinson, Michael M., and Robert A. Nigol. "Selecting Policy Instruments: Neo-Institutional and Rational Choice Interpretations of Automobile Insurance in Ontario." *Canadian Journal of Political Science* 22 (1989): 107–135.

"A-12 Contractors Awarded $12B in Damages for Pentagon's Improper Default Termination." *Federal Contracts Report* 69 (23 February 1998).

Austen, James. *The Collaboration Challenge: How Nonprofits and Businesses Succeed through Strategic Alliances.* San Francisco: Jossey-Bass, 2000.

Axelrod, Donald. *Shadow Government: The Hidden World of Public Authorities.* New York: Wiley, 1992.

Ayres, Ian, and John Braithwaite. *Responsive Regulation: Transcending the Deregulation Debate.* Oxford and New York: Oxford University Press, 1992.

Bailey, Robert W. "Uses and Misuses of Privatization." In *Prospects for Privatization,* edited by Steve Hanke. *Proceedings of the American Academy of Political Science* 36, no. 3 (1987): 138–150.

Bandura, Albert. *Social Foundations of Thought and Action: A Social Cognitive Theory.* Englewood Cliffs, N.J.: Prentice-Hall, 1986.

Banfield, Edward K. *Government Project.* New York: Free Press, 1951.

Bang, Hae-Kyong. "Analyzing the Impact of the Liquor Industry's Lifting of the Ban on Broadcast Advertising." *Journal of Public Policy and Marketing* 17 (1998): 132–138.

Bardach, Eugene. "Social Regulation." In *Beyond Privatization: The Tools of Government Action,* edited by Lester M. Salamon, pp. 197–229. Washington, D.C.: Urban Institute Press, 1989.

———. *The Implementation Game: What Happens after a Bill Becomes a Law.* Cambridge, Mass.: MIT Press, 1977.

Bardach, Eugene, and Robert A. Kagan. *Going by the Book: The Problem of Regulatory Unreasonableness: A Twentieth-Century Fund Report.* Philadelphia: Temple University Press, 1982.

———. *Going by the Book: The Problem of Regulatory Unreasonableness: A Twentieth-Century Fund Report,* pp. 123–151. Philadelphia: Temple University Press, 1982.

Bargh, John A. "The Automaticity of Everyday Life." In *The Automaticity of Everyday Life: Advances in Social Cognition,* edited by Robert S. Wyer, Jr., vol. 10, pp. 1–61. Mahwah, N.J.: Erlbaum, 1997.

Barnard, Chester. *The Functions of the Executive.* Cambridge, Mass.: Harvard University Press, 1938.

Barnow, Burt S. "Vouchers for Federal Targeted Training Programs." In *Vouchers and the Provision of Public Services,* edited by C. Eugene Steuerle, Van Doorn Ooms, George Peterson, and Robert D. Reischauer, pp. 224–250. Washington, D.C.: The Brookings Institution Press, Committee for Economic Development, and Urban Institute Press, 2000.

Barnow, Burt S., and Christopher King, eds. *Improving the Odds: Increasing the Effectiveness of Publicly Funded Training.* Washington, D.C.: Urban Institute Press, 2000.

Barry, Peter J. *The Effects of Credit Policies on U.S. Agriculture.* Washington, D.C.: American Enterprise Institute, 1995.

Barzelay, Michael. *Breaking through Bureaucracy.* Berkeley: University of California Press, 1992.

Baumgartner, Frank, and Bryan Jones. *Agendas and Instability in American Politics.* Chicago: University of Chicago Press, 1993.

Behn, Robert D., and Peter A. Kant. "Strategies for Avoiding the Pitfalls of Performance Contracting." *Public Productivity and Management Review* 22 (June 1999): 470–489.

Bemelmans-Videc, Marie-Louise, Ray C. Rist, and Evert Vedung. *Carrots, Sticks and Sermons: Policy Instruments and Their Evaluation.* New Brunswick, N.J.: Transaction Books, 1998.

Bendick, Jr., Marc. *Quality Control in a Federal-State Public Assistance Program.* Washington, D.C.: Urban Institute, 1979.

Bennis, Warren. Foreword to *The Human Side of Enterprise,* edited by Douglas McGregor. New York: McGraw-Hill, 1985.

Benston, George, and George Kaufman. "Is the Banking and Payments System Fragile?" *Journal of Financial Services Research* 9 (December 1995): 209–240.

Bergin, Christopher. "Spending through the Tax Code: The Top Ten Tax Expenditures." *Tax Notes* 82, no. 8 (1999): 1100.

Bernstein, Marver. *Regulating Business by Independent Commission.* Princeton, N.J.: Princeton University Press, 1955.

Bernstein, Susan R. *Managing Contracted Services in the Nonprofit Agency.* Philadelphia: Temple University Press, 1991.

Besharov, Douglas J., and Nazanin Samari. "Child Care Vouchers and Cash Payments." In *Vouchers and the Provision of Public Services,* edited by C. Eugene Steuerle, Van Doorn Ooms, George Peterson, and Robert D. Reischauer, pp. 195–223. Washington, D.C.: The Brookings Institution Press, Committee for Economic Development, and Urban Institute Press, 2000.

Birnbaum, Jeffrey H., and Alan S. Murray. *Showdown at Gucci Gulch: Lawmakers, Lobbyists, and the Unlikely Triumph of Tax Reform.* New York: Vintage, 1987.

Blais, André, Donald Blake, and Stéphane Dion. *Politics, Elections and Public Employment.* Pittsburgh: University of Pittsburgh Press, 1998.

Blau, Peter M. *On the Nature of Organizations.* New York: Wiley, 1974.

Blough, Roy. *The Federal Taxing Process.* New York: Prentice-Hall, 1952.

Bonnen, James T. "Historical Sources of U.S. Agricultural Productivity: Implications for R and D Policy and Social Science Research." *American Journal of Agricultural Economics* 65, no. 5 (December 1983): 958–966.

Bonser, Charles F., Eugene B. McGregor, Jr., and Clinton V. Oster, Jr. *Policy Choices and Public Action.* Upper Saddle River, N.J.: Prentice-Hall, 1996.

Booz Allen and Hamilton. *Management Audit of the Government Printing Office, Executive Summary.* Submitted to the General Accounting Office 21 May 1998.

Bosso, Christopher J. *Pesticides and Politics: The Life Cycle of a Public Issue.* Pittsburgh: University of Pittsburgh Press, 1987.

Boston, Jonathan, and June Pallot. "Linking Strategy and Performance: Developments in the New Zealand Public Sector." *Journal of Policy Analysis and Management* 16 (1997): 382–404.

Boston, Jonathan, John Martin, June Pallot, and Pat Walsh. *Public Management: The New Zealand Model.* Auckland: Oxford University Press, 1996.

Bovens, Mark A. P., Paul 't Hart, and B. Guy Peters. "Policy Success and Failure." Paper presented at Workshops of European Consortium for Political Research, Mannheim, Germany, 1999.

Bradbury, Darcy. Deputy Assistant Secretary of the Treasury for Federal Finance. Statement before the Subcommittee on Postsecondary Education, Training and Lifelong Learning, Committee on Economic and Educational Opportunities, and the Subcommittee on National Economic Growth, Natural Resources and Regulatory Affairs, Committee on Government Reform and Oversight, U.S. House of Representatives. Washington, D.C., 3 May 1995.

Bradford, Calvin. "Financing Home Ownership: The Federal Role in Neighborhood Decline." *Urban Affairs Quarterly* 14, no. 3 (March 1979): 313–335.

Bradford, David F., and Daniel N. Shaviro. "The Economics of Vouchers." In *Vouchers and the Provision of Public Services,* edited by C. Eugene Steuerle, Van Doorn Ooms, George Peterson, and Robert D. Reischauer, pp. 40–91. Washington, D.C.: The Brookings Institution Press, Committee for Economic Development, and Urban Institute Press, 2000.

Brehm, John, and Scott Gates. *Working, Shirking and Sabotage: Bureaucratic Response to a Democratic Public.* Ann Arbor: University of Michigan Press, 1999.

Bressers, J. Th. A., H. Pullen, and J. Schuddeboom. *Toetsing van beleidsinstrumenten.* Enschede: Universiteit Twente, 1990.

Brickman, Ronald, Sheila Jasnoff, and Thomas Ilgen. *Controlling Chemicals: The Politics of Regulation in Europe and the United States.* Ithaca, N.Y.: Cornell University Press, 1985.

de Bruijn, Hans A., and Hans A. M. Hufen. "The Traditional Approach to Policy Instruments." In *Public Policy Instruments: Evaluating the Tools of Public Administration,* edited by B. Guy Peters and Frans K. M. van Nispen, pp. 11–32. Cheltenham, U.K.: Edward Elgar, 1998.

de Bruijn, J. A., and E. F. ten Heuvelhof. "Instruments for Network Management." In *Managing Complex Networks: Strategies for the Public Sector,* edited by Walter J. M. Kickert, Erik-Hans Klijn, and Joop F. M. Koppenjan, pp. 119–136. London: Sage Publications, 1997.

———. *Sturingsinstrumenten voor de overheid (Governance Instruments for the Government).* Leiden: Stenfert Kroese, 1991.

Brunori, David. "Principles of Tax Policy and Targeted Tax Incentives." *State and Local Government Review* 29 (1997): 50–61.

Budget of the United States Government: Fiscal Year 2001. Washington, D.C.: Government Printing Office, 2000.

Burby, Raymond J. "Baton Rouge: The Making and Breaking of a Petrochemical Paradise." In *Transforming New Orleans and Its Environs: Centuries of Change,* edited by Craig E. Colten, pp. 160–177. Pittsburgh: University of Pittsburgh Press, 2000.

Burby, Raymond J., and Peter J. May. *Making Governments Plan: State Experiments in Managing Land Use.* Baltimore: Johns Hopkins University Press, 1997.

Burby, Raymond J., and Robert C. Paterson. "Improving Compliance with State Environmental Regulations." *Journal of Policy Analysis and Management* 12, no. 4 (1993): 753–772.

Burby, Raymond J., Peter J. May, and Robert C. Paterson. "Improving Compliance with Regulations: Choices and Outcomes for Local Government." *Journal of the American Planning Association* 64, no. 3 (1998): 324–334.

Burki, Shahid J., and Guillermo E. Perry. *Beyond the Washington Consensus: Institutions Matter.* World Bank Latin American and Caribbean Studies Viewpoints. Washington, D.C.: The World Bank, 1998.

Burton, Scott, and Abhijit Biswas. "Preliminary Assessment of Changes in Labels Required by the Nutrition Labeling and Education Act of 1990." *Journal of Consumer Affairs* 27 (1993): 127–144.

Burton, Thomas. "Operation That Rated Hospitals Was Success, but the Patience Died." *Wall Street Journal* (23 August 1999): 1.

Butler, Stewart. *Privatizing Federal Spending: A Strategy to Eliminate the Deficit.* New York: Universe Books, 1985.

Calabresi, Guido. *The Costs of Accidents.* New Haven: Yale University Press, 1970.

Calhoun, Craig. "Indirect Relationships and Imagined Communities: Large-Scale Social Integration and the Transformation of Everyday Life." In *Social Theory for a Changing Society*, pp. 95–130. New York: Russell Sage Foundation, 1991.

Calista, Donald J. "Policy Implementation." In *Encyclopedia of Policy Studies*, edited by Stuart Nagel, pp. 118–140. New York: Marcel Dekker, 1994.

Calomiris, Charles, and Joseph Mason. "Contagion and Bank Failures during the Great Depression: The June 1932 Chicago Banking Panic." *American Economic Review* 87, no. 5 (1997): 863–883.

Campbell, John. "Cataclysm." *St. Louis Federal Reserve Regional Review* (summer 1997): 5–11.

Caprio, Jr., Gerard, and Daniela Klingebiel. "Bank Insolvencies: Cross-Country Experience." World Bank Policy Research Working Paper 1620 (1996).

Caswell, Julie A., and Eliza Mojduszka. "Using Informational Labeling to Influence the Market for Quality in Food Products." *American Journal of Agricultural Economics* 78 (1996): 1248–1253.

Caswell, Julie A., and Daniel I. Padberg. "Toward a More Comprehensive Theory of Food Labels." *American Journal of Agricultural Economics* 74 (May 1992): 460–468.

Cell, Charles P. *Revolution at Work: Mobilization Campaigns in China.* New York: Academic Press, 1977.

Center for Strategic and International Studies. *Integrating Commercial and Military Technologies for National Strength.* Washington, D.C.: CSIS, 1992.

Chase, Gordon. "Implementing a Human Services Program: How Hard Will It Be?" *Public Policy* 27 (fall 1979): 385–435.

Chassin, Mark R., Edward L. Hannan, and Barbara A. DeBuono. "Benefits and Hazards of Reporting Medical Outcomes Publicly." *The New England Journal of Medicine* 334, no. 6 (1996): 394–398.

Cheit, Ross. *Setting Safety Standards: Regulation in the Public and Private Sector.* Berkeley and Los Angeles: University of California Press, 1990.

Chi, Fulin. *Pressing Tasks of China's Economic Transition.* Beijing: Foreign Languages Press, 1996.

Chi, Keon S. *The States and Business Incentives: An Inventory of Tax and Financial Incentive Programs.* Lexington, Ky.: Council of State Governments, 1989.

Chisholm, Donald. *Coordination without Hierarchy: Informal Structures in Multiorganizational Systems.* Berkeley: University of California Press, 1989.

Chubb, John. "The Political Economy of Federalism." *American Political Science Review* 79 (1985): 994–1015.

Chubb, John E., and Terry M. Moe. *Politics, Markets, and America's Schools.* Washington, D.C.: The Brookings Institution, 1990.

Church, Thomas, and Robert Nakamura. "Beyond Superfund: Hazardous Waste Cleanup in Europe and the United States." *Georgetown International Environmental Law Review* 7, no. 1 (1994): 15–57.

Cialdini, Robert B. *Influence: Science and Practice.* 3d ed. New York: HarperCollins, 1993.

Cibinic, Jr., John, and Ralph C. Nash. *Administration of Government Contracts*. 3d ed. Washington, D.C.: George Washington University Press, 1995.

Cibulka, James, and Roberta Derlin. "State Educational Performance Reporting Policies in the U.S." In *Accountability Research in Education: Current Developments*. Elsevier, 1996.

Cigler, Beverly. "A Sampling of Introductory Public Administration Texts." *Journal of Public Affairs Education* 6, no. 1 (January 2000): 45–53.

Clarke, Jeanne Nienaber, and Daniel McCool. *Staking Out the Terrain: Power Differentials among Natural Resources Management Agencies*. 2d ed. Albany: State University of New York Press, 1996.

Claxton, John D., J. R. Brent Ritchie, and Gordon H. G. McDougall. "Evaluating Acceptability and Effectiveness of Consumer Energy Conservation Programs." *Journal of Economic Psychology* 4, nos. 1 2 (1983): 71–83.

Clotfelter, Charles T. "The Impact of Tax Reform on Charitable Giving: A 1989 Perspective." In *Do Taxes Matter? The Impact of the Tax Reform Act of 1986*, edited by Joel Slemrod, pp. 203–235. Cambridge, Mass.: MIT Press, 1990.

———. *Federal Tax Policy and Charitable Giving*. Chicago: University of Chicago Press, 1985.

Cobb, Roger W., and Charles D. Elder. *Participation in American Politics: The Dynamics of Agenda-Building*. Baltimore: Johns Hopkins University Press, 1972.

Cohen, Bernard C. *The Press and Foreign Policy*. Princeton, N.J.: Princeton University Press, 1963.

Cohen, Steven, and Ronald Brand. *Total Quality Management in Government*. San Francisco: Jossey-Bass, 1993.

Coleman, Kevin. *Tax Issues: National Public Opinion*. Washington, D.C.: Congressional Research Service, 1998.

Collett, Merrill. "The Federal Contracting Process." *The Bureaucrat* 10, no. 2 (1981): 18–19.

Coltrane, Scott, Dane Archer, and Elliot Aronson. "The Social Psychological Foundations of Successful Energy Conservation Programmes." *Energy Policy* (April 1986): 133–148.

Congressional Budget Office. *Assessing the Public Costs and Benefits of Fannie Mae and Freddie Mac*. Washington, D.C.: Government Printing Office, 1996.

———. *Controlling Losses of the Pension Benefit Guaranty Corporation*. Washington, D.C.: Government Printing Office, 1995.

———. *Controlling the Risks of Government-Sponsored Enterprises*. Washington, D.C.: Government Printing Office, 1991.

———. *The Economic Effects of the Savings and Loan Crisis*. Washington, D.C.: Government Printing Office, 1995.

Conlan, Timothy J. *From New Federalism to Devolution, Twenty-five Years of Intergovernmental Reform*. Washington, D.C.: The Brookings Institution Press, 1998.

Conlan, Timothy J., Margaret T. Wrightson, and David Beam. *Taxing Choices: The Politics of Tax Reform*. Washington, D.C.: Congressional Quarterly, 1990.

Cooper, Phillip J., and Chester A. Newland, eds. *Handbook of Public Law and Administration*. San Francisco: Jossey-Bass, 1997.

Cortner, Hanna J., and Margaret Moote. *The Politics of Ecosystems Management*. Washington, D.C.: Island Press, 1999.

Council of State Governments and the National Association of State Purchasing Officials. *State and Local Government Purchasing*. 3d ed. Lexington, Ky.: The Council of State Government, 1988.

Covello, Vincent T. "Risk Communication: An Emerging Area of Health Communication Research." In *Communication Yearbook/15*, edited by S. A. Deetz, pp. 359–373. Newbury Park, Calif.: Sage, 1992.

Covello, Vincent T., and Jeryl Mumpower. "Risk Analysis and Risk Management: An Historical Perspective." *Risk Analysis* 5, no. 2 (1985): 103–120.

Cox, Eli P., Michael S. Wogalter, Sara L. Stokes, and Elizabeth J. Tipton Murff. "Do Product Warnings Increase Safe Behavior? A Meta-Analysis." *Journal of Public Policy and Marketing* 16 (1998): 195–204.

Craig, C. Samuel, and J. M. McCann. "Assessing Communication Effects on Energy Conservation." *Journal of Consumer Research* 5 (1978): 82–88.

Crewdson, John. *The Tarnished Door: The New Immigrants and the Transformation of America.* New York: Times Books, 1983.

Curwen, Peter. "The United Kingdom." In *Corporatization, Divestment and the Public-Private Mix: Selected Country Studies,* edited by Ian Thynne, pp. 10–35. Hong Kong: Asian Journal of Public Administration, 1995.

Czerwinski, Stanley. "Flood Insurance: Information on Financial Aspects of the National Flood Insurance Program." Testimony of the General Accounting Office before the House Subcommittee on Housing and Community Opportunity, Committee on Banking and Financial Services, October 1999.

Dahl, Robert, and Charles E. Lindbloom. *Politics, Economics, and Welfare: Planning and Politico-Economic Systems Resolved into Basic Social Processes.* New York: Harper and Row Publishers, 1953.

Datta, Lois-Ellin, and Patrick G. Grasso, eds. *Evaluating Tax Expenditures: Tools and Techniques for Assessing Outcomes.* San Francisco: Jossey-Bass, 1998.

Davie, Bruce F. "Tax Expenditures: The Basics." In *Evaluating Tax Expenditures: Tools and Techniques for Assessing Outcomes,* edited by Lois Ellin Datta and Patrick G. Grasso, pp. 9–23. San Francisco: Jossey-Bass, 1998.

Davies, J. Clarence, and Jan Mazurek. *Pollution Control in the United States: Evaluating the System.* Washington, D.C.: Resources for the Future, 1998.

Davis, Karen. *Medicare Reform: Assuring Health and Economic Security for Beneficiaries.* Testimony before the Committee on the Budget of the United States Senate, 23 January 1997.

Davis, Nuel Pharr. *Lawrence and Oppenheimer.* New York: Simon and Schuster, 1968.

Day, Kathleen. "Fear of What Fannie May Do: Lenders Say the Federally Chartered Company Is Out to Steal Their Business." *The Washington Post* (8 August 1999): H01.

Day, Patricia, and Rudolf Klein. "The Regulation of Nursing Homes: A Comparative Perspective." *The Milbank Quarterly* 65, no. 3 (1987): 303–347.

DeHoog, Ruth Hoogland. "Competition, Negotiation, or Cooperation?: Three Models for Service Contracting." *Administration and Society* 22, no. 3 (November 1990): 317–340.

———. *Contracting out for Human Services: Political, Economic, and Organizational Perspectives.* Albany: State University of New York Press, 1984.

———. "Human Service Contracting: Environmental, Behavioral, and Organizational Conditions." *Administration and Society* 16 (1985): 427–454.

DeLeon, Peter. "The Missing Link Revisited: Contemporary Implementation Research." Paper presented at the 1997 Annual Meeting of the American Political Science Association. Washington, D.C., 1997.

Della Cananea, Giacinto. *Indirizzo e controllo della finanza pubblica.* Bologna: Il Mulino, 1996.

Delli Carpini, Michael X., and Scott Keeter. *What Americans Know About Politics and Why It Matters.* New Haven: Yale University Press, 1996.

Demirguc-Kunt, Asli. Does Deposit Insurance Increase Banking System Stability?: An Empirical Investigation, unpublished manuscript.

Demirguc-Kunt, Asli, and Enrica Detragiache. "The Determinants of Banking Crises: Evidence from Developing and Developed Countries." IMF Working Paper WP/97/106 (1997).

Demirguc-Kunt, Asli, and Harry Huizinga. "Market Discipline and Financial Safety Net Design." World Bank Policy Research Working Paper 2183 (1999).

Demo, David H. "The Self-Concept over Time: Research Issues and Directions." *Annual Review of Sociology* 18 (1992): 303–326.

Demone, Jr., Harold W., and Margaret Gibelman, eds. *Services for Sale: Purchasing Health and Human Services.* New Brunswick, N.J.: Rutgers University Press, 1989.

Denhart, Robert, and Janet Vinzant. "The New Public Service." *Public Administration* 60, no. 6 (2000): 549–559.

Dente, Bruno, ed. *Environmental Policy in Search of New Instruments.* Dordrecht and Boston: Kluwer Academic Publishers, 1995.

Derthick, Martha. *Policy Making for Society Security.* Washington, D.C.: The Brookings Institution Press, 1979.

Dervarajan, Shantayanan, and Jeffrey Hammer. "Risk Reduction and Public Expenditures." World Bank Policy Research Working Paper 1869 (1997).

Dervin, Brenda. "Mass Communicating: Changing Conceptions of the Audience." In *Public Communication Campaigns,* edited by R. Rice and W. Paisley, pp. 71–87. Beverly Hills, Calif.: Sage, 1981.

DeTocqueville, Alexis. *Democracy in America.* New York: Harper Perennial, 1969.

Diamond, Jr., Douglas B., and Michael J. Lea. "Housing Finance in Developed Countries: An International Comparison of Efficiency." *Journal of Housing Research* 3, no. 1 (1992): 1–14.

Dicke, Lisa A., and J. Steven Ott. "Public Agency Accountability in Human Services Contracting." *Public Productivity and Management Review* 22 (June 1999): 502–516.

DiIulio, John J., Gerald Garvey, and Donald F. Kettl. *Improving Government Performance: An Owner's Manual.* Washington, D.C.: The Brookings Institution Press, 1993

DiIulio, John J., et al. "The Public Administration of James Q. Wilson: A Symposium on Bureaucracy." *Public Administration Review* 51, no. 3 (May/June 1991): 193–201.

Dodson, Charles. "Is More Credit the Best Way to Assist Beginning Low-Equity Farmers?" Economic Research Service, U.S. Department of Agriculture. Agriculture Information Bulletin No. 724–04. August 1996.

Doig, James W., and Erwin C. Hargrove, eds. *Leadership and Innovation: A Biographical Perspective on Entrepreneurs in Government.* Baltimore: Johns Hopkins University Press, 1987.

Donahue, John D. *The Privatization Decision: Public Ends, Private Means.* New York: Basic Books, 1989.

Donohew, Lewis, Elizabeth Lorch, and Philip Palmgreen. "Applications of a Theoretic Model of Information Exposure to Health Interventions." *Human Communication Research* 24 (1998): 454–468.

Doorn, Jac A. A. van, and C. J. M. Schuyt, ed. *De Stagnerende Verzorgingsstaat (Stagnating Welfare State).* Meppel/Amsterdam: Boom, 1978.

Drew, Elizabeth. *Politics and Money: The New Road to Corruption.* New York: Macmillan, 1983.

Drucker, Peter. "The Deadly Sins in Public Administration." *Public Administration Review* (March/April 1980): 103–106.

———. *Management: Tasks, Responsibilities, Practices.* New York: Harper and Row, 1973.

Dryzek, John S. *Democracy in Capitalist Times: Ideals, Limits, and Struggles.* New York: Oxford University Press, 1996.

———. *Discursive Democracy: Politics, Policy, and Political Science.* New York: Cambridge University Press, 1990.

Duncan, Joseph W., and William C. Shelton. *Revolution in U.S. Government Statistics 1926–76.* Washington, D.C.: U.S. Department of Commerce, 1978.

Dunlop, John T. "The Limits of Legal Compulsion." *Labor Law Journal* 27, no. 1 (1976): 67–74.

Durkin, Thomas, and Gregory Elliehausen. "The Issue of Market Transparency: Truth-in-Lending Disclosure Requirements as Consumer Protections in the U.S." In *Enhancing Consumer Choice,* edited by R. Mayer, pp. 225–265. Columbia, Mo.: American Council on Consumer Interests, 1990.

Dyckman, Lawrence. "Crop Insurance: Further Actions Could Strengthen Program's Financial Soundness." U.S. General Accounting Office Testimony before the U.S. Senate Committee on Agriculture, Nutrition and Forestry, 21 April 1999.

Dyer, Robert, and Thomas Maronick. "An Evaluation of Consumer Awareness and Use of Energy Labels in the Purchase of Major Appliances: A Longitudinal Analysis." *Journal of Public Policy and Marketing* 7 (1988): 83–97.

Easterbrook, Frank, and Daniel Fischel. "Mandatory Disclosure and the Protection of Investors." *Virginia Law Review* 70 (1984): 669–715.

Edelman, Murray. *Constructing the Political Spectacle.* Chicago: University of Chicago Press, 1988.

Eijde, A. P. J. van der. *Public Management of Society in France.* In press, 2001.

Eisner, Marc Allen. *Regulatory Politics in Transition.* Baltimore and London: Johns Hopkins University Press, 1993.

Elazar, Daniel. *American Federalism: The View from the States,* p. 3. New York: Thomas Y. Crowell, 1973.

Ellmore, Richard. "Backward Mapping." *Political Science Quarterly* 94 (winter 1981): 601–616.

———. "Instruments and Strategy in Public Policy." *Policy Studies Review* 7, no. 1 (1987): 174–186.

Ellul, Jacques. *Propaganda: The Formation of Men's Attitudes,* translated by Konrad Kellen and Jean Lerner. New York: Knopf, 1965.

Ellwood, David T. *Poor Support: Poverty in the American Family.* New York: Basic Books, 1988.

Employment and Training Administration. *Implementing the Workforce Investment Act of 1998: A White Paper.* Washington, D.C.: Government Printing Office, 1998.

Enthoven, Alain. "Health Tax Policy Mismatch." *Health Affairs* 4, no. 4 (1985): 5–14.

Environmental Law Institute. *NEPA in Action: Environmental Offices in Nineteen Federal Agencies.* A Report to the Council on Environmental Quality, 1981.

Esping-Andersen, Gøsta. *The Three Worlds of Welfare Capitalism.* Cambridge: Polity Press in association with Basil Blackwell, 1990.

Evans, Jr., George Heberton. *British Corporation Finance 1775–1850: A Study of Preference Shares.* Baltimore: Johns Hopkins University Press, 1936.

Fairfax, Sally K. "Coming of Age in the Bureau of Land Management: Range Management in Search of a Gospel, in National Research Council/National Academy of Sciences." In *Developing Strategies for Rangeland Management: A Report,* prepared by the Committee on Developing Strategies for Rangeland Management, National Research Council/National Academy of Sciences, pp. 1715–1759. Boulder: Westview Press, 1984.

Farquhar-Pilgrim, Barbara, and F. Floyd Shoemaker. "Campaigns to Affect Energy Behavior." In *Public Communication Campaigns,* edited by Ronald E. Rice and Charles K. Atkin. Beverly Hills, Calif.: Sage, 1981.

Fefferman, Hilbert. "The Redlining of Neighborhoods by Mortgage Lending Institutions and What Can Be Done About It." *Redlining: A Special Report by FNMA,* pp. 25–40. Washington, D.C.: Federal National Mortgage Association, 1976.

Ferguson, Ronald F., and Sara Stoutland. "Recovering the Community Development Field." In *Urban Problems and Community Development,* edited by Ronald F. Ferguson and William T. Dickens, pp. 33–75. Washington, D.C.: The Brookings Institution Press, 1999.

Ferris, James M. "The Double-Edged Sword of Social Service Contracting: Public Accountability Versus Nonprofit Autonomy." *Nonprofit Management and Leadership* 4 (summer 1993): 363–376.

Fiorina, Morris P. *Congress: The Keystone of the Washington Establishment,* rev. ed. New Haven: Yale University Press, 1992.

Fiorino, Daniel. "Toward a New System of Environmental Regulation: The Case for an Industry Sector Approach." *Environmental Law* 26, no. 2 (1996): 457–488.

Fisher, Jeffrey, and William Fisher. "Changing AIDS-Risk Behavior." *Psychological Bulletin* 111 (1992): 455–474.

Fisher, Louis. *Conflicts between Congress and the President.* Princeton, N.J.: Princeton University Press, 1985.

———. "Lobbying with Appropriated Monies Act." In *General Management Laws: A Selective Compendium,* pp. 239–241. Congressional Research Service, Library of Congress, 1999.

Fiske, Susan T., and Shelley E. Taylor. *Social Cognition.* 2d ed. Reading, Mass.: Addison-Wesley, 1990.

Flay, Brian R. *Selling the Smokeless Society: Fifty-six Evaluated Mass Media Programs and Campaigns Worldwide.* Washington, D.C.: American Public Health Association, 1987.

Flora, June A., Nathan Maccoby, and John W. Farquhar. "Communication Campaigns to Prevent Cardiovascular Disease." In *Public Communication Campaigns.* 2d ed. Edited by Ronald E. Rice and Charles K. Atkin, pp. 233–252. Newbury Park, Calif.: Sage, 1989.

Follett, Mary Parker. "The Giving of Orders." Originally published in *Scientific Foundations of Business Administration,* edited by Henry C. Metcalf, pp. 132–149. Baltimore: Williams and Wilkins Co., 1926. Reprinted in *Classics of Public Administration.* 4th ed. Edited by Jay M. Shafritz and Albert C. Hyde, pp. 58–60. Chicago: Dorsey Press, 1997.

Forman, A., and S. Lachter. "The National Institute on Drug Abuse Cocaine Prevention Campaign." In *Communication Campaigns About Drugs,* edited by P. J. Shoemaker. Hillsdale, N.J.: Lawrence Erlbaum Associates, 1989.

Fortin, Y. *La contractualisation dans le secteur public des pays industrialises depuis 1980.* Paris: L'Harmattan, 1999.

Foulke, Roy A. *The Sinews of American Commerce.* New York: Dun & Bradstreet, 1941.

Fox, Edward A. Statement before the Subcommittee on Education, Arts and Humanities, Committee on Labor and Human Resources, United States Senate. *Oversight of Student Loan Marketing Association (Sallie Mae).* Washington, D.C.: Government Printing Office, 12 August 1982.

Frederickson, H. George. "The Repositioning of Public Administration." The John Gaus Lecture, American Political Science Association, 3 September 1999.

———. *The Spirit of Public Administration.* San Francisco: Jossey-Bass, 1997.

Freimuth, Vicki S., and J. P. Van Nevel. "Reaching the Public: The Asbestos Awareness Campaign." *Journal of Communications* 31 (1981): 155–167.

Froot, Kenneth A. "The Evolving Market for Catastrophic Event Risk." *NBER Working Paper* 7287 (1999).

Fung, Archon, and Dara O'Rourke. "Reinventing Environmental Regulation from the Grassroots Up: Explaining and Expanding the Success of the Toxics Release Inventory." *Environmental Management* 25 (2000): 115–127.

Futterman, Jack S. "The Social Security Administration's Recent Reorganizations and Related Administrative Problems." National Commission on Social Security, *Social Security in America's Future,* Appendix E, March 1981.

Galanter, Marc. "Real World Torts: An Antidote to Anecdote." *Maryland Law Review* 55 (1996): 1093–1160.

Galbraith, Jay R. *Organization Design.* Reading, Mass.: Addison-Wesley, 1977.

Gale, William. "Tax Credits: Social Policy in Bad Disguise." *Christian Science Monitor* (16 February 1999): 11.

Gansler, Jacques S. *Defense Conversion: Transforming the Arsenal of Democracy.* Cambridge, Mass.: MIT Press, 1995.

Garcia, Gillian. "Deposit Insurance: A Survey of Actual and Best Practices." *International Monetary Fund Working Paper* 99/54 (1999).

Garin, C. "Comment l'allocation-logement finance le marche des taudis." *Le Monde* 24 (April 1999).

Garrett, G. "Capital Mobility, Trade, and the Domestic Politics of Economic Policy." *International Organization* 49 (1995): 657–687.

Garvey, Gerald. *Facing the Bureaucracy: Living and Dying in a Public Agency.* San Francisco: Jossey-Bass, 1993.

Gebers, C. *New Instruments for Sustainability: The New Contribution of Voluntary Agreements to Environmental Policy.* Darmstadt: Oko-Institut, 1998.

Gentry, Celestea. Federal Credit Programs: An Overview of Current Programs and Their Beginnings in the Reconstruction Finance Corporation. Washington, D.C.: U.S. Department of the Treasury, Office of Corporate Finance, 18 July 1980.

George, Jr., Claude S. *History of Management Thought.* 2d ed. Englewood Cliffs, N.J.: Prentice-Hall, 1972.

Ghali, William A., Arlene S. Ash, Ruth E. Hall, and Mark A. Moskowitz. "Statewide Quality Improvement Initiatives and Mortality after Cardiac Surgery." *Journal of the American Medical Association* 277, no. 5 (1997): 379–382.

Gidron, Benjamin, Ralph M. Kramer, and Lester M. Salamon, eds. *Government and the Third Sector: Emerging Relationships in the Third Sector.* San Francisco: Jossey-Bass, 1992.

Gilboy, Janet. "Compelled Third-Party Participation in the Regulatory Process: Legal Duties, Culture, and Noncompliance." *Law and Policy* 20, no. 4 (1998): 135–155.

Ginsberg, Benjamin. *The Captive Public: How Mass Opinion Promotes State Power.* New York: Basic Books, 1986.

Glenn, Heidi. "List of Tax Expenditures Not Shrinking, JCT Report Shows." *Tax Notes* 82, no. 1 (1999): 7–9.

Glied, Sherry. *An Assessment of Strategies for Expanding Health Insurance Coverage.* Menlo Park, Calif.: Henry J. Kaiser Family Foundation, 1997.

Goetze, Rolf. "Housing, Inflation, and Taxes." *New York Times* (18 March 1981): A27.

Goodrich, Carter. *Government Promotion of American Canals and Railroads 1800–1890.* New York: Columbia University, 1960.

Goodsell, Charles. *The Case for Bureaucracy: A Public Administration Polemic.* 3d ed. Chatham, N.J.: Chatham House Publishers, 1994.

Goodwin, Barry, and Vincent Smith. *The Economics of Crop Insurance and Disaster Aid.* Washington, D.C.: AEI, 1994.

Gore, Al. *Common Sense Government: Works Better and Costs Less.* New York: Random House, 1995.

———. *From Red Tape to Results: Creating a Government That Works Better and Costs Less.* Government Printing Office, 1993.

Gorham, William, and David L. Weimer. *Organizational Report Cards.* Cambridge, Mass.: Harvard University Press, 1997.

Gormley, Jr., William T. "Food Fights: Regulatory Enforcement in a Federal System." *Public Administration Review* 52, no. 3 (1992): 271–280.

———. "Regulatory Enforcement Styles." *Political Research Quarterly* 51, no. 2 (1998): 363–383.

Gormley, Jr., William T., and B. Guy Peters. "National Styles of Regulation: Child Care in Three Countries." *Policy Sciences* 25, no. 3 (1992): 381–399.

Gormley, Jr., William T., and David L. Weimer. *Organizational Report Cards.* Cambridge, Mass.: Harvard University Press, 1990.

———. *Organizational Report Cards.* Cambridge, Mass.: Harvard University Press, 1999.

Graber, Doris. *Public Sector Communication.* Washington, D.C.: Congressional Quarterly Press, 1999.

Grabosky, Peter N. "Regulation by Reward: On the Use of Economic Incentives as Regulatory Instruments." *Law and Policy* 17, no. 3 (1995): 257–282.

———. "Using Non-Governmental Resources to Foster Regulatory Compliance." *Governance: An International Journal of Policy and Administration* 8, no. 4 (1995): 527–550.

Graetz, Michael J. *The Decline (and Fall?) of the Income Tax.* New York: W. W. Norton, 1997.

Graham, Mary. *The Morning after Earth Day: Practical Environmental Politics,* p. 11. Washington, D.C.: Governance Institute/The Brookings Institution Press, 1999.

———. "Regulation by Shaming." *Atlantic Monthly* (April 2000): 36–40.

Gravelle, Jane G. *Corporate Tax Welfare.* Washington, D.C.: Congressional Research Service, 1997.

Gray, Barbara. *Collaborating: Finding Common Ground for Multiparty Problems.* San Francisco: Jossey-Bass, 1989.

Gray, Wayne B., and John T. Scholz. "Analyzing the Equity and Efficiency of OSHA Enforcement." *Law and Policy* 13, no. 3 (1991): 185–214.

Green, Donald P., and Ian Shapiro. *Pathologies of Rational Choice Theory: A Critique of Applications in Political Science.* New Haven: Yale University Press, 1994.

Greenstein, Robert, and Isaac Shapiro. *New Research Findings on the Effects of the Earned Income Tax Credit.* Washington, D.C.: Center on Budget and Policy Priorities, 1998.

Greve, Bent. "The Hidden Welfare State, Tax Expenditure, and Social Policy." *Scandinavian Journal of Social Welfare* 3, no. 4 (1994): 203–211.

Gulick, Luther. "Notes on the Theory of Organization." In *Papers on the Science of Administration,* edited by Luther Gulick and Lyndall Urwick, pp. 1–20. New York: Institute for Public Administration, 1937.

Gullo, Theresa A., and Janet M. Kelly. "Federal Unfunded Mandate Reform: A First-Year Retrospective." *Public Administration Review* 58, no. 5 (1998): 379–387.

Gunningham, Neil, and Joseph Rees. "Industry Self-Regulation: An Institutional Perspective." *Law and Policy* 19, no. 4 (1997): 363–414.

Gunningham, Neil, Peter Grabosky, and Darren Sinclair. *Smart Regulation: Designing Environmental Policy.* Oxford and New York: Oxford University Press, 1998.

Guttman, Daniel. "Public Purpose and Private Service: The Twentieth Century Culture of Contracting Out and the Evolving Law of Diffused Sovereignty." *Administrative Law Review,* 52, no. 3 (summer 2000): 859–926.

Haas, Peter M. "Do Regimes Matter? Epistemic Communities and Mediterranean Pollution Control." *International Organization* 43 (1989): 377–403.

———. "Introduction: Epistemic Communities and International Policy Coordination." *International Organization* 46 (1992): 1–37.

Habermas, Jurgen. *Theorie des Kommunikativen Handelns (The Theory of Communicative Action).* Frankfurt am Main: Suhrkamp, 1981.

———. *The Theory of Communicative Action,* translated by Thomas McCarthy. Boston: Beacon Press, 1984.

Hadden, Susan G. *Read the Label: Reducing Risk by Providing Information.* Boulder: Westview Press, 1986.

Hafkamp, Wilhelmus A., Monique Hozee, and Arthur B. Ringeling, eds. *The Effectiveness of Instruments for Environmental Policies in the Field of Industry.* Rotterdam: Erasmus University Rotterdam, 1999.

Hahn, Robert W., and John A. Hird. "The Costs and Benefits of Regulation: Review and Synthesis." *Yale Journal on Regulation* 8, no. 1 (1991): 233–280.

Hahn, Robert W., and Robert N. Stavins. "Incentive-Based Environmental Regulation: A New Era from an Old Idea?" *Ecology Law Quarterly* 18, no. 1 (1991): 1–42.

Hall, P. A. "Policy Paradigms, Social Learning and the State: The Case of Economic Policymaking in Britain." *Comparative Politics* 25 (1993): 275–296.

Hall, R. G., and W. J. Klepczynski. "Time Service." *Naval Research Reviews* (October 1976): 28–36.

Hamilton, Edward K. "On Nonconstitutional Management of a Constitutional Problem." *Daedalus* 107 (1978): 110–131.

Hamilton, James T. "Exercising Property Rights to Pollute: Do Cancer Risks and Politics Affect Plant Emission Reductions?" *Journal of Risk and Uncertainty* 18, no. 2 (1999): 105–124.

Hammond, Thomas H., and Jack H. Knott. *A Zero-Based Look at Zero-Base Budgeting.* New Brunswick, N.J.: Transaction Books, 1980.

Handler, Joel F. *Down from Bureaucracy.* Princeton, N.J.: Princeton University Press, 1996.

Handlin, Oscar, and Mary Handlin. *Commonwealth.* Cambridge, Mass.: Harvard University Press, 1948.

Hanf, Kenneth, and Ben Soetendorp, eds. *Adapting to European Integration.* London: Longman, 1998.

Hankin, Janet, James Sloan, and Robert Sokol. "The Modest Impact of the Alcohol Beverage Warning Label on Drinking during Pregnancy among a Sample of African-American Women." *Journal of Public Policy and Marketing* 17 (1998): 61–69.

Hannan, Edward L., Harold Kilburn, Jr., Michael Racz, Eileen S. Shields, and Mark R. Chassin. "Improving the Outcomes of Coronary Artery Bypass Surgery in New York State." *Journal of the American Medical Association* 271 (1994): 761–766.

Hannan, Edward L., Dinesh Kumar, Michael Racz, Albert L. Siu, and Mark R. Chassin. "New York State's Cardiac Surgery Reporting System: Four Years Later." *Annals of Thoracic Surgery* 58, no. 6 (1994): 1852–1857.

Hannan, Edward L., Albert L. Siu, Dinesh Kumar, Harold Kilburn, Jr., and Mark R. Chassin. "The Decline in Coronary Artery Bypass Graft Surgery Mortality in New York State: The Role of Surgeon Volume." *Journal of the American Medical Association* 273 (1995): 209–213.

Hardin, Charles M. *The Politics of Agriculture: Soil Conservation and the Struggle for Power in Rural America.* Glencoe, Ill.: Free Press, 1952.

Hargrove, Erwin. *The Missing Link: The Implementation Challenge in Policy Research.* Washington, D.C.: Urban Institute Press, 1975.

Harrington, Scott, and Gregory Niehaus. *Risk Management and Insurance.* Boston: McGraw-Hill, 1999.

Hartz, Louis. *Economic Policy and Democratic Thought: Pennsylvania 1776–1860.* Cambridge, Mass.: Harvard University Press, 1968.

Hasenclever, Andreas, Peter Mayer, and Volker Rittberger. *Theories of International Regimes.* Cambridge: Cambridge University Press, 1997.

Hauptman, Arthur M. "Vouchers and American Higher Education." In *Vouchers and the Provision of Public Services,* edited by C. Eugene Steuerle, Van Doorn Ooms, George Peterson, and Robert D. Reischauer, pp. 336–367. Washington, D.C.: The Brookings Institution Press, Committee for Economic Development, and Urban Institute Press, 2000.

Havemann, Joel. "Tax Expenditures: Spending Money without Expenditures." *National Journal* 9, no. 50 (1977): 1908–1911.

Heclo, Hugh. "Hyperdemocracy." *The Wilson Quarterly* 23, no. 1 (1999): 62–71.

Hedge, David M., Donald C. Menzel, and Mark A. Krause. "The Intergovernmental Milieu and Street-Level Implementation." *Social Science Quarterly* 70, no. 2 (1989): 285–299.

Hedge, David M., Donald C. Menzel, and George H. Williams. "Regulatory Attitudes and Behavior: The Case of Surface Mining Regulation." *Western Political Quarterly* 41, no. 2 (1988): 323–340.

Henderson, William D. *Cohesion, The Human Element in Combat: Leadership and Societal Influence in the Armies of the Soviet Union, the United States, North Vietnam, and Israel.* Washington, D.C.: National Defense University Press, 1985.

Henig, Jeffrey R. *Rethinking School Choice.* Princeton, N.J.: Princeton University Press, 1994.

Henig, Jeffrey R., Joseph J. Cordes, and Eric C. Twombly. "Human Service Nonprofits in an Era of Privatization: Toward a Theory of Political and Economic Response." Paper presented at the Annual Conference of the Urban Affairs Association, Louisville, Kentucky, 15 April 1999.

Herzlinger, Regina. *A Managerial Analysis of Federal Income Redistribution Mechanisms: The Government as a Factory, Insurance Company, and Bank.* Cambridge, Mass.: Ballinger Publishing Company, 1979.

Hilton, Michael E. "An Overview of Recent Findings on Alcoholic Beverage Warning Labels." *Journal of Public Policy and Marketing* 12 (1993): 1–9.

Hinds, Michael deCourcy. "A Tale of Two Cities: The Jobs Initiative in Milwaukee and St. Louis." *Advocasey* 1 (1999): 32–36.

Hird, John. *Superfund.* Baltimore: Johns Hopkins University Press, 1994.

Hoffman, Jr., William H., James E. Smith, and Eugene Willis, eds. *West's Federal Taxation: Individual Income Taxes.* Minneapolis/St. Paul: West Publishing, 1997.

Holyoak, Keith J., and Barbara A. Spellman. "Thinking." *Annual Review of Psychology* 44 (1993): 265–315.

Hondeghem, A. *Ethics and Accountability in a Context of Governance and New Public Management.* Amsterdam: IOS Press, 1998.

Hood, Christopher C. *The Tools of Government.* Chatham, N.J.: Chatham House, 1986.

Hood, Christopher C., and Michael Jackson. *Administrative Argument.* Aldershot, U.K. and Brookfield, Vt.: Dartmouth Publishing, 1991.

Hornik, Robert C. "Channel Effectiveness in Development Communication Programs." In *Public Communication Campaigns.* 2d ed. Edited by R. E. Rice and C. K. Atkin, pp. 309–330. Newbury Park, Calif.: Sage, 1989.

———. *Development Communication: Information, Agriculture, and Nutrition in the Third World.* New York: Longman, 1988.

Howard, Christopher. "Happy Returns: How the Working Poor Got Tax Relief." *The American Prospect* 17 (1994): 46–53.

———. *The Hidden Welfare State: Tax Expenditures and Social Policy in the United States.* Princeton, N.J.: Princeton University Press, 1997.

Howlett, Michael. "Policy Instruments, Policy Styles, and Policy Implementation: National Approaches to Theories of Instrument Choice." *Policy Studies Journal* 19, no. 2 (spring 1991): 1–21.

Howlett, Michael, and M. Ramesh. "Patterns of Policy Instrument Choice: Policy Style, Policy Learning and the Privatization Experience." *Policy Studies Review* 12 (1993): 3–24.

Hughes, Owen E. "New Public Management." In *International Encyclopedia of Public Policy and Administration,* edited by Jay M. Shafritz, pp. 1489–1490. Boulder: Westview Press, 1998.

Huntington, Samuel P. *The Soldier and the State: The Theory and Politics of Civil-Military Relations.* Cambridge, Mass.: Harvard University Press, 1957.

Huppes, Gjalt, and Robert A. Kagan. "Market-Oriented Regulation of Environmental Problems in the Netherlands." *Law and Policy* 11, no. 2 (1989): 215–239.

Hurst, James Willard. *The Legitimacy of the Business Corporation.* Charlottesville: University Press of Virginia, 1970.

Hutton, R. B. "Advertising and the Department of Energy's Campaign for Energy Conservation." *Journal of Advertising* 11 (1982): 27–39.

Hyman, Herbert, and P. Sheatsley. "Some Reasons Why Information Campaigns Fail." *Public Opinion Quarterly* 11 (1947): 412–423.

Ingraham, Patricia W. *The Foundation of Merit: Public Service in American Democracy.* Baltimore: Johns Hopkins University Press, 1995.

Ingram, Helen. "Implementation: A Review and Suggested Framework." In *Public Administration: The State of the Discipline,* edited by Naomi B. Lynn and Aaron Wildavsky, pp. 462–480. Chatham, N.J.: Chatham House Publishers, 1990.

————. "Policy Implementation through Bargaining: The Case of Federal Grants-in-aid." *Public Policy* 25 (1977): 499–526.

Ingram, Helen, and A. Schneider. "The Choice of Target Populations." *Administration and Society* 23 (1991): 333–356.

Ingram, Helen, and Steven Rathgeb Smith, eds. *Public Policy for Democracy.* Washington, D.C.: The Brookings Institution Press, 1993.

Innes, Judith E. "Information in Communicative Planning." *Journal of the American Planning Association* 64 (1998): 52–63.

Institute of Administrative Management (IAM). *Administrative Management and Reform in Japan: Summary of the 1998 Annual Report of Management and Coordination Agency.* Tokyo: IAM, 1999.

Insurance Information Institute. "Insurance Issues Update: Residual Markets." March 1999.

Ippolito, Richard. *The Economics of Pension Insurance.* Homewood, Ill.: Irwin, 1989.

James, Colin. *The State Ten Years on from the Reforms.* Wellington: State Services Commission, 1998.

Jensen, Michael C. "Self-Interest, Altruism, Incentives, and Agency Theory." *Journal of Applied Corporate Finance* 7, no. 2 (summer 1994).

Jenson, Laura. "The Early American Origins of Entitlements." *Studies in American Political Development* 10 (1996): 360–404.

John, Richard R. *Spreading the News: The American Postal System from Franklin to Morse.* Cambridge, Mass.: Harvard University Press, 1995.

Johnson, H. Thomas, and Robert S. Kaplan. *Relevance Lost: The Rise and Fall of Management Accounting.* Boston: Harvard Business School Press, 1987.

Johnson-Laird, Philip N. "Deductive Reasoning." *Annual Review of Psychology* 50 (1999): 109–135.

Jones, Charles O. *Clean Air: The Policy and Politics of Pollution Control.* Pittsburgh: University of Pittsburgh Press, 1975.

Joyce, Philip G. "Using Performance Measures for Budgeting: A New Beat, or Is It the Same Old Tune?" *New Directions for Evaluation* 75 (1997): 45–61.

Kagan, Robert A. "Regulatory Enforcement." In *Handbook of Regulation and Administrative Law,* edited by David H. Rosenbloom and Richard D. Schwartz, pp. 383–422. New York: Marcel Dekker, 1994.

Kagan, Robert A., and John T. Scholz. "The 'Criminology of the Corporation' and Regulatory Enforcement Strategies." In *Enforcing Regulation,* edited by Keith Hawkins and John Thomas, pp. 67–95. Boston: Kluwer-Nijhoff Publishing, 1984.

Kahneman, Daniel, and Amos Tversky. "Choices, Values, and Frames." *American Psychologist* 39 (1984): 341–350.

Kaiser, Mary K., Dennis R. Proffitt, and Kenneth Anderson. "Judgments of Natural and Anomalous Trajectories in the Presence and Absence of Motion." *Journal of Experimental Psychology: Learning, Memory, and Cognition* 11 (1985): 795–803.

Kane, Edward J. *The S & L Insurance Mess: How Did It Happen?* Washington, D.C.: Urban Institute Press, 1989.

Kanter, Rosabeth Moss. "Power Failure in Management Circuits." *Harvard Business Review* 57, no. 4 (July–August 1979): 65–75.

Karniol, Rachel, and Michael Ross. "The Motivational Impact of Temporal Focus: Thinking About the Future and the Past." *Annual Review of Psychology* 47 (1996): 593–620.

Kaufman, Herbert. *The Forest Ranger: A Study in Administrative Behavior.* Baltimore: Johns Hopkins University Press for Resources for the Future, 1960.

Kaul, Mohan. "The New Public Administration: Management Innovations in Government." *Public Administration and Development* 17 (1997): 13–26.

Kearns, Kevin P. *Managing for Accountability: Preserving the Public Trust in Public and Nonprofit Organizations.* San Francisco: Jossey-Bass, 1996.

Kelman, Steven J. "Adversary and Cooperationist Institutions for Conflict Resolution in Public Policymaking." *Journal of Policy Analysis and Management* 11 (1982): 178–206.

———. "Deregulating Federal Procurement: Nothing to Fear but Discretion Itself?" In *Deregulating the Public Service,* edited by John J. DiIulio, Jr., pp. 102–128. Washington, D.C.: The Brookings Institution Press, 1994.

———. "The Grace Commission: How Much Waste in Government?" *The Public Interest* 78 (1985): 62–82.

———. *Procurement and Public Management: The Fear of Discretion and the Quality of Government Performance.* Washington, D.C.: AEI Press, 1990.

———. "Public Choice and Public Spirit." *The Public Interest* 87 (1987): 80–94.

———. *Regulating America, Regulating Sweden.* Cambridge, Mass.: MIT Press, 1981.

———. *What Price Incentives?* Boston: Auburn House Publishing, 1981.

Kemerer, Frank R., and Stephen D. Sugerman, eds. *School Choice and Social Controversy: Politics, Policy, and Law.* Washington, D.C.: The Brookings Institution Press, 1999.

Kennedy, Duncan. "Form and Substance in Private-Law Adjudication." *Harvard Law Review* 89 (1978): 1685–1788.

Kennickell, Arthur, Myron Kwast, and Martha Starr-McCluer. "Households' Deposit Insurance Coverage: Evidence and Analysis of Potential Reforms." *Journal of Money, Credit and Banking* 28, no. 3 (August 1996, Part 1): 311–322.

Kerwin, Cornelius M. *Rulemaking: How Government Agencies Write Law and Make Policy.* 2d ed. Washington, D.C.: Congressional Quarterly Press, 1999.

Kessler, David. "Building a Better Food Label." *FDA Consumer* 25 (1991): 10–13.

Kettl, Donald F. "The Global Revolution in Public Management: Driving Themes and Missing Links." *Journal of Policy Analysis and Management* 16, no. 3 (1997): 446–462.

———. *Government by Proxy: (Mis?)Managing Federal Programs.* Washington, D.C.: Congressional Quarterly Press, 1988.

———. *The Regulation of American Federalism.* Baltimore: Johns Hopkins University Press, 1987.

———. *Reinventing Government: A Fifth-Year Report Card.* Washington, D.C.: The Brookings Institution Press, 1998.

———. *Sharing Power: Public Governance and Private Markets.* Washington, D.C.: The Brookings Institution Press, 1993.

———. "The Three Faces of Reinvention." In *Setting National Priorities: The 2000 Election and Beyond,* edited by Robert D. Reischauer and Henry J. Aaron, pp. 421–447. Washington, D.C.: The Brookings Institution Press, 1999.

Kettl, Donald F., Patricia W. Ingraham, Ronald P. Sanders, and Constance Horner. *Civil Service Reform: Building a Government That Works.* Washington, D.C.: The Brookings Institution Press, 1996.

Kettner, Peter M., and Lawrence L. Martin. "Making Decisions About Purchase of Service Contracting." *Public Welfare* 44 (1986): 30–37.

———. "Purchase of Service at 20: Are We Using It Well?" *Public Welfare* 52, no. 3 (1994): 14–22.

———. "Purchase of Service Contracting in the 1990s: Have Expectations Been Met?" *Journal of Sociology and Social Welfare* 20, no. 2 (1993): 89–103.

Kickert, Walter J. M. et al. *Aansturing van Verzelfstandigde Overheidsdiensten (Governance of Autonomous Government Services).* Alphen aan den Rijn, Netherlands: Samsom, 1998.

Kickert, Walter J. M., Erik-Hans Kliin, and Joop F. M. Koppenjan. "Introduction: A Management Perspective on Policy Networks." In *Managing Complex Networks: Strategies for the Public Sector,* edited by Walter J. M. Kickert, Erik-Hans Kliin, and Joop F. M. Koppenjan, pp. 1–13. London: Sage Publications, 1997.

———, eds. *Managing Complex Networks: Strategies for the Public Sector.* Thousand Oaks, Calif.: Sage, 1997.

Kilman, Scott. "Food Fright: Biotech Scare Sweeps Europe and Companies Wonder If U.S. Is Next." *Wall Street Journal* (7 October 1999): A1.

Kingdon, John W. *Agendas, Alternatives and Public Policies.* 2d ed. New York: HarperCollins College Publishers, 1995.

Kirchhoff, S. "House Clears Agriculture Bill Restoring Food Stamps to Legal Immigrants." *CQ Weekly* (6 June 1998).

Klijn, Erik-Hans. "Policy Networks: An Overview." In *Managing Complex Networks: Strategies for the Public Sector,* edited by Walter J. M. Kickert, Erik-Hans Kliin, and Joop F. M. Koppenjan, pp. 14–34. London: Sage Publications, 1997.

Klimschot, Jo Ann. *The Untouchables: A Common Cause Study of the Federal Tax Expenditure Budget.* Washington, D.C.: Common Cause, 1981.

Klok, Pieter-Jan. *Convenanten als Instrument van Milieubeleid (Covenants as Instruments of Environmental Policy).* Enschede, Netherlands: Universiteit Twente, 1989.

Komesar, Neil K. *Imperfect Alternatives: Choosing Institutions in Law, Economics, and Public Policy.* Chicago: University of Chicago Press, 1994.

Koopmans, T. *Vergelijkend Publiekrecht (Comparative Public Law).* Deventer, Netherlands: Kluwer, 1978.

Kotler, Philip, and Eduardo Roberto. *Social Marketing: Strategies for Changing Public Behavior.* New York: Free Press, 1989.

Kotowitz, Y. "Moral Hazard." In *Allocation, Information and Markets,* edited by John Eatwell, Murray Milgate, and Peter Newman, pp. 207–213. New York: W. W. Norton, 1992.

Kotz, Nick. *Wild Blue Yonder: Money, Politics, and the B-1 Bomber.* New York: Pantheon Books, 1988.

Kraft, Michael. *Environmental Policy and Politics.* New York: HarperCollins, 1996.

Kraft, Michael E., and Denise Scheberle. "Environmental Federalism at Decade's End: New Approaches and Strategies." *Publius: The Journal of Federalism* 28, no. 1 (1998): 131–146.

Kramer, Ralph M. "Voluntary Agencies and the Personal Social Services." In *The Nonprofit Sector: A Research Handbook,* edited by W. M. Powell, pp. 240–257. New Haven: Yale University Press, 1987.

———. *Voluntary Agencies in the Welfare State.* Berkeley: University of California Press, 1981.

Kramer, Ralph, and Bernard Grossman. "Contracting for Social Services: Process Management and Resource Dependencies." *Social Service Review* (March 1987): 32–55.

Kreuter, M. W., L. K. Brennan, D. P. Scharff, and S. N. Lukwago. "Do Nutrition Label Readers Eat Healthier Diets? Behavioral Correlates of Adults' Use of Food Labels." *American Journal of Preventive Medicine* 13, no. 4 (1997): 277–283.

Kubasek, Nancy. *Environmental Law.* Englewood Cliffs, N.J.: Prentice-Hall, 1990.

Kubasek, Nancy K., and Gary S. Silverman. *Environmental Law.* 3d ed. Upper Saddle River, N.J.: Prentice-Hall, 1999.

Kunreuther, Howard, and Richard Roth, eds. *Paying the Price: The Status and Role of Insurance against Natural Disasters in the United States.* Washington, D.C.: Joseph Henry Press, 1998.

Kuttner, Robert. "The Limits of Markets." *The American Prospect* 31 (1997): 28–36.

Kvist, Jon, and Adrian Sinfield. *Comparing Tax Routes to Welfare in Denmark and the United Kingdom.* Copenhagen: Danish National Institute of Social Research, 1996.

Landis, James M. *The Administrative Process.* New Haven: Yale University Press, 1938.

Landy, Marc K. "Public Policy and Citizenship." In *Public Policy for Democracy,* edited by Helen M. Ingram and Steven Rathgeb Smith, pp. 19–44. Washington, D.C.: The Brookings Institution Press, 1993.

Landy, Marc, Marc J. Roberts, and Stephen R. Thomas. *The Environmental Protection Agency: Asking the Wrong Questions.* New York: Oxford University Press, 1990.

Langbein, Laura, and Cornelius Kerwin. "Implementation, Negotiation and Compliance in Environmental and Safety Regulations." *Journal of Politics* 47, no. 3 (1985): 854–880.

Lardy, Nicholas. *China's Unfinished Economic Revolution*. Washington, D.C.: The Brookings Institution Press, 1998.

Lazarsfeld, Paul, and Robert Merton. "Mass Communication, Popular Taste, and Organized Social Action." In *The Communication of Ideas,* edited by L. Bryson. New York: Harper and Row, 1948.

Leach, Jim. "Dissenting Views of Representative Jim Leach." In *Government-Sponsored Housing Enterprises Financial Safety and Soundness Act of 1991.* House Report 102–206. pp. 112–115. Washington, D.C.: Committee on Banking, Finance and Urban Affairs, U.S. House of Representatives, 17 September 1991.

Lemaine, David. "The Stick: Regulation as a Tool of Government." In *Carrots, Sticks and Sermons: Policy Instruments and Their Evaluation,* edited by Marie-Louise Bemelmans-Videc, Ray C. Rist, and Evert Vedung, pp. 59–76. New Brunswick, N.J.: Transaction Publishers, 1998.

Leman, Christopher K. "The Concepts of Public and Private and Their Applicability to North American Lands." In *Land Rites and Wrongs: The Management, Regulation and Use of Land in Canada and the United States,* edited by Elliot J. Feldman and Michael A. Goldberg, pp. 23–37. Cambridge, Mass.: Lincoln Institute of Land Policy, 1987.

———. "The Forgotten Fundamental: Success and Excesses of Direct Government." In *Beyond Privatization: The Tools of Government Action,* edited by Lester M. Salamon, pp. 53–87. Washington, D.C.: Urban Institute Press, 1989.

———. "Political Dilemmas in Evaluating and Budgeting Soil Conservation Programs: The RCA Process." In *Soil Conservation Policy, Institutions, and Incentives,* edited by Harold Halcrow, Melvin Cotner, and Early Heady, pp. 47–88. Ankeny, Ia.: Soil Conservation Society of America, 1982.

———. "The Revolution of the Saints: The Ideology of Privatization and Its Consequences for the Public Lands." In *Selling the Federal Forests,* edited by Adrien E. Gamache, pp. 93–162. Seattle, Wash.: College of Forest Resources, University of Washington, 1984.

Leman, Christopher K., and Robert H. Nelson. "The Rise of Managerial Federalism: An Assessment of Benefits and Costs." *Environmental Law* 12, no. 4 (summer 1982): 981–1029.

Leonard, Herman B. *Checks Unbalanced: The Quiet Side of Public Spending.* New York: Basic Books, 1986.

Lerman, Robert, and C. Eugene Steuerle. "Structured Choice Versus Fragmented Choice: The Bundling of Vouchers." In *Vouchers and the Provision of Public Services,* edited by C. Eugene Steuerle, Van Doorn Ooms, George Peterson, and Robert D. Reischauer, pp. 471–502. Washington, D.C.: The Brookings Institution Press, Committee for Economic Development, and Urban Institute Press, 2000.

Leroy, Greg. "The Terrible Ten: Corporate Candy Store Deals of 1998." *The Progressive* 63, no. 5 (1999): 27–30.

Lester, James P. "Federalism and State Environmental Policy." In *Environmental Politics and Policy.* 2d ed. Edited by James P. Lester, pp. 39–62. Durham, N.C.: Duke University Press, 1995.

Letts, Christine W., William P. Ryan, and Allen Grossman. *High Performance Nonprofit Organizations: Managing Upstream for Greater Impact.* New York: Wiley, 1999.

Levi, Margaret. *Of Rule and Revenue.* Berkeley and London: University of California Press, 1988.

Levine, Robert A. *Public Planning: Failure and Redirection.* New York: Basic Books, 1972.

Levy, Reynold. *Give and Take: A Candid Account of Corporate Philanthropy.* Boston: Harvard Business School Press, 1999.

Lewis, Eugene. *Public Entrepreneurship: Toward a Theory of Bureaucratic Political Power.* Bloomington: Indiana University Press, 1980.

Lichter, S. Robert, Linda S. Lichter, and Dan Amundson. *Images of Government in TV Entertainment.* Washington, D.C.: Center for Media and Public Affairs, 1999.

Light, Paul C. *Thickening Government: Federal Hierarchy and the Diffusion of Accountability.* Washington, D.C.: The Brookings Institution Press and the Governance Institute, 1995.

———. *The Tides of Reform: Making Government Work 1945–1995.* New Haven: Yale University Press, 1997.

———. *The True Size of Government.* Washington, D.C.: The Brookings Institution Press, 1999.

Ligteringen, J. J. *The Feasibility of Dutch Environmental Policy Instruments.* Enschede, Netherlands: Twente University Press, 1999.

Lijphart, A. *The Politics of Accommodation.* Berkeley: University of California Press, 1968.

Lindblom, Charles E. *Inquiry and Change: The Troubled Attempt to Understand and Shape Society.* New Haven: Yale University Press, 1990.

———. *Politics and Markets: The World's Political-Economic Systems.* New York: Basic Books, 1977.

Linder, Stephen H., and B. Guy Peters. "Conceptual Frames Underlying the Selection of Policy Instruments." In *Public Policy Instruments: Evaluating the Tools of Public Administration,* edited by B. Guy Peters and Frans K. M. Van Nispen. Cheltenham, U.K.: Edward Elgar, 1998.

———. "The Design of Instruments for Public Policy." In *Policy Theory and Policy Evaluation,* edited by Stuart S. Nagel and William Dunn, pp. 103–119. Westport, Conn.: Greenwood Press, 1990.

———. "From Social Theory to Policy Design." *Journal of Public Policy* 4, no. 3 (1984): 237–259.

———. "Instruments of Government: Perceptions and Contexts." *Journal of Public Policy* 9, no. 1 (1989): 35–58.

———. "Relativism, Contingency, and the Definition of Success in Implementation Research." *Policy Studies Review* 7, no. 1 (1987): 116–127.

———. "The Study of Policy Instruments: Four Schools of Thought." In *Public Policy Instruments: Evaluating the Tools of Public Administration,* edited by B. Guy Peters and Frans K. M. van Nispen, pp. 33–45. Cheltenham, U.K.: Edward Elgar, 1998.

Lipsky, Michael. *Street-Level Bureaucracy: Dilemmas of the Individual in Public Services.* New York: Russell Sage Foundation, 1980.

Litan, Robert E., ed. *Verdict: Assessing the Civil Jury System.* Washington, D.C.: The Brookings Institution Press, 1993.

Loconte, Joe. *Seducing the Samaritan: How Government Contracts Are Reshaping Social Services.* Boston: Pioneer Institute for Public Policy Research, 1997.

Longo, Daniel R., Garland Land, Wayne Schramm, Judy Fraas, Barbara Hoskins, and Vicky Howell. "Consumer Reports in Health Care: Do They Make a Difference in Patient Care?" *Journal of the American Medical Association* 278, no. 19 (1997): 1579–1784.

Loomis, Burdett. "The Politics of Vouchers." In *Vouchers and the Provision of Public Services,* edited by C. Eugene Steuerle, Van Doorn Ooms, George Peterson, and Robert D. Reischauer, pp. 92–118. Washington, D.C.: The Brookings Institution Press, Committee for Economic Development, and Urban Institute Press, 2000.

Loose, Cynthia. "5 D.C. Housing Employees Charged; Only 10 of 400 New Rent Vouchers Issued Since 1990 Didn't Involve Bribery, Probe Finds." *The Washington Post* (13 April 1994).

Lowi, Theodore J. "American Business, Public Policy, Case Studies, and Political Theory." *World Politics* 16 (1964): 677–715.

———. *The End of Liberalism: The Second Republic of the United States.* 2d ed. New York: W. W. Norton, 1979.

———. "Four Systems of Politics, Policy and Choice." *Public Administration Review* 32, no. 11 (1972): 298–310.

———. "Public Policy, Case Studies and Political Theory." *World Politics* 17 (1964): 677–715.

Lubick, Donald, and Gerard Brannon. "Stanley S. Surrey and the Quality of Tax Policy Argument." *National Tax Journal* 38, no. 3 (1985): 251–259.

Luna, Yvone. "Social Construction of Welfare Mothers: Political Messages and Recipient Response." Paper presented at the annual meeting of the Western Political Science Association, San Jose, California, March 2000.

Lundquist, Lennart J. *The Hare and the Tortoise: Clean Air Policies in the United States and Sweden.* Ann Arbor: University of Michigan Press, 1980.

————. *The Hare and the Tortoise: Implementing Environmental Policy.* Ann Arbor: University of Michigan Press, 1985.

Lynch, Robert G. *Do State and Local Tax Incentives Work?* Washington, D.C.: Economic Policy Institute, 1996. Accessed via http://www.epinet.org/.

Lynn, Laurence. *Managing the Public's Business: The Job of the Government Executive.* New York: Basic Books, 1981.

MacKinnon, David P., Mary Ann Pentz, and Alan W. Stacy. "The Alcohol Warning Label and Adolescents." *American Journal of Public Health* 83, no. 4 (1993): 585–587.

Macrae, C. Neil, and Galen V. Bodenhausen. "Social Cognition: Thinking Categorically About Others." *Annual Review of Psychology* 51 (2000): 93–120.

Magat, Wesley A., and W. Kip Viscusi. *Informational Approaches to Regulation.* Cambridge, Mass.: MIT Press, 1992.

Majone, G. *Evidence, Argument and Persuasion in the Policy Process.* New Haven and London: Yale University Press, 1989.

Majone, G., ed. *Regulating Europe.* London and New York: Routledge, 1996.

Mann, M. "Has Globalization Ended the Rise and Rise of the Nation State?" *Review of International Political Economy* 4 (1997): 477–496.

Mansfield, Harvey. "Accountability and Congressional Oversight." In *Improving the Accountability and Performance of Government,* edited by B. L. R. Smith and J. Carroll. Washington, D.C.: The Brookings Institution Press, 1982.

March, James. *A Primer on Decision Making.* New York: Free Press, 1994.

March, James G., and Johan P. Olsen. "The New Institutionalism: Organizational Factors in Political Life." *American Political Science Review* 78 (1984): 738–749.

————. *Rediscovering Institutions: The Organizational Basis of Politics.* New York: Free Press, 1989.

March, James, and Herbert Simon. *Organizations.* New York: Wiley, 1958.

Marsh, David, and R. A. W. Rhodes. *Policy Communities in British Politics.* Oxford: Oxford University Press, 1992.

Marshall, Martin, Paul Shekelle, Sheila Leatherman, and Robert Brook. "The Public Release of Performance Data: What Do We Expect to Gain?" *Journal of the American Medical Association* 283, no. 14 (2000): 1866–1874.

Marshall, Thomas Humphrey. "Citizenship and Social Class." In *Class, Citizenship and Social Development: Essays,* pp. 71–134. New York: Doubleday, 1964.

Mashaw, Jerry L. *Bureaucratic Justice: Managing Social Security Disability Claims.* New Haven: Yale University Press, 1983.

Masse, Marcel. "Economic, Financial, Political and Technological Pressures Shaping Public Sector Reform." Proceedings of the Canada South-East Asia Colloquium: Transforming the Public Sector. Ottawa, Canada: Institute on Governance, 1993.

Massey, Andrew. *Managing the Public Sector: A Comparative Analysis of the United Kingdom and the United States.* Aldershot, U.K.: Edward Elgar, 1993.

Mathios, Alan D. "Socioeconomic Factors, Nutrition, and Food Choices." *Journal of Public Policy and Marketing* 15 (1996): 45–54.

Matlack, Carol. "Zap! You're Taxed." *National Journal* 22, no. 5 (1990): 267–269.

May, Peter J. "Can Cooperation Be Mandated? Implementing Intergovernmental Environmental Management in New South Wales and New Zealand." *Publius: The Journal of Federalism* 25, no. 1 (1995): 89–113.

————. "Mandate Design and Implementation: Enhancing Implementation Efforts and Shaping Regulatory Styles." *Journal of Policy Analysis and Management* 12, no. 4 (1993): 634–663.

————. "State Regulatory Roles: Choices in the Regulation of Building Safety." *State and Local Government Review* 29, no. 2 (1997): 70–80.

May, Peter J., and Raymond J. Burby. "Making Sense Out of Regulatory Enforcement." *Law and Policy* 20, no. 2 (1998): 157–182.

May, Peter J., and Søren Winter. "Regulatory Enforcement and Compliance: Examining Danish Agro-Environmental Policy." *Journal of Policy Analysis and Management* 18, no. 4 (1999): 625–651.

May, Peter J., Raymond J. Burby, Neil J. Ericksen, John W. Handmer, Jennifer E. Dixon, Sarah Michaels, and D. Ingle Smith. *Environmental Management and Governance: Intergovernmental Approaches to Hazards and Sustainability.* London and New York: Routledge, 1996.

Mazmanian, Daniel A., and David Morell. *Beyond Superfailure: America's Toxics Policy for the 1990s.* Boulder: Westview Press, 1992.

Mazmanian, Daniel A., and Paul A Sabatier. *Implementation and Public Policy.* Glenview, Ill.: Scott, Foresman, 1983.

McConnell, Grant. *Private Power and American Democracy.* New York: Knopf, 1967.

McCubbins, Matthew D., and Thomas Schwartz. "Congressional Oversight Overlooked: Police Patrols and Fire Alarms." *American Journal of Political Science* 28 (1984): 165–179.

McCurdy, Howard E. *Public Administration: A Bibliographic Guide to the Literature.* New York: Marcel Dekker, 1986.

McDaniel, Paul R. "Tax Expenditures as Tools of Government Action." In *Beyond Privatization: The Tools of Government Action,* edited by Lester M. Salamon, pp. 167–196. Washington, D.C.: Urban Institute Press, 1989.

McDiarmid, John. *Government Corporations and Federal Funds.* Chicago: University of Chicago Press, 1938.

McDonnell, Lorraine M. "Policy Design as Instrument Design." Paper presented at the annual meeting of the American Political Science Association, Washington, D.C., 1–4 September 1988.

McDonnell, Lorraine M., and Richard F. Elmore. "Getting the Job Done: Alternative Policy Instruments." *Educational Evaluation and Policy Analysis* 9, no. 2 (summer 1987): 133–152.

McGuire, William J. "Theoretical Foundations of Campaigns." In *Public Communication Campaigns.* 2d ed. Edited by R. Rice and C. Atkin. Newbury Park, Calif.: Sage, 1989.

McKinley, Charles W. *The Management of Land and Related Water Resources in Oregon: A Case Study in Administrative Federalism.* Washington, D.C.: Resources for the Future, 1965.

McKinley, Charles W., and Robert W. Frase. *Launching Social Security: A Capture-and-Record Account, 1935–37.* Madison: University of Wisconsin Press, 1970.

McLaughlin, Milbrey. *Evaluation and Reform.* Cambridge, Mass.: Ballinger, 1975.

McNamara, E. F., T. Kurth, and D. Hansen. "Communication Efforts to Prevent Wildfires." In *Public Communication Campaigns,* edited by R. Rice and W. Paisley, pp. 143–160. Beverly Hills, Calif.: Sage, 1981.

McNeill, Dennis L., and William L. Wilkie. "Public Policy and Consumer Information: Impact of the New Energy Labels." *Journal of Consumer Research* 6, no. 1 (1979): 1–11.

McPherson, James M. *Battle Cry of Freedom.* New York: Ballantine Books, 1988.

McPherson, Michael S., and Morton Owen Schapiro. *Keeping College Affordable.* Washington, D.C.: The Brookings Institution Press, 1991.

Meier, Kenneth J. *The Politics of Sin.* Armonk, N.Y.: M.E. Sharpe, 1994.

Meier, Kenneth J., and E. Thomas Garman. *Regulation and Consumer Protection.* 2d ed. Houston: Dame Publications, 1995.

Mellers, B. A., A. Schwartz, and A. D. J. Cooke. "Judgment and Decision Making." *Annual Review of Psychology* 49 (1998): 447–477.

Merton, Robert. "Structural Analysis in Sociology." In *Approaches to the Study of Social Structure,* edited by Peter Blau, pp. 21–52. New York: Free Press, 1975.

Mettler, Suzanne. Bringing the State Back into Civic Engagement: World War II Veterans, the G.I. Bill, and American Citizenship. Unpublished paper, Department of Political Science, Syracuse University, 2000.

———. *Dividing Citizens: Gender and Federalism in New Deal Public Policy.* Ithaca, N.Y.: Cornell University Press, 1998.

Meyer, John W., and Brian Rowan. "The Structure of Educational Organizations." In *Environments and Organizations,* edited by Marshall W. Meyer and associates, pp. 78–109. San Francisco: Jossey-Bass, 1978.

Meyer, Marshall W., et al. *Change in Public Bureaucracies.* New York: Cambridge University Press, 1979.

Mikesell, James J., and George B. Wallace. *Are Revolving Loan Funds a Better Way to Finance*

Rural Development? Economic Research Service, U.S. Department of Agriculture. Agriculture Information Bulletin No. 724–05, October 1996.

Mikesell, John L. "Tax Administration: The Link between Tax Law and Tax Collections." In *Handbook of Public Finance,* edited by Fred Thompson and Mark T. Green, pp. 173–198. New York: Marcel Dekker, 1998.

Milward, H. Brinton, and Keith G. Provan. "Measuring Network Structure." *Public Administration* 76 (summer 1998): 387–407.

———. "Principles for Controlling Agents: The Political Economy of Network Structure." *Journal of Public Administration Research and Theory* 8 (1998): 203–221.

Minarik, Joseph J. *Making America's Budget Policy: From the 1980s to the 1990s.* Armonk, N.Y.: M. E. Sharpe, 1990.

Ministry of Finance, Financial Bureau, Government of Japan. *FILP Report '98.* Online at http://www.mof.go.jp/zaito/zaito98e.htm.

Mintzberg, Henry. *The Structuring of Organizations.* Englewood Cliffs, N.J.: Prentice-Hall, 1979.

Mishkin, Frederic. "Moral Hazard and Reform of the Government Safety Net." Forthcoming in *Journal of Financial Services Research.*

Mitchell, Jerry. *The American Experiment with Government Corporations.* Armonk, N.Y.: M.E. Sharpe, 1999.

Mitnick, Barry. *The Political Economy of Regulation.* New York: Columbia University Press, 1980.

Modeen, Tore, and Allan Rosas, eds. *Indirect Public Administration in Fourteen Countries.* Åbo, Finland: Åbo Akademi University Press, 1988.

Moe, Ronald C. "Exploring the Limits of Privatization." *Public Administration Review* 47 (1987): 453–460.

———. *Managing the Public's Business: Federal Government Corporations.* Washington, D.C.: Committee on Governmental Affairs, United States Senate. S. Prt. 104–18, April 1995.

———. "The President's Role as Chief Manager." In *The Managerial Presidency.* 2d ed. Edited by James P. Pfiffner, pp. 265–284. College Station: Texas A&M Press, 1999.

Moe, Ronald C., ed. *General Management Laws: A Selective Compendium.* Congressional Research Service, CRS Report RL 30267, Washington, D.C., 1999.

Moe, Ronald C., and R. S. Gilmour. "Rediscovering Principles of Public Administration: The Neglected Foundation of Law." *Public Administration Review* 55 (1995): 135–142.

Moe, Terry M. "The New Economics of Organization." *American Journal of Political Science* 28 (November 1984): 739–777.

Moffitt, Robert A. "Lessons from the Food Stamp Program." In *Vouchers and the Provision of Public Services,* edited by C. Eugene Steuerle, Van Doorn Ooms, George Peterson, and Robert D. Reischauer, pp. 119–138. Washington, D.C.: The Brookings Institution Press, Committee for Economic Development, and Urban Institute Press, 2000.

Moneypenny, Philip. "Federal Grants-in-Aid to State Governments: A Political Analysis." *National Tax Journal* 13 (1960): 1–16.

Moon, Marilyn, Len Nichos, Korbin Liu, Genvieve Kenney, Margaret Sulvetta, Stephen Zuckerman, and Crystal Kintz. *Searching for Savings in Medicare.* Washington, D.C.: Urban Institute Press, 1995.

Moore, Mark H. *Creating Public Value: Strategic Management in Government.* Cambridge, Mass.: Harvard University Press, 1995.

Moorman, Christine. "A Quasi Experiment to Assess the Consumer and Informational Determinants of Nutrition Information Processing Activities: The Case of the Nutrition Labeling and Education Act." *Journal of Public Policy & Marketing* 15 (1996): 28–44.

Morris, Milton. *Immigration: The Beleaguered Bureaucracy.* Washington, D.C.: The Brookings Institution Press, 1985.

Morrison, Ellen Earnhardt. *Guardian of the Forest: A History of the Smokey Bear Program.* New York: Vantage Press, 1976.

Morrissey, John. "HEDIS to Expand Performance Guidelines." *Modern Healthcare* (22 July 1996): 2–3.

Mosher, Frederick C. "The Changing Responsibilities and Tactics of the Federal Government." *Public Administration Review* 40, no. 6 (1980): 541–548.

Mucciaroni, Gary. *Reversals of Fortune: Public Policy and Private Interests.* Washington, D.C.: The Brookings Institution Press, 1995.

Mukamel, Dana B., and Alvin I. Mushlin. "Quality of Care Information Makes a Difference: An Analysis of Market Share and Price Changes after Publication of the New York State Cardiac Surgery Mortality Reports." *Medical Care* 36, no. 7 (1998): 945–954.

Munnell, Alicia. "The Current Status of Our Social Welfare System." *New England Economic Review* (1987): 4–12.

Nagle, James F. *A History of Government Contracting.* Washington, D.C.: George Washington University Press, 1992.

Nakamura, Robert, and Frank Smallwood. *The Politics of Policy Implementation.* New York: St. Martin's Press, 1980.

Nash, Ralph C. *Formation of Government Contracts.* Washington, D.C.: George Washington University Press, 1998.

Nathan, Richard. "State and Local Governments under Federal Grants: Toward a Predictive Theory." *Political Science Quarterly* 98, no. 1 (1983): 47–57.

National Academy of Public Administration. *The Environment Goes to Market: The Implementation of Economic Incentives for Pollution Control.* Washington, D.C.: NAPA, 1994.

———. *Report on Government Corporations,* vol. 1. Washington, D.C.: NAPA, 1981.

———. *Resolving the Paradox of Environmental Protection: An Agenda for EPA, Congress, and the States.* Washington, D.C.: NAPA, 1997.

———. *Setting Priorities, Getting Results: A New Direction for EPA.* Washington, D.C.: NAPA, 1995.

National Association of State Budget Officers (NASBO). *Budget Processes in the States.* Washington, D.C.: NASBO, 1997. Accessed via http://www.nasbo.org/pubs/ budpro/frame.htm.

———. "State Tax Expenditure Reports." *NASBO Information Brief* 2, no. 3. Washington, D.C.: NASBO, 1994.

"New Homes Sold by Financing." *Inside Mortgage Finance* 13 (5 June 1998).

Newton, Robert. "Toward an Understanding of Federal Assistance." *Public Administration Review* 35, no. 4 (1975): 372–377.

Nightingale, Demetra Smith, and Nancy Pindus. "Privatization of Public Social Services: A Background Paper." Washington, D.C.: The Urban Institute, 15 October 1997. Online at http:// www.urban.org/pubman/privitz.html.

Niskanen, William. *Bureaucracy and Representative Government.* Chicago: Aldine, 1971.

Nohria, Nitin. "Is a Network Perspective a Useful Way of Studying Organizations?" In *Networks and Organizations: Structure, Form, and Action,* edited by Nitin Nohira and Robert G. Eccles, pp. 4–8. Boston: Harvard Business School Press, 1992.

North, Douglas. "The New Institutional Economics." *Journal of Institutional and Theoretical Economics* 142 (1986): 231.

Nowland-Foreman, Garth. "Purchase-of-Service Contracting, Voluntary Organizations, and Civil Society." *American Behavioral Scientist* 42, no. 1 (1998): 108–124.

Oberg, Joh H. "Testing Federal Student-Aid Fungibility in Two Competing Versions of Federalism." *Publius: The Journal of Federalism* 27, no. 1 (1997): 115–134.

O'Connell, Jeffrey, and Peter A. Bell. *Accidental Justice: The Dilemmas of Tort Law.* New Haven: Yale University Press, 1997.

Office of Federal Housing Enterprise Oversight. *2000 Report to Congress.* Washington, D.C.: OFHEO, 15 June 2000.

Office of Management and Budget, Executive Office of the President (OMB). *Analytical Perspectives, Budget of the United States Government, Fiscal Year 2001.* Washington, D.C.: OMB, 2000.

———. *Credit Supplement, Budget of the United States Government, Fiscal Year 2001.* Washington, D.C.: OMB, 2000.

———. *Memorandum for Heads of Executive Departments and Agencies: Government Corporations.* M-96–05. Washington, D.C.: OMB, 8 December 1995.

———. *Policies for Federal Credit Programs and Non-Tax Receivables.* Circular A-129. Washington, D.C.: OMB, 1993.

Okun, Arthur M. *Equality and Efficiency: The Big Tradeoff.* Washington, D.C.: The Brookings Institution Press, 1975.

O'Leary, Rosemary, Tracy Yandle, and Tamilyn Moore. "The State of the States in Environmental Dispute Resolution." *Ohio State Journal on Dispute Resolution* 14 (1999): 515–613.

Olsen, J. P., and B. Guy Peters. *Lessons from Experience: Experiential Learning in Administrative Reform.* Oslo: Scandinavian University Press, 1997.

Olson, James Stuart. *Herbert Hoover and the Reconstruction Finance Corporation 1931–1933.* Ames: Iowa State University, 1977.

Organisation for Economic Co-operation and Development (OECD). *Governance in Transition, Public Management Reforms in OECD Countries.* Paris: OECD, 1995.

———. *Tax Expenditures: Recent Experiences.* Paris: OECD, 1996.

Osborne, David, and Ted Gaebler. *Reinventing Government: How the Entrepreneurial Spirit is Transforming the Public Sector.* Reading, Mass.: Addison-Wesley, 1992.

Osborne, David, and Peter Plastrik. *Banishing Bureaucracy: The Five Strategies for Reinventing Government.* Reading, Mass.: Addison-Wesley, 1997.

Ostroff, Frank. *The Horizontal Organization: What the Organization of the Future Actually Looks Like and How It Delivers Value to Customers.* New York: Oxford University Press, 1999.

Ostrom, Vincent. *The Intellectual Crisis in American Public Administration.* University: University of Alabama Press, 1973.

O'Toole, Jr., L. J. K. I. Hanf, and P. L. Hupe. "Managing Implementation Processes in Networks." In *Managing Complex Networks: Strategies for the Public Sector,* edited by Walter J. M. Kickert, Erik-Hans Klijn, and Joop F. M. Koppenjan, pp. 37–151. London: Sage Publications, 1997.

Ouchi, William G. "Markets, Bureaucracies, and Clans." *Administrative Science Quarterly* 25 (March 1980): 129–140.

Owens, Jeffrey P. "Tax Expenditures and Direct Expenditures as Tools of Government Action." In *Comparative Tax Studies,* edited by Sijbren Cnossen, pp. 171–197. Amsterdam: North-Holland, 1983.

Padberg, Daniel I. "Nutritional Labeling as a Policy Instrument." *American Journal of Agricultural Economics* 74 (1992): 1208–1212.

Page, Benjamin I., and Robert Y. Shapiro. *The Rational Public: Fifty Years of Trends in Americans' Policy Preferences.* Chicago: University of Chicago Press, 1992.

Paget, Karen M. *The State Fiscal Analysis Initiative.* Washington, D.C.: Center on Budget and Policy Priorities, 1997.

Paulson, Robert I. "People and Garbage are NOT the Same." *Community Mental Health Journal* 24 (1988): 91–102.

Pear, R. "Now, Special Tax Breaks Get Hidden in Plain Sight." *The New York Times* (1 August 1997).

Pechman, Joseph A. "Tax Reform: Theory and Practice." *Journal of Economic Perspectives* 1, no. 1 (1987): 11–28.

Perrow, Charles. *Complex Organizations: A Critical Essay.* Glenview, Ill.: Scott, Foresman, 1979.

Peters, B. Guy. *The Future of Governing: Four Emerging Models.* Lawrence: University Press of Kansas, 1996.

———. *Institutional Analysis in Political Science: The New Institutionalism.* London: Cassells, 1998a.

———. "Is It the Institutions? Explaining Health Care Reform in the United States." *Public Policy and Administration* 11, no. 1 (1996).

———. "Policy Problems and Policy Design." Paper presented at the annual conference of the Southern Political Science Association, Atlanta, Georgia, 4 November 1998.

———. *The Politics of Taxation: A Comparative Perspective.* Cambridge: Blackwell, 1991.

Peters, B. Guy, and Frans K. M. van Nispen. "Prologue." In *Public Policy Instruments: Evaluating the Tools of Public Administration,* edited by B. Guy Peters and Frans K. M. van Nispen, pp. 1–10. Cheltenham, U.K.: Edward Elgar, 1998a.

———, eds. *Public Policy Instruments: Evaluating the Tools of Public Administration.* Cheltenham, U.K.: Edward Elgar, 1998b.

Petersen, John. "A Primer on State Bond Banks in the United States." First conference on Capital

Market Development at the Subnational Level: Local Strategies to Access Financial Markets. Santander, Spain, 15 October 1998.

Peterson, Eric D., Elizabeth DeLong, James G. Jollis, Lawrence H. Muhlbaier, and Daniel B. Mark. "The Effects of New York's Bypass Surgery Provider Profiling on Access to Care and Patient Outcomes in the Elderly." *Journal of the American College of Cardiology* 32, no. 4 (1998): 993–999.

Peterson, Paul E. *The Price of Federalism*. Washington, D.C.: The Brookings Institution Press, 1995.

Peterson, Paul E., Barry G. Rabe, and Kenneth K. Wong. *When Federalism Works*, pp. 21–23. Washington, D.C.: The Brookings Institution Press, 1986.

Pettit, Philip. "Institutional Design and Rational Choice." In *The Theory of Institutional Design*, edited by Robert E. Goodin, pp. 54–89. New York: Cambridge University Press, 1996.

Pew Research Center for People and the Press. *Deconstructing Distrust: How Americans View Government*. Washington, D.C.: Pew Research Center for People and the Press, 1998.

Pierson, P. *Dismantling the Welfare State?* Cambridge: Cambridge University Press, 1994.

Plumptre, Tim. "Public Sector Reform: An International Perspective." In *Proceedings of the Canada South-East Asia Colloquium: Transforming the Public Sector*. Ottawa, Canada: Institute on Governance, 1993.

Polackova, Hana. "Government Contingent Liabilities: A Hidden Risk to Fiscal Stability." World Bank Policy Research Working Paper 1989 (1999).

Pollitt, C. *Managerialism and the Public Services*. Oxford: Basil Blackwell, 1993.

Posner, Paul L. "Federal Grant Design: What Washington Should Know and Why It Should Know It." Paper presented at the annual meeting of the American Political Science Association. Boston, 1–4 September 1998.

———. *The Politics of Unfunded Mandates: Whither Federalism?* Washington, D.C.: Georgetown University Press, 1998.

Posner, Paul L., and Margaret Wrightson. "Block Grants: A Perennial but Unstable Tool of Government." *Publius: The Journal of Federalism* 26, no. 3 (1996): 87–108.

Posner, Paul, Robert Yetvin, Mark Schneiderman, Christopher Spiro, and Andrea Barnett. "A Survey of Voucher Use: Variations and Common Elements." In *Vouchers and the Provision of Public Services*, edited by C. Eugene Steuerle, Van Doorn Ooms, George Peterson, and Robert D. Reischauer, pp. 503–540. Washington, D.C.: The Brookings Institution Press, Committee for Economic Development, and Urban Institute Press, 2000.

Powell, Walter W., and DiMaggio, Paul J. "Introduction." In *The New Institutionalism in Organizational Analysis*, edited by Walter W. Powell and Paul J. DiMaggio, pp. 1–40. Chicago: University of Chicago Press, 1991.

Prahalad, C. K., and Gary Hamel. "The Core Competence of the Corporation." *Harvard Business Review* 68 (1990): 79–91.

Pratt, John W., and Richard J. Zeckhauser. "Principals and Agents: An Overview." In *Principals and Agents: The Structure of Business*, edited by John W. Pratt and Richard J. Zeckhauser, pp. 1–35. Boston: Harvard Business School Press, 1987.

———. *Principals and Agents: The Structure of Business*. Boston: Harvard Business School Press, 1987.

Pressman, Jeffrey L. *Federal Programs and City Politics: The Dynamics of the Air Process in Oakland*. Berkeley: University of California Press, 1975.

Pressman, Jeffery L., and Aaron B. Wildavsky. *Implementation*. Berkeley: University of California Press, 1973.

———, eds. *Implementation*. 2d ed. Berkeley: University of California Press, 1979.

———, eds. *Implementation*. 3d ed. Los Angeles: University of California Press, 1983.

Price Waterhouse. *An Actuarial Review for Fiscal Year 1997 of the Federal Housing Administration's Mutual Mortgage Insurance Fund: Final Report*. Washington, D.C.: 19 February 1998.

Proffitt, Dennis R., Mary K. Kaiser, and Susan M. Whelan. "Understanding Wheel Dynamics." *Cognitive Psychology* 22, no. 3 (1990): 342–373.

Provan, Keith G., and H. Brinton Milward. "A Preliminary Theory of Interorganizational Network Effectiveness: A Comparative Study of Four Community Mental Health Systems." *Administrative Science Quarterly* 40 (1995): 1–33.

Puska, Pekka. "The North Karelia Project: Health Promotion in Action." In *Strategies for Public Health,* edited by L. K. Y. Ng and D. L. Davis, pp. 317–335. New York: Van Nostrand Reinhold, 1981.

Putnam, Robert D. *Bowling Alone: The Collapse and Revival of American Community.* New York: Simon and Schuster, 2000.

———. *Making Democracy Work.* Princeton, N.J.: Princeton University Press, 1993.

Radin, Beryl A. "The Government Performance and Results Act and the Tradition of Federal Management Reform: Square Pegs in Round Holes?" Paper presented at the National Public Management Conference, Texas A&M University, 3–4 December 1999.

Rainey, Hal G. *Understanding and Managing Public Organizations.* San Francisco: Jossey-Bass, 1991.

Redburn, F. Stevens. "Measuring Revenue Capacity, Effort and Spending: How Should the Government Measure Spending? The Uses of Accrual Accounting." *Public Administration Review* 53 (1993): 228–236.

Redwood, J. *Public Enterprise in Crisis.* Oxford: Blackwell, 1980.

Rees, Joseph. "Development of Communitarian Regulation in the Chemical Industry." *Law and Policy* 19, no. 4 (1997): 477–528.

Regier, D. A., R. M. A. Hirschfield, F. K. Goodwin, J. D. Burke, J. B. Lazar, and L. L. Judd. "The NIMH Depression Awareness, Recognition, and Treatment Program: Structure, Aims, and Scientific Basis." *The American Journal of Psychiatry* 145 (1988): 1351–1357.

Rehfuss, John A. *Contracting Out in Government: A Guide to Working with Outside Contractors to Supply Public Services.* San Francisco: Jossey-Bass, 1989.

Reich, Robert. "Balanced Budget Easier If Corporate Welfare Ended." *USA Today* (22 December 1995): A12.

———. *The Power of Public Ideas.* Cambridge, Mass.: Harvard University Press, 1990.

Reischauer, Robert D. "Medicare Vouchers." In *Vouchers and the Provision of Public Services,* edited by C. Eugene Steuerle, Van Doorn Ooms, George Peterson, and Robert D. Reischauer, pp. 407–437. Washington, D.C.: The Brookings Institution Press, Committee for Economic Development, and Urban Institute Press, 2000.

Reiss, Jr., Albert. "Selecting Strategies of Social Control over Organizational Life." In *Enforcing Regulation,* edited by Keith Hawkins and John Thomas, pp. 23–25. Boston: Kluwer-Nijhoff Publishing, 1984.

Reppucci, N. D., J. L. Woolard, and C. S. Fried. "Social, Community, and Preventive Interventions." *Annual Review of Psychology* 50 (1999): 387–418.

Resnik, Judith. "Managerial Judging." *Harvard Law Review* 96 (1982): 374.

Rhyne, Elisabeth Holmes. *Small Business, Banks, and SBA Loan Guarantees.* New York: Quorum, 1986.

Rice, Ronald E. "Smokey Bear." In *Public Communication Campaigns.* 2d ed. Edited by Ronald E. Rice and Charles K. Atkin. Beverly Hills, Calif.: Sage, 1989.

Richardson, J. *Policy Styles in Western Europe.* Boston: Allen and Unwin, 1982.

Ringeling, Arthur B. *Het Imago van de Overheid (The Image of Government).* 's-Gravenhage: VUGA, 1993.

———. *De Instrumenten van Het Beleid (The Instruments of Government Policy).* Alphen aan den Rijn, Netherlands: Oratie Erasmus University Rotterdam and Samsom, 1983.

———. "Instruments in Four." Paper presented at the annual meeting of the Southern Political Science Association, Atlanta, Georgia, 1998.

———. "Policy Design and the Selection of Policy Instruments." Paper presented at the annual meeting of the Southern Political Science Association, Atlanta, Georgia, 4 November 1998.

Roberts, Donald F., and Nathan Maccoby. "Effects of Mass Communication." In *The Handbook of Social Psychology.* 3d ed. Edited by G. Lindzey and E. Aronson. New York: Random House, 1985.

Roberts, N. C. "Public Entrepreneurship and Innovation." *Policy Studies Review* 11 (1992): 55–73.

Robertson, Peter J., and Muhittin Acar. "Concentrated Hopes, Diffused Responsibilities: Accountability in Public-Private Partnerships." Paper presented at the American Society for Public Administration's 60th National Conference. Orlando, Florida, 10–14 April 1999.

Rogers, Everett M., and J. Douglas Storey. "Communication Campaigns." In *Handbook of Communication Science,* edited by C. R. Berger and S. H. Chaffee, pp. 817–846. Beverly Hills: Sage, 1987.

Rogerson, William P. "Economic Incentives and the Defense Procurement Process." *Journal of Economic Perspectives* 8, no. 4 (1994): 65–90.

———. "Profit Regulation of Defense Contractors and Prizes for Innovation." *Journal of Political Economy* 97, no. 6 (1989): 1284–1305.

Romano, Patrick S., Julie A. Rainwater, and Deirdre Antonius. "Grading the Graders: How Hospitals In California and New York Perceive and Interpret Their Report Cards." *Medical Care* 37, no. 3 (1999): 295–305.

Romzek, Barbara S. "Enhancing Accountability." In *Handbook of Public Administration,* edited by James L. Perry, pp. 97–114. San Francisco: Jossey-Bass, 1996.

Rondinelli, Dennis. "Privatization, Governance, and Public Management: The Challenges Ahead." *Business and the Contemporary World* 10, no. 2 (1998): 167.

Rose, Richard. *Managing Presidential Objectives.* New York: Free Press, 1976.

Rose-Ackerman, Susan. *Controlling Environmental Policy: The Limits of Public Law in Germany and the United States.* New Haven: Yale University Press, 1995.

———. *Corruption and Government: Causes, Consequences, and Reform.* New York: Cambridge University Press, 1999.

Rosen, Bernard. *Holding Government Bureaucracies Accountable.* Westport, Conn.: Praeger, 1998.

Rosenbloom, David H. *Building a Legislative-Centered Public Administration: Congress and the Administrative State, 1946–1999.* Tuscaloosa: University of Alabama Press, 2000.

Rothman, Alexander, and Peter Salovey. "Shaping Perceptions to Motivate Healthy Behavior: The Role of Message Framing." *Psychological Bulletin* 121 (1997): 3–19.

Russo, J. Edward, and France Leclerc. "Characteristics of Successful Product Information Programs." *Journal of Social Issues* 47 (1991): 73–92.

S. 1621. "The Federal Enterprise Regulatory Act of 1991." Drafted by the U.S. General Accounting Office at the request of members of the Senate Committee on Governmental Affairs and introduced on 1 August 1991.

Sabatier, Paul A. "An Advocacy-Coalition Model of Policy Change and the Role of Policy-Oriented Learning Therein." *Policy Sciences* 21 (1988): 129–168.

———. "Top-down and Bottom-up Approaches to Implementation Research: A Critical Analysis and Suggested Synthesis." *Journal of Public Policy* 6, no. 1 (1987): 21–48.

Salamon, Lester M. *America's Non-Profit Sector: A Primer.* New York: The Foundation Center, 1992.

———. "The Changing Partnership between the Voluntary Sector and the Welfare State." In *The Future of the Nonprofit Sector,* edited by Virginia A. Hodgkinson et al. San Francisco: Jossey-Bass, 1989.

———. "The New Governance and the Tools of Public Action: An Introduction," In *The Tools of Government: A Guide to the New Governance,* edited by Lester M. Salamon. New York: Oxford University Press, 2002.

———. "Nonprofit Management Education: A Field Whose Time Has Passed?" In *Nonprofit Management Education: U.S. and World Perspectives,* edited by Michael O'Neill and Kathleen Fletcher, pp. 137–145. Westport, Conn.: Praeger, 1998.

———. *Partners in Public Service: Government-Nonprofit Relations in the Modern Welfare State,* p. 88. Baltimore: Johns Hopkins University Press, 1995.

———. "Rethinking Public Management: Third-Party Government and the Tools of Government Action." *Public Policy* 29, no. 1 (summer 1981): 255–275.

———. "The Rise of the Nonprofit Sector." *Foreign Affairs* 73 (1994): 109–122.

———. "The Rise of Third-Party Government." *The Washington Post* (29 June 1980).

———, ed. *Beyond Privatization: The Tools of Government Action.* Washington, D.C.: Urban Institute Press, 1989.

Salamon, Lester M., and Alan J. Abramson. "The Nonprofit Sector." In *The Reagan Experiment,* edited by John L. Palmer and Isabel V. Sawhill, pp. 223–224. Washington, D.C.: Urban Institute Press, 1982.

Salamon, Lester M., and Helmut K. Anheier. "The Third Route: Government-Nonprofit Collaboration in Germany and the United States." In *Private Action and the Public Good,* edited by Walter W. Powell and Elisabeth S. Clemens, pp. 151–162. New Haven: Yale University Press, 1998.

Salamon, Lester M., and Michael S. Lund. "The Tools Approach: Basic Analytics." *Beyond Privatization: The Tools of Government Action,* edited by Lester M. Salamon, pp. 23–50. Washington, D.C.: Urban Institute Press, 1989.

Salamon, Lester M., et al. *Global Civil Society: Dimensions of the Nonprofit Sector,* p. 14. Baltimore: Johns Hopkins Institute for Policy Studies, 1999.

Sallie Mae. *The Restructuring of Sallie Mae: Rationale and Feasibility.* Washington, D.C.: Government Printing Office, 1994.

Salmi, Jamil. *Student Loans in an International Perspective: The World Bank Experience.* Draft working paper, Washington, D.C.: World Bank, 1999.

Salmon, Charles, ed. *Information Campaigns: Managing the Process of Social Change.* Newbury Park, Calif.: Sage, 1989.

Santomero, Anthony. "Deposit Insurance: Do We Need It and Why?" *Ekonomia* 1, no. 1 (1997): 1–19.

Saulnier, Raymond Joseph, Harold G. Halcrow, and Neil H. Jacoby. *Federal Lending and Loan Insurance.* Princeton, N.J.: Princeton University Press, 1958.

Savas, Emanuel S. *Privatization: The Key to Better Government.* Chatham, N.J.: Chatham House, 1987.

———. *Privatizing the Public Sector.* Chatham, N.J.: Chatham Publishing, 1982.

Scanlon, John. "An Innovative Procurement Effort Where Valuing Time Dramatically Speeds Up Acquisition and Deliveries of Results: Responding to a Crisis—A Federal/State Partnership." A case written for the Council for Excellence in Government, Conference on Real Acquisition Reform: Managing Risk in the New Environment. Washington, D.C.: Council for Excellence in Government, 1995.

———. "Problem Solving Partnerships and Joint Ventures to Share Risks and Benefits in Developing Large System Technology Projects." A case written for the Council for Excellence in Government, Conference on Real Acquisition Reform: Managing Risk in the New Environment. Washington, D.C.: Council for Excellence in Government, 1995.

Schaffer, Bernard, and Geoff Lamb. *Can Equity be Organized?: Equity, Development Analysis and Planning.* Farnborough, Hampshire, U.K.: Gower, 1981.

Scharpf, F. W. *Games Real Actors Play: Actor-Centered Institutionalism in Policy Research.* Boulder: Westview Press, 1997.

Schauer, Frederick. *Playing by the Rules.* Oxford: Clarendon Press, 1991.

Scheberle, Denise. *Federalism and Environmental Policy: Trust and the Politics of Implementation.* Washington, D.C.: Georgetown University Press, 1997.

Scherer, Clifford W., and Napoleon K. Juanillo, Jr. "Bridging Theory and Praxis: Reexamining Public Health Communication." In *Communication Yearbook/15,* edited by S. A. Deetz, pp. 312–345. Newbury Park, Calif.: Sage, 1992.

Schick, Allen. "Contemporary Problems in Financial Control." In *Current Issues in Public Administration.* 2d ed. Edited by Frederick S. Lane, pp. 361–371. New York: St. Martin's Press, 1982.

———. *The Spirit of Reform: Managing the New Zealand State Sector in a Time of Change.* Wellington: New Zealand State Services Commission, 1996.

Schlesinger, Mark, Robert A. Dorwart, and Richard T. Pulice. "Competitive Bidding and State Purchase of Services: The Case of Mental Health Care in Massachusetts." *Journal of Policy Analysis and Management* 8 (1986/1987): 245–259.

Schneider, Anne L., and Helen Ingram. "Behavioral Assumptions of Policy Tools." *Journal of Politics* 52, no. 2 (May 1990): 510–529.

————. *Policy Design for Democracy*, pp. 5–7, 129–135. Lawrence: University Press of Kansas, 1997.

————. "The Social Construction of Target Populations: Implications for Policy and Politics." *American Political Science Review* 87 (1993): 34–47.

Schneider, Eric C., and Arnold M. Epstein. "Use of Public Performance Reports: A Survey of Patients Undergoing Cardiac Surgery." *Journal of the American Medical Association* 279, no. 20 (1998): 1638–1642.

Scholz, John T. "Cooperation, Deterrence, and the Ecology of Regulatory Enforcement." *Law and Society Review* 18, no. 2 (1984): 179–224.

————. "Managing Regulatory Enforcement." In *Handbook of Regulation and Administrative Law,* edited by David H. Rosenbloom and Richard D. Schwartz, pp. 423–463. New York: Marcel Dekker, 1994.

Schon, D. A., and M. Rein. *Frame Reflection: Resolving Intractable Policy Issues.* New York: Basic Books, 1994.

Schooler, Carol, Steven Chaffee, June Flora, and Connie Roser. "Health Campaign Channels: Tradeoffs among Reach, Specificity, and Impact." *Human Communication Research* 24 (1998): 410–432.

Schorr, Lisbeth B. *Common Purpose: Strengthening Families and Neighborhoods to Rebuild America.* New York: Anchor, 1997.

Schuck, Peter H. *Agent Orange on Trial: Mass Toxic Disasters in the Courts.* Cambridge, Mass.: Harvard University Press, 1987.

————. *Foundations of Administrative Law.* New York: Oxford University Press, 1994.

————. *The Limits of Law: Essays on Democratic Governance.* Boulder: Westview Press, 2000.

————, ed. *Tort Law and the Public Interest: Competition, Innovation, and Consumer Welfare.* New York: W. W. Norton, 1991.

Schudson, Michael. *Advertising: The Uneasy Persuasion.* New York: Basic Books, 1984.

Schultze, Charles. *The Public Use of Private Interest.* Washington, D.C.: The Brookings Institution Press, 1977.

Schwartz, Gary T. "Product Liability and Medical Malpractice in Comparative Perspective." In *The Liability Maze: The Impact of Liability Law on Safety and Innovation,* edited by Peter W. Huber and Robert E. Litan, pp. 28–80. Washington, D.C.: The Brookings Institution Press, 1991.

Scott, Graham, Ian Ball, and Tony Dale. "New Zealand's Public Management Reform: Implications for the United States." *Journal of Policy Analysis and Management* 16 (1997): 357–381.

Seidman, Harold. "Organizational Relationships and the Control of Public Enterprise." In *Organization and Administration of Public Enterprises: Selected Papers,* pp. 156–168. New York: United Nations, 1968.

————. *Politics, Position and Power: The Dynamics of Federal Organization.* 5th ed. New York: Oxford University, 1998.

————. "The Quasi World of the Federal Government." *The Brookings Review* 6, no. 3 (1988) 23–27.

Selinger, Mark. "Disaster Insurance Bill Survives House Banking Committee Consideration." *BNA Banking Daily* (1999).

Selznick, Philip. *Leadership in Administration: A Sociological Interpretation.* New York: Harper, 1957.

Sen, Amartya. "Rational Fools: A Critique of the Behavioral Foundations of Economic Theory." In *Beyond Self-Interest,* edited by Jane Mansbridge, pp. 25–43. Chicago: University of Chicago Press, 1990.

Serlin, Michael D. "In the Ring." *Government Executive* (1 September 1997).

Shapiro, Martin. "Administrative Discretion: The Next Stage." *Yale Law Journal* 92 (1983): 1487–1522.

————. "APA: Past, Present, and Future." *Virginia Law Review* 72, no. 447 (1986): 452–533.

Shapiro, Robert J., and Chris J. Soares. *Cut and Invest to Grow: How to Expand Public Investment While Cutting the Deficit.* Policy Report No. 26. Washington, D.C.: Progressive Policy Institute, 1997.

Shapiro, Walter. "GOP Assault on IRS Was a Turning Point." *USA Today* (3 May 2000): 12A.

Shapo, Marshall S. *Basic Principles of Tort Law.* St. Paul, Minn.: West Group, 1999.

Sheils, John, and Paul Hogan. "Cost of Tax-Exempt Health Benefits in 1998." *Health Affairs* 18, no. 2 (1999): 176–181.

Shoemaker, Pamela, ed. *Communication Campaigns About Drugs.* Hillsdale, N.J.: Erlbaum, 1989.

Shover, Neal, John Lynxwiler, Stephen Groce, and Donald Clelland. "Regional Variation in Law Enforcement: The Surface Mining Control and Reclamation Act of 1977." In *Enforcing Regulation,* edited by Keith Hawkins and John Thomas, pp. 121–145. Boston: Kluwer-Nijhoff Publishing, 1984.

Shugart, W. F. *Taxing Choices: The Predatory Politics of Fiscal Discrimination.* New Brunswick, N.J.: Transaction Books, 1997.

Shyles, L., and J. E. Hocking. "The Army's 'Be All You Can Be' Campaign." *Armed Forces and Society* 16 (1990): 369–383.

Silk, Leonard. "Tax Writers' 'Christmas Tree'." *New York Times* (26 June 1981): D2.

Sinfield, Adrian. "Social Protection Versus Tax Benefits." Presented at the Symposium of the European Institute of Social Security, Helsinki, Finland, 4–5 September 1997.

Sirianni, Carmen. *Civic Innovation in America: Community Empowerment, Public Policy, and the Movement for Civic Renewal.* Berkeley: University of California Press, 2001.

Skloot, Edward. "Privatization, Competition, and the Future of Human Services." Unpublished paper prepared for delivery at the Council on Foundations Conference, New Orleans, Louisiana, 21 April 1999.

Slemrod, Joel. "Which Is the Simplest Tax System of Them All?" In *Economic Effects of Fundamental Tax Reform,* edited by Henry J. Aaron and William G. Gale, pp. 355–391. Washington, D.C.: The Brookings Institution Press, 1996.

Slemrod, Joel, and Jon Bakija. *Taxing Ourselves: A Citizen's Guide to the Great Debate Over Tax Reform.* Cambridge, Mass.: MIT Press, 1996.

Smallhout, James H. *The Uncertain Retirement: Securing Pension Promises in the World of Risk.* Chicago: Irwin, 1996.

Smith, David Barton. "Addressing Racial Inequities in Health Care: Civil Rights Monitoring and Report Cards." *Journal of Health Politics, Policy and Law* 23 (1998): 75–105.

Smith, Steven Rathgeb. "Government Financing of Nonprofit Activity." In *Nonprofits and Government: Collaboration and Conflict,* edited by Elizabeth T. Boris and C. Eugene Steuerle, pp. 177–210. Washington, D.C.: Urban Institute Press, 1999.

———. "The New Politics of Contracting: Citizenship and the Nonprofit Role." In *Public Policy for Democracy,* edited by Helen Ingram and Steven Rathgeb Smith, pp. 163–197. Washington, D.C.: The Brookings Institution Press, 1993.

Smith, Steven Rathgeb, and Michael Lipsky. *Nonprofits for Hire: The Welfare State in the Age of Contracting.* Cambridge, Mass.: Harvard University Press, 1993.

Smith, Steven Rathgeb, and Deborah Stone. "The Unexpected Consequences of Privatization." In *Remaking the Welfare State,* edited by Michael K. Brown, pp. 232–252. Philadelphia: Temple University Press, 1988.

Somers, Herman P. *Presidential Agency: The Office of War Mobilization and Reconversion.* Cambridge, Mass.: Harvard University Press, 1951.

Soss, Joe. "Lessons in Welfare: Policy Design, Political Learning, and Political Action." *American Political Science Review* 93, no. 2 (1999): 363–380.

Stanfield, Rochelle L. "Big Money in Low Rents." *National Journal* 26, no. 19 (1994): 1068.

Stanford, John, with Robin Simons. *Victory in Our Schools.* New York: Bantam, 1999.

Stanton, Thomas H. "Credit Scoring and Loan Scoring: Tools for Improved Management of Federal Credit Programs." Arlington, Va.: PricewaterhouseCoopers Endowment, 1999.

———. "Federal Supervision of Safety and Soundness of Government-Sponsored Enterprises." *The Administrative Law Journal* 5, no. 2 (1991) 395–484.

———. "Government-Sponsored Enterprises: Another View." *Public Budgeting & Finance* (1989): 81–86.

———. "Improving the Design and Administration of Federal Credit Programs." *The Financier: Analyses of Capital and Money Market Transactions* 3, no. 2 (1996): 7–21.

————. "Managing Federal Credit Programs in the Information Age: Opportunities and Risks." *The Financier: Analyses of Capital and Money Market Transactions* 5, no. 2; 5, no. 3 (1998): 24–39.

————. "Nonquantifiable Risks and Financial Institutions: The Mercantilist Legal Framework of Banks, Thrifts, and Government-Sponsored Enterprises." In *Global Risk-Based Capital Regulations,* vol. 1. Edited by Charles A. Stone and Anne Zissu, pp. 57–97. Burr Ridge, Ill.: Irwin Professional Publishing, 1994.

————. *A State of Risk.* New York: HarperCollins, 1991.

Steinmo, Sven. *Taxation and Democracy: Swedish, British, and American Approaches to Financing the Modern State.* New Haven: Yale University Press, 1993.

Steinmo, Sven, Kathleen Thelen, and Frank Longstreth, eds. *Structuring Politics: Historical Institutionalism in Comparative Politics.* Cambridge: Cambridge University Press, 1992.

Stern, Paul. "What Psychology Knows About Energy Conservation." *American Psychologist* 47 (1992): 1224–1232.

Steuerle, C. Eugene. "Common Issues for Voucher Programs." In *Vouchers and the Provision of Public Services,* edited by C. Eugene Steuerle, Van Doorn Ooms, George Peterson, and Robert D. Reischauer, pp. 3–39. Washington, D.C.: The Brookings Institution Press, Committee for Economic Development, and Urban Institute Press, 2000.

Steuerle, C. Eugene, Edward M. Gramlich, Hugh Heclo, and Demetra Smith Nightingale. *The Government We Deserve: Responsive Democracy and Changing Expectations.* Washington, D.C.: Urban Institute Press, 1998.

Stevenson, R. W. "The Secret Language of Social Engineering." *The New York Times* (6 July 1997).

Stigler, George. "The Economics of Information." *Journal of Political Economy* 69 (1961): 213–225.

————. "The Optimum Enforcement of Law." *Journal of Political Economy* 70, no. 5 (1970): 526–536.

Stillman, Jr., Richard J. *Preface to Public Administration: A Search for Themes and Direction.* New York: St. Martin's Press, 1991.

————. *Preface to Public Administration: A Search for Themes and Direction.* 2d ed. Burke, Va.: Chatelaine Press, 1999.

Stockwell, Tim. "Influencing the Labeling of Alcoholic Beverage Containers: Informing the Public." *Addiction* 88 (1993): 53–60.

Stoker, Robert P. *Reluctant Partners: Implementing Federal Policy.* Pittsburgh: University of Pittsburgh Press, 1991.

Stoltman, Jeffrey J., and Fred W. Morgan. "Product Safety, Information, and Behavior." *American Behavioral Scientist* 38, no. 4 (1995): 633–645.

Stone, Deborah. *Policy Paradox: The Art of Political Decision Making.* New York: W. W. Norton, 1997.

Stratton, Sheryl. "How Regulations Are Made: A Look at the Reg Writing Process." *Tax Notes* 74, no. 5 (1997): 544–550.

Sugarman, Stephen D. *Doing Away with Personal Injury Law.* New York: Quorum Books, 1989.

Surrey, Stanley S. *Pathways to Tax Reform: The Concept of Tax Expenditures.* Cambridge, Mass.: Harvard University Press, 1973.

————. "Tax Incentives as a Device for Implementing Government Policy: A Comparison with Direct Government Expenditures." *Harvard Law Review* 83, no. 4 (1970): 705–738.

Surrey, Stanley S., and Paul R. McDaniel. *Tax Expenditures.* Cambridge, Mass.: Harvard University Press, 1985.

Sutton, Sharyn, George Balch, and Craig Lefebvre. "Strategic Questions for Consumer-Based Health Communications." *Public Health Reports* 110 (1995): 725–733.

Swaan, A. de. "De Verstatelijking van Verzorgingsarrangementen (Provision Arrangements in the Realm of the State)." *De Gids* (1976): 35–47.

Tarrow, S. *Power in Movement.* 2d ed. Cambridge: Cambridge University Press, 1999.

Taylor, Serge. *Making Bureaucracies Think: The Environmental Impact Statement Strategy of Administrative Reform.* Stanford, Calif.: Stanford University Press, 1984.

Teaford, Jon C. *The Unheralded Triumph: City Government in America, 1870–1900.* Baltimore: Johns Hopkins University Press, 1984.

Telberg, Rick. "Forecast '98: U.S. Firms Poised for Sizzling Growth." *Accounting Today* 12, no. 1 (1998): 1, 38.

Terry, Larry D. "Administrative Leadership, New Managerialism, and the Public Management Movement." *Public Administration Review* 58, no. 3 (May/June 1998): 194–200.

Thalen, Kathleen, Frank Longstreth, and Sven Steinmo. *Structuring Politics: Historical Institutionalism in Comparative Analysis.* New York: Cambridge University Press. 1992.

Thaler, Richard H. *Quasi-Rational Economics.* New York: Russell Sage Foundation, 1991.

Thompson, Boyce. "Managing Our Waste: A Governing Special Report." *Governing* 2 (1989): 5A–26A.

Thurston, John. *Government Proprietary Corporations in the English-Speaking Countries.* Cambridge, Mass.: Harvard University Press, 1937.

Thynne, Ian. "Basic Concepts and Issues." In *Corporatization, Divestment and the Public-Private Mix: Selected Country Studies,* edited by Ian Thynne, pp. 1–9. Hong Kong: Asian Journal of Public Administration, 1995.

———. "The Incorporated Company as an Instrument of Government: A Quest for a Comparative Understanding." *Governance: An International Journal of Policy and Administration* 7, no. 1 (1994): 59–82.

Tooley, James. *The Global Education Industry: Lessons from Private Education in Developing Countries.* Washington, D.C.: International Finance Corporation, 1999.

Transactional Records Access Clearinghouse. *The IRS and Its Responsibilities.* Syracuse, N.Y.: TRAC, 2000. Accessed via http://trac.syr.edu:80/tracirs/findings.

———. *New Findings.* Syracuse, N.Y.: TRAC, 2000. Accessed via http://trac.syr.edu:80/tracirs/findings.

Tsebelis, G. *Nested Games: Rational Choice in Comparative Politics.* Berkeley: University of California Press, 1990.

Tullock, Gordon. *The Politics of Bureaucracy.* Washington, D.C.: Public Affairs Press, 1965.

"Tulsa Race Riot: A Report by the Oklahoma Commission to Study the Tulsa Race Riot of 1921." (28 February 2001). Online at http://www.ok-history.mus.ok.us/trrc/freport.htm.

Twombly, Eric C., and Elizabeth T. Boris. *The Use of Vouchers in the Provision of Human Services and Potential Implications for Nonprofit Organizations.* Paper presented at the Independent Sector Spring Research Forum, Alexandria, Virginia, 26 March 1999.

Tyler, Tom R. *Why People Obey the Law.* New Haven: Yale University Press, 1990.

Ullman, Claire F. "Partners in Reform: Nonprofit Organizations and the Welfare State in France." In *Private Action and the Public Good,* edited by Walter W. Powell and Elisabeth S. Clemens, pp. 163–176. New Haven: Yale University Press, 1998.

Ungar, Sanford. *FBI.* Boston: Little, Brown, 1976.

Urban Institute. "What We Know About Mortgage Lending Discrimination in America." Report to the Department of Housing and Urban Development. September 1999. Online at http://www.hud.gov/pressrel/newsconf/menu.html.

U.S. Bureau of Labor Statistics. *Labor Force Statistics from the Current Population Survey: Union Member Summary.* Washington, D.C.: Department of Labor, 25 January 1999.

U.S. Congress, Office of Technology Assessment. *Are We Cleaning Up?: 10 Superfund Case Studies.* Washington, D.C.: Government Printing Office, 1988.

———. *Coming Clean: Superfund Problems Can Be Solved.* Washington, D.C.: Government Printing Office, 1989.

U.S. Congress. House. Committee on Ways and Means. *Impact of Complexity of the Tax Code on Individual Taxpayers and Small Businesses: Hearings,* 105th Cong., 2d sess., 1998.

U.S. Congress. Joint Committee on Taxation. *Estimates of Federal Tax Expenditures for Fiscal Years 1999–2003.* Washington, D.C.: Government Printing Office, 1998.

U.S. Congress. Senate. Committee on the Budget. *Tax Expenditures: Compendium of Background Material on Individual Provisions,* 102d Cong., 2d sess., 1992. S. Rept. 102–119.

U.S. Congress. Senate. Committee on Finance. *Complexity of the Individual Income Tax: Hearings,* 106th Cong., 1st sess., 1999.

U.S. Congressional Budget Office. *The Changing Business of Banking: A Study of Failed Banks from 1987 to 1992.* Washington D.C.: Congress of the U.S., Congressional Office, 1994.

———. *Controlling Losses of the Pension Benefit Guaranty Corporation.* Washington, D.C.: Congress of the U.S., Congressional Office, 1993.

———. *The Economic Impact of a Solvency Crisis in the Insurance Industry.* Washington, D.C.: Congress of the U.S., Congressional Office, 1994.

———. *The Effects of Tax Reform on Tax Expenditures.* Washington, D.C.: Government Printing Office, 1988.

U.S. Department of Agriculture Office of Inspector General. *Report to the Secretary on Federal Crop Insurance Reform.* No. 05801–2-At. April 1999.

U.S. Department of Health and Human Services. *Caseload Comparison since the Signing of the Welfare Law: Aug. 1996 vs. Dec. 1999.* Washington, D.C.: The Administration for Children and Families, August 2000. http://www.acf.dhhs.gov/news/stats/aug-dec.htm.

U.S. Department of Housing and Urban Development. *Housing in the Seventies.* Report of the National Housing Policy Review, Washington, D.C.: Government Printing Office, 1974.

———. *Opting In: Renewing America's Commitment to Affordable Housing.* Washington, D.C., April 1999. http://www.hud.gov/pressrel/optingin.html.

———. *Studies on Privatizing Fannie Mae and Freddie Mac.* Washington, D.C.: HUD, 1996.

U.S. Department of the Treasury. *FY 1999 National Taxpayer Advocate's Annual Report to Congress.* Washington, D.C.: Internal Revenue Service, 1999. Accessed via http://www.irs.ustreas.gov/ind_info/rpt99–1.html.

———. *Government Sponsorship of the Federal National Mortgage Association and the Federal Home Loan Mortgage Corporation.* Washington, D.C.: U.S. Department of the Treasury, 1996.

———. *Report of the Secretary of the Treasury on Government-Sponsored Enterprises.* Washington, D.C.: Government Printing Office, April 1991.

———. *Tax Reform for Fairness, Simplicity, and Economic Growth.* Washington, D.C.: Government Printing Office, 1984.

U.S. Federal Deposit Insurance Corporation. *History of the Eighties: Lessons for the Future.* Washington, D.C.: FDIC, 1997.

U.S. Federal Emergency Management Agency. National Flood Insurance Program. *Answers to Questions About the National Flood Insurance Program.* Washington, D.C.: National Flood Insurance Program, 1999.

U.S. General Accounting Office. *Agricultural Research: Information on Research System and USDA's Priority Setting.* RCED-96–92, 1996a.

———. *Block Grants: Issues in Designing Accountability Provisions.* Washington, D.C.: GAO, 1998.

———. *Budgeting for Federal Insurance Programs.* Washington, D.C.: GAO, 1997.

———. *Crop Insurance: Additional Actions Could Further Improve Program's Financial Condition.* Washington, D.C.: GAO, 1995.

———. *Crop Insurance: Opportunities Exist to Reduce Government Costs for Private-Sector Delivery.* Washington, D.C.: GAO, 1997.

———. *Crop Insurance: USDA Needs a Better Estimate of Improper Payments to Strengthen Controls over Claims.* Washington, D.C.: GAO, 1999.

———. *Environmental Protection: Collaborative EPA-State Effort Needed to Improve New Performance Partnership System.* GAO/RCED-99–171. Washington, D.C.: GAO, 1999.

———. *Federal Grants: Design Improvements Could Help Federal Resources Go Further.* GAO/AIMD-97–7. Washington, D.C.: GAO, 1996.

———. *Federal Housing Enterprises: HUD's Mission Oversight Needs to Be Strengthened.* GAO/GGD 98–173. Washington, D.C.: GAO, July 1998.

———. *Flood Insurance: Financial Resources May Not Be Sufficient to Meet Future Expected Losses.* Washington, D.C.: GAO, 1994.

———. *Forest Service Management: Little Has Changed as a Result of the Fiscal Year 1995 Budget Reforms.* RCED-99–2, 1998.

———. *Government Contractors: Are Service Contractors Performing Inherently Governmental Functions?* GGD-92–11, 1991.

———. *Government Corporations: Profiles of Existing Government Corporations.* GAO/GGD 96–14. Washington, D.C.: GAO, December 1995.

————. *Government-Sponsored Enterprises: A Framework for Limiting the Government's Exposure to Risks.* GAO/GGD-91–90. Washington, D.C.: GAO, May 1991.

————. *Guidelines for Rescuing Large Failing Firms and Municipalities.* GAO/GGD-84–34. Washington, D.C.: GAO, March 1984.

————. *Higher Education: Restructuring Student Aid Could Reduce Low-Income Student Dropout Rate.* GAO/HEHS 95–48. Washington, D.C.: GAO, March 1995.

————. *High-Risk Series: An Overview.* HR-95–1. Washington, D.C.: Government Printing Office, February 1995.

————. *High-Risk Series: An Update.* HR-99–1. Washington, D.C.: GAO, 1999.

————. H.R. 3078, *The Federal Agency Anti-Lobbying Act.* T-OGC-96–18, 1996b.

————. *Major Management Challenges and Program Risks: A Governmentwide Perspective.* GAO/OCG-99–1. Washington, D.C.: GAO, 1999.

————. *Managing for Results: Using the Results Act to Address Mission Fragmentation and Program Overlap.* Washington, D.C.: GAO, 1997.

————. *Medicaid: States Use Illusory Approaches to Shift Program Costs to the Federal Government.* GAO/HEHS-94–133. Washington, D.C.: GAO, 1994.

————. *Performance Budgeting: Initial Experiences under the Results Act in Linking Plans with Budgets.* AIMD/GGD-99–67. Washington, D.C.: GAO, April 1999.

————. *Proposed Changes in Federal Matching and Maintenance of Effort Requirements.* GAO/GGD-81–7. Washington, D.C.: GAO, 1980.

————. *Recruitment and Retention: Inadequate Federal Pay Cited as Primary Problem by Agency Officials.* GGD-90–117. Washington, D.C.: GAO, September 1990.

————. *The Results Act: Assessment of the Governmentwide Performance Plan for Fiscal Year 1999.* GAO/AIMD/GGD. Washington, D.C.: GAO, 1998.

————. *Tax Credits: Opportunities to Improve Oversight of Low Income Housing.* GAO/GGD/RCED-97–55. Washington, D.C.: GAO, 1997.

————. *Tax Expenditures Deserve More Scrutiny.* Washington, D.C.: GAO, 1994.

————. *Tennessee Valley Authority: Financial Problems Raise Questions About Long-Term Viability.* GAO/AIMD/RCED 95–134. Washington, D.C.: GAO, August 1995.

————. *Toxic Chemicals: EPA's Toxic Release Inventory Is Useful but Can Be Improved.* Washington, D.C.: GAO, June 1991.

U.S. Office of Management and Budget (OMB). *A Citizen's Guide to the Federal Budget: Budget of the United States Government Fiscal Year 2000.* Washington, D.C.: OMB, 1999. Accessed online via http://www.gpo.gov/usbudget/ fy2000/guidetoc.html.

————. *More Benefits, Fewer Burdens: Creating a Regulatory System That Works for the American People.* Washington, D.C.: OMB, Office of Information and Regulatory Affairs, 1996.

————. *Report to Congress on the Costs and Benefits of Federal Regulations.* Washington, D.C.: OMB, Office of Information and Regulatory Affairs, 1997.

————. "Underwriting Federal Credit and Insurance." In *Analytical Perspectives, Budget of the United States Government, Fiscal Year 2000,* pp. 181–200. Washington, D.C.: Government Printing Office, 1999.

————. *Managing Federal Assistance in the 1980s.* Washington, D.C.: OMB, 1980.

U.S. Office of Management and Budget, Office of Federal Procurement Policy. *A Guide to Best Practices Guide for Performance-Based Service Contracting.* Washington, D.C.: OMB, 1996.

U.S. Office of Personnel Management. *Union Recognition in the Federal Government.* Washington, D.C.: Superintendent of Documents, 1997.

U.S. Public Law 344. 93rd Cong., 2d sess., 12 July 1974.

Vandell, Kerry D. "FHA Restructuring Proposals: Alternatives and Implications." *Housing Policy Debate* 6, no. 2 (1995): 291–393.

van der Doelen, F. C. J. "The 'Give and Take' Packaging of Policy Instruments: Optimizing Legitimacy and Effectiveness." In *Carrots, Sticks and Sermons: Policy Instruments and Their Evaluation,* edited by Marie-Louise Bemelmans-Videc, Ray C. Rist and Evert Vedung, pp. 129–146. New Brunswick, N.J.: Transaction Books, 1998.

Van Meter, Donald S., and Carl E. Van Horn. "The Policy Implementation Process: A Conceptual Framework." *Administration and Society* 6, no. 1 (February 1975): 447–474.

Varone, F. *Le choix des instruments des politiques publiques.* Bern, Switzerland: Verlag Paul Haupt, 1999.

Vaughn, Emmett, and Therese Vaughn. *Fundamentals of Risk and Insurance.* 8th ed. New York: Wiley, 1999.

Vedung, Evert. "Policy Instruments: Typologies and Theories." In *Carrots, Sticks and Sermons: Policy Instruments and Their Evaluation,* edited by Marie-Louise Bemelmans-Videc, Ray C. Rist, and Evert Vedung, pp. 21–58. New Brunswick, N.J.: Transaction Publishers, 1998.

Vedung, Evert, and Frans C. J. van der Doelen. "The Sermon: Information Programs in the Public Policy Process: Choice, Effects, and Evaluation." In *Carrots, Sticks and Sermons: Policy Instruments and Their Evaluation,* edited by Marie-Louise Bemelmans-Videc, Ray C. Rist, and Evert Vedung. New Brunswick, N.J.: Transaction Publishers, 1998.

Verba, Sidney, Kay Lehman Schlozman, and Henry Brady. *Civic Voluntarism in American Politics.* Cambridge, Mass.: Harvard University Press, 1995.

Victor, D. G., K. Raustiala, E. B. Skolnikoff, eds. *The Implementation and Effectiveness of International Environmental Commitments.* Cambridge, Mass. and London: MIT Press, 1998.

Vidmar, Neil. "The Performance of the American Civil Jury: An Empirical Perspective." *Arizona Law Review* 40 (1998): 849–899.

Viscusi, W. Kip. *Fatal Tradeoffs: Public and Private Responsibilities for Risk.* New York: Oxford University Press, 1992.

———. *Product-Risk Labeling.* Washington, D.C.: American Enterprise Institute Press, 1993.

Viscusi, W. Kip, and Richard Zeckhauser. "Hazard Communication: Warnings and Risk." *Annals of the American Academy of Political and Social Science* 545 (1996): 106–115.

Visser, J., and A. Hemerijck. *A Dutch Miracle.* Amsterdam: Amsterdam University Press, 1997.

Vogel, David. *National Styles of Regulation: Environmental Policy in Great Britain and the United States.* Ithaca, N.Y. and London: Cornell University Press, 1986.

Wallace, H., and W. Wallace. *Policy-Making in the European Union.* Oxford: Oxford University Press, 1996.

Wallack, Lawrence. "Improving Health Promotion: Media Advocacy and Social Marketing Approaches." In *Mass Communication and Public Health: Complexities and Conflicts,* edited by C. Atkin and L. Wallack, pp. 147–164. Newbury Park, Calif.: Sage, 1990.

Walsh, A. H. *The Public's Business.* Cambridge, Mass.: MIT Press, 1978.

Wang, Guijing, Stanley M. Fletcher, and Dale H. Carley. "Consumer Utilization of Food Labeling as a Source of Nutrition Information." *The Journal of Consumer Affairs* 29 (1995): 368–380.

Warner, Kenneth E. "The Effects of the Anti-Smoking Campaign on Cigarette Consumption." *American Journal of Public Health* 67 (1977): 645–650.

Warwick, Donald P. *A Theory of Public Bureaucracy: Politics, Personality, and Organization in the State Department.* Cambridge, Mass.: Harvard University Press, 1975.

Weaver, Carolyn. "Government Guarantees of Private Pension Benefits: Current Problems and Market-Based Solutions." In *Public Policy Toward Pensions,* edited by Sylvester Schieber and John Shoven, pp. 151–195. Cambridge, Mass.: MIT Press, 1997.

Weaver. R. K., and B. A. Rockman. *Do Institutions Matter?: Government Capabilities in the United States and Abroad.* Washington, D.C.: The Brookings Institution Press, 1993.

Weber, Edward P. *Pluralism by the Rules: Conflict and Cooperation in Environmental Regulation.* Washington, D.C.: Georgetown University Press, 1998.

Weber, Max. "Bureaucracy." In *From Max Weber: Essays in Sociology,* edited by H. H. Gerth and C. Wright Mills, pp. 196–244. New York: Oxford University Press, 1946. Originally published in German in 1919.

Weick, Karl. "Cognitive Processes in Organizations." In *Research in Organizational Behavior,* edited by Barry Staw, vol. 1, pp. 41–74. Greenwich, Conn.: JAI Press, 1979.

———. *Sensemaking in Organizations.* Thousand Oaks, Calif.: Sage Publications, 1995.

Weimer, David L., and Aidan R. Vining. *Policy Analysis: Concepts and Practice.* 2d ed. Englewood Cliffs, N.J.: Prentice-Hall, 1998.

———. *Policy Analysis: Concepts and Practice.* 3d ed., pp. 196–252. Upper Saddle River, N.J.: Prentice-Hall, 1999.

Weiss, Janet A. "Ideas and Inducements in Mental Health Policy." *Journal of Policy Analysis and Management* 9 (1990): 178–200.

———. "Policy Design for Democracy: A Look at Public Information Campaigns." In *Public Policy for Democracy,* edited by Helen Ingram and Steven Smith, pp. 99–118. Washington, D.C.: The Brookings Institution Press, 1993.

———. "The Powers of Problem Definition: The Case of Government Paperwork." *Policy Sciences* 22 (1989): 97–121.

———. "Psychology." In *The State of Public Management,* edited by Donald F. Kettl and H. Brinton Milward, pp. 118–142. Baltimore: Johns Hopkins University Press, 1996.

———. "Theoretical Foundations of Policy Intervention." In *Public Management Reform and Innovation,* edited by H. G. Frederickson and J. M. Johnston, pp. 37–69. Tuscaloosa: University of Alabama Press, 1999.

Weiss, Janet A., and Judith E. Gruber. "Deterring Discrimination with Data." *Policy Sciences* 17, no. 1 (1984): 49–66.

Weiss, Janet A., and Mary Tschirhart. "Public Information Campaigns as Policy Instruments." *Journal of Policy Analysis and Management* 13, no. 1 (1994): 82–119.

Weiss, L. *The Myth of the Powerless State.* Cambridge: Cambridge University Press, 1998.

Welborn, David M. "Conjoint Federalism and Environmental Regulation in the United States." *Publius: The Journal of Federalism* 18, no. 1 (1988): 27–43.

West, Darrell M., and Burdett A. Loomis. *The Sound of Money: How Political Interests Get What They Want.* New York: W. W. Norton, 1998.

West, George P. "Report on the Colorado Strike." Excerpted in *American Violence: A Documentary History,* edited by Richard Hofstadter and Michael Wallace, pp. 160–164. New York: Knopf, 1970.

White, Eugene N. "The Legacy of Deposit Insurance: The Growth, Spread, and Cost of Insuring Financial Intermediaries." National Bureau of Economic Research Working Paper 6063. Cambridge, Mass.: NBER, 1997.

Wildavsky, Aaron B. *Budgeting: A Comparative Theory of Budgetary Processes.* Boston: Little, Brown, 1975.

———. "Choosing Preferences by Constructing Institutions: A Cultural Theory of Preference Formation." *American Political Science Review* 81 (1987): 3–21.

Wildavsky, Ben. "Taking Credit." *National Journal* 29, no. 13 (1997): 610–612.

Wilensky, Harold L. *The Welfare State and Equality.* Berkeley: University of California Press, 1975.

Williams, Fred O. "Facing the IRS: How to Act, What to Do If the IRS Audits You." *Buffalo News* (23 May 2000): D1.

Williamson, Oliver E. *The Economic Institutions of Capitalism: Firms, Markets, Relational Contracting.* New York: Free Press, 1987.

———. *Markets and Hierarchies: Analysis and Antitrust Implications, A Study in the Economics of Internal Organization.* New York: Free Press, 1975.

Willoughby, Woodbury. *The Capital Issues Committee and War Finance Corporation.* Baltimore: Johns Hopkins University Press, 1934.

Wilson, James Q. *American Government.* Lexington, Mass.: D.C. Heath, 1979.

———. "The Bureaucracy Problem." *The Public Interest* 6 (1967): 3–9.

———. *Bureaucracy: What Government Agencies Do and Why They Do It.* New York: Basic Books, 1989.

———. *The Investigators: Managing FBI and Narcotics Agents.* New York: Basic Books, 1978.

———. *Political Organizations.* New York: Basic Books, 1973.

———. "The Politics of Regulation." In *The Politics of Regulation,* edited by James Q. Wilson, pp. 357–394. New York: Basic Books, 1980.

———, ed. *The Politics of Regulation.* New York: Basic Books, 1980.

Witte, John F. *The Politics and Development of the Federal Income Tax.* Madison: University of Wisconsin Press, 1985.

Wolfe, Barbara L. "Reform of Health Care for the Nonelderly Poor." In *Confronting Poverty:*

Prescriptions for Change, edited by Sheldon H. Danziger, Gary D. Sandefur, and Daniel H. Weinberg, pp. 253–288. Cambridge, Mass.: Harvard University Press, 1994.

Wood, Wendy. "Attitude Change: Persuasion and Social Influence." *Annual Review of Psychology* 51 (2000): 539–570.

Woodward, C. Vann. *The Strange Career of Jim Crow.* 2d ed. New York: Oxford University Press, 1966.

Woolcock, Michael. "Managing Risk, Shocks, and Opportunities in Developing Economies: The Role of Social Capital." Online at http://www.worldbank.org/poverty/scapital/library.htm.

World Bank. *Bureaucrats in Business: The Economics and Politics of Government Ownership.* New York: Oxford University Press, 1995.

———. *World Development Report, 1997: The State in a Changing World.* New York: Oxford University Press, 1997.

Wright, Deil. *Understanding Intergovernmental Relations.* Monterey, Calif.: Brooks/Cole Publishing, 1982.

Yaffee, Steven Lewis. *Prohibitive Policy: Implementing the Federal Endangered Species Act.* Cambridge, Mass.: MIT Press, 1982.

Yates, Jessica. "Performance Management in Human Services." *The Welfare Information Network.* October 1997. Online at http://www.welfareinfo.org/perfman.htm.

Young, Stephen. "A Comparison of the Industrial Experiences." In *Planning, Politics, and Public Policy: The British, French, and Italian Experience,* edited by Jack Hayward and Michael Watson, pp. 141–154. Cambridge: Cambridge University Press.

Yu, Chilik, Laurence O'Toole, James Cooley, Gail Cowie, Susan Crow, and Stephanie Herbert. "Policy Instruments for Reducing Toxic Releases." *Evaluation Review* 22 (1998): 571–589.

Yudof, Mark. *When Government Speaks.* Berkeley: University of California Press, 1983.

Zaller, John. "The Myth of Massive Media Impact Revived: New Support for a Discredited Idea." In *Political Persuasion and Attitude Change,* edited by Diana Mutz, Paul Sniderman, and Richard Brody, pp. 17–78. Ann Arbor: University of Michigan Press, 1996.

Zarkin, Gary A., and Donald W. Anderson. "Consumer and Producer Responses to Nutrition Label Changes." *American Journal of Agricultural Economics* 74 (1992): 1202–1207.

Zitner, Aaron. "Tax Code Gives Companies a Lift." *Boston Globe* (8 July 1996): 1.

Zito, A. *Epistemic Communities and Environmental Policies in Europe.* London: Macmillan, 1999.

647